Encyclopedia
of the
American Constitution

Editorial Board

Encyclopedia

of the

American Constitution

LEONARD W. LEVY, Editor-in-Chief
Claremont Graduate School, Claremont, California

KENNETH L. KARST, Associate Editor
University of California, Los Angeles

DENNIS J. MAHONEY, Assistant Editor
Claremont Graduate School, Claremont, California

MACMILLAN PUBLISHING COMPANY
A Division of Macmillan, Inc.
NEW YORK

Collier Macmillan Publishers
LONDON

74132

Macmillan Publishing Company
A Division of Macmillan, Inc.
866 Third Avenue, New York, NY 10022

Collier Macmillan Canada, Inc.

Printed in the United States of America

printing number
1   2   3   4   5   6   7   8   9   10

Library of Congress Catalog in Publication Data

Encyclopedia of the American Constitution.

Includes index.
1. United States—Constitutional Law—Dictionaries.
I. Levy, Leonard Williams, 1923–   II. Karst,
Kenneth L.   III. Mahoney, Dennis J.
KF4548.E53   1986   342.73′023′03   86–3038
ISBN 0–02–918610–2   347.3022303

STAFF:

Charles E. Smith, *Publisher*

Elly Dickason, *Project Editor*

Morton I. Rosenberg, *Production Manager*

Joan Greenfield, *Designer*

SACCO AND VANZETTI CASE

See: *Commonwealth v. Sacco and Vanzetti*

SAN ANTONIO INDEPENDENT SCHOOL DISTRICT v. RODRIGUEZ
411 U.S. 1 (1973)

Rodriguez was the BURGER COURT's definitive statement on the subject of EQUAL PROTECTION guarantees against WEALTH DISCRIMINATION—and the statement was that the Court wanted the subject to go away.

Under Texas law, the financing of local school districts relies heavily on local property taxes. Thus a district rich in taxable property can levy taxes at low rates and still spend almost twice as much per pupil as a poor district can spend, even when the poor district taxes its property at high rates. A federal district court, relying on WARREN COURT precedents, concluded that wealth was a SUSPECT CLASSIFICATION, that education was a FUNDAMENTAL INTEREST, and thus that strict judicial scrutiny of the state-imposed inequalities was required. The trial court also concluded that, even if the permissive RATIONAL BASIS standard of review were appropriate, the Texas school finance system lacked any reasonable basis. The Supreme Court reversed, 5–4, in an opinion by Justice LEWIS F. POWELL that was plainly designed as a comprehensive pronouncement about equal protection doctrine.

The opinion was definitive, as a coffin is definitive. Despite what the Court had said in BROWN V. BOARD OF EDUCATION (1954) about education as the key to effective citizenship, here it said that education was not a fundamental interest in the sense that triggered STRICT SCRUTINY—at least not when some minimal level of education was being provided. Indeed, said the majority, the courts lacked power to create new substantive rights by defining interests as "fundamental," unless those interests were already guaranteed elsewhere in the Constitution. Here was formal recognition of the Burger Court's zero-population-growth policy for fundamental interests.

Nor was wealth a suspect classification. Decisions such as GRIFFIN V. ILLINOIS (1956) and DOUGLAS V. CALIFORNIA (1963) had involved INDIGENTS "completely unable to pay" for the benefits at stake, who "sustained an absolute deprivation" of the benefits. Here, the deprivation was only relative; pupils in poor districts were receiving some education. Furthermore, although the trial court had found a significant correlation between district wealth and family wealth, the Supreme Court held the proof of that correlation insufficient; poor children, after all, might live in the shadows of a rich district's factories. In any case, Justice Powell concluded, the evidence was mixed on the question whether school spending affected the quality of education.

Because there was no occasion for strict scrutiny, the Court employed the rational basis standard of review. Contrary to the district court's conclusion, the Texas financing scheme was rationally designed to maintain local control over school spending and educational policy. Justice BYRON R. WHITE, dissenting, attacked this asserted rationality. If "local control" flowed from control over the spending of money, then Texas, by relying heavily on the property tax and by drawing its district lines, had parceled out that choice in an irrationally selective way, to rich districts and not to poor ones.

Justice THURGOOD MARSHALL's dissent was the most powerful equal protection opinion of the Burger Court era. He elaborated on his DANDRIDGE V. WILLIAMS (1970) dissent, rejecting a two-tier system of standards of review in favor of a "sliding-scale" approach tying the level of judicial scrutiny to the importance of the interests at stake and the degree to which the state's classification bore on the powerless. Here, on both counts, judicial scrutiny should be heightened well above the level of requiring only minimal rationality. In any case, the Court had not, in the *Griffin/ Douglas* line of cases, insisted on a showing of absolute deprivation as a condition of strict scrutiny of wealth discrimination; the problem in those cases was the *adequacy* of an appeal, as affected by a discrimination between rich and poor. The Texas scheme could not survive any heightened judicial scrutiny—as the majority itself had virtually conceded.

Justice Powell, a former school board president, surely feared judicial intrusion into the decisions of local school officials. Beyond that narrow concern, the majority undoubtedly worried about judicial intrusion into the allocation of state resources. These are legitimate concerns. The question was, and remains, what kinds of economic inequality, *imposed by the state itself*, can be tolerated in the face of a constitutional guarantee of the equal protection of the laws.

KENNETH L. KARST

(SEE ALSO: *Education and the Constitution; Plyler v. Doe, 1982.*)

Bibliography

MICHELMAN, FRANK I. 1969 The Supreme Court, 1968 Term—Foreword: On Protecting the Poor Through the Fourteenth Amendment. *Harvard Law Review* 83:7–59.

SANFORD, EDWARD T.
(1865–1930)

Edward Terry Sanford was the last of WARREN HARDING's four Supreme Court appointments. He had served fifteen years as a federal judge in Tennessee and, as with many of Harding's judicial appointments, he was chosen in large part because of Chief Justice WILLIAM HOWARD TAFT's lobbying activities.

For nearly seven years, Sanford loyally followed and served Taft. He began his tenure by joining a rare Taft dissent when the Court invalidated the DISTRICT OF COLUMBIA MINIMUM WAGE LAW in ADKINS V. CHILDREN'S HOSPITAL (1923). He was a regular member of the Chief Justice's Sunday afternoon extracurricular conferences, which excluded the Court's more liberal members such as OLIVER WENDELL HOLMES, LOUIS D. BRANDEIS, and HARLAN F. STONE. In a final coincidence, Sanford died on March 8, 1930, the same day as Taft.

Sanford's most important contribution to constitutional law during his brief tenure came in the area of CIVIL LIBERTIES. In GITLOW V. NEW YORK (1925) he led the Court in sustaining New York's criminal anarchy statute. Sanford's opinion largely reiterated the Court's BAD TENDENCY TEST regarding FREEDOM OF SPEECH, arguing that the state had a right to protect itself against speech that called for the overthrow of government. The state could not, he said, "reasonably be required to measure the danger from every such utterance in the nice balance of a jeweler's scale." But Sanford also acknowledged that the FOURTEENTH AMENDMENT incorporated the FIRST AMENDMENT's guarantees of free speech and FREEDOM OF THE PRESS against STATE ACTION. That INCORPORATION DOCTRINE had momentous consequences for the Court's later views of CIVIL RIGHTS and LIBERTIES.

In WHITNEY V. CALIFORNIA (1927) Sanford again sustained a criminal anarchy conviction. But the same day, in *Fiske v. Kansas*, he spoke for the Court when for the first time the Justices overturned a state conviction on the ground that a criminal anarchy statute had been applied to deny the defendant his freedom of speech, as guaranteed by the First and Fourteenth Amendments. Sanford found that the state had failed to provide evidence of the organization's criminal or violent purposes. Shortly after Sanford's death, the Court nullified a state criminal anarchy statute and a state law sanctioning the suppression of certain newspapers, with both decisions (STROMBERG V. CALIFORNIA, 1931; NEAR V. MINNESOTA, 1931) implementing Sanford's *Gitlow* incorporation doctrine.

Sanford generally concurred with the Court's decisions involving national and state ECONOMIC REGULATION. For example, he joined in approving ZONING laws in EUCLID V. AMBLER REALTY CO. (1926), and he agreed that a Pennsylvania statute requiring drugstore owners to be registered pharmacists was unconstitutional in *Lambert v. Yellowley* (1926). But in *Ma-

ple Floor Association v. United States (1925) Sanford joined Taft's dissent protesting the Court's holding that trade associations did not violate the SHERMAN ANTITRUST ACT. In *Tyson v. Banton* (1927) Sanford, dissenting from a ruling that invalidated regulations of theater ticket brokers, invoked the STATE POLICE POWER doctrine of the GRANGER CASES (1877); he argued that because the brokers' business was AFFECTED WITH A PUBLIC INTEREST, the legislature could protect "the public from extortion and exorbitant rates."

Sanford's Supreme Court tenure was, on the whole, unremarkable. There is irony in that his *Gitlow* opinion, despite its antilibertarian result, laid the foundation for the mid-twentieth-century libertarian revolution and the nationalization of American CIVIL RIGHTS and CIVIL LIBERTIES.

STANLEY I. KUTLER

Bibliography
RAGAN, ALLEN E. 1943 Mr. Justice Sanford. *East Tennessee Historical Society Publications* 15:74–88.

SAN MATEO COUNTY v. SOUTHERN PACIFIC RAILROAD

See: Person

SANTA CLARA COUNTY v. SOUTHERN PACIFIC RAILROAD

See: Person

SAWYER, LORENZO
(1820–1891)

In 1870 ULYSSES S. GRANT commissioned Lorenzo Sawyer of California judge of the Ninth Circuit Court, a position he filled until his death. Throughout these years, Sawyer shared circuit court duties with Supreme Court Justice STEPHEN J. FIELD.

Sawyer formulated a narrow interpretation of the PUBLIC PURPOSE DOCTRINE and STATE POLICE POWERS. He declared that a state could not, consistently with the FOURTEENTH AMENDMENT, define the public purpose to permit mining companies to cause flooding of private lands. Sawyer also resisted local efforts to discriminate against the Chinese under the guise of the POLICE POWER. In 1890 he struck down a San Francisco ordinance, which required Chinese to live and work in a designated area of the city, as an "arbitrary confiscation of property without DUE PROCESS or any process of law." Sawyer also invalidated other suspect uses of the police power that sought to harass the Chinese by outlawing the operation of laundries and opium parlors. Such measures, he ruled, placed "an unlawful inhibition upon the inalienable rights and liberties of [all] citizens. . . ."

Sawyer subscribed to the doctrine of DUAL FEDERALISM, but in *In Re Neagle* he forcefully recited the supremacy of the federal government. David Neagle, a United States marshal and bodyguard for Justice Field, had killed a man to protect Field. Sawyer issued a writ of HABEAS CORPUS releasing Neagle from custody by California officials on charges of murder. He held that the marshal had acted in pursuance of the laws of the United States and that "a state law, which contravenes a valid law of the United States, is, in the nature of things, necessarily void—a nullity."

Justice Field cast a large shadow over jurisprudence of the Ninth Circuit, but Sawyer also significantly shaped American constitutional law. His opinions were a major source of authority on the police powers of the states, the public purpose doctrine, and the Fourteenth Amendment.

KERMIT L. HALL

Bibliography
SWISHER, CARL BRENT 1930 *Stephen J. Field, Craftsman of the Law.* Pages 325–326, 332, 337, 342, 352, 353, 355, 358–359. Washington, D.C.: Brookings Institution.

SCALES v. UNITED STATES
367 U.S. 203 (1961)

The Supreme Court, always careful to avoid declaring the Smith Act unconstitutional, instead employed statutory interpretation to emasculate its provisions. Here the Court held that the act's clause banning "membership" in certain organizations applied only to members active in the organization's affairs, knowing that its purpose was to bring about the overthrow of the government by force and violence as speedily as circumstances would permit, and with the specific purpose to bring about that overthrow. In the *Scales* case itself, the Court affirmed a conviction under the membership clause. Since that time, however, the act's forbidding BURDEN OF PROOF has discouraged further prosecutions.

MARTIN SHAPIRO

SCHAD v. MOUNT EPHRAIM
452 U.S. 61 (1981)

The Supreme Court, 7–2, reversed the conviction of the operators of an "adult" bookstore for violating a ZONING ordinance of a residential town by presenting live entertainment in the form of nude dancing. The state courts had construed the ordinance to forbid all live entertainment; so read, it fell afoul of the FIRST AMENDMENT doctrine of OVERBREADTH. The Court concluded that the state's asserted justifications (limiting commerce to residents' "immediate needs," and avoiding problems with parking, trash, and the like) were unsupported by the record, which showed that live entertainment was offered in three other establishments. The dissenters argued that, although banning other entertainment might present First Amendment problems, banning nude dancing did not.

KENNETH L. KARST

SCHALL v. MARTIN
467 U.S. 253 (1984)

This is one of several cases showing that legal fictions infect JUVENILE PROCEEDINGS involving criminal conduct. *Schall* reflected the fictions that juveniles, unlike adults, "are always in some form of custody" and that PREVENTIVE DETENTION is not punitive and is designed to protect the youthful offender as well as society from the consequences of his uncommitted crimes. New York, without distinguishing first offenders from recidivists and without distinguishing trivial offenses from major crimes of violence, allowed juveniles, aged seven to sixteen, to be jailed for up to seventeen days pending adjudication of guilt. Justice WILLIAM H. REHNQUIST, for a 6–3 Supreme Court, ruled that preventive detention in the case of juveniles is compatible with the FUNDAMENTAL FAIRNESS required by the FOURTEENTH AMENDMENT's guarantee of DUE PROCESS OF LAW. Rehnquist found adequate procedural safeguards in the New York statute, noted that every state permitted preventive detention of juveniles accused of crime, and declared that the juveniles' best interests were served because preventive detention disabled them from committing other crimes prior to the date of court appearance. Justices THURGOOD MARSHALL, WILLIAM J. BRENNAN, and JOHN PAUL STEVENS, dissenting, insisted that the majority's factual argument did not survive critical scrutiny any more than did the statute provide due process.

LEONARD W. LEVY

SCHECHTER POULTRY CORP. v. UNITED STATES
295 U.S. 495 (1935)

After the decision in this case, striking down the NATIONAL INDUSTRIAL RECOVERY ACT, a conservative gave thanks that the Constitution still stood, while a liberal wondered whether it stood still. The Supreme Court's "horse and buggy" interpretation, as President FRANKLIN D. ROOSEVELT called it, imperiled the power of the United States to control any part of the economy that the Court regarded as subject to the exclusive control of the states. Chief Justice CHARLES EVANS HUGHES, for the Court, first held the statute void because it improperly delegated legislative powers. Private business groups might frame codes governing their industries as long as NRA officials approved and the president promulgated them. Hughes said the president's discretion was "unfettered," and even Justice BENJAMIN N. CARDOZO, who had dissented in PANAMA REFINING CO. V. RYAN (1935), separately concurred and spoke of "delegation running riot." Improper DELEGATION [of power] could have been rectified by new legislation, but the Court also held the act unauthorized by the COMMERCE CLAUSE, leaving the impression that labor matters and trade practices were beyond the scope of congressional power unless in INTERSTATE COMMERCE or directly affecting it.

The government argued that although Schechter sold only in the local market, its business was in the STREAM OF COMMERCE. Ninety-six percent of the poultry sold in New York City came from out of state. Hughes rejected that argument by ruling that the flow of interstate commerce had ceased, because the poultry had come to a permanent rest in the city: it was sold locally and did not again leave the state. The government also invoked the SHREVEPORT DOCTRINE, arguing that even if the commerce here were local, it had so close and substantial a relationship to interstate commerce that its federal regulation was necessary to protect interstate commerce. Schechter's preferential trade practices, low wages, and long hours, in violation of the poultry code, enabled it to undersell competitors, diverting the interstate flow of poultry to its own market, injuring interstate competitors, and triggering a cycle of wage and price cutting that threatened to extend beyond the confines of the local market. This entire line of reasoning, Hughes said, proved too much. It laid the basis for national regulation of the entire economy, overriding state authority. It also ignored the fundamental distinction between direct and indirect effects upon interstate commerce. What that distinction was Hughes did not explain, but he asserted that Schechter's violations of the code only indirectly affected interstate commerce and therefore stood beyond national reach. Even Cardozo, joined by Justice HARLAN FISKE STONE, declared that "to find immediacy or directness here is to find it almost everywhere."

Schechter temporarily ended national regulation of industry and allowed Roosevelt to blame the Court, even though the NRA's code programs were cumbersome, unpopular, and scheduled for political extinction. The Court's views of the commerce clause made no substitute constitutionally feasible.

LEONARD W. LEVY

SCHENCK v. UNITED STATES
249 U.S. 47 (1919)

The FREEDOM OF SPEECH provisions of the FIRST AMENDMENT played a singularly retiring role in American constitutional law until the time of World War I or, more precisely, until the Russian Revolution and the Red Scare that it generated in the United States. The Sedition Act of 1798 (see ALIEN AND SEDITION ACTS) obviously posed serious First Amendment questions but was not tested in the Supreme Court and was soon repealed. A scattering of free speech claims and oblique pronouncements by the federal courts occurred after 1900, but speech issues, even when they did arise, typically appeared in state courts in the contexts of OBSCENITY prosecutions and labor disputes. The Court did not declare the First Amendment applicable to the states through the due process clause of the FOURTEENTH AMENDMENT (see INCORPORATION DOCTRINE) until GITLOW v. NEW YORK (1925). Furthermore, in its most direct pronouncement on the freedom of speech provision of the First Amendment, *Patterson v. Colorado* (1907), the Court, speaking through Justice OLIVER WENDELL HOLMES, had suggested that the provision barred only prior restraints, a position that Holmes abandoned in *Schenck.*

In 1917 Congress passed an ESPIONAGE ACT making it a crime to cause or attempt to cause insubordination in the armed forces, obstruct recruitment or enlistment, and otherwise urge, incite, or advocate obstruction or resistance to the war effort. Although there had been much bitter debate about U. S. entry into World War I, the speakers whose prosecutions raised First Amendment issues that ultimately reached the Supreme Court were not German sympathizers. They were left-wing sympathizers with the Russian Revolution who were provoked by the dispatch of Allied expeditionary forces to Russia. If the American war machine was to be turned on the Revolution, it must be stopped.

Prosecutions of such revolutionary sympathizers triggered three important federal court decisions that initiated the jurisprudence of the First Amendment: MASSES PUBLISHING COMPANY V. PATTEN (1917), *Schenck v. United States,* and ABRAMS V. UNITED STATES (1919). *Schenck* was the first major Supreme Court pronouncement on freedom of speech.

Schenck was general secretary of the Socialist Party which distributed to prospective draftees a leaflet denouncing CONSCRIPTION and urging recipients to assert their opposition to it. He was convicted of conspiracy to violate the Espionage Act by attempting to obstruct recruiting. Following his own earlier writing on attempts, Holmes, writing for a unanimous Court, said: It seems to be admitted that if an actual obstruction of the recruiting service were proved, liability for words that produced that effect might be enforced. The statute of 1917 . . . punishes conspiracies to obstruct as well as actual obstruction. If the act (speaking, or circulating a paper), its tendency and the intent with which it is done are the same, we perceive no ground for saying that success alone warrants making the act a crime. In response to Schenck's First Amendment claims, Holmes said:

We admit that in many places and in ordinary times the defendants in saying all that was said in the circular would have been within their constitutional rights. But the character of every act depends upon the circumstances in which it is done. The most stringent protection of free speech would not protect a man in falsely shouting fire in a theatre and causing a panic. . . . The question in every case is whether the words used are used in such circumstances and are of such a nature as to create a CLEAR AND PRESENT DANGER that they will bring about the substantive evils that Congress has a right to prevent. It is a question of proximity and degree.

That the clear and present danger test was first announced in a context in which speech was treated as an attempt to commit an illegal act rather than in a situation in which the statute declared certain speech itself criminal was important for several reasons. First, the attempts context necessarily drew the judicial focus to the nexus between speech and criminal action and thus to the circumstances in which the speech was uttered rather than to the content of the speech itself. Questions of intent and circumstances, crucial to the law of attempts, thus became crucial to the danger test. Second, if the link between speech and illegal act was necessarily a question of degree, then much discretion was necessarily left to the judge. The clear and present danger test has often been criticized for leaving speakers at the mercy of judicial discretion. Having invoked the danger test, the Court affirmed Schenck's conviction. Third, supporters of judicial self-restraint subsequently sought to narrow the scope of the danger test by insisting that it was to be employed only in situations where the government sought to prosecute speech under a statute proscribing only action. In this view, the test was inapplicable when the legislature itself had proscribed speech, having made its own independent, prior judgment that a certain class of speech created a danger warranting suppression.

Although Holmes wrote in Schenck for a unanimous court, he and Justice LOUIS D. BRANDEIS were the danger test's sole supporters in the other leading cases of the 1920s: *Abrams, Gitlow,* and WHITNEY v. CALIFORNIA (1927). A comparison of these cases indicates that Holmes's "tough guy" pose was deeply implicated in his clear and present danger decisions. In the later cases, Holmes seemed to be saying that a self-confident democracy ought not to descend to the prosecution of fringe-group rantings about socialist revolution. In *Schenck,* however, where the speech was concretely pointed at obstructing war time recruitment, Holmes said: "When a nation is at war, many things that might be said in time of peace are such a hindrance to its effort that their utterance will not be endured so long as men fight and that no Court could regard them as protected by any constitutional right."

MARTIN SHAPIRO

Bibliography
CHAFEE, ZECHARIAH 1941 *Free Speech in the United States.* Cambridge, Mass.: Harvard University Press.

SCHEUER v. RHODES
416 U.S. 236 (1974)

This decision established that high state officers are not absolutely immune from suit for constitutional violations. Ohio National Guard troops shot and killed four students demonstrating against the VIETNAM WAR. The deceased students' representatives sued Governor James Rhodes and other state officials, alleging reckless deployment of the Guard and unlawful orders to the Guard which led to the shootings. The Supreme Court held Rhodes not to be absolutely im-

mune from suit. The Court did indicate that officials with substantial discretionary responsibilities are to be given greater deference than officials with more limited tasks. *Rhodes* connects the first SECTION 1983 case on EXECUTIVE IMMUNITY, PIERSON V. RAY (1967), with later decisions such as WOOD V. STRICKLAND (1975) and *Procunier v. Navarette* (1978).

THEODORE EISENBERG

SCHICK v. REED
419 U.S. 256 (1974)

In a 5–4 decision, the Supreme Court upheld the President's right to grant conditional clemency. Maurice Schick, convicted of murder in 1954 by a court-martial, was sentenced to death. In 1960, under Article II, section 2, clause 1, of the Constitution, President DWIGHT D. EISENHOWER commuted the sentence to life imprisonment without parole. Citing FURMAN V. GEORGIA (1972), Schick asked the Court to hold the no-parole condition unconstitutional. But the court held that the PARDONING POWER flows from the Constitution alone and may not be limited except by the Constitution itself.

DENNIS J. MAHONEY

SCHMERBER v. CALIFORNIA
384 U.S. 757 (1966)

Justice WILLIAM J. BRENNAN, for a 6–3 majority of the Supreme Court, ruled that the taking of a blood sample from the petitioner over his objections, to prove his guilt for driving under the influence of alcohol, did not constitute TESTIMONIAL COMPULSION and therefore did not violate the RIGHT AGAINST SELF-INCRIMINATION, nor did it constitute an invalid WARRANTLESS SEARCH under the EXIGENT CIRCUMSTANCES.

LEONARD W. LEVY

SCHNECKLOTH v. BUSTAMONTE
412 U.S. 218 (1973)

The police may conduct a search without a warrant when consent is freely given. Before *Schneckloth,* some lower courts had taken the position that consent was not voluntary unless the prosecution could demonstrate that the person was aware of his right to refuse consent. Others held that knowledge of the right to refuse was merely one element to be considered, and that consent was established by the totality of the circumstances. In *Schneckloth* the Supreme Court adopted the latter position.

The Court distinguished the FOURTH AMENDMENT from other constitutional guarantees (for example, the RIGHT TO COUNSEL) for which the Court had required an intentional relinquishment of the right. The other guarantees intend to promote the ascertainment of truth in a trial; the Fourth Amendment, on the other hand, does not promote pursuit of truth but secures PRIVACY. The requirement of MIRANDA RULE warnings prior to POLICE INTERROGATION was also an inapposite analogy, for the coercion inherent in a custodial environment is unlikely to be duplicated "on a person's own familiar territory."

Justice LEWIS POWELL, concurring, set forth views later adopted by the Court in STONE V. POWELL (1976), proposing radical restrictions on the use of HABEAS CORPUS to review Fourth Amendment violations by state officers. Three dissenting Justices took the position that mere absence of coercion is not the equivalent of a meaningful choice; that "a decision made without actual knowledge of available alternatives" is not "a choice at all."

JACOB W. LANDYNSKI

SCHNELL v. DAVIS
336 U.S. 933 (1949)

In a PER CURIAM opinion, the Supreme Court affirmed a district court JUDGMENT. Davis had brought a CLASS ACTION, arguing that enforcement of Alabama's "Boswell Amendment" violated the VOTING RIGHTS of blacks. The amendment, adopted in 1946 to circumvent the decision in SMITH V. ALLWRIGHT (1944), made the ability to "understand and explain" the Constitution a requirement for voter registration. The record showed that this "understanding clause" was used exclusively to deny registration to blacks. The Court held that the requirement violated the FIFTEENTH AMENDMENT because it was used to deny the right to vote on account of race or color.

DENNIS J. MAHONEY

SCHOOL BUSING

Before BROWN V. BOARD OF EDUCATION (1954–1955) was decided, many a southern child rode the bus to school, passing on the way a bus headed in the other direction, loaded with children of another race. The busing of children was "one tool" used to maintain a system of school SEGREGATION. As late as 1970, before the Supreme Court had approved a single busing order, about forty percent of the nation's children rode buses to school. The school bus had permitted the replacement of rural one-room schoolhouses with consolidated schools; in the city, riding the bus had been thought safer than walking. School busing did not become the object of majoritarian anger until the 1970s, when the Supreme Court described it as "one tool" for dismantling a segregated system and affirmed its use not only in the South but also in the cities of the North and West.

In a rural southern county, the simplest form of DESEGREGATION might drastically reduce school busing; racial living patterns would permit integration of the schools through the discontinuation of racial assignments and assignment of children to the schools nearest their homes. In the cities, however, residential segregation had been so thorough that the abandonment of racial assignments and the substitution of a neighborhood school policy would not end the separation of school children by race. The question was asked: Would the Supreme Court insist on more than the end of racial assignments—on the actual mixing of black and white children in the schools—by way of dismantling segregation produced by deliberate official policy? In SWANN V. CHARLOTTE-MECKLENBURG BOARD OF EDUCATION (1971), the Court answered that question affirmatively. Then, in KEYES V. SCHOOL DISTRICT NO. 1 (1973) and COLUMBUS BOARD OF EDUCATION V. PENICK (1979), the Court extended *Swann*'s commands to the North and West, in ways that blurred the DE FACTO/DE JURE distinction. Once a constitutional violation is found, even in remote acts of deliberate segregation by a school board, then as a practical matter the district court's remedial goal becomes "the greatest possible degree of actual desegregation"—and that, in a large city, means the busing of massive numbers of children for the purpose of achieving the maximum practicable RACIAL BALANCE.

Apart from the busing ordered by courts, some busing for integration purposes has resulted from voluntary programs, mostly involving the busing of minority children to schools formerly populated by non-Hispanic whites. Political resistance has been directed not to those programs but to busing ordered by a court over the opposition of the school board and of large numbers of parents and children. The most outspoken protest has come from white parents. The responses of school board majorities have varied, from political warfare in Boston and Los Angeles to the "let's-make-it-work" attitude in Columbus.

President RICHARD M. NIXON, whose first electoral campaign adopted a "Southern strategy" and whose campaign for reelection included an attack on school busing, proposed congressional legislation to restrict busing. In 1974 Congress purported to forbid a federal court to order a student's transportation to a school "other than the school closest or next closest to his place of residence." This statute's constitutionality would have been dubious but for a proviso that canceled its effect: the law was not to diminish the authority of federal courts to enforce the Constitution.

The school busing issue has forced a reevaluation of the goals of desegregation. In *Brown* the chief harm of school segregation imposed by law was said to be the stigma of inferiority, which impaired black children's motivation to learn. The fact of separation of the races in urban schools may or may not have the same stigmatic effect—even though deliberately segregative governmental actions have contributed to residential segregation in cities throughout the nation. Stigma aside, it is far from clear that racial isolation alone impairs minority children's learning. In communities with substantial Hispanic or Asian-American populations, concerns about the maintenance of cultural identity are apt to be expressed in opposition to taking children out of neighborhood schools and away from bilingual education programs. The call for "community control" of schools is heard less frequently in black communities today than it was around 1970, but some prominent black CIVIL RIGHTS leaders have placed increasing emphasis on improvement of the schools and decreasing emphasis on the busing of children.

Part of the reason for this shift in emphasis surely is a sense of despair over the prospects of busing as an effective means of achieving integration. Social scientists disagree on the amount of "white flight" that has resulted from court-ordered busing. Some demographic changes are merely extensions of a long-established pattern of middle-class migration to the suburbs. The Supreme Court in MILLIKEN V. BRADLEY (1974) made clear that metropolitan relief, combining city and suburban districts for purposes of school integration, was allowable only in rare circumstances. "White flight" can also take the form of withdrawal of children from public schools; recent estimates suggest that about one-fifth of the students in the nation's private schools have fled from desegregation orders. In this perspective, the neighborhood school is seen not only as a focus for community but also, less appe-

tizingly, as a means for controlling children's associations and passing social advantage from one generation to the next. Either strategy of "white flight" costs money. It is no accident that the hottest opposition to court-ordered school busing has come from working-class neighborhoods, where people feel that they have been singled out to bear a burden in order to validate an ideal they have come to doubt.

School busing for integration purposes has come under strong political attack. Neither Congress nor a state can constitutionally prohibit busing designed to remedy *de jure* segregation. However, state measures limiting busing designed to remedy *de facto* segregation may or may not be upheld, depending on the legislation's purposes and effects. (See WASHINGTON V. SEATTLE SCHOOL DISTRICT NO. 1, 1982; CRAWFORD V. LOS ANGELES BOARD OF EDUCATION, 1982.)

Sadly, it is realistic to assume the continuation of urban residential segregation, which has diminished only slightly since 1940, despite nearly half a century of civil rights litigation and legislation. (Even the migration of increasing numbers of middle-class black families to the suburbs has not significantly diminished residential segregation.) Given that assumption, the nation must choose between accepting racially separate schools and using school busing to achieve integration. The first choice will seem to many citizens a betrayal of the promise of *Brown*. The second choice faces opposition strong enough to threaten not only the nation's historic commitment to public education but also its commitment to obedience to law. The resolution of this dilemma is a challenge not only to courts but also to school board members and citizens, demanding imagination, patience, and good will in quantities far beyond their recent supply.

KENNETH L. KARST

Bibliography

BELL, DERRICK A., JR. 1976 Serving Two Masters: Integration Ideals and Client Interests in School Desegregation Litigation. *Yale Law Journal* 85:470–516.

DIMOND, PAUL R. 1985 *Beyond Busing: Inside the Challenge to Urban Segregation.* Ann Arbor: University of Michigan Press.

FISS, OWEN M. 1975 The Jurisprudence of Busing. *Law and Contemporary Problems* 39:194–216.

WILKINSON, J. HARVIE, III 1979 *From Brown to Bakke.* New York: Oxford University Press.

SCHOOL DESEGRATION

See: Desegregation

SCHOOL PRAYER

See: Religion in Public Schools

SCHOULER, JAMES
(1839–1920)

Massachusetts-born James Schouler, while a Union officer in the Civil War, contracted a fever that left him nearly deaf. He nevertheless rose to national prominence as an attorney and historian. Although his law practice was successful—his first Supreme Court victory was *Hosmer v. United States,* 1872)—he gave it up (because of his disability) in favor of teaching. His main historical work was the nationalistic *History of the United States under the Constitution* (7 volumes, 1880–1913), which he conceived as the first comprehensive account of American political and legal history. He also wrote *Constitutional Studies: State and Federal* (1897) and biographies of THOMAS JEFFERSON and ALEXANDER HAMILTON.

DENNIS J. MAHONEY

SCHROEDER, THEODORE
(1864–1953)

Before World War I, Theodore Schroeder, as FELIX FRANKFURTER said, was the foremost authority in the field of FIRST AMENDMENT rights. A prosperous lawyer, he could afford to be a full-time publicist in the cause of opposing all censorship and prosecutions for seditious, blasphemous, and obscene libels. In 1902 he founded the Free Speech League, the mainstay of CIVIL LIBERTIES until the founding of the AMERICAN CIVIL LIBERTIES UNION. ROGER BALDWIN, one of the many civil libertarians whom Schroeder influenced, declared that Schroeder "was the Free Speech League." Schroeder was an uncompromising First Amendment absolutist who defended anarchists, freethinkers, and pornographers. He also advocated equal rights for women and defended Emma Goldman and Margaret Sanger. His major works include *"Obscene" Literature and Constitutional Law* (1911), *Free Speech for Radicals* (1916), *Constitutional Free Speech Defined and Defended* (1919), and *Free Speech Bibliography* (1922).

LEONARD W. LEVY

Bibliography

AUERBACH, JEROLD 1972 (1911) Introduction to Schroeder, Theodore, *"Obscene" Literature and Constitutional Law.* New York: Da Capo Press.

SCHWARE v. NEW MEXICO BOARD OF BAR EXAMINERS
353 U.S. 232 (1957)

Schware was one of the early cases in which state bar examiners refused bar admission to persons suspected of communism. The Court overturned the refusal on DUE PROCESS grounds, holding that a finding that the applicant was a Communist party member before 1940 was constitutionally insufficient to overcome evidence of his later good moral character.

MARTIN SHAPIRO

SCHWIMMER, UNITED STATES v.
279 U.S. 644 (1929)

When Rosiki Schwimmer applied for NATURALIZATION, officials questioned whether she could take the oath to "uphold and defend the Constitution against all enemies" without reservation. She opposed war in all forms.

The question before the Supreme Court was whether Congress had intended to require willingness to perform combatant military service as a condition of naturalization. Justice PIERCE BUTLER spoke for the Court and held that Congress had. Justice OLIVER WENDELL HOLMES dissented, joined by Justice LOUIS D. BRANDEIS. Holmes noted that Schwimmer, a woman of almost sixty years, would never actually be called upon to serve. Furthermore, taking a position against resort to armed forces was simply a reform objective no different from favoring a unicameral legislature. Justice EDWARD T. SANFORD also dissented.

Schwimmer was overruled by GIROUARD v. UNITED STATES (1946).

RICHARD E. MORGAN

SCOPES v. STATE OF TENNESSEE

See: *State of Tennessee v. Scopes*

SCOTT v. ILLINOIS

See: Right to Counsel

SCOTTSBORO CASES

See: *Norris v. Alabama; Powell v. Alabama*

SCREWS v. UNITED STATES
325 U.S. 91 (1945)

Southern law enforcement officers were prosecuted under section 242 of Title 18, United States Code, a federal CIVIL RIGHTS statute, for beating to death a black arrestee. Because section 242 proscribes only action "under COLOR OF LAW," and because congressional power to enforce the FOURTEENTH AMENDMENT was assumed to be limited to reaching STATE ACTION, the question arose whether behavior not authorized by state law could be either state action or action under color of law. The Court's affirmative answer, which relied in part on UNITED STATES V. CLASSIC (1941), both established section 242 as a weapon against police misconduct and nourished the post-1960 expansion of noncriminal civil rights litigation. MONROE V. PAPE (1961), relying on *Screws* and *Classic*, similarly interpreted the "under color of" law requirement for noncriminal civil rights actions brought under SECTION 1983, TITLE 42, UNITED STATES CODE. Exclusive reliance on state law to remedy police misconduct, a position advocated in dissent in *Screws* by Justices OWEN ROBERTS, FELIX FRANKFURTER, and ROBERT H. JACKSON, would never again be the rule.

Screws also raised the question whether federal criminal civil rights statutes are unconstitutionally vague. Section 242 outlaws willful deprivations of rights secured by the Constitution. Because constitutional standards change constantly, there was doubt that section 242 provided potential defendants with adequate warning of proscribed behavior. In *Screws*, the Court sought to avoid this difficulty by holding that the word "willfully" in section 242 connotes "a purpose to deprive a person of a specific constitutional right." The Court's remand of the case to reinstruct the jury on the meaning of "willful" prompted Justice FRANK MURPHY to dissent, pointing out that the officers had contrived to beat their victim for fifteen minutes after he lost consciousness and arguing that the right to "life" protected by the Fourteenth Amendment surely included a right not to be murdered by state officials. The specific intent requirement has generated confusion in subsequent interpretations of the criminal civil rights statutes.

THEODORE EISENBERG

SEARCH, UNREASONABLE

See: Unreasonable Search

SEARCH AND SEIZURE

The FOURTH AMENDMENT has the virtue of brevity and the vice of ambiguity. It does not define the PROBABLE CAUSE required for warrants or indicate whether a WARRANTLESS SEARCH or seizure is inevitably "unreasonable" if made without probable cause, so that the factual basis required for a constitutional search or seizure is unclear. The amendment does not define the relationship of the word "unreasonable" to the clause setting forth the conditions under which warrants may issue; it is thus unclear when a judicial officer's approval must be obtained before an ARREST or search is made. There is also uncertainty as to what official conduct is subject to the amendment's restraints, that is, just what actions amount to "searches and seizures" and threaten the "right of the people to be secure." Finally, there is ambiguity concerning how that right is to be enforced; unlike the Fifth Amendment RIGHT AGAINST SELF-INCRIMINATION, no mention is made of barring from EVIDENCE the fruits of a violation of the amendment. The Supreme Court has had to respond to each of these four fundamental questions. (See RIGHT–PRIVILEGE DISTINCTION.)

The warrant clause of the Fourth Amendment makes it apparent that a valid ARREST WARRANT or SEARCH WARRANT may issue only upon a showing of probable cause to the issuing authority. This requirement is intended to prohibit resort to GENERAL WARRANTS and arrest and search on suspicion. As the Court noted in BRINEGAR V. UNITED STATES (1949), it is also intended "to give fair leeway for enforcing the law in the community's protection," and thus is best perceived as "a practical, nontechnical conception affording the best compromise that has been found for accommodating these often opposing interests" of individual privacy and collective security.

Though a literal reading of the Fourth Amendment does not compel this result, the prohibition upon "UNREASONABLE" SEARCHES and seizures has been construed to mean that even searches and seizures conducted without a warrant require probable cause. As explained in WONG SUN V. UNITED STATES (1963), "the requirements of reliability and particularity of the information on which an officer may act . . . surely cannot be less stringent [when an arrest is made without a warrant] than where an arrest warrant is obtained. Otherwise, a principal incentive now existing for the procurement of arrest warrants would be destroyed." But the amount of probable cause required for with-warrant and without-warrant searches is not exactly the same; the Court stated in *United States v. Ventresca* (1965) that because of the preference accorded to warrants, "in a doubtful or marginal case a search under a warrant may be sustainable where without one it would fail."

The same quantum of evidence is required whether one is concerned with probable cause to arrest or to search. Thus in SPINELLI V. UNITED STATES (1969), concerning probable cause for a search warrant, the Court found its earlier decision in DRAPER V. UNITED STATES (1959), concerning probable cause to arrest, to be a "suitable benchmark." But the arrest and search situations differ in important respects. For arrest, it must be sufficiently probable that an offense has been committed and that the particular individual to be arrested has committed it; for a search, it must be sufficiently probable that specified items are evidence of criminal activity and are to be found in the specified place. On a given set of facts one type of probable cause may be present but not the other.

The probable cause test is an objective rather than a subjective one. "If subjective good faith alone were the test," the Supreme Court said in *Beck v. Ohio* (1964), "the protections of the Fourth Amendment would evaporate, and the people would be 'secure in their houses, papers, and effects,' only in the discretion of the police." The question, therefore, is not what the arresting or searching officer thought but rather what a reasonable person with the experience and expertise of the officer would have thought. That assessment is to be made on all available information regardless of its admissibility in a criminal trial because, as the Court said in *Brinegar,* the probable cause test is "not technical" and involves "the factual and practical considerations of everyday life on which reasonable and prudent men, not legal technicians, act." Thus credible HEARSAY may be considered, but a person's reputation, at least when stated in terms of unsubstantiated conclusions, cannot.

Although *Brinegar* declares that probable cause requires "less than evidence which would justify . . . conviction" but yet "more than bare suspicion" and also that the question is one of "probabilities," it gives no indication as to what degree of probability is required. Some of the Court's decisions—for example, *Johnson v. United States* (1948), holding that the smell of burning opium from within a hotel room did not amount to probable cause to arrest a particular occupant because until the subsequent entry she was not known to be the sole occupant of the room—suggest a more-probable-than-not standard. But the Supreme Court has never explicitly held that the Fourth Amendment requires this standard, and the lower courts have understandably found such an interpreta-

tion too stringent in at least some circumstances. Thus, it is not uncommon to find an appellate decision holding that an arrest near a crime scene was lawful even though the victim's description was not exact or detailed enough to single the arrested person out from all other persons in the vicinity, or that a search of a number of different places under a suspect's control is permissible even though no one of them is the more-probable-than-not location of the evidence sought.

Most of the Supreme Court's probable cause cases involve information from police informants, denizens of the criminal milieu who provide information in exchange for money or informal immunity regarding their own criminal conduct. In AGUILAR V. TEXAS (1964), where the search warrant affidavit merely recited that the affiants had "received reliable information from a credible person" that "narcotics and narcotics paraphernalia are being kept at the above described premises," the Court adopted a two-pronged test. This affidavit was held insufficient because, first, it did not disclose how the informant knew what he claimed to know concerning what was in the house; and second, it did not disclose how the affiants concluded that their informer was reliable. The first prong of this test has usually been met with details about how the informant acquired his knowledge (for instance, that he had just been inside the house and saw there a cache of narcotics from which the occupant made a sale), though it can be indirectly satisfied by self-verifying detail. As explained in *Spinelli,* if the informant gives a great many details about the criminal scheme (the precise amount of narcotics in the house, how it is wrapped, exactly where it is stored), then it may be inferred "that the informant had gained his information in a reliable way."

The second or "veracity" prong of *Aguilar* has typically been met on the basis of past performance, that is, by a recitation that this same informant previously has given information that turned out to be correct. Alternatively, it has sufficed to show, as in UNITED STATES V. HARRIS (1971), that the informant's statement included an admission against penal interest ("I bought some narcotics while I was in that house"), as people "do not lightly admit a crime and place critical evidence in the hands of the police in the form of their own admissions." The Supreme Court sometimes stressed that the informer's tale was partly corroborated, but there was considerable uncertainty as to just what deficiencies under the *Aguilar* two-pronged test this corroboration overcomes. (Because the use of informants raises special concerns not present in other situations, no comparable showing of veracity is needed when the information has been obtained from a police officer or a cooperative citizen.)

The *Aguilar* test was abandoned in ILLINOIS V. GATES (1983) in favor of a more general "totality of the circumstances" approach. The *Aguilar* factors of veracity and basis of knowledge remain as "relevant considerations," but are no longer two independent requirements; "a deficiency in one may be compensated for . . . by a strong showing as to the other." This is an unfortunate development, for the *Aguilar* rule provided a necessary structure and more precise guidance to police and judges. Moreover, the *Gates* approach is unsound, for surely—as the Court has often held—a conclusory allegation ("there are narcotics in that house") is insufficient even when it comes from a source of unquestioned reliability. *Gates* will doubtless make it easier to establish probable cause than it has been previously; the Court deemed it sufficient that the police had received an anonymous letter with a conclusory assertion of drug trafficking and then had corroborated the letter with certain predicted behavior that was not otherwise suspicious.

One extremely important question regarding the Fourth Amendment probable cause test is whether it is fixed or variable, that is, whether it always requires the same quantum of evidence or whether this compromise between privacy and law enforcement interests may be struck differently on a case-by-case basis. For example, may it be concluded that the solution of an unsolved murder is of greater public concern than the solution of an unsolved shoplifting, so that an arrest or search concerning the former would require less evidence than one respecting the latter offense? When confronted with that question in *Dunaway v. New York* (1979), the Court answered in the negative, saying such a variable standard would be impracticable: "A single, familiar standard is essential to guide police officers, who have only limited time and expertise to reflect on and balance the social and individual interests involved in the specific circumstances they confront."

Another supposed variable in *Dunaway* was that the police action at issue was a brief detention of the suspect at the police station, not recorded as an arrest. Though the Court there found the detention "indistinguishable from a traditional arrest" and thus subject to the usual probable cause requirement, on other occasions the Supreme Court has used a BALANCING TEST: when the police action is significantly less intrusive than the usual arrest or search, there is a corresponding reduction in the required factual basis justifying that action. The leading decision is the STOP AND FRISK case, TERRY V. OHIO (1968), which with later decisions may be taken to mean, first, that

a brief on-the-street detention of a suspect, a distinct police practice significantly less intrusive than a full-fledged arrest, is lawful upon a reasonable suspicion of criminality falling short of that needed to arrest; and second, that a frisk of that suspect for purposes of self-protection, a distinct police practice significantly less intrusive than a complete search of the person, is lawful upon a reasonable suspicion that the suspect is armed falling short of the probable cause required for a full search.

Although this balancing in *Terry* upheld a limited seizure and search on a watered-down version of probable cause, in other situations the Supreme Court has permitted very limited routine seizures or searches even absent any case-by-case showing of suspicion. Thus CAMARA V. MUNICIPAL COURT (1967) allowed a safety inspection of a dwelling, without any showing of the likelihood of code violations in that particular dwelling, where the inspection followed "reasonable legislative or administrative standards," such as those authorizing periodic inspection. And in *Delaware v. Prouse* (1979) the Court indicated its approval of stopping a vehicle for a driver's license and vehicle registration check, even absent suspicion that the driver was unlicensed or the car unregistered, as part of a roadblock conducted under standardized procedures.

Still another line of cases requires no factual basis for a particular seizure or search provided it is conducted in connection with some other search or seizure for which there is a sufficient basis. Where such relationships exist, the law would be very complex and difficult to apply if multiple factual bases were required, and thus sophistication has been rejected in favor of certain "bright lines" clearly marking the boundaries of permissible police conduct. Illustrative is UNITED STATES V. ROBINSON (1973), holding that a search of a person is permissible whenever that individual has just been subjected to a lawful custodial arrest. Though the Court in *Robinson* understood that search of the arrestee's person serves only to ensure that he does not have a weapon by which to make an escape or evidence of the crime which he might try to destroy or dispose of, it was not thought realistic to require separate police determinations whether there were grounds for arrest and whether the arrestee might be armed or in possession of evidence. Rather, the right to search was "piggybacked" onto the authority to arrest. By like reasoning, the Court held in *New York v. Belton* (1981) that the search of an automobile's passenger compartment can be piggybacked onto the contemporaneous arrest of an occupant, and in MICHIGAN V. SUMMERS (1981) that the brief detention of an occupant of a house can be piggybacked onto the contemporaneous execution of a search warrant for contraband there.

The Supreme Court has often expressed a preference for searches and seizures made pursuant to a warrant, reasoning that the warrant process protects Fourth Amendment rights by ensuring that critical decisions are made by "a neutral and detached magistrate." Thus the warrant-issuing authority may not be given to a prosecutor (COOLIDGE V. NEW HAMPSHIRE, 1971), or to a justice of the peace who receives a fee for warrants issued (*Connally v. Georgia*, 1977), but at least as to minor offenses may be granted to a clerk of the court acting under the supervision of a judge (*Shadwick v. City of Tampa*, 1972). The magistrate's responsibility is to make the critical probable cause decision which otherwise would be left to the police, and to ensure, as the Fourth Amendment requires, that the warrant describes the place to be searched and the person or things to be seized with such specificity that an officer can, as the Court put it in *Steele v. United States* (1925), "with reasonable effort ascertain and identify" the place, person, or thing intended.

Despite this preference for warrants, in many circumstances a search or seizure may constitutionally be made without a warrant. For one thing, no warrant need be obtained when EXIGENT CIRCUMSTANCES make a detour to a magistrate impracticable. Illustrative is the seminal AUTOMOBILE SEARCH case of CARROLL V. UNITED STATES (1925), where it was stressed that "it is not practicable to secure a warrant because the vehicle can be quickly moved out of the locality or jurisdiction in which the warrant must be sought." However, the Court has not always dealt with the exigent circumstances issue in a consistent fashion. In CHAMBERS V. MARONEY (1970) the Court extended the *Carroll* rule to a vehicle that was in police custody and inaccessible to anyone else. On the other hand, in *Vale v. Louisiana* (1970) the Court chastised the police for not having obtained a search warrant a day earlier, though the probable cause needed for its issuance had unexpectedly come to the attention of the officer for the first time just minutes before the warrantless search of the arrestee's dwelling.

These different attitudes suggest that considerations other than "exigent circumstances" are at play. For example, the Court is less willing to recognize exceptions to the warrant requirement for dwelling searches than for vehicle searches. Apparently perceiving that its expanded vehicle search rule could not be explained in terms of exigent circumstances, the Court in *United States v. Chadwick* (1977) offered another explanation: vehicles have a "diminished ex-

pectation of privacy" which makes them unworthy of the usual Fourth Amendment warrant requirement. Yet in *Arkansas v. Sanders* (1979) the Court found no such diminished expectation in a suitcase, even when placed in a vehicle. It is not immediately apparent why placing one's personal items in the trunk of a car manifests less of a privacy expectation than placing those same items in some other type of container. Perhaps that is why the Court responded in *United States v. Ross* (1982) with this curious rule for the container-in-a-car cases: the *Chambers* no-warrant rule applies if there is probable cause to search the entire vehicle, but the *Sanders* warrant rule applies if there is probable cause to search only the container in the vehicle.

Some decisions reflect the Court's belief that certain police intrusions are more serious than others and that the warrant process is necessary only for the more serious ones. Intrusions upon a possessory interest are generally viewed as less serious than intrusions into a privacy interest; the former alone do not require warrants. *Coolidge v. New Hampshire* teaches that if the police are lawfully present in a place executing a search warrant and find items they believe are subject to seizure but which are not named in the warrant, they usually may make a warrantless seizure of them and need not return to the magistrate for another warrant. By contrast, when the police come into lawful possession of a closed container, for example, one which was turned over to them because misdelivered, as in *Walter v. United States* (1980), further intrusion into the privacy of the container ordinarily requires a warrant.

Similar analysis partly explains the rule of UNITED STATES V. WATSON (1976) that an arrest in a public place may be made without a warrant even if there was ample opportunity to obtain one. The Court did not consider such a seizure as great a threat to Fourth Amendment values as, say, the search of a dwelling. Thus the situation changes if the arrest can be made only by entering private premises; the Court held in PAYTON V. NEW YORK (1980) that a warrant is then required absent true exigent circumstances. The situation also changes if the seizure of the person becomes more intrusive. As the Court explained in *Gerstein v. Pugh* (1975), no warrant is needed merely for "a brief period of detention to take the administrative steps incident to arrest," but if the arrestee is not promptly released then "the Fourth Amendment requires a judicial determination of probable cause as a prerequisite to extended restraint on liberty following arrest."

Yet another theme runs through the Court's decisions: no warrant is necessary when there is little for the magistrate to decide. The most obvious illustration is the rule that no search warrant is required for an inventory of an impounded vehicle because there are no special facts for the magistrate to evaluate. The point is also illustrated by comparing *Payton* with STEAGALD V. UNITED STATES (1981). Together the two cases stand for the proposition that an arrest warrant alone justifies entry into the intended arrestee's home to arrest him but not entry into a third party's home, which usually requires a search warrant. In the former situation, unlike the latter, there is no substantial need for a magistrate to determine on a case-by-case basis whether the suspect will probably be found in his own home. Sometimes, as in *Camara v. Municipal Court,* requiring warrants for housing inspections but permitting their issuance without a case-by-case probable cause showing, the Court has been sharply divided on the question of whether resort to the warrant process would be meaningful.

Still another consideration in the warrant cases of the Court is the need for "bright lines," the notion that case-by-case assessments simply are not feasible as to certain matters, so that a general rule applicable to all cases of a certain type is necessary. An example is *United States v. Watson,* holding that no warrant is required to arrest in a public place; a contrary holding, the Court said, would "encumber criminal prosecutions with endless litigation with respect to the existence of exigent circumstances, whether it was practicable to get a warrant, whether the suspect was about to flee, and the like." But in CHIMEL V. CALIFORNIA (1969) the Court overruled cases permitting a warrantless search of premises contemporaneous with a lawful arrest therein, rejecting the dissenters' claim that the earlier "bright line" rule was necessary because there often is "a strong possibility that confederates of the arrested man will in the meanwhile remove the items for which the police have probable cause to search."

The probable cause and warrant requirements of the Fourth Amendment limit the government only. They have no application to private illegal searches and seizures, as where a private person breaks into premises, seizes evidence of crime found therein, and turns that evidence over to the authorities. But if a government official should instigate or participate in such an activity, that involvement would make the private person an agent of the government. Though most Fourth Amendment cases involve the actions of police officers, the amendment unquestionably applies to other government officials as well.

The limitations of the Fourth Amendment extend only to "searches" and "seizures." The term "seizure" is considerably broader than "arrest"; thus the fact that a particular detention is not called an arrest or is less intrusive than an arrest does not mean the amendment is inapplicable. As the Court put it in *Terry v. Ohio,* "whenever a police officer accosts an individual and restrains his freedom to walk away, he has 'seized' that person." That formulation leaves unresolved an issue of perspective: is the question whether the officer intended to restrain, or whether the suspect believed he was restrained? Either of these subjective states of mind would be difficult to prove apart from the self-serving statements of the officer and suspect, respectively, and thus an objective test is preferable. The courts, including the Supreme Court, have given insufficient attention to this matter. In *Florida v. Royer* (1983) a majority of the Court expressed the view "that a person has been 'seized' within the meaning of the Fourth Amendment only if, in view of all of the circumstances surrounding the incident, a reasonable person would have believed that he was not free to leave." But few people feel free to walk away during a police–citizen encounter, and thus a workable test may require consideration whether the officer added to the inherent pressures by engaging in menacing conduct significantly beyond that accepted in social intercourse. Some governmental pressure causing a person to be in a certain place at a certain time, such as the GRAND JURY subpoena upheld in UNITED STATES V. DIONISIO (1973), does not amount to a Fourth Amendment seizure.

More difficult is the definition of a "search" within the meaning of the Fourth Amendment. The view requiring a physical intrusion into "a constitutionally protected area" was finally abandoned in KATZ V. UNITED STATES (1967), which involved ELECTRONIC EAVESDROPPING upon one end of a telephone conversation with a device attached to the outside of a public telephone booth. The Court held that this conduct was a search because the government "violated the privacy upon which [Katz] justifiably relied while using the telephone booth." Justice JOHN MARSHALL HARLAN, concurring in *Katz* in an opinion often relied upon by lower courts, enunciated "a twofold requirement, first that a person have exhibited an actual (subjective) expectation of privacy and, second, that the expectation be one that society is prepared to recognize as 'reasonable.'"

The first of these two requirements clearly deserves no place in a theory of what the Fourth Amendment protects. Were it otherwise, as Anthony Amsterdam aptly put it, "the government could diminish each person's subjective expectation of privacy merely by announcing half-hourly on television . . . that we were all forthwith being placed under comprehensive electronic surveillance." Justice Harlan later came around to this position, counseling in his dissenting opinion in UNITED STATES V. WHITE (1971) that analysis under *Katz* must "transcend the search for subjective expectations," because our expectations "are in large part reflections of laws that translate into rules the customs and values of the past and present." A majority of the Court continues to use the "actual (subjective) expectation of privacy" formulation, but cautioned in *Smith v. Maryland* (1979) that in some situations it "would provide an inadequate index of Fourth Amendment protection."

The Court has sometimes referred to the second *Katz* requirement simply as the "reasonable 'expectation of privacy'" test. From this, it might be assumed that investigative activity constitutes a search whenever it uncovers incriminating actions or objects which the law's hypothetical reasonable man would have expected to remain private, that is, those which as a matter of statistical probability were not likely to be discovered. But such an approach is unsound. Rather, as Justice Harlan later explained in his *United States v. White* dissent, the question here must "be answered by assessing the nature of a particular practice and the likely extent of its impact on the individual's sense of security balanced against the utility of the conduct as a technique of law enforcement." In Amsterdam's words, at the heart of the matter is "a value judgment": "whether, if the particular form of surveillance practiced by the police is permitted to go unregulated by constitutional restraints, the amount of privacy and freedom remaining to citizens would be diminished to a compass inconsistent with the aims of a free and open society."

Although *Katz*, so viewed, offers a useful approach to the question of what the Fourth Amendment protects, the Court's application of the test has been neither consistent nor cautious, as can be seen by comparing MARSHALL V. BARLOW'S INC. (1978) with *Smith v. Maryland* (1979). In *Marshall*, holding unconstitutional the warrantless inspection of business premises, the Court expressly rejected the government's claim that a businessman lacked any privacy expectation vis-à-vis the government when there was no such expectation as to others (in this instance, his employees). Rather, the Court reached the sensible conclusion that an unconsented entry would be a Fourth Amendment search even though the area entered was regularly used by the company's employees. But a year later, in *Smith*, rejecting the claim that there was a "legitimate expectation of privacy" in the numbers one dials

on his telephone, the Court, though asserting that "our lodestar is *Katz*," concluded there was no such privacy expectation vis-à-vis the government because the telephone company's switching equipment had the capacity to record that information for certain limited business purposes. This unfortunate all-or-nothing view of privacy, as Justice THURGOOD MARSHALL noted in dissent, means that "unless a person is prepared to forego use of what for many has become a personal or professional necessity, he cannot help but accept the risk of surveillance."

In still another situation the Fourth Amendment's probable cause and warrant requirements are not applicable. This situation is most commonly called a CONSENT SEARCH, although when the facilitating party is active rather than passive it may be characterized as involving no search at all. At one time the consent doctrine was assumed to be grounded on the concept of waiver, but in SCHNECKLOTH V. BUSTAMONTE (1973) the Court, saying such an approach "would be thoroughly inconsistent with our decisions," held that the underlying issue was whether the person's consent was "voluntary." One reason the concept of waiver is inappropriate here is because it has long been recognized that sometimes one party may give a consent that will be effective against another. As the Court put it in *United States v. Matlock* (1974), where two or more persons have joint access to or control of premises "it is reasonable to recognize that any of the coinhabitants has the right to permit the inspection in his own right and that the others have assumed the risk that one of their number might permit the common area to be searched." The Court in *Matlock* found it unnecessary to pass upon the correctness of a position taken by several lower courts, namely, that the Fourth Amendment's reasonableness requirement is met if the police reasonably but mistakenly conclude that the consenting person has such authority.

The Fourth Amendment was a largely unexplored territory until BOYD V. UNITED STATES (1886), where the Supreme Court, weaving together the Fourth and Fifth Amendments, concluded that "the seizure of a man's private books and papers to be used in evidence against him" was not "substantially different from compelling him to be a witness against himself" and thus held that physical evidence the defendant was required to produce was inadmissible. *Boyd* was later confined by *Adams v. New York* (1904) to the situation in which a positive act was required of the defendant, but in WEEKS V. UNITED STATES (1914) the Court ruled that the "effect of the 4th Amendment" is to forbid federal courts to admit into evidence the fruits of Fourth Amendment violations. The same could not be said of the state courts, the Supreme Court decided in WOLF V. COLORADO (1949); whether exclusion of evidence was the best way to enforce the Fourth Amendment was "an issue as to which men with complete devotion to the protection of the RIGHT OF PRIVACY might give different answers." *Wolf* was overruled in MAPP V. OHIO (1961), where the majority concluded that other remedies for Fourth Amendment violations had proven worthless. Without an EXCLUSIONARY RULE operative at both the state and the federal level, the Constitution's assurance against unreasonable searches and seizures "would be 'a form of words,' valueless and undeserving of mention in a perpetual charter of inestimable human liberties."

Over the years the Court has given various explanations of the rationale for this exclusionary rule. In ELKINS V. UNITED STATES (1960) the Court emphasized "the imperative of judicial integrity"—that the courts not become "accomplices in the willful disobedience of a Constitution they are sworn to uphold." A second purpose, articulated by Justice WILLIAM J. BRENNAN, dissenting in UNITED STATES V. CALANDRA (1974), is that "of assuring the people—all potential victims of unlawful government conduct—that the government would not profit from its lawless behavior, thus minimizing the risk of seriously undermining popular trust in government." This second purpose is reflected in opinions as early as *Weeks*. Yet a third purpose, not explicitly mentioned in the earlier cases, is that of deterring unreasonable searches and seizures. Thus, in *Elkins* the Court emphasized: "The rule is calculated to prevent, not to repair. Its purpose is to deter—to compel respect for the constitutional guaranty in the only effectively available way—by removing the incentive to disregard it." In recent years the Court has relied almost exclusively upon this deterrence rationale.

Over the years the deterrence issue has occasioned intense debate; some claim the exclusionary rule does not deter and should be abandoned, and others claim that it does and should be retained. Hard evidence supporting either claim is unavailable, but some argue that a deterrent effect may be assumed because of such post-exclusionary-rule phenomena as the dramatic increase in the use of warrants and stepped-up efforts to educate the police on the law of search and seizure. The debate has recently centered on a proposed "good faith" exception to the Fourth Amendment exclusionary rule, allowing admission of illegally obtained evidence if the searching or seizing officer acted in a reasonable belief that his conduct

was constitutionally permissible. A limited version of the exception was adopted by the Court in UNITED STATES V. LEON (1984), where the exclusionary rule was "modified so as not to bar the use in the prosecution's case-in-chief of evidence obtained by officers acting in reasonable reliance on a search warrant issued by a detached and neutral magistrate but ultimately found to be unsupported by probable cause." The majority reasoned that exclusion for purposes of deterrence was unnecessary in such circumstances, as exclusion would have no significant deterrent effect on the magistrate who issued the warrant, and there is no need to deter the policeman who justifiably relied upon the prior judgment of the magistrate. Whether *Leon* will be a stepping-stone to adoption of a broader (and, it would seem, less justifiable and more difficult to apply) "good faith" exception, applicable also in without-warrant cases, remains to be seen.

The current dimensions of the Fourth Amendment exclusionary rule are mostly tailored to the deterrence rationale. The rule is not used in certain settings on the assumption that the incremental gain in deterrence is not worth the cost. Illustrative are *United States v. Calandra,* refusing to compel exclusion at the behest of a grand jury witness because it "would achieve a speculative and undoubtedly minimal advance in the deterrence of police misconduct at the expense of substantially impending the role of the grand jury"; and *United States v. Janis* (1976), declining to require exclusion in federal tax litigation of evidence uncovered in a state criminal investigation of gambling because "common sense dictates that the deterrent effect of the exclusion of relevant evidence is highly attenuated when the 'punishment' imposed upon the offending criminal enforcement officer is the removal of that evidence from a civil suit by or against a different sovereign." Even in the context of a criminal trial the deterrent objective of the exclusionary rule is sometimes perceived as outweighed by competing considerations. This explains the rule in *Walder v. United States* (1954) that the government may use illegally obtained evidence to impeach the defendant's testimony, so that the defendant cannot "turn the illegal method by which evidence in the Government's possession was obtained to his own advantage, and provide himself with a shield against contradiction of his untruths."

Who may invoke the exclusionary rule? The rule of STANDING generally is that a constitutional challenge may be raised only by those who have an interest in the outcome of the controversy, and who are objecting to a violation of their own rights. A defendant in a criminal case against whom illegally obtained evidence is being offered certainly meets the first requirement, but he does not necessarily meet the second. As to the latter, the fundamental question is whether the challenged conduct intruded upon his freedom or expectation of privacy or only that of someone else, as *Rakas v. Illinois* (1978) illustrates. The Court held that passengers in a car did not have standing to object to a search under the seats and in the glove compartment of that vehicle. Essential to the holding were the conclusions that these passengers were not claiming that the car had been illegally stopped, that they "asserted neither a property nor a possessory interest in the automobile, nor an interest in the property seized," and that the areas searched were ones "in which a passenger *qua* passenger simply would not have a legitimate expectation of privacy." The Supreme Court refused in ALDERMAN V. UNITED STATES (1969) to adopt a rule of "target standing" allowing a defendant to object to any Fourth Amendment violation committed for the purpose of acquiring evidence for use against him. This refusal limits to some extent the deterrent effect of the exclusionary rule, for police sometimes deliberately direct an illegal search at one person because they are seeking evidence to use against another person they know will not be able to question their conduct.

What evidence is subject to challenge under the exclusionary rule? Under the FRUIT OF THE POISONOUS TREE doctrine, the exclusionary rule applies not only to the immediate and direct fruits of a Fourth Amendment violation (the physical evidence found in a search), but also to secondary or derivative evidence (a confession acquired by confronting a person with that physical evidence). Of course, in a criminal investigation the discovery of one fact often plays some part in the discovery of many others, and they in turn contribute to the uncovering of still others, and so on, but the fruits doctrine is not pushed this far. Even the fact first discovered by an illegal act does not become forever "inaccessible" for court use: it may still be proved "if knowledge of [the fact] is [also] gained from an independent source," as in SILVERTHORNE LUMBER CO. V. UNITED STATES (1920). The "inevitable discovery" doctrine accepted in *Nix v. Williams* (1984), whereunder illegally obtained evidence is admissible if "the prosecution can establish by a preponderance of the evidence that the information ultimately or inevitably would have been discovered by lawful means," likewise serves to put the police in no worse position than they would have been

if their misconduct had not occurred. Another limitation is provided by the test in *Wong Sun v. United States*: "whether, granting establishment of the primary illegality, the evidence to which instant objection is made has been come at by exploitation of that illegality or instead by means sufficiently distinguishable to be purged of the primary taint." In that case the taint of one defendant's illegal arrest was deemed dissipated by his release on his own recognizance, so that the taint did not reach a subsequently given confession. Considerations close to the deterrent function of the exclusionary rule also come into play here. Thus, suppression of derivative evidence is much more likely if it appears that the primary illegality was a clearly unconstitutional act or that it was undertaken for the purpose of acquiring that derivative evidence. For example, a confession will be deemed the fruit of an obviously illegal arrest made in the hope of acquiring a confession.

It cannot be denied that there is ample room for reasonable disagreement regarding the rationales and results of a number of the Supreme Court's Fourth Amendment decisions. In the main, however, the Court's response to the four fundamental questions just discussed has been indisputably appropriate and sound. The decisions on the requisite factual basis for a seizure or search have generally struck a fair balance between privacy and law enforcement interests. The Court's rulings regarding the warrant requirement have prevented the warrant process from becoming so overburdened as to become a mechanical and meaningless routine, yet have provided added protection to those Fourth Amendment interests that are valued most. The decisions defining the activities to which the amendment applies—especially *Katz* and its justified expectation of privacy test—provide an approach that should enable the Court to protect against new threats to the individual's right to be free of intrusive government surveillance. Finally, it is the Court's insistence upon an exclusionary rule as an enforcement mechanism that has kept the Fourth Amendment from being reduced to "a form of words."

WAYNE R. LaFAVE

Bibliography

AMSTERDAM, ANTHONY G. 1974 Perspectives on the Fourth Amendment. *Minnesota Law Review* 58:349–477.

GRANO, JOSEPH D. 1978 Perplexing Questions about Three Basic Fourth Amendment Issues: Fourth Amendment Activity, Probable Cause, and the Warrant Requirement. *Journal of Criminal Law and Criminology* 69:425–463.

KAMISAR, YALE 1983 Does (Did) (Should) the Exclusionary Rule Rest on a "Principled Basis" Rather Than an "Empirical Proposition"? *Creighton Law Review* 16:565–667.

LAFAVE, WAYNE R. 1978 *Search and Seizure: A Treatise on the Fourth Amendment,* 3 vols. St. Paul, Minn.: West Publishing Co.

LANDYNSKI, JACOB W. 1966 *Search and Seizure and the Supreme Court.* Baltimore, Md.: Johns Hopkins University Press.

OAKS, DALLIN H. 1970 Studying the Exclusionary Rule. *University of Chicago Law Review* 37:665–757.

UNITED STATES, CONGRESS, SENATE COMMITTEE ON THE JUDICIARY, SUBCOMMITTEE ON CRIMINAL LAW 1982 *The Exclusionary Rule Bills,* 97th Cong., 1st & 2d sess.

SEARCH INCIDENT TO ARREST

WEEKS V. UNITED STATES (1914) recognized, as an exception to the FOURTH AMENDMENT's requirement of a SEARCH WARRANT, the authority of police to search a person incident to his arrest in order to discover concealed weapons or evidence. This principle has remained essentially unchallenged, although its application to a person arrested for a minor offense, such as a traffic violation, involving small likelihood of danger to the officer, was severely criticized by some Justices in UNITED STATES V. ROBINSON (1973). Extension of the allowable search from the person of the arrestee to include the area "in his control," in AGNELLO V. UNITED STATES (1925), planted the seed of conflict between those Justices who would allow a complete search of the premises and those who would limit the search to the area from which the arrestee could conceivably reach for weapons to wield or evidence to destroy.

Marron v. United States (1927) allowed the search to cover "all parts of the premises," but in *Go Bart v. United States* (1931) and *United States v. Lefkowitz* (1932) the Court condemned wholesale "rummaging of the place." Again, *Harris v. United States* (1947) upheld the search of an entire apartment, but *Trupiano v. United States* (1948) forebade even the seizure of contraband in PLAIN VIEW of the arresting officers. The pendulum again swung in *United States v. Rabinowitz* (1950), which authorized search of the whole place. By now the field was "a quagmire," as Justice TOM C. CLARK exclaimed, dissenting in CHAPMAN V. UNITED STATES (1961). One group of Justices took the position, essentially, that once officers are legitimately on premises to make an arrest, the accompanying search, no matter how extensive, is only a minor additional invasion of privacy and therefore reasonable. They conceded that the arrest must not serve as a pretext for the search, and that the search must be limited to objects for which the arrest was made, but these limitations are easily evaded. Justice FELIX FRANKFURTER provided intellectual leadership for the opposing view, arguing that when a search incident to arrest is allowed to extend beyond the need that gave rise to it, the exception swallows up the rule that a warrant must be obtained save in EXIGENT CIRCUMSTANCES. Moreover, because a warrant often will strictly limit the area to be searched, to authorize search of the entire premises has the novel effect of allowing searches incident to arrest a broader scope than searches under warrant.

So the matter stood until CHIMEL V. CALIFORNIA (1969). There the Court restored the balance between theory and practice by overruling *Harris* and *Rabinowitz* and limiting the scope of incident searches to the person of the arrestee and his immediate environs. Still, the *Chimel* limitation may not always apply. Where the police have strong reason to believe that confederates of the arrestee are hidden on the premises, they are presumably entitled, under the "hot pursuit" doctrine of WARDEN V. HAYDEN (1967), to make a "sweep" of the place in order to minimize the danger. The reverse would also seem to follow: once the arrestee has been subdued (assuming there is no reason to suspect the presence of confederates), the police no longer have authority to search even a limited area.

An important legal difference between search of the person's clothing and search of property within the area of his reach should be noted. Property under the arrestee's control, which might have been searched without a warrant immediately following the arrest, may not be searched later; to be lawful under *United States v. Chadwick* (1977) the search must be substantially contemporaneous with the arrest. However, in a radical departure from the spirit, if not the letter, of the *Chimel* rule, the Court held in *United States v. Edwards* (1974) that authority to search the arrestee's clothing is not lost by the passage of time and may be exercised hours later, following his incarceration. The rationale for this difference appears to be that the arrestee's expectation of privacy in property not associated with his person remains undiminished. Absent a warrant, the property search must therefore be carried out promptly, as an exigency measure, or not at all.

Under ILLINOIS V. LAFAYETTE (1983), an arrestee's

possessions may be inventoried in the police station prior to his incarceration so as to safeguard them against theft and protect the officers against spurious claims. Because it is considered a reasonable administrative procedure, "the inventory search constitutes a well-defined exception to the warrant requirement."

JACOB W. LANDYNSKI

Bibliography

LAFAVE, WAYNE R. 1978 *Search and Seizure: A Treatise on the Fourth Amendment.* Vol. 2:406–466. St. Paul, Minn.: West Publishing Co.

LANDYNSKI, JACOB W. 1966 *Search and Seizure and the Supreme Court.* Pages 87, 98–117. Baltimore: Johns Hopkins University Press.

———— 1971 The Supreme Court's Search for Fourth Amendment Standards. *Connecticut Bar Journal* 45:2–30.

SEARCH WARRANT

The FOURTH AMENDMENT to the Constitution prohibits unreasonable SEARCHES AND SEIZURES and provides that "No Warrants shall issue, but upon PROBABLE CAUSE, supported by Oath or Affirmation, and particularly describing the place to be searched, and the persons or things to be seized." The Framers adopted the warrant clause in response to the use by British customs officers of GENERAL WARRANTS, known as WRITS OF ASSISTANCE, to enforce British trade laws.

A writ of assistance conveyed virtually unbridled discretion to search under the authority of the Crown. The writ was not required to be based on any facts giving reason to believe that a crime had been committed. Nor did it contain an inventory of things to be taken, the names of alleged offenders, or any limitation on the places to be searched. Once issued, a writ remained valid during the lifetime of the reigning sovereign.

Judicial interpretations of the warrant clause have expressed a strong preference for the use of a neutral and detached magistrate over the "hurried action" of a police officer engaged in the often competitive enterprise of ferreting out crime. Since COOLIDGE v. NEW HAMPSHIRE (1971) searches conducted outside the judicial process have been considered by the Supreme Court to be unreasonable per se unless they fall within one of the exceptions to the warrant requirement.

A magistrate who issues a search warrant may not occupy a dual role, both reviewing the facts presented to justify the warrant and actively participating in the criminal investigation or prosecution. Such a dual role creates a conflict of interest that is inimical to the objectives of the warrant clause. As the Supreme Court observed in UNITED STATES v. UNITED STATES DISTRICT COURT (1972), the Fourth Amendment protections cannot be properly guaranteed if searches "may be conducted solely within the discretion of the Executive Branch."

An important part of the Fourth Amendment's proscription against general warrants is that a warrant may be issued only upon probable cause. This requirement necessarily limits each warrant to a particular set of circumstances relating to a suspected criminal offense. The alleged facts must establish a reasonable basis to believe that the offense was committed and that contraband or EVIDENCE of the offense is located at the place to be searched. Although a finding of probable cause may rest upon HEARSAY or other evidence that would not be admissible at trial, the issuing magistrate must nonetheless carefully consider the reliability of such evidence. According to ILLINOIS v. GATES (1983), in assessing probable cause, a magistrate must make a "practical, commonsense" decision in view of all the circumstances set forth in the affidavit, including the "veracity" and "basis of knowledge" of the persons supplying the information.

The information that forms the basis for the search warrant must be sworn to by "oath and affirmation" at the time the warrant is issued. To ensure an independent review by the magistrate, the oath must attest to facts and circumstances, not merely to the affiant's conclusion that he believes he has probable cause for the search. Moreover, an insufficient affidavit cannot be rehabilitated later by testimony concerning facts known by the affiant or otherwise available, but not disclosed to the magistrate at the time of issuance of the warrant. A contrary rule, of course, would render the warrant requirement meaningless.

An important issue that remained unresolved until *Franks v. Delaware* (1978) was whether the accuracy of the information relied on to justify a search warrant may be challenged. In *Franks* the Supreme Court held that if it can be shown that the affiant intentionally or recklessly gave false or misleading information to the magistrate, a reviewing court may invalidate the warrant if the magistrate's finding of probable cause was based on the misinformation.

The warrant clause also precludes the issuance of general search warrants, for it commands that the warrant describe with particularity the place to be searched and the objects to be seized. In *Gouled v. United States* (1921) the Supreme Court held that law enforcement officers could not seize property, even though particularly described in a search warrant, when the property was merely of evidentiary value in a criminal proceeding. This MERE EVIDENCE RULE, which attempted to distinguish between mere evidence and contraband or other property that was a fruit or instrumentality of a crime, was both unsound and lacking in reason and historical support. The Court abandoned the rule in WARDEN V. HAYDEN (1967).

The purpose of the particularity requirement is to limit implicitly the scope of what the officer executing the warrant may do. As the Court stated in *Marron v. United States* (1927): "The requirement that warrants shall particularly describe the things to be seized makes general searches under them impossible and prevents the seizure of one thing under a warrant describing another. As to what is to be taken, nothing is left to the discretion of the officer executing the warrant." With respect to the place to be searched, the description must be such that the officer executing the warrant can, with reasonable effort, ascertain and identify the place intended.

As a practical matter, of course, law enforcement officers may not be completely divested of all discretion in executing search warrants. Moreover, notwithstanding the language in *Marron*, the Court has held that incriminating evidence not listed in a search warrant may be seized when observed in plain view by officers executing the warrant, provided that the officers inadvertently come upon the evidence. The particularity requirement, however, greatly circumscribes the officer's discretion and therefore plays an important role in minimizing the likelihood of police abuse.

JAMES R. ASPERGER

Bibliography

LAFAVE, WAYNE R.   1978   *Search and Seizure: A Treatise on the Fourth Amendment.* Vol. 2:1–213. St. Paul, Minn.: West Publishing Co.

LASSON, NELSON B.   1937   *The History and Development of the Fourth Amendment to the United States Constitution.* Baltimore: Johns Hopkins University Press.

SECESSION

Secession, the withdrawal of a state from the American Union, first appeared as an impulse rather than an articulated constitutional doctrine. Inchoate secessionist movements agitated the southwestern frontier after the signing of JAY'S TREATY (1794). AARON

BURR's alleged conspiracy was linked to them. Massachusetts Federalists who were disgruntled about the rising political power of the South and the western territories between 1803 and 1814 contemplated secession in correspondence among themselves. Before the Civil War, Garrisonian abolitionists developed doctrines of disunion, calling for both individual disallegiance and the withdrawal of the free states from a union with the slave states. Southern political leaders, uneasy about the spread of abolitionist and Free Soil sentiment in the north, occasionally voiced threats of secession.

JOHN C. CALHOUN developed the theoretical framework for secession, though ironically, he did so in order to avoid secession through the alternatives of INTERPOSITION and NULLIFICATION. Drawing on the thought of earlier STATES' RIGHTS ideologues such as JOHN TAYLOR of Caroline, JOHN RANDOLPH, and THOMAS COOPER, as well as the concepts of state sovereignty and the Union broached in the VIRGINIA AND KENTUCKY RESOLUTIONS of 1798–1799, Calhoun insisted that SOVEREIGNTY in America resided not in the nation but severally in the people of each of the states. The states created the national government, giving it only limited, specific, and delegated powers. The national government was thus the agent or the trustee for the people of the states, and the federal Constitution was merely a "compact" among sovereign states. If the national government abused its delegated powers by unconstitutional legislation or executive acts, the states could interpose their authority between the federal government and their people and could nullify federal legislation within their territory. But if enough other states ratified an amendment to the federal Constitution that authorized the nullified act, then the states had only the option of submitting to or withdrawing from the Union.

After the election of ABRAHAM LINCOLN in 1860, South Carolina radicals induced the legislature to call a convention to consider secession. The convention voted unanimously for secession, and in the "Declaration of the Immediate Causes [of] Secession" (1860) they asserted that the free states had violated the constitutional compact by failing to enforce the Fugitive Slave Acts vigorously and by enacting PERSONAL LIBERTY LAWS that impeded the recapture of fugitive slaves. The free states also had denied slaveholders' right of transit through their territory with their slaves, agitated against slavery, tolerated abolitionist societies, and permitted dissemination of abolitionist propaganda. They had permitted blacks to vote and had elected a sectional presidential candidate determined to effect the eventual abolition of slavery. Thus South Carolina, in order to protect its people and its peculiar institution, severed the union binding it to the other states and reassumed its status as "a separate and independent state."

Though all slave states were deeply divided over the wisdom and constitutionality of secession, Mississippi, Florida, Alabama, Georgia, Louisiana, and Texas also seceded by February 1, 1861. These seven states formed the Confederate States of America in February. After the firing on Fort Sumter, Virginia, North Carolina, Tennessee, and Arkansas seceded. A proslavery rump session of the Missouri legislature and a convention of Kentucky Confederate soldiers declared their states seceded, but both states, as well as the other border slave states, remained in the Union. After the defeat of southern forces in 1865, most of the Confederate states repudiated secession, but diehards in South Carolina merely repealed their secession ordinance instead of nullifying it. Nonetheless, secession as a constitutional remedy was dead, and the United States was thenceforth "one nation, indivisible."

WILLIAM M. WIECEK

SECOND AMENDMENT

However controversial the meaning of the Second Amendment is today, it was clear enough to the generation of 1789. The amendment assured to the people "their private arms," said an article which received JAMES MADISON's approval and was the only analysis available to Congress when it voted. Subsequent contemporaneous analysis is epitomized by the first American commentary on the writings of WILLIAM BLACKSTONE. Where Blackstone described arms for personal defense as among the "absolute rights of individuals" at COMMON LAW, his eighteenth-century American editor commented that this right had been constitutionalized by the Second Amendment. Early constitutional commentators, including JOSEPH STORY, William Rawle, and THOMAS M. COOLEY, described the amendment in terms of a republican philosophical tradition stemming from Aristotle's observation that basic to tyrants is a "mistrust of the people; hence they deprive them of arms." Political theorists from Cicero to JOHN LOCKE and Jean-Jacques Rousseau also held arms possession to be symbolic of personal freedom and vital to the virtuous, self-reliant citizenry (defending itself from encroachment by outlaws, tyrants, and foreign invaders alike) that they deemed indispensable to popular government.

These assumptions informed both sides of the debate over RATIFICATION OF THE CONSTITUTION. While Madison, in THE FEDERALIST #46 assured Americans that they need never fear the federal government because of "the advantage of being armed, which you possess over the people of almost every other nation," opponents of ratification such as PATRICK HENRY declaimed: "The great principle is that every man be armed. Everyone who is able may have a gun." SAMUEL ADAMS proposed that "the Constitution never be construed . . . to prevent the people of the United States who are peaceable citizens from keeping their own arms." As much of this debate used the word "militia," it is necessary to remember that in the eighteenth century the militia was coextensive with the adult male citizenry. By colonial law every household was required to possess arms and every male of military age was required to muster during military emergencies, bearing his own arms. The amendment, in guaranteeing the arms of each citizen, simultaneously guaranteed arms for the militia.

In contrast to the original interpretation of the amendment as a personal right to arms is the twentieth-century view that it protects only the states' right to arm their own military forces, including their national guard units. This view stresses the Anti-Federalists' bitter opposition to the provisions of Article I, section 8, authorizing a standing army and granting the federal government various powers over state militias. Both textual and historical difficulties preclude acceptance of this exclusively STATES' RIGHTS view. For instance, Madison's proposed organization for the provisions of the BILL OF RIGHTS was not to append them, but to interpolate each amendment into the Constitution following the provision to which it pertained. Had he viewed the amendment as modifying the military-militia clauses of the Constitution (which he strongly defended against Anti-Federalist criticism), he would have appended it to those clauses in section 8. Instead, he planned to place what are now the First and Second Amendments in Article I, section 9, along with the original Constitution's guarantees against BILLS OF ATTAINDER and EX POST FACTO LAWS and against suspension of HABEAS CORPUS.

The states' rights interpretation simply cannot be squared with the amendment's words: "right of the people." It is impossible to believe that the First Congress used "right of the people" in the FIRST AMENDMENT to describe an individual right (FREEDOM OF ASSEMBLY), but sixteen words later in the Second Amendment to describe a right vested exclusively in the states. Moreover, "right of the people" is used again to refer to personal rights in the FOURTH AMENDMENT and the NINTH AMENDMENT, and the TENTH AMENDMENT expressly distinguishes "the people" from "the states."

Interpreting the Second Amendment as a guarantee of an individual right does not foreclose all gun controls. The ownership of firearms by minors, felons, and the mentally impaired—and the carrying of them outside the home by anyone—may be limited or banned. Moreover, the government may limit the types of arms that may be kept; there is no right, for example, to own artillery or automatic weapons, or the weapons of the footpad and gangster, such as sawed-off shotguns and blackjacks. Gun controls in the form of registration and licensing requirements are also permissible so long as the ordinary citizen's right to possess arms for home protection is respected.

DON B. KATES, JR.

Bibliography

HALBROOK, STEVEN 1984 *That Every Man Be Armed: The Evolution of a Constitutional Right.* Albuquerque: University of New Mexico Press.

KATES, DON B., JR. 1983 Handgun Prohibition and the Original Meaning of the Second Amendment. *Michigan Law Review* 82:204–273.

MALCOLM, JOYCE 1983 The Right of the People to Keep and Bear Arms: The Common Law Tradition. *Hastings Constitutional Law Quarterly* 10:285–314.

SHALHOPE, ROBERT E. 1982 The Ideological Origins of the Second Amendment. *Journal of American History* 69:599–614.

SECONDARY BOYCOTT

See: Boycotts and the Constitution

SECOND EMPLOYERS' LIABILITY CASES

See: Employers' Liability Cases

SECTION 1983, TITLE 42, UNITED STATES CODE
(Judicial Interpretation)

Few statutes have fluctuated in importance as wildly as section 1983. From near total disuse—twenty-one reported cases from 1871 to 1920—it became one of the most litigated provisions of federal law. This drastic change is attributable both to developments in constitutional law and to developments peculiar to section 1983.

Section 1983's ascension matches the twentieth-century expansion of constitutional rights. As originally enacted in the Civil Rights Act of 1871, section 1983 at most provided a cause of action for deprivations, under color of state law, of constitutional rights. Until relatively recently, citizens had few constitutional rights enforceable against the states. In section 1983's early years, the modern expansions of the EQUAL PROTECTION and DUE PROCESS clauses had not occurred, the STATE ACTION doctrine immunized a broad range of activity from constitutional scrutiny, and the FOURTH AMENDMENT was in the infancy of its constitutional development.

An ill-considered dichotomy between classes of constitutional rights also hindered section 1983's growth. In an influential separate opinion in HAGUE v. CIO (1939), Justice HARLAN FISKE STONE argued that section 1983's jurisdictional counterpart, section 1343(3), should be interpreted to authorize federal courts to hear cases involving personal rights but not to hear cases involving mere property rights. This view influenced many courts' interpretations of section 1983 itself, again with limiting effect. In *Lynch v. Household Finance Corporation* (1972) the Court rejected the personal rights/property rights distinction. Paradoxically, a similar dichotomy between personal interests and economic interests continues to shape, indeed govern, interpretation of the equal protection clause.

Section 1983's text generated interpretive problems that might have hindered its widespread use even if the Constitution had enjoyed a broader scope. As enacted, section 1983 protected "rights, privileges or immunities" secured by the Constitution. Its scope therefore depended upon what were viewed as rights, privileges, or immunities secured by the Constitution. Until the SLAUGHTERHOUSE CASES (1873), one might have thought the rights, privileges, or immunities so secured simply to be all constitutional rights. But the *Slaughterhouse Cases* narrowly interpreted the FOURTEENTH AMENDMENT's privileges or immunities clause to protect only a small subclass of constitutional rights. Some courts adopted a similar interpretation of section 1983. In addition, section 1983 reaches only deprivations "under color of" state law. Not until well into the twentieth century was it clearly recognized that behavior not authorized by state law might constitute action under COLOR OF LAW. A narrowly construed Constitution, the shadow cast by the *Slaughter-*

house Cases, the state action doctrine, and section 1983's text combined to minimize section 1983's importance.

In the 1920s, section 1983 provided actions for some deprivations of VOTING RIGHTS. Perhaps the Court relied on the section when, in NIXON V. HERNDON (1927), it allowed a damage action to go forward against state officials. In *Lane v. Wilson* (1939), another voting rights case, the Court expressly referred to section 1983 in approving a damage action. But these cases did not erode the important limitations on section 1983.

The erosion process commenced with early twentieth-century cases that construed state action to include some actions taken in violation of state law, and with EX PARTE YOUNG (1908), which held that the ELEVENTH AMENDMENT does not bar injunctive actions against state officials. In the 1940s, criminal CIVIL RIGHTS decisions also interpreted the phrase "under color of" law to include some unauthorized action. MONROE V. PAPE (1961) capped the process by interpreting section 1983 to protect at least all constitutional rights embodied in the Fourteenth Amendment and by holding the color of law requirement in section 1983 to be satisfied by the unauthorized action of police officers. *Monroe*, together with the wide expansion of constitutional rights of the 1950s and 1960s, assured section 1983's importance.

But section 1983's growth triggered a reaction, one that began with *Monroe* itself. If every constitutional violation generated a cause of action for damages there must be limits as to when defendants actually would be held liable. In *Monroe*, the Court, giving a questionable reading to section 1983's history, held that the section was not meant to render cities liable for constitutional violations. This limitation survived until MONELL V. DEPARTMENT OF SOCIAL SERVICES (1978), when the Court held that cities may be liable under section 1983 but that, in yet another questionable reading of the section's history, Congress did not intend cities to be liable for acts of city officials unless the acts constituted "official policy," a phrase destined to be the subject of much litigation. The reaction also includes some sentiment to impose an EXHAUSTION OF REMEDIES requirement in one or more classes of section 1983 cases.

With respect to individual defendants, the Court in a series of cases read into section 1983 an array of LEGISLATIVE, JUDICIAL, prosecutorial and EXECUTIVE IMMUNITIES. And in QUERN V. JORDAN (1979) the Court held that section 1983 was not meant to abrogate the Eleventh Amendment immunity of states. In OWEN V. CITY OF INDEPENDENCE (1980),

however, the Court declined to extend to municipalities the good faith defense available to executive officials. The reaction to section 1983's expansion may also encompass a series of cases, including *Parratt v. Taylor* (1981), PAUL V. DAVIS (1976), INGRAHAM V. WRIGHT (1977), and *Estelle v. Gamble* (1976), narrowly interpreting constitutional rights. If a private cause of action accompanies every constitutional right, the Court may be hesitant to "constitutionalize" many rights. Finally, the Court held in *Carey v. Piphus* (1978) that a violation of PROCEDURAL DUE PROCESS, standing alone, will not support a substantial recovery of damages; to recover more than nominal damages a plaintiff in such a case must show actual harm. The Court left open the question whether this rule would apply to other types of constitutional violation.

For many years, courts disagreed over whether section 1983 provided a cause of action for violations of federal statutes by state officials. The REVISED STATUTES of 1874, which were not supposed to make substantive changes in the law, expanded section 1983's wording to include "laws." Over a century later, in *Maine v. Thiboutot* (1980), the Court interpreted section 1983 to provide a cause of action for at least some federal statutory claims.

THEODORE EISENBERG

Bibliography

EISENBERG, THEODORE 1982 Section 1983: Doctrinal Foundations and an Empirical Study. *Cornell Law Review* 67:482–556.

——— 1981 *Civil Rights Legislation.* Charlottesville, Va.: Michie Co.

FRIENDLY, HENRY J. 1973 *Federal Jurisdiction: A General View* Pp. 87–107. New York: Columbia University Press.

NAHMOD, SHELDON H. 1979 *Civil Rights & Civil Liberties Litigation.* Colorado Springs, Colo.: Shepard's.

NOTE 1977 Developments in the Law: Section 1983 and Federalism. *Harvard Law Review* 90:1133–1361.

SECURITIES LAW AND THE CONSTITUTION

Following the 1929 stockmarket crash and the ensuing economic depression, Congress enacted the Securities Act of 1933 and the Securities Exchange Act of 1934 to restore investor confidence and provide for more efficient securities markets. Although both disclosure and regulatory provisions of the two statutes were challenged during the 1930s on constitutional grounds, the lower federal courts consistently held that both statutes were within Congress's power to regulate INTERSTATE COMMERCE and did not violate any other constitutional guarantees. In *Electric Bond & Share Co. v. Securities and Exchange Commission* (1937) the Supreme Court rejected constitutional attacks on certain provisions of the PUBLIC UTILITY HOLDING COMPANY ACT similar to the disclosure and registration requirements of the 1933 and 1934 acts, although the Court did not discuss the general validity of federal securities regulation.

Because both the states and the federal government regulate the securities markets, the Supreme Court has periodically undertaken to define the relationship between federal and state regulatory schemes by interpreting federal securities statutes. The first such case to raise constitutional questions of FEDERALISM grew out of the dramatic increase in hostile corporate takeover attempts in the late 1960s. In 1968 and 1970 Congress amended the 1934 act by adding certain provisions, known as the Williams Act, to regulate tender offers. A number of states immediately adopted takeover statutes of their own, presumably in order to protect local businesses from hostile takeovers. Because the state statutes gave more protection to target companies than did the Williams Act, tender offerors immediately challenged the state statutes as either invalid under the COMMERCE CLAUSE or preempted by the Williams Act.

In *Edgar v. Mite Corporation* (1982) the Supreme Court held that the Illinois takeover statute impermissibly burdened interstate commerce because the statute's nationwide reach significantly interfered with the economic benefits of tender offers while providing few benefits to Illinois. The Court's opinion was limited to the commerce clause holding, although three Justices also argued that the Williams Act preempted the Illinois regulatory scheme. A number of similar state takeover laws have subsequently been invalidated by lower federal courts on either commerce clause or PREEMPTION grounds.

Recent constitutional developments have suggested the possibility of FIRST AMENDMENT restraints on the disclosure aspects of securities regulation. Both the 1933 and 1934 acts regulate extensively the speech of corporate issuers and securities professionals by mandating some disclosures, prohibiting others, and by policing the content of various disclosure documents, all in the interest of preventing securities fraud, facilitating corporate suffrage, and providing investors with full and accurate information about securities and the securities markets. In VIRGINIA STATE BOARD OF PHARMACY V. VIRGINIA CITIZENS CONSUMER COUNCIL (1976) the Court extended First Amendment protection to COMMERCIAL SPEECH, and

in FIRST NATIONAL BANK OF BOSTON V. BELLOTTI (1978) the Court confirmed that corporate speakers could claim the benefits of the First Amendment. In CENTRAL HUDSON GAS & ELECTRIC CORP. V. PUBLIC SERVICE COMMISSION (1980) the Court indicated that while misleading commercial speech may be regulated, remedies must be "no broader than reasonably necessary to prevent the deception."

In 1985, the Supreme Court confronted the question of First Amendment constraints on federal securities regulation. In *Lowe v. Securities and Exchange Commission* the petitioner argued that First Amendment notions of prior restraint barred the SEC from enjoining publication of petitioner's securities newsletter under the Investment Advisers Act of 1940 after petitioner's investment adviser registration was revoked because of his illegal conduct. The Court avoided the First Amendment issue by holding that the petitioner was the publisher of a "bona fide newspaper" and thus statutorily exempt from regulation under the 1940 act. Justices BYRON R. WHITE and WILLIAM H. REHNQUIST and Chief Justice WARREN E. BURGER concurred in the result but argued that the First Amendment question should have been reached and decided. They indicated that the total bar on publication required by the 1940 act was too drastic a remedy for possibly deceptive speech, whether that speech was fully protected or merely commercial speech.

Although many of the disclosure provisions of the 1933 and 1934 acts presumably satisfy the *Central Hudson* tests, those aspects of both statutes requiring prepublication clearance of disclosure by the SEC or limiting informational activities by securities professionals may be regarded as sweeping too broadly to meet First Amendment requirements. In some areas, moreover, as in the application of the proxy rules to corporate and shareholder speech concerning issues of social and political significance, corporate speech may be entitled to full First Amendment protection. All these issues remain to be raised in the courts.

ALISON GREY ANDERSON

SEDITION

Sedition is a comprehensive term for offenses against the authority of the government not amounting to TREASON. Such offenses might include the spreading of disaffection or disloyalty, conspiracy to commit insurrection, or any SUBVERSIVE ACTIVITY. Sedition tends toward treason, but does not reach the constitutionally defined offense of "levying war against the

United States or adhering to their enemies, giving them aid and comfort."

Historically, the broad category of "sedition" has comprised several kinds of activity, although there has not always been consistency about which constituted criminal offenses. SEDITIOUS LIBEL, the uttering of words bringing the government or its officers into ridicule or disrepute, was an offense at COMMON LAW and under the ALIEN AND SEDITION ACTS of 1798. Seditious membership, that is, active, knowing, and purposeful membership in an organization committed to the overthrow of the government by unlawful means, is an offense under the Smith Act. Seditious advocacy, the public promotion of insurrection or rebellion, and seditious conspiracy, combining with others to subvert the government, violate several statutory provisions; but those offenses must be very carefully defined lest the statutes exert a CHILLING EFFECT on legitimate criticism of government.

The possibility of sedition poses a particular problem for constitutional democracy. Democratic governments, no less than any other kind, need to protect themselves against seditious activity. But measures taken in self-defense must not be so broad in their scope as themselves to become a threat to individual liberty. In the United States, the FIRST AMENDMENT to the Constitution protects FREEDOM OF SPEECH, FREEDOM OF THE PRESS, and FREEDOM OF ASSEMBLY AND ASSOCIATION; these specific constitutional guarantees limit the power of Congress and of the states to legislate against sedition.

For most of American history, the national and state governments exercised a CONCURRENT POWER to define and punish sedition. The power of Congress to legislate against sedition does not derive from any of the specific ENUMERATED POWERS, but is NECESSARY AND PROPER for the carrying out of several of them. In PENNSYLVANIA V. NELSON (1956) the Supreme Court held that Congress, by enacting a pervasive scheme of regulation, had preempted the field of legislation concerning sedition against the United States.

DENNIS J. MAHONEY

(SEE ALSO: Sedition Act of 1918.)

SEDITION ACT
40 Stat. 553 (1918)

As World War I progressed, enthusiastic war supporters argued more and more that the ESPIONAGE ACT OF 1917 did not adequately restrict domestic critics of the war effort. Advocates of additional restriction argued that weakness of the existing loyalty legislation forced citizens to take the law into their own hands. If firmer federal policies could be established, such distasteful forms of repression might be averted. Thus a more restrictive amendment to the Espionage Act was proposed and, despite strong congressional protest that the measure virtually terminated freedom of expression, was signed into law on May 16, 1918. The amendment, called the Sedition Act, defined eight offenses punishable by $10,000 fine or more than twenty years in prison, or both. The new offenses included: uttering, printing, writing, or publishing any disloyal, profane, scurrilous, or abusive language intended to cause contempt, scorn, contumely or disrepute as regards the form of government of the United States, or the Constitution, or the flag, or the uniform or the Army or Navy, or any language intended to incite resistance to the United States or to promote the cause of its enemies; urging any curtailment of production of anything necessary to the prosecution of the war with intent to hinder its prosecution; advocating, teaching, defending, or suggesting the doing of any of these acts; and words or acts supporting or favoring the cause of any country at war with the United States, or opposing the cause of the United States therein.

The 1918 act also enlarged the censorship functions of the postmaster general, empowering him to refuse to deliver mail to any individual or business employing the mails in violation of the statute. He was to order a letter that he deemed undeliverable to be returned to the sender with the phrase "Mail to this address undeliverable under the Espionage Act" stamped on the envelope. Thus the postmaster general was empowered to damage or destroy the business or reputation of any American citizen.

Enforced extensively in the period from May to November 1918, the measure virtually terminated wartime criticism until the Armistice. While efforts were made to reenact its provisions in a peace-time sedition statute during the A. MITCHELL PALMER "red scare" period, Congress balked and ultimately took the act off the books in March 1921.

The extremely broad language of the act would today make it vulnerable to attack on the grounds of OVERBREADTH. In 1919, however, the Supreme Court upheld the conviction of five anarchists for circulating a leaflet urging curtailment of war production and encouraging resistance to the participation of U.S. forces in opposition to the Russian revolution. Justice OLIVER WENDELL HOLMES wrote a famous dissent, joined by Justice LOUIS D. BRANDEIS, in ABRAMS V.

UNITED STATES (1919). (See CLEAR AND PRESENT DANGER.)

PAUL L. MURPHY

Bibliography

MURPHY, PAUL L. 1979 *World War I and the Origin of Civil Liberties in the United States.* New York: Norton.

SEDITIOUS LIBEL

Though its scope has varied greatly with time and place, the heart of the doctrine of seditious libel is the proposition that government may punish its critics for words it perceives as a threat to its survival. The offending words may be criticism of the government itself, or, more often, of its leaders. What constitutes seditious libel tends to be whatever the government fears most at the time. In fifteenth-century England, where reverence for the crown was considered essential to the safety of the realm, it was a crime to call the king a fool or to predict his death. In colonial America the most frequent offense was criticizing local representatives of the crown. In 1798, the Federalist party feared that Jeffersonian attacks would so undermine public confidence that the fledgling Republic would fall—or at least that the Federalists would lose the election of 1800. They therefore made it a crime to publish any false, scandalous, and malicious writing about either house of Congress or the President of the United States.

In England, seditious libels were once prosecuted as treason, punishable by death. Thus in 1663 William Twyn, who printed a book endorsing the right of revolution, was hanged, emasculated, disemboweled, quartered, and beheaded. Not until the eighteenth century did the law clearly distinguish seditious libel from treason; the latter then was confined to cases in which the seditious words were accompanied by some overt act. Seditious libel became a misdemeanor, punishable by fines, imprisonment, and the pillory. Prosecutions were common in England until the mid-nineteenth century.

Seditious libel was part of the received law in the American colonies, but it was received unenthusiastically. There probably were no more than a dozen seditious libel prosecutions in the entire colonial period, and few were successful. Although no one seems to have doubted that government should have some power to protect itself from verbal attacks, many complained that the doctrine as it had evolved in England allowed legitimate criticism to be swept within the ambit of the seditious libel proscription. The law allowed no defense of truth; the objective was to preserve respect for government, to which truthful criticism was an even greater threat than falsehood. And because the interests to be protected were the government's, it would hardly do to let a jury decide whether the words were actionable. The judges therefore kept for themselves the power to determine whether the speaker's intent was seditious; the jury was only allowed to decide whether he had uttered the words charged.

As ideas of POPULAR SOVEREIGNTY grew, critics on both sides of the Atlantic attacked these rules. In America the issue jelled in the 1735 trial of John Peter Zenger, a New York printer who had criticized the royal governor. Zenger's lawyer, Andrew Hamilton, argued that he should be allowed to defend Zenger by proving the truth of the publication, and that the jury should be allowed to decide whether the words were libelous. The judge rejected both arguments, but the jury acquitted Zenger anyway, even though he had admitted publishing the words. (See ZENGER'S CASE.)

The case made popular heroes of Zenger and Hamilton and destroyed the effectiveness of seditious libel law as a tool for English control of American dissent. There were few, if any, successful common law prosecutions in the colonies after *Zenger.* Colonial legislatures sometimes punished their critics for breaches of "parliamentary privilege," but public resentment eventually made this device ineffective, too.

The intended effect of the FIRST AMENDMENT on the law of seditious libel is still in dispute. It is clear that seditious libel was still the law in 1789, and that the Framers expressed no intent to preclude prosecutions for seditious libel. They certainly did not intend to prevent the states from prosecuting seditious libels; all agreed that the First Amendment was a limitation on federal power only. And within a decade, Congress passed the Sedition Act of 1798, under which the Federalists prosecuted a number of prominent Republican editors. Several Justices of the Supreme Court, sitting as circuit judges, enforced the act. This evidence has persuaded some modern scholars that the Framers had no intention of abolishing seditious libel.

Others have argued that the Framers had at least a nascent understanding that some freedom to criticize government was a prerequisite to self-government, and that England's rigorous concept of seditious libel was inconsistent with that need. Their failure explicitly to condemn it might be explained by the fact that seditious libel prosecutions had not been a serious threat in their lifetimes. The Sedition Act may have been an unprincipled effort by desperate Federalist partisans to keep control of the government, rather than a considered affirmation of the constitutionality of seditious libel.

The Supreme Court has never squarely held that the First Amendment forbids punishment of seditious libels. From World War I through the McCarthy era, state and federal governments prosecuted numerous anarchists, socialists, and communists for advocating draft resistance, mass strikes, or overthrow of the government. Although the statutes authorizing these prosecutions were not called seditious libel acts, they had much the same effect. The Court generally upheld these convictions (usually over the dissents of the more libertarian Justices) until the 1960s, when in BRANDENBURG V. OHIO (1969) it adopted the view that punishment of mere advocacy is unconstitutional unless it is intended to produce imminent lawless action and is likely to do so.

Garrison v. Louisiana (1964) closely resembled a traditional seditious libel prosecution. A district attorney had been convicted of criminal libel for accusing local judges of laziness and corruption. The Court reversed his conviction, but implied that the prosecution might have been permissible if the state had proved that the defendant spoke with reckless disregard of the truth or falsity of his statements.

Nevertheless, the judgment of history is that seditious libel laws are inconsistent with FREEDOM OF SPEECH and FREEDOM OF THE PRESS. JAMES MADISON and THOMAS JEFFERSON argued in 1799 that the Sedition Act was unconstitutional. Justice OLIVER WENDELL HOLMES, dissenting in ABRAMS V. UNITED STATES (1919), wrote, "I wholly disagree with the argument of the Government that the First Amendment left the common law as to seditious libel in force. . . . I had conceived that the United States through many years had shown its repentance for the Sedition Act . . . by repaying the fines that it imposed." And in NEW YORK TIMES V. SULLIVAN (1964) the Court said, "Although the Sedition Act was never tested in this Court, the attack upon its validity has carried the day in the court of history."

DAVID A. ANDERSON

(SEE ALSO: *Alien and Sedition Acts.*)

Bibliography

ANDERSON, DAVID A. 1983 The Origins of the Press Clause. *University of California at Los Angeles Law Review* 30:455–537.

LEVY, LEONARD W. 1984 *Emergence of a Free Press.* New York: Oxford University Press.

NELSON, HAROLD L. 1959 Seditious Libel in Colonial America. *American Journal of Legal History* 3:160–172.

SEEGER, UNITED STATES v.
380 U.S. 163 (1965)

At issue in the *Seeger* case was Section 6(j) of the Universal Military Training and Service Act. Originally enacted in 1940, the act exempted those who, as a matter of "religious training and belief," were opposed to participation in a war. In 1948, Congress amended this provision and defined religious belief as "an individual's belief in a relation to a supreme being involving duties superior to those arising from any human relation, but [not including] essentially political, sociological, or philosophical views. . . ."

Despite the textual evidence of a congressional intent to condition exemption on the theistic belief, Justice TOM C. CLARK, for the Supreme Court, interpreted the provision as requiring only a sincere and meaningful belief occupying in the life of its possessor a place parallel to that filled by the belief in God of those admittedly qualified for the exemption. Seeger had argued that if section 6(j) granted exemptions only on the basis of conventional theistic belief, it amounted to an ESTABLISHMENT OF RELIGION. Facing the unattractive alternatives of finding section 6(j) unconstitutional or reading it in a sufficiently broad fashion so as to secularize the exemption, the majority chose the latter.

RICHARD E. MORGAN

(SEE ALSO: *Conscientious Objection.*)

SEGREGATION

From the beginning, RACIAL DISCRIMINATION in America has been a national phenomenon. Jim Crow was a southern name for the segregation of the races as part of a system of caste. But segregation antedated Jim Crow, and it began in the North and the West. The leading judicial decision upholding school segregation before the Civil War bears a name Northerners prefer to forget: ROBERTS V. BOSTON (1850). Blacks were either excluded entirely from PUBLIC ACCOMMODATIONS such as hotels, railroads, and theaters, or given separate accommodations. They were segregated in prisons and in churches. Several northern and western states even sought to bar the immigration of blacks; such a legal provision was adopted by Oregon voters by an eight-to-one margin.

Nor has this country's segregation been limited to blacks. As late as 1947, a federal court of appeals held that the segregation of Chicano children in a school district in California was invalid. The decision's ground was itself depressing: the state's statute authorized only the segregation of children whose ancestry was Indian, Chinese, Japanese, and Mongolian.

Still, it was the postabolition South that carried the segregation of the races to its fullest development, and blacks were the chief victims of the practice. Before slavery was abolished, of course, the dominance of whites was assured without any call for segregation. After abolition, the southern states adopted severe legal restrictions on blacks, which served to maintain white supremacy. (See BLACK CODES.) When the CIVIL RIGHTS ACT OF 1866 and the FOURTEENTH AMENDMENT not only ended these legal restrictions but also positively declared the CITIZENSHIP of the freed slaves, segregation was the southern response. By 1870, Tennessee had forbidden interracial marriages (see MISCEGENATION), and later came the "Jim Crow car" laws segregating railroad passenger seating.

Segregation was not, however, merely a creature of state legislation. It also resulted from private action: a hotel would refuse to take black guests; homeowners in a neighborhood would agree not to sell to black buyers. In such cases law played a role that was less obvious on the surface of events but was vital nonetheless. A black who sought the aid of the state courts in overcoming private discrimination would simply be turned away; state laws would deny any remedy.

Late in the nineteenth century, the Supreme Court gave its support to this system of interlocking discriminations. In the CIVIL RIGHTS CASES (1883), the Court held invalid a congressional statute forbidding racial discrimination by railroads, hotels, theaters, and restaurants. (See STATE ACTION.) And in PLESSY V. FERGUSON (1896) the Court upheld a Jim Crow car law against an EQUAL PROTECTION attack. (See SEPARATE BUT EQUAL DOCTRINE.) By the early twentieth century, the South was racially segregated to extremes that were at once tragic and ludicrous: separate telephone booths for blacks in Oklahoma; separate storage for textbooks used by black children in North Carolina and Florida schools; separate elevators for blacks in Atlanta; separate Bibles for swearing black witnesses in Georgia courts. The point of all this was nothing less than the denial to blacks of membership in a white-dominated society—the denial of citizenship itself, in defiance of the Fourteenth Amendment.

Some of the harms caused by racial segregation are harms to material interests: a black is denied accommodation at a hotel, or admission to a state university medical school (and thus to the medical profession), or the chance to live in a particular neighborhood or be a factory foreman. These material harms are serious, but the worst harms of segregation are psychic harms. The primary reason for segregating railroad passengers, of course, is to symbolize a caste system. The stigma of inferiority is a denial of a person's humanity, and the result is anguish and humiliation. The more the races are separated, the more natural it is for members of the dominant white race to see each black person not as an individual but simply as a black. Ralph Ellison, in his novel *Invisible Man* (1952), makes the point: "I am invisible, understand, simply because people refuse to see me. . . . When they approach me they see only my surroundings, themselves, or figments of their imagination—indeed, everything and anything except me. . . . You ache with the need to convince yourself that you do exist in the real world." To be a citizen, on the other hand, is to be respected as a person and recognized as a participating member in the society.

Jim Crow was a complex living system, and its dismantling would be no simple task. The field of segregation in housing exemplifies the difficulties. The NAACP's first major victory against segregation came in BUCHANAN V. WARLEY (1917), when the Supreme Court struck down a local ZONING ordinance aimed at maintaining segregated residential neighborhoods. But the decision by no means ended housing segregation, which continued as a result of private conduct. When the private discrimination was sufficiently connected with state action, as in the case of racially RESTRICTIVE COVENANTS enforced by state courts, the Fourteenth Amendment was an effective weapon against residential segregation. (See SHELLEY V. KRAEMER, 1948.) But in the absence of such state support, a landowner might simply refuse to rent or sell to blacks, and the would-be buyers would be without remedy. Two events in 1968 altered this portion of the doctrinal landscape. In JONES V. ALFRED H. MAYER CO. the Supreme Court concluded that the Civil Rights Act of 1866 forbade private discrimination in the sale of property. In the same year, Congress adopted a comprehensive fair housing law as part of the CIVIL RIGHTS ACT OF 1968. The new law forbade various forms of racial discrimination by lenders and brokers as well as private landlords and sellers. The combination of constitutional litigation and legislation aimed at ending housing segregation had achieved a radical restructuring of the law.

The restructuring of racial patterns in the neighborhoods where people live, however, has proved to be quite another matter. Middle-class blacks have largely left the core cities to live in suburbs, but the degree of racial segregation in residences has changed only slightly since 1940. The term "white flight," coined in the context of school desegregation, seems even more clearly applicable to residential patterns. It is hard to find stable interracial neighborhoods in any large city in the country, at any income level. (For discussion of related questions concerning the public schools—where continued patterns of segregation are related directly to residential segregation—see DESEGREGATION.)

In contrast, racial segregation in transportation and other public accommodations has come to an end. (See SIT-IN; CIVIL RIGHTS ACT OF 1964.) And laws forbidding interracial marriage collapsed under the double weight of equal protection and DUE PROCESS in LOVING V. VIRGINIA (1967). (See FREEDOM OF INTIMATE ASSOCIATION.) EMPLOYMENT DISCRIMINATION, too, is in retreat—including the segregation of job categories by race—as a result of enforcement of the fair employment portions of the 1964 Act.

The segregation that remains in American society, then, is chiefly residential segregation—with its concomitant, a substantial extent of separation of the races in the public schools. There is irony here: the decision in the school segregation case, BROWN V. BOARD OF EDUCATION (1954), was the critical event in the demise of Jim Crow, but our big city schools are the one set of public institutions in which the races remain largely separated. Yet *Brown*'s impact on American life was important. The decision began more than a doctrinal movement; its implicit affirmation of the equal citizenship of all our people accelerated forces that have markedly changed not only race relations but also a wide range of other relationships formerly characterized by dominance and dependency.

It is easy now to see the social and economic changes in the country that permitted the success of the movement to end officially sponsored segregation. World War II was the great watershed. By the time the war began, there was a critical mass of educated blacks, enough to provide a national movement not only with its great chiefs but with local leadership as well—and with a trained cadre of lawyers. The war produced waves of migration of blacks out of the rural South and into the cities of the North and West, where they very soon found a political voice. In part, too, the war had been billed as a war against Nazi racism—whatever we might be doing on the home front. (See JAPANESE AMERICAN CASES, 1943–1944.) The expected postwar depression failed to appear, and the 1950s and 1960s were a time of economic expansion, conducive to a sympathetic reception for egalitarian claims. All this is familiar learning. Yet in the early 1950s there was no sense of inevitability

surrounding the assault on segregation. If the sudden collapse of Jim Crow now seems inevitable, that in itself is a measure of the distance we have come. And if the end of segregation did not end a system of racial caste, that is a measure of the distance we have yet to travel.

KENNETH L. KARST

Bibliography

BELL, DERRICK 1980 Brown v. Board of Education and the Interest-Convergence Dilemma. *Harvard Law Review* 93:518–533.

LEVY, LEONARD W. and JONES, DOUGLAS 1972 Jim Crow Education: Origins of the "Separate but Equal" Doctrine. In Levy, Leonard W., *Judgments: Essays on American Constitutional History.* Chicago: Quadrangle Books.

LITWACK, LEON F. 1961 *North of Slavery.* Chicago: University of Chicago Press.

MYRDAL, GUNNAR 1944 *An American Dilemma.* New York: Harper & Brothers.

WOODWARD, C. VANN 1966 *The Strange Career of Jim Crow,* 2nd rev. ed. New York: Oxford University Press.

SELDEN, JOHN
(1584–1654)

A jurist, antiquary, and occasional member of Parliament, John Selden wrote extensively on the history of English law. With Sir EDWARD COKE he championed individual liberties and helped frame the PETITION OF RIGHT. He contended that Parliament's rights were secured by COMMON LAW and not enjoyed at the Crown's discretion.

DAVID GORDON

SELECTIVE CONSCIENTIOUS OBJECTION

See: Conscientious Objection

SELECTIVE DRAFT LAW CASES
Arver v. United States
245 U.S. 366 (1918)

In 1917, Congress authorized CONSCRIPTION as a means of rapidly increasing the strength of the armed forces. All males between twenty-one and thirty were to register for the draft, and up to one million were selectively to be called up. The six petitioners were all convicted of failure to register.

A unanimous Supreme Court, speaking through Chief Justice EDWARD D. WHITE, rejected each of several constitutional arguments against the draft law. Since the power to raise armies is specifically granted, the Court held that Congress might adopt any means necessary to call the required number of men into service. Compulsion might be used since "a governmental power which has no sanction to it . . . is in no substantial sense a power." A number of ingenious arguments based on the historic nature and uses of the militia were rejected because the power to raise armies is distinct from the militia clause.

For the argument that conscription violated the THIRTEENTH AMENDMENT, White had only eloquent scorn: "We are unable to conceive upon what theory the exaction by the government from the citizen of his supreme and noble duty of contributing to the defense of the rights and honor of the nation . . . can be said to be the imposition of involuntary servitude."

DENNIS J. MAHONEY

SELECTIVE EXCLUSIVENESS

Selective exclusiveness, or the *Cooley* doctrine, derives from the opinion of Justice BENJAMIN R. CURTIS for the Supreme Court in COOLEY V. BOARD OF PORT WARDENS (1852). Before that case, conflict and confusion characterized the Court's decisions in COMMERCE CLAUSE cases. Some Justices believed that Congress's power to regulate interstate and FOREIGN COMMERCE was an EXCLUSIVE POWER and others that the states shared CONCURRENT POWER over commerce. Some believed that a distinction existed between the national power over commerce and the STATE POLICE POWER.

Cooley provided a compromise doctrine that transformed judicial thinking. The Court recognized that commerce embraces a vast field of diverse subjects, some demanding a single uniform rule that only Congress might make, and others best served by state regulations based on local needs and differences. Thus the doctrine treated congressional power as exclusive on a selective basis—in only those cases requiring uniform legislation; and the states shared a concurrent power in other cases. In cases of conflict, of course, congressional action would prevail.

The *Cooley* formulation necessarily failed to provide a means by which the Court could discern which subjects were national and which local. Accordingly the Justices were able to manipulate the doctrine to sustain or invalidate state legislation as they wished.

In time, judicial analysis focused on the purposes of the legislation and the degree to which it adversely affected the flow of commerce, rather than on the nature of the subject regulated. No formulation could diminish the free play of judicial discretion.

LEONARD W. LEVY

Bibliography

FRANKFURTER, FELIX 1937 *The Commerce Clause under Marshall, Taney, and Waite.* Chapel Hill: University of North Carolina Press.

SELECTIVE INCORPORATION

See: Incorporation Doctrine

SELECTIVE SERVICE ACT
40 Stat. 76 (1917)

In the National Defense Act of 1916, the General Staff prepared a blueprint for increasing the military, but it failed to recruit adequate personnel through a voluntary system. With war declared, President WOODROW WILSON in April 1917 sent to Congress a bill to "Authorize the President to Increase Temporarily the Military Establishment." After a six-week debate, the Selective Service Act of 1917 was enacted. The measure vested the President with the power to raise an army by CONSCRIPTION. Enrollment and selection were to be carried out by 4,000 local civilian boards, appointed by the President and organized under federally appointed state directors. Although these boards operated under uniform federal regulations, they were given considerable discretion in meeting quotas and handling deferment applications. The manpower requirements for the war period were developed by the army General Staff and apportioned to the states. The order of induction was determined by lottery. Over twenty-four million American males were registered under the law. Nearly three million were selected and inducted.

The constitutionality of the law was early challenged by its opponents on the grounds of illegal DELEGATION OF POWER and a violation of the THIRTEENTH, Fifth, TENTH, and FIRST AMENDMENTS. The Supreme Court brushed aside such challenges in the SELECTIVE DRAFT LAW CASES (1918), determining that the powers of the central government to make war and support armies encompass the authority to impose compulsory military service.

PAUL L. MURPHY

Bibliography

DUGGAN, JOSEPH S. 1946 *Legislative and Statutory Development of the Federal Concept of Conscription for Military Service.* Washington: Catholic University Press.

SELECTIVE SERVICE ACTS

Conscription Act
12 Stat. 731 (1863)

Burke-Wadsworth Selective Training and
Service Act
54 Stat. 885 (1940)

Universal Military Training and Service Act
62 Stat. 604 (1948)

The Constitution gives Congress the power to "raise and support armies" and to "provide and maintain a navy." The traditions of the American people have dictated that throughout most of our history peacetime military service has been voluntary and emergencies have been met, in the first instance, by activating the organized state militias. CONSCRIPTION, drafting men for compulsory military duty, is available for the gravest emergencies. During the War of 1812, Congress considered, but did not adopt, a Draft Bill.

The first federal military draft in American history was authorized by the Conscription Act of 1863. That act required registration of all able-bodied male citizens eighteen to forty-five years old, and provided that whenever a congressional district failed to provide its quota of volunteers the deficiency should be made up by drawing from the pool of registrants. The act further provided that the draftee could avoid service by providing a substitute or by paying $300. The first draft under the act, in July 1863, was the occasion of a week-long riot in New York City, in which over one thousand people were killed and over one-and-a-half million dollars worth of property was destroyed.

The first peacetime selective service law was the Burke-Wadsworth Act of 1940, requiring registration in anticipation of American entry into World War II. The act, also known as the Selective Training and Service Act, was patterned after the SELECTIVE SERVICE ACT OF 1917: universal registration and classification administered by local boards. The 1940 act expired in 1947 and was replaced by the Universal Military Training and Service Act of 1948, which continued the basic scheme of the 1917 and 1940 statutes. The first draft under this act was in 1950, and conscription for the KOREAN WAR and VIETNAM WAR was done under provisions of that act. Registration under the act (renamed the Military Selective Service Act in 1967) ceased in 1975.

President Jimmy Carter in 1980 sought and received congressional authorization to reimplement peacetime draft registration, but the 1980 measure provided for registration only, not for classification or conscription. (See ROSTKER V. GOLDBERG, 1981.)

DENNIS J. MAHONEY

SELF-INCRIMINATION

See: Right against Self-Incrimination

SEPARATE BUT EQUAL DOCTRINE

The first type of racial SEGREGATION law to spread over the South was the "Jim Crow car" law, requiring blacks and whites to be seated separately in railroad passenger cars. When the Supreme Court held such a law valid in PLESSY V. FERGUSON (1896), the majority concluded that, so long as the facilities for each race were equal, the enforced separation of the races did not itself impose any inequality on black persons. In support of this separate but equal DOCTRINE, the Court drew on a pre-Civil War decision in Massachusetts, upholding racial segregation in the public schools. (See ROBERTS V. BOSTON, 1850.)

Although the doctrine originated in the context of state regulation of private conduct, it was soon extended to validate segregation in state-operated facilities. The races were separated by the law's command in courtrooms; in the public schools (see GONG LUM V. RICE, 1927); in state offices; in public parks, beaches, swimming pools, and golf courses; in prisons and jails. Some state institutions, such as universities, simply excluded blacks altogether; in most southern states there were separate state colleges for blacks. Throughout this system of segregation, the formal assumption was that facilities for blacks and whites might be separate, but they were equal.

Given the undoubted fact that segregation was imposed for the purpose of maintaining blacks in a condition of inferiority, the very term separate but equal is internally inconsistent. But the *Plessy* opinion had rejected the claim that racial separation itself imposed on blacks an inequality in the form of inferiority. (See BADGES OF SERVITUDE.) Yet *Plessy* set the terms of judicial inquiry in a way that ultimately undermined the separate but equal principle. The question of *justifications* for inequality was largely neglected; the Court focused on the question whether inequality *existed*.

In railroad cars, it was easy to achieve a rough equality of physical facilities. Similarly, a public swimming pool might be reserved for whites three days a week, reserved for blacks three days, and closed the other day. In education, however, inequalities of enormous proportion persisted up to the decision in BROWN V. BOARD OF EDUCATION (1954) and beyond. Black colleges lacked professional schools; black high schools emphasized vocational training and minimized preparation for college. In physical plants, teachers' salaries, levels of teacher training, counseling services, curricula—in every measurable aspect— the separate education offered blacks was anything but the equal of the education offered whites.

One strategy devised by the NAACP for ending school segregation was thus the filing of lawsuits aimed at forcing school boards to equalize spending for black education—at crushing expense. At the same time, a direct assault was made on segregation in higher education, and especially graduate education, where it was easiest to prove the inequality of facilities. (See MISSOURI EX REL. GAINES V. CANADA, 1938; SWEATT V. PAINTER, 1950.) These decisions, following *Plessy's* lead, focused on the bare question of inequality. Inevitably, these cases came to touch the question whether segregation itself implied unequal education. The *Brown* opinion pursued that inquiry, found educational inequality in the fact of enforced separation, and—without discussing any purported justifications for segregation—held school segregation unconstitutional.

Separate but equal thus ended its doctrinal sway in the field of education. Within a few years the Supreme Court, in a series of PER CURIAM opinions consisting entirely of citations to *Brown*, had invalidated all state-sponsored segregation. The separate but equal doctrine was laid to rest.

KENNETH L. KARST

Bibliography

LEVY, LEONARD W. and JONES, DOUGLAS 1972 Jim Crow Education: Origins of the "Separate but Equal" Doctrine. In Levy, Leonard W., *Judgments: Essays on American Constitutional History*. Chicago: Quadrangle Books.

OBERST, PAUL 1973 The Strange Career of *Plessy v. Ferguson. Arizona Law Review* 15:389–418.

WOODWARD, C. VANN 1966 *The Strange Career of Jim Crow*, 2nd rev. ed. New York: Oxford University Press.

SEPARATION OF CHURCH AND STATE

The first provision of the BILL OF RIGHTS—known as the establishment clause—states that "Congress shall make no law respecting an ESTABLISHMENT OF RELIGION. . . ." This constitutional mandate seeks to assure the separation of church and state in a nation characterized by religious pluralism.

Justice WILEY B. RUTLEDGE observed in EVERSON V. BOARD OF EDUCATION (1947) that "no provision of the Constitution is more closely tied to or given content by its generating history than the religious clause of the FIRST AMENDMENT." Justice HUGO L. BLACK recounted in *Everson* that in the old world, "with the power of government supporting them, at various times and places, Catholics had persecuted Protestants, Protestants had persecuted Baptists, Protestant sects had persecuted other Protestant sects, Catholics of one shade of belief had persecuted Catholics of another shade of belief, and all of these had from time to time persecuted Jews." And, he added, "these practices of the old world were transplanted to and began to thrive in the soil of the new America." For example, in Massachusetts, Quakers, Baptists, and other religious minorities suffered harshly and were taxed for the established Congregational Church. In 1776, the Maryland "Declaration of Rights" stated that "only persons professing the Christian religion" were entitled to religious freedom, and not until 1826 were Jews permitted to hold public office. The South Carolina Constitution of 1778 stated that "the Christian Protestant religion shall be deemed . . . the established religion of this state."

The specific historical record, rather than disclosing a coherent "intent of the Framers," suggests that those who influenced the framing of the First Amendment were animated by several distinct and sometimes conflicting goals. Thus, THOMAS JEFFERSON believed that the integrity of government could be preserved only by erecting "a wall of separation" between church and state. A sharp division of authority was essential, in his view, to insulate the democratic process from ecclesiastical depradations and excursions. JAMES MADISON shared this view, but also perceived church–state separation as benefiting religious institutions. Even more strongly, ROGER WILLIAMS, one of the earliest colonial proponents of religious freedom, posited an evangelical theory of separation, believing it vital to protect the sanctity of the church's "garden" from the "wilderness" of the state. Finally, there is evidence that one purpose of the establishment clause was to protect the existing state-established churches from the newly ordained national government. (Indeed, although disestablishment was then well under way, the epoch of state-sponsored churches did not close until 1833 when Massachusetts separated church and state.)

Even if the Framers' intent were unanimous and unambiguous, it still could not provide ready answers for many contemporary problems. First, a number of present-day church–state issues were not foreseen by the founders. For example, public education was virtually unknown in the eighteenth century; the Framers could have no position on the matter of RELIGION IN PUBLIC SCHOOLS—one of the most frequently adjudicated modern establishment clause questions. Second, implementing the Framers' precise thinking, even if discernible, might jeopardize values now considered secured by the establishment clause. As Justice WILLIAM J. BRENNAN speculated in ABINGTON TOWNSHIP SCHOOL DISTRICT V. SCHEMPP (1963), perhaps because the nation has become more religiously heterogeneous, "practices which may have been objectionable to no one in the time of Jefferson and Madison may today be highly offensive to . . . the deeply devout and the non-believers alike."

The varied ideologies that prompted the founders do, however, disclose a dominant theme: according constitutional status to RELIGIOUS LIBERTY and the integrity of individual conscience. Moreover, one of the main practices seen by many Framers as anathema to religious freedom was forcing the people to support religion through compulsory taxation. Jefferson viewed this as "sinful and tyrannical," and Madison found it abhorrent to compel "a citizen to contribute three pence only of his property" to a religious cause. The founders recognized that although government subsidy of religion may not directly influence people's beliefs, it coerces citizens either to contribute to their own religions or, worse, to support sectarian doctrines antithetical to their convictions.

By its terms, the establishment clause applies only to the federal government ("*Congress* shall make no law . . ."), but in *Everson* (1947) the Court ruled that the FOURTEENTH AMENDMENT made the clause applicable to the states. Before then, only two Supreme Court decisions had produced any significant consideration of the establishment clause. *Bradfield v. Roberts* (1899) had upheld federal appropriations to a Roman Catholic hospital for care of indigent patients. *Quick Bear v. Leupp* (1908) had sustained federal disbursement of funds, held in trust for the Sioux Indians, to Roman Catholic schools designated by the Sioux for payment of tuition. Neither opinion, however, attempted any comprehensive definition of the nonestablishment precept, an effort first undertaken in *Everson* where the Court stated:

The "establishment of religion" clause of the First Amendment means at least this: Neither a state nor the Federal government can set up a church. Neither can pass laws which aid one religion, aid all religions, or prefer one religion over another. Neither can force nor influence a person to go to or to remain away from church against his will or force him to profess a belief or disbelief in any religion. No person can be punished for entertaining or professing religious beliefs or disbeliefs, for church attendance or nonattendance. No tax in any amount, large or small, can be levied to support any religious activities or institutions, whatever they may be called, or whatever form they may adopt to teach or practice religion. Neither a state nor the Federal Government can, openly or secretly, participate in the affairs of any religious organization or groups and *vice versa*. In the words of Jefferson, the clause against establishment of religion by law was intended to erect "a wall of separation between church and state."

Since then, there has been little agreement among the Justices, lower courts, and scholars as to what constitutes impermissible "aid" to, or "support" of, religion.

Beginning in the early 1960s and culminating in LEMON V. KURTZMAN (1971), the Court developed a three-part test for reviewing establishment clause challenges: "First, the statute must have a secular legislative purpose; second, its principal or primary effect must be one that neither advances nor inhibits religion . . . ; finally, the statute must not foster 'an excessive government entanglement with religion.' " The *Lemon* test, despite its consistent invocation by the Court, has not been a model of coherence. Indeed, in an unusually candid OBITER DICTUM in COMMITTEE FOR PUBLIC EDUCATION V. REGAN (1980) the Court conceded that its approach "sacrifices clarity and predictability for flexibility," a state of affairs that "promises to be the case until the continuing interaction between the courts and the states . . . produces a single, more encompassing construction of the Establishment Clause." A better approach would read the establishment clause to forbid government action when its purpose is religious *and* it is likely to impair religious freedom by coercing, compromising, or influencing religious beliefs.

One of the nation's most politically divisive issues has been the proper place of religion in public schools. Decisions in the early 1960s, holding that prayer and Bible reading violate the establishment clause, precipitated serious efforts to reverse the Court by constitutional amendment. Later legislative proposals have sought to strip the federal courts of JURISDICTION over cases challenging voluntary school prayer.

The first cases concerning religion in public schools involved RELEASED TIME. In McCOLLUM V. BOARD OF EDUCATION (1948) the Court invalidated an Illinois program of voluntary religious instruction in public school classrooms during school hours by privately employed teachers. Students whose parents signed "request cards" attended weekly classes in religion; others pursued secular studies elsewhere in the school during this period. The Court's opinion emphasized use of "the state's tax-supported public school buildings" and "the state's compulsory public school machinery." Four years later, in ZORACH V. CLAUSEN (1952), the Court upheld a New York City "off-premises" released time program. Released students attended classes at their respective religious centers; neither public funds nor public classrooms directly supported religion. In a much quoted and controversial passage, the Court observed: "We are a religious people whose institutions presuppose a Supreme Being. We guarantee the freedom to worship as one chooses. We make room for as wide a variety of beliefs and creeds as the spiritual needs of man deem necessary. . . . When the state encourages religious instruction or cooperates with religious authorities by adjusting the schedule of public events to sectarian needs, it follows the best of our traditions."

Neither *McCollum* nor *Zorach* propounded any specific STANDARD OF REVIEW. A decade later, in EN-GEL V. VITALE (1962), the Court invalidated a New York law providing for recitation of a state-composed prayer at the beginning of each public school day. Although the prayer was denominationally "neutral," and students could remain silent or leave the room, the Court declared that this "breaches the constitutional wall of separation between Church and State," because "it is no part of the business of government to compose official prayers."

The Court's approach soon underwent a dramatic revision. In *Abington Township v. Schempp* the Court held it unconstitutional for public schools to conduct daily exercises of reading student-selected passages from either the Old or New Testaments (without teacher comment) and recitation of the Lord's Prayer. Drawing on its rationale in the SUNDAY CLOSING CASES (1961), the Court articulated a "test" for government action challenged under the establishment clause: "[W]hat are the purpose and the primary effect of the enactment? If either is the advancement or inhibition of religion then the enactment exceeds the scope of legislative power as circumscribed by the Constitution. That is to say that to withstand the stric-tures of the Establishment Clause there must be a secular legislative purpose and a primary effect that neither advances nor inhibits religion." The Court ruled that the "opening exercise is a religious ceremony," emphasizing, however, that "objective" study of the Bible (presumably for its literary and historical value) was constitutionally permissible.

There are two difficulties with the Court's declared willingness—reaffirmed regularly since *Schempp*—to invalidate government action solely on the basis of a nonsecular "purpose." First, although *Schempp* emphasized the establishment clause's requirement of a "wholesome neutrality" by the state toward religion, the Court has also made clear that the Constitution does not mandate an "untutored devotion" to this precept. Indeed, it has sometimes held that the free exercise clause *obliges* government to act with a nonsecular purpose—actually, to give a preference to religion—when the action is necessary to permit the unburdened exercise of religion.

Second, despite the *Schempp* test's condemnation of laws whose purpose is to "advance religion," the Court in *Zorach* had previously conceded that the released time program upheld had a nonsecular purpose: facilitation of religious instruction. *Zorach* has been specifically reaffirmed since *Schempp* was decided. Thus, the Court itself is not fully committed to its articulated doctrine that a religious purpose alone is sufficient to invalidate government action.

Although both *Engel* and *Schempp* declared that religious coercion was irrelevant under the establishment clause, the Court has nevertheless often carefully analyzed the elements of coercion and influence in programs it has considered. For example, in *Engel* the Court remarked on "the indirect coercive pressure upon religious minorities to conform to the prevailing officially approved religion." In *Zorach*, the Court emphasized its questionable conclusion that there was no "coercion to get public school students into religious classrooms." And in WIDMAR V. VINCENT (1981), in requiring a state university to provide student religious groups equal access to its facilities, the Court noted: "University students are . . . less impressionable than younger students and should be able to appreciate that the university's policy is one of neutrality towards religion."

The Court's sensitivity to religious coercion and influence in establishment clause challenges, its doctrinal pronouncements to the contrary notwithstanding, comports with an approach that recognizes that in accommodating the values underlying both the establishment and free exercise clauses, a nonsecular purpose cannot always be avoided, and that the primary offense to the establishment clause is some meaningful intrusion upon religious liberty.

Nearly two decades elapsed between *Schempp* and the BURGER COURT's first major decision on religion in public schools. In *Stone v. Graham* (1980) a Kentucky statute required posting a copy of the Ten Commandments (purchased with private funds) in all public school classrooms, with the notation: "The secular application of the Ten Commandments is clearly seen in its adoption as the fundamental legal code of Western Civilization and the COMMON LAW of the United States." Although the state court found that the legislature's purpose was not religious and sustained the law, the Supreme Court reversed.

The *Stone* opinion is significant for several reasons. First, it sheds further light on how the Court decides whether a legislative purpose is secular or religious. In *Schempp*, when the school board contended that the Bible reading program was not instituted for religious reasons (but rather to promote moral values, teach literature, and inspire student discipline), the Court brusquely replied that "surely, the place of the Bible as an instrument of religion cannot be gainsaid." In *Stone*, the Court stated that the Ten Commandments were not confined to "arguably secular matters" such as prohibition of murder and adultery but also prescribed religious duties such as observing the Sabbath and avoiding idolatry—adding that the law did not integrate the Bible or the commandments into an ethics, history, or comparative religion course. It quite peremptorily concluded that the program "serves no . . . educational function" and that "the Ten Commandments is undeniably a sacred text in the Jewish and Christian faiths, and no legislative recitation of a supposed secular purpose can blind us to that fact." *Stone* also reaffirms that a nonsecular purpose is itself enough to condemn a law under the establishment clause. Although the Court briefly considered the state program's potential for coercing or influencing children—observing that "if the posted copies of the Ten Commandments are to have any effect at all, it will be to induce the school children to read, meditate upon, perhaps to venerate and obey, the Commandments"—it nevertheless held that the law lacked a secular purpose and was invalid on that basis alone. This doctrine was vigorously reinforced in WALLACE V. JAFFREE (1985), which invalidated an Alabama statute authorizing a period of silence in public schools "for meditation or voluntary prayer," because the law was "entirely motivated by a purpose to advance religion." (The Justices plainly indicated that only a slightly different statutory formulation "protecting every student's right to engage in volun-

tary prayer during an appropriate moment of silence during the school day" would pass constitutional muster.)

Although regulatory laws allegedly enacted to aid religion have generated only a few Supreme Court decisions, they have significantly affected establishment clause jurisprudence. In MCGOWAN V. MARYLAND (1961) the Court upheld prohibition of the sale of most merchandise on Sundays. The Court conceded that the original purpose of Sunday closing laws was to encourage observance of the Christian Sabbath. But it found that, as presently written and administered, most such laws "are of a secular rather than of a religious character," seeking "to set one day apart from all others as a day of rest, repose, recreation and tranquility." The choice of Sunday, "a day of particular significance for the dominant Christian sects," did not "bar the state from achieving its secular goals."

McGowan emphasized that a Sunday closing law might violate the establishment clause if its purpose were "to use the State's coercive power to aid religion." This warning was fulfilled in EPPERSON V. ARKANSAS (1968), when the Court invalidated a law that excised the theory of human biological evolution from public school curricula. Reviewing the circumstances of its adoption in 1928, the Court found that "fundamentalist sectarian conviction was and still is the law's reason for existence."

Although Arkansas probably exceeded what the free exercise clause required for "accommodation" of fundamentalist religious doctrine, there was no indication that its anti-evolution statute coerced, compromised, or influenced school children to embrace fundamentalist doctrine. The Arkansas statute thus satisfied religious needs with no meaningful threat to religious liberty—the chief danger the establishment clause was intended to avoid. Yet, as in the Ten Commandments and moment-of-silence cases, a religious purpose alone proved fatal.

The Court first gave plenary consideration to the problem of public aid to church-related schools in *Everson v. Board of Education* (1947). A New Jersey township reimbursed parents for the cost of sending their children on public buses to and from schools, including Roman Catholic parochial schools. Although the Court asserted that "no tax . . . can be levied to support any religious activity or institution," it upheld the New Jersey program by a 5–4 vote. The majority conceded that without the program's subsidy some children might not be sent to church schools. But it reasoned that funding bus transportation for all pupils in both public and sectarian schools accomplished the "public purpose" of aiding parents in getting their children "safely and expeditiously to and from accredited schools." In this respect, New Jersey's aid program was similar to providing all schools with basic municipal services, such as fire and police protection. Furthermore, the state could not constitutionally exclude persons from its aid "because of their faith, or lack of it." (The *Everson* majority indicated that bus transportation might be the limit of permissible assistance.) The dissenters protested that the program aided children "in a substantial way to get the very thing which they are sent to [parochial schools] to secure, namely, religious training and teaching."

The Court did not again confront the issue of aid to church-related schools until BOARD OF EDUCATION V. ALLEN (1968). During the intervening two decades, the Court had developed the "secular purpose-secular effect" standard. *Allen* held that New York's lending secular textbooks, approved by local school boards, to all secondary school students, including those in church-related schools, had the secular purpose of furthering education and a primary effect that benefited students and parents, not religious schools.

The "excessive entanglement" prong of the Court's establishment clause test emerged two years later. WALZ V. TAX COMMISSION (1970) rejected the claim that New York's tax exemption for "real or personal property used exclusively for religious, educational or charitable purposes" supported religion in violation of the establishment clause. After finding that the exemption had the nonreligious purpose of avoiding inhibition on the activities of charities and other community institutions, the Court continued: "We must also be sure that the end result—the effect—is not an excessive government entanglement with religion. The test is inescapably one of degree. Either course, taxation of churches or exemptions, occasions some degree of involvement with religion. . . . [The question is] whether it is a continuing one calling for official and continuing surveillance leading to an impermissible degree of entanglement." The Court conceded that tax exemption accorded an indirect economic benefit to religion, but concluded that it gave rise to less government involvement than nonexemption. Taxing the churches would occasion "tax valuation of church property, tax liens, tax foreclosures, and the direct confrontations and conflicts that follow in the train of those legal processes."

In LEMON V. KURTZMAN (1971) the Court returned to the problem of church-related schools. Rhode Island subsidized public and private school teachers of secular subjects (not to exceed fifteen percent of their salaries); parochial school teachers agreed not to teach religion during the subsidy. The legislature had found that "the quality of education available in nonpublic elementary schools has been jeopardized [by] rapidly rising salaries." Pennsylvania reimbursed nonpublic schools for the salaries of teachers of "secular" subjects such as mathematics, physical science, physical education, and foreign languages. Church-related schools maintained accounts, subject to state audit, that segregated the costs of "secular educational service." Reimbursement for religiously oriented courses was prohibited.

The Court held that both programs violated the establishment clause. It acknowledged a secular purpose, but reasoned that the states' efforts to avoid a primary effect that advanced religion produced "excessive entanglement between government and religion." In the Court's view, church-related elementary and secondary schools had as their mission the inculcation of religious doctrine, especially among "impressionable" primary school pupils. Continuing state evaluation of school records "to establish the cost of secular as distinguished from religious instruction," and the state "surveillance necessary to ensure that teachers play a strictly nonideological role" were "pregnant with dangers of excessive government direction of Church schools and hence of Churches." Although this "administrative" entanglement was fatal, both laws risked another sort of entanglement: their "divisive political potential" along religious lines, given the likely demand for continuing and ever increasing annual appropriations.

The excessive entanglement criterion has been prominent in establishment clause adjudication since 1970; but it does not represent a value that either can or should be judicially secured by the establishment clause. The major fear of administrative entanglement between government and religion is that state regulation impairs the ability of religious groups to pursue their mission. This concern, however, is unfounded both doctrinally and empirically. At least since PIERCE V. SOCIETY OF SISTERS (1925) it has been understood that the Constitution permits the state to regulate church-related institutions whether or not it provides them financial assistance. Parochial school curricula, for example, have long been regulated without significant evidence of infringement of religious values. And if there were, the regulation would be invalid whether or not tied to monetary aid.

Another form of administrative entanglement regularly occurs when the state seeks to distinguish religion from nonreligion in order to grant an exemption from civil regulations. Although government scrutiny of religious beliefs is a sensitive task, the need for that scrutiny springs from the Constitution's explicit definition of religion as a subject for special treatment.

Similar objections can be raised to using "avoidance of political strife along religious lines" as a criterion for establishment clause adjudication. Indeed, if government were to ban religious conflict in the legislative process, serious questions of First Amendment political liberty would arise. But practical considerations, more than doctrinal ones, demonstrate the futility of making "political divisiveness" a constitutional determinant. Legislation does not violate the establishment clause simply because religious organizations support or oppose it. Religious groups have frequently differed on secular political issues—gambling, OBSCENITY, drug and gun control, CONSCRIPTION, PROHIBITION, abolition of slavery, racial integration, prostitution, sterilization, abortion, BIRTH CONTROL, divorce, the VIETNAM WAR, the EQUAL RIGHTS Amendment, and CAPITAL PUNISHMENT, to name but a few. Churches and other religious groups have markedly influenced resolution of some of these matters. In the early 1980s, they actively debated the question of the nation's nuclear arms policy. Although a law may in fact promote a religious purpose, if the law serves genuinely secular ends—and impairs no one's religious liberty by coercing, compromising, or influencing religious beliefs—it should not be unconstitutional simply because its proponents and antagonists were divided along religious lines.

Moreover, even if government could or should eliminate religious fragmentation in the political arena, the establishment clause is an ineffective tool for the task. For example, forbidding aid to parochial schools does not effect a truce, but only moves the battleground; if children in parochial schools are excluded from school aid, their parents will tend to oppose increased funding of public schools.

The Court has viewed aid to church-related higher education more favorably than it has viewed aid to elementary and secondary schools. *Tilton v. Richardson* (1971), a companion case to *Lemon,* upheld federal construction grants to colleges for buildings and facilities that applicants agreed not to use for religious instruction. The government enforced this promise by on-site inspections. The Court easily found a secular purpose in the expansion of higher education opportunities. In reasoning that the subsidy's primary effect did not advance religion, it stated that, unlike elementary and secondary schools, church-related colleges were not "permeated" by religion. Their dominant motive is secular education; they normally afford

a high degree of ACADEMIC FREEDOM for faculty and students; and their students are less susceptible to religious indoctrination than are school children. In sharp contrast to its generalized appraisal of parochial schools, the Court rejected a "composite profile" of a "typical sectarian" college. Instead, the Court found, on the record before it, that courses at the four recipient Roman Catholic institutions were taught according to professional academic standards. Moreover, the aid took the form of a one-time, single-purpose construction grant. Thus no appreciable governmental surveillance was required. Finally, the Court found the potential for "religious fragmentation in the political arena" lessened by the religious colleges' geographically diverse student bodies and the absence of religious affiliation of a majority of recipient colleges.

Decisions since *Tilton* have continued to sustain aid to religiously affiliated colleges. In *Hunt v. McNair* (1973) the Court upheld the use of South Carolina tax-exempt bonds to finance facilities for all colleges, so long as the facilities were limited to nonsectarian purposes. The Court placed the burden on those challenging the aid to establish that recipient colleges are "permeated" with religion. And in *Roemer v. Board of Public Works* (1976) the Court upheld Maryland grants of fifteen percent of the student cost in the state college system to all private colleges, if they certified that they used the funds for nonreligious purposes.

Subsequent decisions on aid to elementary and secondary schools have generally, but not unexceptionally, followed the path of *Lemon. Meek v. Pittenger* (1975) involved a program under which Pennsylvania lent instructional materials (such as maps, films, projectors, and laboratory equipment) to private schools, seventy-five percent of which were church-related. The Court agreed that the aid was ideologically neutral, but held that "when it flows to an institution in which religion is so pervasive that a substantial portion of its functions are subsumed in the religious mission," it has the primary effect of advancing religion. The Court also invalidated "auxiliary services" (such as standardized testing, speech therapy, and psychological counseling) by public employees for private school children on their schools' premises: "To be certain that auxiliary teachers remain religiously neutral . . . the State would have to impose limitations . . . and then engage in some form of continuing surveillance to ensure that those restrictions were being followed." In addition to this "administrative entanglement," the Court observed that the program promised to generate "political entanglement" in the form of "continuing political strife." (The Court reaffirmed this holding as to auxiliary services in 1985 in the COMPANION CASES of *Grand Rapids School District v. Ball* and AGUILAR V. FELTON.)

Two years after *Meek*, *Wolman v. Walter* (1977) illustrated how constitutionality may turn on slight changes in form. The Court upheld Ohio's provision of (1) speech, hearing, and psychological diagnostic services by public employees on private school premises; (2) therapeutic and remedial services by public employees at a "neutral site off the premises" of the private school (even if in an adjacent mobile unit); and (3) payment for standardized tests used in private schools (the dispositive factor being that the tests were drafted and scored by public employees). The Court distinguished *Meek* on paperthin grounds relating to the closeness of the connection between the services provided and the religious school's educational mission and to the likelihood that public employees would "transmit ideological views" to children.

Wolman invalidated state payment for field trips of private school pupils, distinguishing *Everson* on the basis of the school's control over the expenditure of the funds and the close relation of the expenditure to the school's curriculum. The Court also invalidated a program for lending instructional materials to students, but, as in *Meek*, reaffirmed *Allen* and upheld lending students secular textbooks.

COMMITTEE FOR PUBLIC EDUCATION V. REGAN (1980) upheld New York's reimbursing private schools for performing testing and reporting services mandated by state law. The tests were prepared by the state, but, unlike those in *Wolman*, some were administered and scored by private school personnel. Nevertheless, because the tests were mostly objective, the Court concluded that there was little risk of their religious use. The Court distinguished *Levitt v. Committee for Public Education* (1973), which had invalidated a similar New York statute because it did not provide for state audits to ensure that the public funds did not exceed the nonpublic school's actual cost. In *Regan*, the occasional audits were found adequate to prevent a religious effect but not so intrusive as to produce excessive entanglement.

As of the mid-1980s, the most effective way for government to assist elementary and secondary parochial schools is through the tax system. In COMMITTEE FOR PUBLIC EDUCATION V. NYQUIST (1973) the Court invalidated a New York program, which the Court agreed had a "secular purpose," that gave tuition grants to low-income parents and tax relief to middle-income parents of children in private schools. The

Court held that this had the effect of aiding the religious functions of sectarian schools. The Court distinguished *Walz* on several grounds. First, unlike the *Nyquist* programs, tax exemptions for church property had ample historical precedent, being "widespread during colonial days" and currently "in force in all 50 states." Second, although property tax exemption tended to lessen involvement between church and state, the programs in *Nyquist* tended to increase it. Finally, the tax exemption in *Walz* went to a broad class of charitable, religious, and educational institutions, but the record in *Nyquist* showed that eighty-five percent of the children benefited attended sectarian schools, practically all run by the Roman Catholic Church.

A decade later, in MUELLER V. ALLEN (1983), the Court upheld a Minnesota program granting a state income tax deduction for parents with children in *any* nonprofit school, public or private. This deduction could be used for expenditures for tuition and transportation, as well as for textbooks and instructional materials and equipment (so long as they were not used to teach religion). The Court conceded that the "economic consequences" of the Minnesota program were "difficult to distinguish" from the New York program in *Nyquist*. But that it was difficult did not make it impossible. One difference the Court found was that *Mueller* involved "a genuine tax deduction," whereas the *Nyquist* tax credit was more like a direct grant than a tax benefit. The Court found most significant that the *Mueller* plan was available to all parents, not just those with children in private schools. Thus, the plan was "facially neutral" and its "primary effect" did not advance religion. The Court reached this conclusion even though ninety-six percent of the Minnesota deductions were taken by parents who sent their children to parochial schools—mainly Roman Catholic and Lutheran. As for the other four percent, there were only seventy-nine public school students who deducted tuition, which they paid because they attended public schools outside their districts for special reasons. Of course, children who attended public schools in their districts did get some deductions—for the cost of pencils, notebooks, and other incidentals not customarily provided.

The lesson to be drawn from all the elementary and secondary school decisions is that states wishing to provide significant financial assistance may do so simply by adopting the proper form. For example, New York could successfully revive its program invalidated in *Nyquist* by providing a tax benefit to all parents, including those whose children attend public schools, knowing that this would not appreciably increase the cost of the plan. But New York might be required to use the form of a tax deduction (rather than a tax credit or direct grant as in *Nyquist*), a difference of vital importance to parents with low incomes, who would obtain little benefit from a tax deduction.

Application of the Court's three-part test to the problem of GOVERNMENT AID TO RELIGIOUS INSTITUTIONS has generated ad hoc judgments incapable of being reconciled on a principled basis. The Court has assumed that the entire program of parochial schools is "permeated" with religion. But there is much dispute as to the facts. Some "secular" subjects in some parochial schools are unquestionably courses of religious indoctrination; other courses are truly secular; many probably fall between these polar characterizations. Thus, public aid incidentally benefits religion. But virtually all government services to church-related facilities—whether bus transportation, police and fire protection, sewage connections, sidewalks, tuition grants, or textbooks—incidentally benefit their sectarian functions by releasing church funds for religious purposes.

The critical inquiry should be whether direct or indirect government assistance to parochial schools exceeds the value of the secular educational service the schools render. If it does not, there is no use of tax-raised funds to aid religion, and thus no danger to religious liberty. This inquiry differs from the Court's approach, which has often invalidated laws with secular purposes because of their effects in advancing religion. A state program with both a secular purpose and a secular effect does not threaten values underlying the establishment clause. Furthermore, when the Court invalidates such a law simply because it incidentally furthers religious interests, the Justices assert the power to assess the multiple impacts of legislation, to separate religious from secular effects, and then to determine which are paramount. Ultimately the Justices must then rely on their own subjective notions of predominance.

In the mid-1980s, the Court was twice confronted with the problem of government practices that specifically acknowledge religion. MARSH V. CHAMBERS (1983) upheld Nebraska's paying a chaplain to open each legislative session with a prayer. Proceeding unusually, the Court did not apply its three-part test. Rather, it relied first on history and tradition—pointing out that paid legislative chaplains and opening prayers existed in the Continental Congress, the First Congress, and every Congress thereafter, as well as in most states today and in colonies such as Virginia and Rhode Island, both of which were bastions of religious liberty. Second, the Court rested on the intent of the Framers, noting that just three days after the First Congress had authorized paid chaplains it approved the Bill of Rights; this made it difficult to believe that the Framers could conceive of the establishment clause as prohibiting legislative chaplains. Thus, the practice survived challenge even though Nebraska's purpose was unquestionably religious and the Court's doctrine is that such purpose alone produces an establishment clause violation.

A year later, in LYNCH V. DONNELLY (1984), the Court sustained Pawtucket, Rhode Island's inclusion of a nativity scene in the city's annual Christmas season display. The cost was nominal, unlike the $320 expended monthly for Nebraska's chaplain in *Marsh*. The Court reasoned that the purpose and effect were not exclusively religious but, rather, that "the creche in the display depicts the historical origins of this traditional event long recognized as a National Holiday." The opinion also emphasized that our history was replete with government recognition of religion's role in American life and with government expressions of religious belief. As examples, it pointed to presidential proclamations of national days of prayer and of Thanksgiving and Christmas as national holidays, public funding of a chapel in the Capitol and of chaplains in the legislature and in the military, "In God We Trust" as our statutorily prescribed national motto, the language "One Nation under God" as part of the Pledge of Allegiance, and the plethora of religious paintings in publicly supported galleries and in public buildings. Stating that "this history may help explain why the Court consistently has declined to take a rigid, absolutist view of the Establishment Clause," the Court strongly suggested that all these deeply ingrained practices were constitutional.

The final important church–state separation issue concerns the tension between the First Amendment's two religion clauses, one forbidding government to promote or "establish" religion, the other forbidding government to abridge the "free exercise" of religion. As observed in *Walz*, both "are cast in absolute terms, and either . . . if expanded to a logical extreme, would tend to clash with the other." Charting a course that offends neither provision presents a continual challenge for the Court; yet its few direct confrontations with the problem have been unsatisfying.

The two most celebrated free exercise clause decisions illustrate the inherent conflict. In SHERBERT V. VERNER (1962) a Seventh-Day Adventist was discharged by her employer because she would not work on Saturday, her Sabbath. South Carolina denied her unemployment compensation for refusing "suitable work," that is, a job requiring Saturday labor. The

Court held that this denial violated the free exercise clause by conditioning benefits on a violation of her religious faith. Although the Court's decision implements the free exercise clause, the purpose of its ruling—like the purpose of the released time program in *McCollum*—is clearly to facilitate religious practice. Thus, the exemption required by the Court in the name of the free exercise clause appears to violate the Court's establishment clause doctrine, which renders invalid any government action with a nonsecular purpose. The Court's conclusory response was that "plainly we are not fostering the 'establishment' of the Seventh-day Adventist religion" but rather governmental "neutrality in the face of religious differences."

In WISCONSIN V. YODER (1971) the Court held that application of school attendance requirements to the Old Order Amish violated the free exercise clause. In characterizing this as an "accommodation" for the Amish, the Court rejected the contention that this religious exemption violated the establishment clause: "The purpose and effect of such an exemption are not to support, favor, advance or assist the Amish, but to allow their centuries-old religious society . . . to survive free from the heavy impediment compliance with the Wisconsin compulsory-education law would impose."

In THORNTON V. CALDOR, INC. (1985), however, the Court ruled that a state had gone too far in "accommodating" religion. It held that a Connecticut law that required employers to give a day off to employees on their Sabbath, "no matter what burden or inconvenience this imposes on the employer or fellow workers," had the "primary effect" of advancing "a particular religious practice" and thus violated the establishment clause. The Court emphasized the "absolute and unqualified right not to work" afforded the employees, although this appeared to be little different from the exemption that the Court itself had ordered in *Sherbert*.

Although there is considerable overlap in the purposes of the establishment and free exercise clauses—their central function being to secure religious liberty—the decisions disclose that each has an identifiable emphasis. In the main, the free exercise clause protects adherents of religious faiths from secularly motivated laws whose effect burdens them because of their particular beliefs. When the Court finds a violation of the free exercise clause, the law is normally held invalid as applied; all that is required is an exemption for the claimant from the law's otherwise proper operation. In contrast, the principal thrust of the establishment clause concerns religiously

motivated laws that pose the danger to believers and nonbelievers of being required to support their own religious observance or that of others. When the Court finds a violation of the establishment clause, ordinarily the offensive provision is entirely invalid and may not be enforced at all.

A better approach would reconcile the conflict between the clauses by interpreting the establishment clause to forbid only those laws whose purpose is to favor religion, and then only if such laws tend to coerce, compromise, or influence religious beliefs. Under this standard, the religious exemption that the Court required in *Sherbert* would itself be unconstitutional because it impairs religious liberty by supporting religion with funds raised by taxation. Although the core value of religious liberty may forbid government to interfere with Sherbert's practice of Seventh-Day Adventism, it similarly forbids forcing other citizens to subsidize a religious practice. On the other hand, the proposed alternative approach probably would not change the result in *Yoder*; it is doubtful that exempting the Amish from the compulsory education law (or giving employees a day off on their Sabbath, as in *Thornton*) would tend to coerce, compromise, or influence religious choice. Finally, the alternative approach would distinguish *Yoder* from those decisions—such as *McCollum*, *Engel*, and *Schempp*—that have invalidated religious practices in public schools. Neither these programs nor the exemption in *Yoder* had a "secular" purpose. But, unlike *Yoder* and *Thornton*, the public school programs threatened religious liberty and were thus properly held to abridge the constitutional separation of church and state.

JESSE H. CHOPER

Bibliography

ANTIEAU, CHESTER J.; DOWNEY, ARTHUR T.; and ROBERTS, EDWARD C. 1964 *Freedom from Federal Establishment.* Milwaukee, Wisc.: Bruce Publishing Co.

CHOPER, JESSE H. 1963 Religion in the Public Schools: A Proposed Constitutional Standard. *University of Minnesota Law Review* 47:329–416.

——— 1968 The Establishment Clause and Aid to Parochial Schools. *California Law Review* 56:260–341.

——— 1980 The Religion Clauses of the First Amendment: Reconciling the Conflict. *University of Pittsburgh Law Review* 41:673–701.

CURRY, THOMAS 1986 *The First Freedoms.* New York: Oxford University Press.

HOWE, MARK D. 1965 *The Garden and the Wilderness.* Chicago: University of Chicago Press.

KURLAND, PHILIP B. 1962 *Religion and the Law.* Chicago: Aldine Publishing Co.

LEVY, LEONARD W. 1986 *An Establishment of Religion.* New York: Macmillan.

MURRAY, JOHN C. 1960 *We Hold These Truths.* Chap. 2. New York: Sheed & Ward.

NOWAK, JOHN E.; ROTUNDA, RONALD D.; and YOUNG, J. NELSON 1983 *Handbook on Constitutional Law,* 2nd ed. Pages 1229–1281. St. Paul, Minn.: West Publishing Co.

PFEFFER, LEO 1984 *Religion, State, and the Burger Court.* Buffalo, N.Y.: Prometheus Books.

SCHWARTZ, ALAN 1968 No Imposition of Religion: The Establishment Clause Value. *Yale Law Journal* 77:692–737.

STOKES, ANSON PHELPS 1950 *Church & State in the United States.* 3 Vols. New York: Harper.

TRIBE, LAURENCE H. 1978 *American Constitutional Law.* Chap. 14. Mineola, N.Y.: Foundation Press.

SEPARATION OF POWERS

Any system of constitutional government must have as one of its central principles some degree of separation of powers. A system of government in which all legal power and authority is exercised by one person or group of people must depend entirely upon their self-restraint in the exercise of that power. The history of government does not suggest that such self-restraint is likely this side of heaven or utopia, and efforts to prevent the abuse of the powers of government have therefore focused on constitutional arrangements that divide and limit the powers of government.

The doctrine of the separation of powers consists of a number of elements: the idea of three separate branches of government, the legislature, the executive, and the judiciary; the belief that there are unique functions appropriate to each branch; and the assertion that the personnel of the branches of government should be kept distinct, no one person being able to be a member of more than one branch of government at the same time. The more pure or extreme the form of the doctrine, the greater the extent to which all three of these elements are insisted upon without reservation or modification. In past centuries political writers have proposed such extreme solutions in France, Britain, and America, and attempts have been made, unsuccessfully, to approximate as closely as possible to this extreme in practice. The spirit of the doctrine was expressed clearly in the Constitution of Virginia in 1776: "The legislature, executive and judiciary departments shall be separate and distinct, so that neither exercise the powers properly belonging to the other: nor shall any person exercise the powers of more than one of them at the same time. . . ."

A further aspect of the doctrine is the concern with the method by which the members of the executive and judicial branches are selected, for this will have implications for the extent to which the members of one branch may be able to influence the behavior of members of another. The more extreme versions of the doctrine therefore demand the direct election of members of all three branches of government in order that they should be responsible directly to the people, and not dependent upon each other. In the words of Samuel Williams, historian of Vermont, in 1794, "the security of the people is derived not from the nice ideal application of checks, balances, and mechanical powers, among the different parts of the government, but from the responsibility, and dependence of each part of the government, on the people."

The doctrine of the separation of powers, standing alone, however, has never been able to provide the kind of safeguards against the abuse of governmental power which it claims to provide. In practice we find that CHECKS AND BALANCES are required to prevent one or another branch of government from becoming too dominant. The idea of internal checks, exercised by one branch of government over the others, is drawn from the ancient theory of mixed government, and from the eighteenth-century "mixed and balanced constitution" of Great Britain. Thus JAMES MADISON, in THE FEDERALIST #48, undertook to show that unless the branches of government "be so far connected and blended as to give each a constitutional control over the others, the degree of separation which the maxim requires, as essential to a free government, can never in practice be duly maintained." All constitutional systems of government are therefore an amalgam of the separation of powers and checks and balances. The exact composition of this mixture was a central problem for the Framers of the federal Constitution, and their solution distinguished presidential-congressional government from parliamentary systems.

The emergence of a full-blown doctrine of the separation of powers was the result of a long process of development, involving the refinement of a set of concepts, including the idea of law itself, which today we largely take for granted. In early times the idea of law was very different from the modern concept of legislation or statute law. The latter view of law, consciously drafted and adopted by human rather than divine will, did not emerge clearly until the battle between king and parliament in seventeenth-century England sharpened the perception of law, lawyers, and politicians. The more radical opponents of royal power conceived of a parliament that was representative of the people, making laws which the king, or some other executive power, should put into effect. In the turmoil of civil war, this doctrine of the separation of powers was fashioned by a number of writers until it reached a recognizably modern form.

As the British constitutional crisis deepened, the doctrine was refined by those who, like John Milton, pointed to the arbitrary character of the Long Parliament, Henry Ireton in the Whitehall debates of 1649, and JOHN LILBURNE in *The Picture of the Councel of State* asserting that "the House itself was never (neither now, nor in any age before) betrusted with a Law executing power, but only with a Law making power." John Sadler in his *The Rights of the Kingdom* of 1649 asserted the basis of the separation of powers very clearly. The three powers of government, legislative, judicial, and executive, "should be in Distinct Subjects; by the Law of Nature, for if Lawmakers be judges, of those that break their Laws; they seem to be judges in their own cause: which our Law, and Nature itself, so much avoideth and abhorreth, so it seemeth also to forbid, both the Lawmaker, and the Judge to Execute."

The execution of Charles I and the establishment of republican government stripped away the remaining vestiges of mixed government and left the separation of powers as the sole constitutional principle for the organization of the government of Great Britain. The Commonwealth produced the first written constitution of modern times, the Instrument of Government of 1653, and the doctrine of the separation of powers clearly inspired its authors. This document vested the supreme legislative authority in the lord protector and the people assembled in Parliament, but in effect the role of the protector in legislation was to be limited to a suspensive veto of twenty days. The Instrument also provided that "the exercise of the Chief Magistracy and the administration of the Government . . . shall be in the Lord Protector, assisted with a Council." Although the Instrument of Government was never an effective basis for government, from that time on the theory of the separation of powers emerged and reemerged whenever demands were made to limit the power of governments. The official defense of the Instrument, *A True State of the Case of the Commonwealth*, published in 1654, and probably written by Marchamont Nedham, expressed the theory behind the constitution when it criticized earlier institutional arrangements "which placing the legislative and executive powers in the same persons is a marvellous in-let of corruption and tyranny." At this point the idea of a judicial power distinct from the executive was still relatively unde-

veloped, to emerge more fully at the end of the seventeenth century, and then to blossom in the work of MONTESQUIEU and WILLIAM BLACKSTONE, and to be embodied in the Constitution of the United States.

With the restoration of Charles II in 1660 the basis of a new theory of the constitution was required. The principle of the separation of powers must be reasserted, as it was by JOHN LOCKE, but in the context of a "mixed and balanced" constitution, incorporating a role for the monarch and for the House of Lords. This amalgam of the separation of powers and checks and balances, the constitution of the Augustan Age of British politics, was lauded as the model of "a constitution of liberty." Montesquieu is popularly credited with a major role in the development of the separation of powers, but the theory was developed a hundred years before the publication of *The Spirit of the Laws* (1748). Indeed it is the influence of his work, particularly in the American colonies, rather than any intellectual contribution to the separation of powers, that gives such significance to the work of Montesquieu. Montesquieu's contribution to the separation of powers was essentially his modern emphasis upon the three powers of government and the clear recognition of the importance of the power to judge, a point driven home by Blackstone in his *Commentaries on the Laws of England* (1765–1769). Blackstone, whose work was known to every lawyer in the American colonies, took Montesquieu's rather feeble notion of the judicial power and clothed it with the majesty of the English judges.

From the time of the first English settlements in America there was a continual interplay between ideas and events in the home country and the developing politics of the colonies. Mixed government and the separation of powers were common subjects of discussion in Massachusetts in the seventeenth century, and the constitutional debates over the role of king and parliament in England had their repercussions in America. In 1644, the elders of the church described the government of Massachusetts Bay as not a "pure aristocracy, but mixt of an aristocracy and democracy" and defended the "negative voice" which the governor and assistants exercised over decisions of the legislature. In 1679 the elders affirmed that the government of Massachusetts consisted in the "distribution of differing interest of power and privilege between the magistrates and freemen, and the distinct exercise of legislative and executive power." This statement preceded by eleven years the publication of Locke's *Second Treatise*. In the eighteenth century American thought fell into the same mold as that of other eulogists of the English constitution, adapting the terminology where necessary to fit the circumstances of colonial governments, until the increasing conflict between the English Parliament and the colonists brought to the foreground those aspects of the English system that were attracting criticism both at home and abroad, the cabinet system and the corrupt and unrepresentative House of Commons. In the colonies, Americans saw the mixing of legislative, executive, and judicial functions in the governors' councils and in the abuse of power by royal governors. With the upsurge of revolutionary fervor the doctrine of the separation of powers lay ready to hand, both as a stick with which to beat the British and as the basis for a truly American system of government.

The American achievement was to transform the theory of the mixed constitution, in which the powers of government were distributed among monarchy, aristocracy, and democracy, into a functionally divided system in which king and peers had no part, turning a class-based structure into one in which all the different branches of government drew their authority from the people. The first step in this process was taken when the revolutionary state constitutions were established in 1776 and succeeding years. These constitutions contained broad affirmations of the separation of powers, but the checks and balances of the British model were out of favor. Consequently, popularly elected legislatures became the dominant branch of government.

The state legislatures soon began to act in ways that raised fears that the separation of powers, if not buttressed in some other way, meant that in practice, in THOMAS JEFFERSON's words, "All the powers of government, legislative, executive, and judiciary, result to the legislative body." The need for positive checks to the exercise of power was increasingly apparent. The *Essex Result* of 1778, recommending the form which the new constitution for Massachusetts should take, noted that "Each branch is to be independent, and further, to be so balanced, and able to exert such checks upon the others, as will preserve it from dependance on, or a union with them." Madison summed up the situation in *The Federalist* #48: "The conclusion that I am warranted in drawing from these observations is, that a mere demarcation on parchment of the constitutional limits of the several departments is not a sufficient guard against those encroachments which lead to a tyrannical concentration of all the powers of government in the same hands."

It was necessary therefore that the departments of government should "be so far connected and blended as to give to each a constitutional control over the others": the President to have a qualified VETO POWER and the PARDONING POWER, the Senate to play a part in appointments and in the ratification of treaties, and the Supreme Court, by implication at least, to have the power to declare legislative acts to be unconstitutional. As Madison observed in *The Federalist* #48, the three branches of government, although separate, must be "connected and blended" to ensure that each has some "constitutional control over the others."

Thus the separation of powers was not destroyed but rather reinforced by the adoption in the Constitution of a number of checks and balances. Although in some degree this represented a reversion to the pattern of the English Constitution, there was one vital respect in which no one wished to see the English model adopted. The popular denigration of George III as a tyrant in the revolutionary situation was understandable, but the members of the CONSTITUTIONAL CONVENTION had a much deeper understanding of the British political system. They understood the nature of the "*Cabinet Council* composed entirely of the principal officers of the great departments," they understood the role of the king's ministers in the legislature, and they knew well the system of crown influence and the role of unqualified members of the House of Commons. Their rejection of the whole basis of linking the executive and legislative branches of government in this way was complete, and Article I, section 6, of the Constitution, which provided that "no Person holding any Office under the United States, shall be a Member of either House during his Continuance in Office," was adopted without hesitation.

What then have been the practical effects of the separation of powers on the legal and political system of the United States? These effects can be seen in two broad, related areas: the decisions of the Supreme Court relating to "the powers of government," and the political articulation of the American system.

The Supreme Court has faced a number of difficulties which arise from the confusions inherent in the way the "separation of powers" evolved. The term "separation of powers" is sometimes used, as here, to refer to the doctrine that the major branches of government should be kept separate and limited to their own functions, but quite often the term is also used to include the checks and balances in the Constitution, which derive their rationale from a different source. Second, the word "power" is used ambiguously to mean both "branch" and "function." Finally, most of the Court's problems arise from the need to define the functions of government when it is argued that a particular branch has engaged in an activity outside its "proper" function. When the Constitution itself makes what the Court in BAKER V. CARR (1962) called "a textually demonstrable commitment" of an issue to a coordinate branch of government, then the Court has only to determine that to be the case, but what does the text demonstrate when it refers to "the legislative power" or "the executive power"? Such terms are vague indeed. The nub of the problem is that the functions of government can be defined only in the broadest conceptual terms—making rules, carrying rules into effect, and settling disputes arising out of the application of rules—but few activities of government fall unambiguously into such categories. The difficulty is particularly acute in any effort to categorize the exercise of the discretionary powers of government which the traditional doctrine of the separation of powers did not encompass. Indeed, the doctrine had been developed largely to render ineffective the exercise of such discretion in the form of the prerogatives of the Crown in England, or in the exercise of the powers of the governors in the American colonies.

As a consequence of these difficulties the Court has generally followed a pragmatic course in its decisions on the separation of powers. In practice the Court has generally accepted that no precise "watertight definition of government powers is possible." The first major issue facing the Supreme Court was to define its own role in the system of separation of powers and checks and balances. The Anti-Federalist and Jeffersonian interpretations of the Constitution looked back to the strict view that each branch of government not only should be separate from the others but also should not be dependent upon them, and therefore not subject to their control. Such an interpretation would rule out JUDICIAL REVIEW as it has come to be exercised in the United States, and faint echoes of this attempt to escape the JURISDICTION of the Court have been heard as recently as President RICHARD M. NIXON's claim to an absolute EXECUTIVE PRIVILEGE for tape recordings of his conversations with his aides. However, in MARBURY V. MADISON (1803) Chief Justice JOHN MARSHALL emphatically asserted that it was "the province and duty of the judicial department to say what the law is"—and, in the course of doing so, to rule upon the extent of the power and functions of the other branches of government. Respect is due to the interpretations put on the Constitution by other branches, but in the end, as the Court said in UNITED STATES V. NIXON (1974), "the 'JUDICIAL POWER OF THE UNITED STATES' vested in the federal courts by Art. III Sec. 1, of the Constitution can no more be shared with the Executive Branch than the Chief Executive, for example, can share with the Judiciary the power to override a Presidential veto. Any other conclusion would be contrary to the basic concept of separation of powers and checks and balances that flow from the scheme of a tripartite government." The Court has, of course, accepted that interference in the activities of the other branches of government, in particular the Congress, is a delicate and sensitive matter. The POLITICAL QUESTIONS doctrine protects the Court against becoming embroiled in matters that could drag it down into the morass of day-to-day politics, but the Court itself retains the right to determine what is, and what is not, a political question.

The Supreme Court has set limits to the exercise of the legislative powers of Congress either to interfere directly in litigation, to interpret earlier legislation, or to set aside decisions of courts already made. It has also ruled that, as in HAYBURN'S CASE (1792) and *United States v. Ferreira* (1853), Congress cannot impose upon the courts duties not considered to be judicial in character. In two major decisions the Supreme Court announced that the houses of Congress could not properly appropriate to themselves a judicial function. In KILBOURN V. THOMPSON (1881) the Court concluded that in committing a witness to prison for refusing to testify before a committee the House of Representatives had "not only exceeded the limit of its own authority, but assumed power which could only be properly exercised by another branch of the government, because the power was in its nature clearly judicial." And OBITER DICTUM in WATKINS V. UNITED STATES (1957), the Court said, "Nor is the Congress a law enforcement or trial agency. These are functions of the executive and judicial departments of government."

The Supreme Court has also prevented Congress from trenching upon the powers of the executive branch. In MYERS V. UNITED STATES (1926) the Court held that Congress could not limit by statute the President's power to remove executive officers, although in HUMPHREY's EXECUTOR V. UNITED STATES (1935) it upheld congressional restrictions on the President's power to dismiss officers of independent regulatory agencies; and in BUCKLEY V. VALEO (1976) the Court invalidated the attempt by Congress itself to make appointments to the Federal Elections Commission. The Court quoted with approval the decision in *Springer v. Philippine Islands* (1928): "Legislative power, as distinguished from executive power, is the authority to make laws, but not to enforce them or appoint the agents charged with the duty of such enforcement. The latter are executive functions."

In general the Supreme Court has been generous in its interpretation of the powers of the President. However, in two important instances the Court has checked presidential power. In YOUNGSTOWN SHEET AND TUBE COMPANY V. SAWYER (1951) the Court held unconstitutional President Harry S. Truman's attempt to take over steel mills by EXECUTIVE ORDER, on the ground that "the President's power to see that the laws are faithfully executed refutes the idea that he is to be a lawmaker. The Constitution limits his functions in the lawmaking process to the recommending of laws he thinks wise and the vetoing of laws he thinks bad." And in *United States v. Nixon* (1974) the Court rejected the President's claim of executive privilege against a court order to produce tapes and documents relating to the Watergate investigations.

The area in which the Supreme Court has been subjected to the greatest degree of criticism for failing to maintain the spirit and practice of the separation of powers has been the way in which it has handled the question of the DELEGATION OF POWER by Congress to the executive branch and to independent regulatory commissions. In the modern administrative state, complex regulatory activities on the part of government necessitate agencies that will make rules (subordinate to statute law), apply those rules, and decide disputes arising out of their actions. The United States Congress, in establishing a large number of such agencies, has created a "headless fourth branch" of government. These agencies, in the words of Justice ROBERT H. JACKSON in *Federal Trade Commission v. Ruberoid Company* (1952), "have been called quasi-legislative, quasi-executive or quasi-judicial, as the occasion required, in order to validate their function within the separation of powers scheme of the Constitution. The mere retreat to the qualifying 'quasi' is implicit with confession that all recognized classifications have broken down, and 'quasi' is a smooth cover which we draw over our confusion as we might use a counterpane to conceal a disordered bed." Although the Court has said "that the legislative power of Congress cannot be delegated," in practice it has allowed very broad and ill-defined delegations of power to administrative agencies. In two instances such delegation of power has been disallowed: PANAMA REFINING CO. V. RYAN (1935) and SCHECHTER POULTRY CORP. V. UNITED STATES (1935). In the latter case the Court asserted that the proper delegation of power required Congress to establish "standards of legal obligation, thus performing its essential legislative function." Failure to enact such standards for the administrative agency to follow would be an attempt to transfer the legislative function of Congress to others. However, in numerous cases the Court has allowed delegation with little in the way of effective standards set by Congress, and giving to the administrative agency, as in the *Permian Basin Area Rate Cases* (1968), a wide and uncontrolled discretion. In the field of FOREIGN AFFAIRS the delegation of legislative power to the President and his ability to negotiate with foreign powers and make EXECUTIVE AGREEMENTS with them, are very wide indeed, as the Court recognized in UNITED STATES V. CURTISS-WRIGHT EXPORT CORP. (1936).

In all these areas of tension between the branches of government, therefore, the Supreme Court, despite the broad generalizations which appear from time to time in its opinions, has followed a pragmatic approach to the separation of power. However, in IMMIGRATION AND NATURALIZATION SERVICE V. CHADHA (1983) the Court, in the opinion of some, adopted a more theoretical and formal line of argument. In *Chadha* the Court invalidated the use of the LEGISLATIVE VETO, the device by which Congress reserved to itself the right to review administrative regulations and decisions taken under some 200 different statutes. The opinion, written by Chief Justice WARREN E. BURGER, concentrated on the narrow constitutional issues of "presentment" of legislation and BICAMERALISM, but referred to the theory of the separation of powers in the Constitution as dividing the powers of government into "three defined categories, legislative, executive and judicial" which are "functionally identifiable." An alternative approach was put by Justice LEWIS F. POWELL in a CONCURRING OPINION. His objection to the use of the legislative veto in this particular instance was that the House of Representatives had improperly exercised a judicial power by ruling on the case of a particular individual rather than making a general rule. In taking this position Justice Powell was appealing to an element of the separation of powers of long standing and of great importance: the generality of law, restricting the legislative power to the general rather than the particular.

Some critics of the Supreme Court argue with Philip Kurland that as a consequence of its decisions "the ancient concept of the separation of powers and checks and balances has been reduced to a slogan, to be trotted out by the Supreme Court from time to time as a substitute for reasoned judgment." Whether or not this assessment of the judicial history of the separation should be considered too harsh, the impact of the concept upon the day-to-day working of the American political system has undoubtedly been enormous in terms of the relationship between the administration and the Congress. The prohibition on simultaneous membership of the legislative and executive branches in Article I, section 6, of the Constitution distinguishes the American system from the vast majority of genuinely democratic regimes in the world, most of which follow the parliamentary model. The fact that the President and his administration must operate from outside the legislature, rather than from within it, makes a vast difference to the techniques that must be employed to gain the acquiescence of the legislature to policies proposed by the executive. Much more important than the distinction between legislative and executive functions is the fact of two distinct branches of government with no overlapping of personnel (the VICE-PRESIDENT of the United States excepted). This strict separation of the personnel of government is certainly not the only reason why American political parties are so decentralized, diffuse, and undisciplined, but it is certainly a very important factor. The consequences for the way in which government policies are formulated, evolved, enacted, and implemented are immeasurable.

M. J. C. VILE

Bibliography

BARBER, SOTIRIOS A. 1975 *The Constitution and the Delegation of Congressional Power.* Chicago: University of Chicago Press.
ELLIOTT, E. DONALD 1984 INS v. Chadha: The Administrative Constitution, the Constitution, and the Legislative Veto. *Supreme Court Review* 1983:125–176.
GWYN, W. B. 1965 *The Meaning of the Separation of Powers.* New Orleans: Tulane University Press.
KURLAND, PHILIP B. 1978 *Watergate and the Constitution.* Chicago: University of Chicago Press.
SCHWARTZ, BERNARD 1963 *A Commentary on the Constitution of the United States.* New York: Macmillan.
VILE, M. J. C. 1967 *Constitutionalism and the Separation of Powers.* Oxford: Oxford University Press.

SERIATIM

(Latin: "Severally" or "in series.") Members of multi-judge courts sometimes deliver individual opinions seriatim rather than joining in a single "OPINION OF THE COURT." Before JOHN MARSHALL became Chief Justice, the Supreme Court followed this practice, requiring each Justice to explain his DECISION. Opinions delivered seriatim are necessarily less authoritative than those that carry the weight of the full Court or a majority of the Justices. For that reason Marshall abandoned the established practice in favor of giving an opinion of the court. THOMAS JEFFERSON, both in 1787 and later as President, favored a constitutional requirement that Supreme Court opinions be rendered seriatim.

DENNIS J. MAHONEY

SERRANO v. PRIEST
5 Cal. 3d 584, 487 P.2d 1241, 96 Cal. Rptr 601 (1971)

This decision of the California Supreme Court produced a flurry of hope that the disgraceful inequalities in the financing of public schools might fall to an EQUAL PROTECTION attack. Two years after the *Serrano* decision, the Supreme Court of the United States dashed that hope in SAN ANTONIO INDEPENDENT SCHOOL DISTRICT V. RODRIGUEZ (1973).

Public schools throughout the nation are financed in major part through reliance on the local property tax. School districts that are property-wealthy thus can levy relatively low taxes and support their schools at high levels of spending per pupil. Poor districts, however, must levy taxes at much higher rates in order to spend at much lower levels per pupil. The California court in *Serrano* held this system unconstitutional, 6–1, both under the equal protection clause of the FOURTEENTH AMENDMENT and under parallel provisions of the state constitution. Because the decision merely reversed a trial court's determination that the complaint had not stated a valid constitutional claim, and remanded the case for trial, it was not a FINAL JUDGMENT and was not reviewable by the United States Supreme Court. Similarly, the ruling on state constitutional law was an ADEQUATE STATE GROUND, insulating the case from Supreme Court review.

The California court's opinion was devoted mainly to a discussion of the equal protection clause. Two grounds were found for subjecting the school finance scheme to STRICT SCRUTINY: the interest in education was held to be a FUNDAMENTAL INTEREST, and WEALTH DISCRIMINATION was held to be a SUSPECT CLASSIFICATION. Absent a showing of a COMPELLING STATE INTEREST justifying the inequalities in the state's statutory scheme, that scheme must fall.

The Supreme Court's *Rodriguez* decision, rejecting both the California court's bases for strict scrutiny, ended *Serrano*'s brief influence on the course of federal constitutional DOCTRINE. But other state courts reached similar results on the basis of their own state constitutions, and in California itself *Serrano* produced significant efforts to restructure public school finance.

KENNETH L. KARST

SEVENTEENTH AMENDMENT

Proposed by Congress on May 16, 1912, the Seventeenth Amendment went into effect on May 31, 1913. The amendment provided for DIRECT ELECTION of United States senators by the people of the states. Previously, under the first clause of Article I, section 3, senators had been chosen by the state legislatures.

Selection of United States senators by state legislatures had been an object of criticism for many years. Direct election of senators was first proposed in 1826; and after 1893 a constitutional amendment to establish direct election was proposed in Congress every year. Even without a constitutional amendment, popular choice of senators was becoming the rule. By 1912, twenty-nine of the forty-eight states had provided either for nomination by party primaries, with the individual legislators bound to vote for their party's nominee, or for a statewide general election, the result of which was binding on the legislature.

The objectives of direct election included reducing corruption in selection of senators, elimination of national-party domination of state legislatures, and immediate representation of the people in the Senate. But there was actually little change in the characteristics of persons elected to the Senate or in the proceedings and activities either of the Senate or of the state legislatures as a result of the Seventeenth Amendment.

The amendment has not occasioned much litigation. In 1915, the Supreme Court held that the right to vote for United States senators was a privilege of United States CITIZENSHIP, protected by the PRIVILEGES AND IMMUNITIES clause; and in 1946 it held that that right could not be denied on account of race. The Court has also held that the Seventeenth Amendment does not require that a candidate receive a majority of the votes cast in order to be elected.

DENNIS J. MAHONEY

SEVENTH AMENDMENT

An unexpectedly controversial provision of the document that emerged from the CONSTITUTIONAL CONVENTION OF 1787 was that giving the Supreme Court APPELLATE JURISDICTION "both as to law and fact." Anti-Federalists argued that the provision worked to abridge or deny the COMMON LAW right of TRIAL BY JURY in civil cases. Some, including PATRICK HENRY, went so far as to contend that it introduced the continental European civil law into the American court system. Although the convention had considered a clause protecting the right to a jury trial in civil cases, the clause was omitted; because the jury system varied somewhat from state to state, the meaning of the clause would not be certain. In the course of the RATIFICATION OF THE CONSTITUTION, five state conventions recommended an amendment to give the right explicit constitutional status.

The Seventh Amendment was proposed by Congress in 1789 and was ratified in 1791, as part of the BILL OF RIGHTS. As originally introduced by JAMES MADISON, the restriction on review of a jury's findings would have been inserted in Article III immediately after the definition of the Supreme Court's appellate jurisdiction. When the Bill of Rights was reorganized into a series of new articles, the restriction was joined to the general guarantee of a jury trial in federal civil cases.

The purpose of the amendment was not to extend the right to a jury trial but to preserve it as it then existed. The phrase "common law" did not purport to exclude cases arising under federal statutes but rather those cognizable in EQUITY or under ADMIRALTY AND MARITIME JURISDICTION. The word "jury" originally meant the common law jury of twelve men; but the Supreme Court held in *Colegrove v. Battin* (1973) that a jury of six members satisfied the general intent of the amendment. The Seventh Amendment is one of the very few provisions of the Bill of Rights not made applicable to the states under the INCORPORATION DOCTRINE. State courts would thus be free, under federal constitutional law, to dispense with juries altogether in civil cases.

Since the FEDERAL RULES OF CIVIL PROCEDURE in 1934 united the formerly discrete procedures of law and equity, new questions have emerged under the Seventh Amendment. In BEACON THEATRES INC. v. WESTOVER (1959) and DAIRY QUEEN INC. v. WOOD (1962) the Supreme Court held that the right to jury trial attached to all issues of law of the type formerly triable to a jury at common law, even when those issues were "incidental" to equitable issues. In *Ross v. Bernhard* (1970) this principle was extended to STOCKHOLDER'S SUITS, which previously had been heard only under the rules of equity.

DENNIS J. MAHONEY

SEVERABILITY

A court determines whether a statute is severable (or separable) in order to decide one of two different questions: When part of the law is unconstitutional, should the court hold the entire statute invalid, or merely the offending part? When the law can be applied validly to the litigant in court, should the court nonetheless hold the law invalid because it is capable of being applied unconstitutionally to others?

The first question was presented in CARTER V. CARTER COAL CO. (1936). Congress had regulated coal prices and the wages and hours of coal miners. After holding the wage and hour regulations invalid, the Supreme Court posed the severability issue in the usual way, as a question of LEGISLATIVE INTENT: if Congress had known the wage and hour provisions would be held invalid, would it still have regulated prices? Congress had stated plainly that if any part of the coal act were held invalid, the rest of the law remained effective. Nonetheless, the Court said, the price controls were so closely related to the labor provisions that Congress would not have enacted them alone. The price controls were thus invalid, whether or not they would have been valid if considered by themselves. The issue of severability calls into play the same kind of judgment employed in JUDICIAL REVIEW of the constitutionality of LEGISLATION.

Carter involved a federal statute. When a state law presents a similar question of severability, the Supreme Court ordinarily leaves that question to the state courts. However, a state statute may present the Court with the second type of severability issue. When a state law is INVALID ON ITS FACE—for example, under the FIRST AMENDMENT doctrine of OVERBREADTH—the Court refuses to enforce the law because of its potential unconstitutional application to persons not in court. This practice moderates the effect of the rule denying a litigant STANDING to raise other persons' legal rights.

KENNETH L. KARST

Bibliography

MONAGHAN, HENRY P. 1982 Overbreadth. *Supreme Court Review* 1982:1–39.
NOTE 1984 Severability of Legislative Veto Provisions: A Policy Analysis. *Harvard Law Review* 97:1182–1197.
STERN, ROBERT L. 1937 Separability and Separability Clauses in the Supreme Court. *Harvard Law Review* 51:76–128.

SEWARD, WILLIAM H.
(1801–1872)

William Henry Seward was a New York lawyer, governor (1838–1842), United States senator (1849–1861), and secretary of state (1861–1869). As governor he prevented the extradition to Virginia of three men accused of helping a slave escape, and thus set off a minor interstate squabble. In *Jones v. Van Zandt* (1847) Seward, as cocounsel with SALMON P. CHASE, unsuccessfully appealed the conviction of an Ohio Quaker accused of aiding fugitive slaves. In the Senate, Seward opposed the COMPROMISE OF 1850, asserting that on the issue of slavery there was "HIGHER LAW than the Constitution." He supported the admission of Kansas as a free state, attacked the Supreme Court's decision in DRED SCOTT V. SANDFORD (1857), and in 1858 declared that slavery had created "an irrepressible conflict" for the Union. During the SECESSION crisis Seward served on the Committee of Thirteen, and proposed that Congress guarantee to protect slavery wherever it existed. Seward thought secession was illegal, but he urged Lincoln to evacuate Fort Sumter and negotiate with Confederate officials. Seward initially opposed the EMANCIPATION PROCLAMATION and successfully urged Lincoln to delay it until after a Union military victory. In FOREIGN AFFAIRS he deftly negotiated to keep Britain and France out of the war, and avoided a conflict with Britain over the *Trent* affair. He also laid out the legal argument that led to a successful damage claim against Britain over the *Alabama*. During Reconstruction, Seward supported ANDREW JOHNSON's policies, and drafted many of his veto messages. He also negotiated the acquisition of Alaska (1867) from Russia.

PAUL FINKELMAN

Bibliography

VAN DEUSEN, GLYNDON G. 1967 *William Henry Seward.* New York: Oxford University Press.

SEX DISCRIMINATION

The application of constitutional principle to government action that distinguishes on the basis of sex is a late-twentieth-century development. From the 1860s until 1971, the record remained unbroken: the Supreme Court rejected every effort to overturn sex lines in the law. Equalizing the rights, responsibilities, and opportunities of men and women was not considered a judicial task; without offense to the Constitution, women could be kept off juries and barred from occupations ranging from law to bartending. Women could also be "protected" from long hours, night work, and hazardous jobs, as in MULLER V. OREGON (1908), but protection of this order limited women's opportunities and relied upon the notion that a woman "looks to her brother and depends upon him."

The Court explained its position in *Fay v. New York* (1947). The NINETEENTH AMENDMENT's ratification in 1920 gave women the vote, but only that; in other respects, the Constitution remained an empty cupboard for sex equality claims. Nearly a decade and a half later, in *Hoyt v. Florida* (1961), a unanimous bench reaffirmed the traditional view. The Court held that a volunteers-only system for females serving on juries encountered no constitutional shoal; it was rational to spare women from the obligation to serve in recognition of their place at the "center of home and family life."

Pervasive social changes following World War II undermined the *Hoyt* assumptions. That period saw unprecedented growth in women's employment outside the home, a revived feminist movement, changing marriage patterns, and a decline in necessary home-centered activity. Expansion of the economy's service sector opened places for women in traditional as well as new occupations. Curtailed population goals, facilitated by more effective means of controlling reproduction, and extended lifespans counted as well among important ingredients in this social dynamic. These last two developments created a setting in which the typical woman, for the first time, was experiencing most of her adult years in a household not dominated by child care requirements. Columbia economics professor Eli Ginzberg appraised the sum of these changes as "the single most outstanding phenomenon of our century." The BURGER COURT, not noted for its activism in other areas, responded.

Through the 1960s, the Supreme Court had explained its EQUAL PROTECTION rulings in terms of a two-tier model. Generally, challenged legislation was ranked at the lower tier and survived judicial inspection if rationally related to a permissible government objective. Exceptional cases, ranged on the upper tier, involved FUNDAMENTAL RIGHTS (voting is a prime example) or SUSPECT CLASSIFICATIONS (race is a paradigm). Review in these exceptional cases was rigorous. To survive inspection, the legislative objective had to be compelling, and the classification, necessary to its accomplishment. (See STRICT SCRUTINY; COMPELLING STATE INTEREST.)

Equal protection adjudication in gender discrimination cases prompted "in between" standards. As the 1970s wore on, the STANDARD OF REVIEW for sex-based classification inched up toward the higher tier. The process commenced with *Reed v. Reed* (1971). A unanimous Court held that an Idaho estate administration statute, giving men preference over similarly situated women, denied would-be administrator Sally Reed the equal protection of the laws. *Reed* attracted headlines; it marked the first solid break from the Supreme Court's consistent affirmation of government authority to classify by sex. The terse *Reed* opinion acknowledged no departure from precedent, but Court-watchers recognized something new was in the wind.

Less than a year and a half after the laconic *Reed* decision, the Court came within one vote of declaring sex a "suspect" category. In FRONTIERO V. RICHARDSON (1973) the Justices held 8–1 that married women in the uniformed services were entitled to the same fringe benefits as married men. Under the laws declared unconstitutional, men received a housing allowance and health care for their civilian wives automatically; women received these family benefits only if they supplied over three-fourths of the couple's support.

Four of the Justices ranked sex a suspect classification. Justice LEWIS F. POWELL, concurring, articulated a prime reservation of the remaining five Justices: our eighteenth- and nineteenth-century Constitution-makers had evidenced no concern at all about the equality of men and women before the law. The Court must tread lightly, Justice Powell cautioned, when it enters the gray zone between CONSTITUTIONAL INTERPRETATION, a proper judicial task, and constitutional amendment, a job for the people's elected representatives.

No fifth vote has emerged for explicit placement of sex at the top tier of equal protection analysis, although the Court has repeatedly acknowledged that it applies a standard considerably more exacting than the lower tier RATIONAL BASIS test. If a classification based upon gender is to withstand constitutional challenge, the defender of the sex criterion must establish what the Court in *Kirchberg v. Feenstra* (1981) called "exceedingly persuasive justification"; the sex-based distinction will be condemned unless it "substantially furthers an important government interest." In MISSISSIPPI UNIVERSITY FOR WOMEN V. HOGAN (1982) the Court noted that it was unnecessary to "decide whether classifications based upon gender are inherently suspect," for the classification challenged there could not survive even intermediate tier scrutiny. If the Court continues to review categorization by gender with the rigor displayed in many of its 1973–1982 decisions, however, the "suspect" seal may eventually be placed on accumulated precedent.

Despite the absence of a majority opinion, the 8–1 *Frontiero* JUDGMENT was a notable way-paver for challenges to statutes that openly disadvantage or denigrate women. First, the Court did not invalidate the flawed legislation; it repaired it. Congress provided benefits for the military man's family; the Court, in effect, extended the same benefits to families in which the service member was female. Second, in contrast to the statute that figured in *Reed*—a nineteenth-century hangover repealed prospectively months before the Court heard Sally Reed's appeal—post–World War II legislation was at issue in *Frontiero*. Most significantly, *Frontiero* invalidated the type of gender line found most frequently in federal and state legislation. Wives were deemed dependent regardless of their own economic circumstances. Husbands were ranked independent unless they contributed less than one-fourth of the couple's support. In disallowing resort to this particular stereotype the Court set the stage for its subsequent disallowance of similar stereotypes in other settings.

Since *Frontiero*, with few exceptions, the Court has regularly overturned legislation explicitly invoking a male/female criterion and perceived by the Justices as denigrating women. A Utah statute that required a parent to support a son until age twenty-one but a daughter only until eighteen was struck down in *Stanton v. Stanton* (1975). Using DUE PROCESS analysis, the Court invalidated laws excluding all women from jury duty save those who volunteered (TAYLOR V. LOUISIANA, 1975) or chose not to opt out (*Duren v. Missouri*, 1979). In *Kirchberg v. Feenstra* (1981) a unanimous bench condemned Louisiana's "head and master" law, which gave the husband alone a unilateral right to dispose of property jointly owned with his wife.

Even a noncontributory welfare program—the type of governmental largess generally left untouched by the judiciary—has been revised by Court decree to eliminate the law's discrimination against women. Congress had provided for public assistance benefits to families where dependent children had been deprived of parental support because of the father's unemployment; no benefits were allowed when mother, rather than father, qualified as the unemployed parent. "Congress may not legislate 'one step at a time' when that step is drawn along the line of gender, and the consequence is to exclude one group of families [those in which the female spouse is a wage earner] altogether from badly needed subsistence benefits," Justice HARRY BLACKMUN concluded for a Court unanimous on the constitutional issue in CALIFANO V. WESTCOTT (1979). Although the Justices divided 5–4 on the appropriate remedy (the majority extending the benefit to families of unemployed mothers, the dissenters preferring to invalidate the entire program), all subscribed solidly to the equal protection ruling.

In 1837 Sarah Grimke made this plea: "I ask no favors for my sex, I surrender not our claim to equality. All I ask of our brethren, is that they . . . take their feet . . . off our necks. . . ." Does the equal protection principle operate with the same bite when men rather than women are the victims of explicit gender-based discrimination? Constitutional doctrine after *Reed* has evolved, with some insecurity, through three stages. In the first, statutes ostensibly favoring women were upheld if they were seen as "compensatory," even if that rationalization was entirely post hoc. Then the Court recognized more consistently that gender-based classifications rooted in "romantic paternalism" reinforce stereotypes and perpetuate anachronistic social assumptions that confine women's opportunities. In the third stage, the Court attempted a reconciliation of these two strands of doctrine: a classification that favors women can survive an equal protection attack, but only if it reflects a conscious legislative choice to compensate for past, gender-based inequities.

In two first-stage decisions the Court upheld laws that appeared to favor women. *Kahn v. Shevin* (1974) involved a $15-per-year state property tax saving for widows (along with the blind and the totally disabled) but not widowers. The classification, as the Court appraised it, was genuinely "benign"—it helped some women and harmed none. Following on the heels of *Kahn*, the Court ruled, in *Schlesinger v. Ballard* (1975), that it was not a denial of equal protection to hold a male naval officer to a strict "up or out" (promotion or discharge) system, while guaranteeing a female officer thirteen years of duty before mandatory discharge for lack of promotion.

Kahn and *Ballard* were greeted by some in a Panglossian manner. The decisions could be viewed as offering women the best of both worlds—a High Court ready to strike down classifications that discriminate against females, yet vigilant to preserve laws that prefer or favor them. But this analysis was uncritically optimistic. The classification attacked in *Kahn* was barely distinguishable from other products of paternalistic legislators who had regarded the husband more as his wife's guardian than as her peer. And in *Ballard*, neither contender challenged the anterior discrimination that accounted, in large measure, for the navy's promoting men more rapidly than women —the drastically curtailed opportunities and assignments available to navy women.

Sex as a proxy for need, or as an indicator of past discrimination in the marital unit, is a criterion too gross to survive vigorous equal protection scrutiny. The Court eventually demonstrated its appreciation that discrimination by gender generally cuts with two edges, and is seldom, if ever, a pure favor to women. A young widower whose wage-earning wife had died giving birth to the couple's son brought suit in *Weinberger v. Wiesenfeld* (1975). The unanimous Court declared unconstitutional the SOCIAL SECURITY ACT's provision of a mother's benefit for the caretaker of a deceased wage-earner's child. As in *Frontiero*, the remedy was extension of the benefit in question to the entire class of similarly situated individuals, males as well as females. In effect, the *Wiesenfeld* judgment substitutes functional description (sole surviving parent) for the gender classification (widowed mother) employed in the statute.

The government had urged that the sex differential in *Wiesenfeld* operated "to offset the adverse economic situation of women." But the Court read the legislative history closely and rejected "the mere recitation of a benign, compensatory purpose" as a hindsight apology for laws in fact based on twin assumptions: that man's primary place is at work, woman's at home; and that a gainfully employed woman is a secondary breadwinner whose employment is less crucial to her family than her husband's.

Wiesenfeld's focus on actual legislative purpose set a penetrating standard for sex classifications defended as "benign" or "compensatory." Gender classifications superficially favoring women and affecting interests ranging from the purchase of beer to attendance at a nursing school have accordingly been struck down.

CRAIG V. BOREN (1976) held unconstitutional an Oklahoma law allowing young women to purchase 3.2 percent beer at age eighteen, but requiring young men to wait until age twenty-one. *Orr v. Orr* (1979) declared violative of equal protection a statute that required husbands, but never wives, to pay alimony. CALIFANO V. GOLDFARB (1977) rejected social security classifications qualifying a widow for survivor's benefits automatically, a widower only upon proof that his wife supplied three-fourths of the couple's support.

The 4–1–4 judgment in *Goldfarb,* in contrast to the *Wiesenfeld* decision on which *Goldfarb* built, was a cliffhanger. The PLURALITY OPINION concentrated on discrimination against women as breadwinners. Justice JOHN PAUL STEVENS, who cast the swing vote in favor of widower Goldfarb, focused on the discrimination against the surviving male spouse. Why this discrimination against a class of men? Like the plurality, Justice Stevens refused to accept the government's hindsight compensatory justification for the

scheme. Congress, the record suggested, had ordered different treatment for widows and widowers out of longstanding "habit"; the discrimination encountered by widower Goldfarb was "merely the accidental by-product of [the legislators'] traditional way of thinking about females." Four members of the Court, in dissent, repeated a long rehearsed argument: the sex-based classification accurately reflects the station in life of most women, it operates benignly in women's favor, and it is administratively convenient. In 1980, however, the Court adhered to *Goldfarb* with a clearer (8–1) majority, in WENGLER V. DRUGGISTS MUTUAL INSURANCE CO.

The most emphatic reaffirmation of *Wiesenfeld's* skeptical view of benign gender-based classification came in 1982, one day after expiration of the extended deadline for ratification of the proposed EQUAL RIGHTS AMENDMENT. The Court decided, 5–4, in *Mississippi University for Women v. Hogan,* that Mississippi's single-sex admissions policy for a nursing school failed to meet the heightened standard of review. Justice SANDRA DAY O'CONNOR, who, a century earlier under BRADWELL V. ILLINOIS (1873), could have been barred from practicing law without offense to the Constitution, wrote the majority opinion.

Challengers in most of the cases just surveyed contended against gross assumptions that females are (and should be) concerned primarily with "the home and the rearing of the family," males with "the marketplace and the world of ideas" (*Stanton v. Stanton,* 1975). The complainants did not assail the accuracy of these assumptions as generalizations. Rather, they questioned each law's erroneous treatment of men and women who did not fit the stereotype, and the fairness of gender pigeonholing in lieu of neutral, functional description. The traditional legislative slotting, they argued, amounted to self-fulfilling prophecy. A Court that in 1948, in GOESAERT V. CLEARY, had declared "beyond question" the constitutionality of legislation "drawing a sharp line between the sexes," was receptive in the 1970s to argument to which it would not "give ear" a generation earlier.

The Court has left a narrow passage open, however, for compensatory legislation that does not rest on traditional role-typing. In *Califano v. Webster* (1977) the Court distinguished from habitual categorization by sex a law designed, at least in part, to ameliorate disadvantages women experienced. A social security benefit calculation, effective from 1956 to 1972, established a more favorable formula for retired female workers than for retired male workers. The legislative history indicated that this scheme, unlike those in *Wiesenfeld* and *Goldfarb,* had been conceived in light of the discrimination commonly encountered by gainfully employed women, specifically, depressed wages for "women's work" and the early retirement that employers routinely forced on women but not on men. While tilting toward a general rule of equal treatment, the *Webster* PER CURIAM opinion approves genuinely compensatory classifications that are adopted for remedial reasons rather than out of prejudice about "the way women are," and are trimly tailored in scope and time to match the remedial end.

Neutrally phrased laws that disproportionately affect one sex have not attracted the heightened scrutiny generally accorded explicit gender-based classifications that serve as a proxy for a characteristic or condition susceptible of individual testing. Citing RACIAL DISCRIMINATION precedent, the Court has held that facially neutral classifications that disproportionately affect members of one sex are not necessarily sex-based. The Court has not yet considered in a constitutional setting whether official lines may be drawn based on actuarial differences, but statutory precedent indicates the answer will be "no."

"[G]ood intent or absence of discriminatory intent" does not immunize an employment practice from the equal opportunity requirement of Title VII of the CIVIL RIGHTS ACT OF 1964, which now covers both public and private employment. GRIGGS V. DUKE POWER CO., a notable 1971 Title VII race discrimination decision, so held. But in WASHINGTON V. DAVIS (1976) the Court held the *Griggs* principle inapplicable to race discrimination claims invoking the Constitution rather than Title VII. PERSONNEL ADMINISTRATOR OF MASSACHUSETTS V. FEENEY (1979) expanded the *Washington v. Davis* reasoning. *Feeney* involved an assault on exorbitant veterans' preferences in civil service as impermissibly gender-biased. Helen Feeney challenged the nation's most extreme veterans' preference—an absolute lifetime preference Massachusetts accorded veterans in a range of civil service positions. The preference had "a devastating impact upon the employment opportunities of women"; it operated to reserve top jobs for a class almost exclusively male. The purpose? Purely to aid veterans, surely not to harm women, Massachusetts (and the United States, AMICUS CURIAE) maintained. Of course, to become a veteran one must be allowed to serve her country, and the military had maintained highly restrictive quotas and more exacting qualification standards for females. When litigation in *Feeney* commenced, over ninety-eight percent of Massachusetts veterans were male.

Feeney sought accommodation of the conflicting interests—aiding veterans and opening to women civil service employment beyond the "pink-collar" ghetto. The typical "points-added" preference, she said, was not at issue, only the extreme arrangement Massachusetts had legislated, which placed a veteran with a minimum passing grade ahead of a woman with a perfect score, and did so for each promotion as well as for initial hiring. A preference so large, she argued, took too much from Pauline to pay Paul.

The Court rejected the proffered distinction between moderate and exorbitant preferences. The "discriminatory purpose" hurdle could not be surmounted absent proof that the Massachusetts preference "was originally devised or subsequently re-enacted because it would accomplish the collateral goal of keeping women in a stereotypic and predefined place in the Massachusetts Civil Service." The lawmaker must *want*, not merely anticipate, the consequences. Alone, disparate impact on one sex, however "devastating" and "inevitable," does not violate equal protection.

The discriminatory purpose requirement, as elaborated in *Feeney*, leaves a slack rein for legislative choices with foreseeable but undesigned adverse effects on one of the sexes. Suppose, for example, that the social security payments at issue in *Wiesenfeld* or *Goldfarb* had turned not on sex but on the deceased wage-earner's status as the family's principal breadwinner. In most families, husbands would fit that neutrally phrased description, wives would not. May Congress, without violating equal protection, resort to a "principal breadwinner" standard in social welfare legislation in the interest of fiscal economy? Would use of a "principal breadwinner" criterion survive constitutional review as a measure enacted "in spite of," rather than "because of" its practical effect—its reduction of the value to the family of the wife's earnings? The only, uncertain, guide is an obiter dictum from *Feeney*, in which the Court accepted that "covert" sex classifications, ostensibly neutral but in fact a pretext for sex-based discrimination, are vulnerable to equal protection attack.

Can actuarial differences, for example, in life expectancies, health records, or accident experiences, provide constitutionally valid grounds in any context for gender-based categorizations? Sex averaging has not fared well in post-1970 constitutional litigation. Thus, *Reed v. Reed* and *Frontiero v. Richardson* rejected as a basis for government action the generalization that "men [are] as a rule more conversant with business affairs than women"; *Craig v. Boren*, the fact that more 18–20-year-old males than females drink and drive; *Orr v. Orr* (1979), the reality that wives far more often than husbands "need" alimony. Legislation resting on characteristics, attributes, habits, or proclivities of the "typical man" or "typical woman" have been rejected for two reasons: they reinforce traditional restrictive conceptions of the social roles of men and women; and they burden members of one sex by employing gender as a proxy for a characteristic susceptible to individual testing or at least capable of sex-neutral description. But actuarial tables, their defenders point out, are used in situations in which individual testing is not feasible. The Court has not yet explicitly confronted actuarial tables in a constitutional context, but a Title VII decision may indicate the position the Court will take in an equal protection challenge to government action.

Los Angeles Department of Water and Power v. Manhart (1978) raised the question whether women could be required to pay more currently in order to receive monthly benefits on retirement equal to those received by men. The majority held the two-tier charges inconsistent with Title VII's prohibition of sex-based classification. All recognized in *Manhart* that the statement, "on the average, women live longer than men," is accurate, and that an individual's lifespan generally cannot be forecast with precision. But the majority refused to countenance a break from the general Title VII rule against sex averaging. Unquestionably, for pension purposes, women destined to die young are burdened by placement in an all-female class, and men destined to live long are benefited by placement in an all-male class. Moreover, Justice Stevens suggested for the majority, the group insurance context may not be an ideal setting for urging a distinction other than age: "To insure the flabby and the fit as though they were equivalent risks may be more common than treating men and women alike; but nothing more than habit makes one 'subsidy' seem less fair than the other." The Court adhered to *Manhart,* when invited to reconsider, or contain the holding, in *Arizona Governing Committee v. Norris* (1983).

Are women to have the opportunity to participate in full partnership with men in the nation's social, political, and economic life? Kenneth L. Karst has identified this overarching question, in its constitutional dimension, as one ripe for synthesis in the final quarter of the twentieth century. The synthesis envisioned would place within an encompassing sex equality framework cases involving explicit male/female classification as well as cases on REPRODUCTIVE AUTONOMY and pregnancy-linked regulation. That synthesis, however, may well depend on the clarity of directions from the political arena. The Court has treated reproductive choice cases under a "personal autonomy," not a "sex equality" rubric, and it has resisted argument that separate classification of pregnant women is sex-based.

In a bold 1973 ruling, ROE V. WADE, the Court struck down an anti-abortion law as unwarranted state intrusion into the decision of a woman and her doctor to terminate a pregnancy. *Roe v. Wade* has been typed aberrational—an extraordinarily activist decision issued from a bench reputedly deferential to legislative judgments. It bears emphasis, however, that the Court bypassed an equal protection argument presented for the female plaintiffs. Rather, the Court anchored stringent review to a concept of personal autonomy derived from the due process guarantee. Two decisions, particularly, had paved the way: GRISWOLD V. CONNECTICUT (1965), which held inconsistent with due process Connecticut's ban on use of contraceptives even by married couples, and EISENSTADT V. BAIRD (1972), which extended *Griswold* to strike down Massachusetts' prohibition on sales of contraceptives except to married persons by prescription.

Some speculated that *Roe v. Wade* and a companion 1973 decision, *Doe v. Bolton,* were motivated, at least in part, by concerns about unwanted children born into impoverished families. But in MAHER V. ROE (1977) the Court indicated that such speculations had been mistaken. The Court declined to extend the 1973 rulings to require state support for an indigent woman's elective abortion.

The impoverished women, on whose behalf constitutional claims to public assistance for abortion were pursued, relied primarily on the equal protection principle. They maintained that, so long as government subsidized childbirth, it could not withhold subsidy for abortion, a far less expensive, and, at least in the first trimester, less risky procedure. If government pays for childbirth but not abortion, then, the *Maher* plaintiffs argued, government intrudes upon a choice *Roe v. Wade* said the state must leave to doctor and patient. The Court, however, distinguished government prohibition from government support. Though the state could not bar access to a woman able to pay for an abortion, it was not required to buy an admission ticket for the poor woman. Rather, government could pursue a policy of encouraging childbirth (even if that policy would affect only the poor) by refusing Medicaid reimbursement for non-therapeutic abortions and by banning such abortions in public hospitals. Though widely criticized in the reproductive-choice context, the distinction between government stick and government carrot had been made in other settings to which the Court referred in its 1977 ruling.

The *Maher* logic was carried further in HARRIS

v. McRae (1980). The federal law at issue excluded even medically needed abortions from a medical benefits program. In holding, 5–4, that this exclusion violated neither the due process nor the equal protection clause, the Court reiterated the distinction drawn in *Maher*: though the government may not proscribe abortion, it need not act affirmatively to assure a poor woman's access to the procedure.

Following after the intrepid 1973 abortion decisions, the later public-funding-of-abortion rulings appear incongruous. The *Roe v. Wade* decision was not easy to reach or explain. Social and economic conditions that seem irreversible, however, suggest that the ruling made by the Court in 1973 will remain with us in the long run, while the later dispositions may eventually succumb to a different legislative view of state and national policy, and of the centrality of choice with respect to childbearing to a woman's control of her life's course.

When does disadvantageous treatment of pregnant workers operate to discriminate on the basis of sex? High Court decisions on that question display less than perfect logic and consistency.

School teachers may not be dismissed or placed on forced leave arbitrarily at a fixed stage in pregnancy well in advance of term. Such a rule conflicts with due process, the Court ruled in Cleveland Board of Education v. LaFleur (1974). Similarly invoking due process, the Court held in *Turner v. Department of Employment Security* (1975) that pregnant women willing and able to work may not be denied unemployment compensation when jobs are closed to them. It is unlawful under Title VII, as interpreted by the Court in *Nashville Gas Co. v. Satty* (1977), for an employer to deprive women disabled by pregnancy of accumulated job-bidding seniority when they return to work.

But *Geduldig v. Aiello* (1974) held that a state-operated disability income protection plan could exclude pregnancy without offense to the equal protection principle. And in an analogous Title VII case, *General Electric Company v. Gilbert* (1976), the Court held that a private employer's exclusion of pregnant women from disability coverage did not discriminate on the basis of sex because all "nonpregnant persons," women along with men, were treated alike.

Lawyers may attempt to square the apparently contradictory constitutional decisions by referring to the different principles employed in the Court's analyses—equal protection in *Aiello*, due process in both *LaFleur* and *Turner*. But the particular due process theory of irrebuttable presumptions the Court pressed into service in *LaFleur* has lost favor with

the Justices in other contexts. A factor not fully acknowledged in the written opinions, and based more on the Justices' experience than on legal analysis, may account for the divergent responses. Perhaps the able pregnant woman seeking only to do a day's work for a day's pay, or the woman seeking to return to her job relatively soon after childbirth, is a credible figure to the Court, while the woman who asserts she is disabled by pregnancy is viewed with suspicion. Is she really incapacitated physically or is she malingering so that she may stay "where she belongs"—at home tending baby?

With respect to Title VII, Congress in 1978 simplified the judicial task by prospectively overruling *General Electric*. It amended the statute to say explicitly that classification on the basis of sex includes classification on the basis of pregnancy. The Court gave the amended statute a cordial reception in *Newport News Shipbuilding of Drydock Co. v. EEOC* (1983). The congressional definition placed in Title VII is not controlling in constitutional adjudication, but the Court may be stimulated by the legislature's action to revise its view, expressed in *Aiello* and *General Electric*, that singling out "pregnant persons" is not a sex-based action. Coming full circle, there will be pressure on the Court not simply to check regulation disadvantageous to pregnant women but to uphold new-style protective legislation—for example, laws requiring employers to grant to pregnant women a voluntary leave period not accorded others with temporarily disabling physical conditions.

In what areas does the Constitution allow explicit male/female classification? A few idiosyncratic problems survive.

According to current doctrine, the Constitution affords some leeway for discrimination with respect to parental rights and relationships, at least when children are born out of wedlock. A unanimous Court held in *Quilloin v. Walcott* (1978) that an unwed father who "has never exercised actual or legal custody over his child" has no constitutional right to block adoption approved by the mother. (In contrast, the Court held in *Caban v. Mohammed* [1979] that a state statute discriminated on the basis of sex in violation of equal protection when it permitted adoption of a child born out of wedlock solely on the mother's consent, even when the father's parental relationship with the child was substantial.) And according to *Parham v. Hughes* (1979) a state may condition an unwed father's (but not an unwed mother's) right to recover for wrongful death upon his legitimation of his child by court order. The main theme of the *Parham* opinion had been sounded earlier: women and men were not similarly situated for the purpose at hand—maternity is rarely in doubt, but proof of paternity is often difficult. Hence, as the Court held in LALLI V. LALLI (1978), the state may erect safeguards against spurious filiation claims. Those safeguards may be applied even when, as in *Parham*, father and child had a close and constant relationship.

MICHAEL M. V. SUPERIOR COURT (1981) upheld, 5–4, California's "statutory rape" law, under which a male who engages in sexual intercourse with an underage female commits a crime; a female who engages in sexual intercourse with an underage male does not. Both participants in the act that precipitated the prosecution in *Michael M.* were underage.

There was no majority opinion in *Michael M.* Justice WILLIAM H. REHNQUIST wrote for the Court's plurality. He postulated as the statute's purpose, as California had argued, the prevention of teenage pregnancy, and reasoned that males and females were not similarly situated in this setting. Nature inhibited the female, for she would suffer the consequences. The law could legitimately take into account this fact of life by punishing the male, who lacked a biological deterrent. Moreover, the plurality found persuasive California's further contention that sparing the female from criminal liability might encourage her to report the unlawful activity.

Given the ancient roots of the California law, Justice WILLIAM J. BRENNAN pointed out in dissent, it was plain that the sex classification "was initially designed to further . . . outmoded sexual stereotypes" (young women are not capable of consenting to an act of sexual intercourse, young men can make such decisions for themselves). For Justice Stevens, who dissented separately, the critical question in *Michael M.* was whether "the sovereign . . . govern[s] impartially" under a statute that authorizes punishment of the male, but not the female, even "when they are equally responsible" for the disfavored conduct, indeed even "when the female is the more responsible of the two." The answer, it seemed to Justice Stevens, was clearly "no."

Although by 1980 many states had amended all of their sex crime laws to render them equally applicable to males and females, *Michael M.* touched a sensitive nerve. In view of the 4–1–4 division, the decision may well remain an isolated instance.

ROSTKER V. GOLDBERG (1981) presented the politically loaded question whether Congress could confine draft registration to males. Congress had thought about the matter and decided it in 1980. It considered, on the administration's recommendation, authorizing the President to require registration by both sexes.

But it decided on registration for males only. The Court's 6–3 decision upheld the sex classification. The opinion, written by Justice Rehnquist, underlined the special deference due congressional judgments in the areas of national defense and military affairs.

The *Rostker* opinion asserted that men and women were not similarly situated for the purpose at hand because women were excluded from combat service, an exclusion "Congress specifically recognized and endorsed . . . in exempting women from registration." Reminiscent of *Schlesinger v. Ballard*, where no party challenged the dissimilar promotion opportunities for male and female naval officers, no party challenged the combat exclusion in *Rostker*. Even so, the executive branch had estimated that in the event of a major mobilization there would be a substantial number of noncombat positions in the armed services that conscripted women could fill. Against this backdrop *Rostker* may be explained as a WAR POWERS case, unlikely to have a significant influence in future sex discrimination cases.

Constitutional doctrine relating to gender discrimination, although still evolving, and variously interpreted, is nonetheless a remarkable judicial development. In contrast to race discrimination, an area in which constitutional interpretation is tied to amendments drawn with a view to the eradication of the legacy of black slavery, gender discrimination was not a concern to which the Reconstruction Congress (or the Founding Fathers) adverted. Nonetheless, the Court, since 1970, has creatively interpreted clauses of the Constitution (equal protection and, less securely, due process) to accommodate a modern vision of sexual equality in employment, in access to social benefits, in most civic duties, in reproductive autonomy. Such interpretation has limits, but sensibly approached, it is consistent with the grand design of the Constitution-makers to write a charter that would endure as the nation's fundamental instrument of government.

RUTH BADER GINSBURG

Bibliography

BABCOCK, BARBARA A.; FREEDMAN, ANN E.; NORTON, ELEANOR H.; and ROSS, SUSAN C. 1974 *Sex Discrimination: Causes and Remedies* (Wendy Williams, Supplement 1978). Boston: Little, Brown.

GINSBURG, RUTH BADER 1978 Sex Equality and the Constitution. *Tulane Law Review* 52:451–475.

—— 1979 Sexual Equality under the Fourteenth and the Equal Rights Amendments. *Washington University Law Quarterly* 1979:161–178.

—— 1983 The Burger Court's Grapplings with Sex Discrimination. In V. Blasi, ed. *The Burger Court: The*

Counter-Revolution That Wasn't. Pages 132–156. New Haven, Conn.: Yale University Press.

GUNTHER, GERALD 1972 Foreword: In Search of Evolving Doctrine on a Changing Court: A Model for a Newer Equal Protection. *Harvard Law Review* 86:1–48.

KANOWITZ, LEO 1981 *Equal Rights: The Male Stake.* Albuquerque: University of New Mexico Press.

———— 1969 *Women and the Law.* Albuquerque: University of New Mexico Press.

KARST, KENNETH L. 1976 Book Review. *Harvard Law Review* 89:1028–1036.

———— 1977 Foreword, Equal Citizenship under 'the Fourteenth Amendment. *Harvard Law Review* 91:1–68.

———— 1984 Woman's Constitution. *Duke Law Journal* 1984:447–508.

KAY, HERMA H. (1974)1981 *Sex-Based Discrimination,* 2nd ed. St. Paul: West Publishing Co.

———— 1985 Models of Equality. *University of Illinois Law Review* 1985:39–88.

LAW, SYLVIA 1984 Rethinking Sex and the Constitution. *University of Pennsylvania Law Review* 132:955–1040.

TRIBE, LAURENCE H. 1978 *American Constitutional Law.* Pages 1060–1077. Mineola, N.Y.: Foundation Press.

WASSERSTROM, RICHARD A. 1977 Racism, Sexism, and Preferential Treatment: An Approach to the Topics. *UCLA Law Review* 24:581–622.

SEXUAL PREFERENCE AND THE CONSTITUTION

Since the 1960s both legislation and judicial decisions have moved toward decriminalization of homosexual conduct and toward increased acceptance of homosexuals as parents, professionals, and public employees. A number of legal restrictions remain, however, mostly concerning employment and other material benefits. The Supreme Court has not fully considered the constitutional issues raised by these restrictions. In DOE v. COMMONWEALTH'S ATTORNEY (1976) the Court summarily affirmed, 6–3 and without opinion, a federal district court's dismissal of a constitutional challenge to Virginia's sodomy law, brought by two adult males who lived in a stable homosexual relationship. The absence of any serious threat of prosecution suggests that the Court's decision may have rested on a RIPENESS ground. In any case, *Doe* surely is not the Court's last word on the subject—although it provides an object lesson for anyone who would ignore the influence of conventional morality on the development of coherent constitutional principle.

Doe had been argued on the theory of a RIGHT OF PRIVACY, by analogy to the Court's decisions on BIRTH CONTROL and abortion. But "privacy," in its ordinary usage, fails to capture the essence of the constitutional claim. A middle-class homosexual couple need fear no prosecution if they keep their relationship private. It is precisely the public expression of homosexuality that produces sanctions; the interest at stake is in some sense the opposite of privacy, more akin to a FIRST AMENDMENT freedom of expression. Similarly, the issue of homosexual marriage, which has been addressed by some commentators as an issue of SEX DISCRIMINATION, seems better approached as a problem in symbolic expression of a homosexual couple's identity.

Recognition of homosexual relationships within a FREEDOM OF INTIMATE ASSOCIATION would place on government the burden of justifying its interference with those relationships. If a state had to prove that homosexuality alone disqualified a person from child custody or employment as a school teacher, its efforts to do so would demonstrate that the operative factor in the law's disqualifications was not risk of harm but stigma. Commentators have suggested that homosexuality be added to the list of SUSPECT CLASSIFICATIONS calling for STRICT SCRUTINY under the EQUAL PROTECTION clause, and there is force to the argument. Whether the problem be seen as one of equality or as an aspect of SUBSTANTIVE DUE PROCESS, most laws regulating homosexual conduct seem unlikely to survive serious constitutional scrutiny. What remains in question is the willingness of a majority of Justices for the Supreme Court to engage in that scrutiny.

KENNETH L. KARST

Bibliography

PROJECT 1966 The Consenting Adult Homosexual and the Law: Empirical Study of Enforcement and Administration in Los Angeles County. *UCLA Law Review* 13:643–832.

RIVERA, RHONDA R. 1979 Our Straight-Laced Judges: The Legal Position of Homosexual Persons in the United States. *Hastings Law Journal* 30:799–955.

SYMPOSIUM 1985 The Legal System and Homosexuality—Approbation, Accommodation, or Reprobation? *University of Dayton Law Review* 10:445–813.

SHAPIRO v. THOMPSON
394 U.S. 618 (1969)

Two states and the DISTRICT OF COLUMBIA denied WELFARE BENEFITS to new residents during a one-year waiting period. The Supreme Court, 6–3, held that the state schemes denied the EQUAL PROTECTION OF THE LAWS and that the District's law violated the

Fifth Amendment's equal protection component, as recognized in BOLLING V. SHARPE (1954).

Justice WILLIAM J. BRENNAN wrote for the Court. The RIGHT TO TRAVEL from one state to settle in another was a FUNDAMENTAL INTEREST, whose impairment was justified only on a showing of a COMPELLING STATE INTEREST. These statutes served to deter the entry of INDIGENTS and to discourage interstate travel for the purpose of obtaining increased welfare benefits, but those objectives were constitutionally illegitimate efforts to restrict the RIGHT TO TRAVEL. Equal protection considerations forbade a state to apportion its benefits and services on the basis of past tax contributions. The saving of welfare costs similarly could not "justify an otherwise invidious classification." Various arguments addressed to administrative convenience were also insufficiently compelling.

The Court also hinted that WEALTH DISCRIMINATION against the indigent might constitute a SUSPECT CLASSIFICATION, or, alternatively, that minimum subsistence might be a fundamental interest. Both these suggestions were sidetracked in later decisions such as SAN ANTONIO INDEPENDENT SCHOOL DISTRICT V. RODRIGUEZ (1973).

Chief Justice EARL WARREN dissented, joined by Justice HUGO L. BLACK. Warren argued that Congress had approved the one-year waiting periods in the SOCIAL SECURITY ACT. The majority rejected this statutory interpretation but added that in any event "Congress may not authorize the States to violate the Equal Protection Clause."

Justice JOHN MARSHALL HARLAN, in a long dissent, mounted a frontal attack on the WARREN COURT'S expansion of the judicial role in equal protection cases through its heightening of the STANDARDS OF REVIEW in cases involving fundamental interests and suspect classifications. Here, as in other decisions of the same period, the Harlan dissent illuminates the Court's doctrinal path more effectively than does the majority opinion. It has always been possible for a Justice to combine clarity of vision with the wrong conclusion.

KENNETH L. KARST

(SEE ALSO: *Invidious Discrimination.*)

SHAUGHNESSY v. UNITED STATES ex rel. MEZEI
345 U.S. 206 (1953)

Over the dissent of four Justices, the VINSON COURT upheld the authority of the ATTORNEY GENERAL to exclude and detain indefinitely an ALIEN without a

hearing at Ellis Island solely on the basis of confidential information, "the disclosure of which would be prejudicial to the public interest." Justice ROBERT H. JACKSON, dissenting, wrote that he could not imagine how a hearing "would menace the security of this country."

MICHAEL E. PARRISH

SHAW, LEMUEL
(1781–1861)

Lemuel Shaw was chief justice of Massachusetts from 1830 to 1860, during which time he wrote a record number of opinions, over 2,200, only one in dissent. He dominated his court as no other judge has. His opinions were often comprehensive, ponderous, analytical treatises. He often explained guiding principles in terms of policy or social advantage, placing his decisions on the broadest grounds. Justice OLIVER WENDELL HOLMES, attributing Shaw's influence to his "accurate appreciation of the requirements of the community," declared that "few have lived who were his equals in their understanding of the grounds of public policy to which all laws must be ultimately referred. It was this which made him . . . the greatest magistrate which this country has produced."

Before his appointment to the Supreme Judicial Court, Shaw had been a Federalist lawyer, a member of both branches of the state legislature, and a bank director. Shaw did not, however, fit the stereotype of the conservative Whig judge seeking DOCTRINES of VESTED RIGHTS to ward off legislative controls over business enterprise. He was the foremost champion of the power of government to promote and regulate the economy in the public interest. To call the POLICE POWER Shaw's invention would be an exaggeration, but not a great one. Unlike JOHN MARSHALL and ROGER B. TANEY, who viewed the police power as the residual powers of the state, Shaw defined it as the power of government "to trench somewhat largely on the profitable use of individual property" for the public good, and he distinguished the police power from other state powers. Shaw laid the foundations for the legal character of power companies, railroads, and water suppliers as public utilities, privately owned but subject to regulation for the public benefit. He would even have included manufacturers and banks. He was the first to hold that the power of EMINENT DOMAIN cannot be restrained by or contracted away under the CONTRACT CLAUSE. At a time when that clause had become a bulwark of vested rights, making it a link between capitalism and constitutionalism, Shaw voided legislative alterations of chartered rights in only three cases, and in each the essential regulatory powers of the state were undiminished. Shaw was profoundly committed to JUDICIAL RESTRAINT. He held statutes unconstitutional in only nine reported cases, most often to protect the rights of the criminally accused. In as many cases Shaw repudiated the doctrine of SUBSTANTIVE DUE PROCESS drawn from WYNEHAMER V. NEW YORK (1856). Community rights rather than vested ones were Shaw's foremost concern.

In his COMMERCE CLAUSE opinions, too, Shaw sustained state powers. The Supreme Court agreed with him in the LICENSE CASES (1847) but reversed him in the PASSENGER CASES (1849), despite the sagacity of his empirical test to determine whether state and federal laws actually conflicted in their operation. In the absence of a federal law, Shaw would have sustained state legislation. He handed down the leading opinion on the constitutionality of the Fugitive Slave Act of 1850 in SIMS' CASE (1851), though he freed every sojourner slave (not a runaway) who reached Massachusetts. (See COMMONWEALTH V. AVES, 1836.) He originated the SEPARATE BUT EQUAL DOCTRINE that became the legal linchpin of racial SEGREGATION, and he upheld a conviction for BLASPHEMY in an opinion that abridged RELIGIOUS LIBERTY. In such cases he carried his doctrine of judicial restraint too far, but he towered over class and party, and his name became a synonym for judicial integrity and impartiality.

LEONARD W. LEVY

Bibliography

ADLOW, ELIJAH 1962 *The Genius of Lemuel Shaw.* Boston: Court Square Press.
LEVY, LEONARD W. 1957 *The Law of the Commonwealth and Chief Justice Shaw.* Cambridge, Mass.: Harvard University Press.

SHAYS' REBELLION
(1786–1787)

The economic depression following the Revolutionary War fell especially harshly upon small farmers who relied on borrowed money to finance their crops. Falling prices led to default and foreclosure. Seven states resorted to deliberate inflation (through large issues of unsecured paper currency), stay laws, and other forms of DEBTOR'S RELIEF LEGISLATION.

The Massachusetts legislature, however, defeated all such proposals. Beginning in August 1786, mobs of impoverished farmers in central and western Massachusetts prevented the courts from functioning and ordering foreclosures. In September an armed force assembled at Springfield under Daniel Shays, a farmer and one-time Revolutionary army captain. On January 25, 1787, Shays attempted to seize the federal arsenal at Springfield, but his men were repulsed by artillery. On February 4, the rebels were routed and the leaders captured by the state militia.

Meanwhile, Massachusetts had applied to Congress for assistance. Although Congress authorized raising a small force to protect the arsenal, no aid was actually sent.

The effect of the rebellion was to raise the specter of disintegration of civil government and so to hasten the process of constitutional reform. Less than three weeks after the collapse of Shays Rebellion, Congress passed a resolution giving official sanction to the Annapolis Convention's call for the CONSTITUTIONAL CONVENTION OF 1787.

DENNIS J. MAHONEY

Bibliography

SZATMARY, DAVID P. 1980 *Shays' Rebellion: The Making of an Agrarian Insurrection.* Amherst: University of Massachusetts Press.

SHELLEY v. KRAEMER
334 U.S. 1 (1948)
HURD v. HODGE
334 U.S. 24 (1948)

In 1926, in CORRIGAN V. BUCKLEY, the Supreme Court rejected a constitutional attack on judicial enforcement of racially RESTRICTIVE COVENANTS—contractual agreements between neighboring residential landowners limiting the occupancy of their houses to white persons. From that time forward, the NAACP sought to persuade the Court to reconsider and find the covenants' enforcement to constitute STATE ACTION in violation of the FOURTEENTH AMENDMENT. Finally, in *Shelley*, the Court granted review in two such cases, one from Missouri and one from Michigan. In both, white neighbors obtained INJUNCTIONS forbidding black buyers to occupy houses subject to racial covenants. The decision was widely anticipated to be important, both doctrinally and practically. Eighteen AMICUS CURIAE briefs supported the NAACP's position, and on the other side three white "protective associations" filed briefs, as did the National Association of Real Estate Boards. Counsel for the NAACP included CHARLES HOUSTON and THURGOOD MARSHALL.

The time was ripe for an overruling of *Corrigan's* casual acceptance of racially restrictive covenants as a "private" means of imposing residential segregation. The armed forces had integrated at the end of the World War II; in 1947 the President's Committee on Civil Rights had published a report calling attention to the importance of judicial enforcement to the effectiveness of the covenants; and President HARRY S. TRUMAN, a strong CIVIL RIGHTS advocate, had placed the weight of the executive branch on the NAACP's side by authorizing the SOLICITOR GENERAL to file an AMICUS CURIAE brief. The Supreme Court held, 6–0, that state courts could not constitutionally enjoin the sale to black buyers of property covered by restrictive covenants.

Shelley's result seems inescapable. Yet hardly anyone has a kind word for the *Shelley* opinion, written by Chief Justice FRED VINSON. *Corrigan* was not overruled but was characterized as a case involving only the validity of restrictive covenants and not their enforcement in courts. Standing alone, said Vinson, the racial covenants violated no rights; their enforcement by state court injunctions, however, constituted state action in violation of the Fourteenth Amendment. Taken for all it is worth, this reasoning would spell the end of the state action limitation—a loss many could cheerfully bear. But it is plain the Court had no such heroics in mind. The Justices were not ready to find state action in any private conduct the state might fail to prohibit. Yet the opinion never quite explained why, given the *Shelley* result, those larger doctrinal consequences do not follow. The opinion's elusive quality led Philip Kurland to call it "constitutional law's *Finnegans Wake.*"

Two decades later, in EVANS V. ABNEY (1970), the Court picked up the first shoe. *Shelley* was limited severely, and the power of a private owner to call on the courts to enforce his or her control over property was largely freed from constitutional limitations.

A companion case to *Shelley, Hurd v. Hodge* (1948), involved a racial covenant covering land in the DISTRICT OF COLUMBIA. Without reaching the question whether the Fifth Amendment guaranteed EQUAL PROTECTION (see BOLLING V. SHARPE, 1954), the Court held the judicial enforcement of the covenant to violate "the public policy of the United States."

KENNETH L. KARST

Bibliography
HENKIN, LOUIS 1962 Shelley v. Kraemer: Notes for a Revised Opinion. *University of Pennsylvania Law Review* 110:473–505.
HOROWITZ, HAROLD W. 1957 The Misleading Search for "State Action." *Southern California Law Review* 30:208–221.

SHELTON v. TUCKER

See: Least Restrictive Means Test

SHEPPARD-TOWNER MATERNITY ACT
42 Stat. 224 (1921)

FEDERAL GRANTS-IN-AID to the states began in the mid-nineteenth century. As the federal government, in its new capacity as a welfare state, funded important social services, some congressmen and senators considered this form of federal spending socialistic and questioned its constitutionality.

In 1921, Congress passed the Maternity Act, a measure recommended by President WARREN G. HARDING, allocating funds to the states for health service for mothers and children, particularly in rural communities. This welfare measure sought to reduce maternal and infant mortality. Critics argued that federal funds could lawfully be spent only in connection with the ENUMERATED POWERS of Congress, and they asserted that the grant-in-aid was a subtle method of extending federal power and usurping functions properly belonging to the states. Further, since the formal acceptance of such grants by state legislatures brought federal supervision and approval of the funded state activities, the measure placed too much potentially coercive power in the hands of federal bureaucracies.

The Supreme Court was asked to rule on the act's constitutionality in separate suits brought by a taxpayer and the Commonwealth of Massachusetts. The Court did not rule on the merits in either case, holding that the state presented no justiciable controversy and that the taxpayer lacked STANDING to sue. (See TAXPAYERS' SUITS; FROTHINGHAM V. MELLON, 1923.) Still, many states refused to avail themselves of the provisions of the act, and Congress failed to renew it in 1929. Nonetheless, the projects of this period were a political precedent for much of the modern system of federally dispensed welfare.

PAUL L. MURPHY

Bibliography

LEMONS, J. STANLEY 1960 The Sheppard-Towner Act: Progressivism in the 1920's. *Journal of American History* 55:776–786.

SHERBERT v. VERNER
374 U.S. 398 (1963)

Sherbert, a Seventh-Day Adventist, lost her job after the mill at which she had been working went on a six-day work week and she refused Saturday work. She filed for unemployment compensation, was referred to a job, but declined it because it would have required Saturday work. By declining proffered employment she was no longer "available for work" under South Carolina's rules and hence no longer eligible for unemployment benefits.

Justice WILLIAM J. BRENNAN, speaking for the Supreme Court, concluded that the disqualification imposed a burden on Mrs. Sherbert's free exercise of religion. The FIRST AMENDMENT, he declared, protected not only belief but observance. Even an incidental burdening of religion could be justified only if the state could show a COMPELLING STATE INTEREST in not granting an exemption.

This decision was a significant departure from the secular regulation approach to free exercise claims which had been affirmed by the Court as recently as *Braunfeld v. Brown* (1961). Brennan made little attempt to distinguish *Sherbert* from *Braunfeld*. Justice WILLIAM O. DOUGLAS, concurring, rejected the secular regulation approach.

Justice POTTER STEWART concurred in the result, disassociating himself from Brennan's reasoning. Stewart saw tension developing between the Court's interpretation of the free exercise and establishment clauses. To grant free exercise exemptions from otherwise valid secular regulations preferred religious over nonreligious people. In establishment clause cases, however, any governmental action that had the effect of advancing religion was forbidden. Stewart would have relieved the tension by relaxing the establishment clause rule.

Justice JOHN MARSHALL HARLAN, joined by Justice BYRON R. WHITE, dissented. For Harlan, the notion of a constitutional compulsion to "carve out an exception" based on religious conviction was a singularly dangerous one.

RICHARD E. MORGAN

SHERMAN, ROGER
(1721–1793)

Roger Sherman was one of the leading members of the founding generation. For more than two decades he was simultaneously mayor of New Haven, Connecticut, a member of the state legislature, and a judge of the Superior Court. He was a delegate to the Continental Congress almost continuously from 1774 to 1784. He signed the DECLARATION OF INDEPENDENCE, the ARTICLES OF CONFEDERATION, and the Constitution, the only person to sign all these founding documents.

At the CONSTITUTIONAL CONVENTION OF 1787, Sherman was a respected elder statesman. He distrusted a large and ill-informed populace and wanted all elections to national office mediated by the state legislatures. He formally introduced the GREAT COMPROMISE and argued strongly for its passage. He wrote the contingency provision prescribing election of the President by the House of Representatives if there was no majority in the ELECTORAL COLLEGE. He opposed giving the President an absolute VETO POWER and erecting a system of federal courts inferior to the Supreme Court. He originally favored, but later gave up, a unicameral national legislature chosen by the state legislatures. He strongly supported the prohibitions on export duties and BILLS OF CREDIT

After the Convention, Sherman worked hard for RATIFICATION OF THE CONSTITUTION, writing newspaper articles (as "A Countryman") and attending the state ratifying convention. He was a member of the first House of Representatives (1789–1791) and of the United States Senate (1791–1793). In Congress, as in the Convention, Sherman opposed as unnecessary and unwise the enactment of a federal BILL OF RIGHTS.

DENNIS J. MAHONEY

Bibliography

BOARDMAN, ROGER SHERMAN 1938(1971) *Roger Sherman: Signer and Statesman.* Philadelphia: University of Pennsylvania Press. (Reprint, New York: Da Capo).

SHERMAN ANTITRUST ACT
26 Stat. 209 (1890)

This concisely worded law represented the first congressional attempt at antitrust legislation. Neither the reasons for its approval nor its framers' intent are clear, but several circumstances ordained its passage.

Individual state attempts to regulate monopoly were often unsuccessful; a federal statute would satisfy the need for uniform national policy as well as consistent practice. In addition, a heritage of antimonopoly sentiment and an economic depression combined to inflame public opinion against the industrial giants. Consequently, the platforms of both major parties contained antimonopoly planks in 1888, and, following his election, President BENJAMIN HARRISON asked Congress to redeem this pledge. Of sixteen bills introduced into the next Congress, one, sponsored by Senator John Sherman (Republican, Ohio), was briefly debated and then referred to the Judiciary Committee. Six days later the committee reported out a completely rewritten bill which received only cursory debate and passed 52–1 in the Senate and 242–0 in the House. The lack of debate, particularly over such a potentially controversial bill, has never been satisfactorily explained. Often-cited possibilities include fierce interparty competition for support from the vigorously antimonopoly West and an underestimation of the act's importance. Contemporaries paid it little attention—the trusts and their congressional allies did not even bother to oppose the bill. Its proponents conceded that the act was an experimental entry into a new field of ECONOMIC REGULATION. In fact, it contained nothing new.

Although Senator Sherman was the moving force behind the bill, Senator George Edmunds (Republican, Vermont), chairman of the Senate Judiciary Committee, wrote most of it. Despite Edmunds's claim that it was "clear in its terms . . . [and] definite in its definitions," the act failed to define the two most important concepts in it: monopoly and restraint of trade. Although there is a debate over the (Anglo-American) COMMON LAW underpinnings of the act, most scholars agree that the common law forbade agreements in restraint of trade and CRIMINAL CONSPIRACY to monopolize. The controversy arises over these doctrines' application in America and the extent of their incorporation into the Sherman Act. The final bill also omitted any specific exemption for labor or farm organizations. Congress either meant to leave the issue to the courts (see LOEWE V. LAWLOR, 1908) or, more likely, believed an exemption was self-evident from the text.

The first section of the act outlawed "every contract, combination . . . or conspiracy, in restraint of trade" or INTERSTATE COMMERCE and was directed against joint action. Section 2—equally applicable to individuals—outlawed any means of achieving monopoly. Broader than section 1, this clause declared void any attempt, combination, or conspiracy to monopolize. It did not outlaw monopoly per se. Among the remaining provisions were those granting JURISDICTION to the CIRCUIT COURTS, providing for EQUITY proceedings, and authorizing treble damage suits.

Even with public support, the Sherman Act proved ineffective initially. The economic depression of the 1890s adversely affected business, and the general terms of the act required interpretation which could only come with time. The Court hamstrung the act in UNITED STATES V. E. C. KNIGHT (1895), holding that it did not apply to manufacturing. Even though a bare majority of the Court resuscitated the act against pooling arrangements in UNITED STATES V. TRANS-MISSOURI FREIGHT ASSOCIATION (1897), the government would not achieve any notable success until PHILANDER C. KNOX became ATTORNEY GENERAL under THEODORE ROOSEVELT. Then, in quick succession, the government won major victories in NORTHERN SECURITIES CO. V. UNITED STATES (1904) and SWIFT & CO. V. UNITED STATES (1905). The next decade saw a limitation on antitrust policy as the Court formulated the RULE OF REASON and additional implementation by Congress which passed the CLAYTON and FEDERAL TRADE COMMISSION ACTS.

DAVID GORDON

Bibliography
NEALE, A. D. and GOYDER, D. G. 1980 *The Antitrust Laws of the United States of America,* 3rd ed. Cambridge: At the University Press.
THORELLI, HANS B. 1955 *The Federal Antitrust Policy.* Baltimore: Johns Hopkins University Press.

SHIELD LAWS

In BRANZBURG V. HAYES (1972) and later decisions relating to an asserted REPORTER'S PRIVILEGE, the Supreme Court rejected the claim that the FIRST AMENDMENT should privilege reporters from having to respond to proper inquiries incident to legal proceedings. However, before and after *Branzburg,* more than half the states have passed legislation, called shield laws, that give reporters such a privilege. These laws vary considerably, as has their reception in the state courts. Some laws privilege reporters as to all information gathered in the course of their journalistic activities. Others privilege reporters only as to information gathered from confidential informants. Some laws make an exception to the privilege if a reporter has witnessed the commission of a crime.

A number of state courts have found state constitutional grounds for cutting back on shield laws. Thus one California decision held that a shield law could not immunize a reporter from having to answer a judge's questions about who had violated a judicial GAG ORDER against informing the press about evidence in a notorious criminal trial. And New Jersey's supreme court held that the state's law could not shield a reporter from inquiries by a defendant in a criminal case concerning information relevant to his defense.

BENNO C. SCHMIDT, JR.

SHIRAS, GEORGE, JR.
(1832–1924)

George Shiras, Jr., was appointed to the Supreme Court by BENJAMIN HARRISON in 1892 and served for slightly more than a decade. A native of Pittsburgh and a Yale graduate, Shiras had maintained an independent, yet prosperous and varied law practice for nearly forty years before his appointment. He came to the Court without previous experience in public life and charted an independent course. His voting record suggests that he remained aloof from the era's policy debates yet maintained a fundamental distrust of institutional change. His unadorned and cool style and his emphasis on precedent and conventional rules of interpretation reflected his personality as well as his conception of the judicial function.

The 1890s were a transitional period in American public life, and the questions that crowded the Court's docket indicated the increasing scope and intensity of governmental interventions in economy and society. Three major classes of constitutional issues came up during Shiras's tenure. The first involved petitioners who sought enlarged judicial protection under the FOURTEENTH AMENDMENT for FREEDOM OF CONTRACT in the face of state laws regulating labor relations and the price of essential services. They got no encouragement from Shiras. In *Brass v. North Dakota* (1894), a grain elevator case, he refused to restrict the range of "businesses AFFECTED WITH A PUBLIC INTEREST" to those with a "virtual monopoly" at a particular location; he also spoke for the Court in *Knoxville v. Harbison* (1901), sustaining a Tennessee statute that required employers to pay their workers in cash or company-store scrip redeemable in cash. Justices DAVID J. BREWER and RUFUS PECKHAM, the FULLER COURT's leading apostles of laissez-faire, dis-

sented in each instance. Yet Shiras was consistently aligned with Brewer and Peckham in the second class of cases, including UNITED STATES V. E. C. KNIGHT CO. (1895) and CHAMPION V. AMES (1903), involving federal authority under the COMMERCE CLAUSE in policy domains traditionally reserved to the states. Congressional regulation of manufacturing CORPORATIONS and public morals, like federal JUDICIAL REVIEW of STATE POLICE POWER regulations under the Fourteenth Amendment, necessitated new and, in Shiras's view, illegitimate departures in the organization of constitutional power.

Shiras wrote his most powerful opinions in the third class of cases, involving petitioners whose liberty or property was jeopardized by intensified federal activity in areas of acknowledged federal competence. He complained repeatedly about the majority's penchant for narrow construction of the Fifth Amendment's JUST COMPENSATION clause when riparian land was damaged by federal construction of dams and other river improvements. He also dissented sharply in BROWN V. WALKER (1896), contending that a federal immunity statute for persons required to testify before the Interstate Commerce Commission was an inadequate substitute for the Fifth Amendment RIGHT AGAINST SELF-INCRIMINATION. And in *Wong Wing v. United States* (1896) Shiras spoke for a unanimous Court that finally curbed Congress's draconian anti-Chinese program at the point where immigration officials were authorized to sentence illegal aliens to as much as one year of hard labor prior to deportation. The sentence of hard labor was an "infamous" one, Shiras explained. Consequently it could be invoked only after the Fifth and Sixth Amendment requirements of due process and TRIAL BY JURY had been met.

Shiras had determined at the time of his appointment to retire at seventy to avoid burdening his brethren because of age. He underscored his habitual divergence from conventional norms by carrying through his resolve. His retirement in 1903 attracted little notice, and his death more than twenty years later even less. Shiras's constitutional jurisprudence was simply too idiosyncratic to generate a significant following at the bar, in the law schools, or among the general public.

CHARLES W. MCCURDY

Bibliography

PAUL, ARNOLD 1969 George Shiras, Jr. Pages 1577–1591 in Leon Friedman and Fred L. Israel, eds., *The Justices of the United States Supreme Court, 1789–1969: Their Lives and Major Opinions.* New York: Chelsea House.

SHIRAS, WINFIELD 1953 *Justice George Shiras, Jr. of Pittsburgh*. Pittsburgh: University of Pittsburgh Press.

SHOPPING CENTERS

By the 1960s, shopping centers accounted for more than one-third of the nation's retail sales. Crowds of shoppers made the centers attractive places for the exercise of FIRST AMENDMENT rights such as PICKETING, leafleting, and the circulation of petitions. Two decades earlier, in MARSH V. ALABAMA (1946), the Supreme Court had assimilated the "company town" to the First Amendment DOCTRINE governing the use of an ordinary city street as a PUBLIC FORUM. When shopping center owners sought to prevent the use of their property for communications they had not approved, the question arose whether the centers, too, would be assimilated to the public forum doctrine.

The problem first came to the Supreme Court near the zenith of WARREN COURT activism in the defense of CIVIL LIBERTIES. In *Amalgamated Food Employees Union v. Logan Valley Plaza, Inc.* (1968), a bare majority held that union picketing of a store in a shopping center was protected by the First Amendment. Justice THURGOOD MARSHALL, for the Court, described the shopping center as the functional equivalent of the business district of the company town in *Marsh*. The author of the *Marsh* opinion, Justice HUGO L. BLACK, led the four dissenters.

When the issue returned to the Court, President RICHARD M. NIXON's four appointees were sitting. A new 5–4 majority now held, in *Lloyd Corp v. Tanner* (1972), that the distribution of leaflets opposing the VIETNAM WAR could be forbidden by a shopping center's private owner. Justice LEWIS F. POWELL, for the majority, distinguished *Logan Valley:* the leafleting here had no relation to the center's activities, and here alternative means of communication were reasonably available on nearby streets. Justice Marshall led the dissenters.

The circle closed four years later, when a 7–2 majority, speaking through Justice POTTER STEWART (a *Lloyd Corp.* dissenter), said that *Lloyd Corp.* really had overruled *Logan Valley*. HUDGENS V. N.L.R.B. (1976), like *Logan Valley*, was a union picketing case. Justice Stewart pointed out that *Lloyd Corp.* had drawn an untenable distinction based on the content of messages being conveyed; because that distinction failed, it was necessary to make a yes-or-no decision on the assimilation of shopping centers to the doctrine governing company towns—and the majority's answer was "no."

Some passages in the *Lloyd Corp.* opinion had suggested that a shopping center owner had a constitutionally protected property right to exclude leafleters. That argument was flatly rejected by the Court in PRUNEYARD SHOPPING CENTER V. ROBBINS (1980). California's supreme court had ruled that the state constitution protected the right to collect signatures for a petition in a shopping center. The U.S. Supreme Court unanimously held that this principle of state constitutional law did not violate any federal constitutional rights.

KENNETH L. KARST

Bibliography

TRIBE, LAURENCE H. 1978 *American Constitutional Law*. Pages 693–696, 1163–1167. Mineola, N.Y.: Foundation Press.

SHREVEPORT DOCTRINE

In the early twentieth century, the Supreme Court employed several DOCTRINES to sustain federal regulation of INTRASTATE COMMERCE. Among these, the Shreveport doctrine enjoyed a long tenure in the service of the COMMERCE CLAUSE. Since its elaboration, the Court has approved its use as a means of reaching a variety of activities, including professional football, minimum wages, crop control, and RACIAL DISCRIMINATION.

First announced in HOUSTON, EAST & WEST TEXAS RAILWAY V. UNITED STATES—the Shreveport Rate Case—(1914), the doctrine permitted congressional regulation of purely local freight rates when, unmodified, they would have impeded INTERSTATE COMMERCE. The doctrine drew sustenance from the Court's distinction between direct and indirect EFFECTS ON COMMERCE in UNITED STATES V. E. C. KNIGHT COMPANY (1895) but reflected a new economic pragmatism. The Court recognized the integrated nature of the railroad system before it in the Shreveport Rate Case. It asserted that the commerce power "necessarily embraces the right to control . . . [intrastate] operations in all matters having such a close and substantial relation to interstate traffic that the control is essential or appropriate" to maintain a free flow of interstate commerce. The Court applied the doctrine throughout the 1920s in railroad cases such as DAYTON-GOOSE CREEK RAILWAY V. UNITED STATES (1924).

The judicial "revolution" of 1937 enhanced the use of the Shreveport doctrine. Earlier, the Court had struck down federal regulation in CARTER V. CARTER COAL COMPANY (1936) as an attempt to control activities only indirectly affecting interstate commerce, but it soon held that the WAGNER (NATIONAL LABOR RELATIONS) ACT legitimately regulated PRODUCTION (heretofore considered local), reiterating the "close and substantial relation" test of the Shreveport doctrine. (See N.L.R.B. V. JONES & LAUGHLIN STEEL CORP., 1937.)

The doctrine continued to grow in the 1940s. After several predictable decisions allowing federal regulation of intrastate milk prices (UNITED STATES V. WRIGHTWOOD DAIRY, 1942), the Court greatly expanded the doctrine in WICKARD V. FILBURN (1942) by subjecting to federal control a local wheat crop "where no part of the product is intended for interstate commerce or intermingled with the subjects thereof." The Court declared that even local activity that "may not be regarded as commerce . . . may still . . . be reached by Congress if it exerts a substantial economic effect on interstate commerce . . . irrespective of whether such effect is what might at some earlier time have been defined as 'direct' or 'indirect'." This interpretation invited increasing use of the doctrine in antitrust cases, particularly under the SHERMAN ANTITRUST ACT, where, along with the STREAM OF COMMERCE DOCTRINE, it became a test of the law's applicability.

Congress and the Supreme Court continued this expansion in the 1960s. The CIVIL RIGHTS ACT OF 1964, based on the commerce clause, prohibits racial discrimination in PUBLIC ACCOMMODATIONS. The Court sustained application of the act to a local restaurant because "the absence of direct evidence connecting discriminatory restaurant service with the flow of interstate food . . . is not . . . a crucial matter." (See KATZENBACH V. MCCLUNG, 1964; *Daniel v. Paul*, 1969.) Criminal activity, too, fell within the doctrine's scope when the Court found ties between local loan-sharking and interstate commerce in PEREZ V. UNITED STATES (1971). The Court also included firearms in the doctrine's reach, sustaining a conviction under the OMNIBUS CRIME CONTROL AND SAFE STREETS ACT for illegal possession, despite a minimal demonstration of the requisite connection with commerce (*Scarborough v. United States*, 1977).

The Shreveport doctrine helped bring about the demise of DUAL FEDERALISM. Because of the Justices' willingness to accede to congressional determinations, the Court's application of the doctrine has consistently followed its statement in *Board of Trade v. Olsen* (1923) that "this court will certainly not substitute its judgment for that of Congress in such a matter unless the relation of the subject to interstate commerce, and its effect upon it, are clearly nonexistent."

DAVID GORDON

SIBRON v. NEW YORK

See: *Terry v. Ohio*

SIERRA CLUB v. MORTON
405 U.S. 727 (1972)

Acting as a public defender of the environment, the Sierra Club sued the secretary of the interior to enjoin approval of a ski resort development at Mineral King Valley in Sequoia National Forest. The Supreme Court, 4–3, denied the Club's right to JUDICIAL REVIEW of claimed statutory violations, for failure to allege harm to its members in their personal use of Mineral King. Significantly, however, the Court declared aesthetic and environmental interests, though widely shared, to be as deserving of judicial protection as economic interests. Thus, persons whose individual enjoyment of the environment is impaired by government action have STANDING to contest the action's legality.

JONATHAN D. VARAT

SILVERMAN v. UNITED STATES
365 U.S. 505 (1961)

To investigate gambling, DISTRICT OF COLUMBIA police officers inserted a microphone into a wall. The device touched a heating duct, enabling the police to overhear conversations throughout the house.

In *Goldman v. United States* (1942) the Court had afforded no constitutional protection against a microphone placed *against* a wall. By 1961 the Court, concerned about new methods of electronic surveillance, ruled that because there was a physical penetration, albeit only a few inches, the overhearing was subject to the FOURTH AMENDMENT with no need to reconsider *Goldman* or earlier cases; that reconsideration occurred in KATZ V. UNITED STATES (1967).

HERMAN SCHWARTZ

(SEE ALSO: *Electronic Eavesdropping.*)

SILVER PLATTER DOCTRINE

WEEKS V. UNITED STATES (1914), which formulated the EXCLUSIONARY RULE for federal prosecutions, made an exception for EVIDENCE seized by state officers in searches that did not meet FOURTH AMENDMENT standards. The evidence was usable in a federal trial when it was handed by the state to federal officers on "a silver platter" (Justice FELIX FRANKFURTER's phrase in *Lustig v. United States,* 1949). Participation by federal officers in the state search, no matter how minor, rendered the evidence inadmissible in federal cases under *Byars v. United States* (1927), as did even a search conducted by state officers alone if its purpose was the gathering of evidence for the federal government under *Gambino v. United States* (1927).

A combination of several factors led to the overruling of the silver platter doctrine in ELKINS V. UNITED STATES (1960). First, in WOLF V. COLORADO (1949), the Supreme Court had applied "the core" of the Fourth Amendment's standard (which did not, however, include the exclusionary rule) to the states. It therefore became incongruous to admit in federal court evidence which state officials had seized in violation of the Constitution. In addition, about half the states had adopted an exclusionary rule for unlawfully seized evidence; to allow federal authorities to use evidence which would have been excluded in the state courts served to frustrate the exclusionary policies of those states and to undermine the principle of FEDERALISM on which the silver platter doctrine was itself premised. The expansion of federal criminal law also undermined the vitality of the doctrine: a growing catalogue of crimes punishable by both federal and state governments evidently alerted the Court to the attendant possibilities of abuse by cooperative law enforcement.

Thus far the *Elkins* principle applies only to evidence in criminal cases. In *Janis v. United States* (1976), the Court held that evidence unlawfully seized by state officers can be used by the federal government (and vice versa) in civil proceedings (for instance, in a tax assessment case). The Court reasoned that the main purpose of the exclusionary rule is to deter unlawful searches, and that application of the rule should be tailored to this end. When the officer is prevented from using the seized evidence to further a criminal prosecution, the principle of deterrence is amply served; exclusion of the evidence in a civil case would provide no significant reinforcement for Fourth Amendment values.

JACOB W. LANDYNSKI

(SEE ALSO: *Two Sovereignties Rule.*)

Bibliography

LANDYNSKI, JACOB W. 1966 *Search and Seizure and the Supreme Court.* Pages 70–73, 149–158. Baltimore: Johns Hopkins University Press.

SILVERTHORNE LUMBER CO. v. UNITED STATES
251 U.S. 385 (1920)

Silverthorne was the first case to test the scope of the EXCLUSIONARY RULE, formulated in WEEKS V. UNITED STATES (1914), requiring exclusion from a federal trial of EVIDENCE obtained in an unconstitutional search.

Federal officers searched the Silverthorne Company's office; "without a shadow of authority," in Justice OLIVER WENDELL HOLMES's words, they "made a clean sweep of all the books, papers, and documents found there." Compounding the "outrage," the records were copied and photographed, and an INDICTMENT was framed on the basis of the information uncovered. The district court ordered the return of the originals but allowed the copies to be retained by the government, which then subpoenaed the originals. The Supreme Court reversed.

Holmes asserted that to allow the government to use the derivatively acquired evidence would mean that "only two steps are required [to render the evidence admissible] instead of one. In our opinion such is not the law. It reduces the 4th Amendment to form of words." Holmes added: "The essence of a provision forbidding the acquisition of evidence in a certain way is that not merely evidence so acquired shall not be used, but that it shall not be used at all." On this principle, an admission made by a suspect while he is under illegal arrest, as in WONG SUN V. UNITED STATES (1963), like a lead furnished by an illegally placed wiretap, as in NARDONE V. UNITED STATES (1939), may not be introduced into evidence because it is directly derived from an unlawful act. In *Nardone,* Justice FELIX FRANKFURTER dubbed the doctrine of the *Silverthorne* case as the FRUIT OF THE POISONOUS TREE.

JACOB W. LANDYNSKI

SIMON v. EASTERN KENTUCKY WELFARE RIGHTS ORGANIZATION
426 U.S. 26 (1976)

In 1969 the Internal Revenue Service (IRS) amended its regulations governing nonprofit hospitals' obligations to provide care for INDIGENTS. A number of individuals and service organizations sued to set aside the modifications, claiming they would cause the denial of services to indigents. Following WARTH V. SELdin (1975), the Supreme Court held that the plaintiffs lacked standing. Justice LEWIS F. POWELL, for the Court, declared that it was "purely speculative" whether any denials of hospital service to the plaintiffs could be traced to the IRS changes, or whether judicial relief against the IRS would increase the availability of such services to them. The plaintiffs thus could not meet Article III's requirement of CASES OR CONTROVERSIES. Justice WILLIAM J. BRENNAN, joined by Justice THURGOOD MARSHALL, argued that the plaintiffs had alleged a cognizable injury, but concurred in the result on grounds of RIPENESS.

DAVID GORDON

SIMOPOULOS v. VIRGINIA

See: Reproductive Autonomy

SIMS' CASE
7 Cushing (Mass.) 285 (1851)

Chief Justice LEMUEL SHAW of Massachusetts, denying a writ of HABEAS CORPUS for a fugitive slave, delivered the first and most influential opinion sustaining the constitutionality of the Fugitive Slave Act of 1850. The case, which riveted national attention, had political and moral as well as constitutional significance; it reproduced hateful scenes of slavery in the North. The capture and rendition of a black man provoked denunciations of the COMPROMISE OF 1850. Without military force to execute the rendition, Shaw's decision would have been a dead letter in Massachusetts.

LEONARD W. LEVY

(SEE ALSO: *Fugitive Slavery.*)

SINKING FUND CASES
Union Pacific Railroad Co. v. United States
99 U.S. 700 (1879)
Central Pacific Railroad Co. v. Gallatin
99 U.S. 727 (1879)

Congress authorized the construction of transcontinental railroads and made massive grants and loans to them. Following the exposure of enormous corruption in the management of the roads, Congress enacted a statute requiring that twenty-five percent of the annual net earnings of the CORPORATIONS be paid into a sinking fund to guarantee payment of the debts owed to the federal treasury. The Supreme Court sustained the second statute on ground that Congress had reserved the power to alter or amend its original grant. However, Chief Justice MORRISON R. WAITE, for a 6–3 Court, said in an OBITER DICTUM that the United States binds itself by its contracts and that, although the CONTRACT CLAUSE applied only to the states, the Fifth Amendment's DUE PROCESS clause effectuated the binding by preventing the deprivation of property. Three Justices, WILLIAM STRONG, JOSEPH P. BRADLEY, and STEPHEN J. FIELD, wrote dissenting opinions based on Waite's dictum; they believed that the sinking-fund statute violated the Fifth Amendment. The decision is significant, therefore, because of the strong boost it gave to the emerging concept of SUBSTANTIVE DUE PROCESS. In effect, too, the Court incorporated contract clause reasoning into the due process clause as a means of protecting property when Congress "improperly interferes with VESTED RIGHTS." This strange doctrine operated, though infrequently, as late as 1936. (See LOUISVILLE JOINT STOCK LAND BANK V. RADFORD.)

LEONARD W. LEVY

SIPUEL v. OKLAHOMA STATE BOARD OF REGENTS
332 U.S. 631 (1948)

PER CURIAM, reaffirming MISSOURI EX REL. GAINES V. CANADA (1938), the Supreme Court ordered Oklahoma to provide a black applicant with legal education in a state law school. Rather than admit her to the state university, the state roped off part of the state capitol, called it a law school for blacks, and provided three instructors. The Supreme Court avoided ruling on this mockery, saying the case had not presented the issue whether separate law schools satisfied the Constitution.

KENNETH L. KARST

(SEE ALSO: *Sweatt v. Painter, 1950.*)

SIT-IN

The CIVIL RIGHTS movement of the 1960s embraced more than lawsuits aimed at ending racial SEGREGATION in southern public institutions. It also included several forms of direct action, such as "freedom rides," in which blacks would ride on buses and trains, refusing to confine themselves to places set aside for black passengers. The quintessential form of direct action was the sit-in demonstration. The practice began in Greensboro, North Carolina, in 1960. Four black college freshmen went to a dime store lunch counter and ordered coffee. When they were told they would not be served, they sat at the counter, waiting, in silent protest against the indignity of RACIAL DISCRIMINATION. The next week they returned, joined by increasing numbers of students, white and black. Soon the sit-in technique spread to lunch counters throughout the South.

The impact of the sit-ins was enormous. Many stores and restaurants abandoned their discriminatory policies within a matter of weeks. Most, however, held out, and called the police. Sit-in demonstrators by the hundreds were arrested and charged with criminal TRESPASS. From 1960 to 1964, the problem of the sit-ins came to the Supreme Court over and over again.

When the segregating restaurant was a state operation (for example, a lunch counter in a courthouse), the Court could reverse the conviction by analogy to BROWN V. BOARD OF EDUCATION (1954). Even when the lunch counter was privately owned, the Court would reverse the conviction if it could find some public policy in the background, requiring or encouraging segregation. During the early 1960s the Court was pressed to abandon, or drastically alter, the STATE ACTION limitation, so as to create an equivalent FOURTEENTH AMENDMENT right to be free from racial discrimination in all privately owned PUBLIC ACCOMMODATIONS, irrespective of any state participation. The issue reached a climax—but not a resolution—in BELL V. MARYLAND (1964), when the Court again struck down a conviction on a narrow ground, without deciding the larger constitutional issue.

The Court was relieved of the need to face that issue when Congress adopted the CIVIL RIGHTS ACT OF 1964, which included a broad prohibition against racial discrimination in public accommodations. The Supreme Court quickly upheld the law's constitutionality in HEART OF ATLANTA MOTEL V. UNITED STATES (1964). Further, the Court held that the 1964 act applied with retroactive force, invalidating trespass convictions for sit-ins at public accommodations before the law's effective date (*Hamm v. City of Rock Hill*, 1964).

KENNETH L. KARST

Bibliography

LEWIS, THOMAS P. 1963 The Sit-In Cases: Great Expectations. *Supreme Court Review* 1963:101–151.
PAULSEN, MONRAD G. 1964 The Sit-In Cases of 1964: But Answer Came There None. *Supreme Court Review* 1964:137–170.

SIXTEENTH AMENDMENT

The Sixteenth Amendment was designed to circumvent POLLOCK V. FARMERS' LOAN AND TRUST CO. (1895), in which the Supreme Court had held that a federal tax on income from property was a DIRECT TAX on that property and therefore invalid for want of apportionment among the states on the basis of population (Article I, sections 2 and 9). Following *Pollock*, powerful political forces continued to press for an income tax to replace the regressive consumption taxes then employed to finance the federal government. Indeed, an amendment might have been unnecessary, given the Supreme Court's philosophical shift in *Flint v. Stone Tracy Co.* (1911), upholding a corporate income tax as an excise on doing business in corporate form, not a tax on property.

Although there was sentiment for challenging *Pollock* by reenacting a personal income tax, President WILLIAM HOWARD TAFT urged a constitutional amendment. The Sixteenth Amendment was speedily passed and ratified in 1913. It provides: "The Congress shall have power to lay and collect taxes on incomes, from whatever source derived, without apportionment among the several States, and without regard to any census or enumeration."

Since the enactment of a new income tax statute in 1913, only a single Supreme Court decision has held an income tax provision unconstitutional. EISNER V. MACOMBER (1920) ruled that a stock dividend of common stock on common stock was not "income" because the element of "realization" was lacking. *Macomber* has been greatly undermined by subsequent cases, such as *Helvering v. Bruun* (1940) which treated the return of a lessor's property to him at the termination of a lease as a realization of income. Indeed, the current Court would probably dispense entirely with any constitutional requirement of a realization (or alternatively view a stock dividend as a realization). In *Helvering v. Griffiths* (1943) three dissenters would have overruled *Macomber* but the majority held that the constitutional issue had not been presented by the statute.

Eisner v. Macomber also purported to define "income" for constitutional purposes as "the gain derived from capital, from labor, or from both combined." This definition proved far too narrow; in *Commissioner v. Glenshaw Glass Co.* (1955), the Court rejected all considerations of source, holding a windfall constitutionally taxable as income.

Unlike *Macomber,* modern decisions go to considerable lengths to uphold the constitutionality of income tax provisions. For example, the lower courts upheld an income tax provision that taxed mutual insurance companies on their gross receipts in *Penn Mutual Indemnity Co. v. Commissioner* (1976). Because no deductions were allowed, the tax might have been levied even though the taxpayer had no gain. Similarly, lower courts have upheld a Code section that values property received for services by ignoring value-depressing restrictions on the property (*Sakol v. Commissioner,* 1978). Although the Supreme Court has not had occasion to confirm these broad holdings, the modern approach to claims of constitutional invalidity of tax statutes is to uphold them as indirect taxes or alternatively to define "income" with sufficient breadth to accommodate the provision in issue within the Sixteenth Amendment.

MICHAEL ASIMOW

Bibliography

PAUL, RANDOLPH 1954 *Taxation in the United States.* Boston: Little, Brown.

SIXTH AMENDMENT

See: Confrontation, Right of; Counsel, Right to; Criminal Procedure; Fair Trial; Speedy Trial

SKINNER v. OKLAHOMA
315 U.S. 535 (1942)

In *Skinner* the Supreme Court laid a doctrinal foundation for two of the most important constitutional developments of the twentieth century: the expansion of the reach of the EQUAL PROTECTION clause and the reemergence of SUBSTANTIVE DUE PROCESS as a guarantee of personal freedoms. The case arose out of an Oklahoma law authorizing STERILIZATION of a person convicted three times of "felonies involving moral turpitude." Skinner, convicted first of chicken stealing and then twice of armed robbery, was ordered sterilized by the state courts. The Supreme Court unanimously reversed, holding the sterilization law unconstitutional. Surely the decision seemed easy; no doubt the only serious question was the appropriate ground for decision.

The opinion of the Court, by Justice WILLIAM O. DOUGLAS, rested on equal protection grounds. The sterilization law contained an exception for violations of "prohibitory [liquor] laws, revenue acts, embezzle-

ment, or political offenses." Although the state might constitutionally impose different penalties on embezzlement and other forms of stealing, it could not use so artificial a distinction as the basis for depriving someone of the right of procreation, "one of the basic civil rights of man." Because sterilization permanently deprived a person of a "basic liberty," said Justice Douglas, the judiciary must subject it to "STRICT SCRUTINY." Here the state had offered no justification for the belief that inheritability of criminal traits followed the line between embezzlement and chicken stealing.

Surely the Court also recognized that the sterilization law's exceptions were white collar crimes. Justice Douglas said, "In evil or reckless hands" sterilization could "cause races or types which [were] inimical to the dominant group to wither and disappear." (The year was 1942; the Nazi theory of a "master race" was a major ideological target in World War II.) Sterilization of some but not all who commit "intrinsically the same quality of offense" was "INVIDIOUS" DISCRIMINATION in the same way that RACIAL DISCRIMINATION was.

Chief Justice HARLAN FISKE STONE, concurring, found the Court's equal protection rationale unpersuasive, but found a denial of PROCEDURAL DUE PROCESS in the sterilization law's failure to give a three-time felon like Skinner an opportunity to show that his criminal tendencies were not inheritable. Given the prevailing scientific opinion that criminal traits were not generally inheritable, an individual should have a chance to contest the law's assumption. (This style of reasoning was in vogue briefly during the 1970s under the name of IRREBUTTABLE PRESUMPTIONS.) Justice ROBERT H. JACKSON agreed with both the Douglas and the Stone approaches.

Close to the surface of both the Douglas and the Stone opinions was a strong skepticism that any criminal traits were inheritable. Such an objection would seem fatal to Oklahoma's law on substantive due process grounds. But the Court had very recently abandoned substantive due process as a limit on ECONOMIC REGULATION, and in doing so had used language suggesting the complete demise of substantive due process. Both Douglas and Stone seemed to be avoiding the obvious ground that the law arbitrarily deprived Skinner of liberty. But *Skinner* can be seen today as not only a forerunner of a later Court's strict scrutiny analysis of equal protection cases involving FUNDAMENTAL INTERESTS and SUSPECT CLASSIFICATIONS but also a major early precedent for the development of a constitutional RIGHT OF PRIVACY as a branch of substantive due process.

KENNETH L. KARST

(SEE ALSO: *Reproductive Autonomy; Freedom of Intimate Association.*)

Bibliography

KARST, KENNETH L. 1969 Invidious Discrimination: Justice Douglas and the Return of the "Natural-Law-Due-Process Formula." *UCLA Law Review* 16:716–750.

SLANDER

See: Libel and the First Amendment

SLAUGHTERHOUSE CASES
16 Wallace 36 (1873)

Most histories of the Constitution begin consideration of the judicial interpretation of the THIRTEENTH and FOURTEENTH AMENDMENTS with the *Slaughterhouse* decision of 1873. The decision is, to be sure, of vast significance. Justices JOSEPH P. BRADLEY and STEPHEN J. FIELD, dissenting, expressed embryonic DOCTRINES of FREEDOM OF CONTRACT and SUBSTANTIVE DUE PROCESS that were to dominate American jurisprudence for two generations.

In 1869, Louisiana, ostensibly as a public health measure, incorporated the Crescent City Stock Landing and Slaughterhouse Company and granted it a monopoly of licensed butchering in New Orleans. Butchers not parties to the lucrative arrangement, after failing to crack the monopoly in the state courts, employed as counsel, in an appeal to the federal courts, former Supreme Court Justice JOHN A. CAMPBELL, who more recently had been a Confederate assistant secretary of war. Campbell argued before the Supreme Court that the excluded butchers had been deprived of their livelihoods by the state's deliberate discrimination, although Louisiana had disguised the corrupt monopoly as a health measure. Therefore the disputed statute violated the Thirteenth Amendment's ban on involuntary servitude, the 1866 CIVIL RIGHTS ACT's enforcements of that ban, and the Fourteenth Amendment's guarantees of PRIVILEGES AND IMMUNITIES, EQUAL PROTECTION OF THE LAWS, and due process.

Among prominent counsel for the state, Senator MATTHEW HALE CARPENTER responded to Campbell's innovative brief. Carpenter easily assembled case law that sustained state restrictions on private economic relationships. He insisted that the STATE POLICE POWER amply undergirded the Louisiana statute. No federal constitutional question existed, Car-

penter asserted. Both the Thirteenth and the Fourteenth Amendments were irrelevant to the litigants' rights and remedies. And, he prophesied, the federal system would be virtually revolutionized if the Court accepted Campbell's notions and legitimized a federal interest in individuals' claims to be exempt from state regulation.

Speaking through Justice SAMUEL F. MILLER, a majority of the Court was unready to accept Campbell's view that federal guarantees to individuals extended to trades (although, in the TEST OATH CASES, 1867, the Court had extended other federal guarantees to lawyers, ministers, and teachers). Instead, having accepted Carpenter's arguments, Miller reviewed the tradition of judicial support for state determination of ways to meet POLICE POWER responsibilities. Miller denied that exclusion from butchering deprived the appellants of federally protected rights to freedom, privileges and immunities, equal protection, or due process; the "one pervading purpose" of the postwar amendments, he said, was to liberate black slaves, not to enlarge whites' rights. The monopoly created by the state law could not be perceived as imposing servitude; the Thirteenth Amendment was irrelevant as a protection for livelihoods.

Turning to the Fourteenth Amendment, Miller separated federal from state privileges and immunities. He assigned to the states the definition of ordinary marketplace relationships essential to the vast majority of people. More important, he assigned to state privileges and immunities all basic CIVIL LIBERTIES and rights, excluding them from federal protection. Miller's sweeping interpretation relegated everyone, including Negroes, who had assumed that the Fourteenth Amendment had assigned the federal government the role of "guardian democracy" over state-defined CIVIL RIGHTS, to the state governments for effective protection. The national government could protect only the few privileges and immunities of national citizenship: the RIGHT TO TRAVEL, access to Washington, D.C., FREEDOM OF ASSEMBLY and PETITION, and HABEAS CORPUS. Miller and the majority ignored contemporary evidence that many of the framers of both amendments and of the 1866 Civil Rights Act did perceive federally protectable privileges and immunities in broad terms; did assign to federal courts the duty to protect those rights; did envision national civil rights as the essential bridge connecting individuals and states to the nation in a more perfect union. And the majority overlooked earlier contrary case law that spoke directly to the point of the amendments as requirements for federal protection against both state and private discriminations: *In re Turner* (1867) and *Blyew v. U.S.* (1872).

Ignoring also prewar uses of due process in DRED SCOTT V. SANDFORD (1857) and in LAW OF THE LAND clauses in state constitutions, and shrugging off the equal protection argument Campbell had advanced for the appellants, Miller reiterated his position that the postwar amendments protected only blacks against STATE ACTION. The federal protection the Court allowed was minimal and virtually irrelevant to the needs of freedmen, and, for all Americans, left the protection of rights fundamentally unchanged from the prewar condition.

Dissenting, Justices Joseph P. Bradley and Stephen J. Field dredged up Justice SAMUEL CHASE's 1798 opinion in CALDER V. BULL and that of Justice BUSHROD WASHINGTON in his much-quoted 1823 circuit opinion in CORFIELD V. CORYELL, plus the augmented emphases on judicial discretion in a long line of decisions. Bradley emphasized the Fourteenth Amendment's due process clause. Advancing beyond the views of Chief Justice ROGER B. TANEY in *Dred Scott*, he justified judicial intervention to defend substantive due process rights and insisted that a right to choose a calling is a property, a FUNDAMENTAL RIGHT that no state might demean casually. That right was the base for all liberty. The federal courts must repel any state attack on that right, even though the attack might be disguised as a health measure under police powers.

Field argued that the butchering monopoly created servitudes forbidden by the Thirteenth Amendment, but he concentrated on the Fourteenth's privileges and immunities clause. It embraced all the fundamental rights belonging to free men. The national Constitution and laws affirmed those rights. Arbitrary state inhibitions on access to a trade or professions demeaned national rights. Field conceded that states were free to exercise their police powers, even to regulate occupations. But state regulations must apply equally to all citizens who met the standards of the state regulations.

Later, jurists less respectful than Field of state-based FEDERALISM were to cut his *Slaughterhouse* dissent free of its privileges and immunities moorings. Combining his views with Bradley's emphases on the broad effect of the Fourteenth Amendment, later jurists and legal commentators were to transform them into doctrines of freedom of contract and substantive due process. Those doctrines, which were to reign until the twentieth century was well advanced, constrained needful state actions in numerous areas of life and labor.

HAROLD M. HYMAN

Bibliography

BETH, LOREN P. 1963 The Slaughter-House Cases—Revisited, *Louisiana Law Review* 23:487–505.
FAIRMAN, CHARLES 1971 Reconstruction and Reunion, 1864–1868. Chap. 21 in Vol. VI, part 1, of the *Oliver Wendell Holmes Devise History of the Supreme Court of the United States.* New York: Macmillan.
HAMILTON, WALTON H. 1938 The Path of Due Process of Law. Pages 167–179 in Conyers Read, ed., *The Constitution Reconsidered.* New York: Columbia University Press.
HYMAN, HAROLD M. and WIECEK, WILLIAM M. 1982 *Equal Justice under Law: Constitutional Development 1835–1875.* Pages 472–483. New York: Harper & Row.

SLAVERY AND THE CONSTITUTION

Long before the CONSTITUTIONAL CONVENTION OF 1787 the question of slavery had become the prime concern of many Americans. In the first and second Continental Congresses, the matter arose when several groups of slaves petitioned for their manumission. Nothing came of their pleas, of course. In THOMAS JEFFERSON's draft of the DECLARATION OF INDEPENDENCE, he accused the king of waging cruel war against human nature itself, "violating its most sacred rights of life and liberty in the persons of a distant people . . . captivating and carrying them into slavery in another hemisphere. . . ." Although slavery existed throughout the English colonies in 1776, the southern slaveholders in Congress forced rejection of this indictment of the king. If they won their independence on the basis of such an argument, they feared that there would no longer be any justification for slavery.

In some colonies the sentiment against slavery grew during the war for Independence; and the eventual use of slaves as soldiers in the war contributed to the feeling that they should be free. As the states gained their independence some prohibited the slave trade. Some went beyond that enacting legislation looking to the abolition of slavery altogether. Pennsylvania and Massachusetts passed such laws in 1780, followed by Connecticut and Rhode Island in 1784, New York in 1785, and New Jersey in 1786. While no states south of Pennsylvania abolished slavery during this period, several enacted laws facilitating manumission by slaveholders.

Meanwhile, the Continental Congress began to look at the question of slavery as it undertook to develop a national land policy. When Thomas Jefferson framed the ORDINANCE OF 1784 for the organization of government in the western territory, he included a provision that after the year 1800 there should be no slavery or involuntary servitude in any of the states to be organized. That provision was rejected. The idea persisted, however, that slavery should not be extended indefinitely. In the NORTHWEST ORDINANCE of 1787 Jefferson's language of 1784 was adopted with the caveat that fugitive slaves escaping into the Northwest Territory from one of the original states "may be lawfully reclaimed and conveyed to the person claiming his or her labor or service. . . ." The Ordinance did not apply south of the Ohio River, where slaveholders were more likely to settle than in the Northwest Territory.

It was inevitable that slavery should have been an important consideration at the Constitutional Convention. At a time when slavery was waning in the North, the southern states saw in slavery an increasing source of wealth both in the market value of slaves and in what slaves could produce. An economic interest so important could not be ignored by a convention one of whose major concerns was to protect property and to advance the economic interests of those who were to live within the new frame of government. Although there were numerous points at which the emerging document affected the institution of slavery, four were of prime significance to the future of slavery and, indeed, the fate of the Constitution.

One point had to do with the TAXING POWER of Congress. Southern delegates generally feared that in levying taxes, especially POLL TAXES, the federal government might discriminate against the South in the way it counted slaves. Closely connected with this was the perception that in apportioning representation, the South would suffer from any arrangement that did not recognize and count slaves as people. After considerable debate, some of it acrimonious, a compromise was reached. Direct taxes were to be apportioned among the several states according to population, thus making it impossible to raise a major portion of federal revenue by taxing property that existed only in one section of the country. In determining the basis of taxation *and* representation, five slaves were to be counted as equal to three free persons. The cryptic language in Article I, Section 2, reads: "Representatives and direct Taxes shall be apportioned among the several States which may be included within this Union, according to their respective Numbers, which shall be determined by adding to the whole Number of free Persons, including those bound to Service for a Term of Years, and excluding Indians not taxed, three fifths of all other persons."

The other two points regarding slavery were handled with some dispatch, not because they were unimportant but because they did not come up until late in the session, when the weary delegates were eager to return to their homes. On the slave trade, several southern delegates were uncompromising. While those from Virginia and Maryland appeared to favor a prohibition of the trade, those from South Carolina and Georgia were unalterably opposed to the prohibition. To avoid a rupture between the delegates of the upper South and the North, who favored prohibition, and those of the lower South, the compromise was reached that the slave trade could not be ended before twenty years had elapsed. This language was added in Article II, Section 9: "The Migration or Importation of such Persons as any of the States now shall think proper to admit, shall not be prohibited by the Congress prior to the Year one thousand eight hundred and eight, but a Tax or duty may be imposed on such Importation, not exceeding ten dollars for each Person."

Significantly, there was almost no opposition to the proposal that fugitive slaves be returned to their masters. The public obligation to return slaves, which had already been provided for in several Indian treaties between 1781 and 1786, was established in the Northwest Territory in 1787 along with the prohibition of slavery in that region. When the provision came before the Convention in late August, the delegates were in no mood for a protracted debate. The slaveholders had already won such sweeping constitutional recognition of slavery, moreover, that the question of fugitive slaves was something of an anticlimax. Without serious challenge, the provision was inserted in Article IV, Section 2: "No person, held to Service or Labour in one State, under the Laws thereof, escaping into another, shall, in Consequence of any Law or Regulation therein, be discharged from such Service or Labour, but shall be delivered up on Claim of the party to whom such Service or Labour may be due."

In dealing with slavery the delegates to the Convention made certain, as if out of a sense of guilt or shame, never to use the word "slave" or any of its variations in the Constitution itself. "Three fifths of all other persons," "Persons held to Service or Labour," and "Migration or Importation of Such Persons," were all mere euphemisms. Everyone knew what they meant. They were meant to shield the consciences of the delegates just as the clauses themselves were meant to protect the institution of slavery. In none of the deliberations did the delegates give serious consideration to abolishing slavery, even though slavery made a mockery of freedom, equality, and the rights of man. It did not make a mockery, however, of the rights of property. American independence and the new Constitution had the effect of giving slavery a longer life than it was to have in the British Empire.

It was the business of the Congress to enact legislation to carry out the objectives set forth in the Constitution. As far as slaves were concerned, this meant the enactment of legislation to facilitate the recovery of runaway slaves by their masters. The impetus for legislation came, however, not from concerns about fugitive slaves but in the call for a statute to facilitate the surrender of FUGITIVES FROM JUSTICE. When the governor of Pennsylvania was unable to persuade the governor of Virginia to give up three white men accused of kidnapping a Pennsylvania free Negro, he presented the facts in the case to President GEORGE WASHINGTON. When the President transmitted the matter to Congress, it responded by passing the Fugitive Slave Act of 1793. After dealing with the matter of the surrender of fugitives from justice in the first two sections, the law turned to the rendition of fugitive slaves.

Under the law a slaveholder could apply to a federal district or circuit judge for a certificate authorizing him to return his slave to the state from which he had fled. This certificate was to be granted after the master had captured his slave, and there were few federal judges at the time; therefore, the master was compelled to go to considerable expense and travel before enjoying the protection of the federal courts. The law did not authorize judges to issue warrants for the arrest of slaves and it did not compel federal authorities to aid in the pursuit of fugitive slaves. The lack of such provisions generated criticism by slaveholders for years to come.

Although under the law of 1793 many fugitives were recaptured and returned to the places from which they had fled, masters continued to complain about the difficulties of reclaiming their human property. Meanwhile, as antislavery sentiment gained momentum in the first decade of the century, opponents of slavery placed additional obstacles in the way of slaveholders seeking the return of their runaways. They began actively to aid fugitives, to urge federal judges not to issue certificates for the return of runaways, and to persuade local officers not to cooperate in their rendition. Slavemasters soon called for a more effective law, and in 1818, a stronger bill was introduced in the House of Representatives. As it made its way through Congress, it was burdened with amendments introduced by antislavery legislators re-

quiring proof of ownership before a court of record and making masters criminally liable for false claims. Although a version of the proposed law passed both houses, it was tabled when the conference committee was unable to resolve the problem of amendments.

As the new century began, many Americans turned their thoughts to the provision of the Constitution prohibiting Congress from closing the slave trade before 1808. The slave trade was flourishing, and the slave interests faced a curious dilemma. If the trade continued they risked increasing the chances of violence as unruly blacks from Africa or revolutionary and resourceful blacks from the Caribbean were imported. On the other hand, they required a larger number of slaves to tend their burgeoning plantations. Hoping that the national and state governments would provide safeguards against uprisings and insurrections, they were tempted to favor the continued importation of slaves. At least, they wished to keep their options open.

Ending the slave trade under the provision set forth in the Constitution was not a foregone conclusion, and the antislavery forces knew it. All through the decade they pressed for stringent federal legislation to end the trade. In January 1800, a group of free Negroes in Philadelphia called on Congress to revise its laws on the slave trade and on fugitives. When South Carolina reopened its ports to the trade in 1803, antislavery groups began to press Congress to act. Several resolutions were introduced in Congress condemning the slave trade, but that body took no conclusive steps. The question was brought dramatically before the country in December 1805, when Senator Stephen R. Bradley of Vermont introduced a bill to prohibit the slave trade after January 1, 1808, but the bill was indefinitely tabled. This measure set the stage for President Jefferson to address the issue in his annual message to Congress in December 1806. He called attention to the approaching date when Congress could constitutionally prohibit "all further participation in those violations of human rights which have been so long continued on the unoffending inhabitants of Africa, and which the morality, the reputation, and the best interests of our country have long been eager to proscribe."

Pursuant to the President's eloquent call, which was reminiscent of his draft of the Declaration of Independence, Congress proceeded to consider legislation outlawing the trade. Every provision of the proposed law was debated vigorously. Slaveholders, fearing that Africans smuggled into the United States would not be under the control of the law, wanted them seized and sold into slavery. The antislavery members of

Congress strongly objected. The PROHIBITION OF THE SLAVE TRADE ACT (1807) was a compromise. It directed federal officers to be "governed by the provisions of the laws, now existing, of the several states prohibiting the admission or importation . . . of any Negro, mulatto, or other person of color."

In 1818 in the first supplementary act to the law of 1807, Congress sought to make the trade less attractive by increasing the penalty for anyone engaged in it. For example, a fine of $20,000 was replaced by a lowered fine and imprisonment for three to seven years. There were stiffer penalties for persons who knowingly purchased illegally imported Negroes; one-half of all forfeitures and fines were to go to informers. In 1819 Congress directed the President to use armed cruisers on the coasts of the United States and Africa to suppress the trade. Half the proceeds of a condemned ship would go to the captor as bounty, and the captured slaver was to be returned to the port from which it sailed. In the following year Congress provided that direct participation in the slave trade was an act of piracy, punishable by death.

The slave trade was profitable, and it continued despite federal legislation. State laws on the disposition of illegally imported Africans varied. North Carolina directed that such Africans "be sold and disposed of for the state." Georgia directed that the Africans either be sold or given to the Colonization Society for transportation to Africa, with the Society bearing all expenses. Despite these laws, most imported slaves seem to have escaped capture. There were so few captures and the federal officials did so little to enforce the statute of 1807 that it was nearly a dead letter. Slavers introduced their cargo into the United States from Galveston, then a part of Mexico, from Amelia Island in Florida, until 1819 a part of the Spanish Empire, and at various ports on the eastern and southern coasts of the United States. Secretary of the Treasury William H. Crawford confessed that the United States had failed to enforce the law.

Estimates regarding the numbers involved in the illicit slave trade varied. In the decades following passage of the supplementary acts, slavers easily evaded federal authorities, and enforcement received no more than lip service in Washington. In 1839 President MARTIN VAN BUREN called for revision of the laws covering the slave trade in order that "the integrity and honor of our flag may be carefully preserved." A decade later President Zachary Taylor invited the attention of Congress "to an amendment of our existing laws relating to the African slave trade, with a view to the effectual suppression of that barbarous traffic." Nothing happened, and the trade continued

down through the Civil War. Because of its clandestine nature, precise figures are impossible; a recent student of the trade estimates that some 51,000 slaves were illegally imported by 1860.

Shortly after the United States purchased Louisiana in 1803, inhabitants from the older states began to settle in the newly acquired territory. When Louisiana entered the Union in 1812 as a slave state, eastern and northern interests began to appreciate the political and economic consequences of slave states entering the Union. They believed that under the Constitution the federal government could prevent the creation of slave states in the territories. They were determined, therefore, to prevent slave states from entering the Union, or, failing that, to limit the number of new slave states. When Missouri sought admission in 1818, northern members of Congress said that they would agree only on condition that the Missouri constitution forbid slavery. Southerners claimed that the restriction was discriminatory; some threatened disunion. After bitter debate, the impasse was resolved when Maine sought admission. Congress admitted Maine as a free state and Missouri as a slave state and declared that in the Louisiana territory slavery should not exist north of the southern boundary of Missouri.

The MISSOURI COMPROMISE stimulated the rivalry between the slave and free states, with each side searching for ways to enhance its advantage. While southern spokesmen insisted that the problems of slavery were local, they relied on the federal Constitution and laws to protect slavery in defiance of the FIRST AMENDMENT; they demanded that antislavery petitions to Congress be laid on the table without receiving notice. At the same time they demanded that Congress act to facilitate the return of fugitive slaves. As antislavery sentiment in the North increased and abolitionists became more active in obstructing the return of fugitives, the Southerners' demands for protection became more shrill. There were numerous dramatic moments between 1830 and 1860, when abolitionists seized fugitive slaves from their captors or interrupted court proceedings to give accused fugitives the opportunity to flee.

In some northern states residents feared that the Fugitive Slave Law of 1793 would operate to the disadvantage of kidnapped whites and free Negroes accused of being runaway slaves. Consequently, state legislatures empowered state courts to rule in matters arising out of the 1793 law. The Pennsylvania statute of 1826 required the master to present to a magistrate proof of his claim to the alleged fugitive. If the magistrate was convinced the claim was well founded, he was to issue a certificate authorizing the removal of the runaway from the state. If, on the other hand, anyone had seized a person suspected of being a runaway and wrongfully removed him, he would, upon conviction, be deemed guilty of a felony and suffer fine and imprisonment. In due course and by amicable arrangement the Supreme Court ruled on the constitutionality of the Pennsylvania statute in PRIGG V. PENNSYLVANIA (1842), thereby significantly affecting the slavery question for the next two decades.

Edward Prigg, a slave catcher, seized a Negro woman and her children in Pennsylvania with the intention of returning them to their alleged owner in Maryland. When Prigg sought a certificate authorizing their removal, the magistrate, dissatisfied with the proof of ownership, declined to issue the certificate. Prigg took them anyway and was subsequently convicted for violating the 1826 law. The Supreme Court reversed the state court in a decision that had far greater significance than merely exonerating Prigg. Speaking for the Court, Associate Justice JOSEPH STORY declared the Pennsylvania PERSONAL LIBERTY LAW unconstitutional, because it invaded a field placed within the exclusive domain of the federal government by the Fugitive Slave Act of 1793 and by the Constitution itself. "Under the Constitution," said Story, the right to seize a runaway and the duty to deliver him pervaded "the whole Union with an equal and supreme force, uncontrolled and uncontrollable by State SOVEREIGNTY or State legislation." States could enforce the law of 1793, if they wished; but they could not be required to do so, Story added. Further, if an owner recaptured his fugitive slave he did not need a state magistrate's permission to return him to his place of abode.

By placing the fugitive slave question within the exclusive JURISDICTION of the federal government, Justice Story implicitly encouraged northern states that did not wish to cooperate in the enforcement of federal legislation on the subject. The decision promoted the belief, moreover, that antislavery forces could work through sympathetic state and local officials to prevent the recovery of fugitive slaves. Accordingly ten free states enacted personal liberty laws.

When slaveholders felt the impact of *Prigg* in relieving states of responsibility in enforcing the Fugitive Slave Law, they agitated for a more stringent federal law that neither abolitionists nor hostile state laws could nullify. Because the annual pecuniary loss in fugitive slaves was in the hundreds of thousands of dollars, slaveholders increased their pressure on Congress to act. Despite its validation in *Prigg*, the Act of 1793 was inadequate. State courts seemed to

vie with abolitionists in their disregard for federal authority. What was needed was a new act of Congress providing effective federal machinery for its successful enforcement. Early in 1850, Senator James Mason of Virginia introduced a bill to that end. Thus began the long and tortuous route by which a new fugitive slave law made its way through Congress.

The debate on the bill was extensive and, at times, acrimonious, connected as it was with other matters that were to constitute the COMPROMISE OF 1850. In the Senate, WILLIAM H. SEWARD of New York wanted to guarantee to every alleged fugitive slave the right to TRIAL BY JURY. HENRY CLAY of Kentucky, on the other hand, wished to emphasize the right of the aggrieved master to recover his property from any place, including a free state, where the slave had fled. DANIEL WEBSTER of Massachusetts, to the surprise of many Northerners and Southerners, agreed with Clay and declared that "in regard to the return of persons bound to service, who have escaped into the free States . . . it is my judgment that the South is right, and the North is wrong." After the bill passed both houses, President Millard Filmore signed it on September 18, 1850.

The new fugitive slave law undertook to establish adequate federal machinery for its enforcement. Circuit courts were to appoint commissioners who, concurrently with circuit and district judges, had authority to grant certificates for the return of fugitive slaves. United States marshals were to execute warrants issued under the act, and a failure of diligent execution was punishable by a $1,000 fine. If a fugitive should escape from a marshal's custody, the marshal was liable for the slave's full value. When the marshal or claimant brought the slave before the court to request a certificate for his return, the alleged fugitive was not permitted to testify in his own behalf. Court disturbances, aiding or abetting fugitives, and harboring or concealing fugitives were punishable by a $1,000 fine and six months imprisonment.

Abolitionists and others attacked the Fugitive Slave Law as unconstitutional. Horace Mann said that it made war on the fundamental principles of human liberty. CHARLES SUMNER called it a "flagrant violation of the Constitution, and of the most cherished rights—shocking to Christian sentiments, insulting to humanity, and impudent in all its pretensions." Others argued that the fugitive slave clause of the Constitution did not confer on Congress any power to enact laws for the recovery of fugitive slaves. They questioned the power of Congress, moreover, to give commissioners authority to render judgments that only United States judges could properly render under the

Constitution. The denial to fugitives by the law of 1850 of the right to trial by jury and to CONFRONT and cross-examine witnesses was itself an unconstitutional denial of DUE PROCESS, its opponents argued. The fact that commissioners received fees instead of fixed salaries meant that they were themselves interested parties in fugitive slave cases. If the commissioner turned over the fugitive to his claimant, he received a ten dollar fee. If he freed the fugitive, the commissioner received only five dollars. What commissioner could be trusted to render impartial justice when his income depended on the kind of decision that he rendered?

The flight into Canada from northern cities of numerous free Negroes and fugitive slaves dramatized for many Northerners the new role of the federal government in obstructing the efforts of those who sought freedom. Many Northerners vowed to prevent enforcement of the new fugitive slave law. Fugitive slave cases increased, but so did rescues, accompanied by denunciations of federal officials. Friends of fugitives resorted to desperate measures such as kidnapping slave hunters and poisoning their bloodhounds. They organized vigilance committees not only to engage in action but also to express their moral revulsion to every effort to enforce the new law. In 1852 the Boston committee unsuccessfully attempted to prevent the rendition of Thomas Sims, an alleged fugitive from Georgia. Composed of such men as Theodore Parker, Wendell Phillips, Horace Mann, and Charles Sumner, the committee, on April 13 at 3 A.M., watched as the United States marshal walked Sims down State Street, past the spot where Crispus Attucks fell and to the wharf where the ship was waiting to take him back to Savannah. Six days later Sims was publicly whipped in Savannah, the first slave Massachusetts had returned.

Opponents of the Fugitive Slave Law of 1850 challenged it in the same way that opponents had challenged its predecessor. The Supreme Court ruling in STRADER V. GRAHAM (1851) could well have controlled the problem for years to come. After Jacob Strader, a citizen of Kentucky, helped several Negroes leave Kentucky, their alleged master sued Strader for damages. Strader claimed that the blacks were not slaves and that they made regular visits to Ohio where they worked as entertainers. These visits, Strader claimed, had caused them to become free even if they had previously been slaves because the Ordinance of 1787 forbade slavery in the Northwest Territory of which Ohio had been a part. When the case reached the Supreme Court, Chief Justice ROGER B. TANEY, speaking for the entire bench, declared that whatever

the status of the blacks while outside Kentucky, they were subject to Kentucky laws upon their return. Nothing in the Constitution, he insisted, could control the law of Kentucky on this subject.

Meanwhile, opposing forces in Kansas were attempting to settle the issue in their own way. The bill to organize Kansas and Nebraska as territories had repealed the Missouri Compromise and left to the inhabitants of the respective territories the decision whether the states-to-be would be slave or free. Abolitionists, believing there should be no more slave states under any circumstances, were determined to make Kansas as well as Nebraska free states. To that end, they undertook first to settle Kansas with persons who would vote for a free constitution and thus to discourage slaveholders from settling in Nebraska, which they were certain would become a free state. Proslavery forces were determined at least to make Kansas a slave state. Both sides were certain they had the Constitution on their side. After bitter arguments and bloody battles, Kansas voted for a free constitution. The South felt that its ambitions had been frustrated and its rights under the Constitution violated as well.

The antislavery forces would not let the decision in *Strader* stand without challenge. They hoped it might be modified, or even overruled, in another decision offering some protection to slaves who had been in free states. Soon another case, DRED SCOTT V. SANDFORD (1857), presented an ideal opportunity, they thought, to secure an unequivocal statement on the status of slaves in the free states and in the territories. Dred Scott, a Missouri slave, traveled with his master to the free state of Illinois, where they lived for a time, then to Minnesota, a free territory under the provisions of the Missouri Compromise. Upon their return to Missouri, his master sold Scott to a New York resident in a vain attempt to establish federal DIVERSITY JURISDICTION when Scott subsequently sued for his freedom. When the Supreme Court announced its decision on March 6, 1857, Chief Justice Taney was again the spokesman.

Taney declared that because Negroes had been viewed as belonging to an inferior order at the time that the Constitution was ratified, they were not citizens within the meaning of the Constitution's provision defining the permissible JURISDICTION of federal courts in cases between citizens of different states. Moreover Scott had not become free by virtue of the Missouri Compromise, because the Compromise was unconstitutional; Congress had no authority to prohibit slavery in the territories. In any case, Taney concluded, once Scott returned to Missouri his status was determined by Missouri law. In Missouri he was still a slave, and thus not a citizen of any state. The case was dismissed for want of jurisdiction.

The decision gave the proslavery forces more support than they could possibly have expected. Slavery's opponents called the decision wicked, atrocious, and abominable. Others hoped the decision would settle once and for all the grievous sectional issues that were about to destroy the Union. But the decision remained controversial. Its impact on events of the next few years is unclear. Perhaps it did not contribute significantly to the critical disputes and eventual divisions in the Democratic party. Perhaps the decision did not greatly stimulate the growth of the Republican party. Yet, as Don E. Fehrenbacher, the leading historian of the decision, has said, "it was a conspicuous and perhaps an integral part of a configuration of events and conditions that did produce enough changes of allegiance to make a political revolution and enough intensity of feeling to make that revolution violent."

The abolitionists, although embittered by the decision, did not relent in their effort to secure judicial support for their position. In a Wisconsin case, which came to the Supreme Court as ABLEMAN V. BOOTH (1859), they attempted once again to have the Fugitive Slave Law of 1850 declared unconstitutional. Sherman M. Booth, an abolitionist editor in Milwaukee, had been arrested for helping a Negro escape from a United States deputy marshal. The state courts pronounced the law unconstitutional and ordered Booth released. When the case reached the Supreme Court in 1859, Chief Justice Taney reversed the state courts, censured them for presuming to pass judgment on federal laws, and held that the Fugitive Slave Law was fully authorized by the Constitution.

Booth was the last opportunity the abolitionists would have to take their cause to the Supreme Court. They would win local victories, such as the denial of the right of transit by slaves through a free state, but the Fugitive Slave Law remained intact until the Civil War. It would take much more than court challenges or even local disturbances to dislodge the institution of slavery. The fact remained that slavery was so deeply imbedded in the Constitution itself and so firmly protected by it that both violent action and a constitutional amendment would be required to effect far-reaching and lasting change.

The violent action was not long in coming, but the outbreak of the Civil War did not put an end to slavery. President ABRAHAM LINCOLN insisted that the Confederate states were still in the Union and continued to enjoy the constitutional protection of slave property. Once the war began in earnest, however, there was no enforcement of the fugitive slave laws, and as slaves escaped to the Union lines, their emancipation became increasingly a part of the war's objectives. Congress early took steps to free certain slaves. The CONFISCATION ACT of August 6, 1861, declared that owners forfeited slaves engaged in hostile military service. In July 1862 Congress took additional steps in the Second Confiscation Act by granting freedom to slaves of traitors. Furthermore, the slaves of all persons supporting the rebellion were "forever free of their servitude. . . ." Although Lincoln had serious doubts about the constitutionality of the act, he signed it.

Meanwhile, Congress was moving speedily to emancipate the slaves whom it constitutionally could. It could not pass a universal emancipation bill, but it could and did abolish slavery in the DISTRICT OF COLUMBIA and the TERRITORIES. The emancipation bill for the District of Columbia precipitated a lengthy debate, during which President Lincoln persuaded the lawmakers to include an appropriation of $1,000,000 for compensation to owners not exceeding $300 for each slave and for the removal and colonization of the freedmen. Even so, Lincoln was reluctant to sign the bill. He signed it after Senator CHARLES SUMNER of Massachusetts and Bishop Daniel A. Payne of the African Methodist Episcopal Church pleaded with him to approve it. On June 19, 1862, Congress passed and sent to the President a bill abolishing slavery in the territories, with no provision for the compensation of owners, and Lincoln signed it.

The President continued to argue that the federal government could not emancipate the slaves unless it also compensated the owners and colonized the freedmen. Unfortunately for him, his arguments convinced neither the representatives of the border slave states nor the Negro delegations that visited him. Consequently, he was compelled to face the mounting pressures to free the slaves without any apparent constitutional means of doing so. Even as he moved toward an emancipation policy, Lincoln kept his own counsel. He listened patiently to the constant stream of delegations, some urging him to free the slaves, others insisting that he do nothing. The only thing he revealed was that the matter was on his mind, day and night, "more than any other."

In the late spring of 1862 Lincoln decided that he would emancipate the slaves by proclamation. The bleak military outlook pressed the decision on Lincoln. In July he read to the Cabinet a recently completed draft and solicited suggestions regarding language and timing. The members confined their remarks to possible political and military consequences. Lincoln agreed that a propitious moment to issue it would be in the wake of a Union victory, lest some view it as an act of desperation.

Although the battle of Antietam, September 17, 1862, was not the clear-cut victory for which Lincoln had been waiting, he decided to act anyway. On September 22, 1862, he issued the Preliminary EMANCIPATION PROCLAMATION, to take effect on January 1, 1863. Abandoning the notion of colonization, the President, in the final Proclamation, declared free those slaves in states or parts of states under Confederate control. He further declared that the freedmen would be received into the armed service of the United States "to garrison forts, positions, stations, and other places, and to man vessels in said service." Even without a comprehensive emancipation policy, Lincoln is reported to have said as he signed the document, "I never, in my life, felt more certain that I was doing right than I do in signing this paper."

Lincoln realized, of course, that his proclamation, primarily a war measure, did not actually free the slaves. Although military action set many of them free, either state or federal action or both were needed to achieve real and permanent freedom in law and practice. By early 1865, Tennessee, West Virginia, Maryland, and Missouri had taken steps to free their slaves. Delaware and Kentucky, like the Confederate states, had taken no such action by the end of the war.

It early became clear that only national action, preferably through a constitutional amendment, could provide a uniform emancipation policy. Yet some doubted the wisdom or even the prudence of using the Constitution to reform a domestic institution such as slavery. Others questioned the legality of amending the Constitution while eleven states remained outside the Union. The latter circumstance was a major reason why the proposed amendment to forbid slavery throughout the nation initially failed to get the necessary two-thirds approval of the House after it had passed the Senate in the spring of 1864. After the election of 1864 and with the war winding down, the House finally approved the amendment on January 31, 1865. The following day, Lincoln was pleased to sign the resolution submitting the amendment to the states for ratification.

By December 18, 1865, twenty-seven states, including eight former Confederate states, had ratified the THIRTEENTH AMENDMENT, and it became part of the Constitution. One of the ironies was that the amendment could not have been ratified without the concurrence of the slave states whose governments Congress did not recognize in 1865. This seemed an appropriate way to end slavery, which was itself the most remarkable anomaly in the history of the country.

JOHN HOPE FRANKLIN

Bibliography

BECKER, CARL (1942)1953 *The Declaration of Independence: A Study in the History of Political Ideas.* New York: Knopf.
BOWEN, CATHERINE DRINKER 1966 *Miracle at Philadelphia: The Story of the Constitutional Convention May to September 1787.* Boston: Little, Brown.
CURTIN, PHILIP 1969 *The Atlantic Slave Trade: A Census.* Madison: University of Wisconsin Press.
DuBois, W. E. BURGHARDT (1896)1954 *The Suppression of the African Slave Trade to the United States of America.* New York: Social Science Press.
FEHRENBACHER, DON E. 1978 *The Dred Scott Case: Its Significance in American Law and Politics.* New York: Oxford University Press.
FINKELMAN, PAUL 1981 *An Imperfect Union: Slavery, Federalism, and Comity.* Chapel Hill: University of North Carolina Press.
FRANKLIN, JOHN HOPE 1963 *The Emancipation Proclamation.* Garden City, N.Y.: Doubleday.
LEVY, LEONARD W. 1950 Sims' Case: The Fugitive Slave Law in Boston in 1851. *Journal of Negro History* 35:39–74.
ZILBERSMIT, ARTHUR 1967 *The First Emancipation: The Abolition of Slavery in the North.* Chicago: University of Chicago Press.

SLAVERY IN THE TERRITORIES

Slavery was confirmed by statute or royal decree in all the English, Spanish, and French colonies of North America. After American Independence, slavery therefore enjoyed a legal existence in all the states. In the NORTHWEST ORDINANCE of 1787, the Confederation Congress prohibited slavery in the Northwest Territory, although it also provided for the recapture of slaves escaping there. The First Congress reenacted this ban, but in legislation for the area southwest of the Ohio River it omitted the exclusion of slavery, so that slavery was free to penetrate into the TERRITORIES ceded by Virginia, New York, North Carolina, South Carolina, and Georgia. Slavery also existed in the French settlements that were to become Louisiana, Missouri, Illinois, and Indiana. The treaty of cession with France (1803), by which the United States acquired the LOUISIANA PURCHASE, guaranteed extant property rights, thus assuring slavery's perpetuation in those territories.

Despite the ban of the Northwest Ordinance, settlers in Ohio (particularly in the Virginia Military Reserve in the southwest quadrant of the territory), Indiana, and Illinois tried to introduce slavery, with the connivance of Indiana territorial governor William Henry Harrison in the case of Ohio, and at least the tacit consent of President THOMAS JEFFERSON. They failed in Ohio and Indiana, but in Illinois slavery continued in subterfuge forms in the lead mines of Galena and the salt mines of Shawneetown, and only a vigorous abolitionist effort prevented its legalization throughout the state in 1822.

The Constitution contained no direct allusion to slavery in the territories; the new states and territories clauses did not refer to it, although the fugitive slave clause permitted recapture of fugitives only from the states, not the territories. Consequently, when Missouri sought admission as a slave state in 1819, Congress had no textual guidance, and for the first time it had to extrapolate from what it could determine of the Framers' intent concerning the territories. The result was a long and bitter debate in which restrictionists argued that slavery was hostile to the spirit of republican government and should not be extended to the new lands, while slavery's supporters insisted that Congress lacked power to exclude slavery from any territory. Jefferson at the time joined the antirestrictionists, arguing that as slavery spread it would diffuse to the point where the black population, relative to the white, would dwindle in both the old states and the new territories. The Missouri controversy was settled by admitting Missouri as a slave state and Maine as a free state, while prohibiting slavery in all the Louisiana Purchase territory north of Missouri's southern boundary (36°30'). (See MISSOURI COMPROMISE.) Jefferson likened the Missouri debates to a "firebell in the night," the "knell of the union."

As the confrontation over slavery intensified in the 1830s, abolitionists and defenders of slavery amplified their constitutional and policy arguments about slavery's future in the territories. Abolitionists found two sources of congressional power to exclude slavery. They saw the territories clause (Article IV, section 3) as a plenary grant of power to the national government to regulate all matters of property and personal status in the territories. Further, the new states clause (Article IV, section 3) implicitly permitted restriction because it gave Congress power to prohibit a state's admission if it recognized slavery. Abolitionists also maintained that slavery was contrary to the principles of a republican form of government, which the United States must guarantee to each of the states.

Alarmed by such doctrines, JOHN C. CALHOUN in the period 1837–1847 elaborated doctrines that denied any exclusionary power to Congress. He insisted that the territories were the common property of all the states, and that it would be unjust to the slave states to exclude one form of property and its owners (slaves) when all other forms of property were not similarly restricted. Calhoun regarded Congress as the agent of the states (they being the principals) or as their trustee (they being the beneficiaries). By either legal metaphor, Congress lacked power to exclude slavery because that would discriminate against one group of states. He maintained that slavery was not only a positive good but also an essential element in the domestic and political structure of the slave states. Efforts to impede its spread were therefore not only insulting but threatening to the security of the states themselves.

This debate remained academic until 1845. Arkansas had been admitted as a slave state in 1836, the unorganized Indian Territory (modern Oklahoma) was not then targeted for white settlement, and many still considered the remainder of the Louisiana Purchase uninhabitable. But Texas's independence, followed by its request for admission, thrust the territorial debates to center stage, and for over a decade after the outbreak of the Mexican War the territorial issue eclipsed all other topics of the slavery controversy except the problem of fugitive slaves. Texas, a slaveholding Republic that had struck for Independence partly because the Mexican constitution had abolished slavery, presented the potential for more than one slave state; the JOINT RESOLUTION admitting it to statehood recognized its potential subdivision into five states.

When war with Mexico broke out in 1846, the future of the territories to be acquired from that country became a more urgent issue. A few persons suggested that the United States acquire no new territories, but that idea was lost in the tide of Manifest Destiny flooding the country in the 1840s. In 1846, Representative David Wilmot, a Pennsylvania Democrat, offered a proviso to an appropriations bill that used the language of the Northwest Ordinance to exclude slavery from all territories acquired as a result of the Mexican War. Democrats and other defenders of slavery were alarmed by the WILMOT PROVISO's popularity in the North (nearly all free state legislatures endorsed it), and especially by the Proviso's appeal to Northern Democrats, who resented Southern dictation of party policy on slavery-related subjects and wanted to preserve the new territories for free white settlement.

The Proviso's opponents introduced four alternative proposals. Many Southerners at first found the idea of extending the Missouri Compromise line attractive. The Polk administration, Justice JOHN CATRON of Tennessee, the NASHVILLE CONVENTION of 1850, and Senator JOHN J. CRITTENDEN of Kentucky in 1860 all suggested extrapolating the 36°30′ line as a simple and arbitrary solution to the Gordian knot of slavery in the territories. Despite its simplicity, the idea repeatedly failed. One of the reasons for its failure was that other Southern leaders, more determined to protect the South than to compromise the territorial issue, revised their 1820 position and insisted that any exclusion of slavery from the territories was unconstitutional. Their theories for a time were subsumed under the shorthand term "non-intervention," a name for a cluster of doctrines that adopted Calhoun's premises and went on to demand that the federal government protect slavery in all the territories and even establish it there by a federal territorial slave code if necessary.

Northern Democrats rejected this position, but they did not want to split the party by endorsing the Wilmot Proviso. Under the leadership of Lewis Cass of Michigan and STEPHEN A. DOUGLAS of Illinois, they proposed a third alternative: the doctrine of territorial sovereignty, more often but less accurately referred to as POPULAR SOVEREIGNTY or squatter sovereignty. Cass and Douglas insisted that the future of slavery in the territories be decided by the settlers of the territories themselves, not by Congress. After 1850, they also began to adopt the Southern position that slavery's exclusion was not only unnecessary and gratuitously offensive to the South but also unconstitutional. Territorial sovereignty contained a central ambiguity: when were the settlers to decide? If, as Southern spokesmen demanded, territorial settlers could not exercise this prerogative until the eve of statehood, then slavery would establish a foothold, as it had in Missouri, and be impossible to dislodge. Northern proponents of territorial sovereignty, on the other hand, insisted that the settlers had a right to exclude slavery at any point after the organization of the territory. This view, in turn, forced Southerners to another doctrinal redoubt, when they claimed that just as Congress could not exclude slavery, neither could its creature, the territorial legislature. In this view, slavery could establish itself anywhere in American territories.

The Free Soil coalition of 1848, made up of New York Democrats, antislavery Whigs, and former political abolitionists, adopted the Wilmot Proviso as a principal plank in their program. But the COMPROMISE OF 1850 decisively rejected the Wilmot Proviso. In admitting California as a free state and organizing New Mexico and Utah Territories without restrictions as to slavery, Congress also rejected the Missouri Compromise line. But it also adopted the fourth alternative to the Wilmot Proviso, the "Clayton Compromise." Senator John Clayton of Delaware had proposed that all questions arising in TERRITORIAL COURTS concerning title to slaves or a black's claim to freedom be appealable directly to the United States Supreme Court, in effect inviting the Justices of the high court to try their hand at resolving the seemingly insoluble territorial issue. By adopting the Clayton Compromise, Congress admitted its inability to deal with the most exigent political issue of the day. Its desperate grasp at nonpolitical solutions not only confessed its impotence but also assumed the finality of an unpredictable resolution of a question that was ultimately metajudicial.

The KANSAS-NEBRASKA ACT of 1854 adopted the principle of territorial sovereignty, along with some vague and ambiguous allusions to nonintervention. It declared the Missouri Compromise defunct and implied that it was unconstitutional, thus representing a victory for both northern Democrats and Southerners. But this accommodation did not last long, as Kansas filled with authentic settlers and Missouri sojourners. Because most of the former hoped to see Kansas free and because all the latter were determined to make it a slave state, political controversy erupted into guerrilla warfare in the period known as "Bleeding Kansas." President JAMES BUCHANAN tried to force the proslavery LECOMPTON CONSTITUTION on the territory, over the wishes of a large majority of bona fide settlers, and thereby split the Democratic party into Southern-dominated and Douglas wings.

Meanwhile, Chief Justice ROGER B. TANEY and his colleagues took up the invitation tendered by Congress in DRED SCOTT V. SANDFORD (1857). Taney held, in the latter part of his opinion, that the Missouri Compromise was unconstitutional, and that Congress could not exclude slavery from a territory. He adopted three Calhounite positions in OBITER DICTA: the federal government had to protect slavery in the territories; territorial legislatures could not exclude slavery at any time before statehood; and the federal government was the trustee of the states or the territories. In passing, Taney suggested that congressional exclusion would deprive a slaveowner of rights to property protected by the DUE PROCESS clause of the Fifth Amendment. This adumbration of SUBSTANTIVE DUE PROCESS was merely a passing allusion, however, the emphasis of Taney's opinion lying instead in his interpretation of the new states clause.

In the LINCOLN–DOUGLAS DEBATES of 1858, ABRA-

HAM LINCOLN challenged Douglas to explain what was left of territorial sovereignty after *Dred Scott*. Douglas suggested the FREEPORT DOCTRINE: that Congress could for all practical purposes exclude slavery from a territory simply by not enacting a territorial slave code or extending any other protection for it there. Under one interpretation of SOMERSET v. STEWART (1772), there being no positive law to keep a person enslaved, slavery effectively could not establish itself. This led Mississippi Senator JEFFERSON DAVIS to demand that the federal courts protect slavery in the territories somehow, and, if this proved unavailing, that Congress enact a territorial slave code.

The Constitution of the Confederate States of America extended full federal protection to slavery in any territories the Confederacy might acquire. The Congress of the United States abolished slavery in all federal territories in 1862 (Act of June 19, 1862).

WILLIAM M. WIECEK

(SEE ALSO: *Constitutional History, 1829–1848.*)

Bibliography

BESTOR, ARTHUR 1961 State Sovereignty and Slavery: A Reinterpretation of Proslavery Constitutional Doctrine, 1846–1860. *Journal of the Illinois State Historical Society* 54:117–180.

QUAIFE, MILO M. 1910 *The Doctrine of Non-Intervention with Slavery in the Territories.* Chicago: Chamberlin.

RUSSEL, ROBERT R. 1966 Constitutional Doctrines with Regard to Slavery in the Territories. *Journal of Southern History* 32:466–486.

SLOAN v. LEMON

See: Committee v. Nyquist

SMITH, J. ALLEN
(1860–1924)

Lawyer, economist, and political scientist James Allen Smith was an influential spokesman for PROGRESSIVE CONSTITUTIONAL THOUGHT. His most important book was *The Spirit of American Government* (1901), subtitled "A Study of the Constitution: Its Origins, Influence and Relation to Democracy." Smith contended that the Constitution represented a reactionary and undemocratic retreat from the revolutionary principles of the DECLARATION OF INDEPENDENCE. He proposed to make the Constitution more democratic by eliminating CHECKS AND BALANCES, curbing the SU-PREME COURT, and introducing DIRECT ELECTIONS for the President and Senate along with INITIATIVE, REFERENDUM, and RECALL.

DENNIS J. MAHONEY

SMITH v. ALLWRIGHT
321 U.S. 649 (1944)

In 1935 the Supreme Court had held in GROVEY v. TOWNSEND that the Texas Democratic party convention's rule excluding black voters from PRIMARY ELECTIONS was not STATE ACTION and thus violated no constitutional rights. *Allwright* involved the same question, raised in the same manner; Smith alleged that he was excluded from the Texas Democratic primary because of his race and sought damages from election officials under federal CIVIL RIGHTS laws. The case had become a plausible candidate for Supreme Court review because in UNITED STATES v. CLASSIC (1941) the Court had reconsidered the nature of a primary election by way of upholding Congress's power to forbid fraud in primary elections of nominees for federal offices. In *Classic*, the Court had concluded that Louisiana primary elections were, by law, an integral part of the machinery for electing officers.

Applying the *Classic* reasoning in *Allwright*, the Court overruled *Grovey v. Townsend* and held that the state's provision of machinery for primary elections was sufficiently connected with the party's conduct of those elections to satisfy the state action limitation of the FIFTEENTH AMENDMENT. Because that amendment forbade a state to deny or abridge the right to vote on account of race, Smith was entitled to damages if he could prove his allegations. Justice STANLEY F. REED wrote for the Court.

Justice OWEN ROBERTS, who had written for a unanimous Court in *Grovey*, dissented, complaining that the OVERRULING of a DECISION after only nine years tended "to bring adjudications of this tribunal into the same class as a restricted railroad ticket, good on this day and train only." The obvious question was: why had Roberts joined in the *Classic* decision? Contemporary accounts suggest that at least some of the other Justices thought Roberts had been "duped" into concurring in *Classic*, and that Roberts knew they thought so. In the years between *Grovey* and *Allwright*, President FRANKLIN D. ROOSEVELT had made seven appointments to the Court. Justice Roberts's lone companion from the earlier days was Chief Justice HARLAN FISKE STONE, who had written the *Classic* opinion.

KENNETH L. KARST

SMITH ACT

See: Alien Registration Act

SMYTH v. AMES
169 U.S. 466 (1898)

A unanimous Supreme Court, in this arrogation of power, proclaimed its acceptance of SUBSTANTIVE DUE PROCESS in rate regulation. The Court refused to "shrink from the duty" of exercising its judgment in a highly technical area of ECONOMIC REGULATION best left to experts. For the next forty years, the Court would review the rate schedules of REGULATORY COMMISSIONS seeking to accommodate shifting and illusory judicial standards of fairness.

In 1893 a Nebraska statute prescribed maximum rail rates for intrastate transportation. William Jennings Bryan defended the state legislature's power to fix reasonable rates for INTRASTATE COMMERCE; JAMES COOLIDGE CARTER urged that the Court limit the power when unreasonable rates effectively divested a railroad of its property. The question presented by the three cases consolidated here was whether those rates amounted to a TAKING OF PROPERTY without JUST COMPENSATION, thereby depriving the railroads of their property without DUE PROCESS OF LAW. Justice DAVID J. BREWER, sitting as a circuit judge in one of the cases, invented a "FAIR RETURN ON FAIR VALUE" test. He struck down the rates because they failed to provide a fair return on a fair valuation of the railroad property and thereby they effectively destroyed property.

Accepting Brewer's opinion, Justice JOHN MARSHALL HARLAN, for the Court, asserted that REAGAN V. FARMERS' LOAN & TRUST COMPANY (1894) demonstrated the appropriateness of a judicial determination of the question. Courts, he said, must be free to inquire into the sufficiency of the rates set by the state legislature, even though the Nebraska constitution only granted the legislature the power to prescribe " 'reasonable' maximum rates." Admitting that the question could be "more easily determined by a commission" of experts, Harlan pursued the "considerations" which, "given such weight as may be just and right in each case," would allow a determination of reasonable rate. He declared that the "basis of all calculations . . . must be the fair value of the property being used." Then he listed a number of various aids to determine fair value: original construction costs, replacement or reproduction costs, stock values, the cost of permanent improvements, earning power under the prescribed rate structure, operating expenses, and other unspecified matters. The company, he concluded, was justified in asking a "fair return upon the value of that which it employs for the public convenience." The Nebraska statute had failed to provide that fair return and so deprived the railroad of its property without just compensation, thereby depriving it of due process of law under the FOURTEENTH AMENDMENT.

In *Smyth* the Court readily substituted its judgment on a question of policy for other branches of government. Regulatory commissions of all sorts would spend four decades attempting to second-guess the courts' efforts to determine what constituted a "fair return" on "fair value." Over those decades, the Court manipulated the fair value standards to the benefit of corporations. The Court relied primarily on two of Harlan's factors in assessing fair value. Until about 1918, high original costs governed the Court's determination of fair value. When the war ended and both costs and prices rose, the Court turned to replacement costs as a means of deciding fair value, again keeping rates high. The Court consistently avoided using earnings—perhaps the best economic measure—as a guide. Justices LOUIS D. BRANDEIS and OLIVER WENDELL HOLMES denounced the fair return rule throughout the 1920s and 1930s; their views gained adherents by the early 1940s. In *Federal Power Commission v. Natural Gas Company* (1942) the Court asserted that property value was not an essential factor in calculating a fair return, and the Supreme Court finally disavowed a judicial control of the question in FEDERAL POWER COMMISSION V. HOPE NATURAL GAS COMPANY (1944).

DAVID GORDON

Bibliography

HALE, ROBERT LEE 1952 *Freedom through Law: Public Control of Private Governing Power.* Pages 461–500. New York: Columbia University Press.

SNEPP v. UNITED STATES
444 U.S. 507 (1980)

A former Central Intelligence Agency (CIA) employee, Frank W. Snepp III, published a book containing unclassified information about CIA activities in South Vietnam. Snepp did not submit the book to the CIA for prepublication review, in breach of his express employment agreement not to publish any information without the agency's prior approval or to disclose any *classified* information. In a decision remarkable for its procedural setting and for its failure to meet head-on the FIRST AMENDMENT issues implicated by the prior restraint, the Supreme Court, PER CURIAM, sanctioned the imposition of a constructive trust on all proceeds from the book's sales.

The Court recognized, as the government conceded, that Snepp had a First Amendment right to publish unclassified information. The Court found, however, that by virtue of his employment as a CIA agent, Snepp had entered a fiduciary relationship with the agency. Snepp breached the special trust reposed in him by failing to submit *all* material, whether classified or not, for prepublication review. That breach posed irreparable harm to the CIA's relationships with foreign governments and its ability to perform its statutory duties. The constructive trust remedy was thereby warranted.

Justice JOHN PAUL STEVENS, joined by Justices WILLIAM J. BRENNAN and THURGOOD MARSHALL, dissented, arguing that the remedy was unsupported by statute, the contract, or case law. He urged that the contract be treated as an ordinary employment covenant. On this theory, its enforcement would be governed by a rule of reason that would require a balancing of interests, including Snepp's First Amendment rights, and might justify an equity court's refusal to enforce the prepublication review covenant. Further, the alleged harm suffered by the government did not warrant the Court's "draconian" remedy, especially because the government had never shown that other remedies were inadequate. Stevens noted that the Court seemed unaware that it had fashioned a drastic new remedy to enforce a species of prior restraint on a citizen's right to criticize the government.

KIM MCLANE WARDLAW

(SEE ALSO: *Prior Restraint and Censorship.*)

SOCIAL COMPACT THEORY

An invention of political philosophers, the social contract or social compact theory was not meant as a historical account of the origin of government, but the theory was taken literally in America where governments were actually founded upon contract. The words "compact" and "contract" are synonymous and signify a voluntary agreement of the people to unite as a political community and to establish a government. The theory purports to explain why individuals should obey the law: each person, in a government that exists with the consent of the governed, freely and, in effect, continuously gives consent to the constitution of his community.

The theory hypothesizes a prepolitical state of nature in which people were governed only by the law of nature, free of human restraints. From the premise that man was born free, the deduction followed that he came into the world with God-given or NATURAL RIGHTS. Born without the restraint of human laws, he had a right to possess liberty and to work for his own property. Born naked and stationless, he had a right to equality. Born with certain instincts and needs, he had a right to satisfy them—a right to the pursuit of happiness. These natural rights, as JOHN DICKINSON declared in 1766, "are created in us by the decrees of Providence, which establish the laws of our nature. They are born with us; exist with us; and cannot be taken from us by any human power without taking our lives."

When people left the state of nature and compacted for government, the need to make their rights secure motivated them. ALEXANDER HAMILTON observed that "Civil liberty is only natural liberty modified and secured by the sanctions of civil society. . . . The origin of all civil government, justly established, must be a voluntary compact between the rulers and the ruled, and must be liable to such limitations as are necessary for the security of the absolute rights of the latter." The most detailed exposition of this theory was by JOHN LOCKE, the most brief and eloquent by THOMAS JEFFERSON in the preamble of the DECLARATION OF INDEPENDENCE. One of the self-evident truths in the latter is "That to secure these rights, Governments are instituted among Men, deriving their just powers from the consent of the governed. . . ."

The compact theory of government colored the thought and action of Americans during the colonial period and through the period of constitution making. The new world actually seemed like a state of nature, and Americans did in fact compact with each other; the theory seemed to fit the circumstances under which American political and constitutional institutions grew. Our system developed as a self-conscious working out of some of the implications of the compact theory.

The related but distinct idea, so important in Puritan thought, that people covenant with each other to make a church for their ecclesiastical polity, was extended to their secular polity. Even before the founding of Virginia a Separatist leader asked, "What agreement must there be of men? For church governors there must be an agreement of the people or commonwealth." A half century before Locke's *Second Treatise*, THOMAS HOOKER, a founder of Connecticut, explained that in any relationship that involved authority there must be free agreement or consent. "This," he said, "appears in all covenants betwixt Prince and People, Husband and Wife, Master and Servant, and most palpable is the expression of this in all confederations and corporations . . . They should first freely engage themselves in such covenants. . . ." The first concrete application of the covenant theory to civil government was the Mayflower Compact (1620). The Pilgrims, putting theory into practice, solemnly did "covenant and combine . . . into a civil body politick," an experience multiplied over and again with the founding of numerous settlements in New England. (See FUNDAMENTAL ORDERS OF CONNECTICUT.)

The colonists also regarded their charters as compacts. As Hamilton said later, George III was "King of America, by virtue of a compact between us and the Kings of Great Britain." These colonies, Hamilton explained, were settled under charters granted by kings who "entered into covenants with us. . . ." Over a period of a century and a half, Americans became accustomed to the idea that government existed by consent of the governed, that the people created government, that they did it by written compact, and that the compact constituted their FUNDAMENTAL LAW. From practical experience as well as from revolutionary propaganda, Americans believed in the compact theory and they acted it out.

It was a useful tool, immediately at hand and lending historical and philosophical credibility, for destroying the old order and creating a new one. William Drayton, the chief justice of South Carolina, echoed a commonplace idea when he said that George III had "unkinged" himself by subverting the "constitution of this country, by breaking the original contract. . . ." The compact theory legitimated the right of revolution, as the Declaration of Independence made clear. Even before that declaration, colonial radicals contended that the Coercive Acts (see FIRST CONTINENTAL CONGRESS) "have thrown us into a state of nature," and justified contracting for a new government. After Independence a town orator in Boston declared that the people had reclaimed the rights "attendant upon the original state of nature, with the opportunity of establishing a government for ourselves. . . ." The colonies became states by a practice that mirrored the theory; they drew up written constitutions, often phrased as compacts, and purposefully

put formal statements of the compact theory into those documents. The MASSACHUSETTS CONSTITUTION OF 1780 (still operative) declares: "The body politic is formed by a voluntary association of individuals; it is a social compact by which the whole people covenants with each citizen and each citizen with the whole people. . . ." A minister, Jonas Clark, said in a sermon that just government is founded in compact "and in compact alone." The new state constitution, he declared, was "a most sacred covenant or contract. . . ." The state CONSTITUTIONAL CONVENTION that framed that constitution was devised to institutionalize the compact theory.

Although the ARTICLES OF CONFEDERATION do not formally state that theory, letters of the members of the Continental Congress that framed the Articles show that they regarded themselves as making a compact for the union of states, and THE FEDERALIST #21 refers to "the social compact between the States. . . ." Similarly, at the Philadelphia CONSTITUTIONAL CONVENTION OF 1787, JAMES MADISON declared that the delegates had assembled to frame "a compact by which an authority was created paramount to the parties, and making laws for the government of them." GEORGE WASHINGTON, on behalf of the "Federal Convention," when sending the new Constitution to the Congress of the Confederation for submission to the states, drew an analogy from compact theory: individuals left a state of nature by yielding up some liberty to preserve the rest, and the states surrendered some of their SOVEREIGNTY to consolidate the union. Some of the states, when formally ratifying the new Constitution, considered themselves to be "entering into an explicit and solemn compact," as New Hampshire declared. Chief Justice JOHN JAY observed, in CHISHOLM V. GEORGIA (1793), that every state constitution "is a compact . . . and the Constitution of the United States is likewise a compact made by the people of the United States to govern themselves."

The compact theory answers one of the most profound questions of political philosophy: why do people submit to the compulsions of government? The answer is that when they established government they consented to its exercise of power and agreed to obey it if it secured their rights. The compact theory has been remarkably fecund. From government by consent it led to political democracy. It also led to CONSTITUTIONALISM AS LIMITED GOVERNMENT, to a concept of a constitution as fundamental law, to constitutions as written documents, to the constitutional convention as a way of writing the document, to the right of revolution when the government is destructive of the ends of the compact, and to concepts of civil liberty and written BILLS OF RIGHTS.

LEONARD W. LEVY

Bibliography

MCLAUGHLIN, ANDREW C. 1932 *The Foundations of American Constitutionalism.* New York: New York University Press.

ROSSITER, CLINTON 1953 *Seedtime of the Republic: The Origin of the American Tradition of Political Liberty.* New York: Harcourt, Brace.

TATE, THAD W. 1965 The Social Contract in America, 1774–1787: Revolutionary Theory as a Conservative Instrument. *William and Mary Quarterly* 22:375–391.

WOOD, GORDON S. 1969 *The Creation of the American Republic, 1776–1787.* Chapel Hill: University of North Carolina Press.

SOCIAL SCIENCE IN CONSTITUTIONAL LITIGATION

All litigation, including constitutional litigation, resolves issues of law and fact. Social science research can help to clarify the facts on which a case may turn; and it can help the resolution of legal issues by laying before the courts data and analyses that bear on the choice of an appropriate legal rule.

Legal lore has it that the rise of social science in the law began with the BRANDEIS BRIEF, in which LOUIS D. BRANDEIS, special counsel for the state of Oregon, successfully bolstered the state's claim in MULLER V. OREGON (1908) that its statute limiting the working hours for women was constitutional. Although in theory the state merely had to show that such a regulation was not unreasonable, previous decisions had struck down laws regulating working hours of other employees as unreasonable invasions of the liberty of contract. The brief supported the reasonableness of the law in part by showing that a great many American states and even more countries abroad had similar statutes. It was an effective if modest social science effort.

More sophisticated techniques are to be found in contemporary constitutional litigation. Sampling, the most powerful tool of social science research, is now firmly established as an appropriate means of gathering EVIDENCE. If the survey was conducted without bias and if the technical requirements are met, a sample may be accepted as a reasonably accurate representation of the sampled universe. For instance, in support of a motion for change of VENUE in a criminal case, a sample survey measures the extent and depth of pretrial prejudice in the community. If a voluminous body of communications is at issue, sampling may be combined with a technique called content analysis. Thus, when the constitutionality of the work of the House Committee on Un-American Activities was litigated, a sample of the committee's public hearings was examined. This approach yielded a numerical statement of the frequency with which the committee asked its witnesses questions that transcended its constitutional authority. Similar content analysis has sometimes been used in support of a motion for change of venue, documenting the charge that a substantial part of the pretrial publicity originated in the prosecutor's office.

Proof of racial or other discrimination in jury selection, employment, and other contexts frequently employs sampling and subsequent statistical analysis. Such proof involves an analysis of the differences between the actual outcome of the selection process and the outcome that would have been expected if discrimination had no role in the process.

In *United States v. Hazelwood School District* (1977), for instance, the Supreme Court made its own probability computations to determine whether excluding the metropolitan area from the labor market in which a suburban school district hired its teachers would substantially weaken the government's statistical proof that the district had engaged in discrimination. Although the Court's statistical performance in *Hazelwood* was flawed in certain respects, similar methods in proving discrimination have become accepted in both federal and state courts.

Of particular interest are the cases in which the judicial system itself is charged with discrimination. The two main targets here are the administration of the death penalty and the selection of jurors. Evidence has been mounting, and finally has drawn the attention of the Supreme Court, that the death penalty is administered with bias, discriminating against black offenders who killed white victims. The major technical problem in distilling this evidence is to assure comparability of the homicides under analysis.

In the jury selection area, the statistical analysis of discrimination has had more impact. Despite substantial efforts in this direction, the lower courts have rejected these efforts. In *Castandeda v. Partida* (1977), for instance, the Court used a standard statistical formula to compute the probability that the disparity between the proportion of Mexican-Americans serving on GRAND JURIES and their proportion in the county population could have arisen if grand jurors had been selected at random. The majority found the probability to be so minute (about one in a number with 140 zeros) that the discrepancy was sufficient to establish discrimination even though there were problems with the data used to estimate these proportions and even though the majority of jury commissioners were themselves Mexican-Americans.

In the trial of Dr. Benjamin Spock and others accused of conspiring to obstruct the draft, the alleged discrimination involved female jurors. The allegation of bias in that case was directed not against the system but against the particular judge who consistently selected juries with significantly fewer women than those of his colleagues, although all drew from the same pool of potential jurors.

At times experimental social science research is offered to aid a court in assessing the consequences of its legal options or in ascertaining facts relevant to the choice of these options. When the Supreme Court in BROWN V. BOARD OF EDUCATION (1954) held that segregated education was inherently unequal, the Court quoted with approval a lower court's finding that school segregation with the sanction of law produced feelings of inferiority among black children, affecting their motivation to learn. The Court remarked that its conclusion was "amply supported by modern authority." That authority, cited in a footnote, consisted of seven items. Five, such as Gunnar Myrdal's *American Dilemma*, dealt generally with problems of black education. Two bore more directly on the issue: a statement by thirty-two leading social scientists and an experiment conducted by the psychologist Kenneth Clark. Clark had given sixteen black children in a South Carolina elementary school a sheet of paper on which two dolls were drawn, identical in every respect except that the one was black, the other white. The children were asked, "Which doll would you like to play with?" "Which is the nice and which the bad doll?" "Which doll looks like you yourself?" Ten of the children liked the white doll best; eleven called the black doll the "bad" one; seven of the black children, when asked which doll was like themselves, picked the white one. From these answers and earlier research, Clark concluded "that these children . . . like other human beings who are subjected to an obviously inferior status in the society in which they live, have been definitely harmed in the development of their personalities. . . ."

Later, scholars disputed both the evidentiary power of that study and the weight the Justices had attached to it. The study, obviously limited in size and structure, today would hardly survive cross-exam-ination. Most likely its major function was to buttress a position the Justices had reached on their own.

Social science research has provided more solid evidence in litigation over the constitutionality of juries with fewer than twelve members. In the two decisions that affirmed the legality of such juries, the Court cited a number of empirical studies purporting to show that these modifications did not affect the quality of the verdicts rendered by the smaller juries. Subsequently these studies were severely criticized, and five years later BALLEW V. GEORGIA held five-member criminal juries unconstitutional. Justice HARRY A. BLACKMUN's opinion repeatedly cited these critical views.

Most social science operations suffer from some imperfection, partly because their subject matter is so complex, and partly because of methodological flaws. Even if such imperfections are minor, courts may hesitate to accept social science findings that threaten to dislodge established rules. One type of effort to compensate for imperfection is "triangulation"—the confluence of evidence from independent studies that approach the same problem from different angles. An example is the series of studies of "death qualified" juries.

At one time, a New York statute allowed New York City to try murder and other crimes of public notoriety before specially selected BLUE RIBBON JURIES, whose members, among other qualifications, were required to have no objection to the death penalty. When the Court was asked to declare these juries unconstitutional because of alleged bias in favor of the prosecution, it declined by a bare majority on the ground that there was no proof of such bias. Speculation as to how such proof might be established led to the first study which found that jurors who were in favor of the death penalty were indeed more likely to convict, not only in capital trials, but generally. Six other studies followed, with different approaches; each replicated the result.

Witherspoon v. Illinois (1968), decided halfway through these studies, did not reach the issue. Although the Court agreed that merely having scruples about the death penalty was not sufficient cause for eliminating jurors, it dismissed the first few research findings, indicating that the exclusion of jurors with scruples against the death penalty would bias the jury in favor of conviction, as "too tentative and fragmentary." Subsequent efforts to convince other courts that the post-*Witherspoon* juries, too, were biased in favor of convicting defendants failed until 1983 and 1984 when two federal district courts in HABEAS CORPUS proceedings accepted the evidence provided in these studies and invalidated the convictions. Although the federal Courts of Appeals have divided on this issue and the Supreme Court has agreed to review one of these cases, these two decisions mark a preliminary acceptance of proof by triangulation.

The role of social science research in litigation is bound to grow in spite of deep-seated hesitancy on the part of the courts to look at statistical evidence. It is difficult to predict how fast and where the use of social science techniques will increase in constitutional litigation. Much will depend on the resourcefulness of social scientists in developing new research and the initiative of attorneys in presenting evidence that can sharpen the perception of litigated facts and aid courts in judging the consequences of their legal options.

                                        HANS ZEISEL
                                        DAVID KAYE

Bibliography

BALDUS, D. and COLE, J. 1980 *Statistical Proof of Discrimination.* Colorado Springs, Colo.: Shepard's.

CAHN, EDMOND 1962 A Dangerous Myth in the School Segregation Cases. In Kenneth Clark, ed., *Confronting Injustice.* Pages 329–345. Boston: Little, Brown.

KAYE, DAVID 1980 And Then There Were Twelve: Statistical Reasoning, the Supreme Court, and the Size of the Jury. *California Law Review* 68:1004–1043.

——— 1982 Statistical Evidence of Discrimination. *Journal of the American Statistical Association* 77:773–783.

LEMPERT, RICHARD O. 1975 Uncovering "Nondiscernible" Differences: Empirical Research and the Jury-Size Cases. *Michigan Law Review* 73:643–708.

LOH, WALLACE D. 1984 *Social Research in the Judicial Process: Cases, Readings and Text.* New York: Russell Sage Foundation.

SAKS, MICHAEL J. 1974 Ignorance of Science Is No Excuse. *Trial* 10:18–20.

WALBERT, DAVID 1971 The Effect of Jury Size on the Probability of Conviction: An Evaluation of *Williams v. Florida. Case Western Law Review* 22:529–554.

ZEISEL, HANS 1971 And Then There Were None: The Diminution of the Federal Jury. *University of Chicago Law Review* 38:710–724.

——— 1980 Reflections on Experimental Techniques in the Law. *Journal of Legal Studies* 2:107–124.

——— 1968 *Some Data on Juror Attitudes Towards Capital Punishment.* Chicago: University of Chicago Center for Studies in Criminal Justice.

——— 1985 *Say It with Figures,* 6th ed. Chap. 14. New York: Harper & Row.

——— and DIAMOND, SHARI 1974 "Convincing Empirical Evidence" on the Six-Member Jury. *University of Chicago Law Review* 41:281–295.

SOCIAL SECURITY ACT
49 Stat. 620 (1935)

The Social Security Act of 1935, as subsequently amended, is the primary source of federal and federal–state cooperative social welfare programs. In addition to the program popularly denominated "social security," which now includes old age, survivors, and disability insurance, and the fiscally related medical assistance program for the aged (Medicare), the current Social Security Act also provides grants to states for many federally regulated programs, such as unemployment compensation, services to poor families with children (Aid to Families with Dependent Children), services to the aged, blind, and disabled (Supplementary Security Income), health care for the poor (Medicaid), and maternal and child welfare services.

The act has been a fertile source of constitutional litigation. The cooperative federal-state unemployment compensation scheme was narrowly sustained as a legitimate congressional exercise of the power "to lay and collect taxes . . . to . . . provide . . . for the GENERAL WELFARE of the United States" in STEWARD MACHINE CO. V. DAVIS (1937). In a companion case, HELVERING V. DAVIS (1937), seven Justices agreed that the federal social security old age retirement benefits program was well within the purview of Congress's TAXING AND SPENDING POWER.

The act has generated a number of important PROCEDURAL DUE PROCESS cases. GOLDBERG V. KELLY (1970) held that due process requires an evidentiary hearing *prior* to the termination of WELFARE BENEFITS. Justice WILLIAM J. BRENNAN, writing for a majority of six, reasoned that a subsequent hearing would be inadequate to protect the interests of the eligible recipient deprived of basic subsistence while she awaited her opportunity to challenge termination of benefits. *Goldberg v. Kelly* was narrowly construed in MATHEWS V. ELDRIDGE (1976), which held that due process does not require a prior evidentiary hearing when social security disability benefits are terminated after a Social Security Administration determination that the worker is no longer disabled. The Court distinguished *Goldberg* on two grounds: *Goldberg* involved public assistance for the INDIGENT while social security disability benefits are not based on financial need; and the opportunity for a prior hearing is less valuable to the recipient when the administrative conclusion is based on expert medical testimony, as in a disability termination case, rather than on a wide variety of facts and witness credibility, as in a public assistance case.

The social security program embodied a number of gender-based assumptions about economic dependence that were challenged as violative of the EQUAL PROTECTION guarantee in *Weinberger v. Wiesenfeld* (1975) and CALIFANO V. GOLDFARB (1977). In *Wiesenfeld*, the Court required that "mother's benefits," payable to an insured worker's widow who cares for the worker's child, be extended equally to similarly situated widowers. In *Goldfarb*, the Court held invalid a requirement that widowers but not widows prove actual dependency on the deceased insured worker.

In another group of cases prospective social welfare beneficiaries have constitutionally challenged the substantive conditions of individual grants. In *Flemming v. Nestor* (1960), *Weinberger v. Salfi* (1975), and *Mathews v. DeCastro* (1976), the Supreme Court rejected such challenges.

GRACE GANZ BLUMBERG

Bibliography

ALTMEYER, ARTHUR 1968 *The Formative Years of Social Security.* Madison: University of Wisconsin Press.

DEPARTMENT OF HEALTH, EDUCATION AND WELFARE 1960 *Basic Readings in Social Security: The 25th Anniversary of the Social Security Act.* Washington, D.C.: Government Printing Office.

WITTE, EDWIN 1962 *The Development of the Social Security Act.* Madison: University of Wisconsin Press.

SOCIOLOGICAL JURISPRUDENCE

Sociological jurisprudence is one of the most important schools of legal thought in the twentieth century. Its major proponent in the United States was ROSCOE POUND (1870–1964), a prolific writer who was dean of the Harvard Law School from 1916 to 1936. A number of other legal educators and judges also contributed in varying degrees to the theory or practice of sociological jurisprudence. They included five former members of the Supreme Court—OLIVER WENDELL HOLMES, LOUIS D. BRANDEIS, HARLAN FISKE STONE, BENJAMIN N. CARDOZO, and FELIX FRANKFURTER. Even though the doctrines of these jurists were anything but uniform, they shared a number of important attitudes and ideas.

The movement for a sociological jurisprudence emerged during the Progressive Era. Pound interpreted it as the "movement for pragmatism as a philosophy of law," the purpose of which was to facilitate legal reform and social progress. Although legal change should take place under the leadership of lawyers, the agenda of sociological jurisprudence did not focus on changes in legal institutions. Rather, it stressed reform of prevailing conceptions of the study, interpretation, and application of law.

This emphasis reflected a particular diagnosis of the ills of the American legal system at the outset of the twentieth century. These problems included judicial hostility to laws designed to protect workers, which courts often construed narrowly or held unconstitutional. Decisions of the Supreme Court applying the doctrine of SUBSTANTIVE DUE PROCESS are a classic example of the tendency. The advocates of sociological jurisprudence assailed this judicial response to social legislation, which they attributed to several factors. One was the isolation of the study of law from the social sciences. This condition allegedly fostered an ignorance of social realities and needs that contributed to unjust decisions. "Unless we know the facts on which legislators may have acted," Justice Brandeis pointed out in BURNS BAKING CO. V. BRYAN (1924), "we cannot properly decide whether they were . . . unreasonable, arbitrary, or capricious. Knowledge is essential to understanding; and understanding should precede judging."

Pound maintained that another factor contributing to judicial decisions that obstructed social progress was MECHANICAL JURISPRUDENCE, or the rigid deduction of decisions from established principles without regard to their practical effects. He argued that this kind of syllogistic reasoning not only obscured judges' wide range of choice in selecting premises but also contributed to their intolerance of laws limiting FREEDOM OF CONTRACT. The very different attitude of Justice Holmes was one reason why advocates of sociological jurisprudence held him in such high esteem.

These criticisms were the basis of the characteristic reform objectives of sociological jurisprudence. A fundamental goal was the development of a better factual understanding of the practical effects of legal precepts and institutions. Cardozo proposed a Ministry of Justice which would study and observe the "law in action." In "The Living Law" Brandeis recommended "broader education . . . continued by lawyer and judge throughout life: study of economics and sociology and politics which embody the facts and present the problems of today." This idea strongly conditioned the unorthodox BRANDEIS BRIEF in MULLER V. OREGON (1908), an approach that Brandeis and other lawyers such as Felix Frankfurter used in a number of subsequent cases. Only two of the 113 pages of this brief presented the traditional kind of legal argument, while the rest consisted largely of factual evidence of the bad effects on women of excessive hours of work. Brandeis argued that these data showed that the Oregon law, which limited women's working hours to ten per day, was a reasonable limitation of freedom of contract. His argument favorably impressed the Justices, who unanimously upheld the law.

The prescription for abandoning "mechanical jurisprudence" was a more pragmatic approach to judicial decision making. No one expressed this idea better than Cardozo, who insisted that law is a means to the end of "social welfare" or "social justice." He argued that judges should interpret general constitutional limitations to serve this end. The changing meaning of the word "liberty" in the due process clauses of the Fifth and FOURTEENTH AMENDMENTS is an example. (See INCORPORATION DOCTRINE.) Similar beliefs conditioned Frankfurter's suggestion that constitutional law "in its relation to social legislation, is . . . but applied politics, using the word in its noble sense."

These ideas reflected a justifiable dissatisfaction with the content of American constitutional law earlier in this century. The adequacy of the sociological jurists' diagnosis of and reforms for these evils is another matter. To begin with, they tended to exaggerate the causal significance of "mechanical jurisprudence" and judicial ignorance of social needs. Neither of these factors ordinarily influence the actual decisions of the Justices or their choice of premises as much as their policy preferences or attitudes. Furthermore, conservative Justices might (and did) use Cardozo's "method of sociology" for their own purposes. "Social welfare" and "social justice" are subject, after all, to a multitude of interpretations. In some cases a majority of the Justices invalidated laws defended by a "Brandeis brief." The extent to which that technique influenced them to uphold other laws is uncertain, but its impact may have been corroborative rather than decisive. The use of social science evidence in BROWN v. BOARD OF EDUCATION (1954) illustrates this tendency. Finally, social scientists often disagree about the interpretation of the facts or their implications for public policy.

To say this is not to imply that the value of sociological jurisprudence was negligible. Its greatest contribution to constitutional law was that it served as a positive force for upholding social legislation. If its efficacy in this regard was limited, at least it provided support for judges inclined to hold such legislation constitutional. Moreover, knowledge of the actual effects of legal precepts and institutions is essential for informed evaluations of them. The call of sociological jurisprudence for studies of these effects was, thus, a step in the right direction.

WILFRID E. RUMBLE

Bibliography

BRANDEIS, LOUIS D. 1916 The Living Law. Address before the Chicago Bar Association, January 3, 1916.

CAHILL, FRED V. 1952 *Judicial Legislation*. New York: Ronald Press.

ROSEN, PAUL L. 1972 *The Supreme Court and Social Science*. Urbana: University of Illinois Press.

RUMBLE, WILFRID E. 1968 *American Legal Realism*. Ithaca, N.Y.: Cornell University Press.

WHITE, G. EDWARD 1978 *Patterns of American Legal Thought*. Indianapolis: Bobbs-Merrill.

SOLEM v. HELM
463 U.S. 277 (1983)

Expanding the coverage of the Eighth Amendment's CRUEL AND UNUSUAL PUNISHMENT clause, the Supreme Court held that in addition to barbaric sentences it prohibits criminal sentences that are disproportionate to the crime for which a defendant is convicted. Jerry Helm, a habitual offender, passed a bad check and received the most severe punishment—life imprisonment without possibility of parole—that South Dakota could impose for any crime. A 5–4 Court decided that because Helm's six prior FELONY convictions were for relatively minor nonviolent crimes against property and because he was treated more severely than other criminals who had committed more serious crimes, his sentence was significantly disproportionate to his crime. The dissenting Justices saw "judicial usurpation" of state sentencing discretion, especially in cases of incorrigible recidivists.

LEONARD W. LEVY

SOLICITOR GENERAL

The solicitor general is a senior officer of the United States Department of Justice with special responsibilities in the representation of the United States and its officers and agencies before the Supreme Court, and in the administration of justice in the federal appellate courts.

The title—solicitor general—like that of ATTORNEY GENERAL is derived from English usage, but the functions of the offices are quite different in the United States. In England, both offices are political in the sense that they are filled by members of Parliament. In the United States, neither the attorney general nor the solicitor general is a member of Congress. The attorney general is a member of the Cabinet. He advises the President, works with members of Congress on legislative matters and judicial appointments, holds press conferences and is otherwise responsible for governmental and public relations. He is also charged with administering a large department which includes the Federal Bureau of Investigation, the Bureau of Prisons, the Immigration and Naturalization Service, and other important agencies. Though he has policy and administrative responsibilities of great importance, he has virtually no time to be a lawyer in the traditional sense.

Until 1870, the attorney general functioned alone with only a small staff, and in association with the United States attorneys in the various states, over whom he had little authority. In 1870, apparently as an economy device (to eliminate the cost of retaining private lawyers in the increasing number of cases), Congress established the Department of Justice, with the attorney general as its head. The statute provided that there should be in the Department "an officer learned in the law, to assist the Attorney-General in the performance of his duties, to be called the solicitor-general." Under the statute the solicitor general was authorized in the attorney general's discretion to argue "any case in which the government is interested" before the Supreme Court, or in any federal or state court." These statutory provisions remain to the present day, essentially unchanged.

In the years since 1870, the duties of the Department of Justice have greatly increased. Until 1953 the solicitor general was the second officer in the Department of Justice and served as acting attorney general in the attorney general's absence. The responsibilities of the attorney general have made it necessary to add a deputy attorney general and an associate attorney general, so that the solicitor general is now the fourth ranking officer in the department. But the solicitor general's responsibilities have remained essentially unchanged in substance—though greatly increased in volume—over the past sixty years. He remains the leading officer in the department functioning primarily as a lawyer.

As the pattern has developed, the solicitor general is not a politician, and he has only a minimum of political responsibility. His function is to be the government's top lawyer in the courts, particularly the Supreme Court, and by well-established tradition he is allowed considerable independence in carrying out this role. Bent and Schloss, describing the office as "the bridge between the Executive and the Judiciary," have said that "[t]he Solicitor General must often choose between incongruous roles and differing loyalties. He is still the government's lawyer, and he most frequently acts as an advocate. On the other hand, he also functions as a reviewer of government policies, an officer of the Court, and . . . a protector of the public interest."

In more specific terms, the organization of the Department of Justice assigns to the solicitor general four areas of responsibility. Two of these are of primary importance. First, the solicitor general is responsible for the representation of the United States and its officers and agencies in all cases before the Supreme Court of the United States. The BRIEFs which are filed on behalf of the government in the Supreme Court are prepared by him or under his direction. He argues the most important cases himself, and assigns the argument in other cases to members of his staff, to other lawyers in the Department of Justice or to lawyers for the agencies which may be involved in the cases before the Court. Second, the Solicitor General decides whether the United States will APPEAL in any case which it loses in any court, state or federal, or indeed in foreign courts. This function is not widely known, even in the legal profession. It is, however, a very important means of coordinating and controlling the government's litigation, so that cases of little importance are not taken to the appellate courts. It also serves to minimize the taking of inconsistent positions before the various appellate courts.

This function includes determining whether any case will be taken by the government to the Supreme Court. This is probably the most important responsibility assigned to the solicitor general. With few exceptions, no case can now be taken to the Supreme Court except on application for review—called a petition for a WRIT OF CERTIORARI. In recent years, some four thousand such applications are made to the Court by all parties each year. Yet the Court can hear on the merits only about a hundred and fifty cases a year. This means that it is of great importance for the solicitor general to select with care the relatively small number of cases in which the government will file petitions. A high proportion of the solicitor general's petitions are in fact granted by the Court, which means that he has, as part of his responsibility, carried out an important part of the selection process necessarily confronting the Court.

In addition to the two functions just outlined, the solicitor general has two other responsibilities. These assist him in carrying out his role as overall controller of Government APPELLATE JURISDICTION. First his authorization must be obtained before the United States or one of its officers or agencies files a brief as friend of the court—AMICUS CURIAE—in any appellate court. Second his authorization must be obtained before a petition for REHEARING *en banc*—before the whole court—is filed in any UNITED STATES COURT OF APPEALS. The courts of appeals are overburdened, and hearings EN BANC present serious logistical problems. Requiring authority from the solicitor general means that such petitions are rarely filed, and only in the most important cases.

The solicitor general's office is a relatively small one, though it has grown slowly in recent years. At the present time it numbers about twenty lawyers in addition to the solicitor general himself; and, including secretaries and aides, the total number of personnel in the office is about fifty. Thus it can operate in much the same way as a moderate-sized law firm. There is considerable pressure in the office as the cases keep coming in, from all parts of the country, and almost all of them are subject to relatively short deadlines.

In the nature of things, the solicitor general cannot be a specialist. The cases coming to his desk involve every field of law—constitutional law, ADMINISTRATIVE LAW, criminal law, tax law, antitrust law, labor law, international law, ENVIRONMENTAL PROTECTION, energy, and every other field with which the government is concerned. Inevitably, the staff in the office specialize to some extent, and there are four deputy solicitors general, each of whom has special responsibilities for particular areas. But there are no rigid lines, and all lawyers in the office are available to handle the various types of cases as they come in.

The solicitor general's role in the Supreme Court is limited to the representation of the United States, its officers, and its agencies. Other cases which may be of great importance involve private parties, or states or their subsidiaries. Thus, the cases involving BIRTH CONTROL (GRISWOLD V. CONNECTICUT, 1965) and abortion (ROE V. WADE, 1973) were not handled by the solicitor general. But more than half of the cases before the Supreme Court (particularly those heard by the Court on the merits) are "government cases," that is, cases in which the United States, or its officers or agents, are parties. It is important to the Court to have these cases handled in competent fashion, and the research and ideas, and policy decisions, lying behind the solicitor general's advocacy before the Supreme Court can influence the decisions reached by the Court.

Much of the government's litigation before the Supreme Court, though important, does not attract wide public attention. From time to time, though, cases coming before the Court are rather spectacular in terms of public interest. Reference may be made, for example, to YOUNGSTOWN SHEET & TUBE CO. V. SAWYER (1952), where the Court invalidated the action of President HARRY S. TRUMAN in seizing the steel industry during the KOREAN WAR, the Pentagon Papers case (NEW YORK TIMES CO. V. UNITED STATES, 1971), and UNITED STATES V. NIXON (1974), where the Court held that the White House tapes made under the direction of President RICHARD M. NIXON must be turned over in response to a SUBPOENA from a GRAND JURY. For the most part, though, the work of the solicitor general and his staff is rather straightforward professional work.

It is important to recognize that in all cases the solicitor general is an advocate and not a judge. However, he is a very special sort of advocate. There are some positions which he will not support because he thinks the government's position is clearly wrong in law. On rare occasions, in such cases, he "confesses error" before the Court. The Court is not bound by such a confession, but it usually accepts the solicitor general's conclusion. There are other cases where the solicitor general will not himself defend the government's position, but he thinks a "respectable" defense can be made, and he assigns another government lawyer who is willing to do so to present that defense. Illustration of this may be found in *Peters v. Hobby* (1955), involving the LOYALTY-SECURITY PROGRAM during the 1950s, and in *Gutknecht v. United States* (1970), involving "delinquency reclassification" under the SELECTIVE SERVICE ACT. But the solicitor general will frequently advocate a position which he believes to be worthy of presentation to the Court even though he might not decide in favor of that position if he were a judge. Laymen sometimes have difficulty in accepting this, but, within limits, it is inherent in the role of a lawyer, and it is inherent in the position of the solicitor general. For he is the government's chief advocate. The function of deciding cases is assigned to others.

In this situation, the solicitor general's role is sometimes a difficult one. Whenever he decides not to take a case before the Supreme Court, he is in effect depriving the Court of the opportunity to decide it. This is, indeed, an important part of his function, in view of the fact that many more applications come to the Court than it can possibly accept. The solicitor general's judgment that the chances of success in a particular case are slim is obviously a relevant consideration. Yet there are cases of such importance that he should take the case to the Court, in order to obtain a definitive decision, even though he has little faith in the government's position.

An illustration is found in UNITED STATES V.

UNITED STATES DISTRICT COURT (1972). This involved the validity of so-called national security WIRE-TAPS, made on executive authority (the President or the attorney general) alone, without a judicial warrant. As the cases before the Supreme Court developed, it seemed unlikely that the Court would uphold such wiretaps, at least in cases of domestic security. Yet the attorney general needed to know. If he had such authority, cases might develop where he would need to use it. If he did not have the authority, he should have the definitive decision of the Supreme Court, by which he would, of course, abide. A petition was filed with the Court in order that the question might be definitively settled, and the Court granted the petition. In due course, the Court held that domestic "national security" wiretaps are illegal under the FOURTH AMENDMENT, when made without a court warrant. Thus the solicitor general, though himself dubious about the government's case, played his appropriate role in obtaining a definitive decision on an important public question.

In the daily routine of his office the solicitor general has many decisions to make. In making these decisions, he may be subject to various pressures. These pressures may be wholly legitimate professional pressures from other lawyers in the government seeking to persuade him to accept their view. He frequently gives hearings, too, to opposing lawyers. There may also be various forms of political pressure—rarely presented as such—from Capitol Hill, or from other officers of the government. The solicitor general should be able to receive such representations and come to his own conclusions. Attorneys general have usually been firm in their support of the solicitor general. And, indeed, the fact that the decision is assigned to the solicitor general may serve to protect the attorney general from such pressures. But the attorney general and the President are the solicitor general's superiors, and if he receives an order from above he must decide whether the matter is one of principle for him; if it is, he must resign. As far as is known, no solicitor general has ever resigned for such a reason. But this is what happened to Attorney General Elliott Richardson and Deputy Attorney General William Ruckelshaus, when they refused to comply with President Nixon's order to discharge Archibald Cox as Special Prosecutor in 1973.

Special problems arise when officers or agencies differ from the position of the solicitor general, and especially when two or more agencies have different interests or points of view which they present vigorously to the solicitor general or his staff. A situation of this sort arose in the case of *Fortnightly Corp. v.* *United Artists Television, Inc.* (1968), involving cable television. The Copyright Office in the Library of Congress had one view about the case. The Federal Communications Commission had another. And the Antitrust Division in the Department of Justice had still a third. All views were strongly advocated. The solicitor general negotiated separately with the lawyers for each office concerned. None would yield. Then he held a meeting at which all interested lawyers were present, hoping that some sort of a consensus would emerge. Unfortunately, none did, and the solicitor general concluded that he had no alternative but to formulate his own view, which he submitted to the Court.

This case exemplifies one of the important roles of the solicitor general, in resolving differences within the government, so that a single position may be presented to the Court. When these differences arise within the Justice Department, or between the several executive departments, the solicitor general seeks to persuade but eventually may have to make his own decision. The situation is somewhat more difficult when the difference is with one of the "independent agencies," such as the Federal Trade Commission or the Securities and Exchange Commission.

For historical reasons, it has long been settled that the Interstate Commerce Commission and the Maritime Commission can appear before the Supreme Court through their own lawyers. With respect to the other agencies, however, the statutory provisions are not explicit. Though there is occasionally some tension, the solicitor general has been able to maintain effective control over agency cases in the Supreme Court. In this process, various devices are used. He sometimes advises the Court that the agency has a different view. He sometimes authorizes the agency to file a brief stating its view. By and large, the agencies believe that the solicitor general's support is important and helpful, and this belief is reinforced by the standing of the solicitor general before the Court. Cases of this sort are carefully considered in the solicitor general's office, and full hearings are given to the lawyers from the agencies involved. In this way problems of real difficulty have been resolved with substantial satisfaction on the part of all concerned.

There is a final role of the solicitor general which, though long an important one, has been of increasing significance in recent years. This is the preparation and filing of briefs in the Supreme Court as a friend of the Court—amicus curiae. Under the Rules of the Supreme Court, the solicitor general is authorized to file such a brief without consent of the parties or special leave of the Court. Frequently a case between private parties, or a state criminal prosecution, may raise a question of great interest to the federal government, though the latter is not a party. An example is TERRY v. OHIO (1968), involving the validity of a STOP AND FRISK by local police. The solicitor general filed an amicus brief in that case because of the great interest of the federal government in law enforcement. Through such briefs, the solicitor general protects the interests of the federal government, aids the Court by furnishing information and relevant legal materials, facilitates the handling of difficult questions with the "independent agencies" of the government, and, on occasion, presents his own views on novel constitutional questions.

In this way, the solicitor general has participated in cases involving SCHOOL DESEGREGATION, legislative REAPPORTIONMENT, CAPITAL PUNISHMENT, CIVIL RIGHTS, and many other important questions of developing constitutional and statutory law. Within wide limits, the solicitor general has freedom to develop his own position in such briefs. The solicitor general and his staff have great experience in Supreme Court cases, and well-considered and carefully prepared briefs can be of considerable assistance to the Court through impartial and informed analysis of novel questions.

Indeed, a high proportion of briefs amicus filed by the solicitor general are prepared because of direct invitation from the Court. Such invitations are always treated as commands, and great care is taken in determining the position to be taken and in developing the materials to be included in the brief. In many ways, such briefs are the purest expression of the relation of trust and confidence which has long been established between the solicitor general and the Court.

It is this trust and confidence on which the position of the solicitor general before the Court, and his effective representation of the United States, in the long run depend.

ERWIN N. GRISWOLD

Bibliography

NOTE 1969 Government Litigation in the Supreme Court: The Roles of the Solicitor General. *Yale Law Journal* 78:1442–1481.

SOMERSET'S CASE
98 Eng. Rep. 499 (K.B., 1772)

The case of *Somerset v. Stewart*, decided by King's Bench (the highest COMMON LAW court in England) in 1772, profoundly affected the constitutional status of slavery in England and in the United States after independence (because the precedent had become part of American common law). In a brief opinion, Lord Mansfield, Chief Justice, held that slavery "must be recognized by the law of the country where it is used." He further declared that "the state of slavery is of such a nature, that it is incapable of being introduced on any reasons, moral or political; but only [by] positive law." *Somerset's Case* did not abolish slavery in England or America, but until the 1850s it was interpreted to mean that slavery did not exist where it was not established by positive law (which, according to Chief Justice JOHN MARSHALL in *The Antelope* [1825], might include custom as well as statutory law). Abolitionists construed Mansfield's words to mean either that slavery was universally illegitimate or that it had a legal existence only where affirmatively established by a slave code. They denied that the federal government had power to establish slavery in any territory or district, or to protect it anywhere. (See ABOLITIONIST CONSTITUTIONAL THEORY.) This argument became the basis of the Republican "Freedom national, slavery local" slogan of the 1850s and was reflected in STEPHEN A. DOUGLAS's FREEPORT DOCTRINE of 1858. *Somerset's Case* also complicated interstate relations in the matter of fugitive and sojourning slaves; some free states in the 1850s refused to recognize the continuation of an individual's slave status in a free JURISDICTION. (See FUGITIVE SLAVERY.) Southern jurists responded by repudiating the liberating potential of the *Somerset* doctrine after 1851, dismissing Mansfield's words as OBITER DICTA or error.

WILLIAM M. WIECEK

SONZINSKY v. UNITED STATES
300 U.S. 506 (1937)

The unanimous opinion in this case indicated that the spirit animating the decision in BAILEY v. DREXEL FURNITURE CO. (1922) was dead: the Supreme Court would no longer inquire into Congress's motives in enacting a tax measure. The National Firearms Act of 1934 imposed an annual EXCISE TAX on manufacturers and dealers of firearms, excepting handguns. The Court refused to consider that the tax was not imposed to raise a revenue and was a penalty to suppress traffic in a commodity normally subject only to state regulation. Compulsory registration provisions of such statutes, however, were later held unconstitutional in MARCHETTI v. UNITED STATES (1968).

LEONARD W. LEVY

SOSNA v. IOWA
419 U.S. 393 (1975)

Iowa limited access to its divorce court to persons who had resided in the state for one year. Sosna, denied a divorce under this law, brought suit in a federal court challenging the one-year limitation's constitutionality. By the time her case reached the Supreme Court, the year had passed. Because the case had been properly certified as a CLASS ACTION, however, the Court rejected the state's invitation to dismiss the action for MOOTNESS. On the merits, a six-Justice majority, speaking through Justice WILLIAM H. REHNQUIST, upheld the statute.

Justice Rehnquist breathed no word concerning "penalties" on the exercise of the RIGHT TO TRAVEL interstate. Instead, he merely noted that previous decisions had struck down durational RESIDENCE REQUIREMENTS only when they were justified entirely on the basis of budgetary or record-keeping considerations. Here, he said, the state had an interest in protecting the rights of defendant spouses and of any minor children. Further, the state might wish to avoid "officious intermeddling" in another state's primary concerns and to protect its own divorce decrees against COLLATERAL ATTACK. "A state such as Iowa may quite reasonably decide that it does not wish to become a divorce mill." In any event, an Iowa plaintiff was merely delayed in getting a divorce, not denied one altogether.

Justice BYRON R. WHITE dissented, arguing that the case was moot. Justice THURGOOD MARSHALL dissented on the merits, joined by Justice WILLIAM J. BRENNAN: The Court's analysis did not subject this penalty on exercise of the right to travel to the STRICT SCRUTINY it deserved but improperly employed a functional equivalent of the RATIONAL BASIS standard of review. Iowa's most important interest, protecting the integrity of its decrees, could be achieved by the less restrictive means of merely requiring a divorce plaintiff to be domiciled in the state. And the delay/denial distinction was false; a plaintiff would be denied marital freedom (and the freedom to remarry) during an entire year.

KENNETH L. KARST

SOUNDTRUCKS AND AMPLIFIERS

When the Framers of the FIRST AMENDMENT wrote a ban on laws "abridging" FREEDOM OF SPEECH into the Constitution, the range of the human voice was relatively limited. The invention of electronic sound amplification equipment in the twentieth century potentially extended that range even into distant buildings and behind locked doors. Loudspeakers and bullhorns, whether stationary or mobile, present a particular problem of speech regulation: to what extent does the right to speak override the expectation of peace and privacy enjoyed by members of the public? Especially troubling are soundtrucks, amplifier-equipped motor vehicles that blare political slogans or advertising messages while roving the streets of residential neighborhoods.

The problem of soundtrucks and amplifiers was addressed by the Supreme Court in two famous cases. In *Saia v. New York* (1948) a 5–4 Court struck down a city ordinance requiring permission of the chief of police before a soundtruck could be used within the city limits. The ordinance provided no standard for the police chief to apply in granting or withholding permission. Eight months later, in KOVACS V. COOPER (1949), a five-Justice majority (including the *Saia* dissenters) upheld an ordinance prohibiting the operation within a city of soundtrucks that emitted "loud or raucous noises." The plurality thought the "loud and raucous" test an adequate standard of regulation, while two concurring Justices understood the ordinance as a ban on all soundtrucks.

The danger of public regulation of amplified speech is that restrictions ostensibly directed to the time, place, and manner of speaking will be used as a pretext for controlling the content of speech. But, as technology makes the outside world ever more intrusive into the realm of individual privacy, the right of the people to provide themselves freedom from loud and raucous utterance, whatever its content, can only become more valuable.

DENNIS J. MAHONEY

SOUTH CAROLINA v. KATZENBACH
383 U.S. 301 (1966)

This decision upheld the constitutionality of portions of the VOTING RIGHTS ACT OF 1965. Southern states attacked, as an intrusion upon state SOVEREIGNTY and on other grounds, portions of the act suspending tests or devices used to measure voter qualifications, barring new voter qualifications pending approval by federal authorities, providing for the appointment of federal voting examiners to register voters, and determining which states and political subdivisions were subject to the act's coverage. In sustaining the legislation under the FIFTEENTH AMENDMENT, the Supreme Court, in an opinion by Chief Justice EARL WARREN, rejected the argument that Congress could do no more than forbid violations of the Fifteenth Amendment and must leave the fashioning of remedies for violations to the courts. Congressional findings that case-by-case litigation was inadequate to vindicate VOTING RIGHTS justified the decision "to shift the advantage of time and inertia from the perpetrators of the evil to its victims."

THEODORE EISENBERG

SOUTH CAROLINA EXPOSITION AND PROTEST

See: Exposition and Protest

SOUTH CAROLINA ORDINANCE OF NULLIFICATION
(1832)

South Carolinians' objections to the expansion of federal authority focused on protective tariffs enacted in 1828 and 1832. They were most concerned, however, about potential external threats to the security of slavery, including threats from the federal government. Inspired by constitutional theories of JOHN C. CALHOUN, the South Carolina legislature called a convention to nullify the tariff.

On November 24, 1832, the convention adopted the Ordinance of Nullification, which declared that Congress lacked power to adopt a protective tariff. The tariff measures were therefore "null, void, and no law, nor binding upon this State, its officers or citizens." The ordinance voided all contracts and judicial proceedings designed to collect the tariff, prohibited state officials from enforcing it, required the state legislature to enact legislation that would "prevent the enforcement and arrest the operation" of the tariffs, prohibited appeals of tariff-related cases to the Supreme Court, required all public officials and jurors to take an oath to support the ordinance and supportive legislation, and warned that any coercive federal act would trigger the state's SECESSION. South Carolina also subsequently nullified the federal FORCE ACT that empowered President ANDREW JACKSON to collect the tariff. Though the Nullification Ordinance produced a major constitutional crisis in 1832, it was

a short-term failure. President Jackson and all the Southern states denounced it, and South Carolina never found occasion to put its requirements to the test. But the Ordinance was a major step in implementing the theory of NULLIFICATION and, as such, pointed to secession.

WILLIAM M. WIECEK

Bibliography

CURRENT, RICHARD N. 1963 *John C. Calhoun.* New York: Washington Square Press.

SOUTH CAROLINA ORDINANCE OF SECESSION
(1860)

JOHN C. CALHOUN, the foremost theorist of SECESSION, had argued that the United States Constitution was a compact among sovereign states. When one of the parties to the compact (federal government or other state) had violated its terms by enacting or condoning unconstitutional acts, and other remedies such as INTERPOSITION and NULLIFICATION proved futile, an aggrieved party could withdraw from the compact and resume the independent status it enjoyed previously.

In response to ABRAHAM LINCOLN's election, the South Carolina legislature called a convention to consider secession. On December 20, 1860, the convention, meeting at Charleston, unanimously adopted the Ordinance of Secession, a brief statement declaring that "the union now subsisting . . . is hereby dissolved." Four days later, the Convention approved the "Declaration of the Causes of Secession," a brief exposition of secessionist and compact theory. In it, the Carolinians accused the free states of violation or half-hearted enforcement of the Fugitive Slave Acts, tolerating abolitionist agitation, and electing a presidential candidate pledged to the eventual abolition of slavery. Therefore South Carolina declared itself an "independent state, with full power to levy war, conclude peace, contract alliances, establish commerce, and to do all other acts and things which independent States may of right do."

WILLIAM M. WIECEK

Bibliography

POTTER, DAVID M. 1976 *The Impending Crisis,* 1848–1861. New York: Harper & Row.

SOUTH DAKOTA v. NEVILLE
459 U.S. 553 (1983)

In this case the Supreme Court answered a question left unresolved by earlier decisions: can a state use as evidence the fact that a person arrested for drunk driving refused to take a blood-alcohol test? GRIFFIN V. CALIFORNIA (1965) had held that adverse comment on a defendant's refusal to testify impermissibly burdened the RIGHT AGAINST SELF-INCRIMINATION, and SCHMERBER V. CALIFORNIA (1966) had held that a state could compel the taking of a blood-alcohol test without violating that right, which protected against testimonial compulsion only, not compulsion of physical evidence drawn from the body. In *Neville* the Court ruled that a state that authorized a driver to refuse a blood-alcohol test could introduce that refusal as evidence against him. The Court relied not on the earlier distinction between TESTIMONIAL AND NON-TESTIMONIAL COMPULSION but on the fact that the element of compulsion was altogether absent here because the state did not require the test.

LEONARD W. LEVY

SOUTH-EASTERN UNDERWRITERS ASSOCIATION v. UNITED STATES
322 U.S. 533 (1944)

The statement in PAUL V. VIRGINIA (1869) that insurance did not constitute INTERSTATE COMMERCE underlay seventy-five years of acquiescence and spawned an intricate network of state regulation. The question of federal regulation did not come before the Court until this indictment of an underwriters' association for violating the SHERMAN ANTITRUST ACT. A 4–3 Court, led by Justice HUGO L. BLACK, declared that insurance was commerce subject to federal regulation. Moreover, the Sherman Act applied, and the underwriters could properly be convicted for its violation. Justice ROBERT H. JACKSON, dissenting in part, conceded the fact of interstate commerce but felt obliged to follow the well-established legal fiction to the contrary until Congress acted to regulate. Chief Justice HARLAN FISKE STONE dissented, predicting chaos when state regulation was discontinued because federal controls did not exist. Justice FELIX FRANKFURTER joined Stone, admitting the reach of federal power but denying that the Sherman Act was intended to extend to insurance.

DAVID GORDON

(SEE ALSO: *Prudential Insurance Company v. Benjamin,* 1946.)

SOUTHERN MANIFESTO
(March 11, 1956)

Southern politicians generally opposed the Supreme Court's ruling in BROWN V. BOARD OF EDUCATION (1954). Virginia and other states resurrected the doctrine of INTERPOSITION, and Georgia threatened NULLIFICATION. The most considered statement of segregationist constitutional theory was the declaration against INTEGRATION made by ninety-six southern congressmen and senators, in March 1956, led by Senator Harry F. Byrd of Virginia. The manifesto argued: *Brown* represented a clear abuse of judicial power; the FOURTEENTH AMENDMENT, which did not mention education, was not intended to affect state educational systems; PLESSY V. FERGUSON (1896) was still good law; DESEGREGATION would cause chaos and confusion in the states affected. The manifesto called upon the people of the states to "resist forced integration by any lawful means" and concluded with a pledge "to use all lawful means to bring about a reversal of this decision which is contrary to the Constitution, and to prevent the use of force in its implementation." Federal response to such abstract defiance was notably lacking, although a group of distinguished leaders of the American bar denounced attacks on the Supreme Court as "reckless in their abuse, . . . heedless of the value of JUDICIAL REVIEW and . . . dangerous in fomenting disrespect for our highest law."

PAUL L. MURPHY

Bibliography
MUSE, BENJAMIN 1964 *Ten Years of Prelude: The Story of Integration Since the Supreme Court's 1954 Decision.* New York: Viking.

SOUTHERN PACIFIC CO. v. ARIZONA
325 U.S. 761 (1945)

Arizona prohibited operation of a railroad train more than fourteen passenger cars or seventy freight cars long. The Supreme Court, 7–2, held the law an unconstitutional burden on INTERSTATE COMMERCE. Chief Justice HARLAN FISKE STONE, for the Court, emphasized the magnitude of that burden; the law forced the railroad to operate thirty percent more trains in the state, and to break up and remake trains; its total yearly cost to both railroads operating in the state was a million dollars. Stone also noted that requiring more trains would produce more accidents; the state's safety argument was weak. This interest-balancing analysis was far more demanding than the "RATIONAL BASIS" STANDARD OF REVIEW Stone had employed in *South Carolina State Highway Department v. Barnwell Bros., Inc.* (1938), upholding limits on truck widths and weights. *Southern Pacific* set the standard for future challenges to STATE REGULATIONS OF COMMERCE in the transportation field.

KENNETH L. KARST

SOVEREIGN IMMUNITY

At COMMON LAW the sovereign, although subject to the law, was immune from the JURISDICTION of its own courts. The English doctrine of sovereign immunity was established at an early time, probably in the thirteenth century; but long before the American Revolution the jurisdictional exemption of the sovereign, though remaining theoretically absolute, was riddled with exceptions. Judicial process against the sovereign was available through petition of right and other procedures resting upon waiver of immunity, and subordinate officers could be sued for damages attributable to official acts and were subject to process by prerogative writ.

Because sovereign immunity was part of the common law heritage existing when the Constitution was adopted, the courts later embraced the doctrine as an implicit limitation upon their jurisdiction. Hence, some provisions of Article III of the Constitution were interpreted as subject to this qualification. The immunity of the United States, first acknowledged by the Supreme Court in *United States v. McLemore* (1846), became a complete exemption, protecting the federal government and its agencies from unconsented suit in any court by any plaintiff. State immunity was initially rejected by the Court in CHISHOLM V. GEORGIA (1793), but that unpopular HOLDING was quickly reversed by the ELEVENTH AMENDMENT. The amendment, in juxtaposition with Article III, was subsequently construed to immunize the states from unconsented suits by private plaintiffs and by foreign governments in federal court.

The states, however, are not immune from suit by either the United States or other states. As a matter of state law, states commonly have claimed immunity from suit by private plaintiffs in state court. The power of Congress to lift the states' common law immunity seems restricted only by the limitations of the JUDICIAL POWER OF THE UNITED STATES as defined in Article III, the general limitations of congressional power, and—arguably—some core notion of state sov-

ereignty. (See NATIONAL LEAGUE OF CITIES V. Usery, 1976.)

The immunity doctrine is in tension with the RULE OF LAW, and pragmatic justifications for its perpetuation are unpersuasive. By means of statutes waiving immunity and through judicial interpretation, the ambit of the exemption has been drastically reduced. Congressional legislation creating the COURT OF CLAIMS in 1855 and later enactments, such as the Tucker Act (1887) and the FEDERAL TORT CLAIMS ACT (1946), subject the United States to suit on many kinds of claims. The states, by state constitutional provision or statute, have abolished completely or restricted their own immunity—often in state judicial proceedings only, less commonly in federal court actions. Moreover, as a practical matter, the impact of the doctrine is significantly restricted by differentiating suits against public officers for official acts done or threatened pursuant to unconstitutional or legally deficient authorization from suits against the government itself. Although the courts permit state and federal officers to assert sovereign immunity where the suit against them is adjudged to be substantially against the government itself, such cases are generally limited to suits seeking damages or restitution for past acts where judgment will expend itself upon the public treasury, those seeking to dispossess the government of property, and some suits seeking specific performance. As a consequence of these developments, sovereign immunity has become a narrow and ill-defined jurisdictional bar, whose contemporary legitimacy and utility are doubtful.

CLYDE E. JACOBS

Bibliography

DAVIS, KENNETH C. 1970 Supp. *Administrative Law Treatise.* Pages 895–940. St. Paul, Minn.: West Publishing Co.

HOLDSWORTH, SIR WILLIAM S. 1944 *A History of English Law.* Vol. 9 of 15. London: Methuen.

SOVEREIGNTY

The single term "sovereignty" is used to denote two distinct (although related) concepts of constitutional significance. It refers both to the autonomy of a state with respect to its legislative JURISDICTION and to the supreme authority within the state. There are historical reasons why the same term is used for both, but to confound them is a serious and all-too-common error. The term itself comes from the Latin *superans* (meaning "rising above" or "overcoming") through the French *souverain*.

Sovereignty, in the first sense, is a concept derived from international law. A state is sovereign if it is independent of other states and possesses the authority to determine its relationship to other states and to regulate its own internal affairs. Sovereignty, in this sense, is the essential condition required for membership in the family of nations. Sovereign states do not ordinarily make treaties or wage formal war except with other states recognized as sovereign. International law also recognizes some communities as semisovereign, that is, as possessing certain, but not all, of the attributes of sovereignty. The member states of a federal union are in this category.

Internally the several states of the United States are legally sovereign in this sense insofar as they possess jurisdiction, the legitimate authority to declare the law within their territory. But this sovereignty is not unlimited. As the Supreme Court said in PARKER V. BROWN (1943), "The governments of the states are sovereign within their territory save only as they are subject to the prohibitions of the Constitution or as their action in some measure conflicts with powers delegated to the National Government, or with Congressional legislation enacted in the exercise of those powers." The jurisdiction of the states is constitutionally limited by subject as well as by territory, but within their sphere the state governments are as supreme as the national government is within its sphere. This is the meaning of what JAMES MADISON in THE FEDERALIST #39 called the "compound republic."

The states enjoy some other attributes of sovereignty: they may not without their consent be sued in their own courts or in the courts of the United States (see SOVEREIGN IMMUNITY; ELEVENTH AMENDMENT) and they possess independent and plenary authority to lay and collect taxes on persons, things, or transactions within their jurisdiction. Among themselves, also, the states are sovereign. The jurisdiction of a state is exclusive of the other states. Disputes between or among states in cases not governed by the Constitution, an INTERSTATE COMPACT, or a federal statute are resolved according to the principles of international law. But the sovereignty of the states does not limit or diminish the sovereignty of the Union. In all international affairs and in domestic affairs properly subject to it, the government of the United States is sovereign. Without its consent, the United States may not be sued in the courts either of the United States or of the several states.

In political theory sovereignty is generally held to be indivisible; careful writers thus distinguish between the indivisible sovereignty of the people and the powers or attributes of sovereignty that are divided between the national and state governments. Hence ALEXANDER HAMILTON, in The Federalist #32, wrote of "the division of the sovereign power." But not all political actors are so careful; it is not uncommon for politicians, judges, or commentators to refer to a "division of sovereignty" in the federal system.

The second meaning of sovereignty as the single, supreme authority within a state, above the law and uncontrollable except by its own will, was introduced into political theory by Jean Bodin in his Six Bookes of the Commonwealth (1576). Its most extreme expression was given by Thomas Hobbes who, in Leviathan (1651), asserted that opposition to tyranny was identical with opposition to sovereignty, or, in other words, that there is no standard except its own will against which the actions of the sovereign can be judged. A democratic, but no less radical, form was given to this concept of sovereignty by Jean-Jacques Rousseau in The Social Contract (1762).

Originally an analytical or explanatory formulation, the notion of a single, indivisible power in the state became a prescriptive article of the Tory political creed. WILLIAM BLACKSTONE identified the King-in-Parliament as the sovereign in England. Governor THOMAS HUTCHINSON, in his famous dispute with the Massachusetts Assembly in 1773, ascribed that same status to Parliament within the British Empire—denying that the provincial legislatures of America had any power or authority except by Parliament's grace. To the Whigs of America the Hobbesian idea of sovereignty, as it was stated by Hutchinson, represented a threat to the liberty they had inherited and the self-government they had established. As an empirical assertion the indivisibility of sovereignty seemed to be disproved by the federal systems of Germany, Switzerland, and the Netherlands, as well as by the British imperial system as it existed in the mid-eighteenth century; and as a prescriptive formula it was all too clearly intended to subvert American home rule.

The social contract theory expressed in the DECLARATION OF INDEPENDENCE and the first state constitutions was a rejection of the Tory doctrine of sovereignty. Neither the government nor any branch or officer of the government justly exercises any power except by the consent of the governed. The doctrine of equality of rights means that no person or body of persons is above the law. The claim of the Declaration, our most fundamental constitutional document, is that there can be no sovereign but the people. This doctrine of POPULAR SOVEREIGNTY was identified by ALEXIS DE TOCQUEVILLE as the defining characteristic of American constitutionalism. Both the national and state governments derive their powers from the people through the Constitution. Each exercises jurisdiction, but neither possesses sovereignty in the absolute, Hobbesian sense.

The Hobbesian notion of sovereignty was translated from a political to a legal concept in the nineteenth century by the British jurist John Austin, who argued that there was no HIGHER LAW against which the decrees of the state could be measured, and so the power of the legislature was absolute. In this revived form it was brought to America as part of the intellectual baggage of legal positivism.

Throughout American history a favorite rhetorical device has been to identify one level of government—usually the state—as sovereign. The success of this device depends upon the ambiguity of the term. That a political body exercises jurisdiction, is supreme within its sphere, and is autonomous in its internal affairs does not mean that it, its government, or its legislature is immune to the sanctions of the law or is free of the constraints of higher law. To speak of the "sovereign states" is not entirely inaccurate if the speaker refers to their autonomy within their own sphere, but it derives its force by evoking the notion of indivisibility and illimitability drawn from the other sense of the term. The rhetoric seemingly denies that the sovereign states are comprised within a sovereign Union.

Within the American regime the ultimate power and authority to alter or abolish the constitutions of government of state and Union resides only and inalienably with the people. If it be necessary or useful to use the term "sovereignty" in the sense of ultimate political power, then there is no sovereign in America but the people.

DENNIS J. MAHONEY

Bibliography

DIAMOND, MARTIN (1970)1981 *The Founding of the Democratic Republic.* Itasca, Ill.: F. E. Peacock.

JAFFA, HARRY V. 1965 *Equality and Liberty: Theory and Practice in American Politics.* New York: Oxford University Press.

LASKI, HAROLD J. 1921 The Foundations of Sovereignty. Pages 1–29 in *The Foundations of Sovereignty and Other Essays.* New Haven, Conn.: Yale University Press.

SPAIGHT, RICHARD DOBBS
(1758–1802)

Richard Dobbs Spaight represented North Carolina at the CONSTITUTIONAL CONVENTION OF 1787 and signed the Constitution. An infrequent speaker,

Spaight favored strong national government. He was a leader of the RATIFICATION movement in North Carolina and was later elected governor and congressman. In a controversy with JAMES IREDELL over BAYARD V. SINGLETON (1787), he denounced JUDICIAL REVIEW as undemocratic.

DENNIS J. MAHONEY

SPECIAL MASTER

A special master is an officer appointed by a court to assist it in a particular proceeding. When the Supreme Court exercises its ORIGINAL JURISDICTION, normally it appoints a special master to take EVIDENCE, make findings of fact, and submit a draft decree. The master's recommendations are advisory; decision rests with the Court. Many of the Supreme Court's special masters are former federal judges.

KENNETH L. KARST

SPEECH OR DEBATE CLAUSE

The Constitution's speech or debate clause provides that "for any Speech or Debate in either House, [members of Congress] shall not be questioned in any other Place." Despite its narrow phrasing, the clause was read in GRAVEL V. UNITED STATES (1972) and other cases as protecting all integral parts "of the deliberative and communicative process by which Members participate in committee and House proceedings with respect to the consideration and passage or rejection of proposed legislation." The clause also protects members' aides in performing tasks that would be protected if performed by members. An act protected by the clause may not be the basis of a civil or criminal judgment against a member of Congress. Under *Doe v. McMillan* (1973), actions by private citizens are barred even though the English PARLIAMENTARY PRIVILEGE from which the clause derives was concerned with executive encroachments on legislative prerogatives.

There are three inroads upon the speech or debate clause's protection. First, criminal prosecutions for corrupt behavior, such as accepting a bribe to influence legislation, may go forward, as in BREWSTER V. UNITED STATES (1972), on the theory that even if legislative acts were performed in exchange for payment, accepting a bribe is not a legislative act. But this area is not without difficulty, as was evidenced by the Court's refusal in *United States v. Johnson* (1966) and *United States v. Helstoski* (1979) to allow the use of legislative acts as evidence in corruption cases.

Second, in *Gravel v. United States* and HUTCHIN-
SON V. PROXMIRE (1979), the Court implicitly held
that communications with a member's constituents
are not legislative functions and expressly held that
members of Congress could be made to answer for
words, written or spoken, or deeds done, outside formal congressional communications channels. Thus
Senator Mike Gravel (or his aide) could be interrogated about republishing the Pentagon Papers with
a private publisher, even though he could not be asked
about reading the papers into the record of a committee hearing (see NEW YORK TIMES CO. V. UNITED
STATES, 1971). And Senator William Proxmire could
be held liable for defamatory communications.

Third, a citizen aggrieved by a subpoena to appear
before, or furnish documentary evidence to, a congressional committee may challenge the subpoena by
refusing to comply and defending any resulting contempt citation on the ground that the subpoena was
unconstitutional or otherwise defective.

The speech or debate clause also plays a central
but somewhat confusing role in delineating state legislators' immunity from suit under SECTION 1983, TITLE
42, UNITED STATES CODE. (See LEGISLATIVE IMMU-
NITY.) In TENNEY V. BRANDHOVE (1951) the Court
relied in part on the speech or debate clause, which
by its terms applies only to members of Congress,
to find state legislators absolutely immune from damages actions under section 1983. In *United States v.
Gillock* (1980), however, the Court held that in a federal criminal prosecution of a state legislator, the
speech or debate privilege does not bar using legislative acts as evidence.

THEODORE EISENBERG

Bibliography

REINSTEIN, ROBERT J. and SILVERGATE, HARVEY A.
    1973   Legislative Privilege and the Separation of Pow-
    ers. *Harvard Law Review* 86:1113–1182.
YANKWICH, LEON R.   1951   The Immunity of Congres-
    sional Speech—Its Origin, Meaning and Scope. *Univer-
    sity of Pennsylvania Law Review* 99:960–977.

SPEEDY TRIAL

The Sixth Amendment provides that "in all criminal
prosecutions, the accused shall enjoy the right to a
speedy . . . trial." The Supreme Court in KLOPFER
V. NORTH CAROLINA (1967) held that the guarantee
is applicable to the states through the DUE PROCESS
clause of the Fourteenth Amendment. The origin of
the right can be traced back at least to MAGNA CARTA
(1215) and perhaps to the Assize of Clarendon (1166).
On different occasions the Supreme Court has described it as "fundamental," "slippery," and "amor-
phous."

Denial of a speedy trial may result in prolonged
incarceration prior to trial and exacerbation of the
anxiety and concern that normally accompany public
accusations of crime. Prolonged incarceration before
trial inevitably involves a disruption of normal life
and imposition of a substantial sanction at a time when
innocence is still presumed. It causes loss of productive labor, normally without opportunity for training or rehabilitation, and frequently interferes with
preparation of a defense.

Pretrial release can ameliorate these conditions,
but a defendant who achieves pretrial release may
be subject to significant restraints on his freedom of
action, his job may be threatened, his resources may
be dissipated, and he and his family may suffer from
understandable concern about his future while his
reputation in the community is impaired. For these
reasons courts have enforced the right in a variety
of contexts. Charges were dismissed in *Smith v. Hooly*
(1969) when a state failed to bring a defendant to
trial on state charges while he was serving a federal
sentence despite demands for trial by the accused,
and in *Klopfer* when a state suspended prosecution
indefinitely although the defendant was not in custody.

Not all defendants want a speedy trial; many want
no trial at all. Delay is a common defense tactic and
in some cases an accused may benefit from prolonged
delay, particularly when pretrial release has been
achieved. In such cases, although only the defendant
has a right to demand a speedy trial, the state may
desire a speedy trial. Prolonged delay contributes to
court backlog and places pressure on prosecutors to
make concessions in PLEA BARGAINING. Defendants
released pending trial may commit additional crimes.
Witnesses may die. Memories fade. The risk of escape
or bail-jumping cannot be ignored.

Not infrequently, delay may serve the interests of
both an accused and a prosecutor for different reasons.
Even if public interest would be better served by a
prompt trial, there may be no effective way of expedit-
ing trial. Nor is the public interest served by dismissing charges if a trial is not held promptly.

One answer to the problem would be a requirement that trial take place within a specified time. The
variety of factual situations confronting prosecutors
and defense counsel has prevented agreement on an
appropriate time interval between charge and trial
that should govern all cases. The absence of such a

litmus test has deterred the Court from proclaiming any single period of delay as the maximum permitted by the constitutional imperative.

There are good reasons for requiring a defendant to make an appropriate demand before he can complain of a denial of his right to speedy trial, but the Court has also declined to place such an obligation upon a defendant as an absolute requirement. Instead, in BARKER V. WINGO (1972), it chose to consider the facts of each case, examining the length of the delay, the prejudice it might cause, the presence or absence of a demand for trial by the defendant, and the justification asserted by the state for its failure to try the accused earlier.

Courts have been remarkably receptive to government justification for significant delays. For example, in *Barker* a delay of five and one half years and sixteen state-requested continuances was permitted because of the need to convict a co-defendant before proceeding against the accused, illness of the chief investigating officer, and acquiescence by the defendant during most of the period. The willingness of a court to accept government assertions of good cause may be influenced by recognition that a dismissal of pending charges is required by the Supreme Court holding in *Strunk v. United States* (1973) if it decides a speedy trial has been denied. Unlike the EXCLUSIONARY RULE or other sanctions for violation of rights, dismissal resulting from a finding of a deprivation of the right to speedy trial may fully immunize a defendant from prosecution.

According to the Court's holding in *United States v. Marion* (1971) only "an accused" may assert a right to speedy trial and a prosecution must have been initiated by arrest and filing of charges before the right attaches. The period between the charge and trial is crucial. Delay between commission of the crime and formal charge is not significant to a claim of a Sixth Amendment violation, although the identity of the accused was or might have been known and PROBABLE CAUSE for arrest or INDICTMENT may have existed. In UNITED STATES V. MacDONALD (1982) the Supreme Court held that prosecutorial delay between dismissal of initial charges by military authority and reassertion of the charges in a civilian forum at a later time was beyond the purview of the Sixth Amendment.

Many of the disadvantages caused an accused by unreasonable delay between charge and trial also ensue when there is an unreasonable delay before charges are brought against him. In *United States v. Lovasco* (1977) the Supreme Court indicated that, in unusual cases, an accused may be able to establish a violation of the due process clause as a result of oppressive pretrial delay where actual prejudice can be demonstrated and inadequate justification exists. Government "bad faith," as when a charge is delayed, or dismissed and subsequently asserted at a later time in order to "forum shop," stockpile charges, or achieve some other tactical advantage, might also constitute a denial of due process. But the degree of protection afforded to an accused against unreasonable delay between commission of an offense and formal charges will depend on the applicable statute of limitations in most cases.

Statutory provisions implement the constitutional provision in many states and in federal prosecution. Encouraged by the *American Bar Association Standards for Criminal Justice, Speedy Trial* (1968), many jurisdictions have set specific legislative time limits within which a defendant must be brought to trial. Perhaps the most important of these statutes is the federal Speedy Trial Act of 1974, defining in detail permissible time periods in different types of cases and setting forth grounds for dismissal of charges with and without prejudice. Assertion of rights under these statutes is more likely to provide effective protection to an accused than reliance on the Constitution except in extraordinary cases.

A. KENNETH PYE

Bibliography

AMSTERDAM, ANTHONY G. 1975 Speedy Criminal Trial: Rights and Remedies. *Stanford Law Review* 27:525–543.
GODBOLD, JOHN C. 1972 Speedy Trial—Major Surgery for a National Ill. *Alabama Law Review* 24:265–294.
LaFAVE, WAYNE R. and ISRAEL, JEDD H. 1985 *Criminal Procedure.* St. Paul, Minn.: West Publishing Co.
WHITEBREAD, CHARLES H. 1980 *Criminal Procedure.* Mineola, N.Y.: Foundation Press.

SPEISER v. RANDALL
357 U.S. 513 (1958)

The Supreme Court invalidated on DUE PROCESS grounds a noncommunist oath required for a California property tax exemption. *Speiser* is a leading early case in the series breaking down the RIGHT–PRIVILEGE DISTINCTION and establishing that due process must be strictly observed where FUNDAMENTAL RIGHTS are infringed.

MARTIN SHAPIRO

SPENDING POWER

See: Taxing and Spending Power

SPINELLI v. UNITED STATES
393 U.S. 410 (1969)

In *Spinelli* the Supreme Court explicated and expanded the PROBABLE CAUSE standards for SEARCH WARRANTS set forth in AGUILAR V. TEXAS (1964).

Spinelli was convicted under federal law of crossing state lines to conduct gambling operations. A detailed FBI affidavit, on which the search warrant was based, stated in part that Spinelli was "known" to law enforcement officers as a bookmaker, and that a confidential informant had established that Spinelli was operating as a bookmaker.

The Court ruled that the INFORMANT's testimony could not count toward the establishment of probable cause, because the affidavit failed to establish the informant's reliability or to clarify his relationship to Spinelli. The Court rejected the government's claim that the tip gave "suspicious color" to Spinelli's activities, and that, conversely, the surveillance helped corroborate the informant's tip (he had, for example, provided the correct numbers of two telephones listed in someone else's name in an apartment frequented by Spinelli). Such a "totality of the circumstances" approach, said the Court, painted "with too broad a brush." The *Spinelli* approach was abandoned in ILLINOIS V. GATES (1983).

JACOB W. LANDYNSKI

SPOT RESOLUTIONS
(1847)

Congressman ABRAHAM LINCOLN (Whig, Illinois) introduced a series of eight resolutions in the House of Representatives on December 22, 1847. Intended to show the illegality of the Mexican War, the resolutions were in the form of interrogatories, challenging President JAMES K. POLK to name the exact spot upon which American blood was first shed in the war and to concede that that spot was on soil rightfully claimed by Mexico. The contention of the northern Whigs, including Lincoln, was that Polk had used his power as COMMANDER-IN-CHIEF of the Army to provoke the Mexicans into war in order to seize new territory into which SLAVERY could be extended.

In a brilliant speech in January 1848 Lincoln explained that accurate answers to his interrogatories would demonstrate that "the War with Mexico was unnecessarily and unconstitutionally commenced by the President." He claimed that the President had usurped Congress's constitutional power to declare

war and disputed Polk's claim that Congress, by appropriating money for the conduct of the war, had sanctioned its commencement.

The Spot Resolutions, like the WILMOT PROVISO, were meant to embarrass the administration by linking the Mexican War with the slave power in the public mind. The House tabled Lincoln's resolutions but passed another resolution condemning Polk's conduct.

DENNIS J. MAHONEY

Bibliography
JOSEPHY, ALVIN M., JR. 1975 *History of the Congress of the United States.* Pages 188–193. New York: American Heritage Publishing Co.

SPRINGER v. UNITED STATES
102 U.S. 586 (1881)

Springer contested the constitutionality of a federal income tax statute on ground that it was a DIRECT TAX not apportioned on the basis of state population. The Supreme Court unanimously upheld the tax on ground that the only direct taxes are taxes on land and CAPITATION TAXES.

LEONARD W. LEVY

(SEE ALSO: *Pollock v. Farmers' Loan and Trust Co.*)

STAFFORD v. WALLACE
358 U.S. 495 (1922)

Seventeen years after SWIFT & COMPANY V. UNITED STATES (1905), the Supreme Court again approved the extension of federal authority to local activities. A nationalistic exposition of the COMMERCE CLAUSE ran through the opinion in which the Court not only reaffirmed but also extended the STREAM OF COMMERCE DOCTRINE. Commission men, who sold animals on consignment, sued to enjoin enforcement of the PACKERS & STOCKYARDS ACT. They asserted that because they provided only "personal services" and were not engaged in INTERSTATE COMMERCE, they were not subject to the act. For a 7–1 Court, Chief Justice WILLIAM HOWARD TAFT followed Justice OLIVER WENDELL HOLMES's opinion in *Swift* and sustained the act. Congress had acted reasonably in securing an "unburdened flow" of interstate commerce. Moreover, the stockyards were "not a place of rest or final destination . . . but a throat through which the current [of commerce] flows." Because the commission men were essential to maintaining this flow, their activities were properly part of interstate commerce and subject to the act. Justice JAMES C. MC-REYNOLDS dissented without opinion. By reviving and reapplying the stream of commerce doctrine, the Court built a foundation on which the New Deal would later support its ECONOMIC REGULATIONS.

DAVID GORDON

STAMP ACT CONGRESS, RESOLUTIONS OF
(October 19, 1765)

These resolutions, adopted by the delegates of nine American colonies meeting in an intercolonial congress, expressed the basis of the American constitutional position in the quarrel with Great Britain leading to the American Revolution. The mother country, financially exhausted by a great war from which the American colonies stood to gain the most, decided to retain an army in America and to require the colonists to pay a small fraction of the cost of their defense. Parliamentary legislation aimed at raising a revenue in America was, however, unprecedented before the Sugar Act of 1764. That act provoked the first constitutional protests from the colonies. In form the 1764 legislation had regulated their ocean trade, thus imposing an "external" tax. The Stamp Act of 1765 imposed "internal" taxes on every sort of legal document and most business documents; on college diplomas, liquor licences, and appointments to offices; and on playing cards, newspapers, advertisements, almanacs, books, and pamphlets. Admiralty courts, which operated without juries and used inquisitional procedures, had JURISDICTION over offenses against the act. American opposition was so vehement and widespread that the act proved to be unenforceable.

The Stamp Act Congress addressed itself to two constitutional issues raised by the act of Parliament. After asserting that the colonists were entitled to all the rights and liberties of Englishmen, the congress resolved that Parliament, a body in which the colonists were not represented and which could not represent them, had no constitutional authority to tax them. Several resolutions condemned TAXATION WITHOUT REPRESENTATION and endorsed the principle that only their own assemblies could constitutionally tax the American colonists. The congress also endorsed the right to TRIAL BY JURY and condemned the unprecedented extension of admiralty court jurisdiction as subversive of colonial liberties.

The Stamp Act was in force for only four months before Parliament repealed it, not because of the American constitutional protests but because of the protests of British merchants who suffered from a boycott of their goods by American importers. To save face, Parliament accompanied its repealer with the Declaratory Act of 1766, which insisted that Great Britain had full power to make laws for America "in all cases whatsoever." The American position, that "no taxes . . . can be constitutionally imposed . . . but by their respective legislatures," was founded on a different view of the British constitution, even a different understanding of the meaning of a CONSTITUTION and of the word "unconstitutional." A local court in Virginia gratuitously condemned the Stamp Act as unconstitutional and therefore not binding.

LEONARD W. LEVY

Bibliography

MORGAN, EDMUND S. and HELEN M. 1953 *The Stamp Act Congress.* Chapel Hill: University of North Carolina Press.

STANBERY, HENRY S.
(1803–1881)

An Ohio lawyer and United States attorney general (1866–1868), Henry Stanbery opposed congressional reconstruction and prepared many of President ANDREW JOHNSON's veto messages. Nevertheless, in MISSISSIPPI V. JOHNSON (1867) Stanbery successfully defended executive enforcement of congressional statutes by arguing that the SEPARATION OF POWERS barred the Supreme Court from issuing an INJUNCTION against the President. Similarly, in *Georgia v. Stanton* (1868) he successfully argued that the case involved POLITICAL QUESTIONS beyond the Court's JURISDICTION. In 1868 Stanbery resigned his office to defend Johnson at his IMPEACHMENT trial. Stanbery's insistence on DUE PROCESS slowed the trial and helped achieve Johnson's acquittal.

PAUL FINKELMAN

Bibliography

MENEELY, A. HOWARD 1935 Henry Stanbery. In *Dictionary of American Biography*, Vol. 27:498–499. New York: Scribner's.

STANDARD OF REVIEW

Some constitutional limitations on government are readily susceptible to "interpretation," in the sense of definition and categorization. Once a court categorizes a law as a BILL OF ATTAINDER, for example, it holds the law invalid. Other limitations, however, are expressed in terms that make this sort of interpretation awkward: the FREEDOM OF SPEECH, the EQUAL PROTECTION OF THE LAWS, DUE PROCESS OF LAW. The judicial task in enforcing these open-ended limitations implies an inquiry into the justifications asserted by government for restricting liberty or denying equal treatment. The term "standards of review," in common use since the late 1960s, denotes various degrees of judicial deference to legislative judgments concerning these justifications.

The idea that there might be more than one standard of review was explicitly suggested in Justice HARLAN FISKE STONE's opinion for the Supreme Court in UNITED STATES v. CAROLENE PRODUCTS CO. (1938). Confirming a retreat from the JUDICIAL ACTIVISM that had invalidated a significant number of ECONOMIC REGULATIONS over the preceding four decades, Stone concluded that such a law would be valid if the legislature's purpose were legitimate and if the law could rationally be seen as related to that purpose. Stone added, however, that this permissive RATIONAL BASIS standard might not be appropriate for reviewing laws challenged under certain specific prohibitions of the BILL OF RIGHTS, or laws restricting the political process, or laws directed at DISCRETE AND INSULAR MINORITIES. Such cases, Stone suggested, might call for a diminished presumption of constitutionality, a "more exacting judicial scrutiny."

The WARREN COURT embraced this double standard in several doctrinal areas, most notably in equal protection cases. The permissive rational basis standard continued to govern review of economic regulations, but STRICT SCRUTINY was given to laws discriminating against the exercise of FUNDAMENTAL INTERESTS such as voting or marriage and to laws employing SUSPECT CLASSIFICATIONS such as race. The strict scrutiny standard amounts to an inversion of the presumption of constitutionality: the state must justify its imposition of a racial inequality, for example, by showing that the law is necessary to achieve a COMPELLING STATE INTEREST. Today active judicial review of both the importance of legislative purposes and the necessity of legislative means is employed not only in some types of equal protection cases but also in fields such as the freedom of speech and RELIGIOUS LIBERTY. It has even attended the rebirth of SUBSTANTIVE DUE PROCESS.

Inevitably, however, cracks appeared in this two-tier system of standards of review. The Court used the language of "rational basis" to strike down some laws, and in cases involving SEX DISCRIMINATION it explicitly adopted an intermediate standard for reviewing both legislative ends and means: discrimination based on sex is invalid unless it serves an "important" governmental purpose and is "substantially related" to that purpose. A similar intermediate standard is now part of the required analysis of governmental regulations of COMMERCIAL SPEECH. In practical effect, the Court has created a "sliding scale" of review, varying the intensity of judicial scrutiny of legislation in proportion to the importance of the interests invaded and the likelihood of legislative prejudice against the persons disadvantaged. The process, in other words, is interest-balancing, pure and simple. Justice WILLIAM H. REHNQUIST, writing for the Court in ROSTKER V. GOLDBERG (1981), remarked accurately that the Court's various levels of scrutiny "may all too readily become facile abstractions used to justify a result"—a proposition well illustrated by the *Rostker* opinion itself.

KENNETH L. KARST

Bibliography

GUNTHER, GERALD 1972 The Supreme Court, 1971 Term—Foreword: In Search of Evolving Doctrine on a Changing Court: A Model for a Newer Equal Protection. *Harvard Law Review* 86:1–48.

STANDARD OIL COMPANY v. UNITED STATES
221 U.S. 1 (1911)
UNITED STATES v. AMERICAN TOBACCO COMPANY
211 U.S. 106 (1911)

John D. Rockefeller, owner of the nation's first, largest, and richest trust and controller of the nation's oil business, scorned his competitors and contemned the law. His disregard for the SHERMAN ANTITRUST ACT helped earn him, in 1909, a dissolution order which the trust appealed to the Supreme Court. Rockefeller thereby provided Chief Justice EDWARD D. WHITE with the occasion to celebrate the conversion of a majority of the Court to his viewpoint, enabling him to write the RULE OF REASON into antitrust law. After nearly fifteen years of effort, White had managed to enlarge judicial discretion in antitrust cases, even though the oil trust did not urge the doctrine upon the Court; indeed, it was unnecessary to the case's disposition.

Chief Justice White, leading an 8–1 Court, ruled that only an "unreasonable" contract or combination in restraint of trade would violate the law. White had effectively amended the law to insert his test: section 1 of the Sherman Act would henceforth be interpreted as if it said, "Every unreasonable contract, combination . . . or conspiracy in restraint of trade . . . is hereby declared to be illegal."

Standard Oil, however, lost the case. The record, said White, showed clearly and convincingly that this trust was unreasonable. Systematic attempts to exclude or crush rivals and the trust's astounding success demonstrated the violation beyond any doubt.

Justice JOHN MARSHALL HARLAN concurred in the result but dissented from the Court's announcement of the rule of reason. Harlan observed that Congress had refused to amend the act to incorporate the rule of reason, and he lashed out at the majority's "judicial legislation," predicting that the new policy would produce chaos. His call echoed in Congress where Democratic pressure grew to write the rule of reason out of the Sherman Act. That pressure would eventually find partial release in supplementary antitrust legislation, passage of the CLAYTON ACT in 1914. The rule of reason prevailed, however, although the Court applied a double standard. When massive business combinations such as United States Steel Corporation, United Shoe Machinery Company, and International Harvester came before the Court, they were found to have acted reasonably, restraints of trade notwithstanding. In antitrust action against labor unions, however, the Court ignored that rule.

In the companion *American Tobacco* case, Chief Justice White attempted to mitigate a too vigorous federal antitrust policy by ordering reorganization, not dissolution, of the Tobacco Trust. He thereby heartened business interests by showing solicitousness for property rights and a stable economy.

DAVID GORDON

Bibliography
BRINGHURST, BRUCE 1979 *Antitrust and the Oil Monopoly: The Standard Oil Cases, 1890–1914.* Westport, Conn.: Greenwood Press.

STANDING

In the United States, unelected, life-tenured federal judges may decide legal issues only when they are asked to do so by appropriate litigants. Such litigants are said to have standing to raise certain legal claims, including constitutional claims, in the federal courts.

A litigant's standing depends on two sets of criteria, one constitutionally required and one not, each ostensibly having three parts. The constitutional criteria derive from Article III's job description for federal judges, which permits them to declare law only when such a declaration is necessary to decide CASES AND CONTROVERSIES. These criteria center on the notion of an injured person's asking a court for a remedy against the responsible party, and each criterion corresponds to one of the three participants—to the plaintiff, the defendant, and the court, respectively. The plaintiff must assert that he suffered a cognizable personal injury; that the defendant's conduct caused the injury; and that the court's judgment is substantially likely to relieve it. The three nonconstitutional criteria for standing are "prudential" rules, self-imposed by the courts for their own governance, rules which Congress can eliminate if it chooses. These criteria, too, serve to diminish the frequency of substantive pronouncements by federal judges, but they focus on the legal basis of the suit, not on the plaintiff's actual injury. The first nonconstitutional criterion concerns representation: to secure judicial relief, injured litigants normally must assert that the injurious conduct violated their own legal rights, not the rights of third parties. The second assumes that government violations of everyone's undifferentiated legal rights are best left to political, not judicial, response: no one has standing if his or her legal position asserts "only the generalized interest of all citizens in constitutional governance." The third "prudential" criterion for standing seeks assurance that the law invoked plausibly protects the legal interest allegedly invaded: whatever interest is asserted must be "arguably within the zone of interests to be protected or regulated by the statute or constitutional guarantee in question."

Standing issues rarely surface in traditional suits, but federal courts applying these guidelines frequently deny standing to "public interest" plaintiffs anxious to challenge the legality of government behavior. The aim is not only to prevent federal judges from proclaiming law unless such declarations are needed to resolve concrete disputes, but also to promote proper conditions for intelligent adjudication (including adversary presentation of the facts and legal arguments) and to foster adequate representation of affected interests. When litigants ask federal courts to restrict the constitutional authority of politically accountable public officials, moreover, apprehension about unwise or excessive judicial intervention heightens, and the standing limitations may be applied with particular force.

Collectively, the Supreme Court's standing criteria often overlap; they are applied flexibly—sometimes inconsistently—to give the Supreme Court considerable discretion to exercise or withhold its power to declare law. The way that discretion is exercised reflects any particular Court's ideology of JUDICIAL ACTIVISM AND RESTRAINT and the substantive, constitutional rights it is either eager or reluctant to enforce.

The refinements of standing doctrine illustrate this flexibility and discretion. The core requirement of cognizable personal injury, for example, demands that the plaintiff have suffered injury to an interest deemed deserving of judicial protection. Over time, the Court has expanded the category of judicially acknowledged injuries beyond economic harm to include reputational, environmental, aesthetic, associational, informational, organizational, and voter harms, among others. Because of its vision of constrained judicial power in a representative democracy, however, the Court steadfastly forbids TAXPAYERS' SUITS and citizens' suits asserting purely ideological harm, particularly the harms of frustration, distress, or apprehension born of unlawful government conduct. Resting on lack of cognizable injury, the ban on citizen standing thus appears constitutionally compelled, although it effectively duplicates the nonconstitutional barrier to asserting generalized grievances, which appears to rest on the absence of a cognizable legal interest. Less diffuse, but in ALLEN V. WRIGHT (1984) nonetheless held an insufficiently personal injury, is the feeling of stigma arising from discrimination directed, not personally, but against other members of the plaintiff's race. If the type of injury is judicially approved and the plaintiff personally suffered it, however, the fact that many others have suffered it will not negate standing. For example, in UNITED STATES V. SCRAP (1973) a student activist group was deemed to have standing based on widespread environmental injury.

Flexibility also characterizes the Court's degree of insistence on the remaining constitutional criteria. The closeness of the causal link between defendant's conduct and plaintiff's injury has varied from *United States v. SCRAP*, which accepted a loose connection between the Interstate Commerce Commission's approval of freight rate increases for scrap materials and increased trash problems in national parks, to *Allen v. Wright* (1984), which found too attenuated a seemingly closer link between the Internal Revenue Service's allegedly inadequate enforcement of the law requiring denial of tax exemptions to racially discriminatory private schools and "white flight" in public school districts undergoing DESEGREGATION. Similarly, insistence that judicial relief be substantially likely to redress plaintiff's injury has varied from *Linda R. S. v. Richard D.* (1973), where mothers of illegitimate children seeking to force prosecution of the fathers for nonsupport were denied standing because a court order supposedly would result only in

jailing the fathers, not in increased support, to *Duke Power Co. v. Carolina Environmental Study Group* (1978), where neighbors of nuclear power plants, seeking relief from present injury caused by normal plant operation, were granted standing to contest (unsuccessfully) the constitutional validity of a federal statute limiting recovery of DAMAGES for potential nuclear disasters, despite considerable uncertainty that a legal victory for the plaintiffs would stop the plants' normal operations.

Of the nonconstitutional criteria, only the usual prohibition against representing third-party rights needs elaboration, primarily because of its different forms and its significant exceptions. When a personally injured plaintiff seeks to argue that the injurious conduct violated the legal rights of others, the prohibition, beyond serving the usual objectives of standing, serves also to protect nonlitigants who may not wish to assert their own rights or would do so differently (and perhaps more effectively) if they became litigants. Major exceptions to that prohibition respond to this policy by allowing representation, even of constitutional rights, when the Court concludes that the absent third parties would benefit rather than suffer from a substantive decision. One important example of this exception is the case in which third parties would have difficulty asserting their own rights, as in NAACP V. ALABAMA (1958), where the CIVIL RIGHTS group was permitted to assert its members' right to remain anonymous. Another example is the case in which the disputed conduct affects special plaintiff–third party relationships in ways suggesting that the plaintiff and third-party interests coincide. Under this exception doctors can represent patient rights to abortion, private schools can represent parent rights to choose private education, and sellers can represent the rights of young consumers to buy beer or contraceptives.

The Court generally denies standing when persons constitutionally subject to regulation urge that the regulation would be unconstitutional in application to others. This rule preserves legislative policy in cases where the law is applied constitutionally. Again, however, there is an exception, invoked most often in FIRST AMENDMENT challenges of VAGUENESS and OVERBREADTH, when the law's very existence would significantly inhibit others from exercising important constitutional rights and thus deter them from mounting their own challenge.

A final example is the case in which uninjured representatives seek to champion the legal rights of injured persons they represent outside of litigation. Thus, associations, not injured themselves, may sue on behalf of their members' injuries, provided that the members would have standing, the associations seek to protect interests germane to their purposes, and the claims and requested relief do not require individual member participation. And a state, which normally lacks standing as *parens patriae* to represent the claims of individual citizens, or even of all its citizens in opposition to the federal government, may represent its citizens when the injury alleged substantially affects the state's general population, especially if suit by individual citizens seems unlikely.

Like other JUSTICIABILITY doctrines, standing rules often thwart attempts to induce federal courts to make or reform constitutional or other law. How often the rules have that result will depend not only on the articulated criteria of standing but also on the Supreme Court's receptivity to the substance of the underlying claims and its judgment of the desirability and likelihood of political solutions.

JONATHAN D. VARAT

Bibliography

NICHOL, GENE R., JR. 1984 Rethinking Standing. *California Law Review* 72:68–102.
SCOTT, KENNETH E. 1973 Standing in the Supreme Court: A Functional Analysis. *Harvard Law Review* 86:645–692.
VINING, JOSEPH 1978 *Legal Identity: The Coming of Age of Public Law.* New Haven, Conn.: Yale University Press.

STANLEY v. GEORGIA
394 U.S. 557 (1969)

Authorized by a SEARCH WARRANT, federal and state agents entered and searched Stanley's home for evidence of bookmaking activities. Instead they found film, which was used to convict him for possession of obscene material. The Supreme Court reversed, holding that mere possession of obscenity in one's home cannot constitutionally be made a crime.

Prior OBSCENITY decisions had recognized a legitimate state interest in regulating public dissemination of obscene materials. In *Stanley*, however, the Court recognized two fundamental constitutional rights that outweighed the state interest in regulating obscenity in a citizen's home: the FIRST AMENDMENT right to receive information and ideas, regardless of their social worth, and the constitutional right to be free from unwanted government intrusion into one's privacy.

As justification for interfering with these important individual rights, the state asserted the right to protect individuals from obscenity's effects. The Court rejected that argument, viewing such "protection" as an attempt to "control . . . a person's thoughts," a

goal "wholly inconsistent with the philosophy of the First Amendment."

Justices POTTER J. STEWART, WILLIAM J. BRENNAN, and BYRON R. WHITE concurred in the result, on the ground that the SEARCH AND SEIZURE were outside the lawful scope of the officers' warrant, and thus violated Stanley's FOURTH AMENDMENT rights.

KIM MCLANE WARDLAW

STANTON, EDWIN M.
(1814–1869)

A prominent antebellum attorney, Edwin McMasters Stanton was an active member of the Supreme Court bar and was the chief government investigator and counsel in the California land claims cases. In 1859 he successfully defended Congressman Daniel Sickles in a murder trial with the then novel defense of temporary insanity.

In 1860 Stanton became JAMES BUCHANAN's lame duck ATTORNEY GENERAL. An ardent Unionist, Stanton urged support for the garrison at Fort Sumter and the arrest for TREASON of the South Carolina commissioners. During the interregnum Stanton secretly met with Republican senators informing them of the administration's complicity with secessionists. He also worked secretly with General Winfield Scott to move troops to protect Washington while preventing the shipment of arms to the South.

As secretary of war (1862–1868) Stanton vastly reduced corruption and political influence on promotions, while building a highly efficient military. Stanton was an early advocate of emancipation and the use of black troops. Zealous in supporting the Union, Stanton used the War Department to arrest civilians suspected of treason, disloyalty, or disrupting recruitment and rigorously enforced internal security. During the 1863 and 1864 elections Stanton furloughed troops so they could return home to vote, used the army to intimidate opponents, and allowed officers to campaign.

After ABRAHAM LINCOLN's assassination Stanton was ruthless in finding and prosecuting anyone connected with John Wilkes Booth's plot. Despite President ANDREW JOHNSON's opposition, Stanton supported the CIVIL RIGHTS ACT OF 1866 and the FREEDMAN'S BUREAU, while working closely with Congress to support MILITARY RECONSTRUCTION. Stanton's backing of generals sympathetic to congressional goals prevented Johnson from implementing his reconstruction program. Fear that Johnson would fire Stanton led to the TENURE OF OFFICE ACT and then to IMPEACHMENT proceedings when Johnson tried to replace Stanton. Stanton aided the impeachment managers by giving them war department documents and information, lobbying wavering senators, and writing "anonymous" editorials denouncing Johnson. After Johnson's acquittal Stanton resigned. In 1869 President ULYSSES S. GRANT nominated Stanton to the Supreme Court, but he died before confirmation.

PAUL FINKELMAN

Bibliography

THOMAS, BENJAMIN P. and HYMAN, HAROLD M. 1962 *Stanton: The Life and Times of Lincoln's Secretary of War.* New York: Knopf.

STARE DECISIS

(Latin: "to stand by decided [cases].") The DOCTRINE of *stare decisis,* one of the key elements of Anglo-American COMMON LAW, embodies the principle that PRECEDENTS are to be followed in the adjudication of cases. The substance of the law is revealed through the decisions of courts in cases between individuals or between an individual and the government, and adherence to precedent transforms the decisions in those cases into a settled body of public law. Once an issue of law has been resolved in a case by a court of competent JURISDICTION, the HOLDING in the case is determinative of the issue for that court and subordinate courts; and it offers guidance, as well, to courts of coordinate jurisdiction. Courts proceed, as a general rule, by following and applying precedents or else by distinguishing them (that is, by showing how the facts of the instant case render the precedent inapposite). Most frequently a court faces the question of which of two or more lines of precedent to follow. The doctrine of *stare decisis* lends stability and predictability to the legal order, but it is not absolute: courts may dispose of precedents that are outdated, or that have undesirable consequences, by OVERRULING them. The federal courts, and especially the Supreme Court, have tended in recent years to diminish the force of *stare decisis* in constitutional cases.

DENNIS J. MAHONEY

STATE

The DECLARATION OF INDEPENDENCE declares that the "united colonies" are, as they ought to be, "free and independent states." The term "states" was cho-

sen to indicate their status as autonomous political communities. The state was the result of the SOCIAL COMPACT, binding man to man and subjecting all to rule by some part of the community. The term also carried a connotation, already obsolescent in England, of a republican form of government; the seventeenth-century British political writers with whose works the Americans were familiar had generally contrasted "state" with "monarchy" or "principality."

But the Declaration of Independence was, after all, the unanimous declaration of the *united* states. Although the Declaration proclaims that the states are "free and independent," they were not thereby made independent of one another. By the Declaration, the one American people assumes among the powers of the earth the separate and equal station to which it is entitled by natural and divine law. Thus is the American people declared to possess SOVEREIGNTY, and not the several states, although in the common usage, of the eighteenth as well as of the twentieth century, the term "state" refers to a sovereign entity.

The central paradox of American politics has always been, from the time of the Declaration and of the Constitution, the existence of ineradicable states within an indissoluble Union. The sovereignty of the people, from whom both the national and the state governments derive their just powers, is the basis for the distinctively American form of FEDERALISM. Neither is the central government the creature of the states nor do the states exist at the mercy of the central government, but both exercise those limited and delegate powers that are assigned them by the sovereign people.

Each of the original thirteen states had been founded and administered as a British colony prior to 1776. They had, therefore, established forms of government under their COLONIAL CHARTERS. During the Revolution, most of them adopted CONSTITUTIONS providing for government of the same persons and territory as the colonies had comprised. The fourteenth and fifteenth states, Vermont and Kentucky, had experienced provisional self-government before they were admitted to the Union. Before the ANNEXATION OF TEXAS, that state had revolted against Mexico and governed itself as an independent republic. California's brief existence as the "Bear Flag Republic" (1846) scarcely qualifies as independence or self-government; but, when the controversy over slavery prevented Congress from organizing the lands won in the Mexican War, California proceeded to adopt a constitution (1849) and to govern its own affairs until its admission to the Union (1850). Hawaii was an independent kingdom for centuries before American immigrants revolted against the native monarchy and engineered the annexation of those islands by the United States.

All of the rest of the states—thirty-two to date—have been formed out of the national dominion of the United States and have been admitted to the Union as states following a probationary period as TERRITORIES. The process by which the national dominion was to be settled and transformed into states was devised by THOMAS JEFFERSON and adopted by the CONTINENTAL CONGRESS as the ORDINANCE OF 1784, although that ordinance was never actually enforced. Essentially the same scheme was enacted in the NORTHWEST ORDINANCE (1787), which was the model for all subsequent treatment of the territories of the United States. At the CONSTITUTIONAL CONVENTION OF 1787 the delegates rejected GOUVERNEUR MORRIS's proposal that states formed from the western territories should have a status inferior to the original states, and they provided instead that new states should be admitted to the Union on terms of full equality with the existing states.

Under the ARTICLES OF CONFEDERATION the national government was entirely the creature of the state governments. The confederation derived its formal existence from a compact among the states, and the members of Congress were chosen by the state legislatures. Most of the delegates to the Constitutional Convention were convinced of the necessity of creating a national government directly responsible to the people of the nation. JAMES MADISON, for one, arrived in Philadelphia prepared to argue for a pure separation of state from national government, according to which the two tiers of government would be separately elected and separately responsible to the people in their respective spheres. But the Convention chose instead to give the institutions of the states a share in the government of the nation, and to provide, in the national constitution, for certain guarantees to the people of the states, including guarantees against their state governments.

In the Constitution, representatives in Congress are allocated to the states on the basis of population, and the state governments are left free to apportion them among districts and to provide for their election. Each state is allotted two senators, and until adoption of the SEVENTEENTH AMENDMENT (1913) the senators were chosen by the state legislatures. The President and vice-president are chosen by an ELECTORAL COLLEGE whose members are apportioned to, chosen by, and convened in the several states. The Constitution became effective only upon ratification by conven-

tions in the several states, and amendment of the Constitution is impossible without the concurrence of the legislatures of (or conventions in) three-fourths of the states. And the TENTH AMENDMENT, adopted in 1791 as part of the BILL OF RIGHTS, reserves all governmental power not delegated to the national government by the Constitution to the states or the people.

On the other hand, Article I, section 10, prohibits the states from entering into treaties or alliances or granting LETTERS OF MARQUE AND REPRISAL; coining money, issuing BILLS OF CREDIT to circulate as currency, or making anything but gold or silver legal tender for payment of obligations; enacting EX POST FACTO laws or BILLS OF ATTAINDER, legislating to impair the OBLIGATION OF CONTRACTS, or conferring TITLES OF NOBILITY. The exercise of certain other powers by the states is made contingent upon the consent of Congress: taxation of imports or exports, maintenance of armies or navies, entering into INTERSTATE COMPACTS, and making war (unless actually invaded or imminently threatened by a foreign power). Moreover, the SUPREMACY CLAUSE subordinates the enactments of the states to the Constitution and to laws and treaties of the national government, and all state officers and judges are bound by oath to follow these, as the supreme law, whenever there is a conflict with state enactments or decisions.

But a proposal that the national Congress should have the power to review and "negative" state legislation failed to win a majority at the Constitutional Convention; and more drastic proposals that the states be abolished, or realigned, or reduced to the status of provinces or administrative districts were rejected almost without discussion. The Convention did not adopt the VIRGINIA PLAN's wording, granting the national Congress the power to legislate in any field wherein the states were "incompetent," which would effectively have made Congress the only judge of the limits of its own power, and instead listed the fields in which national legislation was, or might be, required.

The sphere of state authority that the Constitution left untouched was vast, and included almost every governmental function with which most citizens were likely to come into direct contact. The laws of property, of inheritance, of marriage, of contract, of debt, of liability for civil wrongs, of employer–employee (or master–servant) relations, of commercial transactions, of banking, of business incorporation, and of common police were left to the states. The law of crimes and punishments, except for crimes against the national government, on the high seas, or in the armed forces, was left to the states. The nineteenth-century French political scientist ALEXIS DE TOCQUE-VILLE referred to these as functions of "administration," distinguishing them from such high political functions as national defense, foreign affairs, and acquisition and settlement of territory. But, precisely because the administrative functions of government are those with which the people are in daily contact, Tocqueville concluded that the affections and loyalties of the people would always be directed first to the states in preference to the national government.

The primary loyalty to the state, rather than to the Union, was one of the chief problems of American politics at least until the end of the Civil War. When regional interests, particularly regional economic interests, ran contrary to the course of national legislation, politicians at the state level frequently attempted to rally the people to the cause of disunion. There were many delegates to the HARTFORD CONVENTION (1814) who advocated the SECESSION of the New England states to protest the War of 1812, and the TARIFF ACT OF 1828 led to South Carolina's attempt at NULLIFICATION. Politicians attempted to justify such acts by resort to THEORIES OF THE UNION that regarded the national government as the product of a compact among the states, the breach of which freed the offended states from their obligations.

The great tragedy of American constitutional history was the coincidence of state loyalties with attachment to the peculiar institution of human slavery. In 1861 eleven states attempted to secede from the federal union and to form a confederacy in which the existence of both slavery and state sovereignty would be permanently guaranteed. Some adherents of ABOLITIONIST CONSTITUTIONAL THOUGHT were content to permit the secession on the ground that the Union was better off without the slave states. Some national politicians, including President JAMES BUCHANAN, were willing to tolerate the secession on the ground that the national government lacked constitutional authority to coerce the states.

President ABRAHAM LINCOLN rejected Buchanan's position, arguing that the federal Union was the permanent creation of the whole American people and dating the creation of the Union from the Declaration of Independence. In this way, Lincoln tied the preservation of the Union to the antislavery cause, making the Civil War not a mere war between the states but a struggle to complete the constitution of the Republic upon the foundation of natural rights and the consent of all the governed, in accordance with the principles of the Declaration. The completion of the Constitution required the addition of the THIRTEENTH AMENDMENT (abolishing slavery), the FOURTEENTH AMENDMENT (guaranteeing individual rights against state interference), and the FIFTEENTH AMENDMENT (prohibiting RACIAL DISCRIMINATION as a limitation on VOTING RIGHTS). The settlement of the crisis that had caused the Civil War necessitated these additional constitutional guarantees to the people against abuses by the state governments.

However, neither the Civil War nor the constitutional amendments adopted in its aftermath transferred significant additional power to the national government. Although there were new constitutional restrictions on the states, and although the national Congress was given power to enforce those restrictions, the distribution of substantive powers within the federal system remained essentially unaltered. What did change was the attitude of the people toward the two levels of government: CITIZENSHIP of the United States became, in most of the country, the primary source of political allegiance, and state citizenship became secondary. Constitutional expression of this change was embodied in the SIXTEENTH AMENDMENT (authorizing an income tax as an independent source of revenue for the national government) and the SEVENTEENTH AMENDMENT (providing for DIRECT ELECTION of United States senators).

In PROGRESSIVE CONSTITUTIONAL THOUGHT it was fashionable to speak of the states as the "laboratories" of the federal system, where experiments in political reform could be carried out. Like the abolition of slavery, all of the important reform measures of the Progressive era began at the state level and were enacted at the national level, if at all, only after successful adoption in the states. Such measures included women's suffrage, direct elections, and the PROHIBITION of alcoholic beverages.

In the twentieth century the states suffered a radical change of relative status. That change had two aspects: the expansion of national power into fields previously regarded as belonging to the states, and the subordination of the states in the administration of national programs. The change of relative status was probably an inevitable consequence of the shift of loyalties as well as of the increased mobility, communication, and interaction attendant upon industrialization.

World War I and the Great Depression of the 1930s were great national emergencies, and the national government strained the limits of its power to effect national measures in response. Ultimately, the COMMERCE CLAUSE became the source of constitutional authority for comprehensive national regulation of the economy, and ECONOMIC REGULATION based on that authority received the approbation of the Supreme Court beginning with the WAGNER ACT CASES (1937). The last vestiges of limitation inherent in the concept of INTERSTATE COMMERCE were swept away in WICKARD V. FILBURN (1941). By the middle of the twentieth century it was no longer true that state law alone governed most ordinary economic relationships. In the 1960s the commerce power became the basis for national CIVIL RIGHTS legislation and had already become the basis for a NATIONAL POLICE POWER generally.

If there is any type of activity that could with certainty be distinguished from "commerce," that would be the activity of governing. Whether on the basis of that distinction, or on some more general basis in the idea of federalism, the state and local governments were long excluded from national regulation under the commerce clause. NATIONAL LEAGUE OF CITIES V. USERY (1976) made that exclusion a matter of constitutional law, at least insofar as the activity that the national government sought to regulate was traditionally or inherently a governmental function and not just a publicly operated business. However, over vigorous dissent, a narrow majority overruled *Usery* in GARCIA V. SAN ANTONIO METROPOLITAN TRANSIT AUTHORITY (1984), and the exclusion was thereby judicially abolished.

The TAXING AND SPENDING POWER and the GENERAL WELFARE CLAUSE form the constitutional basis for coopting the states as administrators of national programs. The Constitution gives Congress the power to lay and collect taxes for the purpose of providing for the general welfare of the United States. Under this authority, Congress may appropriate public monies, raised through taxation, for programs beyond the scope of the ordinary legislative power and may make the appropriation conditional on compliance with nationally established guidelines. Beginning with the SHEPPARD-TOWNER ACT (1921), Congress has appropriated money to the states to support programs conforming to national standards. Such appropriations, and the standards upon which they are conditioned, are virtually immune to constitutional challenge because of judicial rules of STANDING. Thus in cases like FROTHINGHAM V. MELLON (1923) and HELVERING V. DAVIS (1937) neither states nor taxpayers could state a case permitting review of FEDERAL GRANTS-IN-AID or the regulations accompanying them. One result of this is that by the mid-1980s federal grants made up a significant share of the revenues of the state governments and federal regulations dictated the operation of state programs in highway construction, traffic control, driver licensing health care, public relief, education, and most other areas.

Twentieth-century court decisions have also served to change the status of the states. The Fourteenth Amendment's guarantee that the states could not deprive persons of life, liberty, or property without due process of law has formed the basis for federal court intervention in many substantive areas. At the beginning of the century, state economic regulation was often held unconstitutional when it was found to conflict with the due process clause. Later in the century, through the INCORPORATION DOCTRINE, the Supreme Court extended SUBSTANTIVE DUE PROCESS protection to most of the rights that the first ten amendments protect against national government intrusion. In the 1950s and 1960s the Supreme Court used the concept of PROCEDURAL DUE PROCESS effectively to rewrite the state codes of criminal procedure, and in the 1970s and 1980s it expanded SUBSTANTIVE DUE PROCESS to preclude state interference with such RIGHTS OF PRIVACY as abortion and REPRODUCTIVE AUTONOMY.

Nevertheless, the twentieth century did not herald a radical reduction of state power and influence. Government power and government expenditure have grown continuously at all levels; but the states have been largely displaced or coopted in the exercise of some functions as they have expanded their reach into other areas previously left to private activity and enterprise. Although both President RICHARD M. NIXON and President RONALD REAGAN publicly advocated a "new federalism" in which the states and their governments would enjoy greater freedom of action, the tendency toward centralization has continued, and state governments have attempted to maintain their importance not by recovering autonomy in old areas but by expanding their activity into new areas.

DENNIS J. MAHONEY

Bibliography

ELAZAR, DANIEL J. 1972 *American Federalism: A View from the States*, 2nd ed. New York: Thomas Y. Crowell Co.

GOLDWIN, ROBERT, ED. 1962 *A Nation of States*. Chicago: Rand-McNally.

GRODZINS, MORTON 1966 *The American System: A New View of Government in the United States*, ed. Daniel J. Elazar. Chicago: Rand-McNally.

HAWKINS, ROBERT B., ED. 1982 *American Federalism: A New Partnership for the Republic*. San Francisco: Institute for Contemporary Studies.

MORLEY, FELIX 1959 *Freedom and Federalism*. Chicago: Henry Regnery Co.

SANFORD, TERRY 1967 *Storm over the States*. New York: McGraw-Hill.

VILE, M. J. C. 1961 *The Structure of American Federalism*. Oxford: Oxford University Press.

STATE ACTION

The phrase "state action," a term of art in our constitutional law, symbolizes the rule—or supposed rule—that constitutional guarantees of human rights are effective only against *governmental* action impairing those rights. (The word "state," in the phrase, denotes any unit or element of government, and not simply one of the American states, though the "state action" concept has been at its most active, and most problematic, with respect to these.) The problems have been many and complex; the "state action" doctrine has not reached anything near a satisfactory condition of rationality.

A best first step toward exploring the problems hidden in the "state action" phrase may be a look at its development in constitutional history. The development has revolved around the first section of the FOURTEENTH AMENDMENT, wherein the problem is in effect put forward by the words here italicized:

All persons born or naturalized in the United States, and subject to the jurisdiction thereof, are citizens of the United States and of the State wherein they reside. *No State* shall make or enforce any law which shall abridge the privileges or immunities of citizens of the United States; *nor shall any State* deprive any person of life, liberty, or property, without due process of law; nor deny to any person within its jurisdiction the equal protection of the laws.

An early "state action" case under this section, *Ex parte Virginia* (1880), raised an audacious claim as to the limiting effect of the words emphasized above. A Virginia judge had been charged under a federal statute forbidding racial exclusion from juries. He was not directed by a state statute to perform this racial exclusion. The judge argued that the action was not that of the state of Virginia, but rather the act of an official, proceeding wrongfully on his own. On this theory, a "state" had not denied EQUAL PROTECTION. The Fourteenth Amendment, the judge contended, did not therefore forbid the conduct charged, or authorize Congress to make it criminal. The Supreme Court, however, declined to take such high ground. "The constitutional provision," it said, ". . . must mean that no agency of the state, or of the officers or agents by whom its powers are exerted, shall deny . . . equal protection of the laws." But probably the only fully principled and maximally clear rule as to "state action" would have been that the "state," as a state, does not "act" except by its official enactments—and so does not "act" when one of its officers merely abuses his power. "Fully principled and maximally clear"—but, like so many such "rules," aridly

formalistic, making practical nonsense of any constitutional rule it limits. There were gropings, around the year of this case, toward a "state action" requirement with bite, but the modern history of the concept starts with the CIVIL RIGHTS CASES of 1883, wherein many modern problems were foreshadowed. In the CIVIL RIGHTS ACT OF 1875, Congress had enacted "[t]hat all persons . . . shall be entitled to the full and equal enjoyment of the accommodations, advantages, facilities, and privileges of inns, public conveyances on land or water, theatres, and other places of public amusement . . . [regardless of race]."

Persons were indicted for excluding blacks from hotels, theaters, and railroads. The Court considered that the only possible source of congressional power to make such a law was section 5 of the Fourteenth Amendment: "The Congress shall have power to enforce, by appropriate legislation, the provisions of this article." This section the Court saw as authorizing only those laws which *directly* enforced the guarantees of the amendment's section 1 (quoted above), which in turn referred only to a *state*. The amendment therefore did not warrant, the Court held, any congressional dealing with racially discriminatory actions of individuals or CORPORATIONS.

Few judicial opinions seem to rest on such solid ground; at the end of Justice JOSEPH BRADLEY's performance, the reader is likely to feel, "Q.E.D." But this feeling of apparent demonstration is attained, as often it is, by the passing over in silence of disturbing facts and thoughts. Many of these were brought out in the powerful dissent of Justice JOHN MARSHALL HARLAN.

One of the cases involved racial discrimination by a railroad. The American railroads, while they were building, were generally given the power of EMINENT DOMAIN. Eminent domain is a sovereign power, enjoyed par excellence by the state, and given by the state to "private" persons for public purposes looked on as important to the state; the Fifth Amendment's language illustrates the firmness of the background assumption that "private property" shall be taken, even with JUST COMPENSATION, only for PUBLIC USE. The American railroads were, moreover, very heavily assisted by public subsidy from governmental units at all levels. Both these steps—the clothing of railroad corporations with eminent-domain power, and their subsidization out of public funds—were justified, both rhetorically and as a matter of law, on the grounds that the railroads were *public instrumentalities*, fulfilling the classic state function of furnishing a transportation system. Regulation of railroads was undertaken under the same theory.

Railroads and hotel-keepers, moreover, followed the so-called common callings, traditionally entailing an obligation to take and carry, or to accommodate, all well-behaved persons able to pay. The *withdrawal* of protection of such a right to equal treatment might be looked on as "state action," and Congress might well decide, as a practical matter, either that the right had been wholly withdrawn as to blacks (which was in many places the fact of the matter) or that the state action supporting these rights of access was insufficient and required supplementation; only the most purposefully narrow construction could deny to such supplementation the name of "enforcement."

Indeed, this line of thought, whether as to the *Civil Rights Cases* or as to all other "equal protection" cases, is fraught with trouble for the whole "state action" doctrine, in nature as in name. "Action" is an exceedingly inapt word for the "denial" of "protection." Protection against lynching was, for example, usually "denied" by "inaction." Inaction by the state is indeed the classic form of "denial of protection." The Civil Rights Cases majority did not read far enough, even for the relentless literalist; it read as far as "nor shall any State . . ." but then hastily closed the book before reading what follows: ". . . *deny* to any person . . . the equal *protection* of the laws." Contrary to the majority's reading, the state's affirmative obligation of protection should have extended to the protection of the traditional rights of resort to public transport and common inns; it was notorious that the very people (blacks) whose "equal protection" was central to the Fourteenth Amendment were commonly the only victims of nominally "private" denial of these rights.

Justice Harlan pointed out that in its first sentence, conferring CITIZENSHIP on the newly emancipated slaves, the first section of the Fourteenth Amendment did not use any language in any way suggesting a "state action" requirement, so that there was not even the verbal support for the "state action" requirement that the Court had found in the other phrases of that section. The question then became, in Harlan's view, what the legal consequences of "citizenship" were; for purposes of the particular case at hand, he said:

But what was secured to colored citizens of the United States—as between them and their respective States—by the national grant to them of State citizenship? With what rights, privileges, or immunities did this grant invest them? There is one, if there be no other—exemption from race discrimination in respect of any civil right belonging to citizens of the white race in the same State. . . . Citizenship in this country necessarily imports at least equality of civil rights among citizens of every race in the same State. It is fundamental in American citizenship that, in respect of such rights, there shall be no discrimination by the State, or its officers, or by individuals or corporations exercising public functions or authority, against any citizen because of his race or previous condition of servitude. . . .

There is a third, most interesting aspect to Harlan's dissent. The majority had summarily rejected the argument that under the THIRTEENTH AMENDMENT—forbidding SLAVERY and involuntary servitude and giving Congress enforcement power—racial exclusion from public places was one of the "badges and incidents" of slavery. Harlan argued that forced segregation in public accommodations was a BADGE OF SERVITUDE, and he pointed out that no "state action" requirement could be found in the words of the Thirteenth Amendment. This argument was plowed under and was heard from no more for many decades, but it is of great interest because it was revived and made the basis of decision in a leading case in the 1960s, JONES V. ALFRED H. MAYER CO. (1968).

The *Civil Rights Cases,* in the majority opinion, brushed past contentions that were in no way frivolous. Very many discriminatory actions of public scope are taken by persons or corporations enjoying special favor from government and heavily regulated by government; one cannot easily see their actions as isolated from public power. "Denial of equal protection," the central constitutional wrong in racial cases, seems to refer at least as naturally to inaction as it does to action. If any positive rights at all inhere in citizenship—and if there are no such rights, the citizenship clause is a mere matter of nomenclature—these rights are set up by the Fourteenth Amendment without limitation as to the source of their impairment. Nevertheless, the holdings and doctrine of the *Civil Rights Cases* fell on a thirstily receptive society. The "state action" doctrine became one of the principal reliances of a racist nation, North as well as South.

In a society where so much of access to goods and values is managed by nominally "private" persons and corporations—railroads, restaurants, streetcars, cinemas, even food and clothing—a protection that runs only against the government, strictly defined, can work out to very little effective protection. If the official justice system is hampered by inconvenient constitutional safeguards, the sheriff can play cards while the lynch mob forms, and there is "no state action." A nightclub may refuse to serve a black celebrity, and there is "no state action." The "state action" doctrine protected from constitutional scrutiny an enormous network of racial exclusion and humiliation, characterizing both North and South.

Paradoxically, the "state action" requirement may

for a long time have been more important to the maintenance of northern racism than to that of the cruder racism of the South. The South developed SEGREGATION by law, in all phases of public life, and this regime was broadly validated by the notorious 1896 decision in PLESSY V. FERGUSON. For complex political reasons—and perhaps because of a faintly lingering adherence to scraps of Civil War idealism—segregation by official law was not widely imposed in the North. But the practices of real-estate agents, mortgage lenders, restaurant keepers, and a myriad of other "private" people and corporations added up to a pervasive custom of racial segregation in many phases of life, a custom less perfectly kept than the official legal dictates of the southern regime, but effectively barring most blacks from much of the common life of the communities they lived in.

A striking case in point was *Dorsey v. Stuyvesant Town Corporation* (1949–1950). The Metropolitan Life Insurance Company, having much money to invest, struck a complicated deal with the State and the City of New York. The contemplated end-result was the conversion of a large section of New York City—from 14th to 23rd Streets, and from Avenue A to the East River—into a vast complex of apartments, to be owned and run by a Metropolitan subsidiary. By formal statute and ordinance, the State and City acquiesced in this scheme, agreeing to use (and later using) the sovereign "eminent domain" power to acquire title to all the needed land, which was, as prearranged, later transferred to Metropolitan. Again by formal arrangement, a quarter-century tax exemption was granted on "improvements"—that is to say, on the immensely valuable apartment buildings. The public easement on certain streets was extinguished, and control over them turned over to Stuyvesant Town Corporation, a Metropolitan subsidiary; various water, sewage, and fire-protection arrangements were altered to suit the needs of the project. And all this was done, visibly and pridefully, as a joint effort of public and "private" enterprise; politicians as well as insurance men took bows. Then, when the whole thing was built, with "title" safely vested in "private" hands, Stuyvesant Town Corporation announced that no blacks need apply for apartments. The suit of a black applicant reached the highest court of New York, and that court held, 4–3, that there was not enough "state action" in all this to make applicable the Fourteenth Amendment prohibition of racial discrimination. The Supreme Court of the United States denied CERTIORARI.

The *Stuyvesant Town* case illustrates very well what could be done with the "state action" formula.

With the fullest cooperation from government at all levels, as much of any city as might be desired (strictly public buildings alone excepted) could be turned into a "whites only" preserve. With the necessary cooperation, the process could be extended to a whole county, or a whole state. If they were prudent, the political partners in such deals would not put anything in writing about the racial exclusion contemplated.

But the essentiality of the "state action" formula to the success of northern racism must not obscure its considerable strategic importance even in the South. Segregation by law had in the main been validated, and this was the South's main reliance, but there were gaps, and the "state action" formula filled them in.

First, there was the role of nominally "private" violence against blacks, as the ultimate weapon of the racist regime—with lynching at the top of the arsenal's inventory. At this point the disregard of the Fourteenth Amendment's words, "nor shall any State *deny* . . . equal *protection* of the laws," is most surprising. But for a long time a whole lot of seemingly serious people saw no "denial of protection" in the de facto denial of protection to blacks against a great deal of "private" violence.

Second, outright racial residential zoning by law—just one form of segregation—had been struck down by the Supreme Court, in the 1917 case of BUCHANAN V. WARLEY. The opinion in that case does not adequately distinguish *Plessy v. Ferguson*, but it was the law, and nominally "private" methods of racial zoning had often to be resorted to in the South—just as they were, pervasively, in the North. Real-estate agents and mortgage banks played their accustomed part; until astonishingly recent times, the actually published codes of "ethics" of "realtors" forbade (under some transparent euphemism) actions tending toward spoiling the racial homogeneity of any neighborhood. But more was needed, and that more was found—South and North—in the "racially RESTRICTIVE COVENANT." These "covenants" were neither necessarily nor commonly mere casual contractual arrangements between parties dickering at random. Very commonly, when an "addition" was "subdivided," all the first deeds restricted ownership or occupancy, or both, to whites only—or to white Gentiles only, or to white Gentiles of northern European extraction. These covenants, recorded at the courthouse in a registry furnished by the State for this purpose, were ordained by many states' laws to "run with the land"—that is, they had to be put in all subsequent deeds forever, and usually were binding whether so inserted or not, since any buyer, examining title, could find them in the title-chain. These "covenants"—often functionally equivalent to racial zoning by law, enforced by court orders, and kept on file at the courthouse—were for a long time looked on as "merely private" action, in no way traceable to the state, and so not amenable to constitutional command.

A third and even more important use of the "state action" doctrine (or a doctrine closely akin) was peculiar to the South, and was the rotting-out base of southern politics for generations. The FIFTEENTH AMENDMENT forbade racial exclusions from voting—but, like the Fourteenth, it directed its prohibition at governments: "The right of citizens of the United States to vote shall not be denied or abridged by the United States or by any State on account of race, color, or previous condition of servitude."

The general response in the South to this politically inconvenient constitutional mandate was the all-white Democratic PRIMARY ELECTION. This primary was colloquially known as "the election"; its nominees virtually always won in the November balloting, when all the whites who had voted in the Democratic primary were expected to vote for its nominee, and enough did so to wipe out any scattered Republican votes, including the votes of those blacks who could surmount the other barriers to their voting—LITERACY TESTS, difficult registration procedures, and even more violent discouragements. This plain fraud on the Constitution did not rest wholly on the concept that the action of the Democratic party was not "state action," but the even bolder idea behind it—the idea, namely, that the practical substitution of a "party" election for the regular election could altogether escape the Fifteenth Amendment mandate, even when the State commanded the all-whiteness of the Party—was related in more than spirit to the "state action" doctrine as illustrated in the Stuyvesant Town case. Its basis was the thought that racial voting requirements were not "official" if a nominally "private" organization was put in as a buffer between the wrong done and state power. And the all-white primary in the end had to rely (vainly, as at last it turned out) on the "state action" requirement.

The "state action" doctrine is not a mere interesting footnote in constitutional law. It has served as an absolutely essential and broadly employed component in the means by which black equality, theoretically guaranteed by the post-Civil War amendments, was made to mean next to nothing. It could do this because of the fact that, in our society, vast powers over all of life are given to formally private organizations—the Democratic party, the realtors' association, the mortgage bank, the telephone company, and so

on—and because, further and indispensably, the courts were (as is illustrated by a line of decisions from the *Civil Rights Cases* to the Stuyvesant Town case) willing in case after case to gloss over the fact that large organized enterprises can rarely if ever be successfully conducted without very considerable help from the government. Intermixed in these racial cases was, moreover, the disregard of the Fourteenth Amendment's textual condemnation of governmental *inaction*, where that inaction amounted to *denial of equal protection,* as inaction obviously may. And constitutional guarantees that were implicit rather than explicit as limits on government were mostly ignored. A doctrine that went to the length of seeming to make of lynching a thing untouched by the Constitution and (as in UNITED STATES V. CRUIKSHANK, 1875) untouchable by Congress was and could be again a powerful tool indeed for bringing national human rights, nationally enjoyed, to nothing, on the plane of life as lived.

The "state action" requirement thus served the major strategic goal of a nation to which racism, in practice, was utterly essential. But even outside the field of race, its incidence, though spotty, was wide-ranging. As late as 1951, in *Collins v. Hardyman,* the Supreme Court, obviously under the influence of the doctrine though not directly relying on it, forcibly construed a federal statute, in plain contradiction to the law's clear terms, as not to reach the "private" and violent breaking up of a political meeting of citizens.

But a strong countercurrent developed in the 1940s. Without entire consistency, the Supreme Court uttered a striking series of decisions that promised to clip the claws of the "state action" requirement. The Court declared the all-white Democratic primary unlawful in SMITH V. ALLWRIGHT (1944) and extended this ruling in TERRY V. ADAMS (1953) to a local primary serving the same function under another name and form. MARSH V. ALABAMA (1946) held that the FIRST AMENDMENT, as incorporated into the Fourteenth, forbade the barring of Jehovah's Witnesses from distributing leaflets in a company-owned town. And SHELLEY V. KRAEMER (1948) held that judicial enforcement of restrictive covenants was unlawful.

In the "white primary" cases the Court was doing no more than refusing to persevere in self-induced blindness to an obvious fraud on the Fifteenth Amendment. But *Marsh v. Alabama* suggested that the formality of "ownership" could not immunize from constitutional scrutiny the performance of a governmental function—an idea big with possibility. And the

Shelley case even more profoundly stirred the foundations. Of course it was difficult to say that judicial enforcement of a racial-restrictive covenant, recorded at the courthouse, with the attendant implication that such covenants are not (as some others are) "against public policy," did not amount to "state action of some kind"—the requirement as worded in the fountainhead *Civil Rights Cases* of 1883. The difficulty in assimilation of *Shelley* arose from the fact that "state action of some kind" underpins and in one way or another enforces every nominally "private" action; the states had facilitated and lent their aid, indeed, to the very acts of discrimination considered in the 1883 cases. *Shelley*, therefore, forced a more searching analysis of the theory of "state action"; academic commentators became exceedingly eager and thorough, and in later decisions the Court became more willing to find "state action" and to move toward a fundamental doctrinal revision.

This process was accelerated by the civil rights movement that gained strength in the late 1950s, and grew to major force in the 1960s. In 1954, the famous case of BROWN V. BOARD OF EDUCATION had outlawed racial segregation in the public schools; a number of other decisions had extended this rule to all forms of segregation imposed by law or by uncontestable official action. Though enforcement of these decisions was to be difficult, the first of two principal jural supports of American racism—legal prohibition of participation by blacks in the common society—had crumbled. Naturally attention turned—whether with the aim of continuing racism or of completing its demolition—to the second of the pillars of American racism, the "state action" requirement.

Segregation and state action were now clearly seen to have a close functional similarity. Before the decisions following *Brown*, the blacks in a typical southern town could not eat in the good restaurants because state law commanded their exclusion. After these decisions, the proprietors of the restaurants, by and large, went on excluding blacks. (In this they were simply following a practice widely followed in the North already). There was a difference in legal theory, but no difference to the black people. The city-owned bus system could not make black people sit in the back—but most bus companies were "private" in form; seating in the back was "privately" commanded.

The resistance to this widespread public segregation under "private" form was led (actively in part and symbolically throughout) by Dr. Martin Luther King, Jr. Thousands of black people—most, but not all, young—defied the system by "sitting-in"—insisting upon service at "private" establishments open to the general public. They were in great numbers convicted of "crimes" selected with careful attention to the appearance of neutrality, such as "trespass after warning" or BREACH OF THE PEACE, and their cases reached the Supreme Court in some number.

The net result up to about 1965 was a considerable practical loosening up of the "state action" requirement, but no satisfactory theoretical reworking of that doctrine. A very few examples must be selected from the abundant case law.

The 1961 case of BURTON V. WILMINGTON PARKING AUTHORITY is an interesting example. The parking authority, a state agency, leased space in its parking building to a restaurateur, who forthwith refused to serve blacks. One might have thought it all but frivolous to contend that "state action of some kind" was absent here. The state had gone with open eyes into a transaction that empowered the restaurateur to insult and inconvenience citizens, in a public building owned by itself, and its police stood ready to make his rule stick. The state had done this—in effect certainly, if not in intent—for rent money. It had had the easy recourse of inserting in the lease a provision against racial discrimination; one has to wonder how the omission of that provision, obviously available under "the laws," can be anything but a "denial" of "equal protection of the laws," on the part of government. Yet the Court majority, though striking down the discrimination in the very case, roamed back and forth amongst the minutiae of facts—gas, service for the boiler-room, responsibility for structural repairs—and carefully confined its ruling to a lease of public property "in the manner and for the purpose shown to have been the case here. . . ." Still, the Wilmington case might have contributed toward some generality of constitutional theory.

As the "sit-in" issue heated up, however, the Court became even more evasive of the central issues. As cases reached the Court in great numbers, no "sit-in" conviction was ever affirmed. But neither the whole Court nor any majority ever reached and decided the central issue—whether *Shelley v. Kraemer* fairly implied that the knowing state use of state power to enforce discrimination, in publicly open facilities, constituted such action of the state as "denied equal protection of the laws." Instead the cases were decided on collateral grounds peculiar to each of them.

The culminating case was BELL V. MARYLAND (1964). Trespass convictions of Maryland civil-rights "sitters-in" were reversed, on the grounds (available by chance) that a newly enacted Maryland antidiscrimination statute might be held, in the state courts, to "abate" prosecution for prior attempts to get the service now guaranteed; nothing was actually decided on the more fundamental issues. Six Justices reached the "state action" issue, but of those six, three would have found it and three would not.

At this dramatic moment, with indefinite postponement of a major doctrinal decision seemingly impossible, Congress stepped in and solved the immediate problem, by passing the CIVIL RIGHTS ACT OF 1964, Title 2 of which made unlawful nearly all the discriminatory exclusions that had generated the sit-in prosecutions, making future prosecutions of sit-ins impossible. Then, in 1964, in *Hamm v. City of Rock Hill*, the Court held that the act compelled dismissal of all such prosecutions begun before its passage. Thus vanished the immediate problem of the sit-ins, and of many other claims to nondiscrimination previously based purely on the Constitution. It is noteworthy that Congress chose to base this Title 2, dealing with PUBLIC ACCOMMODATIONS, mainly on the COMMERCE CLAUSE rather than on the Fourteenth Amendment. This legislative decision reflected uncertainty as to whether the Court could be persuaded to overrule the 1883 *Civil Rights Cases*, which had severely limited congressional power to enforce the Fourteenth Amendment. In HEART OF ATLANTA MOTEL V. UNITED STATES (1964) and KATZENBACH V. MCCLUNG (1964) the Court construed the 1964 provisions broadly, and upheld them under the commerce clause theory that Congress had emphasized. The public accommodations crisis was over, and with it the really agonizing social crisis as to "state action."

Nevertheless, important problems continued to present themselves after 1964. It seemed for a time that, though no longer under the intense pressure of the public accommodations issue, the Court might be moving along the road toward relaxation of the state action requirement—a road along which travel had begun at least as early as the cases of *Smith v. Allwright* (1944—knocking out the all-white Democratic primary), *Marsh v. Alabama* (1946—the "company-town" case), and *Shelley v. Kraemer* (1948—the case of the racial-restriction covenants). (Indeed, no case actually denying relief on the "no-state-action" ground was decided by the Supreme Court from 1906 to 1970, except the 1935 case upholding the white primary, overruled nine years later).

In 1966 the Court held, in *Evans v. Newton*, that a huge public park in the center of Macon, Georgia, could no longer be operated as a park "for whites only," pursuant to the directions in the 1911 will of the man who had given it to the city, even though the city, for the purpose of seeing this all-white status maintained, had resigned as trustee, and had acquiesced in the appointment of a set of "private" trustees. In *Amalgamated Food Employees v. Logan Valley Plaza* (1968) the Court applied *Marsh v. Alabama* to hold a large SHOPPING CENTER subject to the First Amendment, and REITMAN V. MULKEY (1967) struck down under the Fourteenth Amendment a California constitutional amendment that would have forbidden state or local "fair" (i.e., anti-racist) housing ordinances until such time as the state constitution might be amended again—a process substantially more difficult than the enactment of ordinary legislation. This opinion, by Justice BYRON R. WHITE, encouraged much hope, because it explicitly undertook to judge this state constitutional amendment "in terms of its 'immediate objective,' its 'ultimate effect,' and its 'historical context and the conditions existing prior to its enactment.'" This attitude, if adhered to, would in every case bring the "state action" question down to the earth of reality. The Court would recognize the impact of formal state "neutrality" on the actual patterns of American racism, and would ask in each case whether such seeming "neutrality" operated as a *denial of equal protection* to the group principally marked for protection. This hope was further encouraged in 1969 in *Hunter v. Erickson* wherein the Court struck down an Akron, Ohio, requirement that fair-housing ordinances run an especially difficult gauntlet before they became effective; it was especially striking that Justices JOHN MARSHALL HARLAN and POTTER STEWART, who had dissented in *Reitman*, found the Akron provision too much, because on its face it discriminated against anti-racist laws.

But the current of doctrine changed after President RICHARD M. NIXON made the most of his chance to put his stamp on the Court. The change was signaled by the 1970 decision in EVANS V. ABNEY, a follow-up to the first Macon park case, *Evans v. Newton*, above. After the Newton decision, the heirs of the donor of the park applied for a reverter to them. The Court held this time that the state court's decision in their favor, in effect imposing a penalty on the citizens of Macon for their being unable under the Fourteenth Amendment to keep the park all-white, did not constitute "such state action" as to implicate the equal protection clause.

In 1971, in PALMER V. THOMPSON, the Court upheld the City of Jackson in its closing the city swimming pools and leasing one of them to the "private" YMCA, rather than having blacks swim in them. Here the Court found no state encouragement of discrimination, although the pools had been closed in response to a desegregation order. This was a total turn-about, in just four years, from the *Reitman v. Mulky* resolution to tie the operation of state-action law to the facts of life, and Justice White, the author of the *Reitman* opinion, dissented, with three other pre-Nixon Justices.

In 1974 the Court decided JACKSON V. METROPOLITAN EDISON COMPANY. A heavily regulated "private" electric company, enjoying a monopoly and a state-issued certificate of public convenience, terminated service to a customer without offering her any chance to be heard. This practice was allowed by a "tariff" on file with and at the least acquiesced in by the Public Utilities Commission. Justice WILLIAM H. REHNQUIST's opinion for the Court found insufficient "state action" in any of this to implicate the DUE PROCESS clause. This opinion and judgment, if adhered to in all their implications, would put us at least as far back as the 1883 Civil Rights Cases. Then, in 1976, HUDGENS V. NATIONAL LABOR RELATION BOARD explicitly overruled the *Logan Valley Shopping Center* case and made authoritative for the time being a very narrow view of *Marsh v. Alabama*.

Meanwhile, however, a new doctrinal thread had become visible. In the 1883 *Civil Rights Cases* the first Justice Harlan had argued that the Thirteenth Amendment, which contains no language to support a state-action requirement, proscribes all "badges and incidents" of slavery—which, historically, would mean a great many if not all racially discriminatory and degrading actions. This argument was a long time in coming into its own, but in 1968, in *Jones v. Alfred H. Mayer Co.*, the Court made it the ground of a decision upholding an old act of Congress which the Court interpreted to command nondiscrimination in the sale of housing. And in 1976, GRIFFIN V. BRECKENRIDGE, overruling *Collins v. Hardyman*, based decision solidly on the Thirteenth Amendment, holding that the amendment authorizes Congress to secure its beneficiaries against "racially discriminatory private action aimed at depriving them of . . . basic rights. . . ." Under the very formula of the 1883 *Civil Rights Cases* themselves—Congress may "enforce" only that which is substantively there—this should imply a large substantive content in the Thirteenth Amendment, far beyond literal "slavery." In RUNYON V. MCCRARY (1976) the Court extended much the same rationale to the condemnation of racial exclusion from a "private, commercially operated, nonsectarian" school.

"State action" doctrine has remained intractable to being made rational. What is wanted is attention to these points:

1. In almost any impingement by one person or more on another person or more, there is some contribution by the state: empowerment, support, or threatened support. Thus the presence or absence of "state action" is not a "test" at all; this has led to the spinning out of enormous series of subtests, hard to express and even harder to comprehend, none of which has much if any warrant in law.

2. Concomitantly, "state action" may not legitimately be confined—as the Supreme Court's recent opinions have confined it—to one or more neatly defined categories such as "command," "encouragement," or "public function." One may identify ten ways in which so infinitely complicated and subtle a being as the "state" may act—and the "state" may then act in an eleventh and then in a twelfth way—*all* "state action."

3. There is no warrant whatever in law for the assumption that "state action," to be significant, must be at a *high level* of involvement, or that a *very close* "nexus" must be found between "state action" and the wrong complained of.

4. Many constitutional guarantees do not explicitly require "state action" as a component. The modern "state action" requirement purported to draw its life from the words of the Fourteenth Amendment. Many rights and relationships set up by the Constitution and enforceable by Congress do not refer to the state at all, for example, the prohibition of slavery (and, as now held, its badges and incidents), the right to vote for congressmen and senators, the RIGHT TO TRAVEL. It is only custom-thought, which usually means half-thought, that would think it obvious that an impediment to INTERSTATE COMMERCE would be unconstitutional only if it were state-created.

5. A citizen of the United States should be regarded as having *relational* rights—rights of membership in the organized community—which nobody, state or private person, may interfere with. This principle has some life in the cases; in *Bewer v. Hoxie School District* (8th Cir. 1956), for example, an INJUNCTION was upheld that restrained private persons from interfering with state officials' attempts to comply with the national Constitution. But the principle deserves a greater generality. Anybody who tries forcibly to keep another person from getting his mail is interfering with a legitimate relation between citizen and government, even though the wrongdoer's own actions may not be "state action" at all. (See also UNITED STATES V. GUEST, 1966.)

6. There is broad scope in the natural meaning of the Fourteenth Amendment's words: "deny to any person within its jurisdiction the equal protection of

the laws." These words, even as a matter of "narrow verbal criticism," do not require "action."

7. Above all, while much of the defense of the "state action" requirement is conducted in the name of the private, personal lives of people whose conduct, it is said, ought not to be constitutionalized, it is very, very rare that any real "state action" case involves these values at all. The conduct of public transportation and restaurants, the operation of carnivals and parks, dealings with city swimming pools, the way the light company collects its bills, the character of a whole section of town—these are the usual stuff of "state action" problems in real life. If anybody ever files a lawsuit praying a mandatory injunction that he be included on somebody else's dinner list, that will be time enough to begin devising a well-founded "rule of reason" fencing constitutional prohibition out of the genuinely private life. This "genuinely private" life may be hard to define, but surely no harder to define than the "state action requirement" has turned out to be, and continues to be. And at least one would be trying to define the right thing.

CHARLES L. BLACK, JR.

Bibliography

BLACK, CHARLES L., JR. 1962 The Constitution and Public Power. *Yale Review* 52:54–66.

BLACK, CHARLES L., JR. 1967 "State Action," Equal Protection, and California's Proposition 14. *Harvard Law Review* 81:69–109.

HALE, ROBERT L. 1952 *Freedom through Law.* Chap. 11. New York: Columbia University Press.

HOROWITZ, HAROLD W. 1957 The Misleading Search for "State Action" under the Fourteenth Amendment. *Southern California Law Review* 30:208–221.

VAN ALSTYNE, WILLIAM W. 1965 Mr. Justice Black, Constitutional Review, and the Talisman of State Action. *Duke Law Journal* 1965:219–247.

STATE ACTION—BEYOND RACE

For most of its century-long existence, the STATE ACTION limitation of the reach of the FOURTEENTH AMENDMENT and FIFTEENTH AMENDMENT has had its chief importance in cases involving RACIAL DISCRIMINATION. From the CIVIL RIGHTS CASES (1883) until the 1940s, the state action barrier impeded both judicial and congressional protection of CIVIL RIGHTS. As the civil rights movement gathered force in the years following World War II, relaxation of the state action limitation was essential to the vindication of the rights of blacks and others who were making

claims to constitutional equality. The WARREN COURT accelerated the erosion of the state action barrier, bringing more and more private conduct within the reach of the Fourteenth Amendment. ALEXANDER M. BICKEL accurately described the effects of the Court's decisions as "egalitarian, legalitarian, and centralizing." By the late 1960s some commentators were predicting the state action doctrine's early demise.

Those predictions missed the mark; today the state action limitation remains very much alive. Yet the doctrine's revival has not signaled a return to a restricted role for the national government in protecting rights of racial equality. By the time the BURGER COURT set about rebuilding the state action barrier, the Court had provided Congress with a firm basis for federal civil rights legislation in the THIRTEENTH AMENDMENT, which has never been interpreted to contain a state action limitation. Furthermore, the Court had generously interpreted various federal civil rights laws to forbid most types of private racial discrimination that had flourished behind the state action barrier in the prewar years.

Although the revival of the state action doctrine has offered little new support for private racial discrimination, that revival has diminished the "legalitarian" and "centralizing" effects of the Warren Court's decisions. Indeed, recent Supreme Court majorities have explicitly extolled the Court's use of the state action doctrine to promote the values of individual autonomy and FEDERALISM. The Warren Court had blurred the distinction between state and society, between what is "public" and what is "private." In so doing, the Court assumed that the force of law underlay all private dealings. It is only a short step from this assumption to the judicial creation of a great many constitutional rights of private individuals against other private individuals. Justice JOHN MARSHALL HARLAN, deploring the trend, argued in UNITED STATES V. GUEST (1966) that "[the] CONSTITUTIONAL CONVENTION was called to establish a nation, not to reform the COMMON LAW."

The Burger Court has viewed its revival of the state action barrier in precisely these terms, as a contraction of the reach of the Constitution—and especially the reach of the federal judiciary—with a corresponding expansion of both individual autonomy and state SOVEREIGNTY. The Court's recent majorities have drawn a sharp distinction between society's "public" and "private" spheres, and two implications have followed. First, the Constitution limits governmental, but not private, conduct. Second, if private conduct is to be regulated by government, the preferred regulator is the state government, and not Congress or the federal courts. The result has been a marked reduction in the Fourteenth Amendment's potential applications to private conduct, even when that conduct is carried on with what the Warren Court used to call "significant state involvement."

Indeed, the very search for "significant state involvement" has been replaced by a new analytical approach. Where the Warren Court determined the existence of state action by considering the totality of interconnections between government and private conduct, today's majority separately examines various arguments for finding state action underpinning private conduct—and typically, as in JACKSON V. METROPOLITAN EDISON COMPANY (1974) and BLUM V. YARETSKY (1982), rejects those arguments one by one.

In doctrinal terms, the current majority of the Supreme Court has narrowed both of the principal avenues for finding state action in private conduct. First, the "public function" theory that informed the "white primary" cases from NIXON V. HERNDON (1927) to TERRY V. ADAMS (1953) and the "company town" decision in MARSH V. ALABAMA (1946) has been confined to cases in which the state has delegated to a private party a function traditionally performed exclusively by the state. In FLAGG BROTHERS, INC. V. BROOKS (1978) the Court even tightened its rhetoric for such cases, referring to "the sovereign function doctrine."

Second, the various types of state support that previously contributed to findings of "significant state involvement" in private conduct, having been disaggregated in the Court's analysis, have been strictly limited in their separate meanings. Thus: heavy state financial aid to a private school was insufficient to establish state action in RENDELL-BAKER V. KOHN (1982); the theory of REITMAN V. MULKEY (1967) that the state had "encouraged" private racial discrimination has yet to be employed to find state action in another case; the state's licensing and comprehensive regulation of a public utility was insufficient to establish state action in *Jackson v. Metropolitan Edison Company;* the precedent of BURTON V. WILMINGTON PARKING AUTHORITY (1961) has been restricted to cases in which government and private actors are so intimately interconnected that their relationship can be called one of "symbiosis"—or, as in LUGAR V. EDMONDSON OIL COMPANY (1982), "joint participation"; and the RESTRICTIVE COVENANT precedent of SHELLEY V. KRAEMER (1948) has become a one-case category. Even a public defender, employed by the state to represent indigent defendants in criminal cases, was held in *Polk County v. Dodson* (1981) not to be

acting under COLOR OF LAW as required by SECTION 1983, TITLE 42, OF THE U.S. CODE, statutory words that are interpreted to track the state action limitation.

The insight that law—and thus the coercive power of the state—provides the foundation for claims of right in human society is not new. Indeed, the proposition teeters on the edge of tautology. To say that a person owns land, for example, is mainly a shorthand statement about the readiness of state officials to employ force to protect that person's exercise of certain rights to control the use of that land. To speak of law itself is to speak of a power relationship. In a large and complex society the point may sometimes become diffused, but the potential application of coercive power, wielded by governmental officials, is one of the chief features differentiating interactions in nearly all human societies from those in a jungle. The public/private distinction may have its uses, but candid description is not one of them.

Nonetheless, Justice WILLIAM H. REHNQUIST, writing for the Supreme Court in the *Flagg Brothers* case, reaffirmed "the 'essential dichotomy' between public and private acts" as a feature of American constitutional law. State action, for purposes of interpreting the Fourteenth Amendment, could not be found on the potential enforcement of law by state officials, but only on its actual enforcement. To rule otherwise, Rehnquist said, would "intolerably broaden" the notion of state action. Unquestionably, the public/private distinction is secure in American constitutional law.

The appeal of the public/private distinction for the judges and commentators who create constitutional DOCTRINE is readily identified. If any one value lies at the core of American CONSTITUTIONALISM, it is the protection of individual freedom against arbitrary exercises of governmental power. A central assumption in this value scheme is that a "neutral" body of law is no more than the playing field on which individuals autonomously pursue their own goals. The same assumption is also reassuring about autonomy itself—not just that autonomy is valuable, but that autonomy exists. It is hard to see how American constitutionalism could get along without some form of the public/private distinction, absent a fundamental transformation of the idea of constitutionalism.

Plainly, the public/private distinction would be compatible with a definition of state action much broader than the current one. The present restrictive interpretation of the state action limitation, in other words, serves purposes beyond the maintenance of a zone of individual freedom against arbitrary governmental interference. Those purposes are not far below the surface of the Supreme Court's recent state action opinions. The Supreme Court's current restrictive readings of the state action limitation are congenial to Justices who want to preserve state power against the intrusion of the federal government, and who want to restrict the role of the judiciary in second-guessing the political process. One's attitude toward the state action issue, as toward a great many constitutional issues in the last generation, will reflect one's general views about JUDICIAL ACTIVISM AND RESTRAINT. The consequences of these choices are not merely institutional; they affect substantive rights of liberty and equality. Every decision reinforcing the Fourteenth Amendment's state action barrier is a decision not to vindicate a claim of Fourteenth Amendment rights.

KENNETH L. KARST

Bibliography

NOTE   1974   State Action: Theories for Applying Constitutional Restrictions to Private Activity. *Columbia Law Review* 74:656–705.
SYMPOSIUM   1982   The Public/Private Distinction. *University of Pennsylvania Law Review* 130:1289–1608.
TRIBE, LAURENCE H. 1985 *Constitutional Choices.* Pages 246–268. Cambridge, Mass.: Harvard University Press

STATE AID TO PAROCHIAL SCHOOLS

See: Government Aid to Religious Institutions

STATE AND LOCAL FISCAL ASSISTANCE ACT

See: Revenue Sharing

STATE CONSTITUTIONAL LAW

American constitutionalism is more than the United States Constitution as interpreted by the United States Supreme Court. Each of the fifty states has its own constitution, which is the chief charter of government and of limitations on government in that state. State constitutions offer contrasts to common assumptions, based only on the United States Constitution, concerning both government and constitutional law.

State constitutions preceded the Constitution of the United States. State governments had to be formed when colonial governments were displaced in the move to American independence. The CONTINENTAL CONGRESS called upon each colony to establish its own government, but the Congress decided not to propose a single model for all. Eleven of the original thirteen states adopted written constitutions between 1776 and 1780; Connecticut and Rhode Island established their governing institutions without adopting constitutions until well into the nineteenth century. The generation that drafted the United States Constitution and the BILL OF RIGHTS first applied many of its political theories to forming the state constitutions.

One tradition dating from the early state constitutions is to place the declaration of rights at the beginning of the document. The rights so declared differed among the states, but together they covered virtually all of the guarantees later added to the United States Constitution. As to the structure of government, all states except Pennsylvania adopted bicameral legislatures (today only Nebraska's is unicameral), but they diverged on how and by whom representatives were elected. The theory of a separation of legislative, executive, and judicial powers was widely approved and expressly incorporated in Virginia's and other constitutional texts, but the legislatures were dominant in most states, electing governors, other executive officers, and judges.

By 1800 most of the original state constitutions had been replaced by revised documents. Nineteenth-century constitutions reflected the changing political concerns of old and new states as the nation expanded westward. Jeffersonian and Jacksonian views of democracy and equality broadened political participation and extended popular election from legislative to virtually all executive, administrative, and judicial offices. By mid-century, legislative profligacy with public credit in pursuit of economic development led to constitutional restraints on taxing and borrowing, on "lending the state's credit" or granting special PRIVILEGES OR IMMUNITIES to private persons, and on individual incorporation acts or other special or local laws. New governmental programs such as public education and regulation of banks, railroads, and public utilities were not left to ordinary legislation but were added to state constitutions, often to be administered by separately elected officials. State constitutions address such social problems as alcoholic beverages, gambling, and lotteries. The movement toward populist government reached its climax at the beginning of the twentieth century when many states provided for referenda on legislation and constitutional amendments upon petition by the requisite numbers of voters. Eventually many states had constitutions resembling haphazard legal codes.

After World War II a number of states adopted substantially new or modernized constitutions, including Missouri (1945), New Jersey (1947), Hawaii and Alaska (1959), Michigan (1960), Connecticut (1965), Florida and Pennsylvania (1968), Illinois and Virginia (1970), Montana (1972), Louisiana (1974), California (1976), and Georgia (1982). Others retain their original constitutions as revised by individual amendments. Altogether the fifty states have had a total of nearly 150 constitutions, with corresponding diversity among the states.

Although guarantees of individual rights dominate judicial and public attention, the primary function of constitutions is the organization and allocation of governmental authority. When this is done in a written constitution, the legitimacy of actions even by the highest elected officials depends upon compliance with the constitution and can be challenged for failure to comply. A comparison shows that in a number of respects the constitutional law of state government is more complex than that of the United States, although in one respect it is not.

The authority of states as such is not derived from their constitutions, as the early examples of Connecticut and Rhode Island show; unless limited, state authority is as plenary as that of the British Parliament. State constitutions therefore have no need for lists of legislative "powers" like those granted Congress in the United States Constitution. The great residue of the COMMON LAW concerning private transactions and property is state law. Although elected officials of local governments exercise lawmaking, taxing, and executive powers, their relation to the state is the reverse of that between the state and the federal government insofar as local governments have only the powers defined in state law. The "home rule" provisions found in many state constitutions, however, introduce one complexity comparable to the constitutional problems of FEDERALISM.

There are other contrasts. Federal executive officers are appointed by the President and must trace their actions to some act of Congress except for those powers given the President directly by the Constitution. Although the typical state constitution refers to an executive department of government, many executive officials, such as state treasurers, attorneys general, superintendents of public instruction and prose-

cutors, are separately elected to carry out functions described in the constitution. In fiscal matters many state constitutions, unlike the United States Constitution, require a balanced budget and allow the governor an item veto. Constitutional issues arise from provisions governing uniformity and limits on taxes and procedures for issuing bonds. Others arise in the administration of the election laws, especially the popular initiative and referendum. They result in a body of constitutional law that has no federal parallel.

When parallels do exist, experience under state constitutional law often provides a test for conceptions assumed at the national level or accepted by the United States Supreme Court, for instance, in questions of executive power and privileges. The Alaska court in *State v. A.L.I.V.E.* (1980) invalidated the LEGISLATIVE VETO device before the United States Supreme Court did so in IMMIGRATION AND NATURALIZATION SERVICE V. CHADHA (1983).

The role of state judges in reviewing acts of government developed early and was generally accepted. New York's first constitution included judges in a Council of Revision that exercised the power to veto legislation. Under seven state constitutions the judges of the highest courts may be called upon to render ADVISORY OPINIONS.

Constitutional entrenchment of individual rights began with the earliest state constitutions in 1776 and is universal throughout the states, though the statements of rights differ. The common tradition includes procedural guarantees such as speedy and public trial by jury upon known charges, the right to call and to confront witnesses, freedom from warrantless and unreasonable searches and seizures and from compelled self-incrimination, as well as guarantees of property rights and freedom of expression, assembly, and petition. Many constitutions prescribed the law governing libel actions. The equality posited in the DECLARATION OF INDEPENDENCE was not translated into general state constitutional doctrine, being denied to slaves, women, and unpropertied citizens. But hereditary inequality was proscribed, as were, in the words of the Virginia Bill of Rights (1776), "exclusive or separate emoluments or privileges from the community, but in consideration of public services."

Differences among state provisions were not accidental. The status of religion varied among the early states, some favoring Protestant denominations or Christianity generally. Different views of punishment resulted in different provisions on that subject. Some states limited the right to bear arms to public defense; others extended it to self-defense. Conventions debated such issues as the role of GRAND JURIES. New states adopting constitutions throughout the nineteenth century drew their models not from the United States Constitution but from earlier states.

In the catalogue of guaranteed rights, too, many state provisions have no federal parallel. They may command open court proceedings, a result that the United States Supreme Court has strained to develop indirectly from FREEDOM OF THE PRESS. Many guarantee legal remedies for private injuries, a subject not generally within the powers granted to Congress. Some prescribe humane treatment of prisoners. In modern times some states have added guarantees of workers' rights, environmental values, rights of privacy, and equal rights of men and women. Constitutional rights, in the sense of rights guaranteed by constitutions rather than other law, are by no means identical throughout the United States.

State constitutions have provided almost the only guarantees against the states' laws through most of the nation's history. The United States Constitution denied the states authority to enact BILLS OF ATTAINDER, EX POST FACTO LAWS, and laws impairing the obligation of contracts, but the first ten amendments that are commonly called the Bill of Rights were addressed only to the federal government. When a Maryland property owner in 1833 sought to invoke the just compensation clause of the Fifth Amendment against the City of Baltimore, Chief Justice JOHN MARSHALL wrote in BARRON V. BALTIMORE (1833) that adoption of these amendments "could never have occurred to any human being, as a mode of doing that which might be effected by the state itself"; Congress would not engage in "the extraordinary occupation of improving the constitutions of the several states, by affording the people additional protection from the exercise of power by their own governments, in matters which concerned themselves alone."

After the Civil War, Congress began a process of constitutional amendments that did afford new protections to people who were excluded from political power in their own states. The THIRTEENTH AMENDMENT ended slavery, and the FOURTEENTH AMENDMENT defined CITIZENSHIP and restrained states from denying their own residents as well as other persons national privileges and immunities, DUE PROCESS, or the EQUAL PROTECTION OF THE LAWS. Thereafter, the FIFTEENTH, NINETEENTH, TWENTY-FOURTH, and TWENTY-SIXTH AMENDMENTS, respectively, forbade all states to deny voting rights to any citizen by reason of race or color, or sex, or failure to pay a tax, or to eighteen-year-old citizens. Except for this progressive expansion of the franchise, the Thirteenth and Fourteenth Amendments are the only federal constitutional provisions since 1789 to guarantee individual rights against the states.

With the turn of the twentieth century, the United States Supreme Court began to construe the Fourteenth Amendment's guarantee of "due process" so as to strike down substantive state regulations, first of property and economic activities, and later of activities involving speech, press, assembly, and religion that the FIRST AMENDMENT would protect against federal infringement. Theoretically, each state's bill of rights remained the primary and independent guarantee against oppressive action by that state, but state courts had provided little protection in interpreting and enforcing these guarantees. In the thirty years after 1935, claims to rights equivalent to those under the First Amendment and federal restraints on the criminal law process were increasingly pressed upon and accepted by the United States Supreme Court under the Fourteenth Amendment, until practically all provisions of the federal Bill of Rights were incorporated into "due process" under that amendment. (See INCORPORATION DOCTRINE.)

Because most state constitutions are easily amended, they often reflect the shifting popular concerns of an era as the United States Constitution does not. Although a federal EQUAL RIGHTS AMENDMENT proposed in 1972 failed to win ratification, similar texts were adopted by twelve states. Eight states incorporated guarantees of "privacy" into their bills of rights, creating new conundrums about the intended meaning and scope of that term. Some states sought to halt or reverse the ending of racial SEGREGATION by constitutional amendments, futile in the face of the Fourteenth Amendment, to forbid the operation of integrated public schools or the enactment of OPEN HOUSING LAWS. Some sought to stem the costs of social programs by new limits on taxes and spending.

State constitutions also were amended in reaction to judicial decisions under state bills of rights. The record of state constitutional amendments must be considered in any theory that would locate changing social values in the changeless terms of the Fourteenth Amendment.

State courts have a mixed record in enforcing their states' guarantees of liberty, equality, and fair procedures. Defendants' procedural rights in principle were well protected at trial, but not in police investigations and prearraignment procedures. About half the states followed the federal rule to exclude illegally seized evidence before the United States Supreme Court mandated exclusion under the Fourteenth Amendment. State courts gave some force to constitutional clauses concerning the SEPARATION OF CHURCH AND STATE but practically none to FREEDOM OF SPEECH or of the press, the latter often being threatened as much by orders of the courts themselves as by legislation. Much of the United States Supreme Court's case law after 1930 responded to state court failures to protect individual rights. With the growth of this case law, lawyers began to argue only under the developing federal jurisprudence, and state courts gave no independent application to their states' own guarantees, with one exception: They continued to strike down state regulations of business and property under notions of SUBSTANTIVE DUE PROCESS long after the Supreme Court disavowed this practice under the Fourteenth Amendment.

Since the 1970s, however, there has been a dramatic revival of state court decisions under state constitutions. Some of these were independent of any decision of the United States Supreme Court; many others turned to state constitutions in reaction to Supreme Court holdings or doctrines denying claims under the United States Constitution. The revival was encouraged in a 1977 speech by Justice WILLIAM J. BRENNAN, himself a former member of the New Jersey Supreme Court. The theme was taken up by other Justices and state judges.

The result is a rapidly growing diversity of constitutional decisions among state and federal courts. The California court in SERRANO V. PRIEST (1977) and the New Jersey court in *Robinson v. Cahill* (1973) held that equal rights under their states' constitutions required equalization of financial support to public schools after the Supreme Court denied this claim under the Fourteenth Amendment in SAN ANTONIO SCHOOL DISTRICT V. RODRIGUEZ (1972). Similar holdings followed when the Supreme Court allowed the exclusion of abortion from state-paid medical services. After the United States Supreme Court limited rights of access to shopping centers in *Lloyd Corp., Ltd. v. Tanner* (1972), several state courts found such rights in their state constitutions, some on the far-reaching premise that their state's speech guarantees did not run only against government. State decisions have invalidated services to parochial school students that pass muster under the First Amendment. The Oregon Supreme Court in *Wheeler v. Green* (1979) forbade punitive damages for defamation, though the United States Supreme Court has indicated that they are permissible.

The most numerous and most controversial constitutional guarantees apply to criminal law. Their protection is not so generally valued by twentieth-century citizens as it was by those who gave them

constitutional stature. State supreme courts have struck down the death penalty as cruel or unusual punishment and have departed from federal holdings on such issues as DOUBLE JEOPARDY, right to jury trial and to counsel for petty offenses, and SEARCHES INCIDENT TO ARREST. The response has included constitutional amendments by INITIATIVES to reinstate CAPITAL PUNISHMENT and to tie state provisions relating to police seizures to FOURTH AMENDMENT holdings of the United States Supreme Court.

Before the United States Supreme Court bound the states to most federal constitutional rights through the Fourteenth Amendment, courts had to decide only whether and how to apply each state's bill of rights. After the Supreme Court's incorporation doctrine decisions, most courts again applied only a single body of law, the federal case law. The revival of state constitutional guarantees raised problems inherent in the dual legal system of federalism that had long been forgotten. Some of these are procedural problems; others concern the substance of constitutional interpretation.

When state law, including state constitutional law, protects whatever right a person claims, it cannot logically be said that the state violates any federal guarantee that the person otherwise might invoke. Logical procedure, therefore, requires that the state's ordinary law and thereafter its constitutional law be determined before reaching any claim that the state falls short of federally mandated standards. This principle has been recognized by some state courts, for example Oregon's in *Sterling v. Cupp* (1981), Maine's in *State v. Cadman* (1984), and New Hampshire's in *State v. Ball* (1983). Other courts, however, apply their own state constitutions selectively when they perceive a reason to differ from federal doctrine or to insulate a decision from review by the United States Supreme Court, or they cite both federal and state constitutions for the same holding. These hybrid practices have been criticized as unprincipled because state constitutions are invoked only when necessary to diverge from less protective decisions of the United States Supreme Court, or because citation of both constitutions simultaneously prevents further review by the United States Supreme Court and discourages amendment of the state constitution. In 1983 the United States Supreme Court and some state courts called for "clear statements" whether the claimed right was grounded in the state or the federal constitution.

Many lawyers and judges routinely use contemporary Supreme Court pronouncements on federal constitutional law as benchmarks also for interpretation of state constitutions, particularly when similar texts are involved. But state courts need not regard these pronouncements as authoritative in state constitutional interpretation, whether or not the texts are the same. The fact that state and federal texts were adopted with the same intent or purpose does not make the federal interpretation presumptively correct; a difference in texts only makes this point easier to see. The principle is true both for results and for methodology; many state decisions do not follow the mid-century Supreme Court's formulas for analyzing and resolving constitutional issues, while others do so.

Responsible interpretation of state constitutions often presents problems unique to the state. Historical records are not readily available to lawyers; sometimes none were preserved. When old texts are repeated in successive constitutions, it is debatable which generation's understanding should matter. The uneven quality of opinions requires reliance on precedents to be selective yet not capricious. The ever present temptation held out to courts is to act as pragmatic policymakers in the guise of constitutional interpreters, without excessive scruple whether anyone placed the supposed principle of decision into the constitution, or whether the principle as stated can be given consistent application.

For many reasons constitutional law has long been equated with the decisions of the Supreme Court of the United States. The Court as an institution is the subject of extensive and continuing writings by social scientists and journalists as well as by legal scholars. Only its decisions apply throughout the nation. The Court's nationalization of individual rights in mid-twentieth century, coinciding with the development of dominant national news media and with the emphasis of professional education on national materials, obscures the fact that the federal system makes the states responsible for large and important areas of law over which the Supreme Court has no jurisdiction unless a state administers this responsibility in a manner contrary to the United States Constitution or laws.

The late-twentieth-century revival of state constitutions has served to remind the general public as well as legal professionals of the essentials of the federal system. Its importance is not measured by the instances in which state courts have enforced individual rights beyond decisions of the United States Supreme Court. Many important functions, problems, and innovations of state constitutions do not concern individual rights. Moreover, citizens sometimes were quick to repeal constitutional guarantees of rights when these were enforced by their courts. State constitutions provide no security for dispensing with the national guarantees of the Fourteenth Amendment.

Even debates over repealing guaranteed rights, however, brought citizen responsibility for these rights close to home as no United States Supreme Court decision could do. Although citizens in some states amended their constitutions to revive capital punishment and relinquish protections against police abuses, similar proposals were defeated in other states.

Experience in the states, in the conduct of state government as well as in state court decisions of constitutional issues, continues to offer alternative models and concepts by which to test, and sometimes to gain, ideas for the nation. After two centuries, independent constitutional thought and action in the states remains an essential strength of federalism as well as a guarantee of individual freedom.

HANS A. LINDE

Bibliography

ABRAHAMSON, SHIRLEY S. 1982 Reincarnation of State Courts. *Southwestern Law Journal* 36:951–974.

BRENNAN, WILLIAM J. 1977 State Constitutions and the Protection of Individual Rights. *Harvard Law Review* 90:459–504.

DOUGLAS, CHARLES G. 1978 State Judicial Activism—The New Role for State Bills of Rights. *Suffolk University Law Review* 12:1123–1150.

ELAZAR, DANIEL J. and SCHECHTER, STEPHEN L., eds. 1982 State Constitutional Design in Federal Systems. *Publius* 12:1–185.

LINDE, HANS A. 1984 E Pluribus—Constitutional Theory and State Courts. *Georgia Law Review* 18:165–200.

McGRAW, BRADLEY D. 1984 *Developments in State Constitutional Law.* St. Paul, Minn.: West Publishing Co.

POLLOCK, STEWARD G. 1983 State Constitutions as Separate Sources of Fundamental Rights. *Rutgers Law Review* 35:705–722.

PORTER, MARY C. and TARR, G. ALAN, eds. 1982 *State Supreme Courts.* Westport, Conn.: Greenwood Press.

UTTER, ROBERT F. 1984 Freedom and Diversity in a Federal System. *University of Puget Sound Law Review* 7:491–525.

STATE FREIGHT TAX CASE

See: *Philadelphia & Reading Railroad Co. v. Pennsylvania*

STATE OF . . .

See entry under name of state

STATE OF EMERGENCY

See: Emergency Powers

STATE OF TENNESSEE v. SCOPES
289 SW 363 (1925)

In 1925 Dayton, Tennessee, authorities arrested a local high school teacher, John T. Scopes, for violating the state's Butler Act, which prohibited public school instructors from teaching "any theory that denies the story of the Divine Creation of man as taught in the Bible, and to teach instead that man has descended from a lower order of animals." Scopes admitted to teaching about evolution from George Hunter's *Civic Biology,* a book approved by Tennessee's textbook commission. The Scopes trial, soon known throughout the nation as "the monkey trial," came in the middle of a decade punctuated by the Red Scare, increased urban–rural tensions, and the resurgence of the Ku Klux Klan. The Dayton courtroom soon became an arena of cultural and political conflict between fundamentalist Christians and civil libertarians.

The former, led by William Jennings Bryan, a three-time presidential candidate and ardent prohibitionist who joined the prosecution staff, argued that the Butler Act was a traditional exercise of STATE POLICE POWER with respect to public education, little different from mandating other curricula and fixing the qualifications of teachers. They also saw the statute as a defense of traditional folk values against the moral relativism of modern science and other contemporary religious beliefs. Scopes's defenders, including the AMERICAN CIVIL LIBERTIES UNION (ACLU) and the celebrated criminal lawyer Clarence Darrow, saw in the Butler Act a palpable threat to several constitutional guarantees, including SEPARATION OF CHURCH AND STATE and FREEDOM OF SPEECH.

The trial judge, John T. Raulston, rejected all constitutional attacks against the statute; he also declined to permit testimony by scientific and religious experts, many of whom hoped to argue the compatibility between evolution and traditional religious values, including the belief in a supreme being. The only issue for the jury, Raulston noted, was the narrow one of whether or not John Scopes had taught his class that man had descended from a lower form of animals. Because Scopes has already admitted doing so, the jury's verdict was never in doubt. Darrow and the defense gained a public relations triumph by putting Bryan on the stand to testify as an expert about the Bible. The Great Commoner, who collapsed and died several days after the trial ended, affirmed his faith in biblical literalism, including the story of Jonah and the whale. The jury, however, found Scopes guilty and Raulston fined him the statutory minimum of $100.

Darrow and the ACLU encountered only frustration when they attempted to APPEAL the conviction. The state supreme court, with one judge dissenting, upheld the constitutionality of the Butler Act. However, they reversed Scopes's conviction on a technicality, holding that the Tennessee constitution prohibited trial judges from imposing fines in excess of $50 without a jury recommendation. The state supreme court also urged Tennessee officials to cease further prosecution of John Scopes—advice which the attorney general followed. The Butler Act remained on the Tennessee statute books but was not enforced against other educational heretics.

MICHAEL E. PARRISH

Bibliography
GINGER, RAY 1958 *Six Days or Forever? Tennessee v. John Thomas Scopes.* New York: Oxford University Press.

STATE OF WAR

The existence of a "state of war" for various purposes of domestic and international law is not generally controlled by the existence or absence of a congressional DECLARATION OF WAR. The federal courts, including the Supreme Court, have often held that hostilities, not accompanied by any formal declaration of war (as has been the case in all but five of the approximately 160 occasions in which American armed forces have been committed to combat), were "war" and, conversely, that "peace" existed despite the fact that war had been declared and not terminated by a peace treaty or legislative action. Sometimes the same hostilities have been treated as "war" for one purpose and "peace" for another. Examples can describe the judicial approach better than generalities.

The undeclared naval combat with France in 1798–1799 was treated as war for the purpose of a statute rewarding those who recaptured American vessels "from the enemy" (*Bas v. Tingy,* 1800) but (many years later) as peace under the Franco-American treaty of 1778 (*Gray v. United States,* 1884). The Civil War, though of course never declared by Congress, created a state of war under international law, so that neutral vessels running the Union blockade of Confederate ports could lawfully be captured and sold as prizes. (See PRIZE CASES, 1863). American forces sent to China to help suppress the Boxer Uprising of 1900 were engaged in war under Article of War 58, which permitted courts-martial to try charges of murder only "in time of war" (*Hamilton v. McClaughry*, 1905). But although on June 10, 1949, a declared war still existed between the United States and Germany and Japan, the Supreme Court held that, since there were no hostilities, that date was "time of peace" under a similar Article of War (*Lee v. Madigan*, 1959; the decision effectively overruled *Kahn v. Anderson*, 1921). The COURT OF MILITARY APPEALS and at least one civilian court held that the Korean and Vietnam conflicts, though not declared wars, were nonetheless "war" under provisions of the Uniform Code of Military Justice, which suspended the statute of limitations and increased penalties for certain military offenses in wartime (*Broussard v. Patton*, 1972; *United States v. Bancroft*, 1953; *United States v. Anderson*, 1968). But the Court of Military Appeals and the COURT OF CLAIMS also held that only a declared war could trigger a provision of the Code which gives courts-martial JURISDICTION "in time of war [over] persons serving with or accompanying an armed force in the field." The principle that emerges from examination of these and many similar cases is that the existence of a "state of war" depends principally on the amount of violence, unless a holding that "war" existed would raise serious constitutional questions, as by giving courts-martial jurisdiction over civilians.

The question can, of course, be of profound importance, for war is chief among the great emergencies that may be held to justify actions of the executive and the legislature which would in normal times be plainly unconstitutional. The most extreme example is the Supreme Court's refusal to strike down the 1942 exclusion of American citizens of Japanese descent from the West Coast and their confinement in "relocation centers," under an EXECUTIVE ORDER of President FRANKLIN D. ROOSEVELT, which had been ratified by an act of Congress. (See EXECUTIVE ORDER 9066; JAPANESE AMERICAN CASES.) As a general proposition it may be said that the Supreme Court's unwillingness to hold unconstitutional the actions of the President and Congress in such emergencies varies in inverse ratio to the size of the emergency and the decision's chronological closeness to it. It has been the practice of the Court to scrutinize emergency measures much more closely and to give the executive and legislature much less leeway if the case reaches the Court after the war is over. (See EX PARTE MILLIGAN, 1866; DUNCAN V. KAHANAMOKU, 1946.)

JOSEPH W. BISHOP, JR.

Bibliography

BISHOP, JOSEPH W., JR. 1974 *Justice under Fire: A Study of Military Law.* Pages 178–180, 192–201. New York: Charterhouse.

RATNER, LEONARD G. 1971 The Coordinated Warmaking Power—Legislative, Executive and Judicial Roles. *Southern California Law Review* 44:461–489.

STATE POLICE POWER

The POLICE POWER of the states is one of the most important concepts in American constitutional history; yet, like PRIVACY or FREEDOM OF CONTRACT, its historic significance derives from usage and application, not from the language of the Constitution itself. Nowhere in the Constitution does the term appear.

In his *Commentaries on the Laws of England* (1769) WILLIAM BLACKSTONE provided a definition of public police as "the due regulation and domestic order of the kingdom, whereby the inhabitants of the State, like members of a well-governed family, are bound to conform their general behavior to the rules of propriety, good neighborhood, and good manners, and to be decent, industrious, and inoffensive in their respective stations." Some of the early American treatises quoted this definition, but in fact it serves badly as a guide to constitutional doctrine and governmental realities in the United States in the 1790s or the early nineteenth century. Nor was the Supreme Court much more effective in providing guidance as to the substance and limits of the police power. Chief Justice JOHN MARSHALL verged perilously near outright tautology in GIBBONS V. ODGEN (1824), when he referred to the police power of the states as "that immense mass of legislation, which embraces every thing within the territory of a State, not surrendered to the general [national] government," and as the "acknowledged power of a State to regulate its police, its domestic trade, and to govern its own citizens." Left entirely open, of course, was the matter of what indeed had not been "surrendered" in the way of state powers as well as the matter of what was "acknowledged" as a legitimate part of residual state SOVEREIGNTY in light of the Constitution. The Court itself, clearly, would acknowledge positive powers and define the terms of "surrender." As late as 1847, in his opinion in the LICENSE CASES, Chief Justice ROGER B. TANEY was referring to the state police power in terms that hardly improved upon Marshall's, so far as specificity was concerned, but that at least had a more positive (if not to say sweeping) rhetorical thrust: that power was, Taney declared, "nothing more or less than the powers of government inherent in every sovereignty to the extent of its dominions." Not until the post-Civil War years, when FOURTEENTH AMENDMENT litigation paraded state regulatory laws before the Supreme Court for review, did the Court begin to grapple more tellingly with the problem of definition. Even in contemporary times, however, fitting the police power into the constellation of constitutional ideas has remained one of the Court's most perplexing concerns. There was as much critical acumen as despair in Justice WILLIAM O. DOUGLAS's plaint, in *Berman v. Parker* (1954), that "an attempt to define its reach or trace its outer limits is fruitless, for each case must turn on its own facts." In the last analysis, Douglas contended, "the definition is essentially the product of legislative determinations. . . ."

The Marshall and Taney approach to definition of the police power was sufficient, in a sense, because it sought only to place some sort of label on the powers that remained with the states once the Court had determined the legitimate reach of the CONTRACT CLAUSE and of the COMMERCE CLAUSE; the police power was what the states had left when such determinations had been made. From the standpoint of state lawmakers, however, the approach of the two great Chief Justices was not at all sufficient. First, it did not make even the most basic conceptual distinctions among the fundamental types of governmental power; and so defining the police power as coextensive with sovereignty meant that police subsumed the powers of taxation and EMINENT DOMAIN. Second, the Marshall-Taney approach did not come to grips with power and its legitimate reach in a positive sense. What were the sources of state authority in its exercise of sovereign power? On what basis could a state court, for example, weigh the legitimacy of a regulatory law (even if clearly not beyond the bounds set by federal contract clause and commerce clause rules) against state constitutional limitations such as those prohibiting TAKINGS without JUST COMPENSATION?

It fell to one of the nation's greatest state judges, Chief Justice LEMUEL SHAW of Massachusetts, to produce a doctrinal exposition on the police power that would establish the framework for subsequent adjudication and debate. Shaw's formulation was set forth in *Commonwealth v. Alger* (1851), in which the Massa-

chusetts high court upheld as a proper exercise of "the police power" (so explicitly called) a statute that forbade construction of any wharf in specified areas of Boston harbor. Shaw's great achievement was twofold. He broke out of the *cul de sac* to which Marshall and Taney had driven, addressing the legitimacy of the police power in terms liberated from boundaries set by commerce and contract clause doctrine; and he offered a jurisprudential foundation for positive governmental action.

Shaw conceded at the outset that the police power challenged head-on any efforts to tame it and bring it within bounds. Yet, while it was "not easy to mark its boundaries, or prescribe limits to its exercise," the police power must be acknowledged as superior in some reasoned way to private rights and claims. It was so, Shaw contended, as "a settled principle, growing out of the nature of well-ordered civil society." And so he turned to the task of giving substance to what the Supreme Court had lately termed "the police power belonging to the states, in virtue of their general sovereignty" (Justice JOSEPH STORY in PRIGG v. PENNSYLVANIA, 1842). One of the foundations of that power was the COMMON LAW rule *sic utere tuo ut alienum non laedas* (use your own property in such manner as not to injure that of another). Historically, the rule had been invoked to justify private nuisance and PUBLIC NUISANCE actions alike; in either way, however, it had been used in essentially defensive modes. Shaw linked the *sic utere* concept with a positive obligation of government to impose a system of reasonable restraints on private property uses. "Rights of property," he contended, are properly subject "to such reasonable restraints and regulations established by law, as the legislature, under the governing and controlling power vested in them by the Constitution, may think necessary and expedient." As Leonard W. Levy, the biographer of Shaw, has shown, Shaw thus advanced doctrine well beyond the old common law framework; although Shaw held out the possibility of judicial overturning of laws that were not "reasonable" and violated private VESTED RIGHTS, he stressed the propriety of the legislature's acting when necessary and expedient to impose restraints for the public good.

But Shaw also undertook to define a related, yet in some measure conceptually distinct, foundation for the police power: the concept of "rights of the public." Thus Shaw insisted on the "expediency and necessity of defining and securing the rights of the public," and elsewhere on "the acknowledged public right." Even acts not necessarily punishable by common law might properly be declared illegal by regulatory legislation, Shaw wrote, "for the sake of having a definitive, known and authoritative rule which all can understand and obey." Thus, from the Shaw court in 1851, American police power doctrine emerged in its essentials. As in an earlier decision in 1837 (*Commonwealth v. Blackington*), Shaw asserted the legislature's power to act for the public good to be "the general rule," whereas restraint of the legislature should be the "specific exception."

The next step in elaboration of police power doctrine was the specification of positive purposes, more detailed than the public good or "rights of the public" broadly stated, for which the power would justify regulatory legislation. Early efforts at specification along these lines, before Shaw reformulated the whole issue, had tended simply to codify the common law categories of behavior and property uses constituting nuisance. (Such, for example, is what one finds in Chancellor JAMES KENT's *Commentaries.*) Here again, the arsenal of the common law held an instrument potentially powerful—the principle *salus populi suprema lex* (the welfare of the people is the supreme law), which in the seventeenth and eighteenth centuries in England had often been invoked to assert the plenary powers of Parliament restricted only by accumulated constitutional liberties. In an influential Vermont decision, handed down three years after Shaw's great effort, Chief Justice Isaac Redfield declared that "the general comfort, health, and prosperity of the State" warranted state regulatory powers on the same basis of power as "resides in the British parliament, except where they are restrained by written constitutions" (*Thorpe v. Rutland Railroad*, 1855).

In some other state courts, judges proved reluctant to endorse wholly such broad definitions of legitimate intervention; yet even these more conservative jurists, while looking for principles on which to support JUDICIAL REVIEW, contributed to specification of the bases of positive authority. Thus one of the Michigan judges in *People v. Jackson & Co.* (1861) contended that powers "which can only be justified on [the] specific ground" of the police power or general legislative power must be "clearly necessary to the safety, comfort and well being of society." This line of reasoning was reflected in the 1877 decision of the Supreme Court in BOSTON BEER CO. V. MASSACHUSETTS, in which Justice JOSEPH P. BRADLEY stated for the Court that a PROHIBITION statute against sale of alcoholic beverages did not violate the rights of a brewery company, for clearly such legislation was warranted under the police power: "However difficult it may be to render a satisfactory definition of it," Bradley wrote,

"there seems to be no doubt that it does extend to the protection of the lives, health, and property of the citizens, and to the preservation of good order and the public morals."

Two other doctrinal arguments found their way into antebellum state jurisprudence on the police power. The first, which was rooted in the notion that the power was part of the residuary sovereignty and of legislative authority comparable to that of Parliament, was that the police power was inalienable. That is, states could not bargain away their power—and obligation—to look after the public interest. (See INALIENABLE POLICE POWER.) The second, a pragmatic strain that would doubtless frighten those who believed that vested rights in property deserved more rigid protection, was the view that the police power needed to be consonant with the changing character and needs of the society. This latter, expansive view of the police power found vivid expression in decisions of the 1850s upholding new regulations which permitted railroads to use the public streets to gain access to urban centers. How the imperatives of material progress inspired this expansive doctrine was illustrated in the language of an Illinois decision in 1859 (*Moses v. Railroad*) declaring that to deny a railroad the use of public streets, "no matter how much the general good may require it, simply because streets were not so used in the days of Blackstone, would hardly comport with the advancement and enlightenment of the present age."

Although the antebellum state courts had provided them with a doctrinal foundation for expanded regulatory initiatives, the state legislatures in fact were slow to extend the range or increase the intensity of regulation. Still, grist for judicial mills was provided by laws that were challenged in the long-established areas of state intervention—that is, in such matters as the regulation of streams to protect navigation and fisheries, marketing regulations and standards, laws requiring the fencing-in of livestock, rudimentary safety legislation (especially against fire dangers), and the control of operations on public works such as bridges, highways, and canals. In the late 1840s and the 1850s, police-power measures proliferated as both the regulation of railroad operations and prohibition of alcoholic beverages became common. Astute lawyers were quick to resist expansive claims for the police power, especially when they limited the freedom that powerful economic interests enjoyed in the use of their property. Prior to 1833, challenges to the police power were often based on the Fifth Amendment as well as on comparable provisions of the state constitutions; but the decision of BARRON V. BALTIMORE cut off that line of defense for propertied interests. Still, lawyers continued to rely on the DUE PROCESS provisions of state constitutions; and they contended regularly that regulations took away the value of private property without just compensation—in other words, that the regulations effectively were "takings" and amounted to INVERSE CONDEMNATION. Despite the doctrinal contribution of Chief Justice Shaw and others in the 1850s, moreover, lawyers resorted commonly to the view that only uses of property that were actionable under the common law (as noxious uses, nuisances, or trespasses) could be reached by state regulations. In few cases did courts respond favorably to such arguments. Still, the intellectual and to some degree political groundwork was thereby laid for future attacks on the police power.

Adoption of the Fourteenth Amendment gave new impetus and hope to defenders of private property, who presented arguments in the courts that the PRIVILEGES AND IMMUNITIES clause and the due process clause alike afforded new protections against interventions under the police power. Simultaneously with adoption of the amendment, in 1868, came publication of THOMAS M. COOLEY's treatise, *Constitutional Limitations,* in its first edition. Of basic importance to Cooley's view of the limitations that ought to confine the power of state legislatures was his premise that the "due bounds of legislative power" were not set alone by "express constitutional provisions." The implied limitations that he believed ought to apply all hinged on a generalized "due process" concept. Due process, he contended, forbade enactment of what he termed "class legislation" (laws imposing burdens or granting privileges to specific groups or interests that were arbitrarily singled out instead of being "reasonably" classified). Moreover, his generous definition of due process would forbid laws that were "arbitrary and unusual [in] nature," and as such "unknown to the law of the land." The champions of laissez-faire, if given reason for optimism by the Fourteenth Amendment and the views in Cooley's treatise, were provided with a source of unbounded joy by publication in 1886 of CHRISTOPHER G. TIEDEMAN's *Limitations of the Police Power in the United States.* Tiedeman's great contribution was his attempt to turn the clock back altogether, to negate the principal contribution the Shaw Court had made in *Alger,* by resurrecting wholesale the doctrine that the old common law limits also constituted the proper limits of the positive police power. In effect, Tiedeman attempted to fuse the concept of due process, in the Constitution, with the traditional common law limits of *sic utere.* By the late 1870s, the Supreme Court itself had become divided on the crucial question: how far could state regulation go in limiting the actions of private persons and corporations in the marketplace?

The subsequent battle was not confined to the courts; it extended to the legislatures and the political hustings. Indeed, the question of regulatory power was at the very vortex of the storm in both national and state politics for three-quarters of a century. Three issues were involved in the debates. The first was whether specific types of regulatory actions by government abridged, unconstitutionally, what came to be called FREEDOM OF CONTRACT. The second was whether the courts or, instead, the legislatures were supreme in determining whether specific regulations were constitutionally permissible. Finally, there was the issue of what standards the courts should apply generally—if indeed the judicial branch had the power to review specific regulatory measures—to distinguish constitutional measures from those that were unconstitutional. All these issues centered on the rights of property.

Supreme Court doctrine continued to echo pre-Civil War formulations, even expanding them (rhetorically, at least) at the height of conservative, property-minded influence on the Court. Thus in *Barbier v. Connolly* (1884) Justice STEPHEN J. FIELD declared that neither the Fourteenth Amendment nor any other "was designed to interfere with the power of the State, sometimes termed its police power, to prescribe regulations to promote the health, peace, morals, education, and good order of the people, and to legislate so as to increase the industries of the State, develop its resources, and to add to its wealth and prosperity." Going as far, but in terms perhaps even more open-ended and expansive, Justice JOHN MARSHALL HARLAN asserted in *Chicago, Burlington & Quincy Railway v. Commissioners* (1906) that the legitimate police power of the state "embraces regulations designed to promote the public convenience or the general prosperity, as well as regulations designed to promote the public health, the public morals or the public safety." Despite such assertions of legitimacy for regulatory power, virtually every new or proposed regulation threatening to impose costs or restraints on private interests met with resistance in the state legislatures and the courts. Regulation varied in scope and effectiveness, from one state to another. The latitude and potential for diversity within the legal system offered by FEDERALISM was never more apparent. Nonetheless, the emergent industrial order, the rapid growth of population and absorption of millions of immigrants, urbanization, and the social dislocations that attended the acceleration of technological change and the growth of large-scale firms with enormous leverage over their employees and markets all served to focus political and legislative attention on expansion of the states' regulatory activities. Soon the courts were crowded with cases challenging regulative innovations.

The threshold question, of course, was whether legislative discretion should be permitted or whether the courts should impose constitutional standards that went to questions of substance such as "reasonableness." Before the Civil War, "due process" had been understood as referring to procedural requirements (right to a FAIR HEARING, specification of procedural steps and forms, NOTICE, and the like). In the 1870s, counsel in both the SLAUGHTERHOUSE CASES of 1873 and *Munn v. Illinois* and the other GRANGER CASES of 1877 argued that state regulatory legislation should be overturned on grounds of "due process" deprivation now defined as deprivation of substantive rights in violation of the Fourteenth Amendment. However, the right to regulate private interests, the Court declared in *Munn*, is one "which may be abused," to be sure; but "for protection against abuses by legislatures the people must resort to the polls, not to the courts."

Within a short time, though, the Court reversed itself and began to review state legislation under the police power with a view toward deciding whether "abuse" had occurred. Expansion of the concepts of SUBSTANTIVE DUE PROCESS and freedom of contract, in the hands of a Court whose personnel and social philosophy had changed radically by the 1890s, brought the Court into the business of acting regularly as censor of legislation on substantive grounds. Despite the continued ascendancy in national politics of Republican and conservative-Democratic regimes that resisted pressures for sweeping social-reform legislation, still a flood of new state legislation came forth in such areas as municipal public health, franchise law affecting public utilities, factory and mining safety, maximum hours, child labor, building codes, and railroad safety and operating practices. Neither the state courts nor the Supreme Court lacked for opportunities to play the role of censor and apply the new substantive due process reading of the Fourteenth Amendment.

Thus the courts turned to the last of the great questions regarding constitutional definition of the police power and its limits in the post-Civil War era: the question of standards or formulae for determining constitutionality. One of those standards emerged early in the period—ironically, in *Munn v. Illinois*, in which the new Fourteenth Amendment claims

were decisively rejected by the Court. In deciding the case, however, the Court set forth the new principle of AFFECTATION WITH A PUBLIC INTEREST, asserting that warehouses and railroad companies were subject to regulation because they were virtual monopolies. They were comparable to bridges and ferries, long held by the common law to be a special category of business dedicated to service to the public, standing athwart essential lines of commerce and travel. Citizens were compelled, in effect, to resort to them; hence they were classified by the Court as being in the regulable category. The "affectation" doctrine was a Trojan horse. If there was a line to be drawn between businesses regulable because of their essential character—that is, because the public was compelled to use them for vital activities—then on the other side of that line were types of business immune from regulation. Such was the logic of *Munn*. In later years, the Court struck down a great variety of state regulatory laws on the grounds they were aimed at businesses not affected with a public interest. Indeed, not until 1934 in NEBBIA V. NEW YORK did the Court finally abandon the affectation distinction, ruling that a state could properly regulate any economic interest. "It is clear," the Court declared, "that there is no closed class or category of businesses affected with a public interest."

"Freedom of contract" similarly served as a standard for the Court to strike down regulatory legislation. Thus in LOCHNER V. NEW YORK (1905) and ADKINS V. CHILDREN'S HOSPITAL (1923), as well as in other decisions, the Court invalidated various state laws that regulated the terms of industrial employment. Like the "affectation" standard, however, the freedom of contract formulation as a restriction on the police power was destined to be discarded in the course of the New Deal period of the Court's history.

Other limitations on state exercise of the police power proved to be more enduring. They are, in part, the limitations rooted in the older, antebellum concept of due process as a procedural concept, reinforced by the terms of the EQUAL PROTECTION clause of the Fourteenth Amendment. Not only the Supreme Court but also the state courts—both in periods when many courts were inclined to invalidate social-reform legislation on the grounds of freedom of contract and in periods when they were more inclined to be deferential to legislatures—have contributed to the formulation of continuing restraints on the police power. Thoroughly accepted in American constitutional law, in recent decades, is Justice OLIVER WENDELL HOLMES's warning, in *Noble State Bank v. Haskell* (1911), that regulatory legislation by its definition will "more or less limit the liberty of the individual or . . . diminish property to a certain extent"—but government would be paralyzed if such limitations should regularly fall afoul of constitutional objections. Yet Holmes himself conceded in his opinion in the controversial case of *Pennsylvania Coal Company v. Mahon* (1922) when the Court invalidated a Pennsylvania law curbing mining companies' property rights in an effort to save urban structures from collapsing, that there must be some definable "limits" to the police power: "While property may be regulated to a certain extent, if regulation goes too far it will be recognized as a taking." Thus a line must be drawn between the police power, which permits diminution of property or liberty, and the power of eminent domain, which authorizes a taking only for a public purpose and on payment of adequate compensation.

To this specific consideration of when regulation encroaches on the realm of eminent domain taking, the Supreme Court and state courts have welded the more traditional procedural concerns. Exemplary of the latter was the doctrine of the Tennessee high court in *Vanzant v. Waddel* (1829) to the effect that to be valid a regulation must be "a general public law, equally binding upon every member of the community . . . under similar circumstances." Chief Justice Shaw of Massachusetts elaborated the theme in decisions upholding forfeiture of property deemed unwholesome or a PUBLIC NUISANCE, but requiring TRIAL BY JURY and judicial process. So long as the legislature established a precise statutory rule, applied it evenhandedly, and provided traditional procedural safeguards, the Shaw court would uphold police power regulation. Later, from the Supreme Court opinion in MUGLER V. KANSAS (1887), came the formulation that to be valid a police power regulation must have a "real or substantial relation" to public health, morals, safety, and welfare; and in 1936 (*Treigle v. Homestead Association*) the Court also declared that a regulation must be enacted "for an end which is in fact public and the means adopted must be reasonably adapted to the accomplishment of that end." These considerations of due process, too, have survived even though the restraining concepts to which they were once wedded—the "affectation" idea, and substantive due process concepts such as judicial determination of reasonableness—have largely been stripped from them.

In recent times, and particularly since the expansion of the positive state in the New Deal era, constitutional challenges to the police power have come to a focus on the question of how much administrative discretion ought to be allowed to state regulatory agencies. Agricultural marketing commissions, fish and game control agencies, mining-safety authorities, factory inspection boards, fire- and building-code enforcement agencies, air and water pollution control boards, and other regulatory agencies of government have been held to standards of administrative due process. Their substantive powers of regulation, however, have been generally upheld broadly by state and federal courts.

Emblematic of modern police power issues in the law is the history of land-use ZONING. Even prior to the decision in 1926 of EUCLID V. AMBLER REALTY, in which the Supreme Court upheld zoning that excluded industrial use, several of the states' appellate courts had validated such legislation. In each instance, they rejected claims that property owners had suffered from an effective "taking," hence ought to be compensated. As the Supreme Court itself noted in *Euclid*, such regulations a half century earlier "probably would have been rejected as arbitrary and oppressive"; now they were found necessary and valid because they were consonant with the magnitude of emergent industrial and urban problems. As the California Supreme Court declared in *Miller v. Board of Public Works* (1925), widely cited in other cases involving expansion of administrative discretion: "The police power, as such, is not confined within the narrow circumspection of precedents, resting upon past conditions which do not cover and control present-day conditions. . . . [It] is elastic and, in keeping with the growth of knowledge and the belief in the popular mind in the need for its application, capable of expansion. . . ."

The presumption of constitutionality against claims based on due process was explicitly stated in opinions of the Supreme Court again in the 1930s, echoing the majority's views in *Munn*. In *Nebbia*, for example, the Court not only laid to rest "affectation with a public interest" as a limitation on the police power; it also held that a regulation should be accorded "every possible presumption . . . in favor of its validity . . . unless palpably in excess of legislative power." When the Court upheld a statute regulating prices charged by employment agencies, in OLSEN V. NEBRASKA (1941), it couched its holding in terms that made its new posture unmistakable: "We are not concerned," wrote Justice William O. Douglas, "with the wisdom, need, or appropriateness of the legislation. . . . There is no necessity for the state to demonstrate before us that evils persist." In FERGUSON V. SKRUPA (1963) the Court refused to strike down a state law that prohibited anyone from engaging in the business of debt-adjusting except as incidental to the practice of law.

Justice HUGO L. BLACK, writing for the Court, acknowledged that good arguments doubtless could be made for the social utility of the activity thus restricted. But he concluded that though the regulation might be "wise or unwise," this substantive issue was not the Court's concern; it belonged to the state legislature. In *Agins v. Tiburon* (1980) a municipal zoning ordinance severely limited development of openspace lands; the Court again upheld a sweeping use of the police power and turned away due process arguments against the ordinance. So long as even a greatly reduced use of the land was permitted, the Court ruled, claims that "justice and fairness" had been denied would not be upheld. Although the Court still imposed commerce power limitations on the states' regulatory activities, by the 1980s it seemed that the presumption of constitutionality against due process, contract clause, and inverse condemnation claims was firmly entrenched.

A decision ostensibly on a narrow technical point yet vitally important for expansion of discretionary power's real-life effectiveness was *Morrissette v. United States* (1951). In this decision the Court reaffirmed state court rulings dating back to pre-Civil War years that when criminal penalties are used to enforce police power regulations regarding "public health, safety and welfare," the state is not constitutionally required to prove criminal intent, as in ordinary criminal cases.

In response to the emergence of the modern state police power, there has been abundant scholarly debate and legal controversy regarding its impact on private economic rights. Some have welcomed the enlarged regulatory power and administrative discretion, declaring them to be indispensable in the complex world of modern economic and social change. These same features of the modern police power have been condemned heatedly by others, however, as unfair in their application. That eminent domain takings, which do require compensation, and actions under the police power, which do not, are on a continuous spectrum of state power has long been recognized. Numerous scholarly formulations have been offered to distinguish the two powers. The classic distinction was given in ERNST FREUND's great treatise, *The Police Power: Public Policy and Constitutional Rights*, published in 1904. Freund contended that "the state takes property by eminent domain because it is useful to the public, and under the police power because it is harmful." Modern critics of the expanded police power and the positive state deplore restrictions upon uses of property that impose costs upon a private owner in order to benefit the public, rather than to prevent harm to the public; thus, the person prevented from building on his or her land where it stands in the flight path of an airport's runway is said by these critics to be harmed unfairly, forced in effect to bear alone the cost of a public benefit.

There are some, indeed, who take a hard-line position on the police power by arguing that virtually all restraints—but certainly those that deprive private property owners of what previously had been "reasonable expectations" of use and profit from regulated property—ought to be accompanied by reasonable compensation. Only the narrowest sort of regulation, based on common law nuisance and *sic utere* doctrine, would be exempt as these property-minded conservatives formulate their theory. The possibility that paralysis of the regulatory process might be caused by the sheer volume of government compensation payments required by this theory is a source of satisfaction rather than dismay to the most doctrinaire proponents of this view. Posed against it, and in favor of a definition of police power broad in its terms and consonant with recent decisions, is a theory that when government undertakes the role of "enterpriser" (creating parks, building highways, sponsoring urban renewal projects) it ought to compensate owners whose property is taken or damaged; but in its role as "arbiter" of contending social interests, as Joseph Sax has written, its actions for regulation of private uses of property should require no compensation. Other commentators, taking a middle position, urge that courts should give fresh recognition to considerations of "fairness" in these matters—for example, guarding against the possibility of a property owner's becoming the victim of more or less systematic deprivation, and also distinguishing degrees of harm and damage to the private owners affected by a STATE ACTION. These commentators also urge that administrators and legislators should be aware of "demoralization costs" when no effort is made to ameliorate the suffering of those hit hardest by regulatory activities.

The conflict between claims of the public under the police power and the claims of private property thus constitutes one major area of constitutional adjudication and current debate. Another area, no less turbulent and controversial, is the conflict between the police power and personal freedoms. Virtually all confrontations between persons and the state on matters of FREEDOM OF SPEECH, FREEDOM OF THE PRESS, FREEDOM OF ASSEMBLY, SEPARATION OF CHURCH AND STATE, or discrimination based on sex or religion or race are confrontations involving the police power. The whole corpus of constitutional doctrine based on the BILL OF RIGHTS and on the Fourteenth Amendment, in this area, together with such federal statutes as the various CIVIL RIGHTS acts, serve as a comprehensive set of limitations upon exercise of the state police power. The states remain free, however, to impose a higher standard in regard to constitutional liberties than is required by prevailing Supreme Court doctrine based on the federal Constitution.

As the uses of the federal regulatory powers have expanded, especially since 1933, there has been increasing need for the courts to examine the question of PREEMPTION—that is, the supersession of state laws when federal regulation has occupied a given policy area. In cases such as PARKER V. BROWN in 1943, and *Florida Avocado Growers v. Paul* twenty years later, the Supreme Court has upheld state marketing regulations affecting agricultural products even though both federal antitrust regulation and federal farm policies presented serious preemption questions. In the fields of labor law and transportation regulation, however, the Court has been more inclined to curb the scope of state activity in fields regulated by federal statutes and administrative regulations. Since the mid-1960s, a wave of consumer-oriented, industrial safety, and environmental legislation enacted by Congress has brought national power into regulatory areas previously occupied largely by state law. These initiatives have occasioned considerable litigation centering on preemption and congressional intent. In a few instances, the new federal statutes specifically authorize imposition of higher regulatory standards by individual states; other statutes have provided for federal preemption after a specified period, in states that do not meet certain minimum standards of regulation and enforcement.

The complexities of the preemption issue in modern constitutional law concerning the state police power are emblematic of the differences between government intervention in the present day and intervention on the modest scale of the eighteenth and nineteenth centuries. In 1836 Justice Joseph Story summarized the limited functions of the state in his day: to protect the persons and property of citizens from harm, to guard personal rights; to establish courts of justice and enforce laws against crimes, to enforce contracts, and to encourage moral behavior. These functions, together with state promotion of economic development, were justified because they were "conducive to the strength and the happiness of the people." What Story could not anticipate—and what is at the core of the modern constitutional history of the state police power—is the enormous expansion of regulatory activity and the accompanying shift toward enlarged administrative discretion in the mod-

ern state. Recent decisions and treatises are no longer much concerned with issues concerning the legitimacy of the police power as such issues were defined in Field's and Cooley's day, or even in the early years of the New Deal. Nonetheless, changing values as to equality, fairness, and rights of the public—and, to an increasing degree in the 1980s, a revival of issues concerning efficiency criteria and the wisdom of regulatory policies—continue to be expressed both in policy debates and in scholarly dialogue on the place of the state police power in the constitutional system.

HARRY N. SCHEIBER

Bibliography

FREUND, ERNST 1904 *The Police Power: Public Policy and Constitutional Rights.* Chicago: Callaghan.

HASTINGS, W. A. 1900 The Development of the Law as Illustrated by the Decisions Relating to the Police Power of the State. *Proceedings of the American Philosophical Society* 39:359–554.

LEVY, LEONARD W. 1957 *The Law of the Commonwealth and Chief Justice Shaw.* Cambridge, Mass.: Harvard University Press.

REZNICK, SCOTT M. 1978 Empiricism and the Principle of Conditions in the Evolution of the Police Power: A Model for Definitional Scrutiny. *Washington University Law Quarterly* 1978:1–92.

SCHEIBER, HARRY N. 1982 Law and the Imperatives of Progress: Private Rights and Public Values in American Legal History, *Nomos: Yearbook of the American Society for Political and Legal Philosophy* 24:303–320.

SCHWARTZ, BERNARD 1965 *A Commentary on the Constitution of the United States, Part II: The Rights of Property.* New York and London: Macmillan.

STOEBUCK, WILLIAM V. 1980 Police Power, Takings, and Due Process. *Washington and Lee Law Review* 37:1057–1099.

STATE REGULATION OF COMMERCE

When the Framers of the Constitution granted Congress the power "to regulate Commerce with foreign Nations, and among the several States, and with the Indian Tribes," they did not specify what regulatory powers were to be left to the states. Did they intend simply to grant a power to Congress which left the states free to regulate until such time as Congress acted? Were states restrained only from enacting statutes inconsistent with federal statutes? Or was the grant of power to Congress intended to be exclusive, forbidding the states to regulate commerce among the states even though Congress had not acted?

These questions troubled the Court several times

during JOHN MARSHALL's tenure as Chief Justice. As a strong nationalist, he was attracted by the argument presented by DANIEL WEBSTER in GIBBONS V. OGDEN (1824) that the word "regulate" implied full power over the thing to be regulated and necessarily excluded the power of the states to regulate the same thing. But Congress could not be expected to regulate all commerce among the states. Most transportation was by water. Inland transportation was slow and difficult. It could take a week or ten days to travel from Boston to New York, and in practical effect Georgia was more remote from New York than from the ports of Europe.

Marshall's solution was to suggest that Congress had full power to regulate INTERSTATE COMMERCE but that in the absence of conflicting federal regulations, the states had power to enact local police laws—inspection laws, quarantine laws, health laws, laws respecting turnpike roads and ferries—even though such laws might affect commerce. After Marshall's death the Justices were sharply divided between those advocating the position that exclusive power to regulate interstate commerce was vested in Congress and those, led by the new Chief Justice, ROGER B. TANEY, advocating the position that states had full power to regulate interstate commerce so long as Congress had not acted.

In 1851, in COOLEY V. BOARD OF WARDENS OF PHILADELPHIA, the Court arrived at a compromise of the conflicting views. In upholding a state law requiring vessels in interstate and FOREIGN COMMERCE to accept local pilots, the Court said that when the subjects being regulated "are in their nature national, or admit only of one uniform system, or plan of regulation" they "require exclusive legislation by Congress." On the other hand, when the subjects were local, as in the case of pilotage regulations attuned to individual conditions of the various ports, the states could regulate until Congress might intervene.

During the next half century the Court struggled to limit the negative implications of its notion of broad federal powers to regulate during a time when the federal government regulated little outside of water transportation. Some theory was needed to support the necessary state regulation of commerce. One way to do this was to narrow the definition of interstate commerce. In PAUL V. VIRGINIA (1868) the Court held that the insurance business was not commerce among the states and so could be regulated by the states. In KIDD V. PEARSON (1888) it upheld an Iowa statute forbidding the manufacture of intoxicating beverages as applied to a manufacturer who sold all his output in other states. The Court said that manufacturing

was not commerce. If it were commerce, the Court assumed, "Congress would be invested, to the exclusion of the States, with the power to regulate not only the manufacturers, but also agriculture, horticulture, stock raising, domestic fisheries, mining—in short, every branch of human industry." In other cases the Court decided when an interstate journey began (when the goods had been actually shipped, or delivered aboard a common carrier for shipment, across state borders) and when it ended (when it came to rest at the end of its journey available for final disposition or use).

Toward the end of the century the Court devised another method for enabling states to regulate in areas Congress had not chosen to regulate. In *Cooley* the Court had said that a federal statute consenting to all present and future state pilotage regulations was invalid insofar as it incorporated future regulations because the division of power between state and nation was fixed in the Constitution and Congress could not change it. In LEISY V. HARDIN (1890) the Court held that one state could not forbid the sale of liquor brought in from another state while still in its ORIGINAL PACKAGE, but added that "so long as Congress does not pass any law to regulate it, or allowing the States so to do, it thereby indicates its will that such commerce shall be free and untrammelled." Congress took the hint and enacted a law permitting states to regulate such traffic in liquor, and the Court upheld the law in *In re Rahrer* (1891). Since then it has been settled that Congress may, if it wishes, permit states to regulate in areas otherwise reserved for Congress.

But even these rules did not result in agreement on the principles to be used in deciding individual cases. Despite the fact that *Cooley* appeared to have established that the states sometimes could regulate, the Court continued to refer from time to time to the "exclusive" power of Congress to regulate interstate commerce. In other cases the Court suggested that the test of validity of a state regulation of interstate commerce was whether it imposed a forbidden "direct" burden on commerce or a permitted "indirect" burden. By the beginning of the twentieth century there was clear agreement on only one principle: state regulations that clearly discriminated against interstate commerce by imposing burdens on such commerce beyond those imposed on comparable INTRASTATE COMMERCE were invalid.

During the first third of this century the Court dealt with a large mass of state regulations of transportation. A fair characterization of the cases would be one of doctrinal confusion. While the Court affirmed that states could not ban interstate transportation or discriminate against it for economic reasons, it had great difficulty in deciding when formally nondiscriminatory state regulations might be invalid because of the burdens they cast on commerce.

Today the Court does not get transportation cases involving state discrimination against interstate commerce. Instead, it is asked to determine that even nondiscriminatory regulations may be invalid if they impose substantial burdens on commerce without compensatory state advantages. *South Carolina State Highway Department v. Barnwell Bros.* (1938) involved a state statute prohibiting the use on state highways of any trucks wider than ninety inches. Although nondiscriminatory, the statute had a major impact on interstate commerce; all other states permitted a width of ninety-six inches, and thus most trucks engaged in interstate commerce would not be able to enter South Carolina. The Court said that few matters of state regulation were "so peculiarly of local concern" as was the use of state highways. The problem was one of determining whether local conditions demanded the regulation in the interests of safety. That determination was "a legislative, not a judicial choice," and the state's conclusion that the regulation was necessary was presumed correct unless "upon the whole record . . . it [was] without a RATIONAL BASIS."

But seven years later, in SOUTHERN PACIFIC V. ARIZONA EX REL. SULLIVAN (1945), the Court indicated that the courts rather than the state legislatures would have the final say in such commerce cases. A state statute limited the length of all trains in Arizona to fourteen passenger cars or seventy freight cars. The Court declared that Congress could "permit the states to regulate the commerce in a manner which would otherwise not be permissible . . . or exclude state regulations even of matters of peculiarly local concern which nevertheless affect interstate commerce." But when Congress had not acted, the final determination was for the courts. The question was whether the state interest in preventing injuries to railroad employees due to the slack action of cars on longer trains was outweighed by the burden the statute would have upon interstate commerce. The Court concluded that the state justification was weak and the burden heavy and so invalidated the statute. *Barnwell* was said to be different because it had dealt with the peculiarly local nature of state highways.

In recent years the Court has struggled with the question whether the *Barnwell* or the *Southern Pacific* approach should be used to judge state regulations of highways. In BIBB V. NAVAJO FREIGHT LINES, INC. (1959) the Court held invalid an Illinois statute requiring trucks to use contour mudguards when all other states permitted, and Arkansas required, straight mudflaps. The Court reaffirmed *Barnwell*, saying that courts should not engage in rebalancing the interests which the state legislature had, but added that this was "one of those cases—few in number—where local safety measures that are nondiscriminatory place an unconstitutional burden on interstate commerce." The Court has also dealt with state laws forbidding the use of trucks pulling double trailers as applied to interstate carriers. In RAYMOND MOTOR TRANSPORTATION, INC. V. RICE (1978) the Court unanimously invalidated a Wisconsin statute, noting that extensive evidence showed the law's heavy burden on interstate commerce and that the state had made no effort to demonstrate any safety interest. In *Kassel v. Consolidated Freightways Corp.* (1981) the Court invalidated a similar Iowa statute but was unable to agree upon an opinion or upon the way in which such regulations should be judged. Only four Justices clearly applied the *Southern Pacific* approach in highway regulation cases; the others were willing to leave the matter to the states when the safety interests at stake were substantial.

Cases involving regulation of production and trade also give the Court difficulty in arriving at consistent standards. Some governing rules are fairly straightforward. A state cannot ban the importation of goods, except in the rare case when goods must be excluded to avoid substantial damage to persons or property. So the Court in GREAT ATLANTIC & PACIFIC TEA CO. V. COTTRELL (1976) held that Mississippi could not forbid the importation of milk from Louisiana which had refused to sign a reciprocity agreement with Mississippi. In PHILADELPHIA V. NEW JERSEY (1978) the Court held invalid a state law banning importation of garbage destined for private landfills. The Court said: "[W]here simple economic protectionism is effected by state legislation, a virtually *per se* rule of invalidity has been erected. . . . The clearest example of such legislation is a law that overtly blocks the flow of interstate commerce at a State's borders."

Nor can a state ban the exportation of goods, even for the purpose of conserving scarce goods for use by citizens of the state. Thus in HOOD & SONS V. DU MOND (1949) the Court held that New York could not deny a milk dealer the right to purchase milk and ship it out of state, even though milk was short for a nearby city. In *Hughes v. Oklahoma* (1979) the Court said the commerce clause forbade the state from preventing the transportation or sale outside the state of minnows procured within the state. And an attempt by New Hampshire to make sure that electricity generated by water power served first the needs of local citizens, by forbidding the export of such power without permission of the state, was invalidated in *New England Power Co. v. New Hampshire* (1982). The Court said that the regulation was "precisely the sort of protectionist regulation that the COMMERCE CLAUSE declares off-limits to the States." However, *Sporhase v. Nebraska* (1982) suggests that a state restriction on the exportation of ground water may be upheld when done "to conserve and preserve for its own citizens this vital resource in times of severe shortage."

Regulations which discriminate against interstate commerce or otherwise operate to protect local commerce against competition are also invalidated. In *Baldwin v. G. A. F. Seelig, Inc.* (1935) the Court held unconstitutional a New York statute that made it unlawful to sell milk purchased from out-of-state producers at prices less than those paid local producers. The Court said: "If New York, in order to promote the economic welfare of her farmers, may guard them against competition with the cheaper prices of Vermont, the door has been opened to rivalries and reprisals that were meant to be averted by subjecting commerce between the states to the power of the nation." A Louisiana statute forbidding the export of shrimp unless the heads and hulls had been removed was held invalid in *Foster-Fountain Packing Co. v. Haydel* (1928) because the effect was to favor the canning of meat and the manufacture of bran in Louisiana.

Much more difficult for the Court have been cases that do not overtly discriminate against interstate commerce. In DEAN MILK CO. V. MADISON (1951) the Court invalidated a city ordinance forbidding the sale of milk as pasteurized unless it had been processed and bottled at an approved plant located within five miles of the center of Madison. Although the criterion excluded in-state as well as out-of-state milk, the Court said it discriminated against interstate commerce. The Court recognized that Madison had a legitimate interest in the purity of milk, but held it could not give an economic preference to local businesses if there were reasonable nondiscriminatory alternatives, such as inspection outside the state.

In *Pike v. Bruce Church, Inc.* (1970) the Court held unconstitutional, as applied to a grower with a substantial packing plant in California, an Arizona statute forbidding shipment of fruit out of the state unless it was packed in containers bearing the name of Arizona. The court set out a series of tests which have been frequently referred to in later cases: "Where the statute regulates even-handedly to effectuate a legitimate local public interest, and its effects on interstate commerce are only incidental, it will be upheld unless the burden imposed on such commerce is clearly excessive in relation to the putative local benefits. . . . If a legitimate local purpose is found, then the question becomes one of degree. And the extent of the burden that will be tolerated will of course depend on the nature of the local interest involved, and on whether it could be promoted as well with a lesser impact on interstate activities."

The Court has difficulty in applying the *Pike* formula. The major problem comes in deciding whether a case presents a nondiscriminatory statute with an incidental EFFECT ON COMMERCE or one which can be characterized as discriminatory, hence requiring the higher STANDARD OF REVIEW. In *Hunt v. Washington State Apple Advertising Commission* (1977) a North Carolina statute requiring all closed containers of apples sold in the state to bear no grade other than the applicable U.S. grade or standard was challenged by Washington, which marketed under its own grades which were equivalent or superior to the U.S. grades. Even though the statute applied equally to local and out-of-state shippers of apples, the Justices found that the statute discriminated against the Washington apples and held it invalid. The principal difficulty appeared to be that the statute took from Washington the market advantages it had earned through its own grading system.

The next year, in *Exxon Corp. v. Maryland* (1978), however, the Court upheld a state law forbidding a producer or refiner of petroleum products to operate any retail service station within the states. Maryland had no in-state oil production or refining. The Court said that the act did not affect the interstate transportation of gasoline—presumably the same volume would come in after the statute as before—but merely the structure of retailing. Further, since owners of multi-state chains of retail stations who did not produce gas could continue to compete, there was not even a preference for locally owned stations. The Court said that *Hunt* was different because there the statute favored in-state operators over out-of-state ones.

More recently, in MINNESOTA V. CLOVER LEAF CREAMERY CO. (1981), the Court upheld a Minnesota statute banning the retail sale of milk in plastic nonreturnable, nonrefillable containers while permitting such sale in other nonreturnable, nonrefillable containers such as paperboard milk cartons. The Court noted that the statute did not discriminate. The burden imposed on commerce was very slight since most dairies packaged their milk in various kinds of containers, and the shifts in the business would not be distributed on in-state, out-of-state lines.

Finally, the Court has held that when the state itself is in the market producing or selling goods, the commerce clause does not restrict the state. Thus in *Reeves, Inc. v. Stake* (1980) the Court upheld, 5–4, a decision by South Dakota to cease selling cement which the state manufactured to out-of-state customers in order to supply the needs of South Dakota customers. The Court said that the state, as a market participant, was free to prefer its own citizens, even though it could not order private businesses to do the same. The Court distinguished the manufacture of cement from regulating private use of natural resources such as coal, timber, wild game, or minerals. The cement was the end product of a complex process in which a physical plant and human labor of the state had acted on raw materials. The dissenters said the policy upheld was "precisely the kind of economic protectionism that the Commerce Clause was intended to prevent."

Today, as in 1824, the Court has great difficulty in defining its place with reference to state regulation of interstate commerce. States can regulate commerce in the absence of conflicting federal regulation so long as they do not go too far. The Court will strike down clear discriminations or economic preferences for local economic interests. But, when confronted with a nondiscriminatory regulation that imposes an incidental burden on commerce, the Court will sometimes let the regulation stand until Congress acts and in other cases will intervene to protect commerce. This uncertainty is likely to persist.

EDWARD L. BARRETT, JR.

Bibliography

DOWLING, NOEL T. 1940 Interstate Commerce and State Power—Revised Version. *Virginia Law Review* 27:1–28.

NOWAK, JOHN E.; ROTUNDA, RONALD D.; and YOUNG, NELSON J. 1978 *Handbook on Constitutional Law.* Pages 243–266. St. Paul, Minn.: West Publishing Co.

RIBBLE, F. D. G. 1937 *State and National Power over Commerce.* New York: Columbia University Press.

TRIBE, LAURENCE H. 1978 *American Constitutional Law.* Pages 319–344. Mineola, N.Y.: Foundation Press.

VARAT, JONATHAN D. 1981 State "Citizenship" and Interstate Equality. *University of Chicago Law Review* 48:487–572.

STATES' RIGHTS

"States' rights" is better understood not as a term of art denoting a constitutional principle but as a slogan with tactical value in political controversy. The slogan of states' rights has been raised at one time or another by advocates from every region of the country and by partisans of every political persuasion. The phrase emphasizes one element of FEDERALISM, but it is a serious error to equate federalism with states' rights.

Although the states' rights are often asserted in terms of state SOVEREIGNTY, the claim of states' rights is really a claim on behalf of the sovereignty of the people. No government, national or state, properly exercises any power that has not been delegated to it by the people. The assertion of states' rights is most often made by those who oppose a policy of the national government and who claim that the people have not delegated to the national government the power to implement the policy. Less often the assertion is made by those who believe that the states, or at least their own states, are more likely than the federal government to implement a desired policy.

The idea of states' rights is as old as the Republic. The jealousy with which the colonial legislatures guarded their limited local powers against the British Parliament and the royal government was carried over into ANTI-FEDERALIST CONSTITUTIONAL THOUGHT. To the extent that the argument for states' rights is one of principle, it is based on the classical notion that public virtue flourishes only in relatively small political communities. The French political philosopher MONTESQUIEU, whom JAMES MADISON called the "oracle" for American constitutionalists of the Founding Era, restated the classical view in modern terms and maintained that the best practical regime was a small republic confederated for military and commercial purposes with similar small republics. Many Anti-Federalists opposed the Constitution from a genuine fear of consolidation into a continental empire that only a despot could govern effectively.

But there was also a practical factor in the Anti-Federalist opposition. In the years between 1776 and 1789, the state governments had assumed responsibility for their internal affairs to a far greater degree than the colonial governments had ever done. Individual leaders, parties, cliques, and factions had arisen and assumed their places in state politics; creation of a national political environment was bound to reduce the power of most of them. Familiar ways of dealing with problems would be replaced with strange ones.

After the RATIFICATION OF THE CONSTITUTION, the erstwhile opponents of the new frame of government, along with some of its defenders, sought to interpret it in Anti-Federalist, or Montesquian, terms. The Constitution, according to this interpretation, was a compact between the people of each state and the people of the other states. When the Federalist-dominated national government adopted the ALIEN AND SEDITION ACTS (1798), "states' rights" became the battle cry of the Republican party, whose leaders, JAMES MADISON and THOMAS JEFFERSON, gave the slogan substantive expression in the VIRGINIA AND KENTUCKY RESOLUTIONS (1799).

In the nineteenth century the growing sectional rivalry between the commercial, and increasingly industrial, North and the agrarian South was reflected in competing THEORIES OF THE UNION. The states' rights position came to be identified in public discourse with the interest of the slave power. It found its champion in JOHN C. CALHOUN, who, in the South Carolina EXPOSITION AND PROTEST (1828–1829), announced the doctrine of NULLIFICATION as a logical consequence of the state compact theory. Nullification, of course, was an empty threat unless it was backed up by the possibility of SECESSION.

One attempt was made to implement Calhoun's doctrine, the SOUTH CAROLINA ORDINANCE OF NULLIFICATION directed against the TARIFF ACT OF 1828, and that was a failure. In 1861, when the election of ABRAHAM LINCOLN as President clearly signaled that slavery had been belatedly set upon its course of ultimate extinction, eleven southern states withdrew from the Union. Lincoln denied not only the legitimacy but also the very possibility of secession, and the victory of the Union in the Civil War vindicated his position for all practical purposes. Whatever rights the states have they have as members of the Union.

The FOURTEENTH AMENDMENT, adopted after the Civil War, proved an obstacle to state regulation of economic activity begun under the influence of the Populist and Progressive movements. Because the BILL OF RIGHTS applied only to the federal government, individuals whose rights were infringed by actions of the state governments (unless they were the victims of BILLS OF ATTAINDER, EX POST FACTO LAWS, or laws impairing the OBLIGATION OF CONTRACTS) previously had been able to rely only on the state constitution, political system, or courts for redress. In the late nineteenth and early twentieth centuries, however, the Supreme Court held the substantive guarantees (life, liberty, and property) of the Fourteenth Amendment's due process clause to be effective limitations on state legislative power. In the rhetoric of the reformers, the federal government (or at least its judicial branch) had infringed on the states' right to regulate their internal affairs.

In the 1920s the cry of "states' rights" was raised both by those who opposed federal intrusions into areas of state legislative concern and by those states that were frustrated in the attempt to expand state regulatory power. It is instructive that states' rights claims were raised in both MASSACHUSETTS V. MELLON (1923) and PIERCE V. SOCIETY OF SISTERS (1925), the first in the interest of less and the second in the interest of more governmental regulation.

Between the late 1940s and the late 1960s, the cause of states' rights became virtually identified with the cause of southern opposition to CIVIL RIGHTS legislation. The national commitment to abolishing racial SEGREGATION, first in publicly owned facilities and then in private establishments dealing with the public, aroused fierce opposition among those who were destined to lose their privileged position. Despite its long history of service to every shade of political opinion, the slogan of "states' rights" may have been permanently tarnished by its association with state-sponsored RACIAL DISCRIMINATION.

If the states, as states, have a valid claim of right to any particular field of legislation, that field would seem to be legislation concerning the internal workings of the governmental apparatus of the state. In the twentieth century the federal government undertook to regulate the compensation and working conditions of state employees, incidentally to its regulation of compensation and working conditions of private employees under the COMMERCE CLAUSE. In NATIONAL LEAGUE OF CITIES V. USERY (1976) the Supreme Court struck down such regulation insofar as the employees concerned were involved in the essential governmental operations of the states. The distinction was undermined in EQUAL EMPLOYMENT OPPORTUNITY COMMISSION V. WYOMING (1983), and discarded as unworkable in GARCIA V. SAN ANTONIO METROPOLITAN TRANSIT AUTHORITY (1985). In *Garcia* a 5–4 Supreme Court explicitly overruled *Usery*, and—unless the dissenters were accurate in predicting that the *Usery* doctrine would one day be revived—effectively put an end to the last vestige of states' rights in constitutional law.

DENNIS J. MAHONEY

(SEE ALSO: *Tenth Amendment.*)

Bibliography

ELAZAR, DANIEL J. 1972 *American Federalism: A View from the States,* 2nd ed. New York: Thomas Y. Crowell Co.
GRODZINS, MORTON 1966 *The American System: A New View of Government in the United States,* ed. Daniel J. Elazar. Chicago: Rand-McNally.
SANFORD, TERRY 1967 *Storm over the States.* New York: McGraw-Hill.

VILE, M. J. C. 1961 *The Structure of American Federalism.* Oxford: Oxford University Press.

STATES' RIGHTS AMENDMENTS
(1963–1967)

The decisions of the WARREN COURT radically altered the constitutional balance of power to the disadvantage of the several states. In 1963, the Council of State Governments recommended three constitutional amendments that would, respectively, have established a third variation of the AMENDING PROCESS by which the states could alter the Constitution without the participation of Congress; denied the Supreme Court JURISDICTION over apportionment of state legislatures; and created a Court of the Union, comprising all the state chief justices, with power to overrule the Supreme Court on questions of federal–state relations.

The amendments were introduced in Congress by Senator J. Strom Thurmond of South Carolina but were buried in committee. Supporters hoped to have two-thirds of the state legislatures petition Congress and thereby oblige Congress to call an amending convention. The first and third proposals encountered widespread opposition—including public denunciation by Chief Justice EARL WARREN. But the 1964 REAPPORTIONMENT decisions, REYNOLDS V. SIMS and *Lucas v. Forty-Fourth General Assembly,* spurred the legislatures to act on the remaining proposal. By the time the agitation ceased in 1967, thirty-three states (only one less than necessary) had petitioned for an amending convention on the apportionment issue.

DENNIS J. MAHONEY

STATE SUICIDE THEORY

Massachusetts Senator CHARLES SUMNER, like most abolitionists and all Republicans before the Civil War, believed that the federal government lacked constitutional power to abolish slavery in the states. By early 1862, however, he and some other Republicans sought a theoretical basis for the exercise of congressional authority to govern occupied areas of the Confederacy and to eliminate slavery there. While other Republicans flirted with theories of territorialization or the CONQUERED PROVINCES concept of Representative THADDEUS STEVENS, Sumner developed his own unique amalgam of constitutional ideas for Reconstruction, which came to be known as the state suicide theory.

Sumner believed that the Confederate states, by seceding, had committed a sort of constitutional suicide, dissolving their "peculiar local institutions" (that is, slavery) and leaving their territory and inhabitants to be governed by Congress. This conception derived from three constitutional sources. The idea that the seceded states had reverted to the condition of TERRITORIES was widely discussed among Republicans after the outbreak of war. The belief that slavery, because it required positive law for its existence, would expire when that law expired, was derived from implications of the doctrine of SOMERSET'S CASE (1772) and had appeared in abolitionists' constitutional arguments before the war. Abolitionists also found a basis of congressional power to govern the states (including the power to abolish slavery there) in the clause of Article IV, section 4, that requires the United States to guarantee a REPUBLICAN FORM OF GOVERNMENT to each of the states. (See ABOLITIONIST CONSTITUTIONAL THEORY.)

Democrats, conservatives, and even moderate Republicans deplored the state suicide theory, regarding it as unconstitutional because it recognized the validity, or at least effectiveness, of SECESSION. Sumner abandoned his insistence on the constitutional death of the states but continued to maintain that Congress had plenary governmental power in the occupied states.

WILLIAM M. WIECEK

Bibliography
DONALD, DAVID 1970 *Charles Sumner and the Rights of Man.* New York: Knopf.

STATE TAXATION OF COMMERCE

Since BROWN V. MARYLAND in 1827 the Supreme Court has decided hundreds of cases determining the extent to which the COMMERCE CLAUSE immunizes from state taxation property moving in INTERSTATE COMMERCE or businesses engaged in such commerce. From the outset, agreement has existed on one principle—state taxes that discriminate against interstate commerce are invalid. In WELTON V. MISSOURI (1876) the Court held invalid a state tax on local sales because it applied only to goods produced outside the state. Recently, in *Boston Stock Exchange v. State Tax Commission* (1977), the Court stated that the "fundamental principle" that no state may impose a tax that discriminates against interstate commerce "follows inexorably from the basic purpose of the [Commerce] Clause. Permitting individual states to enact laws that favor local enterprises at the expense of out-of-state businesses 'would invite a multiplication of preferential trade areas destructive' of the free trade which the Clause protects."

The Supreme Court recognized early, however, that even formally nondiscriminatory taxes might put interstate commerce at a competitive disadvantage. In PHILADELPHIA & READING RAILROAD V. PENNSYL- VANIA (1873) a tax on transportation companies measured by cents per ton of freight carried within the state (but not apportioned to distance) was held invalid as applied to goods in interstate commerce even though local commerce paid the same tax. The Court noted that if one state could impose this tax all states could and commercial intercourse between states remote from each other might be destroyed. Interstate commerce could bear the imposition of a single tax but "it would be crushed under the load of many." To avoid such burdens the Court formulated broad prophylactic rules. States were not permitted to tax interstate commerce by laying taxes on property in transit in interstate commerce, the business which constituted such commerce, the privilege of engaging in it, or the receipts derived from it.

The Supreme Court did not go so far, however, as to hold that states could never secure revenue from interstate businesses. An immunity that broad would have placed the states in the position of being required to provide governmental services to interstate property and businesses within their borders without being able to secure from them any contribution to the costs of such governmental services. Hence the Court came to recognize a variety of avenues through which states could derive revenue from interstate commerce.

The principal state revenue producer in the last century was the *ad valorem* property tax. Although property taxes on goods actually moving in interstate commerce were forbidden (because of the risk that they would be applied by more states than one), states were permitted to impose property taxes upon railroad cars and barges if they were apportioned (usually by mileage) so as to apply, in effect, only to the average number of cars present in the state on any one day. The Supreme Court even went so far as to permit states to levy property taxes on the intangible values of interstate transportation companies by permitting the imposition of taxes upon the proportion of the total going-concern value of the companies that track mileage within the state bore to total track mileage.

In other cases activities were characterized as intrastate in order to permit state taxation. Manufacturing, mining, and PRODUCTION were held to be IN- TRASTATE COMMERCE and taxes upon such activities were permitted even though substantially all of the goods produced were shipped in interstate commerce. Sales involving the transfer of goods from seller to buyer within the state were regarded as intrastate while sales involving no more than solicitation of orders within the state followed by delivery from without were interstate sales. Hence, states could impose nondiscriminatory license taxes on peddlers who carried with them the goods they sold but not on drummers who merely took orders. Later, when modern sales taxes came into existence, the Court applied the same principles. A sales tax could not be imposed when the seller outside the state shipped goods to the purchaser inside the state, but it could be imposed upon the local retailer who brought the goods from outside and then sold and delivered them to customers. In order to protect local merchants from competition by out-of-state sellers, states imposed on purchasers a tax on the "first use" within the state of goods purchased, with an exemption for goods on which the sales tax had been paid. The Supreme Court sustained such taxes on the theory that they were imposed on a local transaction—the use—rather than upon the interstate sale.

Another major boost to the power of states to secure revenues from interstate commerce came in *United States Glue Co. v. Town of Oak Creek* (1918). The Supreme Court upheld the power of a state to impose taxes measured by net income derived within the state, including net income from interstate activities. The Court distinguished earlier decisions forbidding the imposition of taxes on gross income from commerce by saying that such taxes burdened commerce directly while net income taxes, applied only to the taxpayers' net profits, bore only indirectly upon commerce. The power of the states to impose net INCOME TAXES was initially limited only by two principles. First, a net income tax could not be collected if the taxpayer did only interstate commerce within the state, because it would constitute an imposition on the privilege of engaging in interstate commerce—a privilege that the state did not grant. Second, the tax could be imposed only upon that portion of the net income fairly attributable to activities within the taxing state. A rational apportionment formula was required.

In *Western Livestock v. Bureau of Revenue* (1938), Justice HARLAN FISKE STONE sought to derive from the cases a general principle that would abrogate the general rule that interstate commerce itself could not be taxed. He said that it was not the purpose of the commerce clause "to relieve those engaged in interstate commerce from their just share of state tax burden even though it increases the cost of doing business." He noted that gross receipts taxes had often been held invalid. "The vice characteristic of those which have been held invalid is that they have placed on commerce burdens of such a nature as to be capable in point of substance, of being imposed . . . or added to . . . with equal right by every state which the commerce touches, merely because interstate commerce is being done, so that without the protection of the commerce clause it would bear cumulative burdens not imposed on local commerce."

The decision in *Western Livestock* did not mark an end to the older idea that interstate commerce itself could not be directly taxed. As recently as 1946 in *Freeman v. Hewit*, Justice FELIX FRANKFURTER speaking for the Court said:

Nor is there any warrant in the constitutional principles heretofore applied by this Court to support the notion that a State may be allowed one single-tax-worth of direct interference with the free flow of commerce. An exaction by a State from interstate commerce falls not because of a proven increase in the cost of the product. What makes the tax invalid is the fact that there is interference by a State with the freedom of interstate commerce. . . . Trade being a sensitive plant, a direct tax upon it to some extent at least deters trade even if its effect is not precisely calculable.

For nearly three decades after *Western Livestock* the cases continued to reflect first one and then the other of these conflicting approaches.

Recently, however, the Supreme Court has cleared out most of the underbrush of the cases from the past and has established some relatively simple guidelines for the future. In *Complete Auto Transit, Inc. v. Brady* (1977) the Court said that it considers not the "formal language" of the tax statute but its "practical effect" and sustains "a tax against commerce clause challenge when the tax is applied to an activity with a substantial nexus with the taxing state, is fairly apportioned, does not discriminate against interstate commerce, and is fairly related to the services provided by the State."

With respect to *ad valorem* property taxation, the Court continues to forbid such taxes on goods moving in interstate commerce while reaffirming the rule that properly apportioned taxes may be imposed upon the instrumentalities of commerce such as railroad cars and airplanes. In *Japan Line, Ltd. v. County of Los Angeles* (1979), however, the Court limited this rule as applied to foreign-owned instrumentalities. It held that a country could not impose even an apportioned tax on the value of shipping containers owned by a Japanese shipping company because Japan was taxing the entire value of the containers. The Court said

that its rule permitting apportioned property taxation was based on its ability to force apportionment on all potential taxing jurisdictions. Since Japan could not be required to apportion, the county could not tax at all even though it provided governmental services to the containers when they were in the state.

The distinction between taxes measured by gross income and those by net income has been abolished, along with the rule that states may not tax the privilege of engaging in interstate commerce. In the *Brady* case and in *Department of Revenue of Washington v. Association of Washington Stevedoring Companies* (1978) the Court upheld privilege taxes measured by gross receipts derived from exclusively interstate commerce within the taxing state. The Court indicated that the key is apportionment, which avoids multiple burdens. In *Washington Stevedoring*, for example, it upheld a tax on the gross receipts of a stevedoring company which had as its entire activity loading and unloading in Washington ships engaged in interstate and FOREIGN COMMERCE. It said that the state had "a significant interest in exacting from interstate commerce its fair share of the cost of state government. . . . The Commerce Clause balance tips against the tax only when it unfairly burdens commerce by exacting more than a just share from interstate activity."

A 1959 federal statute (section 381, Title 18, United States Code) provides that a state may not impose a net income tax if the taxpayer does no more within the state than solicit orders. Beyond that limit the major, current problems relate to the apportionment of an interstate business's income among the states having JURISDICTION TO TAX it. Nearly half of the states are adherents to the Multistate Tax Compact which calls for net income to be apportioned by a three-factor formula based on property, payroll, and sales. Most states, whether or not adherents to the Compact, utilize similar three-factor formulas. Iowa, however, applies a formula under which it taxes that proportion of net income that gross sales within the state bear to total gross sales. In *Moorman Manufacturing Co. v. Blair* (1978) a challenge to this formula was rejected. The taxpayer argued that to permit Iowa to use a single-factor formula when other states in which it did business used a three-factor formula would result in the taxation by Iowa of income that had been taxed in other states. The Supreme Court would go no further than to examine the particular formula to see that it is reasonable and does not allocate disproportionate amounts of income to the taxing state, leaving to Congress the question whether a uniform formula should be imposed on all states. The

Court has also recently rejected challenges to the application of apportionment formulas to the entire net income of integrated companies engaged in production, refining, and distribution of petroleum products. In *Exxon Corporation v. Wisconsin Department of Revenue* (1980) the Court held that so long as the taxpayer is engaged in a "unitary business" any state in which it does business may apply its apportionment formula to the entire net income of the business without regard to how the taxpayer's own accounting system allocates profits and losses.

With respect to taxes on the sales transaction, existing doctrines permit the state in which goods are sold to tax through either a sales or a use tax. However, collection of the use tax is often impossible if the state cannot compel the seller to collect the tax from the purchaser and remit it to the state. Recent concern has been with the DUE PROCESS jurisdictional problem. The state must show some definite link, some minimum connection, between the seller and the state, before it can impose the duty of collection.

A century and a half after *Brown v. Maryland* the Supreme Court's approach to state taxation of interstate commerce is relatively simple: so long as the state taxes do not discriminate against such commerce or create a risk of multiplication of similar levies on the same property or activity, they will be upheld. States will be given wide latitude in devising formulas for apportioning income and allocating values. If more protection for commerce is desired, it will have to come from Congress.

EDWARD L. BARRETT, JR.

(SEE ALSO: *Excise Taxes; Import-Export Clause; Imposts; Original Package Doctrine; State Regulation of Commerce.*)

Bibliography
BARRETT, EDWARD L., JR. 1953 "Substance" vs. "Form" in the Application of the Commerce Clause to State Taxation. *University of Pennsylvania Law Review* 101:740–791.

HARTMAN, PAUL J. 1953 *State Taxation of Interstate Commerce.* Buffalo, N.Y.: Dennis Co.

NOTE 1975 Developments in the Law: Federal Limitations on State Taxation of Interstate Business. *Harvard Law Review* 75:956–1036.

STATUS OF FORCES AGREEMENT

Following World War II, as a consequence of entering into a series of mutual defense pacts, the United States established a continuing military presence in a number of foreign countries. To deal with the legal questions that inevitably arose because of this presence, the United States entered into a number of agreements—known as "status of forces agreements"—with the receiving (that is, host) countries involved.

Typically, status of forces agreements exempt visiting forces from the receiving state's passport and immigration regulations, and from its customs duties and taxes on personal property also. Further, the sending state is permitted to issue driving permits and licenses to members of its forces, to purchase goods locally for local consumption, and to employ indigenous civilian labor. In addition, provision usually is made for the settlement of claims for property damage allegedly caused by the visiting forces.

The heart of a status of forces agreement, however, is its allocation of JURISDICTION in respect of criminal offenses putatively committed by the members and accompanying civilians of the visiting forces. In general, the sending state and the receiving state retain exclusive jurisdiction over offenses not punishable by the laws of the other. Where an offense is punishable by the laws of both states, concurrent jurisdiction prevails, with either the sending state or the receiving state retaining the primary right to exercise criminal jurisdiction, depending on the nature of the offense and the circumstances of its occurrence. Where the receiving state exercises jurisdiction, it ordinarily guarantees a prompt and speedy trial, timely notice of charges, the right to confront hostile witnesses, satisfactory legal representation, and a competent interpreter. The accused is usually guaranteed the right to communicate with her or his governmental representatives and to have them present at trial, if possible.

BURNS H. WESTON

(SEE ALSO: *North Atlantic Treaty; Treaty Power.*)

Bibliography
LAZAREFF, S. 1971 *Status of Military Forces under Current International Law.* Leyden, Netherlands: A. W. Sijthoff.

SNEE, J. and PYE, A. K. 1957 *Status of Forces Agreements and Criminal Jurisdiction.* Dobbs Ferry, N.Y.: Oceana Publications.

STATUTORY CONSTRUCTION

See: Legislation

STAY OF EXECUTION

A stay of execution is an order commanding that the enforcement (execution) of a lower court JUDGMENT be suspended (stayed) pending further proceedings before that court or an appeal of the judgment to a higher court. The entry of such an order is essentially a matter of judicial discretion, tempered by various principles developed in court rules and judicial precedents. In a civil case, a stay order may be conditioned on the posting of a bond to protect the interests of the prevailing party; in a criminal case a stay of a prison sentence raises the question of the defendant's entitlement to release or continued freedom, often conditioned on posting a bail bond.

In the federal court system, stays can be sought in district courts, courts of appeals, and ultimately in the Supreme Court. Generally speaking, a litigant must exhaust all possibilities of securing a stay from a lower court or courts before applying to a higher court. Stays are of two categories: a stay of a district court judgment pending an appeal to a court of appeals, and a stay of a court of appeals judgment or mandate pending application to the Supreme Court to review the judgment of the court of appeals. The Supreme Court or an individual Justice has statutory authority to grant both types of stays, provided that all efforts to secure a stay from the lower courts have failed.

Most stay applications in the Supreme Court are addressed to and resolved by individual Justices, acting in their capacity as circuit Justices "in chambers," although application can be made to the entire Court for reconsideration of an individual Justice's denial of a stay. Generally, a stay will be granted when there is a "reasonable probability" that four Justices, the minimum needed to grant review, will vote to review the case; that there is "a fair prospect" that the decision below will be reversed; that irreparable harm to the applicant will likely result if a stay is denied; and that the balance of equities, to the parties and to the public, favors a stay.

EUGENE GRESSMAN

Bibliography
STERN, ROBERT L.; GRESSMAN, EUGENE; and SHAPIRO, STEPHEN M. 1986 Supreme Court Practice, 6th ed. Chap. 17. Washington, D.C.: Bureau of National Affairs.

STEAGALD v. UNITED STATES
451 U.S. 204 (1981)

A 7–2 Supreme Court extended to third parties the rule of PAYTON V. NEW YORK (1980) that, absent consent or exigent circumstances, law enforcement officers may not enter a home to make an arrest without a SEARCH WARRANT. Here the officers sought to execute an ARREST WARRANT for one person by entering the home of another and found EVIDENCE that served to convict that other party. The Court supported his contention that the FOURTH AMENDMENT required a warrant for the search of his home, reasoning that privacy, especially in one's home, outweighed the inconvenience to the officers of having to obtain a search warrant.

LEONARD W. LEVY

STEEL SEIZURE CONTROVERSY

In the latter part of 1951, a dispute arose between the nation's steel companies and their employees over terms and conditions of employment. On December 18, the steelworkers union gave notice of intention to strike when existing agreements expired on December 31. On December 22, President HARRY S. TRUMAN referred the dispute to the federal Wage Stabilization Board and the strike was canceled. The Board's subsequent report produced no settlement. Early in April 1952, the United Steel Workers of America called a nationwide strike to begin April 9.

President Truman and his advisers feared that the interruption of production would jeopardize national defense, particularly in Korea. The President thus issued EXECUTIVE ORDER 10340 to Secretary of Commerce Charles Sawyer, instructing him to take possession and operate the steel mills in the name of the United States government. Truman's authority to take such action was not granted specifically by the statute, and he cited none, although the Selective Service Act of 1948 and the Defense Production Act of 1950 authorized the seizure of industrial plants failing to give priority to defense orders. Although the TAFT-HARTLEY ACT of 1947 had a procedure for injunctive relief in a strike situation affecting an entire industry, or imperiling the national health and safety, it did not contain seizure provisions. Truman preferred to act on the basis of what Department of Justice attorneys assured him was the INHERENT POWER in the office of the President, stemming from his authority as COMMANDER-IN-CHIEF and "in accordance with the Constitution and the laws of the United States."

The steel companies obeyed Secretary Sawyer's order under protest but brought suit to enjoin the seizure in the District Court for the District of Columbia. There Judge David Pine granted a preliminary injunction restraining the secretary from continuing the seizure. Pine's ruling on the merits and the stay of the injunction by the United States Court of Appeals compelled the Supreme Court to face the constitutional issue also, on final appeal. (See YOUNGSTOWN STEEL AND TUBE V. SAWYER, 1952.)

PAUL L. MURPHY

Bibliography

MARCUS, MAEVA 1977 *Truman and the Steel Seizure Case: The Limits of Presidential Power.* New York: Columbia University Press.

STEPHENS, ALEXANDER H.
(1812–1883)

A successful self-taught Georgia lawyer, Alexander Hamilton Stephens was a congressman (1843–1859, 1873–1882), vice-president of the Confederacy (1861–1865), and a lifelong defender of STATES' RIGHTS. As a southern Whig, Stephens sought to protect state SOVEREIGNTY and preserve the Union. These objectives led to apparent inconsistencies. Thus, he opposed JOHN C. CALHOUN and NULLIFICATION while arguing for the abstract right of SECESSION. Similarly, Stephens was a slaveowner who declared that "I am no defender of slavery in the abstract." He supported ANNEXATION OF TEXAS to preserve the balance of free and slave states, but he did not support slave extension generally. He opposed the Mexican War because of his unrelenting hatred of President JAMES K. POLK, his honest belief that the war was unjust, and his fear that it would reopen the divisive issue of SLAVERY IN THE TERRITORIES. But once the war was over he advocated opening the Mexican Cession to slavery. Ironically, he successfully moved to table the Clayton Compromise (1848), even though he supported its purpose, because he believed the Supreme Court would declare that existing Mexican law prohibited slavery in the new territories.

Stephens opposed the COMPROMISE OF 1850, warning: "Whenever this Government is brought in hostile array against me and mine, I am for disunion—openly, boldly and fearlessly for *revolution.*" Nevertheless, once the compromise passed, Stephens supported it in Georgia, and at the state's secession convention of 1850 he helped write the Georgia Platform which denounced disunion. Stephens then joined ROBERT TOOMBS and Howell Cobb in organizing a Union Party in Georgia.

In 1854 Stephens became a Democrat. He was the floor manager for the KANSAS-NEBRASKA ACT (1854) and worked closely with STEPHEN A. DOUGLAS. As chairman of the House Committee on the Territories Stephens supported the LECOMPTON CONSTITUTION, unlike his Senate counterpart (Douglas). Despite Douglas's apostasy on this issue, Stephens supported his presidential nomination in 1860 and futilely campaigned for Douglas in Georgia.

In November 1860 Stephens opposed secession in Georgia, arguing that Southerners and northern Democrats could block any bill that threatened slavery or the South. His pro-Union speech, reprinted throughout the North, led to a brief correspondence with President-elect ABRAHAM LINCOLN. As a delegate to the Georgia secession convention (January 1861), Stephens supported the creation of a southern nation, provided that it adopted a CONSTITUTION similar to that of the United States. In the provisional Confederate Congress Stephens helped draft the CONFEDERATE CONSTITUTION, which owing in part to his influence resembled the Constitution of 1787. Stephens was then chosen vice-president of the Confederacy. As a moderate who had long opposed secession, Stephens gave the new government legitimacy. On slavery, Stephens was by this time quite "sound." As early as 1855 he had defended slavery on biological and biblical grounds, as well as its role in creating southern society, which Stephens believed was the greatest in history. By 1860 he owned more than thirty slaves. In March 1861 he told the South and the world, in his most famous speech, that slavery was the "cornerstone of the Confederacy."

Throughout the Civil War Stephens's relationship with JEFFERSON DAVIS was stormy. Stephens opposed CONSCRIPTION, martial law, and the suspension of the writ of HABEAS CORPUS. He accused Davis of becoming a dictator and advocated that Georgia seceded from the confederacy to seek peace and sovereignty on its own. Stephens urged that the Confederacy support George McClellan's presidential bid and then seek peace with the United States. He made numerous peace overtures, and in early 1865 met with Lincoln in an unrealistic attempt to negotiate a peace that would preserve a separate southern nation.

Arrested for TREASON in May 1865, Stephens was incarcerated at Fort Warren (Boston) until President ANDREW JOHNSON pardoned him in October. He then returned to Georgia where an unreconstructed state legislature elected him to the United States Senate. The Senate responded to this affront by denying Stephens his seat.

In a ponderous and tedious book, *A Constitutional View of the Late War Between the States* (2 vols., 1868, 1870), Stephens presented an elaborate and unconvincing defense of secession. He responded to his many hostile critics with an even duller book, *The Reviewers Reviewed* (1872). Reelected to Congress in 1873, Stephens remained for nearly a decade as an ineffectual and somewhat scorned relic of the past. He continued to defend slavery and states' rights, while opposing reconstruction and black rights.

PAUL FINKELMAN

Bibliography

VON ABELE, RUDOLPH 1946 *Alexander H. Stephens: A Biography.* New York: Knopf.

STERILIZATION

Late in the nineteenth century, when simple and safe medical procedures for sterilization became available, the eugenics movement began to promote compulsory sterilization laws. A few laws were enacted specifying sterilization as punishment for sex crimes, but they were rarely enforced. In 1907 Indiana adopted a law authorizing sterilization of persons deemed "feebleminded," or, as one leading proponent put it, "socially defective." Other states soon followed. The Supreme Court lent both practical and moral support in its 1927 decision in BUCK V. BELL, upholding the constitutionality of Virginia's law. By 1935 more than thirty states had adopted forced sterilization laws, and 20,000 "eugenic" sterilizations had been performed. The victims of such laws tended to be poor; indeed, in the view of eugenics proponents, poverty and other forms of dependence were the marks of the "socially inadequate classes" that needed eradication.

Times have changed, and constitutional law has changed. Concurring in GRISWOLD V. CONNECTICUT (1965), Justice ARTHUR GOLDBERG said, "Surely the Government, absent a showing of a COMPELLING subordinating STATE INTEREST, could not decree that all husbands and wives must be sterilized after two children have been born to them." After SKINNER V. OKLAHOMA (1942) the point seems incontestable. Yet some state courts, following *Buck,* still uphold laws authorizing the involuntary sterilization of institutionalized mental patients. Although only fifteen years separated the *Buck* and *Skinner* decisions, their doctrinal foundations were worlds apart. *Skinner,* calling procreation "one of the basic civil rights of man," insisted on STRICT SCRUTINY by the Court of the justifications supporting a compulsory sterilization law. *Buck,* on the other hand, had employed a deferential form of RATIONAL BASIS review, analogizing forced sterilization to forced VACCINATION.

Skinner's crucial recognition was that sterilization was more than an invasion of the body; it was an irrevocable deprivation of the right to define one's life and one's identity as a biological parent. Vaccination implies no such consequences for one's self-identi-

fication and social role. The constitutional issues presented by sterilization thus bear a strong analogy to the issues raised by laws restricting other forms of BIRTH CONTROL and abortion. (See FREEDOM OF INTIMATE ASSOCIATION.) The Supreme Court has characterized all these forms of state interference with REPRODUCTIVE AUTONOMY as invasions of FUNDAMENTAL INTERESTS, and has subjected them to close scrutiny in the name of both EQUAL PROTECTION, as in *Skinner,* and that form of SUBSTANTIVE DUE PROCESS that goes by the alias of a RIGHT OF PRIVACY, as in *Griswold* and ROE V. WADE (1973).

The issue of *Buck* seems certain to return to the Supreme Court one day, to be decided on the basis of a much heightened STANDARD OF REVIEW. Similarly, a state law requiring consent of a spouse before a person could be sterilized would surely be held invalid, on analogy to PLANNED PARENTHOOD OF MISSOURI V. DANFORTH (1976). If a law calling for involuntary sterilization must pass the test of strict scrutiny, and if a competent adult has a corresponding right to choose to be sterilized, then the critical ingredient is choice. An "informed consent" requirement thus seems defensible against constitutional attack, provided that the required "informing" procedure does not unreasonably burden the decision to be sterilized. (An informed consent requirement for abortion was upheld by the Supreme Court in *Danforth.*)

As Justice WILLIAM O. DOUGLAS noted in his *Skinner* opinion, sterilization in "evil or reckless hands" can be an instrument of genocide. Even the most devoted partisan of reproductive choice cannot be entirely comfortable knowing that the percentage of sterilized nonwhite women in the United States is almost triple that for white women, or that among public assistance recipients blacks are twice as likely to "choose" sterilization as are whites. Under current interpretations the Constitution has nothing to say about the bare fact of this disparity; yet it reflects a condition of constitutional dimension that deserves to be addressed, at least in the domain of PROCEDURAL DUE PROCESS. And if nonwhite women are led by government officers to believe that sterilization is voluntary in theory but somehow compulsory in fact, that form of "engineering of consent" appears reachable in actions for damages under SECTION 1983, TITLE 42, UNITED STATES CODE, based on the deprivation of substantive due process.

KENNETH L. KARST

Bibliography

KELLY, MARY E. 1979 Sterilization Abuse: A Proposed Regulatory Scheme. *DePaul Law Review* 28:731–768.

KEVLES, DANIEL J. 1985 *In the Name of Eugenics: Genetics and the Uses of Human Heredity.* New York: Knopf.

PILPEL, HARRIET F. 1969 Voluntary Sterilization: A Human Right. *Columbia Human Rights Law Review* 7:105–119.

STETTLER v. O'HARA
243 U.S. 629 (1917)

An Oregon Supreme Court decision sustained that state's minimum wage law for women on the basis of the STATE POLICE POWER argument approved in MULLER V. OREGON (1908). A 4–4 Supreme Court affirmed that ruling in *Stettler.* Several state courts drew the inference that a properly drawn law regulating women's wages would be upheld and sustained such laws in reliance on *Stettler.* The DISTRICT OF COLUMBIA MINIMUM WAGE ACT nonetheless fell, 5–3, in ADKINS V. CHILDREN'S HOSPITAL (1923).

DAVID GORDON

STEVENS, JOHN PAUL
(1920–   )

When President GERALD R. FORD named him to the Supreme Court in 1975, John Paul Stevens had all the conventional qualifications for the job. He had served for five years on the UNITED STATES COURT OF APPEALS for the Seventh Circuit, had been a distinguished antitrust law practitioner, a law school teacher, and a law clerk to Justice WILEY B. RUTLEDGE. But those who expected this conventional background to yield a conventional Justice soon learned better. Most new Justices write first for a unanimous Court; Justice Stevens's maiden effort, HAMPTON V. MOW SUN WONG (1976), included a combination of EQUAL PROTECTION and DELEGATION OF POWERS doctrine so novel that only four other Justices joined in it—and two of those added their own concurrence. In the terms that followed, Justice Stevens found it necessary to write separately far more often than any of his colleagues.

Many of his concurrences and dissents were sparked by disagreement with the substance of the BURGER COURT's decisions. He is the only Justice appointed since 1968 who does not regularly vote against criminal defendants, and his strong defense of PRISONERS' RIGHTS clearly runs counter to the majority's thinking. So too does his STRICT CONSTRUC-

TION of the ESTABLISHMENT OF RELIGION clause; and he is among the least receptive of the Justices when states assert local interests against the workings of a national economy, let alone the voice of Congress.

Overall, however, his moderate pragmatism puts him close to the center of the Court on most issues. What divides him from his colleagues is not so much substance as his fundamental dissatisfaction with the Court's judicial style. That style was summed up in UNITED STATES V. NIXON (1974), the year before Stevens's appointment. It is "emphatically the province and duty" of the judiciary, the Court quoted from MARBURY V. MADISON (1803), "to say what the law is." Left, right, and center, the Court he joined was nearly unanimous in wanting to say as much as possible about what the law is.

Stevens came from a different school. His first constitutional law professor, Nathaniel Nathanson, taught him that abstract talk about constitutional issues is usually misleading. In Nathanson's words, "we are the sworn enemies of the glittering half-truths, the over-simplified explanations. We are constantly at war with . . . the black-letter law, the restatements, the horn books." Another teacher soon reinforced the lesson; years after his clerkship, Stevens remembered: "Justice Rutledge exhibited great respect for experience and practical considerations. He was critical of broadly phrased rules which deceptively suggested that they would simplify the decision of difficult questions."

To a degree, this focus on the practical, the concrete, makes Stevens a spokesman for judicial restraint and narrow opinions. He can be relied upon, for example, to protest when the Court reaches out to decide constitutional issues on an insufficient record, as in *Globe Newspaper Co. v. Superior Court* (1982); when it leaps to interpret the Constitution despite a statute that would do the job, as in REGENTS OF THE UNIVERSITY OF CALIFORNIA V. BAKKE (1978); when it insists on reviewing for federal error a state court decision that will likely be restored on ADEQUATE STATE GROUNDS, as in *Michigan v. Long* (1983); or when it invokes the OVERBREADTH DOCTRINE to discuss facts not before the Court, as in *Metromedia, Inc. v. San Diego* (1981). And despite his reputation for unorthodox and strongly held views, some of Stevens's best work has been done in painstaking opinions such as *NAACP v. Claiborne Hardware Co.* (1982), where he held together a diverse group of Justices by saying no more than was necessary to resolve the case.

But Stevens's rejection of glittering half-truths and over-simplified explanations is no mere passive virtue. It has a radical side. In YOUNG V. AMERICAN MINI THEATRES, INC. (1976), for example, where Stevens defended the constitutionality of special ZONING for theaters showing sexually explicit movies, he did so by launching a frontal attack on that most glittering of half-truths—the assertion that government must ignore the content of the speech that it regulates. Only three other Justices joined him in *Mini Theatres,* but he persisted, pointing out in case after case that the principle of "content neutrality" was plainly too sweeping, that content-based distinctions had been employed for years in OBSCENITY, libel, and COMMERCIAL SPEECH cases. Ultimately he prevailed. In *New York v. Ferber* (1982) the Court explicitly endorsed Stevens's *Mini Theatres* analysis in the course of making child PORNOGRAPHY a new class of unprotected speech. Perhaps characteristically, Stevens refused to join the Court's opinion; in his view, the *Ferber* Court had fallen victim to an equally egregious half-truth—the notion that some kinds of speech are wholly beyond the scope of the FIRST AMENDMENT'S protection.

By stripping away the slogans that obscured the First Amendment, Justice Stevens left himself free to follow what he had so admired in Rutledge: he could seek "a practical solution to a practical problem," exercising "the faculty of judgment and not merely the logical application of unbending principles." Recognizing that even obscene speech is still speech, he looked at the practical effect of criminal obscenity prosecutions. In an analysis strikingly parallel to his CAPITAL PUNISHMENT opinions, he concluded that the Court's obscenity decisions had produced laws so vague that they supplied juries with little or no guidance. The result was that, for most pornography, criminal penalties were applied too arbitrarily to withstand scrutiny.

At the same time, it was plain to him that the reasons for restricting sexually offensive speech do not die at the indistinct boundary between the obscene and the merely indecent. Although speech bordering on obscenity cannot be wholly suppressed, Stevens concluded, the practical—and so the constitutionally permissible—solution was to confine such speech to contexts that minimize or even eliminate its offensiveness. Thus, in SCHAD V. VILLAGE OF MT. EPHRAIM (1981) he would have allowed the town to bar nude dancing from quiet shopping centers and neighborhoods—but apparently not from "a local replica of Place Pigalle." In FEDERAL COMMUNICATIONS COMMISSION V. PACIFICA FOUNDATION (1978) he would have let the government keep four-letter words off afternoon radio—but not out of the United States Reports.

This insistence that constitutional issues be examined context by context marks all of Stevens's campaigns against the artificiality of black-letter constitutional law. When he joined the Court, for example, EQUAL PROTECTION analysis had split into two tiers, each with its own set of incantations; the prevailing doctrinal dispute was whether and where to add yet a third, "intermediate" tier between STRICT SCRUTINY and RATIONAL BASIS review. Again Justice Stevens's solution was a striking doctrinal departure: not more tiers but fewer. "There is only one Equal Protection Clause," he wrote in CRAIG V. BOREN (1976), and so only one basic STANDARD OF REVIEW. By demanding that legislative classifications be genuinely relevant to a legitimate purpose, Justice Stevens produces results not unlike those that emerge from the clanking operation of two- or even three-tiered review. The difference is that Stevens candidly exercises judgment, taking account of the context, the offensiveness of the classification, and the credibility of the legislative purpose.

Though his approach pays dividends in candor and flexibility, it has its costs. Among the first casualties, ironically, are some of the pieties of judicial restraint. Stevens's equal protection analysis, for example, does not allow him to pretend that laws are invalidated by some brooding three-tiered omnipresence in the sky. Instead, it demands a far more skeptical and probing look at legislative politics than is usual for advocates of restraint. His First Amendment analysis, for example, would replace the discredited "content neutrality" standard with a narrower requirement that government not display bias against a particular viewpoint. This practical and pointed inquiry would save some laws that do not survive the Court's more abstract standard. But the price of this restraint is high. To uphold some lawmakers' actions, as in *FCC v. League of Women Voters* (1984), he must bluntly accuse others of actions "obviously directed at spokesmen for a particular point of view."

Perhaps it is a recognition of these costs that makes Stevens adroit at using such techniques as "legislative remand," particularly when federal policies are at stake. His opinion in *Hampton v. Mow Sun Wong* (1976), for example, struck down a civil service rule barring ALIENS from federal employment—not because the asserted federal purposes were insufficient but because they were none of the Civil Service Commission's business. If the President or Congress adopted the same rule, he suggested, it might well withstand review. Similarly, in FULLILOVE V. KLUTZNICK (1980) he would have invalidated a federal law reserving ten percent of certain construction grants for minority-owned businesses—not because such a set-aside was necessarily unconstitutional but because it raised profound constitutional questions that Congress had failed even to consider in its "slapdash" rush to enactment.

What does this unique mix of radicalism and restraint mean for Stevens's role on the Court? It seems clear, first, that his candor will always make him something of an outsider; it shows a glint of cheerful mischief too often for him to be a classic majority-building centrist. It may be true, as Stevens said in *Lakeside v. Oregon* (1978), that "most people formally charged with crime are guilty" or that "most people who remain silent in the face of serious accusations have something to hide and therefore are probably guilty." It may also be true, as Stevens wrote in *Fullilove*, that so-called benign racial preferences make it easier for "representatives of minority groups to disseminate patronage to their political backers." But as bracing as these unwelcome truths can be in the opinions of a single Justice, they will not, and probably should not, find their way soon into opinions of the Court.

More important over the long run is Stevens's campaign to win back broad fields of constitutional judgment from the logicians and their half-truths. Here he has had occasional victories, but he is battling uphill. Justices write opinions that leave much unsaid only when they have faith in the wisdom of those who will finally fill the gaps—the lower courts, their colleagues, future Justices. So long as most members of the Court lack that faith, Stevens's campaign for institutional humility will face long odds. Even when the Court adopts his practical, contextual approach, as it essentially has in equal protection cases, its opinions are likely to cling to the words and forms of a more MECHANICAL JURISPRUDENCE.

Of course no Justice can expect to impose the full range of his or her views on the Supreme Court. It is when one looks at individual doctrines that the impact of Stevens's iconoclastic creativity becomes clear. At times the power of his attack has swept away entrenched dogma and cleared the way for new thinking, as it did in *Ferber*. More important still is his ability to come fresh to new constitutional problems and to tailor new solutions for them. This talent showed even on the Seventh Circuit, where, for example, he preceded the Court in declaring that the First Amendment is a safeguard against patronage dismissals and that state tort remedies are a way of providing due process to a prisoner deprived of his property. On the Court, by joining with other Justices in the center, Stevens has set new terms of constitutional debate in areas as diverse as the death penalty, SEARCH AND SEIZURE, and gerrymandering. As new

Justices and new issues come to the Court, as the shock of his challenge to the old bromides fades, it is this practical creativity that will ultimately make his mark upon the law.

STEWART ABERCROMBIE BAKER

Bibliography

STEVENS, J. P. 1956 Mr. Justice Rutledge. Pages 176–202 in Allison Dunham and Philip B. Kurland, eds., *Mr. Justice*. Chicago: University of Chicago Press.
——— 1985 Judicial Restraint. *San Diego Law Review* 22:437–452.

STEVENS, THADDEUS
(1792–1868)

A Pennsylvania lawyer, state legislator (1833–1841), and congressman (1849–1853, 1859–1868), Thaddeus Stevens was the most powerful Republican congressman throughout the Civil War and beginning of Reconstruction. During this period Stevens was the earliest and most consistent congressional supporter of black rights and opponent of slavery. Stevens initiated, sponsored, or helped pass all key Reconstruction acts from 1865 to 1868. More than any other individual, Stevens was responsible for making the ex-slaves citizens.

After reading law, Stevens began practicing in 1816. In 1817 his unsuccessful defense of an accused murderer with the then novel plea of insanity brought Stevens fame and clients. After an initial case in which he represented a master in regaining fugitive slaves, Stevens never again defended slavery. Throughout the rest of his career Stevens took numerous cases on behalf of fugitive slaves, free blacks, and abolitionists. As one congressman said after his death, Stevens "was an abolitionist before there was such a party name." By 1831 he was one of Pennsylvania's most successful lawyers and a national leader of the Anti-Masonic movement. In 1835 Stevens single-handedly convinced the legislature to create a system of free public education for Pennsylvania. His passionate defense of public education stemmed from his own poverty-stricken background.

In 1848 Stevens was elected to Congress as a Whig, campaigning against slavery in lands ceded by Mexico. In Congress he was an acerbic, sarcastic, unrelenting opponent of slavery. Opposing the COMPROMISE OF 1850, he predicted it would be "the fruitful mother of future rebellion, disunion, and civil war." One of the first bloody fruits of the Compromise was the Christiana Riot, in Stevens's own county; a slaveowner was killed attempting to seize his fugitive slaves. Stevens helped organize the successful defense of Caster Hanway who was indicted for TREASON for refusing to help the master. A backlash against the riot and abolition cost Stevens his congressional seat the following year. After a short time in the Know-Nothing Party, he became a Republican in early 1855. In 1858 he was again elected to Congress, as a staunch opponent of his fellow Pennsylvanian, President JAMES BUCHANAN.

At the beginning of the Civil War Stevens became a leader of congressional Republicans. As chairman of the House Ways and Means Committee he influenced all legislation requiring appropriation of funds. Stevens was largely responsible for the Internal Revenue Act of 1862 and the Legal Tender Acts which were necessary to finance the war. As a member of the Joint Committee on the Conduct of the War Stevens helped insure that civilian, and not military, authority would be pre-eminent during the war. Stevens used this position, as well as his Ways and Means chairmanship, to press ABRAHAM LINCOLN's administration to stop the military from returning fugitive slaves and to allow blacks to enlist.

In 1861 Stevens was one of the few men in Washington who publicly recognized that slavery was the root cause of SECESSION and that the war required its destruction. In July 1861 he was one of two House members to oppose the Crittenden resolution, which declared that the North had no interest in interfering with slavery. In December 1861 Stevens helped defeat a reaffirmation of that resolution. From the outbreak of hostilities Stevens argued that the seceding states should be dealt with according to the "laws of war." He asserted that constitutional obligations and protections—such as those involving fugitive slaves, the protection of private property, or the writ of HABEAS CORPUS—should not be "binding on one party while they are repudiated by the other." Thus, he supported the creation of the new state of West Virginia on the theory that Virginia had ceased to exist as a state when it left the Union, so that it was unnecessary for Virginia to agree to the division of the state. Stevens's theory of STATE SUICIDE was never fully adopted by the Congress or the courts, but it was influential in persuading many congressmen to support his legislation during both the war and Reconstruction.

As early as August 1861 Stevens urged the abolition of slavery as a war measure. In 1862 he tried to secure legislation that would lead to the confiscation of plantations in the rebel states. He believed that such land could be constitutionally seized, not because it was owned by men who could be convicted of treason, but because it was the fruit of war. He subsequently introduced legislation to end slavery in the DISTRICT OF COLUMBIA, prevent the Army from returning fugitive slaves, and provide equal pay for black soldiers. He was a leader in securing other legislation that protected blacks and allowed them to serve in the military, even if they were owned by loyal masters.

During Reconstruction Stevens was the House Republican whip, a member of the Joint Committee on Reconstruction, and probably the most powerful politician in Washington. In early 1866 Stevens introduced legislation for the continuation of the FREEDMEN'S BUREAU, the adoption of the FOURTEENTH AMENDMENT to protect the freedmen, and the enfranchisement of blacks in Washington, D.C. President ANDREW JOHNSON's unexpected veto of the Freedmen's Bureau Bill, his subsequent attempts to prevent ratification of the Fourteenth Amendment, and his vehement opposition to voting by blacks led to congressional Reconstruction. Stevens sponsored legislation that prevented the former Confederate states from sending representatives to Congress without congressional approval. The legislation was specifically aimed at Johnson's home state of Tennessee, but applied to all the Confederate states.

During the election of 1866 Stevens openly argued for complete racial equality while campaigning for Republicans and against Andrew Johnson's administration. Johnson, meanwhile, publicly accused Stevens, CHARLES SUMNER, and the abolitionist Wendell Phillips of treason and suggested they ought to be hanged. The election gave the Republicans more than a two-thirds majority in both houses. Although ill through much of the Fortieth Congress, Stevens nevertheless sponsored the TENURE OF OFFICE ACT, which set the stage for Johnson's IMPEACHMENT, and the MILITARY RECONSTRUCTION ACT of 1867, which placed all former Confederate states, except Tennessee, under military rule. Stevens successfully backed many CIVIL RIGHTS measures introduced by others. He was the prime mover in requiring the former Confederate states to ratify the Fourteenth Amendment and enfranchise blacks. He supported legislation authorizing the army to protect the freedmen from white vigilantes. Virtually all this legislation was enacted over Johnson's veto, with Stevens, as majority whip, guiding it through Congress. Stevens failed, however, to persuade Congress to confiscate Southern plantations and provide land for the freedmen.

In 1866 and 1867 Stevens unsuccessfully supported Congressman James Ashley's motions for impeachment. In early 1868 Stevens himself sought Johnson's impeachment, but could not get committee support for it. However, after Johnson fired Secretary of War EDWIN M. STANTON, in violation of the Tenure of Office Act, an impeachment committee was quickly formed. Stevens, as a member of that committee, helped draft the ARTICLES OF IMPEACHMENT and later was a manager of the prosecution. However, he was quite ill by then and took little part in the trial. Ten weeks after the trial Stevens died.

PAUL FINKELMAN

Bibliography

BRODIE, FAWN M. 1959 *Thaddeus Stevens: Scourge of the South.* New York: Norton.
KORNGOLD, RALPH 1955 *Thaddeus Stevens.* New York: Harcourt Brace & World.

STEWARD MACHINE COMPANY v. DAVIS
301 U.S. 548 (1937)

Plaintiff, an employer, challenged the 1935 SOCIAL SECURITY ACT unemployment compensation provisions, which imposed a payroll tax on employers and directed that the tax receipts be paid to the general revenue. To offset part of this tax, the act granted employers a credit for taxes paid to a state unemployment fund conforming to federal benefit and solvency requirements. One such requirement was that state funds be held for safekeeping by the secretary of the treasury and invested in federal government securities. Plaintiff invoked UNITED STATES v. BUTLER (1936), which had invalidated AGRICULTURAL ADJUSTMENT ACT price support provisions that enabled the secretary of agriculture to contract with farmers to reduce agricultural production in exchange for payments funded by a federal tax levied on agricultural commodity processing. *Butler* had generally addressed the scope of Congress's power "to lay and collect taxes . . . to . . . provide . . . for the GENERAL WELFARE of the United States." While ostensibly rejecting the narrowest reading of the clause, originally proposed by JAMES MADISON, that the taxation power could be exercised only to carry out specifically ENUMERATED POWERS, and purporting to adopt a broader, though undefined, interpretation of the TAXING AND SPENDING POWER, *Butler* nevertheless had treated the TENTH AMENDMENT as a limitation on the federal taxation power. In *Steward Machine Co.,* plaintiff argued that the unemployment taxation scheme, like the agricultural price support provisions, exceeded congressional powers because it infringed

the Tenth Amendment's reservation to the states of power not delegated by the Constitution to the United States.

The unemployment compensation scheme was sustained, 5–4. Justice BENJAMIN N. CARDOZO, writing for the majority, distinguished *United States v. Butler* on two grounds: the unemployment tax proceeds were to be used for the "general welfare" because they were not earmarked for any special group; and the unemployment compensation plan did not infringe state prerogatives because state participation in this cooperative federal-state program was entirely voluntary. The Court described unemployment as a "problem . . . national in area and dimensions." Many states wished to develop unemployment compensation programs but feared economic competition from those states without such plans. Hence a federal tax was necessary to enable states to accomplish their general welfare goals.

In its permissive, though vague, interpretation of the term "general welfare," *Steward Machine Co.* and its companion case, HELVERING V. DAVIS (1937), seem to repudiate the *United States v. Butler* view that Congress, in exercising its power to tax for the general welfare, is required by the Tenth Amendment to eschew regulation of matters historically controlled by the states. *Steward Machine Co.* is also noteworthy for its sympathetic appraisal of joint federal-state welfare ventures. Justice Cardozo amply demonstrated that the competitive pressures of a national economy make it increasingly difficult for the states to perform traditional welfare functions without the national uniformity made possible by federal assistance and regulation.

GRACE GANZ BLUMBERG

STEWART, POTTER J.
(1915–1985)

When DWIGHT D. EISENHOWER nominated Potter Stewart to the United States Supreme Court, the President was recognizing the perfect embodiment of Midwest Republican civic virtues. Born in Cincinnati, Stewart was the son of a popular reformist and Republican mayor who was later appointed to the Ohio Supreme Court. Stewart went from Cincinnati to Yale College where he was a class leader, then to Harvard for graduate study, and then back to Yale Law School. He returned to Cincinnati, after service in the Navy and on Wall Street to practice law and engage in civic affairs. In 1954, at the age of thirty-nine, he was named to the Court of Appeals for the Sixth Circuit. In October 1958, as a recess appointment, Stewart became an Associate Justice of the Supreme Court.

Stewart's tenure on the Court—more than twenty-three years—was atypically long. Only eighteen Justices have served a longer term. Yet Stewart did not seek to place a sharp imprint on the work of the Court, an imprint of the sort Justice HUGO L. BLACK or Justice FELIX FRANKFURTER had brought to their work. Nor did he seek to build a constituency within the Court or outside it. During two periods, at the outset of his tenure and shortly after the transition to the BURGER COURT, Stewart's vote was of great significance in determining the outcome of the Court's work. Because he was not a member of a dominant and consistent majority, it would not be the case, under the customs of the Court, that the most significant cases of the quarter-century were his to write.

Stewart was guided in his decisions and his actions as a judge by a sense of decency and proportion. He believed in a nation in which order, partially derived from privately inculcated values, offered the opportunity for advancement, creativity, and freedom. His sense of propriety led him to decline the possibility of becoming Chief Justice, according to then-President RICHARD M. NIXON, because Stewart thought it inappropriate for a sitting Justice to aspire to a presidential elevation. Even his resignation was characteristic. Stewart resigned not out of illness, nor out of ambition, nor for alternative appointment, but merely because he felt that limited service was correct.

These themes of propriety, of respect for structure and rules, permeate the jurisprudence of Justice Stewart. He was a firm adherent to the principles of STARE DECISIS, even when its application led to a result varying from his own previously expressed view. In a 1974 DISSENTING OPINION he wrote: "A basic change in the law upon a ground no firmer than a change in our membership invites the popular misconception that this institution is little different from the two political branches of the Government. No misconception could do more lasting injury to this Court and to the system of law which it is our abiding mission to serve."

An elegant and careful treatment of the facts was often at the core of a Stewart opinion because an understanding of the facts was central to the way he approached the issues in a case. Regularly, he would indulge his belief that a decision should be of appropriately narrow scope by stating what the case was not about. For him, a deep understanding of context was a prophylactic against undue haste in constitutional decision making. Dissenting in ESTES V. TEXAS (1965),

for example, Stewart sought to demonstrate that the use of television cameras in the courtroom in that criminal case did not provide the factual predicate for the sweeping pronouncements in the Court's opinion concerning rights of defendants. Context yielded DOCTRINE, and not the reverse. If the result of an understanding of the facts was increased doctrinal complexity, then that could not be helped. "The time is long past when men believed that development of the law must always proceed by the smooth incorporation of new situations into a single coherent analytical framework," he wrote in COOLIDGE V. NEW HAMPSHIRE (1971). He thought it wrong that doctrine, sometime encapsulated in a "sterile metaphor" should seem to substitute for careful analysis, a point he made in his dissenting opinion in ABINGTON SCHOOL DISTRICT V. SCHEMPP (1963).

Much of Stewart's most significant work dealt with defining those rules, especially the FIRST AMENDMENT and the FOURTH AMENDMENT, which constrain the activities of government. There was a sharp tinge of the radical in Stewart's protection of the individual from government intervention. He celebrated the Fourth Amendment's warrant clause as a carefully conceived limitation on precipitate government searches and persistently opposed a reading that cheapened the clause. According to his colleague Justice LEWIS F. POWELL, Stewart's opinion in KATZ V. UNITED STATES (1967) "revitalized the fourth amendment" by rejecting the notion first espoused in OLMSTEAD V. UNITED STATES (1928) that the amendment applied only to physical trespass by police officers. In *Katz*, the court held that private conversations even outside the home must be secure from unwarranted police interception. "The Fourth Amendment," Stewart declared in characteristically pithy style, "protects people not places." Thus a Federal Bureau of Investigation microphone placed against the wall of a telephone booth was held to be an invasion of the RIGHT OF PRIVACY. Similarly, Stewart led the Court in a series of opinions that valued the doctrinal purity of a judicially sanctioned warrant requirement for a valid police search. Stewart sought to place the doctrine and its numerous exceptions in proper balance. At the same time, Stewart strongly recognized that in the field of ECONOMIC REGULATION legislatures should not be subject to similar constraints. He especially admired Justice ROBERT H. JACKSON and was fond of quoting Jackson's aphorism that "[t]he view of JUDICIAL SUPREMACY . . . has been its progressive closing of the avenues to peaceful and democratic conciliation of our social and economic conflicts."

Stewart's opinions gave important strength to the First Amendment guarantee of FREEDOM OF SPEECH and FREEDOM OF THE PRESS. He set as a task for himself a clearer and longer-lasting basis for the protection of the press so that it could monitor the government and inform the populace. In NEW YORK TIMES CO. v. UNITED STATES (1971) he wrote that only material that would cause "direct, immediate, and irreparable harm to the nation or its people" could be subject to prior restraint through court-ordered publication restrictions. In an early opinion for the Court, *Shelton v. Tucker* (1960), Stewart proclaimed that government cannot pursue even a legitimate end "by means that broadly stifle fundamental personal liberties when the end can be more narrowly achieved."

Stewart could be bold as well as forceful. It was his influence that led the Court to revitalize the THIRTEENTH AMENDMENT, validating Congress's power to establish a sweeping ban on RACIAL DISCRIMINATION in private housing. In JONES V. ALFRED H. MAYER CO. (1967) a land developer refused to sell a house to Joseph Lee Jones because Jones was black. By invoking the Thirteenth Amendment, Stewart's far-reaching opinion bypassed the limited and often confusing STATE ACTION requirement of the FOURTEENTH AMENDMENT and held that discrimination in private housing violated a previously dormant Reconstruction-era CIVIL RIGHTS statute, the CIVIL RIGHTS ACT OF 1866. In general, his civil rights opinions had a refreshing simplicity and directness that avoided temporizing and recognized statutory and constitutional imperatives.

Stewart was influential in other areas as well. For a time, his was one of the most original and radical views on the freakishness of the imposition of CAPITAL PUNISHMENT. It was his reconception of the criminal law in *Robinson v. California* (1962) that established new categories of thinking about sanctions and stigma. In *Carrington v. Rash* (1965) he broke new ground in his constitutional measure of state-imposed vote eligibility restrictions based on occupation, residency, and similar grounds.

Earlier than many of his colleagues Stewart brought to his analyses of the antitrust laws a keen sense of the economic impact of various approaches to the CLAYTON ACT and the SHERMAN ACT: his perceptions about the inappropriateness of a "per se" approach in vertical integration cases, stated in dissent in *United States v. Arnold, Schwinn & Co.* (1967), became the view of the Court in *Continental T.V. Inc. v. GTE Sylvania Inc.* (1977); his scorn for mechanical reliance on market shares as a test for invalidating mergers, articulated in dissent in *United States v. Von's Grocery*

Co. (1966), became the text of his majority opinion in *United States v. General Dynamics Corp.* (1973).

Stewart was a bridge, a point of continuity from the Court of the late 1950s to the Court of the 1980s. Throughout, he prized what he viewed as the qualities of being a judge. In HARRIS V. MCRAE (1980) he wrote—upholding the constitutionality of a law restricting federal funding for abortions—that it was not the mission of the Court to decide whether "the balance of competing interests" in that legislation, or any other, "is wise social policy." Citing one of his favorite cases, WILLIAMSON V. LEE OPTICAL, INC. (1955), Stewart concluded that "we cannot, in the name of the Constitution, overturn duly enacted statutes simply 'because they may be unwise, inprovident, or out of harmony with a particular school of thought.'" Stewart's philosophy of law, his jurisprudence of appropriateness, his respect for the role of the Court, transcend categories as his devoted service on the Court transcended categorization.

MONROE E. PRICE

Bibliography

FRIEDMAN, LEON 1978 Potter Stewart. In Leon Friedman and Fred L. Israel, eds., *The Justices of the United States Supreme Court: Their Lives and Major Opinions*, 2nd ed. New York: Chelsea House.

MERESMAN, BARNETT, MERESMAN GOLDMAN & MORRIS 1982 A Lawyer's Lawyer, A Judge's Judge: Justice Potter Stewart and the Fourth Amendment. *University of Chicago Law Review* 51:509–544.

STEWART, POTTER 1975 Or of the Press. *Hastings Law Journal* 26:631–637.

STOCKHOLDER'S SUIT

Stockholders suing their CORPORATIONS rarely raise constitutional questions, although the Supreme Court accepted jurisdiction of a case involving such a suit as early as 1856. (See DODGE V. WOOLSEY.) Yet several celebrated constitutional decisions in review of acts of Congress have come in stockholder actions brought to prevent corporate compliance with tax or regulatory programs the stockholders deemed unconstitutional. Having failed to convince management to challenge the programs' constitutionality, dissenting stockholders have used the device of a stockholder's action to accomplish the same result. In most nonconstitutional cases, dissenting stockholders are not permitted to bypass the business judgment of corporate managers and sue on the corporation's behalf, but—ironically, and controversially—this rule has not always prevailed in constitutional cases. The device has not been used effectively since the New Deal era, but when it was used, the Supreme Court seemed eager to render major constitutional decisions, an orientation perennially opposed to the Court's professed practice.

Three celebrated examples tell the story. In POLLOCK V. FARMERS' LOAN & TRUST CO. (1895) the Supreme Court held a federal income tax law unconstitutional. The corporate taxpayer had planned to accept the tax obligation, and a federal statute prevented an INJUNCTION suit by the corporation, but the dissenting stockholders were permitted to seek an injunction preventing compliance. No one objected to the stockholders' right to sue; the plaintiff asserted that the suit was not a COLLUSIVE SUIT between the stockholder and the company; and the Court rendered its controversial decision on the merits—a decision subsequently overturned by the SIXTEENTH AMENDMENT (1913). In ASHWANDER V. TENNESSEE VALLEY AUTHORITY (1936) preferred stockholders of the Alabama Power Company sued to prevent their corporation from performing a contract with the TVA, claiming that Congress lacked constitutional power to authorize the TVA to develop and contract for the sale of electricity. The Supreme Court, over Justice LOUIS D. BRANDEIS's famous objection that the stockholders lacked STANDING to sue and that the Court generally should seek to avoid constitutional questions, permitted the suit. The Court held the TVA's action constitutional, thereby ending a major legal threat to an important New Deal program. A few months later, however, in CARTER V. CARTER COAL CO. (1936), another stockholder suit, the Court invalidated the Guffey Act of 1935, an important anti-Depression measure. The president of Carter Coal, whose parents were majority stockholders and who had set company policy in compliance with the act, initiated the suit as a dissenting stockholder the day after the law was enacted.

These stockholder actions raise several questions of JUSTICIABILITY. One is similar to that raised in taxpayers' and citizens' suits: are they suits to prevent individual injury, suits that incidentally necessitate constitutional interpretation, or are they public actions to assure constitutional governance for the whole citizenry? The allegation that corporate compliance with the questioned law will injure the corporation's (and therefore the stockholders') financial interests, may distinguish stockholder from taxpayer or citizen standing, despite a similar element of remoteness. A second question is raised by the possibility of a collusive suit, with both the dissenting stockholder and the corporate management desiring the same result.

The possibility is real, but the drawbacks of collusive suits have not been a serious problem in stockholder suits. Despite the trumped-up appearance of *Carter v. Carter Coal Co.*, for example, the federal government vigorously opposed Carter. There was strongly adversary presentation, and, in a COMPANION CASE, another company directly challenged the government's enforcement of the new act. The most significant danger may be that the stockholder suit is really a request for a premature advisory opinion, because stockholder, corporation, and government all want a constitutional ruling when the corporation plans to comply with the law and no present controversy exists. The Court was eager to rule in *Pollock, Carter,* and *Ashwander.* The first two produced substantial interferences with congressional power, both subsequently overturned, and the last consciously legitimated government policy. Plainly, the stockholder suit has been used as an instrument of the Supreme Court's judicial activism in the exercise of JUDICIAL REVIEW.

JONATHAN D. VARAT

STONE, HARLAN F.
(1872–1946)

After finishing Amherst College and Columbia Law School (where in 1906 he became dean), Harlan F. Stone divided his time between teaching and practice in New York City. In 1923, President CALVIN COOLIDGE, a former college mate from Amherst, appointed him attorney general of the United States. Less than a year later he became Associate Justice of the United States Supreme Court. In 1941 President FRANKLIN D. ROOSEVELT, ignoring party labels, appointed him Chief Justice.

Experience gained as a teacher at the Columbia Law School had contributed directly to his preparation for the supreme bench. At the university, where he had time and opportunity for study and reflection, he developed ideas about the nature of law and the function of courts. Before donning judicial robes, Stone had argued only one case, *Ownbey v. Morgan* (1921), before the Supreme Court, adumbrating what was to become the major theme of his constitutional jurisprudence—judicial self-restraint. The correction of outmoded processes, he argued, ought to be left to legislatures rather than assumed by courts.

It seems ironical that Stone, a solid, peace-loving man, should have been in the crossfire of controversy throughout his judicial career. On the TAFT COURT, and also during a good part of Chief Justice CHARLES EVANS HUGHES's regime, he differed from colleagues on the right who interposed their economic and social predilections under the guise of interpreting the Constitution. During his own chief justiceship Stone was sometimes at odds with colleagues on the left who were equally intent on using their judicial offices to further particular preferences.

Stone's moderate approach is revealed in his consideration of INTERGOVERNMENTAL IMMUNITIES from taxation—a vexing problem throughout the chief justiceships of Taft and Hughes. Rejecting the facile reciprocal immunities doctrine established in McCULLOCH V. MARYLAND and COLLECTOR V. DAY, respectively, he held that the federal system does not establish a total want of power in one government to tax the instrumentalities of the other. For him, the extent and locus of the tax burden were the important considerations. No formula, no facile "black and white" distinctions sufficed to determine the line between governmental functions that were immune from taxation and those that were not. Stone elaborated these views in *Helvering v. Gerhardt* (1938) and GRAVES V. NEW YORK EX REL O'KEEFE (1939). Similarly, in cases concerning state regulations of economic affairs and STATE TAXATION OF COMMERCE, Stone rejected question-begging formulas such as "business AFFECTED WITH A PUBLIC INTEREST" or "direct and indirect effects."

Though habitually a Republican, Stone believed that increased use of governmental power was a necessary concomitant of twentieth-century conditions. "Law," he said, "functions best only when it is fitted into the life of a people." He made this point specific in his law lectures. This conviction sometimes aligned him with OLIVER WENDELL HOLMES and LOUIS D. BRANDEIS. Uniting the triumvirate was their view that a Justice's personal predilections must not thwart the realization of legislative objectives not clearly violative of the Constitution.

Stone's constitutional jurisprudence crystallized during 1936, the heyday of the Court's resistance to President Roosevelt's program of government control and regulation. In the leading case of UNITED STATES V. BUTLER (1936) the Court voted 6–3 to invalidate the AGRICULTURAL ADJUSTMENT ACT (AAA). Justice OWEN J. ROBERTS and dissenting Justice Stone were about equally skeptical of the wisdom of the AAA. Their differences concerned the scope of national power and the Court's role in the American system of government. Stone thought that the majority had come to believe that any legislation it considered "undesirable" was necessarily unconstitutional. The Court

had come to think of itself, as Stone said, as "the only agency of government that must be assumed to have capacity to govern."

The majority was haunted by the possibility that Congress might become "a parliament of the whole people, subject to no restrictions save such as are self-imposed." But, Stone countered, "consider the status of our own power." The President and Congress are restrained by the "ballot box and the processes of democratic government," and "subject to judicial restraint. The only check on our own exercise of power is our own sense of self-restraint."

Butler was neither the first nor the last time a dissenter expressly accused the court of "torturing" the Constitution under the guise of interpreting it. But no other Justice had previously used such strong language in condemning the practice.

In ADKINS V. CHILDREN'S HOSPITAL (1923) the Court had declared unconstitutional the minimum wage for women. Justice GEORGE H. SUTHERLAND was the spokesman. Holmes dissented as did Chief Justice Taft. *Adkins* was still in good standing in MOREHEAD V. NEW YORK EX REL. TIPALDO (1936) when Stone repeated his indictment: "It is not for the Court to resolve doubts whether the remedy by regulation is as efficacious as many believe, or better than some other, or is better even than blind operation of uncontrolled economic forces. The legislature must be free to choose unless government is rendered impotent. The Fourteenth Amendment has no more imbedded in the Constitution our preference for some particular set of economic beliefs, than it has adopted in the name of liberty the system of theology which we happen to approve."

In his war on the recalcitrant four (PIERCE BUTLER, JAMES C. MCREYNOLDS, Sutherland, and WILLIS VAN DEVANTER) Stone was sometimes allied with Holmes and Brandeis. Chief among points of agreement was their recognition of the need for a living law. As Holmes put it: "A slumber when prolonged means death." The essence of their creed was judicial self-restraint, recognized as a desirable rather than a realizable role.

The bond uniting them strengthened as the majority's doctrinaire approach became increasingly reactionary. Differences were exposed when Holmes, Brandeis, and Stone sometimes filed separate opinions in support of the same decision. In dissent Holmes, a gifted essayist addicted to generalization, often avoided the tough issues and "failed to meet the majority on its own ground." "This is a pretty good opinion," Stone remarked on one occasion, "but the old man leaves out all the troublesome facts and ignores all the tough points that worried the lower courts." "I wish," he once observed in grudging admiration, "I could make my cases sound as easy as Holmes makes his."

Stone's divergence from Brandeis was likewise most vividly portrayed in dissent. When the Court struck down legislation Brandeis favored in terms of policy, the erstwhile "People's Attorney" did not hesitate to use the Court as a forum to persuade others of its wisdom. "I told him [Brandeis] long ago," Holmes commented in 1930, "that he really was an advocate rather than a judge. He is affected by his interest in a cause, and if he feels it, he is not detached." Stone took specific exception to Brandeis's JUDICIAL ACTIVISM. In reply to a note in which Brandeis invited Stone to join his dissent in *Liggett Co. v. Lee* (1931), Stone said: "Your opinion is a very interesting and powerful document. But it goes further than I am inclined to go, because I do not think it necessary to go that far in order to deal with this case. . . . I think you are too much an advocate of this particular legislation. I have little enthusiasm for it, although I think it constitutional. In any case, I think our dissents are more effective if we take the attitude that we are concerned with power and not with the merit of its exercises. . . ."

Without minimizing the great contributions of Holmes and Brandeis, it seems fair to conclude that in a logical as well as a chronological sense Stone was the one who, in both the old and the new Court, carried their tradition to fulfillment. Perforce it fell to him, as his former law clerk, Herbert Wechsler, said, "to carry through to victory and consolidate the gain."

Chief Justice Taft paid high tribute to Stone's pioneering, even as he warned of the danger in the former law teacher's method. Said Taft: "He is a learned lawyer in many ways, but his judgement I do not altogether consider safe and the ease with which he expresses himself, and his interest in the whole branch of the law in which he is called upon to give an opinion on a single principle makes the rest of the Court impatient and doubtful. . . . Without impeaching at all his good faith in matters of that sort, we find we have to watch closely the language he uses."

Viewing Stone's dissent in *United States v. Butler* as a "lodestar for due regard between legislative and judicial power," some commentators interpreted the 1937 judicial about-face as signifying well-nigh complete withdrawal of the Court from the governing process.

After 1937, when the Court's Maginot Line crumbled, Justice Stone feared that the guarantees of CIVIL LIBERTIES might be wanting in effective safeguards. At first glance it does seem paradoxical that the leader of the campaign for judicial self-restraint in cases involving governmental ECONOMIC REGULATION should have articulated the PREFERRED FREEDOMS doctrine. In an otherwise obscure case, Stone suggested in the body of the opinion that he would not go so far as to say that no economic legislation would ever violate constitutional restraints, but he did indicate that in this area the Court's role would be strictly confined. Attached to this opinion is a famous footnote suggesting special judicial responsibility in the orbit of individual liberties. (See UNITED STATES V. CAROLENE PRODUCTS COMPANY, 1938.)

Two years later, in *Minersville School District v. Gobitis* (1940), the Court voted 8–1 to uphold Pennsylvania's compulsory flag salute as applied to Jehovah's Witnesses schoolchildren against their parents' religious beliefs. Justice FELIX FRANKFURTER, who spoke for the majority, wrote privately to Stone: "We are not the primary resolver of the clash. What weighs strongly on me in this case is my anxiety that while we lean in the direction of the libertarian aspect, we do not exercise our judicial power unduly, and as though we ourselves were legislators by holding too tight a rein on organs of popular government." (See FLAG SALUTE CASES.)

When Frankfurter learned that Stone was the lone dissenter, he was deeply disturbed. He pleaded: "That you should entertain doubts has naturally stirred me to an anxious re-examination of my own view. . . . I can assure you that nothing has weighed as much on my conscience since I came on this Court as has this case. . . . I'm aware of the important distinction which you so skillfully adumbrated in your footnote 4 in the *Carolene Products Co.* Case. I agree with that distinction: I regard it as basic. I have taken over that distinction in its central aspect."

Adolph Hitler had already unleashed his diabolical forces in Europe, and a widening conflict seemed inevitable. Frankfurter continued: "For time and circumstances are surely not irrelevant in resolving the conflict that we have to resolve in this particular case. . . . But certainly it is relevant to make the adjustment that we have to make within the framework of present circumstances and those that are clearly ahead of us."

Reflecting his New England heritage of RELIGIOUS LIBERTY, Stone was not convinced. He replied: "I am truly sorry not to go along with you. The case is peculiarly one of the relative weight of imponderables and I cannot overcome the feeling that the Constitution tips the scales in favor of religion."

Stone won this battle in a second case involving

the compulsory flag salute, *West Virginia State School Board of Education v. Barnette* (1943). By 1943 three other justices, HUGO L. BLACK, WILLIAM O. DOUGLAS, and FRANK MURPHY, who had joined Frankfurter in upholding the compulsory flag salute in *Gobitis*, changed their minds. Two new appointees, ROBERT H. JACKSON and WILEY B. RUTLEDGE, agreed with Stone's dissent in the earlier case, thus transforming a vote of 8–1 to uphold the compulsory salute to a vote of 6–3 striking it down. Speaking through Justice Jackson, the Court declared: "If there is any fixed star in our constitutional constellation, it is that no official, high or petty, can prescribe what shall be orthodox in politics, nationalism, religion, or other matters of opinion, or force citizens to confess by word or act their faith therein. If there are any circumstances which permit an exception, they do not occur to us."

Stone had initially expressed the "preferred freedoms" doctrine tentatively, merely raising the question whether in the case of legislation touching rights protected by the FIRST AMENDMENT there may be "narrower scope for the operation of the presumption of constitutionality" and whether such legislation might not be "subjected to more exacting judicial scrutiny." He first used the expression "preferred freedoms" in JONES V. OPELIKA (1942).

After Stone's death in 1946, the passing of Justices Murphy and Rutledge in 1949, and the intensification of the Cold War, the "preferred freedoms" doctrine fell into a constitutional limbo. Justice Frankfurter, still smarting from the second flag salute case, attacked the doctrine fiercely in KOVACS V. COOPER (1949) where, referring to "preferred freedoms," he wrote: "This is a phrase which has crept into some recent decisions of the Court. I deem it a mischievous phrase if it carries the thought, which it may subtly imply, that any law touching communication is infected with invalidity. . . . I say that the phrase is mischievous because it radiates a constitutional doctrine without avowing it."

DENNIS V. UNITED STATES (1951), a case involving the last stage of the 1949 trial of eleven leaders of the Communist party of the United States for violation of the Smith Act of 1940, dealt the doctrine a serious blow. Yet even after *Dennis* some substance of the doctrine remained. In dissent Justice Black expressed the hope "that in calmer times, when present pressure, passions, and fear subside, this or some later Court will restore the First Amendment liberties to the high preferred place where they belong in a free society."

Stone's guiding rule was judicial self-restraint, not self-abnegation. Before 1937 he criticized right-wing colleagues who equated what they considered economically undesirable legislation with unconstitutionality. After Roosevelt had reconstructed the Court, he was at loggerheads with judges on the left, equally intent, he thought, on reading their preferences into the constitution.

Repeated conflicts with Black and Douglas, who, he felt, were prone to resolve all doubt in labor's favor, alienated him. Stone's creativity was confined by the boundaries of the known. Any marked departure from existing principles left him "a little hurt, a little bewildered and sometimes even a little angry." When in 1945 he found himself pitted against judicial activists on the left, he dolefully reminisced: "My more conservative brethren in the old days enacted their own economic prejudices into law. What they did placed in jeopardy a great and useful institution of government. The pendulum has now swung to the other extreme, and history is repeating itself. The Court is now in as much danger of becoming a legislative Constitution making body, enacting into law its own predilections, as it was then. The only difference is that now the interpretation of statutes, whether 'over-conservative' or 'over-liberal' can be corrected by Congress."

Stone's conception of judicial conduct was almost monastic. He strove against almost insuperable odds to keep the Court within what he considered appropriate bounds. A judge should limit himself precisely to the issue at hand. Contradictory precedents should usually be specifically overruled. The Court ought "to correct its own errors, even if I help in making them." Stone's judicial technique recognized complexity. "The sober second thought of the community," he urged, "is the firm base on which all law must ultimately rest."

Stone advocated restraint, not because he believed a judge's preference should not enter law, but precisely because it inevitably did. The sharp barbs of his thought were intended for the flesh of judges, both right and left, who, without weighing social values, prematurely enforced private convictions as law. He strove not to eliminate subjectivity but to tame it.

As Chief Justice he was less impressive. In 1929, when it was rumored that President HERBERT C. HOOVER might elevate Stone as Taft's successor, the Chief Justice had opposed it, saying that the Associate Justice was "not a great leader and would have a great deal of trouble in massing the Court." Years later, Taft's assessment proved true. The bench Stone headed was the most frequently divided, the most quarrelsome in history. If success be measured by the

Chief's ability to maintain harmony, he was a failure. Solid convictions handicapped him. Nor would he resort to the high-pressure tactics of Chief Justices Taft and Hughes. Believing profoundly in freedom of expression for others, no less than himself, he was slow to cut off debate.

Stone had an abiding faith in free government and in JUDICIAL REVIEW as an essential adjunct to its operation. He believed that radical change was neither necessary not generally desirable. Drastic change could be avoided "if fear of legislative action, which Courts distrust or think unwise, is not overemphasized in interpreting the document." A free society needed continuity, "not of rules but of aims and ideals which will enable government in all the various crises of human affairs, to continue to function and to perform its appointed task within the bounds of reasonableness."

ALPHEUS THOMAS MASON

Bibliography

DOUGLAS, WILLIAM O. 1946 Chief Justice Stone. *Columbia Law Review* 46:693–695.
DOWLING, NOEL T. 1941 The Methods of Mr. Justice Stone in Constitutional Cases. *Columbia Law Review* 41:1160–1181.
DOWLING, NOEL T.; CHEATHAM, E. E.; and HALE, R. L. 1936 Mr. Justice Stone and the Constitution. *Columbia Law Review* 36:351–381.
FRANK, JOHN P. 1957 Harlan Fiske Stone: An Estimate. *Stanford Law Review* 9:621–632.
HAND, LEARNED 1946 Chief Justice Stone's Conception of the Judicial Function. *Columbia Law Review* 46:696–699.
KONEFSKY, S. J. 1946 *Chief Justice Stone and the Supreme Court.* New York: Macmillan.
MASON, ALPHEUS THOMAS 1956 *Harlan Fiske Stone: Pillar of the Law.* New York: Viking.
WECHSLER, HERBERT 1946 Stone and the Constitution. *Columbia Law Review* 46:764–800.

STONE v. FARMERS' LOAN & TRUST CO.
116 U.S. 307 (1886)

This case marks a transition in our constitutional law from the Supreme Court's use of the CONTRACT CLAUSE as a bastion of VESTED RIGHTS protected by corporate charter to its use of SUBSTANTIVE DUE PROCESS as a check on state regulation of business. Here, however, the Court sustained the regulation before it even as it laid the basis for the new DOCTRINE. The facts seemingly constituted an open-and-shut case

for a victory of the contract clause. A railroad company's charter explicitly authorized the railroad to set rates for carrying passengers and freight. Thirty-eight years after granting the charter, the state of Mississippi empowered a railroad commission to revise rates. The trust company, a stockholder of the railroad, sued to enjoin Stone and other members of the commission from enforcing the state rate regulations. In past rate cases, whenever the contract clause argument had lost, the RESERVED POLICE POWER doctrine had prevailed; in this case the state had reserved no power to alter the company's charter. The INALIENABLE POLICE POWER doctrine had defeated the contract clause argument only in cases involving the public health, safety, or morals. Yet the Court, by a vote of 7–2, held that the state had not violated the company's charter.

Chief Justice MORRISON R. WAITE, in his opinion for the Court, reasoned that the explicit grant of rate-making powers to the railroad did not imply either a grant of exclusive powers or that the state had surrendered a power to revise rates set by the railroad. The state's power to regulate rates, Waite declared, cannot be "bargained away" except by a positive grant. Never before had the Court construed a contract so broadly in favor of the public and so strictly against a corporation.

Waite added, however, that the regulatory power was not unlimited: under pretense of regulating rates, the state could not require the railroad to carry persons or property free, and "neither can it do that which in law amounts to a taking of private property . . . without DUE PROCESS OF LAW. What would have this effect we need not now say, because no tariff has yet been fixed by the commission." Waite also declared that state rate-making does "not necessarily" deny due process. In effect he undercut his own proposition, asserted in *Munn v. Illinois* (1877), that the question of the reasonableness of rates is purely legislative in nature. (See GRANGER CASES.) In *Stone* the implied principle was that reasonableness was subject to JUDICIAL REVIEW. Moreover, the references to due process of law in effect reflected substantive due process, because a rate regulation could not violate due process except in a substantive sense. *Stone* heralded a new era in constitutional law, which the Court entered during the next decade.

LEONARD W. LEVY

STONE v. GRAHAM

See: Religious Liberty

STONE v. MISSISSIPPI
101 U.S. 814 (1880)

Chief Justice MORRISON R. WAITE for a unanimous Supreme Court held that the state might revoke the chartered right of a lottery company to do business in the state, without violating the CONTRACT CLAUSE. Because the company was not subject to the state's reserved POLICE POWER to alter or repeal the contract, the Court relied on the doctrine of INALIENABLE POLICE POWER, here the power to protect the public morals by outlawing gambling.

LEONARD W. LEVY

STONE v. POWELL
428 U.S. 465 (1976)

By act of Congress, a state prisoner may petition a federal court for a writ of HABEAS CORPUS on a claim that he was imprisoned in violation of his constitutional rights. In *Stone,* however, the Supreme Court ruled that federal courts should not entertain habeas corpus claims by prisoners who charge that they were convicted on unconstitutionally seized EVIDENCE, when the prisoner has had an opportunity for a full and fair hearing on the issue in the state courts.

The Court differentiated, for habeas corpus purposes, between the guarantees of the Fifth and Sixth Amendments, which are vital to the trustworthiness of the fact-finding process, and the FOURTH AMENDMENT, which is not. Exclusion of evidence is not a personal right of the defendant but a judicial remedy designed to deter the police from unlawful searches. Thus the EXCLUSIONARY RULE is not an "absolute" but must be balanced against competing policies. Indiscriminate application of the rule, far from fostering respect for constitutional values, might generate disrespect for the judicial system. On the other hand, denying the right to raise SEARCH AND SEIZURE claims in habeas corpus proceedings would not seriously diminish the educational effect of the rule; it was scarcely likely that police would be deterred by the possibility that the legality of the search would be challenged in habeas corpus proceedings after the state courts had upheld it.

Dissenting Justices WILLIAM J. BRENNAN and THURGOOD MARSHALL averred that the exclusionary rule is a right of the defendant and not a "mere utilitarian tool" which turns on its deterrent value.

JACOB W. LANDYNSKI

STONE COURT
(1941–1946)

When Associate Justice HARLAN FISKE STONE moved over to the central seat of the Chief Justice in October 1941, he presided over a bench seven of whose nine members had been appointed to the Court by President FRANKLIN D. ROOSEVELT. All seven, who were sympathetic to the mass of new regulatory laws and welfare measures sponsored by the President, could be expected to develop approvingly the constitutional revolution of 1937. Surely they would sustain vast congressional expansion of federal power under the COMMERCE CLAUSE and drastically curtail the scope of JUDICIAL REVIEW. Stone himself had been appointed Associate Justice by President CALVIN COOLIDGE, but he had long advocated newly dominant constitutional principles in dissenting opinions. OWEN J. ROBERTS, now the senior Associate Justice, was a Republican appointed by President HERBERT C. HOOVER, but it was the shift of his vote, along with Chief Justice CHARLES EVANS HUGHES's, that had tipped the scales for change. Outside observers expected "a new unity in Supreme Court DOCTRINE, based upon a clearer philosophy of government than has yet been expressed in the swift succession of decisions rendered by a Court standing in the shadow of political changes."

But there was no unity. The new Chief Justice soon came to view his brethren as "a team of wild horses." DISSENTING OPINIONS and CONCURRING OPINIONS proliferated in numbers previously inconceivable. The controversies ranged from major jurisprudential differences to unworthy personal squabbles over such matters as the phrasing of the Court's letter to Justice Roberts upon his retirement.

The sources of disunity were both philosophical and temperamental. All but one or two of the Justices were highly individualistic, each was accustomed to speak his mind. All, with the possible exception of Justice Roberts, accepted the new regulatory and welfare state; but there were sharp differences over the proper pace and extent of change. The Chief Justice and Justices Roberts, STANLEY F. REED, JAMES F. BYRNES, and to a lesser degree Justices FELIX FRANKFURTER and ROBERT H. JACKSON, were more conservative in disposition than Justices HUGO L. BLACK, WILLIAM O. DOUGLAS, FRANK MURPHY, and Justice Byrnes's successor, WILEY B. RUTLEDGE. The temperamental differences were sometimes matched by differences in legal philosophy. The Chief Justice, Justice Frankfurter, and to a lesser degree Justice Jackson, were craftsmen of the law deeply influenced by a strong sense of the importance of the judge's loyalty to a growing, changing, but still coherent set of legal principles. For them, such institutional concerns were often more important than immediate, practical consequences. Justices Black, Douglas, and Murphy gave far more emphasis to the redistribution of social and economic power and to progressive reform. In conflicts between the individual and his government outside the economic area, the conservatives' instinct for order would often clash with the progressive liberals' enthusiasm for CIVIL LIBERTIES and CIVIL RIGHTS. The marked dissension indicates the difficulty any President of the United States faces in stamping one pattern upon the work of the Court.

Viewed in the sweep of constitutional history, the Stone years, 1941–1946, were the first part of a period of transition also encompassing the VINSON COURT, 1946–1953. By 1940 the main lines of CONSTITUTIONAL INTERPRETATION under the commerce clause and GENERAL WELFARE CLAUSE had been adapted to centralized ECONOMIC REGULATION and the welfare state. After 1953, when EARL WARREN became Chief Justice of the United States, the driving force would be a new spirit of libertarianism, egalitarianism, and emancipation. It remained for the Stone Court to complete the reinterpretation of the commerce clause and to pursue the philosophy of judicial deference to legislative determinations, whether state or federal. But harbingers of the new age of reform by constitutional adjudication also began to appear. The first explicit challenges to an across-the-board philosophy of judicial self-restraint were raised in the Stone Court. From the seeds thus scattered would grow the doctrinal principles supporting the subsequent vast expansion of constitutionally protected civil liberties and civil rights.

In interpreting the commerce clause, the Stone Court, whenever faced with a clear assertion of congressional intent to exercise such wide authority, did not shrink from pressing to its logical extreme the doctrine that Congress may regulate any local activities that in fact affect INTERSTATE COMMERCE. For example, in WICKARD V. FILBURN (1942) the Court sustained the imposition of a federal penalty upon the owner of a small family farm for sowing 11.9 acres of wheat in excess of his 11.1 acre federal allotment, upon the ground that Congress could rationally conclude that small individual additions to the total supply, even for home consumption, would cumulatively affect the price of wheat in interstate markets. The reluctance of the more conservative Justices to sanction unlimited expansion of federal regulation into once local affairs took hold when federal legislation was couched in terms sufficiently ambiguous to permit limitation. Decisions putting marginal limits upon the coverage of the federal wage and hour law are the best examples. Only a bare majority of four of the seven Justices participating could be mustered in UNITED STATES V. SOUTHEASTERN UNDERWRITERS ASSOCIATION (1944) for holding the insurance industry subject to the SHERMAN ANTITRUST ACT. In PAUL V. VIRGINIA (1879) the Court had first ruled that writing an insurance policy on property in another state was not interstate commerce. Later decisions and an elaborate structure of regulation in every state were built upon that precedent. Congress had essayed no regulation of insurance. The executive branch had not previously sought to apply the Sherman Act. Justices Black, Douglas, Murphy, and Rutledge seemed not to hesitate in sustaining the Department of Justice's novel assertion of federal power, a position supportable by the literal words of the statute and the logic of the expansive view of the commerce power. Respect for precedent and a strong sense of the importance of institutional continuity led the Chief Justice and Justices Frankfurter and Jackson to protest so sharp a departure from the status quo in the absence of a specific congressional directive: "it is the part of wisdom and self-restraint and good government to leave the initiative to Congress. . . . To force the hand of Congress is no more the proper function of the judiciary than to tie the hands of Congress." Congress responded to the majority by limiting the application of the Sherman Act to the insurance business, and by confirming the states' powers of regulation and taxation.

New constitutional issues that would lead to the next major phase in the history of constitutional adjudication began to emerge as wartime restrictions and the multiplication of government activities stirred fears for personal liberties. The war against Nazi Germany reinvigorated ideals of human dignity, equality, and democracy. As more civil liberties and civil rights litigation came upon the docket, a number of Justices began to have second thoughts about the philosophy of judicial deference to legislative determinations. That philosophy had well fitted the prevailing desire for progressive social and economic reform so long as the states and the executive and legislative branches of the federal government were engaged in the redistribution of power and the protection of the disadvantaged and distressed. The recollection of past judicial mistakes and the need for consistency of institutional theory cautioned against activist judicial ventures even in so deserving an area as civil liberty. On the other hand, continued self-restraint would leave much civil liberty at the mercy of executive or legislative oppression. The libertarian judicial activist could achieve a measure of logical consistency by elevating civil liberties to a PREFERRED POSITION justifying stricter standards of judicial review than those used in judging economic measures. The older dissenting opinions by Justices OLIVER WENDELL HOLMES and LOUIS D. BRANDEIS pleading for greater constitutional protection for FREEDOM OF SPEECH pointed the way even though they had failed to rationalize a double standard.

Stone himself, as an Associate Justice, had suggested one rationale in a now famous footnote in UNITED STATES V. CAROLENE PRODUCTS CO. (1938). Holding that the Court should indulge a strong presumption of constitutionality whenever the political processes of representative government were open, he nonetheless suggested that stricter judicial review might be appropriate when the challenge was to a statute that interfered with the political process—for example, a law restricting freedom of speech—or that was a result of prejudice against a DISCRETE AND INSULAR MINORITY—for example, a law discriminating against black people.

The issue was first drawn sharply under the FIRST and FOURTEENTH AMENDMENTS in the FLAG SALUTE CASES (1940, 1943). The substantive question was whether the constitutional guarantees of the freedom of speech and free exercise of religion permitted a state to expel from school and treat as truants the children of Jehovah's Witnesses, who refused to salute the United States flag. In the first case, the expulsions were sustained. Speaking for the Court, Justice Frankfurter invoked the then conventional rationale of judicial self-restraint. National unity and respect for national tradition, he reasoned, were permissible legislative goals. The compulsory flag salute could not be said to be an irrational means of seeking to secure those goals, even though the Court might be convinced that deeper patriotism would be engendered by refraining from coercing a symbolic gesture. To reject the legislative conclusion "would amount to no less than the pronouncement of pedagogical and psychological dogma in a field where courts possess no marked and certainly no controlling competence." The lone dissent came from Stone, who was still an Associate Justice.

Three years later the Court reversed itself. Justice Jackson, for the Court, summarized the core philosophy of the First Amendment: "If there is any fixed star in our constitutional constellation, it is that no official, high or petty, can prescribe what shall be or-

thodox in politics, nationalism, religion, or other matters of opinion or force citizens to confess by word or act their faith therein." First Amendment freedoms, the Court reasoned, rejecting Justice Frankfurter's plea for consistent application of the principle of judicial self-restraint, might not be curtailed for "such slender reasons" as would constitutionally justify restrictions upon economic liberty. Freedom of speech, of assembly, and of religion were susceptible of restriction "only to prevent grave and immediate danger to interests that the State may lawfully protect. We cannot because of modest estimates of our competence in such specialities as public education, withhold the judgment that history authenticates as the function of this Court when liberty is infringed."

Even in the 1980s, the deep and pervasive cleavage between the advocates of judicial self-restraint and the proponents of active judicial review in some categories of cases still divides both the Justices and constitutional scholars. It is now pretty clear, however, that judicial review will be stricter and there will be little deference to legislative judgments when restrictions upon freedom of expression, religion, or political association are at stake. (See JUDICIAL ACTIVISM AND RESTRAINT.)

In later years the Court would come also to scrutinize strictly, without deference to the political process, not only some laws challenged as denials of the EQUAL PROTECTION OF THE LAWS guaranteed by the Fourteenth Amendment but even statutes claimed to infringe FUNDAMENTAL RIGHTS in violation of the DUE PROCESS clauses of the Fifth and Fourteenth Amendments. The Stone Court broke the ground for STRICT SCRUTINY of statutory classifications prejudicing an "insular minority" in a opinion in one of the JAPANESE AMERICAN CASES declaring that "all legal restrictions which curtail the civil rights of a single racial group are immediately suspect . . . the courts must subject them to the most rigid scrutiny." In later years the constitutional standard thus declared became the basis for many decisions invalidating hostile RACIAL DISCRIMINATION at the hands of government, segregation laws, and other "invidious" statutory classifications.

Earlier the Stone Court opened the door to strict review in a second and still highly controversial class of cases under the equal protection clause. An Oklahoma statute mandated the STERILIZATION of persons thrice convicted of specified crimes, including grand larceny, but not of persons convicted of other crimes of much the same order and magnitude, such as embezzlement. The somewhat obscure opinion by Justice Douglas in SKINNER V. OKLAHOMA (1942), holding the differential treatment to violate the equal protection clause, emphasized the need for "strict scrutiny" of classifications made in a sterilization law, and referred to procreation as "a basic liberty." Later reforms by constitutional adjudication in the area of VOTING RIGHTS and legislative REPRESENTATION would be based upon the proposition that a legislative classification is subject to strict scrutiny not only when it is invidious but also when it differentiates among individuals in their access to a basic liberty. The precedent would also be invoked to support still later controversial decisions upholding claims of individual liberty in matters of sexual activity, childbirth, and abortion.

The Stone Court also sharpened the weapons for challenging crucial discrimination in the processes of representative government. In most of the states of the Old South, nomination as the candidate of the Democratic party still assured election to office. A political party was regarded as a private organization not subject to the equal protection clause of the Fourteenth Amendment or to the FIFTEENTH AMENDMENT's prohibition against denial or abridgment of VOTING RIGHTS by reason of race or color. Even after PRIMARY ELECTIONS regulated by state law became the standard method for nominating party candidates, "white primaries" remained an accepted method of excluding black citizens from participation in self-government.

The first step in upsetting this neat device was taken in an opinion by Justice Stone just before he became Chief Justice. Interference with the right to cast an effective ballot in a primary held to nominate a party's candidate for election as senator or representative was held in UNITED STATES V. CLASSIC (1938) to interfere with the election itself and thus to be punishable under legislation enacted by Congress pursuant to its power to regulate the time, place, and manner of holding elections under Article I, section 4. Next, in SMITH V. ALLWRIGHT (1944) the Stone Court ruled that if black citizens are excluded because of race or color from a party primary prescribed and extensively regulated by state law, their "right . . . to vote" has been denied or abridged by the state in violation of the Fifteenth Amendment. Opening the polls to effective participation by racial minorities throughout the South, in accordance with the promise of the Fifteenth Amendment, would have to await the civil rights revolution and the enactment of the VOTING RIGHTS ACT OF 1965, but these decisions eliminating "white primaries" were the first major steps in that direction.

While marking its contributions to the mainstream of constitutional history, one should not forget that the Stone Court was a wartime court subject to wartime pressures as it faced dramatic cases posing the underlying and unanswerable question, "How much liberty and judicial protection for liberty may be sacrificed to ensure survival of the Nation?" Economic measures were uniformly upheld, even a scheme for concentrating the review of the legality of administrative price regulations in a special EMERGENCY COURT OF APPEALS, thus denying a defendant charged in an ordinary court with a criminal violation the right to assert the illegality of the regulation as a defense. Extraordinary deference to military commanders under wartime pressures alone can account for the Court's shameful decision sustaining the constitutionality of a military order excluding every person of Japanese descent, even American-born United States citizens, from most of the area along the Pacific Coast.

More often, the majority resisted the pressures when individual liberty was at stake. In DUNCAN V. KAHANAMOKU (1946), an opinion with constitutional overtones, the substitution of military tribunals for civilian courts in Hawaii was held beyond the statutory authority of Army commanders. Prosecution of a naturalized citizen of German descent who had befriended a German saboteur landed by German submarine and who took his funds for safekeeping was held in CRAMER V. UNITED STATES (1945) not to satisfy the constitutional definition of TREASON because the only overt acts proved by the testimony of two witnesses—meetings with the enemy saboteur in public places—were not shown to give aid and comfort to the enemy. In *Schneiderman v. United States* (1943) the Court held that proof that a naturalized citizen was an avowed Marxist and long-time active member, organizer, and officer of the Communist Party of the United States, both before and after his NATURALIZATION, was insufficient to warrant stripping him of CITIZENSHIP on the ground that, when naturalized, he had not been "attached to the principles of the Constitution . . . and well disposed to the good order and happiness of the United States."

The delicate balance that the Stone Court maintained between the effective prosecution of the war and the constitutional safeguards of liberty is perhaps best illustrated by the dramatic proceedings in EX PARTE QUIRIN (1942). In June 1942 eight trained Nazi saboteurs were put ashore in the United States by submarine, four on Long Island and four in Florida. They were quickly apprehended. President Roosevelt immediately appointed a military commission to try the saboteurs. The President was determined upon swift military justice. The proclamation declared the courts of the United States closed to subjects of any nation at war with the United States who might enter the United States and be charged with sabotage or attempt to commit sabotage. The trial was prosecuted with extraordinary speed and secrecy. Before the trial was complete, counsel for the saboteurs sought relief by petition for HABEAS CORPUS. By extraordinary procedure the case was rushed before the Supreme Court. The Justices broke their summer recess to hear oral argument. An order was promptly entered denying the petitions and promising a subsequent opinion. Within a few days the military tribunal passed sentence and six of the saboteurs were executed.

In the post-execution opinion the Court explained that the offense was triable by military commission; that the military commission was lawfully constituted; and that the proceedings were conducted without violation of any applicable provision of the Articles of War. The Justices were greatly troubled upon the last question. Some realized that in truth the swift and secret procedure ordained by the President left them with little ability to give meaningful protection to the saboteurs' legal rights in the military proceedings. Yet, even while recognizing that wartime pressures bent traditional legal safeguards in this as in other instances before the Stone Court, one should not conclude "inter arma silent leges." The hard core of the Court's decision was that judicial review of the saboteurs' constitutional contentions could not be barred even by the President as COMMANDER-IN-CHIEF. One may therefore hope that, if similar circumstances again arise, the Stone Court's basic defense of CONSTITUTIONALISM in time of war will prove more significant than its occasional yielding to the pressures of emergency.

ARCHIBALD COX

Bibliography

MASON, ALPHEUS 1956 *Harlan Fiske Stone, Pillar of the Laws.* Chaps. 34–42. New York: Viking Press.
ROSTOW, EUGENE 1945 The Japanese American Cases: A Disaster. *Yale Law Journal* 54:489–533.
SWINDLER, WILLIAM F. 1970 *Court and Constitution in the Twentieth Century,* Vol. 2, chaps. 6–10. Indianapolis: Bobbs-Merrill.
WOODWARD, J. 1968 *Mr. Justice Murphy.* Chaps. 11–13. Princeton, N.J.: Princeton University Press.

STOP AND FRISK

Most courts recognize that a police officer has the authority to detain a person briefly for questioning even without PROBABLE CAUSE to believe that the person is guilty of a crime. The Supreme Court first addressed the "stop and frisk" issue in TERRY V. OHIO (1968). In *Terry,* an experienced police officer observed three unknown men conducting themselves in a manner that suggested the planning of an imminent robbery. With his suspicion aroused—but clearly without probable cause to make an ARREST—the officer stopped and patted the men down, finding weapons on two of them. The holders of the two guns were arrested and convicted of possession of a concealed weapon. The Supreme Court ruled that the officer's actions in stopping the suspects were constitutional.

Terry, therefore, authorized law enforcement officials, on the grounds of reasonable suspicion, to stop briefly a suspicious person in order to determine his identity or to maintain the status quo while obtaining more information. Such a "stop" is proper when: the police observe unusual conduct; the conduct raises reasonable suspicion that criminal activity may be afoot; and the police can point to specific and articulable facts that warrant that suspicion. A "frisk" is proper when the following prerequisites are met: a "frisk" cannot be justified on "inchoate and unparticularized suspicion or 'hunch'," but must be grounded on facts which, in light of the officer's experience, support "specific reasonable inferences" that justify the intrusion; a "frisk" is proper only after "reasonable inquiries" have been made, although such inquiries need not be extensive; and a "frisk" is authorized where an officer reaches a reasonable conclusion that the person stopped for questioning may be armed and presently dangerous.

Further clarifying the test permitting a valid "stop and frisk," the Supreme Court has stated that the totality of the circumstances must be taken into account. Looking at the whole picture, the detaining officers must have a particularized and objective basis for suspecting the particular person stopped of criminal activity. The Court has emphasized that the process of assessing all the circumstances often will not involve hard certainties but rather probabilities; the evidence to justify the stop must be weighed in accordance with the understanding and experience of law enforcement personnel.

Applying that standard in UNITED STATES V. CORTEZ (1981), the Court upheld the propriety of stopping a defendant whose camper van was observed late at night near a suspected pick-up point for illegal ALIENS. The size of the vehicle, the lateness of the hour, and the remoteness of the spot all combined to make the stop reasonable.

Moreover, in *Adams v. Williams* (1972) the Supreme Court extended the *Terry* DOCTRINE in the following ways: (1) a "stop and frisk" is authorized for such offenses as possession of illegal drugs or a concealed weapon; (2) an informant's tip may provide reasonable cause for a "stop and frisk" even where no unusual conduct has been observed by an officer; and (3) the "identification" and "reasonable inquiries" requirements of the *Terry* decision are no longer absolute prerequisites. The *Terry* doctrine was again extended in *Michigan v. Long* (1983) where a "frisk" for weapons was not restricted to the person but was extended to any area that might contain a weapon posing danger to the police. A search of the passenger compartment of a car was held reasonable due to the observance of a hunting knife, the intoxicated state of the defendant, and the fact that the encounter took place at night in an isolated rural area.

In *Pennsylvania v. Mimms* (1977) the Court held that, whenever a vehicle is lawfully detained for a traffic violation, the police officer may order the driver out of the vehicle for questioning without violating the proscriptions of the FOURTH AMENDMENT.

In SIBRON V. NEW YORK (1968) a patrolman observed Sibron with a group of known drug addicts. The officer approached Sibron in a restaurant and ordered him outside. During a brief conversation with the officer, Sibron reached into his pocket. The patrolman promptly thrust his hand into the same pocket and found several glassine envelopes containing heroin.

The Supreme Court found the search to be unlawful on several grounds, including the fact that the "mere act of talking with a number of known addicts" was not enough to produce a reasonable inference that a person was armed and dangerous. The officer's motive, which was clearly to search for drugs, not for a weapon, invalidated the search as well. The *Sibron* decision is important because it made clear that *Terry* established only a narrow power to search on less than probable cause to arrest, and that the right to frisk is not an automatic concomitant to a lawful stop. *Sibron* also established proper motive as a prerequisite to a proper frisk.

In *Peters v. New York* (1968), *Sibron*'s companion case, an off-duty policeman saw through the peephole of his apartment door two strangers tiptoeing down the hallway. After calling the police station, dressing, and arming himself, the officer pursued the men and questioned Peters. Peters said he was visiting a married girlfriend but would not identify her. The officer then patted down Peters and felt in his pocket a hard, knife-like object. He removed the object, which turned out to be a plastic envelope containing bur-

glar's tools. Peters was charged with unlawful possession of burglar's tools. The search was held proper as incident to a lawful arrest because the circumstantial EVIDENCE available to the officer reached the level of probable cause to arrest Peters for attempted burglary.

After *Sibron* and *Peters*, the issue arises as to the legal consequences when a police officer pats down a suspect, reaches into the suspect's pocket, and pulls out evidence of a crime but not a weapon. The questions are whether the officer could reasonably have believed the item was a weapon, and whether the item was visible even without removing it. Using *Sibron* and *Peters* as models, a box of burglar's tools would satisfy the test (*Peters*), while a soft bag of heroin would not be admissible (*Sibron*).

The lower courts have expanded the scope of a constitutionally permissible frisk beyond a limited patdown of a suspect's outer clothing. Courts have included within the scope of a permissible frisk the area under a suspect's car seat, after the suspect appeared to hide something there, and a glove compartment within the reach of a suspect. In addition, the lower courts have relaxed their supervision over police judgments concerning objects that seem to be weapons when suspects are frisked, allowing officers to search after they have touched objects such as razor blades, cigarette lighters, and even lipstick containers.

The Supreme Court has declined to impose a rigid time limit for stop and frisk situations. In *United States v. Sharpe* (1985), where a pickup truck involved in drug trafficking was detained for twenty minutes, the Court determined that the length of the stop was reasonable by considering the purpose of the stop, the reasonableness of the time in effectuating the purpose, and the reasonableness of the means of investigation. In *United States v. Hensley* (1985) the Court widened the application of permissible investigative stops to include investigations of completed crimes. The Court also articulated that a police officer's reliance on a "wanted flyer" issued by another police department provided reasonable basis to conduct a stop if the flyer was based on "specific and articulable facts."

Finally, courts have handled the special case of airport "stop and frisk" situations in three ways. The first treats the problem through a straightforward application of the *Terry* test. The second method involves courts lowering the *Terry* level of "reasonable suspicion" to a less stringent standard. The third approach overtly abandons the *Terry* formula, opting for an ADMINISTRATIVE SEARCH consent rationale which does not even require reasonable suspicion. Today, the use of electronic scanning devices at most airports has diminished this area of "stop and frisk" concern.

CHARLES H. WHITEBREAD

Bibliography
WHITEBREAD, CHARLES H. 1980 *Criminal Procedure.* Mineola, N.Y.: Foundation Press.

STORING, HERBERT J.
(1928–1977)

Herbert Storing established the American Founding as a special field of study, both in his teaching at the University of Chicago and in his scholarship. Storing's monumental work, *The Complete Anti-Federalist,* contains introductions to and annotated, accurate texts of all substantial Anti-Federalist writings, along with the essay, "What the Anti-Federalists were *For.*" This material plus his essay on "The 'Other' Federalist Papers," facilitates a full study of the dialogue over RATIFICATION OF THE CONSTITUTION in 1787–1788. It also explains why the Constitution's opponents "must be seen as playing an indispensable, if subordinate, part in the founding process." Storing argued that the Anti-Federalists lost the debate, ultimately, because they could not reconcile the contradiction of supporting union while opposing adequate powers for the federal government, but he regarded as well taken their criticism of the Constitution as not providing for, and even undermining, republican virtue.

Elsewhere, in essays on slavery, CIVIL DISOBEDIENCE, the political thought of black Americans, and statesmanship, and in congressional testimony concerning the ELECTORAL COLLEGE, Storing demonstrated the continuing relevance of the founding dialogue for American politics.

MURRAY DRY

Bibliography
STORING, HERBERT J. 1981 *The Complete Anti-Federalist.* 7 Vols. Chicago: University of Chicago Press. (Volume 1 was also published separately under the title, *What the Anti-Federalists were For.*)
_____ 1976 "The 'Other' Federalist Papers." *Political Science Reviewer* 6:215–247.

STORY, JOSEPH
(1779–1845)

Joseph Story's contributions to American nationalism were as great as those of any other figure in American judicial history. The record of his career—his thirty-four years as an associate Justice of the Supreme Court, his hundreds of opinions delivered from the First Circuit Court (of Appeals), his many influential *Commentaries,* his contributions to the creation of admiralty and commercial law and EQUITY jurisprudence, his re-creation of the Harvard Law School—is more abundant, more distinguished, and more fertile than that of any jurist of his generation. Imbued with a deep pride in the American nation, Story believed that nationalism should proclaim itself in the might of the government and the majesty of the law, and in the expression of this philosophy he was articulate beyond any of his fellow jurists. Ceaselessly—in Congress, on the bench, from the professor's podium and the speaker's platform, in his study, and through his voluminous correspondence—he admonished the American people to exalt the nation and to preserve the Constitution and adapt it to the exigencies of history.

Born in Marblehead, Massachusetts, in 1779, Story graduated from Harvard College in 1798, read law, and began legal practice in Salem in 1801. In 1807 New England land speculators retained him to protect their interests in the notorious Yazoo lands controversy; his argument before the Supreme Court in their behalf was accepted by Chief Justice JOHN MARSHALL for the Court in FLETCHER V. PECK (1810).

A conservative Republican in a predominantly Federalist state, Story served for three years (1805–1808) in the Massachusetts legislature and then briefly (1808–1809) in the national House of Representatives. Though nominally a Republican, Story early displayed his independence by openly challenging President THOMAS JEFFERSON'S policies on naval preparedness and on the Embargo; Jefferson blamed the "pseudo-Republican," Story, for the repeal of that Embargo, which he had hoped would be a substitute for war. On returning to Massachusetts, Story reentered the state legislature and in 1811 was elected its speaker. When Justice WILLIAM CUSHING of Massachusetts died in 1810, Story was one of four candidates proposed to President JAMES MADISON as Cushing's successor. Not having forgiven Story's opposition to the Embargo, Jefferson protested to Madison that Story was "unquestionably a tory . . . and too young." Only after three other prospective nominees—LEVI LINCOLN, Alexander Wolcott, and JOHN QUINCY ADAMS—had declined the nomination or were rejected by the Senate did Madison turn to Story. At thirty-two, he was—and remains—the youngest appointee in the history of the Court.

When Story took his seat on the Bench in 1812, he was already an ardent nationalist. From the beginning he endorsed that BROAD CONSTRUCTION of the Constitution that we associate with Marshall, and throughout Marshall's life he was not so much a disciple of as a collaborator with the Chief Justice. For the next quarter century, these two magisterial jurists presented a united front on most major constitutional issues; only on the issue of PRESIDENTIAL POWERS in wartime, raised in *Brown v. United States* (1814), and a few issues of admiralty, international, and prize law did they ever disagree. Yet throughout his judicial career, Story's was an independent and original mind different in style if not in philosophy from Marshall's. Story respected and even venerated the Chief Justice, and the respect was mutual. If Story looked to Marshall for authoritative exposition of the Constitution, Marshall looked to Story for the substantiation of his logic and for help in other areas of law—notably in admiralty, conflict of laws, and equity. And when Story spoke on constitutional issues, it was in no mere imitative tones; frequently he pointed the way that Marshall later followed, as when his great opinion in MARTIN V. HUNTER'S LESSEE (1816) anticipated Marshall's opinion in COHENS V. VIRGINIA (1821). Although in some areas—such as the interpretation of the COMMERCE, NECESSARY AND PROPER, and CONTRACT CLAUSES of the Constitution—Marshall blazed the way, in others—notably those concerning the proper realms of executive and judicial power, issues of concurrent state and national power, and the creation of a uniform national commercial law—Story's was the greater overall achievement.

What emerges most strikingly from a study of Story's constitutional opinions is his passionate commitment to the authority of the national government in the federal system. He was quick to counter any attack or limitation upon its powers; he was alert to the potentialities of the concept of IMPLIED POWERS; he was ambitious to extend federal JURISDICTION by judicial opinion, legislation, or doctrinal writing. His ambitions were chiefly for the judiciary, for whose authority he was acquisitive and even belligerent, but he made bold claims for the national executive and legislative powers as well.

Story's solicitude for national executive authority was early asserted in *Brown v. United States* (1814), one of the few constitutional cases where he and Marshall disagreed. The issue presented was the validity of the confiscation of enemy property during the War of 1812 by the local United States district attorney without express legislative authority. Marshall, speaking for the Court, held such seizures illegal absent express authority granted by Congress. Story claimed that under the WAR POWER, the executive had full

authority to direct such seizures, for in the absence of legislation he was bound only by international law, which countenanced such action. Not content to vindicate the executive power merely under the rules of international law, Story rested his case upon the doctrine of implied powers in the Constitution, here anticipating Marshall's statement of that doctrine in McCULLOCH V. MARYLAND (1819). Story later seized the opportunity to restate and expand on his views on the implied powers of the executive in national emergencies in MARTIN V. MOTT (1827), which established the constitutional authority of the President to use his discretion as to the exigency that justified calling out the militia.

Though Story was not as jealous for legislative as for executive authority, in cases where the distribution of powers in the federal system was at issue he ranged himself strongly on the nationalist side. Thus, in PRIGG V. PENNSYLVANIA (1842), which presented the grave question whether authority to enforce the FUGITIVE SLAVE ACT of 1793 was vested exclusively in the national government or concurrently in the national and state governments, the Court held unconstitutional a Pennsylvania statute setting up parallel state enforcement machinery and imposing heavy penalties on any person who should seize or remove from the state anyone who had not been adjudged a fugitive from service. Story held for the Court that Congress had preempted the field by passing the 1793 act. This general argument was nothing new, being derived from Marshall's statement of the PREEMPTION doctrine in GIBBONS V. OGDEN (1824), but Story went further, arguing in dictum that the Constitution's fugitive slave clause did not impose upon the states any obligation to carry it into effect. Congressional authority was exclusive, so that the states not only could not cooperate with it through parallel legislation but might even prohibit their officials from acting under it. This was nationalism with a vengeance—as well as an escape hatch for northern states' PERSONAL LIBERTY LAWS. Only Justice JAMES M. WAYNE accepted Story's reasoning entirely; Chief Justice ROGER B. TANEY and Justices PETER V. DANIEL and HENRY BALDWIN agreed that the state statute was unconstitutional but denied that a state could release its officers from the obligation to enforce a federal law, while Justice JOHN McLEAN dissented *in toto*, upholding the state statute's constitutionality.

Story's ambiguous views on slavery, exemplified by his opinion in *Prigg*, merit special discussion. Story detested slavery and denounced it in charges to federal GRAND JURIES, and it was the source of his sole extrajudicial public statement on political issues—his condemnation of the MISSOURI COMPROMISE. Yet he generally yielded to the countervailing pull of his belief in the necessity to support and sustain the authority of the legal system. Thus, his opinion in *The Amistad* (1841), while upholding the claims for freedom of Africans who had liberated themselves from captivity and seized control of the slave ship carrying them to Latin America, rested solidly upon principles of international law, not on the noble rhetoric of John Quincy Adams's argument in the Africans' behalf. And while his OBITER DICTUM in *Prigg* might be read as flowing from hostility to slavery, his appeals in his lectures at the Harvard Law School that all citizens faithfully obey the Fugitive Slave Act indicate that it was his zeal for the RULE OF LAW and for exclusive national authority rather than sympathy for the fugitive slave that dictated the ingenious reasoning in *Prigg*.

Story's support for exclusive congressional authority extended to other areas as well. In *Houston v. Moore* (1820) he argued (in dissent) that by providing for the trial and punishment of offenses against the federal militia act, Congress had preempted the field, thereby precluding the states from making similar provisions; it followed that the criminal jurisdiction of the United States in this area could not be delegated in whole or in part to state tribunals. In his dissent in MAYOR OF NEW YORK V. MILN (1837) Story asserted that congressional authority to regulate commerce was supreme and exclusive and that a state law requiring the master of a foreign vessel to supply elaborate information about his passengers was an unconstitutional regulation of commerce rather than a constitutional exercise of the STATE POLICE POWER. Similarly, in *United States v. Coombs* (1838), he expanded the reach of federal power under the commerce clause, holding for the Court that a federal statute prohibiting as a crime against the United States the theft of goods from wrecked or stranded ships was a constitutional regulation of commerce, even though it might not fall within federal admiralty jurisdiction.

Ready as Story was to vindicate national executive and legislative powers, it was the judicial prerogative that was closest to his heart. In his eyes the judiciary was the bulwark of the Constitution, and the courts' role in maintaining the balance of the departments and the federal system was of supreme importance.

Key to this balance was Section 25 of the JUDICIARY ACT OF 1789, which provided for APPEALS from state to federal courts, guaranteeing the harmonious interpretation of the Constitution throughout the United States. In *Martin v. Hunter's Lessee* (1816), Story upheld the constitutionality of Section 25. In one form or another, this case had dragged its tortuous way through the courts for almost a quarter of a century. While the legal issues were complicated, the constitutional question was comparatively simple: was the authoritative interpretation of the Constitution lodged finally in the Supreme Court or did it share this prerogative with the highest state courts? The Court had already decided the legal issues in *Fairfax v. Hunter's Lessee* (1813), but the Virginia courts refused to be bound by that decision. Marshall disqualified himself from the case for reasons of judicial propriety, so Story spoke for the Court in his first great opinion. To him the case presented the simple question of national versus state supremacy, and his answer was equally simple, in contrast to his opinion's verbosity: the national government was supreme. Appeals from state to national courts did not involve any infringement upon the SOVEREIGNTY of the state, for the people of the state, acting in their sovereign capacity, had already provided for such appeals through their ratification of the Constitution. Building on *Martin*, Marshall later seized his chance to vindicate Section 25 anew in *Cohens v. Virginia*.

Story's other efforts to expand federal judicial power were to prove no less significant than *Martin*. While early in his judicial career he had unsuccessfully advocated common-law jurisdiction for the federal courts, Story achieved that goal indirectly in SWIFT V. TYSON (1842). In *Swift*, Story held that Section 34 of the Judiciary Act of 1789, which provided that "the laws of the several States, except where the Constitution, treaties, or statutes of the United States shall otherwise require or provide, shall be regarded as rules of decision in trials at common law in the courts of the United States," did not always bind federal courts to follow the decisions of state courts. He contended rather that Section 34 required federal courts to follow state court decisions only in strictly state matters, and that federal courts were free in cases posing "questions of general commercial law" to follow "the general principles and doctrines of commercial jurisprudence."

Swift was the entering wedge for the gradual creation of a FEDERAL COMMON LAW, but the decision had a troubled history until, after repeated challenge and criticism, the Court overruled it in ERIE RAILROAD CO. V. TOMPKINS (1938). Despite *Erie*, the need for uniformity of interpretation in contracts, sales, commercial paper, secured transactions, and other branches of commercial law resulted in the gradual though somewhat disorderly creation of a common commercial law. Through federal legislation, uniform state laws (such as the Uniform Commercial Code), the American Law Institute's promulgation of Restatements of the various branches of the law, and the publication of authoritative treatises and reports of decisions, Story's dream of a national commercial law has been substantially vindicated.

Story helped to establish uniformity in many areas of commercial law. Almost single-handed, he shaped American admiralty law in his opinions on the First Circuit Court and the Supreme Court. More important, however, were his many authoritative *Commentaries*, which he composed as part of his responsibilities as Dane Professor of Law at Harvard, a position which he held from 1829 until his death. Story was "driven to accept" this post by his old friend Nathan Dane, who conditioned his gift to the near moribund Harvard Law School on Story's acceptance of the chair. His lectures gave rise to commentaries on *Bailments* (1832), the *Constitution* (3 vols., 1833), *Conflict of Laws* (1834), *Equity Jurisprudence* (1836), *Equity Pleading* (1838), *Agency* (1839), *Partnership* (1841), *Bill of Exchange* (1843), and *Promissory Notes* (1845), which together comprise the most impressive body of scholarship on commercial law ever to come from the pen of one scholar. These commentaries, together with his authority and prestige, made the Harvard Law School the largest and most distinguished in the nation.

To three fields particularly Story's contributions were of outstanding importance. His *Commentaries on the Constitution* molded constitutional law and history for half a century; in light of their influence on DANIEL WEBSTER and ABRAHAM LINCOLN, it might be said that it was Story who triumphed in the Civil War and the FOURTEENTH AMENDMENT. His works on equity established its popularity in the American legal system by giving equity (in the words of an English commentator) "a philosophical character with which it never had been invested by any preceding author." His *Conflict of Laws*, the most original and learned of all his books, opened up a relatively new subject and revealed the possibilities of Continental to American and—even more remarkable—of American to English and Continental law, as well as winning for Story a distinguished international reputation.

Equally characteristic of Story's zeal for national authority and uniformity was his legal and judicial conservatism. His belief in natural law—that laws are discovered rather than made—was part and parcel

of the thinking of his generation, as of that earlier generation which had fought the American Revolution and framed state and national constitutions. Of the talismanic trio of life, liberty, and property, Story emphasized property—an emphasis peculiarly congenial to his temperament. The society in which Story lived was acquisitive and speculative—more fully so than the society that produced Marshall and Taney—and Story, along with JAMES KENT, came to be its most persuasive legal representative.

TERRETT V. TAYLOR (1816) gave Story his first opportunity to uphold property rights from the bench; writing for the Court, he struck down Virginia's attempt to revoke grants of glebe lands to the Episcopal Church, on the HIGHER LAW ground that legislative grants of land could not constitutionally be revoked by a subsequent legislative act. Similarly, Story's learned concurring opinion in DARTMOUTH COLLEGE v. WOODWARD (1819) supported Marshall's conclusion that the Constitution's contract clause forbade the revision or revocation by a state legislature of a college's charter. In the hands of Marshall and Story, the contract clause proved a powerful weapon for the maintenance of the status quo and the frustration of legislative experiments.

Marshall's death in 1835 and his replacement by Taney created a situation in which Story was increasingly uncomfortable. In three cases in the 1837 Term—*Mayor of New York v. Miln* (discussed above), CHARLES RIVER BRIDGE CO. v. WARREN BRIDGE, and BRISCOE v. BANK OF KENTUCKY—Story found himself in lonely and eloquent dissent, mourning the passing of the "old law." In *Charles River Bridge*, Story's most famous dissent, he bitterly countered the Court's decision upholding the Massachusetts legislature's grant of a permit to a new bridge company to build a bridge across the Charles River in competition with an existing bridge authorized by an earlier charter. Story's opinion ransacked the history of the COMMON LAW to establish that public grants were to be construed in the same manner as private grants—against the grantor; thus, the earlier grant of permission to build the first bridge should be read as granting an irrevocable monopoly. In *Briscoe*, Story dissented from a decision upholding Kentucky's creation of a state bank authorized to issue bank notes. Invoking the departed Marshall, Story argued that because a state could not do through an agent what it was barred from doing directly, Kentucky had violated the constitutional prohibition against the issuing by a state of BILLS OF CREDIT. These three cases dramatized the contrast between the Story-Marshall interpretation of the Constitution and that advanced by Taney and his colleagues; they illustrate the TANEY COURT's modification of the MARSHALL COURT's earlier positions to favor the states' police powers and a greater exercise of judicial continence.

Although Story died suddenly in 1845, leaving unwritten his projected works on admiralty and insurance and his memoirs, he had in large part succeeded in his determination to create a rounded system of law not only through judicial opinions but also through systematic treatises and teaching. His judicial opinions helped to formulate our constitutional, equity, PATENT, COPYRIGHT, admiralty, insurance, and commercial law. His *Commentaries* did more than those of any other expositor until our own day to mold popular ideas about the American constitutional system and to influence professional ideas about law, while they all but created the fields of commercial law and conflict of laws. And from the great law school which was so largely of his making and the extension of his shadow, he sent forth lawyers, judges, and teachers imbued with his nationalist philosophy of law and politics. Nor, indeed, did his influence end here; through such disciples as CHARLES SUMNER, TIMOTHY WALKER, and FRANCIS LIEBER, he handed on a vital and persistent tradition.

HENRY STEELE COMMAGER
RICHARD B. BERNSTEIN

Bibliography

COMMAGER, HENRY STEELE 1953 Joseph Story. In *Gaspar G. Bacon Lectures on the Constitution of the United States, 1940–1950.* Boston: Boston University Press.
DUNNE, GERALD T. 1970 *Justice Joseph Story and the Rise of the Supreme Court.* New York: Simon & Schuster.
McCLELLAN, JAMES 1971 *Joseph Story and the American Constitution: A Study in Political and Legal Thought.* Norman: University of Oklahoma Press.
NEWMYER, R. KENT 1985 *Supreme Court Justice Joseph Story: Statesman of the Old Republic.* Chapel Hill: University of North Carolina Press.
STORY, WILLIAM W. 1851 *Life and Letters of Joseph Story,* 2 vols. Boston: Little, Brown.

STRADER v. GRAHAM
10 Howard (51 U.S.) 83 (1851)

In a suit under a Kentucky statute making an abettor of fugitive slaves liable to the master for their value, defendant attempted to evade liability by arguing that the slaves, who had previously been permitted by their master, the plaintiff, to sojourn in free states, became free there and retained that status upon their return to their slave-state domicile. Defendant sought a reversal of the Kentucky Court of Appeals' determination that their slave status reattached.

On the central question, Chief Justice ROGER B. TANEY held that a state court's determination of the status of blacks was conclusive on federal courts. But he went on to assert in dictum that every state had the right to determine the status of persons within its territory "except in so far as the powers of the states in this respect are restrained, or duties and obligations imposed on them" by the federal Constitution, thus suggesting that the Constitution might somehow invalidate northern abolition statutes or statutes regulating the permissible stay of sojourning slaves. He also insisted that the NORTHWEST ORDINANCE was defunct, its famous sixth article no longer a basis for the exclusion of slavery from the five states of the former Northwest Territory, thus suggesting that Congress might not be able to impose an enforceable antislavery condition on a territory's admission as a state.

Had the United States Supreme Court in 1857 wished to evade the controversial question raised in DRED SCOTT V. SANDFORD of the constitutionality of congressional prohibition of SLAVERY IN THE TERRITORIES, it might have used *Strader* to hold that the determination of Scott's status by the Missouri Supreme Court was binding on federal courts. Justice SAMUEL NELSON's concurrence in *Dred Scott,* originally intended to be the opinion for the Court, did in fact adopt this approach.

WILLIAM M. WIECEK

STRAUDER v. WEST VIRGINIA
100 U.S. 303 (1880)
VIRGINIA v. RIVES
100 U.S. 313 (1880)
EX PARTE VIRGINIA AND J. D. COLES
100 U.S. 339 (1880)

On a day in 1880 the Supreme Court handed down three opinions that fixed the constitutional law of JURY DISCRIMINATION for over half a century. The effect of the three, taken collectively, barred overt state denial of the rights of blacks to serve on juries and effectively barred blacks from jury service in the South. Anything so crude as an announced and deliberate effort to exclude persons on ground of race was unconstitutional; but if official policy did not refer to race and yet blacks were systematically excluded by covert practices, the Constitution's integrity remained unimpaired. No estimate can be made of the miscarriages of justice that occurred in the South and border states where only whites sat in judgment in civil cases involving the property of blacks or in criminal cases involving their life and liberty over a period of at least fifty-five years.

Strauder was a case in which official state policy was overtly discriminatory on racial grounds. West Virginia by statute declared that only whites might serve on juries. Justice WILLIAM STRONG, for the Court, holding the act to be a violation of the EQUAL PROTECTION clause of the FOURTEENTH AMENDMENT, declared that denying citizens the right to participate in the administration of justice solely for racial reasons "is practically a brand upon them, affixed by law; an assertion of their inferiority, and a stimulant to that race prejudice which is an impediment to securing to individuals of the race that equal justice which the law aims to secure to all others." The Court also sustained the constitutionality of a section of the CIVIL RIGHTS ACT OF 1866 by which Congress authorized the removal of a case from a state court to a federal court in order to prevent the denial of CIVIL RIGHTS by the state court. Justice STEPHEN J. FIELD and NATHAN CLIFFORD dissented without opinion.

In *Ex Parte Virginia and J. D. Coles*, the Court sustained the constitutionality of an act of Congress which provided that no qualified person should be disqualified because of race for service as a grand or petit juror in any court, state or federal. Coles, a county court judge of Virginia charged with selecting jurors, excluded from jury lists all black persons. He was indicted by the United States and was liable to be fined $5,000. On petition for a writ of HABEAS CORPUS, he alleged that the federal court had no JURISDICTION over him and that the act of Congress was unconstitutional. Strong declared that under the Fourteenth Amendment, Congress could reach any act of a state that violated the right of black citizens to serve on juries or their right to be tried by juries impartially selected without regard to race. The act of Judge Coles was the act of the state of Virginia, for a state acts through its officers and agents, none of whom may deny the equal protection of the laws. By so ruling, the Court prepared the ground for the doctrine of STATE ACTION. Field and Clifford, again dissenting, thought the act of Congress regulated purely local matters and destroyed state autonomy.

The effects of *Strauder* and *Ex Parte Virginia* were vitiated by the *Rives* decision. Two black men, indicted for the murder of a white man, sought to have their cases removed from a state court to a federal court on the ground that the GRAND JURY that indicted them and the PETIT JURY summoned to try them were composed entirely of whites. The prisoners claimed that the jury lists should include one third blacks, in proportion to the population, and, most important, that no blacks had ever been allowed to serve on juries in the county where they were to be tried. In this case the record did not show, as it did in the other two, overt and direct exclusion of blacks. Strong, for the Court, this time supported by Field and Clifford concurring separately, simply stated, without further ado, that the "assertions" that no blacks ever served on juries in the county "fall short" of showing the denial of a civil right or the existence of racial discrimination. The defendants might still be tried impartially. Similarly, they had no right to a jury composed in part of members of their race. A mixed jury, said the Court, is not essential to the equal protection of the laws. There was no "unfriendly legislation" in this case. In effect the Court placed upon black prisoners the burden of proving deliberate and systematic exclusion on ground of race. As a result, blacks quickly disappeared from jury service in the South.

LEONARD W. LEVY

(SEE ALSO: *Neal v. Delaware*, 1881; *Norris v. Alabama*, 1935.)

Bibliography
SCHMIDT, BENNO C. 1983 Juries, Jurisdiction, and Race Discrimination: The Lost Promise of *Strauder v. West Virginia*. *Texas Law Review* 61:1401–1499.

STREAM OF COMMERCE DOCTRINE

The Supreme Court introduced the "stream" or "current" metaphor in SWIFT & CO. V. UNITED STATES (1905) to represent the movement of goods in INTERSTATE COMMERCE. The DOCTRINE is significant because it marks the Court's first recognition that commercial markets ignored state lines; the Justices departed from decades of CONSTITUTIONAL INTERPRETATION in which economic reality had yielded to formal legal discrimination. The doctrine itself may be stated as follows: what appears, when out of context, to be INTRASTATE COMMERCE comes within the reach of the interstate commerce power if that commerce is but an incident related to an interstate continuum. Thus Congress can regulate the local aspects of commerce that are inseparably related to the current of interstate commerce, even though the flow has been temporarily interrupted by a kind of whirl-pool or eddy while the product goes through some stage in the transformation of the raw material into the finished goods before being shipped again in the interstate stream to reach its final destination.

In *Swift* the government charged the nation's largest meat packers with conspiring to monopolize inter-state commerce in violation of the SHERMAN ANTI-TRUST ACT. The packers asserted that their activities took place at the stockyards—solely within the bound-aries of a single state—and thus involved only local or intrastate commerce. Justice OLIVER WENDELL HOLMES, for a unanimous Court, rejected the packers' contentions.

[C]ommerce among the states is not a technical legal con-ception, but a practical one drawn from the course of busi-ness. When cattle are sent for sale from a place in one state, with the expectation that they will end their transit, after purchase, in another, and when in effect they do so, with only the interruption necessary to find a purchaser at the stock yards, and when this is a typical, constantly recurring course, the current thus existing is a current of commerce among the states, and the purchase of cattle is a part and incident of such commerce.

The opinion struck hard at the rigid separation be-tween PRODUCTION and commerce approved in UNITED STATES V. E. C. KNIGHT & CO. (1895). In recognizing that the United States no longer com-prised a group of small, discrete markets, the Court began to confront the legal implications of the trans-portation and communications revolutions.

Although Holmes did not create the pithy meta-phor, it stuck. In STAFFORD V. WALLACE (1922) Chief Justice WILLIAM HOWARD TAFT declared that the stockyards were "a throat through which the current flows, and the transactions which occur therein are only incident to this current." The doctrine marked the "inevitable recognition of the great central fact" that such streams of commerce are interstate "in their very essence."

By the 1930s, as the circumstances that had given rise to the doctrine disappeared, the doctrine's prag-matism became increasingly well-accepted. Though the stream of commerce terminology made frequent appearances, the Court began to ignore the doctrine itself. In SCHECHTER POULTRY CORP. V. UNITED STATES (1935) and CARTER V. CARTER COAL CO. (1936) the Court refused to apply it. When a 5–4 Court sustained government regulation of interstate com-merce in NLRB v. Jones & Laughlin Steel Corp. (1937), the Justices still chose not to base their opinion

merely on the stream of commerce doctrine. Drawing upon both *Stafford* and HOUSTON, EAST & WEST TEXAS RAILWAY CO. V. UNITED STATES (1914), Chief Justice CHARLES EVANS HUGHES declared that only those intrastate activities that had "such a close and substantial relation" to interstate commerce would be subject to congressional control.

The Supreme Court continued to use Holmes's lan-guage into the 1940s, but the doctrine almost disap-peared. Indeed, although the phrase "stream of com-merce" has enjoyed renewed use in the 1970s and 1980s, the Court almost never invokes the doctrine. Instead, the Justices have echoed Holmes's rejection of technical legal inquiries.

DAVID GORDON

Bibliography
GORDON, DAVID 1984 Swift & Company v. United States: The Beef Trust and the Stream of Commerce Doctrine. *American Journal of Legal History* 28:244–279.

STRICT CONSTRUCTION

This phrase purports to describe a method of CONSTI-TUTIONAL INTERPRETATION. Those using it, however, often are not referring to the same interpretive method. Classically, a strict construction is one that narrowly construes Congress's power under Article I, section 8. But some use strict construction to mean interpretations that limit the situations to which a con-stitutional provision applies, without regard to the in-terpretations' effect on the scope of federal power. Despite the existence of these and other definitions, one theme unites many uses of the phrase. Most users employ strict construction to support political posi-tions by portraying them as the result of what at least sounds like a value-neutral interpretive technique. The phrase's political use now outweighs any techni-cal legal significance it may have.

The term's greatest historical importance stems from its use to describe restrictive interpretations of the federal government's constitutional powers. Mod-ern constitutional interpretations render strict con-struction of federal power a remnant of the past. In the nation's early years, however, the question of strict versus BROAD CONSTRUCTION of federal power was as critical as any question facing the country. The dispute over whether to establish a BANK OF THE UNITED STATES provided the setting for the first de-bate over the construction to be afforded Congress's powers. THOMAS JEFFERSON and JAMES MADISON, who both opposed the Bank, "strictly construed" the federal government's powers and concluded that Congress lacked power to create the Bank. ALEXANDER HAMILTON, who favored the Bank, advocated a more flexible view of federal power. In disputes over federal power, the phrase would continue to characterize these early Jeffersonian positions opposed by Federalists.

Chief Justice JOHN MARSHALL's reputation as a non-strict-constructionist owes much to his opinion for the Court sustaining the validity of the act creating the second Bank of the United States. In MCCULLOCH V. MARYLAND (1819) Marshall endorsed Hamilton's view of Congress's powers in an opinion that included the oft-quoted passage, "Let the end be legitimate, let it be within the scope of the constitution, and all means which are appropriate, which are plainly adapted to that end, which are not prohibited, but consist with the letter and spirit of the constitution, are constitutional." In GIBBONS V. OGDEN (1824), again speaking through Marshall, the Court expressly rejected strict construction of federal power as a proper method of interpretation. It found not "[o]ne sentence in the Constitution . . . that prescribes this rule."

Strict construction becomes a much more complex concept when offered, as it has been, as a method of interpreting the entire Constitution. Strict construction then means interpretations that restrict the situations in which constitutional grants of power, or limitations on them, are deemed applicable. A strict construction simply limits the cases in which the Constitution applies. In this sense, a strict construction need not correspond to a constitutional interpretation that limits federal power. This difference results from the variable structure of constitutional provisions.

Some constitutional provisions are phrased positively in the sense that they confer powers upon Congress, the President, or the courts. Other provisions, such as the FIRST AMENDMENT, are phrased negatively. A strict construction—in the sense of limiting the Constitution's applicability—of the positive powers limits federal authority, as Marshall did in MARBURY V. MADISON (1803), when he construed Article III not to authorize the Supreme Court to issue original writs of MANDAMUS. But strict (that is, narrow) construction of a negative provision such as the First Amendment expands governmental authority. Even if strict construction had become the accepted technique for interpreting grants of power to Congress, it is questionable whether, in a government of limited powers, strict construction would be an appropriate

technique for interpreting express constitutional limitations on Congress's power.

When used to interpret the entire Constitution, strict construction fails as a guiding principle in the large class of cases in which one constitutional provision can be interpreted narrowly only by broadly interpreting another provision. DRED SCOTT V. SANDFORD (1857) highlights this problem. *Dred Scott*, which restricted Congress's power to regulate slavery in the territories and assured Chief Justice ROGER B. TANEY's reputation as a strict constructionist, is the Court's most famous strict construction of federal power. Yet, while Taney construed strictly Congress's power, he simultaneously construed broadly constitutional limitations on Congress's authority and the constitutional rights of slaveholders.

A similar problem undermines efforts to embrace strict construction as a politically conservative technique for judicial decision making. The conservative Supreme Court of the late nineteenth and early twentieth centuries did limit Congress's powers by, among other things, invalidating federal statutes as exceeding Congress's power under the commerce clause and by finding, in UNITED STATES V. BUTLER (1936), short-lived limitations on Congress's TAXING AND SPENDING POWER. But in relying on the due process clauses to invalidate many federal and state enactments, the same Court offered broad interpretations of those limitations on government power.

The ambiguity attending strict construction has not deterred many from trying to exploit the concept for political advantage. Even in the early disputes between Federalists and Jeffersonians, when strict construction may have had its clearest meaning, there is a hint of hypocrisy in the reliance placed on strict construction. It is unlikely that insufficient strictness is what really troubled early critics of Marshall's and other Federalists' loose constructions. When it suited their goals, Marshall's critics supported loose construction. For example, to justify an administrative and legislative program imposing an embargo on France and England, President Jefferson interpreted broadly presidential and congressional authority to terminate and influence commerce. And Marshall did not always generously interpret the federal government's powers. At AARON BURR's treason trial, Marshall strictly, that is to say, narrowly, construed Article III, section 3, the constitutional provision on treason.

Although many have tried to rely on strict constructionism to political advantage, this trend reached its modern peak under President RICHARD M. NIXON. He referred to strict construction as a characteristic he sought in a Supreme Court appointee. Nixon probably did not primarily mean one who narrowly construed the federal government's powers. He was most dissatisfied with the Supreme Court's CRIMINAL PROCEDURE decisions. In his 1968 campaign, Nixon announced his preference for Supreme Court appointees who would aid the society's peace forces in combating criminals. In this context strict construction was a double negative: limiting the situations in which the Constitution restricted states' criminal procedures. Only coincidentally would such constructions reduce the federal government's role.

Like previous users of the term, Nixon employed strict construction for political advantage, not to facilitate discussion of theories of CONSTITUTIONAL INTERPRETATION. He never articulated his understanding of the phrase, and Justice HARRY BLACKMUN, one of his Supreme Court appointees, disclaimed an understanding of it. Nixon once described Justice FELIX FRANKFURTER as exemplifying what he sought in a Justice, yet Frankfurter delivered nonstrict criminal procedure opinions. In ROCHIN V. CALIFORNIA (1952) he wrote that forcing an emetic into a suspect's stomach to gather recently swallowed evidence shocked the conscience and, therefore, violated the DUE PROCESS CLAUSE of the FOURTEENTH AMENDMENT. And Frankfurter dissented from the Court's decision upholding the admissibility of conversations overheard by means of ELECTRONIC EAVESDROPPING. In addition, in assessing a president's constitutional powers, Nixon was anything but a strict constructionist. The impoundment of funds appropriated by Congress, the invasion of Cambodia, the assertion of EXECUTIVE PRIVILEGE, and many of Nixon's domestic security measures all suggest an expansive, nonstrict view of a president's constitutional authority.

Finally, "strict construction" may have other sensible meanings that do not refer to narrow interpretations. Justice HUGO BLACK may have thought himself to be construing the Constitution strictly when he applied it literally, as in First Amendment cases. Another plausible meaning is strict adherence to the letter and spirit of the Constitution. Under this view, everyone can claim to be a strict constructionist, adhering to what he or she ascertains to be the principles embodied in the Constitution. Strict construction also may characterize a passive judiciary. For example, many believe legislative apportionment to be a POLITICAL QUESTION, a matter of concern only for the legislative and executive branches. A judge who invades the area is deemed active and, therefore, not a strict constructionist. Judge LEARNED HAND may have used strict construction in this sense when he stated that

the Supreme Court's failure to define political questions is "a stench in the nostrils of strict constructionists."

THEODORE EISENBERG

Bibliography

BLACK, CHARLES L., JR. 1960 *The People and the Court.* New York: Macmillan.

KELLY, ALFRED H.; HARBISON, WINFRED A., and BELZ, HERMAN 1983 *The American Constitution,* 6th ed. New York: Norton.

KOHLMEIER, LOUIS M., JR. 1972 *God Save This Honorable Court.* New York: Scribner's.

MURPHY, WILLIAM P. 1967 *The Triumph of Nationalism.* Chicago: Quadrangle Books.

STRICT SCRUTINY

In its modern use, "strict scrutiny" denotes JUDICIAL REVIEW that is active and intense. Although the "constitutional revolution" of the late 1930s aimed at replacing JUDICIAL ACTIVISM with a more restrained review using the RATIONAL BASIS formula, even that revolution's strongest partisans recognized that "a more exacting judicial scrutiny" might be appropriate in some cases. Specific prohibitions of the BILL OF RIGHTS, for example, might call for active judicial defense, and legislation might be entitled to a diminished presumption of validity when it interfered with the political process itself or was directed against DISCRETE AND INSULAR MINORITIES. (See UNITED STATES V. CAROLENE PRODUCTS CO., 1938.) The term "strict scrutiny" appears to have been used first by Justice WILLIAM O. DOUGLAS in his opinion for the Supreme Court in SKINNER V. OKLAHOMA (1942), in a context suggesting special judicial solicitude both for certain rights that were "basic" and for certain persons who seemed the likely victims of legislative prejudice.

Both these concerns informed the WARREN COURT's expansion of the reach of the EQUAL PROTECTION clause. "Strict scrutiny" was required for legislation that discriminated against the exercise of FUNDAMENTAL INTERESTS or employed SUSPECT CLASSIFICATIONS. In practice, as Gerald Gunther put it, the Court's heightened scrutiny was " 'strict' in theory and fatal in fact." The Court took a hard look at both the purposes of the legislature and the means used for achieving them. To pass the test of strict scrutiny, a legislative classification must be "necessary to achieve a COMPELLING STATE INTEREST." Thus the state's objectives must be not merely legitimate but of compelling importance, and the means used must be not merely rationally related to those purposes but necessary to their attainment.

The same demanding standard of review has emerged in other areas of constitutional law. Thus even some "indirect" regulations of the FREEDOM OF SPEECH—that is, regulations that do not purport to regulate message content—must be strictly scrutinized. Similarly, strict scrutiny is appropriate for general legislation whose application is attacked as a violation of the right of free exercise of religion. (See RELIGIOUS LIBERTY.) And in those places where SUBSTANTIVE DUE PROCESS has made a comeback—notably in defense of liberties having to do with marriage and family relations, abortion and contraception, and more generally the FREEDOM OF INTIMATE ASSOCIATION—the same strict judicial scrutiny is the order of the day.

The Court has developed intermediate STANDARDS OF REVIEW falling between the rational basis and strict scrutiny standards. Not every heightening of the intensity of judicial review, in other words, implies strict scrutiny. Most critics of the Supreme Court's modern activism reject not only its employment of the strict scrutiny standard but also its use of any heightened standard of review. For these critics, there is little room in the Constitution for any judicial inquiry into the importance of governmental goals or the utility of governmental means. Some action by the state is forbidden by the Constitution, more or less explicitly. Beyond these prohibitions, say these critics, lie no principled guides to judicial behavior.

Yet strict judicial scrutiny of legislation is almost as old as the Constitution itself. From one season to another, the special objects of the judiciary's protection have varied, but from JOHN MARSHALL's day to our own the courts have always found *some* occasions for "a more exacting judicial scrutiny" of the political branches' handiwork. It is hard to imagine what our country would be like if they had not done so.

KENNETH L. KARST

Bibliography

GUNTHER, GERALD 1972 The Supreme Court, 1971 Term—Foreword: In Search of Evolving Doctrine on a Changing Court: A Model for a Newer Equal Protection. *Harvard Law Review* 86:1–48.

STROMBERG v. CALIFORNIA
283 U.S. 359 (1931)

A California law made it a crime to display a red flag or banner "as a sign, symbol or emblem of opposition to organized government or as an invitation or stimulus to anarchistic action or as an aid to propaganda that is of a seditious character. . . ." A member of the Young Communist League who ran a summer camp where the daily ritual included the raising of "the workers' red flag" was convicted for violating the statute, although a state appellate court noted that the prohibition contained in the first clause—"opposition to organized government"—was so vague as to be constitutionally questionable. That court nonetheless upheld the conviction on the grounds that the defendant had been found guilty of violating the entire statute and that the other two clauses relating to "anarchistic action" and "seditious character" were sufficiently definite.

Chief Justice CHARLES EVANS HUGHES and six other members of the Supreme Court reversed the conviction. In his opinion, Hughes pointed out that, the jury having rendered a general verdict, it was impossible to know under which clause or clauses the defendant had been convicted. If any of the three clauses were invalid, the conviction could not stand. The Court found the first clause "so vague and indefinite" that it violated the DUE PROCESS clause of the FOURTEENTH AMENDMENT because it prohibited not only violent, illegal opposition to organized government but also "peaceful and orderly opposition to government by legal means. . . ." Justices JAMES C. MCREYNOLDS and PIERCE BUTLER dissented.

MICHAEL E. PARRISH

STRONG, WILLIAM
(1808–1895)

Strong was a learned, able, hard-working Supreme Court Justice who competently handled the tedious routine of COMMON LAW, admiralty, PATENT, and revenue law cases. Except for sustaining legal tenders and invalidating state-authorized exclusion of blacks from jury service, he rarely spoke for the Court in constitutional matters during his ten-year career. Strong's appointment in 1870 was viewed as part of an alleged court-packing scheme to reverse a recent decision invalidating legal tender legislation. But President ULYSSES S. GRANT had decided to nominate Strong and JOSEPH P. BRADLEY in January 1870, a month before an eight-man court, including a Justice who already had resigned, narrowly decided *Hepburn v. Griswold*. Grant, meanwhile, was well aware that Strong had written an opinion for the Pennsylvania Supreme Court sustaining the laws.

Strong did not disappoint Grant. In May 1871, he

wrote the majority opinion in *Knox v. Lee* and *Parker v. Davis*, reversing *Hepburn*. He largely based his argument on the NECESSARY AND PROPER clause, finding the legal tender legislation a necessary concomitant to the WAR POWER. He also refuted the *Hepburn* argument that the laws violated the "spirit of the Constitution" because they impaired the OBLIGATION OF CONTRACTS. All contracts, Strong contended, had to anticipate the rightful exercise of congressional power.

Strong generally defended vested contractual and property rights, the LEGAL TENDER CASES notwithstanding. He joined Justice STEPHEN J. FIELD's dissent in *Munn v. Illinois* (1877). In his own dissent in the SINKING FUND CASES (1879), he maintained that the government could not require railroads to divert part of their earnings into a special fund for payment of their federal debts. The original railroad grant contained no such provision, but Congress had reserved the right to alter, amend, or repeal the act. Strong nevertheless insisted that the new requirement was "plainly transgressive of legislative power" for it violated an implied contractual promise not to call for debt payment before 1897. Strong's dissent, along with those by JOSEPH BRADLEY and Field, heralded the procorporation, antistatist tendencies that dominated the Court for several decades.

The Court's concern with state economic regulation inevitably provoked operations of national authority. In the *State Freight Tax Case* (1873) (see PHILADELPHIA AND READING R.R. CO. V. PENNSYLVANIA) Strong offered a significant commentary on the scope of the COMMERCE CLAUSE when it conflicted with traditional state power. Pennsylvania had imposed a tonnage tax on railroad freight carried within and out of the state, but Strong held that the transportation of goods was a "constituent of commerce" and the tax's "effect" unduly burdened INTERSTATE COMMERCE. In a comparison case, Strong held valid a tax on corporate gross receipts irrespective of whether they came from interstate or intrastate businesses (*State Tax on Railway Gross Receipts,* 1873). In effect, the commerce clause was not a shield for private enterprise against STATE TAXATION.

Strong's record on CIVIL RIGHTS was mixed. He joined the Court's majority in the SLAUGHTERHOUSE CASES (1873) to restrict the scope of the FOURTEENTH AMENDMENT. Similarly, he voted to limit federal guarantees for voting and civil rights. In *Blyew v. United States* (1872), he wrote the Court's first opinion restricting the CIVIL RIGHTS ACT OF 1866. The act authorized federal trials for crimes "affecting persons"

denied rights secured by law. Strong held, however, that federal courts lacked JURISDICTION over a defendant accused of murdering three blacks on the ground that the dead persons could not be affected by any prosecution. Although Strong favored upholding a state statute requiring equal access in public transportation, he silently acquiesced when the Court held that the law unduly burdened interstate commerce (HALL V. DeCUIR, 1878). But he spoke for the Court in a series of cases that marked some exceptional, however limited, victories for blacks.

In STRAUDER V. WEST VIRGINIA (1880) the Court invalidated a state statute excluding blacks from juries. Strong conceded that blacks were not entitled to have other blacks sit on their juries, but he held that they had a right to have juries selected impartially. The protection of one's life and liberty against racial prejudice was, Strong contended, a "legal right" under the Fourteenth Amendment and therefore the state's exclusion law constituted a denial of EQUAL PROTECTION OF THE LAWS. In a companion case, *Ex parte Virginia* (1880), Strong upheld a section of the 1875 CIVIL RIGHTS ACT which prohibited RACIAL DISCRIMINATION in jury selection. Although state law forbade such discrimination, a state judge had refused to call blacks as jurors. Strong brushed aside arguments that the judge's refusal was not the same as STATE ACTION, which Congress concededly could prohibit. The judge, he insisted, held state office and acted for the state; as such he was obligated to obey the federal constitution and law. But in a third case decided that day, *Virginia v. Rives* (1880), Strong denied a plea for removal of a cause to a federal court on the ground of JURY DISCRIMINATION. Here blacks had been excluded as a result of discretionary action by jury commissioners, not as a result of state law as in *Strauder*. The decision in effect condoned the practical exclusion of blacks from southern juries for the next seventy-five years. Nevertheless, Strong's opinion in *Ex Parte Virginia* preserved a vestige of federal power that was revived in the CIVIL RIGHTS ACT OF 1957, the first such legislation since Reconstruction.

Strong did not have the domineering intellectual force of a Bradley, Field, or Miller, but he performed capably during his career. He was admired and respected by his diverse colleagues, and he managed to avoid the intense personal and ideological conflicts that characterized the period. He abruptly resigned in 1880. Strong was in good health, but he supposedly stepped down as an example to NATHAN CLIFFORD, WARD HUNT, and NOAH SWAYNE who were ill and frequently absent from the bench. Within two years, the three resigned. In retirement, Strong publicized the Court's burdensome workload, and his efforts contributed to the creation of new courts of appeal in 1891. (See CIRCUIT COURTS OF APPEALS ACT.)

STANLEY I. KUTLER

Bibliography

KUTLER, STANLEY I. 1969 William Strong. In Friedman, Leon, and Israel, Fred L., eds., *The Justices of the United States Supreme Court, 1789–1969: Their Lives and Major Opinions,* pages 1153–1178. New York: Chelsea House.

STUART v. LAIRD
1 Cranch 299 (1803)

The JUDICIARY ACT OF 1802, having repealed the JUDICIARY ACT OF 1801 before it could go into operation, abolished the new CIRCUIT COURTS and returned the Justices of the Supreme Court to circuit duty under the JUDICIARY ACT OF 1789. The *Stuart* case raised the constitutionality of the repeal act of 1802. Although Chief Justice JOHN MARSHALL despised the repeal act and believed it to be unconstitutional, on circuit duty he sidestepped the constitutional issue. When the case came before the Court on a WRIT OF ERROR, Justice WILLIAM PATERSON for the Court, with Marshall abstaining, ruled that the practice of riding circuit had begun under the act of 1789 and that long acquiescence "has fixed the construction. It is a contemporary interpretation of the most forcible nature." Thus the Court avoided holding unconstitutional an act of THOMAS JEFFERSON's administration.

LEONARD W. LEVY

(SEE ALSO: *Marbury v. Madison.*)

STUDENTS CHALLENGING REGULATORY AGENCY PROCEDURES (SCRAP), UNITED STATES v.
412 U.S. 669 (1973)

Environmentalists sued to force the Interstate Commerce Commission to suspend a freight rate surcharge announced by the nation's railroads. Plaintiffs claimed the surcharge would raise the cost of transporting recyclable materials and thus injure their recreational and aesthetic use of areas around Washington, D.C., by increasing pollution from waste disposal and causing greater consumption of natural resources.

In one of its most generous rulings on STANDING, the Court held that environmental advocates could raise a statutory claim that, according to three dissenters, was based on injuries that were too remote, speculative, and insubstantial to confer standing. Justice POTTER J. STEWART followed the implications of SIERRA CLUB V. MORTON (1972): environmental harm, however widespread, satisfies the "injury in fact" requirement of standing, and the case will be heard if those who complain allege harm to themselves. The harm need not be "substantial." Nor did it matter that the line of causation between the challenged government act and the asserted environmental harm was "attenuated." Several subsequent decisions, such as *Warth v. Seldin* (1975) and SIMON V. EASTERN KENTUCKY WELFARE RIGHTS ORGANIZATION (1976), differ from *SCRAP,* insisting that the causal link between act and harm be more clearly shown. *SCRAP's* relaxed view of causal nexus in standing may reflect a special judicial receptivity to environmental litigation.

JONATHAN D. VARAT

STUMP v. SPARKMAN
435 U.S. 349 (1978)

This decision confirmed judges' absolute immunity from damage suits for alleged constitutional violations. At the request of a mother who was displeased with her "somewhat retarded" fifteen-year-old daughter's behavior, and in EX PARTE proceeding in which the child was not represented, Judge Stump ordered the child to be sterilized. The girl was told she was having an appendectomy, and she discovered some years later she had been sterilized. In an action brought by the sterilization victim and her husband, the Supreme Court held, 5–3, that the judge was immune from liability. Because signing the sterilization order was a judicial act, and because there was no express statement in state law that judges lacked JURISDICTION to entertain sterilization requests, the judge's behavior was covered by the doctrine of JUDICIAL IMMUNITY. In the name of judicial independence, the majority immunized conduct that the three dissenters aptly called "lawless," "beyond the pale of anything that could sensibly be called a judicial act."

THEODORE EISENBERG

STURGES v. CROWNINSHIELD
4 Wheaton 122 (1819)

This was the first of the very rare CONTRACT CLAUSE cases decided by the Supreme Court involving private executory contracts. The case arose during a depression, when many states had enacted bankruptcy or insolvency statutes. Chief Justice JOHN MARSHALL, for a unanimous Court, agreed that the states possessed a concurrent power to enact such statutes in the absence of the exercise by Congress of its power to establish uniform bankruptcy laws but held that New York's act violated the contract clause. Crowninshield had declared his bankruptcy under that state's act to protect himself from paying a debt contracted before its passing. The doctrine of the case is that a state act cannot operate retroactively on previously existing contracts; a statute that relieves the debtor from imprisonment is valid but not one that cancels the obligation of his contract. The case left uncertain the constitutionality of bankruptcy acts that operate prospectively on contracts formed after their enactment. (See OGDEN V. SAUNDERS, 1827.)

LEONARD W. LEVY

SUBJECTS OF COMMERCE

A chief purpose of the COMMERCE CLAUSE of the federal Constitution is to assure the free movement of the subjects of commerce among the several states. What are these subjects? Essentially, the term refers to things sold or transported in INTERSTATE COMMERCE. But they need not be articles of trade or even of value. Nor are they confined to objects as such. They may include PERSONS. All are included as subjects or articles of commerce when they begin to move from one state to another. They remain articles of commerce until they fall into the possession of the ultimate buyer or reach their final stage of repose within a given state. Thus, at any point between the beginning and the end of their journey among the states, they are legitimate candidates for congressional regulation. With respect to these subjects, as with interstate commerce generally, Congress may, in the words of GIBBONS V. OGDEN (1824), "prescribe the rule by which commerce is to be governed."

Congress ordinarily exerts its power over the subjects of commerce in order to protect their free movement across state borders. But this power has also been construed to permit Congress to divest some subjects of their interstate character. Divestment occurs when Congress prohibits the interstate transpor-

tation of certain goods or persons. Examples of such subjects are stolen automobiles, intoxicating beverages, forged checks, convict-made goods, explosives, prostitutes, firearms, lottery tickets, and kidnaped children. Federal laws prohibiting commerce in such subjects are usually designed to assist the states in fighting crime or protecting their citizens against social, moral, or economic harm. (See NATIONAL POLICE POWER.) But Congress has also banned the interstate shipment of ordinary objects of trade, like lumber, in opposition to state policy. Any such federal law must of course bear a reasonable relationship to interstate commerce. Thus, according to UNITED STATES V. DARBY (1941), Congress may validly bar the interstate shipment of goods produced in violation of a federal MAXIMUM HOUR AND MINIMUM WAGE law so that "interstate commerce [does not become] the instrument of competition in the distribution of goods produced under substandard labor conditions."

The commerce clause, however, is not merely an authorization to Congress to enact laws for the protection of the subjects of commerce. It serves also by its own force to prevent the states from erecting trade barriers or passing any legislation that would obstruct the movement of goods from state to state. As a practical matter the states, not Congress, regulate most subjects (and aspects) of commerce. They may do so out of a legitimate concern for the health, welfare, and safety of their own citizens. Yet, the exercise of this valid STATE POLICE POWER is often in tension with the value of free and open borders that informs the commerce clause. (See STATE REGULATION OF COMMERCE; STATE TAXATION OF COMMERCE.)

A central development in modern commerce clause jurisprudence is the Supreme Court's identification as legitimate articles of commerce many subjects historically regarded as the exclusive preserve of the states. Such subjects include insurance contracts, natural resources, fish and wild game, and even valueless material such as solid and liquid wastes. Prevailing DOCTRINE holds that the shipment in and out of the states of these subjects of commerce is protected by the commerce clause unless Congress ordains otherwise. Most recently, in *Sporkase v. Nebraska* (1982), the Supreme Court added ground water to its list of legitimate subjects of commerce. As the Court noted in PHILADELPHIA V. NEW JERSEY (1978), no object of interstate trade is excluded by definition from this list.

Still the tension between state power and the commerce clause remains. In the watershed case of COOLEY V. BOARD OF WARDENS (1851) the Court tried to resolve this tension by declaring that states may not regulate a subject of commerce the *nature* of which requires a single (national) uniform plan of regulation, even in the absence of any federal law. The *Cooley* rule has not yielded a long list of particular subjects requiring exclusive national regulation. It has been applied mainly to identify subjects whose number and diversity might require, when regulated, local knowledge and experience. State or local regulation of such subjects, whether justified to facilitate trade or to protect the public, is valid unless it conflicts with a law of Congress. *Cooley* itself upheld state regulation of harbor traffic, over commerce clause objections, because of the local peculiarities of port facilities.

Today, however, the Court rarely finds the *Cooley* rule applicable. The modern approach to commerce clause analysis applies a "balancing" test that weighs the interest served by a local regulation of a subject of commerce against the regulation's burden upon interstate commerce. If the burden substantially outweighs the local benefit, even if the legislation is nondiscriminatory, the regulation is unlikely to survive constitutional analysis. (If the *Cooley* rule forbids state regulation there is of course no balancing.) Generally, an article of commerce, although it may be taxed or regulated by the state, may not be so burdened as to prevent or seriously to obstruct its transportation in interstate commerce.

Yet the states do bar some "subjects of commerce" from entering their borders. Local inspection laws, for example, may exclude goods such as diseased cattle, adulterated food, and infectious plants. Such articles do not fall within the Court's classification of *legitimate* subjects of commerce. Correspondingly, the states may validly prevent some goods from leaving their borders. Certain natural resources, like rare birds and fish, may be withheld from commercial exploitation altogether. Such resources assume the character of subjects of commerce, however, when they are permitted legally to be sold or are reduced to personal possession. At that point, even though the private acquisition of such resources may be regulated by law in the interest of their preservation, the states are generally forbidden to restrict their use or sale to their own citizens.

DONALD P. KOMMERS

Bibliography

BENSON, PAUL R., JR. 1970 *The Supreme Court and the Commerce Clause, 1937–1970.* Cambridge, Mass.: Dunnellen.

CORWIN, EDWARD S. 1936 *The Commerce Power Versus States Rights.* Princeton, N.J.: Princeton University Press.

SCHWARTZ, BERNARD 1979 Commerce, the States, and the Burger Court. *Northwestern University Law Review* 74:409–439.

SUBPOENA

A subpoena is a court order that compels a person to appear for the purpose of giving testimony at a trial or a pretrial proceeding, such as a preliminary examination or pretrial deposition. A court also can issue a subpoena for documents or other items of tangible EVIDENCE. Parties to civil suits, and the prosecution in criminal cases, had a COMMON LAW right to compel testimony before the creation of the Constitution. The Sixth Amendment provides defendants in criminal cases a basis for fairly presenting their defense by giving them the power to subpoena witnesses. The government in some circumstances may have an affirmative duty to help a defendant find a witness, such as a government informer, or to refrain from restricting the defendant's ability to locate a witness essential to the presentation of a defense.

The Sixth Amendment, in part, provides that accused persons have the right of witnesses and the right "to have compulsory process" for obtaining witnesses in their behalf. The confrontation and compulsory process clauses permit the defendant to use the power of the courts to obtain witnesses and they limit governmental interference with the defendant's ability to examine witnesses at trial. These clauses have been incorporated into the FOURTEENTH AMENDMENT by the Supreme Court; thus they govern both federal and state prosecutions.

A defendant may compel a person to testify in a court proceeding by applying to the court for a subpoena ordering the person to appear in court or at a pretrial hearing. However, the defendant's ability to use the court's subpoena power is not unlimited. A court can require a defendant to provide it with information that justifies the production of the witness.

When a defendant has a court issue a subpoena to a witness, the witness normally is entitled to a statutory fee to offset his expenses for attendance at the judicial proceeding. An INDIGENT defendant may use the court's subpoena power to compel witnesses to testify in his behalf even though he cannot pay the witness fee. In these circumstances, however, a court may require the indigent defendant to show that the persons whom he subpoenas are likely to give testimony relevant to the charge.

An indigent defendant may try to use the subpoena power to compel an expert (such as a psychiatrist or a ballistics expert) to attend court to testify on the defendant's behalf. Whether the government must pay the cost for providing the defendant with an expert witness is primarily a DUE PROCESS, rather than a subpoena power, issue. However the issue be phrased, courts must determine whether, under the circumstances of the case, a fair trial depends on government provision of the expert witness.

The Sixth Amendment's confrontation clause, together with the compulsory process clause, restricts the government's ability to limit the testimony of potential defense witnesses and the cross-examination of prosecution witnesses. If a person who has received a subpoena to give testimony believes that his testimony would not be relevant to the trial, or that his testimony is subject to an EVIDENTIARY PRIVILEGE, he may move to quash the subpoena. A witness may assert a constitutionally based privilege, such as the RIGHT AGAINST SELF-INCRIMINATION, or a common law or statutory privilege, such as a doctor–patient privilege. One who has no such privilege may not refuse to respond to the subpoena or refuse to give testimony.

JOHN E. NOWAK

Bibliography

LaFave, Wayne R. and Israel, Jedd H. 1984 *Criminal Procedure*. Section 23.3. St. Paul, Minn.: West Publishing Co.

Wright, Charles Alan and Graham, K. 1980 *Federal Practice and Procedure: Evidence*. Section 5436. St. Paul, Minn.: West Publishing Co.

SUBSTANTIVE DUE PROCESS OF LAW

To say that governmental action violates "substantive due process" is to say that the action, while adhering to the forms of law, unjustifiably abridges the Constitution's fundamental constraints upon the content of what government may do to people in the name of "law." As the Supreme Court put the matter most succinctly in HURTADO V. CALIFORNIA (1884), "Law is something more than mere will exerted as an act of power. . . . [It] exclud[es], as not due process of law, acts of attainder, bills of pains and penalties, acts of confiscation . . . and other similar special, partial and arbitrary exertions of power under the forms of legislation. Arbitrary power, enforcing its edicts to the injury of the persons and property of its subjects, is not law, whether manifested as the decree of a personal monarch or of an impersonal multitude."

Substantive due process thus restricts government power, requiring coercive actions of the state to have public as opposed to merely private ends, defining certain means that government may not employ absent the most compelling necessity, and identifying certain aspects of behavior which it may not regulate without a clear showing that no less intrusive means could achieve government's legitimate public aims.

The phrase DUE PROCESS OF LAW derives from King John's promise in MAGNA CARTA to abide "by the law of the land," as translated four centuries later by Sir EDWARD COKE. But the belief that even the sovereign must follow a HIGHER LAW can be traced further back still. Even before the Middle Ages, kings symbolically acknowledged their limitations when they accepted their crowns; royal coronations were religious rites in which the rulers supposedly received power directly from God. The medieval notion of a divine law that even the sovereign might not transgress lay at the heart of English COMMON LAW and of the barons' demands at Runnymede. By the eighteenth century, the idea was phrased in terms of a natural law philosophy of SOCIAL COMPACT between sovereign and citizen. Although individuals were thought to surrender certain freedoms to the state, other rights were considered so much a part of personhood that they lay outside the scope of the social compact. Indeed, protection of such rights had to be the aim of any valid government; a state would abrogate its essential function were it to deny its citizens these fundamental freedoms.

The most famous articulation of that social compact philosophy in American history is the statement in the DECLARATION OF INDEPENDENCE that "all men . . . are endowed by their Creator with certain unalienable Rights . . . among these are Life, Liberty and the Pursuit of Happiness . . . to secure these Rights, Governments are instituted among Men, deriving their just Powers from the Consent of the Governed." Although the Declaration of Independence does not, of course, use the words "due process," the notion that substantive limits may be implied from the character of our society and from our reasons for ceding coercive authority to the state underlies both that document and the system of law and politics structured by our Constitution. The Fifth and FOURTEENTH AMENDMENTs to the Constitution provide, respectively, that neither the federal government nor the states may deprive persons "of life, liberty, or property, without due process of law." The Supreme Court has long recognized that STATE ACTION that follows fair procedures and thus satisfies PROCEDURAL DUE PROCESS may nonetheless violate substantive due process by exceeding the limits of the proper sphere of government. In the name of substantive due process, the Supreme Court has accordingly struck down hundreds of statutes governing matters ranging from wages and hours to sexual conduct.

Some commentators have called "substantive due process" a contradiction in terms. But a dismissal on semantic grounds of the very notion of substantive due process is unwarranted. First, the very idea of "process" has often been taken to include concerns as to the nature of the body taking an action, and legislatures have at times been understood as structurally improper sources of particular kinds of public actions. Second, the Constitution guarantees "due process *of law*," and, as the passage quoted above from *Hurtado* suggests, the term "law" can itself be taken to imply various normative requirements. Third, even the purest "procedural" norms inevitably embody substantive choices. Finally, the choice of the constitutional phrase on which substantive review has been pinned is to a large degree accidental; the Fourteenth Amendment's "privileges or immunities" clause might have been a happier selection—but the real question is whether and how individual rights not explicitly guaranteed by the Constitution should be protected under that document taken as a whole, not whether courts have picked a felicitous phrase to describe that protective task.

The Constitution, however, does not specify the essential rights of personhood; the BILL OF RIGHTS lists only certain rights that particularly warranted articulation in 1791, and the NINTH AMENDMENT makes clear that the list is not to be taken as exhaustive. It is on a largely open landscape that courts, including the Supreme Court, have had to mark out our fundamental freedoms. The process has necessarily been one of continual redefinition, responding to the changing—one hopes evolving—values and concerns of the Justices and the nation. Due process, as FELIX FRANKFURTER noted, has a "blessed versatility."

Not until the adoption of the Fourteenth Amendment in 1868 did the Constitution explicitly require state deprivations of liberty or property to comply with "due process of law"; BARRON V. BALTIMORE (1833) had interpreted the parallel Fifth Amendment bar to limit only the federal government. Well before 1868, however, both the Supreme Court and various state courts had begun to articulate inherent, judicially enforceable bounds on governmental interference with individual autonomy. Insofar as these limits were announced and enforced by federal judges, such holdings occurred in cases not involving specific provisions of the United States Constitution but falling within the DIVERSITY JURISDICTION of federal courts because the opposing parties were citizens of different states. The liberties the courts protected were almost exclusively economic: the ability to contract as one wished and to do as one pleased with one's own property.

Thus, as early as 1798, Justice SAMUEL CHASE wrote in CALDER V. BULL that any law that "takes property from A. and gives it to B." is invalid as contrary to "general principles of law and reason," even if it is not "expressly restrained" by the Constitution. Justice Chase reasoned that such a law would usurp judicial authority if intended to correct an injustice A had done to B, and, if intended simply to improve matters, would not be "law" at all but would instead transgress limitations implied by the very notion of representative government: "the nature, and ends of legislative power will limit the exercise of it."

From time to time throughout the nineteenth century, the Supreme Court struck down state statutes it judged to exceed these inherent limits on legislative power. Typically, however, the Court left unclear whether the limits derived from the purpose and character of legislatures, as Justice Chase had argued; or from an ahistorical body of natural law; or from specific, if unnamed, provisions of the Constitution. In FLETCHER V. PECK (1810), for example, the Supreme Court invalidated a Georgia statute that attempted to revoke state land grants. Writing for the Court, Chief Justice JOHN MARSHALL explained only that the statute was rendered invalid "either by general principles which are common to our free institutions, or by the particular provisions of the Constitution." Similarly, when the Supreme Court in TERRETT V. TAYLOR (1815) struck down Virginia's attempt to divest the Episcopal Church of its property, it rested its holding on "principles of natural justice" and "fundamental laws of every free government," as well as on the "spirit and letter" of the Constitution.

Within a decade or so after the Civil War, however, the Supreme Court more clearly embraced a theory of implied limitations. When, in LOAN ASSOCIATION V. TOPEKA (1875), the Court invalidated a tax designed to finance a bonus for local industry, it did not mention the Constitution at all; exercising the common law power of a federal court sitting in a diversity case, the Court simply found the tax "purely in aid of private or personal objects" and hence "beyond the legislative power and . . . an unauthorized invasion of private right." Echoing *Calder v. Bull*, the *Loan Association* Court declared that there are "rights in every free government beyond the control of the state" and that limitations on sovereign power "grow out of the essential nature of free governments."

Ironically, it was a notion of intrinsic limits on proper government action, including judicial action—a notion similar to that underlying the Court's invalidation of state and local laws in *Fletcher v. Peck, Terrett v. Taylor,* and *Loan Association v. Topeka*—that initially constrained substantive review of state legislation under the Fourteenth Amendment. By prohibiting state laws that "abridge the PRIVILEGES OR IMMUNITIES of citizens of the United States," the amendment's framers may have intended to provide federal protection against state encroachment of fundamental rights, but the Supreme Court in the SLAUGHTERHOUSE CASES (1873) construed the clause narrowly to safeguard only rights peculiarly associated with national CITIZENSHIP, such as the right to vote in national elections. In the Court's view, the clause did not protect the essential freedoms traditionally protected by the states themselves in intrastate disputes and protected by federal courts under Article IV, section 2, only from state laws unjustly discriminating against out-of-staters. Upholding the constitutionality of a state-granted monopoly on slaughterhouses around New Orleans, the *Slaughterhouse* Court held that the right to pursue one's trade was a right of state not national citizenship.

Writing for the Court in *Slaughterhouse*, Justice SAMUEL F. MILLER—who two years later penned the majority opinion in *Loan Association v. Topeka*—made clear that the main motivation for the *Slaughterhouse* decision lay in the Court's fear that a more expansive interpretation of the Fourteenth Amendment would allow the federal government to exceed the proper bounds of its authority and to intrude on the regulatory domain of the states. Construing the amendment's privileges or immunities clause or its due process clause to protect all fundamental rights, Miller explained, "would constitute this Court a perpetual censor upon all legislation of the states" and, by virtue of the affirmative enforcement power granted Congress in section 5 of the Fourteenth Amendment, would allow Congress to "pass laws in advance, limiting and restricting the exercise of legislative power by the states in their most ordinary and useful functions." In contrast, the largely nonconstitutional review carried out in *Fletcher, Terrett,* and *Loan* was seen by the Court as guided and constrained by well-developed common law notions of the inherent limits of legitimate state action, gave no affirma-

tive power to Congress, and fell within one of the federal government's clearly proper roles: adjudicating cases in which diversity of citizenship cast doubt on the impartiality of state tribunals.

But the doctrinal distinction between constitutional and common law review of the substantive legitimacy of state legislation was internally unstable: if natural law limitations on government could guide and constrain the Court in diversity-of-citizenship cases, they could do the same in cases brought pursuant to the Fourteenth Amendment. Moreover, the Court could apply common law principles to invalidate any congressional attempt under the guise of the Fourteenth Amendment to prohibit perfectly legitimate state activity.

Partly because of this doctrinal instability, and partly because of strong pressure from the organized bar for a more expansive review of state ECONOMIC REGULATION, the Court moved rapidly in the years following *Loan Association* and *Slaughterhouse* toward substantive review of state legislation under the Fourteenth Amendment's due process clause. Throughout the last quarter of the nineteenth century, the Court often warned in OBITER DICTA that the due process clause prohibited states from transgressing common law limitations on legitimate governmental action. In particular, the Court gave notice that unreasonable state deprivations of property or of the FREEDOM OF CONTRACT would be struck down as unconstitutional. In ALLGEYER V. LOUISIANA (1897) this line of dicta finally ripened into a landmark HOLDING: the Court there invalidated a Louisiana restriction on insurance contracts as substantively incompatible with due process of law. By barring companies not licensed by the state from insuring Louisiana property, the Court held, Louisiana had exceeded its STATE POLICE POWER and had unconstitutionally impaired the freedom of contract.

In the four decades following *Allgeyer*, the Supreme Court scrutinized socioeconomic legislation more aggressively and persistently than ever before or since, striking down scores of federal and state statutes as violative of substantive due process. The period from 1897 to 1937 has come to be known as "the *Lochner* era," after its most infamous product, LOCHNER V. NEW YORK (1905). *Lochner* invalidated a New York law limiting the work week of bakery employees to sixty hours; the Court found the statute an unreasonable infringement of the freedom of contract. In dissent, Justice OLIVER WENDELL HOLMES protested that "[t]he fourteenth amendment does not enact Mr. Herbert Spencer's *Social Statics.*"

Throughout the *Lochner* era, the Court closely examined both the means and the ends of socioeconomic legislation. The Court required that the relationship between a statute and its legitimate objectives be "real and substantial," and it repeatedly invalidated laws that it deemed to burden individual economic liberty more than strictly necessary to accomplish the goals of such laws. Thus, the majority in *Lochner* reasoned that regulation of bakery work hours exceeded the proper bounds of the police power in part because the state could protect the health of bakery employees without infringing so fundamentally on contractual freedom. Similarly, ADKINS V. CHILDREN'S HOSPITAL (1923) struck down minimum wage laws for women partly because the Court deemed narrower wage regulations sufficient to achieve the legislature's legitimate ends, and *Liggett Co. v. Baldridge* (1928), which invalidated Pennsylvania restrictions on corporate ownership of pharmacies, noted less objectionable regulatory means the state could employ to protect the same interests in public health.

In addition to demanding a tight fit between ends and means, the *Lochner* Court required that the statutory ends themselves fit its sense of the proper aims of lawmaking. Informed by earlier doctrines of implied limitations, as well as by the popular notions of social Darwinism and the writings of conservative legal COMMENTATORS ON THE CONSTITUTION such as THOMAS M. COOLEY and CHRISTOPHER G. TIEDEMAN, the Court viewed protection of individual common law rights and advancement of the general health, safety, and moral welfare to be the only valid objectives of government regulation. Laws aimed at redistributing economic and social power—giving A's property to B—by their very nature fell outside the realm of legitimate legislative action. Thus, for example, in ADAIR V. UNITED STATES (1908) and COPPAGE V. KANSAS (1915), the Court invalidated prohibitions against YELLOW DOG CONTRACTS that conditioned employment on workers' promises not to join unions. Writing for the majority in *Coppage*, Justice MAHLON PITNEY rejected the argument that inequality of bargaining power could justify infringing contractual liberty: it is "impossible to uphold freedom of contract and the right of private property without at the same time recognizing as legitimate those inequalities of fortune that are the necessary result of the exercise of those rights."

Although the Court in the *Lochner* era struck down close to 200 statutes under the due process clauses, it upheld even more. Many of the laws sustained were distinguished from invalidated statutes only by subtle factual differences supporting findings that they served the Court's narrow vision of the general welfare. After repeatedly striking down price controls, for example, the Court in NEBBIA V. NEW YORK (1934) upheld regulation of milk prices, concluding that the regulation was plausibly connected to public health on the theory that price competition encouraged suppliers to cut corners on sanitation. Other statutes, however, were sustained for a more specific reason: the Court exempted from its general liberty-of-contract approach statutes designed to protect especially disadvantaged or vulnerable groups. Thus, in HOLDEN V. HARDY (1897), the Court upheld restrictions on the hours worked by coal miners; the Court stressed the ultrahazardous nature of coal mining and the ability of coal companies in company-run towns virtually to dictate the terms of employment. Similarly, the Court in MULLER V. OREGON (1908), moved in part by the supposed physical vulnerability of women and by sexist notions of their maternal mission, permitted Oregon to limit women's hours of work outside the home.

Just as prior doctrinal instabilities had helped to usher in the *Lochner* era, so these exceptions to the regime of laissez-faire presaged the era's close. By acknowledging that a state could protect at least some groups at the expense of others, *Holden* and *Muller* made available in every substantive due process case the argument that the legislature might reasonably have determined that the class protected by the challenged statute was unable to, or should not be forced to, fend for itself. Indeed, *Lochner v. New York* was itself drastically limited *sub silentio* in 1917, when the Court in BUNTING V. OREGON (1917) relied on *Muller* in upholding a state law limiting to ten hours the work day of manufacturing employees.

With the onset of the Depression, moreover, it became progressively more difficult to view the relative wealth of A and B as a matter of purely private concern, outside the domain of proper governmental authority. Increasingly, economic transactions were seen as interrelated, and the general welfare was understood as intimately linked to the welfare of disadvantaged groups. The Supreme Court's persistent invalidation of redistributive legislation was sharply criticized by labor unions, the liberal press, and New Deal politicians, all of whom argued that extensive economic regulation, both state and federal, was necessary to alleviate the Depression. The perceived legitimacy of such regulation was further bolstered by the work of "realist" legal scholars such as MORRIS R. COHEN and Robert Hale, who portrayed distributions of private wealth and power as the results of public choices expressed, for example, in the law of property and contract.

After much outcry, the Supreme Court parted dramatically with *Lochner* in WEST COAST HOTEL V. PARRISH (1937), which abandoned earlier precedent and upheld a statutory minimum wage for women as reasonable in light of women's vulnerability to economic exploitation and the public interest in minimizing the number of workers requiring government relief. In the years that followed, the Court confirmed its abandonment of *Lochner* by repeatedly rejecting challenges to expansive New Deal regulation of private economic arrangements, and in 1949 the Court unanimously and explicitly rejected the *"Allgeyer-Lochner-Adair-Coppage* constitutional doctrine."

Never, however, did the Supreme Court explicitly abandon *Lochner*'s substantive theory of what constitutes legitimate legislation; it remains the official dogma to this day that regulatory power may not be exercised solely to transfer property from one private party to another. Instead, the Court relaxed the STANDARD OF REVIEW it applied to socioeconomic regulation: the close scrutiny of the *Lochner* era was replaced with extreme deference to legislative determinations. Thus, in UNITED STATES V. CAROLENE PRODUCTS CO. (1938) the Court promised to uphold socioeconomic legislation if any known or reasonably inferable state of facts supported the legislature's judgment.

In the intervening decades, this extreme deference has become virtually complete judicial abdication. Although substantive scrutiny has occasionally been smuggled in through the privileges or immunities clause of Article IV or the CONTRACT CLAUSE, in due process review the Court has required of economic regulation only "minimum rationality" and has shown itself willing to uphold laws on the basis of purely hypothetical facts or objectives, or on blind trust in legislative rationality. Justice WILLIAM H. REHNQUIST carried the Court's approach to its logical extreme in his opinion for the majority in *Railroad Retirement Board v. Fritz* (1980). Rejecting a due process challenge to legislation that phased out the eligibility of long-retired railroad employees to receive both social security and railroad retirement benefits, but preserved the similar eligibility of more recently retired employees of equally long (or longer) tenure, the majority reasoned that the statute was clearly a rational way to accomplish its precise result: cutting off the dual benefits of the very employees adversely affected by the law. "The plain language" of the statute, Justice Rehnquist wrote, "marks the beginning and end of our inquiry."

The Supreme Court has not been entirely without textual guidance in its post-1937 effort to define the fundamental freedoms protected by the Fourteenth Amendment's due process clause. Although the Bill of Rights formally applies only to the federal government, the Court has relied heavily on the first eight amendments in determining which rights—both procedural and substantive—are so essential that governmental action abrogating them violates due process of law. Most of the guarantees in the Bill of Rights have now been "selectively incorporated" into the Fourteenth Amendment, although the Court has decisively repudiated the view, espoused by Justice HUGO L. BLACK, that the Fourteenth Amendment applies the Bill of Rights to the states *in toto*.

At the close of the *Lochner* era, the Justices laid down a fairly restrictive rule for determining which provisions of the Bill of Rights were "incorporated." Writing for the Court in PALKO V. CONNECTICUT (1937), Justice BENJAMIN N. CARDOZO limited incorporation to those rights "implicit in the concept of ORDERED LIBERTY." Eventually recognizing the irrelevance of an inquiry into whether "a civilized system could be imagined that would not accord the particular protection," the Court in the late 1960s adopted a more contextual approach, asking whether a particular right was essential to the American political order. Thus, in DUNCAN V. LOUISIANA (1968) the Court held that criminal trial safeguards provided by the Bill of Rights are absorbed by the Fourteenth Amendment if they are "fundamental in the context of the criminal processes maintained by the American states." Over time, *Duncan* has come to stand for the more general proposition that guarantees in the Bill of Rights should be incorporated—and guarantees not expressly mentioned should be added—if they are necessary to protect values basic to our society. (See INCORPORATION DOCTRINE.)

Although substantive due process protection of implied rights to contractual liberty virtually vanished with the close of the *Lochner* era, judicial solicitude has grown in the ensuing years for a different set of liberties not expressly protected by the Constitution—a diverse group of claims to personal autonomy that have been collectively labeled the RIGHT OF PRIVACY. In contrast to the narrow contractual liberty to which the *Lochner* Court devoted the bulk of its concern, the right of privacy has come to embrace a wide array of freedoms, including rights of association and reproduction as well as of seclusion and intellectual independence. Some of these freedoms have been derived by extrapolation (or, perhaps, excavation) from the Bill of Rights or other clauses of the Fifth and Fourteenth Amendments. Yet the stirring rhetoric that has typically accompanied the elaboration of these personal freedoms testifies to a judicial perception that they are in some way more fundamental than the textual provisions to which they are pegged.

The Supreme Court made clear the essential nature of these "privacy" or "personhood" rights when it gave them their earliest articulation during the *Lochner* era itself. Striking down a state law that forbade the teaching of foreign languages before the eighth grade, the Court in MEYER V. NEBRASKA (1923) stressed the importance of allowing teachers to pursue their calling and parents to raise their children as they saw fit. Justice JAMES C. MCREYNOLDS's majority opinion gave broad scope to the liberty protected by the due process clauses: "Without doubt, [it] denotes not merely freedom from bodily restraint but also the right of the individual to contract, to engage in any of the common occupations of life, to acquire useful knowledge, to marry, establish a home and bring up children, to worship God according to the dictates of his own conscience, and generally to enjoy those privileges long recognized at common law as essential to the orderly pursuit of happiness by free men." Two years later, in PIERCE V. SOCIETY OF SISTERS (1925), the Court marshaled similar rhetoric in invalidating a state requirement that all students attend public schools. Still more sweeping—and perhaps of more lasting influence—was Justice LOUIS D. BRANDEIS's formulation in his dissent in OLMSTEAD V. UNITED STATES (1928): "The makers of our Constitution . . . sought to protect Americans in their beliefs, their thoughts, their emotions, and their sensations. They conferred, as against the government, the right to be let alone—the most comprehensive of rights and the right most valued by civilized men."

Despite the broad language of these early opinions, *Meyer* and *Pierce* evinced special judicial solicitude primarily for family autonomy—freedom from government intrusion into the traditionally intimate realms of marriage, reproduction, and child-rearing. That emphasis, along with recognition of personal autonomy rights as fundamental, was furthered by the watershed case of SKINNER V. OKLAHOMA (1942), the Supreme Court's first important privacy decision following the demise of *Lochner.* Invalidating a state statute providing for the STERILIZATION of persons convicted two or more times of "felonies involving moral turpitude," the Court termed the right to reproduce "one of the basic civil rights of man." Part of the Court's concern stemmed from fear of the invidious and possibly genocidal ways in which government control over reproduction might be exercised: the Court observed that the "power to sterilize, . . . [i]n evil or reckless hands . . . can cause races or types

which are inimical to the dominant group to wither and disappear."

The right to REPRODUCTIVE AUTONOMY recognized in *Skinner* has since been elaborated and considerably expanded. As recently as 1978, the Court in ZABLOCKI V. REDHAIL "reaffirm[ed] the fundamental character of the right to marry," holding that a state may not forbid marriage of parents unable to meet their child support obligations. More controversial has been the extension of *Skinner* to BIRTH CONTROL practices. In GRISWOLD V. CONNECTICUT (1965) the Supreme Court ruled that a married couple's decision to purchase and use contraceptives is a private matter beyond the proper reach of government authority. Perhaps not surprisingly, Justice WILLIAM O. DOUGLAS's majority opinion focused on the intimacy of marital choices, invoking "a right of privacy older than the Bill of Rights" and defending the "sacred precincts of marital bedrooms." The freedom to practice contraception was not freed of its familial trappings until 1972, when Justice WILLIAM J. BRENNAN wrote for the Court in EISENSTADT V. BAIRD that, if "the right of privacy means anything, it is the right of the *individual,* married or unmarried, to be free from unwarranted governmental intrusions into matters so fundamentally affecting a person as the decision whether to bear or beget a child." That *Baird* singled out as decisive in *Griswold* the element of reproductive autonomy was made clear by CAREY V. POPULATION SERVICES INTERNATIONAL (1977), which invalidated a state statute allowing contraceptives to be sold only by licensed pharmacists and only to persons over sixteen.

When the Court assessed the constitutionality of ABORTION laws in ROE V. WADE (1973), its commitment to reproductive autonomy collided with an equally basic concern for the sanctity of human life. Writing for the majority, Justice HARRY L. BLACKMUN reasoned that the liberty protected by the due process clauses includes a woman's fundamental right to decide, with her physician, whether to end or to continue a pregnancy, but that certain state interests are sufficiently compelling to override that right. During the final trimester of pregnancy, the state's interest in preserving the fetus, by then viable, justifies a ban on abortions; before the third trimester, however, abortions may not be prohibited and may be regulated only as necessary to protect the woman's health; and, before the second trimester, the state may require only that abortions be performed by licensed physicians.

As an element of substantive due process, the right to privacy has received its doctrinally purest exposition in reproductive autonomy cases. Equally important rights to personal autonomy, however, have been found in the "penumbras" of constitutional provisions less abstract than the requirement of "due process of law," most notably the FIRST AMENDMENT. In *West Virginia State Board of Education v. Barnette* (1943) the Court construed the First Amendment, along with the Fifth and the Fourteenth, to establish for each individual a sphere of intellectual and spiritual independence. Striking down a compulsory flag salute in public schools, Justice ROBERT H. JACKSON wrote for the Court that, "[i]f there is any fixed star in our constitutional constellation, it is that no official, high or petty, can prescribe what shall be orthodox in politics, nationalism, religion, or other matters of opinion or force citizens to confess by word or act their faith therein." The Court appealed to the same notion when it held, in *Wooley v. Maynard* (1977), that New Hampshire could not punish a person for obscuring the words "Live Free or Die" on his license plate because he found it religiously or philosophically repugnant to display the state's slogan on his car. The Court reasoned that the state had impermissibly invaded the private "sphere of intellect and spirit" by requiring individuals "to use their private property as a 'mobile billboard' for the State's ideological message."

In NAACP v. ALABAMA (1958) and *Talley v. California* (1960) the Court found in the First Amendment guarantees of associational and expressive freedom correlative rights to anonymity. And in MOORE v. CITY OF EAST CLEVELAND (1977) the Court protected a special right to familial association by invalidating a single-family zoning ordinance that prevented a woman from living with her son and two grandsons. Renewing its special commitment to traditional visions of family autonomy, the Court distinguished the zoning law upheld in *Village of Belle Terre v. Boraas* (1974) on the basis that "the ordinance there affected only *unrelated* individuals," whereas East Cleveland had "chosen to regulate the occupancy of its housing by slicing deeply into the family itself."

Other penumbral rights to personal autonomy have been found in the intersection of several textual provisions, or in the constitutional system taken as a whole. In SHAPIRO V. THOMPSON (1969), for example, the Court alluded to the COMMERCE CLAUSE, the privileges or immunities clause of the Fourteenth Amendment, and the similar language in Article IV, section 2, as well as to the Fifth Amendment's due process clause and "the nature of our Federal Union" in finding that "our constitutional concepts of personal liberty" imposed a general requirement that "all citizens

be free to travel throughout the length and breadth of our land uninhibited by statutes, rules, or regulations which unreasonably burden or restrict this movement." The newly vitalized RIGHT TO TRAVEL had earlier been recognized in the context of international mobility, at least when other First Amendment rights were also at stake: the Court in APTHEKER V. SECRETARY OF STATE (1964) had struck down a congressional denial of passports to members of the Communist party. In HAIG V. AGEE (1981) the Court sustained revocation of the passport of a former intelligence agent who was engaged in exposing undercover agents stationed abroad. In *Haig* the Court distinguished sharply between the "right" of inter*state* travel and the "freedom" of inter*national* travel, refusing to extend to congressional regulation of the latter the close scrutiny it had given state regulation of the former.

The Supreme Court attempted to unify some of these disparate doctrinal threads in WHALEN V. ROE (1976), its most comprehensive treatment thus far of the right of privacy. Writing for a unanimous Court, Justice JOHN PAUL STEVENS upheld a carefully crafted state scheme for maintaining computerized records of prescriptions for certain dangerous drugs, but only after examining the statute's implications for what he described as the two components of the right to privacy: an interest in confidentiality—"avoiding disclosure of personal matters"—and an interest in free choice—"independence in making certain kinds of important decisions."

Despite this seemingly broad formulation, the Court has resisted the creation of a generic right to choose how one lives. In *Kelley v. Johnson* (1976), for example, the Court upheld police department rules regulating officers' hair styles and prohibiting them from having beards. Writing for the majority, Justice Rehnquist argued that the rules did not violate the right of privacy recognized in *Roe, Baird,* and *Griswold;* he distinguished those cases as involving "substantial claims of infringement on the individual's freedom of choice with respect to certain basic matters of procreation, marriage, and family life." Nor is the Court apparently prepared to protect even all intimate decisions central to one's self-definition; the Justices have, for example, passed up several opportunities to review statutes punishing or burdening private homosexual activity between consenting adults. (See FREEDOM OF INTIMATE ASSOCIATION.)

Some lower courts have been more willing to expand the protected sphere of personal autonomy, recognizing broad rights of lifestyle choice as well as, in some cases, freedom to decide how and when one will die. The Supreme Court, however, appears unlikely to follow very quickly. Not only are some Justices concerned about the open-ended and potentially radical nature of such decisions, but the Court has repeatedly dropped unsubtle hints that there are fairly sharp limits to its tolerance. The "blessed versatility" of substantive due process is limited by the Justices' awareness that the Supreme Court is an institution of government.

LAURENCE H. TRIBE

Bibliography

BLACK, CHARLES L. 1969 *Structure and Relationship in Constitutional Law.* Baton Rouge: Louisiana State University Press.

BREST, PAUL and LEVINSON, SANFORD 1983 *Processes of Constitutional Decisionmaking: Cases and Materials.* Boston: Little, Brown.

CHOPER, JESSE H. 1980 *Judicial Review and the National Political Process: A Functional Reconsideration of the Role of the Supreme Court.* Chicago: University of Chicago Press.

ELY, JOHN HART 1980 *Democracy and Distrust: A Theory of Judicial Review.* Cambridge, Mass.: Harvard University Press.

GUNTHER, GERALD 1975 *Cases and Materials on Constitutional Law.* Mineola, N.Y.: Foundation Press.

KENNEDY, DUNCAN 1980 Toward an Historical Understanding of Legal Consciousness: The Case of Classical Legal Thought in America 1850–1940. *Research in Law & Sociology* 3:3–57.

LOCKHART, WILLIAM B., KAMISAR, YALE, and CHOPER, JESSE H. (1964)1980 *Constitutional Law: Cases—Comments—Questions.* St. Paul, Minn.: West Publishing Co.

PENNOCK, ROLAND J. and CHAPMAN, JOHN W., eds. 1977 *Due Process.* New York: New York University Press.

TRIBE, LAURENCE H. 1978 *American Constitutional Law.* Mineola, N.Y.: Foundation Press.

—— 1985 *Constitutional Choices.* Cambridge, Mass.: Harvard University Press.

SUBVERSIVE ACTIVITIES CONTROL BOARD

The INTERNAL SECURITY ACT of 1950 created the Subversive Activities Control Board (SACB). This agency was to determine, on request of the ATTORNEY GENERAL, whether a particular organization was a communist-action, communist-front, or communist-infiltrated organization. After SACB had issued an order so designating an organization and after the order had been sustained by the courts, various disabilities and sanctions could be imposed on the group and its members. These included being barred from federal jobs, being denied employment in defense-related industries, and being prohibited from using United States passports.

Eleven years after SACB's creation, the Supreme Court sustained its findings that the Communist party was a communist-action organization as defined by the act and upheld an order requiring the party to register. (See COMMUNIST PARTY V. SACB, 1961.) The Court subsequently declared unconstitutional attempts to implement the sanctions of the act, and in 1965 (ALBERTSON V. SACB) it ruled that the forced registration of individual members of the party would violate the RIGHT AGAINST SELF-INCRIMINATION. By the late 1960s, SACB was moribund. Congress, attempting salvage, gave it authority to register with the attorney general the names of persons it had determined were members of communist organizations, and SACB eventually declared seven persons to be in this category. Such limited action, as well as a 1967 decision holding unconstitutional provisions barring members of registered organizations from jobs in defense-related industries, further limited SACB's utility. In 1974, the RICHARD M. NIXON administration, bowing to SACB's critics, requested no further funding, effectively ending its life.

PAUL L. MURPHY

Bibliography

MURPHY, PAUL L. 1972 *The Constitution in Crisis Times, 1918–1969.* New York: Harper & Row.

SUBVERSIVE ACTIVITY

Activity is "subversive" if it is directed toward the overthrow of the existing form of government by force or other unlawful means. Subversive activity comprises TREASON, SEDITION, insurrection, and sabotage, as well as other unlawful acts committed with the requisite intent. Although individuals may engage in subversive activity, concerted or organized subversion is more common and excites more public concern. Active, purposive membership in subversive organizations—such as the Communist party, the American Nazi party, or the Ku Klux Klan—is a federal crime, and between 1950 and 1974 the ATTORNEY GENERAL'S LIST was maintained as an official catalog of such groups.

In twentieth-century America, the suppression of subversion has been controversial where the "activity" has seemed to consist primarily of SUBVERSIVE

ADVOCACY. But the controversy should not obscure the fact that there is such a thing as subversive activity and that the survival of constitutional government requires that such activity be controlled.

The critical distinction is not between words and deeds, speech and action. Even the staunchest defenders of CIVIL LIBERTIES agree that INCITEMENT TO UNLAWFUL CONDUCT may be punished by law, at least when the speaker has the intention and capability of inducing his hearers to engage in insurrection, riot, or disobedience of law. Some forms of subversive activity—for example, the attack on the House of Representatives by Puerto Rican nationalists in 1954—are extreme forms of SYMBOLIC SPEECH, known in revolutionary jargon as "propaganda of the deed." The political goal toward which it is aimed is precisely what distinguishes subversive activity.

Because the government of the United States is one of limited and ENUMERATED POWERS, its authority to define and punish subversive activities as crimes is not entirely clear. Treason is defined in Article III, section 2, of the Constitution, and as the same section limits the range of punishment for treason, it implies the power of Congress to prescribe punishment within the permitted range. The Constitution does not define any lesser degree of subversive activity, nor does it expressly grant to Congress the power to define and punish such crimes. Instead, the power must be an IMPLIED POWER incidental to the power to punish treason or else NECESSARY AND PROPER for the carrying out of one or more of the enumerated powers.

In the absence of statutes against insurrection or rebellion, the perpetrators of FRIES' REBELLION and the WHISKEY REBELLION were tried for treason. The prosecutors argued that an armed rising to prevent the execution of federal law—the normal definition of insurrection—was at least a constructive treason as the COMMON LAW had understood the term. Similarly, when AARON BURR assembled an armed force in the Western territories, for purposes that are still not entirely clear, the only federal offense for which he could be tried was treason. But a charge of treason seems manifestly to have been inappropriate in each of these cases.

On the other hand, the ALIEN AND SEDITION ACTS, enacted when the country was on the brink of war with France, generously defined offenses against the United States. Although section 2, defining SEDITIOUS LIBEL, is more famous, section 1 of the Sedition Act proscribed certain subversive activities: combination or conspiracy to impede the operation of law or to intimidate government officials, procuring or counsel-

ing riot or insurrection—whether or not the activity was successful. The ESPIONAGE ACT OF 1917, enacted while the country was fighting World War I, treated as criminal any attempt to procure draft evasion or to interfere with military recruitment while the Sedition Act of 1918 proscribed all advocacy of revolution, however remote the prospect of success.

In the latter half of the twentieth century, the phenomenon of political terrorism raised new problems. Frequently directed from outside the United States, terrorist activity, like the extreme forms of subversive activity, employs politically motivated violence. Although the aim of terrorism may not be the overthrow of the American government, terrorism shares with the more extreme forms of subversive activity the substitution of violence for public deliberation and constitutional government.

DENNIS J. MAHONEY

Bibliography

GRODZINS, MORTON 1956 *The Loyal and the Disloyal: Social Boundaries of Patriotism and Treason.* Chicago: University of Chicago Press.

HURST, JAMES WILLARD 1971 *The Law of Treason in the United States.* Westport, Conn.: Greenwood Press.

SUBVERSIVE ADVOCACY

The quest for NATIONAL SECURITY has placed strains on the FIRST AMENDMENT when the country has been at war, or threatened by war, or torn by fear of an external enemy or domestic social unrest. Federal and state governments have sought to silence those regarded as "subversives" and internal enemies because they supported a foreign cause or advocated revolutionary change in American institutions.

The ALIEN AND SEDITION ACTS, passed only seven years after ratification of the First Amendment, were the most extreme of these measures in our history. President JOHN ADAMS and the Federalist Congress used them to stifle the opposition Republicans who were accused of being "servile minions" of France, with which war seemed imminent in early 1798. Seventeen prosecutions were instituted against Republican newspaper editors, officeholders, and adherents, with only one acquittal.

The constitutionality of the Sedition Act was never tested in the Supreme Court, which then had no JURISDICTION to review federal criminal convictions. But the act was sustained by the lower federal courts, including three Supreme Court Justices sitting as trial judges. The modern Supreme Court, in NEW YORK

TIMES CO. V. SULLIVAN (1964), has stated that the First Amendment bars prosecution for SEDITIOUS LIBEL. Opposition to the government in power, accompanied by criticism of official policy and conduct, cannot constitutionally be proscribed as "seditious" or "subversive."

During the nineteenth century there was no federal legislation limiting FREEDOM OF SPEECH or FREEDOM OF THE PRESS. No official efforts were made to silence the Federalist denunciation of the War of 1812. Abolitionist sentiment did not fare so well in the succeeding decades of bitter controversy over slavery. Southern states passed laws limiting the freedom to criticize slavery. During the Civil War no sedition act was passed to suppress the widespread opposition to the war in the North. But President ABRAHAM LINCOLN suspended the writ of HABEAS CORPUS, controlled the mails, telegraph, and passports, and approved military detention of thousands of persons accused of disloyalty.

The rapid industrialization and urbanization of the country after the Civil War was accompanied by social unrest. The Haymarket Square bombing in Chicago in 1886, the violent Homestead and Pullman strikes in the 1890s, the assassination of President WILLIAM MCKINLEY in 1901 by a presumed "anarchist," and the militant tactics of the Industrial Workers of the World led to the passage of the first state Criminal Anarchy Law in New York in 1902. By 1921, thirty-three states had enacted similar laws making it a crime to advocate the overthrow of existing government by force or violence. Unlike the Sedition Act of 1798, these laws forbade only the advocacy of illegal means to effect political change.

Together with the federal ESPIONAGE ACT of 1917, these state laws were used to suppress opposition to World War I voiced by pacifists, sympathizers with Germany, and international socialists. The 1917 act made it criminal to obstruct recruiting, cause insubordination in the armed forces, or interfere with military operations. Amendments to the Espionage Act (the SEDITION ACT of 1918) made it an offense, among other things, to say or do anything that would favor any country at war with the United States, oppose the cause of the United States in the war, or incite contempt for the American form of government or the uniform of the Army or Navy. Under the Espionage Act 877 people were convicted, almost all for expressing opinions about the merits and conduct of the war. The Supreme Court sustained these convictions, rejecting the contention that they violated the First Amendment.

SCHENCK V. UNITED STATES (1919) was the first of the Espionage Act cases to reach the Supreme Court. Justice OLIVER WENDELL HOLMES wrote the Court opinion affirming the conviction and, for the first time, enunciated the CLEAR AND PRESENT DANGER test to determine when advocacy of unlawful conduct is protected by the First Amendment. Holmes also wrote the opinions of the Court in FROHWERK V. UNITED STATES (1919) and DEBS V. UNITED STATES (1919), sustaining the convictions of a newspaper editor for questioning the constitutionality of the draft and charging that Wall Street had dragged the country into the war, and of Eugene V. Debs, the railroad union and Socialist party leader, for denouncing the war as a capitalist plot. Just what the "clear and present danger" was in these cases was doubtful, and Holmes and Brandeis soon began to dissent from the way the majority used the test.

Their first great dissent came in ABRAMS V. UNITED STATES (1919). In his dissenting opinion, which Brandeis joined, Holmes gave new content to the clear and present danger test by emphasizing the immediacy of the danger that must exist. Although Holmes would have softened this requirement, permitting punishment of speech with the specific intent to bring about the danger even if the danger itself was not "immediate," he did not think the necessary intent had been shown in Abrams.

The Red Scare of 1919 and 1920 was induced not only by fear of the Bolshevik revolution and the Communist International but also by the economic and social insecurity that accompanied demobilization after World War I. The PALMER RAIDS expressed the federal government's fears and antiradical sentiments. The states resorted to their criminal anarchy laws and the Supreme Court sustained convictions under these laws in GITLOW V. NEW YORK (1925) and WHITNEY V. CALIFORNIA (1927).

In Gitlow the Court assumed that freedom of speech and press, protected by the First Amendment from abridgment by Congress, was a "liberty" protected by the DUE PROCESS clause of the FOURTEENTH AMENDMENT against state impairment. In both Gitlow and Whitney the Court refused to apply the clear and present danger test because the state legislatures had prohibited a particular class of speech—the advocacy of the doctrine that the government should be overthrown by violence. Gitlow's advocacy of violent revolution violated the law even if there were no clear and present danger of revolution. The legislature might reasonably seek "to extinguish the spark without waiting until it has enkindled the flame or blazed into the conflagration."

Dissenting in Gitlow, Holmes argued for application of the clear and present danger test, but did not confront the majority's position. But Brandeis, concurring in *Whitney*, insisted that courts and juries must be free to decide whether, under the circumstances of each case, "the evil apprehended is [relatively serious and its incidence] so imminent that it may befall before there is opportunity for full discussion. . . . Only an emergency can justify repression."

From the end of the Red Scare to the outbreak of World War II, federal action against alleged subversives was limited to deportation of alien communists. State prosecutions under criminal anarchy laws were infrequent after the middle 1920s. The Sedition Act of 1918 was repealed in 1921 and has never been revived.

The Smith Act of 1940 was modeled on the New York Criminal Anarchy law. During World War II, twenty-eight pro-Nazi individuals were prosecuted under it for conspiring to cause insubordination in the armed forces, but the judge died and the prosecution was dropped. Eighteen members of the Trotskyist Socialist Workers party, which opposed the war, were convicted of conspiracy to cause insubordination in the armed forces and to advocate violent overthrow of the government.

On the whole, the country supported World War II. After the Nazi invasion of the Soviet Union, in June 1941, communists became the staunchest supporters of the war. But as soon as the war was won, the activities of the international communist movement resumed. In 1949 eleven leaders of the Communist party were convicted under the Smith Act for conspiring to advocate violent overthrow of the United States government and establishment of a dictatorship of the proletariat, and to organize the Communist party to advocate these goals. The Supreme Court affirmed the convictions, 6–2, in DENNIS V. UNITED STATES (1951).

In 1948 the Soviet Union had blockaded Berlin and engineered the communist coup that overthrew the parliamentary regime in Czechoslovakia. By the time the Supreme Court decided *Dennis,* several Soviet spy rings in the West had been exposed, the communists had taken control in China, and Americans were dying in the KOREAN WAR. The domestic and foreign policies of the American Communist party were consistent with Soviet policies and directives. In light of these events, a plurality of four Justices, speaking through Chief Justice FRED M. VINSON, reformulated the clear and present danger test into a BALANCING TEST that weighed the seriousness of the danger, discounted by its improbability, against the degree of invasion of freedom of speech.

Justice FELIX FRANKFURTER concurred, deferring to Congress's judgment regarding the extent of the danger posed by the Communist party and the world communist movement. With the experience of the Nuremberg war crimes trials still fresh in his memory, Justice ROBERT H. JACKSON also concurred, joining Frankfurter in rejecting the appropriateness of the clear and present danger test to the communist conspiracy.

Though not purporting to overrule *Dennis,* the Supreme Court, in YATES V. UNITED STATES (1957), reversed convictions of the officers of the Communist party in California. Justice JOHN MARSHALL HARLAN's plurality opinion read the Smith Act as requiring proof that the defendants had advocated "unlawful action" and not merely "abstract doctrine" that the United States government should be overthrown. *Yates* did not represent a return to the Holmes-Brandeis version of the clear and present danger test. It emphasized the content of the advocacy, not its consequences. On this view, advocacy of unlawful action was punishable, irrespective of the immediacy of the danger.

After *Yates* was decided, the government concluded that it could not satisfy the requirements of proof demanded by the Supreme Court and abandoned all prosecutions under the Smith Act. Altogether twenty-nine communists were convicted under that act, including the leaders involved in *Dennis* and the only person convicted under the provision proscribing membership in the Communist party. His conviction was upheld in SCALES V. UNITED STATES (1961) because he was an "active member" who knew of the Party's unlawful goals and had a "specific intent" to achieve them.

In 1950, shortly after the outbreak of the Korean War, Congress enacted the SUBVERSIVE ACTIVITIES CONTROL ACT, which required communist organizations to register with the ATTORNEY GENERAL. When the Communist party failed to register, the attorney general asked the Subversive Activities Control Board to order it to register and list its members. In COMMUNIST PARTY V. SUBVERSIVE ACTIVITIES CONTROL BOARD (1961) the Court upheld the board's finding that the party was a communist-action organization and its order requiring the party to register. Only Justice HUGO L. BLACK dissented from the majority view that the First Amendment did not prohibit Congress from removing the party's "mask of anonymity."

The Supreme Court in 1961 did not pass upon the contention that compulsory registration would violate the RIGHT AGAINST SELF-INCRIMINATION afforded by the Fifth Amendment because it would subject party members to prosecution under the Smith Act and the

1954 COMMUNIST CONTROL ACT. This contention was eventually sustained in ALBERTSON V. SUBVERSIVE ACTIVITIES CONTROL BOARD (1965). As a result, neither the Communist party nor any of its members ever registered under the act, and no organization ever registered as a communist front. In 1968, Congress removed the registration obligation. Instead, the Subversive Activities Control Board was authorized to keep records, open to public inspection, of the names and addresses of communist organizations and their members. But in 1969 and 1970 the courts held that mere membership in the party was protected by the First Amendment, and the board was disbanded in 1973.

The Communist Control Act of 1954 purported to deprive the Communist party of the "rights, privileges, and immunities attendant upon legal bodies." It was not clear whether Congress intended this provision to dissolve the party as a legal organization or only to bar it from the ballot and benefits such as mailing privileges. Though the Supreme Court has not passed upon its constitutionality, the act has become a dead letter.

Although the Espionage Act and the Smith Act remained in force during the VIETNAM WAR, no prosecutions were brought under either measure. In *Bond v. Floyd* (1966) the Supreme Court assumed that opposition to the war and the draft was protected by the First Amendment.

In 1967 a Ku Klux Klan leader was convicted of violating the Ohio CRIMINAL SYNDICALISM LAW by making a speech at a Klan rally to which only television newsmen had been invited. The speech was derogatory of blacks and Jews and proclaimed that if the white race continued to be threatened, "it's possible that there might have to be some revengence [sic] taken." In a PER CURIAM opinion in BRANDENBURG V. OHIO (1969) the Supreme Court reversed the conviction and held the Ohio statute unconstitutional. In so doing, it overruled *Whitney v. California* and again reformulated the clear and present danger doctrine: "constitutional guarantees of free speech and free press do not permit a State to forbid or proscribe advocacy of the use of force or of law violation except where such advocacy is directed to inciting or producing such action." Although the Court purported to follow *Dennis*, commentators generally conclude that *Brandenburg* overruled *Dennis*. In *Communist Party of Indiana v. Whitcomb* (1974) the Supreme Court held that it was unconstitutional for Indiana to refuse a place on the ballot to the Communist party of Indiana because its officers had refused to submit an oath that the party "docs not advocate

the overthrow of local, state or national government by force or violence."

The *Brandenburg* formula, the most speech-protective standard yet evolved by the Supreme Court, has been criticized from opposing sides. Concurring in *Brandenburg*, Justices WILLIAM O. DOUGLAS and Black would have abandoned the clear and present danger test in favor of a distinction between ideas and overt acts. Some critics reject even this concession on the ground that an incitement-of-overt-acts test can be manipulated by the courts to cut off speech just when it comes close to being effective.

Others argue that advocacy of the forcible overthrow of the government, or of any unlawful act, is not protected by the First Amendment. Such advocacy is not political speech because it is a call to revoke the results that political speech has produced; violent overthrow destroys the premises of our system. An organization that seeks power through illegal means refuses to abide by the legitimate conditions of party competition in a democracy.

Furthermore, in suppressing totalitarian movements, even if they purport to reject illegal means, a democratic society is not acting to protect the status quo but the very same interest which freedom of speech itself seeks to secure—the possibility of peaceful progress under freedom. In this view, the *Brandenburg* formula would deny our democracy the constitutional right to act until it might be too late to prevent a totalitarian victory.

Although one may disagree with the view that the problem of a totalitarian party's competing for political power in a democracy is solely one of "freedom of expression," the reasons for toleration—to keep even the freedom of expression open to challenge lest it become a "dead dogma," and to allow extremist groups to advocate revolution because they may represent real grievances that deserve to be heard—must be seriously considered by legislators in determining whether suppression is a wise policy. But if wisdom may sometimes dictate toleration, that conclusion does not imply that the Constitution gives the enemies of freedom the right to organize to crush it.

CARL A. AUERBACH

Bibliography

GUNTHER GERALD 1975 Learned Hand and the Origins of Modern First Amendment Doctrine: Some Fragments of History. *Stanford Law Review* 27:719–773.
LEVY, LEONARD W. 1985 *Emergence of a Free Press.* New York: Oxford University Press.
LINDE, HANS A. 1970 "Clear and Present Danger" Reexamined: Dissonants in the Brandenburg Concerto. *Stanford Law Review* 22:1163–1186.

NATHANSON, NATHANIEL L. 1950 The Communist Trial and the Clear-and-Present-Danger Test. *Harvard Law Review* 63:1167–1175.

SUGARMAN v. DOUGALL
413 U.S. 634 (1973)
GRIFFITHS, IN RE
413 U.S. 717 (1973)

In *Sugarman*, the Supreme Court held, 8–1, that New York's law making ALIENS ineligible for civil service employment was unconstitutional. In *Griffiths*, the Court held, 7–2, that Connecticut could not constitutionally bar resident aliens from the practice of law. Both decisions rested on EQUAL PROTECTION grounds. Justice LEWIS F. POWELL, writing for the Court in *Griffiths*, concluded that the state had not shown that excluding aliens from law practice was necessary to serve an interest sufficiently substantial to justify the rule. In *Sugarman*, Justice HARRY A. BLACKMUN wrote for the Court, repeating what he had said in GRAHAM V. RICHARDSON (1971), that discrimination against aliens must survive STRICT SCRUTINY by the courts. Here the bar to aliens was not necessary to achieve any substantial interest. Justice Blackmun added that some discrimination against aliens would be justified in the name of "political community": the right to vote or to hold high public office, for example, might be limited to citizens. These OBITER DICTA assumed importance in the later cases of FOLEY V. CONNELIE (1978) and AMBACH V. NORWICK (1979).

KENNETH L. KARST

SUGAR TRUST CASE

See: *Knight Co., E. C., United States v.*

SULLIVAN, UNITED STATES v.
332 U.S. 689 (1948)

In no other case has the Supreme Court more sweepingly construed the COMMERCE CLAUSE. To protect consumers the Federal Food, Drug, and Cosmetic Act of 1938, passed under the NATIONAL POLICE POWER, prohibited the misbranding of drugs "held for sale after interstate shipment." Nine months after a bottle of sulfathiazole tablets had been shipped from Chicago to Atlanta, a retail druggist in Columbus, Georgia, who had purchased the bottle, properly labeled with a warning that the drug could be toxic, sold twelve tablets in a box without the mandatory warning. The local druggist thereby committed a federal crime. A federal court of appeals reversed his conviction on the ground that the words "held for sale after interstate shipment" extended only to the first intrastate sale and could not apply to all subsequent local sales after any lapse of time.

The Supreme Court, in an opinion by Justice HUGO L. BLACK for a bare majority, reversed and sustained the constitutionality of the statute. Black declared that it prohibited misbranding no matter when the drug was sold and without regard to how many local sales intervened; the statute remained in force "to the moment of . . . delivery to the ultimate consumer" in an intrastate transaction. Sullivan, the druggist, had contended that the statute so construed exceeded the commerce power and invaded powers reserved to the states under the TENTH AMENDMENT. Black replied merely that a 1913 precedent, *McDermott v. Wisconsin*, which had sustained the misbranding provision of the PURE FOOD AND DRUG ACT of 1906, controlled the case. He thought that the "variants" between the two cases were "not sufficient" to distinguish *McDermott*, although he conceded that the retailer in *McDermott* had been the direct consignee of an interstate shipment. That fact should have made the precedent inapplicable. Black did not take notice that in *McDermott* the Court had reversed the state conviction of a grocer who misbranded under state law but complied with federal law. Black did not consider that under the ORIGINAL PACKAGE DOCTRINE the druggist sold local merchandise. Justice WILEY RUTLEGE concurred without reaching the constitutional issue and like the three dissenters wrote only on the construction of the statute.

After *Sullivan* the commerce power seemed to have no statable limits, though the rationale of the decision is unclear. The transaction involved in *Sullivan* was neither INTRASTATE COMMERCE that affected INTERSTATE COMMERCE, nor the PRODUCTION of goods for interstate commerce. The reach of the national police power, which began with CHAMPION V. AMES (1903), seems to have no end.

LEONARD W. LEVY

SUMNER, CHARLES
(1811–1874)

In 1833 Charles Sumner, a protégé of JOSEPH STORY, graduated from Harvard Law School. Until 1851 he practiced law, taught at Harvard Law School, annotated Vesey's Chancery Reports, and became a well-known lecturer advocating, among other reforms, world peace and abolition of slavery. In 1848 Sumner was an unsuccessful Free Soil candidate for Congress, campaigning against the "lords of the lash and the lords of the loom." In ROBERTS V. BOSTON (1849) Sumner unsuccessfully challenged government compulsion of SEGREGATION in Boston schools, arguing that racially separate schools denied equality. In upholding segregation, Massachusetts Chief Justice LEMUEL SHAW enunciated, for the first time, the doctrine of SEPARATE BUT EQUAL.

In 1851 Sumner won the Senate seat once held by DANIEL WEBSTER. In his first speech, "Freedom National, Slavery Sectional," Sumner attacked the fugitive slave law and congressional support of slavery for nearly four hours. In an 1856 speech, "The Crime Against Kansas," Sumner vilified senators who had supported the KANSAS-NEBRASKA ACT. He described STEPHEN A. DOUGLAS as "the squire of slavery, its very Sancho Panza, ready to do all its humiliating offices." South Carolina's Andrew Butler was, in Sumner's view, the Don Quixote of slavery who had "chosen a mistress to whom he has made his vows, and who, though ugly to others . . . is chaste in his sight; I mean the harlot slavery." Two days later Congressman Preston Brooks, a relative of Butler, repaid Sumner for these remarks by beating him insensible with a cane. Many Northerners viewed this incident as a symbol of a violent slavocracy which threatened the Constitution and the nation. After a three-and-a-half-year convalescence Sumner returned to the Senate in 1860, renewing his crusade against bondage with a four-hour oration, "The Barbarism of Slavery." This speech became a Republican campaign document in 1860.

From the beginning of the Civil War Sumner urged the abolition of slavery. He argued that secession was STATE SUICIDE, that the Confederate States had reverted to territorial status, and that, despite the decision in DRED SCOTT V. SANDFORD, Congress had the power to end slavery in these TERRITORIES. On a less theoretical level Sumner successfully sponsored legislation to repeal the fugitive slave laws and to allow black witnesses to testify in federal courts. Sumner was unsuccessful, however, in his attempts to gain congressional support for the integration of Washington's street railroads and other facilities. As chairman of the Senate Foreign Relations Committee, Sumner was constantly at odds with Secretary of State WILLIAM SEWARD, and often served as President ABRAHAM LINCOLN's unofficial adviser on foreign policy. Sumner exploited that position to gain diplomatic recognition for Haiti and Liberia and to secure a passport for a black constituent. As chairman of the Select Committee on Slavery and Freedmen, Sumner laid the groundwork for the FREEDMEN'S BUREAU.

During Reconstruction, Sumner was the Senate's most vociferous advocate of black rights and an early opponent of ANDREW JOHNSON. Sumner's increasingly moralistic and uncompromising posture undermined his legislative effectiveness during Reconstruction. Sumner initially opposed the THIRTEENTH and FOURTEENTH AMENDMENTS because they failed to give blacks enough rights. He gave little support to the FIFTEENTH AMENDMENT because he believed the Constitution embodied the highest moral principles and thus enabled Congress under existing constitutional powers to enfranchise blacks. After 1870 Sumner devoted himself to a comprehensive CIVIL RIGHTS bill, which would give the freedmen complete equality. Its passage, in a somewhat truncated form, as the CIVIL RIGHTS ACT OF 1875 was a posthumous tribute to Sumner's integrity and his passionate devotion to racial equality.

PAUL FINKELMAN

Bibliography

DONALD, DAVID HERBERT 1960 *Charles Sumner and the Coming of the Civil War.* New York: Knopf.
—— 1970 *Charles Sumner and the Rights of Man.* New York: Knopf.

SUNDAY CLOSING LAWS

The first compulsory Sunday observance law in what is now the United States was promulgated in Virginia in 1610. It made absence from church services punishable by death for the third offense. Although there is no record of any person suffering the death penalty, lesser penalties, including whipping, were in effect in all the colonies and were continued after independence. Implicit constitutional recognition of Sunday observance is found in Article I, section 7, which excepts Sundays from the ten days wherein the President is required to exercise his veto of bills adopted by Congress.

Before the Supreme Court ruled that the FIRST AMENDMENT was applicable to the states, it held, in *Hennington v. Georgia* (1896), that Georgia had not unconstitutionally burdened INTERSTATE COMMERCE by regulating the movement of freight trains on Sundays. Four years later, it held, in *Petit v. Minnesota* (1900), that the state had not denied DUE PROCESS in refusing to classify barbering as an act of necessity or charity that could legally be performed on Sundays.

In 1961, after the Court had ruled the First Amendment applicable to the states, it considered the constitutionality of three state Sunday closing laws under that Amendment in four cases, known collectively as the Sunday Closing Law Cases. Two, *McGowan v. Maryland* and *Two Guys from Harrison-Allentown, Inc. v. McGinley,* concerned owners of highway discount stores that were open for business seven days a week. The other two, *Gallagher v. Crown Kosher Super Market* and *Braunfeld v. Brown,* involved stores owned by Orthodox Jews, who, by reason of religious convictions, abstained from all business activities on Saturdays.

In these cases the statutes were challenged on three principal grounds: that the laws violated the ban on the ESTABLISHMENT OF RELIGION; that the statutes' crazy-quilt pattern of exemptions was arbitrary, constituting a denial of due process and the EQUAL PROTECTION OF THE LAWS (for example, in one of the states it was legal to sell fish and food stuffs wholesale, but not at retail; in another, merchandise customarily sold at beaches and amusement parks might be sold there, but not elsewhere); that, at least in respect to Jews, Seventh-Day Adventists, and others whose religions required rest on Saturday, the laws violated the constitutional protection of RELIGIOUS LIBERTY by making it economically difficult if not impossible for them to observe their own Sabbath when their competitors operated six days each week.

In all four cases the Court upheld the constitutionality of the challenged laws, with all the prevailing opinions written by Chief Justice EARL WARREN. He recognized that the laws challenged in these cases had been enacted in colonial times with the purpose of ensuring observance of the majoritarian Christian Sabbath as a religious obligation. However, he said, the religious origin of these statutes did not require their invalidation if their present purpose was secular.

Warren said that the modern purpose of the challenged statutes was to set aside a day for "rest, repose, relaxation, tranquillity"; the purpose was therefore secular rather than religious. The Maryland statutes, for example, permitted such Sunday activities as the operation of bathing beaches, amusement parks, and even pinball and slot machines, as well as the sale of alcoholic beverages and the performance of professional sports. That such exemptions are directly contrary to the religiosity of the Sabbath indicated clearly that the Sunday laws' present purpose was not religious.

Viewed as welfare legislation, the Sunday laws presented little constitutional difficulty. The Chief Justice noted in *McGowan* that numerous federal and state laws affecting public health, safety, conditions of labor, week-end diversion at parks and beaches, and cultural activities of various kinds, had long been upheld. To forbid a state from prescribing Sunday as a day of rest solely because centuries ago such laws had their genesis in religion would be a CONSTITUTIONAL INTERPRETATION based on hostility to the public welfare rather than the SEPARATION OF CHURCH AND STATE.

The Court had more difficulty in sustaining laws applied against persons observing a day other than Sunday as their divinely ordained day of rest. Six Justices agreed that state legislatures, if they so elected, could constitutionally exempt Sabbatarians from complying with Sunday law restrictions, but the free exercise clause did not mandate that they do so. However, a majority of the Court could not agree upon one opinion to that effect. The Chief Justice, speaking for a plurality of four, noted that while the clause secured freedom to hold any belief, it did not forbid regulation of secular practices merely because some persons might suffer economically if they obeyed the dictates of their religion. Income tax laws, for example, did not violate the clause even though they limited the amount of deductions for religious contributions. If a state regulated conduct by a general law, the purpose and effect of which were to advance secular goals, its action was valid despite its indirect burden on the exercise of religion unless the purpose could practicably be otherwise accomplished. A sabbatarian exemption would be hard to enforce, and would interfere with the goal of providing a uniform day of rest that as far as possible eliminated the atmosphere of commercial activity. The laws thus did not violate the free exercise clause.

In THORNTON V. CALDOR, INC. (1985) the Court went even further. It ruled unconstitutional, under the effect aspect of the purpose-effect-entanglement test of constitutionality under the establishment clause, a Connecticut law that accorded employees an absolute right not to work on their chosen Sabbath.

LEO PFEFFER

Bibliography

PFEFFER, LEO (1953)1967 *Church, State and Freedom.* Boston: Beacon Press.
———— 1975 *God, Caesar, and the Constitution.* Boston: Beacon Press.
STOKES, ANSON PHELPS 1950 *Church and State in the United States.* New York: Harper & Brothers.

SUPREMACY CLAUSE

The supremacy clause of Article VI, clause 2, declares: "This Constitution and the Laws of the United States which shall be made in Pursuance thereof; and all

Treaties made, or which shall be made, under the authority of the United States, shall be the supreme law of the Land." This principle of national supremacy was a radical departure from the constitutional order that prevailed under the ARTICLES OF CONFEDERATION. Whereas the Articles created a short-lived confederation of states—according to its terms a mere "league of friendship" founded on the good faith of sovereign states—the Constitution established a federal union designed to last in perpetuity. The distinguishing feature of the "more perfect union" created by the Constitution was a strong national government capable of dealing with the problems and complexities of a growing nation and strong state governments acting within their sphere of authority. The Constitution does not establish the supremacy of the national government in all things. National supremacy is limited to laws made PURSUANT TO THE CONSTITUTION. What is not granted to the national government under its ENUMERATED POWERS is, as a general rule, reserved to the people or to the states under the TENTH AMENDMENT.

The supremacy clause may truly be regarded as the linchpin of American FEDERALISM. It holds the republic together by providing a principle for the resolution of conflicts between the states and the nation. Valid national law is clearly paramount in the face of conflicting state law. But whether a state law conflicts with federal law or a federal constitutional provision is not always clear. When doubts exist over the compatibility of federal and state law, and a real controversy arises from these doubts, the judiciary is usually called upon to work out the implications of the supremacy clause through interpretation. The outcome of such cases often depends on inferences drawn by the courts from the structure of the federal system and the values it represents.

The problems of interpretation generated by the supremacy clause have taken two forms epitomized by the celebrated cases of MCCULLOCH V. MARYLAND (1819) and GIBBONS V. OGDEN (1824). In the first Maryland taxed a national bank doing business within its borders; in the second New York granted a monopoly over steamboat navigation on its internal waterways. The supremacy clause operated to invalidate both measures. *McCulloch* stands for the principle that even a power reserved to the states—here the ordinary and indispensable power of taxation—may not be exercised in such a way as to impede or unduly burden a federal agency or activity; *Gibbons* stands for the principle that the state's regulation of a subject matter within its territory, and normally under its control, must give way before a conflicting, and valid,

federal statute. "It is of the very essence of [national] supremacy," wrote Chief Justice JOHN MARSHALL, "to remove all obstacles to its action within its own sphere, and to so modify every power vested in subordinate governments as to exempt its own operation from . . . their influence." In both cases, Marshall underscored the plenary nature of the enumerated powers of Congress; they admit of no limitations save those prescribed in the Constitution. When combined with *McCulloch*'s doctrine of IMPLIED POWERS, fortified by the NECESSARY AND PROPER CLAUSE, the reach of federal power cuts a potentially deep furrow into the field of state SOVEREIGNTY.

This expansive view of federal power was for almost a century strongly contested by the doctrine of DUAL FEDERALISM. It held that nation and states were essentially equal in their respective spheres of influence. The doctrine did not hold that the states could decide for themselves the extent of their sovereign powers. Once again this was a judicial task, for dual federalism was an axiom of CONSTITUTIONAL INTERPRETATION. Beginning roughly in 1835, shortly after ROGER B. TANEY replaced Marshall as Chief Justice, the Supreme Court deployed and developed the concept of STATE POLICE POWER—broadly characterized as the power of a state to provide for the general welfare of its people—to limit the reach of national law. This movement attained its apogee in the first third of the twentieth century when the Supreme Court used the Tenth Amendment to invalidate numerous federal laws, all of them regulating various aspects of the economy. Most of these decisions supported the ideology of individualism and capitalism. The national statutes struck down by the Court were deemed to interfere with state police power yet arguably enacted pursuant to the delegated powers of Congress and clearly not expressly forbidden by the Constitution.

The year 1937 marks the collapse of the doctrine that state sovereignty constitutes a limitation on the exercise of power delegated by the Constitution to Congress. Since then the Supreme Court has returned and held steadfastly to the spirit of *McCulloch* and *Gibbons*. Even activities sponsored or operated by the state are subject to federal regulation when imposed pursuant to a delegated power. NATIONAL LEAGUE OF CITIES V. USERY (1976) is the only exception to this principle: in striking down a federal wage and hour provision as applied to state and local public employees, a closely divided Supreme Court ruled that such power—in this instance the federal commerce power—may not be exercised to interfere with "functions essential to the separate and independent existence" of the "states as states." The ghost of dual federalism lurks in *Usery.* In 1985, however, a closely divided Court overruled *Usery* in GARCIA V. SAN ANTONIO METROPOLITAN TRANSIT AUTHORITY.

In interpreting the supremacy clause today, the Supreme Court has given up the search for bright lines separating federal and state authority. The two levels of government are no longer perceived as antagonistic rivals, whatever the tensions between them. The supremacy clause once operated to immunize persons closely related to the federal government from most forms of state taxation. The pre-1937 doctrine of federal tax immunity, based on the generalized notion of federal supremacy rooted in *McCulloch,* was construed to invalidate such levies as state or local taxes on the income of federal employees, on interest income from federal bonds, on income derived from property leased by the federal government, and on sales to the United States. Since 1937, however, the Supreme Court with the help of Congress has wiped out most of this RECIPROCAL TAX IMMUNITY. The prevailing doctrine today, particularly after *United States v. New Mexico* (1982), is that a nondiscriminatory state tax even upon private contractors with close and intricate relationships with the federal government will not violate the supremacy clause unless the tax is imposed *directly* upon the United States.

In the field of regulation, too, sharp lines between federal and state authority are often difficult to find. Modern government is complex, involving the entanglement of federal and state policy in fields once regarded as exclusively state concerns. Education, conservation, aid to the poor and the handicapped, and environmental protection are prominent examples of such fields. The relationship between levels of government in all these areas today is one of cooperation and reciprocity. By means of FEDERAL GRANTS-IN-AID and other funding programs the national government, pursuant to its power of taxing and spending for the GENERAL WELFARE, has actually encouraged the states to pass laws and adopt policies in response to local needs. This new context of COOPERATIVE FEDERALISM does not mean, however, that the supremacy clause has lost its bite. Indeed, it has operated to establish the primacy of the national government even in some of the aforementioned fields. An example is *Blum v. Bacon* (1982), where the Supreme Court invalidated a New York law excluding recipients of a federal program aiding poor families with dependent children from receiving aid under the state's federally funded emergency welfare program. (*Blum* involved a state statutory policy that conflicted with a federal administrative regulation.)

As the preceding suggests, contemporary supremacy clause analysis is largely a matter of statutory interpretation. The supremacy clause has not been interpreted to prevent federal and state governments from regulating the same subject, partly out of the judiciary's recognition of the reality of cooperative federalism. The nature of some subjects (e.g., IMMIGRATION and NATURALIZATION, bankruptcy, PATENTS, and some articles of commerce) may require national uniform legislation. But most problems of American national life are valid topics of both national and state legislation (e.g., air and water pollution, motor carrier transportation, labor relations, consumer protection, and CIVIL RIGHTS). States and nation may legislate on these topics for similar or different reasons. The key to the validity of such concurrent or parallel legislation is whether both federal and state regulations can be enforced without impairing federal superintendence of the field. Even apparently conflicting state legislation may survive supremacy clause analysis if the state law deals with a field traditionally occupied by the state and the state's interest is substantial enough to offset any presumption that Congress may have intended to occupy the field all by itself. A principle of comity has thus replaced the earlier antagonism between nation and states characteristic of dual federalism. Today, as a general rule, unless Congress statutorily declares its intent to occupy a field, federal regulation preempts state law only where the latter seriously impedes the former.

Jones v. Roth Packing Company (1977) is a leading example of a case in which federal policy displaced state law notwithstanding the absence of explicit preemptive language in the congressional statute. Here the federal Fair Packaging and Labeling Act, enacted under the COMMERCE CLAUSE, was construed to conflict with a state consumer protection law dealing with the weight of certain goods packaged for sale. The Supreme Court read into the federal statute a congressional intent to supersede state law. Supersession was inferred from the supremacy clause because the enforcement of the state law was an obstacle to the full accomplishment and execution of the congressional purpose. In other cases federal PREEMPTION has been inferred because "[t]he scheme of federal regulation may be so pervasive as to make reasonable the inference that Congress left no room for the states to supplement it" or because "the Act of Congress may touch a field in which the federal interest is so dominant that the federal system will be assumed to preclude enforcement of state laws on the same subject." The supremacy clause thus remains a vital operative principle of American constitutional law even though the Supreme Court tends to presume the validity of concurrent state legislation, barring proof of its interference with federal policy.

DONALD P. KOMMERS

Bibliography

CORWIN, EDWIN S. 1913 *National Supremacy: Treaty Power versus State Power.* New York: Holt.

SCHMIDHAUSER, JOHN R. 1958 *The Supreme Court as Final Arbiter of Federal–State Relations.* Chapel Hill: University of North Carolina Press.

SUPREME COURT
(History)

The only court whose existence is mandated by the Constitution is the Supreme Court. Article III states: "The judicial power of the United States shall be vested in one supreme court, and in such inferior courts as the Congress may from time to time ordain and establish." Besides its existence, a few attributes are constitutionally entrenched by Article III. The tenure of the judges is to be "during GOOD BEHAVIOR," and their compensation "shall not be diminished during their continuance in office." These provisions, modeled on English law and made applicable to all federal judges, were obviously intended to assure the independence of a judiciary appointed, pursuant to Article II, by the President with the ADVICE AND CONSENT of the Senate.

Other features having a bearing on the character and independence of the Court were not addressed, presumably to be left at large or determined from time to time by Congress. Qualifications for membership on the Court were not specified; nor were the size of the Court, the period of its TERMS, or the level of the judges' compensation. The Court was to have both ORIGINAL JURISDICTION and APPELLATE JURISDICTION, but the latter was subject to "such exceptions, and under such regulations, as the Congress shall make." Nothing was said concerning the relation of the Supreme Court to the courts of the STATES.

Thus from the outset the Court was only partially sheltered from the politics of republican government. The status of the Court was one of those creative ambiguities that have marked the Constitution as no less an organism than a mechanism, Darwinian as well as Newtonian. The position of the Court may have been in the mind of an eminent modern foreign-born mathematician who, contemplating American CITIZENSHIP, regretted that he could not swear allegiance to the Constitution because "it is full of inconsistencies." In a self-governing nation, to be sure, the Court is detached but not disengaged, distant but not remote. Therein lay its potential either for popular neglect and scorn or for power and prestige.

The need for a federal judiciary, and so for an ultimate tribunal, was felt by the Framers as part of the transition from a confederation to a federal union. The ARTICLES OF CONFEDERATION supplied no such institution, except a supreme tribunal for prize and admiralty cases. A system of federal courts, parallel to those of the states, was one of the innovative conceptions of 1787. Their function was to serve as impartial tribunals, free of local bias, in suits between states, or controversies involving citizens of different states or a foreign country; to establish a uniform interpretation of federal laws; and to maintain the supremacy of federal law in cases where a state law conflicted with the Constitution, federal statutes, or treaties of the United States. In sum, the JURISDICTION OF THE FEDERAL COURTS could rest on the nature of the parties or of the question presented. Only in cases where a state, or a foreign country or its diplomatic representative, was a party was the Supreme Court given original (nonappellate) jurisdiction.

These skeletal provisions of Article III were fleshed out by Congress in the JUDICIARY ACT OF 1789. That act set the number of Supreme Court Justices at five associate Justices and one CHIEF JUSTICE, with salaries of $3,500 and $4,000, respectively. (The monetary differential remained at $500 until 1969, when it was increased to $2,500.) Three provisions of the act led to developments that proved to be of seminal importance for the prestige and power of the Supreme Court: a requirement that the Justices serve on regional CIRCUIT COURTS ("circuit riding"); a provision in section 13 that seemed to grant original jurisdiction to the Court to issue WRITS OF MANDAMUS; and a grant of power in section 25 to review the decisions of state supreme courts in cases turning on the Constitution, laws, or treaties of the United States. Each of these merits attention.

The circuit duties meant sitting with a federal district judge to form a circuit court, which heard appeals from district courts and had original jurisdiction in diversity of citizenship cases. In the early years circuit riding consumed the greater part of a Justice's time and surely his energy; travel by carriage or horseback over rough roads and stopovers at uncomfortable inns resulted in a weariness of flesh and spirit, against which the Justices complained bitterly, but which they forbore to resist. Yet these excursions into the local courthouses brought them into touch with lawyers, journalists, and townspeople, and gave a reality to the Supreme Court that its functioning in the capital city could not match. Moreover, the assignment of each Justice to a particular circuit affected significantly the appointments to the Court, for a vacancy on the Court would normally be filled by an appointment from the same circuit, and so at any time the practical range of nominees was limited and the influence of a small group of senators was proportionately great. Not until 1891, with the passage of the CIRCUIT COURTS OF APPEALS ACT, were the Justices fully relieved of circuit-riding duties. Thereafter geography played a decreasing role in appointments. A striking instance was the widely acclaimed appointment by President HERBERT C. HOOVER in 1932 of Judge BENJAMIN N. CARDOZO of New York to succeed Justice OLIVER WENDELL HOLMES of Massachusetts, although two New Yorkers, Chief Justice CHARLES EVANS HUGHES and Justice HARLAN FISKE STONE, were already on the Court. A comparable instance was the appointment by President Reagan in 1981 of Judge SANDRA DAY O'CONNOR of Arizona to succeed Justice POTTER STEWART of Ohio even though another Arizonan, Justice WILLIAM H. REHNQUIST, was already serving.

As circuit riding was a cardinal factor in gaining popular recognition of the Court (at considerable cost to the Justices) and in determining appointments, so did the practice furnish an early opportunity for the Court to judge the validity of an act of Congress. In the waning days of the Federalist administration, Congress passed the JUDICIARY ACT OF 1801, compounded of partisanship and principle, which created new judgeships and abolished circuit riding. When the Jeffersonians took office, however, they countered with the JUDICIARY ACT OF 1802, which abolished the judgeships and restored circuit riding. Chief Justice JOHN MARSHALL, sensing a political crisis for the Court, solicited the opinions of his brethren on the question of complying with the law or treating it as beyond the authority of Congress. The Justices had serious doubts about the law's validity, and a strong distaste for the resumption of the burden it imposed, yet a majority counseled compliance, in accord with Marshall's own inclination. But a private litigant, defeated in a circuit court in Virginia at which Marshall himself presided, appealed to the Supreme Court, arguing the unconstitutionality of the 1802 act. The Congress, fearing a judgment voiding the act, had abolished the 1802 term of the Supreme Court. When the case, STUART V. LAIRD, was decided, in February of 1803, the Court, with Marshall not participating, surprised and gratified the Jeffersonians by upholding the act, in a brief opinion which simply declared that acquiescence by the Court in circuit duty for twelve years under the Judiciary Act of 1789 had given a practical construction of the Constitution that would not now be disturbed. That the Court would at least consider the validity of an act of Congress had been resolved just six days earlier in the landmark case of MARBURY V. MADISON (1803).

That case, establishing the power of JUDICAL REVIEW of acts of Congress, marked the second of the three germinal developments from the Judiciary Act of 1789. Section 13, which gave the Court power to issue mandamus and other writs, might have been read simply as conferring the power where the jurisdiction of the Court rested on one of the grounds specified in Article III. But the Court was not of a mind for so narrow a reading. When William Marbury of Maryland invoked the original jurisdiction of the Court to enforce a right to an office of justice of the peace pursuant to an appointment by President JOHN ADAMS, and sought a mandamus to compel Secretary of State JAMES MADISON to deliver his commission, the Court regarded section 13 as conferring jurisdiction, and as so construed beyond the ambit of original jurisdiction defined in Article III. The suit for mandamus was therefore dismissed, again to the gratification of the Jeffersonians, but in the process the Court had declared the far more significant principle that in the decision of a case where a federal law was arguably incompatible with the Constitution, the Court, in deciding what "the law" was, must, if necessary, vindicate the HIGHER LAW and treat the legislative act as ineffectual.

Despite some provocative language in Marshall's opinion (the executive branch cannot "sport away" the rights of others), the Jeffersonians focused on the immediate result and regarded it as a victory at the hands of a still-Federalist Court. Indeed, judicial review was not then the divisive party issue; the Jeffersonians would have welcomed a Supreme Court decision holding the Sedition Act of 1798 unconstitutional. Whether Marshall's doctrine of judicial review was a usurpation later became a subject of heated debate, scholarly and unscholarly. Although the Constitution contains no specific mention of the power, and although Marshall's opinion, resting on the logic of the decisional process, can be said to beg the question of who is to decide, the debates in the CONSTITUTIONAL CONVENTION do indicate obliquely an acceptance of the power, in explaining the rejection of attempts to involve judges in an extrajudicial power of veto of legislation. But the debates were not cited in Marbury; MADISON'S NOTES, the most authoritative source, pursuant to the policy of secrecy, were not published until fifty years after the Convention.

The third of the salient projections from the Judiciary Act of 1789, involving section 25, produced more immediate partisan repercussions. Section 25 empowered the Court to review decisions of state courts that denied rights claimed under the federal Constitution, statutes, or treaties. Again, no constitutional provision explicitly conferred such power on the Supreme Court, although Article VI does declare the supremacy of federal law: "the judges in every state shall be bound thereby." By their silence, the Framers may have sought to avoid confrontations in the ratifying process, as in forbearing to be explicit about a national power to issue paper money or to establish a national bank.

The storm over the Court's power to review state court decisions was precipitated by its decision in MARTIN V. HUNTER'S LESSEE (1816) sustaining the validity of section 25. The case was a contest over title to the extensive Fairfax estate in the northern neck of Virginia, turning on the intricate interrelations of Virginia land law and treaties of the United States with Great Britain concerning ownership of land by British nationals. Holding that the Virginia court had misapplied both Virginia and federal law, the Supreme Court in 1813, through Justice JOSEPH STORY, reversed the state court's judgment and remanded the case to that court. A number of factors weakened the force of the decision. Story's opinion controverted the state court's even on points of the interpretation of state law, although section 25 itself limited review to federal questions. At a time when seven Justices constituted the Court, only four participated in the decision; the vote was 3–1, and the mandate to the Virginia court was unfortunately in the traditional form addressed to an inferior court, "you are hereby commanded, etc." The Virginia court was outraged and refused to obey the mandate. On a new WRIT OF ERROR to the Supreme Court, Story elaborated the justification of Supreme Court review in terms of the need for uniformity and supremacy of national law. The nature of the cause, not the court, was determinative of the Supreme Court's power to review (though critics wondered, no doubt unfairly, if the Supreme Court could then be given authority to review certain decisions of the House of Lords). John Marshall could not have uttered a pronouncement more nationalistic than that of the New England Republican appointed by President JAMES MADISON. (Marshall had excused himself because of his family's ownership of part of the land. Story, appointed in 1811 at the age of thirty-two, one of the most learned

and powerful of Justices and a firm ally of Marshall, had been Madison's fourth choice to succeed WILLIAM CUSHING of Massachusetts: LEVI LINCOLN declined the nomination, Alexander Wolcott was rejected by the Senate, and JOHN QUINCY ADAMS also declined. Thus are the inevitabilities of history determined.)

In a sequel to the decision, the Court took the further step of sustaining its power to review even criminal judgments of state courts where a federal question, such as the interpretation of a federal law, was implicated. The opinion by Chief Justice Marshall in COHENS V. VIRGINIA (1821) was the climactic realization of the Court's vision of a uniform federal law and a Constitution that was supreme in reality as well as in principle.

Reaction to the *Cohens* decision by Jeffersonians, particularly in Virginia, was intense. Judge SPENCER ROANE, who instead of Marshall would probably have become Chief Justice if OLIVER ELLSWORTH had not resigned before Jefferson took office, published a series of bitter letters under pseudonyms, paying his respects to "A most monstrous and unexampled decision. It can only be accounted for from that love of power which all history informs us infects and corrupts all who possess it, and from which even the upright and eminent Judges are not exempt." The Court's "extravagant pretension" reached "the zenith of despotic power." In the following years a series of bills were introduced in Congress to repeal, in whole or in part, the appellate jurisdiction of the Supreme Court. Under these genial auspices was thus established a particularly sensitive and probably the most crucial power of the highest court in our federal union: the review of decisions of state courts in the interest of vindicating rights secured by the Constitution.

Conflicts between the Supreme Court, on the one hand, and the executive or legislative branches, or both, on the other, have occurred continually. The other branches have utilized the full spectrum of measures made available by the constitution. The most drastic of these, IMPEACHMENT, was the first to be tried; indeed it was designed as a trial run by Jefferson to prepare the way for a similar attack on Chief Justice Marshall. The immediate target was Justice SAMUEL CHASE, ardent Federalist, whose partisan outbursts in charges to the grand jury in Maryland furnished the occasion. The attempt misfired, however; Chase was narrowly acquitted in the Senate, owing probably to comparable overreaching by the fiery JOHN RANDOLPH, who managed the case for the Jeffersonians.

A milder form of resistance to the Court was the doctrine of departmental independence, whereby the

President was as free to act on his view of constitutional authority as the Court was to act on its own. Despite the prospect of endless oscillation that this theory implied, it was espoused in some form by Jefferson, ANDREW JACKSON, and ABRAHAM LINCOLN. President JACKSON'S VETO OF THE BANK BILL (1832) was based partly on grounds of unconstitutionality, although the earlier law creating the bank had been sustained by the Supreme Court. In his message justifying the veto, Jackson had the advice and aid of his attorney general, ROGER B. TANEY. By an irony of history, when President Lincoln in his first inaugural address dealt with Taney's opinion in DRED SCOTT V. SANDFORD (1857), he adopted something of the Jackson-Taney philosophy, maintaining that although he offered no resistance to the decision as a settlement of the lawsuit he could not regard it as binding on the political branches for the future.

The indeterminate size of the Court became a weapon in the contest between President ANDREW JOHNSON and Congress over Reconstruction. By successive statutory changes, following the admission of new states and the creation of new circuits, the authorized membership of the Court had been increased to ten. A radical Congress, distrustful of Johnson and wishing to deprive him of the power to make new appointments to the Court, reduced the number of seats prospectively to seven. (Contributing to the move was a plan of Chief Justice SALMON P. CHASE to induce a reluctant Congress to increase the Justices' salaries in return for a decrease in the number to be compensated. That plan failed, but Chase did succeed in having the title of his office changed from Chief Justice of the Supreme Court to Chief Justice of the United States.) The actual number of Justices did not fall below eight, and in 1869 the number was fixed at nine.

More famous is the action of the same Congress in withdrawing the appellate jurisdiction of the Supreme Court in cases under a HABEAS CORPUS act, giving rise to the decision in EX PARTE MCCARDLE in 1869. While the immediate issue in the case was whether a military commission in Mississippi could try a newspaper editor for inflammatory writings urging citizens not to cooperate with the military government, Congress was fearful that a politically minded majority on the Court would hold the entire plan of Reconstruction unconstitutional. The Court, which had already heard argument in the case, bowed to the withdrawal of jurisdiction, but carefully pointed out that another appellate route remained unaffected by the repealing statute. Consequently the value of

McCardle as a PRECEDENT, which is the centerpiece of constitutional argument on the extent of congressional power to limit the Court's jurisdiction, is at best doubtful.

The post-Reconstruction Court alienated labor and progressives by decisions taking a narrow view of state power to regulate and tax business; the COMMERCE CLAUSE and FREEDOM OF CONTRACT protected by SUBSTANTIVE DUE PROCESS served as shields for industry. The Progressive party platform in 1912, under the aegis of THEODORE ROOSEVELT, advocated the RECALL of judges and judicial decisions by popular vote. Although this thrust was aimed at state courts rather than the Supreme Court, the latter had set a tone for judicial review in a triad of decisions in 1895. UNITED STATES V. E. C. KNIGHT CO. held that a combination of sugar refiners controlling ninety percent of sugar production in the nation was not subject to the SHERMAN ANTITRUST ACT because processing is not commerce. IN RE DEBS held that a labor leader could be imprisoned for violating a federal court's INJUNCTION in a railroad labor strike, without judicial reliance on any statutorily defined offense. POLLOCK V. FARMERS LOAN AND TRUST CO. held the federal income tax law unconstitutional as applied to income from real property, stocks, and bonds, though valid as applied to wages, because an income tax is tantamount to a tax on its source, and where the source is property in some form the tax is a DIRECT TAX which under the constitution is forbidden to Congress unless apportioned according to population.

The most serious conflict with the Court, certainly since Marshall's time, culminated in President FRANKLIN D. ROOSEVELT's Court reorganization plan in early 1937. The Court had held unconstitutional a series of major New Deal measures designed for economic recovery and reform: the NATIONAL INDUSTRIAL RECOVERY ACT; AGRICULTURAL ADJUSTMENT ACT; Railway Pension Act; Farm Mortgage Act; Guffey-Snyder Bituminous Coal Act; Municipal Bankruptcy Act; and a state minimum wage law for women. Still to be decided was the validity of the WAGNER NATIONAL LABOR RELATIONS ACT, the SOCIAL SECURITY ACT, the PUBLIC UTILITY HOLDING COMPANY ACT, and the TENNESSEE VALLEY AUTHORITY ACT in its full scope. The administration was persuaded that the barrier did not inhere in the Constitution but was the handiwork of Justices who were out of sympathy both with the New Deal and with the best traditions of constitutional decision. Apparently accepting the validity of this analysis, Chief Justice Hughes, appointed by President Hoover, though he greatly disliked 5–4 decisions, nevertheless joined Justices LOUIS D. BRANDEIS, Stone, and Cardozo as dissenters in the last five of the cases listed above as holding measures invalid. During his first term President Roosevelt had no opportunity to make an appointment to the Court.

The reorganization plan, which was formulated by Attorney General HOMER S. CUMMINGS, called for the appointment of an additional member of the Court for each Justice who did not retire at the age of seventy, up to a maximum membership of fifteen. Despite the President's sweeping electoral victory in 1936, and intensive political efforts by the administration for four months, the plan failed to pass the Senate. A number of factors contributed to the result. The argument based on age and inefficiency, stressed by proponents at the outset, was transparently disingenuous. A letter from Chief Justice Hughes, joined by Justices WILLIS VAN DEVANTER and Brandeis, to Senator Burton K. Wheeler, at the latter's request, effectively refuted the charge that the Court needed additional members to keep abreast of its docket. The Court itself, while the bill was pending, sustained a state minimum wage law, the National Labor Relations Act, an amended Farm Bankruptcy Act, and the Social Security Act. As one senator remarked, "Why keep on running for the bus after you've caught it?" Moreover, Congress enacted a new retirement act for Supreme Court Justices, which made retirement more acceptable. Since 1869 a full pension had been provided for, but as retirement was equivalent to resignation under the statute, the pension was subject to the will of Congress and in 1932, as an economy measure, it had been reduced by half and was later restored. The act of 1937, by enabling retired Justices to serve on the lower federal courts, placed their retirement compensation under constitutional protection against diminution. Justice Van Devanter availed himself of this new law, giving the President his first opportunity to make an appointment and lessening further the need for enactment of his plan. But perhaps the most powerful factor leading to its defeat was a pervasive feeling, even among groups holding grievances against particular decisions, that the independence of the judiciary was too important a principle to be sacrificed, even under the extreme provocation furnished by a majority of the Court itself.

The appellate jurisdiction of the Court became a target of attack in 1958, as it had been in the early nineteenth century. Senator William E. Jenner of Indiana, reacting against decisions curtailing governmental actions in the field of loyalty investigations, introduced a series of bills withdrawing Supreme Court jurisdiction in this and related classes of cases. Passage was narrowly averted by the efforts of the then majority leader, Senator LYNDON B. JOHNSON. Comparable bills were introduced in 1982 to preclude review of decisions concerning abortion and school prayers. Such efforts, if successful, would produce chaotic results. In the name of the federal Constitution, varying decisions, for and against local laws, would stand unreconciled; the Supreme Court would have no opportunity to reconsider or modify its precedents; state and federal judges would be left to take different positions on the binding effect of prior Supreme Court decisions.

It is apparent that in the recurrent clashes of party, section, and class that have marked American history, the Court, whose role, in principle, is that of an arbiter, has not escaped the role of participant. In these judicial involvements, extraordinary force on one side has induced similar force on the other. A dramatic example is the contest over the production of the White House tapes for use as evidence in the prosecutions growing out of the Watergate break-in. President RICHARD M. NIXON refused to comply with a subpoena issued by the district court, on the ground of EXECUTIVE PRIVILEGE. The tension between the rule of law and presidential immunity from suit had been resolved in part by bringing suit against a subordinate who was carrying out presidential orders, as in the steel seizure case, YOUNGSTOWN SHEET AND TUBE CO. v. SAWYER (1952), where the named defendant was the secretary of commerce. President Nixon, however, forced the issue by taking sole custody of the tapes. On appeal, the Supreme Court responded with the countervailing measure of holding the President amenable to the process of a court where the need of EVIDENCE in a criminal trial outweighs a generalized claim of privilege. The unanimity of the decision (with one abstention) was doubtless a factor impelling the President to yield, thus avoiding an ultimate confrontation.

That the supreme judicial tribunal, without the power of purse or sword, should have survived crises and vicissitudes and maintained its prestige can be ascribed partly to its own resourcefulness and partly to the recognition by a mature people of the Court's necessary functions in the American constitutional democracy. The Court's resourcefulness owes much to the central paradox of its work: it decides issues of great political moment, yet it does so in the context of a controversy between ordinary litigants in a conventional lawsuit. That setting provides a test of concreteness in the formulation of DOCTRINE, allows flexibility of development, and enables the Court to adapt and refine doctrine as new factual and procedural settings may suggest.

The Supreme Court's essential functions, performed within the framework of conventional lawsuits, are fourfold: to resolve controversies between states; to assure the uniform application of national law; to maintain a common market in a continental union; and to enforce the guarantees of liberty and equality embodied in the BILL OF RIGHTS, the post-Civil War Amendments, and other provisions of the Constitution.

Although the Court's jurisdiction over suits between states is statistically insignificant, the function is of practical and symbolic importance, serving as a substitute for diplomacy and war in disputes over boundaries, allotment of waters, and the like. Because these cases originate in the Supreme Court, factual disputes are referred to a SPECIAL MASTER for hearings, findings, and recommendations, which are then presented to the Court for argument and decision.

The uniform interpretation and application of national law has become increasingly important with the proliferation of federal regulatory statutes and administrative rules. For almost a century, until 1938, the Supreme Court essayed a broader concept of uniformity in the COMMON LAW itself, in fields such as commercial law and torts, under the doctrine of SWIFT V. TYSON (1842), which empowered the federal courts to pronounce a FEDERAL COMMON LAW without regard to the common law of particular states. Sweeping as it was, the doctrine was truncated, for the federal common law could have no binding authority in state courts, and thus a bifurcated system of common law developed, along with a practice of forum shopping by lawyers as between federal and state courts. The doctrine was repudiated by the Court in ERIE RAILWAY V. TOMPKINS (1938) in an opinion by Justice Brandeis that branded as unconstitutional the course theretofore pursued by the federal courts. With the demise of *Swift v. Tyson* the rationale for retaining DIVERSITY OF CITIZENSHIP JURISDICTION in the federal courts, for the decision of matters of state law, was materially weakened.

The maintenance of a common market is a modern description of a historic function of the Court, exercised since Marshall and his colleagues decided in GIBBONS V. OGDEN (1824) that the constitutional power of Congress over commerce among the states implied a negative on state power, even when Congress has not acted, and that the Supreme Court would enforce that implied prohibition. For a generation these commerce clause cases elicited a series of decisions upholding or setting aside state regulations—of quarantine, pilotage, intoxicating liquors, entry fees—by classifying them as either regulations of commerce, and so invalid, or regulations of local health or safety, and so valid as POLICE POWER measures. This effort at classification obscured the process of judgment by treating a conclusory label as if it were a premise for reasoning. A pivotal change in methodology occurred in COOLEY V. BOARD OF WARDENS (1852), a pilotage case where the opinion by Justice BENJAMIN CURTIS recognized that commercial regulation and police power were not mutually exclusive categories, and that decision should turn on an empirical judgment, weighing the necessity of the local law, the seriousness of the impact on commerce, the need for uniformity of treatment, and the possible discriminatory impact on out-of-state enterprise. This kind of scrutiny, and comparable analysis of local taxation when challenged by multistate business, have been staples of Supreme Court adjudication and exemplars for other economic federations struggling to accommodate local interests and those of a union.

The most intensive, acclaimed, and in some quarters questioned, aspects of the Court's work has been the elaboration of fundamental human rights. While in England the great expressions of these rights are found in the writings of philosophers and poets—the secular trinity of John Milton, JOHN LOCKE, and John Stuart Mill—in America the pronouncements are embodied—Jefferson apart—in the judicial opinions of Holmes, Brandeis, Hughes, Stone, ROBERT H. JACKSON, HUGO L. BLACK, and other Justices. The development of a body of CIVIL LIBERTIES guarantees, mainly under the Bill of Rights and the FOURTEENTH AMENDMENT, reached its fullest flowering during the Chief Justiceship of EARL WARREN (1953–1969), though the seeds were planted in the HUGHES COURT.

During the 1930s, while public attention was focused on the Court's struggle with national power over the economy, path-breaking advances were made in a series of decisions applying federal constitutional guarantees against the states. It is more than coincidence that this development occurred at a time of rising totalitarianism abroad. FREEDOM OF THE PRESS and FREEDOM OF ASSOCIATION AND ASSEMBLY were unmistakably put under the protection of the liberty secured by the Fourteenth Amendment in NEAR V. MINNESOTA (1931) and DEJONGE V. OREGON (1937), respectively. The principle that a conviction in a state court following the use of a coerced confession is a violation of DUE PROCESS OF LAW was announced for the first time BROWN V. MISSISSIPPI (1936). A state's duty to afford racial equality in education was sharpened in MISSOURI EX REL. GAINES V. CANADA (1938): it could not be satisfied by resort to a neighboring state. Mayors and governors were subjected to the reach of federal judicial process in HAGUE V. CIO (1939) and *Sterling v. Constantin* (1932), an accountability that came to be important in later contests over desegregation.

If the drama of these seminal developments was largely overlooked, the same cannot be said of the great expansion of civil liberties and CIVIL RIGHTS by the WARREN COURT. The leading decisions have become familiar landmarks. BAKER V. CARR (1962), requiring substantial equality of population in electoral districts within a state, asserted judicial power over what had previously been deemed a POLITICAL QUESTION; Chief Justice Warren regarded it as the most important decision of his tenure, because of its potential for redistributing basic political power. BROWN V. BOARD OF EDUCATION (1954, 1955) was both the culmination and the beginning in the long drive against RACIAL DISCRIMINATION: doctrinally a climax, practically a starting point in the devising of remedies. MIRANDA V. ARIZONA (1966), limiting POLICE INTERROGATION of suspects in custody and giving suspects the RIGHT TO COUNSEL during interrogation, has become a symbol of the Court's intense concern for standards of CRIMINAL PROCEDURE, a concern that has sometimes been viewed as an index to a society's civilization. The EQUAL PROTECTION guarantee, which Justice Holmes in 1927 could call the last refuge of a constitutional lawyer, was revitalized in the service not only of racial minorities but of other stereotyped groups: ALIENS, illegitimates, and women. Freedom of the press was extended well beyond freedom from restraint on publication: In actions for LIBEL brought by PUBLIC FIGURES following NEW YORK TIMES V. SULLIVAN (1964), the defendant publisher would be liable only if he acted with legal malice, that is, with knowledge of the publication's falsity or with reckless disregard for its truth or falsity.

A constitutional RIGHT OF PRIVACY, of uncertain scope, extending beyond the explicit SEARCH AND SEIZURE guarantee to encompass at least certain conjugal intimacies, was established in GRISWOLD V. CONNECTICUT (1965). The religion clauses of the FIRST AMENDMENT were given new vitality in decisions rejecting organized prayer in the public schools, such as ENGEL V. VITALE (1962).

On any measure, it is an impressive performance.

The momentum was somewhat slackened during the first decade and a half of Chief Justice WARREN E. BURGER's tenure, particularly in the areas of criminal procedure and nonestablishment of religion; yet during this period the Court reached the high-water mark of constitutionally protected autonomy in ROE V. WADE (1973), upholding freedom of choice respecting abortion in the first two trimesters of pregnancy.

Criticism of the modern Court has taken diverse directions. Some critics have complained that the Court has been unfaithful to the historic meaning of constitutional provisions. But the argument begs the question of "meaning." If the term signifies denotative meaning, the particular instances that the Framers envisioned as comprehended in the text, the original meaning has indeed been departed from. If, however, the purposive meaning is accepted, and the application does not contradict the language of the text, there is no infidelity. Such an analysis will not disapprove, for example, the "meaning" ascribed to the freedom of the press in the First Amendment.

Another criticism charges defenders of the Court with a double standard: the modern Court is a mirror image of the pre-1937 Court, the judicial vetoes coming now from the left instead of the right. The asserted parallel, however, is inexact. The problem is to identify the appropriate role for judicial review in a representative democracy. The older Court set aside such products of the political process as minimum wage, price control, and tax legislation. The modern Court, by and large, has given its intensive scrutiny to two areas of law that are of peculiarly legitimate concern to the judiciary. One is the field of procedure, in a large sense, civil and criminal. The other is the set of issues concerning representation of interests in the formation of public opinion and lawmaking. This category would include FREEDOM OF SPEECH and press and association, VOTING RIGHTS, education, and the interests of groups underrepresented in the formulation of public policy. This approach gives a certain coherence to constitutional theory: as the commerce clause protects out-of-state enterprise against hostility, open or covert, the Bill of Rights and the Civil War amendments especially protect the political, social, or ethnic "outsider" against official neglect or ostracism.

A more qualified criticism is addressed to two tendencies of the modern Court. One is a perceived disposition to carry a constitutional safeguard to excessive lengths, as in BUCKLEY V. VALEO (1976), which held invalid, in the name of freedom of expression, statutory limits on expenditures by or on behalf of candidates for federal offices. The other, illustrated by the abortion and police interrogation cases, is an inclination, when holding a state law or practice invalid, to prescribe only a single form of corrective that will not offend constitutional standards.

A problem faced by the Court throughout much of its history, one that has again become acute, is the burden of an expanding caseload. In the last hundred years two statutory jurisdictional revisions brought temporary relief. The Circuit Courts of Appeals Act of 1891, by establishing a system of regional appellate courts, assured litigants of one opportunity for review without resort to the Supreme Court. The JUDICIARY ACT OF 1925, sponsored by the Justices themselves and promoted by Chief Justice WILLIAM HOWARD TAFT, made discretionary review by WRIT OF CERTIORARI, instead of APPEAL as of right, the normal mode of access to the Supreme Court.

Each solution, however, has in time become part of the problem. With thirteen courts of appeals, and the burgeoning of federal statutory law, there is a growing incidence of conflicting decisions calling for review. Moreover, the disposition of petitions for certiorari has occupied an increasing amount of the Justices' time, with more than 4,000 filed each term. Of these, approximately 175 are granted and the cases decided with full opinion after oral argument.

A study group appointed under the auspices of the Federal Judicial Center reported in 1972 that the caseload was reaching the saturation point. Certain ameliorative measures had already been taken. The normal time allowed for oral argument had been reduced from an hour to a half hour for each side. The number of law CLERKS had been increased in stages from one to four for each Justice. The study group expressed disquiet at what it viewed as a bureaucratic movement, and recommended the creation of a national court of appeals to review decisions that warranted review but not necessarily by the Supreme Court. Others proposed variations on this plan, notably one or more courts of appeals having specialized jurisdiction, in tax or criminal or regulatory cases. Sixty years after the 1925 act, the problem has not been resolved. And yet without adequate time for reflection, collegial discussion, critical scrutiny, mutual accommodation, and persuasive exposition, the Court cannot function at its best.

At its best, the Court can recall the legal profession and the people to an appreciation of their constitutional heritage, by translating the ideals and practices embodied in an eighteenth-century charter of the Enlightenment into the realities of a modern industrial democracy.

PAUL A. FREUND

Bibliography

BICKEL, ALEXANDER M. 1962 The Least Dangerous Branch. Indianapolis: Bobbs-Merrill.
CONGRESSIONAL QUARTERLY 1981 The Supreme Court and Its Work. Washington, D.C.: Congressional Quarterly.
FREUND, PAUL A. 1961 The Supreme Court of the United States. Cleveland and New York: Meridian Books.
FREUND, PAUL A. and KATZ, STANLEY N. 1971– The Oliver Wendell Holmes Devise History of the Supreme Court of the United States. 11 Vols. New York: Macmillan. The following volumes have been published: vol. I, GOEBEL, JULIUS, JR. 1971 Antecedents and Beginnings to 1801; vol. II, HASKINS, GEORGE L. AND JOHNSON, HERBERT A. 1981 Foundations of Power: John Marshall, 1801–1815; vol. V, SWISHER, CARL B. 1974 The Taney Period, 1836–1864; vols. VI and VII, FAIRMAN, CHARLES 1971 Reconstruction and Reunion, 1864–1888, Part One; 1986 Part Two; vol. IX, BICKEL, ALEXANDER M. and SCHMIDT, BENNO C., JR. 1984 The Judiciary and Responsible Government, 1910–1921.
FRIEDMAN, LEON and ISRAEL, FRED L., eds. 1969–1978 The Justices of the United States Supreme Court, 1789–1969. 5 Vols. New York: Chelsea House.
LEWIS, ANTHONY 1964 Gideon's Trumpet. New York: Random House.
POLLAK, LOUIS H., ed. 1966 The Constitution and the Supreme Court: A Documentary History. 2 Vols. Cleveland: World Publishing Co.
SWINDLER, WILLIAM F. 1970 Court and Constitution in the Twentieth Century: The New Legality, 1932–1968. Indianapolis: Bobbs-Merrill.
WARREN, CHARLES 1926 The Supreme Court in United States History. 2 Vols. Boston: Little, Brown.
WESTIN, ALAN, ed. 1961 The Supreme Court: Views from Inside. New York: Norton.

SUPREME COURT
(Role in American Government)

The Supreme Court is the only court in the United States whose existence is mandated by the Constitution, yet the Constitution designates no number of judges for the Supreme Court and sets no qualifications for judicial service. So far as the Constitution is concerned, the Supreme Court could as readily consist of two or of twenty-two judges, rather than of nine as has been the case since 1870. And so undemanding is the Constitution in setting qualifications for appointment to the Supreme Court that its members could consist entirely of persons not qualified to serve in either House of Congress, for which at least a few minimum standards of eligibility (of age and of CITIZENSHIP) are constitutionally prescribed. The Constitution speaks simply to the vesting of the JUDICIAL POWER OF THE UNITED STATES in "one supreme court, and in such inferior Courts as the Congress may from time to time ordain and establish," but it leaves much else to discretion and a great deal to chance.

The role of the Supreme Court in American government is much like this overall. Some impressions of what the Court's role was meant to be can be gained from what the Constitution says and from the immediate history of 1789, as well as from the categories of JURISDICTION assigned to the Court by Article III. But much of that role is also the product of custom and of practice about which the Constitution itself is silent.

The constitutional text itself suggests several ways of describing the Supreme Court's role, in conformity with Article III's prescriptions of the Court's jurisdiction. The useful jurisdictional distinctions are of four principal kinds, each providing some insight into what the Court was originally expected to do.

First mentioned is the Supreme Court's jurisdiction as a trial court, an ORIGINAL JURISDICTION invocable by certain parties in particular (states and representatives of foreign states) but by no one else. Second is that branch of its appellate jurisdiction applicable also solely because of who the parties are, irrespective of the nature of the dispute between them. Third is the Court's appellate jurisdiction that attaches solely because the case involves a federal statute or treaty of the United States, or arises under ADMIRALTY AND MARITIME LAW, without regard to who the parties may be and whether or not any constitutional question may be involved. Finally, the Court may exercise an appellate jurisdiction over "all cases arising under [the] Constitution," a phrase construed broadly to include any case in which the outcome may be affected by a question of constitutional law. It is the application of this phrase, of course, that tends to fix the Supreme Court's most important role, but as can be seen from the foregoing larger enumeration, it is not by any means the sole business to which the Court was expected to attend.

The role of the Supreme Court as a court of original jurisdiction has been useful but minor. Ordinarily, the Court's small complement of original jurisdiction has merely expedited its speedy examination of certain legal issues raised by states against other states (typically involving boundary or interstate river claims) or against the national government, as in OREGON V. MITCHELL—a 1970 decision holding unconstitutional one portion of an act of Congress that sought to override state voting age restrictions. Because Congress can provide for expedited Supreme Court review of cases originating in other courts, however, it is doubtful whether this feature of Article III has been terribly vital. Its one theoretical importance may be that the original jurisdiction it provides to the states is guaranteed against elimination by Congress—for unlike the Court's appellate jurisdiction, its original jurisdiction is not subject to the "exceptions" clause of Article III.

Dwarfing the Court's role as a court of original jurisdiction is its much larger and more familiar role as the ultimate appellate court in the United States for a vastly greater number and variety of disputes, although the Court is not obliged to review all such cases and in fact hears but a small fraction of those eligible for review. The cases eligible for review, some on APPEAL and a larger number on petition for a WRIT OF CERTIORARI, are divisible into two principal categories: those in which the character of the contesting parties makes the case reviewable, and those in which the nature of the legal issue raised by the case makes the case reviewable.

In the first category of cases within the Court's appellate jurisdiction there are many that raise no constitutional questions and indeed need not raise any kind of federal question. As these cases are within the Court's power of review solely because of the parties, regardless of the subject in dispute between them, they may involve very ordinary legal issues (for example, of contract, tort, or property law) as to which there is no special expertise in the Supreme Court and no obvious reason why they need be considered there. And in practice, they are not reviewed.

Part of the original interest in providing the Supreme Court as the ultimate appellate tribunal in the United States reflected the Framers' desire to provide an appellate court for litigants likely to be sued in hostile jurisdictions—cases, for instance, arising in state courts which nonresident defendants might fear would be inclined to favor local parties as against outsiders. Since the furnishing of lower federal courts (to hear such cases) was left entirely optional with Congress to provide or not provide as it liked, the Supreme Court's appellate jurisdiction even from state court diversity cases was directly provided for in Article III. Nonetheless, in the course of 200 years the felt need for such cases to be heard in the Supreme Court has never materialized—although such cases remain a staple of lower federal court jurisdiction. (Efforts in Congress to repeal this entire category of lower federal court jurisdiction are more than a half-century old, but they have been only partly successful, largely in restricting such cases to those involving sums in excess of $10,000.) In the meantime, however, the Supreme Court does not review such cases and, by act of Congress, it is under no obligation to take them. This particular anticipated role of the Supreme Court, as an active court in hearing appeals in ordinary diversity cases presenting no federal question and implicating no general interest of the United States, has never been significant in fact.

In contrast, the second branch of the Supreme Court's appellate jurisdiction—identified not by the parties but by the nature of the legal questions—remains intensely active. Indeed, the principal role the Court plays today as an appellate court undoubtedly arises almost entirely from this subject matter assignment of appellate jurisdiction of cases involving disputes of national law. In these cases the Court interprets acts of Congress and treaties of the United States as well as the Constitution as the ultimate source of governing law in the United States.

Specifically, these cases may raise any of the following four kinds of basic conflicts: conflicts between claims relying upon mutually exclusive interpretations of concededly valid acts of Congress or treaties of the United States; between constitutional claims of state power and claims of federal power (FEDERAL-ISM conflicts); between constitutional claims by Congress and claims by the President or claims by the judiciary (SEPARATION OF POWERS conflicts); or between constitutional claims of personal right and claims of either state or of national power (personal rights conflicts). A principal function of Article III was to establish the Supreme Court as the ultimate national court of appeals to provide finality and consistency of result in the interpretation and application of all federal and constitutional law in the United States, within the full range of these four fundamental and enduring concerns.

For nearly the first hundred years (1789–1875), almost all appeals to the Supreme Court on such federal questions as these came from state courts rather than from lower federal courts. Not until 1875, in the aftermath of the Civil War, were lower federal courts given any significant original (trial) jurisdiction over private civil cases arising under acts of Congress or treaties of the United States. Since 1875, moreover, many federal question cases still proceed from state courts to the Supreme Court, because reliance on some federal law or on the Constitution often arises only in answer to some claim filed in a state court and thus emerges only by way of defense rather than as the basis of complaint.

The fact that this arrangement of the Court's appellate jurisdiction places the Supreme Court in appellate command over all other courts in the United States in all federal question cases is exactly what makes the Supreme Court supreme. In constitutional matters, for instance, this fact is the basis of Justice ROBERT H. JACKSON's observation, in speaking of the Court, that "[w]e are not final because we are infallible, but we are infallible only because we are final," that is, superior in constitutional authority to review the determinations of other courts and in turn unreviewable by any other court. It likewise animates the 1907 observation by CHARLES EVANS HUGHES (later Chief Justice of the United States). "We are under a Constitution," Hughes acknowledged, "but the Constitution is what the judges say it is," since it is their view and, most important, the Supreme Court's view, that ultimately controls in each case. And even when no constitutional issue is present, but the issue is how an act of Congress shall be interpreted and applied, the finality of the Supreme Court's appellate jurisdiction is equally pivotal; it is the Americanized version of Bishop Hoadley's observation in 1717, in reference to the power of the English courts in interpreting acts of Parliament. "Whoever hath an absolute authority to interpret any written or spoken laws," Hoadley observed, "it is he who is truly the lawgiver, to all intents and purposes, and not the person who first spoke or wrote them." From an early time Americans seem to have believed in the wisdom of reposing in the courts—and ultimately in the Supreme Court—the responsibility of substantive constitutional review, and it seems clear (despite some scholars' qualified doubts) that the Supreme Court was indeed meant to exercise that responsibility. (See JUDICIAL REVIEW.) It is unquestionably this role of substantive constitutional review that marks the special position of the Supreme Court.

The Supreme Court's decisions in constitutional cases may be roughly divided into three kinds, according to which its role in American government is occasionally assessed or described. The three kinds of decisions are these: legitimizing, braking, and catalytic.

A decision is said to be legitimizing whenever the Court examines any act of government on constitutional grounds and finds it not wanting. In holding that the act as applied is in fact authorized by the

Constitution and not offensive to any of its provisions (for example, the BILL OF RIGHTS or the FOURTEENTH AMENDMENT), the Court thus vouches for its constitutional legitimacy. A decision may be called a braking decision whenever its immediate effect is necessarily to arrest the further application of an act of Congress because the Court holds the act either inapplicable or unconstitutional, or whenever OBITER DICTA accompanying the decision serve notice of constitutional barriers in the way of similar legislation. Finally, a decision may be called catalytic when its immediate practical effect is to compel highly significant action of a sort not previously forthcoming from national or state government.

A significant and controversial example of the legitimizing sort is PLESSY V. FERGUSON (1896), the case sustaining certain state racial SEGREGATION laws as not inconsistent with the Fourteenth Amendment, despite intense argument to the contrary. A modern example of the same sort may be FULLILOVE V. KLUTZNICK (1980), a case sustaining a limited form of RACIAL DISCRIMINATION in favor of certain minority contractors as not inconsistent with the Fifth Amendment, despite intense argument as well. In each case, the Court considered a previously untested kind of race-related law. In each, the Supreme Court's decision could be said effectively to have impressed the operative law with a judicial imprimatur of constitutional legitimacy, given that in each case the challenged statute was sustained.

Examples of the braking sort may be found in the Court's early New Deal decisions holding Congress unauthorized by the COMMERCE CLAUSE to supplant state laws with its own much more sweeping and detailed ECONOMIC REGULATIONS. In this instance, the critical decisions of the Court forced a momentary pause in the onrush of legislation, compelling more deliberate attention to what the nation had been and what it meant to become. As it happened, the braking effect of these cases was eventually overcome, but it is nonetheless true that in the meantime the position taken by the Court played a sobering role. In a few other instances, the braking effect of equivalent cases was overcome by formal amendment of the Constitution itself: the SIXTEENTH AMENDMENT, for instance, was adopted principally to overcome the effect of the Court's decision in POLLOCK V. FARMERS' LOAN & TRUST (1895); the Thirteenth Amendment and Fourteenth Amendment displaced the Court's decision in DRED SCOTT V. SANDFORD (1857); and the TWENTY-SIXTH AMENDMENT displaced the decision in *Oregon v. Mitchell.* These reactions are by themselves not an indication that the Court has erred, of course, since

the Constitution itself separates the role of the Court from the formal processes of constitutional modification. (See AMENDING PROCESS.) Any decision in the Supreme Court holding a statute unconstitutional may provide occasion to activate the AMENDING PROCESS provided for in Article V. Amendments by themselves are not proof that the decisions they effectively overrule were necessarily poorly conceived. They may, rather, but mark new Cambrian rings in what is meant to be a living constitution.

An example of a catalytic decision would be one holding certain prison conditions to be so inadequate as to constitute a form of CRUEL AND UNUSUAL PUNISHMENT, such that either the prisoners must be released (which public authorities are loath to do), or large sums must be raised and less congested prisons must be built. The change-forcing nature of the Court's catalytic decision is but descriptive of its practical implications. By itself it thus carries no suggestion that the Court acted from impulse rather than from obligation, in ruling as it did. The same observation may apply equally to the other two categories of decisions.

Thus, in the "legitimizing" decision there is no necessary insinuation that the measure that has been sustained is on that account also necessarily desirable or well-taken legislation; such questions are ordinarily regarded as no proper part of the judicial business. Adjudicated constitutionality properly vouches solely for an act's consistency with the Constitution, which consistency may still leave much to be desired, depending upon one's own point of view and one's feeling of constitutional adequacy. Similarly, it does not follow that an act's adjudicated unconstitutionality necessarily implies its undesirability or, indeed, that there would be anything terribly wrong were the Constitution amended so that similar legislation might subsequently be reenacted and sustained. It means merely that the act does not pass muster under the Constitution as it is and as the judges are oath-bound to apply it until it is altered.

So also with catalytic decisions: such forced change as a particular decision may produce is required simply to bring the conduct of government back within constitutional lines as they are, and not as they need be. As conscientiously applied by the Court, the Constitution thus speaks to such constitutional boundaries as were put in place sometime in the past, from a considered political judgment of the time that such boundaries would be important. The judgment is wholly an inherited one, however, and contemplates the possibility of amendment to cast off such restraints as subsequent extraordinary majorities may find unendurable. Viewed in this way, the Constitution is a device by means of which past generations signal to subsequent generations their cumulative assessment of what sorts of restraints simple majoritarianism needs most. The Supreme Court is the ultimate judicial means by which the integrity of those restraints is secured against the common tendency to think them ill-conceived or obsolete, sustaining them when pressed by proper litigants with suitable standing, until instructed by amendment to acknowledge the change. It is a signal responsibility and an unusual power—one which few other national supreme courts have been given.

On the other hand, the phrases "legitimizing," "braking," and "catalytic" are not always used so descriptively, however well they capture the by-products of the Court's work. Rather, they are sometimes used prescriptively, and thus in an entirely different sense. In this different usage they presume to provide a more jurisprudential blueprint for the role of the Supreme Court: that it is appropriate for the Court actively to serve these three functions politically as it were, and to involve the Constitution only instrumentally in their service. Employed in this different locution, they are phrases used to express faith in a specific kind of judicial activism, according to which the right role of the Court is to identify the needs of efficient and humane government and to adjust its own adjudications accordingly.

In this view, it is in fact the proper role of the Supreme Court to legitimate (by holding constitutional) such laws as circumstances persuade it ought not be disapproved, to brake (by adverse construction or by holding unconstitutional) such developments as it determines to have been precipitously taken or otherwise to have been ill-advised, and to catalyze (by artful action) such changes it deems highly desirable but unlikely to be forthcoming from government unless the Court so requires. The persuasive justification for the Supreme Court lies in what it can do best as a distinct institution, in this view, and only secondarily in adhering to the Constitution. And what the Supreme Court can do better than others is to compensate for such gaps as it finds in the Constitution or in the political process, and to take such measured steps as it can to repair them. Accordingly, the more appropriate role of the Supreme Court is to conduct itself institutionally as best it can to contribute actively to a better political quality of life in the United States: in deciding which cases to hear, when to hear them, on what grounds to decide them, and how to make them come out in ways most in keeping with these three vital functions of granting legitimacy to the

good, putting brakes on the bad, and compelling such changes as are overdue.

As an original jurisprudence of proposed judicial role, this perspective on the Supreme Court has had considerable occasional support. In the concrete, moreover, there is good reason to believe that certain Justices—probably a nontrivial number—have embraced it in selected aspects of their own work. At the least, there are a large number of constitutional decisions that appear to reflect its view of what judges should seek to do, as indeed some Justices have virtually absorbed it as an articulate feature of proper judicial review; their decisions seem sometimes to be based on little else.

Still, and for obvious reasons, it remains deeply problematic, for at bottom it would have the judges struggle against the obligation of their oaths. Insofar as cases such as *Plessy* or *Fullilove* were to any extent self-conscious efforts by a Supreme Court majority simply to legitimate race-based arrangements it thought desirable, and not decisions reporting a difficult judicial conclusion respecting the lack of constitutional restrictions on the legislative acts at issue, for instance, it is doubtful whether the "legitimacy" thus established was appropriate or, indeed, constitutionally authorized. Likewise, insofar as the early New Deal cases were to any extent simply a deliberate institutional attempt by the majority Justices to arrest what they thought to be ill-advised varieties of market intervention, and not decisions reflecting an attentive interpretation respecting the limits of Congress's commerce power, it is debatable whether the "braking" thus applied was appropriate or authorized. So, too, with such decisions as may be catalytic, but which may be driven more by a judicial desire to see changes made than by a mere firm resolve that the Constitution shall be obeyed.

Without doubt, however, the tendency to urge the Supreme Court to compose its interpretations of the Constitution in subordination to allegedly significant social tasks remains widespread. Moreover, the malleability of many constitutional clauses invites it, and the political staffing mechanism (provided by Article III) for selecting the judges may appear obliquely to legitimate it. The tendency to rationalize its propriety is deeply entrenched.

Even so, the conscious treatment of constitutional clauses as but textual or pretextual occasions for judicial legitimation, braking, or social catalysis, does tend to pit the Court against itself in its disjunction of fundamentally incompatible roles. The resulting tension has split the Court virtually from the beginning. It divides it even now: between these two visions of the Court, as a professional court first of all or as a political court first of all, lie two centuries of unsteady swings of actual judicial review. The history of the Supreme Court in this respect but reiterates a classic antinomy in American constitutional law. It doubtless reflects the conflicts Americans tend to sense within themselves—as to what role they genuinely wish this Court to fulfill.

With certain highly notable exceptions (including West Germany, Japan, Australia, and most recently Canada), the written CONSTITUTIONS of most modern nation-states serve merely as each nation's explanation of itself as a government. Such a constitution typically presents a full plan of government, a statement of its purposes and powers, and an ample declaration of rights. Yet, unlike the Constitution of the United States, such a constitution cannot be invoked by litigants and does not require or even permit courts of law to use it as against which all other laws may be examined. It is, rather, a nonjusticiable document. It is intended to be taken seriously (at least this is the case generally), but only in the political sense that legislative and executive authorities are meant to reconcile their actions with the constitution at the risk of possible popular disaffection should they stray too far from what the constitution provides. Whether the authorities have thus strayed, however, and what consequences shall follow if they have, is not deemed to be the appropriate business of courts of law.

The enormous distinction of American constitutional law has thus rested in the very different and exceptional role of the judiciary, from the most unprepossessing county courts through the hierarchy of the entire federal court system. The unique role of the Supreme Court has been its own role as the ultimate appellate court in reference to that judiciary, most critically in all constitutional cases. The arrangement thus established does not lessen the original obligation of other government officials separately to take care that their own actions are consistent with the Constitution, but it is meant to provide—as effectively as human institutions can arrange—an additional and positive check. When official action is not consistent with the Constitution, as ultimately determined under the Supreme Court's authority, the courts are given both the power and the obligation to intercede: to interpose such authority as they have and to provide such redress as appears to be due. Judged even by international standards, this is an ample role. It is not this role that now appears fairly open to question, moreover, but rather the definition of role that would assume something more or accept something less.

WILLIAM VAN ALSTYNE

Bibliography

ABRAHAM, HENRY J. 1986 *The Judicial Process.* 5th ed. New York: Oxford University Press.

AGRESTO, JOHN 1984 *The Supreme Court and Constitutional Democracy.* Ithaca, N.Y.: Cornell University Press.

BICKEL, ALEXANDER M. 1962 *The Least Dangerous Branch: The Supreme Court at the Bar of Politics.* Indianapolis, Ind.: Bobbs-Merrill.

COX, ARCHIBALD 1976 *The Role of the Supreme Court in American Government.* New York: Oxford University Press.

ELY, JOHN HART 1980 *Democracy and Distrust: A Theory of Judicial Review.* Cambridge, Mass.: Harvard University Press.

FREUND, PAUL 1961 *The Supreme Court of the United States.* Cleveland, Ohio: World Publishing Company.

HOROWITZ, DONALD L. 1977 *The Courts and Social Policy.* Washington, D.C.: The Brookings Institution.

JACKSON, ROBERT H. 1955 *The Supreme Court in the American System of Government.* New York: Harper & Row.

MASON, ALPHEUS THOMAS 1979 *The Supreme Court from Taft to Burger.* 3d ed. Baton Rouge: Louisiana State University Press.

MCCLOSKEY, ROBERT G. 1960 *The American Supreme Court.* Chicago: University of Chicago Press.

WOLFE, CHRISTOPHER 1986 *The Rise of Modern Judicial Review.* New York: Basic Books.

SUPREME COURT, 1789–1801

On January 8, 1801, twelve days before President JOHN ADAMS appointed JOHN MARSHALL as Chief Justice, a Jeffersonian newspaper reported: "JOHN JAY, after having thru' decay of age become incompetent to discharge the duties of Governor, has been appointed to the sinecure of Chief Justice of the United States. That the Chief Justiceship is a sinecure needs no other evidence than that in one case the duties were discharged by one person who resided at the same time in England, and by another during a year's residence in France." The one in France was OLIVER ELLSWORTH, sent there by President Adams as a special ambassador to negotiate peace. Ellsworth had recently resigned, and Jay, whose appointment as Ellsworth's successor had been confirmed by the Senate, had himself been the first Chief Justice, whom President GEORGE WASHINGTON had sent to England to negotiate a treaty that bore Jay's name. The chief justiceship was no sinecure: although the Supreme Court then met for only two short terms a year, the Justices also served as circuit court judges, and riding circuit was extremely arduous. When Jay was offered the position again, he declined it because of the circuit responsibilities and because the Court had neither "the energy, weight and dignity" necessary for it to support the national government nor "the public confidence and respect."

Jay's judgment was harsh although the Court did have problems, some of its own making. All the Justices were Federalists; their decisions EN BANC or on circuit seemed partisan—pro-Administration, pro-English, or procreditor—and they presided at trials under the infamous Sedition Act, whose constitutionality they affirmed. But the Court was not responsible for most of its difficulties. It had no official reporter (ALEXANDER J. DALLAS's unofficial reports first appeared in 1798) and the press publicized only a few of the Court's decisions. The public knew little about the Court, and even members of its own bar were unfamiliar with its decisions. Nothing better symbolizes the nation's neglect of the Court than the fact that when the United States government moved to Washington, D.C., in late 1800, the Court had been forgotten. Not only did it lack a building; it had no courtroom. Congress hastily provided a small committee room in the basement of the Senate wing of the Capitol for the Court to meet.

The Court's beginnings were hardly more auspicious, however distinguished its membership. At its first term in February 1790 it had nothing to do except admit attorneys to its bar, and it shortly adjourned. It began as a court without a reporter, litigants, a docket, appeals, or decisions to make. It was chiefly an appellate court whose APPELLATE JURISDICTION scarcely matched the breadth of the JUDICIAL POWER OF THE UNITED STATES stated in Article III. Congress in the JUDICIARY ACT OF 1789 had authorized the Court to review state court decisions that denied claims based on federal law, including the Constitution. Review was not authorized when the state court upheld a claim of federal right. The system of appellate jurisdiction thus permitted the Supreme Court to maintain federal law's supremacy but not its uniform interpretation. The Court's review of civil decisions of the lower federal courts was limited to cases involving more than $2,000 in controversy, and it could not review criminal cases from those courts. Congress had stingily authorized the Court to hear cases in its appellate capacity in order to keep it weak, to prevent centralization of judicial powers, to preserve the relative importance of state courts, and to insulate the Court from many matters that concerned ordinary citizens. For its first two years it heard no cases, and it made no substantive decisions until 1793. Its docket never got crowded. Dallas reported less than seventy cases for the pre-Marshall Court, and

fewer than ten percent of them involved constitutional law. The Court was then first a COMMON LAW court, second a court of ADMIRALTY AND MARITIME JURISDICTION.

Although its members were able, the pre-Marshall Court had difficulty attracting and keeping them. When Marshall became Chief Justice, only WILLIAM CUSHING of the original six Justices appointed by Washington remained. Robert H. Harrison, one of the original six, was confirmed but declined appointment, preferring instead the chancellorship of Maryland. JAMES IREDELL accepted Harrison's place, so that the first Court consisted of Chief Justice Jay and Justices Cushing, JOHN BLAIR, JOHN RUTLEDGE, JAMES WILSON, and Iredell. Rutledge performed his circuit duties but had never attended a session of the Court when he resigned after two years to become chief justice of South Carolina. CHARLES C. PINCKNEY and Edward Rutledge declined appointment to John Rutledge's seat, preferring to serve in their state legislature. THOMAS JOHNSON accepted that seat but resigned it in less than two years because circuit riding was too strenuous. WILLIAM PATERSON succeeded him. The February 1794 term was Jay's last. That he reentered New York politics after negotiating JAY'S TREATY says something about the Court's prestige at the time. So too does the fact that ALEXANDER HAMILTON preferred private practice to the chief justiceship. At that point, John Rutledge, who had quit the Court, applied for the post vacated by Jay. Washington appointed Rutledge, who attended the August 1795 term of the Court when it decided only two cases. The Senate, having reconvened, rejected him because of his opposition to Jay's Treaty. Washington offered the chief justiceship to PATRICK HENRY who declined it. The President then named Justice Cushing, whom the Senate confirmed; but he too declined, preferring to remain Associate Justice. In 1796, Oliver Ellsworth became Chief Justice but quit after four years. John Blair retired early in 1796 and Washington again had to fill a vacancy on the Court. After EDMUND RANDOLPH refused the position, SAMUEL CHASE accepted. In 1798, Wilson became the first Justice to die in office. RICHARD PETERS refused to be considered for the position, and John Marshall also declined. Adams then appointed BUSHROD WASHINGTON, and after Iredell died in 1798, he appointed ALFRED MOORE, who resigned within five years. When Ellsworth resigned and Jay declined reappointment, even though the Senate confirmed him, Adams turned to Marshall. The rapid turnover in personnel during the Court's first decade did not ease its work or enhance its reputation.

Jeffersonians grumbled about the Court's Federalist constitutional theories, but Jay kept his Court out of politics and established its independence from the other branches of the government. That achievement and the Court's identification of its task as safeguarding the supreme law of the land kept the Court a viable institution, despite its many problems during the first decade, and laid the groundwork for the achievements of the MARSHALL COURT.

Late in 1790, Virginia's legislature denounced as unconstitutional the bill for national assumption of state debts. Washington allowed Hamilton to send a copy of the Virginia resolves to Jay and to inquire whether the various branches of the government should employ their "collective weight . . . in exploding [Virginia's STRICT CONSTRUCTION] principles." Hamilton warned that Virginia had shown "the first symptom of a spirit which must either be killed or it will kill the Constitution of the United States." However, Jay, who privately advised Washington and drafted his PROCLAMATION OF NEUTRALITY, recognized the difference between a judicial pronouncement and an extrajudicial one. The Court, strongly believing in the principle of SEPARATION OF POWERS, would not express ex officio opinions except in judicial cases before it. Jay calmly declined the executive's invitation.

Similar principles motivated the Justices when confronted by Congress's Invalid Pensioners' Act of 1792 which required the circuit courts to pass on the pension applications of disabled veterans, subject to review by the secretary of war and Congress. Justices Wilson and Blair together with Judge Peters on circuit in the district of Pennsylvania, having refused to pass on an application from one Hayburn, explained their conduct in a letter to the President. They could not proceed because first, the business directed by the statute was not judicial in nature, there being no constitutional authority for it, and second, because the possible revision of the Court's judgment by the other branches of government would be "radically inconsistent with the independence" of the judiciary. In their circuits, Jay, Cushing, and Iredell similarly explained that a judicial decision must be a final decision. HAYBURN'S CASE (1792), which was not really a "case" and in which nothing was judicially decided, was important because the Court, in Wilson's words, affirmed "a principle important to freedom," that the judicial branch must be independent of the other branches.

Similarly, Jay established another principle vital to the Court's independent, judicial, and nonpolitical character when he declined Washington's request for an ADVISORY OPINION. That request arose out of apparent conflicts between American treaty obligations to France and the Proclamation of Neutrality. The French commissioned privateers in American ports and established prize courts to condemn vessels captured by those privateers. Washington sought the Court's opinion on twenty-nine questions involving international law and treaty interpretation, in connection with the French practices. Jay, relying again on the principle of separation of powers, observed that the Court should not "extra-judicially" decide questions that might come before it in litigation. Thus, by preserving its purely judicial character, the Court was free to decide some of those questions when real cases posed them. From the beginning, the Court staked its power and prestige on its special relationship to the supreme law of the land, which it safeguarded, expounded, and symbolized.

The pre-Marshall Court also exercised the power of JUDICIAL REVIEW. The Justices on circuit quickly held state acts unconstitutional for violating the supreme law of the land. Jay and Cushing on circuit in the district of Connecticut held that that state, by adversely affecting debts owed to British creditors, had violated the treaty of peace with Britain; Iredell in Georgia and Paterson in South Carolina made similar decisions. The Justices held that United States treaties were superior to state laws. The Supreme Court confronted the issue in WARE V. HYLTON (1796). With Iredell alone dissenting, the Court rejected the arguments of John Marshall, making his only appearance before the Justices, as counsel for the debtor interests of Virginia. He opposed "those who wish to impair the sovereignty of Virginia" and contended first that the Constitution had not authorized the Court to question the validity of state statutes and, second, that a treaty could not annul them. SERIATIM opinions by Chase, Paterson, Wilson, and Cushing held otherwise.

In *Clarke* v. *Harwood* (1797) the Court ruled that *Ware* "settled" the question before it. *Clarke* was the Court's first decision against the validity of a state act in a case arising on a WRIT OF ERROR to a state court under section 25 of the Judiciary Act of 1789. Section 25 authorized the Court to reverse or affirm state decisions that denied rights claimed under United States treaties. Maryland's high court, relying on a state statute sequestering debts owed to British creditors, had barred a claim based on the treaty of peace with Britain. By reversing the Maryland court, the Supreme Court in effect voided the state act. However, the Court rarely heard cases on a writ of error to a state court. Indeed, it had not decided its first such case until shortly before *Clarke*. In *Olney v. Arnold* (1796) the Court had reversed a Rhode Island decision that misconstrued a revenue act of Congress. The Court's power of reviewing state decisions under Section 25 did not become controversial until 1814. (See MARTIN V. HUNTER'S LESSEE, 1816.) During the Court's first decade, judicial review of state legislation was uncontested, and it was exercised.

On circuit the Justices also struck down state acts as violating the CONTRACT CLAUSE of the Constitution. The first such decision occurred in 1792 in CHAMPION AND DICKASON V. CASEY, which voided a Rhode Island state law. Given the hullaballoo in that state when its own judiciary was suspected of having voided a state act in TREVETT V. WEEDEN (1787), the meek acceptance of the 1792 decision showed the legitimacy of judicial review over the states.

In HYLTON V. UNITED STATES (1796) the Court for the first time determined the constitutionality of an act of Congress, ruling that an EXCISE on carriages, not being a DIRECT TAX, was valid even if not apportioned among the states. Those hoping for the Court to hold the federal excise unconstitutional were Jeffersonians; they did not then or at any time during the Court's first decade challenge the legitimacy of the Court's power to refuse to enforce an unconstitutional statute. Until the debate on the repeal of the JUDICIARY ACT OF 1801 (see JUDICIARY ACTS OF 1802), scarcely anyone opposed judicial review, whether over state or over congressional legislation. *Hayburn's Case* in 1792 was misunderstood throughout the nation. Not only did Attorney General Randolph believe that the Court had annulled an act of Congress; so did Congress. The House established an investigating committee, "this being the first instance in which a Court of Justice had declared a law of Congress unconstitutional." Jeffersonians gleefully praised the Justices and hoped the Court would extend the precedent by holding unconstitutional other congressional legislation that promoted Hamilton's economic programs. Later, Jeffersonians in Sedition Act trials sought to persuade the Justices on circuit that they should declare the statute void. Repeatedly during the first decade, bills arose in Congress that provoked members in both houses to state that the Court should and would hold them unconstitutional. The way to the doctrine of judicial review announced in MARBURY V. MADISON (1803) was well paved, and the opposition to the Court's opinion did not derive from its assumption of a power to void an act of Congress.

Another major theme in the work of the Court during its first decade was nationalism. Once again, the Marshall Court built on what the Jay and Ellsworth Courts had first shaped. The early Courts helped vindicate the national character of the United States government, maintain the supremacy of the nation over the states, and keep the states from undermining the new constitutional system. On circuit duty the Justices frequently lectured federal GRAND JURIES, inculcating doctrines from THE FEDERALIST, and these grand jury charges were well publicized in the newspapers. In one of his charges, Jay, in 1790, having declared, "We had become a Nation," explained why national tribunals became necessary for the interpretation and execution of national law, especially in a nation accustomed only to state courts and state policies. Circuit court opinions striking down state laws in violation of the contract clause or federal treaties preached nationalism and national supremacy. Many of the criminal prosecutions before the federal circuit courts during the first decade were connected with national suppression of the WHISKEY REBELLION and the FRIES REBELLION. Similarly, prosecutions under the Sedition Act were intended to vindicate the reputations of Congress and the President.

The development of a FEDERAL COMMON LAW OF CRIMES, expanding the jurisdiction of the national courts, fit the nationalist pattern. Whether the courts could try nonstatutory offenses was a question that first arose in Henfield's case (1793). Wilson maintained that an American citizen serving on a French privateer commissioned in an American port and attacking ships of England, with whom the United States was at peace, had committed an indictable offense under the Proclamation of Neutrality, the law of nations, and the treaty with England, even though Congress had not made his act a crime.

The same nationalist pattern unified several of the Court's opinions in cases dealing with various issues. In CHISHOLM V. GEORGIA (1793) the Court's holding, that its jurisdiction extended to suits against a state by citizens of another state, was founded on nationalist principles as well as on the text of Article III. Wilson, for example, began with the principles that the people of the United States form a nation, making ridiculous the "haughty notions of state independence, state SOVEREIGNTY, and state supremacy." "As to the purposes of the Union," he said, "therefore, Georgia is not a sovereign state." Jay's opinion also stressed "the national character" of the United States and the "inexpediency" of allowing state courts to decide questions that involved the performance of national treaties. The denunciation of the Court for its "consolidation of the Union" and its "annihilation of the sovereignty of the States" led to the ELEVENTH AMENDMENT, which was intended to nullify *Chisholm*.

In *Glass v. Sloop Betsy* (1794) the Court supported

the government's neutrality policy by ruling that France, after capturing a neutral ship, could not hold or award her as a prize in an American port. Only the United States courts could determine the lawfulness of prizes brought into its ports, and no foreign nation controlled its admiralty law or could subvert American rights under international law. In *Penhallow v. Doane* (1795) the Court resolved an old dispute over the ownership of a prize. One party's claims relied on decisions of a New Hampshire court, the other's on a decision of a prize court established by the old Congress of the Confederation. Paterson, in the Supreme Court's principal opinion, upheld the lower federal courts, which had decided against the state court and claimed jurisdiction. No nation, he said, had recognized the states as sovereign for the purpose of awarding prizes. The old Congress had been the supreme council of the nation and center of the Union, he claimed, whose sovereignty was approved by the people of America and recognized by foreign nations. The federal courts succeeded to that sovereignty in prize matters. New Hampshire angrily remonstrated against the "destruction" of its sovereignty but the Court's ruling prevailed.

Its decision in *Hylton v. United States* gave life to the government's revenue powers. When the Court upheld federal treaties as paramount to state laws, in *Ware v. Hylton* (1796), Chase, in the principal opinion for the Court, indulged in fanciful nationalism when declaring, "There can be no limitation on the power of the people of the United States. By their authority the State Constitutions were made."

Other notable cases of the first decade were VAN HORNE'S LESSEE V. DORRANCE (1794) and CALDER V. BULL (1798), in which the Court laid the foundation for the judicial doctrine of VESTED RIGHTS, which it developed further in contract clause and HIGHER LAW decisions during Marshall's chief justiceship. Although the Court was left out of the planning for the new national capital, it had been enunciating doctrines—of judicial review, national supremacy, and vested rights—that helped shape the United States and would in time make the judicial branch of government impossible to ignore.

LEONARD W. LEVY

Bibliography

CURRIE, DAVID P. 1981 The Constitution in the Supreme Court: 1789–1801. *University of Chicago Law Review* 48:819–885.
GOEBEL, JULIUS 1971 *Antecedents and Beginnings.* Vol. I of the *Oliver Wendell Holmes Devise History of the Supreme Court,* ed. Paul Freund. New York: Macmillan.
HAINES, CHARLES GROVE 1944 *The Role of the Supreme Court in American Government and Politics, 1789–1835.* Berkeley: University of California Press.
HENDERSON, DWIGHT F. 1971 *Courts for a New Nation.* Washington, D.C.: Public Affairs Press.
WARREN, CHARLES 1923 *The Supreme Court in United States History.* Vol. I. Boston: Little, Brown.

SUPREME COURT PRACTICE

The SUPREME COURT is the only judicial body created by the Constitution. Article III, Section 1, specifies that "The JUDICIAL POWER OF THE UNITED STATES, shall be vested in one supreme Court, and in such inferior Courts as the Congress may from time to time ordain and establish." The judges of that "one supreme Court," like the judges of the inferior courts created by Congress, are to hold their offices "during GOOD BEHAVIOUR" and to suffer no diminution of compensation during their continuance in office. Supreme Court Justices can be impeached, however. And it is not constitutionally clear that their "good Behaviour" term of office is the equivalent of a life term, as generally thought.

In practice, this "one supreme Court" has always acted as a unitary body. That means that the Court never divides into panels or groups of Justices for purposes of resolving matters submitted to the Court. All petitions and briefs are circulated to, and considered by, all participating Justices; and all Court decisions are rendered on behalf of the Court as a unit of nine Justices.

Article III of the Constitution, in establishing the judicial institution known as the Supreme Court, vests in the Court two basic kinds of jurisdiction: ORIGINAL JURISDICTION and APPELLATE JURISDICTION. The Court's original jurisdiction is its power to decide certain cases and controversies in the first instance. Its appellate jurisdiction is its power to review certain cases and controversies decided in the first instance by lower courts.

In COHENS V. VIRGINIA (1821), Chief Justice JOHN MARSHALL stated that the Court "must decide" a case before it that is properly within one of these two areas of jurisdiction, and that the Court has "no more right to decline the exercise of jurisdiction which is given, than to usurp that which is not given . . . [either of which] would be treason to the Constitution." But in the Court's judicial world, Marshall's proposition is no longer universally true, if it ever was. The modern need to control and limit the voluminous number of cases clamoring for review has forced the Court to resist demands that every facet of the Court's vested jurisdiction be exercised. Limitations of time and human energy simply do not permit the luxury of resolving every dispute that comes before the Court. Notions of judicial prudence and sound discretion, given these limitations, have thus become dominant in the Court's selection of those relatively few cases it feels it can afford to review in a plenary fashion and to resolve the merits. Such factors are evident in the Court's control of both its original docket and its appellate docket.

Section 2 of Article III specifies that the Supreme Court "shall have original jurisdiction" in all cases "affecting Ambassadors, other public Ministers and Consuls, and those in which a State shall be Party." Compared with cases on the appellate docket, cases on the original docket are quite few in number. Indeed, cases involving ambassadors, ministers, and consuls have never been common and have virtually disappeared from the original docket. The typical original case has thus become that in which a state is the plaintiff or defendant; most frequent are suits between two or more states over boundaries and water rights, suits that cannot appropriately be handled by any other tribunal. States have also sued each other over state financial obligations, use of natural resources, multistate domiciliary and escheat problems, breaches of contracts between states, and various kinds of injuries to the public health and welfare of the complaining state.

States can also invoke the Court's original jurisdiction to sue private nonresident citizens, or ALIENS, for alleged injuries to the sovereign interests of the complaining state. And a state may bring such suits on behalf of all its citizens to protect the economy and natural resources of the state, as well as the health and welfare of the citizens. The ELEVENTH AMENDMENT bars an original action against a defendant state brought by a private plaintiff who is a citizen of another state; and the sovereign immunity principle recognized by that Amendment also bars such an action by a citizen of the defendant state. Because that amendment does not apply to the federal sovereign as plaintiff, the United States can bring an original action in the Supreme Court against a defendant state. All cases brought by a state against a private party defendant, however, fall within the nonexclusive category of the Court's original jurisdiction; such suits can alternatively be brought in some other federal or state court. The Court in recent years has sought to reduce its original docket workload by rejecting some nonexclusive causes of action and requiring the parties to proceed in an available alternative forum.

Original cases often involve factual disputes. In processing such cases, the Court considers itself the equivalent of a federal trial court, though with significant differences. The Court's rules and procedures in this respect are not very specific, and practices may vary from case to case. The case starts with a motion for leave to file a complaint, a requirement that permits the Court to consider and resolve jurisdictional and prudential objections. If the Court denies the motion for leave to file, the case terminates. If the motion is granted, the complaint is ordered filed, the defendant files an answer, and in most instances a trial ensues.

The Justices themselves do not conduct trials in original cases. Instead, they appoint a member of the bar or a retired lower court judge to serve as a special master. The special master then takes evidence, hears witnesses, makes fact-findings, and recommends legal conclusions. But all rulings, findings, and conclusions of the special master are subject to review by the Court. That review occurs after parties aggrieved by the special master's actions have filed exceptions thereto; all parties then brief and orally argue the exceptions before the entire Court, which decides the case by written opinion. A complicated case may require more than one hearing before the special master and more than one opinion by the Court, prolonging the case for years.

The Court itself has admitted that it is "ill-equipped for the task of factfinding and so forced, in original cases, awkwardly to play the role of factfinder without actually presiding over the introduction of evidence." Original cases take away valuable time and attention from the Court's main mission, the exercise of its appellate jurisdiction, where the Court serves as the prime overseer of important matters of federal constitutional and statutory law. The Court is thus increasingly disposed to construe its original jurisdiction narrowly, exercising that jurisdiction only where the parties cannot secure an initial resolution of their controversy in another tribunal. If there is such an alternative proceeding, the Court prefers to REMAND the parties to the lower court and to deal with any important issues in the case on review of the lower court's determination.

The Court's appellate jurisdiction is also defined and vested by Article III, Section 2. That jurisdiction extends to all categories of CASES AND CONTROVERSIES, decided in the first instance by lower federal courts or state courts, that fall within the JUDICIAL POWER OF THE UNITED STATES. Those categories include: cases arising under the Constitution, laws, and treaties of the United States; cases affecting ambassadors, ministers, and consuls; cases of ADMIRALTY AND MARITIME JURISDICTION; controversies to which the United States is a party; controversies between two or more states; and controversies between a state and citizens of another state, between citizens of different states, between citizens of the same state claiming lands under grants of different states, or between a state or its citizens and foreign states or citizens. The Court's appellate jurisdiction extends "both as to Law and Fact, with such Exceptions, and under such Regulations as the Congress shall make."

The exceptions clause in Section 2 contains within it a constitutional enigma, as yet unsolved. The problem is the extent of Congress's power to control and limit the Supreme Court's appellate jurisdiction. The Court has never held that its appellate jurisdiction is coterminous with the Section 2 categories of judicial power. Consistently since *Wiscart v. Dauchy* (1796) the Court has said, albeit often by way of OBITER DICTUM, that it can exercise appellate jurisdiction only to the extent permitted by acts of Congress, and that a legislative denial of jurisdiction may be implied from a failure by Congress to make an affirmative grant of jurisdiction. The Court, in other words, assumes that its appellate jurisdiction comes from statutes, not directly from Section 2 of Article III. The assumption is that Congress cannot add to the constitutional definitions of appellate jurisdiction, but that Congress can subtract from or make exceptions to those definitions.

It is clear that Congress has made broad statutory grants of jurisdiction to the Court, though not to the full extent permitted by Section 2. These affirmative grants have always been sufficient to permit the Court to fulfill its essential function of interpreting and applying the Constitution and of insuring the supremacy of federal law. So far, the statutory omissions and limitations have not hobbled the performance of that function.

At the same time, periodic proposals have been made in Congress to use the exceptions clause to legislate certain exclusions from the appellate jurisdiction previously granted by Congress. Such proposals usually spring from displeasure with Court decisions dealing with specific constitutional matters. The proponents would simply excise those areas of appellate jurisdiction that permit the Court to render the objectionable decisions. Many commentators contend that the exceptions clause was not designed to authorize Congress to strip the Court of power to perform its essential function of overseeing the development of constitutional doctrines and guarantees. Objections are also raised that such legislative excisions are mere subterfuges for overruling constitutional rights established by the Court, a most serious infringement of the separation of powers doctrine. Because no jurisdictional excisions of this broad nature have been enacted, the Court has yet to speak to this constitutional conundrum. (See JUDICIAL SYSTEM.)

Whatever the outer limits of the exceptions clause, Congress since 1789 has vested in the Court broad appellate power to review lower court decisions that fall within the constitutional "case or controversy" categories. Statutes permit the Court to review virtually all decisions of lower federal appellate courts, as well as a limited number of decisions of federal trial courts. And Congress has from the start given the Court jurisdiction to review decisions of the highest state courts that deal with federal constitutional, treaty, or statutory matters.

An ingredient of most jurisdictional statutes are legislative directions as to the mode by which the Court's appellate powers are to be invoked. In modern times, most lower court decisions are made reviewable by way of WRIT OF CERTIORARI or, in a declining number of specialized instances, by way of APPEAL. Congress permits the Court to issue its own extraordinary writs, such as HABEAS CORPUS or MANDAMUS, and to review certain matters not otherwise reviewable on certiorari or appeal; and there is a rarely used authorization for lower federal appellate court CERTIFICATION of difficult questions to be answered by the Supreme Court.

At COMMON LAW, the term "certiorari" means an original writ commanding lower court judges or officers to certify and transfer the record of the lower court proceedings in a case under review by a higher court. In the Supreme Court lexicon, the common law meaning of the term has been modified and expanded. Certiorari refers generally to the entire process of discretionary review by the Supreme Court of a lower court decision. Such review is sought by filing a petition for writ of certiorari. That document sets forth in short order the reasons why the questions presented by the decision below are so nationally important that the Court should review the case and resolve those questions on the merits. In most cases, the record in the court below is not routinely filed in the Court along with the petition.

Each Justice, after reviewing the petition for certiorari, the brief in opposition, and the opinion below, makes his or her own subjective assessment as to the appropriateness of plenary review by the entire Court. Such review is granted only if at least four Justices vote to grant the petition, a practice known as the RULE OF FOUR. If the petition is granted, a formal order to that effect is entered; copies of the order are sent to the parties and to the court below, which is then requested to transmit a certified copy of the record. But at no time does any writ of certiorari issue from the Court. The parties proceed thereafter to brief and argue orally the questions presented in the petition.

An appeal, on the other hand, refers to a theoretically obligatory type of review by the Supreme Court. That means that once the appeal is properly filed and docketed, the Court must somehow consider and dispose of the case on its merits. There is said to be no discretion to refuse to make such a decision on the merits of the appeal, which serves to distinguish an appeal from a certiorari case.

To invoke the Court's review powers by way of appeal, the aggrieved party first files a short notice of appeal in the lower court and then dockets the appeal in the Supreme Court by filing a document entitled "jurisdictional statement." Apart from the different title, a jurisdictional statement is remarkably like a petition for writ of certiorari. Like a petition, the jurisdictional statement sets forth briefly the reasons why the issues are so substantial, or important, "as to require plenary consideration, with briefs on the merits and oral argument, for their resolution." The Rule of Four is followed in considering whether to grant plenary consideration of an appeal. Such a grant takes the form of an order to the effect that "probable jurisdiction is noted," although if there remains any question as to whether the case complies with the technical jurisdictional requirements of an appeal, the order is changed to read: "further consideration of the question of jurisdiction is postponed to the hearing of the case on the merits." The appeal then follows the pattern of a certiorari case with respect to obtaining the record from the lower court(s), briefing the questions presented, and arguing orally before the Court.

As if to underscore the similarity between a jurisdictional statement and a petition for writ of certiorari, Congress has directed the Court, in situations where a party has "improvidently" taken an appeal "where the proper mode of review is by petition for certiorari," to consider and act on the jurisdictional statement as if it were a petition for writ of certiorari, and then either granting or denying certiorari. Thus a party cannot be prejudiced by seeking the wrong mode of Supreme Court review.

There is, however, one historical and confusing difference in the Court's summary disposition of certiorari cases and appeals, a difference springing from the notion that the Court is obliged to dispose of all appeals on their merits. When a petition for writ of certiorari is denied, the order denying the petition has no precedential value. It means only that fewer than four Justices, or perhaps none at all, want to hear and decide the merits of the questions presented. That is the end of the case.

But when fewer than four Justices wish to hear an appeal in a plenary manner, the long-held theory is that the Court is still compelled to dispose of the appeal on the merits of the questions presented. To comply with this theory, which is judge-made and not dictated by Congress, the Court has constructed a number of one-line orders, any one of which can be used to dismiss or dispose of the appeal without further briefing or oral argument. A typical order of this nature, used particularly in appeals from state court decisions, reads: "the appeal is dismissed for want of a substantial FEDERAL QUESTION." Such summary orders, which are devoid of explanation of the insubstantiality of the question involved, consistently have been held to be precedents. The Court has said that they must be understood and followed by state and lower federal courts.

In 1978, all nine Justices publicly conceded to the Congress that, while these summary dispositions of appeals are decisions on the merits, experience has shown that they "often are uncertain guides to the courts bound to follow them and not infrequently create more confusion than clarity." The Justices accordingly asked Congress to eliminate virtually all appeals, thereby recognizing formally that the Court's appellate jurisdiction is almost wholly discretionary. Congress has yet to respond.

At the start in 1789 and for a century thereafter, the Court was authorized to exercise only mandatory jurisdiction, either by way of appeal or a closely related process known as WRIT OF ERROR. But as the nation expanded and matured, litigation proliferated. It became evident toward the end of the nineteenth century that the Court could not keep up with its growing docket if it had to continue resolving the merits of every case that was filed. Gradually, Congress began to withdraw some of this mandatory jurisdiction from the Court, replacing it with discretionary jurisdiction by way of certiorari. But it was not until 1925 that Congress decreed a major shift toward discretionary review powers. At that time the dockets of the Court were so clogged with mandatory appeals and writs of error that litigants had to wait two and three years to have their cases decided. In the JUDICIARY ACT OF 1925, written largely at the suggestion of the Court, Congress transferred large segments of appellate jurisdiction from the obligatory to the discretionary category. Fully eighty percent of the

Court's docket thereafter was of the certiorari variety.

But the 1925 transfer proved insufficient. During the 1970s, Congress eliminated many of the remaining appeals that could be taken from lower federal courts, leaving only a handful within the federal sector of Supreme Court jurisdiction. The largest pocket of mandatory appeals left untouched consists of appeals from state court decisions validating state statutes in the face of federal constitutional challenges. The caseload explosions in the 1970s and 1980s, which saw the Court's annual case filings rising near the 5,000 mark, created pressure to eliminate all significant remnants of mandatory appeal jurisdiction.

Nearly one-half of these filed cases are petitions and applications filed by prisoners, petitions that are often frivolous and thus quickly disposed of. But from the overall pool of some 5,000 cases the Justices select about 150 cases each term for plenary review and resolution. The Justices feel that time limitations do not permit them to dispose of many more than 150 important and complex controversies, although they do manage to dispose of another 200 or so cases in a summary fashion, without briefs or oral arguments. In any event, the number of cases granted full review has hovered around the 150 mark for many of the last fifty years. This constancy is largely the product of the discretion and the docket control inherent in the certiorari jurisdiction. Without discretion to deny review to more than ninety-five percent of the certiorari petitions filed each year, the Court's ability to function efficiently would soon cease.

The procedures by which the Court achieves this docket control and makes this vital selection of cases for plenary review are simple but not well understood by the public. And some of the processes change as workloads increase and issues tend to become more difficult of resolution. As of the 1980s, the procedures may be summarized as follows:

By law, the Supreme Court begins its annual TERM, or working session, on the first Monday in October. Known as the October Term, this session officially runs for a full year, eliminating the prior practice of convening special sessions during the summer to hear urgent matters. But for most administrative purposes, each term continues for about nine months, October through June, or until all cases considered ready for disposition have been resolved. At that point, the Court normally recesses without formally adjourning until the following October.

The Court usually disposes of requests for review, hears oral arguments, and issues written opinions only during the nine-month working portion of the term. But the Court never closes for purposes of accepting new cases, as well as briefs and motions in pending cases. That means that filing time requirements are never waived during the summer recess; parties must respect those requirements in all seasons. In most civil cases, certiorari petitions and jurisdictional statements must be filed within ninety days from the entry of judgment, or from the denial of rehearing, in the court below. This filing period is only sixty days in criminal cases, federal or state.

As soon as opposing parties have filed briefs or motions in response to a certiorari petition or jurisdictional statement, these documents are circulated to all nine Justices. These circulations occur on a weekly basis all year round. The circulated cases are then scheduled by the Court's clerk for disposition by the Justices at the next appropriate CONFERENCE. Cases circulated during the summer recess accumulate for consideration at a lengthy conference held just before the opening of the new October term. Cases circulated during term time are considered at a conference held about two weeks after a given weekly circulation.

The massive numbers of case filings make it impossible for every Justice personally to examine these thousands of documents, although some may try. Most are aided in this task by law CLERKS, each Justice being entitled to employ four. The clerks often have the task of reading these documents and reducing them to short memoranda for the convenience of their respective Justices. In recent years, a number of Justices have used a "cert pool" system, whereby law clerk resources in several chambers are pooled to produce memoranda for the joint use of all the participating Justices. But whether a Justice reads all these matters or is assisted by law clerk memoranda, the ultimate discretionary judgments made respecting the grant or denial of review are necessarily those of each Justice. Law clerks simply do not make critical judgments or cast votes.

Law clerks are selected personally by each Justice, a practice dating back to 1882 when Justice HORACE GRAY first employed a top Harvard Law School graduate. In modern times, clerks are invariably selected from among recent law school graduates with superior academic records. And many Justices require that their clerks also have clerked for lower court judges. The clerks normally stay with their Justices for one term only, though some have served longer. Many law clerks have gone on to distinguished legal careers of their own. Three of them have become Supreme Court Justices: Justices BYRON R. WHITE, WILLIAM H. REHNQUIST, and JOHN PAUL STEVENS.

An important element of each Justice's workload is to act in the capacity of Circuit Justice, a vestigial remnant of the earlier circuit-riding tasks. For this purpose, each Justice is assigned one or more federal judicial circuits, which divide the nation into twelve geographical areas. The Justice assigned to a particular circuit handles a variety of preliminary motions and applications in cases originating in the area covered by the circuit. Included are such matters as applications for stays of lower court judgments pending action on a petition for certiorari, applications in criminal cases for bail or release pending such action, and applications to extend the time for filing certiorari or appeal cases. Law clerks frequently assist in processing these applications, and on occasion an application may be disposed of by a written "in chambers" opinion of the Circuit Justice.

The Court no longer discusses every certiorari petition at conference. The excessive number of petitions makes it necessary and appropriate to curtail collegial discussion of petitions at the formal conferences of the Justices. At present, the Chief Justice circulates a "discuss list," a list of cases in a given weekly circulation deemed worthy of discussion and formal voting at conference. All appeals are discussed at conference, but rarely more than thirty percent of the certiorari cases are listed for discussion. Any Justice may add an omitted case to the list, however. Review is then automatically denied to any unlisted case, without conference consideration.

Decisions whether to grant or deny review of cases on the "discuss list" are reached at one of the periodic secret conferences. During term time, conferences are normally held each Friday during the weeks when oral arguments are heard, and on the Friday just before the commencement of each two-week oral argument period. Conferences can be held on other days as well. Only the Justices are present at these conferences; no law clerks or secretaries are permitted to attend.

Conferences are held in a well-appointed room adjacent to the Chief Justice's chambers, which are to the rear of the courtroom. The conference begins with exchanges of handshakes among the Justices, a custom originating in 1888. Coffee is available from a silver urn. The typical conference begins with discussion and disposition of the "discuss list" cases, appeals being considered first. The Chief Justice leads the discussion of each case, followed by each associate Justice in order of seniority. Any formal voting takes place in reverse order of seniority. Then, if there are argued cases to be decided, a similar order of discussion and voting is followed. Argued cases, however, may be discussed at other conferences scheduled immediately after a day or two of oral arguments, thus making the Friday conferences less lengthy.

Using the Rule of Four at these conferences, the Court selects from the pool of "discuss list" cases those that it will review and resolve on the merits, following full briefs and oral argument. A few cases, however, may be granted review and then resolved immediately in a summary manner without briefs or oral argument, by way of a PER CURIAM written opinion. Such summary disposition has been much criticized by those who lose their cases without being fully heard, but the practice has been codified in the Court's rules. The important point is that it is the cases that are selected at these conferences for plenary review that account for the 150 or so cases at the core of the Court's workload each term.

The cases thus selected for full review reflect issues that, in the Justices' view, are of national significance. It is not enough that the issues are important to the parties to the case; they must be generally important. But the Court rarely if ever explains why review is denied, or why the issues were not deemed important enough to warrant plenary attention. There are occasional written explanatory dissents from the denial of review, but these can only express the views of a minority. Review is granted only when four or more Justices are subjectively convinced that there are special and important reasons for reviewing the questions presented, which may or may not involve a conflict among lower courts as to how to resolve such questions. It bears emphasis that the exercise of this kind of discretionary judgment enables the Court to control its docket and to limit the extent of its plenary workload.

When a "discuss list" case is granted review, the petitioning party has forty-five days in which to file a brief on the merits, together with a printed record appendix. The opposing party then has thirty days to file a brief on the merits. Briefs of intervening parties and AMICI CURIAE, if there are any in a given case, are filed during these periods. When all briefs are in, the case is ready to be scheduled for oral argument.

Oral argument before the Justices occurs only on Monday, Tuesday, and Wednesday of a scheduled week of argument, leaving the other weekdays available for work and conferences. Usually, fourteen weeks of oral argument are scheduled, in two-week segments from October through April. One hour of argument is allowed in most cases, one-half hour for each side. Arguments start promptly at 10 A.M. and end at 3 P.M., with a lunch adjournment from noon to 1

P.M. The Justices are well prepared, having read the briefs. Some may also be aided by "bench memos" prepared by their law clerks, memoranda that outline the critical facts and the opposing arguments. Counsel arguing a case may thus expect sharp and penetrating questions from the bench; and counsel are warned by the Court's rules not to read arguments from a prepared text.

Sometime during the week in which a particular case has been argued, the Court meets in secret conference to decide the merits of that case. With the Chief Justice presiding and leading the discussion, the normal pattern of collegial discussion and voting takes place. But the vote reached at conference is necessarily tentative and subject to change as work begins on opinion writing. Shortly after the vote is taken, the case is assigned to one of the Justices to draft an opinion for the Court. The assignment is made by the senior Justice in the majority, if the vote is split. Normally, the assignment is made by the Chief Justice, unless he is in dissent.

The Justice assigned to write an opinion for the Court then begins work on a draft. This is essentially a lonely task. Following the conference discussion, there is little time for further collegial consultation among the Justices in the preparation of an opinion. Depending upon the work patterns of a particular Justice, the law clerks may engage in much of the research and analysis that underlie scholarly opinions; some clerks may be assigned the task of producing drafts of an opinion, while some Justices may do all the drafting themselves. Since 1981, drafting of opinions has been mechanically made easier by the installation of word processors in each Justice's chambers.

Once the draft of the majority opinion has been completed, it is circulated to all other members of the Court. The other Justices may suggest various changes or additions to the draft. To become an opinion of the Court, the draft opinion must attract the adherence and agreement of a majority of five Justices, which sometimes requires the author of the draft to accept modifications suggested by another Justice as the price of the latter's adherence. One or more of the Justices who cannot accept the reasoning or the result of the draft opinion then may produce their own drafts of CONCURRING or DISSENTING OPINIONS. The circulation of these separate opinion drafts may in turn cause the author of the majority draft to make further changes by way of answer to arguments made in a draft concurrence or dissent. Thus nothing is truly final until the collegial exchange of opinions is complete, the votes are set in concrete, and the result is

considered ready for public announcement. Even then, there are cases in which the Court cannot reach a majority consensus, resulting in simply an announcement of the judgment of the Court accompanied by a number of PLURALITY, concurring, and dissenting opinions. The difficulty sometimes encountered in reaching a clear-cut majority result, while distressing to the bar and the lower courts, is generally reflective of the difficulty and complexity of some of the momentous issues that reach the Court.

The opinions and judgments of the Court in argued cases are announced publicly in the courtroom. At one time, opinions were uniformly announced on what became known as Opinion Monday. But the Court found that too many opinions announced on a Monday, particularly toward the end of a term, made it difficult for the press to give adequate media coverage to important Court rulings. The Court now announces opinions on any day it sits, thereby spreading out opinion announcements. In weeks in which oral arguments are scheduled for three days, the practice is to announce opinions only on a Tuesday or Wednesday, leaving Monday for the announcement of summary orders. Opinions may still be announced on a Monday, particularly if no oral arguments are scheduled for that day. After all oral arguments have been heard, usually by the end of April, opinions can be announced on any given Monday, when the Court sits to announce summary orders, or on any other day of the week that the Court wishes to sit solely to announce opinions.

The practices regarding the announcement of opinions in open court change from time to time. At one time, many opinions were read by the authors in full or in substantial part. More recently the Justices have tended merely to give short summaries save in the most important cases; in some less important cases only the result is announced. All opinions and orders are made available to the public and the news media a few moments after the courtroom announcements. Eventually, opinions and orders appear in bound volumes known as the United States Reports.

When the Court first convened in February of 1790, one of its first actions was to prescribe qualifications for lawyers wishing to practice before the Court. The original rule, in language very like that of the present rule, established two requirements: the attorney must have been admitted to practice in a state supreme court "for three years past," and the attorney's "private and professional character" must appear to be good.

Nearly 200,000 attorneys have been admitted to

the Supreme Court bar since the Court was established. In recent times, as many as 6,000 have been admitted in a year. Prior to 1970, an attorney could be admitted only on motion of a sponsor in open court, before all the Justices. But the Court found that so much time was taken in listening to these routine motions and admissions and that it was often so expensive for a lawyer to travel to Washington from afar just to engage in this briefest of ceremonies, that an alternative "mail-order" procedure should be made available. Most attorneys today are admitted by mail, although some prefer to follow the earlier practice of being admitted in open court.

The modern Supreme Court bar has no formal structure or leadership. It is largely a heterogeneous collection of individual lawyers located in all parts of the nation. Many members of the bar never practice before the Court, and even fewer ever have the opportunity to argue orally. Most private practitioners who do have occasion to argue orally do so on a "once-in-a-lifetime" basis. Those who appear with some regularity before the Court are usually connected with an organization or governmental group specializing in Supreme Court litigation, such as the office of the SOLICITOR GENERAL of the United States. Gone are the days when private legal giants, such as DANIEL WEBSTER, were repeatedly employed specially by litigants to present oral arguments before the Court.

While a lay litigant may prepare and file petitions and briefs on the litigant's own behalf, without the aid of a member of the bar, the complexities and subtleties of modern practice make such self-help increasingly inadvisable. Only in the rarest of circumstances will the Court permit a lay litigant to present oral argument. Those imprisoned have frequently filed their own petitions for certiorari, seeking some sort of review of their criminal convictions. Indeed, about half of the nearly 5,000 case filings per year can be ascribed to prisoner petitions. The Court catalogues these petitions on its IN FORMA PAUPERIS docket but gives them the same careful treatment it gives petitions filed on behalf of clients who can afford to pay filing and printing costs.

The Court will, on application by an impecunious litigant or prisoner, appoint a member of the Court's bar to prepare briefs on the merits and to present oral arguments, once review has been granted in the case. But the Court will not appoint a lawyer to aid in preparing and filing a petition for certiorari or jurisdictional statement. Legal aid programs operating in most lower courts usually insure that a lawyer appointed or volunteering to represent a prisoner in

the lower courts will be available to file such documents in the Supreme Court.

Such are the basic processes and procedures that enable the Court to perform its historic missions. As the Court approaches its third century, the Justices are deeply concerned with the Court's growing workload and the resulting effect upon the quality of its decision making. The Court's internal and external procedures have been streamlined and perfected about as much as possible. Some restructuring of its jurisdiction and functions seems necessary. Yet despite these perceived shortcomings, the Court has managed to maintain its prime role in the evolving history of the American legal system. The Court's effective performance of that role is due in no small part to the procedures and rules established for those who practice before it.

EUGENE GRESSMAN

Bibliography
STERN, ROBERT L.; GRESSMAN, EUGENE; and SHAPIRO, STEPHEN M. 1986 Supreme Court Practice, 6th ed. Washington, D.C.: Bureau of National Affairs.

SUSPECT CLASSIFICATION

Long before the term "suspect classification" gained currency, Justice HARLAN FISKE STONE captured the idea in his opinion for the Supreme Court in UNITED STATES V. CAROLENE PRODUCTS CO. (1938). While insisting on RATIONAL BASIS as the appropriate STANDARD OF REVIEW for cases involving ECONOMIC REGULATION, Stone suggested that "prejudice against DISCRETE AND INSULAR MINORITIES [that is, religious, or national, or racial minorities] may be a special condition, which tends seriously to curtail the operation of those political processes ordinarily to be relied upon to protect minorities, and which may call for a correspondingly more searching judicial inquiry." In modern idiom, to call a legislative classification "suspect" is to suggest the possibility that it resulted from prejudice against the group it burdens, a possibility that justifies strict judicial scrutiny to assure that it is necessary to achieve a COMPELLING STATE INTEREST. In practice, most laws subject to this exacting standard are held invalid.

Irony attends the origins of the expression. Justice HUGO L. BLACK, writing for a majority in Korematsu v. United States (1944), one of the JAPANESE AMERICAN CASES, found no denial of EQUAL PROTECTION in an EXECUTIVE ORDER excluding American citizens of Japanese ancestry from the West Coast. Along the way to this extraordinary conclusion, however, he said: "all legal restrictions which curtail the civil rights of a single racial group are immediately suspect. That is not to say that all such restrictions are unconstitutional. It is to say that courts must subject them to the most rigid scrutiny." In *Korematsu* itself, the Court did no such thing; it paid the greatest deference to a "military" judgment that was chiefly political and steeped in racial prejudice. Yet *Korematsu*'s main doctrinal legacy was that racial classifications were suspect.

In one view, this two-stage analysis, first identifying a classification as suspect and then subjecting it to STRICT SCRUTINY, is a roundabout way of addressing the issue of illicit legislative motives. (See LEGISLATION; WASHINGTON V. DAVIS, 1976.) Strict scrutiny is required in order to allay the suspicion that a law was designed to disadvantage a minority that lacked effective power in the legislature. That suspicion is laid to rest only by a showing that the law is well designed to achieve a legitimate purpose that has real importance. In another view, a classification based on race should be subjected to strict scrutiny because the immutable characteristic of race lends itself so well to a system thought dominated by stereotype, which automatically consigns a person to a general category, often implying inferiority. This concern for stigmatic harm is part of the substantive core of the equal protection clause, the principle of equal citizenship; the concern retains vitality even in an era when members of racial minorities have become electoral majorities in many of our major cities.

A number of egalitarian decisions in the later years of the WARREN COURT suggested a wide range of classifications that were candidates for inclusion by the Supreme Court in the "suspect" category: alienage, sex, ILLEGITIMACY, age, indigency. In the event, none of these candidates was accepted fully. Some classifications disadvantaging ALIENS were held "suspect," but many were not. The Court did significantly heighten the standard of review for most cases involving claimed denials of SEX DISCRIMINATION and gave some "bite" to the rational basis standard in cases involving illegitimacy. On the whole, however, the Court's behavior since the late 1970s suggests a determination to limit expansion of the list of suspect classifications, and thus to limit the occasions for active judicial supervision of legislation.

Some racial classifications are adopted as remedies for past societal discrimination based on race. Such an AFFIRMATIVE ACTION program presents neither of the principal dangers that have been said to require strict judicial scrutiny of racial classifications. There is less reason to suspect an illicit motive when a majoritarian body such as a legislature discriminates in favor of a historically disadvantaged minority, and the risk of stigmatic harm to a racial group is much reduced. Thus, varying majorities of the Supreme Court have consistently agreed that the appropriate standard of review for such remedial legislation, including RACIAL QUOTAS, is considerably less exacting than the strictest form of strict scrutiny.

The whole "suspect classifications" idea would seem to have outlived its usefulness. Surely the Supreme Court no longer needs the doctrine to justify its highest levels of intensity of judicial review. In race cases, for example, the Court needs no such locution in order to continue imposing on government a "heavy burden of justification" of laws imposing invidious racial discrimination. Abandonment of the rhetoric of suspect classifications would promote candor, by easing the way for open recognition of the sliding scale of standards of review now serving to cloak the Court's interest balancing. It would also remove a barrier, built into the very language of suspect "classifications," to doctrinal growth in the direction of affirmative governmental responsibility to alleviate those inequalities that prevent the realization of the principle of equal citizenship.

KENNETH L. KARST

Bibliography

BREST, PAUL A. 1976 The Supreme Court, 1975 Term—Foreword: In Defense of the Antidiscrimination Principle. *Harvard Law Review* 90:1–54.

ELY, JOHN HART 1980 Democracy and Distrust: A Theory of Judicial Review. Cambridge, Mass.: Harvard University Press.

SUTHERLAND, GEORGE
(1862–1942)

George Sutherland, Supreme Court Justice from 1922 to 1938, was born in England in 1862. A year thereafter, he was brought by his parents to Brigham Young's Utah. Although he himself was never a Mormon, Sutherland attended a Mormon academy; in 1882–1883, he studied at the law school at the University of Michigan. On leaving the university, Sutherland was admitted to the Utah bar. He attained immediate prominence, both professionally and politically. He was elected to the House of Representatives as a Republican in 1900 and to the Senate in 1905, where he remained until 1917.

Sutherland's tenure in Congress forced him to confront issues in a political context that he would later deal with as a Supreme Court Justice. Generally he supported a conservative position. Yet his most enduring legislative achievements centered on improving conditions for seamen; advancing a federal WORKER'S COMPENSATION program; and promoting woman suffrage. Sutherland's congressional tenure enabled him as early as 1910 to establish his credentials for appointment to the Supreme Court. The 1920 election of Warren Harding, attributed in considerable part to Sutherland in his role of principal confidential adviser to the candidate, virtually assured him the nomination. The nomination was sent to an approving Senate on September 5, 1922.

Anyone interested in the new Justice's approach to legal and political problems had not far to look. In the five years since his retirement from the Senate, Sutherland had delivered major addresses setting forth his conservative philosophy. In his presidential address to the American Bar Association in 1917, he chose to speak on "Private Rights and Government Control." The message was clear. "Prying Commissions" and "governmental intermeddling" were unnecessary and at war with the "fundamental principle upon which our form of government depends, namely, that it is an empire of laws and not of men." Four years later Sutherland was telling the New York State Bar Association "that government should confine its activities, as a general rule, to preserving a free market and preventing fraud." He further explained that "fundamental social and economic laws" were beyond the "power of official control."

Once on the Court, Sutherland readily joined his conservative colleagues invoking SUBSTANTIVE DUE PROCESS to strike down exertions of governmental power. His first major opinion, in ADKINS V. CHILDREN'S HOSPITAL (1923), was directed at the minimum wage. Here, in the area of FREEDOM OF CONTRACT, no presumptive validity could be accorded to the exercise of legislative power. Rather, its legitimacy could be established only by "exceptional circumstances" and certainly not by considerations of a worker's needs or bargaining power. In short order, state attempts to regulate prices of gasoline, theater tickets, and employment agency services were similarly condemned. Other forms of state regulation fared no better. Nor was substantive due process the sole doctrinal reliance. In the Court's continuing battle with state legislatures, Sutherland led his colleagues in discovering hitherto unrealized prohibitions in the EQUAL PROTECTION, COMMERCE, and CONTRACT CLAUSES. And, under his hand, the PRIVILEGES AND IMMUNITIES clause of the FOURTEENTH AMENDMENT, neglected and forgotten for decades, sprang to life as a restraint on state power in COLGATE V. HARVEY (1935).

Eventually, of course, the Court repudiated the Sutherland approach to state legislative power and little of it remains. Yet, in at least two respects, his contribution in this area is of continuing significance. The first has to do with his seminal opinion in *Frost and Frost Trucking v. Railroad Commission* (1926) where he elaborated the theory of unconstitutional conditions. This theory destroyed the notion that a state's power to withhold a privilege somehow gives it authority to discriminate without check in granting the privilege. The second is his opinion for a divided court in EUCLID V. AMBLER REALTY (1926) which furnishes the constitutional foundation for the modern law of ZONING.

When Sutherland came to deal with the actions of Congress and the President, he exhibited the same jealousy of authority that characterized his response to state legislatures. Accordingly, he remained to the end unconvinced of the constitutionality of many of the New Deal enactments and in time was overwhelmed by the arrival of our modern-day Constitution of "powers." Even so, Sutherland's lasting impact will be found on close examination to have been highly significant. Particularly, he made highly personalized contributions to our *structural* Constitution; he had a distinctive role in shaping the Constitution as a guarantor of CIVIL RIGHTS; and he, more than anyone else, supplied the intellectual underpinnings for the FOREIGN AFFAIRS power.

As for the structural Constitution, Sutherland's opinion in *Massachusetts v. Mellon* (1923), and its companion case of FROTHINGHAM V. MELLON (1923), is still, despite scores of intervening qualifying decisions, the basic starting point in determining when a federal "taxpayer" has STANDING to raise a constitutional question in actions in the federal courts. Here plainly is one of the most telling limitations on federal judicial power. In a number of cases, Sutherland wrote opinions enforcing restraint on Supreme Court review of state decisions that were found to rest on independent and ADEQUATE STATE GROUNDS. In still others, he resisted effectively the pleas of reformers to whittle down guarantees of the right to TRIAL BY JURY, in civil as well as criminal cases. And in the highly technical matter of the relationship between state and federal courts, Sutherland's influence continues. Finally, Sutherland's views have been decisive in regard to the President's power to remove federal office holders. Early in his judicial career he concurred in Chief

Justice WILLIAM HOWARD TAFT's unnecessarily wide-ranging opinion in MYERS V. UNITED STATES (1926), sanctioning a presidential power to remove without restraint. In HUMPHREY'S EXECUTOR V. UNITED STATES (1935) he started the Court on the way to new DOCTRINE. The removal power must take account of the nature of the office involved.

Sutherland's tenure on the Court spanned the years in which the Court began to take the BILL OF RIGHTS seriously as a check on STATE ACTION. His role in this development was not all of one piece. But he did write a leading opinion, in GROSJEAN V. AMERICAN PRESS COMPANY (1936), condemning a state tax on the press because of the levy's impermissible *motive* to make costly the criticism of public officials. And in POWELL V. ALABAMA (1932), he charted for the Court the first steps a state must take to assure counsel in legal proceedings. His problem there was counsel in a capital case. But Sutherland's opinion was not so confined in its implications and has proved influential even beyond the bounds of the criminal law.

Long before he went on the Court, Sutherland was given to speculation about the foreign relations powers, producing in 1919 a book on the subject, *Constitutional Power and World Affairs.* In his book and elsewhere, Sutherland developed the theory that the powers of the United States in respect to foreign affairs were largely unrelated to any grant from the states and existed as an incident of SOVEREIGNTY devolved directly on the United States from Great Britain. Their employment and their distribution were to be governed by rules not applicable to the specific delegations of the Constitution. In 1936, in CURTISS-WRIGHT EXPORT CORP. V. UNITED STATES, Sutherland was able to incorporate these views in an opinion for a unanimous Court.

Sutherland retired from the Court in 1938. He died in 1942.

FRANCIS PASCHAL

Bibliography

PASCHAL, JOEL FRANCIS 1951 *Mr. Justice Sutherland: A Man against the State.* Princeton, N.J.: Princeton University Press.

SWAIN v. ALABAMA
380 U.S. 202 (1965)

A 6–3 Court, speaking through Justice BYRON R. WHITE, rejected the claim of a black defendant to proportional representation of his race on grand and petit juries. Although blacks were substantially under-represented on the jury panel, and although the prosecutor had used his peremptory challenges to exclude blacks in this case (there had been eight blacks on the venire), the Court found no evidence on the record of purposeful discrimination. The Court hinted that systematic use of peremptory challenges to exclude blacks from all juries would be unconstitutional, but it said that the record in *Swain* failed to show such systematic discrimination. In *Batson v. Kentucky* (1986) the Court partially overruled *Swain*, holding that a prosecutor cannot constitutionally use peremptory challenges to exclude potential jurors solely on account of their race.

DENNIS J. MAHONEY

(SEE ALSO: *Jury Discrimination.*)

SWANN v. CHARLOTTE-MECKLENBURG BOARD OF EDUCATION
402 U.S. 1 (1971)

Three years before *Swann* was decided, the Supreme Court had established a school board's affirmative duty to dismantle a school system that had been racially segregated by the command of law or by the board's deliberate actions. (See GREEN V. COUNTY SCHOOL BOARD, 1968.) In *Swann,* the Court was asked to apply this standard to a large metropolitan school district including the city of Charlotte, North Carolina, and its surrounding county. President RICHARD M. NIXON had made two appointments to the Court in the intervening years, and some observers expected the Justices' previous unanimity in school DESEGREGATION cases to be shattered in this case. In the event, no such thing happened; a unanimous Court affirmed a sweeping order by the federal district judge, James B. McMillan, calling for districtwide busing of children for the purpose of improving the schools' RACIAL BALANCE. (After issuing this order, Judge McMillan received death threats and was given police protection.) The *Swann* opinion was signed by Chief Justice WARREN E. BURGER. However, internal evidence strongly suggests that the opinion was a negotiated patchwork of drafts, and investigative journalists have asserted plausibly that Justice POTTER STEWART contributed its main substantive points.

Once a constitutional violation was found, the Court said, the school board had an obligation to take steps to remedy both present de jure segregation (see DE FACTO/DE JURE) and the present effects of past de jure segregation. These steps must achieve "the greatest possible degree of actual desegregation, taking into account the practicalities of the situation." The Court thus approved Judge McMillan's use of districtwide racial percentages as "a starting point" in shaping a remedy and placed on the school board the very difficult burden of showing that the continued existence of one-race schools was not the result of present or past de jure segregation. Finally, the Court approved the busing of children to schools not in their own neighborhoods as one permissible remedy within a court's discretion. The matter of busing, however, was not left to lower court discretion. In a COMPANION CASE from Mobile, Alabama, *Davis v. Board of School Commissioners,* the Court *required* busing the lower courts had not ordered.

Swann set the pattern for school desegregation litigation not only in southern cities but in the North and West as well. Once a court finds deliberate acts of segregation, *Swann's* affirmative duties arise.

KENNETH L. KARST

(SEE ALSO: *Keyes v. School District No. 1, 1973; Columbus Board of Education v. Penick, 1979; School Busing.*)

Bibliography

FISS, OWEN M. 1974 School Desegregation: The Uncertain Path of the Law. *Philosophy & Public Affairs* 4:3–39.

WOODWARD, BOB and ARMSTRONG, SCOTT 1979 *The Brethren: Inside the Supreme Court.* Pages 96–112. New York: Simon & Schuster.

SWAYNE, NOAH H.
(1804–1884)

Noah Haynes Swayne was the first of President ABRAHAM LINCOLN's five Supreme Court appointees. Geography, antislavery credentials, and support for the Union constituted Lincoln's chief criteria when he made his first appointments to the Court. Swayne fulfilled these qualifications.

Because of his hostility to slavery, Swayne left his native Virginia and in 1823 moved to Ohio, where he served in the state legislature. In 1830 President ANDREW JACKSON named him United States Attorney. During the next several decades, he continued his active political career, and he appeared as counsel in a number of FUGITIVE SLAVERY cases. In 1855, he joined the fledgling Republican party and became a leading figure in the Ohio group. His close friend, Justice JOHN MCLEAN, had suggested Swayne as his successor. When McLean died early in 1861, Swayne

quickly marshaled support from leading Ohio Republicans; Lincoln appointed him in January 1862.

On the Supreme Court, Swayne enthusiastically supported the administration, approving of Lincoln's blockade of southern ports in the PRIZE CASES (1862), upholding the Legal Tender Act of 1862 in *Roosevelt v. Meyer* (1863), and sustaining military trials in EX PARTE VALLANDIGHAM (1864). After the war, in EX PARTE MILLIGAN (1866), he joined the Court's minority faction which declined to discuss the question of congressionally authorized military tribunals.

During Reconstruction, Swayne again demonstrated consistent support for the congressional Republican program. For example, he dissented in the TEST OATH CASES (1867), and he voted to decline JURISDICTION in the unreported case of *Mississippi v. Stanton* (1868), when the Court divided evenly on whether to take another case that might have decided the fate of the Reconstruction program. Perhaps Swayne's clearest deference to congressional determination of Reconstruction was expressed in his dissent in TEXAS V. WHITE (1869). He rejected the majority fiction that Texas was not out of the Union and insisted that Texas's relationship to the Union must be determined by Congress. Swayne recognized that the FOURTEENTH AMENDMENT had been designed in part to benefit the freedmen, as evidenced by his vote in STRAUDER V. WEST VIRGINIA (1880), striking down RACIAL DISCRIMINATION in jury selection. Yet he repeatedly supported the Court's narrow construction of the FIFTEENTH AMENDMENT, thus limiting black VOTING RIGHTS.

After the Civil War, Swayne continued to back Republican programs. He dissented when the majority struck down the legal tender laws in 1870, but the next year he joined the new majority that reversed that decision. (See LEGAL TENDER CASES.) A decade later, just before his retirement, Swayne delivered the Court's opinion in SPRINGER V. UNITED STATES (1881) upholding the Civil War income tax. He impressively rejected arguments that the tax confiscated property without DUE PROCESS OF LAW and that it was a DIRECT TAX, and therefore need not be apportioned among the states according to population. That decision subsequently was temporarily overruled in POLLOCK V. FARMER'S LOAN AND TRUST (1895), but Swayne's opinion generally is regarded as the more historically valid.

In its time, Swayne's opinion in GELPCKE V. CITY OF DUBUQUE (1864) had enormous influence. Speaking for the Court, Swayne held that a state court could invalidate a lawfully controlled municipal bonding arrangement. The decision left countless municipalities responsible for maintaining railroad financing, despite popular protests against the practice as well as deceitful activities on the part of the railroads. Later, Swayne joined JOSEPH P. BRADLEY, STEPHEN J. FIELD, and SALMON P. CHASE in dissent in the SLAUGHTERHOUSE CASES (1873). Swayne's dissent lacked the elaborate rhetoric and logic of the Bradley and Field dissents, but he invoked the same mystical faith in the sanctity of property.

Swayne ranks as an ordinary Justice, not greatly appreciated even in his own time. His colleagues disapproved of his aggressive campaigning for the Chief Justiceship in 1864 and 1873, and he remained on the bench long after his physical and mental capacities had noticeably declined. He wrote few major opinions in his two decades on the bench.

STANLEY I. KUTLER

Bibliography

FAIRMAN, CHARLES 1939 *Mr. Justice Miller and the Supreme Court, 1862–1890.* Cambridge, Mass.: Harvard University Press.

GILLETTE, WILLIAM 1969 Noah H. Swayne. In Leon Friedman and Fred L. Israel, eds., *The Justices of the Supreme Court,* Vol. 2:789–1010. New York: Chelsea House.

SWEATT v. PAINTER
339 U.S. 629 (1950)
MCLAURIN v. OKLAHOMA STATE REGENTS
339 U.S. 637 (1950)

Texas had established a separate law school for blacks; the state university law school thus rejected Sweatt, a black applicant. In *McLaurin,* the state university admitted a black to graduate study in education but made him sit in segregated classroom alcoves and at separate tables in the library and cafeteria. In both cases, state courts upheld the challenged SEGREGATION. In *Sweatt* the NAACP recruited some law professors to file a brief AMICUS CURIAE urging the Supreme Court to abandon the SEPARATE BUT EQUAL DOCTRINE and hold that state-sponsored segregation was unconstitutional. Eleven states supported the Texas position.

The Court unanimously held the practices of segregation in these cases unconstitutional, but it did not reach the broader issue. Chief Justice FRED M. VINSON wrote both opinions. In *Sweatt* he emphasized the intangibles of legal education: faculty reputation,

influential alumni, traditions, prestige, and—most significant for the doctrinal future—a student body including members of a race that would produce an overwhelming majority of the judges, lawyers, witnesses, and jury members Sweatt might face. Assuming the continued vitality of "separate but equal," the new law school for blacks was not equal to the state university law school, and Sweatt must be admitted to the latter.

The *McLaurin* opinion, too, avoided direct attack on the separate-but-equal principle, but it sapped that principle's foundations: segregation impaired McLaurin's ability to study and learn, to discuss questions with other students and be accepted by them on his merits; thus the state must lift its restrictions on him.

In neither case did the Court discuss segregation's stigmatizing effects. In neither did the Court consider any asserted justifications for segregation. The only question was whether segregation produced significant inequality; affirmative answers to that question ended the Court's inquiries. Taken seriously, these decisions must lead—as they did, four years later—to the conclusion that racial segregation in public education is unconstitutional. (See BROWN V. BOARD OF EDUCATION, 1954.)

KENNETH L. KARST

SWEEZY v. NEW HAMPSHIRE

See: *Watkins v. United States*

SWIFT v. TYSON
41 U.S. (16 Peters) 1 (1842)

In *Swift v. Tyson* the Supreme Court gave to the Rules of Decision Act (JUDICIARY ACT OF 1789, section 34) a construction that was to stand until ERIE RAILROAD CO. V. TOMPKINS (1938), almost a century later. As a result of this construction, the federal courts came to exercise COMMON LAW authority over a wide variety of disputes, some of which involved matters outside the limits of federal legislative power. Because these federal court decisions did not purport to bind state courts, the result was often the parallel existence of two different rules of law applicable to the same controversy.

Proceeding on the basis of diversity of citizenship (see DIVERSITY JURISDICTION), Swift sued Tyson in a New York federal court on a bill of exchange. A critical question in the case was whether, in light of the particular facts, Swift was a "purchaser for value" of that bill. The Supreme Court, in an opinion by Justice JOSEPH STORY, held that he was, resolving the question on the basis of "general principles and doctrines of commercial jurisprudence," not on the basis of the decisional law of New York.

Tyson had argued that although there was no relevant state statute, the decisions of the New York state courts were controlling because the Rules of Decision Act provided that the "laws of the several states . . . shall be regarded as rules of decision . . . in cases where they apply." This provision, the Court replied, was limited in application to "the positive statutes of the state, and the construction thereof by the local tribunals, and to rights and titles to things having a permanent locality." It did not require adherence to state judicial decisions on such matters as "questions of general commercial law, where the state tribunals are called upon to perform the like functions as ourselves, that is, to ascertain, upon general reasoning and legal analogies . . . what is the just rule furnished by the principles of commercial law to govern the case."

Historians disagree on the justification and soundness of the *Swift* decision. But there is general agreement that in the years that followed, *Swift* was expanded well beyond its originally intended scope, and that its OVERRULING, in *Erie*, reflected a very different perception of the proper role of the federal courts.

DAVID L. SHAPIRO

(SEE ALSO: *Federal Common Law, Civil.*)

SWIFT & COMPANY v. UNITED STATES
196 U.S. 375 (1905)

Justice OLIVER WENDELL HOLMES's opinion for a unanimous Supreme Court in *Swift* announced the STREAM OF COMMERCE doctrine, fundamental to constitutional COMMERCE CLAUSE adjudication ever since.

In 1902 Attorney General PHILANDER C. KNOX ordered that an EQUITY complaint be filed against the Beef Trust, the five largest meat-packing concerns in the country. The complaint alleged conspiracy and combination in restraint of interstate trade, suppression of competition, and price-fixing, all in violation of the SHERMAN ANTITRUST ACT. In 1903 federal district court judge PETER S. GROSSCUP issued a perpetual INJUNCTION against the packers. On appeal to the Supreme Court, the packers, though admitting the

truth of the government allegations, contended that they were not involved in INTERSTATE COMMERCE. The entire transaction between the packers and those who purchased meat from them had occurred completely within the state where the packers slaughtered and prepared their meat. The sale had been consumated in-state and thus only INTRASTATE COMMERCE was involved. Knox's successor, WILLIAM H. MOODY, asserted that the restraint of trade directly affected interstate commerce even if no interstate acts were involved. Armed with the packers' admissions, Moody stressed the unity of the transactions, arguing that the operation had to be viewed as a whole.

The Court accepted Moody's view. The trust's "EFFECT UPON COMMERCE is not accidental, secondary, remote, or merely probable," Holmes declared, as he revised the Court's view of interstate commerce, affecting decisions for decades to come: "Commerce among the states is not a technical legal conception, but a practical one, drawn from the course of the business." Livestock moving from the range to the retailer, "with the only interruption necessary to find a purchaser at the stock yards," created "a current of commerce among the states, and the purchase of cattle is a part and incident of such commerce." Thus a local activity might be seen as part of interstate commerce. This stream of commerce doctrine fundamentally redirected the Court's examination of commerce clause questions and brought the Court face-to-face with economic reality, modifying the doctrinal effect of UNITED STATES v. E. C. KNIGHT COMPANY (1895).

DAVID GORDON

Bibliography
GORDON, DAVID 1983 The Beef Trust: Antitrust Law and the Meat Packing Industry, 1902–1922. Ph.D. diss., Claremont Graduate School.

SWISHER, CARL BRENT
(1897–1968)

Carl Brent Swisher taught constitutional history for many years at Johns Hopkins University. A pioneer in the field of judicial biography, Swisher published *Stephen J. Field: Craftsman of the Law* (1930), still highly regarded. His *Roger B. Taney* (1935), the leading biography, and his posthumously published *The Taney Period, 1836–1864* (1974; Vol. 5, Holmes Devise History of the Supreme Court) describe Taney's accomplishments as Chief Justice as well as his failures of judgment and proslavery bias, thereby rescuing Taney from the limbo to which most historians had consigned him in the wake of DRED SCOTT V. SANDFORD (1857). Swisher also published several general studies of constitutional law and the Supreme Court, including *American Constitutional Development* (1943; rev. ed. with E. M. Sait, 1954) and *The Supreme Court in Modern Role* (1958; rev. ed., 1965). In the most influential of these works, *The Growth of Constitutional Power in the United States* (1946; rev. ed., 1963), Swisher questioned the continuing usefulness of the doctrine of SEPARATION OF POWERS, fearing that it prevented government from achieving the ends which society increasingly expected government to achieve; he also urged government supervision of large corporations to check their political and economic power.

RICHARD B. BERNSTEIN

SYMBOLIC SPEECH

Does communication by conduct rather than by words constitute "speech" within the FIRST AMENDMENT's guarantee of FREEDOM OF SPEECH? The status of communicative conduct, as with most free speech questions, is usually presented in an emotion-laden context: does the burning of a flag, or of a draft card, constitute a First-Amendment-protected activity? Is the act of marching in a public DEMONSTRATION (as distinguished from the placards which the marchers carry) a form of protected "speech?" Are school or other governmental regulations of hair styles an abridgment of freedom of speech? Does nude dancing constitute a form of First Amendment "speech?" Although the lower federal and state courts frequently have wrestled with all of these questions, the United States Supreme Court has yet to articulate a theoretical base that explains the status of symbolic speech under the First Amendment.

At least since STROMBERG V. CALIFORNIA (1931), the Supreme Court has assumed that "speech" within the meaning of the First Amendment's guarantee of "freedom of speech" includes more than merely verbal communications. In *Stromberg* the Court declared invalid a California statute that prohibited the public display of "any flag, badge, banner or device . . . as a sign, symbol or emblem of opposition to organized government." Among other decisions applying the First Amendment to nonverbal conduct, perhaps the most striking was TINKER V. DES MOINES INDEPENDENT COMMUNITY SCHOOL DISTRICT (1969). The Court there upheld the right of high school students to wear black armbands as a protest against American

participation in the VIETNAM WAR, calling their conduct "the type of symbolic act that is within the Free Speech Clause of the First Amendment."

But if conduct sometimes constitutes protected "speech," sometimes it does not. UNITED STATES V. O'BRIEN (1968) affirmed a conviction for draft card burning. Chief Justice EARL WARREN, speaking for the Court, answered the defendant's symbolic speech defense by opining, "We cannot accept the view that an apparently limitless variety of conduct can be labeled 'speech' whenever the person engaging in the conduct intends thereby to express an idea."

Any attempt to disentangle "speech" from conduct that is itself communicative will not withstand analysis. The speech element in symbolic speech is entitled to no lesser (and also no greater) degree of protection than that accorded to so-called pure speech. Indeed, in one sense all speech is symbolic. At this moment the reader is observing black markings on paper which curl and point in various directions. We call such markings letters, and in groups they are referred to as words. What is being said in this sentence is meaningful only because the reader recognizes these markings as symbols for particular ideas. The same is true of oral speech which is simply the use of symbolic sounds. Outside the science fiction realm of mind-to-mind telepathic communication, all communications necessarily involve the use of symbols.

But because all expression necessarily requires the use of symbols, it does not necessarily follow as a matter of logic that First Amendment protection is or should be available for all symbolic expressions. The "speech" protected by the First Amendment might be limited to expressions in which the symbols employed consist of conventional words. The Supreme Court has found so restrictive a reading of the First Amendment to be unacceptable. Significantly, in First Amendment cases, the Court often refers to "freedom of expression" as the equivalent of freedom of speech. Justice OLIVER WENDELL HOLMES's "free trade in ideas" may not be reduced to mere trade in words. It is the freedom to express ideas and feelings, not merely the freedom to engage in verbal locutions, that must be protected if the First Amendment's central values are to be realized.

In COHEN V. CALIFORNIA (1971) the Supreme Court held that the emotive form of speech is as entitled to First Amendment protection as is its cognitive content. Emotive expression can be fully as important as intellectual, or cognitive, content in the competition of ideas for acceptance in the marketplace. Of course, most communications encompass both cognitive and emotive content. But even if a communication is substantially devoid of all cognitive content, its emotive content surely lies within the First Amendment scope. Symphonic compositions or nonrepresentational art are protected against governmental censorship, notwithstanding their lack of verbal or cognitive content.

Of course, not all conduct should be regarded as "speech" within the meaning of the First Amendment. Not even the most ardent free speech advocate would contend that all legislation regulating human conduct is subject to First Amendment restrictions. If, as the Court stated in the *O'Brien* opinion, the First Amendment is not to apply to a "limitless variety of conduct," what standards should be applied in determining whether given restrictions on conduct constitute First Amendment abridgment of symbolic speech?

If government's purpose in restricting is to suppress the message conveyed by the conduct, then the state should not be heard to deny the actor's claim that the conduct in question was intended to communicate a message. Such a message-restricting motivation by the state should also establish that the conduct in question constitutes symbolic speech. But such a conclusion does not necessarily imply that the speech is entitled to First Amendment protection. Even speech in words may in some circumstances be subordinated to a counter-speech interest. Likewise, no First Amendment ABSOLUTISM will protect communicative conduct. In some contexts symbolic speech may be overbalanced by counter-speech interests. If, however, the asserted or actual counter-speech interest is simply commitment to a particular view of the world—political, ethical, aesthetic, or otherwise—this interest will not justify abridgment of the right to express a contrary view, either by words or by conduct.

Just as First Amendment principles apply equally to expression in the symbols of the English or French languages, for example, the same principles govern when the symbols are of neither of these languages, nor of any conventional language. The crucial question under the First Amendment is whether meaningful symbols are being employed by one who wishes to communicate to others.

The courts have resisted equating symbolic speech with verbal speech because of a fear of immunizing all manner of conduct from the controls of the law. This fear is unjustifiable; it stems from a false premise as to the First Amendment protection accorded to verbal speech. In fact, speech in words is not immune from regulation. For example, an interest in excluding trespassers will justify abridging the verbal speech of those who wish to speak on property from which they may properly be excluded. Similarly, words that presage an imminent and likely BREACH OF THE PEACE will justify regulation just as much as if the idea be conveyed by nonverbal symbols. These are but two of many instances when verbal speech is subordinated to counter-speech interests.

According full and equal status to symbolic speech under the First Amendment will not open the floodgates to abuses, immunizing *O'Brien's* "apparently limitless variety of conduct" from legal regulation. Recognition of such equality of forms of expression would mean that no one will be penalized because he chooses to communicate—or is able to communicate—only in a language other than conventional words. We shall all be the richer for such recognition.

MELVILLE B. NIMMER

Bibliography

NIMMER, MELVILLE B. 1973 The Meaning of Symbolic Speech to the First Amendment. *UCLA Law Review* 21:29–62.

TAFT, ROBERT A.
(1889–1953)

Senator Robert Alphonso Taft, the son of President and Chief Justice WILLIAM HOWARD TAFT, was a leader of Republican opposition to the New Deal policies of FRANKLIN D. ROOSEVELT. A graduate of Yale University and Harvard Law School, Taft served in the Ohio legislature from 1921 to 1933. His public crusade against the Roosevelt revolution began in 1935; in 1938 he was elected to the United States Senate, sworn to do battle against "the mistaken belief that government can remove all poverty, redistribute all wealth, and bestow happiness on every citizen."

An advocate of STRICT CONSTRUCTION of constitutional provisions that confer power on government, Taft severely criticized Roosevelt's appointees to the Supreme Court for acting as if "constitutional principles are weak as water" by abdicating their duty to keep the government within the limits set by the Constitution. He strongly urged that Congress become the locus of responsible CONSTITUTIONALISM, and he opposed, both in peacetime and wartime, DELEGATIONS OF POWER to the executive branch.

Taft continued to oppose expansion of the executive power after HARRY S. TRUMAN became President. During the STEEL SEIZURE CONTROVERSY Taft argued that if the President could increase his own powers by simply declaring a national emergency the Constitution would become a dead letter. Taft used his position as chairman of the Senate Labor Committee to sponsor a comprehensive reform of federal labor law, now known as the TAFT-HARTLEY ACT.

After a decade and a half of being "Mr. Republican," Taft felt entitled to his party's presidential nomination in 1952. However, the nomination, and election to the presidency, went to General DWIGHT D. EISENHOWER, hero of World War II. Nevertheless, Taft had a major share in formulating the domestic policy of the new administration during its first year in office.

DENNIS J. MAHONEY

Bibliography

KIRK, RUSSEL and MCCLELLAN, JAMES 1967 *The Political Principles of Robert A. Taft.* New York: Fleet Press Corporation.

TAFT, WILLIAM HOWARD
(1857–1930)

William Howard Taft's life was amazing both for length of public service (1881–1930) and for the variety of his activities: prosecuting attorney in his native state of Ohio, superior court judge in Cincinnati, SOLICITOR GENERAL of the United States, federal circuit court judge, governor general of the Philippine Islands, cabinet member, President of the United States (1908–1912), professor of law at Yale, and Chief Justice of the United States (1921–1930).

Taft appeared to be almost the prototype of a Chief Justice. Large of frame and good-natured, weighing well over 350 pounds, he filled out the popular image. His gallantry was famous. "I heard recently," Justice DAVID J. BREWER reported, "that he arose in a street car and gave his seat to three women."

Taft idolized Chief Justice JOHN MARSHALL. One day, passing by the west entrance to the Capitol, he paused in front of the bronze statue of Marshall. "Would you rather have been Marshall than President?" a friend asked. "Of course," Taft answered, "I would rather have been Marshall than any other American unless it had been Washington, and I am inclined to think I would rather have been Marshall than Washington. He made this country." Taft himself became the only man in history to occupy both the White House and the Supreme Court's center chair.

During Roosevelt's administration Taft rejected two opportunities to join the Supreme Court as associate justice. As successor to Roosevelt in the White House, Taft thought longingly about the future and pined to succeed aging Chief Justice MELVILLE W. FULLER. "If the Chief Justice would only retire," Taft lamented, "how simple everything would become!"

As President Taft signed Associate Justice EDWARD D. WHITE's commission as Chief Justice, he grieved: "There is nothing I would have liked more than being Chief Justice of the United States. I can't help seeing the irony in the fact that I, who desired that office so much, should now be signing the commission of another man." Rating Supreme Court appointments as among his most important presidential functions, Taft had the opportunity to appoint five associate Justices as well as the Chief—WILLIS VAN DEVANTER, HORACE H. LURTON, JOSEPH R. LAMAR, CHARLES EVANS HUGHES, and MAHLON PITNEY. Each appointment was a continuing source of pride to Taft, who at every opportunity underscored the importance of the judiciary.

Taft's cordial relations with Roosevelt did not last. Differences developed during Taft's presidency over questions of policy and administration. Finally the clash led to a split in the Republican Party. As a result, when Taft ran for reelection in 1912 Roosevelt ran as a Progressive. The upshot was a Democratic victory and the election of WOODROW WILSON as President.

After Justice Lamar died, rumor began to spread that the new President might, rising above party politics, follow the example of his predecessor's high-mindedness when in 1910 Taft had selected as Chief Justice a southern Democrat and Roman Catholic, Associate Justice Edward D. White. But Wilson appointed LOUIS D. BRANDEIS instead, and Taft, outraged by that appointment, declared that Brandeis was "not a fit person to be a member of the Court."

In 1919, Taft was off the public payroll for the first time. Soon he took a position at Yale, teaching constitutional law. Meanwhile, the chief justiceship seemed a remote possibility. Prospects brightened in 1920 with the smashing Republican victory of WARREN G. HARDING. Shortly after Harding's election the unblushing aspirant made the pilgrimage to Marion, Ohio. Taft was "nearly struck dumb" when the President-elect broached a Supreme Court appointment. Of course, the former President was available, but he made it clear that, having appointed three of the present bench and three others and, having vigorously opposed Brandeis's appointment in 1916, he would accept only the chief justiceship.

Taft's opportunity to achieve his ambition was not altogether accidental. During his presidency, when Chief Justice Fuller died, two choices loomed as possibilities—CHARLES EVANS HUGHES and Edward D. White. The latter, seventeen years Hughes's senior, received the nod. Had Taft chosen Hughes, instead of White, his lifelong ambition would not have been realized.

The office of Chief Justice carries scant inherent power. He manages the docket, presents the cases in conference, and guides discussion. When in the majority, he assigns the writing of opinions. In 1921 Taft remarked: "The Chief Justice goes into a monastery." Yet it is difficult to think of a Chief Justice who more frequently violated the American Bar Association's canons of judicial propriety on so many fronts. During the presidency of CALVIN COOLIDGE he was often a White House visitor. His political activities ranged widely over legislation and judicial appointments at all levels. In his choice of judges his alleged purpose was competence. But Taft even opposed selection of the eminent New York Judge BENJAMIN N. CARDOZO, fearful lest he "herd with [OLIVER WENDELL] HOLMES and Brandeis." At the outset, he had kind words for HARLAN F. STONE, indeed claimed credit for his appointment to the Court. But when Stone began to join Holmes and Brandeis, the Chief Justice became increasingly critical.

As institutional architect, Taft ranks second only to OLIVER ELLSWORTH, the third Chief Justice, who originally devised the judicial system. Taft's best known extrajudicial achievement, "The Judges' Bill" of 1925, giving the Supreme Court control over its docket, passed with only token opposition. Soon Congress authorized other procedural changes Taft had long advocated. To achieve these reforms Taft lobbied Presidents and members of Congress and sought press support. The most striking example of his effectiveness as a lobbyist was his campaign for the marble palace in which the Court now sits. At the cornerstone ceremony, in October 1932, Chief Justice Hughes declared: "For this enterprise progressing to completion we are indebted to the late Chief Justice William Howard Taft more than anyone else. The building is the result of his intelligent persistence."

Taft's goals as Chief Justice were efficiency, prompt dispatch of the Court's business, and harmonious relations among his colleagues. His overwhelming desire was to "mass" the Court. For the ex-President, Brandeis's appointment had been "one of the deepest wounds that I have had as an American and a lover of the constitution and a believer in progressive conservatism." Naturally Taft anticipated strained relations with his new colleague. To smooth this possible difficulty he wrote Brandeis long letters on the desirability of taking prompt steps to make the Court more efficient. Such friendly appeals moved his brother Horace to predict: "I expect to see you and Brandeis hobnobbing together with the utmost good will." Taft's strategy worked. Soon he was able to write: "I've come to like Brandeis very much." The feeling was mutual. Brandeis thought of Taft as "a cultivated man" and enjoyed talking with him. The Chief Justice's brother thought Brandeis "had been taken into camp." Justice JOHN H. CLARKE resigned because he believed that Brandeis could no longer be counted on to uphold the liberal stance.

"Things go happily in the CONFERENCE room with Taft," Brandeis commented. "The judges go home less tired emotionally and less weary physically than in White's day. When we differ, we agree to differ without any ill feelings." It seems likely that certain of Brandeis's unpublished opinions reflect his high regard for the Chief Justice. In one decision in particular, the second child labor case, BAILEY V. DREXEL FURNITURE CO. (1922), Taft writing for the Court invoked the authority of HAMMER V. DAGENHART (1918), a singularly conservative ruling. Yet, Brandeis went along with the majority, explaining: "I can't always dissent. I sometimes endorse an opinion with which I do not agree. I acquiesce." Brandeis's silence may have been the measure of Taft's gift for leadership.

In ALEXANDER BICKEL's volume, *The Unpublished Opinions of Mr. Justice Brandeis* (1957), eight out of eleven were prepared during less than ten years of Taft's chief justiceship. Taft went to great pains to create esprit de corps. Seemingly trivial personal considerations—the sending of a salmon to Justice WILLIS VAN DEVANTER, the customary ride he gave Holmes and Brandeis after the Saturday conference, the Christmas card that always went out to Justice JOSEPH MCKENNA—all such thoughtful attention to highly dissimilar human beings contributed immeasurably to judicial teamwork.

Justice Van Devanter posed a unique problem. He was indispensable in conference where Taft was not always acquainted with judicial technicalities or even facts of the cases. But Van Devanter was "opinion shy." This, however, evoked no complaint from the Chief Justice, even if he wrote no opinions at all. Taft regarded him as "the mainstay of the Court" and dubbed him "my Lord Chancellor."

Taft was determined to make the Court's promptness "a model for the courts of the country." His colleagues, as Holmes said, approved the Chief's "way of conducting business . . . especially his disinclination to put cases over." To accelerate the Court's work, Taft urged cutting vacations from seventeen to twelve weeks and using various time-saving devices.

Taft's first major opinion, TRUAX V. CORRIGAN (1921), involved the constitutionality of an Arizona statute barring state courts from issuing injunctions in LABOR cases, except under special conditions. Owners of a restaurant sought an injunction against a BOYCOTT and PICKETING of their place of business. A majority of five Justices, concluding that the bar against injunctions denied DUE PROCESS OF LAW and EQUAL PROTECTION OF THE LAW, declared the act unconstitutional. "A law which operates to make lawful such a wrong as described in the plaintiff's complaint," the Chief Justice observed, "deprives the owner of the business and the premises of his property without due process of law and cannot be held valid under the FOURTEENTH AMENDMENT. . . . The Constitution was intended, its very purpose was to prevent experimentation with the fundamental rights of the individual."

Taft's next major opinion, STAFFORD V. WALLACE (1922), upheld broad federal power under the COMMERCE CLAUSE, announcing that Congress had a "wide area of discretion, free from judicial second guessing." At issue was the PACKERS AND STOCKYARD ACT of 1929, regulating the business of packers done in INTERSTATE COMMERCE. The "chief evil" Congress aimed at was the monopoly of packers, "enabling them unduly and arbitrarily to lower prices to the shipper who sells, and unduly and arbitrarily to increase the price to the consumer who buys." In deciding *Stafford* Taft relied mainly on Holmes's majority opinion in SWIFT V. UNITED STATES (1905). "That case," wrote the Chief Justice, "was a milestone in the interpretation of the Commerce Clause of the Constitution. It recognized the great changes and development in the business of this vast country and drew again the dividing line between interstate and intrastate commerce where the Constitution intended it to be. It refused to permit local incidents of great interstate movements which, taken alone, were intrastate, to characterize the movement as such. The *Swift* case merely fitted the Commerce Clause to the real and practical essence of modern business growth."

Another example of Taft's effort to keep the Court "consistent with itself" was ADKINS V. CHILDREN'S HOSPITAL (1923) involving an act of Congress fixing the minimum wage for women and minors. Speaking for the Court, Justice Sutherland invalidated the act, relying primarily on Justice RUFUS PECKHAM'S reactionary decision in LOCHNER V. NEW YORK (1905). Refusing to endorse *Lochner,* Taft and Holmes dissented: "It is impossible," the Chief Justice explained, "for me to reconcile the *Bunting* [*v. Oregon*] case of 1917 and the *Lochner* case and I have always supposed that the *Lochner* case was thus overruled *sub silentio.*" Although Sutherland and Taft disagreed in *Adkins,* Taft could not bring himself to endorse Holmes's dissent because of its irreverent treatment of the FREEDOM OF CONTRACT doctrine. And in *Wolff Packing Co. v. Court of Industrial Relations* (1923) Taft for the Court approvingly cited Sutherland's *Adkins* opinion on that doctrine.

The year 1926 witnessed a significant decision in American constitutional history: the 6–3 ruling in MYERS V. UNITED STATES upholding the President's power to remove a postmaster without the consent of the Senate. Said Taft: "I never wrote an opinion that I felt to be so important in its effect." The Chief Justice's unqualified appraisal reflects his White House experience. There were three dissenters—Holmes, JAMES C. MCREYNOLDS, and Brandeis. Brandeis wrote: "The separation of powers of government did not make each branch completely autonomous. It left each in some measure dependent on the other. . . . The doctrine of SEPARATION OF POWERS was adopted by the [CONSTITUTIONAL] CONVENTION OF 1787, not to promote efficiency but to preclude the exercise of arbitrary power. The purpose was not to avoid friction, but by means of the inevitable friction incident to the distribution of governmental powers among the departments, to save the people from autocracy."

Taft did not live to see the Court's later qualification of the President's power to remove executive officers. In HUMPHREY'S EXECUTOR V. UNITED STATES (1935) the President was denied executive power to remove a federal trade commissioner, appointed for seven years with the ADVICE AND CONSENT of the Senate, on the score of inefficiency or neglect of duty. Speak-

ing for the Court in that later case, Justice Sutherland, who had enjoyed most cordial relations with Taft, went out of his way to say that the authority of the *Myers* case remained intact. The Court did not adopt the views of the *Myers* dissenters, but shifted emphasis from the "simple logic" of Article II of the Constitution—that the removal power is inherently "executive"—to the theory that a postmaster "is merely one of the units in the executive department and hence inherently subject to the exclusive and illimitable power of removal by the Chief Executive whose subordinate and aide he is."

As Taft's tenure drew to a close, dissents came more frequently and vehemently. Holmes and Brandeis, who had dissented from Taft's first major opinion in *Truax,* dissented from his last major opinion in OLMSTEAD V. UNITED STATES (1928). Justice Stone and even Justice PIERCE BUTLER joined the dissenters. Taft, a crusader for stricter enforcement of the criminal law, narrowly construed the FOURTH AMENDMENT'S ban on unreasonable searches and seizures by ruling that evidence obtained by wiretapping could be introduced at a criminal trial. In the face of hostile criticism of his *Olmstead* opinion, Taft declared privately, "If they think we are going to be frightened in our effort to stand by the law and give the public a chance to punish criminals, they are mistaken, even though we are condemned for lack of high ideals." Taft thought that Holmes's dissent was sentimental in declaring that "it is a lesser evil that some criminals should escape than that the Government should play an ignoble part."

Near the end, Taft winced nervously whenever he contemplated his probable successor. Knowing that President HERBERT C. HOOVER's attachment to Stone was "very great," Taft feared the worst: "I have no doubt that if I were to retire or die, the President would appoint Stone head of the Court." Once in the Chief Justice's good graces, Stone had fallen into profound disfavor. "He definitely has ranged himself with Brandeis and with Holmes in a good many of our constitutional differences." Nor was Stone's "herding" with the Court's "kickers" his only shortcoming. He was "not a great leader and would have a great deal of trouble in massing the Court." The Chief was not entirely without hope: "With Van and Mac and Sutherland and you and Sanford," he wrote to Justice Butler in 1929, "there will be five to steady the boat. So there would be a great deal of difficulty in working through reversals of present positions, even if I either had to retire or were gathered to my fathers, so that we must not give up at once."

Taft's triumphant march continued to the end, but

the future was clouded with uncertainty. By 1929 the world he had known and the people on whom he relied were in eclipse. As the economy slid rapidly toward the abyss, government intervention was openly advocated. To combat these forces, Taft's determination stiffened. "As long as things continue as they are and I am able to answer in my place," he resolved to "stay on the Court in order to prevent the Bolsheviki from getting control." President Hoover, Taft thought, "would put in some rather extreme destroyers of the Constitution. . . ."

None of Taft's predecessors, with the possible exception of Marshall, entertained so expansive a view of the chief justiceship, or used it so effectively on so many fronts. Taft was a great administrator, a great judicial architect, a skillful harmonizer of human relations. Yet he is not commonly considered a great Chief Justice.

ALPHEUS THOMAS MASON

Bibliography
MASON, ALPHEUS THOMAS 1930 The Labor Decisions of Chief Justice Taft. *University of Pennsylvania Law Review* 78:585–625.
——— 1979 *The Supreme Court from Taft to Burger.* Baton Rouge: Louisiana State University Press.
——— 1964 *William Howard Taft: Chief Justice.* New York: Simon & Schuster.
McHALE, FRANCIS 1931 *President and Chief Justice: The Life and Public Services of William Howard Taft.* Philadelphia: Dorrance.
MURPHY, W. F. 1962 Chief Justice Taft and the Lower Court Bureaucracy. *Journal of Politics* 24:453–476.
——— 1961 In His Own Image: Mr. Justice Taft and Supreme Court Appointments. *Supreme Court Review* 1961:159–193.
PRINGLE, H. F. 1939 *The Life and Times of William Howard Taft.* New York: Farrar & Rinehart.

TAFT COURT
(1921–1930)

WILLIAM HOWARD TAFT became Chief Justice of the United States on June 30, 1921. Never before or since has any person brought such a range of distinguished experience in public affairs and professional qualifications to the bench. Taft presided over a court that included Justices of highly varied abilities and achievements. In 1921, OLIVER WENDELL HOLMES, already a great figure of the law, had served nineteen years on the Supreme Court. He remained on the Court throughout Taft's tenure and beyond. Holmes's only equal on the Court was LOUIS D. BRANDEIS, who

had been on the Court barely five years at Taft's accession. Taft, a private citizen in 1916, had vigorously opposed the appointment of Brandeis to the High Court. Although they remained ideological opponents and although some mistrust persisted on both sides, they maintained cordial relations, carrying on their opposition in a highly civil manner.

The rest of the Court that Taft inherited lacked the stature or ability of Holmes and Brandeis. Three Justices, JOHN J. CLARKE, MAHLON PITNEY, and WILLIAM R. DAY would retire within the first two years of Taft's tenure. Their retirements gave President WARREN C. HARDING a chance to reconstitute the Court. The President appointed his former Senate colleague GEORGE H. SUTHERLAND to one of the vacancies. The other two spots were filled by men strongly recommended by Taft: PIERCE BUTLER and EDWARD T. SANFORD.

The other Justices on the Court in 1921 were WILLIS VAN DEVANTER, JAMES C. McREYNOLDS, and JOSEPH McKENNA. Van Devanter had been appointed to the bench by Taft when he was President. He, like Butler and Sanford, continued to be strongly influenced by the Chief Justice. During the Taft years, he served the Chief Justice in the performance of many important institutional tasks outside the realm of decision making and opinion writing. For example, Van Devanter led the drive to revamp the JURISDICTION of the Supreme Court in the "Judges' Bill," the JUDICIARY ACT OF 1925. McReynolds, a Wilson appointee, was an iconoclastic conservative of well-defined prejudices.

Finally, Taft inherited Joseph McKenna, whose failing health impaired his judicial performance. In 1925, Taft, after consulting the other justices, urged McKenna to retire. McKenna was succeeded by HARLAN F. STONE. Though deferential to Taft at the outset, by the end of the decade Stone became increasingly identified with the dissenting positions of Holmes and Brandeis. From early 1923 through Taft's resignation only that one change took place.

Because of the substantial continuity of personnel the Taft Court can be thought of as an institution with a personality and with well-defined positions on most critical issues that came before it. Outcomes were as predictable as they ever can be, and the reasoning, persuasive or not, was consistent.

Taft was a strong Chief Justice. He lobbied powerfully for more federal judges, for a streamlined federal procedure, for reorganization of the federal judiciary, and for greater control by the Supreme Court over the cases it would decide. The most concrete of Taft's reforms was a new building for the Court itself, though the building was not completed until after his death.

A second major institutional change was completed during Taft's term. In 1925 Congress passed the "Judges' Bill." The Supreme Court's agenda is one of the most important factors in determining the evolution of constitutional law. Until 1891 that agenda had been determined largely at the initiative of litigants. In 1891 the Court received authority to review certain classes of cases by the discretionary WRIT OF CERTIORARI. However, many lower court decisions had continued to be reviewable as of right in the Supreme Court even after 1891. The 1925 act altered the balance by establishing the largely discretionary certiorari jurisdiction of the Supreme Court as it has remained for six decades. The act was one of Taft's major projects. It relieved the docket pressure occasioned by the press of obligatory jurisdiction, and placed agenda control at the very center of constitutional politics.

The successful initiatives of the Court in seizing control of its own constitutional agenda and constructing a new home should not obscure the fact that the Court's institutional position was, as always, under attack during the 1920s. A spate of what were perceived as antilabor decisions in 1921–1922 led to calls from the labor movement and congressional progressives to circumscribe the Court's powers. In the 1924 election Robert LaFollette, running as a third-party candidate on the Progressive ticket, called for a constitutional amendment to limit JUDICIAL REVIEW. Both the Republican incumbent, CALVIN COOLIDGE, and the 1924 Democratic candidate, JOHN W. DAVIS, defended the Court against LaFollette. The upshot of the unsuccessful LaFollette campaign was a heightened sensitivity to judicial review as an issue and a firm demonstration of the consensus as to its legitimacy and centrality in the American constitutional system.

Much of the labor movement had supported LaFollette's initiatives against judicial review, but labor specifically sought limitations on federal court labor INJUNCTIONS. Labor's campaign against injunctions peaked in 1927 after the Supreme Court simultaneously declined to review a series of controversial injunctions in the West Virginia coal fields and approved an injunction in BEDFORD CUT STONE COMPANY V. JOURNEYMAN STONECUTTERS, holding that a union's nationwide refusal to handle nonunion stone should be enjoined as an agreement in RESTRAINT OF TRADE. Between 1928 and 1930 the shape of what was to become the NORRIS-LAGUARDIA ACT OF 1932 emerged in Congress. The impetus behind that law,

the politics of it, indeed, the language and theory of the statute itself are rooted in the Taft years.

A description of the Court's institutional role must consider the relations between CONGRESS AND THE COURT in shaping constitutional law and constitutional politics. During the Taft years a dialogue between Court and Congress persisted on a variety of crucial constitutional issues. The decision of the Court striking down the first Child Labor Act in HAMMER V. DAGENHART (1918) led to congressional interest in using the taxing power to circumvent apparent limitations on the direct regulatory authority of Congress under the COMMERCE CLAUSE. The second Child Labor Act imposed an excise tax on the profits of firms employing child labor. That act was struck down as unconstitutional in 1922.

From 1922 on Congress had before it various versions of antilynching legislation—most notably the Dyer Bill, which had actually passed the House. Opponents of the antilynching legislation argued that it was an unconstitutional federal usurpation of state functions. In *Moore v. Dempsey* (1923), decided shortly after the Dyer Bill had nearly succeeded in passage, the Court held that a state criminal trial dominated by a mob constituted a denial of DUE PROCESS OF LAW, appropriately redressed in a federal HABEAS CORPUS proceeding. *Moore v. Dempsey* did not establish that an antilynching law would be constitutional. Yet a conclusion that mob domination of a criminal trial did *not* deny due process surely would have been a constitutional nail in the coffin of antilynching laws. And, prior to *Moore v. Dempsey* the relatively recent PRECEDENT of FRANK V. MANGUM (1915) had pointed toward just such a conclusion. Considerations concerning the response of Congress regularly influenced the constitutional decision making of the Taft Court. When Taft was appointed, three important labor cases were pending that had been argued but not decided by the WHITE COURT. The Court had reached an impasse. Two of the cases presented questions about the use of injunctions to restrain labor picketing. Section 20 of the Clayton Act appeared to deny the federal courts the power to issue such injunctions subject to certain exceptions, most notably the power to use the injunction to protect property from damage. *American Steel Foundries v. Tri-City Labor Council* presented questions of construction of this section, and TRUAX V. CORRIGAN, involving a state law, presented a constitutional variant of the Clayton Act problem.

In *American Steel Foundries*, Taft's first significant opinion as Chief Justice, the Court read section 20 to encompass protection of the property interest in an ongoing business from unreasonable or intimidating picketing or from illegal BOYCOTTS or strikes. Statutory construction thus preserved the injunction as a restraint on labor.

But not all state courts saw the issue as the Taft Court did. The Arizona Supreme Court read its statute to bar injunctions in labor disputes, at least where actual destruction of physical property was not threatened. In *Truax v. Corrigan,* decided a week after *American Steel Foundries,* Taft wrote for a majority of five, holding that Arizona had unconstitutionally denied employers the injunction in labor disputes. *Truax* in effect created a constitutional *right* to a labor injunction. It did so on two grounds. First, it held that employers were denied the EQUAL PROTECTION OF THE LAWS insofar as their particular type of property interest was denied the same protection afforded other property interests. Second, it held that the failure to protect the interest in the continued operation of a business deprived the business owner of property without due process of law. *Truax v. Corrigan* was the cornerstone of the Taft Court edifice of industrial relations. Not only did the decision suggest that Congress could not constitutionally prevent the federal courts from granting labor injunctions, but it also ushered in a decade of the most intensive use of the labor injunction the country had ever seen. A desperate battle was fought to save the unionized sector of coal from competition from the newer, largely nonunion, southern mines. That union campaign was broken by dozens of labor injunctions upheld by the Fourth Circuit in a consolidated appeal. The Supreme Court's refusal to review those decisions in 1927 attracted larger headlines than all but the most significant of Supreme Court opinions ever get. The Fourth Circuit opinion later cost Circuit Judge John J. H. Parker a seat on the Supreme Court. In fact, however, his conclusion was an all but inevitable consequence of the Supreme Court's position in *Truax v. Corrigan.*

The industrial order that the Taft Court sought to protect from labor insurgency was itself built upon uncertain constitutional foundations. The Taft Court was not committed, unambiguously, to a laissez-faire market. The Court distinguished sharply between legislation regulating the price (wage or rent) terms of a contract and laws regulating other terms. Thus, in the best known of its apparent inconsistencies, the Taft Court held void a District of Columbia law prescribing a minimum wage for women, although only a year later it upheld a New York law establishing maximum hours for women. The Court also struck

down a state statute regulating fees or commissions for employment brokers while intimating that other reasonable regulatory measures directed at employment brokerage would be upheld.

Sutherland, in his peculiar majority opinion in the minimum wage case—ADKINS V. CHILDREN'S HOSPITAL (1923)—seemed preoccupied with the redistributive aspects of the minimum wage law. There was nothing wrong with a legislative preference for a living (minimum) wage; the problem lay in imposing an obligation on the employer to pay it. One person's need, he argued, could not, in itself, justify another's obligation to satisfy it. The regulation of nonprice terms need not be redistributive in effect, for the costs of any such regulation could be recaptured by negotiated changes in price. If the Court was seeking to protect bargains against regulation with redistribution effect, then shielding price terms from governmental interference was the most visible and easily understood way to accomplish its purpose.

In general the Taft Court sought to maintain principled distinctions among three forms of economic activity. Government enterprise was subject to the usual constitutional constraints upon government. This form of economic activity was relatively unimportant in the 1920s, although in cases involving municipal utilities the Court had some opportunity to address such issues as contractual rate structure. The Court spoke more frequently to the problem of transition from private to public or from public to private enterprise. World War I had seen government control of the railroads, shipping, coal, and, to a lesser degree, labor relations generally. The Court had to develop principles of compensation to govern the takeover and return of such large-scale enterprises.

More important than the dichotomy between governmental and private economic activity was the distinction drawn between private activity AFFECTED WITH A PUBLIC INTEREST and the more general run of private economic endeavor. Upon this distinction turned the constitutionality of public regulation—including price regulation in some circumstances—of various forms of economic activity. Although the category of business affected with a public interest had been part of the Court's rhetorical stock in trade for almost half a century when Taft took his seat, it assumed particular significance through the decade beginning with a case from Kansas. In 1920, having survived the effects of a bitter coal strike, Kansas passed its Industrial Court Act, declaring all production and distribution of food, clothing, shelter, and fuel for human consumption or use to be business affected with a public interest. Public transportation and public utilities were also so labeled. The act forbade strikes, lockouts, and plant closings in all such industries except by order of the Kansas Court of Industrial Relations. Moreover, that court upon its own motion or upon the petition of virtually any person could adjudicate the fitness or adequacy of wages and prices in any such business. The act contemplated a form of compulsory arbitration to replace labor bargaining against a background of strikes and lockouts.

In a series of unanimous opinions the Supreme Court struck down one after another of these innovative aspects of the Kansas act. Taft, in the leading opinion, WOLFF PACKING CORPORATION V. COURT OF INDUSTRIAL RELATIONS (1923) held that the state could not, by legislative fiat, declare businesses to be affected with a public interest for purposes so comprehensive as to include supervision of their wage and price structures. Taft's opinion wholly failed to state a principled distinction between those businesses traditionally subject to price regulation (such as grain elevators), on the one hand, and meat packing, on the other. In OBITER DICTUM he suggested that the competitive structure of the industry was not determinative of the legislature's power to regulate. But the opinion did acknowledge that long-established law permitted regulation of publicly conferred monopolies and of common carriers or inns even if not monopolies.

The Taft Court thus rejected a generalization, based on the war experience, that all basic economic activity could be defined as affected with a public interest. But the Court was not unmindful of the war's lessons. Unanimously it upheld the recapture provisions of the [Railroad] Transportation Act of 1920 despite the overt redistributive effect of the law. The act required the payment into a federal trust fund of half the profits earned by strong railroads, for redistribution to failing ones. The Chief Justice, at least, understood the recapture provisions as justified in part because the alternative to such a scheme might have to be nationalization. Furthermore, the Court had already gone to great lengths to uphold other, seemingly inevitable, characteristics of rate regulation in an integrated transportation system. The Interstate Commerce Commission (ICC), if it were to be effective at all, needed power to regulate joint rates over hauls using more than one line for a single journey. It was apparent that the apportionment of joint rates could be used to redistributive effect. In the *New England Divisions Case* (1923) the Court had already upheld the ICC's explicit consideration of the need to strengthen the weaker New England lines when

it apportioned revenues from joint rates. It was a short step from such use of joint rates to the recapture provisions.

The Court's willingness to accept some qualifications of vested property rights in the interest of planning was not confined to such traditional areas of regulation as transportation and public utilities. The Court decided its first cases challenging general ZONING ordinances in the 1920s and, on the whole, upheld the power, though not without significant dissent and important qualifications.

Despite the Court's upholding of zoning and of regulatory initiatives such as the recapture provisions, the Taft Court has long been considered to have been ardent in imposing constitutional limits upon legislation that restricted vested property interests. That reputation is soundly based, although the extent to which the Taft Court differed from predecessor and successor Courts has been substantially exaggerated by FELIX FRANKFURTER and his followers.

Perhaps the best known of the Taft Court pronouncements on the constitutional protection of property is Justice Holmes's opinion for the Court in *Pennsylvania Coal Company v. Mahon* (1923). Pennsylvania's Kohler Act required anthracite coal mining to be done so as to avoid subsidence of surface areas at or near buildings, streets, and other structures used by human beings. The Court held unconstitutional the application of the law to mining in an area where the mining company had conveyed surface rights, expressly reserving to itself and to its successors the subsurface mining rights.

Despite Brandeis's dissenting opinion, Holmes's opinion was moderate in tone and antithetical to the sort of dogmatics that characterized Sutherland's opinions in the wage and price regulation area. Indeed, Holmes's methodology was explicitly one that reduced the takings/regulation distinction to a matter of degree—as Holmes himself once recognized in a flippant reference to "the petty larceny of the police power." Moreover, the Court that decided *Pennsylvania Coal* decided the case of *Miller v. Schoene* (1928) five years later, upholding a Virginia law providing for the uncompensated (or less than fully compensated) destruction of cedar trees infected with cedar rust, a condition harmful only to neighboring apple trees.

The Court also had to face the implications of the constitutional protection of property in considering the methodology of public utility rate regulation. In a series of cases beginning in 1923 and proceeding throughout the Taft period, Justice Brandeis posed a major challenge to the "fair value" methodology of SMYTH V. AMES (1895). Industry during the 1920s argued that the rate base—the "property" upon which the Constitution guaranteed a reasonable rate of permissible return—should be valued according to the replacement cost of capital items—despite a general inflationary trend, accelerated by World War I. Brandeis formulated a comprehensive critique both of this particular windfall calculation and of the rule that produced it. Brandeis first reformulated the problem in a characteristically daring way. The issue was not so much a vested right to a return on capital as it was the necessity for a level of profit that could attract the new capital required for effective operation of the public utility. Brandeis lost the battle for a new approach to rate-making. Yet here, no less than in other arenas for disputes over the constitutional protection of property, doctrinal lines had been drawn that anticipated the issues of the New Deal.

Traditional, genteel conservativism is neither overtly ideological in content nor strident in manner. In most respects the Taft Court was traditionally conservative. The Court was hostile to labor and to any insurgency from the left, but the hostility usually took the form of a neutral defense of civil order. That neutrality, though it almost always worked against the left, was not explicitly one-sided and was, in fact, applied occasionally against rightist militant politics and street activity as well.

The constitutional defense of civil order entailed a strong commitment to ratify the acts of local government and of the national political branches so long as their power and authority were used to put down militant politics and especially politics of the street. Thus, the Court consistently upheld CRIMINAL SYNDICALISM LAWS, even while recognizing, in GITLOW V. NEW YORK (1925), that the FIRST AMENDMENT limited state as well as federal legislative power. Moreover, in a theoretically interesting, though practically less significant case, the Court upheld a New York law requiring the registration and disclosure of names of members of certain secret societies—a measure directed against the Ku Klux Klan. Brandeis and Holmes repeatedly dissented in the criminal syndicalism cases, sketching an alternative version of the political process far more hospitable to insurgent initiatives for change.

A second pillar of the defense of civic order was the reliance upon independent courts as guarantors of vested property rights against street politics. To this end the injunction was elevated to a constitutional pedestal. *Truax v. Corrigan*, which constitutionalized capital's right to a labor injunction, must be seen not only as a part of a larger antilabor *corpus* but also as the link between that work and the principle of civic order.

For traditional conservatives the injunction had much to commend it. It was in the hands of politically independent judges, who were less susceptible than other officials to mass pressure. It was governed—or supposed to be governed—by neutral principles rather than special interests; it permitted the adaptation of principle to local needs and adjusted the level of intervention to that necessary to shore up appropriately sound local elites. No wonder, then, that the issue of the injunction pervaded the constitutional politics of the 1920s.

If Taft was committed to the courts' playing a dominant role in labor discipline and the guarantee of civic order, he was at the same time committed to an efficient, unintimidated, and uncorrupted judiciary to do the job. In *Tumey v. Ohio* (1927) he wrote for a unanimous Court striking down as a denial of due process an Ohio scheme through which a public official judging traffic violations was paid a percentage of the fines collected. Of greater significance was MOORE V. DEMPSEY (1923), in which a divided Court upheld the power of a federal district court in federal HABEAS CORPUS proceedings to go behind the record of a state court murder conviction to determine whether the trial had been dominated by a mob.

Racist justice was a deeply rooted problem, not high on the conservative agenda for reform. Taft was, however, very concerned with the potential for corruption of the courts inherent in the great national experiment of the decade, prohibition. The Chief Justice realized that there were many opportunities for organized crime in the liquor business to buy friendly judges and other officials, especially in states where prohibition was unpopular. The Court refused to extend the protection of the DOUBLE JEOPARDY principle to cases of successive prosecutions under state and federal law for substantially the same conduct. Part of the reason for this limit upon the double jeopardy principle was the potential under any contrary rule of insulating conduct from federal prosecution by securing a state conviction and paying a small fine. The Court's interpretation of FEDERALISM to tolerate structural redundancy was thus a major prophylactic against the dangers of local corruption of courts.

Like all its predecessors, however conservative, the Taft Court paid lip service to the idea that the people are sovereign and, consequently, that popular government is a pervasive and overriding principle in constitutional interpretation. Even though dissenters within the court (Holmes and Brandeis) and critical commentators without (Frankfurter, EDWARD S. CORWIN, and

THOMAS REED POWELL) claimed that the Justices ignored the presumption of constitutionality that ought to attach to the work of the popular branches, the simple fact is that no Justice denied, as an abstract principle, either the presumption of constitutionality or the deference that ought to be paid to legislative judgments. It was the application of the principle that divided the Court.

Most of the Justices were skeptical of the capacity of the masses intelligently to exercise the rights and discharge the obligations of participatory, popular government. Taft himself welcomed a leading role for elites in suppressing, or at least damping, the demands of the rabble and in representing the "better class" of citizens. But Taft's views in these matters were not very different from those of Holmes. Holmes doubted the capacity of the masses and considered a dominant role for elites in politics to be almost a natural law. Brandeis, the only real contrast, was considerably more committed to reform and to its promise. But he, in his own way, also distrusted the masses. He saw hope for change in a shift from a propertied oligarchy to a technically trained meritocracy. At the same time Brandeis understood the limits of this vision. His support of STATES' RIGHTS and localism in politics and his hostility to concentration in industry had common roots: the recognition of limits to techniques of effective organization; the affirmation of political principles limiting concentrations of power; and the affirmation of the principles of maximum participation in public affairs. Chiefly in this last respect, Brandeis stood committed to a principle that the other Justices ignored or rejected.

In what ways did the general attitudes of the Justices to popular government affect the work of the Court? Perhaps the most direct effect was visible in the great, perennial debate over the power of judicial review. The Justices appear to have been unanimous in their private opposition to schemes such as that of LaFollette to limit the power of judicial review by statute or constitutional amendment. Even Brandeis, who was personally close to LaFollette and who supported the Wisconsin senator's positions on many substantive issues, opposed initiatives to curb the Court.

In at least one important area the Taft Court initiated a significant reform in the mechanics of popular government itself. The Court struck down the first version of the Texas system of white primaries which, through official state action, denied blacks the right to vote in statewide PRIMARY ELECTIONS. NIXON V. HERNDON (1927) was the first in a line of cases that ultimately destroyed the white primary device.

The Court upheld the power of Congress to conduct LEGISLATIVE INVESTIGATIONS and to use COMPULSORY PROCESS to that end. The Court also appeared to uphold an enlarged vision of an exclusive PRESIDENTIAL POWER to remove executive officers. A special constitutional status for government of TERRITORIES was approved. Finally, the Court struggled mightily but produced no satisfactory or consistent principles in the area of STATE TAXATION OF COMMERCE and STATE REGULATION OF COMMERCE.

The 1920s saw a determined attack upon the ethnic pluralism, the cultural and ethical relativism, and the absence of traditional controls that characterized a newly emergent urban America. The prohibition movement, resurgent religious fundamentalism, virulent nativism, and racism gave rise to a reactionary program for legal reform. In the area of prohibition the Court did more than give full effect to a constitutional amendment and its implementing legislation. The Justices also decided a host of criminal procedure issues in such a way as to arm the enforcers against what was perceived as a concerted attack on law and order themselves.

But the Court was actively hostile to groups like the "new" Ku Klux Klan. It not only upheld a Klan registration statute but also, in PIERCE V. SOCIETY OF SISTERS (1925), held invalid an Oregon statute that had effectively outlawed private schools. The law was the product of a popular initiative organized and vigorously supported by the Klan as part of its nativist and anti-Catholic crusade. The decision in MEYER V. NEBRASKA (1923) striking down laws forbidding the teaching of German in the schools also reflected the Justices' unwillingness to permit nativist sentiment to cut too deeply into the social fabric.

But the Court did uphold state ALIEN land ownership laws directed principally against Asian immigrants and upheld the disgraceful national discrimination against Asian immigration in the face of constitutional attack. The Court also permitted the continuation of restrictive covenants in housing (CORRIGAN V. BUCKLEY, 1926) and segregation in public schools (GONG LUM V. RICE, 1927), though in each instance it avoided an explicit articulation of constitutional approval for these practices.

The constitutional work of the Taft Court extended over the customary broad area of national life, but it was dominated by the motif of conflict between property and labor. Civil strife, policies toward insurgency, free or regulated markets, confiscation—all were issues that arose principally from the overarching conflict. It is a measure of the Taft Court's achievement that, through Brandeis on the one hand and

Taft on the other, a measure of clarity was achieved in articulating the implications of this conflict for constitutional structure and doctrine over a wide range of subjects. It was Taft's vision alone, however, that dominated the Court's action—consistently hostile to labor and its interests. The traditional conservative structure of property and order was one legacy of Taft's Court to the era of the Great Depression; Brandeis's vision—as yet wholly unrealized—was the other.

ROBERT M. COVER

Bibliography

BERNSTEIN, IRVING 1960 *The Lean Years: A History of the American Worker, 1920–1933.* Boston: Houghton Mifflin.
BICKEL, ALEXANDER M. 1957 *The Unpublished Opinions of Mr. Justice Brandeis: The Supreme Court at Work.* Cambridge, Mass.: Belknap Press of Harvard University Press.
DANELSKI, DAVID J. 1964 *A Supreme Court Justice Is Appointed.* New York: Random House.
FRANKFURTER, FELIX AND GREENE, NATHAN 1930 *The Labor Injunction.* New York: Macmillan.
MASON, ALPHEUS THOMAS 1946 *Brandeis: A Free Man's Life.* New York: Viking.
——— 1956 *Harlan Fiske Stone: Pillar of the Law.* New York: Viking.
——— 1964 *William Howard Taft: Chief Justice.* New York: Simon & Schuster.
MURPHY, WALTER F. 1964 *Elements of Judicial Strategy.* Chicago: University of Chicago Press.
PRINGLE, HENRY F. 1939 *The Life and Times of William Howard Taft.* New York: Farrar & Rinehart.
RABBAN, DAVID M. 1983 The Emergence of Modern First Amendment Doctrine. *University of Chicago Law Review* 50:1205–1355.

TAFT-HARTLEY LABOR RELATIONS ACT
61 Stat. 136 (1947)

Passed over President HARRY S. TRUMAN's veto, the Taft-Hartley Act represented Republican hostility to the power of labor unions and the National Labor Relations Board (NLRB); its provisions limit the authority and conduct of unions and their officials and curtail the Board's authority.

In amending the WAGNER (NATIONAL LABOR RELATIONS) ACT, the measure banned the CLOSED SHOP; permitted employers to sue unions for strike-incurred damages; forbade union contributions to political campaigns; required public disclosure of union finances; required unions to give sixty days notice before inau-

gurating strikes; and allowed the President to halt a major strike by seeking a court INJUNCTION for an eighty-day "cooling off" period. Although the right to COLLECTIVE BARGAINING was further guaranteed, section 14b permitted states to adopt RIGHT-TO-WORK LAWS, forbidding any requirement that workers join unions to hold jobs. Most constitutionally suspect were provisions requiring labor union officials, in order to use the facilities of the NLRB, to sign affidavits denying communist party membership or belief. These noncommunist oath provisions were unsuccessfully challenged in the courts in AMERICAN COMMUNICATIONS ASSOCIATION V. DOUDS (1950).

PAUL L. MURPHY

Bibliography

SUTHERLAND, ARTHUR E. 1948 The Constitutionality of the Taft-Hartley Law. *Industrial and Labor Relations Review* 1:177–205.

TAKAHASHI v. FISH AND GAME COMMISSION
334 U.S. 410 (1948)

Under California law, ALIENS ineligible for CITIZENSHIP (mainly Asians) could not hold commercial fishing licenses. Citing the broad power of Congress to regulate aliens, the Supreme Court held, 7–2, that the PREEMPTION DOCTRINE barred the law. The CIVIL RIGHTS ACT OF 1866 was taken to protect the rights of aliens to pursue their livelihoods under nondiscriminatory state laws. The opinion also conveyed overtones of FOURTEENTH AMENDMENT reasoning.

KENNETH L. KARST

TAKING OF PROPERTY

The authority of government to acquire private property from an involuntary owner (usually called the power of EMINENT DOMAIN) is recognized in the Fifth Amendment to the Constitution, which provides: "nor shall private property be taken for public use, without JUST COMPENSATION." The public use and compensation requirements of the Constitution apply not only to acquisitions by the federal government but—by INCORPORATION in the FOURTEENTH AMENDMENT—to acquisitions by the states as well. Similar provisions appear in the state constitutions, and the state and federal requirements are usually identically interpreted. It is, however, possible that a taking would pass muster under the federal Constitution and still be held to violate the state constitutional provision (or vice versa).

The requirement of PUBLIC USE has been liberally interpreted by the courts, which rarely find that a taking is not for a public use. For example, property may be taken for resale to private developers in an urban renewal project, or for the development of an industrial park. Indeed, the courts have permitted authority to take private property to be vested by LEGISLATION in privately owned public utilities, such as water companies. The test is not ultimate public ownership, or even direct public benefit, but rather the general benefit to the public from projects that are publicly sponsored or encouraged to promote the economy or the public welfare. The only clear limits on the broad interpretation of "public use" would be (1) the grant of the taking authority to a private company simply to improve its private economic position; or (2) the use of the taking power by the government if government itself were simply seeking to make money by engaging in strictly entrepreneurial activities.

The requirement of "just compensation" has been interpreted to mean the amount a willing seller would get from a willing buyer in the absence of the government's desire to acquire the property. The owner is not entitled to receive more for the property simply because the government has an urgent need for it— as for a military base. Neither may the owner receive less compensation because the government's plan for the area—to install a garbage dump, for example, has depressed neighborhood values. Nor is the owner entitled to increased compensation merely because the property has special value to him, such as sentimental or family value, or because he would not sell the property at any price. Compensation must be given in cash immediately upon the taking; government cannot oblige the owner to accept future promises of payment which may be unmarketable, or marketable only at a discount from the just compensation value.

Ordinarily there is no ambiguity about whether a property has been taken. Nor is there any ambiguity about the principle of takings law, stated at the most general level: if the public wants something, it should pay for it and not coerce private owners into contributing their property to the public. If government wants a site for a post office, for example, it is obliged to institute condemnation proceedings in court, leading to an involuntary transfer of title and possession, at which time it will pay the owner just compensation. But in many instances government legislates or behaves in a way that reduces or destroys the value of private property without formally taking title or pos-

session and without instituting condemnation proceedings. If the owner complains, seeking just compensation for a taking, government may reply that it has simply regulated under the POLICE POWER, but has not "taken" the property and thus need not compensate. The great bulk of all legal controversies over the taking of property turn on the question whether there has been a "taking" at all.

Plainly government sometimes gets the benefits of a taking without any of the formal incidents of ownership. A celebrated case, *Causby v. United States* (1946), involved the flight of military planes just above the surface of privately owned farmland adjacent to a military airport. As a result of noise from the overflights the farm was made virtually worthless for agricultural purposes. The farmer claimed that his farm had in practical effect been taken, that government was using it as a sort of extension of the runway, and that government should have to pay for it as it had for the rest of the airport. The Supreme Court agreed that this use of the farmland was a taking in effect, if not in form, and that the farmer was entitled to just compensation for what is called INVERSE CONDEMNATION.

This ruling does not mean that the neighbors of a public airport or highway subjected to noise that reduces their property values will always be compensated. In general such disadvantaged neighbors are not viewed by the courts as having had their property taken in the constitutional sense. The reason is that although a nearly total loss (such as the farmer sustained) is judicially viewed as a taking, some modest diminution of value resulting from neighboring public activities is viewed as one of the disadvantages of modern life that must be accepted by property owners.

The judicial focus on the quantum of loss as a test of a taking is called the diminution of value theory and was put forward many years ago by Justice OLIVER WENDELL HOLMES in *Pennsylvania Coal Co. v. Mahon* (1922). There is no clear line, Holmes believed, between the formal taking of property by government (in which title and possession are acquired) and the various forms of government regulation (such as zoning and pollution control), which do not transfer ownership formally, but restrict private owners' uses and values for the benefit of the general public. In both cases, according to Holmes, the traditional rights of private owners are being restricted for the benefit of the public. If there were no legal limits on such restrictions, he said, private property would be worthless and wholly at the mercy of government. On the other hand, Holmes said, if every value-diminishing regulation were viewed as a compensable taking of property, government would be unable to function, for essentially all of its regulatory activities (speed limits, liquor control, safety standards, rent control) disadvantage property owners to some degree.

He thus devised a practical test. We must all accept some impairment of property values so that society can function in a civilized way, and government must be permitted to make regulations requiring such impairments. If, however, the losses from such regulations become extreme—nearing total destruction of the property's value for any owner—then the society should compensate the owner and bear the losses of the regulation commonly. Thus, under the Holmesian theory, the amount of the loss and the ability of the owner to continue to earn some return from his property after the regulation has been imposed become the critical determinants of the constitutional question: has there been a taking for which compensation must be paid?

Although Holmes's test continues to dominate taking cases, there are a number of other theories that are widely found in the literature and in judicial opinions. One theory holds that prohibitions of certain socially undesirable uses do not qualify as compensable takings despite considerable loss to the owners, because one cannot be viewed as having a property right to engage in "noxious" conduct, and losses flowing from prohibition of such conduct is not a taking away of property. The illegalization of manufacture and sale of a dangerous drug, or of polluting activity, has been so categorized.

Another theory sometimes advanced is that certain government restrictions imposed on property owners are not a taking of property from the owners by the government, but are the merely regulation by the government of activities by which it mediates between various private uses in conflict with each other. Under this theory compensation is required only when the government as an enterprise itself benefits directly from the regulation (it gets additional space for its military airport, for example). The enterprise/regulation theory has sometimes been used to justify ZONING and other LAND USE controls that restrict the amount or type of building permitted to a landowner on his land. Modern historic preservation ordinances as well as safety and environmental controls are sometimes justified on this theory.

Still another view suggests that government may, without compensation, impose much greater restrictions to prevent future additional exploitation of property, while leaving existing uses, than it may cut back on existing uses. Thus, in PENN CENTRAL TRANSPORTATION CO. V. NEW YORK (1978), an important case,

the Supreme Court upheld a historic preservation ordinance prohibiting the owners of Grand Central Station in New York from building a high rise office tower above the railroad station, noting that the existing station did produce some economic return to the owners. The claimed "taking" of a property right to build a bigger building was rejected.

Although no single theory wholly dominates taking law, two guidelines permit safe prediction about the great majority of cases. Courts will find a taking and require just compensation if (1) the government acquires physical possession of the property; or if (2) regulation so reduces the owner's values that virtually no net economic return is left to the proprietor.

JOSEPH L. SAX

(SEE ALSO: *Dames & Moore v. Regan, 1981; Hawaii Housing Authority v. Midkiff, 1984.*)

Bibliography

ACKERMAN, BRUCE A. 1977 *Private Property and the Constitution.* New Haven, Conn.: Yale University Press.

BOSSELMAN, FRED; CALLIES, DAVID; and BANTA, JOHN 1973 *The Taking Issue.* Washington, D.C.: Council on Environmental Quality.

MICHELMAN, FRANK I. 1967 Property, Utility and Fairness: Comments on the Ethical Foundations of "Just Compensation" Law. *Harvard Law Review* 80:1165–1258.

SAX, JOSEPH L. 1971 Taking and the Police Power. *Yale Law Journal* 74:36–76.

———— 1971 Takings, Private Property and Public Rights. *Yale Law Journal* 81:149–186.

TANEY, ROGER BROOKE
(1777–1864)

Roger B. Taney, Chief Justice of the United States from 1836 until his death in 1864, profoundly shaped American constitutional development in cases dealing with states' regulatory powers, corporations, slavery, and the JURISDICTION OF FEDERAL COURTS. His reputation long suffered from invidious and inappropriate comparisons with his predecessor Chief Justice JOHN MARSHALL and because of his disastrous opinion in DRED SCOTT V. SANDFORD (1857). But his influence has been enduring and, on balance, beneficial.

Taney was born in 1777 in Calvert County, Maryland. His father, a well-to-do planter, destined him for a career in law. After graduation from Dickinson College (Pennsylvania), he was admitted to the bar in 1799 and began a thirty-six-year career of politics and law practice in Maryland. He served intermittently in both houses of the state legislature until 1821, at first as a Federalist. But finding that affiliation intolerable because of the conduct of New England Federalists during the War of 1812, he assumed leadership of a local faction known as Coodies and then after 1825 supported ANDREW JACKSON. Practicing first in Frederick, where he maintained his lifelong residence, and then in Baltimore, he became a preeminent member of the Maryland bar, state attorney general from 1827 to 1831, and then attorney general of the United States, a position he held until 1833, when he served for a year as secretary of the treasury.

Taney urged President Jackson to veto the bill to recharter the Bank of the United States and contributed that part of JACKSON'S VETO OF THE BANK BILL in which the President denied that the Supreme Court's opinion on constitutional matters bound the President. As treasury secretary, Taney ordered removal of the federal deposits from the Bank and their distribution to certain "pet banks." In these bank matters, Taney was not the mere pliant tool of Jackson; rather, he acted in accord with his own deep suspicions of centralized and monopolistic economic power.

As attorney general, Taney also had occasion to explore issues involving slavery and free blacks. Upholding South Carolina's Negro Seamen's Act, which prohibited black seamen from disembarking from their vessels while in Carolina waters, Taney insisted that the state's sovereign right to control slaves and free blacks overrode any inconsistent exercise of federal treaty and commerce powers. Presaging his *Dred Scott* opinion, he maintained that blacks were "a separate and degraded people," incapable of being citizens. He also expressed doubt that a Supreme Court decision holding the statute unconstitutional would bind the states.

As Chief Justice of the United States after 1836, Taney left an enduring imprint on the American Constitution. Most of the landmark cases coming before the Court in the first decade of his tenure involved questions of the power of the states to regulate the economic behavior of persons or corporations within their jurisdictions. In CHARLES RIVER BRIDGE V. WARREN BRIDGE (1837) Taney employed a paradigmatic balance between investors' demands for autonomy and the states' insistence on public control of that new legal creature, the private corporation. Refusing to read into a bridge company's charter an implicit grant of a transportation monopoly, Taney held that "in charters, . . . no rights are taken from the public, or given to the corporation, beyond those which the words of the charter, by their natural and

proper construction, purport to convey." (See RESERVED POLICE POWERS.)

Subsequent decisions of the Taney Court confirmed the *Charles River Bridge* DOCTRINE: where the state had explicitly conveyed monopoly rights or otherwise conferred valuable privileges, a majority of the Court honored the grant and held the state to it under CONTRACT CLAUSE doctrines deriving from FLETCHER V. PECK (1810). On the other hand, the Court refused to infer monopoly grants or other restrictions on state regulatory power if they were not explicitly conferred in a corporate charter. Thus in BANK OF AUGUSTA V. EARLE (1839) Taney held that states could regulate the activities of foreign corporations within their jurisdictions, or exclude them altogether, but that such regulations would have to be explicit. Absent express declarations of state policy, the TANEY COURT refused to hold that banking corporations could not enter into contracts outside the state that chartered them.

Yet Taney entertained an instinctive sympathy for states' efforts to control economic activity within their jurisdictions. In another case from his maiden term, BRISCOE V. BANK OF KENTUCKY (1837), Taney supported the majority's holding that a state was not precluded from creating a bank wholly owned by it and exercising note-issuing powers, so long as the state did not pledge its credit to back the notes. Such notes would have been a subterfuge form of the state BILLS OF CREDIT that had been struck down in CRAIG V. MISSOURI (1830). In BRONSON V. KINZIE (1843), however, Taney invalidated state statutes that restricted foreclosure sales and granted mortgagors rights to redeem foreclosed property. Even here, however, he emphasized that states could modify contractual remedies so long as they did not tamper with the substance of existing contracts.

Taney's opinions dealing with the jurisdiction of federal courts proved to be among his most significant. Some of these restricted the autonomy of the states in the interests of protecting the national market. Thus in SWIFT V. TYSON (1842) the Court unanimously supported an opinion by Justice JOSEPH STORY holding that in commercial law matters, federal courts need not look to the forum state's COMMON LAW for rules of decision, but instead might formulate commercial law doctrines out of "the general principles and doctrines of commercial jurisprudence," a principle that survived until *Swift* was overruled in ERIE RAILROAD V. TOMPKINS (1938). (See FEDERAL COMMON LAW.) In PROPELLER GENESEE CHIEF V. FITZHUGH (1851), Taney discarded the English tidewater rule of ADMIRALTY JURISDICTION that Story had imported into American law, and held instead that the inland jurisdiction of federal courts in admiralty matters extended to all navigable waters, tidal or not, thus expanding the reach of federal admiralty jurisdiction to the Great Lakes and the interior rivers. But in LUTHER V. BORDEN (1849), he reasserted the POLITICAL QUESTION doctrine, holding that a challenge to the legitimacy of Rhode Island's government after the Dorr Rebellion of 1842 was to be resolved only by the legislative and executive branches of the national government, not the judicial.

It might be expected that Taney would have been warmly sympathetic to the emerging doctrine of the POLICE POWER, first fully articulated by Massachusetts Chief Justice LEMUEL SHAW in *Commonwealth v. Alger* (1851). But Taney held unspoken reservations about the police power doctrine, fearing that if the states' regulatory powers were defined too explicitly or couched under a rubric, they might somehow be restricted by the federal Constitution. He thus preferred to avoid an explicit definition of the police power, and instead emphasized the states' inherent powers of SOVEREIGNTY over persons and things within their jurisdiction, believing that if the issue were framed in terms of sovereignty rather than regulatory power, the states' autonomy from external interference might be more secure.

This issue of state regulatory power remained sensitive throughout Taney's tenure and was prominent in cases arising out of the attempt of Democratic majorities in the Ohio legislature to levy taxes on banks that had been exempted from certain forms of taxation by their charters. In *Ohio Life Insurance & Trust Co. v. Debolt* (1854) Taney held, in accordance with the *Charles River Bridge* paradigm, that the Court would not read into bank charters an implicit exemption from taxes. But in DODGE V. WOOLSEY (1856), Taney joined a majority in defending an explicit charter exemption against a state constitutional amendment empowering the state to tax exempted banks. Taney was not hostile to banks and corporations as such; he had an alert appreciation of the role that they would play in developing the national market.

Another issue—indeed, the critical one—that kept Taney and his colleagues sensitized to issues of state regulatory power was the protean matter of slavery and black people. This issue, deep in the background, skewed all but one of the Taney Court's COMMERCE CLAUSE decisions. In his first term, the Court skirted slavery complications in a case, MAYOR OF NEW YORK V. MILN (1837), challenging the right of a state to impose some measure of control over the ingress of foreign passengers, by holding that the challenged authority was not a regulation of commerce but rather an exercise of the police power. But this evasion would not dispose of subsequent cases challenging the power of the state to control the importation of liquor or the immigration of persons. In the LICENSE CASES (1847), the Court rendered six opinions, including one by Taney who was with the majority for the result, sustaining the efforts of three New England states to prohibit the importation and sale of liquor. But in the PASSENGER CASES (1849), raising issues similar to *Miln*, the court produced eight opinions, this time with Taney in the minority, striking down state laws regulating or taxing the influx of ALIENS. Taney was consistent throughout, insisting that no federal constitutional restraints existed on the power of the states to control persons or objects coming into their borders. His brush with the controversy over the Negro Seamen's Act as United States attorney general had left him hostile to any constitutional restraints that might inhibit the power of the slave states to control the ingress of free blacks, slaves, abolitionists, or antislavery propaganda.

The Taney Court did manage to filter slavery complications out of one major commerce clause case, thereby producing another paradigm of state regulatory power. In COOLEY V. BOARD OF WARDENS OF PHILADELPHIA (1851) the Court, with Taney in the majority, held that the commerce clause did not restrain the states from regulating matters essentially local in nature (such as, in this case, pilotage fees or harbor regulations) even if they had some impact on interstate or foreign commerce.

Curiously, the Court was more successful, in the short run, in disposing of cases where the question of slavery was overt rather than implicit. Taney, deeply dedicated to the welfare of his state and region, and anxious above all to protect the slave states from external meddling that would threaten their control of the black population, free or slave, or that would promote widespread emancipation, adopted passionate and extremist postures in slavery cases. In GROVES V. SLAUGHTER (1841), which involved the validity of a contract for sale of a slave under a state constitution that prohibited the commercial importation of slaves, Taney was provoked to a sharp reiteration of his attorney general's opinion, insisting that the power of a state to control blacks within its borders was exclusive of all federal power, including that under the commerce clause.

In PRIGG V. PENNSYLVANIA (1842) Taney was again prodded into another concurrence. Though he agreed with most of Justice Joseph Story's opinion for the majority holding unconstitutional a Pennsylvania PERSONAL LIBERTY LAW, he firmly disavowed Story's dictum that states need not participate in the recapture and rendition of fugitive slaves. Taney rejected Story's assertion that states could not enact legislation supplemental to the federal Fugitive Slave Act, and maintained that states must do so; his colleagues PETER V. DANIEL and SMITH THOMPSON merely asserted that a state could adopt such laws.

In STRADER V. GRAHAM (1851) Taney spoke for the Court in a case raising American variants of issues earlier canvassed in SOMERSET'S CASE (1772), a doctrinally seminal English decision that had passed into the mainstream of American constitutional thought. Appellant sought to have the Court overturn a Kentucky Court of Appeals decision that slaves permitted by their master to sojourn in a free state who then returned to their slave domicile did not become liberated because of their free-state sojourn. Taney held that the state court determination of the slaves' status was conclusive on federal courts (a point consistent with his emphasis on state control of blacks and a doctrinal opportunity for evading the issues of *Dred Scott* later). But Taney uttered OBITER DICTA disturbing to the free states. He suggested that the power of states over persons in their jurisdictions was unfettered "except in so far as the powers of the states in this respect are restrained . . . by the Constitution of the United States," thus hinting that there might be some federal constitutional impediment to the abolition statutes of the free states. He further insisted, needlessly, that the antislavery provisions of the NORTHWEST ORDINANCE were defunct, no longer an effective prohibition of the introduction of slavery in the states that had been carved out of the Northwest Territory.

Dred Scott (1857) was Taney's definitive utterance on the slavery question. His opinion, though one of nine, was taken by contemporaries to be for the Court, and Taney himself so considered it. Taney first excluded blacks descended from slaves from the status of "Citizens" as that term was used both in the Article III diversity clause and the Article IV PRIVILEGES AND IMMUNITIES clause. In order to support this conclusion, Taney asserted, incorrectly, that blacks in 1787 had been "considered as a subordinate and inferior class of beings, who . . . had no rights which the white man was bound to respect." Taney further insisted that the meaning of the Constitution does not change over time, so that the connotations of its words in 1787 remained rigid and static, unalterable except by formal amendment.

In the second half of his long opinion, Taney held that the federal government lacked power to exclude slavery from the territories, thus holding the MISSOURI COMPROMISE unconstitutional (even though it had already been declared void by the KANSAS-NEBRASKA ACT of 1854). He grounded this lack of federal power not in the territories clause of Article IV, but in its textual sibling, the new states clause, insisting that Congress could not impose conditions on the admission of new states that would put them in a position inferior to those already admitted. Taney also suggested in passing that the DUE PROCESS clause of the Fifth Amendment prohibited Congress from interfering with the property rights of slaveholders. But the significance of this utterance as a source of the later doctrine of SUBSTANTIVE DUE PROCESS has been overrated. Taney was not a devotee of HIGHER LAW doctrines, such as those enunciated by Justice SAMUEL CHASE in CALDER V. BULL (1798), by Justice Story in cases like TERRETT V. TAYLOR (1815) and *Wilkinson v. Leland* (1829), and by numerous state court judges, most recently in the landmark case of WYNEHAMER V. NEW YORK (1856).

In his *Dred Scott* opinion Taney also adopted three points of proslavery constitutional thought previously voiced in Southern legislatures and doctrinal writings: the federal government had no power over slavery except to protect the rights of slaveholders; the federal government was the "trustee" of the states for the territories, and as such must protect the interests of all of them there; and the territorial legislature could not exclude slavery during the territorial period. His performance in the *Dred Scott* case was widely condemned. Justice BENJAMIN R. CURTIS effectively controverted it in his scholarly dissent in *Dred Scott;* northern legislators, political leaders, attorneys, and polemicists poured forth innumerable rebuttals; and the Vermont legislature and the Maine Supreme Judicial Court flatly rejected its doctrines. ABRAHAM LINCOLN insisted that *Dred Scott*'s doctrine must be overruled.

Taney remained unmoved by such criticism, insisting in private correspondence that his position would be validated in time. Though aged and in intermittent ill health, he continued his judicial labors unabated. In ABLEMAN V. BOOTH (1859), a magisterial treatise on the role of the federal judiciary in the American federal system, Taney held that state courts could not interfere with the judgment of a federal court through use of the writ of HABEAS CORPUS. He adumbrated the doctrine of dual sovereignty: the federal and state governments "are yet separate and distinct sovereignties, acting separately and independently of each other." (See DUAL FEDERALISM.) But he insisted on the unfettered independence of federal courts in their execution of federal laws. In *dictum,* he asserted that the Fugitive Slave Act of 1850 was constitutional.

Taney produced significant published and unpublished opinions during the Civil War. In private communications, he supported SECESSION and condemned Lincoln's resort to force to save the Union. In keeping with such views, he drafted opinions, probably to be incorporated into conventional judicial opinions when the opportunity arose, condemning the EMANCIPATION PROCLAMATION, CONSCRIPTION, and the Legal Tender Acts. He also extended the first half of his *Dred Scott* opinion to exclude all blacks, not just those descended from slaves, from CITIZENSHIP; and he reasserted the obligation of the free states to return fugitive slaves. In an official opinion on circuit he condemned Lincoln's suspension of the writ of *habeas corpus* in EX PARTE MERRYMAN (1861), an opinion Lincoln refused to honor. He also joined the dissenters in the PRIZE CASES (1863), who insisted that because only Congress can declare war, Lincoln's military response to secession and southern military actions was "private" and of no legal effect. His death in 1864 relieved him from the painful necessity of seeing his vision of the constitutional and social order destroyed by the victory of Union arms.

Taney's lasting contributions consisted of his reinforcement of the political question doctrine, his strong defense of the states' regulatory powers, and his vigorous aggrandizement of the jurisdiction of the federal courts. More than his colleagues, he keenly appreciated the role of technological change in American law, a sensitivity apparent in *Charles River Bridge* and *Genesee Chief.* His defense of regional autonomy and his hostility to the power of concentrated capital retain a perennial relevance. His instinct for dynamic balance in the formulation of enduring rules of law, as in the *Charles River Bridge* paradigm, evinced judicial statesmanship of the first rank.

Constitutional problems related to slavery combined with Taney's personal failings to blight his reputation and eclipse his real achievements. *Dred Scott* remains a monument to judicial hubris, and all the slavery cases that came before the Taney Court bear the impress of Taney's determination to bend the Constitution to the service of sectional interest. Though he manumitted nearly all his own slaves and was in his personal relations a kind and loving man, Taney as Chief Justice was immoderate and willful when the times called for judicial caution. His tolerance of multiple opinions permitted dissents and concurrences to proliferate, blurring the clarity of doc-

trine in commerce clause cases. In any case touched directly or indirectly by slavery, Taney's sure instincts for viable doctrine, as well as his nobler personal qualities, deserted him and gave way to a blind and vindictive sectionalism unworthy of the Chief Justice of the United States.

It is the tragic irony of Taney's career that his virtues were so closely linked to his faults, especially in their results. He fully merited FELIX FRANKFURTER's warm appreciation of his role in shaping the American federal system: "the intellectual power of his opinions and their enduring contribution to a workable adjustment of the theoretical distribution of authority between two governments for a single people, place Taney second only to Marshall in the constitutional history of our country." Yet no other Justices have so gravely damaged the federal system because of sectional bias, and the real merits of Taney's defense of localist values have been obscured by his racial antipathies and sectional dogmatism.

WILLIAM M. WIECEK

Bibliography

FEHRENBACHER, DON E. 1979 *The Dred Scott Case: Its Significance in American Law and Politics.* New York: Oxford University Press.

HARRIS, ROBERT J. 1957(1966) Chief Justice Taney: Prophet of Reform and Reaction. Pages 93–118 in Leonard W. Levy, ed., *American Constitutional Law: Historical Essays.* New York: Harper & Row.

LEWIS, WALKER 1965 *Without Fear or Favor: A Biography of Chief Justice Roger Brooke Taney.* Boston: Houghton Mifflin.

SWISHER, CARL B. 1935 *Roger B. Taney.* New York: Macmillan.

——— 1974 *The Taney Period, 1835–64.* Volume 5 of *The Oliver Wendell Holmes Devise History of The Supreme Court of the United States.* New York: Macmillan.

TANEY COURT
(1836–1864)

The Supreme Court under Chief Justice ROGER B. TANEY (1836–1864) has not been a favorite among historians, perhaps because it defies easy generalization. There were few great constitutional moments and no dramatic lawmaking decisions comparable to those handed down by the MARSHALL COURT. The fifteen Justices who served with Taney (not counting ABRAHAM LINCOLN's Civil War appointees) varied immensely in ability—from JOSEPH STORY of Massachusetts who was the leading scholar on the bench until his death in 1845 to JOHN MCKINLEY of Alabama whose twenty-five years on the Court left barely a trace. Institutional unity and efficiency were often disrupted by abrasive personalities like HENRY BALDWIN (who became mentally unstable shortly after his appointment in 1830) and PETER V. DANIEL (whose passion for STATES' RIGHTS drove him into chronic dissent). Division was constant and bitter as the Justices disagreed openly over corporation, banking, and slavery questions—all of which tended to be seen from a sectional point of view. Fortunately for the ongoing work of the Court, most of its members shared a respect for the Constitution and had a common commitment to economic progress and property rights that cut across ideological and sectional differences. All were Democrats, too, except Story, JOHN MCLEAN, and BENJAMIN R. CURTIS. Most of the Court respected the Chief Justice—whose legal mind was of a high order—and responded well to his patient, democratic style of leadership. Still the Court under Taney did not quite cohere. There was no "leading mind," as DANIEL WEBSTER complained, and no clear-cut doctrinal unity.

Clearly the Taney Court was not the Marshall Court—but then again it was not the age of Marshall. The society that conditioned the Taney Court and defined the perimeters within which it made law was democratic in its politics, pluralistic in social composition, divided in ideology, and shaped by capitalist forces which increasingly sought freedom from traditional governmental restraints. Most threatening to judicial unity, because it was directly reflected in the opinions of the Court, was the intensification of sectional rivalry. As northern states committed themselves to commerce and manufacturing, they came to see themselves—taking their cultural cues from the abolitionists—as a section united in defense of liberty and freedom. The South found ideological conservatism an ideal umbrella for an expansive social-economic system based on cotton and organized around plantation slavery. As the sections competed for political power and control of the new West, each came to think of itself as the last best hope of mankind. And each insisted that the Constitution accommodate its policy preferences—a demand that the Supreme Court could satisfy only by compromising doctrinal purity and finally could not satisfy at all.

In short, the political and economic problems of the new age became constitutional problems just as ALEXIS DE TOCQUEVILLE had said they would. Whether the Supreme Court would be the primary agency to resolve those problems was, of course, a matter of debate. ANDREW JACKSON, armed with a mandate from the people, did not believe that the Court had a monopoly of constitutional wisdom. Newly organized POLITICAL PARTIES stood ready to dispute judicial decisions that offended their constituencies. States armed with JOHN C. CALHOUN's theory of NULLIFICATION insisted that they, not the Court, had the final word on the Constitution. Accordingly, the margin of judicial error was drastically reduced. The Court was obliged to make the Constitution of 1787 work for a new age; the high nationalism of the Marshall Court, along with its Augustan style of judging, would have to be toned down. Changes would have to come. The question—and it was as yet a new one in American constitutional law—was whether they could be made without disrupting the continuity upon which the authority of the law and the prestige of the Court rested.

The moment of testing came quickly. Facing the Court in its 1837 term were three great constitutional questions dealing with state banking, the COMMERCE CLAUSE, and corporate contracts. Each had been argued before the Marshall Court and each involved a question of FEDERALISM which pitted new historical circumstances against a precedent from the Marshall period. The Court's decisions in these cases would set the constitutional tone for the new age.

In BRISCOE V. BANK OF KENTUCKY the challenge was simple and straightforward. The issue was whether notes issued by the state-owned Commonwealth Bank were prohibited by Article I, section 10, of the Constitution, which prevented states from issuing BILLS OF CREDIT. The Marshall Court had ruled broadly against state bills of credit in CRAIG V. MISSOURI (1830), but the new Jacksonian majority ruled for the state bank. Justice McLean's opinion paid deference to legal continuity by distinguishing *Briscoe* from *Craig*, but political and economic expediency controlled the decision as Story's bitter dissent made clear. The fact was that, after the demise of the second Bank of the United States, state bank notes were the main currency of the country. To rule against the bank would put such notes in jeopardy, a risk the new Court refused to take.

Policy considerations of a states' rights nature also overwhelmed doctrinal consistency in commerce clause litigation, the Court's primary means of drawing the line between national and state power. Marshall's opinion in GIBBONS V. OGDEN (1824) had conceded vast power over INTERSTATE COMMERCE to Congress, although the Court had not gone so far as to rule that national power automatically excluded states from passing laws touching FOREIGN and INTERSTATE COMMERCE. The new age needed a flexible interpretation of the commerce clause that would please states' rights forces in both the North and the South and at the same time encourage the growth of a national market.

In MAYOR OF NEW YORK V. MILN, the second of the trio of great cases in 1837, the Court struggled toward such a reinterpretation. A New York law required masters of all vessels arriving at the port of New York to make bond that none of their passengers should become wards of the city. The practical need for such a law seemed clear enough; the question was whether it encroached unconstitutionally on federal power over interstate commerce as laid out in the *Gibbons* decision. The Chief Justice assigned the opinion to Justice SMITH THOMPSON who was prepared to justify the New York law as a police regulation and as a legitimate exercise of concurrent commerce power. His narrow definition of STATE POLICE POWER displeased some of his brethren, however, and even more so his position on CONCURRENT POWER. When he refused to compromise, the opinion was reassigned to PHILIP P. BARBOUR, who upheld the state regulation as a valid exercise of state police power. Barbour's contention that police power was "unqualified and exclusive" far exceeded anything that precedent could justify, however, as Story pointed out in his dissent. Indeed, Barbour's opinion, so far as it ruled that states could regulate interstate passengers, went beyond the position agreed upon in CONFERENCE and lacked the full concurrence of a majority.

The *Miln* case settled little except that the New York regulation was constitutional. The Court remained sharply divided over the basic questions: whether congressional power over foreign and interstate commerce was exclusive of the states or concurrent with them and, if it was concurrent, how much congressional action would be necessary to sustain national predominance. The doctrine of state police power had taken a tentative step toward maturity, but its relation to the commerce clause remained unsettled. That the states reserved some power to legislate for the health and welfare of their citizens seemed clear enough, but to establish an enclave of state power prior to, outside the scope of, and superior to powers delegated explicitly to Congress was to beg, not settle the crucial constitutional question.

The uncertainty regarding the questions generated by *Miln* continued throughout the 1840s in such cases as GROVES V. SLAUGHTER (1841) where the Court refused to rule on whether the provision of the Mississippi Constitution of 1832 touching the interstate slave trade was a violation of national commerce power. Confusion increased in the LICENSE CASES (1847) and the PASSENGER CASES (1849), which dealt with state regulation of alcohol and immigration respectively. The Justices upheld state authority in the first and denied it in the second, but in neither did they clarify the relation of state police power to federal authority over interstate commerce.

Not until COOLEY V. BOARD OF WARDENS (1852), which considered the constitutionality of a Pennsylvania law regulating pilotage in the port of Philadelphia, did the Court supply guidelines for commerce clause litigation. Congress had twice legislated on pilotage, but in neither case was there any conflict with the Pennsylvania law. The issue came, therefore, precisely and unavoidably to focus on EXCLUSIVE POWER versus concurrent power: whether the constitutional grant of commerce power to Congress automatically prohibited STATE REGULATION OF COMMERCE or whether the states could regulate commerce as long as such regulations did not actually conflict with congressional legislation.

Justice Curtis's majority opinion upheld the state law and in the process salvaged some doctrinal regularity. Starting from the undeniable premise that the commerce power granted to Congress did not expressly exclude the states from exercising authority over interstate commerce, he ruled that exclusive congressional JURISDICTION obtained only when the subject matter itself required it. The SUBJECTS OF COMMERCE, however, were vast and varied and did not require blanket exclusiveness. Some matters, he said, needed a "single uniform rule, operating equally on the commerce of the United States in every port." Some just as certainly admitted of local regulation. Power, in other words, followed function: if the subject matter required uniform regulation, the power belonged to Congress; if it did not, the states might regulate it. State police power remained to be settled, but the pressure to do so was lessened because the concurrent commerce power of the states was now clearly recognized.

SELECTIVE EXCLUSIVENESS, as the Court's approach in *Cooley* came to be called, was not a certain and final answer to the problem of allocating commerce power between the national government and the states, however. The rule was clear enough but how to apply it was not, which is to say that Curtis gave no guidelines for determining which aspects of commerce required uniform regulation or which permitted diversity. What was clear was that the Court had retreated from the constitutional formalism of the Marshall period. The opinion was short, only ten pages long; it made no reference to precedent, not even *Gibbons*. The Justices now willed to do what they had previously done unwillingly: they decided cases without a definitive pronouncement of DOCTRINE. The important difference in *Cooley* was that the Court devised a rule of thumb recognizing the judicial interest-balancing that previously had been carried on covertly in the name of formal distinctions. Ordered process, not logical categories, would be the new order of the day.

The Court's flexibility also signaled a shift of power in the direction of the states. The constitutional legacy of the Marshall Court had been altered to fit Jacksonian priorities. Still, national authority had not been destroyed. The Taney Court had refused to extend the nationalist principles of MCCULLOCH V. MARYLAND (1819) and *Gibbons,* to be sure, but the principles stood. The Court's new federalism did not rest on new states' rights constitutional doctrine. Neither did the new federalism threaten economic growth, as conservatives had predicted. Agrarian capitalism, for example, fared as well under the Taney Court as it had under its predecessor. The Justices did sometimes resist the most exorbitant demands of land speculators, and occasionally a dissenting Justice spoke for the little man as did Daniel in *Arguello v. United States* (1855). But the majority took their cue from FLETCHER V. PECK (1810), which is to say that plungers in the land market mostly got free rein, as for example in *Cervantes v. United States* (1854) and *Fremont v. United States* (1855). That slaveholding agrarian capitalists were to benefit from this judicial largess was clear from the decision in DRED SCOTT V. SANDFORD (1857).

The Court's promotion of commercial-industrial-corporate capitalism proved more difficult because of the sectional disagreements among the Justices. But there is no doubt that the Taney Court served as a catalyst for the release of American entrepreneurial energies. Its plan for a democratic, nonmonopolistic capitalism, Jacksonian style, was unveiled in CHARLES RIVER BRIDGE V. WARREN BRIDGE, the last of the three landmark decisions of the 1837 term. Here the question was whether the toll-free Warren Bridge, chartered and built in 1828 a few hundred feet from the Charles River Bridge, destroyed the property rights of the old bridge, in violation of its charter as protected by DARTMOUTH COLLEGE V. WOODWARD (1819). The difficulty was that the charter of 1785, although granting the Charles River Bridge the right to collect tolls, had not explicitly granted a monopoly. The fate of the old bridge depended, therefore, on the willingness of the Taney Court to extend the principle of *Dartmouth College* by implication.

Taney, who spoke for the new Jacksonian majority on the Court, refused to do so. The Chief Justice agreed that "the rights of private property are sacredly guarded," but he insisted "that the community also have rights, and that the happiness and well-being of every citizen depends on their faithful preservation." The Court should not venture into the no-man's land of inference and construction when the public interest rested in the balance, Taney argued. He cleverly supported this position by citing Marshall's opinion in PROVIDENCE BANK V. BILLINGS (1830). And the public interest, as Taney saw it, lay in extending equality of economic opportunity. "Modern science," he said with an eye on new railroad corporations, "would be throttled and transportation set back to the last century if turnpike and canal companies could turn charter rights into monopoly grants.

The *Bridge* decision, like the Court's decisions in banking and commerce, revealed a distinct instrumentalist tone as well as a new tolerance for state legislative discretion. The Court also showed its preference for dynamic over static capital. Still, property rights were not generally threatened. To be sure, in WEST RIVER BRIDGE COMPANY V. DIX (1848) the Court recognized the power of state legislatures to take property for public purposes with JUST COMPENSATION, but conservatives themselves were willing to recognize that power. The Court also took a liberal view of state DEBTORS' RELIEF LEGISLATION, especially laws applying to mortgages for land, but even here the Court could claim the Marshall Court's decision in OGDEN V. SAUNDERS (1827) as its guide. There was no doubt, on the other hand, as BRONSON V. KINZIE (1843) showed, that state relief laws that impaired substantial contractual rights would not be tolerated.

Corporate property also remained secure under the *Bridge* ruling. Indeed, corporate expansion was strongly encouraged by the Taney Court despite the resistance of some of the southern agrarian Justices. After 1837 the Court consistently refused to extend charter rights by implication, but it also upheld corporate charters that explicitly granted monopoly rights even though in some cases such rights appeared hostile to community interest. Corporations also greatly profited from BANK OF AUGUSTA V. EARLE (1839), which raised the question whether corporations chartered in one state could do business in another. Taney conceded that the legislature could prohibit foreign corporations from doing business in the state and some such laws were subsequently passed. But such prohibitions, he went on to say, had to be explicit; practically speaking, this limitation assured corporations the right to operate across state lines. Hardly less important to corporate expansion was *Louisville Railroad v. Letson* (1844) which held that corporations could be considered citizens of the states in which they were chartered for purposes of DIVERSITY JURISDICTION—thus removing the increasingly unworkable fiction created in *Bank of United States v. Deveaux* (1809) and assuring corporate access to federal courts where the bias in favor of local interests would be minimized.

The Court's promotion of capitalism showed the basic continuity between the Marshall and Taney periods and the fact that antebellum law followed the contours of economic development. Acknowledgment of this continuity, however, should not obscure the real changes in constitutional federalism as the Taney Court deferred more to state power and legislative discretion. Overall the Court spoke more modestly, too, readily acknowledging former errors and generally toning down its rhetoric. In LUTHER V. BORDEN (1849), it went so far as to promise judicial self-restraint regarding POLITICAL QUESTIONS, though that promise ought not to be confused with a hard-and-fast doctrine, which it clearly was not. Although the Court avoided stridency, it did not claim less power. The constitutional nationalism which the Taney Court reduced was not the same as the judicial nationalism which it actually extended. In short, the Court did things differently, but it did not surrender its power to do them. Although the *Bridge* case conceded new power to state legislatures and promised judicial restraint, the Court still monitored the federal system in corporate contract questions. The Court's commerce clause decisions worked to make the federal system more flexible. But in every case from *Miln* through *Cooley*, the Court retained the right to judge—and often, as in *Cooley*, by vague constitutional standards. This judicial authority, moreover, was used throughout the Taney period to expand the jurisdiction of the Court, often at the expense of state judiciaries which the Court claimed to respect.

Never was federal judicial expansion more striking than in SWIFT V. TYSON (1842), a commercial law case which arose under federal diversity jurisdiction. For a unanimous Court, Story held that, in matters of general commercial law, state "laws," which section 34 of the JUDICIARY ACT OF 1789 obliged the federal courts to follow in diversity cases, did not include state court decisions. In the absence of controlling state statutes, then, federal courts were free to apply general principles of commercial law, which they proceeded to do until *Swift* was overruled in 1938. Almost as expansive was Taney's opinion in PROPELLER

GENESEE CHIEF V. FITZHUGH (1851), which bluntly overturned the tidewater limitation imposed by the Marshall Court and extended the admiralty jurisdiction of the federal courts over the vast network of inland lakes and rivers.

Both these decisions were part of the Court's consistent effort to establish a system of uniform commercial principles conducive to the interstate operation of business. Both paved the way for federal judicial intrusion into state judicial authority. When state courts objected to this judicial nationalism, as the Wisconsin Supreme Court did in the slave rendition case of ABLEMAN V. BOOTH (1859), Jacksonian Roger Taney put them in their place with a ringing defense of federal judicial authority that was every bit as unyielding as was Federalist John Marshall's in COHENS V. VIRGINIA (1821). *Ableman* was an assertion of power that would have astonished conservative critics in 1837 who predicted the imminent decline and fall of the Court. Instead, by 1850 the Taney Court was even more popular than the Marshall Court had been and the Chief Justice was praised by men of all political persuasions. All this would change when the Court confronted the issue of slavery.

Adjudicating the constitutional position of slavery fell mainly to the Taney Court; there was no escape. Slavery was the foundation of the southern economy, a source of property worth billions, a social institution that shaped the cultural values of an entire section and the politics of the whole nation. Moreover, it was an integral part of the Constitution, which the Court had to interpret. At the same time, it was, of all the issues facing the antebellum Court, least amenable to a rational legal solution—and in this respect, it foreshadowed social issues like abortion and AFFIRMATIVE ACTION which have troubled the contemporary Court. No other single factor so much accounts for the divisions on the Taney Court or its inability to clearly demarcate power in the federal system.

Given the slavery question's explosive nature, the Justices not surprisingly tried to avoid confronting it directly. Thus the obfuscation in *Groves v. Slaughter* (1841), where the issue was whether a provision in the Mississippi Constitution prohibiting the importation of slaves for sale after 1833 illegally encroached upon federal power over interstate commerce. The Court circumvented this issue by ruling that the state constitutional clause in question was not self-activating—a position that, while avoiding trouble for the Court, also guaranteed the collection of millions of dollars of outstanding debts owed slave traders and in effect put the judicial seal of approval on the interstate slave trade. The Court also dodged the substantive issue in STRADER V. GRAHAM (1851), which raised the question whether slaves who resided in Kentucky had become free by virtue of their temporary residence in the free state of Ohio. The Court refused jurisdiction on the ground that Kentucky law reasserted itself over the slaves on their return, so that no federal question was involved.

Where the substantive question could not be sidestepped, the Court aimed to decide cases on narrow grounds and in such a way as to please both North and South. Thus in *The Amistad* (1841), Justice Story ruled that Africans on their way to enslavement who escaped their Spanish captors were free by virtue of principles of international law and a close reading of the Treaty of 1794 with Spain. Extremists in neither section were pleased. Even less were they content with Story's efforts to juggle sectional differences, morality, and objective adjudication in PRIGG V. PENNSYLVANIA (1842). There the question was whether and to what extent states were allowed to pass PERSONAL LIBERTY LAWS protecting the rights of free Negroes in rendition cases. The South was pleased when Story declared the Pennsylvania liberty law of 1826 to be a violation of the constitutional and statutory obligation to return fugitive slaves. He went on to say, with his eye on northern opinion (and with doubtful support from a majority on the Court), that the power over fugitives belonged exclusively to the federal government and that states were not obliged to cooperate in their return. The decision encouraged northern states to pass personal liberty laws but also necessitated the more stringent federal fugitive slave law of 1850. Both developments fueled sectional conflict. (See FUGITIVE SLAVERY.)

The Court's strategy of avoidance aimed to keep slavery on the state level where the Constitution had put it, but the slavery question would not stay put. What brought it forth politically and legally as a national question was SLAVERY IN THE TERRITORIES, a problem which confronted the Court and the nation in *Dred Scott*. The nominal issue in that famous case was whether a Negro slave named Scott, who had resided in the free state of Illinois and the free territory of Minnesota (made free by the MISSOURI COMPROMISE of 1820) and who returned to the slave state of Missouri, could sue in the federal courts. Behind this jurisdictional issue lay the explosive political question of whether Congress could prohibit slavery in the territories, or to put it another way, whether the Constitution guaranteed it there. The future of slavery itself was on the line.

The first inclination of the Justices when they confronted the case early in 1856 was to continue the strategy of avoidance by applying *Strader v. Graham* (1851); by that precedent Scott would have become a slave on his return to Missouri with no right to sue in the federal courts. This compromise was abandoned: in part because of pressure from President JAMES BUCHANAN and Congress; in part because northern Justices McLean and Curtis planned to confront the whole issue in dissent; in part because the proslave, pro-South wing of the Court (led by Taney and Wayne) wanted to silence the abolitionists by putting the Constitution itself behind slavery in the territories; in part because the Justices pridefully believed they could put the troublesome question to rest and save the Union.

Taney's was the majority opinion so far as one could be gleaned from the cacophony of separate opinions and dissents. It was totally prosouthern and brutally racist: Scott could not sue in the federal courts because he was not a citizen of the United States. He was not a citizen because national CITIZENSHIP followed state citizenship, and in 1787 the states had looked upon blacks as racially inferior (which the states in fact did) and unqualified for citizenship (which several states did not). Scott's argument that he was free by virtue of residence in a free state was wrong, said Taney, because of *Strader* (which had been relied upon by the Supreme Court of Missouri); Scott's argument that residence in a free territory made him free carried no weight because Congress had no authority to prohibit slavery in the territories—an assertion that ignored seventy years of constitutional practice and permitted Taney to set forth the SUBSTANTIVE DUE PROCESS theory of the Fifth Amendment against the TAKING OF PROPERTY. Scott was still a slave. Congress could not prohibit slavery in the territories, because the Constitution guaranteed it there; neither, as the creatures of Congress, could territorial legislatures prohibit slavery as claimed by proponents of the doctrine of POPULAR SOVEREIGNTY. Taney's Constitution was for whites only.

Instead of saving the Union the decision brought it closer to civil war and put the Court itself in jeopardy. In effect, the decision outlawed the basic principle of the Republican party (opposition to the extension of slavery in the territories), forcing that party to denounce the Court. The Democratic party, the best hope for political compromise, was now split between a southern wing (which in 1860 chose the certainty of *Dred Scott* over the vagueness of popular sovereignty) and northern antislavery forces who, if they did not defect to the Republicans, went down to defeat with STEPHEN DOUGLAS and popular sovereignty. Sectional hatred intensified and the machinery of political compromise was seriously undercut—along with the prestige of the Court. From its peak of popularity in 1850 the Taney Court descended to an all-time low. After SECESSION it served only the section of the Union that ignored *Dred Scott* entirely, condemned the Court as a tool of southern expansionism, and looked upon the Chief Justice as an archtraitor to liberty and national union.

Fortunately, these disabilities were not permanent. Northern hatred focused less on the Court as an institution and more on the particular decision of *Dred Scott*, which was obliterated by the THIRTEENTH and FOURTEENTH AMENDMENTS. *Dred Scott* seemed less important, too, after President Lincoln "Republicanized" the Court with new appointments (five, including a new Chief Justice who had been an abolitionist). More important, the Court brought itself into harmony with the northern war effort by doing what the Supreme Court has always done in wartime: deferring to the political branches of government and bending law to military necessity. Sometimes the Court deferred by acting (as in the PRIZE CASES of 1863 where it permitted the President to exercise WAR POWERS and still not recognize the belligerent status of the Confederacy) and sometimes it deferred by not acting (as when it refused to interfere with the broad use of martial law during the war).

The Taney Court not only survived but it also salvaged its essential powers—and with time even a grudging respect from historians. The memory of *Dred Scott* could not be totally exorcised, of course, but it diminished along with the idealism of the war years and with the recognition that the racism of the opinion was shared by a majority of white Americans. In any case, the reform accomplishments of the Taney Court helped to balance the reactionary ones. Its modest style of judging fit the new democratic age. Through its decisions ran a new appreciation of the democratic nature and reform potential of state action and a tacit recognition as well of the growing maturity of legislative government. The Court's pragmatic federalism, while it could support the evil of slavery, also embodied a tradition of cultural pluralism, local responsibility, and suspicion of power. This it did without destroying the foundations of constitutional nationalism established by the Marshall Court. Change is the essence of American experience. The Taney Court accepted this irresistible premise and accommodated the Constitution to it. The adjustment was often untidy, but the Court's preference for process over substance looked to the modern age and prefigured the main direction of American constitutional law.

R. KENT NEWMYER

Bibliography

COVER, ROBERT M. 1975 *Justice Accused: Antislavery and the Judicial Process.* New Haven: Yale University Press.

FEHRENBACHER, DON E. 1978 *The Dred Scott Case: Its Significance in American Law and Politics.* New York: Oxford University Press.

FRANKFURTER, FELIX 1937 *The Commerce Clause under Marshall, Taney and Waite.* Chapel Hill: University of North Carolina Press.

HARRIS, ROBERT J. 1957 Chief Justice Taney: Prophet of Reform and Reaction. *Vanderbilt Law Review* 10:227–257.

KUTLER, STANLEY 1971 *Privilege and Creative Destruction: The Charles River Bridge Case.* Philadelphia: J. B. Lippincott.

SWISHER, CARL B. 1974 *The Taney Period, 1836–1864.* Volume V of *The Oliver Wendell Holmes Devise History of the Supreme Court of the United States.* New York: Macmillan.

WARREN, CHARLES 1926 *The Supreme Court in United States History,* Vol. 2. New and revised ed. Boston: Little, Brown.

TARIFF ACT
4 Stat. 270 (1828)

Known as the "Tariff of Abominations," this act was designed to embarrass JOHN QUINCY ADAMS and help ANDREW JACKSON win the Presidency. Jacksonians controlling the House Committee on Manufactures wrote a tariff with excessively high duties for iron, hemp, flax, and numerous other raw materials. The bill's authors believed Adams's New England supporters would have to oppose the bill, and that the failure to pass a tariff would cost Adams the Middle States and the election. When New Englanders tried to amend the bill they were voted down by a coalition of southern and Middle State representatives organized by MARTIN VAN BUREN. The plan ultimately failed when representatives from everywhere but the South voted for the bill. Legislatures in South Carolina, Georgia, Mississippi, and Virginia denounced the act. JOHN C. CALHOUN anonymously wrote the South Carolina EXPOSITION AND PROTEST which laid out a theory of state NULLIFICATION of federal laws. While not adopting the Exposition, the South Carolina legislature printed 5,000 copies for distribution and declared the tariff unconstitutional. Although nullification was defeated at this juncture, and the tariff was amended in 1832, the 1828 act set the stage for the nullification crisis of 1832–1833.

PAUL FINKELMAN

Bibliography

FREEHLING, WILLIAM W. 1965 *Prelude to Civil War: The Nullification Controversy in South Carolina, 1816–1836.* New York: Harper & Row.

TAXATION OF INTERSTATE COMMERCE

See: State Taxation of Commerce

TAXATION WITHOUT REPRESENTATION

Taxation without representation was the primary underlying cause of the American Revolution. Taxation by consent, through representatives chosen by local electors, is a fundamental principle of American CONSTITUTIONALISM. From the colonial period, REPRESENTATION had been actual: a legislator was the deputy of his local electors. He represented a particular geographic constituency, and like his electors he had to meet local residence requirements. Thus, representation of the body politic and government by consent of the governed were structurally connected in American thought.

Taxation without representation deprived one of his property contrary to the first principles of the SOCIAL COMPACT and of the British constitution. No Englishmen endorsed the constitutionality of taxation without representation; that it violated FUNDAMENTAL LAW was the teaching of the CONFIRMATIO CARTARUM, the PETITION OF RIGHT, and the BILL OF RIGHTS. Englishmen claimed, however, that Parliament "virtually" represented the colonies—every member of Parliament represented the English nation, not a locality—and therefore could raise a revenue in America. Rejecting the concept of virtual representation, Americans insisted that they were not and could not be represented in Parliament. The argument of virtual representation implicitly conceded the American contention that taxation was the function of a representative body, not merely a legislative or sovereign body. American legislatures, facing parliamentary taxation for the first times in 1764 and 1765, resolved that Parliament had no constitutional authority to raise a revenue in America. Pennsylvania's assembly, for example, resolved "that the taxation of the people of this province, by any other . . . than . . . their representatives in assembly is unconstitutional." Similarly, the STAMP ACT CONGRESS resolved that the colonies could not be constitutionally taxed except by their own assemblies. The resolutions of the colonies, individually and collectively, claimed an exemption from all parliamentary taxation including customs duties and trade regulations whose purpose was to raise revenue.

The American claims were not simply concocted to meet the unprecedented taxation levied by Parliament in 1764 and after. The experience of Virginia, the first colony, was typical. Its charter guaranteed the rights of Englishmen, which Virginia assumed included the exclusive right of its own representative assembly to tax its inhabitants; the assembly so declared in a statute of 1624. In 1652 planters in a county not represented in the assembly protested the imposition of a tax. In 1674, when Virginia sought confirmation from the crown of its exclusive right to tax its inhabitants, the crown's attorney in England endorsed "the right of Virginians, as well as other Englishmen, not to be taxed but by their consent, expressed by their representatives." The Committee for Foreign Plantations and the Privy Council approved, too, but the king withheld approval because of Bacon's Rebellion. Virginia nevertheless persisted in its position. In 1717 the imposition of a royal postal fee produced, in the words of the colony's royal governor, "a great clamor. . . . The people were made to believe that Parliament could not levy any tax (for so they called the rates of postage) here without consent of the General Assembly." In 1753, when Virginia's governor imposed a trivial fee for the use of his seal on each land patent, the assembly lectured him on the theme that subjects cannot be "deprived of the least part of their property but by their own consent: Upon this excellent principle is our constitution funded." The history of any colony would yield similar incidents, showing how entrenched were the claims that Americans advanced when Parliament first sought to tax the colonies.

When the Declaratory Act of 1766 claimed for Parliament a power to "legislate" for America "in all cases whatsoever," some members of Parliament argued the American position that Parliament could tax only in its representative capacity and therefore could not tax America. WILLIAM PITT and Lord Camden (CHARLES PRATT) endorsed that position. Pitt denounced virtual representation as a contemptible idea and declared that taxation "is no part of the governing or legislative power"; he also distinguished taxes levied for revenue from trade regulations that incidentally but not deliberately produced some revenue. The dominant British position, however, assumed that because taxation was inseparable from SOVEREIGNTY, Parliament as the sovereign legislature in the empire had the power to tax in matters of imperial concern, even though the tax fell on unrepresented members of the empire. That position provoked Americans to distinguish the powers belonging to local governments (the idea of FEDERALISM); to develop the concepts of LIMITED GOVERNMENT, fundamental law, and a CONSTITUTION as supreme law over all government; and to frame written constitutions that enumerated the powers of government.

LEONARD W. LEVY

Bibliography

BAILYN, BERNARD 1967 *The Ideological Origins of the American Revolution.* Cambridge, Mass.: Harvard University Press.

MORGAN, EDMUND S. 1976 *The Challenge of the American Revolution.* Chap. 1. New York: W. W. Norton.

MORTON, RICHARD L. 1960 *Colonial Virginia*, 2 vols. Chapel Hill: University of North Carolina Press.

TAX COURT OF THE UNITED STATES

When the Internal Revenue Service determines a deficiency, a taxpayer who disagrees can either pay the additional tax and sue for a refund in a federal district court or withhold payment and petition the Tax Court to set aside the deficiency. Tax Court decisions are reviewed in the UNITED STATES COURTS OF APPEALS.

The Tax Court, until 1942 called the Board of Tax Appeals, was declared by Congress in 1970 to be a "court." It is not, however, a CONSTITUTIONAL COURT created under Article III, but a LEGISLATIVE COURT. Its members do not have life tenure but serve for fifteen-year terms.

KENNETH L. KARST

TAX CREDITS AND RELIGIOUS SCHOOLS

See: Government Aid to Religious Institutions

TAXING AND SPENDING POWER

A principal weakness of the ARTICLES OF CONFEDERATION was that Congress had no power of taxation. It could request the states to contribute their fair shares to the national treasury but it had no power to collect when, as often happened, the states did not pay. Hence, the first grant of power to Congress in the Constitution was to "have Power to Lay and collect Taxes, Duties, Imposts and Excises, to pay the Debts and provide for the common Defense and general Welfare of the United States; but all Duties, Imposts and Excises shall be uniform throughout the United States." The Constitution also imposed two other limitations. Congress could not tax exports nor lay a "Capitation, or other direct, Tax" unless "in Proportion to the Census or Enumeration herein before directed to be taken."

The direct limitations on taxing power pose few problems. Congress does not impose capitation or property taxes, which would be direct taxes and require apportionment among the states in accordance with population. Other taxes must be uniform—which means that the same subject or activity must be taxed at the same rate wherever it is found. Congress, like the states, cannot tax exports to foreign countries.

More difficult problems have risen because taxes not only raise revenue but also regulate. A tax on liquor may be designed to raise money but also to discourage consumption. A deduction for interest in computing income tax encourages home ownership. A tax may be high enough to virtually stop the production and sale of a particular product. Before the Civil War the federal government derived most of its revenue from the customs and in many years had no internal revenue beyond that. But beginning with the Civil War, Congress expanded the scope of federal taxation at a time when the Supreme Court had fairly restrictive views as to congressional powers to regulate local activities. The question became how far Congress could use taxation to achieve policies that were forbidden to it through direct regulation.

When Congress imposed a ten percent tax on local banknotes for the purpose of achieving a federal government monopoly in the issuing of currency, the Court in VEAZIE BANK V. FENNO (1869) indicated that the tax was constitutional but said that in any event no regulatory problem was presented; Congress did have an independent MONETARY POWER, and the tax was merely a means of implementing it. Thirty-five years later the Court faced the problem more directly. Congress had imposed a ten cents per pound tax on oleomargarine that was colored and only one-quarter cent per pound if it was white. The Court in McCRAY V. UNITED STATES (1904) said that even though Congress did not have the power to pass a statute forbidding the sale of colored oleomargarine, it could still tax it and the courts would not interfere merely on the grounds that the tax was too high. And the Court also held that Congress could impose a tax on distributing narcotic drugs and include in the same statute regulations as to how such drugs were to be distributed. The Court in UNITED STATES V. DOREMUS (1919) said that a tax was not invalid just because it had regulatory as well as taxation purposes and that the regulations attached to the tax were constitutional as facilitating the collection of the tax.

But in the Child Labor Tax Case (1922) the Court concluded that a tax might really be a regulation and thus invalid. A federal statute prohibiting interstate transportation of goods made by child labor had been held to exceed Congress's power under the COMMERCE CLAUSE in HAMMER V. DAGENHART (1918). So Congress imposed a tax of ten percent of the net profits for the year for any manufacturing business that employed children within certain age limits. Here, the court said, the challenge was not merely that the tax was too high. Rather, Congress had imposed a regulation and used the tax as a penalty for violation. "[A] court must be blind not to see that the so-called tax is imposed to stop the employment of children within the age limits prescribed. Its prohibitory and regulatory effect and purpose are palpable." In *United States v. Constantine* (1935) the Court similarly held invalid a special tax of $1,000 upon anyone dealing in liquor in a state or locality where such dealing was illegal. The Court said that the law clearly was not a tax but rather a penalty for violating state law.

In a series of later cases, however, the Court upheld the taxes. A heavy tax on sale of special weapons such as sawed-off shotguns was upheld in SONZINSKY V. UNITED STATES (1937). In *United States v. Sanchez* (1950) and *United States v. Kahriger* (1953) the Court upheld taxes on narcotics and gambling in which taxpayers were required to register with the federal government, even though that registration would make it easier for the states to enforce their gambling and narcotics laws. In *Sanchez* the Court said: "It is beyond serious question that a tax does not cease to be valid merely because it regulates, discourages, or even definitely deters the activities taxed. . . . The principle applies even though the revenue obtained is obviously negligible, . . . or the revenue purpose of the tax may be secondary. . . . Nor does a statute necessarily fall because it touches on activities which Congress might not otherwise regulate. . . . These principles are controlling here. The tax in question is a legitimate exercise of the taxing power despite its collateral regulatory purpose and effect." Later, in MARCHETTI V. UNITED STATES (1968), the Court

eliminated the use of the taxing power to compel violators of state laws to register with the federal government on the grounds that it violates the RIGHT AGAINST SELF-INCRIMINATION. And since the power of the federal government to regulate has received such major expansion in modern times, there is little need to use the taxing power to expand federal powers. Even though the Child Labor Tax Case may still be good law in defining when a tax ceases to be a tax and becomes a regulation, it is of minor importance. Congress will almost always have power to regulate and can cast its regulation in the form of a tax.

The spending power has also raised constitutional questions. Before the early 1900s, Congress spent money chiefly to defray its routine powers of government. It made a few grants to the states to encourage the construction of roads and universities, granting the money outright with no matching requirements or federal supervision. In 1902 the grants amounted to only seven million dollars per year. Soon, however, Congress began to see that grants could be used to encourage states to take action meeting federal standards even with respect to parts of the economy then thought to be outside congressional power.

The SHEPPARD-TOWNER MATERNITY ACT of 1921 provided for federal grants to states that would agree to spend the money for reducing maternal and infant mortality. Massachusetts, which had refused the grants, and Frothingham, a citizen and taxpayer, brought suits. The Supreme Court in *Massachusetts v. Mellon* and FROTHINGHAM V. MELLON (1923) held that neither had STANDING to litigate the issue. Massachusetts had no real interest at stake, for it had refused the grant. Frothingham had no standing as a taxpayer because her interest in the funds spent was miniscule and shared with all other federal taxpayers. The result of this suit was to make most government spending programs impossible to challenge in court.

As a result, it was not until 1936 that a major question as to the scope of the spending power was settled. Congress has power to levy taxes "to pay the Debts and provide for the common Defence and general Welfare of the United States." What does the GENERAL WELFARE CLAUSE mean? JAMES MADISON had argued that money could be spent only to carry out the other powers given to Congress—that there was not, in essence, any additional power granted by the general welfare language. ALEXANDER HAMILTON had said that the clause granted a substantive power to tax and spend so long as it was for the general welfare of the United States.

The Court finally had an opportunity to decide the issue in 1936 in UNITED STATES V. BUTLER. The AGRI-

CULTURE ADJUSTMENT ACT of 1933 had provided for agreements between the secretary of agriculture and farmers to reduce acreage in exchange for benefit payments. The money for the payments came from a tax levied on the processors of the commodity concerned with all of the tax proceeds directed to that purpose. The Court held first that the processors upon whom the tax was levied did have standing to challenge the expenditure, because they paid a substantial tax earmarked for that expenditure. Next, the Court adopted the Hamilton position that the power to spend might be exercised for the general welfare and was not limited to the other direct grants of legislative power. Finally, the Court said it did not have to decide whether the expenditure in this case was for the general welfare, because this law was a regulation, not an expenditure, and invalid as going beyond congressional regulatory power.

The *Butler* interpretation of the spending power, however, soon became the basis to uphold expenditures. In HELVERING V. DAVIS (1937) the Court upheld the SOCIAL SECURITY ACT, concluding that expenditures for old age pensions were expenditures for the general welfare. And in BUCKLEY V. VALEO (1976) the Court held that expenditures of funds to finance campaigns of presidential candidates was valid as an expenditure for the general welfare. (See CAMPAIGN FINANCING.) The Court said: "Congress was legislating for the 'general welfare'—to reduce the deleterious influence of large contributions on our political process, to facilitate communication by candidates with the electorate, and to free candidates from the rigors of fundraising. . . . Congress has concluded that the means are 'necessary and proper' to promote the general welfare, and we thus decline to find this legislation without the grant of power in Art. I, § 8."

The use of grants to states as a means of federal regulation has proceeded apace, almost totally free of challenge by the courts. Only where the challenge is based on the ESTABLISHMENT OF RELIGION has the Court recognized standing to challenge by taxpayers. And that holding, in FLAST V. COHEN (1968), is not absolute, as was shown by VALLEY FORGE CHRISTIAN COLLEGE V. AMERICANS UNITED FOR SEPARATION OF CHURCH AND STATE (1982). The seven million dollars of such grants in 1902 had risen to seven billion in 1960 and to over one hundred billion in the early 1980s—about one-third percent of state and local receipts from their own sources. Again, however, the constitutional issues have lost their former importance. If the expenditure can be said to be for the general welfare, the intrusion of the federal government into a local area does not matter. Because con-

gressional powers to spend for the general welfare and to regulate under the commerce clause are so broad, there is little prospect of a successful constitutional challenge to federal spending.

Both as to taxation and as to expenditure, no major constitutional problems remain. Congress has such broad regulatory powers that it no longer needs to attempt to get around power limitations by using taxation and expenditure. These methods of regulation are used today as convenient devices for accomplishing goals within congressional power. The major limitations on them are political. If the increase in federal grants to states appears to be slowing and if some recent Presidents have talked about a New Federalism policy to decrease such federal spending, the reasons lie not in constitutional limitations but in governmental policy.

EDWARD L. BARRETT

(SEE ALSO: *Direct and Indirect Taxes; Economic Regulation; Import-Export Clause; Impoundment of Funds; National Police Power.*)

Bibliography

GRANT, J. A. C. 1936 Commerce, Production, and the Fiscal Powers of Congress. *Yale Law Journal* 45:751–778.
POWELL, THOMAS R. 1922 Child Labor, Congress and the Constitution. *North Carolina Law Review* 1:61–81.
TRIBE, LAURENCE H. 1978 *American Constitutional Law.* Pages 225–227, 244–250. Mineola, N.Y.: Foundation Press.

TAXPAYERS' AND CITIZENS' SUITS

Federal courts will rule on the merits of a legal claim only at the request of one with a "personal stake in the outcome of the controversy." As a corollary of this central, entrenched STANDING doctrine, the federal judiciary turns away attacks on the legality of government behavior by citizens suing only as such. The rule stems from a SEPARATION OF POWERS premise: that federal judges should not review conduct of Congress or the Executive absent the need to protect a plaintiff from distinct personal injury. The rule has been applied mostly to reject challenges by United States citizens to acts of the political branches of the federal government, although it also appears to bar federal court suits by state or local citizens against acts of their governments. In essence, the citizen interest in lawful governance is viewed as an ideological, not a personal, interest, an interest best left to political rather than judicial resolution. Nonetheless, if a plaintiff can show concrete individual injury, as in SIERRA CLUB V. MORTON (1972), the public interest may then be argued in behalf of the personal claim, even if the primary motive for suing is not the personal but the citizen interest.

The law of taxpayer standing is more elaborate, because taxpayers' suits are sometimes deemed sufficiently personal to permit standing and sometimes rejected as disguised citizens' suits. Taxpayers contesting their own tax liability have a "personal stake," of course, but such an individualized interest is less clear for taxpayers disputing how tax revenues are spent. In FROTHINGHAM V. MELLON (1923) the Supreme Court found the pecuniary interest of a federal taxpayer in federal spending too remote to justify JUDICIAL REVIEW of congressional appropriations, but it reaffirmed its previous approval of federal court suits by local taxpayers attacking local spending programs. In FLAST V. COHEN (1968) the Court created an exception, allowing federal taxpayers to challenge congressional spending as an ESTABLISHMENT OF RELIGION because the establishment clause gives taxpayers a special interest in challenging the use of tax dollars to support religion. The dissent objected that the Court was recognizing standing to bring a "public action" having no effect on the suing taxpayer's financial interest.

Since *Flast*, the Court has denied standing to federal taxpayers who raised other constitutional objections in *United States v. Richardson* (1974) and *Schlesinger v. Reservists Committee* (1974). And in VALLEY FORGE CHRISTIAN COLLEGE V. AMERICANS UNITED (1982), a decision that substantially undermines the premise of *Flast*, the Court denied standing to taxpayers who raised establishment clause objections, but challenged federal distribution of surplus property rather than congressional appropriations of money. Even at the state taxpayer level, invoking the establishment clause will not suffice if the claim is not of government financial support of religion but of regulatory support, as in DOREMUS V. BOARD OF EDUCATION (1952). In short, a federal court will recognize taxpayer standing only when there is a tangible financial connection between a local or state taxpayer's interest and government spending, or when a local, state, or federal taxpayer challenges legislative appropriations on establishment clause grounds.

The federal judiciary's rejection of citizen suits and most taxpayer attacks on spending reflects a view that the power of judicial review is only a by-product of the need to apply law, including constitutional law, to decide the rights of those claiming injury. To entertain public actions would be to expand judicial scrutiny of acts of the elected branches of government—usurpation that might bring retaliation, in the eyes of those who take this view. For those who think judicial review is founded on a broader obligation to assure government adherence to the Constitution, such an expanded scrutiny would be desirable. If Congress were to authorize the federal courts to take jurisdiction over public actions, the Supreme Court probably would not find Article III's "case" or "controversy" requirement an insurmountable barrier. But the Court has always been reluctant to entertain public actions on its own authority.

JONATHAN D. VARAT

Bibliography

WRIGHT, CHARLES A.; MILLER, ARTHUR R.; and COOPER, EDWARD H. 1984 *Federal Practice and Procedure.* Vol. 13:634–663. St. Paul, Minn.: West Publishing Co.

TAYLOR, JOHN
(1753–1824)

John Taylor of Caroline read law in the office of his uncle, EDMUND PENDLETON. He became involved early in Virginia revolutionary politics and was a delegate to the FIRST CONTINENTAL CONGRESS. He served as an Army officer and almost continuously as a member of the House of Delegates (1779–1785). In the legislature he supported a measure to end ESTABLISHMENT OF RELIGION in Virginia.

As a delegate to the state convention in 1788 Taylor opposed RATIFICATION OF THE CONSTITUTION, which lacked a BILL OF RIGHTS, gave too much power to the general government, and was insufficiently republican. Even so, he involved himself immediately in the politics of the new government, becoming the foremost publicist of Jeffersonian democracy. Both in the Senate (1792–1794) and in the public press he was a leading opponent of the economic policies of ALEXANDER HAMILTON. In the controversy over the ALIEN AND SEDITION ACTS, Taylor introduced the Virginia Resolutions (written by JAMES MADISON) in the state legislature. (See VIRGINIA AND KENTUCKY RESOLUTIONS.)

An ardent supporter of THOMAS JEFFERSON, Taylor returned briefly to the Senate in 1803. He supported the TWELFTH AMENDMENT and defended the constitutionality of the LOUISIANA PURCHASE when even the President doubted it. Taylor broke with the Republican party over the War of 1812 and the renomination of President Madison, but he did not deviate from its principles. In his final term in the Senate

(1822–1824) and in his last books Taylor denounced the growing power of the federal judiciary, JOHN MARSHALL'S decision in McCULLOCH v. MARYLAND (1819), and HENRY CLAY'S AMERICAN SYSTEM, with its INTERNAL IMPROVEMENTS and protective tariff. He advocated STRICT CONSTRUCTION of constitutional grants of power to the federal government.

Taylor saw himself as the defender of a liberty in constant danger and a republic in perpetual crisis. He thought that, in every generation, the American people were presented with a choice between the political principles and practice of Thomas Jefferson and those of JOHN ADAMS—the former conducive to, and the latter destructive of, self-government and public happiness. He believed that the civic virtue of farmers, tradesmen, and professional persons was the indispensable basis of free institutions; and for him banks and corporations raised the specter of economic oligarchy, undermining both that virtue and those institutions. Big government was the creature and ally of big business; and bigness was the enemy of liberty and equality. Incongruously, for all his concern with liberty and equality he unqualifiedly supported black slavery. Taylor is probably best known as a theorist of STATES' RIGHTS: his ideas bridged the gap between the Virginia and Kentucky Resolutions and JOHN C. CALHOUN'S doctrine of NULLIFICATION.

Taylor's most important books are *An Enquiry into the Principles and Policies of the Government of the United States* (1814), a comprehensive statement of the political theory of agrarian democracy, and *Construction Construed and Constitutions Vindicated* (1820), an attack on the expansion of federal court JURISDICTION and the use of JUDICIAL REVIEW to reduce the independence of the states.

DENNIS J. MAHONEY

Bibliography

HILL, CHARLES W. 1977 *The Political Theory of John Taylor of Caroline.* Rutherford, N.J.: Fairleigh Dickinson University Press.
LLOYD, THOMAS GORDON 1973 *The Danger Not Yet Over: The Political Thought and Practice of John Taylor of Caroline.* Ph.D. dissertation, Claremont Graduate School.

TAYLOR, ZACHARY
(1784–1850)

A professional soldier and hero of the Mexican War, Zachary Taylor was elected President as a Whig in 1848. A moderate on most issues, Taylor was a Louisi-

ana slaveholder who was politically close to New Yorkers Thurlow Weed and WILLIAM SEWARD. Taylor opposed any interference with slavery in the South but also opposed opening the Mexican Cession to slavery. Similarly, he opposed the WILMOT PROVISO but advocated immediate admission of California and New Mexico as free states. He opposed the COMPROMISE OF 1850 and would probably have vetoed most of its provisions, had he not died in July 1850.

PAUL FINKELMAN

Bibliography

HAMILTON, HOLMAN 1941 *Zachary Taylor: Soldier of the Republic.* Indianapolis: Bobbs-Merrill.

TAYLOR v. LOUISIANA
419 U.S. 522 (1975)

Under Louisiana law women were selected for jury service only when they explicitly volunteered for duty; men were selected irrespective of their desires. In *Hoyt v. Florida* (1961), the Supreme Court had employed a RATIONAL BASIS standard of review to uphold a similar law against DUE PROCESS and EQUAL PROTECTION attacks. In *Taylor*, however, the Court invalidated this jury selection system as a denial of the Sixth Amendment right of the accused to "a jury drawn from a fair cross section of the community." That the accused was male was irrelevant to this claim. The vote was 8–1; Justice WILLIAM H. REHNQUIST dissented, and Chief Justice WARREN E. BURGER concurred only in the result.

Writing for the other seven Justices, Justice BYRON R. WHITE declined to follow *Hoyt*; if the fair cross section requirement ever "permitted the almost total exclusion of women, this is not the case today." Women had entered the work force in large numbers, undermining their exemption "solely on their sex and the presumed role in the home." *Taylor* is not only an important JURY DISCRIMINATION precedent but also a strong judicial rejection of laws resting on stereotypical assumptions about "woman's role."

KENNETH L. KARST

TEN BROEK, JACOBUS
(1911–1968)

The major contribution of Jacobus ten Broek to American constitutional scholarship was *The Antislavery Origins of the Fourteenth Amendment* (1951; rev. ed.,

Equal under Law, 1965), in which he described the influence of the abolitionist movement on the drafting and ratification of the FOURTEENTH AMENDMENT. Ten Broek argued that the abolitionists identified the NATURAL RIGHTS of human beings as constitutional rights requiring a national constitutional power of enforcement. He maintained that the PRIVILEGES AND IMMUNITIES clause of the amendment protected these natural rights and the auxiliary rights necessary to their enjoyment; that the EQUAL PROTECTION clause required the states to supply full legal protection to natural rights and authorized Congress to protect these rights if the states failed to do so; and that the amendment applied to the states those provisions of the federal BILL OF RIGHTS guaranteeing natural rights, as well as those natural rights not mentioned in the Bill of Rights. Ten Broek, a lawyer, was a political scientist at the University of California, Berkeley.

RICHARD B. BERNSTEIN

TENNESSEE v. GARNER
105 S.Ct. 1694 (1985)

At the time of this case a majority of police departments in the nation prohibited the use of deadly force against nonviolent suspects, and the Supreme Court sought by its decision to stimulate a uniformity of that practice. Justice BYRON R. WHITE for a 6–3 majority held unconstitutional on FOURTH AMENDMENT grounds a state act authorizing an officer to shoot to kill in order to prevent an escape after he gave notice of an intent to arrest. The DOCTRINE of the case is that to kill a fleeing, unarmed felon as a last resort in order to prevent his getaway constitutes an unreasonable seizure unless the officer believes that failure to use deadly force will result in serious harm to himself or others. Justice SANDRA DAY O'CONNOR, for the dissenters, would have permitted deadly force at least against residential burglars who resist arrest by attempting to flee the scene of the crime.

LEONARD W. LEVY

(SEE ALSO: *Unreasonable Search.*)

TENNESSEE v. SCOPES

See: *State of Tennessee v. Scopes*

TENNESSEE VALLEY AUTHORITY ACT
48 Stat. 58 (1933)

A debate over the best use for an uncompleted defense plant site at Muscle Shoals—in the heart of a chronically depressed region—emerged after World War I, ending with passage of the Tennessee Valley Authority Act. In 1933, President FRANKLIN D. ROOSEVELT urged creation of "a corporation clothed with the power of government but possessed of the flexibility and initiative of a private enterprise" to rehabilitate and develop the resources of the Tennessee River valley.

The resultant act, largely written by Senator GEORGE W. NORRIS, encompassed a variety of objectives including national defense; flood control and the improvement of navigation; the development of agriculture, industry, and electric power; and even reforestation. To accomplish these goals, Congress created the Tennessee Valley Authority (TVA), granting it the power to construct dams and power works in the valley and to increase production of badly needed fertilizers. The act also authorized the TVA to sell any energy produced in excess of its needs, giving preference to publicly owned organizations; the TVA further received authority to build power lines to facilitate sales and transmission of power. A series of amendments in 1935 and 1939 sought to liquidate the system's costs by providing for sales of electric power, producing "gross revenues in excess of the costs of production," to acquire major utility properties, and even to issue credit to assist the distribution of its power.

Supporters of the act relied on arguments including the GENERAL WELFARE CLAUSE, the commerce power, and the WAR POWERS. The Supreme Court sustained a TVA contract for the sale of surplus power in ASHWANDER V. TENNESSEE VALLEY AUTHORITY (1936), thus effectively sustaining the act's constitutionality.

DAVID GORDON

TENNEY v. BRANDHOVE
341 U.S. 367 (1951)

This decision established the absolute immunity of state legislative officials from damages actions, brought under SECTION 1983, TITLE 42, UNITED STATES CODE, alleging violations of constitutional rights. William Brandhove claimed that Senator Jack

B. Tenney and other members of a California state legislative committee had violated his constitutional rights by conducting hearings to intimidate and silence him. In an opinion by Justice FELIX FRANKFURTER, the Supreme Court noted the history of parliamentary immunity in England, and cited the SPEECH OR DEBATE CLAUSE as a recognition of the need for a fearless and independent legislature. It held that, despite the unequivocal language of section 1983, Congress had not meant to "impinge on a tradition so well grounded in history and reason." (See LEGISLATIVE IMMUNITY.)

THEODORE EISENBERG

TEN POUND ACT CASES
N.H. (1786–1787)

These cases, about which little is known (not even the names of the litigants are known), are notable as the first instances in our history of a state court's holding unconstitutional an act of a state legislature. The Inferior Court of Common Pleas of Rockingham County, sitting in Portsmouth, New Hampshire, in 1786 and 1787, voided the "Ten Pound Act," which had been passed in 1785 for the speedy recovery of small debts. Our scanty knowledge of the cases derives from newspaper reports and legislative records. The act of 1785 allowed justices of the peace to try certain civil cases, involving sums less than ten pounds, without juries. The state constitutional guarantee of TRIAL BY JURY extended to all civil cases except those which juries customarily did not try. New Hampshire practice had previously allowed a justice of the peace to try a case without a jury if the sum amounted to less than two pounds. After the court ruled that the act conflicted with the right to trial by jury, petitions to the state House of Representatives demanded IMPEACHMENT of the judges. The house, by a 3–1 majority, voted that the act was constitutional, but the judges stood by their initial decision or reaffirmed it in another case. Following the failure of a motion to impeach the judges, the house capitulated and repealed the Ten Pound Act.

LEONARD W. LEVY

TENTH AMENDMENT

Adopted in 1791 as part of the BILL OF RIGHTS, the Tenth Amendment declares that "powers not delegated to the United States by the Constitution . . . are reserved to the States respectively, or to the people." This language was an attempt to satisfy the public that the new constitution would not make a reality of that most repeated of Anti-Federalist fears: a completely centralized or "consolidated" government. But while the Tenth Amendment reminded Congress that its concerns were limited, the Constitution envisioned the effective exercise of national power, as the NECESSARY AND PROPER CLAUSE and the SUPREMACY CLAUSE indicated. The inevitable question was to be: what happens when Congress's responsibilities require measures the states say are beyond Congress's powers? JOHN MARSHALL attempted the Supreme Court's first answer to this question in McCULLOCH V. MARYLAND (1819). McCulloch is best interpreted as advancing the following propositions: by granting and enumerating powers, the Constitution envisions the pursuit of a limited number of ends (see ENUMERATED POWERS); the framers did not and could not have enumerated all the legislative means appropriate to achieving constitutional ends in changing historical circumstances; Congress can select appropriate means to authorized national ends without regard for state prerogatives; the states, by contrast, cannot enact measures conflicting with lawful congressional policies.

To reach these conclusions Marshall observed that in drafting the Tenth Amendment the First Congress had refused to limit national powers to those "expressly granted," as the ARTICLES OF CONFEDERATION had done, and that a STRICT CONSTRUCTION of national powers would defeat the vital purposes for which the Constitution had been established. By rejecting a rigid line between state and national powers McCulloch opened the way to the future assumption of state responsibilities by the national government as needed to achieve national ends. Critics charged that Marshall would consolidate all power in the national government by permitting unlimited means to an ostensibly limited number of national ends. Marshall defended his theory by insisting that judges should invalidate pretextual congressional acts, that is, congressional acts cloaked in the commerce power and other national powers but actually aimed at state concerns, not at the free flow of commerce or other authorized national ends. The Court did not always conform to this view of McCulloch in upholding the expansions of national power in the twentieth century. The SOCIAL SECURITY ACT, the FAIR LABOR STANDARDS ACT, and the CIVIL RIGHTS ACT of 1964 were good faith exercises of national power because they were plausible as means to the nation's economic health or the ends of the Civil War amendments. The same cannot be said for the MANN ACT, the Little Lindbergh Act, and other uses of national power for POLICE POWER purposes. (See GENERAL WELFARE CLAUSE.)

From the late 1840s to the late 1930s judges unfriendly either to national power or to government generally lapsed into a static conception of state–federal powers that exempted "state instrumentalities" from federal taxation (see INTERGOVERNMENTAL IMMUNITIES) and removed aspects of the nation's economic life (such as labor relations and other incidents of manufacturing) from Congress's reach. (See COMMERCE CLAUSE.) Scholars have imputed a theory of DUAL FEDERALISM to many of the decisions of this period because the Court seemed to say that the RESERVED POWERS of the states constituted a line Congress could not cross in exercising its admitted powers. The most infamous of dual federalist decisions, HAMMER V. DAGENHART (1918), prevented Congress from using its power over INTERSTATE COMMERCE to combat child labor, a practice then considered reserved to state control. After the Depression changed attitudes toward federal power, the Court all but eliminated the tax immunity doctrine, leaving only hypothetical protection from federal taxes that might interfere with "essential state functions," as might a federal tax on a statehouse. And in the landmark case of UNITED STATES V. DARBY (1941) the Court overruled *Hammer*, holding that Congress, regardless of its underlying purposes, could stop any goods from moving in interstate commerce, even though they were produced in conformity to state policies toward child labor and other conditions of manufacturing. For the *Darby* majority Justice HARLAN FISKE STONE said that the Tenth Amendment declared the "truism" that Congress could only exercise granted powers but that it had no effect on the question of what powers had actually been granted. Stone thus returned the Court to Marshall's view that Congress could disregard state prerogatives in the pursuit of what it saw as the nation's economic health in changing circumstances. But by disavowing judicial inquiries into underlying legislative purposes, Stone rejected the view that judges should invalidate pretextual uses of power—the essence of Marshall's defense of *McCulloch* as a decision compatible with the concept of a national government with limited concerns. Time had run out on this concept by the mid-1940s as Congress had advanced far in the use of its commerce, taxing, and spending powers for purposes of admitted state concern. (See NATIONAL POLICE POWER.)

Such was the general picture in the postwar constitutional law of state–federal power until a surprise decision in 1976 invalidated federal wage and hour standards for state employees. A plurality opinion in NATIONAL LEAGUE OF CITIES V. USERY (1976) likened STATES' RIGHTS "regarding the conduct of integral governmental functions" to the rights of individuals protected by the Bill of Rights. Here was an even clearer statement of dual federalism than *Hammer*, and critics charged that this radical departure from *McCulloch* threatened federal standards in areas such as CIVIL RIGHTS and environmental protection. But after evading extension of *Usery* for a decade the Court overruled *Usery* in GARCIA V. SAN ANTONIO METROPOLITAN TRANSIT AUTHORITY (1985), on the theory that representation of state governmental interests in Congress, as opposed to judicial vindication of states' rights, is the constitutionally preferred way to protect state prerogatives. *Garcia* thus abandoned *Usery* without returning to the theory of *McCulloch*.

Beyond fluctuations in judicial doctrine one can attribute the decline of the Tenth Amendment to the social and economic interdependencies of an industrial society and an enhanced public commitment to minority and other fundamental rights with which states' rights historically clashed.

SOTIRIOS A. BARBER

Bibliography
CORWIN, EDWARD S. 1950 The Passing of Dual Federalism. *Virginia Law Review* 36:1–24.
FLAX, KAREN H. 1983 In the Wake of National League of Cities v. Usery: A "Derelict" Makes Waves. *South Carolina Law Review* 34:649–686.
WECHSLER, HERBERT 1954 The Political Safeguards of Federalism: The Role of the States in the Composition and Selection of the National Government. *Columbia Law Review* 54:543–560.

TENURE OF OFFICE ACT
14 Stat. 430 (1867)

After a complete political rupture between President ANDREW JOHNSON and congressional Republicans over Reconstruction policy, Congress enacted the Tenure of Office Act in March 1867, providing that all officials of the executive branch, except cabinet officers whose appointment had required Senate confirmation, would hold office until their successors had likewise been confirmed. Cabinet officers were to hold office only during the term of the president appointing them plus one month. The act also provided for interim appointments while the Senate was not in session.

In February 1868, President Johnson removed Secretary of War EDWIN M. STANTON, who was hostile to his Reconstruction policies, and appointed General Lorenzo Thomas in his place. The House promptly voted to impeach Johnson. Though Republicans sought to remove him from office because of his stubborn obstruction of their Reconstruction program, debates in his Senate trial turned on the constitutionality of the statute. The President's counsel maintained that it was unconstitutional as an interference with the president's removal power, a prerogative distinct from the APPOINTIVE POWER. The Senate could not muster the two-thirds vote necessary for conviction. Congress repealed the act in 1887.

WILLIAM M. WIECEK

Bibliography

BENEDICT, MICHAEL LES 1973 *The Impeachment and Trial of Andrew Johnson.* New York: Norton.

TERM
(Supreme Court)

As prescribed by congressional statute, the Supreme Court holds a regular annual term of court, beginning on the first Monday in October. The term usually concludes in late June or early July of the following year. The Court is also authorized to hold special terms outside the normal October terms but does so only infrequently, in urgent circumstances (EX PARTE QUIRIN, 1942, German saboteurs convicted by military commission; O'BRIEN V. BROWN, 1972, seating of delegates to Democratic National Convention).

Although Congress manipulated the Court's terms to postpone decision of MARBURY V. MADISON (1803) for nearly a year, modern times have seen no similar stratagems.

KENNETH L. KARST

TERMINIELLO v. CHICAGO
337 U.S. 1 (1949)

Terminiello was convicted of disorderly conduct after a meeting in a private hall outside of which a thousand persons violently protested his anti-Semitic, antiblack, and anticommunist harangue. The Court reversed because the jury had been instructed that it might convict on a finding that Terminiello's speech "invite[d] dispute." This instruction failed to require a finding of CLEAR AND PRESENT DANGER of violence. *Termi-niello* frequently is coupled with FEINER V. NEW YORK (1951) as illustrations of the HOSTILE AUDIENCE problem.

MARTIN SHAPIRO

TERRETT v. TAYLOR
9 Cranch 43 (1815)

This was the first case and one of the very few in which the Supreme Court relied exclusively upon the concept of a HIGHER LAW as the sole basis for holding a state act unconstitutional. After adopting THOMAS JEFFERSON'S statute of religious liberty, which separated church and state in Virginia, the legislature confiscated certain Episcopal glebe lands and sold them, using the proceeds for charity. The lands in question having been donated to the church by private persons, no contract and therefore no CONTRACT CLAUSE issue existed. Justice JOSEPH STORY for the Court held the confiscation act void, offering as grounds: "we think ourselves standing upon the principles of natural justice, upon the fundamental laws of every free government, upon the spirit and letter of the constitution. . . ." Story did not mention *which* letter. Usually the Court applied the DOCTRINE of VESTED RIGHTS in a way that absorbed the higher law within express provisions of the Constitution.

LEONARD W. LEVY

TERRITORIAL COURT

From the beginning the United States has held TERRITORIES outside the existing states. Some territories have been destined for statehood, others for independence, and still others for "permanent" territorial status. (See COMMONWEALTH STATUS.) Early in our history Congress established courts to serve the territories, but it did not give their judges the life tenure and salary guarantees demanded by Article III for judges of CONSTITUTIONAL COURTS. The constitutional status of these territorial courts was thus uncertain.

Chief Justice John Marshall sought to resolve the uncertainty in AMERICAN INSURANCE CO. V. CANTER (1828) by inventing a new category called LEGISLATIVE COURTS. Such a court, Marshall said, is not created under Article III, which provides for the establishment of constitutional courts to exercise the JUDICIAL POWER OF THE UNITED STATES. Rather it is created by Congress in carrying out its general legislative powers under Article I, including the power to provide for the government of the territories. Although the case at hand was one of ADMIRALTY AND MARITIME JURISDICTION, plainly within the federal judicial power, the fact that it arose in a territory made it appropriate for disposition by such a "legislative" territorial court. The result made good sense in a territory (Florida) that was to become a state; upon statehood, most of the work of the territorial courts would be taken over by the state courts, and there would be no place for a large body of life-tenured judges in the new federal courts. Furthermore, independence from the President and Congress receded in importance in a territorial government that had essentially the same power as a state to discard the principle of SEPARATION OF POWERS.

Today legislative courts continue to serve in territories such as Guam and the Virgin Islands. In the Commonwealth of PUERTO RICO, Congress has created a dual court system matching that of the DISTRICT OF COLUMBIA: one set of constitutional courts, operating wholly within the terms of Article III, and one set of commonwealth courts roughly equivalent to state courts.

KENNETH L. KARST

Bibliography

WRIGHT, CHARLES ALAN 1983 The Law of Federal Courts, 4th ed. Pages 14–15, 40–42, 49, 139–140. St. Paul, Minn.: West Publishing Co.

TERRITORY

At the time of independence several states had extensive claims to territory on the western frontier. A dispute over whether such territories were to be administered by the claimant states or by and for the United States long delayed ratification of the ARTICLES OF CONFEDERATION. In 1780 Congress passed a resolution urging the states to cede their claims to the United States. The resolution contained three promises which became the basic principles of American CONSTITUTIONALISM as extended to the territories: that the territories would be "disposed of for the common benefit of the United States"; that they would be "settled and formed into distinct republican states"; and that they would eventually "become members of the federal union and have the same rights of SOVEREIGNTY, freedom, and independence as the other states." After the cession was complete and the western boundary was settled by the Treaty of Paris (1783), Congress embodied these three principles in measures for the temporary government of

the territories: the ORDINANCE OF 1784 and the NORTHWEST ORDINANCE OF 1787. The same principles were reaffirmed by the CONSTITUTIONAL CONVENTION OF 1787. Although some delegates advocated maintaining the western lands as a federal colony to be exploited and governed permanently by the existing states, the Constitution provided for the admission of new states on an equal basis with the original states.

The first acquisition of territory beyond the original borders of the nation was the LOUISIANA PURCHASE. After brief debate about the constitutional propriety of such territorial expansion, Congress proceeded to organize the Louisiana Territory following the model of the Northwest Ordinance. Exploration, purchase, and cession, as well as the conquests of the Mexican War, resulted in further territorial expansion.

Congress's power to make rules and regulations for the territories derives from the second clause of Article IV, section 3. In the first important case on territories to be decided by the Supreme Court, AMERICAN INSURANCE COMPANY V. CANTER (1828), Chief Justice JOHN MARSHALL suggested that the power to govern the territories was also implied in the power to acquire them through the use of the TREATY POWER or the WAR POWERS. He added that, whatever its source, Congress's power over the territories was plenary, whether exercised directly or through a local legislature, and extended even to creation of TERRITORIAL COURTS with JURISDICTION beyond the JUDICIAL POWER OF THE UNITED STATES.

In the early nineteenth century the question of SLAVERY IN THE TERRITORIES divided the country and sparked new controversy over the constitutional status of territories. Southerners maintained that the federal government held the territories in trust for the states and that Congress could not properly prohibit slavery in them, while northern Whigs such as ABRAHAM LINCOLN maintained that the territories were national possessions and failure to prohibit slavery in them would constitute a national endorsement of the institution. STEPHEN A. DOUGLAS proposed to avoid the issue by leaving it to a vote of the settlers in each territory. Congress sought to allay sectional contention in the MISSOURI COMPROMISE by permitting slavery in one part of the Louisiana Purchase while prohibiting it in the rest. In the COMPROMISE OF 1850, Douglas's formula (which he called POPULAR SOVEREIGNTY) was adopted for the territory acquired in the Mexican War (except California). In DRED SCOTT V. SANDFORD (1857) the Supreme Court held that Congress did not have the power to exclude slavery from the territories. The Civil War, by eliminating the slavery issue, ended the sectional dispute over the status of territories.

By 1869 American territorial acquisition on the mainland of North America was complete. A new debate about the status of territories began when, at the end of the nineteenth century, the United States started to acquire overseas possessions, not a part of the continent and apparently not destined for statehood. The place of this "colonial empire" in the constitutional system was a subject of political dispute in the 1900 elections; but it was not resolved until the Supreme Court decided the INSULAR CASES. In these cases the Court formulated the doctrine of INCORPORATION OF TERRITORIES, according to which territorial possessions do not become part of the United States until Congress, by some positive action, makes them so.

Territories may be either incorporated or unincorporated, and either organized or unorganized. The former refers to the degree of constitutional protection enjoyed by inhabitants and to Congress's ultimate intention to confer statehood or not; the latter refers to the provision Congress has made for government of the territory. There are now no incorporated territories, but there are both organized and unorganized unincorporated territories. In 1934 the special status of "commonwealth" was created for the Philippines, which became independent after World War II; PUERTO RICO and the Northern Marianas currently have COMMONWEALTH STATUS and enjoy virtually complete internal self-government. After World War II the United States accepted a mandate over the Trust Territory of the Pacific Islands. Authority over that territory was exercised by virtue of the UNITED NATIONS CHARTER until the trusteeship ended in 1981.

DENNIS J. MAHONEY

Bibliography

BLOOM, JOHN PORTER, ed. 1973 *The American Territorial System.* Athens: Ohio University Press.

LIEBOWITZ, A. H. 1979 United States Federalism: States and Territories. *American University Law Review* 28:449–482.

PERKINS, WHITNEY T. 1962 *Denial of Empire.* Leyden, Netherlands: A. W. Sythoff.

TERRY v. ADAMS
345 U.S. 461 (1953)

With confidence, we can call *Terry* the last of the series of "Texas primary cases" beginning with NIXON V. HERNDON (1927). The decision is also a clear modern example of the "public function" strand of STATE ACTION doctrine. In a Texas county, a group called the Jaybird Democratic Association conducted pre-PRIMARY ELECTIONS, from which black voters were excluded. The winners of these elections consistently won both the Democratic primaries and the general elections. The Supreme Court held that black plaintiffs were entitled to a DECLARATORY JUDGMENT that their exclusion from the Jaybird election amounted to state action in violation of the FIFTEENTH AMENDMENT. There was no MAJORITY OPINION. Three Justices said that the state could not constitutionally permit a racial exclusion from the only election that mattered in the county. The electoral process was inescapably public, subject to the Fifteenth Amendment's commands. Four other Justices said the Jaybirds were an auxiliary of the local Democratic party organization, and thus included within the doctrine of SMITH V. ALLWRIGHT (1944). Justice FELIX FRANKFURTER found state action in the participation of state election officials as voters in the Jaybird election. Justice SHERMAN MINTON dissented, calling the Jaybirds nothing but a "pressure group."

KENNETH L. KARST

TERRY v. OHIO
392 U.S. 1 (1968)
SIBRON v. NEW YORK
392 U.S. 40 (1968)

Terry v. Ohio marked the first attempt by the Supreme Court to deal with a pervasive type of police conduct known as STOP AND FRISK. Where an individual's suspicious conduct gives rise to an apprehension of danger, but PROBABLE CAUSE for an arrest does not exist, it is common police practice to stop the suspect for questioning and to pat down (frisk) his outer clothing in a search for concealed weapons. While this may be an effective way to deter crime it is susceptible to abuse. Though far less intrusive on privacy and security than formal arrest and thorough search, a stop and, especially, a frisk can be a frightening and humiliating experience.

It was this consideration that led the Court in *Terry* to hold that stop and frisk is subject to limitations established by the FOURTH AMENDMENT. Chief Justice EARL WARREN declared that the forcible restraint of an individual, however temporary, is a "seizure," and a frisk, though limited in scope, is a "search," within the meaning of the Fourth Amendment. However, the imperative of sound law enforcement, as well as the need of the police to assure their own safety and that of the citizenry, requires that the amendment's reasonableness clause—rather than the probable cause standard of the warrant clause—should govern this type of police conduct. Balancing individual freedom against community needs, Warren concluded that if "a reasonably prudent [officer] in the circumstances [is] warranted in the belief that his safety or that of others [is] in danger," he is, under the reasonableness clause, entitled to stop and frisk the suspect in order to avoid the threatened harm. Any weapon thus seized is admissible at trial. However, in *Terry*'s companion case, *Sibron v. New York* the Court held that where the motivation for the frisk is the discovery of EVIDENCE rather than the confiscation of weapons, the evidence seized is inadmissible.

The officer's apprehension of danger must be based on articulable facts rather than mere hunch; the difference between probable cause and the less strict standard authorized in *Terry* is a difference between reasonable belief and reasonable suspicion. Paradoxically, the case both significantly limited and momentously expanded the police search power: it placed "on the street" police–citizen encounters under the protection of the Fourth Amendment even as it allowed, for the first time, a standard less exacting than probable cause to meet the requirement of reasonableness for searches made in EXIGENT CIRCUMSTANCES.

JACOB W. LANDYNSKI

TEST CASE

Whenever a unit of government, or an interest in the private sector, wants a favorable constitutional decision on a point in question, a test case is often organized to gain a ruling from the Supreme Court. The Court has not defined the term, and need not, as there is no judicial criterion for "test case" under the CASES AND CONTROVERSIES clause of Article III. Scholarship on the judicial process provides the best understanding of the term as a strategy employed by different interests, for differing ends. FLETCHER v. PECK (1810) showed that systematically plotting a test case, so framing it as to elicit particular answers based on prediction concerning how the Justices are likely to respond, and then using the judicial decision for political advantage is not a strategy unique to recent CIVIL RIGHTS cases but a durable aspect of constitutional litigation since the early years of the Republic.

Organizers of test cases sometimes look upon victory in the Supreme Court as a secondary goal. For example, the arguments of the National Woman Suffrage Association that women, as citizens, were already enfranchised by terms of the FOURTEENTH AMENDMENT breathed new life into the organization through publicity of test cases. MINOR V. HAPPERSETT (1875) and two other cases failed but they produced national news.

The Department of Justice took little initiative in enforcing new legislation in the nineteenth century, largely because Congress intended enforcement to come through complaints of individuals entitled to sue violators. An example of this is the CIVIL RIGHTS CASES (1883). Individuals challenged about a hundred violations of the CIVIL RIGHTS ACT OF 1875. Eventually, five came to the Supreme Court as test cases, where they were unsuccessfully argued by the SOLICITOR GENERAL. These test cases were not managed; they simply happened as individual blacks complained.

Business interests may bring test cases to prevent enforcement of new regulatory legislation, as in 1917 when David Clark for the Southern Cotton Manufacturers sought to invalidate the KEATING-OWEN ACT which prohibited shipment in INTERSTATE COMMERCE of designated products manufactured in plants employing children. Stephen Wood reports the advice of a Philadelphia lawyer to the manufacturers:

No legal proceeding will lie until the [Keating-Owen] bill is in operation. Some action must be taken under some provision of the bill so that a real and not a moot question is raised. A court, in order to pass upon any phase of it, must have before it an actual case, and if the measure is to be contested, the case should not only be carefully selected in order that the constitutional principle desired to be raised may be clearly presented, but I believe then that when the issue is raised, if possible, a judicial district should be selected in which the judge is a man of known courage. This is no case to try before a weak character [1968: 87–88].

Clark proceeded to raise money, select suitable counsel, identify Judge James Edmund Boyd as courageous, and locate cotton companies in the western district of North Carolina ready to cooperate. After searching for the "perfect combination of factors," Clark worked up four possible test cases to submit to the attorneys in New York. There the *Dagenhart* case was selected as the best. The Dagenharts, a father and two minor sons, and the company "were mere figureheads" whom Clark persuaded to set up the case. First, the company posted notices that under-age employees would be dismissed when the Keating-Owen law went into effect. The attorneys employed by Clark then prepared a complaint for Dagenhart asserting that this threat would deprive him of his VESTED RIGHTS, because he was entitled to the services of his minor sons and the compensation arising from their labors. By moving before the law became effective, the cotton manufacturers put the Department of Justice on the defensive, trapped within the confines of their test case. Judge Boyd, who ruled the Keating-Owen Act invalid under the Fifth and TENTH AMENDMENTS, was upheld by the Supreme Court in 1918 in HAMMER V. DAGENHART.

Success in managing constitutional litigation requires understanding of both substantive law and litigation practice. Following enactment of the WAGNER ACT in 1935, lawyers for the National Labor Relations Board combined these talents in impressive fashion, gaining a stunning triumph from the Supreme Court in *NLRB v. Jones & Laughlin* in March 1937. (See WAGNER ACT CASES.) Against hostile attacks by the National Lawyers' Committee of the American Liberty League, NLRB lawyers carefully developed cases running the gamut of size and type to make the first tests establishing wide congressional power to regulate labor practices in businesses affecting interstate commerce.

NLRB lawyers, even before the Wagner Act was signed, had designed a "master plan" envisioning test cases built around COMMERCE CLAUSE issues stressing the type of industry, characteristics of individual businesses, the degree of actual or threatened obstruction of commerce, and the type of unfair labor practices charged. In Peter Irons's words, this "master plan" gave clear directions for "sifting through their massive case loads in search of ideal test cases, charting a clear path from the picket line to the Supreme Court." The NLRB staff functioned as legal craftsmen, "as much meticulous technicians as partisan advocates," who "winnowed and selected cases with care; scrutinized records with a fine-tooth comb; chose courts with a shopper's discriminating eye; wrote briefs to draw the issues narrowly and precisely."

Although numerous voluntary associations with litigation programs, such as the Anti-Saloon League of America, the National Consumers' League, and the AMERICAN JEWISH CONGRESS, have sponsored test cases as a way of influencing public policy, the organizations most noted for this practice have been the National Association for the Advancement of Colored People (NAACP), formed in 1909, and the NAACP LEGAL DEFENSE FUND, INC., organized in 1939.

Modern test cases by associations, public interest law firms, or lawyers working *pro bono publico* are often cast as CLASS ACTIONS under the FEDERAL RULES OF CIVIL PROCEDURE. Although they may at-tack conditions that are widespread, these cases rest on particularized explorations of fact, often through discovery and expert testimony. In attacking school segregation in the five cases styled as BROWN V. BOARD OF EDUCATION, the NAACP sought to develop full factual records, building upon the experience of THURGOOD MARSHALL and others as counsel in the earlier white primary cases and racial RESTRICTIVE COVENANT cases. Widespread test cases will continue because both government and private counsel can approach the Supreme Court only by representing particular parties with particular concrete claims.

CLEMENT E. VOSE

Bibliography
CORTNER, RICHARD C. 1964 *The Wagner Act Cases.* Pages 106–141. Knoxville: University of Tennessee Press.
FREUND, PAUL A. 1951 *On Understanding the Supreme Court.* Pages 77–116. Boston: Little, Brown.
IRONS, PETER 1982 *The New Deal Lawyers.* Pages 234–289. Princeton, N.J.: Princeton University Press.
KLUGER, RICHARD 1975 *Simple Justice: The History of Brown v. Board of Education and Black America's Struggle for Equality.* Pages 256–540. New York: Vintage Books.
VOSE, CLEMENT E. 1959 *Caucasians Only: The Supreme Court, the NAACP, and the Restrictive Covenant Cases.* Pages 50–73, 151–176. Berkeley: University of California Press.
WOOD, STEPHEN B. 1968 *Constitutional Politics in the Progressive Era.* Pages 81–110. Chicago: University of Chicago Press.

TESTIMONIAL AND NONTESTIMONIAL COMPULSION

In the 1960s the Supreme Court ruled that the RIGHT AGAINST SELF-INCRIMINATION was not infringed when police compelled the driver of an accident vehicle to give a blood sample for analysis of its alcoholic content, compelled a suspect in a LINEUP to utter before witnesses the words used by a bank robber, and compelled another suspected bank robber to submit a sample of his handwriting for comparison with a note given to a bankteller. In the 1970s the Court held that the right against self-incrimination did not protect a person from the compulsory production of business and tax records in the possession of his or her accountant or lawyer, and did not protect a person from a court order to make a voice recording for a federal GRAND JURY seeking to identify a criminal by the sound of a voice on a legally intercepted telephone conversation. All these decisions shared a thorny problem: if a person is compelled to provide the state with evidence to incriminate him, is he necessarily a witness against himself in the Fifth Amendment sense?

The Court prefers a different formulation: does nontestimonial compulsion force a person to be a witness against himself criminally? The consistent answer has been "no," even if there was a testimonial dimension to the forced admissions. If that testimonial dimension loomed too large, the Court loosened its distinction between testimonial and nontestimonial compulsion and relied on some other distinction. Thus, when the driver of a vehicle involved in an accident was required by state law to stop and identify himself, though doing so subjected him to criminal penalties, the Court saw no Fifth Amendment issue, only a regulation promoting the satisfaction of civil liabilities. Similarly, when a lawyer or accountant was forced to turn over a client's incriminating records, the client had not been compelled at all, though he paid the criminal penalty and lost the chance to make a Fifth Amendment plea. And when the police during the course of a lawful search found incriminating business records, the records were introduced in evidence, although they could not have been subpoenaed directly from the businessman. In these cases, where the compulsion was communicative or testimonial in character, the Court inconsistently discoursed on the need to decide as it did in order to avoid a decision against the introduction of nontestimonial evidence that had been compelled.

More often the Court relied on a supposed distinction between forcing a person to furnish evidence against himself of a testimonial nature and forcing him to be the source of nontestimonial or physical evidence against himself, usually derived from his body. The word "witness" implies giving testimony based on one's knowledge, not displaying one's person. Compulsion to reveal information other than one's physical characteristics is generally unconstitutional, especially if the information is derived directly from the party himself, though not if the police lawfully find his records. The Court's distinction between testimonial and nontestimonial compulsion is obviously a bit porous. That distinction derived from the realistic need to prevent the Fifth Amendment from disabling police identifications based on fingerprints, handwriting, photographs, blood samples, voice exemplars, and lineups. The distinction had its origin in a passing remark by Justice OLIVER WENDELL HOLMES in 1910, when he dismissed as "an extravagant extension of the Fifth Amendment" the claim that requiring a defendant to model a shirt for identification purposes breached the right against self-incrimination.

The trouble with the distinction, apart from the Court's own inconsistency, is that physical or identifying evidence can be communicative in character, as when a laboratory report, the result of a drunken driver's blood sample, is introduced against him, or when a grand jury indicts one whose voice identifies him as the culprit. Whether by writing, speaking, or giving blood involuntarily, an individual has been compelled to furnish evidence against himself. That he has not been forced to "testify" is a distinction less persuasive than semantically catchy. However, some such distinction seems necessary. The fundamental meaning of the Fifth Amendment is that a person need not be the unwilling instrument of his own undoing and that the state must find its own evidence against him without his involuntary cooperation, and a literal reading of the amendment would prevent the police from fingerprinting a suspect or making him stand in a lineup for identification purposes. Thus the Court must find ways around the amendment.

A minority of Justices have sought a compromise by permitting as nontestimonial that evidence which does not require volition or affirmative cooperation; thus, the lineup and taking blood, photographs, and fingerprints require merely passive conduct. If, however, incriminating evidence can be secured only by the active volition of one asked to repeat certain words, model clothing, or give a handwriting sample, these minority Justices would sustain a Fifth Amendment plea. But their distinction between volitional and passive acts is as hairsplitting as the majority's between testimonial and nontestimonial compulsion. Anyone overpowered to give a sample of his blood would scarcely think he affirmatively cooperated.

The Justices in the majority also make unreal distinctions, as between the physical properties of one's voice and the testimonial content of what he says: "This is a stickup" communicates more than pitch and resonance. If the right against self-incrimination protects a defendant at his trial from having to speak up for the benefit of witnesses, why does it not protect him in the grand jury room, the interrogation room, or the lineup?

The distinction between testimonial and nontestimonial compulsion derives from the needs of law enforcement and seems to be a permanent addition to constitutional law. The Court, which can reach whatever results it desires, probably will add to the roster of nontestimonial evidence that can be compelled and will narrow the meaning of testimonial compulsion or find exceptions to it.

LEONARD W. LEVY

Bibliography

BAUER, W. J. 1977 Formalism, Legal Realism, & Constitutionally Protected Privacy under the Fourth & Fifth Amendments. *Harvard Law Review* 90:945–991.

KOONTZ, HAL and STODEL, JEFFREY 1973 The Scope of Testimonial Immunity under the Fifth: *Kastigar v. United States. Loyola* (Los Angeles) *Law Review* 6:350–383.

TESTIMONIAL IMMUNITY

See: Use Immunity

TEST OATH CASES

Cummings v. Missouri
4 Wallace 277 (1867)

Ex Parte Garland
4 Wallace 333 (1867)

Historically test oaths were weapons to inflict penalties and punishments on obnoxious minorities and were enemies of freedom of political and religious thought. A test or LOYALTY OATH should not be confused with an oath of allegiance, which is a promissory oath by which one swears to support the government and, if assuming office, to discharge its duties faithfully. An oath of allegiance concerns future conduct. A test oath is retroactive and purgative, because it is a disclaimer of specific beliefs, associations, and behavior deemed criminal or disloyal.

Missouri by its constitution prescribed a series of disavowals of belief and past conduct in the form of oaths to be taken by all voters, jurors, state officers, clergymen, lawyers, teachers, and corporation officers. All must swear as a condition of voting, holding office, teaching, and the like, that they had never been in armed hostility to the United States, had never by word or deed manifested adherence to the enemies of the country or desired their victory, had never been connected with any organization inimical to the United States, and had never been a Southern sympathizer. Anyone teaching, preaching, voting, or engaging in any of the specified activities without first taking the oaths was subject to fine and imprisonment. Cummings, a Roman Catholic priest, carried on his religious duties without taking the oath and was convicted.

The test oath prescribed by Congress was a disclaimer of having served the Confederacy and applied only to federal officials until extended in 1865 to members of the federal bar. It could be construed as a wartime qualification for office until it was extended to peacetime and to members of the federal bar. Until then it was not passed to inflict punishment for past offenses. The oath disqualified AUGUSTUS H. GARLAND, who had spent the war as a member of the Confederate Congress, from resuming his prewar practice before the Supreme Court, although he had been given a presidential pardon.

The Supreme Court, Justice STEPHEN J. FIELD writing for a bare majority, held unconstitutional both the Missouri requirement of a test oath and the federal requirement of 1865. Field reasoned that each violated the bans against EX POST FACTO laws and BILLS OF ATTAINDER. To conclude that they constituted ex post facto laws, Field had to demonstrate that they retroactively imposed punishment for acts not criminal when committed. Missouri's dragnet covered not only hostile acts against the government but "words, desires, and sympathies also," and some of the acts were not even blameworthy. The federal statute reached acts that under certain circumstances might not have been offenses, such as assisting persons in armed hostility to the United States, serving in innocuous positions in the South, or reluctantly obeying the existing order. Persons who were incapable of truthfully taking the oaths suffered disabilities that constituted punishment, such as the deprivation of civil and political rights, disqualifications from office and from the pursuit of lawful professions, and, in the case of Garland, disbarment. Justice SAMUEL F. MILLER for the dissenters replied that an ex post facto law punished only in a criminal sense by imposing fines and imprisonment, not civil disabilities.

Field described a bill of attainder as a legislative act that inflicts punishment without a judicial trial. Attainders, he insisted, could be directed against whole classes, not just named individuals, and might inflict punishments conditionally, as in these cases. Cummings the priest and Garland the lawyer were presumed guilty until they removed that presumption by their expurgatory oaths; if it was not removed, they faced the punishment of being deprived of their professions without trial and conviction. Miller could see no attainder because the required oaths designated no criminal by name or description, declared no guilt, and inflicted neither sentence nor punishment. He saw merely a qualification for office, a position that Field savaged. Miller accurately argued, however, that Field stretched the conventional meanings of ex post facto laws and bills of attainder to cover the cases before the Court. For that reason, these decisions are today considered triumphs for CIVIL LIBERTIES; in their time, however, they exposed the Court to accusations of sympathizing with the Confederate cause, opposing Reconstruction, and assisting enemies of the Union.

LEONARD W. LEVY

Bibliography

FAIRMAN, CHARLES 1939 *Mr. Justice Miller and the Supreme Court.* Pages 129–136. Cambridge, Mass.: Harvard University Press.

SWISHER, CARL BRENT (1930)1963 *Stephen J. Field: Craftsman of the Law.* Pages 138–154. Hamden, Conn.: Archon Books.

TEXAS v. BROWN
460 U.S. 730 (1983)

This case is significant for Justice WILLIAM H. REHNQUIST'S exposition of the scope and applicability of the PLAIN VIEW DOCTRINE, which had emerged in COOLIDGE V. NEW HAMPSHIRE (1971) as an exception to the warrant requirement for a SEARCH AND SEIZURE. According to Rehnquist, the answer to the question whether property in plain view may be seized depends on the lawfulness of the intrusion that allows the police to see that property. Plain view therefore provides the basis for seizure if an officer's access to the object has a prior FOURTH AMENDMENT justification. The police may seize a suspicious object if they are engaged in a lawful activity; they do not have to know at once that the object inadvertently exposed to their sight is EVIDENCE of a crime. Reasonable suspicion on PROBABLE CAUSE is sufficient even if the property seized was not immediately apparent as evidence of crime. No Justice dissented in this case, but Rehnquist spoke for a mere plurality, and a mere plurality had announced the plain view doctrine in *Coolidge.* Accordingly, judicial controversy about the doctrine will continue, as will controversy about its application to particular facts.

LEONARD W. LEVY

TEXAS v. WHITE
7 Wallace 700 (1869)

In 1867 the Court accepted ORIGINAL JURISDICTION of *Texas v. White* because one party was a state (Article III, section 2). So doing, the Court raised again, as in EX PARTE MILLIGAN (1866) and the TEST OATH cases, a possibility of judicial intervention into military reconstruction. Some decision on the state-status question was needed. Democrats insisted that the nation was not empowered to answer the state-status question and that the South's states, like bottom-weighted dolls, had sprung up, fully restored, with prevailing race hierarchies intact, in the wake of Union Army advances. Almost all Republicans assumed that the South's states, by attempting to secede, had twisted themselves out of their proper federal relations; that the Constitution (Article IV, section 4) imposed a duty on the nation to guarantee every state a REPUBLICAN FORM OF GOVERNMENT; and that the nation also possessed temporary "grasp of war" dominion over the defeated states.

Post-Appomattox Texas wished to recover possession of state bonds that secessionist Texas had sold. Counsel for bond buyers argued in 1869, when the Supreme Court heard *Texas v. White,* that Texas was always a state and the sales were valid. Special counsel for Texas, Unionist George Washington Paschal, author of a recent treatise on the Constitution, insisted that though Texas remained a state, its acts adverse to federal responsibilities invalidated the bond sales; the state should recover the bonds.

Chief Justice SALMON P. CHASE, for the majority of the Court, accepted and restated Paschal's position. The Constitution "looks to an indestructible Union composed of indestructible States." SECESSION was void. Texas's acts supportive of rebellion, performed while seceded, were unsupportable.

Justices ROBERT C. GRIER, SAMUEL F. MILLER, and NOAH SWAYNE insisted that Texas was as much out of the Union in 1869 as in 1861. Therefore the original jurisdiction clause of the Constitution did not apply.

Both the majority and the minority stressed Congress's primacy in defining a state's status. Chase, though insisting that he was not pronouncing upon military reconstruction, by implication approved its constitutional bases and reinforced Court pretensions to at least an equal share, if not more, in implementation of policy, through its review authority.

HAROLD M. HYMAN

TEXAS ANNEXATION

See: Annexation of Texas

THAYER, JAMES BRADLEY
(1831–1902)

American jurist, Harvard law professor, and author of a masterful treatise on EVIDENCE, Thayer is important in constitutional studies for his powerful advocacy of judicial self-restraint, or deference to legislation challenged as unconstitutional. He influenced Justices LOUIS D. BRANDEIS, FELIX FRANKFURTER, and OLIVER WENDELL HOLMES, and Judge LEARNED HAND.

Thayer invoked a supposedly established judicial rule which, recognizing that the Constitution admitted of different interpretations and allowed legislatures a vast range of permissible choice, required that all rational legislative choices be adjudged constitutional. Properly holding legislation unconstitutional only in cases clear beyond REASONABLE DOUBT, courts should not consider their own views on unconstitutionality, but should consider instead whether the legislature could reasonably have thought its actions constitutional. (See RATIONAL BASIS.)

Thayer regarded JUDICIAL REVIEW as a legitimate outgrowth of American experience and as a valuable conservative admixture in popular government. But he warned that this "outside" corrective threatened to curtail the people's political education. His strictures against JUDICIAL ACTIVISM were published just as the Supreme Court was embarking on a course of active defense of FREEDOM OF CONTRACT against ECONOMIC REGULATION. In a later era, when the Court's activism turned to personal liberties of another kind, Thayer's rule came under criticism: it was not an "established rule," but a policy preference; its reasonable doubt standard either would enfeeble judicial review or would be too flexible to restrain courts effectively; its applicability in Supreme Court review of state legislation was unclear; it was particularly inappropriate for legislation affecting specific BILL OF RIGHTS guarantees. Regrettably, Thayer himself had not adequately explored either the strengths and weaknesses of his rule or the broader underlying problem—how to square JUDICIAL REVIEW AND DEMOCRACY.

HOWARD E. DEAN

Bibliography

THAYER, JAMES BRADLEY 1893 The Origin and Scope of the American Doctrine of Constitutional Law. *Harvard Law Review* 7:129–156.

THEORIES OF THE UNION

Political unions are organizations of states possessing specific powers for carrying out purposes of mutual interest to constituent polities. Unions are formed by means of confederation or federation, and by definition are combinative or compound in nature rather than unitary or homogeneous. In American history the Union refers to the general structure of political authority created during the Revolution by the American people, acting through their colonial and state governments, for the pursuit of common purposes as an expression of their incipient nationality. Theories of the Union are explanations of the American state system, descriptive and normative in purpose, which have been formulated to guide political action and resolve controversies among the member states. Especially important in the period from 1789 to 1868, theories of the Union have been concerned with four principal issues: the origin and nature of statehood; the nature and extent of state powers; the origin, nature, and extent of the powers of the central government; and the manner of resolving conflicts between the states and the central authority.

Although intercolonial cooperation occurred intermittently before the Revolution, in an effective political sense the formation by the colonies in 1774 of an assembly to deal with imperial matters of common concern marked the beginning of the American Union. In 1776 this assembly, the CONTINENTAL CONGRESS, issued the DECLARATION OF INDEPENDENCE, proclaiming that the colonies "are, and of right ought to be, free and independent states." Yet the Declaration also referred to the people in the colonies as "one people," and to the colonies as "the United States of America." The practical effect was to announce the existence of a national Union comprising thirteen state governments and a central body, Congress, which, although not constituted as a government and incapable of legislating for individuals in the states, was more than merely the agent of the states. Although theory and principle to explain this new compound political organization were yet to be formulated, the fact of a division of SOVEREIGNTY characterized the American Union from the outset.

The Union thus existed as political reality before it was rationalized in a formal instrument of government, the ARTICLES OF CONFEDERATION (1781). Asserting that "[e]ach State retains its sovereignty, freedom and independence, and every Power, JURISDICTION, and right which is not by this confederation expressly delegated to the United States," the Articles conformed to the model of a league of autonomous states. However, the language of state sovereignty notwithstanding, the states were not perfect states. And Congress, although empowered only to make resolutions and recommendations rather than to make law, in matters submitted to its consideration acted as a real government. In practical effect the Union resembled the operation of the British empire, in which sovereignty had been divided between the colonial governments managing local affairs and the authority of Parliament regulating matters of general interest in the empire.

Theory of the Union was relevant to territorial problems of the 1780s, which raised the question of the origin and nature of statehood. The original colonies based their claim to statehood on their COLONIAL CHARTERS and the fact of succession to previously existing political establishments. This theory of the creation of states implied a fixed or determinate Union, and was useless to those people—either in existing states or outside them—who desired to form new states and join the Union. An alternative approach was to claim a revolutionary right of self-government; Vermont may be said to have employed this principle in its struggle to separate from New York and achieve statehood. A third method of state making was to form a political community and secure recognition from the other states. This technique was developed in the 1780s when Virginia and other states with extensive land claims, desiring to confirm their sovereignty, ceded some of their lands to Congress and secured in return approval of their claims and state boundaries. Implicit in these transactions was an expansive rather than static conception of the Union: although states might proclaim their sovereignty, the determination of statehood—the very existence of the states—depended on the sanction of the other states acting through Congress.

The CONSTITUTIONAL CONVENTION OF 1787 altered the nature and structure of the Union by creating a central government, capable of making law and regulating individuals, in place of the noncoercive authority of the Confederation. Precisely how much and in what ways the restructured Union differed from the Confederation was debated during the process of RATIFICATION OF THE CONSTITUTION. These debates gave rise to the classic theories of the Union expounded by statesmen of the early national period.

In providing for a government based on the SEPARATION OF POWERS and comprising a legislature elected in part by the people, the Framers of the Constitution applied republican principles to the problem of organizing the American Union. They did not, however, completely reject the essential principle of the Confederation, the idea that the states were the constituent power. This principle was retained in the provisions for equal state representation in the Senate and for the contingency plan for electing the President in the House of Representatives, where each state was to have had one vote. The result, as JAMES MADISON wrote in THE FEDERALIST #39, was

a government partly national and partly federal in respect of the source, operation, and extent of its powers; the constituent basis on which it was established; and the nature of the amending authority. Some of these functions embodied the idea that the American people as a single national community were the constituent power; others, the idea that the states as separate political communities were constituting the central government.

In contemporary usage the term "federal" referred to a confederation of sovereign states, and the word "national" to a unitary government operating directly on individuals. Accordingly, the Articles of Confederation were described as a federal government. But the supporters of the new government, combining elements of both a confederation and a unitary national government, called *it* a federal government. In doing so they gave a new definition to FEDERALISM as the division of sovereignty among a central government and separate state governments operating on the same population in the same area.

In the ratification controversy Federalists and Anti-Federalists combined arguments from history, the constitutional text, and political theory to fashion competing theories of the Union in pursuit of their divergent political goals. Denying that sovereignty could be divided, Anti-Federalists warned that the proposed central government would transform the Union into a consolidated state. The Federalists, in order to allay STATES' RIGHTS apprehensions, stressed the division of authority between the states and the central government and the ultimate sovereignty of the people. Although the Federalists glossed over conflicts that were bound to arise in a governmental system based on a division of sovereign authority, their constitutional theory confirmed the main tendencies in the operation of the American Union from its inception.

Perhaps the single most important formulation of Unionist theory was contained in the VIRGINIA AND KENTUCKY RESOLUTIONS of 1798–1799, written by JAMES MADISON and THOMAS JEFFERSON. Seeking a constitutionally legitimate way to prevent the enforcement of the ALIEN AND SEDITION ACTS, the Republican party leaders advanced the compact theory of the Union. On this theory were based all subsequent assertions of states' rights and state sovereignty, including those supporting SECESSION in 1861.

Jefferson and Madison argued that the Union was a compact made by the states, which as the constituent parties retained the right to judge whether the central government had violated the compact. Exercising this right by the accepted practices for implementing compacts, the states, according to Madison, could "interpose" their authority to stop unconstitutional acts of the central government. In the Kentucky Resolutions of 1799 Jefferson declared that a NULLIFICATION by the sovereign states of all unauthorized acts of the federal government was "the rightful remedy." The theory thus propounded held that the states created the Union; the federal government could exercise only delegated powers, not including regulation of speech and press, which were reserved to the states; and the states had authority to question the exercise of central authority and by implication to settle constitutional disputes over federal–state relations.

Whether Madison and Jefferson contemplated peaceful concerted action by the states, or single-state defiance of federal authority (possibly by force, as was later proposed in South Carolina), their action served as precedent and model for one of the basic strategies of constitutional politics throughout the antebellum period. From the standpoint of constitutional law the most significant feature of the compact theory was the proposition that the states had created the Constitution and the Union. The argument could mean any number of things depending on how a state was defined. A state could be considered to be the territory occupied by a political community, the governing institutions and officers of the community, or the people forming the community. In his report to the Virginia legislature in 1800, Madison used the third of these definitions to explain how the states, through the ratification process, had made the Constitution. On this theory, the TENTH AMENDMENT expressed the equivalence of state and people, reserving powers not delegated to the federal government "to the States respectively or to the people." A fixed feature of later states' rights and state sovereignty teaching, this popular conception of statehood enabled compact theorists to define the nation as self-governing political communities founded on common republican principles.

An alternative theory of the Union was propounded by the Federalist party. Federalists held that the Constitution and the Union had been made by the people of the United States, who as the constituent power had divided sovereignty between the states and the central government. The government of the United States possessed limited powers, but within its sphere of action it was supreme. Federalists, and their Whig political descendants in the 1830s, further reasoned that according to the original constitutional design conflicts in federal–state relations were to be resolved by the federal judiciary. In his debate with Robert Y. Hayne of South Carolina in 1830 on the nature of the Union, DANIEL WEBSTER said the judicial article and the SUPREMACY CLAUSE were the "key-stone of the arch" of Union. "With these," he declared, "it is a constitution; without them, it is a confederacy."

Distrusting localism, Federalists identified the nation with the central government, and theirs is often referred to as the nationalist theory of the Union. This reference is misleading, however, insofar as it implies that the compact theory was not a valid expression of American nationality. Properly regarded, the Federalist-Whig doctrine is the central supremacy theory of the Union. Acknowledging divided sovereignty and the limited nature of federal authority, Federalists and Whigs recognized states' rights as essential to the Union. But, believing the nation could act only through the central government, they insisted on the supremacy of federal power when it conflicted with an otherwise legitimate state power. The supremacy clause of the Constitution was the positive expression of the principle of federal paramountcy that its proponents believed was intended to guide national development.

In refuting the compact theory, central supremacy theorists made the popular origins of the Union their most distinctive tenet. They insisted that the Constitution was not a compact made by the states but an instrument of government made by "the people of the United States." The meaning of this term is not self-evident. It might be taken to mean that the American people constituted and could act as a single political community. Webster seemed to have this conception in mind when in the debate with Hayne he argued that the Constitution "pronounces that it is established by the people of the United States in the aggregate," not by the states or even by the people of the several states. JOHN MARSHALL stated the popular-origins thesis more carefully in McCULLOCH V. MARYLAND (1819). Marshall observed that the Constitution was "submitted to the people" for ratification, and they acted on it "by assembling in Convention." In a sense Marshall conceded the compact theorists' main point—that the Constitution had been ratified by the people acting as separate political communities. "It is true," he wrote, "they assembled in their several States." But he discounted the significance of this fact, adding: "and where else should they have assembled? No political dreamer was ever wild enough to think of breaking down the lines which separate the States, and of compounding the American people into one common mass. Of consequence, when they act they act in their States." Thus the same facts on which the compact theorists based their conclusion that the Union was made by the states supported the central supremacy contention that the Union was made by the people of the United States.

From 1830 to 1860 theories of the Union continued to have political significance as Americans expanded territorially and struggled with the slavery question. Two variations of the compact theory were developed to protect slavery within the state system: DUAL FEDERALISM and the nullification theory of JOHN C. CALHOUN of South Carolina. Within the central supremacy theory, meanwhile, the idea of the Union as perpetual and indissoluble was elaborated.

Although formally accepting divided sovereignty, dual federalists in a practical sense sought to remove actual or potential central government restraints on state power, including the power to protect slavery. Insisting that the reserved powers of the states constituted a limitation on the federal government, they regarded the Tenth Amendment as a kind of supremacy clause for the states. Accordingly, in cases such as NEW YORK V. MILN (1837) the Supreme Court under Chief Justice ROGER B. TANEY, reversing the effect of Marshall's central supremacy unionism, held that state powers over matters of "police" had not been surrendered to federal authority.

Calhoun's doctrine of nullification, employed in South Carolina's fight against the tariff in 1832, was a more radical extension of the compact theory of the Union. Calhoun held that federal powers were granted in trust by the states, which he defined as the people exercising indivisible sovereignty in separate political communities. He thus rejected the principle of divided sovereignty. Picking up where Madison and Jefferson had left off, Calhoun sought to devise a constitutional means of obstructing unconstitutional acts of the central government. His ingenious, if ultimately perverse, solution was to transform the creative constituent power of the states, identified in the Article V amending power, into an instrument of negation. Calhoun reasoned that a state, acting in popular convention, might interpose its authority to nullify a federal measure. The states would then be consulted, and if three-fourths of them did not approve the objectionable measure it would be withdrawn. If, however, the states upheld the central government, the nullifying state could secede from the Union.

Placed on the defensive by the nullificationists, central supremacy advocates were moved to insist on the perpetuity of the Union. This idea was implicit in the very creation of the Constitution. The fact that the Articles of Confederation referred to the Union as "perpetual" did not prevent men from believing that a state might withdraw its membership; by the same token the omission from the Constitution of the language of perpetuity did not mean that the Framers considered the Union to be anything less than a permanent government. It is nevertheless significant that while the terms disunion and secession were employed in the early nineteenth century, not until the nullification crisis did central supremacy theorists like Webster and JOHN QUINCY ADAMS explicate the perpetuity idea. Their argument may be described as declaratory in nature. But it was not only Whig keepers of the central supremacy tradition but also Democrats who met the South Carolina challenge by asserting perpetual Unionism. In his Proclamation to South Carolina (1832) President ANDREW JACKSON condemned secession as unconstitutional and affirmed the Constitution as a binding obligation on the states.

Changing little as constitutional doctrine, the central supremacy theory of the Union formed part of a nationalist ideology that emerged in the North in the pre-Civil War period. In contrast to the universalistic, democratic, and decentralized nationalism associated with the compact school, northern nationalism, based on New England Federalist sources and developed by Whig and Republican politicians, was historical, ethnic, cultural, and religious in nature. Whereas President GEORGE WASHINGTON in his Farewell Address had said it was the "unity of government which constitutes you one people," central supremacy theorists such as FRANCIS LIEBER turned the equation around by regarding the American people as forming a sovereign national community, from which emanated the Constitution and the Union. In this sectionally sponsored nationalism, the Union, without ceasing to be a means of securing liberty, became as well an end in itself: an organically rooted thing of absolute and intrinsic value.

Theories of the Union had a configurative as well as causative effect on the Civil War and Reconstruction. The existence of the compact theory—and the reiteration of this theory from 1798 to 1860 as the basis for states' rights, nullification, and disunionist demands—provided an arguably constitutional course of action for Southerners to follow in seceding from the Union in response to the antislavery threat. In the North the tradition of central supremacy constitutionalism was available to rationalize and sustain the Republican party's decision to resist secession. Pronouncing secession "the essence of anarchy," President ABRAHAM LINCOLN in 1861 affirmed the perpetuity of the Union, declared its primacy over the states, and asserted that "the States have their *status* in the Union, and they have no other *legal status*." The war would be fought, Congress resolved in 1861, "to defend and maintain the supremacy of the Constitution and to preserve the Union, with all the dignity, equality, and rights of the several States unimpaired."

Applying central supremacy tenets, the United States government between 1861 and 1868 regarded the Union as unbroken in a constitutional sense. It denied any legal effect to secession, treated the rebellious states as disorganized communities, and adopted measures to form loyal state governments capable of resuming their place in the Union. Acknowledging at most that the seceded states were out of their proper practical relation with the Union, federal authorities were forced to consider the fundamental question in Unionist theory: the origin, nature, and meaning of statehood.

Was a state to be defined as territory, population, governmental institutions and officers, or political community? Federal reconstruction policy held that a state was a body of people constituting a political community whose existence was dependent on and qualified by the Union. Implicit in the history of the state system, this relationship was explicitly rationalized in Article IV, section 4, of the Constitution, which states: "The United States shall guarantee to every State in this Union a Republican Form of Government." In choosing the guarantee clause as a reconstruction basis, Congress rejected the idea that a state was mere territory, or population, or governmental institutions and officers whose acts of disloyalty could destroy the state and cause it to revert to a territorial condition, subject to the plenary power of Congress. The progression to statehood out of the territorial condition, if not a constitutional right enjoyed by the people as a political community, was at least irreversible.

Although compact theorists had long feared the transformation of the Union into a consolidated government, when political conditions in the 1860s were most favorable for this development, reconstruction policymakers evinced a concern for states' rights and divided sovereignty as essential to Unionism. The Supreme Court expressed this outlook in TEXAS V. WHITE (1869), confirming the congressional view of statehood as an irreversible condition. The Court declared that a "State, in the ordinary sense of the Constitution, is a political community of free citizens, occupying a territory of defined boundaries." Without the states in the Union, the Court reasoned, there could be no such political body as the United States. The conclusion therefore followed that "the preservation of the States, and the maintenance of their governments, are as much within the design and care of the Constitution as the preservation of the Union

and the maintenance of the National government. The Constitution, in all its provisions, looks to an indestructible Union, composed of indestructible States."

The triumph of the central government in the Civil War signified the rejection of the compact theory of the Union as a framework for national development. Although aspects of the theory continued to be used in political and constitutional debate, it was repudiated in relation to the practical question that made it a vital element in antebellum politics: the mounting of single or concerted state resistance to central authority, including the possibility of secession. After the war secession was no longer a constitutionally conceivable or politically practical course of action. The central supremacy theory prevailed as the framework for constitutional development.

Although it is doubtful whether the American people, to use John Marshall's formulation, could in a constitutional sense be described as having been compounded into a single common mass as a result of the war, nevertheless in a political and ideological sense the idea of the people as a single national community, rather than as similar yet separate political communities, gained wider acceptance. Moreover, within the central supremacy theory the adoption of the THIRTEENTH, FOURTEENTH, and FIFTEENTH AMENDMENTS greatly altered federal–state relations. The nature and extent of federal and state powers of course continued to be a major issue in constitutional law and politics. But the nature of statehood, the nature of the Union, and the propriety of federal resolution of conflicts in the operation of the state system were now settled issues. Theories of the Union, associated with fundamentally different conceptions of nationalism, ceased to be relevant to basic political choices as Americans entered the period of industrialization.

HERMAN BELZ

Bibliography

ARIELI, YEHOSHUA 1966 Individualism and Nationalism in American Ideology. Baltimore: Penguin Books.

BENNETT, WALTER HARTWELL 1964 American Theories of Federalism. University: University of Alabama Press.

CARPENTER, JESSE T. 1930 The South as a Conscious Minority 1789–1861: A Study in Political Thought. New York: New York University Press.

DAVIS, S. RUFUS 1978 The Federal Principle: A Journey through Time in Quest of Meaning. Berkeley: University of California Press.

DIAMOND, MARTIN 1974 What the Framers Meant by Federalism. In R. A. Goldwin, ed., A Nation of States: Essays on the American Federal System. Chicago: Rand McNally.

ONUF, PETER S. *The Origins of the Federal Republic: Jurisdictional Controversies in the United States, 1775–1787.* Philadelphia: University of Pennsylvania Press.

STAMPP, KENNETH M. 1978 The Concept of a Perpetual Union. *Journal of American History* 65:5–33.

THIRD AMENDMENT

Quartering of troops in private houses, except in cases of military necessity, has long been regarded as contrary to British political traditions. Illegal quartering figured in important controversies between the king and the people, and it was condemned in the PETITION OF RIGHT (1628) and the English BILL OF RIGHTS (1689).

The British government sent regular troops to America in 1765 to discourage resistance to parliamentary taxation. Parliament, in the Quartering Act, required that the soldiers be housed at the expense of the province to which they were sent, and provided that, if existing barracks were insufficient, private buildings would be commandeered for the purpose. This measure was one of the specific grievances cited in the DECLARATION OF INDEPENDENCE.

During the debates over RATIFICATION OF THE CONSTITUTION several state conventions suggested a prohibition against quartering of troops. It was among JAMES MADISON's original proposals for the BILL OF RIGHTS, and the First Congress approved it unanimously and virtually without change. The amendment affirms the sanctity of private property in our constitutional system: the refusal of an individual property owner is an absolute bar to quartering in peacetime. The amendment represents a principle so fundamental that no act of Congress has ever been seriously challenged under it.

DENNIS J. MAHONEY

THIRD-PARTY BUGGING

See: Electronic Eavesdropping

THIRTEENTH AMENDMENT
(Framing)

Scholars and jurists have virtually ignored the Thirteenth Amendment, the Constitution's first formal addition in sixty-one years. Reasons for this indifference seem, initially, to be both obvious and adequate. The Thirteenth Amendment, ratified in December 1865, appears to be a simple, brief statement of the noble, limited effect of the Civil War.

Its succinct text, written by Illinois Senator LYMAN TRUMBULL, echoed clauses of the NORTHWEST ORDINANCE. In the Civil War's last weeks, during the closing session of the 38th Congress, Senator CHARLES SUMNER tried to substitute for the proposed Amendment's second section one specifying that every person was equal before both national and state laws. Trumbull, a constitutional specialist, favored section 2 in its present form. Sumner and many other congressmen assumed that all parts of the Constitution, including amendments, implicitly authorized enforcement; Trumbull wished to have the amendment empower enforcement explicitly. There was almost no other discussion on the amendment. In a sense, abolition had been before the congressmen and the nation since 1861.

Persons who celebrated abolition's arrival in 1865 did not foresee that race problems and derivative strains in federal relations were to require a FOURTEENTH and a FIFTEENTH AMENDMENT plus enforcement legislation, and would lead to the first IMPEACHMENT of a President. Celebrants of 1865 stressed the "war-gulf" that separated the ratified Thirteenth Amendment from one in early 1861 that Congress had proposed and three states had ratified in a desperate effort to seduce the South from seceding. The aborted Thirteenth Amendment would have forbidden the nation perpetually from curtailing slavery in states where it existed. Thereafter the nation steadily raised both its sense of self-interest and its moral sights. Union troops in the South reported that the only trustworthy residents were black. Though few Negroes lived outside the South, most Northern states had long been racist in laws and customs, if never so fiercely as in the slave states. During the war Northern racism softened, partially as a result of pro-Negro reports from Union soldiers and partly from the diffusion of ABOLITIONIST CONSTITUTIONAL THEORY. Before the war, abolitionists, long hard-pressed even in the North, had come to scorn the Constitution, for it did not protect them against unpunished harassments. But once the war started, Union and abolition became identified. Gradually, Congress and ABRAHAM LINCOLN caught up to Union soldiers' needs, constituents' altering race sentiments, and abolitionists' aspirations and perceptions.

In 1861 and 1862, CONFISCATION ACTS threatened disloyal individuals with the loss of their title to property, including slaves, after individual prosecutions in federal courts. In September 1862, Lincoln's EMAN-

CIPATION PROCLAMATION, an executive, war-power order, offered slaveowners ninety days in which to give up the rebellion or lose their slaves. That grace period having expired, Lincoln in January 1863 ordered also the recruitment of Negroes, most of whom lived in the South, into the Union's armies. In December 1863 and July 1864 respectively, Reconstruction policies issued by the President and the Congress provided for emancipation as a prerequisite for state restorations. The fall 1864 election proved the growth of a Northern consensus in favor of irreversible emancipation as a war result, though, save for abolitionists, it had not been an original war aim. Therefore the 38th Congress, with Lincoln's warm support, prepared the present Thirteenth Amendment, and when the war ended it sent it to the states for ratification.

Despite its simplicity, the Thirteenth Amendment was a momentous, perhaps revolutionary change in constitutional relationships. It prohibited not only the national or state governments or officials but every American institution and person from allowing slavery or involuntary servitude to exist, and it specifically authorized Congress to enforce the prohibition. If states, the traditional parents of slavery, did not comply with the prohibition and allowed individuals to hold other people in a slave status, the nation now had authority to punish directly either the oppressing persons or the states.

Democrats strongly opposed ratification. Even before the Civil War, most Democrats rejected a view of the Constitution as an adaptable, organic instrument. The amendment's enforcement clause allowed Congress to initiate changes in race relationships beyond abolition. Some Democrats insisted that abolition was illicit even by means of an amendment; that slave property remained totally a state's right to define; and that the unrepresented Southern states could not properly be asked to ratify the amendment.

Republicans argued for the amendment's ratification, in part because Lincoln's Emancipation Proclamation might have left slavery alive in the unseceded border states and in some Confederate areas earlier reconquered. It was clear also that individual confiscation trials could never reach the millions of slaveholders and slaves. Republicans also worried because the amendment voided the Constitution's THREE-FIFTHS CLAUSE. The South's Negroes were now to count as whole persons in determining the size of a state's congressional representation. Ironically, the South, after initiating and carrying on a civil war for four years, would substantially increase its strength in the House of Representatives. "Radical" Republicans looked at the Thirteenth Amendment as the culmination of abolitionist constitutional theory. Radicals asserted that the amendment, freeing slaves, also equalized all Americans in the protections due to them in their states for the exercise of both public and private rights. The DECLARATION OF INDEPENDENCE and the BILL OF RIGHTS defined the duties all states owed to every resident; the nation's duty was to see to state performance. State justice, down to the remotest hamlet, must protect every resident equally against hurtful positive acts or discriminatory nonacts by public officers and private persons, in both civil and criminal relationships.

No Republicans advocated centralization; all Republicans were STATES' RIGHTS nationalists. State sovereignty was dead but state rights flourished. State wrongs that diminished individuals' rights as defined by state laws, were, however, unacceptable; they again threatened the nation's stability. Republicans assumed that the ex-rebel states would emulate, in their formal law at least, the lessened racism of the rest of the nation, and afford Negroes the same protections that whites enjoyed. But it became apparent from evidence such as the BLACK CODES that the South would not behave as expected.

All through 1865, Democrats criticized the fact that President ANDREW JOHNSON required the reconstructing states to ratify the Thirteenth Amendment, and they insisted that those states were entitled to be represented in Congress. The Johnson provisional states, excepting Florida and Texas where reconstruction proceeded slowly, did ratify the Thirteenth Amendment, though reluctantly, with spokesmen expressing special distaste for the enforcement clause. Johnson pressured recalcitrant states with threats of indefinite military rule if ratification failed; Secretary of State WILLIAM SEWARD calmed Southerners by asserting that the amendment restricted Congress to enforcing only a prohibition of formal slavery, a dubious interpretation. On December 15, 1865, Seward proclaimed the amendment to be in effect. Were the southern states truly states for the purposes of ratification? The question asked in 1865 and again in 1868 and 1870 when the Fourteenth and Fifteenth Amendments were ratified, and repeated endlessly since, has a metaphysical quality. Ratification was a mandate to the nation by a clear majority of the American people, not an act of the national government. Lincoln's insight that the South's states were still states, although out of their proper relationship to the Union of states, neither supported immediate restorations of those states nor diminished their capacities to perform certain state functions including ratification of amendments. In 1865 the southern states ratified in number beyond the Constitution's requirement (Article V) that three-fourths of the states approve an amendment. Additional states ratified subsequently to end all doubts as to the amendment's validity. But in 1865, those doubts existed and enhanced the doubts that Democrats spread, and Republicans also felt, about President Johnson's unlimited authority over the South.

The 39th Congress assembled in December 1865 for its first postwar session. Its Republican members, upon examination of the Black Codes and other evidence from the South of lingering vestiges of servitude, resorted immediately to the just-ratified Thirteenth Amendment's enforcement clause. Sharing a mobile, organic view of the Constitution, Republicans were ready to confirm that the nation had an interest in and a duty to personal equality in states, as defined by state law and customs; their readiness is evident in the quick formulation of the CIVIL RIGHTS BILL (the world's first), the second FREEDMAN'S BUREAU BILL, and the Fourteenth Amendment. Republicans created these measures in light of the Thirteenth Amendment, a far more complex and inclusive statement than most accounts suggest.

HAROLD M. HYMAN

Bibliography

BUCHANAN, SIDNEY G. 1976 *The Quest for Freedom: A Legal History of the Thirteenth Amendment.* Houston: Reprint from *Houston Law Review.*

HOWE, MARK A. DEWOLFE 1965 Federalism and Civil Rights. [Massachusetts Historical Society] *Proceedings* 77:15–67.

HYMAN, HAROLD M. and WIECEK, WILLIAM M. 1982 *Equal Justice under Law: Constitutional Development 1835–1875.* Chaps. 10–11. New York. Harper & Row.

TEN BROEK, JACOBUS 1951 *The Antislavery Origins of the Fourteenth Amendment.* Chap. 13. Berkeley: University of California Press.

THIRTEENTH AMENDMENT
(Judicial Interpretation)

Ratification of the Thirteenth Amendment in 1865 not only diminished the urgency of the debate over the constitutionality of the EMANCIPATION PROCLAMATION but also wrote a new substantive value into the Constitution. The amendment's first section abolished slavery and involuntary servitude throughout the nation, and its second section empowered Congress to enforce abolition. If any of the amendment's framers expected it to end the system of racial domi-

nance and dependence, they were soon divested of that illusion. The persistence of a plantation economy and the adoption in southern states of the BLACK CODES kept blacks in a position of subordination that was not only economic but political and social as well.

The question thus arose whether section 2 of the Thirteenth Amendment gave Congress the power to do more than provide sanctions against slavery or involuntary servitude, narrowly defined. Over a presidential veto, Congress adopted the CIVIL RIGHTS ACT OF 1866, which not only declared the CITIZENSHIP of the freed slaves but also protected them against the sort of RACIAL DISCRIMINATION that had been embodied in the Black Codes, such as disqualification to own property, to make contracts, or to serve on juries. President ANDREW JOHNSON had explained his veto of the bill partly on the ground that the Thirteenth Amendment had not empowered Congress to adopt legislation aimed at such purposes. Reacting to this argument, Congress proposed the FOURTEENTH AMENDMENT as a means of assuring the validity of the 1866 Act and placing beyond doubt the power of Congress to enforce the CIVIL RIGHTS of the freed slaves.

From the beginning it was arguable that the abolition of slavery implied that the persons so freed would take on the status of free citizens—that the amendment should be read broadly as a response to the whole social system of racial subordination associated with slavery. But in the early years, this view did not prosper in the Supreme Court; it was found mainly in OBITER DICTA and in dissenting opinions. All agreed that section 1 of the amendment was self-executing: slavery and involuntary servitude were abolished, whether or not Congress enacted civil or criminal sanctions to enforce the abolition. Because the amendment contained no STATE ACTION limitation, it operated directly, of its own force, against either public or private conduct that imposed slavery. But the Court limited the notion of "involuntary servitude" to personal servitude, refusing to extend it (by analogy to feudal servitudes) to cover the granting of monopolies or other similar privileges. (See SLAUGHTERHOUSE CASES, 1873). By the end of the nineteenth century, the Court was saying that slavery implied no more than "a state of bondage," and the lack of "a legal right to the disposal of [one's] own person, property, and services"; thus the Thirteenth Amendent standing alone did not even forbid a state to impose racial segregation on seating in railroad cars. (See PLESSY V. FERGUSON, 1896.)

This narrow view of the Thirteenth Amendment's self-executing reach was reflected in the Supreme

Court's treatment of the power granted to Congress by section 2. In the CIVIL RIGHTS CASES (1883) the Court, in the face of a powerful dissenting opinion by Justice JOHN MARSHALL HARLAN, held invalid the CIVIL RIGHTS ACT OF 1875, a congressional statute forbidding racial discrimination in such PUBLIC ACCOMMODATIONS as hotels, theaters, and railroads. Both the majority and the dissent agreed that the Thirteenth Amendment was designed to put an end to the "incidents" of slavery as well as slavery itself. The question was whether racially based refusals of access to public accommodations amounted to "badges of slavery and servitude," and the majority held that they did not. This severely restrictive interpretation of the power of Congress to enforce the Thirteenth Amendment culminated in 1906, when the Court decided HODGES V. UNITED STATES. Congress could prohibit no more than the "entire subjection" of one person to another, as in laws forbidding PEONAGE; Congress was not empowered by section 2 to go further in erasing "badges" or "incidents" of slavery.

So matters stood for six decades. The Thirteenth Amendment, like the Fourteenth Amendment's guarantee of the EQUAL PROTECTION OF THE LAWS, lay dormant, offering no effective protection against racial discrimination. The judicial interpretation of the Thirteenth Amendment mirrored the nation's political history; Congress adopted no civil rights legislation from the time of Reconstruction to the late 1950s. The first modern civil rights law of major importance was the CIVIL RIGHTS ACT OF 1964; its public accommodations provisions were upheld by the Supreme Court, but on the basis of the COMMERCE CLAUSE, not the Thirteenth or Fourteenth Amendments. (See HEART OF ATLANTA MOTEL V. UNITED STATES, 1964; *Katzenbach v. McClung,* 1964.) The Court seemed determined to uphold congressional legislation aimed at establishing racial equality, and in UNITED STATES V. GUEST (1966) six Justices agreed in two separate opinions that Congress could reach even private conduct that interfered with the exercise of Fourteenth Amendment rights. The state action limitation, in other words, would not bar congressional enforcement of the equal protection clause of the Fourteenth Amendment's prohibition on private discrimination.

The reach of the equal protection clause, of course, is not limited to racial inequalities. Perhaps some of the Justices were reluctant to pursue the line of doctrinal development suggested by the separate opinions in *Guest,* for fear of giving Congress an invitation without apparent limitation. The solution to this puzzle—if it was a puzzle—came only two years after the *Guest* decision, in the form of a complete turnabout in the interpretation of the power of Congress to enforce the Thirteenth Amendment.

The turnabout came in JONES V. ALFRED H. MAYER CO. (1968), when the Court interpreted the 1866 Civil Rights Act to prohibit all racial discrimination in the sale of property and upheld the act as so construed. The Court overruled the *Hodges* decision and essentially adopted the dissenting views of Justice Harlan in the *Civil Rights Cases.* The Thirteenth Amendment was held to empower Congress not only to eliminate slavery but also to eliminate slavery's "badges and incidents." Furthermore, said the Court, it is for Congress itself "rationally to determine what are the badges and incidents of slavery," and to enact laws to eradicate any such "relic of slavery" it might find.

This broad language is not limited to racial discrimination. Commentators have asked whether the Court, in seeking to avoid an open-ended interpretation of congressional power under the Fourteenth Amendment, has offered Congress a different set of constitutional bootstraps. In the quoted passage from the *Jones* opinion, the Court appears to authorize Congress to define a given right—any right—as one that is essential to freedom, to define its impairment as an incident of slavery, and to enact a law protecting the right against both public and private interference.

When the right in question is a right to be free from racial discrimination, this line of reasoning accords not only with the language of the *Jones* opinion but also with the decision's place in the historical process of constitutional validation of modern civil rights legislation. Outside the racial context, however, the reasoning is unlikely to be adopted by the Supreme Court. Of course the Thirteenth Amendment prohibits the enslavement of anyone, of any race. And the Court has upheld an application of the 1866 act to a case of racial discrimination against whites, evidently (but without discussion) on the basis of Congress's power to enforce the Thirteenth Amendment, in *McDonald v. Santa Fe Trail Transportation Co.* (1976). The decision is defensible, despite the lack of historic links between slavery and discrimination against whites. There is a basis in experience for a congressional conclusion that discrimination against one racial group affects attitudes toward race generally and promotes discrimination against other races. It would be much harder to justify a similar conclusion about the effects of discrimination on the basis of gender, or sexual preference, or physical handicap. Even if the analogy were stronger, the doctrinal context of the *Jones* decision cautions against a prediction that its "badges and incidents" reasoning will be extended beyond cases of racial discrimination. The Thirteenth Amendment seems to have had its main appeal as a basis for congressional power precisely because that power could be contained within the confines of remedies for racial discrimination. The "badges and incidents of slavery" which justify congressional intervention are to be found in racial discrimination if they are to be found at all.

The power of Congress to enforce the Thirteenth Amendment, like any other congressional power, is subject to the limitations of the BILL OF RIGHTS. Without question, the amendment empowers Congress to prohibit racial discrimination in all the public areas of life, including commercial dealings. In RUNYON v. McCRARY (1976), for example, the Supreme Court relied on the Thirteenth Amendment to uphold application of the 1866 act to a private school that accepted applicants from children in the public at large but excluded blacks. The potential limitations of the Bill of Rights found expression in that case. Justice LEWIS F. POWELL, concurring, cautioned that some hypothetical congressional enforcements of the Thirteenth Amendment might violate constitutional rights of PRIVACY or associational freedom, as when a litigant might seek application of the 1866 act to a case of racial discrimination in the selection of a home tutor or babysitter.

The expansion of the power of Congress to enforce the Thirteenth Amendment has not been accompanied by a corresponding expansion of the amendment's reach as a self-executing provision. The *Jones* opinion left open the question whether the amendment "by its own terms did anything more than abolish slavery," and although MEMPHIS v. GREENE (1981) raised the issue, the Court did not reach it. Thus, even though a great many forms of private racial discrimination may constitute "badges and incidents of slavery" justifying congressional action to secure their elimination, if Congress has not acted, these same "badges and incidents" are insufficient to trigger the operation of the amendment's section 1. The practical significance of this difference, however, is slight. The Supreme Court has construed existing civil rights legislation broadly enough to prohibit a wide range of private acts of racial discrimination.

Even assuming that the Thirteenth Amendment's self-executing force is limited to cases of bondage to personal service, there is room for debate about the kinds of compulsion that constitute involuntary servitude. Debt bondage—the requirement that a person work in discharge of a debt—is a classic case of peonage and is plainly forbidden by the amendment.

However, compulsory military service (or alternative service for CONSCIENTIOUS OBJECTORS), hard labor for persons imprisoned for crime, and restrictions on the right to strike all have been sustained against Thirteenth Amendment attacks.

KENNETH L. KARST

Bibliography
CASPER, GERHARD 1968 Jones v. Mayer: Clio, Bemused and Confused Muse. *Supreme Court Review* 1968:89–132.
FAIRMAN, CHARLES 1971 *Reconstruction and Reunion: 1864–1888, Part One.* Chapter XIX. New York: Macmillan Company.
NOTE 1969 The "New" Thirteenth Amendment: A Preliminary Analysis. *Harvard Law Review* 82:1294–1321.

THOMAS v. REVIEW BOARD
450 U.S. 707 (1981)

Reaffirming its decision in SHERBERT V. VERNER (1963), the Supreme Court, 8–1, invalidated Indiana's refusal of unemployment compensation to a Jehovah's Witness who, for religious reasons, had quit his job rather than work on weapons production. The state had not shown that denying benefits was the LEAST RESTRICTIVE MEANS of achieving a COMPELLING STATE INTEREST.

KENNETH L. KARST

THOMAS v. UNION CARBIDE AGRICULTURAL PRODUCTS CO.
473 U.S.   (1985)

The Supreme Court's decision in NORTHERN PIPELINE CONSTRUCTION CO. V. MARATHON PIPE LINE CO. (1982) left considerable confusion about the power of Congress to confer JURISDICTION on administrators or LEGISLATIVE COURTS over cases falling within the JUDICIAL POWER OF THE UNITED STATES. *Thomas* provided some useful clarification.

The Federal Insecticide, Fungicide, and Rodenticide Act (FIFRA) requires a manufacturer, as a condition on registering a pesticide, to supply research data on the pesticide's health, safety, and environmental effects to the Environmental Protection Agency (EPA). These data may be used in evaluating a second manufacturer's registration of a similar product, provided that the second manufacturer offers to compensate the first. If the two manufacturers cannot agree on the compensation, FIFRA requires binding arbitration of the dispute. An arbitrator's decision is reviewable by a court only for "fraud, misrepresentation or other misconduct."

Various pesticide manufacturers sued the EPA administrator challenging the constitutionality of the scheme of binding arbitration with limited court review. The federal district court held that the scheme violated Article III of the Constitution; on direct APPEAL, the Supreme Court unanimously reversed, upholding the law.

Justice SANDRA DAY O'CONNOR, writing for the Court, recognized a broad policy in Article III "that federal judicial power shall be vested in courts whose judges enjoy life tenure and fixed compensation." *Marathon* effectuated a part of that policy but was distinguishable here. Considering the origin of the claims to compensation in federal law, along with the reasons of public policy that persuaded Congress to impose binding arbitration, the manufacturers' claimed rights were properly considered "public rights," the adjudication of which Congress could place in administrative hands. Cases involving "public rights" were not limited to those in which the government itself was a party. Nor, said the Court in an important OBITER DICTUM, is Article III's requirement of independent judges irrelevant merely because the government is a party. Here the assignment of decision to nonjudicial arbitrators was softened somewhat by FIFRA's provision of some minimal review by CONSTITUTIONAL COURTS of arbitrators' decisions. (In some cases, the Court noted, DUE PROCESS considerations might independently require further court review.)

Thomas thus adopted a flexible approach to Article III's limitations on Congress's employment of nonjudicial tribunals—the very approach urged by the *Marathon* dissenters. Justice WILLIAM J. BRENNAN, for three Justices, concurred separately on the basis of his PLURALITY OPINION in *Marathon*. Justice JOHN PAUL STEVENS concurred, saying the manufacturers lacked STANDING to challenge the law's validity.

KENNETH L. KARST

THOMPSON, SMITH
(1763–1843)

Smith Thompson was among the most experienced judges ever appointed to the Supreme Court, and his tenure on the bench (1823–1843) linked the constitutional doctrines of the MARSHALL COURT and the TANEY COURT. After sixteen years on the New York Su-

preme Court (1802–1818), four years as chief justice, Thompson had been secretary of the navy (1818–1823). His experience in JAMES MONROE's cabinet made Monroe feel so comfortable with Thompson, presumably including his constitutional views, that the President insisted that the New Yorker fill the seat vacated by the death of a fellow New Yorker, H. BROCKHOLST LIVINGSTON.

Thompson did not change his jurisprudence significantly during his twenty years on the Court. He remained a black-letter lawyer, whose most interesting contributions to constitutional jurisprudence can be traced to his New York judicial and cabinet experiences. Besides adhering to precedent, Thompson concerned himself with maintaining judicial independence while showing a willingness to let the legislature have free rein. Having served in an era when Congress was relatively inactive, Thompson appears today as a STATES' RIGHTS advocate, or more precisely an adherent to states' responsibilities. Yet his values did not differ greatly from those of his nationalistic brethren on the Marshall Court. He was, for example, aware of the business community's needs. Unlike Livingston, his predecessor on the Marshall Court, Thompson was more willing to express his differences with the rest of the Court.

He was absent when GIBBONS V. OGDEN (1824) was argued, but in *Livingston v. Van Ingen* (1812), decided by the New York court, he had resolved some of the questions involved in *Gibbons* in favor of the steamboat monopoly. Although Thompson's *Van Ingen* opinion did not consider the commerce clause question, that of his colleague, JAMES KENT, did and commerce clause cases subsequent to *Gibbons* show that Thompson subscribed to Kent's doctrine of concurrent powers to regulate commerce. JOHN MARSHALL's language in *Gibbons* was, moreover, sufficiently broad to allow Thompson to render lip service to *Gibbons* while taking a contrary position. In BROWN V. MARYLAND (1827), Thompson dissented from Marshall's majority opinion holding that Maryland's law imposing license taxes on wholesalers of imported goods violated both the import and export and the COMMERCE CLAUSE. Like Kent, Thompson did not examine the nature of the power underlying state regulations. Whether the state regulated commerce or not was immaterial so long as the statute did not conflict with a congressional act. In rejecting Marshall's ORIGINAL PACKAGE DOCTRINE in *Brown*, Thompson set forth the position that goods became subject to a state's jurisdiction upon crossing its borders. Thompson continued his adherence to the doctrine of concurrent commerce powers in MAYOR OF

NEW YORK V. MILN (1837), to the extent that he wrote separately rather than subscribe to the majority's reasoning that regulation of immigrant passengers was simply a valid exercise of the STATE POLICE POWER. Subsequently, the concurrent powers doctrine became an integral part of ROGER B. TANEY's constitutional thought. Taney had not advanced that doctrine while arguing for the state in *Brown,* and it is reasonable to assume that he borrowed it from Thompson.

On the slavery question, Thompson assumed the doughface position later followed by his replacement on the Court, SAMUEL NELSON, of providing support for the peculiar institution, while striving to confine the question at hand and giving the appearance of sticking rigidly to precedent. Typical, in this respect, was GROVES V. SLAUGHTER (1841), where Thompson, speaking for the Court's majority, was able to avoid the question whether Mississippi's constitutional ban on uncontrolled slave shipments from other states violated the commerce clause. In PRIGG V. PENNSYLVANIA (1842), Thompson differed from JOSEPH STORY's opinion that the fugitive slave clause did not prohibit state laws designed "faithfully" to enforce the clause. In contrast with Thompson's adherence to legal formalism in slavery cases was his activism in *Cherokee Nation v. Georgia* (1831). Dissenting, in the most elaborate opinion of his career, he asserted that regardless of their relative weakness to their white neighbors, the Cherokees constituted an independent, foreign, sovereign, nation. The following year, Thompson's dissent became the majority position in WORCESTER V. GEORGIA. (See CHEROKEE INDIAN CASES.)

Thompson's conservative attitude toward government and business sometimes put him at odds with both Marshall and Taney. Perhaps none of his contemporaries had more concern for protecting VESTED RIGHTS than did Thompson. He joined Story's CHARLES RIVER BRIDGE dissent (1837), and in his own WHEATON V. PETERS (1834) dissent he said that as a matter of "sound reason and abstract morality" the COMMON LAW provided COPYRIGHT protection. It was his concern for vested rights alone with his administrative experience that caused Thompson to distinguish between cabinet officers' political and ministerial duties. Only the latter functions were "subject to the control of the law, and the direction of the president," he said in *United States ex rel. Stokes et al. v. Kendall* (1838). Thompson's conservatism meshed with his adherence to states' responsibilities in interpreting the CONTRACT CLAUSE. In his view contracts were subject to the existing law of a place, including insolvency laws. Such laws, like the long-standing New York sys-

tem, were also good for business. These beliefs explain Thompson's opposition to Marshall in OGDEN V. SAUNDERS (1837), and partially explains his CRAIG V. MISSOURI dissent (1830). Thompson's impact on constitutional law was slight, and only a few Whig politicians lamented his death.

DONALD ROPER

Bibliography

DUNNE, GERALD T. 1969 Smith Thompson. In Leon Friedman and Fred L. Israel, eds., *The Justices of the United States Supreme Court.* Pages 475–492. New York: Chelsea House.

THORNHILL v. ALABAMA
310 U.S. 88 (1940)

This case involved a FIRST AMENDMENT challenge to convictions under an Alabama antipicketing statute. Normally one has STANDING only to plead one's own constitutional rights. In *Thornhill,* however, the Supreme Court did not ask whether the particular activity in which the pickets had engaged was constitutionally protected. Instead it asked whether the statute itself, rather than its application to these particular persons, violated the First Amendment. Because the statute was INVALID ON ITS FACE, it could be challenged, even by a union that itself might have engaged in violent picketing not protected by the First Amendment. The theory was that the statute's general ban on all labor dispute picketing would threaten peaceful picketers as well, even though no peaceful picketers had even been prosecuted.

Justice FRANK MURPHY acknowledged that the state legislature legitimately might have written a narrowly drawn statute that condemned only violent or mass picketing. Instead it wrote a general ban on all picketing in labor–management disputes. "The existence of such a statute . . . which does not aim specifically at evils within the allowable area of state control but, on the contrary, sweeps within its ambit other activities that in ordinary circumstances constitute an exercise of freedom of speech . . . readily lends itself to . . . discriminatory enforcement by local prosecuting officials [and] results in a continuous and pervasive unconstitutional restraint on all freedom of discussion." Subsequently the Court was to speak of the unconstitutional CHILLING EFFECT of such "facially overbroad" statutes.

MARTIN SHAPIRO

THORNTON v. CALDOR, INC.
105 S. Ct. 2914 (1985)

The Supreme Court held unconstitutional, on establishment clause grounds, a state act authorizing employees to designate a sabbath day and not work that day. Applying the three-part test of LEMON V. KURTZMAN (1971), Chief Justice WARREN E. BURGER found that by vesting in employees an "absolute and unqualified" right not to work on the sabbath of one's choice, and by forcing employers to adjust work schedules to the religious practices of employees, the act constituted a law respecting an ESTABLISHMENT OF RELIGION. In purpose and effect it advanced religion, preferring those who believe in not working on the sabbath to those who hold no such belief. By implication, a statute giving employers some leeway would be constitutional. Only Justice WILLIAM H. REHNQUIST dissented, without opinion. No member of the Court defended the statute as a state effort to prevent discrimination against sabbath believers by preventing the imposition of employment penalties on those acting in obedience to conscience by refusing to work. (See SHERBERT V. VERNER, 1963.)

LEONARD W. LEVY

THORPE, FRANCIS N.
(1857–1926)

Francis Newton Thorpe, professor of history at the University of Pennsylvania, edited seven volumes of *American Charters and Constitutions.* He also wrote several books on political and constitutional history from a post-Civil War nationalist viewpoint. He emphasized the UNWRITTEN CONSTITUTION by which the written Constitution is continually extended and adapted.

DENNIS J. MAHONEY

THREE-FIFTHS CLAUSE

Article I, section 2, clause 3, of the United States Constitution originally provided that members of the House of Representatives would be apportioned among the states on a formula that added to "free Persons" (including indentured servants but excluding untaxed Indians) "three fifths of all other Persons." The 1840 publication of JAMES MADISON's notes of debates in the CONSTITUTIONAL CONVENTION OF 1787 revealed that the euphemism "all other Persons" referred to slaves.

The clause originated in an unsuccessful 1783 proposal in the Confederation Congress to amend the ARTICLES OF CONFEDERATION by changing the method of apportioning taxes among the states to a per capita basis that would include all free persons and "three-fifths of all other persons." At the Philadelphia convention, JAMES WILSON, a Pennsylvania delegate, resurrected the three-fifths formula as an amendment to the VIRGINIA PLAN and thereby touched off heated debates on counting slaves for apportionment purposes. The underlying conflict of interests between slave and free states provoked a great crisis of the convention. The deadlock was resolved by a complex formula that was part of the GREAT COMPROMISE basing both representation and DIRECT TAXES on the three-fifths formula and, for good measure, making the direct-tax provisions of Article I, section 9, unamendable (Article V).

Madison in THE FEDERALIST #54 defended the clause as an arbitrary but reasonable compromise that roughly reflected the anomalous legal status of a slave, a human for certain purposes and a chattel for others. The slave was "debased by servitude below the equal level of free inhabitants, which regards the slave as divested of two-fifths of the man." NATHANIEL GORHAM of Massachusetts had earlier agreed, accepting the clause as "pretty near the just proportion."

The three-fifths formula gave the slave states an additional political weight in Congress quite close to what they would have enjoyed if they had counted all slaves for purposes of apportionment. In 1811 this produced eighteen slave-state representatives more than the southern states would have had if slaves had been excluded altogether from apportionment. The clause therefore rankled New England and middle-state Federalists, who used the clause as a vehicle to voice their resentment at the Virginia Dynasty and the rising political power of the west. Reviving arguments of 1787 that if Virginia counted its slaves Massachusetts should be able to count its cattle, New Englanders complained with JOHN QUINCY ADAMS that "slave representation has governed the union." The HARTFORD CONVENTION demanded in 1814 that the clause be abrogated.

Later debates during the abolition controversy renewed this dispute. Abolitionists either disingenuously tried to construe the clause as referring to persons other than slaves (indentured servants or ALIENS) or demanded that the clause be expunged. Defenders of slavery and Garrisonian abolitionists both cited the clause as an explicit assurance of the privileged constitutional status of that unique form of property, human chattels.

Though the abolitionist debates proved inconclusive, the clause bedeviled Republicans during Reconstruction. After the abolition of slavery, all blacks became "free Persons" and thus the congressional representation of the former Confederate states would be augmented by perhaps a dozen congressmen, endangering the Republicans' objectives for the war and Reconstruction. To forestall this, Republicans first temporarily excluded ten of the former seceded states from representation in Congress, then forced ratification of the FOURTEENTH AMENDMENT, whose section 2 provides that representatives shall be apportioned simply on "the whole number of persons in each State," and that a state's representation should be reduced in proportion to its denial of the vote to male citizens over twenty-one years old, except for participation in rebellion or crime.

WILLIAM M. WIECEK

Bibliography

OHLINE, HOWARD A. 1971 Republicanism and Slavery: Origins of the Three-Fifths Clause in the United States Constitution. *William and Mary Quarterly* 28:563–594.
SIMPSON, ALBERT F. 1941 The Political Significance of Slave Representation, 1787–1821. *Journal of Southern History* 7:315–342.

THREE-JUDGE COURT

The Supreme Court's decision in EX PARTE YOUNG (1908) made it possible for one federal judge to tie up an entire state legislative program by granting preliminary injunctive relief. In 1910 Congress required certain applications for federal-court INTERLOCUTORY injunctions against state officers to be heard by three judges. Such a court's order was made directly appealable to the Supreme Court. A similar statutory scheme had been devised earlier for certain ANTITRUST and railroad regulation cases. The 1948 revision of the JUDICIAL CODE made clear that the three-judge requirement applied to all hearings on applications for interlocutory or permanent INJUNCTIONS against state officers.

A considerable body of law developed out of this statute. Applications for DECLARATORY JUDGMENTS were not subject to the requirement, although injunctive relief is authorized to enforce a declaratory judgment. Three-judge courts were required only for actions seeking to enjoin state officers in carrying out

statutes of general and statewide application, not local ordinances. While three judges were ordinarily necessary to deny injunctive relief as well as grant it, a single judge could dismiss such an action when it was "insubstantial."

The system of three-judge courts was enormously burdensome, both on the lower federal courts and on the Supreme Court. In 1976, Congress drastically limited the three-judge requirement, retaining it only in certain cases involving legislative REAPPORTIONMENT or VOTING RIGHTS and some cases under the CIVIL RIGHTS ACT OF 1964.

KENNETH L. KARST

Bibliography

WRIGHT, CHARLES ALAN 1983 *The Law of Federal Courts*, 4th ed. Pages 295–299, 728–729. St. Paul, Minn.: West Publishing Co.

TIEDEMAN, CHRISTOPHER G.
(1857–1903)

Christopher G. Tiedeman, a professor of law, published *A Treatise on the Limitations of Police Power in the United States* (1886). Second only to THOMAS COOLEY'S *Constitutional Limitations* in its influence on American constitutional law, Tiedeman's book spurred the conversion of the FOURTEENTH AMENDMENT into a bulwark of VESTED RIGHTS. He believed that liberty found its highest expression in laissez-faire economics and that the POLICE POWER, which he sought to reduce to the role of policeman, was making "socialism, communism, and anarchism . . . rampant in America." He found evidence for that claim in the advocacy of prolabor legislation and state protection of the weak against the strong. Conservatism, he wrote, feared "the advent of an absolutism more tyrannical and more unreasoning than any before experienced by man, the absolutism of a democratic majority." JUDICIAL REVIEW in support of written constitutions that limited government provided the only hope, and Tiedeman's exposition of cases was calculated to assist courts in their task of thwarting invasions of private rights. In 1900, in the preface to a revised second edition, Tiedeman expressed gratification that "the first edition of this book has been quoted by the courts in hundreds of cases."

LEONARD W. LEVY

TILTON v. RICHARDSON

See: *Lemon v. Kurtzman*

TIMBER CULTURE ACT

See: Environmental Regulation

TIMES-MIRROR CO. v. CALIFORNIA

See: *Bridges v. California*

TINKER v. DES MOINES INDEPENDENT COMMUNITY SCHOOL DISTRICT
393 U.S. 503 (1969)

Tinker is a leading modern decision on the subjects of SYMBOLIC SPEECH and CHILDREN'S RIGHTS. A group of adults and students in Des Moines planned to protest the VIETNAM WAR by wearing black armbands during the 1965 holiday season. On learning of this plan, the public school principals adopted a policy to forbid the wearing of armbands. Two high school students and one junior high school student wore armbands to school, refused to remove them, and were suspended until they might return without armbands. They sued in federal court to enjoin enforcement of the principals' policy and for nominal damages. The district court dismissed the complaint, and the court of appeals affirmed by an equally divided court. The Supreme Court reversed, 7–2, in an opinion by Justice ABE FORTAS.

The wearing of these armbands was "closely akin to 'pure speech' " and protected by the FIRST AMENDMENT. The school environment did imply limitations on the freedom of expression, but here the principals lacked justification for imposing any such limitations. The authorities' "undifferentiated fear" of disturbance was insufficient. While student expression could be forbidden when it materially disrupted school work or school discipline, these students had undertaken "a silent, passive expression of opinion, unaccompanied by any disorder or disturbance." Furthermore, only this "particular symbol . . . was singled out for prohibition"; political campaign buttons had been allowed, and even "the Iron Cross, traditionally a symbol of Nazism." (Justice Fortas may have been unaware of the vogue among surfers and their inland imitators.)

Justice HUGO L. BLACK dissented, accusing the majority of encouraging students to defy their teachers and arguing that the wearing of the armbands had,

in fact, diverted other students' minds from their schoolwork. He did not ask how much the principals' reaction to the planned protest might have contributed to that diversion.

KENNETH L. KARST

TITLES OF NOBILITY

In the twentieth century, the idea of a hereditary ruling elite using titles of nobility as a device for maintaining its authority seems a bit frivolous. To the founding generation, however, the threat was only too real. Moreover, the threat that a foreign potentate might suborn an American citizen or official by proffering such a title was also perceived as significant. The ARTICLES OF CONFEDERATION forbade the acceptance of foreign titles by any person holding federal or state office and forbade the granting of titles by the United States or by any state. The prohibitions were carried over into the Constitution, except that there is no longer a ban on state officers accepting foreign titles, and Congress may authorize acceptance of titles by federal officers. In both documents, titles of nobility are treated, along with gifts and offices, as items of value that foreign governments might offer in exchange for favors, and Governor EDMUND RANDOLPH, at the CONSTITUTIONAL CONVENTION, asserted that the provision was designed to guard against corruption.

As it appears in the Constitution, the prohibition against accepting foreign titles applies only to those holding a federal office of trust or profit. On the eve of the War of 1812, Congress proposed to the states a constitutional amendment extending the prohibition to every citizen of the United States. Under the proposed amendment, acceptance of a title of nobility would have caused automatic forfeiture of United States CITIZENSHIP and permanent disqualification from holding federal or state office. The titles-of-nobility amendment was one of only six constitutional amendments ever proposed by Congress to fall short of ratification by the states.

DENNIS J. MAHONEY

TOCQUEVILLE, ALEXIS DE
(1805–1859)

The French magistrate and political theorist Alexis Clerel de Tocqueville spent nine months of 1831 and 1832 in the United States. He believed that democracy was the inescapable destiny of all nations and that America, as the first avowedly democratic nation in the modern world, offered an opportunity for the student of politics to observe democracy in action. One product of Tocqueville's sojourn on our shores was *Democracy in America.*

Tocqueville thought that the main problem of democracy was a tendency toward radical equality of condition which was destructive of the liberty necessary for excellence in human endeavors. He perceived in America two undesirable developments: a pervasive tyranny of the majority and a centrifugal individualism. He proposed, as a solution to democracy's problems, a "new science of politics" based on enlightened self-interest. He emphasized the utility, rather than the beauty or nobility, of virtue and public-spiritedness.

A shrewd observer of political affairs, Tocqueville was one of the first to discern the American tendency toward JUDICIAL SUPREMACY. American judges, he noted, although confined to deciding particular cases, and only those presenting justiciable controversies, possess immense political power. This is possible because "scarcely any political question arises in the United States which is not resolved, sooner or later, into a judicial question," and because of the simple fact that the Americans have acknowledged the right of judges to found their decisions on the Constitution rather than on the laws, or, in other words, they have permitted them not to apply such laws as may appear to them to be unconstitutional. The political power of the judges, arising out of the exercise of JUDICIAL REVIEW, appeared to Tocqueville a salutary check on potential legislative excess. Tocqueville's observation, made when the Supreme Court had voided only a single federal law as unconstitutional, seems all the more perceptive today.

Tocqueville also recognized the unique status of the Constitution in American political life. The English constitution was alterable by ordinary legislation and the constitutions of continental monarchies were immutable save by violent revolution; only in America was the Constitution regarded as an expression of the SOVEREIGNTY of the people, not subject to change at the whim of legislators, but amendable by the common consent of the citizens in accordance with established rules.

Not all of Tocqueville's observations remain valid. For example, he wrote that the states were more powerful than the national government and that Congress was more powerful than the President. In each case, however, he identified the factors that have caused those relationships to be reversed in our own day.

Tocqueville's purpose in writing *Democracy in America* was not merely to describe American institutions. He addressed himself to the universal problems of modern politics—economic and social, as well as governmental. America provided illustrations and examples, and from the American experience he made generalizations applicable to all modern nations. In America Tocqueville learned how to make democracy safe for the world.

DENNIS J. MAHONEY

Bibliography

PIERSON, G. W. 1959 *Tocqueville in America.* New York: Basic Books.
ZETTERBAUM, MARVIN 1965 *Tocqueville and the Problem of Democracy.* New York: Basic Books.

TODD, THOMAS
(1765–1826)

Thomas Todd served as a Justice of the United States Supreme Court for nearly nineteen years, but he had only a small impact on the Court's decisions. Born into a fairly prominent Virginia family, he was orphaned at an early age. Because the bulk of his father's estate went to his eldest brother, he was forced to fend for himself. Following a short enlistment in the army during the Revolutionary War he went to Liberty Hall in Lexington, Virginia (later Washington and Lee University), where he studied the classics and mathematics. Todd then entered the household of his cousin Harry Innes, an accomplished lawyer and respected member of the Virginia legislature, where he served as a tutor in return for room and board. In 1784 Innes and his family removed to Kentucky where he became a judge, and Todd accompanied them. Through his cousin's political connections Todd quickly became involved in the movement to make Kentucky a separate state, serving as secretary and clerk for the various conventions that were called, and helped to write Kentucky's first CONSTITUTION in 1792.

Admitted to the bar in 1788, Todd developed a lucrative law practice, with a specialty in land titles. During the 1790s he served as secretary to the Kentucky legislature and as clerk to the federal district court. In 1799 he was appointed judge of that court, and five years later he became chief judge. In 1807 Congress increased the number of United States Supreme Court Justices from five to six in order to accommodate the newly created western circuit (Ohio, Kentucky, and Tennessee) and to resolve the special problems in land law arising there. As this was Todd's area of expertise and because Todd was popular with the congressmen from the western states, President THOMAS JEFFERSON appointed him to the newly created post.

Although a Republican, Todd invariably supported the strongly nationalist and probusiness decisions of the MARSHALL COURT. Reportedly he was opposed to the Supreme Court's ruling in DARTMOUTH COLLEGE V. WOODWARD (1819), but he was absent when it was handed down. In fact, bad health combined with the difficulties of riding the western circuit forced him to miss many of the Supreme Court sessions. He wrote only fourteen decisions, eleven for the majority, two concurring, and one dissenting in the relatively unimportant case of *Finley v. Lynn* (1810). With the exception of his last opinion, *Riggs v. Taylor* (1824), which dealt with an evidentiary problem, all his opinions dealt with problems involving land titles. He remained active in various local and state civic affairs until his death.

RICHARD E. ELLIS

Bibliography

ISRAEL, FRED L. 1969 Thomas Todd. Pages 407–412 in Leon Friedman and Fred L. Israel, eds., *Justices of the Supreme Court, 1789–1969.* New York: Chelsea House.

TOLERATION ACT
1 William & Mary ch. 18 (1689)

The principle of RELIGIOUS LIBERTY denies that the state has any legitimate authority over the individual's religion or irreligion; the principle of toleration insists that a state which maintains an ESTABLISHMENT OF RELIGION indulge the existence of nonconformist religious groups. Toleration is a step between persecution and liberty. The Toleration Act, which accompanied the Glorious Revolution of 1688–1689, was a political necessity that restored peace to a religiously pluralistic England and ended a period of persecution during which thousands of nonconformist Protestant ministers had died in jail.

The act, entitled "A Bill of Indulgence," exempted most nonconformists from the penalties of the persecutory laws of the Restoration, leaving those laws in force but inapplicable to persons qualifying for indulgence. Subjects who took the requisite oaths to support the new king and reject the authority of the pope might have the privilege of worshiping as they pleased, because they were exempted from the penalties that had suppressed them. Baptists and Quakers

received special indulgences. Thus the act had the effect of permitting the existence of lawful nonconformity, though nonconformists still had to pay tithes to the established church and endure many civil disabilities. One section of the act excluded from its benefits Roman Catholic recusants and Protestant antitrinitarians. England still regarded the former as political subversives, the latter as virtual atheists. For all its faults the statute of 1689 ushered in an era of toleration under the established church and ultimately benefited dissenters in those American colonies that maintained establishments of religion.

LEONARD W. LEVY

Bibliography

SEATON, A. (1911)1972 *The Theory of Toleration under the Later Stuarts.* Pages 92–236. New York: Octagon Books.

TONKIN GULF RESOLUTION

See: Gulf of Tonkin Resolution

TOOMBS, ROBERT A.
(1810–1885)

A Georgia attorney educated at Schenectady's Union College, Robert Augustus Toombs was a congressman (1843–1853) and senator (1853–1861) before becoming a SECESSION leader. Initially a conservative Whig and an ally of ALEXANDER STEPHENS, Toombs became a Democrat, but not a fire-eater, after the COMPROMISE OF 1850. In 1856 he supported the admission of Kansas without slavery, if the settlers there voted for statehood on that basis. In 1860 Toombs worked for a united Democratic Party, but despite this goal and his previous support for STEPHEN A. DOUGLAS in the Senate, Toombs opposed Douglas's presidential aspirations. After ABRAHAM LINCOLN's election Toombs supported the Crittenden Compromise, and he also offered his own. When compromise failed, he returned to Georgia as a secession leader, writing a report for the Georgia Secession Convention explaining why disunion was necessary. Appointed Confederate secretary of state, Toombs resigned after five months to accept a rebel army commission. When he was denied a promotion after Antietam, Toombs left the army and became a critic of JEFFERSON DAVIS's economic inefficiency, confederate violations of CIVIL LIBERTIES, and CONSCRIPTION. In 1865 he escaped to England; he returned in 1867 to lead Georgia's anti-Reconstruction forces. He dominated Georgia's 1877 CONSTITUTIONAL CONVENTION, which paved the way for black disfranchisement, and, at Toombs's insistence, severely limited corporate charters and railroad development. Toombs never petitioned for CITIZENSHIP, and although a successful attorney, never again held public office.

PAUL FINKELMAN

Bibliography

THOMPSON, ROBERT Y. 1966 *Robert Toombs of Georgia.* Baton Rouge: Louisiana State University Press.

TOOMER v. WITSELL
334 U.S. 385 (1948)

South Carolina required state residents to pay a $25-per-boat license fee to gather shrimp in state waters; for nonresidents, the fee was $2,500. The Supreme Court, speaking through Chief Justice FRED M. VINSON, held that this discrimination violated both the PRIVILEGES AND IMMUNITIES clause of Article IV and the COMMERCE CLAUSE. (See STATE REGULATION OF COMMERCE.) The commerce ground was easy and unanimously supported by the Justices. The decision's main importance lay in its approach to the privileges and immunities clause; on this issue the Court divided, 6–3. Earlier decisions had suggested that the clause protected only "fundamental rights." *Toomer* redirected the inquiry: discrimination against nonresidents was permissible only if it bore a substantial relation to solving a problem distinctively presented by nonresidents. South Carolina's discriminatory tax failed this test.

KENNETH L. KARST

TORCASO v. WATKINS
367 U.S. 488 (1961)

The Maryland Constitution provided: "No RELIGIOUS TEST ought ever to be required as a qualification to any office . . . other than a declaration of belief in the existence of God. . . ." For Justice HUGO L. BLACK, speaking for the Supreme Court, the Maryland requirement contravened the ESTABLISHMENT OF RELIGION clause of the FIRST AMENDMENT. Black, quoting his own opinion for the Court in EVERSON V. BOARD OF EDUCATION (1947), repeated that government may not "force a person to profess a belief . . . in any religion."

RICHARD E. MORGAN

TORT CLAIMS ACT

See: Federal Tort Claims Act

TOTH, UNITED STATES ex rel., v. QUARLES
350 U.S. 11 (1955)

Five months after his honorable discharge from the Air Force, Toth was charged with committing murder while on active duty in Korea. Taken to Korea for trial by court martial, Toth sought HABEAS CORPUS in a DISTRICT OF COLUMBIA court. On APPEAL, the Supreme Court held, 6–3, that a civilian was entitled to TRIAL BY JURY in a civilian court established under Article III; court-martial JURISDICTION was constitutionally limited to actual members of the armed forces.

KENNETH L. KARST

(SEE ALSO: *Judicial Power of the United States; Military Justice and the Constitution.*)

TOWNSEND v. SAIN
372 U.S. 29 (1963)

When a state prisoner seeks federal HABEAS CORPUS review of a constitutional error in his or her case, the federal court must decide what weight to give the state court fact findings that are relevant to the prisoner's claim. The fairness and accuracy of such findings are crucial to the proper adjudication of federal constitutional rights, because most habeas corpus petitions raise mixed questions of law and fact, such as the VOLUNTARINESS of a WAIVER OF CONSTITUTIONAL RIGHTS, or the suggestiveness of a LINE-UP identification. In *Townsend,* a unanimous Supreme Court held that a federal court in a habeas corpus proceeding always has the power to try the facts anew, and that it must do so if the defendant did not receive a full and fair evidentiary hearing in any state court proceeding. The Court split 5–4 over the need for more specific directives concerning mandatory hearings, with Chief Justice EARL WARREN setting forth the majority's view that a hearing is required in six particular circumstances.

In 1966, Congress enacted a modified form of the *Townsend* criteria in an amendment to the JUDICIAL CODE, specifying eight circumstances when the validity of state court findings may not be presumed. In other circumstances, the habeas corpus petitioner bears the burden of proving that the state fact findings were erroneous.

CATHERINE HANCOCK

TOWNSHEND ACTS
(1767)

The Townshend Acts imposed duties upon American imports of glass, lead, paint, paper, and tea and authorized WRITS OF ASSISTANCE as one means of enforcing payment. Although "external" in form, the duties were not levied to regulate trade but to raise revenue to help pay for maintaining British soldiers and officials in America. The colonists protested that the levies constituted TAXATION WITHOUT REPRESENTATION. The Townshend Act duties (except that on tea) were repealed in 1770.

DENNIS J. MAHONEY

TRADE UNIONS

See: Labor and the Constitution

TRANSACTIONAL IMMUNITY

See: Immunity Grant

TRANS-MISSOURI FREIGHT ASSOCIATION v. UNITED STATES
166 U.S. 290 (1897)

A 5–4 Supreme Court, holding that the SHERMAN ANTITRUST ACT extended to railroads, rejected the RULE OF REASON advanced by Justice EDWARD D. WHITE in dissent. In 1889, eighteen railroads had combined to form the Trans-Missouri Freight Association "for the purpose of mutual protection, by establishing and maintaining reasonable rates, rules and regulations [over their mutual] freight traffic." Any member's proposed rate reduction for a route shared with another member needed Association approval.

Justice RUFUS PECKHAM, the Court's spokesman, found two questions: Did the Sherman Act apply to railroads and, if so, was the Freight Association agreement a violation of that act? He dismissed the railroads' claim of exemption on two grounds. Their business was commerce, and the lower courts and the

dissenters had relied on a mistaken belief that the Sherman Act could not apply to railroads because the INTERSTATE COMMERCE ACT already regulated carriers. He refused "to read into the act by way of judicial legislation an exception that is not placed there [by Congress]." Policy matters were not questions for judicial determination; any alteration of the law was for Congress to undertake. Peckham concluded that the Sherman Act prohibited all restraints of INTERSTATE COMMERCE; adopting the rule of reason would "substantially . . . leave the question of reasonableness to the companies themselves." Endorsing free competition, the Court declared that intent need not be proved: the Association agreement clearly restrained commerce.

DAVID GORDON

TRAVEL

See: Right to Travel

TREASON

Treason is the only crime defined in the United States Constitution. Article III, section 3, declares that

Treason against the United States shall consist only in levying war against them, or in adhering to their enemies, giving them aid and comfort. No person shall be convicted of treason unless on the testimony of two witnesses to the same overt act, or on confession in open court. The Congress shall have power to declare the punishment of treason, but no ATTAINDER OF TREASON shall work corruption of blood, or forfeiture except during the life of the person attainted.

State constitutions contain similar limiting definitions of treason against a state. However, since national independence there has been little action or development of doctrine under the state provisions. The notable exceptions are the trials of Thomas Wilson Dorr (1844) and of John Brown (1859) which ended in convictions of treason by levying war against the states of Rhode Island and Virginia, respectively. State histories include a few abortive attempts to employ treason INDICTMENTS against people who incurred the wrath of powerful elements in the community. Thus indictments were brought against Mormon leaders in Missouri in 1838 and in Illinois in 1844; for political reasons the Missouri charge was not pressed and the defendants escaped jail; a mob murdered Joseph Smith shortly after his arrest on the Illinois indictment. Such isolated instances aside, the law of treason in the United States has been almost wholly the product of debates over making the national Constitution and decisions of federal courts under Article III, section 3.

As it has developed under the Constitution, the law regarding treason has strikingly mingled concern for the security of government and the legal order and concern for the freedom of private individuals and groups. The crime deals with the most serious threats to the existence of the state. In adopting the Constitution everyone took for granted that, since the people were creating a new SOVEREIGNTY, it must have authority to protect itself. Congress has reflected this judgment of the gravity of the matter by prescribing penalties that may extend to life imprisonment, or perhaps even to execution. Where charges have fallen fairly within the constitutional definition of the offense, judges have not hesitated to make firm application of the law. However, on its face the Constitution takes a limiting approach to the crime. Treason, says Article III, section 3, shall consist "only" in two named types of conduct; Congress is thus barred from adding new categories of treason, as it is also explicitly limited in fixing penalties. Moreover, the treason clause puts a stringent limit on the executive in prosecuting the crime; absent a confession in open court, by constitutional mandate the prosecution must muster testimony of two witnesses to the same overt act that the accused committed in seeking to carry out the treason. Federal judges in cases arising under the treason clause have followed a restrictive approach in marking the outer boundaries of the crime. Thus in one aspect the treason clause guards the security of the government. But in another dimension it sets limitations that make it functionally analogous to provisions of the BILL OF RIGHTS, protecting CIVIL LIBERTIES of private individuals and groups.

The constitutional emphasis on restricting the scope of the crime of treason is a marked departure from the main directions the law had taken in England and in this country before 1789. Before the eighteenth century, in practice, official policy had given clear primacy to the security of government, often more obviously to serve the interests of particular powerholders than to serve the common good.

From the fourteenth to the eighteenth century, English political history included aggressive use of charges of treason as weapons of partisan conflict; prosecution was usually vindictive and pressed with scant regard to fair procedure or careful insistence on clear proof or reliable evidence. The only counterweight to this abusive trend was the continuance of the statute of 25 Edward III (1350), stating seven categories of high treason—notably those of levying war, adhering to enemies, or seeking "to compass or imagine the death of our lord the King"—and asserting that only Parliament might enlarge the definitions of treason, thus forbidding judges to extend the offense by interpretation. The restrictive emphasis of the statute of Edward III was stressed by the English treatise writers from whom lawmakers in the new United States got most of their knowledge of the course of English policy regarding treason. In particular, EDWARD COKE, Matthew Hale, and WILLIAM BLACKSTONE spoke of abuse of vague, extended definitions of the crime as instruments of partisan combat, imperiling the general liberty. Thus Hale warned, "How dangerous it is by construction and analogy to make treasons, where the letter of the law has not done it; for such a method admits of no limits or bounds, but runs as far as the wit and invention of accusers, and the odiousness and detestation of persons accused will carry men." Offsetting such warnings, however, the English treatises also brought to the knowledge of lawmakers in North America a considerable range of decisions in which English judges had, despite the limit declared in Edward III's statute, greatly enlarged the offense of treason by construction.

Security in the most elemental sense was at stake for the English colonies in North America under the threat of French and Indian wars and in the new states torn through the American Revolution by bitter divisions between those loyal to the Crown and those asserting independence. Thus in the colonies and in the new states during the years of the Revolutionary War, statute books included many broadly and sometimes vaguely defined offenses of subversion, in dramatic contrast to the limited definition of treason later written into the national Constitution and thereafter typically included in constitutions of the states. Though colonial and early state legislation sometimes borrowed the language of the act of Edward III, we must realize that at least by the late eighteenth century lawyers here would be familiar, through the standard English treatises, with the expansive readings which English courts had given the old statute.

With adoption of the national Constitution we encounter introduction of a restrictive emphasis to balance the security concerns previously dominant in the law of treason. There is not a great deal about the treason clause in the records of the framing and RATIFICATION OF THE CONSTITUTION. But what there is shows sensitivity to lessons that policymakers here felt they should draw from English experience of the dangers to individual and political liberty of loose resort to treason prosecutions. JAMES WILSON was probably the ablest lawyer on the CONSTITUTIONAL CONVENTION's Committee of Detail, which took the responsibility of adopting a restrictive rather than an extensive approach to defining treason. In the Pennsylvania ratifying convention, Wilson twice—on his own initiative and without any criticisms of the provision voiced by an alert and suspicious opposition—praised the treason clause as including protection of civil liberty along with protection of government. In his law lectures delivered at the College of Philadelphia in 1790 and 1791, Wilson emphasized the constitutional provision by devoting an entire lecture to it. He made the centerpoint of his analysis the importance of carefully bounding the crime: "It is the observation of the celebrated MONTESQUIEU, that if the crime of treason be indeterminate, this alone is sufficient to make any government degenerate into arbitrary power." Two fears were prominent in the limited attention given the treason clause in adopting the Constitution: that holders of official power would use the treason charge to suppress legitimate, peaceful political opposition and to destroy those who were out of official favor, and that popular fear and emotion might be stirred under the dread charge to produce convictions without additional evidence. Subsequent federal court opinions recognized this restrictive background, in decisions limiting extension of the offense. Speaking for the Supreme Court in EX PARTE BOLLMAN AND SWARTWOUT (1807) in a matter indirectly involving a treason charge, Chief Justice JOHN MARSHALL declared that "to prevent the possibility of those calamities which result from the extension of treason to offences of minor importance, that great fundamental law which defines and limits the various departments of our government, has given a rule on the subject both to the legislature and the courts of America, which neither can be permitted to transcend." In the first treason case to reach the Supreme Court, CRAMER V. UNITED STATES (1945), the Court reaffirmed the propriety of this approach, quoting with approval Marshall's further admonition that "It is, therefore, more safe, as well as more consonant to the principles of our constitution, that the crime of treason should not be extended by construction to doubtful cases; and that crimes not clearly within the constitutional definition, should receive such punishment as the legislature in its wisdom may provide."

Three key elements enter into the crime of treason: an obligation of allegiance to the legal order, and intent and action to violate that obligation. First, treason is a breach of allegiance. A citizen owes loyal support to the sovereignty within which he lives or from which he derives his citizen's status. There are circumstances under which by the law of a foreign state an individual may owe it allegiance at the same time that he owes fealty to the United States; thus an individual may be a citizen of the United States because he was born here, and also be a citizen of another nation because he was born to nationals of that country. But dual nationality does not relieve an individual of obligation to refrain from volunteering aid or comfort to the foreign nation when it is at war with the United States. The restrictive tone attending treatment of treason charges had an analogy in World War II decisions which put on the government the burden of proving by clear and convincing evidence that citizens of the United States who had been lawfully present in an enemy country at the outbreak of war and were conscripted into enemy military service on the basis of their dual nationality had not complied under duress. However, in 1961 Congress amended the governing legislation to put the burden of proving duress on the individual claiming to hold United States CITIZENSHIP. The change from the court decisions to Congress's amendment revealed the persistence of tension between values placed on governmental security and on individual security, familiar in the treatment of the treason offense. One other facet of the allegiance element deserves note. Though the matter has not been presented to a court in this country, a resident alien enjoying the nation's protection owes it obedience to its laws while he is a resident. Such an individual is probably guilty of treason if he commits acts that would constitute the offense if done by a citizen.

To convict one of treason, the government must prove that the accused had a treasonable intent to levy war or to adhere to an enemy and to give aid and comfort to that enemy. Since betrayal of allegiance is at the heart of the offense, the requisite wrongful intent must be specific—a focused purpose to bring about a betrayal. In many crimes requiring proof of a guilty mind, the law holds an individual responsible as intending the reasonably foreseeable consequences of his conduct, even though he pleads that he did not intend to bring about the particular outcome for which he is charged. In *Cramer v. United States* the Supreme Court opinion included some incautious language which appeared to adopt that position. But the weight of authority in earlier federal court decisions and in rulings after *Cramer* indicates that the prosecution must prove that the defendant did intend to challenge the full authority of government at home (levy war) or to deliver aid to an enemy, as a substantial, independent element in his purpose, whatever other ends he may have had in mind. To this extent it appears that the prosecution must prove that the accused had a specific intent to levy war or to aid enemies. However, this requirement does not necessitate proof of guilty purpose by explicit statement or direct admission; the prosecution may prove the guilty intent by strong inference from the context of the accused's behavior.

The calculated limitations of the treason clause of the Constitution offer persuasive evidence that proof of the crime should require showing a specific intent. The Constitution obviously narrows the prior scope of treason by omitting any analogue to the offense of "compassing" or "imagining" the death of the king. Under that head, old English doctrine erected "constructive" treasons by inferring the wrongful intent from speech or writings that complaisant judges ruled might have the "natural consequences" of stirring popular discontent out of which violence might erupt to endanger the state. The weight of authority in federal court decisions has recognized that the policy of Article III, section 3, is to prevent expansion of the offense by building upon loose inferences of intention.

The character of the requisite wrongful intent varies according to which of the two heads of the offense is in issue. To be guilty of levying war against the United States, the individual must intend to use organized force to overthrow the government. Under the older English law treason existed if there was intent by collective force to prevent enforcement of a particular statute or other lawful order, or to obtain some particular benefit for a group, contrary to law. This English doctrine was followed in two early instances involving violent group resistance to enforcing particular federal laws—collection of a federal excise on whiskey (the WHISKEY REBELLION in western Pennsylvania in 1794) and collection of a federal property tax (the FRIES REBELLION, also in Pennsylvania, 1799). However, the later weight of authority is that nothing short of intention to overthrow the government suffices to make out the offense. Significant of this trend was the disposition of a late nineteenth-century effort to revive the old English doctrine. Following the Homestead Riot of 1892, several strike leaders were indicted for levying war against the state of Pennsylvania. But the indictments were later quietly dropped, while use of the treason charge met with prompt criticism even from conservative legal commentators. Violent group actions short of challenge to the existence of the government are now treated under heads of INCITEMENT, riot, or unlawful assembly.

Adhering to an enemy requires intent to render the enemy tangible support ("aid and comfort"). Established doctrine has defined "enemies" as only those against whom a legally declared STATE OF WAR exists. However, in the twentieth century, experience of such undeclared shooting hostilities as the Korean POLICE ACTION has raised the question of the continued vitality of the older limitation. The accused does not rebut the existence of the requisite intent for treason by pleading that he acted for mixed purposes, as to make money by selling goods to an enemy, if one of his purposes was in fact to render performance useful to the enemy. However, the accused may seek to persuade the court that he acted solely for a nontreasonable purpose, as when out of parental affection a father gave shelter to his son who was present in the country in wartime as an enemy agent. So, too, one whom the outbreak of war finds in a hostile country probably will not be found to have had treasonable intent merely because he took a job there to meet the necessities of earning a living, though the employment may have made some contributions to the enemy's strength.

In addition to proving wrongful intent, the government must prove that the accused committed some overt act to carry out his treasonable purpose. The calculated omission from the constitutional definition of treason of any counterpart of the English charge of compassing the death of the king underlines the requirement of proving overt action. The function of the overt act element, said the Supreme Court in *Cramer v. United States,* is to ensure "that mere mental attitudes or expression should not be treason." However, the Court's opinion in *Cramer* clouded definition of the requirement thus put on the prosecution; the Court seemed to say that the act must be of such character as itself to be evidence of the treasonable intent—a position apparently contrary to the emphasis common in other court rulings that the intent and the act elements are distinct. But in HAUPT V. UNITED STATES (1947) the Court somewhat clarified the matter: the behavior of the accused proved by the required testimony of two witnesses need not on its face evidence treasonable intent; an act apparently innocent, such as a transfer of money, might suffice if, in the light of other evidence of the context of the action, what the accused did could fairly be understood to aid an enemy. However, *Haupt* indicated that evidence of the context illuminating the significance of the overt act must also be supplied by two witnesses to the same circumstances. On the other hand, by the weight of authority, to prove the offense the prosecution need not establish that the accused succeeded in delivering aid to the enemy; it is enough that he took overt action to attempt delivery, though the *Cramer* opinion also contains language suggesting that effective delivery of aid should be shown. Mindful of abuses of charges of treason to suppress peaceful political opposition, English doctrine, adopted by judges in the United States, declares that a meeting to plan against the government is not a sufficient overt act to establish treason; conspiracy to levy war is not the levy of war, said Coke. But there is no comparable line of authority that a meeting to plan giving aid to an enemy is insufficient as an overt act of adherence to the enemy.

About the constitutional requirement of "testimony of two witnesses to the same overt act" hangs the uncertainty earlier noted, created by the Supreme Court opinion in *Cramer,* whether the act so proved must itself evidence treasonable intent or constitute actual delivery of aid to the enemy. Otherwise, rulings under the two-witness requirement have been straightforward. Courts have shown care to enforce the substance of the requirement, but not with doctrinaire rigidity. Two witnesses must testify directly to the act charged in the indictment; it will not suffice that there is two-witness evidence of a separate act from which it might be inferred that the charged act occurred. Two-witness testimony to the accused's admissions of an act does not meet the requirement of two-witness evidence to the act itself. However, the testimony of the two witnesses need not be identical or precise as to all aspects of the behavior cited as the overt act, nor need the testimony minutely cover every element into which an episode of behavior might be analyzed; the evidence is sufficient if it joins in identifying what reasonable jurors can regard as a connected transaction. Thus in *Haupt* the Supreme Court held that it was not fatal to the government's case that two-witness testimony did not show the enemy agent entering the accused's apartment, where it did show that he entered the building in which the accused had an apartment, and entered only as the accused's licensee, since the prosecution showed by other two-witness testimony that no other tenant in the building sheltered the agent.

This record suggests regard for the restrictive policy embodied in the constitutional history of treason. However, probably in large measure it also indicates that through most of its history the country has enjoyed substantial political stability. In any event the record shows little vindictive resort to the charge and few cases carrying politically controversial tones. Most actions taken against Loyalists in the American Revolution were to confiscate property. Because of the scale of the Civil War and the de facto belligerent status which events assigned the Confederacy, there was no material resort to treason prosecutions in that contest, though clearly those who took arms in behalf of the seceded states levied war against the United States. JEFFERSON DAVIS, President of the Confederacy, was indicted for treason. But the government faced strong arguments that it improperly charged treason against those conducting a rebel government which had achieved the status of a recognized belligerent. Though the government did not formally concede the point, neither did it bring Davis to trial on the indictment. Treason cases arising out of the Whiskey Rebellion (1795), the Fries disturbance (1799–1800), the Burr conspiracy (1807), THOMAS JEFFERSON's embargo (1808), and resistance to enforcement of the Fugitive Slave Law (1850), grew out of difficult domestic political issues but were of limited practical impact. Treason prosecutions by state authorities incident to the Dorr Rebellion in Rhode Island (1844) and John Brown's raid in Virginia (1859) were exceptional for their broad political bearing. Some cases carried tones of domestic ideological disputes over the country's entry into World War I. But this cast was notably absent from treason prosecutions incident to World War II.

By its terms the constitutional definition of treason puts some limits on governmental agencies in dealing with subversion. Congress may not increase the categories of conduct which the government may prosecute under the name of treason, nor may it extend the reach of the offense by including under the heads of adherence to enemies or levying war conduct lacking the historic elements of those crimes, or by mandating an extensive view of the evidence deemed relevant to establishing the elements of such treasons. The treason clause pointedly restricts Congress's authority to fixing penalties for the crime, and the position of the clause in Article III (establishing the JUDICIAL POWER OF THE UNITED STATES) underlines the implication that problems of applying the law of treason are ultimately for the courts. In their turn, federal judges have generally found in the language and history of Article III, section 3, a mandate against extending the range of the offense in doubtful cases. The two-witness requirement implies a further limitation on Congress. In light of that strict limitation on the prosecution's case, Congress should not have authority to avoid the two-witness requirement simply by changing labels and legislating under other names against offenses that involve all the elements of treason within the constitutional definition. However, the Supreme Court's decision in EX PARTE QUIRIN (1942) cast doubt on the validity of this analysis. One of several Nazi agents landed secretly on the east coast of the United States to sabotage war production plants was an American citizen. The Court rejected the argument that he must be prosecuted for treason by adhering to the enemy, and not for an offense against the laws of war incorporated in an act of Congress. Clearly the accused had committed treason. But the Court focused on the fact that the offense under the laws of war included another element—that the accused, having the status of an enemy belligerent, had passed the country's defenses in civilian dress with a hostile purpose.

Though it approaches the borderline of propriety, the Court's decision in *Quirin* might find support in analogues that date from the First Congress. There is no evidence that those who adopted the limiting constitutional definition of "treason" meant thereby to bar legislators from creating other crimes of subversion, the elements of which did not turn on the distinctive character of levying war or adhering to enemies. Congress in fact has defined and provided for punishment of other offenses of subversive or hostile activity against the security of the government, and federal courts have sustained such statutes. *United States v. Rosenberg* (1953) presented charges of conspiracy to violate the Federal ESPIONAGE ACT, which provides penalties for "whoever, with intent or reason to believe that it is to be used to the injury of the United States or to the advantage of a foreign nation," communicates or delivers to any foreign government or its agents information relating to the national defense. The federal court of appeals held that the treason clause did not bar creation of this offense, because "in the Rosenbergs' case, an essential element of treason, giving aid to an 'enemy' is irrelevant to the espionage offense." In *United States v. Drummond* (1965) the same appeals court dealt with a charge of conspiracy to violate the same statute by a serviceman in the United States Navy who between 1957 and 1962 delivered classified military materials to Soviet agents. Reaffirming that the treason clause did not bar creation of the espionage offense, the court found it "unnecessary" to invoke the difference relied on in *Rosenberg*, because it found differences in the required mental element in the crimes of treason and espionage. It pointed out that the espionage act required a showing only (1) that the defendant transmitted information with intent "or reason to believe" that it would be used for a forbidden result; and (2) with intent or reason to believe that it would be used either "to the injury of the United States or to the advantage of a foreign nation." In contrast, the court implied, treason requires proof of a specific intent, and a spe-

cific intent both to aid an enemy and to injure the United States.

Though the constitutional definition of treason may do no more formally than limit the kinds of conduct that may be prosecuted under the name of treason, there are respects in which it may have broader practical effect in restricting action of official agencies. The Constitution abolished the barbarous or oppressive penalties that were once a distinguishing mark of the crime. But legislation still allows heavy penalties for the offense; in light of Supreme Court limitations put on resort to the death penalty in other crimes there may be doubt whether a court may order execution of a convicted traitor, but the law still permits imposing a life sentence. Thus it may be of consequence whether the prosecutor can make out a case of "treason" or is limited to another charge which may carry a lesser penalty. Political history teaches that the mere accusation of treason, rather than of another crime, carries peculiar intimidation and stigma. Federalist treason prosecutions arising out of the Whiskey Rebellion (1794) were designed to stain supporters of Jefferson and JAMES MADISON with the imputation of subversive intent. The Jefferson administration sought to use the charge of treason (1808) to make examples against widespread opposition to the Embargo imposed to press England to respect rights of neutral use of the high seas. Democratic accusations of treason against the HARTFORD CONVENTION protesting the conduct of war with England (1814–1815) helped that venture to weaken a tottering Federalist party structure. A prosecution for treason undertook to discredit opposition to enforcement of the Fugitive Slave Law (1850). To break rank-and-file morale, Pennsylvania authorities brought treason indictments against leaders of the Homestead Strike (1892). In the cold war emotions of the 1950s, epithets of "treason" were employed in reckless attacks on the record of Democratic administrations in conducting relations with communist Russia and China. Such episodes validate the cautions expressed among those who adopted the national Constitution, that the definition of treason be limited so that this country would not repeat the old English experience of using the charge to destroy legitimate, peaceful political competition. Adoption of the FIRST AMENDMENT guarantees of free speech, press, assembly, and petition provided more direct and comprehensive declarations of the values of free political processes, and eventually these guarantees found substantial enforcement in decisions of the Supreme Court. That the First Amendment tended to preempt the field was early indicated when it became the prime reliance of those who attacked the constitutionality of the Sedition Act of 1798. (See ALIEN AND SEDITION ACTS.) However, given the extent to which concern for safeguarding peaceful public policy debate and activity figured in adopting a restrictive definition of treason, constitutional history here offers as yet unrealized possibilities for safeguarding First Amendment values.

JAMES WILLARD HURST

Bibliography
ABRAMS, STUART E. 1976 Threats to the President and the Constitutionality of Constructive Treason. *Columbia Journal of Law and Social Problems* 12:351–392.
CHAPIN, BRADLEY 1964 *The American Law of Treason: Revolutionary and Early National Origins.* Seattle: University of Washington Press.
HILL, L. M. 1968 The Two-Witness Rule in English Treason Trials. *American Journal of Legal History* 12:95–111.
HURST, JAMES WILLARD 1971 *The Law of Treason in the United States.* Westport, Conn.: Greenwood Press.
SIMON, WALTER G. 1961 The Evolution of Treason. *Tulane Law Review* 35:667–704.
STILLMAN, ARTHUR M. AND ARNER, FREDERICK R. 1954 *Federal Case Law Concerning the Security of the United States.* 83rd Congress, 2d session. Printed for the use of the Senate Committee on Foreign Relations. Washington, D.C.: Government Printing Office.
WIENER, FREDERICK BERNAYS 1962 Uses and Abuses of Legal History. *The Law Society's Gazette* 59:311–315.

TREATY OF GUADALUPE HIDALGO
9 Stat. 922 (1850)

In 1821 Mexico, having declared its independence from Spain, took control of the territory that now includes all of California, Arizona, New Mexico, and Texas, and parts of Nevada, Utah, and Colorado. But within twenty-five years, present-day Texas had been annexed by the United States, and at the end of the Mexican War the remaining areas were ceded to the United States under the Treaty of Guadalupe Hidalgo.

The treaty, signed in 1848, was not ratified by the Senate until 1850; the delay was caused by the unsuccessful efforts of Republicans to attach to the treaty the WILMOT PROVISO, banning slavery in the newly acquired territory. For more than a decade an important constitutional issue was debated but not resolved: the question whether the treaty's provisions preserving Spanish or Mexican local law in the territory were themselves sufficient to abolish slavery.

The Treaty of Guadalupe Hidalgo gave all inhabitants of the affected territory the option of becoming United States citizens or of relocating within the new Mexican borders. Although some moved to Mexico, the overwhelming majority remained at home in what had become United States territory. As a result, for the first time in the nation's history United States CITIZENSHIP was conferred on people who were not citizens of any state. This action added fuel to a constitutional debate about the relation of national citizenship to state citizenship, a debate that continued until the FOURTEENTH AMENDMENT was ratified in 1868.

The international border remained unmarked and for most purposes unreal. Until 1894 there was no formal control over the border; United States IMMIGRATION statistics recorded the arrival of Mexicans only at seaports. Many border areas remained integrated economic regions, with workers traveling in both directions to fill fluctuating labor demands. Many Mexicans, especially those in direct conflict with Americans in the border region, continued to think of the southwest as "lost" territory that was rightfully Mexico's. These views, long expressed by the Mexican government, are echoed among today's Chicanos in support of diffuse if underdeveloped positions concerning the legal (including constitutional) effects of the Treaty of Guadalupe Hidalgo: for example, that the territory rightfully belongs to Mexicans or Chicanos, or that United States violations of the treaty have voided its effects. Whatever one may think of such claims, one should appreciate the collective sense of group identification reflected in their public assertion.

GERALD P. LÓPEZ
KENNETH L. KARST

(SEE ALSO: *Compromise of 1850; Slavery in the Territories.*)

TREATY ON THE EXECUTION OF PENAL SENTENCES
24 U.S.T. 7399 (1977)

The Mexican-American Treaty on the Execution of Penal Sentences was signed on November 25, 1976. Legislation implementing the treaty became law on October 28, 1977. Since that time, thousands of prisoners have been exchanged under its provisions.

The treaty, a model for later agreements with countries such as Canada, responded to concerns about the treatment of Americans imprisoned in Mexican jails, concerns that became increasingly acute as the two countries in the 1970s began a crackdown on drug traffic from Mexico to the United States. Preexisting procedures for monitoring and improving the conditions of Americans incarcerated in Mexico, mainly action taken by United States consular offices, had proven unsatisfactory.

Under the treaty, any American imprisoned in Mexico can, with his consent and the consent of Mexico and the United States, be sent to serve his sentence in the American prison system. Mexican prisoners can similarly be transferred from the United States to Mexico. Once transferred, the prisoner's sentence can be reduced by any procedures such as parole or conditional release applicable in the receiving country. The treaty covers only acts criminal in both countries, and does not extend to political crimes or to infractions of IMMIGRATION laws or "purely military" laws.

The attorney general administers the obligations of the United States under the treaty. The implementing legislation requires the attorney general to verify the prisoner's consent to transfer, and also provides a right to appointed counsel during the verification proceedings should the prisoner be unable to pay.

Lower federal courts have held that the treaty does not violate the Constitution despite the fact that under it the United States incarcerates United States citizens whose trials may not have complied with the BILL OF RIGHTS.

GERALD P. LÓPEZ

(SEE ALSO: *Prisoners' Rights.*)

TREATY POWER

To enhance the pledged word of the United States in foreign relations, the Framers of the Constitution granted to the President, in cooperation with the Senate, the power to make and enter into treaties. They also provided that this power should vest exclusively in the federal government. The Framers neglected to define the term "treaty," however, leaving its meaning to subsequent clarification. Today, under international law, the term is used for all manner of formal instruments of agreement between or among nations that, regardless of the titles used, create relationships of reciprocal rights and obligations. Under United States law, the term "treaty" usually denotes only those international agreements that are concluded by the federal government and ratified by the President upon receiving the ADVICE AND CONSENT of the Senate. All other international agreements—EXECUTIVE AGREEMENTS, for example—are brought into force for the United States upon a constitutional basis other than senatorial advice and consent.

The process of treaty making involves negotiation, signature, ratification, exchange of instruments of rati-

fication, publication, and proclamation; but, other than prescribing that two-thirds of the senators present must give their advice and consent to the ratification of a treaty, the Constitution is silent on the subject. In the early days of the Republic, it was thought that the Senate would participate with the President by giving its advice and consent at every negotiating juncture. Today, it is the accepted practice for the President to solicit the advice and consent of the Senate only after a treaty has been negotiated and signed, although in many—especially important—instances, Senate and even House committees play active roles in advance of the conclusion of a treaty, sometimes on their own initiative, sometimes at the behest of the executive branch.

Once the negotiation of a treaty is complete, the President decides whether to sign the treaty and, if so, whether to submit it to the Senate for advice and consent to ratification. If the Senate is perceived as hostile, the President may choose to let the treaty die rather than suffer defeat. If the Senate receives the treaty, it refers the treaty to the Committee on Foreign Relations, which may or may not report the treaty to the full Senate for its advice and consent. Committee inaction is the usual method for withholding consent to controversial treaties. Sometimes the executive branch will request that the committee withhold or suspend action. Few treaties are defeated by direct vote of the full Senate.

After the Senate gives its advice and consent to ratification, often subject to "reservations," "understandings," and "declarations" initiated by the Senate or the executive branch itself (to clarify, alter, or amend the treaty), the treaty is returned to the President for ratification. The President may choose to ratify the treaty or to return it to the Senate for further consideration. The President also may choose not to ratify the treaty at that time.

After a treaty is ratified, which is a national act, some international act—typically the exchange or deposit of instruments of ratification—usually is required to bring the treaty into force. Also upon ratification, the President issues a proclamation making the treaty officially public. There is disagreement over whether proclamation of a treaty is constitutionally required before the treaty takes effect domestically, but it is the norm to issue such a proclamation which, in any event, is useful in determining the date on which the treaty enters into force.

The Constitution does not limit the treaty power explicitly. Moreover, no treaty or treaty provision has ever been held unconstitutional. Nevertheless, it is generally agreed that such limitations exist. For example, the Supreme Court held, in REID V. COVERT (1957), that treaties may not contravene any constitutional prohibition, such as those in the BILL OF RIGHTS or in the THIRTEENTH, FOURTEENTH, and FIFTEENTH AMENDMENTS. Further, although MISSOURI V. HOLLAND (1920) largely disposed of the argument that the subject matter of treaties is limited by the TENTH AMENDMENT, it remains possible, as the Court hinted in *DeGeofroy v. Riggs* (1890), that the treaty power may be limited by "restraints . . . arising from the nature . . . of the states."

Beyond these limitations, however, the treaty power is perceived as a broad power, extending to all matters of "international concern," a phrase that some claim limits the treaty power, but that the courts have used to illustrate the power's broad scope. Ordinarily it is difficult to show that a treaty matter is not of international concern even in the presence of domestic effects.

In addition to granting the power to make and enter into treaties, the Framers of the Constitution provided that resulting treaties, together with the duly enacted laws of the United States, should constitute part of the "supreme law of the land." Thus, as well as giving rise to international legal obligations, treaties have force as domestic law, to be applied as federal statutes and consequently to prevail at all times over inconsistent state laws (assuming no conflict with the Constitution).

Still, not all treaties are automatically binding on American courts. Aside from the general constitutionality requirement, two additional conditions must obtain for treaties to have domestic effect. First, a treaty must not conflict with a subsequent act of Congress. This is in keeping with the judiciary's interpretation of the SUPREMACY CLAUSE, ranking treaties and acts of Congress equally and therefore ruling that the law later in time prevails. With the sole exception of *Cook v. United States* (1933), cases in this area have involved conflicts between an earlier treaty and a later statute, with the latter prevailing. The courts presume, however, that Congress does not intend to supersede treaties, and consequently the courts are disposed toward interpretations that will achieve compatibility between treaties and federal statutes on the same subject.

Second, for a treaty to bind courts it must be "self-executing" or, alternatively, "non–self-executing" but supported by enabling legislation. Such was the holding in *Foster v. Neilson* (1829). Judicial decisions vary widely in their application of this requirement, however. The distinction between "self-executing" and "non–self-executing" treaties is more easily stated

than applied. A determination that a treaty fits one category or the other often may be shown to depend on subjective, at times political, considerations.

Although the Constitution is silent on the question of who has the power to suspend or terminate treaties and under what circumstances, it is generally accepted that the President has such power, *without* the advice and consent of the Senate, based on the President's established constitutional authority to conduct the foreign affairs of the United States. A challenge to the President's authority in this connection has thus far arisen only in the one case of GOLDWATER V. CARTER (1979), and that case was decided, on purely jurisdictional grounds, against the challenge. Were the Senate to consent to a treaty on the condition that its advice and consent would be required for the treaty's suspension or termination, however, such a condition might be binding on the President. Also, based on the power of Congress to declare war, it is arguable that the entire Congress (not just the Senate) might legitimately claim a voice in the termination of a treaty where such termination might threaten war.

BURNS H. WESTON

Bibliography

AMERICAN LAW INSTITUTE 1965 *Restatement of the Law, Second—Foreign Relations Law of the United States.* Pages 361–448. St. Paul, Minn.: American Law Institute.

———— 1980 *Restatement of the Law—Foreign Relations Law of the United States (Revised), Tentative Draft No. 1.* Pages 71–144. Philadelphia: American Law Institute.

FOSTER, J. 1901 The Treaty-Making Power under the Constitution. *Yale Law Journal* 11:69–79.

HENKIN, LOUIS 1972 *Foreign Affairs and the Constitution.* Mineola, N.Y.: Foundation Press.

MCLAUGHLIN, C. H. 1958 The Scope of the Treaty Power in the United States. *Minnesota Law Review* 42:709–771; 43:651–725.

WRIGHT, QUINCY 1919 The Constitutionality of Treaties. *American Journal of International Law* 13:242–266.

TRENCHARD, JOHN

See: Cato's Letters

TRESPASS

A person commits trespass when he or she enters or remains on the property of another without the permission of the property owner. Violation of trespass laws may result in civil action by the property owner or criminal prosecution. Constitutional issues arise in civil or criminal trespass actions when a defendant claims that the basis for his or her exclusion from the property violates the Constitution. A defendant may assert that she was excluded from the property because she engaged in an activity protected by the Constitution (such as the FREEDOM OF SPEECH protected by the FIRST AMENDMENT) or because she is a member of a constitutionally protected class (such as a racial group) disfavored by the property owner.

If a property owner uses the property to perform a public function or if the property owner has become associated with the government in the operation of a business located on the property, the owner may not exclude persons on a basis that is incompatible with constitutional values. A public function is an activity that traditionally has been within the exclusive province of government, such as the operation of a municipality. When a state allowed a private company to own and operate a company town, which included residential and business districts, the First Amendment protection for freedom of speech prohibited exclusion of a woman who wished to distribute religious literature within the town. Operation of a store or SHOPPING CENTER on privately owned property is not held to be a public function. Thus, the First Amendment is not violated when a shopping center owner relies on trespass laws to exclude persons from the shopping mall who wish to engage in speech, PICKETING, or distribution of leaflets.

The Supreme Court will not allow trespass laws to be used to exclude persons from private property because of their race or political activity if the property owner has been directed or encouraged by the government to use the trespass laws in such a discriminatory manner. The Court has held that statutes requiring or specifically allowing a restaurant owner to provide separate areas for customers of different races encouraged racial segregation so that the owner could not use the trespass laws to exclude persons seeking service on a race neutral, integrated basis. Similarly, the owner of a restaurant operated in a government building could not exclude persons from the premises because of their race.

Federal statutes or state law may also limit the use of trespass laws. The National Labor Relations Board, for example, may order store or shopping center owners to allow labor picketers to walk on privately owned sidewalks or parking lots adjacent to businesses involved in a labor dispute. A state supreme court may interpret its state constitution to prohibit shopping center owners from excluding persons who wish to

engage in political speech. These state and federal limitations on property owners' use of the trespass laws to exclude persons from their property do not violate any right guaranteed the property owners by the United States Constitution.

JOHN E. NOWAK

Bibliography

NOWAK, JOHN E.; ROTUNDA, RONALD D.; and YOUNG, J. NELSON 1983 *Constitutional Law.* Pages 497–525. St. Paul, Minn.: West Publishing Co.

VAN ALSTYNE, WILLIAM W. and KARST, KENNETH L. 1961 State Action. *Stanford Law Review* 14:3–58.

TREVETT v. WEEDEN
(Rhode Island, 1786)

A Rhode Island case of 1786, this is the best known of the alleged state precedents for JUDICIAL REVIEW. The Superior Court of Judicature, the state's highest tribunal, did not hold a state act unconstitutional but it did construe it in a manner that left it inoperative. The case arose under a force act passed by the legislature to compel observance of the state paper-money laws; anyone refusing to accept paper money at par with specie was triable without a jury or right of appeal "according to the laws of the land" and on conviction was subject to a 100 pound fine and costs or be committed "till sentence be performed." Trevett filed an INFORMATION before the state chief justice charging that Weeden refused tender of paper money at face value. James Varnum, representing Weeden, argued that the force act violated the right to TRIAL BY JURY, guaranteed by the unwritten state constitution, which was FUNDAMENTAL LAW that limited legislative powers; the legislature could make law "not repugnant to the constitution" and the judiciary had "the sole power of judging those laws . . . but cannot admit any act of the legislative as law, which is against the constitution."

The court refused to decide the issue, ruling that it lacked JURISDICTION. Its JUDGMENT was simply that Trevett's complaint "does not come under the cognizance of the Justices . . . and it is hereby dismissed." Orally, however, some of the judges, according to the newspaper accounts, declared the force act "to be repugnant and unconstitutional," and one of them pointed out that its phrase, "without trial by jury, according to the laws of the land," was self-contradictory and thus unenforceable.

The governor called the legislature into special session, and the legislature summoned the high court judges to explain their reasons, the legislature said, for holding an act "unconstitutional, and so absolutely void," an "unprecedented" judgment that tended "to abolish the legislative authority." Judge David Howell, the court's main spokesman, defended judicial review and judicial independence. Although he summarized Varnum's argument that the act was unconstitutional, Howell insisted that the legislature had confused the argument, for the judgment was just that the complaint was "cognizable."

The legislature, unconvinced by the court's technical distinction, recognized that the judgment made the paper money laws unenforceable; in effect the court had exercised judicial review, which the legislature deemed subversive of its supremacy. Howell, by contrast, had claimed that if the legislature could pass on the court's judgment, "the Legislature would become the supreme judiciary—a perversion of power totally subversive of civil liberty." Anticipating a motion to unseat them, the judges presented a memorial demanding DUE PROCESS OF LAW. Varnum and the attorney general supported them, arguing that they could not be removed except on a criminal charge. The motion to remove the judges failed, and the legislature even repealed the force act, but it revenged itself on the judges by failing to reelect four of the five members when their annual terms expired, and by ousting Congressman Varnum and the state attorney general. Varnum published a one-sided pamphlet on the case, giving it publicity even in Philadelphia while the CONSTITUTION CONVENTION OF 1787 met. Although the pamphlet popularized the doctrine of judicial review, in Rhode Island no judge endorsed it for seventy years after.

LEONARD W. LEVY

TRIAL BY JURY

The right to jury trial is provided in three clauses of the Constitution of the United States. Jury trial in federal criminal cases is required by Article III, which is otherwise given to defining the role of the federal judiciary: "The Trial of all Crimes, except in Cases of IMPEACHMENT, shall be by Jury." This provision is repeated in the Sixth Amendment, which is otherwise given to the rights of the accused: "In all criminal prosecutions, the accused shall enjoy the right to a speedy and PUBLIC TRIAL, by an impartial jury . . ." The BILL OF RIGHTS also included a provision for jury trial in civil matters; this right is embodied in the SEVENTH AMENDMENT: "In Suits at common law, where the value in controversy shall exceed twenty

dollars, the right of trial by jury shall be preserved. . . ."

The federal Constitution makes no explicit provision regarding the right to trial by jury in proceedings in state courts. State constitutions contain many similar provisions, although the interpretations of the right in state courts have varied significantly from the standards applied in federal courts. Substantial variation survived the enactment of the FOURTEENTH AMENDMENT, which for the first time subjected the state courts to the strictures of the DUE PROCESS clause. It was early held, and appears still to be the law, that the Fourteenth Amendment does not incorporate the Seventh, that there is no federal constitutional requirement of a right to jury trial in *civil* cases in state court. (See WALKER V. SAUVINET, 1875.) More recently, the Supreme Court has held that due process does require some form of access to a jury in major criminal prosecutions in state courts. (See DUNCAN V. LOUISIANA, 1968.)

Although the institution of jury trial has been known to American and English courts for a millennium, there have been significant changes in its form and nature over that period. Indeed, the origins of the institution are shrouded in the uncertainties of prehistory. Germanic tribes, like most stable societies, made early use of laymen in official resolution of disputes. Such practices were well known to Saxons and their neighbors at the time of the Norman Conquest in 1066. Nevertheless, at that time and place, more common resort was made to various ordeals, which were essentially religious services purporting to reveal the will of the deity. One variation on trial by ordeal was trial by battle, in which the Saxon disputants, or their champions, waged a ritual struggle to determine the side of the diety. Yet another variation was trial by wager of law, which engaged the services of the neighbors as oath helpers. By their willingness in numbers to risk salvation to stand up for a disputant, the oath helpers were perceived to express a divine will. In some sense witnesses and in some sense decision makers, these laymen can be viewed as early jurors. The nature, origin, and extent of the use of such institutions in the several shires of Saxon England doubtless varied and are the subject of some uncertainty.

The royal judges appointed by Norman kings embraced Saxon traditions, including trial by ordeal, oath helping, wager of law, and the use of laymen to share responsibility for official decisions. A papal decree in 1215, which withdrew the clergy from participation in trials by ordeal, had the effect of withdrawing the imprimatur of the deity from the decisions of the royal courts. This apparently stimulated interest in alternative methods of trial that might deflect some of the odium of decision from the royal surrogate. Thus, the PETIT JURY (to be distinguished from the GRAND JURY) emerged in more nearly contemporary form in the thirteenth century as a feature of the Norman royal courts.

Thirteenth-century jury trial emerged chiefly in proceedings of TRESPASS, a form of action in which the lash of royal power was applied to maintain the peace of the realm. As trespass and its derivative forms of action came to dominate the COMMON LAW, so trial by jury became the dominant method of trial in civil matters coming before the royal law courts. Thus, jury trial was associated with the various forms of trespass on the case (from which the modern law of torts emerged), of assumpsit (from which the modern law of contracts emerged), and of replevin, an action important to the development of personal property rights. Indeed, one reason for the demise of some of the earlier royal writs, such as the writ of right, or even the writ of debt, was dissatisfaction with the mode of trial that accompanied the use of such writs.

A concurrent evolution led to the emergence of the jury as an important element of criminal justice in the royal courts. The royal inquest was a feature of early Norman royal governance; it was an important device for centralizing power in the royal government and was a proceeding for calling local institutions and affairs to account. The grand jury was a group of local subjects of the crown who were called upon to investigate, or answer from their own knowledge, regarding the observance by their neighbors of the obligations imposed upon them by royal command. By stages, the inquest came to be followed by a further proceeding to impose royal punishment on apparent wrongdoers. In the latter half of the twelfth century, the royal government was initiating such enforcement proceedings, thus supplementing the trespass proceedings which had earlier provided protection for the peace of the realm, but only on the initiative of a victim of wrongdoing. By 1164, there was a clear beginning of the use of petit juries in crown proceedings. By 1275, it was established that the petit jury of twelve neighbors would try the guilt of an accused, provided the accused consented to such a means of trial, which he was coerced to do.

One major theme in the evolution of the right to jury trial in royal courts was the development of a system of accountability to constrain lawlessness by juries. For some time, the only method available to royal courts to deal with such behavior was to prosecute (or, more precisely, to attaint) the jurors for rendering a false verdict. If a second jury so decided, a jury could be punished for this offense. The harshness of this remedy led to its demise, for the attaint jurors were reluctant to expose an earlier jury to disgrace and punishment. In the seventeenth century the writ of attaint was gradually replaced by the practice of granting a new trial when the first verdict was against the weight of the evidence. This practice came to be equally applicable to criminal as well as civil proceedings, except insofar as an accused could not twice be placed in jeopardy of conviction. (See DOUBLE JEOPARDY.)

A second major theme in the evolution of the right to jury trial in civil cases was its confinement to the common law courts when the Chancery emerged as an alternative system of adjudicating the use of the royal power. English chancellors were exercising a form of judicial power as early as the fifteenth century. An important feature of the Chancery (or proceedings in EQUITY as they came to be known) was the absence of the jury. Another important feature was the use by the chancellor of a broader range of judicial remedies, most prominently including the INJUNCTION, which were personal commands of the judge under threat of punishment for contumacy.

Nineteenth-century English law reform ultimately brought about the demise not only of equity as a separate judicial system, but also of the right to jury trial in civil cases. In a search for greater efficiency and dispatch, the jury system in the law courts was modified and limited, so that the jury trial is now seldom used in the United Kingdom, or in other parts of the Commonwealth, except in criminal cases.

The right to jury trial took quite a different turn in the United States. At the time of the Revolution, that right came to be celebrated as a means of nullifying the power of a mistrusted sovereign; hence the several constitutional provisions guaranteeing the continued exercise of the right. Moreover, there was a special mistrust of equity (where the English recognized no right to jury trial) in eighteenth-century America, based in large part on its close connection to the royal power. Accordingly, some of the states abolished it, others conferred its powers on their legislatures, while only some retained its colonial forms or created state chanceries to continue the English tradition.

In many parts of the early United States, there was a widely shared mistrust of professional lawyers and of judges drawn from that profession. Mistrust of officials in general and professional judges in particular was a feature of the Jacksonian politics of the first half of the nineteenth century, which was reflected in provisions for the election of judges and the reaffirmation of the importance of jury trial as a means of deprofessionalizing the exercise of judicial power. These political impulses were magnified in the populism of the late nineteenth century.

Indeed, the American legal profession came to be shaped in important degree around the institution of the jury; jury advocacy became in the popular mind the central activity of the American lawyer. During much of the nineteenth century, the most powerful intellectual force in American law was the work of WILLIAM BLACKSTONE, an English scholar of the previous century. Blackstone's *Commentaries* (1776) was the one book read by almost all American lawyers, and perhaps the only law book read by some. By no coincidence Blackstone was a staunch advocate of the right to jury trial in civil cases, an institution already in decline in his own country; his belief in the institution of the lay jury was one of his strongest links to the frontier society which he so significantly influenced.

Beginning as early as 1848 in New York, most American states adopted "merged" systems of procedure in civil cases. Merger united law and equity in a single judicial system; reformers were careful to retain the right to jury trial in actions "at law" and in some states even extended it to some matters properly described under the former system as "suits in equity." Through most of the nineteenth century, the federal courts played a secondary role in the American legal system, and Congress required their procedures to conform "as near as may be" to the procedural legislation of the states in which they sat. For the most part, this conformity seemed to apply to the forms of jury practice as well as to other details of procedure. It was not until 1938 that the FEDERAL RULES OF CIVIL PROCEDURE were promulgated for the federal courts, for the first time formally merging law and equity in federal courts in accordance with national standards. The FEDERAL RULES OF CRIMINAL PROCEDURE soon followed. A national system or method of conducting jury trials in federal courts for defining the scope of the jury's power and the judge's responsibility and for prescribing the limits of the right to jury trial at last emerged.

For a period of several decades following the reform era of the 1930s, the Supreme Court made the protection of the right to jury trial in civil cases a major item on its agenda. A number of its decisions enlarged on previous expectations about the scope of the right and increased the authority of the jury, for example, BEACON THEATERS, INC. V. WESTOVER (1959) and ROGERS V. MISSOURI PACIFIC RAILROAD

Co. (Justice FELIX FRANKFURTER's dissent, 1957). Interest in the right to jury trial became very intense in the mid-1960s as a result of widespread CIVIL RIGHTS litigation, preoccupation with EQUAL PROTECTION, and the possible NULLIFICATION or impairment of federal law by locally selected juries.

In the last decade, there may have been some growth in consciousness of the disadvantages of jury trial in civil cases. Increasing attention has focused on trial efficiency, the effectiveness of the law, and alternative methods of dispute resolution. But it is too early to say that we have entered a period in which the distinctly American institution of jury trial will be seriously reexamined.

As much as for any procedural right, the beauty of the right to jury trial is in the eye of the beholder. For as long as there have been lay decision makers, there have been strong-minded critics and devoted defenders who have disputed the wisdom of the system with equal vehemence. The practice rests on values so basic and so unsuitable to proof or disproof that the debate seems unlikely to terminate. It is at least in part for this reason that so many reforms, from the Seventh Amendment to the Rules Enabling Act, sought to evade debate on the fundamental issues by ostensibly preserving the status quo in regard to the right to jury trial, leaving the issues of the scope of jury trial to other times and other forums. Rarely has Congress or any state legislature been able to address the merit of the right to jury trial without having its deliberative processes impaled on the sharp point of the debate. For the same reason, decisions to expand or contract, preserve or alter, existing practices have been and will continue to be greatly influenced by the predominance of one view or the other of the merits of the institution.

Supporters of the right to jury trial regard it as a keystone of democratic government. It is, indeed, a method of sharing power with those who are governed. It deflects the hostility toward public institutions otherwise engendered by the lash of public power. It is a remedy for judicial megalomania, the occupational hazard of judging. Particularly in regard to criminal legislation, the right to jury trial provides a limit on the power of legislatures who eventually must countenance the nonenforceability of laws which citizens are unwilling to enforce. It is also a means of education: jurors learn about the law and share their learning with families and neighbors. In all these respects, it engenders trust. In general, supporters and critics alike agree that those benefits are more substantial in criminal than in civil litigation.

Critics observe, however, that juries are inefficient

and may well be quite inaccurate in their perceptions and decisions. Involving many people in the making of a decision is inherently inefficient. It is necessary to invest time and expense in the selection of jurors. Trials proceed much more slowly because of the shorter attention span of lay persons in courtroom contexts and because additional participants entail additional interruptions and delays for personal reasons. Because of the inexperience of jurors, there has developed a substantial body of rules governing the admission of EVIDENCE which have as their purpose the protection of the jury from confusion and inflammation of prejudice. These strictures operate at times to increase the complexity of trials and to enlarge the possibility of mistrial or new trial, which is the result of error in the application of such rules of evidence. For these reasons, jury trials take substantially longer than nonjury trials and are substantially more expensive for the participants.

Moreover, as other critics emphasize, the deliberations of juries are undisciplined. Although jurors tend to be conscientious in the application of the governing law, the controlling rules are often dimly understood and not infrequently sacrificed in order to secure the requisite consensus. Whatever guidance or control the trial judge may supply, the chance of erratic decision is greater in jury than in nonjury trials.

Other adverse factors are less frequently mentioned. Jury service is in many cases a substantial burden to jurors; although they receive token payment, they are coerced to perform a duty that can sometimes be onerous. Particularly in communities characterized by disorder and social disintegration, jurors may even be frequent objects of intimidation and bribery; they are, in general, more difficult to protect from these vices than are judges, and they are perhaps also more vulnerable to such pernicious influences.

To a substantial degree, the perceived merits or demerits of the system will depend on particular features of the system which are designed to respond to the problems the system presents. Unfortunately, techniques for diminishing the demerits of jury trial often tend also to diminish its merits: the more control exercised over juries, the less advantage there is in assembling them. In the final analysis, almost every issue regarding the right to jury trial turns on the degree to which power is to be confided in professional officers of the law. Consensus on that basic issue being so distant a prospect, the contours of the institution as described below must be regarded as an unstable compromise, quite subject to change.

Instability is nowhere more clearly exemplified than in regard to JURY SIZE. Perhaps as early as the thirteenth century, Englishmen understood that a jury is a group composed of twelve persons. The method of selecting the jury might have varied, the duties assigned to the group may have been altered, but the one element of stability was their number, twelve. Some states experimented with the use of smaller juries, particularly in the trial of lesser crimes, and the Supreme Court in WILLIAMS V. FLORIDA (1970) held that the use of such groups as six is not itself a deprivation of due process of law. It was, however, long presumed that a common law jury is twelve and that such a number was required in federal courts by the Sixth and Seventh Amendments, unless a smaller number be agreed to by the parties. This presumption is reflected in the language of Federal Rule of Civil Procedure 48, which authorizes parties to agree to smaller juries.

Nevertheless, most federal district courts have in the last decade adopted local rules of court designating civil juries to consist of six persons. The validity of these local rules was sustained by the Supreme Court in *Colegrove v. Battin* (1973). The Court rested its decision on the absence of any straightforward legislative prohibition on juries of less than twelve and on the dubious assumption that there were no solid data demonstrating that twelve-person juries reach substantially different verdicts from six-person juries. The Court also manifested a conviction that six-person juries are more efficient than those composed of larger numbers, a conviction which is itself not amenable to solid empirical proof. However, in BALLEW V. GEORGIA (1978) the Court held that a five-member group was too small to be properly deliberative, representative, and free from intimidation and therefore did not afford due process. The Court's decisions have stimulated increased interest in the scientific examination of judicial institutions; the decisions have also called into question other traditional presumptions about juries, none of which carries more historical weight than did the tradition of twelve.

A second traditional feature of the common law jury has been the requirement of JURY UNANIMITY in reaching a verdict. Some states have experimented with the acceptance of verdicts supported by juries that are less than unanimous. In general, such provisions have called for super-majorities, such as a vote of ten or twelve jurors. The Supreme Court held in *Minneapolis and St. Louis Railway Co. v. Bombolis* (1916) that such provisions were not denials of due process for state court proceedings involving issues of federal law, but later, in BURCH V. LOUISIANA (1979), it invalidated a Louisiana law that authorized verdicts of conviction on the basis of a five-to-one vote of a six-person jury. Despite these variations at the state level, however, the unanimity requirement remains a standard feature of federal jury practice, unless, as the Federal Rules authorize in civil cases, the parties agree on a lesser majority.

One effect of the unanimity requirement is to assure that the jury will deliberate on its decision rather than settle for a mere nose count. A secondary effect is to increase the likelihood that no decision will be reached, with the result that a new trial before a new jury will be required, unless the controversy is privately resolved without further litigation. A third effect is to enhance the role and responsibility of each individual juror, making each an important actor with power to control the ultimate outcome of the process. To the extent that the jury is intended to be a representative body, the unanimity requirement tends to protect litigants and interests that are associated with minority groups.

A third important feature of traditional common law jury practice was the mode of selecting the jury. Using the Norman nomenclature, the court administrative arm assembles a VENIRE of citizens from whom the jury will be selected. Veniremen may be excused or disqualified by the judge and those remaining are then subject to a further process of selection by the parties. The latter process, known as VOIR DIRE examination, proceeds from a questioning of the jurors to their challenge by the parties on grounds of cause, or peremptorily if the parties would simply prefer other members of the venire. Peremptory challenges have perhaps always been limited in number, a somewhat larger number being allowed in criminal than in civil cases.

In recent decades, this traditional process has been subject to substantial criticism and pressure. Criticism proceeds from the premise that the jury should be in some degree representative of the community it helps to govern. Most of the criticism has been directed at the process of selecting veniremen, the usual earlier practice in this country having been to authorize a court administrator to select prospective jurors by methods that were usually elitist in premise and effect. In many communities, the usual method was the "key man" system, which invoked the assistance of community leaders to identify citizens of stature who would be deserving of the trust reposed in jurors. Such systems were common in federal courts. Indeed, it was not uncommon for a federal court to maintain a BLUE RIBBON list of veniremen of more than ordinary intelligence and experience who might be summoned to decide cases requiring more than ordinary skill on the part of the decision maker. Such methods

produced juries that were anything but representative, in the proportional sense, of the communities from which they were selected.

In a legal environment favoring egalitarianism, such practices were doomed. As early as 1945, in *Thiel v. Southern Pacific Co.*, the Supreme Court upheld a challenge by a federal litigant to a venire selection method that seemed likely to result in underrepresentation of the working class in local jurors. In *Carter v. Jury Commission of Greene County* (1970), the Supreme Court refused to declare a state key-man system invalid on its face absent a showing that the scheme was purposefully adopted as a means of preventing some group (usually blacks) from being represented. Nevertheless, when such a scheme underrepresents a group consistently, a prima facie case of JURY DISCRIMINATION is established and the scheme may then be found unconstitutional as applied, as in *Turner v. Fouche* (1970). Congress anticipated these holdings by enacting federal jury selection legislation in 1968. Current legislation does repose some authority in local federal courts to administer jury selection, on condition that their methods produce juries that bear proximate resemblances to randomness. Of course, individual litigants are not entitled under the statute or the Constitution to have a jury that actually reflects the demography of the community; all that is assured is that the method of selection be one that is reasonably likely to produce such a panel.

In recent years, mounting attention has been given to the process of peremptory challenge and the practice of some local prosecutors to use these challenges to prevent minority representation on particular juries, especially those called to try minority members on serious criminal charges. The Supreme Court has held that a prosecutor's use of peremptory challenges in any single case is immune from attack; the Court held in SWAIN V. ALABAMA (1965) that the very concept of peremptory challenges entailed the right to act without explanation. Still, the Court did leave open the possibility that systematic use of peremptories to exclude members of some group might be found to violate the equal protection guarantee of the Fourteenth Amendment. In subsequent cases, however, proving to the Court's satisfaction that systematic discrimination did exist has been virtually impossible. Some state courts have gone beyond the federal standards and ruled that peremptory challenge of veniremen on the basis of membership in any group violates provisions of their state constitutions, for example, California in *People v. Wheeler* (1978).

Partly as a result of the practice of making juries

more representative, a new issue has arisen regarding the competence of juries to deal with intricate technical disputes beyond the ken of ordinary citizens. The Third Circuit Court of Appeals held in *Matsushita Electric Industrial Company v. Zenith Radio Corporation* (1980) that the Seventh Amendment is subject to the Fifth Amendment, that the use of juries in very complex civil cases may be a denial of due process of law. This question, also, has not reached the Supreme Court.

Litigants having a right to jury trial are entitled to a jury decision only on questions of fact, not on matters of law. The distinction between questions of fact and law can be stated clearly enough: the former pertain to the specific events in dispute; the latter to the legal principles to be applied. But the application of the distinction is often problematic. For this reason, juries often have to deal with issues containing substantial elements of legal interpretation. The classic example, which arises in both civil and criminal contexts, is a decision applying a general standard of negligence to the conduct of the accused or the defendant; the general standard takes more specific shape in the minds of jurors as they apply it to the events at hand.

Since the seventeenth century, it has been the responsibility of the trial judge to assure that the controlling law is obeyed by the jury; the trial judge is accountable to the appellate court for the effective performance of this duty. There are several steps in the usual common law jury trial at which the trial judge is obliged to perform this function.

A major function of the judge at a jury trial is to instruct the jury on the controlling law. This instruction is usually the last event before the jury retires to deliberate. If either party makes a timely objection to the judge's statement of law in his charge to the jury, any error in the instructions will be a solid ground for reversal.

In a civil trial, the judge should not instruct the jury at all unless there is a dispute in the evidence presented which might raise some doubt in a reasonable mind or about which jurors might reasonably differ. If the judge finds that there is no such dispute, he should direct the jury to find a verdict for the part entitled under the law to JUDGMENT. In cases of doubt about the application of this standard, the judge may prefer to reserve his ruling on a motion for directed verdict until after the jury has rendered a verdict. If the verdict is rendered contrary to the law, the judge may then enter a judgment notwithstanding the verdict in favor of the verdict loser. The Supreme Court has held in *Baltimore and Carolina*

Line v. Redman (1935) that the judge may not take this latter step unless the motion for directed verdict was timely and the question properly reserved; otherwise, there is a violation of the Seventh Amendment because the judgment notwithstanding the verdict was unknown to English practice at the time of adoption of the Amendment.

In a criminal case the judge should direct a verdict for the accused when the prosecution has failed to offer proof of one or more elements of the offense charged. But the trial judge may not direct a verdict of guilty in a criminal case; to this extent, the Sixth Amendment assures the role of the jury as a bulwark against punishment deemed oppressive by the community, even if the punishment is required by the positive law. An element of natural justice is thereby introduced to the legal system.

In addition to his role as law officer, the trial judge also has some responsibility for the quality of fact-finding done by the jury. In either civil or criminal cases, he may set aside a verdict as contrary to the weight of the evidence. When exercising this prerogative, the trial judge is obliged to order a new trial before a second jury. In a criminal case, the power to order the new trial is confined by the constitutional constraint against double jeopardy. In a civil case, the power to grant a new trial may be exercised conditionally, but this power is subject to constitutional limitations. A conditional order of new trial is likely to occur where the trial judge regards a jury verdict as correct on the matter of liability but excessive in regard to the award of damages.

Some factual issues arising in jury-tried cases may be reserved for the judge. For example, in civil cases, issues of fact arising in a determination of the jurisdiction of the court must be decided by the judge. In criminal cases, sentencing is a function of the judge, not the jury, although the wisdom and propriety of the sentence often require factual determination.

With the exceptions noted, the division of function between judge and jury in federal courts has not been deemed a matter for constitutional adjudication. *A fortiori*, state practice in respect to these issues has not generally been regarded as presenting any constitutional problems of due process of law. The Supreme Court, however, has on occasion intervened to reverse state court judgments in actions arising under federal law on the ground that the federal law posed an issue for a jury which under the state practice was incorrectly left to the decision of a judge. Particularly in cases arising under the federal EMPLOYERS LIABILITY ACT, the Court was strict in limiting the role of the trial judge. Its decisions, based upon statutory grounds, may indicate that state jury practice must meet federal standards when state courts are called upon to enforce federal law. It is even possible that the Seventh Amendment will be found to be applicable to litigation of federal claims in state courts, not by reason of the Fourteenth Amendment, but by an inference of congressional intent.

The Sixth Amendment applies only to criminal proceedings that could have been tried by a jury at the time of its adoption in 1791. Even at that time, it was well understood that "petty" offenses might be tried without a jury. Federal legislation gives specific meaning to such offenses as those involving a punishment of imprisonment for six months or less and fines of $500 or less. In BALDWIN V. NEW YORK (1970) the Supreme Court held that due process requires jury trial in state court prosecutions for offenses involving imprisonment for more than six months. In *Bloom v. Illinois* (1968) the Court applied a similar standard to punishments imposed for contempt of court, although it conceded that there was some historical basis for treating contempt as a matter between litigant and judge, particularly where the contumacious act is committed in the presence of the court. In MCKEIVER V. PENNSYLVANIA (1971), however, the Court held that the right to jury trial is not applicable to a proceeding to determine the delinquency of a juvenile, even though a decision adverse to the juvenile might result in imprisonment for a period significantly in excess of six months; such proceedings, the Court said, are not strictly criminal because they involve less moral judgment about the conduct of the juvenile.

The Seventh Amendment has proved much more complex and troublesome. One major question has been the applicability of the amendment to claims brought under federal legislation enacted after the adoption of the amendment. A narrowly historical view would preclude the application of the right to such legislation-based claims, since they are not strictly actions "at common law." The Court has, however, generally extended the right to jury trial to statutory actions where the remedy pursued in the judicial proceeding was one that resembled a common law remedy. Thus, in *Pernell v. Southall Realty Co.* (1974) the Court held that there was a right to jury trial in a statutory action of eviction that was closely analogous to a common law action for ejectment. And in *Curtis v. Loether* (1974) the Court held that there was a right to jury trial in an action brought under the fair housing provisions of the CIVIL RIGHTS ACT OF 1964 because the remedy sought was compensatory damages of the sort that might have been recoverable in a common law action of trespass on the case.

In other cases, however, the Court has approved legislation creating administrative procedures and remedies that displace common law rights and thus eliminate jury-triable actions. In *National Labor Relations Board v. Jones & Laughlin Steel Corp.* (1937), the Court upheld the award of back pay in proceedings before the board, despite the close analogy to common law contract actions. This decision was extended in *Atlas Roofing Co. v. Occupational Safety and Health Administration* (1977), in which the Court upheld legislation providing for the recovery by a government agency of a civil penalty in a court proceeding where there was no right to jury trial. The Court emphasized that the case involved a "public right," to be distinguished from common law rights of private parties. In *Lorillard v. Pons* (1978) the Court interpreted the legislature to intend a statutory right to jury trial in proceedings brought under the AGE DISCRIMINATION ACT. In that case, as in *Curtis*, the Court avoided any indication of the applicability of the Seventh Amendment to the employment discrimination provisions of the Civil Rights Act, which, like the Age Discrimination Act, provides for back pay awards to be made by courts, not administrative agencies.

The most complex issues of the scope of the right to jury trial arise in complex litigation where matters that are within the compass of the Seventh Amendment coincide with other matters outside that compass. In general, the Supreme Court has tended to insist upon protection of the right to jury trial in such situations, even at the risk of submitting to a jury matters that would not be jury-triable if litigated alone. Illustrative is DAIRY QUEEN, INC. V. WOOD (1962) in which the plaintiff sought both an injunction and compensatory damages. Injunctive relief, unlike compensatory damages, is an equitable rather than a legal remedy and so is not subject to the right of trial by jury. The trial court deemed the injunction to be the primary relief sought and undertook to try the case without a jury, albeit with the intention of seating a jury to decide the measure of damages should it appear that a wrong had been committed. The Supreme Court reversed, holding that the jury-triable claim for damages must be tried first in order to protect the constitutional right to jury trial, leaving it for the judge later to decide on the availability of injunctive relief if the jury should determine that a wrong had been committed. Similarly, in BEACON THEATERS, INC. V. WESTOVER (1959) the Court held that a jury-triable counterclaim would have to be tried first, before a determination could be made on a related claim by the plaintiff that was not jury-triable.

These cases illustrate that the constitutional right to jury trial now tends to depend on the specific substantive right and remedy involved in the litigation, not on the general (common law or equity) context in which that right is disputed. This approach was illustrated in *Ross v. Bernhard* (1970), in which the Court held that a claim brought by a shareholder on behalf of the CORPORATION was jury-triable when the claim would have been triable by a jury had it been brought by the corporation itself; this decision would seem to be applicable as well to claims for damages brought by class representatives. This is so even though the procedures of STOCKHOLDER SUITS and CLASS ACTIONS are derived from the equity tradition, not from the practices of law courts. Thus, the increasingly widespread use of complex procedural devices that unite equitable and legal matters may in fact operate to enlarge the practical scope of the right to jury trial. This seems true despite the disclaimers set forth in such law reforms as the Federal Declaratory Judgment Act and the Federal Rules Enabling Act, which express the intent not to alter the existing scope of the right. That intent was not practicably attainable consistent with achieving the other aims of the procedural reforms, which include efficiency and dispatch.

On the other hand, a rule that the Seventh Amendment right to jury trial depends on the substantive right and remedy involved in the litigation is not always applied. Illustrative is *Katchen v. Landy* (1966), which upholds the power of the court to determine without a jury claims brought against a bankrupt estate, whether or not the claims might have been jury-triable if asserted directly against the bankrupt. The Court emphasized the practical needs of the bankruptcy system for dispatch in making such decisions; it was said that these considerations justified Congress in directing that they be made without juries. Thus, the scope of the constitutional right to jury trial in civil cases is a complex question, drawing heavily on historical analogues but also influenced by considerations of contemporary practicality. It is not a static right, but it is likely to take on new dimensions in the hands of future courts.

It may be concluded that the right of accused persons to a trial by jury has become a deeply entrenched feature of criminal litigation in the United States, broadly protected by the Sixth and Fourteenth Amendments, with the selection and role of the jury being aspects of the right that are themselves subject to constitutional control. The right to jury trial in civil cases, on the other hand, rests upon a different constitutional provision, which is inapplicable in state courts and may be somewhat less rigidly maintained even in federal courts, for the reason that it is less assuredly beneficial to the citizens to be protected.

PAUL D. CARRINGTON

Bibliography

DAWSON, JOHN P.   1962   *A History of Lay Judges.* Cambridge, Mass.: Harvard University Press.
HELLER, FRANCIS H.   1951   *The Sixth Amendment to the Constitution of the United States.* Lawrence: University of Kansas Press.
JAMES, FLEMING   1963   Right to Jury Trial in Civil Cases. *Yale Law Journal* 72:655–693.
KALVEN, HARRY and ZEISEL, HANS   1966   *The American Jury.* Boston: Little, Brown.
MCCART, SAMUEL N.   1964   *Trial by Jury.* Philadelphia: Chilton Books.
SCHULTZ, MARJORIE S., ED.   1980   The American Jury. *Law and Contemporary Problems.* Durham, N.C.: Duke University.
SPOONER, LYSANDER   1852   *An Essay on the Trial by Jury.* Boston: John P. Jewett Co.
VAN DYKE, JON M.   1977   *Jury Selection Procedures.* Cambridge, Mass.: Ballinger.
WOLFRAM, CHARLES   1973   The Constitutional History of the Seventh Amendment. *Minnesota Law Review* 57:639–747.

TRIMBLE, ROBERT
(1776–1828)

Robert Trimble, appointed to the Supreme Court by JOHN QUINCY ADAMS on April 11, 1826, was born in Virginia and raised in Kentucky. He studied law, began practice in Paris, Kentucky, and became one of the leading lawyers of the state with a specialty in land litigation. To the Supreme Court he brought an independence of character, a respect for legality, and considerable judicial experience. From 1807 to 1808 he served on the Kentucky Court of Appeals and from 1817 to 1826 on the federal district court. His years on the district bench corresponded to a period of political-economic upheaval during which Kentucky openly resisted federal ADMIRALTY JURISDICTION and federal judicial interference with state relief measures. Both as district judge and as circuit partner with his friend Justice THOMAS TODD, Trimble held the line for federal judicial authority and objective legality as he saw it—so firmly in fact that he was threatened with IMPEACHMENT.

His integrity, ability, and nationalism won him an appointment to the Court on Todd's death. He served only twenty-seven months before his own death but long enough to have won the respect of JOHN MAR-SHALL and JOSEPH STORY; Story eulogized him as belonging "to that school, of which Mr. Chief Justice Marshall (himself a host) is the acknowledged head and expositor." Trimble spoke for the Court only fifteen times; ironically his lone constitutional opinion in OGDEN V. SAUNDERS (1827) called forth Marshall's only dissent in a constitutional case. The question was whether a state bankruptcy law applying to contracts made after the passage of the law was a violation of the CONTRACT CLAUSE. Trimble's clear-headed, practical opinion upholding state power remained controlling for most of the nineteenth century despite the dissents of Marshall and Story.

R. KENT NEWMYER

Bibliography

STORY, JOSEPH 1829 Memoir of Judge Trimble. *American Jurist and Law Magazine* 1:149–157.

TRIMBLE v. GORDON
430 U.S. 762 (1977)

A year before this decision, the Supreme Court had refused, in *Mathews v. Lucas* (1976), to hold that ILLEGITIMACY was a SUSPECT CLASSIFICATION requiring strict judicial scrutiny. In *Trimble*, a 5–4 majority invalidated an Illinois law that prevented illegitimate children from inheriting from their fathers who had not made wills. Discriminations based on illegitimacy, said Justice LEWIS F. POWELL for the majority, must be "carefully attuned to alternative considerations." Although paternity might be hard to prove in some cases, wholesale disinheritance of illegitimate children was unjustified. In this case a judicial paternity proceeding had determined the decedent to be the father.

Justice WILLIAM H. REHNQUIST dissented at length, criticizing the development of modern EQUAL PROTECTION doctrine. Except for classifications based on race or national origin, he would abandon all forms of STRICT SCRUTINY, requiring no more than a RATIONAL BASIS for legislative discrimination. Laws classifying according to legitimacy of parentage deserved no more heightened judicial scrutiny than did "other laws regulating economic and social conditions."

Only a year later, in LALLI V. LALLI (1978), a fragmented Court made *Trimble*'s precedential status uncertain.

KENNETH L. KARST

TROP v. DULLES
356 U.S. 86 (1958)
PEREZ v. BROWNELL
356 U.S. 44 (1958)

In two cases decided the same day the Supreme Court ruled on the constitutionality of the EXPATRIATION provisions of the Nationality Act of 1940. In *Perez* the Court held (5–4) that revocation of CITIZENSHIP for voting in a foreign election was a valid exercise of governmental control over FOREIGN AFFAIRS.

In *Trop*, however, the Court held unconstitutional (5–4) the involuntary expatriation of a wartime deserter. Chief Justice EARL WARREN, for a plurality, contended that expatriation is CRUEL AND UNUSUAL PUNISHMENT; but WILLIAM J. BRENNAN, the one justice who changed sides, argued only that Congress's power over citizenship is less extensive when foreign affairs are not involved.

DENNIS J. MAHONEY

TRUAX v. CORRIGAN
257 U.S. 312 (1921)

A 1913 Arizona law, similar to the labor provisions of the CLAYTON ANTITRUST ACT, prohibited state court INJUNCTIONS against peaceful PICKETING. Following a dispute with restaurant proprietor William Truax, a local union peacefully picketed and distributed handbills calling for a BOYCOTT. Truax's business receipts dropped dramatically, and after the Arizona courts denied him relief, he appealed to the Supreme Court, contending that the state law deprived him of his property without DUE PROCESS OF LAW and violated the EQUAL PROTECTION clause of the FOURTEENTH AMENDMENT.

Chief Justice WILLIAM HOWARD TAFT, speaking for a 5–4 majority, held the state statute unconstitutional. He reasoned that Truax held a property right in his business; free access to it by employees and customers was incidental to that right. Concerted action that intentionally injured that right was a conspiracy and a tort. In this case, the union's activities constituted an "unlawful annoyance and hurtful nuisance." Such wrongs, Taft concluded, could not be remediless, and he declared that the anti-injunction law deprived Truax of due process. He also ruled that the law violated equal protection by limiting the application of an injunction to a particular class.

JUSTICE LOUIS D. BRANDEIS, dissenting, maintained that even if the employer had a constitutional right to be free from boycotting and picketing, the state was not compelled to protect that right with an injunction, as states were free to expand or control their EQUITY jurisdiction. In a separate dissent, Justice OLIVER WENDELL HOLMES argued that the state law was a valid "social experiment," however "futile or even noxious." Beyond that, he challenged the assumption equating "business" with a property right. Business, he asserted, was "a course of conduct," and like any other was subject to modification regarding what would justify doing it a harm.

STANLEY I. KUTLER

TRUMAN, HARRY S.
(1884–1972)

The thirty-third President began his career in local Democratic politics in Missouri. Truman served in various capacities, including county judge and planning official, and helped coordinate employment and relief programs during the early 1930s. After his election to the United States Senate in 1934, he supported the New Deal programs and specialized in transportation policy. Declining President FRANKLIN D. ROOSEVELT's offer of an appointment to the Interstate Commerce Commission, he was reelected to the Senate in 1940. During the war years he attracted notice as the effective chairman of a Senate investigating committee established to oversee the efficiency and fairness of defense contracting. Elected vice-president in 1944, he succeeded to the presidency the next year when Roosevelt died. He returned to the White House in 1949 for a second term, following an unexpected election victory.

Truman believed in a strong and active presidency, operating within a Constitution sufficiently flexible to accommodate executive initiatives for the public good. The Framers of the Constitution, Truman said, had deliberately left vague the details of presidential power, allowing the "experience of the nation to fill in the outlines." He disagreed with scholars who claimed that history makes the man: "I think that it is the man who makes history." His roster of favorite Presidents included GEORGE WASHINGTON, THOMAS JEFFERSON, ANDREW JACKSON, ABRAHAM LINCOLN, GROVER CLEVELAND, THEODORE ROOSEVELT, WOODROW WILSON, and Franklin Roosevelt.

Although criticized at times by liberals for providing inadequate leadership and action on CIVIL RIGHTS, Truman's record is impressive. In 1946 he created the President's Committee on Civil Rights. A year later it issued an important document, *To Secure These Rights*, that took a firm stand against various forms of RACIAL DISCRIMINATION. In 1948 Truman issued EXECUTIVE ORDER 9981, ending discrimination in the armed services, and in that same year delivered a powerful civil rights message to Congress and supported the inclusion of a civil rights plank in the Democrats' platform.

Truman's commitment to the BILL OF RIGHTS was tested by the issue of subversion that overshadowed his administration. As a student of history he was keenly aware of the hysteria that had fanned repressive episodes, from the Salem witch trials to the Red Scare of 1919. He felt prepared to handle the new cycle that took the form of anticommunism and indiscriminate labeling of "subversives." (See SUBVERSIVE ACTIVITIES AND THE CONSTITUTION.)

EXECUTIVE ORDER 9835, issued by Truman in 1947, established procedures to control subversive infiltration of the federal government. The effect was to deprive agency employees of fundamental elements of DUE PROCESS, including the right to receive specific charges against them and to confront their accusers. Even when an accused received clearance from a loyalty board, the data remained in the files, forcing the employee to answer the same charges with each move to a new job. Truman later admitted that the program, which thrived on secret evidence and secret informers, was filled with defects and injustices.

Truman began to give closer attention to CIVIL LIBERTIES. In a message to Congress on August 8, 1950, he warned that pending legislation on internal security would forbid dissent. When the internal security bill reached his desk in the fall of 1950, he delivered a ringing denunciation, protesting in his veto message that the bill would put government in the "thought control business." Especially objectionable to him was a provision requiring "Communist-front" and "Communist-action" groups to register with the attorney general. This placed on the government the responsibility for probing the "attitudes and states of mind" of organization leaders. Groups could be linked to the Communist party whenever their positions failed to "deviate" from those of the Communist movement. Thus, any organization dedicated to low-cost housing or other humanitarian goals espoused by the party could be branded a communist front. Truman called this feature "the greatest danger to FREEDOM OF SPEECH, press and assembly, since the ALIEN AND SEDITION LAWS of 1798." The veto message, delivered in the midst of an election campaign that featured charges from some Republicans about Democrats being soft on communism, was courageous and principled. Within a day both Houses of Congress easily overrode the veto. (See INTERNAL SECURITY ACT.)

Following North Korea's invasion of the south in June 1950, Truman dispatched American soldiers to Korea without seeking congressional support or approval. A month later the State Department issued a belated memorandum defending the President's legal authority to repel the attack. The memo claimed that Truman's action was justified by international law, the UNITED NATIONS CHARTER, "and the resolution pursuant thereto." However, the United Nations issued *two* resolutions on Korea, one of June 25 calling for the cessation of hostilities and the withdrawal of North Korean forces to the 38th parallel, and a second resolution (adopted two days later) recommending armed force to repel the attack. Truman intervened militarily before passage of the second resolution. (See KOREAN WAR.)

Truman placed General Douglas MacArthur in command of American forces in Korea. MacArthur wanted to widen the military front, probing deeply into North Korea. He objected repeatedly, in public, to the limited war policy adopted by the administration. Eventually he alienated Truman, top cabinet officials, the Joint Chiefs of Staff, and the National Security Council. Over the course of almost a year, Truman became convinced that MacArthur was untrustworthy and insubordinate, but his abrupt dismissal of the general on April 11, 1951, triggered a storm of protest across the nation. In explaining his decision, Truman said it was fundamental that "military commanders must be governed by the policies and directives issued to them in the manner provided by our laws and Constitution."

Only a few members of Congress questioned Truman's authority to send troops to Korea, but as part of a "Great Debate" in 1951, legislators challenged his constitutional power to send ground forces to Europe. Resolutions were introduced in each house to require congressional authorization before military forces could be sent abroad. Although these measures were not enacted, uneasiness about the scope of presidential war-making power persisted. After President LYNDON B. JOHNSON's commitment of American troops to Southeast Asia and subsequent military actions there by President RICHARD M. NIXON, Congress passed the WAR POWERS RESOLUTION of 1973 to restrict the President's military powers. (See EMERGENCY POWER.)

Truman's attitude about presidential power and constitutional constraints is illuminated by his 1952 seizure of steel mills. He believed that a pending strike would prevent production of materials needed for the war in Korea. (See EXECUTIVE ORDER 10340; STEEL SEIZURE CONTROVERSY.) At a news conference on April 17 he was asked whether his INHERENT POWERS permitted seizure of newspapers and radio stations. To the consternation of the press he replied that the President could act "for whatever is for the best of the country." A week later, complaining that speculation about him seizing the press and the radio was "hooey," he stated that he had "difficulty imagining the Government taking over and running those industries." Continuing to respond to concerns about his views of emergency power, on April 27 he wrote in a letter that presidential powers are "derived from the Constitution, and they are limited, of course, by the provisions of the Constitution, particularly those that protect the rights of individuals."

Meanwhile, the Justice Department was developing a different scenario for District Judge David Pine. Assistant Attorney General Homer Baldridge told Pine on April 24 that "there is not power in the Courts to restrain the President. . . ." After Pine had declared the seizure invalid, Truman claimed at a news conference on May 22 that "nobody" (including Congress and the Court) could take from the President his power to seize private property and to protect the welfare of the people. However, he said that he would abide by the Supreme Court's verdict, and when the decision fell on June 2 (see YOUNGSTOWN SHEET & TUBE CO. V. SAWYER, 1952), declaring the seizure invalid, he immediately ordered the government to relinquish possession of the mills.

Often careless with his remarks at press conference, for which he paid dearly, Truman came to the White House with a solid understanding of history and governmental institutions and processes. He maintained a deep respect for individual rights and civilian government. Through his personal integrity and honesty he helped moderate many of the repressive forces that operated during his years in office.

LOUIS FISHER

Bibliography

HAMBY, ALONZO L. 1973 *Beyond the New Deal: Harry S. Truman and American Liberalism.* New York: Columbia University Press.
TRUMAN, HARRY S. 1960 *Mr. Citizen.* New York: Bernard Geis.
_____ 1955 *Year of Decisions.* Garden City, N.Y.: Doubleday.
_____ 1956 *Years of Trial and Hope.* Garden City, N.Y.: Doubleday.

TRUMBULL, LYMAN
(1813–1896)

An Illinois state supreme court judge (1848–1853) and United States senator (1855–1873), Lyman Trumbull opposed all slavery expansion before 1861, and during the SECESSION crisis he argued that the Constitution already adequately protected slavery and no amendments, concessions, or compromises were necessary. A strong supporter of the Union war effort, Trumbull nevertheless believed that the war should be fought within the framework of the Constitution. Thus, he opposed President ABRAHAM LINCOLN's unilateral suspension of HABEAS CORPUS, arbitrary arrests, and the closing of northern newspapers. Nonetheless, he supported legislation authorizing such actions. Trumbull gave mild support to the EMANCIPATION PROCLAMATION but doubted its constitutionality, and thus he introduced the resolution which led to the THIRTEENTH AMENDMENT. As chairman of the Senate Judiciary Committee during the war and Reconstruction, Trumbull initiated the first and second CONFISCATION ACTS, the CIVIL RIGHTS ACT OF 1866, the FREEDMEN'S BUREAU Extension Act (1866), and the first civil service reform legislation (1870). Despite his opposition to slavery and support of CIVIL RIGHTS, Trumbull was at heart a white supremacist and only reluctantly voted for the FIFTEENTH AMENDMENT. He opposed both punitive legislation for southern states that discriminated against blacks and the 1871 Ku Klux Klan Act, because of his lack of sympathy for blacks and his refusal to accept the fact that the Civil War had radically altered the nature of STATES' RIGHTS. He gave unenthusiastic support for ANDREW JOHNSON in 1865–1866, and, although disgusted with Johnson's vetos of his Civil Rights and Freedman's Bureau Bills, Trumbull voted against conviction of Johnson in the trial following IMPEACHMENT because he doubted Johnson had committed an impeachable act under the Constitution. A successful corporate lawyer, Trumbull argued EX PARTE MCCARDLE (1867) at the express request of General ULYSSES S. GRANT and was paid $10,000 for his services, even though he was a senator at the time. In 1876 Trumbull unsuccessfully argued the cause of Samuel Tilden before the Election Commission that considered the disputes over the Tilden-Hayes presidential election. (See COMPROMISE OF 1877.) Late in life he supported populism and the rights of workers, and in his last Supreme Court case he defended the labor organizer Eugene V. Debs in IN RE DEBS (1895).

PAUL FINKELMAN

Bibliography
KRUG, MARK M. 1965 *Lyman Trumbull: Conservative Radical.* New York: A. S. Barnes & Co.

TRUPIANO v. UNITED STATES

See: Search and Seizure; Search Incident to Arrest

TUCKER, HENRY ST. GEORGE
(1780–1848)

A political leader, scholar, and jurist, Henry St. George Tucker studied law under his father, ST. GEORGE TUCKER. He was a congressman (1815–1819), state judge (1824–1841), and professor of law at the University of Virginia (1841–1848). In his classroom lectures and in his textbook entitled *Lectures on Constitutional Law* (1843), he took a moderate STATES' RIGHTS position, steering, as he said, "a middle course between [the] dangerous extremes" of NULLIFICATION and centralization. His book is intended as a refutation of the nationalist position of JOSEPH STORY, but, although he regarded the Constitution as a compact among the states, he rejected nullification and SECESSION as remedies for violations by the federal government.

DENNIS J. MAHONEY

Bibliography
BAUER, ELIZABETH KELLEY 1952 *Commentaries on the Constitution, 1790–1860.* New York: Columbia University Press.

TUCKER, JOHN RANDOLPH
(1823–1897)

A political leader, scholar, and attorney, John Randolph Tucker was the son of HENRY ST. GEORGE TUCKER and the grandson of ST. GEORGE TUCKER. He was attorney general of Virginia (1857–1865), congressman (1875–1887), professor of law at Washington and Lee University (1870–1875, 1888–1897), and president of the American Bar Association (1894). From his retirement from Congress until his death he worked on his two-volume commentary, *The Constitution of the United States,* which was published posthumously in 1899. Tucker continued the family's tradition of STATES' RIGHTS constitutionalism, proposing that the TENTH AMENDMENT was the key to understanding the Constitution. He was strikingly influenced by European political theorists, including J. K. Bluntschli, and rejected the ideas of NATURAL RIGHTS, human equality, and SOCIAL COMPACT in favor of the concept of an organic state.

DENNIS J. MAHONEY

TUCKER, N. BEVERLEY
(1784–1851)

Jurist, scholar, and novelist Nathaniel Beverley Tucker developed his political views under the influence of his half-brother, JOHN RANDOLPH. As a judge and politician in Missouri (1815–1830) he fiercely resisted the MISSOURI COMPROMISE. Later, as a professor of law at William and Mary College (1834–1851) he was one of the most extreme advocates of a STATES' RIGHTS interpretation of the Constitution. He argued that SOVEREIGNTY resided in the several states and that the people of Virginia were obliged to obey federal law only because Virginia commanded them to do so. He defended slavery and supported NULLIFICATION. His novel, *The Partisan Leader* (1836), advocated SECESSION and predicted a civil war.

DENNIS J. MAHONEY

Bibliography

BAUER, ELIZABETH KELLEY 1952 *Commentaries on the Constitution, 1790–1860.* New York: Columbia University Press.

TUCKER, ST. GEORGE
(1751–1827)

St. George Tucker, who became known as the "American Blackstone," wrote the first commentary on the Constitution since THE FEDERALIST, a book that he recommended as a "masterly discussion." After a dozen years as a judge in Virginia, Tucker succeeded GEORGE WYTHE, with whom he had studied law, as professor of law at the College of William and Mary. Using WILLIAM BLACKSTONE's *Commentaries on the Laws of England* as his text, Tucker updated and domesticated Blackstone in his lectures, showing how the English law had changed in the United States and in Virginia. His lectures led in 1803 to the publication in five volumes of an annotated edition of Blackstone. Notwithstanding Tucker's 1,400 notes, the most creative parts of his work are to be found in his appendices, which run to 425 pages in the first volume,

mostly an analysis of the United States Constitution. Although Tucker preferred a "federal" to a "consolidated" Union, he was a moderate who defended the American constitutional system, championed democracy, opposed SLAVERY, and made constructive criticisms. The appendix argued against a FEDERAL COMMON LAW OF CRIMES. Volume two's appendices included an extended proposal for the gradual abolition of slavery and a libertarian essay on FIRST AMENDMENT freedoms, in which Tucker discoursed on the reasons that religion, speech, and press should be "absolute" and "unrestricted," except for laws against personal defamation. Tucker's edition of Blackstone led to his appointment to the highest court of Virginia, where he served with distinction, followed in 1813 by an appointment as a United States district judge. Tucker held that position until shortly before his death. He ranks with the best of Jeffersonian jurists and theorists.

LEONARD W. LEVY

TUCKER ACT
24 Stat. 505 (1887)

Thirty-two years after establishing the Court of Claims, Congress enacted the Tucker Act, expanding that court's JURISDICTION to decide claims against the United States. Henceforth, the court might decide not only contract claims but also claims against the government founded on the Constitution and other damage claims not based on tort. Today the act confers jurisdiction over such cases on the United States CLAIMS COURT, along with jurisdiction over claims founded on various federal statutes and regulations. If the amount in controversy in such a case is less than $10,000, the UNITED STATES DISTRICT COURT exercises CONCURRENT JURISDICTION—thus allowing persons with small claims to bring suit in their home districts rather than in Washington, D.C. The act creates no substantive rights but merely provides jurisdiction in cases in which the government's liability is founded on other principles of law. In effect, however, the act amounts to a waiver of the federal government's SOVEREIGN IMMUNITY, in recognition of the vital principle that government should not be above the law.

KENNETH L. KARST

(SEE ALSO: *Federal Tort Claims Act.*)

Bibliography

WRIGHT, CHARLES A.; MILLER, ARTHUR R.; and COOPER, EDWARD H. 1985 *Federal Practice and Procedure,* 2nd ed. Vol. 14:270–294. St. Paul, Minn.: West Publishing Co.

TUGWELL, REXFORD G.
(1891–1979)

Economist Rexford Guy Tugwell was a member of President FRANKLIN D. ROOSEVELT's "brain trust" and an advocate of centralized economic planning by the federal government. After serving as under-secretary of agriculture and governor of Puerto Rico, he began a second career as a historian and constitutional theorist. His books on the Roosevelt years include *The Democratic Roosevelt* (1957, 1969) and *The Brains Trust* (1968). Tugwell's years as a government official convinced him that only a rewriting of the Constitution, emphasizing provisions for centralization, economic planning, and emergency powers, would produce an effective form of government. He denounced as undemocratic the accepted principles of JUDICIAL REVIEW, FEDERALISM, and SEPARATION OF POWERS, and he stressed the need for total revision of the Constitution rather than gradual evolution through judicial interpretation. Tugwell frequently published his own proposals for a rewritten constitution. In *The Emerging Constitution* (1975) his proposals included: reduction of the states to administrative districts of a unitary national government; expansion of executive power, including EXECUTIVE PRIVILEGE; curtailment of the judiciary's power to pass judgment on actions of the national government to supervise the economy; and periodic revision of the Constitution through a simplified AMENDING PROCESS.

RICHARD B. BERNSTEIN

TUITION GRANTS

While parents have a constitutional right to send their children to private rather than public schools (see PIERCE V. SOCIETY OF SISTERS, 1925), the exercise of that right costs money. Such parents not only bear their share of the taxes that support public schools but also pay tuition to their children's schools. Not surprisingly, a regular item of business in Congress and the state legislatures is a proposal to relieve this "double burden" through some form of governmental relief. Two types of constitutional problems beset such proposals. Governmental aid to private schools may be attacked as STATE ACTION that promotes racial SEGREGATION or as an unconstitutional ESTABLISHMENT OF RELIGION.

Soon after the decision in BROWN V. BOARD OF EDUCATION (1954–1955), a number of southern states adopted a series of devices aimed at evading DESEGREGATION. One such device was the payment of state grants to private schools or to parents of private school children. The assumption was that when public schools were ordered to desegregate, white children would be withdrawn and placed in private schools. Some states went so far as to give local school boards the option of closing public schools and even selling those schools' physical plants to the operators of private schools which would be supported by tuition subsidized by the state. These private schools, it was expected, would be limited to white students. (More recently, federal CIVIL RIGHTS legislation has been applied to forbid that type of "segregation academy" to refuse black applicants. See RUNYON V. MCCRARY, (1976.) The Supreme Court held these tuition grant programs unconstitutional as evasions of *Brown* in cases such as GRIFFIN V. COUNTY SCHOOL BOARD (1964) and *Poindexter v. Louisiana Financial Assistance Commission* (PER CURIAM, 1968).

More recently, private schools in the North and West have acquired new white students following orders desegregating urban school systems. "White flight" means not only the departure of white families for the suburbs but also the transfer of white students from public to private schools. Estimates in the late 1970s suggested that as many as one-fifth of all enrollments in the nation's private schools were the result of "white flight." Proposals for governmental aid to private school children and their parents must therefore face a challenge based on the likely racially discriminatory impacts of various proposed forms of aid. Such impacts would not, of themselves, establish a constitutional violation; they would, however, be some evidence of an improper governmental purpose. (See LEGISLATION.)

Tuition grants limited to low-income parents of children enrolled in religious schools were held to violate the establishment clause in COMMITTEE FOR PUBLIC EDUCATION V. NYQUIST (1973). That decision did not settle the question of the constitutionality of a hypothetical program in which the state gave *all* parents education vouchers, to be used to support schools of their choosing, public or private, religious or secular. (See GOVERNMENT AID TO RELIGIOUS INSTITUTIONS; MUELLER V. ALLEN, 1983.)

Proponents of voucher plans designed to aid private schools and their clienteles have gone to some lengths in an effort to tailor their proposals to meet these two types of constitutional objection. One proposal provides elaborate incentives for racial integration, such as bonuses for integrated schools. In the absence of strong incentives of some kind, it seems obvious that significant aid to private elementary and secondary education will have the effect of increasing racial segregation by increasing the educational mobility of middle class whites.

KENNETH L. KARST

Bibliography

SUGARMAN, STEPHEN D. 1974 Family Choice: The Next Step in the Quest for Equal Educational Opportunity? *Law and Contemporary Problems* 38:513–565.

TWELFTH AMENDMENT

The ELECTORAL COLLEGE, as contemplated in Article II of the Constitution, was to be a kind of "search committee," nominating outstanding men of various regions from among whom Congress would elect the President and vice-president. The Framers expected each elector to cast his first vote for a candidate from his home state and his second for a national figure from another state. The delegates to the CONSTITUTIONAL CONVENTION assumed that the primary electoral divisions in the country were, and would remain, sectional.

The rise of POLITICAL PARTIES, which began almost immediately after the Constitution went into effect, belied that assumption. The parties nominated candidates, and the Electoral College had only to choose between the party slates; sectional loyalties were subordinated to ideological ones. In 1796, when party discipline was still developing, the Electoral College chose a Federalist President and a Republican vice-president. In 1800 straight party voting produced a tie between THOMAS JEFFERSON and AARON BURR, the Republican nominees for President and vice-president, respectively. The disgraceful performance of the House of Representatives, which required thirty-five ballots to ratify the voters' choice, led directly to adoption of the Twelfth Amendment.

The amendment provided that the electors would vote for President and vice-president in separate ballots; if no candidate obtained a majority of electoral votes, the House of Representatives (voting by states) would elect the President and the Senate the vice-president. Introduced by Senator DeWitt Clinton of New York, the amendment faced congressional opposition from Federalists and representatives of small states, each group fearing that its influence on presidential selection would be diminished. Once Congress proposed the Twelfth Amendment in 1804, the necessary thirteen states ratified it in less than six months—only the TWENTY-SIXTH AMENDMENT (1971) was ratified more quickly.

DENNIS J. MAHONEY

TWENTIETH AMENDMENT

Congress proposed the Twentieth Amendment, sponsored by Senator GEORGE W. NORRIS of Nebraska, on March 2, 1932; ratification was completed on January 23, 1933. The amendment provided that the President, vice-president, and Congress begin their terms in the January following their election. Under the old scheme of Article I, section 4, congressmen had not taken their seats until thirteen months after their election, and a short "lame duck" session in election years included members who had already been defeated. The amendment also made provisions for PRESIDENTIAL SUCCESSION and authorized Congress to provide for a situation in which a President-elect or vice-president-elect does not qualify by inauguration day.

DENNIS J. MAHONEY

TWENTY-FIFTH AMENDMENT

Congress proposed the Twenty-Fifth Amendment in July 1965, and ratification by the state legislatures was completed in February 1967. The amendment revised the constitutional provisions dealing with PRESIDENTIAL SUCCESSION, specifically providing that when a vacancy occurs in the office of President the VICE-PRESIDENT becomes (rather than "acts as") President. The amendment also provides for the orderly transfer of executive power in the event of a temporary presidential disability and for filling a vacancy in the office of vice-president.

DENNIS J. MAHONEY

Bibliography

FEERICK, JOHN D. 1976 *The Twenty-Fifth Amendment.* New York: Fordham University Press.

TWENTY-FIRST AMENDMENT

The Twenty-First Amendment repealed the EIGHTEENTH AMENDMENT and rescinded the constitutional mandate for national PROHIBITION of alcoholic beverages. Congress proposed the amendment in February 1933; RATIFICATION was complete in December 1933. To the extent that the VOLSTEAD ACT depended upon the constitutional authority of the Eighteenth Amendment, that statute became inoperative upon the passage of the Twenty-First Amendment.

The second clause of the Twenty-First Amendment prohibits transportation or importation of intoxicating liquors into states or territories in contravention of local law. The clause apparently gives the states power to regulate interstate commerce in alcoholic beverages, including the authority to discriminate against out-of-state producers and distributors, thus freeing the states, as far as liquor is concerned, from COMMERCE CLAUSE restrictions. The Supreme Court has upheld that interpretation in several cases, notably *State Board v. Young's Market* (1936). The Court suggested an even broader scope for state regulatory power under the amendment in *California v. LaRue* (1972), when it upheld a regulation banning sexually explicit entertainment in licensed taverns, and in *Elks' Lodge v. Ingraham* (1973), when it upheld a statute denying liquor licenses to private clubs that practiced RACIAL DISCRIMINATION.

The Twenty-First Amendment is the only constitutional amendment to have been ratified by state conventions rather than by the state legislatures. Congress chose this variant of the AMENDING PROCESS because proponents of repeal feared that antiliquor sentiment was dominant in many state legislatures, because of the overrepresentation of rural areas.

DENNIS J. MAHONEY

TWENTY-FOURTH AMENDMENT

The Twenty-Fourth Amendment, written by Senator Spessard Holland of Florida, was proposed by Congress on August 27, 1962, and became part of the Constitution on February 4, 1964. The amendment provides that the right of United States citizens to vote for federal officers shall not be denied or abridged for nonpayment of a POLL TAX or other tax.

A poll tax is simply a per capita tax and has no necessary relationship to election polling. However, several southern states made payment of the poll tax an electoral qualification in order to diminish the VOTING RIGHTS of black citizens. Bills to abolish the practice were introduced every year from 1939 on, and Holland, who believed statutory abolition to be beyond Congress's power, introduced his amendment every year from 1949 on.

By 1964, only five states retained payment of the poll tax as a qualification for voting. Because the Twenty-Fourth Amendment governed only federal elections, four states divided their elections, continuing to require poll tax payment for voting in state elections; but the Supreme Court held, in HARPER V. VIRGINIA BOARD OF ELECTIONS (1966), that this practice violated the Constitution by denying EQUAL PROTECTION OF THE LAWS.

DENNIS J. MAHONEY

TWENTY-SECOND AMENDMENT

Although, as ALEXANDER HAMILTON explained in THE FEDERALIST #69, the President was "to be re-eligible as often as the people of the United States shall think him worthy of their confidence," a constitutional custom dating back to the administration of GEORGE WASHINGTON limited the President of the United States to two terms in office. In 1940, however, with the Great Depression finally coming to an end and with most of the world already engaged in World War II, FRANKLIN D. ROOSEVELT sought and won election to a third term. He was subsequently elected to a fourth term, although he died sixty days after that term began.

The Twenty-Second Amendment makes the two-term limit a part of the formal Constitution. Congress proposed the amendment in March 1947 and RATIFICATION was complete four years later.

The effect of the amendment on the balance of power between the executive and the legislature is not clear. Hamilton, who personally had advocated a life term for the President, speculated in *The Federalist* #71 that Presidents would become more submissive to Congress as elections approached; and DWIGHT D. EISENHOWER argued during his second term that his ineligibility for reelection was a guarantee that he was more disinterestedly public-spirited than congressmen who opposed him. In the 1980s, on the other hand, journalists and political scientists who had come to see elections as retroactively legitimating, rather than prospectively legitimating, began referring to President RONALD REAGAN as a "lame duck" even before his second inauguration.

The two-term limit is no longer controversial. Ever since the CONSTITUTIONAL CONVENTION OF 1789 there have been proposals for limiting the President to a single term, generally longer than four years, but none of these has ever been seriously considered as a constitutional amendment.

DENNIS J. MAHONEY

TWENTY-SIXTH AMENDMENT

Congress proposed the Twenty-Sixth Amendment on March 23, 1971. Ratification was completed in 107 days, the shortest time ever required to complete the

AMENDING PROCESS. The amendment standardized the voting age in all federal, state, and local elections at eighteen.

Under the Constitution the power to establish qualifications for voting in all elections was left to the states, except that the qualifications to vote for representatives in Congress (and, after the SEVENTEENTH AMENDMENT, for senators) had to be the same as those to vote for members of the most numerous branch of the state legislature. Under various amendments, VOTING RIGHTS could not constitutionally be denied or abridged on account of race, color, previous servitude, sex, or failure to pay taxes; the FOURTEENTH AMENDMENT set twenty-one as the highest minimum age a state could require for voters. Before 1970 only four states had enacted a minimum voting age lower than twenty-one.

In the VOTING RIGHTS AMENDMENTS of 1970, Congress purported to lower the voting age to eighteen for all elections. The Supreme Court, in OREGON V. MITCHELL (1970), upheld the statute, insofar as it pertained to federal elections, under Article I, section 4, which authorizes Congress to regulate the time and manner of elections of its members; but the Court held the act unconstitutional insofar as it pertained to state elections. The decision threatened to throw the 1972 elections into chaos, because in most states the voting age for balloting for federal officials would have been different from the voting age for state races. The rapidity with which the amendment was ratified is attributable to a general desire to avoid such chaos.

Although Congress, in proposing the amendment, expressed confidence in the "idealism and concern and energy" the new voters would bring to the political system, the actual effect of the amendment has been less than revolutionary. Empirical studies have shown that eighteen-to-twenty-one-year-olds have the lowest voter turnout rate of any age group; and those who do vote do not differ markedly from the rest of the population concerning political parties or issues.

DENNIS J. MAHONEY

TWENTY-THIRD AMENDMENT

Proposed by Congress on June 17, 1960, the Twenty-Third Amendment became effective on March 29, 1961. The amendment includes residents of the DISTRICT OF COLUMBIA in the process of electing the President and vice-president by allowing them to choose members of the ELECTORAL COLLEGE. The influence of the district is limited by the proviso permitting it no more electoral votes than the least populous state—in practice fixing the district's electoral votes at three.

As the amendment was introduced by Senator Kenneth Keating, of New York, it would have allocated the District of Columbia as many electoral votes as a state with the same population and would have permitted the district to elect representatives to Congress on the same basis. Representative Emmanuel Celler, of New York, chairman of the House Judiciary Committee, reduced it to its final form in order to insure passage. Celler's committee also separated the District of Columbia suffrage amendment from two other amendments (on Congressional vacancies and POLL TAXES) to which the Senate had linked it.

There was some opposition from Republicans, who predicted the district would inevitably support Democratic candidates, and Southerners, who feared the amendment would increase the political power of blacks.

DENNIS J. MAHONEY

TWINING v. NEW JERSEY
211 U.S. 78 (1908)

Twining formed part of the line of decisions, from HURTADO V. CALIFORNIA (1884) and MAXWELL V. DOW (1900) to PALKO V. CONNECTICUT (1937), in which the Supreme Court denied that the traditional Fifth and SIXTH AMENDMENT rights of accused persons were FUNDAMENTAL RIGHTS protected against state infringement by the FOURTEENTH AMENDMENT. In *Twining*, an eight-man majority, speaking through Justice WILLIAM H. MOODY, held that neither the PRIVILEGES AND IMMUNITIES clause nor the DUE PROCESS clause incorporated the RIGHT AGAINST SELF-INCRIMINATION. The Court also considered whether some of the personal rights safeguarded by the BILL OF RIGHTS might be safeguarded against the states because to deny those rights would be to deny due process of law. That is, apart from the question whether the Fourteenth Amendment's protection of immunities and liberty had the effect of incorporating the Fifth Amendment right, the Court also decided the question whether the concept of due process itself was of such a nature as to include the right against self-incrimination. Was a denial of that right a denial of due process?

Although Moody admitted that the Court would

not allow history to "strait-jacket" constitutional law, he resorted to "every historical test" to determine how history "rated" the right in question. Moody was a pathetically poor historian; his mangling of the little evidence he knew led him wrongly to conclude that the right against self-incrimination was neither a fundamental right nor part of due process of law. On that reading of history he decided that the state had not violated the Constitution by permitting a trial court to instruct the jury that they might draw adverse inferences against a defendant because of his reliance on the right against self-incrimination or his failure to testify.

Justice JOHN MARSHALL HARLAN delivered another lone dissenting opinion, arguing that immunity against self-incrimination, like the right to INDICTMENT by GRAND JURY and the right to TRIAL BY JURY, should be deemed fundamental and applicable to the states. Whether he believed that the privileges and immunities clause or the due process clause, or both, incorporated the right is not clear; but he certainly believed it to be essential to due process.

At the time the Court held a narrower view of PROCEDURAL DUE PROCESS, it used an expanded SUBSTANTIVE DUE PROCESS to protect CORPORATIONS and prevent Congress from protecting trade unions (see ADAIR V. UNITED STATES, 1908). ADAMSON V. CALIFORNIA (1947) reaffirmed *Twining*, but the Court overruled both cases in MALLOY V. HOGAN (1964).

LEONARD W. LEVY

(SEE ALSO: *Incorporation Doctrine.*)

TWO GUYS FROM HARRISON-ALLENTOWN v. MCGINLEY

See: Sunday Closing Laws

TWO-LEVEL THEORY

In an important 1960 article, Harry Kalven, Jr., coined the phrase "two-level theory." As he described it, FIRST AMENDMENT methodology classified speech at two levels. Some speech was so unworthy as to be beneath First Amendment protection: no First Amendment review was necessary. Thus the Court in CHAPLINSKY V. NEW HAMPSHIRE (1942) had referred to "certain well-defined and narrowly limited classes of speech, the prevention and punishment of which has never been thought to raise any constitutional problem. These include the lewd and obscene, the profane, the libelous, and the insulting or fighting words." At the second level, speech of constitutional value was protected unless it presented a CLEAR AND PRESENT DANGER of a substantive evil.

In a subsequent article Kalven observed that in NEW YORK TIMES V. SULLIVAN (1964) neither the two-level approach nor the clear and present danger test was an organizing strategy or guiding methodology. He expressed the hope that the *Sullivan* Court's unwillingness to employ the two-level theory presaged the theory's demise along with the clear and present danger test. Kalven's hopes have been only partially realized. Perhaps partly as a result of his persuasive efforts, the Court has been willing to scrutinize state justifications for regulating some types of speech previously thought to raise no constitutional problem. *Chaplinsky*'s off-hand assumption that each class of speech in its litany raises no constitutional problem is no longer credible. Nonetheless, the Court continues to be impressed by *Chaplinsky*'s famous OBITER DICTUM that speech beneath the protection of the First Amendment occupies that status because its slight contribution to truth is outweighed by the state interests in order and morality.

Kalven's hope for the complete repudiation of the clear and present danger doctrine also remains unfulfilled. A variation of the doctrine occupies a secure doctrinal place in the context of INCITEMENT TO UNLAWFUL CONDUCT, and the DENNIS V. UNITED STATES (1951) version of the test has been employed by the Court in other contexts, as in *Landmark Communications, Inc. v. Virginia* (1978) and NEBRASKA PRESS ASSOCIATION V. STUART (1976).

If doctrine were described today in terms of levels, many levels would be necessary. At one level, there is the question whether a First Amendment problem is presented: an effort to communicate a message by assassination presumably raises no First Amendment problem. If cognizable First Amendment values are present, there remains the question whether any legal protection is appropriate: advocacy of illegal action often is unprotected despite the existence of cognizable First Amendment interests. If some protection is appropriate, further questions remain: what protection in what contexts, at what times, in what places, and concerning what modes of expression? A multitude of doctrinal tests now govern a multitude of contexts. Harry Kalven would appreciate the Court's sensitivity to the vicissitudes of human conduct, but likely would regret the absence of an overall vision.

STEVEN SHIFFRIN

Bibliography

KALVEN, HARRY, JR. 1960 The Metaphysics of the Law of Obscenity. *Supreme Court Review* 1960:1–45.

—— 1964 The New York Times Case: A Note on "The Central Meaning of the First Amendment." *Supreme Court Review* 1964:191–221.

TWO SOVEREIGNTIES RULE

This rule, which the Supreme Court repudiated in *Murphy v. Waterfront Commission* (1964), was a limitation on the RIGHT AGAINST SELF-INCRIMINATION. Based on the federal principle that one sovereignty has no interest in the law enforcement activities of another, the rule was that a person could not refuse to testify on the grounds that his disclosure would subject him to prosecution by another sovereignty or JURISDICTION. Thus he could be convicted of a federal crime on the basis of testimony compelled in a state proceeding or of a state crime on the basis of testimony compelled in a federal proceeding. In matters involving national supremacy, Congress can grant immunity against state prosecutions, but a state cannot immunize against a federal prosecution and one state cannot immunize against prosecution in another.

The rule entered American constitutional law in 1906 in *Hale v. Henkel* as a result of the Court's factual mistakes. In that case the appellant, who had received a grant of immunity against federal prosecution, sought reversal of his conviction for contempt by a federal court for refusing to answer questions that exposed him to state prosecution. The Court needlessly declared that English COMMON LAW had settled the question by a rule that "the only danger to be considered is one arising within the same jurisdiction and under that same sovereignty." The Court cited two English cases, one not in point and the other soon discredited by a decision unknown to the Court. In *United States v. Murdock* (1933), a unanimous Court "definitely settled that one under examination in a federal tribunal could not refuse to answer on account of probable incrimination under state law," a proposition resting on *Hale* and the two English precedents. By 1944 the Court made the two sovereignties rule reciprocal, so that a suspect could be whipsawed into incriminating himself in one jurisdiction by receiving a grant of immunity from another. State and federal authorities sometimes assisted each other, one compelling disclosure, the other prosecuting. So matters stood until the *Murphy* case.

Although granted immunity by New York and New Jersey, Murphy remained silent because his answers might incriminate him under federal law. He won a reversal of his conviction when the Supreme Court, in an opinion by Justice ARTHUR J. GOLDBERG, exposed the erroneous basis of the precedents and concluded that the two sovereignties rule had no support in history or in the policies underlying the Fifth Amendment right. On the same day, in MALLOY V. HOGAN (1964), the Court extended that right to the states. Given that extension and a broad view of the right, the Court held that a state witness is protected against incrimination under both federal and state law and a federal witness is similarly protected. Justices BYRON R. WHITE and POTTER STEWART concurred separately. *Murphy* also stands for the proposition that use immunity rather than TRANSACTIONAL IMMUNITY satisfies the demand of the Fifth Amendment at least in a two sovereignties case.

A two sovereignties rule still operates with respect to DOUBLE JEOPARDY: a person may be prosecuted for both state and federal crimes committed by the same act.

LEONARD W. LEVY

TYLER, JOHN
(1790–1862)

A Virginia lawyer, governor, and United States senator, John Tyler, a Democrat elected vice-president as a Whig in 1840 became America's first accidental President upon the death of WILLIAM HENRY HARRISON in 1841. This peaceful transition of leaders underscored the strength of the Constitution even though it frustrated the Whig politicians who had nominated Harrison. As President, Tyler was usually a constitutional strict constructionist, and many of his policies resembled those of ANDREW JACKSON. Tyler refused to interfere with the SOVEREIGNTY of Rhode Island during Dorr's Rebellion, but he was an early advocate of Texas annexation which was accomplished in the last months of his administration. In 1861 Tyler chaired the Washington Peace Conference, but after its failure he advocated SECESSION. The only former President to serve the Confederacy, Tyler was elected to the provisional Congress and the Confederate House of Representatives.

PAUL FINKELMAN

Bibliography

MORGAN, ROBERT J. 1954 *A Whig Embattled: The Presidency of John Tyler.* Lincoln: University of Nebraska Press.

TYSON & BROTHER v. BANTON
273 U.S. 418 (1927)

Citing Chief Justice WILLIAM HOWARD TAFT's opinion in WOLFF PACKING COMPANY v. COURT OF INDUSTRIAL RELATIONS (1923), Justice GEORGE SUTHERLAND found unconstitutional a New York statute regulating ticket "scalpers." The state based the law on a declaration that theater prices were AFFECTED WITH A PUBLIC INTEREST, but because the theater business did not fit Taft's categories, the law fell as a violation of FREEDOM OF CONTRACT and a denial of DUE PROCESS OF LAW.

Justice OLIVER WENDELL HOLMES dissented: "a state legislature may do whatever it sees fit to do unless it is restrained by some express prohibition in the [federal or state] constitution." Justice LOUIS D. BRANDEIS joined him and Justice HARLAN FISKE STONE wrote a separate dissent. All three urged rejection of the public interest concept—"a fiction intended to beautify what is disagreeable to the sufferers"—in favor of state regulation wherever the public welfare demanded it.

DAVID GORDON

(SEE ALSO: *Ribnik v. McBride, 1928; New State Ice Company v. Liebmann, 1932.*)

U

ULLMANN v. UNITED STATES
350 U.S. 422 (1956)

Ullmann, relying on his right not to be a witness against himself, refused to testify before a federal GRAND JURY concerning his alleged communist activities. Though he received immunity against prosecution for any criminal transaction concerning which he was compelled to testify, he continued pertinacious. Ullmann argued against the constitutionality of the congressional Immunity Act of 1954 on the grounds that it did not immunize him from such disabilities as loss of job, expulsion from labor unions, compulsory registration as a subversive, passport ineligibility, and general public opprobrium. Thus he distinguished his case from BROWN v. WALKER (1896) on the theory that he had not received full transactional immunity. The Court rejected Ullmann's argument, 7–2. Justice FELIX FRANKFURTER for the majority reasoned that the Fifth Amendment's right to silence operated only to prevent the compulsion of testimony that might expose one to a criminal charge. The disabilities to which Ullmann claimed exposure were not criminal penalties. Justices WILLIAM O. DOUGLAS and HUGO L. BLACK, dissenting, would have held the immunity act unconstitutional on the ground that the right of silence created by the Fifth Amendment is beyond the reach of Congress. Douglas contended that the amendment was designed to protect against INFAMY, as well as prosecution, and against forfeitures—those disabilities of which Ull-

mann spoke—as well as criminal fines and imprisonment.

LEONARD W. LEVY

(SEE ALSO: *Right against Self-Incrimination.*)

ULTRA VIRES

(Latin: "Beyond powers.") This term applies either to acts taken by a CORPORATION beyond the limits of its chartered (legally authorized) powers or to acts of a public official beyond his or her delegated authority.

DAVID GORDON

"ULYSSES," ONE BOOK ENTITLED, UNITED STATES v.
5F. Supp. 182 (1933); 72 F.2d 705 (1934)

Although it was not a decision of the Supreme Court, *Ulysses* was not merely a case involving a famous book and prominent judges but also a harbinger of modern decisions on OBSCENITY. Its standards for construing the COMMON LAW terms embodied in federal customs regulations were transmuted in UNITED STATES v. ROTH (1957) into constitutional principles for testing both federal and state legislation on the subject.

The handful of early obscenity cases that reached the Supreme Court mainly presented claims of technical error in the trials below. *Ulysses* presented clear questions of substantive standards for adjudging obscenity and lewdness. The established reputation of the book insured careful attention; Judge John M. Woolsey's lower court opinion was unmistakably written for the anthologies it ultimately graced. Judge AUGUSTUS N. HAND's appellate majority opinion was straightforward, but Judge Martin T. Manton's dissent was somewhat verbose.

Woolsey declared that the book successfully showed "how the screen [sic] of consciousness with its ever-shifting kaleidoscopic impression carries, as it were on a plastic palimpsest, . . . a penumbral zone residual of past impressions . . . not unlike the result of a double or, if that is possible, a multiple exposure on a cinema film. . . ."

The relevant statute on importation of books prohibited not pandering but obscenity. Woolsey announced without discussion that the test for obscenity required examination of the whole work. The standard was the effect on "what the French would call *l'homme moyen sensuel*—who plays, in this branch of legal inquiry . . . the same role . . . as does the "reasonable man in the law of torts. . . ." With this standard he found the book "somewhat emetic, nowhere . . . an aphrodisiac." He also found Joyce to have been sincere and lacking pornographic intent or the "leer of the sensualist."

At the appellate level Augustus Hand for himself and LEARNED HAND managed to come to grips with the central legal issue—whether isolated passages could render a work of art obscene. This was the test derived from *Regina v. Hicklin* (1868), the classic British case, and, they conceded, followed in *United States v. Bennett* (1879), a CIRCUIT COURT decision by Justice SAMUEL BLATCHFORD. They discounted other alleged precedents and argued that the isolated passages concept was not followed for works of science or medicine and should not be followed for literature either. They cited state decisions embracing the "dominant effect" notion, and read that test (together with their definition of the relevant audience) into the statute, concluding that other readings would be impractical and overrestrictive.

Manton, dissenting, insisted that federal decisions in the past had accepted the "isolated passages" test. As literature was for amusement only, the community could reasonably demand that it meet moral standards—those of average, not exceptional, individuals.

SAMUEL KRISLOV

Bibliography

LOCKHART, WILLIAM B. and McCLURE, ROBERT C.   1954 Literature, the Law of Obscenity, and the Constitution. *Minnesota Law Review* 38:295–395.

UNCONSTITUTIONAL CONDITIONS

Although government may not be obligated to provide its citizens with a certain benefit or privilege, it is not free to condition granting the benefit or privilege on the recipient's relinquishing a constitutional right. Likewise, the government may not withhold or cancel the benefit by way of penalizing the assertion of a constitutional right. For example, in SHERBERT V. VERNER (1963) the Supreme Court held South Carolina's unemployment compensation act unconstitutional as applied to exclude a Seventh Day Adventist from benefits when she would not find a job releasing her from work on Saturdays. Withholding the benefits effectively penalized exercise of the claimant's RELIGIOUS LIBERTY.

It has sometimes been argued that a legislature's greater power of withholding a benefit must necessarily include the lesser power of granting the benefit with restrictions. On this theory, the recipient of the benefit is deprived of no right, for the right can be retained simply by rejecting the proffered benefit. This logic leads to drastic consequences as government becomes increasingly involved in supplying such vital needs as jobs, housing, welfare, and EDUCATION.

As early as *Frost & Frost Trucking Company v. Railroad Commission* (1926) the Court recognized the potential for excess conditions on the exercise of constitutional rights: "If the state may compel the surrender of one constitutional right as a condition of its favor, it may, in like manner, compel a surrender of all. It is inconceivable that guarantees embedded in the Constitution of the United States may thus be manipulated out of existence."

Subsequent courts have rarely been persuaded by arguments claiming an absolute power of government to condition and limit the grant of general benefits. Rather, they have generally recognized that the revocation of benefits amounts to regulatory activity by government, for which sufficient justification must be established if constitutional rights are restricted. This doctrine of unconstitutional conditions has been successfully applied to restrain assertions of unlimited governmental power in four major substantial areas: the privilege of out-of-state corporations to engage in local business; the use of public property and facilities; the receipt of entitlements and social service benefits; and government employment.

As early as 1839, the Supreme Court announced that a state might exclude out-of-state corporations from conducting business within its borders. In early cases, this power to exclude was held sufficient to justify highly unreasonable conditions on entry and even the arbitrary revocation of a corporation's license. Subsequent Court decisions, however, have subjected such regulations to DUE PROCESS standards. Given the Court's increasing sensitivity to national interests in economic growth and the smooth functioning of the federal system, it is not surprising that the Court invoked the doctrine of unconstitutional conditions to check a power previously thought to be virtually absolute.

In 1897 the Court upheld an ordinance that prohibited public speaking in a municipal park without a permit from the mayor. The Court reasoned that ownership of the land gave the city the right to withhold access completely; the city therefore could grant access on any conditions, including those restricting FIRST AMENDMENT freedoms. This logic has been invalidated by later decisions which have viewed the manipulation of access to streets and parks as regulatory activity subject to constitutional attack. (See PUBLIC FORUM.)

Given the large number of benefits now provided by government, the imposition of conditions on the recipients of such benefits raises a significant possibility of undermining individual liberties. The Supreme Court has used unconstitutional condition analysis to prevent such a result in cases involving unemployment compensation, WELFARE BENEFITS, public housing, tax exemptions, public education, and the mail services. One leading doctrinal basis for these decisions has been the guarantee of PROCEDURAL DUE PROCESS.

In *McAuliffe v. Mayor of New England* (1892) the Massachusetts Supreme Judicial Court denied the petition of a policeman who had been fined for violating a regulation restricting his political activity. Justice OLIVER WENDELL HOLMES, speaking for the state court, stated: "The petitioner may have a constitutional right to talk politics, but he has no constitutional right to be a policeman. . . . There are few employments for hire in which the servant does not agree to suspend his constitutional right of free speech, as well as of idleness, by the implied terms of his contract. The servant cannot complain, as he takes his employment on the terms which are offered him." More recently, however, courts have found conditions on employees unconstitutional irrespective of any abstract right to public employment. The courts have asked whether the condition restricts employment in a "patently arbitrary and discriminatory manner" in violation of due process, as set forth in WIEMAN V.

UPDEGRAFF (1952), and whether, in withholding or revoking employment under conditions capable of improper application, the state is penalizing specific constitutional freedoms.

Although claims of unconstitutional conditions in these four areas have become less common in recent years, the doctrine has recently emerged in the sphere of CRIMINAL PROCEDURE, particularly in cases involving the guilty plea. PLEA BARGAINING effectively penalizes the exercise of the right to trial by rewarding those who plead guilty. In addition, it denies the individual the RIGHT AGAINST SELF-INCRIMINATION and the right to confront and cross-examine witnesses against him. The Court, however, has endorsed the use of plea bargaining. Rather than address the challenges raised by the unconstitutional conditions doctrine, the Court has insisted only that guilty pleas be "voluntary and intelligent" and that the plea bargaining process conform to certain standards of fairness. The tension between the principle of unconstitutional conditions and the Court's endorsement of plea bargaining seems likely to produce future controversy.

ARTHUR ROSETT

Bibliography

VAN ALSTYNE, WILLIAM W. 1968 The Demise of the Right–Privilege Distinction in Constitutional Law. *Harvard Law Review* 81:1439–1464.

UNCONSTITUTIONALITY

The American concept of unconstitutionality was born before the Constitution was adopted. The STAMP ACT CONGRESS of 1765, for example, declared that acts of Parliament imposing TAXATION WITHOUT REPRESENTATION were unconstitutional and need not be obeyed. Then as now, of course, the British constitution was an unwritten collection of customs and usages, only partly reflected in statutes and COMMON LAW principles. Since the adoption of the earliest state constitutions, however, the statement that a governmental action is unconstitutional has been taken as an assertion that the action violates a written constitution. In common speech, "unconstitutional" normally refers to an action's invalidity under the United States Constitution, but in law the term also refers to invalidity under a state constitution. Legislation is not the only form of governmental action that may be unconstitutional. When police officers conduct unreasonable SEARCHES AND SEIZURES, for example, they act unconstitutionally. Similarly, a state court acts unconstitutionally when it enforces a racially RESTRICTIVE COVENANT.

An assertion of unconstitutionality can be made by anyone: a citizen making a complaint, a newspaper editorial writer, a lawyer arguing a case. The assertion may take on a more authoritative character when it is made by a public officer acting in a governmental capacity. Thus, the President might veto a bill passed by Congress on the ground that it is unconstitutional. (See CIVIL RIGHTS ACT OF 1866; JACKSON'S VETO OF THE BANK BILL.) Or, the President might refuse to enforce an act of Congress on similar grounds. Such a presidential refusal led the House of Representatives to adopt ARTICLES OF IMPEACHMENT against ANDREW JOHNSON, thus registering its view that Johnson's conduct was itself unconstitutional. An executive officer may decline to enforce a law for the purpose of allowing others to frame a TEST CASE, thus allowing the courts to rule on the law's validity. BOARD OF EDUCATION V. ALLEN (1968) resulted from one such refusal.

The official in *Allen* thought it important to get a judicial ruling on the constitutionality of the law in question. In fact, Americans have become accustomed to identifying the idea of unconstitutionality with a judicial declaration of unconstitutionality—and, in particular, with such a declaration by the Supreme Court. A lawyer, asked by a client whether a law is or is not constitutional, ordinarily will respond with a prediction of what the courts will hold.

From MARBURY V. MADISON (1803) forward, American courts have assumed that they have the power to disregard a statute that violates a constitutional norm. When a court holds a statute unconstitutional it refuses to give effect to the law in the case before it. Indeed, the *Marbury* opinion grounded the principle of JUDICIAL REVIEW in the need for a court to decide the case before it according to law, including the Constitution as the supreme law. Federal courts are not permitted to give ADVISORY OPINIONS on the law but make their constitutional rulings only in the context of concrete CASES AND CONTROVERSIES. Yet there is a sense in which any opinion is, in part, advisory. The statement of a reason for decision requires a court to move from the particulars of the case before it to the more abstract level of a rule or principle which can be applied later as a PRECEDENT in deciding another appropriate case. Occasionally, particularly in the area of the FREEDOMS OF SPEECH and of the PRESS, a court may hold a law INVALID ON ITS FACE. But even if the court merely says it is holding the law "invalid as applied," the ruling becomes a precedent for other applications to similar facts.

In a statement now famous for its inaccuracy, the Supreme Court said in *Norton v. Shelby County* (1886) that an unconstitutional law "is not a law; it confers no rights; it imposes no duties; it affords no protection; it creates no office; it is, in legal contemplation, as inoperative as though it had never been passed." The statement is misleading in two respects. First, courts are no better than anyone else at undoing the past. A great many actions may be taken on the basis of a statute in the time between its enactment and its judicial invalidation. Justice often requires that those actions be given effect: a corporation organized under an invalid statute will be bound under its contracts; an official who enforces a law in good faith before the law is held invalid will not be liable in damages for the action. In *Lemon v. Kurtzman II* (1973), the Supreme Court allowed Pennsylvania to reimburse church schools for educational services performed under a statute before the Court had held the law invalid in LEMON V. KURTZMAN I (1971).

Second, the *Norton* statement is misleading in the context of an OVERRULING of a previous decision that has held a statute invalid. In ADKINS V. CHILDREN'S HOSPITAL (1923) the Supreme Court had held the DISTRICT OF COLUMBIA MINIMUM WAGE LAW unconstitutional, but in WEST COAST HOTEL CO. V. PARRISH (1937), the Court overruled *Adkins.* Was it then necessary for Congress to reenact the law for it to be effective? The attorney general issued an opinion answering this question negatively, and no one now challenges that opinion's soundness.

Determining whether a court has actually held a law unconstitutional may prove more difficult than identifying the court's HOLDING on the underlying constitutional law. In dealing with a federal statute, for example, the Supreme Court may make clear its view of the Constitution's command, but it may not make clear whether it has held the statute invalid or construed the statute narrowly to avoid holding it unconstitutional. Such an ambiguity still bemuses collectors of antique trivia when they contemplate HODGSON V. BOWERBANK (1809).

Ultimately, the notion of unconstitutionality refers not so much to a fact—or even an opinion, judicial or otherwise—as to a decisional process. In that process courts play the most prominent role, but now and then they yield the center of the stage to other actors. (See ABRAHAM LINCOLN; THOMAS JEFFERSON; WATERGATE AND THE CONSTITUTION.)

KENNETH L. KARST

Bibliography
BICKEL, ALEXANDER M. 1962 *The Least Dangerous Branch: The Supreme Court at the Bar of Politics.* Indianapolis: Bobbs-Merrill.
FIELD, OLIVER P. 1935 *The Effect of an Unconstitutional Statute.* Minneapolis: University of Minnesota Press.

UNIFORM CODE OF MILITARY JUSTICE ACT

See: Military Justice

UNION PACIFIC RAILROAD COMPANY v. UNITED STATES

See: Sinking Fund Cases

UNITED BUILDING & CONSTRUCTION TRADES COUNCIL v. MAYOR AND COUNCIL OF CAMDEN

See: Privileges and Immunities

UNITED JEWISH ORGANIZATIONS v. CAREY
430 U.S. 144 (1977)

Under the VOTING RIGHTS ACT OF 1965 New York sought approval of the United States attorney general for its REAPPORTIONMENT of voters in state legislative districts in Greater New York City. To increase the nonwhite majorities in certain districts, and thus secure approval, the legislature divided a Hasidic Jewish community into two districts, each with a nonwhite majority. Petitioners claimed that assignment of voters solely on the basis of race violated the FOURTEENTH and FIFTEENTH AMENDMENTS.

By a 7–1 vote, the Supreme Court upheld the race-conscious reapportionment. There was no majority opinion but a series of overlapping alignments. Four Justices, noting that the percentage of nonwhite-majority districts was less than the percentage of nonwhites in the county in question, said that the use of racial criteria to comply with the act was not limited to compensating for past discrimination. Other Justices emphasized the lack of stigma or legislative pur-

pose to disadvantage the Hasidim. Justice WILLIAM J. BRENNAN, in a comprehensive opinion on race-conscious remedies, appeared to look ahead to REGENTS OF UNIVERSITY OF CALIFORNIA V. BAKKE (1978). Chief Justice WARREN E. BURGER dissented.

KENNETH L. KARST

UNITED MINE WORKERS v. CORONADO COAL COMPANY
259 U.S. 344 (1922)
CORONADO COAL COMPANY v. UNITED MINE WORKERS
268 U.S. 295 (1925)

In two nearly identical cases, the Supreme Court provided opposite answers to the same question: does the SHERMAN ANTITRUST ACT apply to local strikes that indirectly restrain commerce? The United Mine Workers (UMW) struck to prevent an employer from closing its mines despite valid union contracts; violence and property damage resulted. The company sued the union claiming a Sherman Act conspiracy to restrain INTERSTATE COMMERCE. In its defense, the UMW claimed that it was exempt from suit because it was unincorporated and, because mining was local, that there had been no Sherman Act violation. On APPEAL to the Supreme Court, Chief Justice WILLIAM HOWARD TAFT declared for a unanimous bench that, although unions (even though unincorporated) could clearly be sued, the union had not violated the Sherman Act here. Mining was merely local; any interference concerned the PRODUCTION rather than the distribution of goods. Taft said no restraint of trade existed, absent an explicit showing of intent to restrain trade, unless the obstruction had "such a direct, material and substantial effect to restrain [commerce] that intent reasonably may be inferred." Taft thus introduced new tests of reasonableness (see RULE OF REASON) and intent.

The company soon appealed with new EVIDENCE. Again unanimous, the Supreme Court now said that when intent to restrain trade attended a decrease in production, a previously "indirect and remote obstruction" became a direct interference in violation of the law. The Court asserted that the evidence at the second trial demonstrated such intent. The Court's near reversal, a finding of intent where none had previously existed, probably resulted from a fear of the implications of the first decision. The effect of the later opinion was to hamper union organizing efforts and cast doubt on the legality of strikes generally; certainly intent could be found by Justices who were looking for it.

DAVID GORDON

(SEE ALSO: *Labor and the Antitrust Laws.*)

UNITED MINE WORKERS v. UNITED STATES
330 U.S. 258 (1947)

When John L. Lewis and the United Mine Workers went on strike in the spring of 1946 against coal operators throughout the country, President HARRY S TRUMAN, acting as COMMANDER-IN-CHIEF, seized the mines by EXECUTIVE ORDER to protect the national interest during the emergency. The failure of subsequent negotiations prompted a call that autumn for a second strike, which the government forestalled by obtaining an INJUNCTION in federal district court. Lewis defied the injunction, incurring contempt citations, a personal fine of $10,000, and a fine against his union of $3,500,000.

Lewis appealed to the Supreme Court. Chief Justice FRED M. VINSON, for a 7–2 majority, held that neither the NORRIS-LAGUARDIA nor the CLAYTON ACT deprived the district court of JURISDICTION to issue the injunction pending judicial interpretation of the contract between the government and the miners. The majority denied the assertion that the "employer" referred to in the acts included the government; neither legislative history nor subsequent policy demonstrated any intent to make those acts applicable to government–employee disputes. Moreover, even if the Norris-LaGuardia Act applied, the Court could legitimately issue an injunction to maintain existing conditions pending the court's decision on its jurisdiction. The Court upheld the contempt findings—asserting that the same conduct might constitute both civil and criminal contempt for which both coercive and punitive measures might be imposed—and the fine against Lewis, but remanded the case for redetermination of the union fine.

DAVID GORDON

UNITED NATIONS CHARTER
59 Stat. 1031 (1945)

The United Nations Charter, a multilateral treaty which serves as the "constitution" of the United Nations Organization, was drafted in San Francisco at the United Nations Conference on International Organization in 1945 and ratified by fifty-one original member states. Like the Constitution of the United States, the charter has proved to be a flexible instrument subject to broad interpretation.

The charter was ratified by the United States Senate, 89–2, and it became law, binding both internally and externally, when it entered into force on October 24, 1945. Treaties, properly executed and ratified, are international law, at least formally, and in the United States they also are domestic law by virtue of the SUPREMACY CLAUSE of Article IV of the Constitution.

Despite the charter's nearly unanimous endorsement by the Senate, it was eagerly suggested that, in removing the right of the United States to go to war at will and in authorizing the Security Council to commit the member states to war in certain circumstances, the charter improperly delegated to the United Nations powers and functions belonging to the federal government, including the power to declare war, vested in Congress, and the power to conduct war, vested primarily in the President as commander-in-chief.

Congress and the President are not, however, deprived by the charter of the powers to declare and conduct war, only of the right to exercise these powers in contravention of international law (including the charter). All treaties, the charter included, limit only the international legal right—not the constitutional authority—of states to do freely that which is within their power to do freely in the absence of a treaty. Moreover, as a sovereign nation, the United States has the final authority to decide how it will comply with the particular terms and requirements of a treaty; and as a permanent member of the Security Council, the United States retains, in any event, an absolute veto over any action that would commit the United States to unwelcome policy. When Congress and the President act to comply with their charter obligations, in accordance with the United Nations Participation Act of 1945, they do so pursuant to the TREATY POWER and to their more general FOREIGN AFFAIRS powers.

Another, more recent, matter of constitutional concern is the question of whether United States courts, state and federal, are bound by the human rights clauses of the charter and related instruments, such as the Universal Declaration of Human Rights. The United States Supreme Court has never addressed the question of whether the charter's human rights provisions are self-executing in the United States; lower courts have answered that question in the negative.

BURNS H. WESTON

Bibliography

CAHILL, J. 1952 "The United Nations Charter as Law of the Land." *Albany Law Review* 15–16:51–57.

Charter of the United Nations and Statute of the International Court of Justice. Office of Public Information, United Nations, New York.

GOODRICH, M. and HAMBRO, E. 1949 *Charter of the United Nations: Commentary and Documents.* Boston: World Peace Foundation.

HENKIN, LOUIS 1972 *Foreign Affairs and the Constitution.* Mineola, N.Y.: Foundation Press.

UNITED RAILWAYS & ELECTRIC CO. OF BALTIMORE v. WEST
280 U.S. 234 (1930)

This obscure case has no significance except to illustrate how the Supreme Court manipulated the FAIR RETURN rule of SMYTH V. AMES (1898) to prevent rate regulation, which the Court disapproved. A public service commission fixed rates that permitted the company to earn a profit of 6.26 percent. The company sought rates returning 7.44 percent. The Court used SUBSTANTIVE DUE PROCESS to void the commission's rates and decided that rates returning "7½ percent, or even 8 percent, on the value of the property" might be "necessary to avoid confiscation." Justices LOUIS D. BRANDEIS, OLIVER W. HOLMES, and HARLAN FISKE STONE dissented.

LEONARD W. LEVY

UNITED STATES v. . . .

See entry under name of other party

UNITED STATES COIN & CURRENCY, UNITED STATES v.

See: *United States v. Marchetti*

UNITED STATES COURT OF APPEALS FOR THE FEDERAL CIRCUIT

This court was created by the FEDERAL COURTS IMPROVEMENT ACT (1982), to take over the JURISDICTION of the COURT OF CUSTOMS AND PATENT APPEALS and the COURT OF CLAIMS. Its first judges were the judges of the superseded courts. It is a CONSTITUTIONAL COURT, whose twelve judges serve for life during good behavior.

The Federal Circuit, like the other UNITED STATES COURTS OF APPEALS, is an intermediate appellate court; its jurisdiction, however, is defined not by region but by subject matter. It has nationwide jurisdiction to hear APPEALS in cases chiefly of the types previously heard by the superseded courts: customs and patent matters, and claims against the United States. In the future, however, other types of cases may be added to the Federal Circuit's jurisdiction—tax appeals, for example. Such developments might relieve some of the pressure on the Supreme Court's docket, effectively removing certain technical and specialized areas from the Court's workload. Many proponents of the 1982 act regard the creation of this opportunity as the act's most important achievement.

KENNETH L. KARST

UNITED STATES COURTS OF APPEALS

The United States Courts of Appeals form the intermediate component of the three-tiered federal judiciary, lying between the UNITED STATES DISTRICT COURTS and the SUPREME COURT of the United States. As such, they normally serve as the first courts of review in the federal JUDICIAL SYSTEM. But because of the natural limitations upon the Supreme Court's capacity, the Courts of Appeals are often also the final courts of review.

Article III, section 1, of the Constitution provides: "The JUDICIAL POWER OF THE UNITED STATES, shall be vested in one supreme Court, and in such inferior Courts as the Congress may from time to time ordain and establish." Thus, in contrast to the Supreme Court, inferior federal courts were not required by the Constitution; rather, their creation was left to the discretion of Congress. Such treatment reflected a compromise between two views, one favoring the mandatory creation of inferior courts, and the other completely opposed to the existence of any such courts.

The Courts of Appeals are relative newcomers to the federal judicial system, having been born with the CIRCUIT COURTS OF APPEALS ACT (Evarts Act) of 1891. The Courts of Appeals were created to solve an acute crisis in the federal judiciary stemming from the limited capacity of the existing system, which had remained largely unchanged since the JUDICIARY ACT

OF 1789. That act had established a bilevel system of inferior federal courts. There were, first of all, single-judge "district courts," generally one per state. The Union was also divided into several "circuits." CIRCUIT COURT was to be held twice a year in each of the districts encompassed by a given circuit. At these sittings, cases would be heard by a three-judge panel consisting of two Supreme Court Justices and the district judge for the district in which the circuit court was being held.

Having determined to avail itself of its constitutional prerogative to establish inferior federal courts, Congress faced the further issue of those courts' appropriate function and JURISDICTION. In the debates over Article III, there had been substantial support for giving Congress the power to create only admiralty courts, rather than inferior courts of general jurisdiction. No such limitation was adopted, however. It has therefore been generally assumed that Congress is constitutionally free to define the role of the inferior federal courts however it chooses.

The manner that Congress selected in the 1789 act is of some interest. The district courts were, and remain today, trial courts or courts of first instance. The circuit courts, in distinct contrast to today's middle-tier courts, also functioned primarily as trial courts. In the area of private civil law, the circuit courts' jurisdiction was largely concurrent with that of the district courts: it encompassed cases within the DIVERSITY JURISDICTION, but not FEDERAL QUESTION cases. (Original federal jurisdiction was not extended to federal question cases until 1875.) Similarly, with respect to civil suits by the United States, both circuit and district courts were given ORIGINAL JURISDICTION, the only difference being that the requisite amount in controversy was higher for circuit court jurisdiction.

The circuit courts even had certain original jurisdiction that the district courts lacked. The first removal jurisdiction was vested in the circuit courts alone. And the circuit courts had exclusive jurisdiction over most federal crimes.

Nonetheless, the seeds of the modern federal courts of appeals were planted by the first Judiciary Act. The early circuit courts had appellate jurisdiction in civil cases involving disputes over amounts exceeding $50, and in admiralty cases exceeding $300. (A district judge sitting as a circuit judge was not, however, permitted to vote on appeals from his own decisions.) Unlike the modern courts of appeals, however, the circuit courts were the final federal forum for many of these cases. In civil suits, circuit court judgments were reviewable only when the amount in dispute

exceeded $2,000. Judgments in criminal cases were categorically unreviewable.

The early circuit courts proved problematic, in the main because of the burden that circuit riding placed on the Supreme Court Justices. Congress attempted to alleviate that hardship by reducing from two to one the number of Justices required to sit on a circuit court, but the benefit of the reduction was more than outweighed by several important augmentations of the High Court's jurisdiction that were enacted by Congress during the century following the 1789 Judiciary Act. Most notable of such legislation was the JUDICIARY ACT OF 1875, which granted the lower courts, as well as the Supreme Court, nearly the full scope of Article III jurisdiction, including original federal question jurisdiction in the district and circuit courts. The federal courts, already vastly overloaded with cases, were virtually submerged after this act. Reform was inevitable.

Indeed, attempts to improve the judicial system had more than once been made. In 1801 Congress had enacted the JUDICIARY ACT OF 1801 (the "Law of the Midnight Judges"), which among other things had established permanent circuit judgeships, three to a circuit. When political tides shifted the following year, however, the act was repealed, and the system reverted essentially to its original condition, except that Congress permitted circuit court to be held by a single judge, rather than three. Much later, in 1869, Congress partially restored the plan of 1801 by creating a single permanent circuit judgeship for each of the nine circuits then in existence. And in 1887 and 1888 Congress passed a series of measures aimed at pruning the expanded jurisdiction of the lower federal courts.

But it was not until the Evarts Act that Congress provided structural reforms adequate to the crisis of judicial overload. The act established three-judge courts of appeals for each of the nine circuits, and increased the number of permanent circuit judgeships to two per circuit. The third appeals judge would in most instances be a district judge (though Supreme Court Justices remained eligible), but the act, following the rule set down by the Act of 1789, barred district judges from reviewing their own decisions.

Curiously, the Evarts Act left the old circuit courts standing, although it did remove their APPELLATE JURISDICTION. Until these courts were abolished in 1911, there thus functioned two sets of federal trial courts.

The Evarts Act provided for direct review by the Supreme Court of the decisions of the district courts and the old circuit courts, in some important cases.

The new circuit courts of appeals would review the remainder. Under the act, a circuit court's decision in an admiralty or diversity case would be final, unless that court certified a question to the Supreme Court or the Supreme Court granted a WRIT OF CERTIORARI in order to review the circuit court's decision. In most other cases, circuit court decisions were appealable as of right.

Since the Evarts Act, only a few significant alterations have been made to the federal judicial system in general, and the courts of appeals in particular. The rules governing Supreme Court review are perhaps the most important arena of change. In 1925, Congress replaced appeal as of right with discretionary review for all circuit court judgments except those holding a state statute unconstitutional. In 1937, Congress passed a law permitting appeal to the Supreme Court from any judgment by a federal court holding an act of Congress unconstitutional in any civil case to which the United States is a party.

In 1948 the circuit courts established by the Evarts Act were renamed; each court is now known as the United States Court of Appeals for the____Circuit. The number of circuits has also been increased; and there is now a "Federal Circuit" court to hear appeals from the CLAIMS COURT and from district courts in patent cases or in cases arising under the TUCKER ACT. Finally, procedures in the various courts of appeals were standardized in 1968 in the Federal Rules of Appellate Procedure. Each circuit, however, retains its own rule-making power for matters not covered by the Federal Rules.

The chief work of the courts of appeals is the review of final judgments of the United States district courts. The courts, however, are also empowered to review certain orders that are not strictly final, essentially when the benefit of such review clearly outweighs any attendant disruption and delay of district court proceedings. In addition, Congress has enabled the appeals courts to issue the extraordinary WRIT OF MANDAMUS and WRIT OF PROHIBITION in cases in which district courts may abuse their constitutional powers. Finally, the statutes governing many of the various federal administrative agencies provide for direct review of agency adjudication and rule-making in the court of appeals for the circuit in which the party seeking review resides, or in the Court of Appeals for the District of Columbia Circuit. The latter circuit court has been a frequent forum for challenges, constitutional and otherwise, to federal agency action.

To understand the role of the courts of appeals in the development of constitutional law, it is necessary to understand the relationship between the appeals courts and the Supreme Court. As was noted above, since the JUDICIARY ACT OF 1925, the "Judges Bill," the Supreme Court has had a discretionary power of review of most circuit court decisions. Again, however, appeal as of right lies in cases in which the appeals court has held a state statute to be repugnant to the Constitution, laws, or treaties of the United States, and in civil cases in which either a court of appeals or a district court has held an act of Congress unconstitutional and the United States is a party. Nonetheless, neither type of case in which appeal is of right bulks very large in the overall volume of appeals from circuit courts, and of those, many are denied Supreme Court review for want of a substantial federal question.

Accordingly, the Supreme Court has the discretion to review or not to review the vast majority of decisions by the courts of appeals. Not surprisingly, because of the limited capacity of the High Court, its discretion is much more often exercised to deny review than to grant it. As a general rule, in fact, the Supreme Court tends not to review appeals court decisions unless the issues involved either have an urgent importance or have received conflicting treatment by different circuits, or both.

One might conclude that, because the Supreme Court does review important cases, the appeals courts have no significant role in the development of constitutional law. Constitutional law, however, is not the product solely of the Supreme Court.

To begin, the Supreme Court can only review a decision that a party seeks to have reviewed; not every losing party in the court of appeals may do so. For example, in *Kennedy v. Sampson* (1974) the District of Columbia Circuit construed the POCKET VETO clause of the Constitution (Article 1, section 7, clause 2) to bar the President from exercising the pocket veto power during brief, intrasession adjournments of Congress. The President then declined to seek review in the Supreme Court; he chose instead to acquiesce in the rule laid down by the appeals court. The court's decision thus became a cornerstone of the law respecting the presentation of laws for presidential approval.

Of course, as a glance at any constitutional law textbook or casebook reveals, the vast majority of important constitutional PRECEDENTS are produced not by the courts of appeals but by the Supreme Court. Decisions like *Kennedy* are thus the exception, not the rule. Nonetheless, in several ways the appeals courts contribute significantly to the development of constitutional law.

Before a constitutional issue is decided by the Supreme Court, it will often have received a thorough ventilation by one or more circuit courts. The Supreme Court thus has the benefit of the circuit judges' consideration of difficult constitutional matters, and may sometimes explicitly adopt the reasoning of the court of appeals. For example, in *United States v. Dennis* (1950) the Second Circuit faced the difficult issue of whether, and if so, how, the CLEAR AND PRESENT DANGER test applied to a conspiracy to advocate the overthrow of the government by force and violence and to organize a political party for the purpose of such advocacy. The Court of Appeals, in an opinion by Judge LEARNED HAND, held that such advocacy was unprotected by the FIRST AMENDMENT even though the actual forceful overthrow of the government was not imminent. The Supreme Court affirmed the decision in DENNIS V. UNITED STATES (1951), and its opinion adopted much of Judge Hand's analysis, including Judge Hand's "clear and present danger" formula, namely, "whether the gravity of the 'evil,' discounted by its improbability, justifies such invasion of free speech as is necessary to avoid the danger."

The role of the courts of appeals in resolving novel issues of constitutional law, however, is only half of the picture. Equally important is the appeals courts' adjudication of cases raising issues on which the Supreme Court has already spoken. Because the High Court can only sketch the broad outlines of constitutional DOCTRINE, it remains for the lower courts to apply precedent, elaborate or clarify it, and extrapolate from it. Because appeal from the district courts to the appeals court is of right, and because most litigation never reaches the Supreme Court, it is in the courts of appeals that the Supreme Court's sketch is worked into a fully drawn landscape.

When the Supreme Court decides not to give plenary review to a case arising from an appeals court, what implication should be drawn concerning the value of the appeals court's opinion as a precedent? By denying a petition for certiorari or dismissing an appeal as of right for want of jurisdiction, the Court formally indicates no view of the merits or demerits of the appeals court's decision. Nonetheless, it is commonly thought that the Supreme Court generally does not decline to review an appeals court decision that it finds clearly incorrect. Similarly, when the Supreme Court summarily affirms an appeals court's decision, it is formally signaling its agreement with the result only, and not necessarily the reasoning of the lower court. Yet, such affirmances are popularly thought to indicate at least the Court's tentative agreement with the substance of the lower court's opinion.

Since the early 1960s, the federal courts at all three levels have experienced a dramatic and continuing increase in their workload. At the district and circuit levels, Congress has responded by adding judges to existing courts. When the number of judges in a circuit has become sufficiently great, Congress has divided the circuit into two. That course is not entirely satisfactory, however, because it tends to push the appeals courts in the direction of being regional, rather than national courts, and increases the likelihood of inter-circuit conflict.

At the Supreme Court level, Congress has made no significant changes. Various proposals for reducing the Court's workload would also affect adjudication at the appeals court level. A frequent suggestion has been to establish a national court of appeals. In one version, the national court would sit only to resolve conflicts among the circuits, thereby eliminating a significant share of the Supreme Court's annual docket. In another version, the national court would screen cases to determine those worthy of Supreme Court review. Another proposal would reduce the Supreme Court's workload by eliminating appeal as of right. One effect of such a measure, of course, would be to increase the number of appeals court decisions that are effectively final.

CARL McGOWAN

Bibliography

BATOR, PAUL M.; MISHKIN, PAUL J.; SHAPIRO, DAVID L.; and WECHSLER, HERBERT 1973 *Hart and Wechsler's The Federal Courts and the Federal System*, 2nd ed. Mineola, N.Y.: Foundation Press.

WRIGHT, CHARLES A. 1983 *Handbook of the Law of Federal Courts*. St. Paul, Minn.: West Publishing Co.

UNITED STATES DISTRICT COURT FOR THE EASTERN DISTRICT OF MICHIGAN, UNITED STATES v.
407 U.S. 297 (1972)

Most Presidents have claimed inherent executive authority to use electronic surveillance for national security purposes without complying with conventional FOURTH AMENDMENT requirements such as prior court approval. In several earlier decisions, such as KATZ V. UNITED STATES (1967), and in the 1968 statute authorizing federal and state officials to use ELECTRONIC EAVESDROPPING, the issue had been left open.

During the VIETNAM WAR, Attorney General John N. Mitchell approved a wiretap "to gather intelligence information deemed necessary to protect the nation from attempts of domestic organizations to attack and subvert the existing structure of the government." The Supreme Court unanimously ruled that where threats by *domestic* organizations were concerned, neither section 2511(3) of the 1968 act nor the Constitution gave the President authority to use electronic surveillance without first obtaining a warrant from a magistrate. The Court thus rejected the President's claim of INHERENT POWER. The Court did not decide whether the Fourth Amendment's warrant requirement applied to activities of foreign powers or their agents; a 1978 statute now governs this. The Court also suggested that Congress could authorize standards for intelligence gathering for domestic security purposes that are less stringent than for law enforcement; Congress has not done so.

HERMAN SCHWARTZ

UNITED STATES DISTRICT COURTS

In enacting Article III, the Framers of the Constitution authorized the establishment of a federal judicial system consisting of a SUPREME COURT and such inferior courts as Congress might decide to establish. In the JUDICIARY ACT OF 1789 Congress created a Supreme Court, divided the country into three circuits, authorized a CIRCUIT COURT to sit in each circuit, and established a federal district court in each of the states. The Supreme Court was the only truly appellate court in the system. Unlike the modern courts of appeal, the old circuit courts, while exercising some appellate jurisdiction, were intended to be the chief federal trial courts. A Supreme Court Justice riding the circuit and judges of the district courts in the circuit manned each of these circuit courts.

The federal district courts were empowered to sit at various times in specified locations within the states where they were located. They were tribunals of very limited JURISDICTION and originally had as their main function the adjudication of admiralty and maritime matters. It was anticipated that the state trial courts or federal circuit courts would handle, as trial courts, the most important legal issues facing the new nation. The federal district courts were empowered to try minor criminal cases. In addition, they had CONCURRENT JURISDICTION with the circuit courts over suits by ALIENS for tort violations of a treaty or the law of nations, suits against consuls, and disputes in which the federal government initiated the proceeding and the matter in controversy was $100 or less. However, district court jurisdiction was exclusive in admiralty,

over seizures of land for violation of federal statutes, and over seizures under import, navigation, and trade statutes.

This limited and specialized jurisdiction has steadily expanded. Today the district court is the only federal nonspecialized court, handling both criminal and civil matters. Among the latter are admiralty cases, federal question cases, and cases within the DIVERSITY JURISDICTION (cases between different states). In a diversity case the matter in controversy must exceed $10,000. No jurisdictional amount is normally required for the other exercises of the district court's civil jurisdiction. Appeals from a district court go to the UNITED STATES COURT OF APPEALS.

The first district court to be organized was the district court of New York. That court began functioning on November 3, 1789, and was the predecessor to the current district court for the Southern District of New York. Even today judges of the Southern District refer to theirs as the "Mother Court."

As the system was originally conceived, each state was to contain at least one federal district and one federal court. There has been no deviation from this pattern as the country has expanded from thirteen to fifty states. In addition, the DISTRICT OF COLUMBIA and the federal TERRITORIES (the Virgin Islands, PUERTO RICO, and Guam) are each organized as a federal district with a district court. In over half the states, although there may be a number of federal district judges who sit in separate locations throughout the state, there is only one federal district. Twelve states are divided into two federal districts; some states have three federal districts; and California, New York, and Texas are subdivided into four federal districts.

As the country has expanded, the number of federal district judges has increased. Since 1954 the roster of federal judges has grown through enactment of legislation authorizing additional judgeships for federal district courts nationwide. The Omnibus Judgeship Act of 1978 raised the number of authorized district judges from 399 to 516. The Southern District of New York has twenty-seven authorized judgeships, the largest number of any district in the country.

Federal district judges are nominated by the President and appointed with the ADVICE AND CONSENT of the Senate. The prevailing practice is for the selection of the nominee to come to the President from the Department of Justice. If one or both of the senators from the state in question belong to the President's party, the candidate for nomination is proposed by one or both senators and submitted to the Department of Justice for approval and recommendation to the President for nomination. Today few candidates are nominated and sent to the Senate for confirmation without first being found qualified by the American Bar Association. When the President decides to nominate a candidate, the Federal Bureau of Investigation undertakes a security check. If the candidate is cleared, the President announces the nomination and sends the name to the Senate. The Senate Judiciary Committee holds hearings, which are usually one-day affairs for candidates for federal district courts. If the Senate Judiciary Committee approves, the nomination is voted on by the full Senate.

An Article III judge has life tenure during GOOD BEHAVIOR, and his salary cannot be diminished while he is in office. The only way to remove a federal district judge from office is by IMPEACHMENT. Of course, a federal judge, like any other person, may be prosecuted for criminal law violations. Bribery has been the most frequent charge, but criminal prosecutions of federal judges are rare and attempts to remove them by impeachment have been infrequent.

When the first change of political power occurred in the United States at the national level, from the Federalist party to the Republican party of THOMAS JEFFERSON, the Jeffersonians commenced impeachment proceedings against two judges appointed by the Federalists and disliked by the Republicans: JOHN PICKERING, a judge of the district court in New Hampshire, and SAMUEL CHASE, an Associate Justice of the Supreme Court. Pickering was convicted by the Senate in 1803, but the requisite two-thirds Senate majority could not be mustered to convict Chase. Since that time impeachment to unseat a federal judge has not been a successful political weapon. Partisan politics has from time to time generated unsuccessful calls for impeachment of various judges.

A federal district court judgeship carries considerable prestige. It is a presidential appointment; it is a national rather than a local office; and federal district court judgeships are limited in number. District judges in the main have had prior careers as prominent or distinguished lawyers before going on the bench. They are drawn for the most part from the middle and upper strata of our society. They are generally alumni of the best known law schools of the nation or of the state in which they will serve. They have generally had successful careers in private practice, often with backgrounds as federal, state, or local prosecutors. A few are former academics, and some come to court from public service careers outside government.

Until the twentieth century, all federal district judges were white males. The first woman to be confirmed as a federal judge was Florence Allen, who was appointed to the Court of Appeals for the Sixth Circuit in 1934. The first woman appointed to the district court was Burneta Matthews, who was given an interim appointment to the District of Columbia bench in 1949. She was confirmed by the Senate in 1950 for a permanent appointment. Constance Baker Motley was the first black woman to be appointed to the federal bench. She was appointed to the District Court for the Southern District of New York in 1966, and in 1982 became chief judge of that court.

WILLIAM HASTIE was the first black to be made a federal judge. He was appointed to the District Court of the Virgin Islands in 1937 and in 1949 was named to the Court of Appeals for the Third Circuit. James Parsons, appointed judge of the Northern District of Illinois in 1961, was the first black named a district judge in the continental United States. Since these initial appointments the number of blacks, women, and members of other ethnic minorities has grown steadily.

The first Judiciary Act authorized each court to make rules for conducting its own business, and in 1842 the Supreme Court was empowered to regulate process, pleading, proof and DISCOVERY in EQUITY, admiralty, and law cases in the district and circuit courts. In 1938 uniform rules for conducting civil cases, entitled the FEDERAL RULES OF CIVIL PROCEDURE, were adopted for the federal system. In 1946 the FEDERAL RULES OF CRIMINAL PROCEDURE were enacted. These rules have achieved uniformity of procedure and practice in the federal district courts throughout the nation.

The typical calendar of civil cases in a federal district court contains a plethora of complex cases involving PATENT, trademark, and COPYRIGHT infringement claims; federal securities law violations; CIVIL RIGHTS infractions; private antitrust claims; shareholders' derivative suits; IMMIGRATION and NATURALIZATION cases; employment, age, and housing discrimination claims; and claims under a variety of other federal statutes, such as the FREEDOM OF INFORMATION ACT, Investment Advisers Act, Commodities Exchange Act, FAIR LABOR STANDARDS ACT, and Federal Employers' Liability Act. In addition, there are seamen's injury and cargo damage claims, HABEAS CORPUS petitions by both state and federal prisoners, and litigation based on diversity jurisdiction. The criminal case load involves a variety of infractions defined in the United States criminal code.

Among the primary functions of the federal district courts are the vindication of federal rights secured by the Constitution and laws of the United States.

UNITED STATES DISTRICT COURTS

1945

The federal district court is often called upon to hold a state law or act unconstitutional because it violates federal constitutional guarantees or has been preempted by federal legislation. Obviously, the exercise of this power by federal district courts has the potential for creating friction and disharmony between state and federal courts. A lower federal court's power to strike down a state law on federal constitutional grounds, in the face of a contrary ruling by the highest court of the state, is not an easy pill for state judges to swallow. Federal courts have devised doctrines of COMITY and ABSTENTION to ease the friction. A growing number of federal judges, recognizing that state judges, too, have a duty to protect and enforce federal rights, have been inclined to give increasing deference to state court determinations of federal constitutional questions.

A burgeoning federal caseload undoubtedly promotes this inclination toward accommodation and also promotes a tightening of limitations on federal habeas corpus review of state court criminal convictions. A habeas corpus petition enables a state prisoner, after unsuccessfully appealing his conviction through the state court system, to have the matter reviewed by the federal district court to determine whether the trial and conviction violated the defendant's federal constitutional rights. Not surprisingly, habeas corpus petitions have inundated the federal courts. While most are without merit, the few petitions of substance that succeed are another cause of federal–state court friction. Rules of limitations have been imposed requiring exhaustion of state remedies and forbidding review if the state court's denial of the appeal of the criminal conviction rests on the defendant's failure to conform to state governing procedure absent a showing of cause and prejudice. (See WAINWRIGHT V. SYKES, 1977.)

Diversity jurisdiction brings to the federal courts issues of state law that would ordinarily be tried in the state courts. The initial justification for giving federal courts jurisdiction over such cases was concern that parochialism would put the out-of-state complainant at a disadvantage in seeking redress in state court against a resident of the forum state.

Exercise of federal diversity jurisdiction was at one time a cause of federal–state confusion if not friction. The district courts in diversity cases have been required to follow applicable state statutes, but until 1938 they were free to disregard state decisional law and decide on the basis of their own notions of what the COMMON LAW was or should be. With the Supreme Court's decision in ERIE RAILROAD V. TOMPKINS (1938) federal courts were no longer free to disregard state court decisions. Federal courts may apply their own rules as to pleading and practice but on substantive issues must function as adjuncts of the state judiciary.

ERIE V. TOMPKINS has made clear that the diversity jurisdiction is a wasteful use of federal judicial resources. State court parochialism is no longer a justifiable basis for federal diversity jurisdiction. Because the federal court must apply state law, apart from federal procedural rules, the litigant is seldom better off in federal court than he would be if relegated to state courts, where increasing numbers of federal judges feel such cases belong. Congress, however, has shown little interest in divesting federal district courts of the diversity jurisdiction.

The federal district court is the place where litigation usually commences to test the constitutional validity of state or federal governmental action with national implication. These TEST CASES usually seek injunctive relief or DECLARATORY JUDGMENTS. These are suits in EQUITY; thus no jury is empaneled, and the district judge must determine both the facts and the law. The judge will articulate his or her findings of the facts and legal conclusions as to the constitutional validity of the governmental action being tested. The trial record and the district court's analysis are thus extremely important for appellate courts, particularly in cases of first impression.

It is the district court that decides in the first instance whether the government is violating a newspaper's FIRST AMENDMENT rights, an accused's RIGHT AGAINST SELF-INCRIMINATION, or a minority citizen's right to the equal protection of the laws. Organizations such as the AMERICAN CIVIL LIBERTIES UNION, the National Association for the Advancement of Colored People, Jehovah's Witnesses, environmental groups, corporations, and individuals initiate litigation in the district court to test the constitutionality of some federal, state, or local legislation or practice. (See TEST CASES.)

Such a case was *McLean v. Arkansas Board of Education* (D. Ark., 1982). The American Civil Liberties Union sought to challenge an Arkansas law requiring that creationism—a biblical story of man's and the world's creation, as opposed to Darwin's evolutionary theory for explaining the genesis of mankind—be taught in the public schools. The issue was tried first in the federal district court, which framed the issue in these terms: is creationism a religious doctrine or a valid scientific theory? The court heard and weighed testimony, chiefly from experts on both sides, and held that the Arkansas statute was an unconstitutional ESTABLISHMENT OF RELIGION.

Sometimes prior DOCTRINE has forecast the outcome. For instance, although the SEPARATE BUT EQUAL DOCTRINE on which school SEGREGATION had been founded was not overruled until BROWN V. BOARD OF EDUCATION (1954), earlier decisions such as SWEATT V. PAINTER (1950) and *McLaurin v. Oklahoma State Regents* (1950) pointed to that overruling. Nonetheless, the record amassed by several district courts, showing the psychological and education deprivation inflicted by segregation on black children, was crucial in enabling the Supreme Court to take the final step of overruling PLESSY V. FERGUSON (1896) and holding that segregated schools violated the right of minority school children to equal protection of the law.

Similarly, a federal district court facing a constitutional challenge to the HYDE AMENDMENT, a congressional provision largely denying Medicaid funds for the cost of abortions, held hearings for about a year. The trial record contained some 400 exhibits and 5,000 pages of testimony. The judge was required to digest this mountain of testimonial and documentary evidence and prepare cohesive findings of facts and conclusions of law. (See HARRIS V. MCRAE, 1980.)

The need for so long a trial and the condensation of so voluminous a record into a coherent decision is not commonplace. However, it is not unusual for a district judge to be required to master the facts in a complex trial lasting many months, and to set forth the facts found and legal conclusions in a comprehensive fashion.

In some cases the district court, as a supplement to its own adjudicative fact-finding, must make findings as to LEGISLATIVE FACTS as well. For instance, in FULLILOVE V. KLUTZNICK (1980) Congress had required at least ten percent of federal funds granted for local public works projects to be set aside for minority businesses. This legislation was attacked as unconstitutional racial discrimination. The district court framed the issue as the power of Congress to remedy past discrimination. The district judge relied on congressional findings that minorities had been denied access to entrepreneurial opportunities provided in building construction works financed by public funds. Based on this legislative finding and Congress's purpose to take remedial action, the district court found the set-aside to be a legitimate remedial act. The Supreme Court adopted this rationale, and upheld the quota.

At times, in a constitutional controversy, the district court, although adhering to judicial precedent requiring it to dismiss the constitutional challenge, may help to bring about a reversal of precedent by recognizing that a wrong exists which should be remedied. BAKER V. CARR (1962) was a challenge to Tennessee's malapportioned legislature. The district court, in its opinion, carefully and sympathetically tracked the contentions of the plaintiffs that the legislators had condoned gross inequality in legislative REPRESENTATION and debased the VOTING RIGHTS of a large number of citizens. The court, however, relied on COLEGROVE V. GREEN (1946) and dismissed the action. On review of this order, the Supreme Court ruled that the plaintiffs' allegations had stated a case within the district court's jurisdiction. Subsequently, REYNOLDS V. SIMS (1964) embodied the Supreme Court's famous ONE PERSON, ONE VOTE principle, requiring legislative districts to be constructed as nearly as possible of an equal number of voters. (See REAPPORTIONMENT.)

Issues of such magnitude are highly charged; it is not unusual, in these controversial circumstances, for the judge who decides a case contrary to the majority's view to face public criticism and in some cases even social ostracism.

Judge Waties Waring's unpopular decision in favor of blacks in voting and school cases led to his social ostracism in Charleston, South Carolina; Judge Skelly Wright became anathema to many whites in New Orleans for the same reason, and escaped that environment through appointment to the Court of Appeals of the District of Columbia Circuit. Similarly, Judge William Ray Overton, who decided the creationism case adversely to local sentiments, and Judge James B. MacMillan, who ordered a complex program of SCHOOL BUSING in Charlotte, North Carolina, were subjected to severe community criticism.

Although not so dramatic as the examples given, public criticism meets almost every district judge at one time or another for rendering an unpopular decision. Because most public controversies have a way of ending up in the federal courts, district judges must decide whether seniority systems must be modified to prevent the employment gains of minorities and women from being wiped out; whether regulations requiring physicians to report to parents abortions performed on teenagers are valid; whether the overcrowding and the rundown conditions of a prison require it to be closed; or whether permitting school authorities to provide for prayer or meditation violates the SEPARATION OF CHURCH AND STATE. The district judge normally sits alone, and does not share decision with others, as do federal appellate judges—and therefore is singularly exposed to abuse and pressure.

Life tenure helps secure the independence of the district judge in facing such issues. This independence is crucial, not only for the judge but also for a constitutional system that seeks to secure the rights of the unpopular and despised.

ROBERT L. CARTER

Bibliography

ADMINISTRATIVE OFFICE OF THE UNITED STATES COURT. *Annual Report of the Director.* Washington, D.C.: Government Printing Office.

CLARK, D. S. 1981 Adjudication to Administration: A Statistical Analysis of Federal District Courts in the 20th Century. *Southern California Law Review* 55:65–152.

HALL, KERMIT 1976 The Antebellum Lower Federal Judiciary, 1829–1861. *Vanderbilt Law Review* 29:1089–1129.

―――― 1981 California's Lower Federal First Judicial Appointments. *Hastings Law Journal* 32:819–837.

HENDERSON, DWIGHT F. 1971 *Courts for a New Nation.* Washington, D.C.: Public Affairs Press.

HOUGH, CHARLES M. 1934 *The U.S. District Court for the Southern District of New York.* New York: Maritime Law Association.

Management Statistic for United States Courts. 1981.

STECKLER, WILLIAM E. 1978 Future of the Federal District Courts. *Indiana Law Review* 11:601–620.

SURRENCY, ERWIN C. 1963 History of Federal Courts. *Missouri Law Review* 28:214–244.

THOMPSON, FRANK, JR. 1970 Impeachment of Federal Judges: A Historical Overview. *North Carolina Law Review* 49:87–121.

UNITED STATES RAILROAD RETIREMENT BOARD v. FRITZ

See: Rational Basis; Substantive Due Process

UNITED STATES TRUST CO. v. NEW JERSEY
431 U.S. 1 (1977)

This decision marked the beginning of the modern revitalization of the CONTRACT CLAUSE as a limitation on state legislative power. New York and New Jersey had promised, on issuing bonds to support their Port Authority, to limit severely their use of Authority revenues to subsidize rail passenger transportation. Twelve years later the states sought to divert commuters from automobiles to railroads; they raised bridge and tunnel tolls and, repealing their earlier promise, authorized use of the increased revenues to subsidize commuter railroads. The Supreme Court, 4–3, held the repeal unconstitutional as an impairment of the OBLIGATION OF CONTRACT.

The dissenters, led by Justice WILLIAM J. BRENNAN, accurately described the decision as the first in nearly forty years to invalidate economic legislation under the contract clause and argued vigorously for maintaining judicial deference to legislative power. For the majority, Justice HARRY A. BLACKMUN commented that the outright repeal had deprived bondholders of an important security interest and could be justified only if it were both "reasonable and necessary to serve an important public purpose." The repeal failed this heightened STANDARD OF REVIEW, because alternative means of diverting commuters to railroads were available: taxing parking or gasoline, for example.

KENNETH L. KARST

(SEE ALSO: *Allied Structural Steel Co. v. Spannaus, 1978.*)

UNITED STEELWORKERS OF AMERICA v. WEBER
443 U.S. 193 (1979)

This was one of an important series of decisions upholding the legality of AFFIRMATIVE ACTION. In *Weber,* the Court held, 5–2, in an opinion by Justice WILLIAM J. BRENNAN, that a private affirmative action plan reserving for blacks fifty percent of the openings in a training program leading to plant employment did not violate Title VII of the CIVIL RIGHTS ACT OF 1964. *Weber* left open important questions about the permissible scope of affirmative action, including whether governments might resort to affirmative action without violating the Fifth or FOURTEENTH AMENDMENT, and the extent to which private affirmative action programs may "trammel the interests" of white employees.

THEODORE EISENBERG

UNREASONABLE SEARCH

"Unreasonable" is the controlling word in the FOURTH AMENDMENT. In its first clause the amendment guarantees the right of the people to be free from unreasonable SEARCHES AND SEIZURES; its second clause stipulates the terms for issuance of a judicial warrant: probable cause, oath or affirmation, particularity of description. What is an unreasonable and therefore forbidden search? Conversely, what is a reasonable and permitted one? The amendment does not say. The answer, in large measure, depends on one's understanding of the relationship of the two clauses.

Two polar positions have dominated debate in the Supreme Court on this matter. The view that was in the ascendancy before 1946 and that has generally prevailed again since CHIMEL V. CALIFORNIA (1969), treats the two clauses in conjunction so that the unreasonable searches forbidden by the first clause are defined by the warrant requirements in the second clause: a reasonable search is one conducted subject to a proper warrant, an unreasonable search is one that is not. A second view, generally dominant between HARRIS V. UNITED STATES (1946) and 1969, holds that reasonableness is an autonomous principle, to be measured by all the circumstances rather than by the securing of a warrant (although this is one factor to be considered).

The conflict between the two readings of "unreasonable" essentially has centered on SEARCH INCIDENT TO ARREST, a recognized "emergency" exception to the warrant requirement since WEEKS V. UNITED STATES (1914). According to the second interpretation, once the privacy of the dwelling has legitimately been invaded to make a lawful arrest, it is reasonable to allow the search (for the purpose of disarming the arrestee and seizing EVIDENCE which he may seek to destroy) to blanket the entire premises in which the arrest was made. This is a matter of the greatest consequence, for the vast majority of searches are carried out incident to arrest. If, however, the warrant requirement is considered to be the core of the amendment, the search must be circumscribed to the extent required by the emergency and therefore confined to the person arrested and the area within his immediate reach.

To treat reasonableness as an independent standard is contrary to both history and logic. On logical grounds there seems little value to stringent warrant requirements that can be readily negated by "reasonable" WARRANTLESS SEARCHES. History, too, sets its face against the notion. The Fourth Amendment's proscription of unreasonable searches, alone among the provisions of the BILL OF RIGHTS to set fair standards for the apprehension and trial of accused persons, has a rich historical background in American, as well as English, experience. The amendment is rooted in the restrictions which seventeenth- and eighteenth-century COMMON LAW judges in England placed on the search power (for example, WILKES CASES, 1763–1770). This power had been abused through the government's relentless hunt for political and religious dissidents during a phase of English history well understood in the colonies. The amendment stems more directly from the public outcry against indiscriminate searches for smuggled goods (autho-rized by GENERAL WARRANTS known as WRITS OF ASSISTANCE) during the last years of the colonial period in America, notably in Massachusetts. The main object of the Fourth Amendment, to prevent the recurrence of the detested general warrant, was to be accomplished by placing strict limits on the issuance of a warrant. The reasonableness clause, as seems clear from the historical record of the amendment's drafting in the first Congress, was meant to reemphasize, and perhaps strengthen, the warrant requirements in the second clause. To detach the reasonableness clause from the warrant clause by infusing it with independent potency serves to dilute the amendment's protection, exactly the opposite of the result its framers intended. It is insufficient to leave the initial determination of reasonableness to the police, with JUDICIAL REVIEW taking place retrospectively when the prosecutor seeks to introduce the fruits of the search in evidence. Many searches will produce no evidence, and even when evidence is found, the pressure on judges to rule against obviously guilty defendants will be great despite the illegality of the searches.

Consonant with the amendment's history, the Court at one time assigned an even broader meaning to "unreasonable" than is taken by the first view. In BOYD V. UNITED STATES (1886) the Court held that private papers are immune to seizure even under warrant—on the theory that one test of the reasonableness of a search is whether or not its purpose is to seize evidence that will force the person to incriminate himself. In contrast, contraband goods and fruits and instrumentalities of crime are deemed seizable because their possessor has no legal property right in them. In *Gouled v. United States* (1921) the Court logically extended the immunity granted private papers to all kinds of evidentiary materials (for example; clothing). However, this MERE EVIDENCE RULE, as it came to be known, was overturned as "wholly irrational" in WARDEN V. HAYDEN (1967), and probably little remains of the immunity granted to private papers (*Fisher v. United States*, 1976).

Other EXIGENT CIRCUMSTANCES, in addition to search incidental to arrest, which, in either view, permit the police to bypass the warrant requirement, include the rule of CARROLL V. UNITED STATES, (1925), which permits the search of a moving vehicle on PROBABLE CAUSE to believe that it is transporting contraband; the ruling in *Schmerber v. California* (1966), which permits the compulsory taking of a blood sample from a driver to measure its alcoholic content where there is probable cause to believe he was intoxicated while driving; and the rule of *Warden v. Hayden* (1967), which permits the "hot pursuit" of a felon into a dwelling. Even in the absence of evidence that a crime has been committed, where the suspicious conduct of an individual leads an officer to believe that he or others are in danger and imminent action is imperative, he may stop the suspect and "frisk" the individual's outer clothing in order to disarm him of weapons he may be carrying. (See TERRY V. OHIO, 1968.)

In the case of search incidental to arrest, hot pursuit, or STOP AND FRISK, the emergency is self-evident, but it is no less genuine in the case of a moving vehicle or a blood test, for the delay involved in the obtaining of a warrant will usually defeat the object of the search. The automobile might by that time be far away, perhaps in another jurisdiction, and the percentage of alcohol in the blood gradually diminishes once intake ceases. These are only examples. Clearly any real emergency, as the sound of a shot or a cry for help coming from behind closed doors, would justify a warrantless search by the police.

The only kinds of searches known to the framers, and to which the Fourth Amendment was originally addressed, contained two elements: (1) entry into the dwelling (2) for the purpose of seizing evidence of crime. At first the Court considered the definition of search to be governed by this experience and maintained that warrants were not required for more modern types of searches that lacked one or the other of these elements. Thus searches for oral utterances conducted by WIRETAPPING which do not involve entry onto premises, as in OLMSTEAD V. UNITED STATES (1928), or inspection of dwellings to uncover nuisances to public health or safety, as in *Frank v. Maryland* (1959), were held not to be covered by the amendment. Subsequently, however, ELECTRONIC EAVESDROPPING (including wiretapping) and ADMINISTRATIVE SEARCHES were both brought under the amendment's protective umbrella in KATZ V. UNITED STATES (1967) and CAMARA V. MUNICIPAL COURT (1967), respectively. But a visit to the home by a caseworker for the purpose of determining whether a public assistance grant is being properly used does not amount to an unreasonable search and requires no warrant, as the Court held in WYMAN V. JAMES (1971).

A court order for the surgical removal of a bullet from the body of a suspect was ruled unreasonable in *Winston v. Lee* (1985)—at least when the need for the evidence is not "compelling"—because of the serious intrusion on privacy and the medical risks entailed.

In order to prevent the Fourth Amendment from being reduced to a mere parchment guarantee, evidence obtained through unreasonable search has since 1914 been excluded from trials in the federal courts (*Weeks v. United States*), and in the state courts as well since MAPP V. OHIO (1961). (See EXCLUSIONARY RULE.) Although the amendment contains no express command of exclusion, it has been construed to authorize the judiciary to apply such sanctions as are necessary to ensure compliance with the standard of reasonableness.

Like the rest of the Bill of Rights, the ban on unreasonable searches was originally intended to place restrictions only on the federal government. That ban became applicable to the states, as an element of FOURTEENTH AMENDMENT due process, in 1961 (*Mapp v. Ohio*), and the same standard of reasonableness now governs searches made by federal and state authorities (KER V. CALIFORNIA, 1963). (See INCORPORATION DOCTRINE.)

JACOB W. LANDYNSKI

Bibliography

FELLMAN, DAVID 1976 *The Defendant's Rights Today.* Pages 277–284. Madison: University of Wisconsin Press.

LaFAVE, WAYNE R. 1978 *Search and Seizure: A Treatise on the Fourth Amendment.* Vol. 2:406–476, 498–609; vol. 3:2–140. St. Paul, Minn.: West Publishing Co.

LANDYNSKI, JACOB W. 1966 *Search and Seizure and the Supreme Court.* Pp. 30–44, 387–417. Baltimore: Johns Hopkins University Press.

———— 1971 "The Supreme Court's Search for Fourth Amendment Standards: The Warrantless Search." *Connecticut Bar Journal* 45:2–39.

LEVY, LEONARD W. 1974 *Against the Law: The Nixon Court and American Justice.* Pages 75–117. New York: Harper & Row.

UNWRITTEN CONSTITUTION

When the American colonists charged that some British colonial policies and practices were unconstitutional, they appealed to what was generally conceived as an unwritten constitutional tradition that combined the practical good sense of English experience with standards of conduct that were simply, or naturally, equitable and right. Though the principles of this constitutional tradition were scattered among state documents, reported cases of the COMMON LAW, treatises, and other writings, their status derived not from having been written or enacted but from their perceived origin in sources like custom, divine will, reason, and nature. These principles were thought superior to acts of Parliament, whose status did depend on their enactment.

While invoking unwritten HIGHER LAW, however, the colonists were implicitly challenging its efficacy. To the charge of TAXATION WITHOUT REPRESENTATION, Parliament responded with the theory of virtual representation. The colonists rejected this DOCTRINE and insisted that as a practical matter responsible government depended on the ballot, not on government's respect for natural justice. Belief in a higher law thus coexisted with a pessimistic view of human nature and a corresponding distrust of government.

Unlike Britain's constitution, the American Constitution was established through RATIFICATION, a form of enactment. As the supreme law of the land this enacted Constitution consigns appeals from its authority to the category of extralegal considerations. But foreclosing the constitutionality of appeals from the highest written law did not depreciate unwritten law as such, for the written or enacted law could still reflect unwritten standards of natural justice and reason whose status did not depend on enactment. This was the claim of those who campaigned for ratification, as was to be expected from the rhetoric typical of public attempts to persuade.

This is not to say that anyone saw the proposed constitution as entirely consistent with the dictates of reason and justice. Slavery and the equal REPRESENTATION in the Senate of small and large states are examples of acknowledged compromises with contingencies that would not bend to principle. Nevertheless, the argument for ratification was full of references to higher norms as standards for evaluating constitutions, as principles behind its rules and institutions, and as objectives of the system as a whole. In THE FEDERALIST #9 and #10, ALEXANDER HAMILTON and JAMES MADISON not only presented the Constitution as an attempt to reconcile democracy with minority rights and the common good, but they also stated that the fate of democracy justly depended on that reconciliation. In *The Federalist* #78 Hamilton defended JUDICIAL REVIEW and recognized the role of judges in "mitigating the severity and confining the operations" of "unjust and partial" enactments. In *The Federalist* #51 Madison said, "Justice is the end of government" and that it "ever will be pursued until it is obtained, or until liberty be lost in the pursuit." And in the same number he described CHECKS AND BALANCES as a "policy of supplying, by opposite and rival interests, the defects of better motives." Taking this statement at face value would require as a prerequisite to a full understanding of the Constitution knowledge of the "better motives" that constituted part of the model for what the Framers wrote.

It is a matter of central importance that appeals to ideas like justice were not expressed as appeals to this or that particular version but to the general idea itself. Aware of the difference, Hamilton urged readers of *The Federalist* #1 to rise above "local prejudices little favorable to the discovery of truth." He recalled the frequent claim that Americans would decide the possibility of rational government for the whole of mankind, a claim that might redouble efforts to rise above parochialism by adding "the inducements of philanthropy to those of patriotism." Equally important, however, was his acknowledgment of the great number and power of "causes which . . . give a false bias to . . . judgement." And he urged "moderation" on those "ever so thoroughly persuaded of their being in the right." This appeal suggests the value of self-critical striving for truth, an attitude more of confidence in progress toward truth than in claims to possess it.

Further indication of the Constitution's dependence on commitments that some theorists believe written constitutions can displace is the fact that properties of the Constitution as a whole influence the interpretation of its parts. In addition to the rhetoric of its PREAMBLE and of its draftsmen, the document reflects a concern for simple justice by virtue of its written character. As written communication to an audience of indefinite composition, size, and duration, the document presupposes that virtually anyone can come to understand what it means. Presupposing a large and lasting community of meaning, it anticipates a community of interests embracing all to whom it would potentially apply or who would accept it as a model.

Because of their content, provisions like the TENTH AMENDMENT and the old fugitive slave clause are at odds with the community of interests presupposed by the Constitution as a whole. They are at odds with themselves by virtue of their enunciation as parts of the whole. This tension justified JOHN MARSHALL's nationalist construction of the Tenth Amendment, ABRAHAM LINCOLN's view that the Constitution had put slavery on the path of ultimate extinction, and the Supreme Court's application of the BILL OF RIGHTS to the states through the INCORPORATION DOCTRINE. Observers have interpreted the acceptance of this kind of construction as a sign that the nation has an unwritten constitution. But therapeutic constructions might as easily indicate the power of a written constitution to undermine the parochial and particularistic aspects of its content, separable as the written word is from the physical presence of its authors and their particular needs and conceptions.

The implications of the Constitution's written character bear on a protracted debate among constitutional theorists over the possibility of limiting the discretion of judges in difficult constitutional cases involving human rights, especially rights to SUBSTANTIVE DUE PROCESS and EQUAL PROTECTION. Many participants in the debate share an academic moral skepticism that finds no meaning in general normative concepts beyond the particular conceptions of historical individuals or communities. They diminish simple justice with quotation marks, and they hold particular conceptions of justice interesting primarily as facts that influence other facts, not as beliefs that can be morally better or worse than other beliefs. Rejecting the object of its quest, they also reject traditional moral philosophy as a method of acquiring knowledge. They treat the beliefs of persons and communities as matters essentially of historical fact, to be established by empirical methods, with some room for conceptual analysis, but not for judgments of right and wrong.

To these commentators, talk of reason and justice is essentially rationalization of personal preference, class interest, community morality, and the like. And because they tend to believe that elected officials have a stronger claim to represent the community, they argue that judicial review often involves the imposition of minority preferences on the majority. In an effort to reconcile judicial review with majoritarianism these theorists have tried to link the meaning of general constitutional norms with the intentions of the Framers, tradition, existing and projected community morality, the institutional prerequisites of democratic decision, and other sources whose content they perceive essentially as matters of fact or uncontroversial inference. The effort has failed largely because each source yields conflicting options, not simple, consistent answers. And when the skeptics make their selections, they inevitably (if covertly and therefore irresponsibly) make normative judgments whose rationality their position would force them to deny.

The failure of these skeptical theorists to extirpate normative judgments from decisions about the meaning of constitutional provisions has strengthened the case for moral philosophy in constitutional inquiry, which, in turn, has exacerbated apprehension of unrestrained judicial power. But renewed concern for natural justice need not threaten hopes for limiting judicial discretion. Those who take seriously the idea of justice as something higher than their particular conceptions will value the self-critical striving for moral and political truth recommended in *The Federalist* #1. This attitude is itself a limitation on discretion

of the most objectionable variety because it is the antithesis of willful assertiveness.

Arguments for taking natural justice seriously might begin by reflecting on the apparent power of ordinary political debate to change minds about justice and related ideas. This familiar fact shows that, as ordinary citizens understand it, political life presupposes simple justice. Moral skeptics err in supposing that continuing disagreement about justice proves that debate is pointless or that there is nothing to debate about. If there are moral truths to be known, as is ordinarily presupposed, agreement is not the test of what is right. Holding that agreement is the test may signal that one abandons ordinary presuppositions, but it is not an argument for doing so. Academic inquiry begins with ordinary presuppositions. And though constitutional theorists have not reached agreement (a good thing, for universal consensus would remove the impetus for reflection and improvement), they have been unable to avoid ordinary presuppositions about justice and the value of reasoning in deciding what the Constitution means. Perhaps this is a reason to value self-critical striving for the best constructions to which constitutional language, tradition, and opinion are open.

SOTIRIOS A. BARBER

(SEE ALSO: *Higher Law; Limited Government; Natural Rights and the Constitution.*)

Bibliography
BREST, PAUL 1981 The Fundamental Rights Controversy: The Essential Contradictions of Normative Constitutional Scholarship. *Yale Law Journal* 90:1063–1109.
GREY, THOMAS C. 1978 Origins of the Unwritten Constitution: Fundamental Law in American Revolutionary Thought. *Stanford Law Review* 30:843–893.
HARRIS, WILLIAM F., II 1982 Bonding Word and Polity: The Logic of American Constitutionalism. *American Political Science Review* 76:34–45.
MOORE, MICHAEL S. 1985 A Natural Law Theory of Interpretation. *Southern California Law Review* 58:277–398.
_____ 1982 Moral Reality. *Wisconsin Law Review* 1982:1061–1156.

UPHAUS v. WYMAN
360 U.S. 72 (1959)

In PENNSYLVANIA V. NELSON (1956) the Court appeared to hold that the Smith Act preempted state antisubversion laws. Here the Court held that state JURISDICTION over sedition against the state, as opposed to sedition against the federal government, was not preempted. In *Sweezy v. New Hampshire* (1956) the Court had invalidated a subversion investigation by the New Hampshire attorney general. Here, using the interest-balancing techniques of BARENBLATT V. UNITED STATES (1959), decided the same day, the Court upheld a similar investigation by him in his capacity as a one-man legislative investigating committee.

MARTIN SHAPIRO

USE IMMUNITY

See: Immunity Grant

UTILITY REGULATION

See: Economic Regulation

VACCINATION

Vaccination is the introduction into the body of a vaccine to prevent disease. In the late nineteenth and early twentieth centuries a number of states made smallpox vaccination compulsory. The Supreme Court upheld the constitutionality of such a law in JACOBSON V. MASSACHUSETTS (1905), and *Jacobson*'s continuing vitality as a PRECEDENT is routinely assumed.

The *Jacobson* opinion was written by Justice OLIVER WENDELL HOLMES, who regarded the case as he regarded LOCHNER V. NEW YORK (1905), decided later the same year over his dissent. For Holmes, the question in both cases was whether the legislative judgment had passed the bounds of reason. For the majority who found a violation of SUBSTANTIVE DUE PROCESS in *Lochner's* sixty-hour limit on bakers' weekly work but validated compulsory vaccination, the difference surely was that they saw vaccination as a soundly based health requirement. Yet the subsequent collapse of substantive due process as a constitutional limit on ECONOMIC REGULATION should not be taken as a return to the Holmes view equating invasions of the body with the general run of restrictions on liberty. Undoubtedly the standard of judicial review in such cases today is far more demanding than it was for Holmes in *Jacobson*.

A patient who refuses medical treatment, for example, surely has a constitutional right to do so, founded on the liberty protected by the due process clauses, absent the most compelling justification for state-ordered intrusion into his or her body. The right may come to be described in the PRIVACY language used to explain the abortion decisions, which really rest not so much on privacy in its ordinary sense as on a woman's control over her own body and her own life. Similarly, the decisions involving invasion of the body to extract blood or other EVIDENCE for use in detecting crime make clear that such invasions must pass the test of strict judicial scrutiny of their justifications. Claims of RELIGIOUS LIBERTY may be added to the constitutional mix, as when a Jehovah's Witness refuses a blood transfusion, but with or without that ingredient the constitutional claim to autonomy over the body is strong.

The strength of the countervailing governmental interest in compelling vaccination would, of course, depend on the degree of danger to the public posed by unvaccinated persons. Now that smallpox is approaching worldwide eradication, the constitutional claim of a latter-day Jacobson would be far more substantial. Many doctors now recommend against smallpox vaccination, because—as Jacobson himself argued—the procedure involves a risk of contracting the disease. Given the vastly reduced public health justification for the inoculation, it is by no means clear that a compulsory smallpox vaccination law would survive constitutional challenge today. Undoubtedly, however, a state could constitutionally require vaccination for other diseases that significantly endanger public health.

KENNETH L. KARST

Bibliography

TRIBE, LAURENCE H. 1978 *American Constitutional Law.* Pages 913–921. Mineola, N.Y.: Foundation Press.

VAGRANCY LAWS

Historically, society has used vagrancy laws to punish undesirable or immoral persons considered to be dangerous because of their potential for engaging in criminal conduct. Such laws differed significantly from traditional criminal statutes in that they made it a crime to be a person of a specified status or condition. In the United States, the types of persons punished as "vagrants" have included rogues, vagabonds, habitual loafers, and others considered to be of immoral character.

The first vagrancy laws, which originated in England, required workers to live in specified locations and proscribed giving assistance to able-bodied beggars who refused to work. Late-fifteenth-century vagrancy laws provided that beggars and idle persons, after punishment, were to be banished.

Vagrancy legislation in the United States began in colonial times and closely followed the English model. In the nineteenth century, the Supreme Court in MAYOR OF NEW YORK V. MILN (1837) implicitly recognized both the objectives and necessity of such laws, stating in OBITER DICTUM: "We think it as competent and as necessary for a state to provide precautionary measures against this moral pestilence of paupers, vagabonds, and possible convicts; as it is to guard against the physical pestilence. . . ." More recently, the Court in EDWARDS V. CALIFORNIA (1941) expressly rejected this notion, observing that "[w]hatever may have been the notion then prevailing, we do not think that it will now be seriously contended that because a person is without employment and without funds he constitutes a 'moral pestilence.' Poverty and immorality are not synonymous."

Edwards, however, was a narrow decision, which struck down under the COMMERCE CLAUSE a California statute making it a misdemeanor to bring an indigent, nonresident alien into the state. Thus, notwithstanding *Edwards*, vagrancy laws continued broadly to proscribe various types of status crimes until the Supreme Court's decision in *Papachristou v. City of Jacksonville* (1972).

In *Papachristou* the Court held under the VAGUENESS DOCTRINE that a vagrancy statute was unconstitutional on its face. The ordinance, a typical example of a traditional vagrancy law, subjected the following persons to criminal penalty because the city deemed them to be "vagrants":

Rogues and vagabonds . . . dissolute persons who go about begging, common gamblers, persons who use juggling or unlawful games or plays, common drunkards, common night walkers, thieves, pilferers or pickpockets, traders in stolen property, lewd, wanton and lascivious persons, keepers of gambling places, common railers and brawlers, persons wandering or strolling around from place to place without any lawful purpose or object, habitual loafers, disorderly persons, persons neglecting all lawful business and habitually spending their time by frequenting houses of ill fame, gaming houses, or places where alcoholic beverages are sold or served, [and] persons able to work but habitually living upon the earnings of their wives or minor children.

Two fundamental constitutional defects arise from the vagueness inherent in traditional vagrancy laws. Initially, the definition of "vagrant" fails to give adequate notice of what criminal conduct is proscribed. As recognized in *Connally v. General Construction Co.* (1926), when a criminal statute "either forbids or requires the doing of an act in terms so vague that men of common intelligence must necessarily guess at its meaning and differ as to its application," the DUE PROCESS CLAUSE requires its invalidation under the vagueness doctrine. This doctrine was first applied to a vagrancy-type statute in *Lanzetta v. New Jersey* (1939), which held unconstitutional for vagueness a New Jersey "gangster" statute punishing any "person not engaged in any lawful occupation, known to be a member of a gang consisting of two or more persons, who has been convicted [of a crime or at least three disorderly person offenses]." *Papachristou* applied this doctrine to traditional vagrancy laws, in which the generalized and all-inclusive definitions may encompass many types of innocent behavior.

The second aspect of the vagueness doctrine, even more important than the requirement of fair notice, is that a criminal statute must set forth minimal guidelines to govern law enforcement. Absent such guidelines, a criminal statute is subject to substantial abuse by police officers, prosecutors, and jurors on the basis of their own personal predilections. Imprecise definitions, like those contained in traditional vagrancy statutes, give law enforcement officers virtually unbridled discretion to make arrests on mere suspicion rather than on PROBABLE CAUSE, and to use such arrests as a law enforcement tool to gather information and to interview persons about unrelated crimes. Moreover, as suggested in Justice HUGO L. BLACK'S dissenting opinion in *Edelman v. California* (1953), they are also easily susceptible of being used against persons expressing unpopular views, as well as against the poor and minorities.

Traditional vagrancy statutes may also suffer from other constitutional defects. For example, *Robinson v. California* (1962) struck down a provision of a California vagrancy statute that made it a crime to be a "narcotics addict," on the ground that the statute violated the CRUEL AND UNUSUAL PUNISHMENT clause of the Eighth Amendment. In *Powell v. Texas* (1968), by contrast, the Court upheld a state statute that proscribed public drunkenness, even though the person so charged might suffer from chronic alcoholism. The Court noted in *Powell* that such a proscription differs from convicting someone for being an addict, a chronic alcoholic, mentally ill, or a leper. Rather than punishing mere status, the proscription focuses on the specific act of appearing drunk in public on a particular occasion—conduct that the state has an interest in prohibiting.

To the extent that vagrancy laws have been used to exclude undesirables from a state or otherwise to confine them geographically, *Edwards* recognizes that they may unreasonably burden INTERSTATE COMMERCE. Moreover, such restrictions also may unconstitutionally impair the RIGHT TO TRAVEL. And provisions of vagrancy laws that prohibit association with known thieves and other undesirables not only suffer from vagueness but also may violate an individual's right of association.

In view of the Supreme Court's decisions in the area of vagrancy laws, most of the antiquated provisions of such laws—which focus on controlling undesirables by proscribing various types of status or condition—no longer can withstand constitutional scrutiny.

JAMES R. ASPERGER

(SEE ALSO: *Kolender v. Lawson, 1983.*)

Bibliography

AMSTERDAM, ANTHONY G. 1967 Federal Constitutional Restrictions on the Punishment of Crimes of Status, Crimes of General Obnoxiousness, Crimes of Displeasing Police Officers, and the Like. *Criminal Law Bulletin* 3:205–241.
FOOTE, CALEB 1956 Vagrancy-Type Law and Its Administration. *University of Pennsylvania Law Review* 104:603–650.
LACEY, FORREST W. 1953 Vagrancy and Other Crimes of Personal Condition. *Harvard Law Review* 66:1203–1226.

VAGUENESS

The Fifth Amendment and FOURTEENTH AMENDMENT respectively prohibit the federal and state governments from taking life, liberty, or property without DUE PROCESS OF LAW. These provisions forbid the enforcement of any law that, in the classic words of *Connally v. General Construction Co.* (1926), "either forbids or requires the doing of an act in terms so vague that men of common intelligence must necessarily guess at its meaning and differ as to its application." Vagueness imperils the fair administration of legal sanctions in several ways. First, it threatens punishment of people who had no fair warning of what conduct to avoid. Second, by creating interpretive latitude for those who apply the law—police, prosecutors, judges, juries, and others—vagueness permits punishment to be inflicted selectively for arbitrary or improper reasons. Third, a law's vagueness hinders the efforts of reviewing courts to control such abuses in the law's enforcement; the less clear the law is, the less visible—and correspondingly more difficult to detect and correct—are irregular instances of its administration.

To minimize these dangers, the due process requirement of reasonable clarity forbids enforcement even if the legislature constitutionally could have prohibited, through a clearer law than it did enact, all the behavior its vague law might have been intended to reach. When the uncertain coverage of a vague law might extend into areas of behavior that are constitutionally protected from regulation, however, the ordinary dangers of arbitrary enforcement are heightened, and two additional concerns emerge: the risk that a vague law, which inevitably poses an uncertain risk of prosecution, will inhibit people from exercising precious liberties that the government has no right to outlaw, and the possibility that the legislature did not explicitly focus on the liberty interest and thus did not actually decide that there was compelling reason to regulate it.

The deterrence of constitutionally guaranteed activity that vagueness may produce is akin to the deterrence produced by overbroad laws that encompass both behavior that legitimately may be regulated and behavior that is constitutionally protected. Vagueness differs from overbreadth in that the source of potential inhibition is the law's lack of clarity, not its excessive reach. Yet in both cases the ultimate threat is that those who wish to exercise constitutional rights will refrain from doing so for fear of being penalized. That vagueness may have the practical effect of overbroad regulation explains the common doctrinal confusion between the two concepts. Vagueness also differs from OVERBREADTH in another way: an uncertain law that addresses, even in its most expansive interpretation, only behavior that constitutionally may be regulated may still be void for vagueness, but, by definition, cannot be void for overbreadth.

Two questions dominate the law of vagueness: how much vagueness is tolerable before the law violates due process, and who may raise the vagueness objection. The Supreme Court appears to give different answers to each question, depending on whether or not the vagueness implicates constitutionally protected activity. Still, the constitutional issue of vagueness is always a question of degree, of how much interpretive uncertainty is tolerable before the legitimate regulatory interests of government must yield to the perils of vagueness. If the constitutional definition of vagueness is itself uncertain, the reason is that language is inherently imprecise. The public interest in regulating antisocial behavior would be sacrificed if due process mandated impossible standards of clarity before laws validly could be enforced.

The starting point for vagueness analysis is to ascertain the nature of the standard that the law sets. This inquiry requires judges to consider not only the statutory language but also all interpretive aids that may add to the law's precision, such as accepted meanings in the relevant community (or in other areas of law) for terms contained in the statute, implementing regulations, past judicial interpretations that have clarified uncertain terms, and even judicial clarification in the very case raising the vagueness objection—if this after-the-fact clarification does not disregard the legislature's intent and if the challenger reasonably could have anticipated that the law could be construed to cover his conduct. The interpretive option often allows the Supreme Court and lower federal courts to avoid invalidating vague federal laws. When federal courts confront state laws, however, they are limited to determining whether state court clarification has cured any constitutional problems of vagueness. This difference largely explains why state laws are stricken for vagueness more often than are federal laws.

Once a law has received the benefit of all available clarification, a wide range of factors affects a court's judgment whether the law's remaining vagueness renders it unconstitutional. In a case in which the vagueness does not bear on constitutionally shielded behavior, only two vagueness objections are permitted: that the law is vague as applied to the particular behavior of the individual challenger, or that the law is INVALID ON ITS FACE for being unduly vague as applied to anyone, including the challenger, because no one who consulted it could derive fair warning of what conduct was prohibited or could determine whether the legislature meant one thing rather than another. In *Hoffman Estates v. Flipside* (1982) the Supreme Court confirmed that in deciding cases in which the latter objection is raised, greater uncertainty is constitutionally permissible when the law

regulates a relatively narrow subject matter; when the law regulates economic behavior (because businesses more reasonably can be expected to consult laws in advance of acting than can individuals); when the law imposes civil rather than criminal penalties (because the consequences of noncompliance are less severe); and when the law applies only to those who intentionally or knowingly violate it (because there is less risk of unfair surprise). Historically, once the Supreme Court determined that ECONOMIC REGULATION posed no significant threat to constitutional freedoms, it became more tolerant of the imprecision in laws banning "unreasonable," "unjust," or "unfair" prices or business practices, as *United States v. National Dairy Products Corp.* (1963) illustrates. Moreover, the Court permits more uncertainty when it perceives the government's regulatory objective to be especially important—as SCREWS V. UNITED STATES (1945) demonstrated in upholding a rather vague CIVIL RIGHTS law protecting individuals—and also when it would be difficult for the legislature to delineate more precisely the penalized behavior.

The Court is especially receptive to a challenge based on vagueness when a law's uncertain coverage risks inhibiting constitutionally safeguarded freedoms. In the last half-century this receptivity has been manifested primarily in FIRST AMENDMENT cases. One indicator of the Court's increased sensitivity is the wide range of people who may now raise the vagueness objection. In cases implicating constitutionally protected activity, the Court not only entertains complaints that a law is vague as applied to the individual litigant or vague in all applications, but it sometimes permits those to whom a law clearly applies to object that it is facially invalid because it is unduly vague as to others. Despite Supreme Court rulings to the contrary both in earlier periods and in cases as recent as PARKER V. LEVY (1974) and BROADRICK V. OKLAHOMA (1973), and despite continuing voices of dissent that this practice allows one as to whom enforcement is fair to assert the hypothetical rights of others and confuses vagueness and overbreadth, the Court currently maintains, in such cases as YOUNG V. AMERICAN MINI THEATRES (1976) and KOLENDER V. LAWSON (1983), that such a person may have the whole law invalidated if the deterrent effect of its vagueness on others is real and substantial.

All of the factors that bear on the acceptable degree of vagueness in laws encompassing only unprotected conduct still apply, some more heavily, to laws that potentially reach constitutionally protected conduct. In addition, the Supreme Court seems to be concerned with other factors: how much protected freedom the vagueness might deter; how important the asserted freedom is; the judges' capacity to preserve the freedom through case-by-case application; the legislature's ability to reformulate the law in less inhibiting fashion; and the extent and importance of legitimate regulation that must be foregone if the law is voided for vagueness.

Although the Court does not always articulate these considerations, they appear to underlie many decisions. In *Baggett v. Bullitt* (1964) and *Cramp v. Board of Public Instruction* (1961), for example, the invalidation of LOYALTY OATH requirements for undue vagueness arrayed important freedoms of association against dubious government needs for assurance. More generally, when the enactment's vagueness risks suppression of unpopular expression or criticism of government, the Court's tolerance level is low. Thus in *Coates v. Cincinnati* (1971) an ordinance barring assembly of three or more persons "annoying" passers-by was held void, as was a law prohibiting "contemptuous treatment" of the American flag in *Smith v. Goguen* (1974).

On the other hand, even vagueness that inhibits valued expression is sometimes indulged if regulatory interests are perceived as powerful. Good examples are the extreme vagueness *Parker v. Levy* permitted the military in punishing "conduct unbecoming an officer and a gentleman" and the lesser, yet undoubted, uncertainty of laws prohibiting partisan political activity by PUBLIC EMPLOYEES that the Court upheld in *Broadrick v. Oklahoma*.

Similarly divergent assessments of the acceptable level of indefiniteness in statutes defining and proscribing OBSCENITY reflect conflict within the Court over the value of sexually explicit, but constitutionally protected, materials. The judgment that deterrence of some sexually explicit adult movies was no cause for alarm led a plurality in *Young v. American Mini Theatres* to uphold a ZONING ordinance restricting the concentration of adult theaters and bookstores in downtown Detroit. A similar judgment underlies the Court's willingness to permit inevitably vague definitions of obscenity to serve as the basis for criminal punishment. By contrast, Justice WILLIAM J. BRENNAN, who is more concerned about the potentially protected sexual expression that might be lost, declared in his important dissent in *Paris Adult Theatre I v. Slaton* (1973) his firm, if belated, conviction that vagueness in defining obscenity is virtually an insuperable problem. Even he, however, did not conclude that the distribution of obscene materials must conse-

quently remain unregulated; rather, he suggested that the protection of juveniles and the privacy of unconsenting adults might render vagueness tolerable, though protection of consenting adults and community mores and aesthetics would not.

The complexity of the vagueness doctrine stems, then, from the dual nature of the constitutional protection that it offers. Individuals are protected in any case from arbitrary enforcement without a fair opportunity to conform their conduct to legitimate law, and the social interest in maximizing constitutional freedoms is central to judgments about vagueness when the law's indefiniteness threatens to inhibit those freedoms.

JONATHAN D. VARAT

Bibliography

AMSTERDAM, ANTHONY B. 1960 The Void-for-Vagueness Doctrine in the Supreme Court. *University of Pennsylvania Law Review* 109:67–116.
BOGEN, DAVID S. 1978 First Amendment Ancillary Doctrines. *Maryland Law Review* 37:679, 714–726.
SCHAUER, FREDERICK 1978 Fear, Risk and the First Amendment: Unravelling the "Chilling Effect." *Boston University Law Review* 58:685.

VALENTINE v. CHRESTENSEN

See: Commercial Speech

VALLANDIGHAM, EX PARTE
1 Wallace 243 (1864)

In 1863, soldiers arrested, tried, and found guilty Negrophobic Democratic congressman Clement L. Vallandigham (Ohio) for violating Army orders against public expressions of Confederate sympathies. After returning to this country from banishment in rebel lines, which ABRAHAM LINCOLN had ordered, Vallandigham applied to the Supreme Court for a WRIT OF CERTIORARI to annul the military proceedings. The Court, accepting JURISDICTION, decided, without dissent, that it had no jurisdiction over appeals from military courts. The likelihood of direct clashes between the Court and the COMMANDER-IN-CHIEF thus receded to revive in EX PARTE MILLIGAN (1867).

HAROLD M. HYMAN

VALLEY FORGE CHRISTIAN COLLEGE v. AMERICANS UNITED FOR SEPARATION OF CHURCH AND STATE
454 U.S. 464 (1982)

Severely limiting the precedent of FLAST V. COHEN (1968), the Supreme Court here tightened the requirements for STANDING in a TAXPAYER'S SUIT against the federal government.

Under a general power from Congress to dispose of surplus federal property, the Department of Health, Education and Welfare (HEW) transferred land and buildings worth over $500,000 to a religious college that trained students for the ministry. Because HEW calculated that the government benefited from the transfer at a rate of 100 percent, the college paid nothing.

Federal taxpayers sued to set aside the transfer, contending that it amounted to an ESTABLISHMENT OF RELIGION. The Supreme Court held, 5–4, that the taxpayers lacked standing. The majority distinguished *Flast*, which had upheld taxpayer standing to challenge federal subsidies to church schools: *Flast* challenged an act of Congress; here plaintiffs challenged a decision by HEW. Furthermore, *Flast* involved injury to the plaintiffs as taxpayers: tax money was to be spent unconstitutionally. Here the Court dealt not with Congress's spending power but with the power to dispose of property.

The dissenters emphasized what everyone knew: absent taxpayer standing, no one has standing to challenge government donations of property to churches. In such cases the establishment clause is enforceable in the consciences of government officials, but not in court.

KENNETH L. KARST

VAN BUREN, MARTIN
(1782–1862)

Martin Van Buren of Kinderhook, New York, was admitted to the bar in 1803 and quickly established himself as a successful lawyer and politician. While serving in the New York legislature, Van Buren and a group of close associates known as the Albany Regency constituted the first political machine with a modern cast in the nation. As such the Regency gave a new direction to American politics.

But Van Buren did not consider the political process an end in itself; he saw in it a mode for achieving his notion of a Jeffersonian republic, in which a judicious division of power and responsibility between the central government and the states turned on a STRICT CONSTRUCTION of the Constitution. Opposition was expressed in BROAD CONSTRUCTION, along Hamiltonian lines. Between these two positions, the one emphasizing state power, the other national, the very essence of SOVEREIGNTY would be in constant conflict over public questions, a conflict he thought essential to the democratic governance of the states and the nation. He carried his ideas of an adversarial party system to Washington when elected a United States senator in 1821, and over the two terms he served, developed, and promoted them. Van Buren bound together into a cohesive program the personal factions that constituted his party. As he had planned, his partisan coalition gave impetus to a specific political opposition. Thus, he played a significant role in the formation of the current two-party system.

Van Buren articulated a historical view of strict construction. He was a frequent critic of the centralizing doctrines of the MARSHALL COURT and supported measures to curb JUDICIAL REVIEW. He drafted ANDREW JACKSON's veto of the MAYSVILLE ROAD BILL, the first comprehensive treatment of the responsibility of the central government to fund INTERNAL IMPROVEMENTS in the various states. Van Buren distinguished projects that were clearly intrastate from those that were interstate in character. In withholding the support of the national government for the economic development of the individual states, he relied partly on JAMES MONROE's veto of the Cumberland Road Bill, but he took care to assert that many projects purely local in character and initiated by a state might deserve support under constitutional provisions that provided for the common defense and the GENERAL WELFARE. His distinction depended upon many variables which could change with time and with circumstance.

Van Buren's second expression of what might be properly called the New Jeffersonianism was in the financial policy he pursued as President (1837–1841): the subtreasury system, which looked to the separation of the federal government from the state deposit banks. The federal government held most of the nation's specie currency, the basis of the paper money supply; thus it would act as a restraint on state banks, curbing their tendencies to speculation and ensuring a more equitable distribution of credit. His means may have been orthodox and deflationary, but they acted as a restriction upon state power, contrary to THOMAS JEFFERSON's ideas on government.

Van Buren's stand on the powers of Congress over

the TERRITORIES, however, was a restatement of Jeffersonian views expressed in the NORTHWEST ORDINANCE of 1787. Van Buren added his own interpretation of Article IV, section 3, of the Constitution, which delegates to the Congress the power "to make needful rules and regulations respecting the territory or other property of the United States." In doing so he went further than JOHN MARSHALL and agreed with JOSEPH STORY who asserted that the power was exclusive and that "rules and regulations" covered all possible contingencies. Van Buren had supported the MISSOURI COMPROMISE as a proper exercise of congressional power even though, as a matter of precedent, he thought the Ordinance of 1787 excluded slavery from all territories. In the United States Senate he voted against the bill organizing a territorial government for Florida because it sustained slavery. The most complete exposition of his stand on the territorial question of the late 1840s and 1850s is expressed in an address he prepared for the New York Democratic legislative caucus. It was the basis for the platform of the Free Soil party in the campaign of 1848 and the spirit and the substance of the Republican party platform in the campaigns of 1856 and 1860.

W. JOHN NIVEN

Bibliography

NIVEN, W. JOHN 1983 *Martin Van Buren and the Romantic Age of American Politics.* New York: Oxford University Press.

VAN DEVANTER, WILLIS
(1859–1941)

Colleagues and contemporary observers agreed that Willis Van Devanter was enormously influential during his twenty-six years on the Supreme Court. Chief Justice WILLIAM HOWARD TAFT, who as President appointed him in 1911, described his Wyoming associate as "my mainstay," "the most valuable man in our court," and the Justice who had "more influence" than any other. Justice LOUIS D. BRANDEIS, Van Devanter's ideological antipode, praised him as a "master of formulas that decided cases without creating precedents." Harvard's Professor FELIX FRANKFURTER aptly dubbed him Taft's "Lord Chancellor."

Van Devanter's backstage prominence contrasted vividly with his well-known "pen paralysis." He rarely spoke for the Court in major constitutional cases. During his tenure, Van Devanter averaged only fourteen written opinions each year; during the 1930s he averaged only three a year.

Van Devanter came to the Court after a career in Wyoming law and politics, followed by five years in the Interior Department. President THEODORE ROOSEVELT appointed him to the Eighth Circuit Court of Appeals in 1903; eight years later, President Taft elevated him to the Supreme Court. Taft, himself a former circuit judge, prized judicial experience as a criterion for appointment to the Supreme Court.

Although Van Devanter was one of the conservative "Four Horsemen" of the New Deal era, two of his earlier opinions aligned him with the "liberal nationalistic" wing of the Court. In the second of the EMPLOYERS' LIABILITY CASES (1913) he upheld a federal statute holding railroads liable for injuries suffered by workers engaged in INTERSTATE COMMERCE. He boldly generalized about the sweep of the COMMERCE CLAUSE, describing the commerce power as "complete in itself," but he added that it did not extend to matters that had no "real or substantial relation to some part of such commerce." The previous year, in *Southern Railway Co. v. United States* (1911), he had written for the Court to sustain federal railroad safety legislation in a case involving an intrastate railroad which carried goods that had passed through interstate commerce. Again, Van Devanter found the commerce power plenary and operative if an intrastate matter affected interstate commerce. The decision anticipated Justice CHARLES EVANS HUGHES's consideration of intrastate effects on the commerce power in the *Shreveport Case* (HOUSTON, EAST AND WEST TEXAS RAILROAD COMPANY V. UNITED STATES, 1914), an opinion Van Devanter supported; yet, in the 1930s he consistently rejected similar arguments to expand the scope of federal ECONOMIC REGULATION.

Van Devanter's most important and enduring contribution to constitutional law came with his opinion broadly approving Congress's investigative powers. In McGRAIN V. DAUGHERTY (1927) the plaintiffs had challenged a Senate committee's investigation of Harding administration scandals. Van Devanter recognized that historically "the power of inquiry—with process to enforce it—is an essential and appropriate auxiliary to the legislative function"; that the power might be abused, he added, was no argument against its existence.

Van Devanter usually supported governmental repression of political dissent in the World War I era. In the early 1930s, however, he deviated from his ideological allies as he joined the majority in invalidating a section of California's criminal anarchy law in STROMBERG V. CALIFORNIA (1931). He also supported

Justice GEORGE H. SUTHERLAND's pathbreaking opinion on Sixth Amendment rights in POWELL V. ALABAMA (1932). But a few years later, when the Court reverted to the CLEAR AND PRESENT DANGER doctrine for FIRST AMENDMENT cases, Van Devanter led the "Four Horsemen" in dissent. In HERNDON V. LOWRY (1937), which involved a black communist who had been convicted under Georgia state law, Van Devanter thought that Herndon's appeal to blacks was especially dangerous; Van Devanter's dissent reflected the suppressive BAD TENDENCY TEST and racist rhetoric, as well.

During the constitutional struggles over the New Deal, Van Devanter opposed the administration in every case except ASHWANDER V. TENNESSEE VALLEY AUTHORITY (1936). Even when his conservative colleagues resurrected the restrictive doctrines of UNITED STATES V. E. C. KNIGHT COMPANY (1895), a decision which he had circumvented in some of his early opinions, Van Devanter steadfastly opposed the expansion of national regulatory power. But he never spoke for that viewpoint, either in the majority or in dissent. Fittingly, however, he played a key role in what may have been FRANKLIN D. ROOSEVELT's most significant political defeat. During the consideration of Roosevelt's court-packing proposal in April 1937, Van Devanter announced his intention to take advantage of a new law allowing Justices to retire at full pay. The impending vacancy offered promise of a shift in the Court's ideological stance, and made the President's plan unnecessary for many administrative supporters. After his retirement from the Supreme Court, Van Devanter apparently was the first retired Justice who served regularly as a reserve judge.

STANLEY I. KUTLER

Bibliography

PASCHAL, JOEL F. 1951 *Mr. Justice Sutherland: A Man Against the State.* Princeton, N.J.: Princeton University Press.

PRINGLE, HENRY F. 1939 *The Life and Times of William Howard Taft.* New York: Farrar & Rinehart.

VAN HORNE'S LESSEE v. DORRANCE
2 Dallas 304 (1795)

Van Horne's Lessee, a circuit court case in the District of Pennsylvania, is memorable because of Justice WILLIAM PATERSON's charge to the jury, instructing them that a state act unconstitutionally violated property rights. His opinion can be read as a roadmap of the direction that constitutional law would take as a law of judicially implied limitations on legislation adversely affecting property rights. In lucid nonlegal language, Paterson spelled out judicial presuppositions and constitutional principles that were to become orthodox for well over a century. In discussing "What is a Constitution?" and analyzing the legislature's authority to pass its act divesting land titles, Paterson joined together the doctrines of JUDICIAL REVIEW and VESTED RIGHTS. Prefiguring FLETCHER V. PECK (1810) as well as the basic principle of MARBURY V. MADISON (1803), Paterson invoked the HIGHER LAW concept and the CONTRACT CLAUSE against the statute.

Having declared that "it will be the duty of the Court to adhere to the constitution, and to declare the act null and void" if it exceeds the legislature's authority, Paterson discoursed on the relationship between FUNDAMENTAL LAW and the rights of property. He found such rights inalienable, their preservation a primary object of "the social compact." Property, when vested, must be secure. For the government to take property without providing a recompense in value would be "an outrage," a "dangerous" display of unlimited authority, "a monster in legislation" that would "shock all mankind." To divest a citizen of his freehold even with compensation was a necessary "despotic" power to be exercised only in "cases of the first necessity." The reason was that the Constitution "encircles, and renders [a vested right] an holy thing. . . . It is a right not *ex gratia* from the legislature, but *ex debito* from the constitution. It is sacred. . . ."

Paterson informed the jury that courts must hold unconstitutional legislative encroachments on sacred property rights even in the absence of a written constitutional limitation on legislative powers. He relied on "reason, justice, and moral recitude," "the principles of social alliance in every free government," and the "letter and spirit of the constitution." The letter, in this instance, turned out to be the clause in Article I, section 10, of the Constitution, prohibiting a state law impairing the OBLIGATION OF A CONTRACT. Paterson assumed that the contract clause extended to contracts to which the state was a party; that a previous state act recognizing a property interest of the original claimant was a contract within the protection of the contract clause; and that the divestiture of the titles, even with compensation, violated the clause. Paterson's charge was a textbook exposition of SOCIAL COMPACT THEORY, CONSTITUTIONALISM, higher law limitations, judicial review, courts as bulwarks of property rights, and the contract clause.

LEONARD W. LEVY

VATTEL, EMERICH DE
(1714–1767)

Emerich de Vattel, the Swiss-born statesman and theorist of LIMITED GOVERNMENT, wrote his *Law of Nations* (1758) as an attempt to explain international law on the basis of NATURAL RIGHTS. He argued that men compacted to form sovereign states, and the state ordained a CONSTITUTION superior to any prince or legislature. Vattel reasoned that because the "legislature derives its power from the constitution, it cannot overleap the bounds of it without destroying its own foundation"—and this maxim was frequently cited by American revolutionary leaders including JAMES OTIS and SAMUEL ADAMS. Even more important for American constitutional thought was his assertion, often quoted by JAMES MADISON, that states joining a federal union retained their SOVEREIGNTY but were nevertheless bound by the terms of the union.

DENNIS J. MAHONEY

VEAZIE BANK v. FENNO
8 Wallace 533 (1869)

During the Civil War, Congress introduced national bank notes, secured by United States bonds, as one form of currency. Congress then decided to make its money supreme by driving out of circulation bank notes issued by state banks, and to that end it imposed a prohibitory ten percent tax on those notes. Veazie Bank objected on the grounds that the tax was not levied for revenue purposes but to drive state notes out of existence by the device of a DIRECT TAX, which must be apportioned among the states on the basis of population. Chief Justice SALMON P. CHASE, for a seven-member majority, upheld the constitutionality of the congressional tax statute. Chase declared that only taxes on land and CAPITATION TAXES were direct taxes. He found the constitutional authority for the statute in Congress's power to control the currency of the nation and for that purpose to restrain "the circulation as money of any notes not issued under its own authority." Without such a restraining power the attempt by Congress to secure a "sound and uniform currency for the country must be futile."

LEONARD W. LEVY

VENUE

"Venue" refers to the location of a trial. Article III of the Constitution specifies that federal crimes be tried "in the State where the said Crimes shall have been committed." This provision is reinforced by the SIXTH AMENDMENT's guarantee of TRIAL BY JURY "of the State and district wherein the crime shall have been committed." Although the INCORPORATION DOCTRINE has made the Sixth Amendment's jury trial guarantee applicable to the states, the Supreme Court has not yet had occasion to decide whether that amendment's venue provision also limits the states. However, state law itself usually provides for trial in the locality where the crime is alleged to have been committed.

Both the FEDERAL RULES OF CRIMINAL PROCEDURE and a number of state laws contemplate a change of venue when trial in the district otherwise appropriate risks prejudicing the fairness of a criminal trial. The availability of a change of venue has been offered by the Supreme Court as one argument against GAG ORDERS forbidding the press to publish information about pending prosecutions. (See FREE PRESS/FAIR TRIAL.)

Some crimes are committed in more than one place: interstate transportation of a stolen automobile, for example, or certain criminal conspiracies. The Supreme Court has upheld congressional legislation allowing prosecution in any of the districts in which such a crime is committed.

Venue in civil actions is not limited by the Constitution. By statute, Congress has established an elaborate set of rules governing venue in federal civil cases. Because these rules are designed for the parties' convenience, the right to assert them can be waived. Thus a defendant in a federal court civil action must raise the objection of improper venue before trial, at the pleadings stage of the case.

KENNETH L. KARST

Bibliography
WRIGHT, CHARLES ALAN 1983 *The Law of Federal Courts*, 4th ed. Chap. 7. St. Paul, Minn.: West Publishing Co.

VERMONT CONSTITUTION OF 1777
(July 8, 1777)

In significant respects Vermont's early constitutional history was unique. It was never a colony, had no charter, and was not recognized as a separate government or state by the original thirteen, although it fully supported the American cause during the Revolution. Vermonters declared their independence not only from Great Britain but also from New York. A "convention" adopted a CONSTITUTION, prefaced by a declaration of rights, that was modeled after the extremely democratic PENNSYLVANIA CONSTITUTION OF 1776, but Vermont added three notable provisions. Its constitution was the first to outlaw slavery, the first to allow all male residents over twenty-one to vote even if they owned no property and paid no taxes, and the first to include a provision for JUST COMPENSATION in cases of EMINENT DOMAIN. Vermont joined the union as the fourteenth state in 1791.

LEONARD W. LEVY

VESTED RIGHTS

"Vested rights" are claims enforceable under law. Early in the history of the Republic, an assertive concept of vested rights became the core of a highly refined legal and constitutional doctrine that was invoked as a shield for private property against regulation by government. In EDWARD S. CORWIN's phrase, this became "the basic doctrine of American constitutional law."

An early expression of the doctrine was Justice WILLIAM PATERSON's opinion in VAN HORNE'S LESSEE V. DORRANCE (1795), stating that preservation of private property is "a primary object of the SOCIAL COMPACT," so that any law taking one person's freehold and vesting it in another without compensation must be seen as "inconsistent with the principles of reason, justice and moral rectitude . . . [and] contrary to the principle of social alliance in every free government." In expounding this doctrine, judges and treatise writers cited general principles of justice from natural law, civil law, and COMMON LAW. In pre-1860 contract and property law, the doctrine served in tandem with the CONTRACT CLAUSE and was regularly invoked by those opposing the expansion of state interventions under the taxation, EMINENT DOMAIN, and POLICE POWERS.

There is a difference between "vested interests" and "vested rights." The former are claims and expectations based on private contractual relationships and upon a property owner's understanding of the privileges, immunities, and responsibilities associated by law with the property in question. Interests become "rights" when courts agree to enforce such contractual relationships and understandings concerning property. This difference was recognized by Justice ROBERT H. JACKSON, in his opinion in *United States v. Willow Run Power Company* (1945), declaring: "Not all economic interests are 'property rights'; only those economic advantages are 'rights' which have the law back of them. . . ." A claim to a right (or "advantage"), Jackson stated, "is really a question to be answered" in judicial proceedings and decisions; it is not something to be taken a priori, even when ancient maxims and rules can be adduced in favor of the claim.

Justice Jackson's robust LEGAL REALISM was not the view that prevailed in legal and constitutional discourse during the nineteenth century. On occasion, individual judges or courts did defend legislative prerogatives against claims of vested rights in terms that foreshadowed Jackson's formulation. For example, a New York judge in 1835 denounced vested rights as an "indefinite" term that was "resorted to when no better argument exists." Any governmental action, he contended, imposed "burthens and duties" that redefined rights. Much more commonly found, however, were views founded on the notion that it was "manifest injustice by positive law" when legislation took away what Justice SAMUEL CHASE described in CALDER V. BULL (1798) as "that security for personal liberty, or private property, for the protection whereof the government was established."

State judges regularly invoked the vested rights doctrine, often explicitly merged with DUE PROCESS declarations, to review and sometimes invalidate legislation. Many judges applied natural-law principles associated with the Fifth Amendment, contending that they were a check upon the abuse of legislative power no less important than explicit state constitutional provisions or than the contract clause. Much relied upon, in such decisions, was Justice JOSEPH STORY's opinion in *Wilkinson v. Leland* (1829), contending that "the fundamental maxims of a free government seem to require that the rights of personal liberty and private property should be held sacred."

During JOHN MARSHALL's tenure as Chief Justice, the court introduced "vested rights" doctrine into contract clause rulings, as in Marshall's opinions in FLETCHER V. PECK (1810) and DARTMOUTH COLLEGE V. WOODWARD (1819). When conservative, property-minded state and federal judges applied Marshall's doctrines in broad terms in the 1830s and 1840s, the debate over vested rights began to center on whether or not corporate privileges, broadly construed, should be given the same protection as property held by individuals and quasi-public institutions. To conservatives such as DANIEL WEBSTER and Justice Story, a corporation's privileges and property rights under a franchise were merely a variant of an individual's rights in fee simple to a house or a tract of farmland. Webster, for example, viewed the action of Massachusetts in CHARLES RIVER BRIDGE COMPANY V. WARREN BRIDGE COMPANY (1837) as part of a "revolution against the foundations on which property rests." He raised the alarm again in his argument in WEST RIVER BRIDGE V. DIX (1848), denouncing broad use of the power of eminent domain as a dangerous kind of agrarian radicalism. There was a pragmatic side, as well, to the arguments of conservatives; both Story and Webster warned on many occasions that to allow legislatures unrestrained use of the police power or eminent domain, in derogation of vested property rights whether personal or corporate, would risk bringing all new investment (and material progress) to a halt.

Beginning with the decision in the *Charles River Bridge* case, the antebellum Supreme Court softened its stand on vested rights; state judges, however, kept the doctrine before the bar and the public. The high-sounding rhetoric of vested rights doctrine can easily obscure one of the important facts of the pre-Civil War period—the irony that in practice the antebellum state courts, as James Willard Hurst has shown, "tended to uphold vested rights only so long as they were felt to yield substantial or present returns in social function." Seldom did the courts support claims of vested rights that were invoked to protect "static" economic interests, attempting to block technological innovation or new forms of investment. Judges favored instead claims of "dynamic" rights that could be seen as forces for change and growth.

The adoption of the FOURTEENTH AMENDMENT opened the way to revival of vested rights doctrine in federal constitutional law. If anything, "vested rights" were now championed in enlarged forms. Leading conservative lawyers such as WILLIAM M. EVARTS, former Justice JOHN A. CAMPBELL, and John N. Jewett seized on the Fourteenth Amendment to forge the new, broader doctrine. Citing the concept of property as an "established expectation," they denied that government could deprive property owners of any expectation unless it paid compensation. They expanded the notion of property to include the right to engage in occupations; and they contended broadly that the rights of ownership included the right to compete freely in the quest for profits. Taking up arguments presented earlier by Campbell, Justice STEPHEN J. FIELD even attempted in his dissenting

opinion in the SLAUGHTERHOUSE CASES (1873) to fuse the Fourteenth Amendment with the DECLARATION OF INDEPENDENCE—and thereby to throw the mantle of vested rights over economic interests and activities that he viewed as embraced by the phrase "pursuit of happiness." As he believed, such rights were beyond the legitimate reach of state regulation. Some conservative jurists and lawyers also found in the amendment's PRIVILEGES AND IMMUNITIES clause another prop for vested rights doctrine.

The newly expanded version of vested rights soon found its way into constitutional law, as Justice Field's views came to prevail with those of his colleagues. The traditional rhetoric of vested rights was harnessed to the FREEDOM OF CONTRACT doctrine, which became standard fare in the Court's decisions concerning the validity of laws regulating labor and business practices. In giving content to the doctrine of SUBSTANTIVE DUE PROCESS in the field of economic and social regulation, the Supreme Court marked out a meandering, uncertain, often absurd boundary between what it found to be legitimate police power and the "sacred" rights of property. The view, as Laurence Tribe has phrased it, "that certain settled expectations of a focused and crystallized sort should be secure against governmental disruption, at least without appropriate compensation" became a powerful weapon in the hands of the new industrial corporate interests—and at the same time became the center of political storms in the Populist and Progressive eras. Only with abandonment of economic due process in the late 1930s, together with the ascendancy of views such as Justice Jackson's harshly realist version of vested rights, did the concept recede in importance in constitutional law and in political strife.

In HOME BUILDING & LOAN ASSOCIATION V. BLAISDELL (1934), the Court gave notice that it was ready to uphold even so dramatic a state abridgment of private rights as a mortgage moratorium law. The Court would not, the majority declared, "throttle the capacity of the States to protect their fundamental interests." The common good, or the public interest, must also be honored in any system allocating constitutional powers and immunities. Thus the career of vested rights in the Webster-Story-Field tradition clearly had run its course. Nor for more than thirty years did debates in legislatures and courts return to the concerns of the conservative era; and even then the notion of "settled expectations" and related vested rights ideas were exhumed for application only in a fairly narrow context, relating to land use regulation and INVERSE CONDEMNATION. To that degree, at least, echoes of a doctrine rooted in natural law do continue to be heard in our own day.

HARRY N. SCHEIBER

Bibliography

CORWIN, EDWARD S. 1914 The Basic Doctrine of American Constitutional Law. *Michigan Law Review* 12:247–276.

HURST, JAMES WILLARD 1956 *Law and the Conditions of Freedom in the Nineteenth Century United States.* Madison: University of Wisconsin Press.

MCCLELLAN, JAMES 1971 *Joseph Story and the American Constitution.* Norman: University of Oklahoma Press.

MCCURDY, CHARLES W. 1975 Justice Field and the Jurisprudence of Government–Business Relations. *Journal of American History* 61:970–1005.

TWISS, BENJAMIN R. 1942 *Lawyers and the Constitution: How Laissez Faire Came to the Supreme Court.* Princeton, N.J.: Princeton University Press.

VETO POWER

After rejecting an absolute veto for the President, the delegates at the CONSTITUTIONAL CONVENTION OF 1787 granted the President a qualified power to veto congressional legislation, subject to an override by a two-thirds majority of each house of Congress. Some anti-Federalists objected to the veto as an encroachment upon the legislative power in violation of the SEPARATION OF POWERS doctrine, but ALEXANDER HAMILTON answered in THE FEDERALIST #73 that the President needed a veto to protect the executive branch from "depredations" by the legislature. The veto was also designed to be used against bills that were constitutionally defective, poorly drafted, or injurious to the community.

The Constitution provides that any bill not returned by the President "within ten Days (Sundays excepted)" shall become law "unless the Congress by their Adjournment prevent its Return, in which Case it shall not be a Law." The latter procedure, known as the POCKET VETO, was first used by President JAMES MADISON in 1812. In the POCKET VETO CASE of 1929, the Supreme Court decided that "adjournment" did not refer merely to final adjournment at the end of a Congress. The pocket veto could be used during any adjournment, final or interim, that "prevented" a bill's return to Congress. However, in *Wright v. United States* (1938) the Court considered a three-day recess by the Senate too short a period to constitute adjournment.

Further clarification of the pocket veto resulted from an action by President RICHARD M. NIXON. In 1970, during an adjournment of Congress for less than a week, he pocket-vetoed the Family Practice of Medicine Bill. An appellate court, in *Kennedy v. Sampson* (1974), held that an *intra*session adjournment of Congress does not prevent the President from returning a bill so long as Congress makes appropriate arrangements to receive presidential messages. The GERALD R. FORD and JIMMY CARTER administrations renounced pocket vetoes during *inter*session adjournments as well. This political accommodation restricted the pocket veto to the final adjournment at the end of the second session. President RONALD W. REAGAN, however, has used the pocket veto between the first and second sessions, provoking renewed litigation.

Other court decisions have clarified the boundaries of the veto power. In 1919, in *Missouri Pacific Railway Co. v. Kansas,* the Supreme Court announced that the Constitution required only two-thirds of a quorum in each House to override a veto, not two-thirds of the total membership. In 1899 the Court decided, in *La Abra Silver Mining Co. v. United States,* that the President could sign a bill after Congress recessed, and in *Edwards v. United States* (1932) the Court ruled that he could sign a bill after a final adjournment of Congress.

Statistics underscore the effectiveness of the President's veto. Of the 1,380 regular (return) vetoes from GEORGE WASHINGTON through Jimmy Carter, Congress overrode only ninety-four. There have also been 1,011 pocket vetoes, more than half of them directed by GROVER CLEVELAND and FRANKLIN D. ROOSEVELT against private relief bills.

Most of the governors of the states have been granted authority to veto individual items of a bill (the "item veto"). Congress has thus far resisted giving this power to the President, despite popular belief that such a power would increase "economy and efficiency" by combating "logrolling" and "pork-barrel" politics in Congress. Prominent among the arguments against the item veto is the danger that Presidents could use the authority to control the votes of individual members of Congress. A project in a member's district or state could be held hostage until he or she agreed to support a nominee or legislative proposal backed by the White House.

An informal type of item veto has evolved because Presidents selectively enforce the law. In signing a bill, Presidents have announced that they would refuse to carry out certain provisions which they considered unconstitutional or undesirable. The IMPOUNDMENT of funds has been a common example, but Presidents have also severed from authorization bills a number of sections they considered a "nullity," without binding force or effect.

                                                    LOUIS FISHER

Bibliography

FISHER, LOUIS 1985 *Constitutional Conflicts between Congress and the President.* Princeton, N.J.: Princeton University Press.

JACKSON, CARLTON 1967 *Presidential Vetoes, 1792–1945.* Athens: University of Georgia Press.

MASON, EDWARD CAMPBELL 1890 *The Veto Power.* New York: Russell & Russell.

VICE-PRESIDENCY

The American vice-presidency has historically occupied an ambiguous position. Although protocol ranks it the nation's second office, the duties assigned it have not been commensurate with that status. Pundits have frequently ridiculed the office and reformers have generously proposed modifying it. Yet for an institution that has engendered so much criticism the vice-presidency has undergone remarkably little constitutional change.

The office was conceived in the final days of the CONSTITUTIONAL CONVENTION OF 1787 for reasons that remain obscure. Some delegates suggested the need for an officer to preside over the Senate and resolve tie votes. Others viewed the vice-presidency as a way to handle unexpected presidential vacancies. Finally, some saw the office as an expedient to ensure the election of a national President. They feared that presidential electors would invariably support their own state's favorite son, thereby frustrating efforts to select a chief executive. By creating a second office and by giving electors a second vote subject to the proviso that one of the votes must go to a person from a state other than the elector's these constitutional architects believed they would overcome provincial tendencies and provide the new nation with a consensus leader. The candidate with the most votes (provided that they constituted a majority) would be President, the runner-up vice-president.

The system provided not only a national President but also vice-presidents of rare ability—JOHN ADAMS, THOMAS JEFFERSON, and AARON BURR. In 1800, however, the electoral votes for Jefferson and Burr deadlocked, although the Republican party had clearly intended Jefferson to be President. The constitutional crisis required thirty-six ballots of the House of Representatives before Jefferson prevailed. The initial system accordingly fell into disfavor, and in 1804 the states ratified the TWELFTH AMENDMENT which provided for separate election of President and vice-president. Many legislators feared that the vice presidency would attract only inferior candidates and accordingly proposed its abolition.

Although the office survived, the high caliber of its occupants did not. Most vice-presidents during the remainder of the nineteenth century were nonentities who brought few credentials to the office, did little while in it, and disappeared from public attention once their term ended. Presidents had little influence on the selection of their running mates. Party leaders typically chose the second candidate from a different wing of the party in order to balance the ticket. Presidents and vice-presidents frequently feuded over policy and personal differences. The vice-president presided over the Senate, but did little else. As WOODROW WILSON wrote, "The chief embarrassment in discussing his office is, that in explaining how little there is to be said about it one has evidently said all there is to say."

The nineteenth century did, however, provide four occasions for vice-presidents to succeed to the presidency on the death of the incumbent. JOHN TYLER, MILLARD FILLMORE, ANDREW JOHNSON, and CHESTER A. ARTHUR all became President when their predecessors died in office. None, however, won a term of his own.

The ambiguous constitutional status of the office was one source of its problem. The office was a hybrid between the legislative and executive branches; its occupant was selected with the President, and yet his only constitutional duty resided in the legislative branch. Neither the Senate nor the President was disposed to give great power to an officer which neither had selected and neither could remove. Some Presidents have viewed the vice-presidency as a legislative office and argued that the principle of SEPARATION OF POWERS precludes delegation of duties. Some vice-presidents have advanced this reasoning (or rationalization) to resist executive assignments. Moreover, since the presidency itself was relatively inactive for much of the nineteenth century, the President typically had little need to delegate duties to a vice-president, especially one not politically or personally compatible.

During the twentieth century, the vice-presidency achieved greater importance. The rise in status of the office occurred primarily because of political change rather than constitutional reform. The presidency became the main beneficiary of increased activity of the federal government, especially from the New Deal onward. The President became the distributor of increased patronage, and therefore other political actors responded more willingly to his influence. Accordingly, presidential candidates, rather than party leaders, began to assume a larger role in selecting the running mate. Presidents thus had a chance to select compatible vice-presidents and an incentive to provide them with some assignments. Moreover, increased demands on the presidency provided opportunities for vice-presidential activity. Presidents have tended to use their vice-presidents as foreign envoys, commission chairmen, party leaders, public spokesmen, legislative liaison, and advisers. Ratification in 1967 of the TWENTY-FIFTH AMENDMENT, which in part provided a means for filling unexpected vice-presidential vacancies, recognized the new significance of the office. With a few notable exceptions, twentieth-century vice-presidents have been men of some accomplishment. Many have been presidential candidates prior to accepting the second position: virtually all subsequently were considered for their party's presidential nomination or received it. Since 1900, five vice-presidents—THEODORE ROOSEVELT, CALVIN COOLIDGE, HARRY S. TRUMAN, LYNDON B. JOHNSON, and GERALD FORD—have succeeded to the presidency upon death or resignation of the incumbent. Each one except Ford subsequently won his own term—and Ford lost but narrowly. Presidents JIMMY CARTER and RONALD REAGAN have done much to enhance the office by granting Vice-Presidents Walter F. Mondale and George Bush, respectively, broad access to, and influence in, decision making.

The vice-presidency's enlarged significance this century has not silenced its critics. Some prominent students of American government recommend abolishing the office: they would generally handle an unexpected presidential vacancy by designating an interim President and holding special elections. Others would retain the vice-presidency but would attempt to augment its powers either by requiring that the vice-president hold a leading cabinet position or have a vote or significant powers in the Senate. Finally, a third group of reformers seeks to change the process of nominating or electing vice-presidents. Proposals range from having presidential and vice-presidential candidates run together during primaries to holding separate elections for President and vice-president. Although these proposals stimulate interesting debates, the prospects of significant formal changes in the vice-presidency are slim. Constitutional change rarely, if ever, comes easily. Proposed reforms of the vice-presidency would tend to create as many problems as they would solve. Growth in the office will probably depend largely on further changes in American politics and on the relation between future Presidents and vice-presidents.

JOEL K. GOLDSTEIN

Bibliography

FEERICK, JOHN 1965 *From Failing Hands.* New York: Fordham University Press.
GOLDSTEIN, JOEL K. 1982 *The Modern American Vice Presidency: Transformation of a Political Institution.* Princeton, N.J.: Princeton University Press.
WILLIAMS, IRVING G. 1956 *The Rise of the Vice Presidency.* Washington, D.C.: Public Affairs Press.

VICINAGE

Of all the features constituting a citizen's right to a TRIAL BY JURY, none is so outdated or less of service than the Sixth Amendment provision guaranteeing "an impartial jury of the State and district wherein the crime [charged] shall have been committed." This specification of the geographic area from which jurors must be drawn should not be confused, however, with VENUE, which fixes the location of the trial itself.

The clause providing for a jury of the vicinage or neighborhood enjoys a time-worn heritage. In the thirteenth century jurors were usually witnesses or had personal knowledge of the event at issue. Although jurors eventually lost their character as witnesses, both EDWARD COKE and WILLIAM BLACKSTONE discussed the precise number of jurors who must come from the immediate locality. Vicinage became an issue in the colonial debate with England, and the Virginia Assembly, in 1769, asserted the colonists' right to "the inestimable Privilege of being tried by a Jury from the vicinage," a position echoed by the Continental Congress and listed as a grievance against the king in the DECLARATION OF INDEPENDENCE. The Sixth Amendment, framed shortly after the JUDICIARY ACT OF 1789, probably refers to the judicial districts established by that act.

Nevertheless, a federal defendant today "does not have a right under the Sixth Amendment to have jurors drawn from the entire district" (*Zicarelli v. Dietz,* 1980), and the Supreme Court has denied that trial juries "must mirror the community and reflect the various distinctive groups in the population" (*Taylor v. Louisiana,* 1975). State courts have generally been willing to narrow the vicinage requirement to a unit as small as an individual county, although federal courts have asserted that the Sixth Amendment clause applies "only to federal criminal trials, not to state criminal trials" (*Zicarelli*).

DAVID GORDON

VIETNAM WAR

Throughout American history, Presidents have dispatched armed forces abroad to protect the lives and property of United States citizens as well as American security interests. However, these military operations usually were limited in scope and duration, were conducted against relatively defenseless nations, and did not involve major powers. Thus, there was little opportunity to test the President's constitutional authority to send armed forces abroad without prior congressional authorization or a DECLARATION OF WAR. For various reasons, the KOREAN WAR did not furnish the occasion to test President HARRY S. TRUMAN's constitutional powers. The Vietnam War (1965–1973) was the first modern undeclared war that provided the opportunity to test the President's authority as COMMANDER-IN-CHIEF.

During the Vietnam War numerous litigants challenged the President's authority to initiate and conduct military hostilities without a congressional declaration of war or other explicit prior authorization. Such litigants denied that the GULF OF TONKIN resolution constituted authorization. Despite these challenges, the federal courts exhibited extreme caution in entering this twilight zone of concurrent power. The federal judiciary's reluctance to decide WAR POWERS controversies reveals a respect for the constitutional SEPARATION OF POWERS, an appreciation for the respective constitutional functions of Congress and the President in FOREIGN AFFAIRS, and a sense of judicial self-restraint. Nevertheless, toward the end of the Vietnam War, several lower federal courts entered the political thicket to restore the constitutional balance between Congress and the President.

Despite factual variations, the Vietnam War cases can be classified into four broad categories. One federal district court asserted categorically that the complaint raised a POLITICAL QUESTION beyond the court's JURISDICTION. A second agreed that the President's authority to conduct military activities without a declaration of war posed a nonjusticiable political question, but proceeded to determine whether the President had acted on his own authority, pursuant to, or in conflict with either the expressed or implied will of Congress. Courts in the third category concluded that the political question doctrine did not

foreclose them from inquiring into the existence and constitutional sufficiency of joint congressional-presidential participation in prosecuting the war. Finally, some district courts decided cases on the substantive merits. Yet the Vietnam War ended without an authoritative Supreme Court decision.

At the war's end Congress enacted the War Powers Resolution (1973), which attempted to resolve the constitutional ambiguities posed by the separation of the congressional war powers from the President's office of commander-in-chief. Under the resolution, Congress can alternatively authorize continuation of military hostilities that the President has initiated or require him to disengage armed forces from foreign combat within sixty to ninety days. Practical problems aside, the resolution seems constitutionally flawed. The Supreme Court's decision in IMMIGRATION AND NATURALIZATION SERVICE V. CHADHA (1983) cast doubt on the constitutionality of the resolution's LEGISLATIVE VETO provision, which states that Congress can direct the disengagement of troops by CONCURRENT RESOLUTION. Moreover, if the Constitution vests the authority to initiate military hostilities exclusively in the Congress, can Congress constitutionally delegate this authority to the President, even for a limited period? Is the War Powers Resolution an undated declaration of war that allows the President to choose the time, the place, and the enemy?

The Framers of the Constitution conferred only a limited set of defensive war powers on the President. As commander-in-chief he superintends the armed forces in war and peace, defending the nation, its armed forces, and its citizens and their property against attack, and directing military operations in wartime. The Framers did not authorize the President to initiate military hostilities, to transform defensive actions into aggressive wars, or to defend allies against attack.

In the Framers' view, only Congress could change the nation's condition from peace to war. Yet neither the constitutional text nor the records of the CONSTITUTIONAL CONVENTION conclusively draw the boundary between congressional power to initiate war and presidential power to defend against attack. In the twentieth century, international terrorism, the Vietnam War, guerrilla and insurgency warfare, wars of "national liberation," and the global conflict between the United States and the Soviet Union have virtually erased the Framers' distinction between defensive and offensive war.

A long history of undeclared war and military hostilities demonstrates that the constitutional questions raised during the Vietnam War are inherent in the American constitutional system. Presidents will be confronted with demands and opportunities to intervene militarily to protect American national security interests and the security interests of the nation's allies. Before yielding to this temptation, future Presidents should recall one of the Vietnam War's most important lessons: the nation should not wage a protracted undeclared war without a continuing agreement between Congress and the President that reflects broad, sustained public support.

EDWARD KEYNES

Bibliography

KEYNES, EDWARD 1982 *Undeclared War: Twilight Zone of Constitutional Power.* University Park: Pennsylvania State University Press.

REVELEY, W. TAYLOR, III 1981 *War Powers of the President and Congress: Who Holds the Arrows and Olive Branch?* Charlottesville: University Press of Virginia.

SOFAER, ABRAHAM D. 1976 *War, Foreign Affairs, and Constitutional Power.* Cambridge, Mass.: Ballinger Publishing Co.

VILLAGE OF . . .

See entry under name of village

VINSON, FRED M.
(1890–1953)

Fred M. Vinson was appointed thirteenth CHIEF JUSTICE of the United States by President HARRY S. TRUMAN in 1946 and served in that office until his death. His appointment followed a distinguished career in all three branches of the federal government. That career profoundly influenced his performance as Chief Justice.

Born and raised in the jail of Louisa, Kentucky—his father was the town jailer—he devoted almost his entire professional career to the public sector. Shortly after his admission to the bar, he served as city attorney and as Commonwealth attorney. Elected to Congress in 1928, he was an influential member of that legislative body during the New Deal years. His judicial experience commenced with appointment as judge of the United States Court of Appeals for the District of Columbia in 1937, and was broadened in 1942 when Chief Justice HARLAN FISKE STONE named him Chief Judge of the EMERGENCY COURT OF APPEALS. His executive branch experience began

with his 1943 appointment as director of Economic Stabilization, followed in 1945 by three posts in rapid succession: Federal Loan administrator, director of War Mobilization and Reconversion, and secretary of the Treasury.

He was appointed Chief Justice in 1946 to a Court widely regarded as ridden not only with the usual ideological disagreements but also with severe personal animosities. One successful aspect of his tenure as Chief Justice was the substantial reduction of public exposure of these conflicts.

In 1949, the deaths of Justices FRANK MURPHY and WILEY B. RUTLEDGE were followed by the appointments of TOM C. CLARK and SHERMAN MINTON. These changes, which occurred just short of the midpoint of his tenure, shifted the balance of the Court to a more conservative position, one more consonant with his own judicial and political philosophy.

That philosophy must be ascertained more by inference than through direct revelation. During his seven years as Chief Justice, the number of cases heard by the Court declined; as Chief Justice he assigned comparatively few opinions to himself. The evidence makes clear, however, that his philosophy reflected his public and political experience, acquired during the New Deal and World War II years, when a strong national government was deemed a *sine qua non* and loyalty to one's party and political confreres was a necessary condition of the success of the political process.

For him, the governmental institutions were democratically based, sound, and trustworthy; they were entitled to the loyalty of those whom they served and to protection from those who would destroy them. The judgments of the President and Congress that communism threatened both from without and from within were entitled to respect. The nation and its people fared better with a stable regime than with one of disruption; government was entitled at least to have time to respond to conflicts. The lowest person could rise to the highest office. Concomitantly—although the enactments of legislatures were normally to be respected—legal restrictions based upon race, disabling handicaps to the realization of the American dream, were disfavored. Even as his extensive federal governmental experience made him sympathetic to a strong central government, so his executive branch experience rendered him unafraid of strong executive power.

His tenure as Chief Justice spanned the Cold War era in which pro-Soviet attitudes that had developed during World War II became suspect. The rise of McCarthyism, the trial of Alger Hiss, the KOREAN

WAR, the theft of atomic secrets, and like events dominated public discussion and government reaction.

These events pervaded the atmosphere in which major constitutional issues were presented. Thus, his views about loyalty are perhaps best represented in those cases that sustained noncriminal deprivations addressed to communists and those considered disloyal, for example, his opinion for the Court in AMERICAN COMMUNICATIONS ASSOCIATION V. DOUDS (1950); denial of TAFT-HARTLEY COLLECTIVE BARGAINING benefits); and his votes in *Bailey v. Richardson* (1951; denial of federal employment) and JOINT ANTI-FASCIST REFUGEE COMMITTEE V. MCGRATH (1951; blacklisting of suspected organizations).

His lack of sympathy for those whose purpose he viewed as destructive of the governmental institutions is evidenced in his plurality opinion in DENNIS V. UNITED STATES (1951), which sustained against a FIRST AMENDMENT claim the criminal convictions of communist leaders under the Smith Act, and his majority opinion in FEINER V. NEW YORK (1951), affirming the conviction of an antigovernment speaker who refused to stop speaking when ordered to do so by a police officer after members of the audience threatened to assault him.

His concern for institutional stability is reflected in his opinion in UNITED STATES V. UNITED MINE WORKERS (1947), sustaining the judiciary's use of the CONTEMPT POWER to halt a disruptive strike, and his dissenting opinion in YOUNGSTOWN SHEET & TUBE CO. V. SAWYER (1951), where he would have sustained the power of the President to seize steel mills to maintain steel production interrupted by a strike.

Overtaken by later cases, several of Vinson's most significant opinions advanced the elimination of RACIAL DISCRIMINATION and in theoretical terms expanded the interpretation of the EQUAL PROTECTION clause. Although the unanimous opinions he authored in SWEATT V. PAINTER (1950) and MCLAURIN V. BOARD OF REGENTS (1950) did not in terms overrule the SEPARATE BUT EQUAL DOCTRINE of PLESSY V. FERGUSON (1896), the rejection of the separate Texas law school in *Sweatt* and of the special treatment of *McLaurin* made the demise of that doctrine inevitable. His most interesting and venturesome equal protection opinion was SHELLEY V. KRAEMER (1948), the RESTRICTIVE COVENANT case, whose doctrinal implications have yet to be satisfactorily delineated.

Vinson accorded the federal government expansive legislative power under the COMMERCE CLAUSE. Perceived conflicts between the federal government and the states were resolved in favor of a strong central government. Where the federal government had not spoken, his concern focused on discrimination against INTERSTATE COMMERCE and the out-of-stater, a position most clearly seen in the STATE TAXATION OF COMMERCE cases and TOOMER V. WITSELL (1948), the path-breaking interpretation of the PRIVILEGES AND IMMUNITIES clause of Article IV, which in effect extended his commerce clause philosophy to areas he thought the clause did not reach.

His general judicial approach inclined Vinson to focus on the particular facts of the case and to eschew promulgation of sweeping legal principles. He was slow to overrule earlier opinions and DOCTRINES. The power of the Court to invalidate federal executive and legislative actions on constitutional grounds was to be used sparingly; he never voted to invalidate an act of Congress or a presidential action. He was as apt as any member of his Court, save perhaps Justice FELIX FRANKFURTER, to avoid constitutional questions and, when those issues were faced, to take an intermediate rather than ultimate constitutional position. Clearly, Fred M. Vinson belonged to the "judicial restraint" school of Supreme Court Justices.

MURRAY L. SCHWARTZ

Bibliography

KIRKENDALL, K. 1969 Fred M. Vinson. In Leon Friedman and Fred L. Israel, *The Justices of the United States Supreme Court.* Vol. 4:2639–2649. New York: Chelsea House.

PRITCHETT, C. HERMAN 1954 *Civil Liberties and the Vinson Court.* Chicago: University of Chicago Press.

SYMPOSIUM 1954 *Northwestern University Law Review* 49:1–76.

VINSON COURT
(1946–1953)

FRED M. VINSON was Chief Justice of the United States from June 24, 1946, until his death on September 8, 1953. During his seven-year period of service the Supreme Court was considerably less interesting, colorful, or originative of significant constitutional DOCTRINE than its predecessor, the STONE COURT, or its successor, the WARREN COURT. However, the Vinson Court did deal with serious and important issues, particularly Cold War challenges to CIVIL LIBERTIES and awakening concerns about RACIAL DISCRIMINATION.

Vinson was a close friend of President HARRY S. TRUMAN and an active Democrat who had had the unique experience of serving in all three branches of the federal government. Immediately preceding his appointment to the Court he had been secretary of the treasury. President Truman had made one previous appointment, naming HAROLD BURTON, a Republican and former Senate colleague of Truman, to replace OWEN ROBERTS in 1945. The other seven justices were of course all holdovers from the Stone Court, which guaranteed a continuation of the judicial dialogue that had pitted the liberal activism of HUGO L. BLACK, WILLIAM O. DOUGLAS, FRANK MURPHY, and WILEY B. RUTLEDGE against the brilliant critiques of FELIX FRANKFURTER and ROBERT H. JACKSON, with the moderate STANLEY F. REED somewhere in the center.

The four-judge liberal bloc had within itself the votes required to grant CERTIORARI petitions, which ensured that civil liberties issues would continue to appear on the Court's agenda. When the liberals agreed, they needed only one additional vote to constitute a majority. But in the summer of 1949 Justices Murphy and Rutledge died, cutting the liberal bloc in half. President Truman filled these two vacancies by the appointment of TOM C. CLARK, his attorney general, and SHERMAN MINTON, who had been a New Deal senator from Indiana. The two new justices joined with Vinson, Reed, and Burton in a moderately conservative bloc which dominated the remaining four terms of the Vinson Court. An indication of the balance of power on the Court is provided by the number of dissents registered by each of the Justices during this four-year period: Clark 15, Vinson 40, Burton 44, Minton 47, Reed 59, Jackson 80, Frankfurter 101, Douglas 130, Black 148.

The most famous decision of the Vinson Court in terms of public reaction, and probably the most noteworthy as a contribution to constitutional theory, was YOUNGSTOWN SHEET & TUBE CO. V. SAWYER (1952), generally known as the Steel Seizure Case. Here the Court by a vote of 6–3 held unconstitutional President Truman's seizure of the nation's steel mills in 1952, an action he justified as necessary to avert a nationwide strike that might have affected the flow of munitions to American troops in Korea. The President had no statutory authority for the seizure, which consequently had to be justified on a theory of inherent presidential power to meet emergencies.

Justice Black, supported by Douglas, flatly denied the existence of any inherent presidential powers. Justices Jackson and Frankfurter were less dogmatic, and the doctrine of the case is generally drawn from their opinions. As they saw it, the controlling factor was that Congress had considered granting the President seizure power to deal with nationwide strikes when adopting the TAFT-HARTLEY ACT in 1947 but had decided against it. In addition, Jackson contributed a situational scale for ruling on claims of executive emergency power. Vinson, in his most famous dissent, upheld the President as having moved in an emergency to maintain the status quo until Congress could act, and he rejected the majority's "messenger boy" concept of the presidential office.

The fact that the Court could have avoided the constitutional issue in the Steel Seizure Case by various alternatives suggested that most of the justices believed it important to announce a check on presidential power. The decision was enormously popular with the press and public and has subsequently been accepted as an authoritative statement on the SEPARATION OF POWERS, establishing that actions of the president are subject to JUDICIAL REVIEW. There had been some doubt on this point since the failure of the post-Civil War suit against the president in MISSISSIPPI V. JOHNSON (1867). It established also that executive claims of power for which statutory authority is lacking, and which must consequently rely on the President's general Article II authority, are subject to strict judicial scrutiny.

Less significant in its doctrine than the Steel Seizure Case but almost as controversial was the Court's contempt ruling against John L. Lewis, leader of the coal miners, in 1947 (UNITED STATES V. UNITED MINE WORKERS). The government had seized the nation's bituminous coal mines in 1946 to end a crippling strike and had entered into a contract with Lewis on wages and working conditions. When Lewis subsequently terminated the contract unilaterally and resumed the strike, the government secured a contempt JUDGMENT and heavy fine against Lewis and the union. In his first major opinion Vinson upheld the conviction for contempt, ruling that the NORRIS-LAGUARDIA ACT limiting the issuance of labor INJUNCTIONS was not binding on the government as an employer.

A significant difference between the Stone and Vinson Courts was that World War II had ended and the Cold War against communism had begun. The hunt for subversives in which the nation was caught up soon after the shooting war was over tainted the entire period of the Vinson Court and created difficult civil liberties issues. The government's principal weapon against suspected subversion was the Smith Act of 1940, which made it unlawful to teach and advocate the overthrow of the United States government by force and violence, or to organize a group for such a purpose.

Convictions of eleven leaders of the American Communist party under the Smith Act were upheld by the Supreme Court in DENNIS V. UNITED STATES

(1951). In the most memorable event of his judicial career, Chief Justice Vinson wrote the Court's majority opinion defending the Smith Act against contentions that it violated the FIRST AMENDMENT. The defendants admittedly had taken no action with the immediate intention of initiating a revolution. But Vinson held that the CLEAR AND PRESENT DANGER TEST, developed by Justice OLIVER WENDELL HOLMES and LOUIS D. BRANDEIS, did not require the government to wait until a "putsch" was about to be executed before acting against a conspiracy. Vinson accepted the reformulation of the test developed by Judge LEARNED HAND: "Whether the gravity of the 'evil,' discounted by its improbability, justifies such invasion of free speech as is necessary to avoid the danger." He considered the communist "evil" to be that grave. Justices Black and Douglas dissented; Douglas pointed out that the prosecution had introduced no evidence of Communist party action aimed at overthrow of the government.

Vinson also wrote the Court's opinion in AMERICAN COMMUNICATIONS ASSOCIATION V. DOUDS (1950), upholding the Taft-Hartley Act noncommunist oath. This statute denied the protections and services of the WAGNER (NATIONAL LABOR RELATIONS) ACT to any labor organization whose officers failed to file affidavits that they were not members of the Communist party. The Chief Justice held that Congress in adopting this statute was acting to prevent the obstruction of commerce by "political strikes." The law was not aimed at speech but rather at harmful conduct carried on by persons who could be identified by their political affiliations and beliefs.

The Vinson Court was caught up in the final moments of the Cold War's most spectacular event, the execution of Julius and Ethel Rosenberg, who were charged with passing atomic "secrets" to the Russians. Review of the lower court conviction and subsequent APPEALS was routinely denied by the Supreme Court in 1952 and early 1953, as were also the initial petitions for STAY OF EXECUTION. But Justice Douglas thought that one final petition filed the day before execution was scheduled raised a new legal issue deserving consideration. He consequently granted a stay which the full Court set aside the next day, and the executions were then carried out. Douglas's action caused a brief furor and a congressman demanded his IMPEACHMENT. In the last opinion before his death Vinson defended Douglas's action as a proper response to protect the Court's JURISDICTION over the case pending a consideration of the legal issue raised. Black and Frankfurter joined Douglas in asserting that the stay should have been granted.

During the era of the Vinson Court, congressional committee investigations of communism developed into major political and media events. Senator Joseph McCarthy's pursuit of "Fifth Amendment Communists" got under way in 1950, too late to create issues for the Vinson Court. But the HOUSE COMMITTEE ON UN-AMERICAN ACTIVITIES had begun operations in 1938, and by 1947 petitions for review of contempt citations against witnesses who had refused to reply to committee interrogation began to reach the Supreme Court. However, it declined review of all the cases that would have required a ruling on the constitutionality of the use of investigatory power, and it dealt only with certain less controversial issues of committee procedure and use of the Fifth Amendment privilege by witnesses.

A prominent feature of the Cold War period was concern about the loyalty of government employees. A LOYALTY OATH fad developed in nearly every state, which the Vinson Court legitimated in GERENDE V. BOARD OF SUPERVISORS OF ELECTIONS (1951) by upholding a Maryland law that required candidates for public office to file affidavits that they were not "subversive persons."

A loyalty program covering federal employees was set up by President Truman in 1947 and was continued by President DWIGHT D. EISENHOWER. It required checking the loyalty of all incumbent employees and all applicants for federal employment. A complex administrative organization of loyalty review boards was created, and to assist the boards the attorney general issued a list of organizations he found to be "totalitarian, fascist, communist, or subversive." Consideration of the constitutionality of this program split the Court 4–4 in Bailey v. Richardson (1951). But in JOINT ANTI-FASCIST REFUGEE COMMITTEE V. MCGRATH (1951), decided the same day, the Court by a vote of 5–3 challenged the attorney general's list as having been drawn up without appropriate investigation or DUE PROCESS. The dissenters were Reed, Vinson, and Minton. In spite of this opinion the list continued to be used for a number of years in government hiring and investigation.

At the state level a New York law providing for the removal of public school teachers on grounds of membership in listed subversive organizations was upheld in ADLER V. BOARD OF EDUCATION OF CITY OF NEW YORK (1952), Justice Minton reasoning that the purpose was constitutional and that procedural protections provided by the statute were adequate. Justices Black and Douglas dissented, and Frankfurter would have denied the appeal on technical grounds of STANDING and RIPENESS.

Apart from Cold War cases, FREEDOM OF SPEECH and FREEDOM OF THE PRESS did not suffer seriously at the hands of the Vinson Court. BURSTYN V. WILSON (1952) was in fact an advance in its holding that a motion picture could not be censored on the ground that it was "sacrilegious." A law censoring magazines featuring bloodshed and lust was struck down in *Winters v. New York* (1948) as void for vagueness. *Poulos v. New Hampshire* (1953) upheld licensing of meetings in public parks and streets, but only if the licenses were granted without discrimination, and the use of licensing ordinances to prevent unpopular religious groups or preachers from holding meetings in public parks was rebuffed in NIEMOTKO V. MARYLAND (1951) and KUNZ V. NEW YORK (1951).

In TERMINIELLO V. CHICAGO (1949) a divided Court reversed on rather technical grounds the conviction of a rabble-rouser for BREACH OF THE PEACE resulting from an incendiary speech. But FEINER V. NEW YORK (1951) upheld the conviction of a soapbox orator even though the situation was much less inflammatory than in *Terminiello*. Moreover, BEAUHARNAIS V. ILLINOIS (1952) approved a state law treating critical comments about racial groups as criminal and subjecting their authors to prosecution for GROUP LIBEL.

The Vinson Court dealt with a number of conflicts between freedom of expression and privacy but without producing any theories justifying or limiting privacy claims such as those subsequently developed in GRISWOLD V. CONNECTICUT (1965) by the Warren Court. Use of sound trucks in streets and parks was initially upheld in *Saia v. New York* (1948) against contentions of infringement on privacy, but in the following year the Court conceded that "loud and raucous" sound trucks could be forbidden (KOVACS V. COOPER). Radio broadcasts including commercial messages in DISTRICT OF COLUMBIA streetcars were permitted to continue by *Public Utilities Commission v. Pollak* (1952), even though CAPTIVE AUDIENCES might suffer, but *Breard v. City of Alexandria* (1951) protected householders by approving an ordinance forbidding door-to-door selling of magazine subscriptions. Justice Black charged that the latter decision violated the "preferred position" for First Amendment freedoms originated by the Roosevelt Court. The severest blow to that philosophy was *United Public Workers v. Mitchell* (1947) which upheld by a vote of 4–3 the HATCH ACT limits on political activity by public employees.

In a 1940 case, THORNHILL V. ALABAMA, the Court had strongly asserted that PICKETING in labor disputes was protected by the First Amendment. Almost immediately, however, the Court found it necessary to announce limits on this holding, a process the Vinson Court continued. The most significant case was GIBONEY V. EMPIRE STORAGE & ICE CO. (1949), where the Court ruled unanimously against a union that was picketing to force an employer to enter into an illegal restrictive contract.

The issue of public financial aid to religious schools required the Vinson Court to make the first significant effort to interpret and apply the First Amendment ban on ESTABLISHMENT OF RELIGION. EVERSON V. BOARD OF EDUCATION (1947) involved a state arrangement under which parents could be reimbursed from public moneys for their children's bus fare to parochial schools. An unusual five-judge majority composed of three liberals (Black, Douglas, and Murphy) and two conservatives (Vinson and Reed) held that the subsidy was simply a social welfare measure and that the First Amendment did not require exclusion of persons of any faith from the benefits of "public welfare legislation." Rutledge's vigorous dissent regarded payment for transportation to church schools as a direct aid to religious education and so unconstitutional.

The following year McCOLLUM V. BOARD OF EDUCATION presented another church–state issue. The case involved a RELEASED TIME program of religious education under which public school children attended classes in Protestant, Roman Catholic, or Jewish religious instruction during school hours and in the school building. The Court's almost unanimous verdict of UNCONSTITUTIONALITY aroused a storm of criticism in church circles, and within four years the Court substantially reversed this ruling, upholding a New York City released time program that differed from *McCollum* only in that the classes were held off the school grounds (ZORACH V. CLAUSEN, 1952.) A similar reluctance to disturb the religious community was seen as the Court avoided on technical grounds of standing a ruling on the constitutionality of Bible-reading in the public schools (DOREMUS V. BOARD OF EDUCATION).

The Vinson Court's civil liberties record was distinctly better than that of its predecessors in one area, protection of minorities from discrimination. The prevailing constitutional rule was that established by PLESSY V. FERGUSON in 1896—that SEGREGATION of the races was constitutional provided treatment or facilities were equal. In practice, they were never equal, but over the years the Court had consistently avoided the difficult task of enforcing the *Plessy* rule. In the field of education, none of the few efforts to challenge unequal facilities had been successful. But in 1938 the HUGHES COURT made a small beginning, ruling in MISSOURI EX REL. GAINES V. CANADA that Missouri, which denied blacks admission to state law schools, must do so or set up a separate law school for blacks. MORGAN V. VIRGINIA (1946) invalidated a state Jim Crow law requiring racial segregation of passengers on public motor carriers, but the constitutional ground given was burden on INTERSTATE COMMERCE rather than denial of EQUAL PROTECTION.

The Vinson Court undertook cautiously to build on these beginnings. The COMMERCE CLAUSE justification used in the Virginia bus case was likewise employed in BOB-LO EXCURSION CO. V. MICHIGAN (1948). But the Vinson Court's boldest action against segregation came shortly thereafter in SHELLEY V. KRAEMER (1948). With Vinson writing the opinion, the Court declared that RESTRICTIVE COVENANTS binding property owners not to sell to minorities, although within the legal rights of property owners, were unenforceable. For a court to give effect to such a discriminatory contract, Vinson held, would amount to STATE ACTION in violation of the FOURTEENTH AMENDMENT.

The separate law school for blacks that Texas had established was declared unequal in SWEATT V. PAINTER (1950). The University of Oklahoma, forced to admit a black graduate student, required him to sit in a separate row in class, at a separate desk in the library, and at a separate table in the cafeteria. MCLAURIN V. OKLAHOMA STATE REGENTS (1950), with Vinson again writing the opinion, held these practices to be an unconstitutional impairment of the student's ability to learn his profession.

Vinson's opinion, however, rejected the opportunity to consider the broader issue of the *Plessy* SEPARATE BUT EQUAL rule. So attacks on the segregation principle continued, and the TEST CASES moved from the universities and graduate schools to the primary and secondary schools. In December 1952 BROWN V. BOARD OF EDUCATION OF TOPEKA and four other school segregation cases were argued for three days before the Court. But instead of a decision in June, the Court set the cases for reargument in October. The Chief Justice died in September, and so the Vinson Court's most momentous issue was passed on to the Warren Court.

Although the Stone Court had broken some new ground in CRIMINAL PROCEDURE, its record was mixed, particularly in guaranteeing the RIGHT TO COUNSEL and protection against UNREASONABLE SEARCHES and seizures. This latter issue surfaced in the Vinson Court's first term. One of the oldest problems in American constitutional law is whether the due process clause of the Fourteenth Amendment "incorporated" and made effective in state criminal proceedings the protections of the Fourth through the Eighth Amendments. As recently as 1937 in PALKO V. CONNECTICUT the Court had reiterated the principle that all state procedures consistent with ORDERED LIBERTY are acceptable.

In ADAMSON V. CALIFORNIA (1947) the *Palko* doctrine survived on the Vinson Court, but by only a 5–4 vote. Justice Black led the minority. He relied on legislative history to establish his version of the intention of the framers of the Fourteenth Amendment and attacked the ORDERED LIBERTY test as substituting natural law and the notions of individual Justices for the precise and protective language of the BILL OF RIGHTS.

Although Black lost in *Adamson*, "ordered liberty" was a standard powerful enough to bring state criminal processes within the ambit of the FOURTH AMENDMENT in WOLF V. COLORADO (1949). However, Justice Frankfurter for the six-judge majority held only that SEARCHES AND SEIZURES by state law officers are bound by the standard of reasonableness; he declined to go further and impose on state prosecutions the EXCLUSIONARY RULE which prevents EVIDENCE secured by unconstitutional means from being offered in federal prosecutions. Justices Murphy, Douglas, and Rutledge, dissenting, contended that the exclusionary rule provided the only effective protection against police violation of the Fourth Amendment, and their view was finally adopted on the Warren Court in MAPP V. OHIO (1961).

With respect to right to counsel, the Vinson Court accepted the rule announced by the Stone Court in BETTS V. BRADY (1942) that the necessity for counsel depended upon the circumstances, such as the seriousness of the crime, the age and mental capacity of the defendant, and the ability of the judge. Applying the "special circumstances" rule in twelve cases, the Vinson Court concluded that in six the absence of counsel had resulted in denial of a FAIR TRIAL. In only one of the twelve was the Court unanimous. This experience was a factor in the Warren Court's decision in GIDEON V. WAINWRIGHT (1963) to abolish the confusing special circumstances rule and make counsel mandatory in all state felony prosecutions.

What was potentially one of the Vinson Court's most significant decisions for the federal system was nullified by Congress. In 1947 the Court ruled that subsurface land and mineral rights in California's three-mile coastal area belonged to the federal government (*United States v. California*), and in 1950 the Court applied the same rule to Texas. Congress retaliated in 1953 by ceding to the states ownership of land and resources under adjoining seas up to a distance of three miles from shore or to the states' historic boundaries.

In summary, the tendency of the Vinson Court was to follow a policy of judicial restraint, rejecting innovation or activism. The number of cases decided by full opinion fell below one hundred during three of the last four years, far less than the number typically decided by earlier Courts. The five justices who dominated the Court in its latter period were capable but lacking in style or originality. The four Justices of intellectual distinction—Black, Douglas, Frankfurter, and Jackson—generally paired off and pulled in opposite directions.

The pall of the Cold War hung over the Court. Confronted with the scandal of McCarthyism, it was quiescent. Facing Smith Act prosecutions, the loyalty inquisition of federal employees, lists of subversive organizations, scrutiny of school teachers' associates, loyalty oaths, and deportation of ex-communists, the Court's response was usually to legitimate the government's action.

But in one field, significantly, there was a different kind of response. The Vinson Court did not evade the issue of racial discrimination. Although moving cautiously, as was appropriate considering the enormity of the problem, the Court nevertheless proceeded to bring denial of equal protection out of the limbo of neglect and unconcern into the focus of national consciousness and thereby prepared the way for its successor's historic decision on May 17, 1954.

C. HERMAN PRITCHETT

Bibliography

FRANK, JOHN P. 1954 Fred Vinson and the Chief Justiceship. *University of Chicago Law Review* 21:212–246.
MURPHY, PAUL L. 1972 *The Constitution in Crisis Times, 1919–1969.* New York: Harper & Row.
PRITCHETT, C. HERMAN (1954)1966 *Civil Liberties and the Vinson Court.* Chicago: University of Chicago Press.
SWINDLER, WILLIAM F. 1970 *Court and Constitution in the Twentieth Century: The New Legality, 1932–1968.* Indianapolis: Bobbs-Merrill.

VIRGINIA, EX PARTE

See: *Strauder v. West Virginia*

VIRGINIA v. RIVES

See: *Strauder v. West Virginia*

VIRGINIA v. TENNESSEE

See: Interstate Compacts

VIRGINIA AND KENTUCKY RESOLUTIONS
(1798–1799)

These resolutions declared the ALIEN AND SEDITION ACTS unconstitutional and sought to arouse political opposition by appealing to the legislatures of the several states. The strategy was devised by THOMAS JEFFERSON, the vice-president, who secretly drafted the resolutions that were adopted by the Kentucky legislature. A similar but milder series was drafted by JAMES MADISON for the Virginia assembly. Both set forth the compact theory of the Constitution, holding that the general government was one of strictly delegated powers; that acts beyond its powers were void; and that, there being no ultimate arbiter of the Constitution, each state had "an equal right to judge for itself, as well of infractions as of the mode and measure of redress." (See THEORIES OF THE UNION.) Jefferson baptized the theory "NULLIFICATION," though the name was omitted by Kentucky; and Virginia spoke instead of the right of each state to "interpose" to arrest the evil.

Five of the nine Kentucky Resolutions were devoted to proving the unconstitutionality of the Alien and Sedition Laws. The Alien Law was attacked for want of power, for violation of a specific constitutional provision (Article I, section 9), and for denial of TRIAL BY JURY and other fair procedures. The Sedition Act was asserted to be outside the scope of the Constitution as well as a direct violation of the FIRST AMENDMENT. The resolutions offered no broadly philosophical plea for FREEDOM OF SPEECH and PRESS but met the threat of the Sedition Law at its most vulnerable point, as an invasion of rights reserved to the states. It belonged to each state, not the general government, to determine "how far the licentiousness of speech and of the press may be abridged without lessening their useful freedom." Kentucky urged the other state legislatures to concur in declaring the acts unconstitutional and void.

Replies to the resolutions, mostly from Northern legislatures under Federalist control, were uniformly unfavorable. Prodded by Jefferson, Kentucky adopted a second set of resolutions in November 1799, reaffirming the principles of the first and, incidentally, introducing the word "nullification." In January 1800 the Virginia assembly adopted Madison's Report, a masterly exposition of the dual sovereignty theory of the federal union and a powerful defense of CIVIL LIBERTIES.

The principal object of the resolutions was to secure the freedom of opposition, of debate, and of change through the political process. This object was secured by the Republican victory in the election of 1800. But in pursuing "a political resistance for political effect," in Jefferson's words, he and his associates were somewhat careless on points of constitutional theory. Whether the resolutions were meant as a declaration of opinion or as a "nullification" of federal law, whether the right claimed for the state was limited to "usurpations" of the compact or extended to "abuses" as well, whether the ultimate recourse was the natural right of revolution or a constitutional right of SECESSION, these points were left unclear. It mattered little in 1800, after the resolutions had done their work and then were forgotten; but it mattered a great deal a generation later when the "Resolutions of '98" were revived and tortured by JOHN C. CALHOUN into a defense, not of liberty, but of slavery.

MERRILL D. PETERSON

Bibliography

KOCH, ADRIENNE and AMMON, HARRY 1948 The Virginia and Kentucky Resolutions: An Episode in Jefferson's and Madison's Defense of Civil Liberties. *William and Mary Quarterly* (3rd. ser.) 5:145–176.

MALONE, DUMAS 1962 *Jefferson and the Ordeal of Liberty.* Boston: Little, Brown.

VIRGINIA CHARTER OF 1606
(April 10, 1606)

This was the first royal charter issued for the planting of a colony in America. Charters were usually issued to private trading companies, as in this case, or to proprietary lords. The charter laid out boundaries, defined the relationship of the colony to the crown, and provided for a government. In this first charter, the government consisted only of a council. Subsequent charters for Virginia in 1609 and 1612 established the office of the governor; by 1619, in accord with a document called the "Great Charter" of 1618, elections were held and the first representative legislature in American history met at Jamestown. The enduring significance of Virginia's first charter lies in its provision that the colonists and their descendants "shall have and enjoy all Liberties, Franchises, and Immunities . . . as if they had been abiding and born,

within this our Realm of England. . . ." Later charters for Virginia contained similar clauses. Their meaning was doubtless restricted at the time to legal rights of land tenure and inheritance, trial by jury, and little else; but the vague language (repeated in numerous other charters for colonies from New England to the South) allowed American colonists to believe that they were entitled to all the rights of Englishmen—their constitutional system and common law. Charters could be revoked and some were, but the American experience eventually led to written constitutions of fundamental law that contained bills of rights.

LEONARD W. LEVY

VIRGINIA DECLARATION OF RIGHTS AND CONSTITUTION OF 1776
(June 12 and 29, 1776)

Virginia, the oldest, largest, and most prestigious of the original states, adopted a Declaration of Rights on June 12, 1776, and two weeks later its "Constitution or Form of Government." Each document was the first of its kind and considerably influenced constitution-making in the other states. The primary draftsman of both documents was GEORGE MASON, although the self-styled "convention" that adopted them included many luminaries, among them JAMES MADISON. The convention was actually an extralegal or provisional legislature similar in membership to the last House of Burgesses under the royal charter before the Revolution. The same convention enacted ordinary legislation and elected a governor under the new CONSTITUTION.

THOMAS JEFFERSON in his *Notes on Virginia*, written in 1781, observed that "capital defects" marred the work of the constitution-makers of 1776 who were acting without precedent. Property qualifications on the right to vote disfranchised about half the men of the state who served in the militia or paid taxes, and gross malapportionment, which benefited the old tidewater counties, diminished the representative character of the new government. The governor was little more than a ceremonial figurehead. The assembly elected him and his councillors as well as the state judges, and the governor had no veto power. Jefferson believed that concentrating the powers of government in the legislature, notwithstanding recognition of the principle of separation of powers, "is precisely the definition of despotic government. . . . An elective despotism was not the government we fought for." In fact, however, legislative supremacy characterized all the new state governments, excepting those of Massachusetts and New York.

The gravest deficiency of the Virginia system, according to Jefferson, was that the legislature, having framed the constitution and declaration of rights without having provided that they be perpetual and unalterable, could change them by ordinary legislation. That was true in theory, although the constitution lasted over half a century and rarely did the legislature enact measures inconsistent with it. In practice it was regarded a FUNDAMENTAL LAW, especially the declaration of rights.

That declaration was the most significant achievement of the convention. As the first such American document, it contained many constitutional "firsts," such as the statements that "all men" are equally free and have inherent rights which cannot be divested even by compact; that among these rights are the enjoyment of life, liberty, property, and the pursuit of happiness; and that all power derives from the people who retain a right to change the government if it fails to secure the people's objectives. The declaration recognized "the free exercise of religion" and FREEDOM OF THE PRESS, and included clauses that were precursors, sometimes in rudimentary form, of the FOURTH through the Eighth AMENDMENTS of the Constitution of the United States. Inexplicably the convention voted down a ban on BILLS OF ATTAINDER and on EX POST FACTO LAWS and omitted the FREEDOMS OF SPEECH, assembly, and petition, the right to the writ of HABEAS CORPUS, GRAND JURY proceedings, the right to compulsory process to secure EVIDENCE in one's own behalf, the right to counsel, and freedom from DOUBLE JEOPARDY. Although RELIGIOUS LIBERTY was guaranteed, the ban on an ESTABLISHMENT OF RELIGION awaited enactment of the VIRGINIA STATUTE OF RELIGIOUS FREEDOM in 1786. Madison's familiarity with his own state's bill of rights strongly influenced his draft of the amendments that became the BILL OF RIGHTS of the Constitution.

LEONARD W. LEVY

Bibliography

LINGLEY, CHARLES R. 1910 *The Transition of Virginia from Colony to Commonwealth.* New York: Columbia University Press.

VIRGINIA PLAN

At the CONSTITUTIONAL CONVENTION OF 1787, EDMUND RANDOLPH, arguing that the government of the union under the ARTICLES OF CONFEDERATION could not defend itself against state encroachments, introduced the alternative of a "national plan," probably the work of JAMES MADISON. In effect Virginia proposed to supersede the Articles by providing for a strong, central government of three branches, each with broad, undefined powers. The plan included a congress of two houses, the first elected by the people and the second by the first, both to be apportioned on the basis of a state's population of free inhabitants or its contributions to the national treasury. The most significant provision empowered congress to legislate in all cases of state incompetency or whenever state legislation might disrupt national harmony. Congress was also empowered to veto state laws. The sole check on congress was a qualified veto power vested in a council consisting of the executive and some judges. One provision required state officers to swear support of the new constitution, and another authorized the use of force against recalcitrant states. The Virginia Plan structured the deliberations of the Constitutional Convention and became the nucleus of the Constitution of the United States.

LEONARD W. LEVY

Bibliography

BRANT, IRVING 1950 *James Madison: Father of the Constitution, 1787–1800.* Pages 23–54. Indianapolis: Bobbs-Merrill.

VIRGINIA PRIVATE SCHOOL CASES

See: *Runyon v. McCrary*

VIRGINIA STATE BOARD OF PHARMACY v. VIRGINIA CITIZENS CONSUMER COUNCIL
425 U.S. 748 (1976)

Traditionally COMMERCIAL SPEECH was assumed to lie outside the FIRST AMENDMENT's protection. This decision made clear that this assumption was obsolete. Virginia's rules governing professional pharmacists forbade the advertising of prices of prescription drugs. The Supreme Court, 7–1, held this rule invalid at the behest of a consumers' group, thus promoting the notion of a "right to receive" in the FREEDOM OF SPEECH. (See LISTENERS' RIGHTS.) The Court's opinion indicated that false or misleading commercial advertising might be regulated—a rule the Court would never apply to political speech. For a few years, this decision stood as the Court's principal commercial speech precedent, only to be assimilated in the comprehensive opinion in CENTRAL HUDSON GAS V. PUBLIC SERVICE COMMISSION (1980).

MARTIN SHAPIRO

VIRGINIA STATUTE OF RELIGIOUS FREEDOM
(1786)

This historic statute, one of the preeminent documents in the history of RELIGIOUS LIBERTY, climaxed a ten-year struggle for the SEPARATION OF CHURCH AND STATE in Virginia. On the eve of the Revolution Baptists were jailed for unlicensed preaching, and JAMES MADISON exclaimed that the "diabolical Hell conceived principle of persecution rages." The Church of England (Episcopal) was the established church of Virginia, supported by public taxes imposed on all. The state CONSTITUTION of 1776 guaranteed that everyone was "equally entitled to the free exercise of religion," but the convention defeated a proposal by Madison that would have ended any form of an ESTABLISHMENT OF RELIGION. By the close of 1776 the legislature, responding to dissenter petitions, repealed all laws punishing any religious opinions or modes of worship, exempted dissenters from compulsory support of the established church, and suspended state taxation on its behalf. But the legislature reserved for future decision the question whether religion ought to be supported by voluntary contributions or by a new establishment of all Christian churches.

In 1779 an indecisive legislature confronted two diametrically opposed bills. One was a general assessment bill, providing that the Christian religion should be "the established religion" supported by public taxation and allowing every taxpayer to designate the church that would receive his money. The other was THOMAS JEFFERSON's Bill for Religious Freedom, which later provided the philosophical basis for the religion clauses of the FIRST AMENDMENT. The preamble, a classic expression of the American creed on intellectual as well as religious liberty, stressed that everyone had a "natural right" to his opinions and that religion was a private, voluntary matter of individual conscience beyond the scope of the civil power to support or restrain. Jefferson rejected the BAD TENDENCY TEST for suppressing opinions and proposed "that it is time enough for the rightful purposes of the civil government for its officers to interfere when

principles break out into overt acts against peace and good order. . . ." The bill, which protected even freedom of irreligion, provided that no one should be compelled to frequent or support any worship. Neither Jefferson's bill nor the other could muster a majority, and for several years the legislature deadlocked.

Each year, however, support for an establishment grew. When a liberalized general assessment bill was introduced in 1784, omitting subscription to articles of faith and giving secular reasons for the support of religion, the Presbyterian clergy backed it. Madison angrily declared that they were "as ready to set up an establishment which is to take them in as they were to pull down that which shut them out." Only Madison's shrewd politicking delayed passage of the general assessment bill until the legislature had time to evaluate the state of public opinion. MADISON'S MEMORIAL AND REMONSTRANCE turned public opinion against the assessment; even the Presbyterian clergy now endorsed Jefferson's bill. Madison reintroduced it in late 1785, and it became law in early 1786, completing the separation of church and state in Virginia and providing a model for a nation.

LEONARD W. LEVY

Bibliography

STOKES, ANSON PHELPS 1950 *Church and State in the United States.* Vol. 1:366–394. New York: Harper & Row.

VIRTUAL REPRESENTATION

See: Representation; Taxation without Representation

VLANDIS v. KLINE
412 U.S. 441 (1973)

A Connecticut statute gave resident students at a state university certain tuition preferences. A student who had entered the university as a nonresident was relegated to that status for his or her full student career. The Supreme Court, 6–3, held the latter provision unconstitutional. A majority of five Justices, speaking through Justice POTTER STEWART, held that the provision created "a permanent and IRREBUTTABLE PRESUMPTION of non-residence." Because this presumption was "not necessarily or universally true in fact," it denied a student PROCEDURAL DUE PROCESS by denying a hearing on the issue of residence. Justice BYRON R. WHITE concurred on EQUAL PROTECTION GROUNDS. The dissenters suggested that the Court had, in fact, drifted into an area of SUBSTANTIVE DUE

PROCESS that the Court had abandoned in the 1930s. The irrebuttable presumptions DOCTRINE had a brief vogue, but *Weinberger v. Salfi* (1975) placed it in mothballs.

KENNETH L. KARST

VOICE SAMPLES

See: Testimonial Compulsion

VOID FOR VAGUENESS

See: Vagueness

VOIR DIRE

Voir dire (Old French: "to speak the truth") refers to the questioning by the court or counsel of prospective jurors to determine their qualification for jury service.

Two types of objections may be raised to disqualify prospective jurors: peremptory challenges and challenges for cause. A peremptory challenge allows dismissal of a juror without cause. Most states provide each side with twenty such challenges for a capital offense, and a lesser number for other felonies and misdemeanors.

A challenge for cause requires the challenging party to prove potential prejudice to the case if the challenged juror should be accepted. There is generally no limit to such challenges. The typical statute permits such an objection if the juror is of unsound mind, lacks the qualifications required by law, is related to a party in the litigation, has served in a related case or GRAND JURY investigation, or has a "state of mind" that will prevent him from acting with impartiality.

In *Wainwright v. Witt* (1985) the Supreme Court stated that the standard to determine when a prospective juror should be excluded for cause is whether the juror's views would prevent or substantially impair the juror's duties in accordance with his/her instructions and oath.

Commonly, a prosecutor calls and examines twelve veniremen, exercises his challenges for cause and peremptory challenges, replaces those excused with others, and then tenders a group of twelve to the defense. The defendant follows a similar procedure. This process continues until the parties have exhausted their challenges or expressed their satisfaction with the jury.

Voir dire proceedings are usually open to the public. In *Press-Enterprise v. Superior Court* (1984) the trial judge had ordered that all but three days of a six-week voir dire for a rape-murder trial of a teenage girl be closed to the public and press and had refused to grant the defendant's pretrial motion for release of the voir dire transcript. The Supreme Court unanimously reversed, holding that voir dire proceedings in criminal trials should be presumptively open to the public, unless fair trial interests would be better served by closure.

Voir dire vests broad authority in the trial judge. A judge may refuse to allow questions deemed irrelevant or inappropriate. The Constitution, however, requires certain inquiries. In *Ham v. South Carolina* (1973) the Supreme Court held that where racial issues permeate or are inextricably bound up in a trial, the defendant is entitled to questioning specifically directed at racial prejudice. In *Ristano v. Ross* (1976), however, the Court held that this right does not extend to all cases in which the victim and the defendant are of different races. Questioning about general bias or prejudice will normally suffice. The Court held in *Rosales-Lopez v. United States* (1981) that judges may decide on a case-by-case basis whether racial overtones justify such questioning.

Finally, voir dire violates DUE PROCESS if its exclusion of a particular group seriously detracts from the jury's impartiality and ability to reflect dominant community values. In *Witherspoon v. Illinois* (1968) the Supreme Court invalidated a statute that had the effect of screening out jurors not enthusiastic about CAPITAL PUNISHMENT, but accepting those who were. Jurors may constitutionally be disqualified, however, by expressing an absolute refusal to impose the death penalty.

CHARLES H. WHITEBREAD

Bibliography

KALVEN, HARRY and ZEISEL, HANS 1966 *The American Jury.* Boston: Little, Brown.

VOLSTEAD ACT
41 Stat. 305 (1919)

Congress passed the Volstead National Prohibition Act, sponsored by Representative Andrew J. Volstead (Republican, Minnesota), on October 28, 1919. The act provided both for the continuation of wartime PROHIBITION and for enforcement of the EIGH-

TEENTH AMENDMENT. It was enacted over the veto of President WOODROW WILSON, who objected to the linking of those "two distinct phases of prohibition legislation."

To enforce the Eighteenth Amendment against private conduct the Volstead Act defined "intoxicating beverages" as any beverages containing at least 0.5% alcohol by volume, and provided stringent penalties for their manufacture, importation, transportation, sale, possession, or use. The constitutionality of the act was upheld in the National Prohibition Cases (*Rhode Island v. Palmer*, 1920), in which the Supreme Court, speaking through Justice WILLIS VAN DEVANTER, held that Congress's power under the amendment was complete and extended to intrastate as well as interstate transactions.

The Beer-Wine Revenue Act of March 1933 amended the Volstead Act by permitting the manufacture and sale of beer and wine with an alcohol content of up to 3.2%. Passage of the TWENTY-FIRST AMENDMENT later the same year rendered the Volstead Act void.

DENNIS J. MAHONEY

VOLUNTARINESS

See: Police Interrogation and Confessions

VON HOLST, HERMANN EDUARD
(1841–1904)

A German immigrant who became chairman of the department of history at the University of Chicago, Hermann E. von Holst published a seven-volume *Constitutional and Political History of the United States* (1876–1892). The work is malproportioned; the last four volumes cover 1850–1861. Intent on condemning the "slavocracy," the author blamed the ANNEXATION OF TEXAS, the Mexican War, the KANSAS-NEBRASKA ACT, and the Civil War on a slaveholders' conspiracy. The decision in DRED SCOTT V. SANDFORD (1857), wrote von Holst, was "an unparalleled prostitution of the judicial ermine." Von Holst believed that centralized sovereignty and a free society stood for morality and national salvation. Despite his valuable use of newspapers and public documents, his style is so turgid and his judgments are so biased that he is no longer read.

LEONARD W. LEVY

VOTING RIGHTS

"The right to vote freely for the candidate of one's choice is of the essence of a democratic society, and any restrictions on that right strike at the heart of representative government." So spoke Chief Justice EARL WARREN, on behalf of the Supreme Court, in REYNOLDS V. SIMS (1964).

The Chief Justice's words were in direct philosophic succession to principles of the primacy of representative political institutions announced by the FIRST CONTINENTAL CONGRESS 190 years before, in the Declaration and Resolves of October 14, 1774:

[T]he foundation of English liberty, and of all free government, is a right in the people to participate in their legislative council: and as the English colonists are not represented, and from their local and other circumstances, cannot properly be represented in the British parliament, they are entitled to a free and exclusive power of legislation in their several provincial legislatures, where their right of representation can alone be preserved, in all cases of taxation and internal policy, subject only to the negative of their sovereign, in such manner as has been heretofore used and accustomed.

The failure of King George III, through his ministers, to recognize the urgency of the colonists' demand for true representative institutions was one of the chief causes of revolution set forth in the DECLARATION OF INDEPENDENCE: "He has dissolved Representative Houses repeatedly, for opposing with manly firmness his invasions in the rights of the people. He has refused for a long time, after such dissolutions, to cause others to be elected; whereby the Legislative Powers, incapable of Annihilation, have returned to the People at large for their exercise."

The severing of the ties with Britain required the establishment, at the state level and at the national level, of new and more representative institutions of government. American constitutional history is characterized in part by the continuing enlargement of the right to vote, the mechanism which, in the American political tradition, has become the *sine qua non* of a valid system of REPRESENTATION. An anomaly presents itself: The Constitution, as amended, addresses aspects of the right to vote with far greater frequency than any other topic. Nonetheless, it has never been the function of the Constitution affirmatively to define the universe of voters. The Constitution's function has been narrower—progressively to limit the permissible grounds of disenfranchisement.

Prior to the American Revolution, eligibility to vote was not uniform among the colonies, but the variations were relatively minor. Broadly speaking, voting for colonial (as distinct from township or borough) officials was reserved to adult (generally meaning twenty-one or older) "freeholders." In equating property ownership and suffrage, the colonies were following a familiar English model. But landowning was far more widely dispersed in the colonies than in the mother country, so the proportion of colonists eligible to vote was larger.

There were not more than a few black or women freeholders in any of the colonies, and pursuant either to convention or to formal legal specification those few did not vote. Religious restrictions were also commonplace but varied somewhat among the colonies and at different times. In general, the franchise was the prerogative of the propertied, Protestant, white male.

With the coming of independence, all of the newly sovereign states except Connecticut and Rhode Island adopted new charters of government—"constitutions." Impelled by the rhetoric of revolution and the eagerness of thousands of militiamen to participate in the processes of governance, the drafters of the new state constitutions relaxed but did not abandon the property and religious qualifications for voting for state officials (and the correlative, and generally more stringent, qualifications for holding state office). As Max Farrand observed, Americans

might declare that "all men are created equal," and bills of rights might assert that government rested upon the consent of the governed; but these constitutions carefully provided that such consent should come from property owners, and, in many of the States, from religious believers and even followers of the Christian faith. "The man of small means might vote, but none save well-to-do Christians could legislate, and in many states none but a rich Christian could be a governor." In South Carolina, for example, a freehold of 10,000 currency was required of the Governor, Lieutenant Governor, and members of the council; 2,000 of the members of the Senate; and, while every elector was eligible to the House of Representatives, he had to acknowledge the being of a God and to believe in a future state of rewards and punishments, as well as to hold "a freehold at least of fifty acres of land, or a town lot."

Under the ARTICLES OF CONFEDERATION, the state delegates in Congress constituted the nation's government. The Articles limited the numbers of delegates (no fewer than two and no more than seven per state) but left each state legislature free to determine the qualifications of those selected and the mode of their annual selection. The Articles did not preclude popular election of delegates, but the word "appointed," in the phrase "appointed in such manner as the legislature of each State shall direct," suggests that it was not anticipated that legislatures would remit to their constituents the power to choose those who would speak and vote for the states in Congress.

At the CONSTITUTIONAL CONVENTION OF 1787, the Framers divided on how the lower house was to be selected. JAMES MADISON told his fellow delegates that he "considered an election of one branch at least of the legislature by the people immediately, as a clear principle of true government." Madison's view carried the day. But then the Convention faced the question whether the Constitution should set the qualifications of those who were to elect representatives. GOUVERNEUR MORRIS of Pennsylvania proposed that only freeholders should vote. Colonel GEORGE MASON of Virginia found this proposal regressive: "Eight of nine States have extended the right of suffrage beyond the freeholders. What will the people there say, if they should be disfranchised." OLIVER ELLSWORTH of Connecticut also challenged Morris's proposal: "How shall the freehold be defined? Ought not every man who pays a tax to vote for the representative who is to levy and dispose of his money?" Morris was unpersuaded: "He had long learned not to be the dupe of words. . . . Give the votes to people who have no property, and they will sell them to the rich who will be able to buy them." But BENJAMIN FRANKLIN took decisive issue with his fellow Pennsylvanian: "It is of great consequence that we should not depress the virtue and public spirit of our common people; of which they displayed a great deal during the war, and which contributed principally to the favorable issue of it." Morris's proposal was decisively defeated. The Convention instead approved the provision that has endured ever since, under which eligibility to vote for representatives is keyed, in each state, to that state's rules of eligibility to vote for members of the most numerous house of the state legislature.

When it came to designing the method of selecting the President and vice-president, the Convention devised the indirect election system of the ELECTORAL COLLEGE. The expectation was that the electors—themselves chosen from among the leading citizens of their respective states—would, through disinterested deliberation, select as the nation's chief executive officials the two persons of highest civic virtue, wholly without regard for the vulgar demands of "politics." According to ALEXANDER HAMILTON in THE FEDERALIST #68, "[t]he mode of appointment of the Chief Magistrate of the United States is almost the only part of the system, of any consequence, which has escaped without severe censure, or which has received the slightest mark of approbation from its opponents." But, measured against its intended purpose, no other structural aspect of the Constitution has wound up wider of the mark. The Framers of the Constitution wholly failed to anticipate the development of national political parties whose chief political goal would be the election of the party leader as President. That development has meant that since the fourth presidential election—that of 1800, in which THOMAS JEFFERSON defeated JOHN ADAMS—the electors in each state have themselves been selected as adherents of the political party prevailing in that state and thus have, with the rarest of exceptions, cast their electoral votes for the party's presidential and vice-presidential candidates. The system of electors remains to this day, but it has been entirely drained of its intended function.

Those who drafted the Constitution in 1787, and who saw it through ratification to the launching of the new ship of state in 1789, were America's aristocracy. The transformation of American politics from 1789 to the Civil War can be measured in the marked shift in class status of those who occupied the Presidency. The Presidents from GEORGE WASHINGTON to JOHN QUINCY ADAMS were all patricians. Most of the Presidents from ANDREW JACKSON to ABRAHAM LINCOLN were not. The growth of national parties, beginning with Jefferson and accelerating with Jackson, democratized politics by putting politicians in the business of seeking to enlarge their voting constituencies. Property qualifications gave way, for the most part, to taxpayer qualifications. And, in many states, these in turn were soon largely abandoned.

The erosion of property tests for voting did not mean that anything approximating universal suffrage was at hand. As one political scientist has summarized the situation:

Apart from a few midwestern states, hungry for settlers, no one was very warm to the prospect of aliens and immigrants at the polls; all the states but Maine, Massachusetts, Vermont, New Hampshire, Rhode Island, and New York explicitly barred free blacks from voting, and New York imposed special property requirements on blacks which, while repeatedly challenged, were repeatedly upheld in popular referenda. Even in the tiny handful of northern states that did not exclude blacks by law, social pressures tended to accomplish the same end. New Hampshire and Vermont in 1857 and 1858 had to pass special laws against excluding blacks from voting. Chancellor James Kent concluded that only in Maine could the black man participate equally with the white man in civil and political rights. Women were universally denied the vote [Elliott 1974, p. 40].

In 1848, a year of revolution in Europe, 300 people gathered in a church in the little upstate New York town of Seneca Falls to consider the status of women. The most revolutionary item on the agenda was voting. Half a century before there had been a small outcropping of female voting in New Jersey, whose 1776 constitution had, perhaps inadvertently, used the word "inhabitants" to describe those who, if they met the property qualifications, could vote. It appears that by 1807, respectable New Jersey opinion had reached the consensus that laxity was slipping into license (at a local election in Trenton even slaves and Philadelphians were said to have cast ballots). At this point, "reform" was clearly called for: the legislature promptly altered the electoral code to bring New Jersey's voting qualifications back into conformity with the white maleness that characterized the electorate in the rest of the country and remained the accepted order of things until Seneca Falls.

The chief driving energies behind the Seneca Falls Convention were Elizabeth Cady Stanton and Lucretia Mott. Stanton drafted the "Declaration of Principles" and the several resolutions which the convention was asked to adopt. The only resolution to receive less-than-unanimous endorsement was the ninth: "Resolved, that it is the duty of the women of this country to secure to themselves their sacred right to the elective franchise." That the franchise was a far more chimerical goal than other concerns (for example, property rights for married women) was recognized by Mott. She had asked Stanton not to submit the ninth resolution for the reason that "Thou will make us ridiculous." The factor that may have tipped the balance in Stanton's decision not to subordinate her principle to Mott's pragmatism was the strong encouragement of Frederick Douglass. The great black leader supported the ninth resolution. He joined the cause of equal rights for women to the cause of abolition.

The women's movement maintained its close association with abolitionism through the Civil War. After the freeing of the slaves, the country's attention focused on the terms on which American blacks were to be brought into the mainstream of American life. The leaders of the women's movement hoped that the drive for women's suffrage would complement and be reinforced by the drive for black suffrage. But that was not to be. As the war neared its end, a number of Republican leaders began to recognize a strong partisan interest in creating black voters to counter the feared resurgence of the Democratic party; there were no comparable reasons for creating women voters. Many of the women leaders, recognizing the political realities, accepted—albeit with no enthusiasm—the priority given to the rights of blacks. But not Elizabeth Cady Stanton and Susan B. Anthony. Said Anthony: "I will cut off this right arm before I will ever work for or demand the ballot for the Negro and not the woman." (Anthony and Stanton then formed the National Woman Suffrage Association, while the other leaders worked through the American Woman Suffrage Association; the split was not to be healed for twenty-five years.)

In 1864 Abraham Lincoln appointed SALMON P. CHASE—Lincoln's former secretary of the treasure and one of his chief rivals for the Republican presidential nomination in 1860—to succeed ROGER B. TANEY as CHIEF JUSTICE of the United States. Chase's elevation to the Court did not abate his presidential ambitions and his attendant interest in promoting a favorable political environment. The new Chief Justice wrote to Lincoln, as he subsequently wrote to President ANDREW JOHNSON, urging that black suffrage be made a condition of the reconstruction of the rebel states. And by 1867 Chase had taken the position that Congress had constitutional authority to enfranchise blacks as a mode of enforcing the THIRTEENTH AMENDMENT: "Can anything be clearer than that the National Legislature charged with the duty of 'enforcing by appropriate legislation' the condition of universal freedom, is authorized and bound to provide for universal suffrage? Is not *suffrage* the best security against *slavery* and *involuntary servitude*? Is not the legislation which provides the *best* security the most *appropriate*?" Chase lost interest in active promotion of black voting when it became apparent that his modest chances of being nominated for the presidency were more likely to be realized in the Democratic party than in the Republican party. In any event, the question whether the Thirteenth Amendment could have been a platform for enlarging the franchise became moot upon the adoption of the two other post-Civil War Amendments, both of which expressly addressed the franchise—for blacks, not for women.

The FOURTEENTH AMENDMENT, ratified in 1868, dealt with black voting by indirection. By declaring that "[a]ll persons born or naturalized in the United States, and subject to the jurisdiction thereof, are citizens of the United States and of the State wherein they reside," the first sentence of the first section of the amendment overruled Roger B. Taney's pronouncement in DRED SCOTT V. SANDFORD (1857), that blacks, whether slave or free, could not be citizens within the contemplation of the Constitution. The second sentence of the first section sought to protect the CIVIL RIGHTS of blacks: First, it guaranteed "the privileges and immunities of citizens of the United States" against state abridgment and, second,

it prohibited state denial to any person, whether citizen or not, of "life, liberty or property without DUE PROCESS OF LAW," or deprivation of the "EQUAL PROTECTION OF THE LAWS." The second section of the amendment spoke to the political rights of blacks. It provided that any state that denied participation in federal or state elections to "any of the male inhabitants of such State, being twenty-one years of age, and citizens of the United States . . . except for participation in rebellion, or other crime," should have its allocation of representatives and of presidential electors proportionately reduced. The framers of the amendment thus preserved the states' entitlement to discriminate but proposed a substantial penalty as the price of discrimination.

By 1869, after General ULYSSES S. GRANT's narrow victory in the 1868 presidential election, the Republican party recognized that black votes were essential to its survival. So the Republican leadership in Congress fashioned the FIFTEENTH AMENDMENT. That amendment, ratified in 1870, addressed the question of black voting directly. A citizen's entitlement to vote could not be "abridged by the United States or by any State on account of race, color, or previous condition of servitude."

Notwithstanding that the express language of the Fourteenth Amendment addressed male voting, and that the express language of the Fifteenth Amendment addressed discriminations rooted in "race, color or previous condition of servitude," some leaders of the women's movement contended that women were constitutionally entitled to vote. Arguing that the right to vote in a federal election was a privilege of national citizenship protected by section 1 of the Fourteenth Amendment, Susan B. Anthony actually persuaded election officials in Rochester, New York, to let her vote in 1872 notwithstanding that the New York constitution limited the franchise to men. Anthony was promptly charged with the crime of casting a ballot in a federal election in which she was not an eligible voter. The presiding judge was Justice WARD HUNT of the Supreme Court. Justice Hunt rejected Anthony's constitutional claim in the following words:

The right of voting, or the privilege of voting, is a right or privilege arising under the constitution of the state, and not under the Constitution of the United States. The qualifications are different in the different states. Citizenship, age, sex, residence, are variously required in the different states, or may be so. If the right belongs to any particular person, it is because such person is entitled to it by the laws of the state where he offers to exercise it, and not because of citizenship of the United States. If the state of New York should provide that no person should vote until he had reached the age of thirty years, or after he had reached the age of thirty years, or after he had reached the age of fifty, or that no person having grey hair, or who had not the use of all his limbs, should be entitled to vote, I do not see how it could be held to be a violation of any right derived or held under the Constitution of the United States. We might say that such regulations were unjust, tyrannical, unfit for the regulation of an intelligent state; but, if rights of a citizen are thereby violated they are of that fundamental class, derived from his position as a citizen of the state, and not those limited rights belonging to him as a citizen of the United States.

Read through the prism of a century of doctrinal hindsight, Justice Hunt's words seem—at least at first blush—somewhat surprising. The surprise is not occasioned by the fact that the Justice gave such short shrift to arguments based on the Fourteenth Amendment's PRIVILEGES AND IMMUNITIES CLAUSE, for we are accustomed to the fact that, ever since the SLAUGHTERHOUSE CASES (1873), the Supreme Court has read the grant of privileges and immunities flowing from national citizenship very restrictively. The surprise stems from Hunt's failure—which may also have been counsel's failure—to approach sex-based denial of the franchise (not to mention the assertedly analogous hypothetical denials based on age, physical handicap, or color of hair) in equal protection terms. The likely explanation is that in *Slaughterhouse* the Court doubted that "any action of a State not directed by way of discrimination against the negroes as a class, or on account of their race, will ever be held to come within the" equal protection clause.

Justice Hunt directed the jury to return a verdict of guilty and imposed a fine of $100.

Justice Hunt's rejection of Anthony's privileges and immunities claim was vindicated two years later by Chief Justice MORRISON R. WAITE'S opinion for the unanimous Court in MINOR V. HAPPERSETT (1875). This was a civil suit brought in a Missouri state court by Virginia L. Minor, and her lawyer husband Francis Minor, to challenge the refusal of a Missouri election official to register her as a voter. The Minors contended that the provision of the Missouri constitution limiting the electorate to male citizens transgressed the privileges and immunities clause. In rejecting the Minors' contention, Chief Justice Waite demonstrated that limitation of the franchise to males had been the norm, despite the fact that women were citizens. Voting had not been a privilege of national citizenship prior to the Fourteenth Amendment. As the amendment "did not add to the privileges and immunities of a citizen," but merely "furnished an additional

guaranty for the protection of such as he already had," Missouri's refusal to let Minor vote was not unconstitutional. *Minor v. Happersett* ended attempts to win the campaign for woman's suffrage by litigation. The road to the ballot box was to be political—persuading male legislators to pass laws giving women the vote.

It was to be a long road. In 1870 Wyoming's territorial legislature enacted a law entitling women to vote. Utah followed suit, but the victory there was temporary. An 1887 congressional statute forbidding Utah's Mormons from practicing polygamy also overrode the territorial legislature's grant of the franchise to women. Three years later Wyoming's first state constitution called for women's suffrage. Thereafter progress was slow. Many state campaigns were fought and most were lost. In the South, votes for women were seen as a harbinger of votes for blacks, and the states resisted accordingly; in the East, many industrialists mistrusted the links between some women's suffragists and trade union and other reform groups; in the Midwest, the women's suffrage movement was seen by the brewing interests as the advance guard of prohibition. By 1913 women could vote in only nine states; in that year Illinois admitted women to participation in presidential elections.

In 1912, THEODORE ROOSEVELT's Progressive party endorsed women's suffrage. This endorsement served as a reminder that Susan B. Anthony and her associates had sought to achieve women's suffrage not state-by-state but by amending the Constitution. Pressure for a women's suffrage amendment mounted during World War I when women entered the work force in record numbers. In 1918 WOODROW WILSON announced support for the proposed amendment, notwithstanding that women's suffrage was anathema to the white Democratic South. In 1919, with Democrats divided and Republicans strongly in favor, Congress submitted to the states a proposed amendment barring denial or abridgment of the right to vote in any election on grounds of sex. In 1920, the NINETEENTH AMENDMENT was ratified. In the 1920 elections one of the voters was Charlotte Woodward Pierce who, as a nineteen-year-old farm girl, had attended the Seneca Falls Convention in 1848.

Following the Civil War, the military occupation of the South ushered in a period in which blacks not only voted but were elected to office. With the adoption of the Fifteenth Amendment, there appeared to be some ground for supposing that black voting had achieved a legal infrastructure which might suffice even after the army departed. However, although the amendment bars race, color, and previous condition of servitude as criteria of eligibility to vote, it does not proscribe other criteria—such as literacy or tax-payer status—susceptible of adaptation as surrogates for racism. The lesson was that most blacks might be prevented from voting by educational or property qualifications.

Following the COMPROMISE OF 1877, which led to the withdrawal from the South of the last military units, the twilight of black participation in the southern political process began. Through the 1880s, some black voting continued—frequently in Populist alliance with poor whites. But in the 1890s, as a corollary of the spreading gospel of Jim Crow, the southern white political leadership forged a consensus to exclude blacks from the ballot box. Some of this was achieved by force, and some by skulduggery, but in large measure the forms of law were utilized. LITERACY TESTS and POLL TAXES were common exclusionary devices, as was closing Democratic primaries—the only real elections in most of the South—to blacks. The underlying rationale was that offered by Senator James Vardaman of Mississippi: "I am just as much opposed to Booker Washington as a voter, with all his Anglo-Saxon reinforcements, as I am to the cocoanut-headed, chocolate-covered, typical little coon, Andy Dottson, who blacks my shoes every morning. Neither is fit to perform the supreme function of citizenship."

By and large, the legal stratagems employed by the southern states to disenfranchise blacks succeeded. Poll taxes and literacy tests which did not on their face show a discriminatory purpose easily passed constitutional muster from BREEDLOVE V. SUTTLES (1937) to *Lassiter v. Northampton Election Board* (1959). To be sure, the Supreme Court did intervene in those rare instances in which the purpose to discriminate was evident on the face of the challenged restraint. A flagrant example was the so-called GRANDFATHER CLAUSE in Oklahoma's 1910 constitution, which exempted from the literacy requirement any would-be voter "who was, on January 1, 1866, or at any time prior thereto, entitled to vote under any form of government, or who at that time resided in some foreign nation, and [any] lineal descendant thereof." In GUINN V. UNITED STATES (1915) the Supreme Court held this literacy test invalid.

Because during the first half of the twentieth century the decisive voting in the South took place in Democratic primaries, not in the general elections, the cases of greatest practical as well as doctrinal consequence were those that challenged devices to maintain the whiteness of the "white primary."

In NIXON V. HERNDON (1927) a unanimous Court, speaking through Justice OLIVER WENDELL HOLMES,

sustained the complaint of L. A. Nixon, who contended that he had been unconstitutionally barred from voting in a Texas Democratic primary through enforcement of a Texas statute that recited that "in no event shall a negro be eligible to participate in a Democratic party primary election held in the state of Texas." The Court held that this statutory racial exclusion contravened the Fourteenth Amendment.

The consequence of this ruling was described by Justice BENJAMIN N. CARDOZO in his opinion in NIXON V. CONDON (1932): "Promptly after the announcement of [the Herndon] decision, the legislature of Texas enacted a new statute . . . repealing the article condemned by this court; declaring that the effect of the decision was to create an emergency with a need for immediate action; and substituting for the article so repealed another bearing the same number. By the article thus substituted, 'every political party in this State through its State Executive Committee shall have the power to prescribe the qualifications of its own members and shall in its own way determine who shall be qualified to vote or otherwise participate in such political party. . . .'" Thereupon the executive committee of the Texas Democratic party voted to limit party membership and participation to whites, and L. A. Nixon was once again barred from voting in the Democratic primary. Once again Nixon brought a lawsuit, and once again he prevailed in the Supreme Court. Justice Cardozo, speaking for a majority of five, concluded that the new Texas statute delegated exercise of the state's power over primaries to party executive committees, with the result that the racial exclusion decided on by the executive committee was in effect the racially discriminatory act of the State of Texas and hence prohibited by the Fourteenth Amendment. Justice JAMES C. MCREYNOLDS, joined by three other Justices, dissented.

Three years later, in GROVEY V. TOWNSEND (1935), the Court considered the next refinement in the Texas Democratic primary—exclusion of blacks by vote of the party convention. Speaking through Justice OWEN J. ROBERTS, the Court this time unanimously concluded that the action taken by the Texas Democratic party was an entirely private decision for which the State of Texas was not accountable; accordingly, neither the Fourteenth nor the Fifteenth Amendment was transgressed.

Nine years later, toward the end of World War II, the Court, in SMITH V. ALLWRIGHT (1944), again considered the *Grovey v. Townsend* question. In the interval, seven of the Justices who had participated in *Grovey v. Townsend* had died or retired. Approaching the matter in a common sense way, the Court, with

Justice Roberts dissenting, concluded that the role of the primary as a formal and vital predicate of the election made it an integral part of the state's voting processes and hence subject to the requirement of the Fifteenth Amendment. Accordingly, the Court in *Smith v. Allwright* overruled *Grovey v. Townsend.*

The resumption, after three-quarters of a century, of significant black participation in the southern political process dates from the decision in *Smith v. Allwright*. But the elimination of the most egregious legal barriers did not mean that all blacks were automatically free to vote. Hundreds of thousands of would-be black voters were still kept from the polls by fraud or force or both. In 1957, three years after the Court, in BROWN V. BOARD OF EDUCATION (1954), held that legally mandated racial SEGREGATION contravened the Fourteenth Amendment, Congress passed the first federal civil rights law enacted since the 1870s: a voting rights law which authorized modest federal supervision of the southern voting process. And the year 1964 witnessed ratification of the TWENTY-FOURTH AMENDMENT, barring exclusion of American citizens from voting in any federal election on grounds of failure to pay any poll tax or other tax. But as black demands for equal treatment multiplied, responsive abuses escalated.

In the spring of 1965, a Boston minister, one of scores of clergymen who had gone to Selma, Alabama, to help MARTIN LUTHER KING, JR., launch a voter registration drive, was murdered. A few days later, on March 15, 1965, President LYNDON B. JOHNSON addressed Congress:

Many of the issues of civil rights are very complex and most difficult. But about this there can and should be no argument. Every American citizen must have an equal right to vote. There is no reason which can excuse the denial of that right. There is no duty which weighs more heavily on us than the duty we have to ensure that right.

Yet the harsh fact is that in many places in this country men and women are kept from voting simply because they are Negroes.

Every device of which human ingenuity is capable has been used to deny this right. The Negro citizen may go to register only to be told that the day is wrong, or the hour is late, or the official in charge is absent. And if he persists and if he manages to present himself to the registrar, he may be disqualified because he did not spell out his middle name or because he abbreviated a word on the application. And if he manages to fill out an application, he is given a test. The registrar is the sole judge of whether he passes this test. He may be asked to recite the entire constitution, or explain the most complex provisions of state laws. And even a college degree cannot be used to prove that he can read and write.

For the fact is that the only way to pass these barriers is to show a white skin.

Experience has clearly shown that the existing process of law cannot overcome systematic and ingenious discrimination. No law that we now have on the books—and I have helped to put three of them there—can ensure the right to vote when local officials are determined to deny it. . . .

This time, on this issue, there must be no delay, or no hesitation or no compromise with our purpose.

We cannot, we must not refuse to protect the right of every American to vote in every election that he may desire to participate in. And we ought not, we must not wait another eight months before we get a bill. We have already waited a hundred years and more and the time for waiting is gone. . . .

But even if we pass this bill, the battle will not be over. What happened in Selma is part of a far larger movement which reaches into every section and state of America. It is the effort of American Negroes to secure for themselves the full blessings of American life.

Their cause must be our cause too. Because it is not just Negroes, but really it is all of us, who must overcome the crippling legacy of bigotry and injustice. And we shall overcome.

As a man whose roots go deeply into Southern soil I know how agonizing racial feelings are. I know how difficult it is to reshape the attitudes and the structure of our society.

But a century has passed, more than a hundred years, since the Negro was freed. And he is not fully free tonight.

It was more than a hundred years ago that Abraham Lincoln, the great President of the Northern party, signed the Emancipation Proclamation, but emancipation is a proclamation and not a fact.

A century has passed, more than a hundred years since equality was promised. And yet the Negro is not equal.

A century has passed since the day of promise. And the promise is unkept.

The time of justice has now come. I tell you that I believe sincerely that no force can hold it back. It is right in the eyes of man and God that it should come. And when it does, I think that day will brighten the lives of every American.

Congress enacted the VOTING RIGHTS ACT OF 1965. The act provided, among other things, for the suspension of literacy tests for five years in states or political subdivisions thereof in which fewer than "50 per cent of its voting-age residents were registered on November 1, 1964, or voted in the presidential election of November, 1964." This and other major provisions of the 1965 act were thereafter sustained in SOUTH CAROLINA V. KATZENBACH (1966), *Rome v. United States* (1980), and KATZENBACH V. MORGAN (1966), as appropriate ways of enforcing the Fifteenth and Fourteenth Amendments. Subsequent amendments to the 1965 act have broadened its coverage.

The 1944 decision in *Smith v. Allwright* was more than a new and hospitable judicial approach to the right of blacks to participate in the American political process. It was a major advance (as, four years later, was SHELLEY V. KRAEMER, 1948) toward the day— May 17, 1954—when a unanimous Court, speaking through Chief Justice Warren, was to hold, in *Brown v. Board of Education,* that the equal protection clause barred the legally mandated racial segregation of school children. Subsequent decisions, building on *Brown v. Board of Education,* soon made it plain that the equal protection clause barred all the legal trappings of Jim Crow. *Brown v. Board of Education* worked a fundamental change in the Court's and the nation's perception of the scope of judicial responsibility to vindicate those values.

In 1962, eight years after *Brown v. Board of Education,* the Court, in *Baker v. Carr,* held that allegations that a state legislature suffered from systematic malapportionment, under which districts of widely different populations were each represented by one legislator, stated a claim cognizable under the equal protection clause. The importance of *Baker v. Carr* cannot be overestimated. Chief Justice Warren thought it the most significant decision handed down by the Court during his sixteen years in the center chair. Even those who rank *Brown v. Board of Education* ahead of *Baker v. Carr* must nonetheless acknowledge that the latter decision set in motion a process that resulted in the redesign of numerous state legislatures and a myriad of local governing bodies, and, indeed, of the House of Representatives. That redesign has been required to meet the Court's pronouncement, in GRAY V. SANDERS (1963), that "[t]he conception of political equality from the Declaration of Independence, to Lincoln's Gettysburg Address, to the Fifteenth, Seventeenth, and Nineteenth Amendments can mean only one thing—one person, one vote." Long-standing patterns of malapportionment in which rural districts with relatively few inhabitants were represented on equal terms with heavily populated urban districts have become a thing of the past. (See REAPPORTIONMENT.)

Guaranteeing the voting rights of women and blacks and overcoming rampant malapportionment have cured the major inexcusable deficiencies of the American political process. In recent decades, certain lesser inequalities have also begun to be addressed.

From the beginning of the republic, Americans residing in the continental United States but not within any state—for example, those who lived in federal territories—had no way of voting in national elections.

In the most egregious of anomalies, residents of the nation's capital were voiceless in the selection of the President who dwelt and governed in their own home town. So matters stood until 1964, when the TWENTY-THIRD AMENDMENT was added to the Constitution, giving the DISTRICT OF COLUMBIA a minimum of three electoral votes in presidential elections.

In the late 1960s, profound divisions in American opinion about America's military involvement in the VIETNAM WAR forced recognition of another anomaly—that tens of thousands of young men were being drafted to fight in an unpopular foreign war although they were not old enough to vote in national elections choosing the officials responsible for making decisions for war or for peace. In 1970, Congress, in amending the Voting Rights Act, included a provision forbidding abridgment of the right of any citizen to vote "on account of age if such citizen is eighteen years or older." The statute was promptly challenged in OREGON V. MITCHELL (1970). Four Justices concluded that Congress had the power to lower the voting age to eighteen. Four Justices concluded that Congress had no such power. The casting vote was that of Justice Hugo L. Black, who held that Congress could regulate the voting age in national elections but not in state elections. Because Americans vote every two years for state and national officials at the same time, *Oregon v. Mitchell* was an invitation to chaos. Within six months, Congress proposed and the requisite three-fourths of the states ratified, the TWENTY-SIXTH Amendment which accomplished by constitutional mandate what Congress had been unable to achieve by statute.

In the course of two centuries law and conscience have combined to make the American suffrage almost truly universal. One massive obstacle remains: apathy. In recent national elections in the European democracies, seventy-two percent of the eligible electorate voted in Great Britain, seventy-nine percent in Spain, eighty-five percent in France, and eighty-nine percent in Italy and West Germany. By contrast, in the American presidential election of 1980, only fifty-three percent of those eligible voted. In America's 1984 presidential election, after both major parties had made massive efforts to register new voters, not more than fifty-five percent of those who could have voted made their way to the ballot box. A fateful question confronting American democracy is whether tens of millions of self-disenfranchised Americans will in the years to come find the energy and good sense to exercise the precious right won at such great labor at the Constitutional Convention, in Congress and state legislatures and the Supreme Court, and at Selma and Seneca Falls.

LOUIS H. POLLAK

(SEE ALSO: *Rogers v. Lodge,* 1982.)

Bibliography

CHUTE, MARCHETTE G. 1969 *First Liberty: A History of the Right to Vote in America, 1619–1850.* New York: Dutton.

DUBOIS, ELLEN CAROL, ed. 1981 *Elizabeth Cady Stanton, Susan B. Anthony: Correspondence, Writings, Speeches.* New York: Shocken.

ELLIOTT, WARD E. Y. 1974 *The Rise of Guardian Democracy: The Supreme Court's Role in Voting Rights Disputes, 1845–1969.* Cambridge, Mass.: Harvard University Press.

FAIRMAN, CHARLES 1971 *Reconstruction and Reunion, 1864–1888.* New York: Macmillan.

FARRAND, MAX, ed 1921 *The Fathers of the Constitution.* New Haven, Conn.: Yale University Press.

——, ed. 1911 *The Records of the Federal Convention of 1787.* New Haven, Conn.: Yale University Press.

FLEXNER, ELEANOR 1975 *Century of Struggle: The Woman's Right to Vote Movement in the United States.* Rev. ed. Cambridge, Mass.: Harvard University Press.

HIGGINBOTHAM, A. L., JR. 1984 "States' 'Rights' and States' 'Wrongs' ": Apartheid, Virginia and South African Style." Dubois Lecture, Harvard University.

MCKAY, ROBERT B. 1965 *Reapportionment: The Law and Politics of Equal Representation.* New York: Twentieth Century Fund.

WILLIAMSON, CHILTON 1960 *American Suffrage from Property to Democracy, 1760–1860.* Princeton, N.J.: Princeton University Press.

WOODWARD, C. VANN 1951 *Origins of the New South, 1877–1913.* Baton Rouge: Louisiana State University Press.

—— 1957 *The Strange Career of Jim Crow.* New York: Oxford University Press.

VOTING RIGHTS ACT OF 1965 AND ITS AMENDMENTS
79 Stat. 437 (1965)

Despite Congress's efforts in the CIVIL RIGHTS ACTS of 1957, 1960, and 1964 to protect the right to vote, the case-by-case approach of these laws proved ineffective in dealing with denials of VOTING RIGHTS to millions of blacks. By 1965, only seventy-one voting rights cases had been filed by the Department of Justice. And in 1964 only 19.4, 6.4, and 31.8 percent of eligible blacks were registered to vote in Alabama, Mississippi, and Louisiana, respectively. In Louisiana, comparable white registration stood at 80.2 percent.

The Voting Rights Act of 1965, amended in 1970, 1975, and 1982, provided additional protection of the right to vote. The 1965 act's most extraordinary features, its preclearance requirements, applied only to states or political subdivisions with low voter registration or participation. In such jurisdictions, most of which were in the South, the act suspended literacy, educational, and character tests of voter qualifications used to deny the right to vote in any elections. In addition, with a view to New York's Puerto Rican population, the act prohibited conditioning the right to vote on any English comprehension requirement for anyone who had completed sixth grade in a school in which the predominant classroom language was other than English. States and political subdivisions subject to the suspension of voting tests were barred from implementing other voting practices that had the effect of denying or abridging the right to vote without obtaining preclearance from a federal court or the ATTORNEY GENERAL.

The Voting Rights Act Amendments of 1970 and 1975 enhanced the preclearance provisions. The 1965 act's coverage had been triggered by low electoral participation in the 1964 election. The 1970 amendments extended the preclearance requirement through 1975 and suspended voting qualification tests or devices until 1975 in all jurisdictions, not just in jurisdictions covered by other provisions of the original 1965 act. The 1975 amendments extended the preclearance requirement through 1982 and suspended tests or devices indefinitely. The 1970 and 1975 amendments also added 1968 and 1972 to 1964 as years in which low electoral participation would trigger the act's coverage. The 1982 amendments imposed new preclearance standards to be effective until 2007.

The Supreme Court has taken an expansive view of the procedures covered by the act's preclearance requirement. In *Allen v. State Board of Elections* (1969), *Dougherty County Board of Education v. White* (1978), and other cases, the Court applied the act to voting practices that might affect minority voter effectiveness, as well as to practices directly limiting voter registration. Under these rulings, the act's preclearance requirements would govern changes in voting districts, or a county board of education's requirement that employees seeking elective office take an unpaid leave of absence.

A change in voting procedure raises the question

whether the change triggers the act's preclearance requirement by having the effect of denying or abridging the right to vote. In deciding whether the requisite effect exists, the Supreme Court has held that the act covers effects even if they are not discriminatorily motivated. This standard, which is more stringent than the purposeful discrimination requirement the Court applies under the FOURTEENTH AMENDMENT and FIFTEENTH AMENDMENT, was upheld against constitutional attack in *Rome v. United States* (1980).

In addition to the preclearance requirements, the 1965 act included a nationwide prohibition upon voting qualifications or standards that deny or abridge voting rights on account of race. This prohibition applies whether the governmental unit is subject to the act's preclearance requirements or not. And, unlike the preclearance requirements, which apply only to changes in voting procedures, it applies to procedures that have long been in effect. A plurality opinion in MOBILE V. BOLDEN (1980) suggested that this provision only proscribed purposeful discrimination prohibited by the Constitution. In the 1982 amendments, however, Congress rejected a purposeful discrimination requirement and set forth standards governing findings of discriminatory effect.

In one of its remedies, the 1965 act continued and expanded a method of guaranteeing voting rights initiated in the FORCE ACT OF 1871. On a showing of widespread denials of voting rights, the act authorized a federal court to appoint federal voting examiners who themselves would examine and register voters for all elections, thereby superseding state election officials.

Addressing problems not covered by the 1965 act, the 1970 amendments lowered from twenty-one to eighteen the minimum voting age for all elections, prohibited states from imposing RESIDENCY REQUIREMENTS in presidential elections, and provided for uniform national rules for absentee voting in presidential elections. The 1975 amendments also sought to overcome linguistic barriers to political participation by requiring bilingual elections in certain political subdivisions. These language provisions brought Texas and Florida under the act's coverage. The 1982 amendments changed the expiration date of these provisions from 1985 to 1992, and added voter assistance provisions for the handicapped.

In general, the 1965 act and amendments have fared well in the Supreme Court. In SOUTH CAROLINA V. KATZENBACH (1966) and KATZENBACH V. MORGAN (1966) the Court upheld the constitutionality of the act. Following the Court's decision in NATIONAL LEAGUE OF CITIES V. USERY (1976) that certain integral state operations are beyond Congress's power to regulate under the COMMERCE CLAUSE, the constitutional attack was renewed. In *Rome v. United States* (1980) the Court held this argument inapplicable to cases involving Congress's power to enforce the Civil War amendments. In UNITED JEWISH ORGANIZATIONS OF WILLIAMSBURGH, INC. V. CAREY (1977) the Court held that use of racial criteria to favor minority voters in an effort to comply with the Voting Rights Act did not violate the Fourteenth or Fifteenth Amendments. In OREGON V. MITCHELL (1970) the Supreme Court sustained most of the 1970 amendments but invalidated lowering the voting age in state and local elections. The latter ruling in *Mitchell*, however, soon was overturned by the TWENTY-SIXTH Amendment.

The Voting Rights Act has been the most measurably successful CIVIL RIGHTS statute. In most southern states the gap between black and white voter registration shrank dramatically, and the number of elected black officials tripled between 1970 and 1975. Overt racial appeals no longer are a routinely successful part of southern political campaigns. The 1975 amendments confirmed a shift in attitude on civil rights matters. For the first time in the twentieth century, a majority of southern congressmen voted in favor of a federal civil rights statute.

THEODORE EISENBERG

Bibliography

BELL, DERRICK A., JR. 1980 *Race, Racism and American Law,* 2nd ed. Boston: Little, Brown.

DORSEN, NORMAN; BENDER, PAUL; NEUBORNE, BURT; and LAW, SYLVIA 1979 Emerson, Haber, and Dorsen's *Political and Civil Rights in the United States,* 4th ed. Vol. 2:609–685. Boston: Little, Brown.

UNITED STATES SENATE, COMMITTEE ON THE JUDICIARY 1982 Senate Report No. 97–417, 97th Congress, 2d Session.

WABASH, ST. LOUIS & PACIFIC RAILWAY v. ILLINOIS
118 U.S. 557 (1886)

Tremendous growth in a national railroad network after the Civil War led to increasingly scandalous and harmful abuses. State efforts to control the problems were generally ineffective until *Munn v. Illinois* (1877). In that case, Chief Justice MORRISON R. WAITE allowed state regulation of railroads where Congress had not yet acted, "even though it may indirectly affect" those outside the state. Illinois had attempted to curb one area of abuse by forbidding LONG HAUL–SHORT HAUL DISCRIMINATION. So pervasive was this evil that it would be outlawed later in the INTERSTATE COMMERCE and MANN-ELKINS ACTS. The state sued the Wabash company to prevent it from charging more for shorter hauls; because significant portions of most long hauls lay outside Illinois, the issue lay in the constitutionality of a state regulation of INTERSTATE COMMERCE.

A 6–3 Supreme Court struck down the Illinois statute, undercutting the decisions in the GRANGER CASES (1877) without impairing the DOCTRINE of AFFECTATION WITH A PUBLIC INTEREST. Justice SAMUEL F. MILLER looked to the COMMERCE CLAUSE as securing a "freedom of commerce" across the country. The imposition, by individual states, of varying patterns of rates and regulations on interstate commerce was "oppressive" and rendered the commerce clause a "very feeble and almost useless provision." Miller then relied on the decision in COOLEY v. BOARD OF WAR-DENS OF PHILADELPHIA (1851) to declare that such regulation was clearly national, not local, in character even though Congress had not yet acted. In so doing, he altered the thrust of the *Cooley* test by examining the impact of state regulation on the nation instead of on the subjects involved. Miller concluded that "it is not, and never has been, the deliberate opinion of a majority of this court that a statute of a state which attempts to regulate the fare and charges by railroad companies [affecting interstate commerce] is a valid law."

Justices HORACE GRAY, JOSEPH P. BRADLEY, and Chief Justice Waite dissented, contending that the *Granger Cases* should have ruled the decision here. Citing WILLSON v. BLACK BIRD CREEK MARSH COMPANY (1829), Gray and his colleagues argued that "in the absence of congressional legislation to the contrary, [the railroads] are not only susceptible of state regulation, but properly amenable to it." They recited the litany of rights and powers granted the railroads by the state: "its being, its franchises, its powers, its road, its right to charge" all confirmed the state's right to regulate the road. The dissenters asserted that the Illinois statute affected interstate commerce only "incidentally" and not adversely. Subject to future congressional action, they would have affirmed the state action.

This decision effectively created a vacuum—Congress had not acted and the states were forbidden to act or even to control intrastate abuses. Together with an increasingly powerful reform movement, *Wabash* helped contribute to the passage of the Interstate Commerce Act in 1887, creating the first national regulatory body.

DAVID GORDON

WADE, UNITED STATES v.
388 U.S. 218 (1967)

Wade's conviction of bank robbery depended heavily on the identification of him as the robber by two bank employees. After he was indicted and counsel appointed for him, the Federal Bureau of Investigation arranged a LINEUP, which included Wade and five or six other people. Wade's counsel was not notified of the procedure; neither he nor anyone else representing Wade's interests was present.

The Supreme Court held that the lineup was a "critical stage" of the proceedings; thus, the Sixth Amendment guarantees a right to the presence of counsel at the pretrial identification if evidence of the lineup were to be used at the trial. The Court reasoned that counsel was necessary at this early stage in order to assure the fairness of the trial itself. The two premises were that eyewitness identification is treacherously subject to mistake, and that police methods in obtaining identifications are often and easily unduly suggestive. If a lawyer has been present at the lineup, later, at the trial, by his questioning of the eyewitnesses he will be able to show how any irregularities have tainted the in-court identification of the defendant.

Wade established a per se rule: if counsel is absent at the pretrial confrontation, the government may not use EVIDENCE that such an event happened. Whether the witness can nevertheless make an in-court identification depends on whether the unfair procedure tainted his present ability to identify: if he had not seen the uncounseled lineup, would he still be able to pick out the defendant?

Finally, the Court suggested that the pretrial confrontation might not be a "critical stage" if other methods were developed to assure against the risk of irreparable mistaken identification. In KIRBY V. ILLINOIS (1972) the Court restricted the holding in *Wade* to lineups held after defendants have been formally charged with crime.

BARBARA ALLEN BABCOCK

WADE-DAVIS BILL
(July 2, 1864)

Republicans worried that under LINCOLN'S PLAN OF RECONSTRUCTION (December 8, 1863), the old state leadership might reverse emancipation. On July 2, 1864, Ohio's Senator Benjamin Wade and Maryland's Representative Henry Winter Davis passed a state-restoration bill that emphasized emancipation's permanence and equalized freedmen's CIVIL RIGHTS.

Their bill, implementing the Constitution's guarantee to each state of a REPUBLICAN FORM OF GOVERNMENT (Article IV, section 4), authorized the President to appoint a provisional governor for each conquered state. When a majority of white male citizens swore future loyalty to the Union, the governor was to initiate a CONSTITUTIONAL CONVENTION. Each new CONSTITUTION must incorporate emancipation, disfranchise high Confederates, and repudiate Confederate debts; then a majority of state voters, the President, and Congress must approve each constitution, and elections could proceed. State laws were to prevail excepting those on slavery. Criminal laws were to apply equally to whites and blacks.

ABRAHAM LINCOLN, unwilling to upset Arkansas's and Louisiana's progress under his 1863 policy, pocket-vetoed the bill. Advocating an abolition constitutional amendment to insure the legitimacy of emancipation, Lincoln suggested that Wade-Davis procedures, though vetoed, were satisfactory.

An election impended. If reelected, LINCOLN would serve until 1869. His educability on race was outstanding. Almost all Republicans, including Wade and Davis, supported him. Had Lincoln signed their bill, it would have committed his successor to equal state justice for all residents.

HAROLD M. HYMAN

Bibliography
HYMAN, HAROLD M. 1963 *A More Perfect Union: The Impact of the Civil War and Reconstruction on the Constitution.* Chap. 16. New York: Knopf.

WAGNER ACT CASES
NLRB v. Jones & Laughlin Steel Corp.
301 U.S. 1 (1937)
NLRB v. Fruehauf Trailer Co.
301 U.S. 49 (1937)
NLRB v. Friedman-Harry Marks Clothing Co.
301 U.S. 58 (1937)
Associated Press Co. v. NLRB
301 U.S. 103 (1937)

The reinvigoration of the COMMERCE CLAUSE as a source of congressional power began with the first cases to reach the Supreme Court under the WAGNER (NATIONAL LABOR RELATIONS) ACT. That statute had been passed in 1935 in an effort to preserve the rights of employees in interstate industries to choose their own representatives and to bargain collectively with their employers. In 1930 the Supreme Court had held that the Railway Labor Act gave such rights to railroad employees. The NATIONAL INDUSTRIAL RECOVERY ACT (NIRA) of 1933 sought to extend such rights to other employees by requiring all codes of fair competition for other industries to contain similar provisions. The code system collapsed when the NIRA was invalidated in SCHECHTER POULTRY CORP. v. UNITED STATES in May 1935. The President and Congress believed that the denial of COLLECTIVE BARGAINING rights would lead to industrial unrest and strikes, which would necessarily obstruct INTERSTATE COMMERCE, and would also aggravate the Great Depression by depressing wage rates and the purchasing power of wage earners. As a result the National Labor Relations Act became law less than six weeks after the *Schechter* decision.

The act authorized the newly created National Labor Relations Board (NLRB), which succeeded similar boards created under the NIRA, to prevent employers from engaging in unfair labor practices "affecting [interstate] commerce," which was defined to mean "in commerce, or burdening or obstructing commerce," or which had led or might lead to a labor dispute burdening or obstructing commerce. These definitions were designed to embody the decisional law upholding the authority of Congress to regulate acts that "directly" obstructed interstate commerce. Congress assumed, correctly as it turned out, that the courts would construe the statute as "contemplating the exercise of control within constitutional bounds."

The NLRB's first cases were brought against employers engaged in interstate transportation and communication (bus lines and the Associated Press) and manufacturers who purchased their supplies and sold their products across state lines. Before these cases were decided, the Supreme Court, in CARTER v. CARTER COAL CO. (1936), held that the substantially identical provisions of the Guffey-Snyder (Bituminous Coal Conservation) Act, enacted shortly after the Labor Relations Act, did not fall within the commerce power of Congress. In the *Carter* case the government had proved that coal strikes would burden not merely the interstate commerce of the immediate employers but also the interstate rail system and many other industries dependent upon coal. No stronger showing could be made under the Wagner Act for employers engaged in mining or manufacturing. As was to be expected, the courts of appeals, though sustaining the act as to companies engaged in interstate transportation and communication, deemed themselves bound

by *Carter*, as well as *Schechter* and UNITED STATES v. BUTLER (1936) to hold that the act did not extend to manufacturers.

The first five NLRB cases to reach the Supreme Court involved a bus line, the Associated Press, and three manufacturers. The cases were argued together, beginning on February 8, 1937. Three days before, President FRANKLIN D. ROOSEVELT had announced his plan to appoint up to six new Supreme Court Justices, one for each justice over 70 years of age. On April 12, the Court affirmed the NLRB's rulings in all five cases. The opinions on the commerce clause issue in the bus and press cases were unanimous, although in the press case, four Justices dissented on FIRST AMENDMENT grounds. The cases against manufacturers—the Jones & Laughlin Steel Corporation, the Fruehauf Trailer Co., and a medium-size men's clothing manufacturer—were decided by a 5–4 vote. The membership of the Court had not changed since *Schechter* and *Carter*. But Chief Justice CHARLES EVANS HUGHES and Justice OWEN ROBERTS, who had been part of the majority of six who had rejected the labor relations provisions of the Guffey Act in *Carter,* now joined with Justices LOUIS D. BRANDEIS, HARLAN FISKE STONE, and BENJAMIN N. CARDOZO. The Chief Justice wrote the opinions in the manufacturers' cases.

In the *Carter* case, the majority opinion of Justice GEORGE SUTHERLAND had not denied the magnitude of the effect of coal strikes upon interstate commerce. The question, he held, was whether the effect was "direct," and that did not turn upon the "extent of the effect" or its "magnitude," but "entirely upon the manner in which the effect has been brought about"; "it connotes the absence of an efficient intervening agency or condition." The effect must "operate proximately—not mediately, remotely, or collaterally." Why "direct" should be so defined was not otherwise explained, except by the need for preserving the power of the states over PRODUCTION, even in interstate industries in which interstate competition would preclude state regulation. (See EFFECTS ON COMMERCE.)

The opinion of Chief Justice Hughes in the *Jones & Laughlin* case flatly rejected the *Butler* approach.

Giving full weight to respondent's contention with respect to a break in the complete continuity of the "STREAM OF COMMERCE" by reason of respondent's manufacturing operations, the fact remains that the stoppage of those operations by industrial strife would have a most serious effect upon interstate commerce. In view of respondent's far-flung activities, it is idle to say that the effect would be indirect or remote. It is obvious that it would be immediate and might be catastrophic. We are asked to shut our eyes to the plainest facts of our national life and to deal with the question of direct and indirect effects in an intellectual vacuum. . . . When industries organize themselves on a national scale, making their relation to interstate commerce the dominant factor in their activities, how can it be maintained that their industrial labor relations constitute a forbidden field into which Congress may not enter when it is necessary to protect interstate commerce from the paralyzing consequences of industrial war? We have often said that interstate commerce itself is a practical conception. It is equally true that interferences with that commerce must be appraised by a judgment that does not ignore actual experience.

The Chief Justice also met head on the argument that the federal power did not extend to activities in the course of production or manufacturing. Citing many antitrust cases, he declared: "The close and intimate effect which brings the subject within the reach of Federal power may be due to activities in relation to productive industry although the industry when separately viewed is local. . . . It is thus apparent that the fact that the employees here concerned were engaged in production is not determinative."

"The fundamental principle," Hughes stated, "is that the power to regulate commerce is the power to enact 'all appropriate legislation' for 'its protection and advancement'; to adopt measures 'to promote its growth and insure its safety'; 'to foster, protect, control and restrain.' That power is plenary and may be exerted to protect interstate commerce 'no matter what the source of the dangers which threatened it.'" Hughes also invoked the SHREVEPORT DOCTRINE he had announced in HOUSTON EAST AND WEST TEXAS RAILWAY V. UNITED STATES (1914): "Although activities may be intrastate in character when separately considered, if they have such a close and substantial relation to interstate commerce that their control is essential or appropriate to protect that commerce from burdens and obstructions, Congress cannot be denied the power to exercise that control."

In deference to his own opinion in *Schechter,* the Chief Justice declared that "undoubtedly the scope of this power must be considered in the light of our dual system of government" so as not to "obliterate the distinction between what is national and what is local." In *Schechter* the effect upon commerce had been too "remote"; "to find 'immediacy or directness' there was to find it 'almost everywhere', a result inconsistent with the maintenance of our Federal system." With little explanation Hughes added that *Carter* was "not controlling."

Within a few weeks the Court sustained the constitutionality of the SOCIAL SECURITY ACT. Soon after

Justices WILLIS VAN DEVANTER and Sutherland retired. And President Roosevelt's court-packing plan, not very surprisingly, got nowhere.

Subsequent Labor Board cases extended the application of the Labor Act far beyond the three manufacturers in the center of the interstate movement; it was sufficient that a strike would interfere with interstate movement of products (for example, *Santa Cruz Fruit Packing Co. v. NLRB,* 1938; *NLRB v. Fainblatt,* 1939; *Consolidated Edison Co. v. NLRB,* 1938). The unanimous opinion of the Court speaking through Justice Stone, with Hughes and Roberts still on the bench, in UNITED STATES V. DARBY (1941) explicitly rejected the concept that the TENTH AMENDMENT limited the powers granted Congress by the Constitution. And other cases by now have extended the commerce power "almost everywhere." Nevertheless, the opinion in *Jones & Laughlin* remains a landmark in the interpretation of the commerce clause, as the definitive acceptance of the modern theories which recognize the power of Congress to control all aspects of the nation's integrated economic system.

ROBERT L. STERN

Bibliography

CORTNER, RICHARD C.   1970   *The Jones & Laughlin Case.* New York: Knopf.
———   1964   *The Wagner Act Cases.* Knoxville: University of Tennessee Press.
DODD, E. MERRICK   1945   The Supreme Court and Organized Labor, 1941–1945. *Harvard Law Review* 58:1018–1071.
GROSS, JAMES A.   1974   *The Making of the National Labor Relations Board: A Study in Economics, Politics, and the Law,* Vol. 1 (1933–1937). Albany: State University of New York Press.
STERN, ROBERT L.   1946   The Commerce Clause and the National Economy, 1933–1946. *Harvard Law Review* 59:645–693, 888–947.

WAGNER (NATIONAL LABOR RELATIONS) ACT
49 Stat. 449 (1935)

Named after the New York senator who introduced and fought for it, the National Labor Relations Act (NLRA) extended the protection of the United States to organized labor. Robert Wagner framed the act to provide a constitutional basis for the protections given to labor by section 7(a) of the NATIONAL INDUSTRIAL RECOVERY ACT (NIRA) and by a National Labor Relations Board, which had been established and was operating under the sole authority of Public Resolution 44 and an EXECUTIVE ORDER. The Supreme Court confirmed the need for new legislation when, eleven days after the NLRA's enactment, it voided the NIRA in SCHECHTER POULTRY CORP. V. UNITED STATES (1935).

Congress based the Wagner Act on the COMMERCE CLAUSE: the denial by employers of employees' rights to organize and bargain collectively caused "strikes and other forms of industrial strife or unrest, which have the intent or necessary effect of burdening or obstructing [interstate] commerce." Congress added that unequal bargaining positions had exacerbated national economic instability. One section of the act guaranteed employees the right to organize, "to bargain collectively through representatives of their own choosing," and to act together to further these ends. Another section reinforced these rights by delineating employers' obligations; it defined and prohibited "unfair labor practices," including interference with the exercise of the above-mentioned rights, or discrimination to encourage or discourage union formation, administration, or membership. This section also outlawed discrimination against an employee for filing a complaint against his employer under the act and made it illegal to refuse to bargain collectively with a union's legal representative.

The act also provided for a National Labor Relations Board with broad supervisory powers to administer its provisions. The Board could issue complaints, hear and determine charges, and issue CEASE-AND-DESIST ORDERS which were enforceable upon application to federal circuit courts. Congress further empowered the board to hold representation elections and to certify the winner.

Wagner drafted the act carefully so that it would withstand scrutiny by the Supreme Court. Section 1—outlining the NLRA's policy—was rewritten after the decision in *Schechter* to specify the burdens placed upon INTERSTATE COMMERCE by labor unrest. The act's policy statement attributed that discord to the denial of workers' rights which this act would secure. Wagner's diligence paid off. A 5–4 majority of the Court upheld the NLRA in *N.L.R.B. v. Jones & Laughlin Steel Corporation* (1937). (See WAGNER ACT CASES.) The Wagner Act provided for strong independent unions in an effort to promote COLLECTIVE BARGAINING. By thus indirectly stimulating higher wages and increased consumer demand, the act helped guarantee a stable national economy and social justice for American labor. The TAFT-HARTLEY LABOR MANAGEMENT RELATIONS ACT, passed in 1947 partly to plug loopholes in the NLRA, governed union conduct much as employers' actions had earlier been regulated.

DAVID GORDON

Bibliography

MILLIS, HARRY A. and BROWN, EMILY C. 1950 *From the Wagner Act to Taft-Hartley: A Study of National Labor Policy.* Chicago: University of Chicago Press.

TAYLOR, BENJAMIN J. and WITNEY, FRED (1970)1975 *Labor Relations Law,* 2nd ed. Pages 134–199. Englewood Cliffs, N.J.: Prentice-Hall.

WAINWRIGHT v. SYKES
433 U.S. 72 (1977)

In *Sykes* the ADEQUATE STATE GROUND bar to federal HABEAS CORPUS, buried in FAY V. NOIA (1963), was unearthed and returned to service with little more than a coat of paint for disguise. *Noia* had held that a state prisoner was not barred from seeking federal habeas corpus relief merely because the applicant had failed to raise his or her federal constitutional claim in the earlier state proceeding as required by state law. *Noia* was attacked within the Supreme Court and by some scholars for sacrificing finality of decision. State judges trumpeted their resentment at giving federal district courts the last word in the state criminal process.

Sykes was the culmination of the attack on *Noia* from within the Court. A state prisoner sought federal habeas corpus, arguing that his rights to a warning under MIRANDA V. ARIZONA (1966) had been violated when his statement was admitted into EVIDENCE at his state trial. He had not objected when the evidence was offered, as state law required. The Supreme Court held, 7–2, that federal habeas corpus was barred.

Justice WILLIAM H. REHNQUIST, for the majority, announced that failure to raise a federal constitutional claim in the manner required by state law bars resort to federal habeas corpus unless the applicant shows "cause" for the procedural default and "prejudice" from the forfeiture of the federal claim. Defendant had asserted no cause for the absence of timely objection, and prejudice was negated by other evidence of his guilt, independent of his statement.

KENNETH L. KARST

WAITE, MORRISON R.
(1816–1888)

Morrison Remick Waite, sixth Chief Justice of the United States, successfully led the Supreme Court in dealing with major constitutional problems concerning Reconstruction and business–government relations between 1874 and 1888.

Son of Henry Matson Waite, Chief Justice of the Connecticut Supreme Court of Errors, Morrison Waite read law after graduating from Yale College in 1837. In 1838 he removed to Ohio, where he built a flourishing legal practice specializing in commercial law, acquired substantial property interests, and joined the Whig party. Although prominent in the legal profession, Waite was virtually unknown in national affairs prior to his appointment as Chief Justice. He served one term in the Ohio legislature and a term on the Toledo city council, was appointed counsel to the Geneva Tribunal to negotiate the *Alabama* claims in 1872, and was elected president of the Ohio CONSTITUTIONAL CONVENTION of 1873.

The circumstances of Waite's appointment to the Court were remarkable, not so much because he lacked national political recognition as because he was the fifth person whom President ULYSSES S. GRANT nominated or asked to serve as Chief Justice. Yet Waite had early been touted for the position by leading Ohio politicians, and Grant had considered him a possibility from the beginning. His effective service at the Geneva Arbitration, professional reputation, and unwavering Republican party loyalty recommended him, and in January 1874 the Senate confirmed him by a 63–0 vote.

Waite's significance in American constitutional history is threefold. He wrote the first Supreme Court opinions interpreting the FOURTEENTH and FIFTEENTH AMENDMENTS in cases involving Negroes' CIVIL RIGHTS. Second, his 1877 opinions in *Munn v. Illinois* and the other GRANGER CASES established the basic principles of constitutional law governing state governments as they attempted to deal with economic changes caused by the industrial revolution. Third, Waite expressed a conception of JUDICIAL REVIEW that summarized dominant nineteenth-century ideas about constitutional adjudication and provided a model for twentieth-century theorists of judicial restraint.

The northern retreat from Reconstruction was well underway when Waite became Chief Justice, and the WAITE COURT did not attempt to reverse this political development. Under the circumstances, and given the circumscribed role of the judiciary in nineteenth-century constitutional politics, it had little choice but to acquiesce. In determining the meaning of the Fourteenth and Fifteenth Amendments and in applying federal civil rights laws, however, the Court could choose among several possible conceptions of national legislative power and federal–state relations. Waite

guided the Court toward a moderate position of STATES' RIGHTS nationalism which upheld national power to protect civil rights within the framework of traditional FEDERALISM.

To understand this development it is necessary to advert to the SLAUGHTERHOUSE CASES (1873) and to Justice JOSEPH P. BRADLEY's circuit court opinion in UNITED STATES v. CRUIKSHANK (1874). In the former, the Supreme Court confirmed the theory of dual American CITIZENSHIP, stated that the Fourteenth Amendment did not add to the rights of national citizenship, and concluded that ordinary civil rights were attributes of state citizenship, regulation of which was beyond the authority of the United States. In the *Cruikshank* case, involving prosecution of whites in Colfax, Louisiana, for violating the civil rights of Negro citizens, Justice Bradley held that although the Fourteenth Amendment prohibited state rather than private denial of civil rights, under certain conditions the federal government was authorized to guarantee civil rights against interference by private individuals. The relevant circumstance, according to Bradley, was state failure to fulfill its affirmative duty to protect citizens' rights.

Chief Justice Waite wrote the majority opinion when *United States v. Cruikshank* (1876) was decided in the Supreme Court. Defendants were indicted under a section of the Force Act of 1870 that declared it a federal crime for two or more persons to deprive any citizen of rights secured by the Constitution or laws of the United States. Like Bradley in the CIRCUIT COURT, Waite found numerous flaws in the INDICTMENTS and on that ground ordered the defendants to be discharged, thus frustrating the federal civil rights enforcement effort. Nevertheless, Waite asserted national authority to enforce civil rights.

The Chief Justice followed the *Slaughterhouse* opinion in positing separate federal and state citizenships and in stating that the federal government could protect only those rights placed within its JURISDICTION. He held further that the FREEDOM OF ASSEMBLY, which the defendants were charged with violating, was a right of state rather than federal citizenship. The indictment, however, had incorrectly stated that denial of freedom of assembly by private persons was a federal crime within the meaning of the Force Act; therefore the indictment was invalid. Yet federal authority was not nugatory in civil rights matters. Waite pointed out that if the indictment had charged a violation of the right to assemble in order to petition the national government, it would have been proper under the act. Thus in protecting a federal right national authority was putatively effective against private individuals as well as states. Waite furthermore asserted an indirect federal power to protect rights of state citizenship against both state and private interference. The ordinary right of assembly was a state right, said Waite, over which "no direct power" was granted to Congress. This appeared to mean that if states failed to uphold civil rights within their jurisdiction, the federal government could provide the needed protection. Finally Waite noted that the indictments did not allege that the full and equal benefit of laws for the protection of whites was denied to blacks on account of race; accordingly the CIVIL RIGHTS ACT OF 1866 was not in point. The implication was that if a racially discriminatory purpose had been alleged, federal authority under the 1866 law could have been employed against private as well as against state denial of rights.

Waite also gave the opinion in UNITED STATES V. REESE (1876), the first Supreme Court case involving Fifteenth Amendment VOTING RIGHTS. State officials in Kentucky were indicted for refusing to accept the vote of a Negro citizen. Again the Court ruled against the federal government. Waite declared two provisions of the Force Act of 1870 unconstitutional because they did not in express terms limit the offense of state officials to denial of the right to vote on account of color. Insisting on the need for STRICT CONSTRUCTION of criminal statutes, he interpreted the act in a strained and technical manner as preventing any wrongful interference with voting rights, rather than simply interferences that were racially motivated. The Fifteenth Amendment authorized the federal government to deal only with the latter. It did not, said Waite, secure the right to vote, but only the right not to be discriminated against in voting on racial grounds. Observing that "Congress has not as yet provided by 'appropriate legislation' for the punishment of the offense charged in the indictment," Waite in effect invited Republican lawmakers to enact a more tightly drawn enforcement act.

Waite's personal sympathies were enlisted in efforts to assist Negroes. As a trustee of the Peabody Fund in 1874 he signed a report endorsing a constitutional argument for federal aid to education, thus breaking the rule against extra-Court political involvement to which he scrupulously adhered throughout his judicial career. Although Waite accepted the abandonment of Reconstruction and held that Congress had no power "to do mere police duty in the States," his opinions nevertheless authorized federal interference against state and in some circumstances private denial of rights when racially motivated. In subsequent cases, most notably UNITED STATES V. HARRIS (1883), the CIVIL RIGHTS CASES (1883), and EX PARTE YARBROUGH (1884), the Waite Court amplified the principles set forth in the *Cruikshank* and *Reese* cases.

In the sphere of government–business relations, Waite was sympathetic to regulatory legislation within a political and legal framework that encouraged industrial expansion and a national free trade area. In the early 1870s, in response to farmers' and merchants' demands for relief from high shipping costs, several midwestern states adopted legislation setting maximum railroad rates. These laws appeared to discourage further railroad construction, and within a few years most of them were repealed or modified. Nevertheless, in the landmark *Granger Cases* the Supreme Court ruled on the constitutionality of these regulatory measures.

Munn v. Illinois (1877), Waite's most famous opinion, sustained an 1871 Illinois law that established maximum rates for grain elevators. Waite based his approval of the legislation on a broad conception of the STATE POLICE POWER, which he said authorized states to regulate the use of private property "when such regulation becomes necessary for the public good." He rejected the contention that state regulation of the rates charged by ferries, common carriers, or bakers was a deprivation of property without DUE PROCESS OF LAW in violation of the Fourteenth Amendment. Support for Waite's conclusion lay in numerous state COMMON LAW precedents asserting a public interest in certain kinds of property, such as lands bordering on watercourses, which were subject to government regulation. Like other judges in similar cases, and influenced by a memorandum prepared by Justice Bradley dealing with the instant case, Waite relied on a treatise of the seventeenth-century English judge Lord Chief Justice Sir Matthew Hale in asserting: "When property is 'AFFECTED WITH A PUBLIC INTEREST, it ceases to be juris privati only.'" The grain elevator companies, Waite explained, exercised a virtual monopoly in the regional market structure; thus, they were affected with a public interest and subject to regulation by the state legislature. In the other *Granger Cases* Waite employed this principle to uphold state regulation of railroad rates.

Waite also approved state regulation of CORPORATIONS in a series of decisions that carried to a logical conclusion the principle by which the CONTRACT CLAUSE of the Constitution did not prevent state legislatures from reserving the power to alter charter grants. These cases included STONE V. MISSISSIPPI (1880), *Ruggles v. Illinois* (1883), and *Spring Valley Water Works v. Schotteler* (1883). This trend culminated in STONE V. FARMERS LOAN AND TRUST CO.

(1886), known as the *Railroad Commission Cases*, in which Waite held that a state charter authorizing railroads to set reasonable rates did not divest a state of the power ultimately to determine what was a reasonable rate.

While generally approving regulatory legislation, Waite placed limitations on the POLICE POWER with a view toward protecting private property. In the *Railroad Commission Cases* he admonished: "This power to regulate is not a power to destroy; and limitation is not the equivalent of confiscation. Under pretence of regulating fares and freights the state cannot require a railroad corporation to carry persons or property without reward; neither can it do that which in law amounts to a TAKING of private property without due process of law." Rather than suggesting an irresistible tendency to accept the argument for SUBSTANTIVE DUE PROCESS that was later adopted by the Supreme Court, these and similar dicta indicate that Waite, like Justice STEPHEN J. FIELD who dissented in *Munn* and the other *Granger* cases, believed the essential constitutional problem in cases involving government–business relations was to determine the extent of the police power. Shortly after the *Munn* decision Waite wrote: "The great difficulty in the future will be to establish the boundary between that which is private, and that in which the public has an interest."

Waite epitomized nineteenth-century thinking about the nature of the judicial function and the power of judicial review. He believed the judiciary should play a subordinate role in public-policy making, and should especially defer to the political branches in questions concerning the reasonableness of legislation. His clearest and most forceful expression of this view appeared in *Munn v. Illinois* when he stated: "For us the question is one of power, not of expediency. If no state of circumstances could justify such a statute, then we may declare this one void, because in excess of the legislative power of the States. But if it could we must presume it did. Of the propriety of legislative interference within the scope of legislative power, the legislature is the exclusive judge." Waite acknowledged that legislative power might be abused. But "[f]or protection against abuses by legislatures," he observed, "the people must resort to the polls, not to the courts."

Waite effectively balanced the competing demands of state and federal authority as constitutional equilibrium was restored after the end of Reconstruction. In addition to the decisions already noted, he wrote the opinions in *Louisiana v. Jumel* (1882) and *New Hampshire v. Louisiana* (1882), both of which held

that the ELEVENTH AMENDMENT prevented suits by bondholders attempting to force a state government to redeem its bonds. These decisions expressed the political logic of the COMPROMISE OF 1877 and marked a significant broadening of states' SOVEREIGN IMMUNITY under the Eleventh Amendment. In another notable case involving state power and women's rights, MINOR V. HAPPERSETT (1875), Waite adhered to a narrow interpretation of the Fourteenth Amendment in deciding that the right to vote was not an attribute of federal citizenship and that states could regulate the suffrage as they saw fit.

On the other hand, Waite upheld federal authority in the controversial SINKING FUND CASES (1879) and in PENSACOLA TELEGRAPH CO. V. WESTERN UNION TELEGRAPH CO. (1878). In the former, the Court confirmed the constitutionality of an act of Congress requiring the Union Pacific and Central Pacific railroads to set aside money from current income for the subsequent payment of its mortgage debts. In the latter case the Court upheld the rights of an interstate telegraph company operating under authority of an act of Congress against the rights of a company acting under a state charter. Waite also voted to strike down state tax legislation when it interfered with INTERSTATE COMMERCE, although he was less inclined than his colleagues to regard STATE TAXATION OF COMMERCE in this light.

Overcoming the resentment of several Justices who had aspired to the Chief Justiceship, Waite performed the administrative and other tasks of his position with great skill. In a larger political sense he was also a successful judicial statesman. During his tenure, as at few times in American constitutional history, the Supreme Court was remarkably free of congressional criticism. Waite achieved this success by confining JUDICIAL POLICYMAKING within limits approved by the nation's representative political institutions and public opinion.

HERMAN BELZ

Bibliography

BENEDICT, MICHAEL LES 1979 Preserving Federalism: Reconstruction and the Waite Court. *Supreme Court Review* 1978:39–79.
FRANTZ, LAUREN B. 1964 Congressional Power to Enforce the Fourteenth Amendment Against Private Acts. *Yale Law Journal* 73:1352–1384.
MAGRATH, PETER C. 1963 *Morrison R. Waite: The Triumph of Character.* New York: Macmillan.
SCHEIBER, HARRY N. 1971 The Road to *Munn*: Eminent Domain and the Concept of Public Purpose in the State Courts. *Perspectives in American History* 5:329–402.
TRIMBLE, BRUCE R. 1938 *Chief Justice Waite: Defender*

of the Public Interest. Princeton, N.J.: Princeton University Press.

WAITE COURT
(1874–1888)

A new age of American constitutional law was at hand when MORRISON R. WAITE became CHIEF JUSTICE of the United States in 1874. Not only had the Civil War discredited many antebellum glosses on the "old" Constitution, consisting of the venerable document framed in 1787 and the twelve amendments adopted during the early republic, but it had also generated a "new" Constitution consisting of the THIRTEENTH AMENDMENT, the FOURTEENTH AMENDMENT, and the FIFTEENTH AMENDMENT. The range of choices at the Court's disposal was virtually unlimited as it reconstituted the old organic law and integrated the new. CHARLES SUMNER said it best just four years before Waite took the Court's helm. The tumultuous events of 1861–1869, he exclaimed, had transformed the Constitution into "molten wax" ready for new impression. An extraordinarily homogeneous group of men made this impression. Of the fourteen associate Justices who sat with Waite between 1874 and his death in 1888, only NATHAN CLIFFORD had been appointed by a Democrat and all but two—SAMUEL F. MILLER and JOHN MARSHALL HARLAN, both of Kentucky—had been born in the free states. All of them were Protestants. Thus the Republican party, which had subdued the South and created the "new" Constitution, had also reconstructed the federal judiciary. As the Waite Court proceeded to refashion the structure of American constitutional law, its work ineluctably reflected the values, aspirations, and fears that had animated the Republican party's northern Protestant constituency since the 1850s.

Fierce opposition to state SOVEREIGNTY concepts was a core element of Republican belief from the party's very inception. Republicans associated state sovereignty with proslavery constitutionalism in the 1850s, with SECESSION in 1861, and ultimately with the tragic war both engendered. Waite and his colleagues shared this aversion to state sovereignty dogma and repeatedly expressed it in controversies involving the IMPLIED POWERS of Congress under the "old" Constitution. In case after case the Court resisted limitations on federal power derived from state sovereignty premises and held, in effect, that Congress's authority to enact statutes deemed NECESSARY AND PROPER for the ENUMERATED POWERS had the same scope under the Constitution as it would if the states did

not exist. On several occasions the Court even revived the idea that Congress might exercise any power inherent in national sovereignty as long as it was not specifically prohibited by the Constitution. This doctrine, first expounded by Federalist congressmen during debate on the SEDITION ACT of 1798, had been regarded as "exploded" by most antebellum statesmen. But its revival after the Civil War did have a certain logic. If there was one impulse that every member of the Waite Court had in common, it was the urge to extirpate every corollary of "southern rights" theory from American constitutional law and to confirm the national government's authority to exercise every power necessary to maintain its existence.

The revival of the implied powers doctrine began in the often overlooked case of *Kohl v. United States* (1876). There counsel challenged Congress's authority to take private property in Cincinnati as a site for public buildings on the ground that the Constitution sanctioned federal exercise of the EMINENT DOMAIN power only in the DISTRICT OF COLUMBIA. Article I, section 8, vested Congress with authority to acquire land elsewhere "for the erection of forts . . . and other needful buildings" only "by the consent of the legislature of the State in which the same shall be." This was by no means a novel argument. JAMES MADISON and JAMES MONROE had pointed to the national government's lack of a general eminent domain power when vetoing INTERNAL IMPROVEMENT bills, and proslavery theorists had invoked the same principle as a bar to compensated emancipation and colonization schemes. In *Pollard's Lessee v. Hagan* (1845), moreover, the TANEY COURT had said that "the United States have no constitutional capacity to exercise municipal jurisdiction, sovereignty, or eminent domain within the limits of a State or elsewhere, except in the cases in which it is expressly granted." But WILLIAM STRONG, speaking for the Court in *Kohl*, refused to take this doctrine "seriously." Congress's war, commerce, and postal powers necessarily included the right to acquire property for forts, lighthouses, and the like. "If the right to acquire property for such uses be made a barren right by the unwillingness of property holders to sell, or by the action of a State prohibiting a sale to the Federal Government," Strong explained, "the constitutional grants of power may be rendered nugatory. . . . This cannot be." Congress's eminent domain power must be implied, Strong concluded, for commentators on the law of nations had always regarded it as "the offspring of political necessity, and . . . inseparable from sovereignty."

HORACE GRAY sounded the same theme in the Legal Tender Cases (*Juilliard v. Greenman*, 1884), where the Court sustained Congress's authority to emit legal tender notes even in peacetime. With only STEPHEN J. FIELD dissenting, Gray asserted that because the power to make government paper a legal tender was "one of the powers belonging to sovereignty in other civilized nations, and not expressly withheld from Congress by the Constitution," it was unquestionably "an appropriate means, conducive and plainly adapted" to the execution of Congress's power to borrow money. In EX PARTE YARBROUGH (1884), decided the same day, the Court spoke the language of national sovereignty in an especially significant case. At issue there was the criminal liability of a Georgia man who had savagely beaten a black voter en route to cast his ballot in a federal election. The Court unanimously sustained the petitioner's conviction under the 1870 CIVIL RIGHTS ACT, which made it a federal crime to "injure, oppress, threaten, or intimidate any citizen in the free exercise or enjoyment of any right or privilege secured to him by the Constitution or laws of the United States." It did so on the ground that Congress's duty "to provide in an ELECTION held under its authority, for security of life and limb to the voter" arose not from its interest in the victim's rights so much as "from the necessity of the government itself." Samuel F. Miller explained that Congress's power to regulate the time, place, and manner of holding federal elections, conferred in Article I, section 4, implied a "power to pass laws for the free, pure, and safe exercise" of the suffrage. "But it is a waste of time," he added, "to seek for specific sources to pass these laws. . . . If this government is anything more than a mere aggregation of delegated agents of other States and governments, each of which is superior to the general government, it must have the power to protect the elections on which its existence depends from violence and corruption."

The Court's decisions in *Kohl*, *Juilliard*, and *Yarbrough* merely jettisoned antebellum canons of STRICT CONSTRUCTION. They did not impair the autonomy of state governments. The eminent domain power of the several states was not threatened by *Kohl*, the Constitution expressly prohibited the states from making anything but gold and silver a legal tender, and *Yarbrough* did not jeopardize Georgia's power to prosecute political assassins for assault or murder. Yet the Waite Court was as quick to defend exercises of Congress's powers in situations where counsel claimed that the states' autonomy was in jeopardy as in cases where their reserved powers remained unimpaired. *Ex parte Siebold* (1880) was the leading case in point. There the Court sustained a conviction for ballot stuffing under the 1871 ENFORCEMENT ACT, which made it a federal crime for any state official at a congressional election to neglect duties required of him by either state or federal law. Counsel for the petitioner argued that in PRIGG V. PENNSYLVANIA (1842) and KENTUCKY V. DENNISON (1861) the Taney Court had held that the principle of divided sovereignty precluded acts of Congress compelling the cooperation of state officials in the execution of national law. "We cannot yield to such a transcendental view of State sovereignty," JOSEPH BRADLEY proclaimed for the Court in *Siebold*. "As a general rule," he said, "it is no doubt expedient and wise that the operations of the State and National Governments should, as far as practicable, be conducted separately, in order to avoid undue jealousies and jars." But the Constitution neither mandated an immutable boundary between spheres of federal and state power nor restricted Congress's choice of means in implementing its enumerated authority to regulate federal elections.

The Court's constitutional nationalism did have limits. Like most Republicans of the age, Waite and his colleagues resisted the idea of centralization with as much ardor as the concept of state sovereignty. They regarded the national government's competence as deriving from the powers specified in the Constitution or fairly implied from it; the residual powers of government, usually called "internal police," belonged exclusively to the several states. Thus decisions like *Kohl* and *Siebold*, as Waite and his associates understood them, did not contract the ambit of state JURISDICTION. Rather the court simply refused to recognize implied limitations on the powers of Congress derived from state sovereignty premises. The *Trade-Mark Cases* (1879) underscored the Waite Court's allegiance to this view of the federal system. There a unanimous Court, speaking through Miller, held that Congress had no authority to enact a "universal system of trade-mark registration." Miller's method of analysis was more revealing than the result. His first impulse was to determine which sphere of government ordinarily had responsibility for such matters in the constitutional scheme. "As the property in trade-marks and the right to their exclusive use rest on the laws of the States, and like the great body of the rights of persons and of property, depend on them for security and protection," he explained, "the power of Congress to legislate on the subject . . . must be found in the Constitution of the United States, which is the source of all the powers the Congress can lawfully exercise." This two-tier method not only reified DUAL FEDERALISM but also put the burden of demonstrating Congress's authority to act on the government. In the *Trade-Mark Cases* it could not do so. Trade-marks lacked "the essential characteristics" of creative work in the arts and sciences, consequently the statute could not be sustained under the COPYRIGHT or PATENT powers. And the commerce power, though admittedly "broad," could not be construed as to permit federal regulation of commercial relations between persons residing in the same state.

When the Waite Court turned to cases involving the "new" Constitution, the instinct to conceptualize rights and powers in terms of dual federalism had fateful consequences. Beginning in UNITED STATES V. CRUIKSHANK (1876), the Court emasculated Congress's power "to enforce, by appropriate legislation," the rights guaranteed by the Fourteenth and Fifteenth Amendments. At issue was the validity of conspiracy convictions under the 1870 Civil Rights Act against a band of whites who had attacked a conclave of blacks in Grants Parish, Louisiana, killing from sixty to one hundred of them. The government claimed that the defendants had deprived the black citizens of their constitutional rights to hold a peaceful assembly, to bear arms, to vote, and to EQUAL PROTECTION OF THE LAWS safeguarding persons and property. The Court unanimously overturned the convictions. The CONSPIRACY law was not voided; indeed, the Court sustained a conviction under that very statute in *Yarbrough*. But Waite and his associates were determined to confine Congress's power to enact "appropriate legislation" in such a way to preserve what Miller called "the main features of the federal system." The Court had no choice in the matter, Joseph Bradley remarked on circuit in 1874, unless it was prepared "to clothe Congress with power to pass laws for the general preservation of social order in every State," or, in short, with a plenary power of "internal police."

Waite's opinion for the Court in *Cruikshank* contained two separate lines of argument. He began the first foray by pointing out that every American citizen "owes allegiance to two sovereigns, and claims protection from both." Because the two levels of government could protect the rights of citizens only "within their respective spheres," federal authorities could assert jurisdiction over perpetrators of violence only if the rights denied to victims were derived from the Constitution and laws of the United States. But in the SLAUGHTERHOUSE CASES (1873), decided ten months before Waite came to the Court, a majority of five had concluded that there were very few PRIVILEGES OR IMMUNITIES of national CITIZENSHIP and that the Fourteenth Amendment had not created any

new ones. Fundamental rights of life, liberty, and property still rested upon the laws of the states, and citizens had to rely upon the states for the protection of those rights. Among the privileges of state citizenship, Waite explained in *Cruikshank*, were the rights to assemble, to bear arms, and to vote. Although guaranteed against infringement by Congress in the BILL OF RIGHTS, the rights to assemble and bear arms were not "granted by the Constitution" or "in any manner dependent upon that instrument for existence." The right to vote in state and local elections stood on the same footing because "the right to vote in the States comes from the States." The Fifteenth Amendment did give citizens a new right under the Constitution— exemption from RACIAL DISCRIMINATION when attempting to vote. Because the Grants Parish indictments did not aver that the defendants had prevented their victims "from exercising the right to vote on account of race," however, that count was as defective as the rest.

Waite's second line of argument in *Cruikshank* was designed to hold the votes of Joseph Bradley, Stephen J. Field, and NOAH SWAYNE. They had dissented in the *Slaughterhouse Cases*, claiming that the Fourteenth Amendment had been designed to reconstruct the federal system by creating a third sphere in the constitutional scheme—that of the individual whose FUNDAMENTAL RIGHTS were now protected against unequal and discriminatory state laws. Waite satisfied them by stating what came to be known as the STATE ACTION doctrine. He not only conceded that "[t]he equality of the rights of citizens is a principle of republicanism" but strongly implied that the Fourteenth Amendment had nationalized this principle under the equal protection clause, if not the privileges or immunities clause. But the amendment, he added, "does not . . . add any thing to the rights which one citizen had under the Constitution against another." The very language of the amendment's first section—"No state shall . . ."—suggested that it must be read not as a grant of power to Congress but as a limitation on the states. It followed that the exercise of fundamental rights did not come under the Constitution's protection until jeopardized by the enactment or enforcement of a state law. "This the amendment guarantees, but no more," Waite declared. "The power of the national government is limited to the enforcement of this guaranty."

The principles announced in *Cruikshank* doomed the rest of Congress's CIVIL RIGHTS program, all of which had been based on the assumption that the "new" Constitution might be employed as a sword to protect any interference with fundamental rights.

A voting rights statute went down in UNITED STATES v. REESE (1876) because Congress had failed to limit federal jurisdiction over state elections to the prevention of racially motivated fraud or dereliction; the antilynching provisions of the 1871 Civil Rights Act were invalidated for want of state action in UNITED STATES v. HARRIS (1883). One latent function of *Cruikshank*, however, was to draw renewed attention to the equal protection clause as a shield for blacks and other racial minorities whose civil rights were imperiled by discriminatory state laws. Soon the docket was crowded with such cases, and the Court was compelled to wrestle with longstanding ambiguities in the Republican party's commitment to racial equality.

Republicans had always been quick to defend equal rights in the market, for it was the rights to make contracts and own property that distinguished free people from slaves. But many Republicans regarded the idea of equality before the law as wholly compatible with legalized race prejudice in the social realm. Words like "nation" and "race" were not merely descriptive terms in the nineteenth century; they were widely understood as objective manifestations of natural communities, the integrity of which government had a duty to maintain. Thus most Republicans never accepted the proposition that blacks ought to be free to marry whites and many denied the right of blacks to associate with whites even in public places. The framers of the "new" Constitution had neither abjured this qualified view of equality not incorporated it into the Fourteenth Amendment. The discretion of Waite and his colleagues was virtually unfettered. They could weave prevailing prejudices into equal protection jurisprudence or they could interpret the equality concept broadly, declare that the "new" Constitution was colorblind, and put the Court's enormous prestige squarely behind the struggle for racial justice.

Exponents of racial equality were greatly encouraged by STRAUDER V. WEST VIRGINIA (1880), the case of first impression. There a divided Court reversed the murder conviction of a black defendant who had been tried under a statute that limited jury service to "white male persons." The Fourteenth Amendment, William Strong explained for the majority, "was designed to secure the colored race the enjoyment of all the civil rights that under the law are enjoyed by white persons." This formulation was acceptable even to the two dissenters. According to Stephen J. Field and Nathan Clifford, however, jury service was not a "civil right." It was a "political right." The only rights Congress intended to protect with the Fourteenth Amendment, they contended, were those enumerated in the Civil Rights Act of 1866—to own prop-

erty, to make and enforce contracts, to sue and give evidence. The equal protection clause, Field said, "secures to all persons their civil rights upon the same terms; but it leaves political rights . . . and social rights . . . as they stood previous to its adoption." But the *Strauder* majority was unimpressed by Field's version of the "original understanding" and it set a face of flint against his typology of rights. "The Fourteenth Amendment makes no attempt to enumerate the rights it designed to protect," Strong declared. "It speaks in general terms, and those are as comprehensive as possible." The very term equal protection, he added, implied "that no discrimination shall be made against [blacks] by the law because of their color."

Strauder seemed to open the door for judicial proscription of all racial classifications in state laws. John R. Tompkins, counsel for an interracial couple that had been sentenced to two years in prison for violating Alabama's antimiscegenation law, certainly read the case that way. But the idea of distinct spheres of rights—"civil" and "social" if no longer "political"—furtively reentered the Waite Court's jurisprudence in PACE V. ALABAMA (1883). Field, speaking for a unanimous Court, held that antimiscegenation laws were not barred by the Fourteenth Amendment as long as both parties received the same punishment for the crime. Equal protection mandated equal treatment, not freedom of choice; antimiscegenation laws restricted the liberty of blacks and whites alike. Underlying this disingenuous view was an unarticulated premise of enormous importance. In settings involving the exercise of "social rights" the equal protection clause did not prohibit state legislatures from enacting statutes that used race as a basis for regulating the rights of persons. The legal category "Negro" was not suspect per se. (See SUSPECT CLASSIFICATION.)

The concept of "social rights" also figured prominently in the CIVIL RIGHTS CASES (1883), decided ten months after *Pace*. There the Court struck down the CIVIL RIGHTS ACT OF 1875, which forbade the owners of theaters, inns, and public conveyances to deny any citizen "the full and equal benefit" of their facilities. Joseph Bradley, speaking for the majority, rejected the claim that the businesses covered by the act were quasi-public agencies; consequently the state action doctrine barred federal intervention under the Fourteenth Amendment. But Bradley conceded that the state action doctrine was not applicable in Thirteenth Amendment contexts. It not only "nullif[ies] all state laws which establish or uphold slavery," he said, but also "clothes Congress with power to pass all laws necessary and proper for abolishing all badges and incidents of slavery in the United States." With the exception of John Marshall Harlan, however, every member of the Waite Court equated the "badges and incidents of slavery" with the denial of "civil rights" and concluded that Congress had nearly exhausted its authority to enact appropriate legislation under the Thirteenth Amendment with the CIVIL RIGHTS ACT OF 1866. "[A]t that time," Bradley explained, "Congress did not assume, under the authority given by the Thirteenth Amendment, to adjust what may be called the social rights of man and races in the community; but only to declare and vindicate those fundamental rights which appertain to the essence of citizenship, and the enjoyment or deprivation of which constitutes the essential distinction between freedom and slavery." Bradley's opinion was circumspect in only one respect. Whether denial of equal accommodation "might be a denial of a right which, if sanctioned by the state law, would be obnoxious to the [equal protection] prohibitions of the Fourteenth Amendment," he said, "is another question." But that was true only in the most formal sense. Once the Court had identified two distinct spheres of rights under the Thirteenth Amendment, one "civil" and another "social," it was difficult to resist the impulse to link that standard with the doctrine expounded in *Pace* when deciding equal protection cases. Stephen J. Field and Horace Gray, the only members of the *Civil Rights Cases* majority still alive when PLESSY V. FERGUSON (1896) was decided, had no qualms about state laws that required SEPARATE BUT EQUAL accommodations for blacks on public conveyances. Harlan was the sole dissenter on both occasions.

Equal opportunity in the market was one civil right that every member of the Waite Court assumed was guaranteed by the equal protection clause. Thus in YICK WO V. HOPKINS (1886) the Court invalidated the racially discriminatory application of a San Francisco ordinance that required all laundries, except those specifically exempted by the board of supervisors, to be built of brick or stone with walls one foot thick and metal roofs. No existing San Francisco laundry could meet such stringent building regulations, but the ordinance had the desired effect. The authorities promptly exempted the city's white operators and denied the petitions of their 240 Chinese competitors. "[T]he conclusion cannot be resisted," STANLEY MATTHEWS asserted for a unanimous Court, "that no reason for [this discrimination] exists except hostility to the race and nationality to which the petitioners belong, and which in the eye of the law is not justified." Yet the type of right divested was at least as important in *Yick Wo* as the fact of discrimination. The Court

described laws that arbitrarily impaired entrepreneurial freedom as "the essence of slavery" while laws that denied racial minorities free choice in the selection of marriage partners and theater seats were not. But that was not all. The court invoked the absence of standards for administering the laundry ordinance as an independent ground for its unconstitutionality. The boundless discretion, or, as Matthews put it, "the naked and arbitrary power" delegated to the authorities was as decisive for the Court as the fact that the ordinance had been applied with "an evil eye and an unequal hand." In the Waite Court's view, however, the same kind of concern about official discretion was neither possible nor desirable in jury-service cases. In *Strauder* Strong conceded that jury selection officials might constitutionally employ facially neutral yet impossibly vague tests of good character, sound judgment, and the like. The Court had no choice but to presume that the jury commissioners had acted properly, Harlan explained in *Bush v. Kentucky* (1883), in the absence of state laws expressly restricting participation to whites. As blacks began to disappear from jury boxes throughout the South, it became clear that although *Strauder* put jury service in the "civil rights" category, in practical application it stood on a far lower plane than the rights enumerated in the Civil Rights Act of 1866. When Booker T. Washington counseled blacks to place economic opportunities ahead of all others in 1895, he expressed priorities that the Waite Court had long since embroidered into equal protection jurisprudence.

The path of DUE PROCESS was at once more tortuous and less decisive than the development of equal protection doctrine. In *Dent v. West Virginia* (1888), decided at the close of the Waite era, the Court conceded, as it had in the beginning, that "it may be difficult, if not impossible, to give to the terms 'due process of law' a definition which will embrace every permissible exertion of power affecting private rights and exclude such as are forbidden." Yet two generalizations about the Waite Court's understanding of due process can be advanced with confidence. First, the modern distinction between PROCEDURAL and SUBSTANTIVE DUE PROCESS had no meaning for Waite and his colleagues. In their view, the Fifth and Fourteenth Amendments furnished protection for fundamental rights against arbitrary action, regardless of the legal form in which the arbitrary act had been clothed. In HURTADO V. CALIFORNIA (1884), where the majority rejected counsel's claim that the Fourteenth Amendment INCORPORATED the Bill of Rights, Stanley Matthews explained that because the due process concept embraced "broad and general maxims of liberty and justice," it "must be held to guaranty not particular forms of procedure, but the very substance of individual rights to life, liberty, and property." Even Miller, the most circumspect member of the Court, agreed in 1878 that a law declaring the property of A to be vested in B, "without more," would "deprive A of his property without due process of law." It is equally clear that the Court assumed that CORPORATIONS were PERSONS within the meaning of the Fifth and Fourteenth Amendments long before Waite acknowledged as much during oral argument in *Santa Clara County v. Southern Pacific Railroad Co.* (1886). As early as the GRANGER CASES (1877) the Court decided controversies in which railroad corporations challenged state regulation on due process grounds, and neither the defendant states nor the Justices breathed a doubt about the Court's jurisdiction. In the SINKING FUND CASES (1879), moreover, Waite stated emphatically in obiter dictum that the Fifth Amendment had always barred Congress "from depriving persons or corporations of property without due process of law."

Although every member of the Court accepted the essential premises of substantive due process, no statute was voided on due process grounds during the Waite era. Conventional assumptions about the boundary between the legislative and judicial spheres were largely responsible for the Court's reticence. In due process cases, at least, most of the period's Justices meant it when they stated, as Waite did in the *Sinking Fund Cases*, that "[e]very possible presumption is in favor of the validity of a statute, and this continues until the contrary is shown beyond a reasonable doubt." The most disarming demonstration of that Court's adherence to this principle came in *Powell v. Pennsylvania* (1888). At issue was an act that prohibited the manufacture and sale of oleomargarine. The legislature had labeled the statute as a public health measure, but it was no secret that the law really had been designed to protect the dairy industry against a new competitor. Harlan, speaking for everyone but Field, conceded that counsel for the oleomargarine manufacturer had stated "a sound principle of constitutional law" when he argued that the Fourteenth Amendment guaranteed every person's right to pursue "an ordinary calling or trade" and to acquire and possess property. Indeed, the Court had furnished protection for those very rights in *Yick Wo.* "But we cannot adjudge that the defendant's rights of liberty and property, as thus defined, have been infringed," Harlan added, "without holding that, although it may have been enacted in good faith for the objects ex-

pressed in its title . . . it has, in fact, no real or substantial relation to those objects." And this the Court was not prepared to do. Defendant's offer of proof as to the wholesomeness of his product was insufficient, for it was the legislature's duty, not the judiciary's, "to conduct investigations of facts entering into questions of public policy." Nor could the Court consider the reasonableness of the means selected by the legislature: "Whether the manufacture of oleomargarine . . . is, or may be, conducted in such a way . . . as to baffle ordinary inspection, or whether it involves such danger to the public health as to require . . . the entire suppression of the business, rather than its regulation . . . are questions of fact and of public policy which belong to the legislative department to determine." Field, dissenting, claimed that the majority had not simply deferred to the legislature but had recognized it as "practically omnipotent."

Field overstated the predisposition of his colleagues, and he knew it. The Court seldom spoke with a luminous, confident voice in due process cases; majority opinions almost invariably revealed lingering second thoughts. Each time the Court said yes to legislatures, it reminded them that someday the Court might use the due process clause to say no. In *Powell,* for example, Harlan warned lawmakers that the Court was ready to intercede "if the state legislatures, under the pretence of guarding the public health, the public morals, or the public safety, should invade the rights of life, liberty, and property." Harlan did not explain how the Court might identify an act that had been passed "under the pretence" of exercising the police power, but he seemed to be confident that the Justices would be able to identify a tainted statute once they saw one. Waite's opinion in *Munn v. Illinois* (1877) was equally ambiguous. In one series of paragraphs he stated that the power to regulate prices was inherent in the police power; in another he suggested that price fixing was legitimate only if the regulated concern was a "business AFFECTED WITH A PUBLIC INTEREST." It followed from the latter proposition, though not from the former, that "under some circumstances" the Court might disallow regulation of prices charged by firms that were "purely and exclusively private." In *Munn* Waite was more certain about the reasonableness of rates lawfully fixed. "We know that it is a power which may be abused," he said; "but . . . [f]or protection against abuses by the legislatures the people must resort to the polls, not the courts." By 1886, however, Waite and some of his colleagues were not so sure. "[U]nder the pretense of regulating fares and freights," Waite declared in the *Railroad*

Commission Cases (1886), "the State cannot require a railroad corporation to carry persons or property without reward; neither can it do that which in law amounts to a taking of private property for public use without JUST COMPENSATION, or without due process of law." This statement, like Harlan's similar remark in *Powell*, warranted many conflicting inferences. At the close of the Waite era, then, the scope of the JUDICIAL POWER under the due process clause was as unsettled as the clause's meaning.

When Waite died in 1888, a St. Louis law journal observed that he had been "modest, conscientious, careful, conservative, and safe." It was a shrewd appraisal not only of the man but of his Court's work in constitutional law. The Court's unwillingness to use judicial power as an instrument of moral leadership evoked scattered protests from racial egalitarians, who accused Waite and his colleagues of energizing bigotry, and from exponents of laissez-faire who complained that the Court had failed to curb overweening regulatory impulses in the state legislatures. But no criticism was heard from the Republican party's moderate center, where the Court had looked for bearings as it reconstructed the "old" Constitution and integrated the "new." In retrospect, it was THOMAS M. COOLEY, not Charles Sumner, who supplied the Waite Court with an agenda and suggested an appropriate style for its jurisprudence. The Republican party had resorted to "desperate remedies" and had treated the Constitution as if it were "wax" during the Civil War, he said in 1867. Now it was time for the bench and bar to ensure that postwar institutions were "not mere heaps of materials from which to build something new, but the same good old ship of state, with some progress toward justice and freedom."

CHARLES W. MCCURDY

Bibliography

BENEDICT, MICHAEL LES 1979 Preserving Federalism: Reconstruction and the Waite Court. *Supreme Court Review* 1978:39–79.

CORWIN, EDWARD S. 1913 *National Supremacy: Treaty Power versus State Power.* New York: Henry Holt.

——— 1948 *Liberty against Government.* Baton Rouge: Louisiana State University Press.

MAGRATH, C. PETER 1963 *Morrison R. Waite: The Triumph of Character.* New York: Macmillan.

MCCURDY, CHARLES W. 1975 Justice Field and the Jurisprudence of Government–Business Relations. *Journal of American History* 61:970–1005.

SCHMIDT, BENNO C. 1983 Juries, Jurisdiction, and Race Discrimination: The Lost Promise of Strauder v. West Virginia. *Texas Law Review* 61:1401–1499.

WAIVER OF CONSTITUTIONAL RIGHTS

A potential beneficiary may waive almost any constitutional claim. Rights not of constitutional dimension also may be waived. The Supreme Court has struggled with the questions whether any special DOCTRINE governs waivers of constitutional rights and, if so, whether the special doctrine applies to all constitutional rights. These waiver issues, like much of the rest of constitutional law, took on massive new proportions with the rapid expansion of constitutional rights in the 1960s and 1970s. Prior to that era, there were relatively few rights eligible for waiver.

Distinctions between waivers of constitutional rights and waivers of other rights do not appear in very early cases. The most frequent waiver issue probably was whether a civil litigant had waived the SEVENTH AMENDMENT right to TRIAL BY JURY. *Hodges v. Easton* (1882), a case raising this issue, was the setting for one of the Supreme Court's important statements concerning waiver. In *Hodges* the Court acknowledged that litigants may waive the right but cautioned, in an oft-quoted statement that seemed to contemplate special treatment for waivers of constitutional rights, that "every reasonable presumption should be indulged against . . . waiver."

Then, as later would be true, there seemed to be a gap between the Court's statement of the waiver standard and its application of the standard in deciding cases. The Court's casual attitude toward waiver emerged in *Pierce v. Somerset Railway* (1898) and *Eustis v. Bolles* (1893), in which the Court found waivers of claims that state laws unconstitutionally impaired the OBLIGATION OF CONTRACT. In each case not only was "every reasonable presumption" against waiver not indulged; the Court went so far as to indicate that a state court's finding of waiver of constitutional rights did not even raise a federal issue reviewable by the Supreme Court. It may be, however, that the Court was insufficiently attentive to differences between the waiver issue and the existence of an independent and ADEQUATE STATE GROUND for decision, which would preclude Supreme Court review of the state court's judgment.

Although the Court had not become deeply involved in waiver issues, the legal community knew that waiver doctrine might have to be attuned to differences among constitutional rights. Through eight editions from 1868 to 1927, THOMAS M. COOLEY's treatise on constitutional law acknowledged that litigants may waive constitutional rights but it stated that in criminal cases this "must be true to a very limited extent only." Subsequent Supreme Court waiver doctrine at first would adhere to, and later partially undermine, Cooley's suggested distinction. But in his time, Cooley, himself a state supreme court justice, was on safe ground. As long as there were few constitutional rights regulating CRIMINAL PROCEDURE, one easily could limit their waivability.

The Court became more involved with waivers of constitutional rights in the 1930s. In *Aetna Insurance Co. v. Kennedy* (1937) and JOHNSON V. ZERBST (1938), cases raising civil and criminal procedure waiver issues, the Court seemed to indulge presumptions against waiver. And *Johnson v. Zerbst* supplied a new guiding rhetoric. Waiver required "an intentional relinquishment or abandonment of a known right or privilege." Again, though, the Court's articulated waiver standard sometimes was difficult to reconcile with the standard it applied. In *Rogers v. United States* (1951) a GRAND JURY witness who answered many questions was held to have waived her Fifth Amendment RIGHT AGAINST SELF-INCRIMINATION with respect to additional information.

The 1930s doctrinal seeds restricting waiver flowered in the 1960s. The most significant waiver developments concerned the question of a state criminal defendant's waiver of the right to assert a federal constitutional claim in a federal HABEAS CORPUS proceeding. A habeas corpus case, FAY V. NOIA (1963), became the touchstone for analysis of waiver of constitutional rights. *Fay* reaffirmed *Johnson v. Zerbst*'s waiver standard and required a conscious decision to forgo the privilege of seeking to vindicate federal rights. On the language of *Fay*, accidental waivers seemed impossible. The Court's reluctance to allow waivers of constitutional rights reached a high point in MIRANDA V. ARIZONA (1966), when the Court required that police inform suspects of their constitutional rights to assure that any waiver would be knowing.

The late WARREN COURT's reluctance to allow waivers of constitutional rights contrasts with the BURGER COURT's attitude. In one respect, a retreat from the 1960s standard seemed inevitable. For *Fay* and *Johnson* soon collided with the realities of the American criminal justice system. Through the PLEA BARGAINING process, the entire system depends upon widespread waivers of constitutional rights. In the trilogy of *McMann v. Richardson* (1970), *Parker v. North Carolina* (1970), and *Brady v. United States* (1970), holdings difficult to reconcile with the *Fay-Johnson* standard, this reality took hold. The trilogy effectively

made a plea of guilty a waiver of nearly all constitutional procedure rights, known or unknown.

Another waiver issue, one with perhaps less of a foregone conclusion, further signaled the Court's shift in attitude. The FOURTH AMENDMENT guarantees the right to be free of UNREASONABLE SEARCHES and seizures and often requires police to obtain a warrant before conducting a search. For many years there was doubt about the relationship between searches conducted with consent, which need not comply with the Fourth Amendment's warrant requirement, and the concept of waiver. If consent were equated with a waiver of Fourth Amendment rights, then the *Johnson* standard seemed applicable. But since few who consent to searches are informed of their Fourth Amendment rights, it was difficult to characterize any waiver as knowing. The widespread practice of CONSENT SEARCHES seemed to hang in the balance.

A Court reluctant to allow waivers of constitutional rights might have adopted the *Miranda*-like solution of generally requiring the police to inform suspects of their Fourth Amendment rights before obtaining consent to a search. In SCHNECKLOTH V. BUSTAMONTE (1973) the Court, opting for a different extreme, preempted most Fourth Amendment waiver problems. It found that the *Johnson* standard had, almost without exception, "been applied only to those rights which the Constitution guarantees to a criminal defendant in order to preserve a FAIR TRIAL." Fourth Amendment claims were held not to be subject to the knowing and intelligent waiver requirement.

Schneckloth's reasoning may have implications for other constitutional rights. It suggests that rights other than those relating to a fair trial are subject to a waiver standard more lenient than the *Johnson* test. But it did not signal a wholesale retreat from *Johnson*. After *Schneckloth*, in cases such as EDWARDS V. ARIZONA (1981), the Court reaffirmed that the *Johnson* standard governs waivers of the RIGHT TO COUNSEL.

In WAINWRIGHT V. SYKES (1977), where the Court squarely confronted *Fay*, it further limited 1960s waiver doctrine. Under *Wainright*, failure to comply with state procedural rules effectively waives the right to raise a constitutional claim on federal habeas corpus. A habeas applicant must both explain his failure to comply with state procedures and show that his case was prejudiced by the constitutional flaw. The Court rejected *Fay*'s requirement of a knowing and deliberate waiver. In effect, the burden of proving nonwaiver had been placed on the defendant.

The waiver question also continued to arise in contexts not involving criminal procedure. In *D. H. Over-*

myer Co. v. Frick Company (1972) and *Swarb v. Lennox* (1972) the Court reconfirmed earlier holdings that at least some civil litigants may contractually waive due process rights to NOTICE and hearing prior to a JUDGMENT and thereby effectively waive the opportunity to contest the validity of a debt. In *Parden v. Terminal Railway* (1964) states may have been surprised to learn that certain activities effectively waived their constitutional immunity from suit in federal court. For many years prior to *Parden,* it appeared that only an express waiver by states would be effective. But the Court found that by operating a railroad in INTERSTATE COMMERCE, a state effectively waived its immunity from employees' suits in federal court under the federal EMPLOYERS LIABILITY ACT. *Parden's* reach was limited by *Employees v. Department of Public Health and Welfare* (1973), which refused to rely on the FAIR LABOR STANDARDS ACT to subject states to federal damage suits by employees. More important, EDELMAN V. JORDAN (1974) held that state participation in a federal program did not amount to consent to suit in federal court on claims relating to the program.

THEODORE EISENBERG

Bibliography

COVER, ROBERT M. and ALEINIKOFF, T. ALEXANDER 1977 Dialectical Federalism: Habeas Corpus and the Court. *Yale Law Journal* 86:1035–1102.

LAFAVE, WAYNE R. 1978 *Search and Seizure: A Treatise on the Fourth Amendment* §§ 8.1, 8.2, 11.1, 11.7 (f). St. Paul, Minn.: West Publishing Co.

TIGAR, MICHAEL E. 1970 Foreword: Waiver of Constitutional Rights: A Disquiet in the Citadel. *Harvard Law Review* 84:1–28.

TRIBE, LAURENCE H. 1978 *American Constitutional Law.* Pages 133–138. Mineola, N.Y.: Foundation Press.

WALKER, TIMOTHY
(1802–1856)

Born in Massachusetts, Timothy Walker attended Harvard College and Harvard Law School where he studied with Justice JOSEPH STORY. He settled in Cincinnati in 1830 and opened a private law school, which eventually became part of the University of Cincinnati. He wrote on various legal subjects, but his primary contribution was his compilation of his lectures, *An Introduction to American Law* (1837), which he dedicated to Story, whose teachings and viewpoint he spread. A third of the work is on constitutional law, strongly nationalist in its orientation. By 1905 the book had gone through eleven editions.

LEONARD W. LEVY

WALKER v. BIRMINGHAM
388 U.S. 307 (1967)

The Supreme Court, 5–4, upheld criminal contempt convictions of eight black ministers, including MARTIN LUTHER KING, JR., for holding a CIVIL RIGHTS protest parade in violation of an INJUNCTION issued by an Alabama state court. The injunction, which forbade them from engaging in street parades without a permit, was issued EX PARTE, two days before the intended march. The order was based on a city ordinance that the Court later held unconstitutional for VAGUENESS in *Shuttlesworth v. Birmingham* (1969), a case arising out of the same events.

For the majority, Justice POTTER STEWART concluded that the ministers, once enjoined by a court order, were not entitled to disregard the injunction even if it had been granted unconstitutionally. Rather, they were obliged to ask the court to modify the order, or to seek relief from the injunction in another court.

Justice WILLIAM J. BRENNAN, for the four dissenters, pointed out that, in the absence of a court order, the FIRST AMENDMENT would have entitled the marchers to disregard the ordinance, which was INVALID ON ITS FACE. It was incongruous, he argued, to let the state alter this result simply by obtaining "the ex parte stamp of a judicial officer on a copy of the invalid ordinance." These views were echoed in separate dissents by Chief Justice EARL WARREN and Justice WILLIAM O. DOUGLAS. The *Walker* principle, though much criticized, remains the DOCTRINE of the Court.

KENNETH L. KARST

(SEE ALSO: *Demonstration.*)

WALKER v. SAUVINET
92 U.S. 90 (1876)

Walker lost a civil judgment in a trial decided by a judge, in conformance with state law, after the jury deadlocked and after Walker had demanded TRIAL BY JURY. The Court held, 7–2, that the SEVENTH AMENDMENT to the Constitution, guaranteeing trial by jury in civil actions at law, applied only in federal courts, and that the right to a jury trial in similar state cases was not a privilege of United States citizenship guaranteed by the PRIVILEGES AND IMMUNITIES clause of the FOURTEENTH AMENDMENT. This was the earliest rejection of the INCORPORATION DOCTRINE. Its result is still good law, long after the latter doctrine's triumph.

LEONARD W. LEVY

WALLACE v. JAFFREE
472 U.S.   (1985)

A 6–3 Supreme Court, in an opinion by Justice JOHN PAUL STEVENS, held unconstitutional an Alabama statute that required public school children to observe a period of silence "for meditation or voluntary prayer." No member of the Court contested the constitutionality of the period of silence for meditation. As Justice SANDRA DAY O'CONNOR said in her CONCURRING OPINION, no threat to RELIGIOUS LIBERTY could be discerned from a room of "silent, thoughtful school children." Chief Justice WARREN E. BURGER added that there was no threat "even if they chose to pray." Burger willfully misunderstood or missed the point. Any student in any public school may pray voluntarily and silently at almost any time of the school day, if so moved. The state, in this case, sought to orchestrate group prayer by capitalizing on the impressionability of youngsters. Compulsory attendance laws and the coercive setting of the school provided a CAPTIVE AUDIENCE for the state to promote religion. Justice JOHN PAUL STEVENS emphasized the fact that the state act was "entirely motivated by a purpose to advance religion" and had "*no* secular purpose." The evidence irrefutably showed that. Accordingly, the Alabama act failed to pass the test of LEMON V. KURTZMAN (1971) used by the Court to determine whether a state violated the FIRST AMENDMENT's prohibition against an ESTABLISHMENT OF RELIGION.

Justice O'Connor, observing that Alabama already had a moment of silence law on its books, noted that during the silence, no one need be religious, no one's religious beliefs could be compromised, and no state encouragement of religion existed. "The crucial question," she wrote, "is whether the State has conveyed or attempted to convey the message that children should use the moment of silence for prayer." The only possible answer was that the state, by endorsing the decision to pray during the moment of silence, sponsored a religious exercise, thereby breaching the First Amendment's principle of SEPARATION OF CHURCH AND STATE.

LEONARD W. LEVY

WALZ v. TAX COMMISSION
397 U.S. 664 (1970)

In this 8–1 decision, the Supreme Court added a new element to the test for the constitutionality of financial aid to religious institutions. Chief Justice WARREN E. BURGER rejected Walz's claim that a state's grant of tax exemption to property used only for religious purposes violated the ESTABLISHMENT OF RELIGION clause of the FIRST AMENDMENT. Adding to tests already elaborated in ABINGTON SCHOOL DISTRICT V. SCHEMPP (1963), Burger required assurance that "the end result—the effect—[of a grant of tax exemption] is not an excessive government entanglement with religion. The test is inescapably one of degree." Commenting that "the course of constitutional neutrality in this area cannot be an absolutely straight line," he said that taxing a church would have involved even more "entanglement" than exempting them. Justice WILLIAM O. DOUGLAS, dissenting, believed that TORCASO V. WATKINS (1961) governed. He concluded that "a tax exemption is a subsidy."

DAVID GORDON

(SEE ALSO: *Government Aid to Sectarian Institutions.*)

WAR, DECLARATION OF

See: Declaration of War

WAR, STATE OF

See: State of War

WARD v. ILLINOIS
431 U.S. 767 (1977)

The Supreme Court upheld, 5–4, a conviction for selling "sado-masochistic" materials. (See MISHKIN V. NEW YORK, 1966). Justice BYRON R. WHITE, for the majority, said that a state law could pass the "patent offensiveness" part of the test of MILLER V. CALIFORNIA (1973) although it did not specifically define the proscribed materials; state court interpretations had followed *Miller*'s guidelines. The dissenters, led by Justice JOHN PAUL STEVENS, argued that the absence of the statutory definition specified by *Miller* left the law unconstitutionally vague.

KENNETH L. KARST

WARDEN v. HAYDEN
387 U.S. 294 (1976)

In *Gouled v. United States* (1921) the Court announced a rule that rings strange to the modern ear; when conducting an otherwise lawful search, police are authorized to search for contraband, fruits of crime, means and instrumentalities of crime, or weapons of escape, but they are not authorized to search for "mere evidence." The rationale for the MERE EVIDENCE RULE was never clear, but its main theme was that police could not take objects from an accused without asserting a superior property interest in the object seized. This requirement spurred judicial creativity in recognizing property interests and in broadly defining their scope.

In *Warden v. Hayden* the Supreme Court rejected this property-centered conception of FOURTH AMENDMENT jurisprudence. Police could seize evidence after all. Questions remained concerning the scope of searches for items previously regarded as mere evidence (such as diaries) and concerning the applicable standards for SEARCHES AND SEIZURES of "mere evidence" belonging to innocent parties.

STEVEN SHIFFRIN

WARE v. HYLTON
3 Dallas 199 (1796)

Ware established the fundamental principle of constitutional law that a state act may not violate a national treaty. An act of Virginia during the Revolution sequestered sterling debts owed by Virginians to British subjects and provided that such debts be discharged on payment (in depreciated currency) to the state. The Treaty of Paris of 1783 provided that creditors should meet with no lawful impediments to the recovery of full value in sterling, and Article VI of the Constitution made treaties of the United States the supreme law of the land. Ware, a British subject, brought an action in a federal court seeking such a recovery from Hylton, a Virginian. The prewar debts of Virginians to British creditors exceeded $2,000,000. Justice JAMES IREDELL, on circuit, ruled that the treaty did not revive any debt that had been discharged, and on the WRIT OF ERROR from the circuit court, JOHN MARSHALL, for Hylton, argued that a United States treaty could not annul a statute passed when the state was sovereign. He also denied the authority of the Supreme Court to question the validity of a state law, arguing that the Constitution had not expressly granted such an authority.

Iredell persisted in his opinion expressed below, but Justice SAMUEL CHASE, supported by the concurring opinions of the remainder of the Justices, declared that the SUPREMACY CLAUSE (Article VI), operating retroactively, nullified the state act, thereby reviving the sterling debt. Chase cloaked his opinion in sweeping nationalist doctrine that twisted history: "There can be no limitations on the power of the people to change or abolish the state constitutions, or to make them yield to the general government, and to treaties made by their authority." A treaty, he ruled, could not be supreme law if any state act could stand in its way; state laws contrary to the treaty were prostrated before it and the Constitution, which was the "creator" of the states. The *Ware* decision intensified Jeffersonian hostility to the consolidating and procreditor opinions of the federal courts. The decision's imperishable principle of the supremacy of national treaties survived its origins—no doubt in part because JAY'S TREATY of 1794 had provided that the United States should assume the payment of the controversial debts.

LEONARD W. LEVY

WAR, FOREIGN AFFAIRS, AND THE CONSTITUTION

The United States became a nation among nations on July 4, 1776, fully endowed with SOVEREIGNTY, that is, the capacity to do whatever nations do in world politics. International law acknowledges that nations have the power to breach their international legal obligations and take the consequences so far as other nations are concerned. Constitutionally, breaches of international law by Congress or the President are binding on courts and citizens alike as official acts within the discretion of the political branches of the government. Thus the FOREIGN AFFAIRS powers, including the WAR POWERS, draw their substance from the matrix of public international law. In the language of PEREZ V. BROWNELL (1958), the Constitution recognizes in the national government "the powers indispensable to its functioning effectively in the company of sovereign nations."

In the CONSTITUTIONAL CONVENTION, a majority led by JAMES WILSON insisted that an "energetic" and independent President was needed to maintain the unity of a country that was already large and destined to become larger, and above all to help assure its safety in a turbulent and dangerous world. As EDWARD S. CORWIN wrote:

[T]he fact is that what the Framers had in mind was not the cabinet system, as yet nonexistent even in Great

Britain, but the "balanced constitution" of [JOHN] LOCKE, MONTESQUIEU, and [WILLIAM] BLACKSTONE, which carried with it the idea of a *divided initiative in the matter of legislation and a broad range of autonomous executive power or "prerogative."* Sir Henry Maine's dictum that "the American constitution is the British constitution with the monarchy left out," is, from the point of view of 1789, almost the exact reverse of the truth, for the presidency was designed in great measure to reproduce the monarchy of George III with the corruption left out, and also of course the hereditary feature [1957, pp. 14–15].

Actually, all comparisons of the British and American constitutions break down. The President is effectively both king and prime minister, but Congress is not Parliament, and its relation to the President is necessarily at arm's length.

The entire authority of the United States to act as a sovereign nation in world politics is confined by the Constitution to the national government and denied to the states. It is divided by the Constitution between the President and Congress.

The President is head of state as well as head of government, and therefore the ultimate embodiment of the nation's sovereignty, especially in times of crisis. ABRAHAM LINCOLN turned to his prerogative and residual powers as the source of much of his authority during the Civil War. In addition, the Constitution endows the President with "the" executive power of the United States, including without limitation the power to conduct diplomacy; to make treaties, with the ADVICE AND CONSENT of the Senate; and to serve as COMMANDER-IN-CHIEF of the armed forces; moreover, he is enjoined to see to it that the laws are faithfully executed.

The constitutional definition of the role of Congress in foreign affairs is comparably broad. Article I provides that "all LEGISLATIVE POWERS herein granted shall be vested in a Congress of the United States." Among the powers expressly granted to Congress are the powers to lay and collect taxes and provide for the common defense; regulate foreign commerce; establish an uniform rule of NATURALIZATION; define and punish piracies and FELONIES committed on the high seas and offenses against the law of nations; declare war, grant LETTERS OF MARQUE AND REPRISAL, and make rules concerning captures on land and water; and raise and support the armed forces, make rules for their government and regulation, and provide for organizing, arming, and disciplining the militia and calling forth the armed forces and the militia to execute the laws of the Union, suppress insurrections, and repel invasions. The problems of CITIZENSHIP and of foreign affairs in their more general aspects are not mentioned, but Congress's authority to legislate on such issues has been readily inferred by the Supreme Court as inherent in national sovereignty.

In short, the Constitution prescribes that the foreign affairs powers of the nation—including the war power—be shared between Congress and the President in accordance with the overriding principle of functional necessity. All the powers the nation requires in the international environment exist. Those which are executive in character are to be exercised by the President. Those which are legislative in nature are reserved for Congress. When in recess, however, Congress can meet only at the President's call, and can act in all cases only subject to the President's VETO POWER. As Corwin concluded, the Constitution invites the President and Congress "to struggle for the privilege of directing American foreign policy."

Sooner or later, most aspects of the conduct of foreign affairs involve both legislative and executive decisions; they are therefore the proper business of both Congress and the President, in a pattern that reflects subtle political judgments about how their cooperation can best be organized under the circumstances. A few functions are unique to each branch. Only the President can command the armed forces, call a special session of Congress, or conduct the diplomacy of the nation; and only Congress can declare war, appropriate money, or make certain conduct criminal. On the other hand, the President sometimes asks members of Congress to serve on diplomatic delegations. And Congress sometimes attempts to restrict the President's power to deploy or use the armed forces, although many constitutional authorities have regarded such restrictions as invasions of the President's executive power.

The flexibility of the constitutional arrangements for making and carrying out foreign policy is not peculiar to the field of foreign affairs. As JAMES MADISON saw from the beginning, the principle of the SEPARATION OF POWERS does not mean that the three branches of the government are really separate. Most of their powers are commingled. The branches are not independent but interdependent, and the preservation of the functional boundaries between the legislative and the executive depends as much on the reflexes of the political system as on rulings of the Supreme Court.

It was realized from the beginning that rigid rules about how Congress and the President should work together in the field of foreign affairs would be undesirable and indeed dangerous. As ALEXANDER HAMILTON wrote in THE FEDERALIST #23, "the authorities essential to the common defense . . . ought to exist without limitation, *because it is impossible to foresee or define the extent and variety of national exigencies or the correspondent extent and variety of the means which may be necessary to satisfy them.* The circumstances that endanger the safety of nations are infinite, and for this reason no constitutional shackles can wisely be imposed on the power to which the care of it is committed."

Diplomacy without force behind it has been and will remain a nullity. The use or the threat of armed force has been a normal instrument of American diplomacy, from secret warnings, "showing the flag," and conducting maneuvers, at one end of the spectrum, to programs of rearmament, partial mobilization, and the actual use of armed force—in times of "war" and of "peace," as international law defines those words—at the other. In the early days of the Republic, raids across the borders were commonplace. The problems of piracy and the slave trade required the frequent use of force, pursuant to treaty, statute, or the decisions of the President acting alone. Then and now, international law recognized the right of all states to use limited force in peacetime to cure forceful breaches of international law when no peaceful remedy was available. The United States has taken advantage of its rights in this regard to protect its borders, its ships, its citizens in peril abroad, and indeed, the rights of citizens whose monetary claims had not been paid by foreign governments. Moreover, the United States and other Western nations have sometimes intervened abroad on humanitarian grounds where organized government has broken down. Such exercises by the United States of its "inherent" right of self-defense have been carried out mainly, but not exclusively, on the authority of the President.

The threat to use force and even the use of force have been familiar features of diplomacy from the opening of Japan to President RICHARD M. NIXON's secret nuclear warnings that induced the Soviet Union not to attack Chinese nuclear installations. At the end of the Civil War, we deployed 50,000 troops along the Mexican border. France heeded our suggestion, withdrew its troops from Mexico, and left Maximilian to his fate. Similarly, in 1962, President JOHN F. KENNEDY assembled some 250,000 troops in Florida, and halted a Soviet vessel carrying military supplies to Cuba; the Soviet Union withdrew its nuclear missiles from Cuba. A few years earlier, at a moment of severe Soviet pressure against Turkey, President HARRY S. TRUMAN ordered the battleship *Missouri* to carry the body of a deceased Turkish ambassador to Istanbul

for burial—manifestly a journey intended to be more than a courteous gesture to the people of Turkey. Such threats of force have been almost entirely within the province of the President.

The list of such incidents is long enough to demonstrate that throughout its history the United States government has called upon its armed forces to perform a wide variety of functions in support of its foreign policy. There have been five DECLARATIONS OF WAR in our national experience, and more than 200 episodes in which the President ordered the armed forces into combat, sometimes with the support of a treaty or of legislation passed before or after the event, more often on his own authority. The number of occasions on which the President secretly threatened to use force in aid of his diplomacy cannot be counted accurately, but is surely considerable.

The pattern of cooperation between the President and Congress with respect to war and foreign affairs has been the same since the first administration of President GEORGE WASHINGTON. This continuity of practice arises from the nature of things. Congress could and did admonish the President to protect frontier settlements from Indian raids but could not meet and vote every time the risk arose. In any event, it was the President's duty to protect the settlements with or without the support of a statute. The circumstances which may require the use of or the threat to use armed force are too protean, and pervade the conduct of foreign affairs too completely, to be compressed within a single procedure.

From the beginning of our government under the Constitution, a great deal of energy has been absorbed by attempts to define the respective roles of the President and of Congress in carrying out these functions. The participants in the debate are divided into two camps.

Hamilton's view of the Presidency dominates the judicial opinions, the pattern of practice, the writings of scholars, and the pronouncements of senators and representatives. To Hamiltonians, all national powers not granted to Congress or the courts are "executive" and therefore presidential, especially if they concern relations with foreign powers or the duties of the nation under international law.

But a dissenting opinion has persisted, based on the fear of executive power as dictatorship in disguise. Corwin calls it the "ultra-Whig" view. It opposes almost all claims to presidential independence, and regards the executive as no more than an obstreperous but indispensable servant of a "sovereign" Congress. This conception of the Presidency has been a mainstay of political attacks on Presidents for unpopular wars.

The Hamiltonian position crystallized during the neutrality controversy of 1793, an episode of immense importance to the formation of the Constitution. France had declared war against Great Britain. The United States was bound to France by the 1778 treaties of perpetual alliance which seemed to require the infant Republic, in the event of war between France and Britain, to give various forms of belligerent aid to France. Any such assistance would have been an act of war against Great Britain, which could easily have snuffed out the new nation. Washington and his cabinet were determined to preserve neutrality despite the treaties with France and the strongly pro-French bias of public opinion. After the Supreme Court refused Washington's request for an ADVISORY OPINION determining whether the President could issue a proclamation of neutrality on his own authority, Washington did so, and took special precautions to assure Great Britain of America's pacific intentions.

The concurrent nature of the foreign relations power was soon demonstrated. Juries would not convict American seamen for violating the President's neutrality proclamation. Congress then grudgingly passed a Neutrality Act, supporting the President's interpretation of the treaties with France. In due course, the Neutrality Act was enforced. Congress had the last word, but acted under circumstances carefully arranged by the President, acting independently.

Hamilton's *Pacificus* papers, defending the President's right to issue the Proclamation of neutrality, are among the most cogent of all our state papers on the conduct of foreign affairs. The President, said Hamilton, has the foreign affairs and war powers of the British monarch minus the limitations on those powers mentioned in the Constitution. Those limitations, being exceptions to the President's executive powers, should be strictly construed.

The President is the sole officer of the government empowered to communicate with foreign nations. This is an executive power. It was therefore the President's role to inform the nations about the position of the United States with respect to the European war. Next, Hamilton argued, it is the President's duty to preserve peace until Congress declares war. In this case, the President's duty required him faithfully to execute the international law of neutrality, and thus avoid giving offense to foreign powers. To carry out that duty, the President had to determine for himself whether a status of neutrality conformed to our national interests and was compatible with our obligations under the French treaties, and then to announce his position diplomatically. Hamilton said that the President has the authority and the duty to determine the operation of treaties in the first instance, an important example of his right as President to decide upon the obligations of the country to foreign nations until Congress does so within its own sphere.

Hamilton's analysis would lead to the conclusion that while only Congress can move the nation into a state of general war, the President can authorize more limited uses of force in peacetime for purposes of self-defense, the protection of citizens abroad, the fulfillment of treaty obligations, and the support of diplomacy.

The Ultra-Whig dissenting view draws an altogether different boundary between the respective war powers of the President and Congress. For the dissenters, Congress's power to "declare" war gives Congress entire control over every aspect of the war power, including neutrality. It means, they contend, that the President can never employ the armed forces, save to repel a sudden attack, unless Congress has first passed a "declaration of war." Some dissenters agree that Congress may authorize limited war in the international law sense, but insist that the declaration of war clause requires congressional action before the President uses force at all, except in cases of sudden attack. A few concede that circumstances may justify congressional approval after the event—after Pearl Harbor, for example, or the firing on Fort Sumter. And some even accept the decision of the Supreme Court in THE PRIZE CASES (1863), which upheld acts of Congress ratifying President Lincoln's blockade of the Confederacy, enacted some months after the President had instituted the blockade. But all the dissenters are dubious about statutes, treaties, or joint resolutions—and many have been put on the books since 1792—that may be invoked to support presidential uses of force years later. The Ultra-Whigs admit that the United States may, like other nations, sign treaties that have military provisions, but they are uneasy about the propriety of such commitments unless they are reiterated by Congress when they become the basis for military action.

There is no reason for such confusion to persist. The "declaration of war" authorized in the Constitution is bracketed in Article I, section 8, with "letters of marque and reprisal" and "captures on land and sea." All are terms of specific meaning in international law. A declaration of war has far-reaching consequences, including: the authorization of unlimited hostilities, the possible internment of enemy ALIENS, the sequestration of enemy property, and the imposition of regulations, such as censorship, that would be unthinkable in peacetime. But many kinds of hostilities recognized as legitimate under international law do not constitute "general war," and can therefore be initiated by official action less sweeping than a declaration of war. Most familiar are exercises of the right of self-defense against certain breaches of international law. Many are short, quick responses to a sudden threat; others become more prolonged conflicts. International law limits all such defensive campaigns to the use of as much force as is reasonably necessary to eliminate the original breach.

Hamilton's theory of presidential power is clearly the operative model of American constitutional law with respect to the international use of force. But the practice has not been nearly so symmetrical as Hamilton's logic. Every American President who has felt obliged to use the armed forces has vividly remembered the political attacks on "JOHN ADAMS' Undeclared War," and therefore sought to obtain congressional support for his policies as soon as it was politically feasible to do so. But such prudence has never helped a President saddled with an unpopular war. John Adams was supported by four successive statutes; they had no effect on the political outcry against him, or the fate of the Federalist party. Presidents Truman and LYNDON B. JOHNSON endured similar trials. As Johnson commented: "I said early in my Presidency that if I wanted Congress with me on the landing of Vietnam, I'd have to have them on the take off. And I did just that. . . . But I failed to reckon with one thing: the parachute. I got them on the take off, but a lot of them bailed out before the end of the flight."

Between the Congress of Vienna and the turn of the twentieth century, the United States was not a major actor in world politics; the central features of American foreign policy were Manifest Destiny and the MONROE DOCTRINE. Nonetheless, there were periods of tension between Congress and the President with respect to the conduct of foreign relations. The most acute of these episodes concerned the expansion of the nation to the Pacific and controversies about problems in Latin America and Canada. Some of the controversies reflected deep divisions between the parties and among the people, others no more than normal rivalry between the political branches of the government.

But the collapse of the old state system in 1914 imposed new burdens on the United States, which in turn gave rise to profound disquiet in American opinion, exacerbating the traditional tension between Congress and the President with respect to the war power, and reaching a climax during the early 1970s. The VIETNAM WAR dragged on, accompanied by antiwar rioting of a kind the nation had not experienced

since the Civil War. At the same time, the controversy over President Nixon's behavior with respect to Watergate poisoned the political atmosphere, and produced so strong a movement for the President's impeachment that he resigned.

In this atmosphere of extreme political excitement, Congress passed the War Powers Resolution of 1973. Its political purpose was to assure the people that Congress could and would protect the nation against future Vietnams. For the first time in nearly two hundred years, the Hamiltonian view of the Presidency and the war power suffered at least a nominal defeat.

The Resolution asserts congressional supremacy with regard to the war power, but it does not adopt an extreme form of the Ultra-Whig view. It does not say, for example, that the President can use force only if Congress has first declared war. Not does it seek to confine the President's use of force without prior congressional approval to cases of "sudden attack."

The Resolution purports to fulfill the intent of the Framers of the Constitution, as summarized in three propositions. First, the armed forces should not be involved in hostilities without the collective judgment of Congress and the President. Second, Congress has the power to pass all laws NECESSARY AND PROPER for carrying into execution the powers of the President. Third, the constitutional powers of the President as Commander-in-Chief can be exercised by him to introduce the forces into hostile situations only pursuant to a declaration of war or a "specific" statute, or in a national emergency created by an attack upon the United States. Clearly, this attempt at restatement omits the nation's obligations under treaties.

The Resolution requires the President to consult with Congress "in every possible instance" before introducing the armed forces into situations where hostilities are an imminent risk, and also to "consult" regularly with Congress after hostilities have begun until they are terminated. The resolution makes no attempt to define the term "consult," which is a word of political but not of constitutional meaning.

The War Powers Resolution requires the President to report to Congress within forty-eight hours and regularly thereafter whenever he has introduced armed forces into situations risking hostilities without a declaration of war. It further requires the President to terminate such a use of the armed forces within sixty days unless Congress has declared war, authorized hostilities in another "specific" form, or extended the sixty-day period to not more than ninety days. Where hostilities are being conducted abroad without a declaration of war or "specific" authorization in another form, the resolution authorizes Congress, by CONCURRENT RESOLUTION, to require the President to terminate hostilities and remove the armed forces.

If the War Powers Resolution were carried out literally, it would constitute the most revolutionary change in the Constitution ever accomplished—far more drastic in its effects than the shift of authority from the states to the national government which began after Civil War. It would subject the President to the orders of an omnipotent Congress. No future President could do what Lincoln did during the Civil War, or rely on the behavior of every strong President between Washington and Lyndon Johnson as precedents. The deterrent influence of American military power and of American treaties, already weakened after Vietnam, would decline even further. The United States would be the only country in the world that lacked the capacity to enter into treaties or conduct secret negotiations contemplating the use of force, and it would be hampered in many other ways in the conduct of its foreign relations. Enforcing the resolution would produce paradoxes. Although no future President could do what President Kennedy did during the Cuban Missile Crisis in 1962, the highly "specific" legal arrangements for the Vietnam War would have satisfied the Resolution's requirements. That war was authorized not only by the United Nations Charter and the Southeast Asia Collective Defense Treaty of 1954, but by the GULF OF TONKIN RESOLUTION of 1963 and other explicit acts of Congress as well. On the other hand, the sponsors of the Resolution have said that it does not affect the President's unique responsibilities with regard to the nuclear weapon. Above all, as has been evident in the decade since it was passed, the Resolution would convert almost every serious foreign policy problem into a debate between Congress and the President about constitutional power, making the conduct of foreign relations even more cumbersome and contentious than is the case already.

The War Powers Resolution is in profound conflict with the necessities of governance in a turbulent world and with the concept of the Presidency that has evolved from the experience of the nation under the Constitution. We can therefore predict that the Hamiltonian conception of the war powers will prevail as the constitutional norm, and that the War Powers Resolution will become a footnote to history, either through repudiation or desuetude.

Institutional pride may keep Congress from repealing the resolution, although repeal disguised as revision is not unthinkable. The courts will almost surely declare the Resolution unconstitutional if an appropriate case should arise. The ruling of the Supreme Court in IMMIGRATION AND NATURALIZATION SERVICE V. CHADHA (1983) is applicable to the chief operative parts of the War Powers Resolution. *Chadha* ruled that congressional action can have legislative effect only through acts or joint resolutions fully subject to the President's veto. If Congress cannot constitutionally terminate a war by passing a concurrent resolution, it can hardly do so by failing to pass such a resolution within sixty or ninety days.

In holding the War Powers Resolution unconstitutional, the Supreme Court may well go beyond *Chadha* to deal with more fundamental aspects of the separation of powers principle: the resolution's effect, for example, on the President's hitherto unquestioned power to conduct secret negotiations, receive surrenders, or negotiate cease-fire agreements; and its attempt, recalling the proposed BRICKER AMENDMENT, to require legislation before treaties can become the supreme law of the land.

Even if the resolution is neither repealed nor declared unconstitutional by the courts, it is unlikely to be an important influence on Presidents. The resolution does not correspond to the nature of the problems of foreign policy and national security with which the government has to deal, and therefore cannot function as effective law. At least eleven episodes involving the use of force or the imminent risk of using force occurred during the first decade after the War Powers Resolution was passed. In each case the President, while protesting that the resolution was unconstitutional, consulted with congressional leaders and kept Congress informed about events. In no case did the procedure mandated by the resolution prove convenient or appropriate, and in no case was it followed. In each case there were some congressional protests that the War Powers Resolution was being violated, and even suggestions that the President be impeached.

The President and Congress, separately and together, have been entrusted by history with sovereign prerogatives in exercising the foreign affairs and war powers of the nation. Those prerogatives have been in uneasy balance for two hundred years, an instance of the friction between the branches of government on which the Founding Fathers relied to preserve the liberties of the people. Over a wide range, the President and Congress can exercise their joint and several political discretion in dealing quickly with complex and swiftly moving events, often on the basis of fragmentary information. Within that zone, the only constitutional restraints on which the people can rely to secure them from the abuse of such political discretion is the electoral process itself, as Chief Justice Marshall remarked in GIBBONS V. OGDEN (1824).

But the choices committed by the Constitution to the care of Congress and the President are not unlimited, even when one gives full weight to the view that the war power is the power to wage war successfully. The foreign affairs and war powers are aspects of a government organized under a written Constitution dominated by the principle of democratic responsibility. Although the Supreme Court has hesitated to pass on many conflicts between the President and Congress, it has intervened where exercises of the war power impinged upon CIVIL RIGHTS, or attempted radically to alter the equilibrium of the constitutional order.

Thus, certain constitutional limits on the President's war power emerged in its first major test—the neutrality crisis of 1793. President Washington could have used the armed forces or called up the militia to keep French privateers at the docks of Philadelphia or Charleston; in the event, he prudently refrained from such action. But he could not get American juries to convict American citizens indicted for violating a presidential proclamation. Similarly, YOUNGSTOWN SHEET & TUBE CO. V. SAWYER (1952) decided that the President had no INHERENT POWERS to seize steel mills as a step toward settling a strike during the Korean War when Congress had rejected such a procedure.

There are comparable constitutional limits on what Congress and the President acting together can do in the name of the war power. Congress can make it an offense to recruit soldiers within the United States for wars in which the United States is neutral, but it is doubtful whether it would be constitutional for Congress to forbid American citizens from going abroad to fight. In *Ex parte Merryman* (1861) and *Ex parte Milligan* (1867) the courts held that even in the midst of the Civil War, courts-martial could not try civilians while the ordinary courts were available. And in REID V. COVERT (1957) and *Kinsella v. United States* (1960) the Supreme Court struck down convictions imposed by courts-martial on the wives of military personnel living on American bases abroad.

The only exceptions to this line of cases are the JAPANESE AMERICAN CASES, decided during World War II. These cases upheld the constitutionality of a statute authorizing the President to exclude citizens of Japanese descent from California, Oregon, and Washington, and requiring their internment in camps until they could be resettled in other parts of the

country. These decisions have been severely criticized, and the Court's opinion in DUNCAN V. KAHANA-MOKU (1946) can be interpreted as overruling them *sub silentio*. Until they are more decisively repudiated, however, they remain, as Justice Jackson said in KOREMATSU V. UNITED STATES (1944), "a loaded weapon ready for the hand of any authority that can bring forward a plausible claim of an urgent need."

EUGENE V. ROSTOW

Bibliography
CORWIN, EDWARD S. (1940)1957 *The President: Office and Powers, 1787–1957.* New York: New York University Press.
HENKIN, LOUIS 1972 *Foreign Affairs and the Constitution.* Mineola, N.Y.: Foundation Press.
RANDALL, JAMES G. (1926)1951 *Constitutional Problems under Lincoln.* Urbana: University of Illinois Press.
REVELY, W. TAYLOR, III 1981 *The War Powers of the President and Congress.* Charlottesville: University Press of Virginia.
ROSTOW, EUGENE V. 1945 The Japanese-American Cases: A Disaster. *Yale Law Journal* 54:489–533, reprinted in *The Sovereign Prerogative* (1962). New Haven: Yale University Press.
——— 1973 Statement, in Appendix to *War Powers,* Hearings before Subcommittee on National Security Policy and Scientific Developments, Committee on Foreign Affairs, House of Representatives, 93rd Congress, 1st Session, March 7–20, 1973, pp. 395–502; also in Rostow, Eugene V. 1972 Great Cases Make Bad Law: The War Powers Act. *Texas Law Review* 50:833–900.
SOFAER, ABRAHAM D. 1976 *War, Foreign Affairs, and Constitutional Power: The Origins.* Cambridge, Mass.: Ballinger Publishing Co.
TURNER, ROBERT F. 1983 *The War Powers Resolution: Its Implementation in Theory and Practice.* Philadelphia: Foreign Policy Research Institute.

WAR POWERS

Not appearing in the Constitution, the phrase "war powers" nonetheless describes a cluster of powers exercised by the President or Congress, together or separately, to combat both domestic insurgency and foreign military enemies. They comprise those activities necessary "to wage war successfully," including the raising of troops, the provision of equipment and supplies, the mobilization of opinion, and the maintenance of security in loyal areas (during civil war or insurgency) or on the home front (during foreign war).

As with all governmental activity, the legitimacy of the war powers depends ultimately on explicit or implicit sources in the Constitution. Among these are the grants to Congress of authority "to declare War," to raise, maintain, and make rules for federal military forces, and "to provide for calling forth the Militia to execute the Laws of the Union, suppress Insurrections and repel Invasions." Other sources include the Article I authorization to suspend the privilege of the writ of HABEAS CORPUS "when in Cases of Rebellion or Invasion the public Safety may require it," the Article II clauses making the President COMMANDER-IN-CHIEF, giving him power to make treaties subject to Senate consent, and charging him to "take Care that the Laws be faithfully executed," and the Article IV commitments guaranteeing "to every State . . . a REPUBLICAN FORM OF GOVERNMENT" and pledging protection against invasion and domestic violence. Magnifying all these grants is the NECESSARY AND PROPER CLAUSE.

Contrariwise, only in exceptional circumstances have officials instituted TREASON prosecutions, for in Article III the Framers laid out strict evidentiary requirements, owing to the crime's draconian connotations. But such seemingly plausible restrictions as the FIRST AMENDMENT and Fifth Amendment, the principle of SEPARATION OF POWERS, and the rule against delegation of power have seldom proved real barriers to effective wartime government; and generally JUDICIAL REVIEW has had little impact on the power to make war.

As early as 1792, Congress empowered the President to call forth state militias when "combinations too powerful to be suppressed by the ordinary course of judicial proceedings" prevented the execution of federal law. Used during the WHISKEY REBELLION (1794), and subsequently modified to include regular military forces and to clarify the President's authority to determine the existence of emergency, this provision later helped undergird President ABRAHAM LINCOLN's response to the siege of Fort Sumter. The ALIEN AND SEDITION ACTS of 1798 provide another early illustration of legislative-executive collaboration; adopted during the Quasi-War with France, they posed the enduring issue of reconciling CIVIL LIBERTIES with the perceived requirements of internal security.

Although Presidents THOMAS JEFFERSON and ANDREW JACKSON confronted serious opposition to enforcement of federal law during the Embargo and NULLIFICATION crises, the Civil War produced the first comprehensive test of the war powers' true potential. With only a slender statutory base—or none at all—for much of his action, Lincoln called out the militia, requested federal volunteer troops, increased the size of the regular army and navy, spent money from the treasury, established a naval blockade of the Confederacy, and suspended the privilege of the writ of habeas corpus. When Congress finally met at Lincoln's call, on July 4, 1861, it confronted not only a program already in place but also the President's explanation that his actions, "whether strictly legal or not, were ventured upon under what appeared to be a popular demand and a public necessity, trusting . . . that Congress would readily ratify them."

Besides retroactively endorsing much of the Lincoln program, Congress voted appropriations and passed confiscation, legal tender, and draft legislation to support the defeat of the rebellion. It also authorized Lincoln's seizure of the Union's telegraphs and railways in January 1862. The general rule of the Civil War, however, was executive initiative under the theory that the Constitution had been intended to provide government adequate to all contingencies. This view built on THE FEDERALIST #23 and LUTHER V. BORDEN (1849) and gained important wartime endorsement in the PRIZE CASES (1863). Its fullest elaboration appeared in *War Powers under the Constitution of the United States,* a massive exposition and compilation by William Whiting, the War Department's solicitor.

Even Lincoln's internal security program, which emphasized military arrest without warrant, detention without trial, and release once danger had passed, escaped serious censure during the war itself, despite the short-term imprisonment of some 13,000 to 25,000 northern civilians. Typical of Court review of war powers disputes, Chief Justice ROGER B. TANEY's attack on the suspension of habeas corpus, in *Ex parte Merryman* (1861), was feeble and futile, while the more serious blow in EX PARTE MILLIGAN came in 1866, after the war had ended.

In World War I, WOODROW WILSON by no means ignored the Lincoln model; such key agencies as the War Industries Board and the Committee on Public Information rested solely on executive authority. But the bulk of the internal effort during 1917–1918 relied on congressional delegation of power. Wilson in turn delegated authority to a host of administrative agencies that exercised direct control of the sinews of war.

The resulting intervention contrasted markedly with the Civil War experience. Bolstering prewar statutes that had given the President power to place mandatory defense contracts with private firms, the Lever Act (1917) constituted the war's largest delegation of power. It allowed sweeping regulation of priorities, production, and prices throughout the economy; yet in only a minor detail did the Supreme Court eventually rule the act unconstitutional, in UNITED STATES V. COHEN GROCERY COMPANY (1921). The Trading with the Enemy Act (1917) permitted control of foreign commodity and currency transactions, encountered no significant judicial challenge, and later provided a statutory base for President FRANKLIN D. ROOSEVELT's "Bank Holiday" during the economic emergency of the Great Depression. (Not until 1977 did Congress limit the law's availability to periods of declared war—and then provided a slightly narrower set of financial powers for use in other crises.) The SELECTIVE SERVICE ACT (1917) gave free rein to Wilson in establishing draft machinery and received strong endorsement in the SELECTIVE DRAFT LAW CASES (1918), a decision supplying precedent for upholding selective service legislation in World War II and the Cold War. The ESPIONAGE ACT (1917) and SEDITION ACT (1918) enlisted the judicial system and were upheld in SCHENCK V. UNITED STATES (1919), ABRAMS V. UNITED STATES (1919), and PIERCE V. UNITED STATES (1920). Over 1,900 prosecutions took place under these two measures, with 930 convictions.

In World War II, President Roosevelt effectively combined the Lincoln and Wilson approaches. He based many actions and agencies on his INHERENT POWERS as commander-in-chief, even when tackling problems of domestic mobilization. The National War Labor Board is an example. Created in January 1942 to insure against labor strife and work stoppages in war industries, its orders were in theory only "informatory," "at most advisory"; yet companies violating the orders were denied federal contracts and needed materials. Recalcitrant workers risked revocation of their draft exemptions and denial of other jobs within the jurisdiction of the United States Employment Service. Although avowedly established under authority vested in Roosevelt "by the Constitution and the statutes of the United States" (a commonly used formula for World War II agencies), until June 1943 the Board actually had no statutory base but rather fell under the Office of Emergency Management, itself a creation within the Executive Office of the President.

Other action rested on legislation. In September 1939, well before American entry into the war, Roosevelt's declaration of a national emergency activated laws, some dating to before World War I, that empowered him to increase the size of the army and navy, regulate banking and currency dealing, take over fac-

tories and power plants, reallocate appropriations among executive departments and agencies, and censor wire and radio communications. The Lend-Lease Act (1941) delegated the broadest procurement powers ever given to a President, yet it was never challenged judicially. The Office of Price Administration, established under the Emergency Price Control Act (1942), provided the major wartime inflation fighting program; like the nonstatutory agencies, it often employed indirect sanction that proved impossible to challenge judicially. Decisions validating the act included YAKUS V. UNITED STATES (1944), *Bowles v. Willingham* (1944), and *Steuart and Brothers v. Bowles* (1944). Not surprisingly, the war's proliferation of alphabetical agencies dwarfed the New Deal's.

In addition, the government had a sedition law available (the Smith Act of 1940), but widespread support for the war meant relatively few prosecutions. The Japanese American relocation program—the single most blatant obstruction of CIVIL LIBERTIES in the nation's history—instead had its own flimsy legislative base and for practical purposes received judicial sanction in the JAPANESE AMERICAN CASES—*Hirabayashi v. United States* (1943) and *Korematsu v. United States* (1944).

The lesson of the two world wars, as Clinton Rossiter accurately summarized, is "that in time of war Congress can pass just about any law it wants as a 'necessary and proper' accessory to the delegated war powers; that the President can make just about any use of such law he sees fit; and that the people with their overt or silent resistance, not the Court with its power of judicial review, will set the only practical limits to arrogance of abuse." Indeed, even popular resistance, real or imagined, generally has proved more of a challenge to be subdued than a restrictive hurdle.

Punctuated by limited wars in Korea and Vietnam, the period of Cold War since 1945 conveys a similar lesson: if Congress and the President act together, little likelihood exists of judicial challenge. In this respect President HARRY S. TRUMAN erred during the KOREAN WAR, when a plant seizure triggered YOUNGSTOWN SHEET AND TUBE CO. V. SAWYER (1952). As for the VIETNAM WAR, Presidents LYNDON B. JOHNSON and RICHARD M. NIXON found that despite flagging public support, Congress kept voting supplies until the main fighting was over. For its part, the judiciary moved only gingerly when limiting use of war-related powers, as in NEW YORK TIMES V. UNITED STATES (1971) (government secrecy), and

UNITED STATES V. UNITED STATES DISTRICT COURT (1972) (national security electronic surveillance). Moreover, the Supreme Court in LAIRD V. TATUM (1972) held that the courts lacked jurisdiction over a challenge to the use of military personnel to gather domestic intelligence pertaining to potential public disorder; and other courts managed to discover executive-legislative *agreement* in Congress's decision finally to cut appropriations for operations in or over Cambodia.

Future Presidents may not benefit so readily from legislative acquiescence. Soon after enacting the War Powers Resolution (1973) to control external warmaking by the President, Congress passed the NATIONAL EMERGENCIES ACT (1976). Recent studies had disclosed that four declarations of national emergency were still in effect, one dating to 1933 and another to 1950; these proclamations activated 470 provisions of federal law, many of which lingered from the two world wars and Korea. The 1976 law ended these existing emergencies two years after its passage, mandated periodic six-month review of any future emergency declarations, and made them terminable by CONCURRENT RESOLUTION—a procedure of doubtful constitutionality under IMMIGRATION AND NATURALIZATION SERVICE V. CHADHA (1983). The act also required Presidents to inform Congress fully of the legislative basis for emergency actions. But subsequent response to President JIMMY CARTER's declaration of national emergency over the Iranian hostage crisis (1979) indicated little congressional desire to adhere rigorously to the new requirements.

Whenever a crisis plausibly justifies their exercise, the war powers seem likely to continue to generate government centered in the executive branch, emphasizing energetic administration that transcends normal restrictions, and on occasion sufficiently vigorous to warrant the label "constitutional dictatorship."

CHARLES A. LOFGREN

Bibliography

CORWIN, EDWARD S. (1957)1984 *The President: Office and Powers, 1787–1984,* 5th ed., revised by Randall W. Bland, Theodore T. Hindson, and Jack W. Peltason. New York: New York University Press.

FISHER, LOUIS 1985 *Constitutional Conflicts between Congress and the President.* Princeton, N.J.: Princeton University Press.

ROSSITER, CLINTON (1948)1963 *Constitutional Dictatorship: Crisis Government in the Modern Democracies.* New York: Harcourt, Brace.

———— (1951)1976 *The Supreme Court and the Commander in Chief.* Expanded edition by Richard P. Longaker. Ithaca, N.Y.: Cornell University Press.

WAR POWERS ACTS
First War Powers Act
55 Stat. 838 (1941)
Second War Powers Act
56 Stat. 176 (1942)

Enacted less than two weeks after the bombing of Pearl Harbor, the First War Powers Act was similar to the World War I Overman Act (1917). It delegated to the President virtually complete authority to reorganize the executive branch, the independent government agencies, and government corporations in any manner he deemed appropriate to expedite prosecution of the war. That power, and reorganizations accomplished under it, were to remain in force until six months after the end of the war. The act also authorized the President to censor mail and other forms of communication between the United States and foreign countries.

The Second War Powers Act, passed three months after the first, further strengthened the executive branch for conduct of the war. It authorized acquisition of land for military or naval purposes, by condemnation if necessary. It also suspended some provisions of the HATCH ACT (1939), relaxed NATURALIZATION standards for ALIENS serving in the armed forces, established procedures for war production contracting, and authorized several other adjustments of governmental affairs.

The War Powers Acts, like their predecessors, represented an attempt to accommodate the concentration of power necessary for the prosecution of the war to the accustomed forms of constitutional government.

DENNIS J. MAHONEY

WARRANT

See: Arrest Warrant; General Warrant; Search Warrant

WARRANTLESS SEARCH

The FOURTH AMENDMENT makes no explicit provision for warrantless searches. The first clause of the amendment provides simply that "the right of the people to be secure in their persons, houses, papers, and effects, against unreasonable SEARCHES AND SEIZURES, shall not be violated." This general prohibition is followed by another clause that provides more particularly for the issuance of SEARCH WARRANTS. The amendment itself does not indicate what connection there is between the two clauses (which are separated only by a comma and the word "and"). Accordingly, its application to various kinds of warrantless searches has depended heavily on which clause the Supreme Court favors. On the one hand, the first clause might be regarded as the main provision, searches pursuant to a warrant being only one type of reasonable search that is authorized. Or, if the second clause be emphasized, the absence of a search warrant might be regarded ordinarily as itself making a search unreasonable, the requirement of a warrant being disregarded only in exceptional circumstances including particularly lack of an opportunity to obtain one.

Some kinds of warrantless search are obviously necessary to the performance of other official duties. A police officer who unexpectedly makes an ARREST of someone committing a violent crime may necessarily search him for weapons. If the Fourth Amendment were deemed to prohibit every search without a warrant, one would be driven to the conclusion that the arresting officer's conduct was not a search at all within its contemplation. Current interpretation of the Fourth Amendment has avoided such an all-or-nothing approach. The amendment is applicable to a very wide range of official conduct interfering with expectations of privacy; within that context, the prevailing rules have established a number of situations in which a warrant to search is unnecessary.

The first such situation is the SEARCH INCIDENT TO AN ARREST. The need for an arresting officer to ensure that the person whom he arrests does not have in his possession a weapon or means of escape is the basis for the most frequently applied exception to the requirement of a warrant. Because police actively engaged in crime prevention often come on circumstances calling for an arrest without advance notice, a search incident to the arrest must be made without a warrant. Although not strictly necessary to effectuate the arrest, another reason for allowing a search is to prevent the arrestee from destroying EVIDENCE in his possession. The Supreme Court said in CHIMEL v. CALIFORNIA (1969) that all three justifications are sufficient to authorize a search of the arrestee's person and the area "within his immediate control" from which he might grab something. That general rule defines an area that may be searched without a warrant following an arrest, whether or not there is particular reason to believe that anything subject to seizure is there to be grabbed and, indeed, whether or not there is reason to believe that the arrestee is likely to grab anything. In effect, the rule authorizes a not-too-intensive search of the arrestee, including small containers on his person like a wallet or purse, and a small area around the place of the arrest. If a person were arrested in his home, the rule would authorize a limited search of the table or desk at which he sat, but not all the contents of the room or the contents of other rooms.

The scope of this rule illustrates a general feature of the exceptions to the warrant requirement. Although from time to time the Court has intimated that such exceptions depend on an emergency that demands a search before a warrant could practicably be obtained, the rule does not depend on a particularized finding of that kind. In some cases, the rule has been applied to uphold a search even though the arresting officers could easily have (or even had) removed the person from the area searched or immobilized him. (One might note also that the rule applies fully to arrests that are not unanticipated, even though in that case a warrant could presumably have been obtained.) The evident rationale is that a warrantless search incident to an arrest is so often necessary that it is impractical to require particular justification in each case.

Warrants are not required for AUTOMOBILE SEARCHES in various circumstances. Although automobiles (and other motor vehicles) as private places enjoy the protection of the Fourth Amendment, two distinct lines of analysis have markedly limited the application to them of the requirement of a search warrant. Automobiles, the Supreme Court has said, are subject to much greater regulation and inspection than dwellings; the expectation of privacy in them is much less. Having reached that judgment, the Court has not modified it to differentiate between areas like the back seat that are generally open to view and closed or concealed areas like the trunk or glove compartment that are not.

If police officers obtain lawful custody of an automobile which they have PROBABLE CAUSE to search for evidence of a crime, a warrantless search is allowed for some period, a few hours at least, after custody is obtained. This rule is based not only on the lesser expectation of privacy attached to an automobile but also on its mobility and the unpredictability with which custody often is obtained. The Supreme Court has not been persuaded that the immobilization of the car while it is in custody ordinarily makes it unnecessary to allow a search until a warrant has been obtained. Second, if officers have lawful custody of an automobile and routinely follow a regular custodial procedure, like an inventory of its contents, a search performed as part of the procedure is permitted. The routine nature of such practices, which are followed by many police departments, has persuaded the Supreme Court that they are reasonable. (Also, the arrest-incident exception authorizes a thorough search of the passenger compartment of an automobile, including all containers within it, as an incident of the arrest of an occupant.)

A search at the time and place of an arrest is likely to be limited by the circumstances to weapons or means of escape and only the most obvious evidentiary items. Later, when the person is about to be placed in detention or while he is in detention, there is opportunity for a more thorough search; sometimes, the evidentiary significance of an item is not plain at the time of the arrest and is revealed as the investigation proceeds. The police have authority to make a very thorough search without a warrant of items removed from the arrested person and held by them while he is lawfully detained temporarily in a jail or similar facility. The arrest, it has been said, being the more significant interference with liberty, includes the lesser intrusion on privacy occasioned by the search. Furthermore, a search is authorized at the time and place of the arrest and it is routine administrative procedure to impound and perhaps inventory a person's effects before he is placed in a cell; therefore, it is reasoned, the fact that some time elapses between the arrest and the search has no constitutional significance.

The most general exception to the requirement of a search warrant allows the police and other public officials to search without a warrant in EXIGENT CIRCUMSTANCES: an emergency furnishing adequate grounds for a search that has to be carried out before a warrant can be obtained. A search incident to the unanticipated arrest of a potentially dangerous person is an example of this more general category, although justified by a special rule. Another example is an entry and search of private premises while in "hot pursuit" of someone who has just committed a crime; police officers are not required to interrupt the chase until they have obtained a warrant. Similarly, officers responding to a cry for help or acting to avert a danger inside private premises need not wait to obtain a warrant. It has usually been held also that if officers have particular, reliable information that specific evidence of crime is about to be destroyed and there is not time to obtain a warrant, they can enter to prevent its destruction.

In such cases, authority to search without a warrant is tailored to the emergency. The officers claiming the authority must not themselves be responsible for the existence of the emergency; if, for example, they unreasonably delayed applying for a warrant until it was too late, they could not then assert their inability to obtain a warrant. Also, the authority extends only as far as the emergency requires. Entering in hot pursuit, officers could also search for weapons that the person whom they are pursuing might use against them; but once having him in custody, they could not continue to search solely for evidence.

The regulation of persons and goods entering or leaving the country has always been understood to provide a special basis for warrantless searches. Public officials who supervise traffic across the border are authorized to inspect goods and to require a person crossing the border to submit to a thorough search. (See BORDER SEARCHES.) Some comprehensive statutory programs for the regulation of industry and commerce have authorized warrantless entries and inspections. Such procedures have been upheld if a requirement of a warrant might be expected to frustrate the regulatory program and the business in question is generally subject to close governmental supervision: for example, gun and liquor dealerships, and mines. Similarly, the Supreme Court has held that inspection visits to the home by a welfare official can be made a condition of receipt of public welfare. In other cases, the Court has concluded that the regulatory purpose of a statute did not require that warrantless (unannounced) searches be allowed.

In some circumstances, a brief invasion of personal privacy less intrusive than a full search is allowed without a warrant. Most common is the protective "frisk" or pat-down of a person whose conduct a police officer has reason to investigate and who he reasonably suspects may be armed. There being no opportunity to obtain a warrant, the safe performance of the officer's investigative duty justifies a limited search for weapons. Likewise, traffic officers are allowed to make routine checks for driver's licenses and automobile registrations, so long as the checks follow an established pattern or there are specific grounds for a departure from the pattern. Routine inspection of passengers and carry-on luggage has been upheld as a regulatory measure to prevent airplane hijacking. In these cases, not only is the procedure in question thought to be less objectionable than a full search; there is no way to accomplish the legitimate objective of the procedure consistently with a requirement of a warrant.

The Fourth Amendment does not insist that persons protect a privacy that they are willing to forego. Accordingly, a warrant to search is not required if a person having authority to do so voluntarily admits public officials and permits them to search. A consensual search that is successful often is challenged later on the grounds that consent was not given fully voluntarily or did not extend to the actual search; or, if the premises are shared by others, it may be claimed that the person who consented did not have the independent authority to do so. While a resolution of such issues may depend on difficult matters of fact, the basic principle that a search with consent does not require a warrant is unquestioned.

Those who believe that the requirement of a search warrant is a significant protection against UNREASONABLE SEARCHES may conclude that the Supreme Court has drawn the categories of lawful warrantless searches too broadly. Categories like the search incident to arrest, automobile search, and jail search appear to depend only on the premises that such searches often are fruitful and sometimes have to be made before a warrant can be obtained. But the categories are general and require neither premise to be fulfilled in the particular case; each of them encourages the police to make a large number of searches routinely, without particular justification. This approach, it can be argued, is inconsistent with the plain purpose of the Fourth Amendment to prohibit *general* searches: unfocused, unlimited rummaging in the privacy of individuals.

Critics of the Court have observed also that its analysis of warrantless searches is to a considerable degree incoherent. Why, for example, should an arrest justify the search of any area surrounding the arrestee, if he can be and often is removed from that place before the search is made? Why should automobiles, which often are used for the same private purposes as dwellings, be treated categorically as less private? Why should an arrest automatically defeat the person's separate interest in the privacy of items in his possession? The Court's failure to provide convincing answers to such questions has rendered this part of Fourth Amendment DOCTRINE only a set of rules without supporting rationale.

A defense of the rules for warrantless searches begins with the premise that warrants are peculiarly appropriate for planned investigative searches and have much less utility in the ordinary unplanned encounters between police or other public officials and private persons. If legitimate police duties justify an encounter, then a search related in purpose is also legitimate. This approach places a great deal of emphasis on the requirement that a search be "reasonable" and construes that term with attention to common police practices as well as the individual interest in privacy. To limit warrantless searches to cases of manifest necessity would blink the natural—and therefore reasonable—impulse of police officers to search whatever is legitimately in their custody and

may furnish evidence of crime. Some explanation for the breadth of the exceptions to the requirement of a warrant may lie also in the fact that the issue is almost always tested in the context of a criminal prosecution, when the defendant seeks the protection of the EXCLUSIONARY RULE to avoid the admission of incriminating evidence that a search has uncovered.

LLOYD L. WEINREB

Bibliography

AMERICAN LAW INSTITUTE 1975 *A Model Code of Pre-Arraignment Procedure.* Philadelphia: American Law Institute.

AMSTERDAM, ANTHONY G. 1974 Perspectives on the Fourth Amendment. *Minnesota Law Review* 58:349–477.

LAFAVE, WAYNE R. 1978 *Search and Seizure.* St. Paul, Minn.: West Publishing Co.

LANDYNSKI, JACOB W. 1966 *Search and Seizure and the Supreme Court.* Baltimore: Johns Hopkins University Press.

WEINREB, LLOYD L. 1974 Generalities of the Fourth Amendment. *University of Chicago Law Review* 42:47–85.

WARREN, CHARLES
(1868–1954)

Charles Warren was a Boston lawyer who, as assistant attorney general of the United States, drafted the ESPIONAGE ACT and argued many cases before the Supreme Court. He became an expert on constitutional and legal history. He wrote excellent books in the tradition of the old school of high-minded conservative nationalists who rejected CHARLES BEARD's economic interpretation. Among his leading books are *A History of the American Bar, A History of Harvard Law School, The Supreme Court in United States History,* which won the Pulitzer Prize, *Congress, the Constitution, and the Supreme Court,* and *The Making of the Constitution.* His works still merit reading and remain influential. His article on the JUDICIARY ACT OF 1789 helped lead the Supreme Court in ERIE RAILROAD V. TOMKINS (1938) to overrule almost a century of decisions based on SWIFT V. TYSON (1842).

LEONARD W. LEVY

WARREN, EARL
(1891–1974)

The fourteenth Chief Justice of the United States, Earl Warren presided over the most sweeping judicial reinterpretation of the Constitution in generations. He served from October 1953 to June 1969. In that time the SUPREME COURT, overruling the doctrine that SEPARATE BUT EQUAL facilities for black persons satisfied the requirement of EQUAL PROTECTION, outlawed official racial SEGREGATION in every area of life. The Court ended the long-established rural bias of legislative representation by opening the question to judicial scrutiny and then ruling that citizens must be represented equally in state legislatures and the national House of Representatives. It imposed constitutional restraints for the first time on the law of LIBEL, hitherto a matter entirely of state concern. It applied to the states the standards set by the BILL OF RIGHTS for federal CRIMINAL PROCEDURE: the right of all poor defendants to free counsel, for example, and the prohibition of unreasonable SEARCHES AND SEIZURES, enforced by the EXCLUSIONARY RULE. It limited government power to punish unorthodox beliefs and enlarged the individual's freedom to express herself or himself in unconventional, even shocking ways.

The WARREN COURT, as it was generally called, had as profound an impact on American life as any Supreme Court since the time of JOHN MARSHALL. It was extraordinary not only in the scale but in the direction of its exercise of power. From Marshall's day to the Court's clash with President FRANKLIN D. ROOSEVELT in the 1930s judges had exercised a conservative influence in the American system. Shortly before his appointment to the Court in 1941 ROBERT H. JACKSON wrote that "never in its entire history can the Supreme Court be said to have for a single hour been representative of anything except the relatively conservative forces of its day." But the Warren Court in its time was perhaps *the* principal engine of American liberal reform.

Earl Warren seemed an unlikely figure to lead such a judicial revolution. He was a Republican politician, the elected attorney general of California and for three terms its phenomenally popular governor. In 1948 he was the Republican candidate for vice-president, on the ticket headed by Thomas E. Dewey. On naming him Chief Justice, President DWIGHT D. Eisenhower emphasized his "middle-of-the-road philosophy." Yet within a few years billboards in the South demanded Warren's IMPEACHMENT, and the paranoid right charged that he was doing the work of communism. Putting aside the rantings of extremists, there was no doubt that as Chief Justice Warren consistently favored liberal values and unembarrassedly translated them into constitutional doctrine. Where did that commitment come from in a man whose appearance was that of a bland, hearty political figure?

There were in fact clues in his life and earlier career. He was born in Los Angeles in 1891, the son of a Norwegian immigrant who worked for the Southern Pacific Railroad. He knew poverty and personal tragedy. As a young man he was a railroad callboy, waking up the gangs, and he saw men with their legs cut off in accidents carried in on planks. His father was murdered, the murderer never found: a traumatic event that must have helped to point Warren in the direction of justice, legal and social. He put himself through college and law school at the University of California. After a brief try at private practice he spent all his life in public office, as a local prosecutor and crusading district attorney before winning statewide office.

In California politics he at first had the support of conservatives. As attorney general he blocked the nomination of Max Radin, a law professor known as a legal realist, to the state supreme court because Radin was a "radical." As attorney general and governor Warren was a leading proponent of the World War II federal order removing all persons of Japanese ancestry from the West Coast and putting them in desolate camps; opposing their return in 1943, he said, "If the Japs are released, no one will be able to tell a saboteur from any other Jap." (In a memoir published after his death, Warren wrote: "I have since deeply regretted the removal order and my own testimony advocating it, because it was not in keeping with our American concept of freedom and the rights of citizens. . . .")

But in 1945 Warren astounded political California by proposing a state program of prepaid medical insurance. Characteristically, he did so not for ideological but for human, practical reasons: he had fallen ill and realized how catastrophic serious illness would be for a person without resources. Then, in his last two terms as governor, he became an apostle of liberal Republicanism. A later Democratic governor, Edmund G. Brown, said Warren "was the best governor California ever had. . . . He felt the people of California were in his care, and he cared for them."

Many Americans and other people around the world saw that same paternal image in Earl Warren the Chief Justice, for he became an international symbol. He represented the hope of authority bringing justice to the downtrodden, an American vision of change by law rather than by rebellion. A single case gave Warren that status: BROWN V. BOARD OF EDUCATION, the 1954 school segregation decision. In recent years the Supreme Court had chipped away at PLESSY V. FERGUSON, the 1896 decision allowing what were termed "separate but equal" facilities but what were almost always in fact grossly inferior schools and other public institutions for blacks. Yet in 1953 seventeen southern and border states, with forty percent of the national enrollment, still confined black children to separate public schools; moreover, there was involved here, unlike higher education, the compulsory daily association of children. The emotional content of the legal question was high. The Court had given the most gingerly handling to the question, restoring the issue to the calendar for reargument.

Warren became Chief Justice before the second argument. The following May he delivered the opinion for a unanimous Court holding public school segregation unconstitutional. The unanimity was itself a striking feature of the result, and a surprising one. Expected southern resistance made unanimity politically essential, but the known attitudes of some members of the Court had suggested the likelihood of dissents. Richard Kluger's exhaustive study has demonstrated that the new Chief Justice played a crucial part in his management of the process inside the Court. After argument he delayed formal discussion of the cases in conference to avoid the development of rigid positions among the nine Justices. Then he stated as his view that the separate-but-equal doctrine could not be maintained unless one thought blacks inherently inferior: an approach likely to induce shame in any judge prepared to argue for that outcome. He persuaded his colleagues even then to avoid a formal vote but to continue discussing the cases, in tight secrecy, among themselves. He wrote an opinion in simple terms. Finally, he persuaded reluctant members of the Court to join for the sake of unanimity. A law clerk present at a late meeting between the Chief Justice and the most reluctant, STANLEY F. REED, remembers him saying, "Stan, you're all by yourself in this now. You've got to decide whether it's really the best thing for the country."

What is known about the process of decision in the school cases throws lights on one question asked during his lifetime: did Chief Justice Warren exercise leadership or have influence in the Court beyond his own vote in conference? He shared that bench with men of strong personality and conviction: in particular HUGO L. BLACK, who said the judicial duty was to follow the literal language of the Constitution and found in it absolutes, and FELIX FRANKFURTER, who scorned absolutes and said the Court should defer to the political branches of government in applying the uncertain commands of the Constitution. Warren came to the Court utterly inexperienced in its work; how could he have effective influence? The school cases show that he did.

No Chief Justice can command his associates' beliefs. If Warren had served with different, more conservative colleagues, many of the views that made history might have been expressed by him in dissent. Changes while he was on the Court greatly affected the trend of doctrine, in particular the retirement of Justice Frankfurter in 1962 and his replacement by ARTHUR J. GOLDBERG, who was much readier to join Warren in intervening on behalf of liberal values. But the identification of that Court with its Chief Justice, for all its logical imperfection, has substantial basis in reality.

Warren wrote the opinions of the Court not only in *Brown* but in later cases that dramatically overturned expectations. The most important of these— Warren himself thought them the weightiest decisions of his years on the Court—were the REAPPORTIONMENT cases. A divided Supreme Court in COLEGROVE V. GREEN (1946) had refused to entertain an attack on numerical inequality in political districts, an opinion by Justice Frankfurter saying that courts must stay out of the "political thicket." In 1962 the Warren Court, in an opinion by Justice WILLIAM J. BRENNAN, overthrew that doctrine of reluctance and said that federal courts could consider issues of fairness in districting. The decision in BAKER V. CARR left open the substantive questions: must the population be the test of equality, or may states weigh geography or other factors in districting? Does the same standard apply to both houses of legislatures? The answers were given by Chief Justice Warren in 1964, in terms so firm that some who listened in the courtroom felt as if they were at a second American constitutional convention. In REYNOLDS V. SIMS Warren said for a 6–3 majority that every house of every state legislature must be apportioned on the basis of population alone, with the districts as nearly equal as practicable. Few cases in any court ever had so direct and immediate an impact on a nation's politics; reapportionment was required in most of the fifty states, ancient legislative expectations were upset, new suburban power vindicated. Justice JOHN MARSHALL HARLAN predicted in dissent, as had Justice Frankfurter in *Baker v. Carr,* that the courts would not be able to manage the apportionment litigation—or to enforce their decisions against political resistance. But the gloomy prediction was wrong. Resistance from political incumbents quickly collapsed; nothing like the emotional public opposition to the school segregation cases developed in any region.

Emotions were aroused by Warren's opinion in MIRANDA V. ARIZONA (1966), holding that before questioning an arrested person the police must warn him that he has a right to remain silent and a right to see a lawyer first—one provided by the state if he cannot afford one—and that a confession obtained in violation of that rule is inadmissible at trial. The decision touched a nerve among police, prosecutors, and others convinced that judges were impeding the fight against crime. *Miranda* climaxed a series of cases holding local police to the standards of the Bill of Rights: for example, MAPP V. OHIO (1961), exclusion of illegally obtained evidence; GIDEON V. WAINWRIGHT (1963), RIGHT TO COUNSEL; GRIFFIN V. CALIFORNIA (1965), RIGHT AGAINST SELF-INCRIMINATION; each overruling an earlier decision. In *Spano v. New York* (1959) Warren commented: "The abhorrence of society to the use of involuntary confessions does not turn alone on their inherent untrustworthiness. It also turns on the deep-rooted feeling that the police must obey the law while enforcing the law; that in the end life and liberty can be as much endangered from illegal methods used to convict those thought to be criminals as from the actual criminals themselves." Impatient with reviewing the facts in case after case of claimed coercion, the Court under Warren sought a general prophylactic rule—and wrote it in *Miranda*.

Objection to the *Miranda* decision came not only from the law enforcement community. More dispassionate critics saw it as an example of overreaching by the Warren Court. The opinion seemed more legislative in character than judicial, laying out what amounted to a code of police procedure with little basis in precedent. Moreover, the Court did not confront a situation in which reform by other means was blocked, as it had with school segregation and malapportioned legislatures; various reformers were working on the confession problem.

Freedom of expression was another subject of fundamental constitutional development during the Warren years. The most important single decision was probably NEW YORK TIMES V. SULLIVAN (1964), holding that a public official may not recover libel damages unless the statement was published with knowledge of its falsity or in reckless disregard of truth or falsity. That opinion was by Justice Brennan. Justice WILLIAM O. DOUGLAS wrote for the Court in LAMONT V. POSTMASTER GENERAL (1965), holding that a statute requiring the post office to detain "Communist political propaganda" from abroad unless the addressee requested its delivery violated the FIRST AMENDMENT—the first federal statute that the Supreme Court ever held invalid under that amendment. Warren joined in these and other expansive decisions. He

wrote for a 5–4 majority in UNITED STATES V. ROBEL (1967), striking down a law that forbade the employment in defense plants of any member of an organization required to register under the Subversive Activities Control Act. Warren's opinion for a unanimous Court in *Bond v. Floyd* (1966) held that the Georgia legislature could not exclude a duly elected member because he had expressed admiration for draft resisters.

The one area of expression in which Warren departed from the majority of his colleagues was OBSCENITY. He thought that local and national authorities should have a relatively free hand to combat what he evidently regarded as a social evil. Thus, while in *Miranda* imposing a national standard for fair pretrial procedures in criminal cases, he argued in dissent in JACOBELLIS V. OHIO (1964) that each local community should be allowed to fix its own standard of obscenity, a view that became the law under Chief Justice WARREN E. BURGER in MILLER V. CALIFORNIA (1973). Another example of a departure from Warren's usual approach came when gambling was involved. He generally favored broad application of the right against self-incrimination; but when the rule was applied for the benefit of a gambler in MARCHETTI V. UNITED STATES (1968), he alone dissented. Once again he saw a social evil.

Scholarly critics of Chief Justice Warren saw the obscenity and gambling cases as illustrating a fundamental shortcoming in a judge: a concern to reach particular results rather than to work out principles applicable whoever the parties in a case might be. In Warren's view, it seemed, justice consisted not in providing a philosophically satisfactory process and basis of decision but in seeing that the right side, the good side, won in each case. Many of the commentators regretted the lack of a consistent doctrinal thread in his opinions. There was nothing like Justice Black's exaltation of the constitutional text, or Justice Frankfurter's institutional concern for self-restraint.

G. Edward White, in a full-length study of Warren's work, rejected the general scholarly view that Warren had no rudder as a judge and lacked craftsmanship. He was an ethicist, White concluded, who saw his craft as "discovering ethical imperatives in a maze of confusion"—and in the Constitution. Thus the prosecutor so hard on corruption that he was called a boy scout, the Californian politician who stood aloof from party machines lest he be sullied, became a judicial enforcer of ethical imperatives. In general his sympathy lay with the little person, with victims, with people excluded from the benefits of our democracy.

But he also was in the tradition of the American Progressives, who thought that government could be made to work for the people. Those two themes came together in the reapportionment cases, decisions designed to make democracy work better by making the electoral process fairer. John Hart Ely, in an analysis of judicial review as practiced in the Warren years, suggested that many of the pathbreaking decisions had a democratic structural purpose: to assure access for the powerless and thus make the system work.

There was a directness, a simplicity in Warren's opinions on the largest issues. "Legislators represent people," he wrote in the reapportionment cases, "not acres or trees. Legislators are elected by voters, not farms or cities or economic interests. . . . The weight of a citizen's vote cannot be made to depend on where he lives." When the Court held unconstitutional a statute depriving a native-born American of his citizenship for deserting the armed forces in time of war, TROP V. DULLES (1958), Warren for a plurality argued that EXPATRIATION was a CRUEL AND UNUSUAL PUNISHMENT in violation of the Eighth Amendment. The death penalty would not have been "cruel," he conceded, but the deprivation of citizenship was, for it caused "the total destruction of the individual's status in organized society" and cost him "the right to have rights."

Warren's whole career suggests that he was a person born not to muse but to act—and to govern. That view provides a connecting thread through all the offices he held. In each he exerted his powerful abilities in the ways open to him. As a prosecutor he fought crime. As wartime attorney general and governor he was a patriot, worrying about spies. In the postwar years, he turned to the social problems of an expanding California. As Chief Justice, too, he was committed to action, to using the opportunities available to make an impression on American life: to break the pattern of malapportionment, to attack local police abuses, to condemn racial discrimination. The instinct to govern did not leave Earl Warren when he put on a robe.

Many regarded him as a heroic figure because he put aside philosophical concerns and technical legal issues and dealt squarely with what he considered outrageous situations. And there were outrages in American life: official racism, political discrimination, abuse of police authority, suppression of free expression. Warren as Chief Justice had the conviction, the humanity, and the capacity for growth to deal effectively with those issues inside that prickly institution, the Supreme Court. But there were those who shared Justice LEARNED HAND's doubts about rule by judges,

however beneficent. "For myself," Hand wrote in 1958, with the contemporary Supreme Court in mind, "it would be most irksome to be ruled by a bevy of Platonic Guardians, even if I knew how to choose them, which I assuredly do not." Earl Warren may have been the closest thing the United States has had to a constitutional Platonic Guardian, dispensing law without any sensed limit of authority except what he saw as the good of society. He was a decent, kindly law-giver. But the exercise of such power by other judges—before and after Warren—has not always had kindly or rational results. The questions about judicial power remain after its extraordinary uses in the Warren years.

ANTHONY LEWIS

Bibliography

ELY, JOHN HART 1980 *Democracy and Distrust: A Theory of Judicial Review.* Cambridge, Mass.: Harvard University Press.
KLUGER, RICHARD 1975 *Simple Justice: The History of Brown v. Board of Education and Black America's Struggle for Equality.* New York: Knopf.
SCHWARTZ, BERNARD 1983 *Superchief.* Garden City, N.Y.: Doubleday.
WHITE, G. EDWARD 1982 *Earl Warren: A Public Life.* New York: Oxford University Press.

WARREN COURT

It was surely the best known Supreme Court in history, and probably the most controversial. Its grand themes—racial equality, REAPPORTIONMENT, the separation of religion and education, DUE PROCESS—became matters of public consciousness. Its leading judges—HUGO L. BLACK, WILLIAM O. DOUGLAS, FELIX FRANKFURTER, JOHN MARSHALL HARLAN, and EARL WARREN—became personages in whom the general public took an interest. When the Warren Court came into being in October 1953, the Supreme Court was the least known and least active of the major branches of government; by the retirement of Chief Justice Warren in June 1969, nearly everyone in American life had been affected by a Warren Court decision, and a great many Americans had firm opinions about the Supreme Court. When Warren was appointed Chief Justice, few commentators took note of the fact that he had had no previous judicial experience and had spent the last twelve years as a state politician. By the time WARREN E. BURGER succeeded Warren as Chief Justice the process of nominating a Justice to the Supreme Court had become an elaborate search for the "experienced," uncontroversial, and predictable nominee, and the Court was to lower its profile again.

The Warren Court years, then, were years in which the Supreme Court of the United States made itself a vital force in American culture. A striking pattern of interchange between the Court and the general public emerged in these years. As public issues, such as CIVIL RIGHTS or legislative malapportionment surfaced, these issues became translated into constitutional law cases. The Court, expanding the conventional ambit of its JURISDICTION, reached out to decide those cases, thereby making an authoritative contribution to the public debate. As the Court continued to reach out, the public came to rely on its presence, and the American JUDICIAL SYSTEM came to be perceived as a forum for the resolution of contemporary social problems. The use of the Supreme Court as an institution for redressing grievances ignored by Congress or state legislatures became common with the Warren Court.

The origins of the Warren Court can officially be traced to September 8, 1953, when Chief Justice FRED M. VINSON died of a heart attack. By September 30, President DWIGHT D. EISENHOWER had named Warren, the governor of California who had been a rival candidate for the Republican presidential nomination in 1952, as Vinson's successor. This nominal creation of the Warren Court did not, however, hint at its character. Indeed that character was not immediately apparent. Even the Court's first momentous decision, BROWN V. BOARD OF EDUCATION (1954), announced in May of its first term, was in some respects a holdover from the VINSON COURT. *Brown* had been argued before the Vinson Court, was based in part on Vinson Court precedents chipping away at RACIAL DISCRIMINATION in education, and was decided by a Court whose only new member was its Chief Justice. It was a cautious decision, apparently assuming that DESEGREGATION would be a long and slow process.

But *Brown* was also the Warren Court's baptism of fire. All the elements that were to mark subsequent major Warren Court decisions were present in *Brown*. *Brown* involved a major social problem, racial discrimination, translated into a legal question, the constitutionality of SEPARATE BUT EQUAL public schools. It posed an issue that no other branch of government was anxious to address. It raised questions that had distinctively moral implications: in invalidating racial SEGREGATION the Court was condemning the idea of racial supremacy. And it affected the lives of ordinary citizens, not merely in the South, not merely

in public education, for the Court's series of PER CURIAM decisions after *Brown* revealed that it did not consider racial segregation any more valid in other public facilities than it had in schools. The Warren Court had significantly altered race relations in America.

The context of the Warren Court's first momentous decision was decisive in shaping the Court's character as a branch of government that was not disinclined to resolve difficult social issues, not hesitant to foster social change, not reluctant to involve itself in controversy. By contrast, the legislative and executive branches appeared as equivocators and fainthearts. The Warren Court was deluged with criticism for its decision in *Brown*, both from persons who resisted having to change habits of prejudice and from scholars who faulted the reasoning of the Court's opinion. This response only seemed to make the Court more resolute.

The deliberations of *Brown* also served to identify some of the Justices whose presence was to help shape the character of the Warren Court. Earl Warren transformed a closely divided Court, which had postponed a decision on *Brown* because it was uncertain and fragmented on the case's resolution, into a unanimous voice. That transformation was a testament to Warren's remarkable ability to relate to other people and to convince them of the rightness of his views. In *Brown* he had argued that those who would support the separate but equal doctrine should recognize that it was based on claims of racial superiority. That argument struck home to at least two Justices, TOM C. CLARK and STANLEY F. REED, who had grown up in the South. When Warren had finished his round of office visits and discussions, he had secured nine votes for his majority opinion and had suppressed the writing of separate concurrences. ROBERT H. JACKSON, a long holdout in *Brown* who was dubious about the possibility of finding a doctrinal rationale to invalidate the separate but equal principle, joined Warren's opinion and left a hospital bed to appear in court the day the decision was announced.

A silent partner in the *Brown* decision had been Felix Frankfurter. By the late 1950s Frankfurter's jurisprudence, which stressed a limited role for judges in reviewing the constitutionality of legislative decisions, had rigidified, isolating Frankfurter from many other justices and identifying him as one of the guardians of a theory of judicial self-restraint. Judicial self-restraint in *Brown* would have supported the separate but equal doctrine, since that doctrine itself signified a judicial reluctance to disturb legislative enactments forcibly separating persons on the basis of race. Frankfurter, however, could not abide the consequences of continued deference to the separate but equal doctrine, but he did not want to expose the lack of "restraint" that his position assumed. He accordingly confided his views on *Brown* only to Warren and worked toward fashioning a decree—containing the controversial phrase ALL DELIBERATE SPEED as a guideline for implementing desegregation—that would temper the shock of the *Brown* mandate. At the appropriate moment he joined Warren's opinion.

The partnership of Warren and Frankfurter in the segregation cases contrasted with the usual posture of both Justices on the Warren Court. Warren's approach to judging, with its relative indifference to doctrinal reasoning and to institutional considerations, its emphasis on the morally or ethically appropriate result, and its expansive interpretation of the Court's review powers, was the antithesis of Frankfurter's. For the most part the two men sharply disagreed over the results or the reasoning of major Warren Court decisions, with Frankfurter enlisting a stable of academic supporters in his behalf and Warren seeking to bypass doctrinal or institutional objections to make broad ethical appeals to the public at large.

The presence of two other significant Warren Court Justices, Hugo Black and William O. Douglas, was also felt in *Brown*. Black, a native of Clay County, Alabama, and fleetingly a member of the Ku Klux Klan, had been an opponent of racial discrimination since being elected to the Senate in 1926. He had supported the Vinson Court precedents crippling "separate but equal," for which he had received outspoken criticism in his home state. His position in *Brown* was well known early on: an uncompromising opposition to discriminatory practices. Such positions were characteristic of Black on the Warren Court. He staked out positions decisively, held them with tenacity, and constantly sought to convert others to his views. His theory of constitutional adjudication, which placed great emphasis on a "literal" but "liberal" construction of BILL OF RIGHTS protections, was a major contribution to Warren Court jurisprudence.

Equally outspoken and tenacious, and even more activist than Black, was William O. Douglas, whose academic experience, which paralleled Frankfurter's, had generated a strikingly different conception of judicial behavior. Douglas did not agonize over issues of institutional deference and doctrinal principle; he took his power to make law as a given and sought to use it to promote values in which he believed. The values were principally those associated with twentieth-century libertarianism and egalitarianism. Douglas spoke out for small business, organized labor, disadvantaged minorities, consumers, the poor, dissidents, and those who valued their privacy and their freedom from governmental restraint. Douglas's role on the Warren Court was that of an ideologue, anxious to secure results and confident that he could find doctrinal justifications. Together, Black and Douglas prodded the Court to vindicate even the most unpopular forms of free expression and minority rights.

While the Warren Court was generally regarded as an activist Court and a liberal Court, it was not exclusively so, and not all its members could be characterized as either activists or liberals. Until his retirement in 1962, at the midway point of Warren's tenure, Frankfurter had vociferously protested against an excessively broad interpretation of the Court's review powers, a position that resulted in his supporting the constitutionality of a number of "conservative" legislative policies. Other Justices on the Warren Court were either disinclined to exercise sweeping review powers or less enthusiastic than Warren, Black, or Douglas about the policies of twentieth-century liberalism. Most influential among those Justices was John Harlan, an Eisenhower appointee who joined the Court in 1955 and remained until 1971.

Harlan frequently and adroitly rejected the assumptions of Warren Court majorities that "every major social ill in this country can find its cure in some constitutional 'principle'" and that the Court could be "a general haven for reform movements." Moreover, in a group of Justices who were often impatient to reach results and not inclined to linger over the niceties of doctrinal analysis, Harlan distinguished himself by producing painstakingly crafted opinions. Often Harlan's quarrels with a majority would be over the method by which results were reached; his concurrences and dissents regularly demonstrated the complexities of constitutional adjudication.

The Warren Court will be best known for its identification with three themes: egalitarianism, liberalism, and activism. From *Brown* through POWELL V. MCCORMACK (1969), Earl Warren's last major opinion, the Court demonstrated a dedication to the principle of equality, a principle that, in Archibald Cox's felicitous phrase, "once loosed . . . is not easily cabined." Race relations were the initial context in which the Court attempted to refine the meaning of equal justice in America. Once the ordeal of *Brown* was concluded, that meaning seemed comparatively straightforward. In a series of *per curiam* opinions, the Court extended *Brown* to public beaches, parks, recreational facilities, housing developments, public buildings, eating facilities, and hospitals. The conception of equality embodied by these decisions was that of equality of opportunity: blacks could not be denied the opportunity of access to public places.

Brown had been rationalized by the Court on similar grounds: the gravamen of the injustice in a segregated school system was a denial of equal educational opportunities to blacks. But equality of opportunity became difficult to distinguish, in the race cases, from the conception of equality of condition. The Court presumed that classifications based on race were constitutionally suspect and seemed to suggest that equal justice in the race relations area required something like color-blindness. Classifications based on race or skin color not only denied black Americans equal opportunities, they also were not based on any rational judgment, since the human condition transcended superficial differences of race. After the *per curiams,* the massive resistance to *Brown,* and the civil rights movement of the 1960s, the Court gradually perceived that equality in race relations necessitated the eradication of stigmas based on skin color. This momentum of egalitarianism culminated in *Loving v. Virginia* (1967), in which the Court invalidated state prohibitions of miscegenous marriages, thereby affirming the absence of fundamental differences between blacks and whites.

Between the *per curiums* and *Loving* had come skirmishes between the Court and groups resisting its mandates for change in race relations. COOPER V. AARON (1963) involved a challenge by the governor of Arkansas to compulsory integration in the Little Rock school system. The Court, in an unprecedented opinion signed individually by all nine Justices, reaffirmed the obligations of Southern schools to integrate. *Goss v. Board of Education* (1963) invalidated minority-to-majority transfer plans whose purpose was to allow students to attend schools outside their districts in which their race was in the majority. HEART OF ATLANTA MOTEL V. UNITED STATES (1964) and *Katzenbach v. McClung* (1964) used the Constitution's COMMERCE CLAUSE and the CIVIL RIGHTS ACT OF 1964 to prevent hotels and restaurants from refusing service to blacks. BURTON V. WILMINGTON PARKING AUTHORITY (1961) and *Evans v. Newton* (1966) showed the Court's willingness to use the DOCTRINE of "STATE ACTION" to compel ostensibly private establishments (restaurants and parks) to admit blacks.

After *Loving* the Court grew impatient with resistance to the implementation of its decrees in *Brown.* In GREEN V. NEW KENT COUNTY SCHOOL BOARD (1968) the Court scrutinized the actual effect of "freedom of choice" plans, where students attended schools of their own choice. The Court found that the system perpetuated segregation when eighty-five percent of the black children in a school district had remained in a previously all-black school and no white child had chosen to attend that school, and advised that "delays are no longer tolerable." Finally, in ALEXANDER V. HOLMES COUNTY BOARD OF EDUCATION (1969) the Court declared that the time for racial integration of previously segregated school systems was "at once." *Green* and *Alexander* compelled integration of schools and other public facilities. Equality of condition had become the dominant means to achieve the goal of equality.

One can see a similar trend in the area of reapportionment. For the first half of the twentieth century, including the early years of the Warren Court, state legislatures were not apportioned solely on the basis of population. Upper houses of legislatures had a variety of means for electing their members, some deliberately unresponsive to demographic concerns, and few states apportioned legislative seats on the basis of ONE PERSON, ONE VOTE. In *Baker v. Carr* (1962), however, the Court announced that it would scrutinize Tennessee's system of electing state legislators to see if it conformed to the population of districts in the state. Justice WILLIAM J. BRENNAN, a former student of Frankfurter's, rejected the POLITICAL QUESTION doctrine Frankfurter had consistently imposed as a barrier to Court determination of reapportionment cases. Frankfurter wrote an impassioned dissent in *Baker,* but the way was clear for constitutional challenges to malapportioned legislatures. By 1964 suits challenging legislative apportionment schemes had been filed in more than thirty states.

Chief Justice Warren's opinion for the Court in REYNOLDS V. SIMS (1964), a case testing Alabama's reapportionment system, demonstrated how the idea of equality had infused the reapportionment cases. "We are cautioned," he wrote, "about the dangers of entering into political thickets and mathematical quagmires. Our answer to this: a denial of constitutionally protected rights demands judicial protection; our oath and our office require no less of us. . . . To the extent that a citizen's right to vote is debased, he is that much less a citizen." Equality did not mean merely an equal opportunity to have representatives from one's district in a state legislature, but that all votes of all citizens were to be treated equally: voting, like race relations, was to be an area in which equality of condition was to prevail.

The Court provided for such equality even where the state's citizens had indicated a preference for another scheme. In LUCAS V. FORTY-FOURTH GENERAL ASSEMBLY (1964), the Court invalidated Colorado's districting plan apportioning only one house of the legislature on a population basis. This plan had been adopted after a statewide referendum in which a majority rejected population-based apportionment for both houses. Warren found that the scheme did not satisfy the equal protection clause because it was not harmonious with the principle of one person, one vote. Voting was a condition of CITIZENSHIP, not just an opportunity to participate in government.

In free speech cases, the Warren Court struggled to move beyond a "marketplace" approach, in which majorities could perhaps suppress speech with distasteful content, to an approach where all speakers were presumed to have an equal right to express their thoughts. The approach was first developed in "communist sympathizer" cases, where a minority of the Court objected to laws making it a crime to be a member of the Communist party or to advocate Communist party doctrine. Eventually, in BRANDENBURG V. OHIO (1969), a unanimous Court distinguished between "mere advocacy" of views and "incitement to imminent lawless action." That case involved statements made by a member of the Ku Klux Klan at a rally that were derogatory of blacks and Jews. The fact that the speaker was known to belong to an organization historically linked to racism and violence was not enough to hinder expression of his views.

Brandenburg united, without entirely clarifying, a number of strands of Warren Court FIRST AMENDMENT doctrine. In the OVERBREADTH cases, such as *NAACP v. Alabama ex rel. Flowers* (1964), APTHEKER V. SECRETARY OF STATE (1964), KEYISHIAN V. BOARD OF REGENTS (1967), and UNITED STATES V. ROBEL (1967), the Court found that legitimate governmental prohibitions on speech that employed "means which sweep unnecessarily broadly" violated the First Amendment, because they might deter the behavior of others who could not legitimately be prohibited from speaking. In the SYMBOLIC SPEECH cases, the Court considered the permissibility of wearing black arm bands (TINKER V. DES MOINES COMMUNITY SCHOOL DISTRICT, 1969) or burning draft cards (UNITED STATES V. O'BRIEN, 1968) or mutilating flags (STREET V. NEW YORK, 1969) as a means of protesting the Vietnam War. Finally, in the "sit-in" and "picketing" cases, such as COX V. LOUISIANA (1964), BROWN V. LOUISIANA (1966), and ADDERLEY V. FLORIDA (1966), the Court sought to distinguish protected "expression" from unprotected but related "conduct." In none of these areas was the Court's doctrinal position clear—draft card burners and picketers were de-

nied constitutional protection, although flag mutilators and "sit-in" demonstrators were granted it—but the decisions revealed the Warren Court's interest in carving out an area of First Amendment protection that was not dependent on public support for the speaker or his actions.

The Warren Court also attempted to extend the First Amendment's reach into other doctrinal areas, notably defamation and OBSCENITY. In NEW YORK TIMES V. SULLIVAN (1964) the Court concluded that common law libel actions could raise First Amendment issues. The Court's opinion, which found that the First Amendment gave rise to a constitutional privilege to make false and defamatory statements about public officials if the statements were not made with recklessness or malice, expressed concern that libel law could be used as a means of punishing "unpopular" speech. Justice Brennan's majority opinion referred to "a profound national commitment to the principle that debate on public issues should be uninhibited, robust, and wide-open," and spoke of the "inhibiting" effects of civil damages on "those who would give voice to public criticism."

Once the First Amendment was seen as relevant to defamation cases, the future of common law principles in the area of libel and slander seemed precarious. *New York Times v. Sullivan* had established a constitutional privilege to publish information about "public officials." *Rosenblatt v. Baer* (1966) widened the meaning of "public official" to include a supervisor of a county-owned ski resort; *Curtis Publishing Co. v. Butts* (1967) and *Associated Press v. Walker* (1967) included "public figures" as well as public officials in the category of those in whose affairs the general public had a special interest; *Time, Inc. v. Hill* (1967) found a privilege to disclose "private" but newsworthy information.

The defamation cases showed the tendency of the equality principle to expand once set in motion: it seemed hard to distinguish different rules for public officials, public figures, and matters of public interest. Such was also true in the area of obscenity. Once the Court recognized, as it did in ROTH V. UNITED STATES (1957), that First Amendment concerns were relevant in obscenity cases, and yet a core of unprotected expression remained, it was forced to define obscenity. Thirteen obscenity cases between 1957 and 1968 produced fifty-five separate opinions from the Justices, but the meaning of "obscene" for constitutional purposes was not made much clearer. Some Justices, such as Black and Douglas, decided that obscene speech was entitled to as much constitutional protection as any other speech, but a shifting majority of the Court continued to deny protection for expressions that, by one standard or another, could be deemed "obscene." Among the criteria announced by Court majorities for labeling a work "obscene" was that it appeal to a "prurient interest," and that it be "patently offensive" and "utterly without redeeming social value." Justice Stewart, in JACOBELLIS V. OHIO (1964), announced a different criterion: "I know [obscenity] when I see it." Eventually, after *Redrup v. New York* (1967), the Court began to reverse summarily all obscenity convictions whenever five Justices, for whatever reason, adjudged a work not to be obscene.

A final area of unprotected expression involved the FIGHTING WORDS doctrine of CHAPLINSKY V. NEW HAMPSHIRE (1942). A series of Warren Court cases, including *Edwards v. South Carolina* (1963), *Gregory v. Chicago* (1969) and even *New York Times v. Sullivan,* with its language about "vehement, caustic, and sometimes unpleasantly sharp attacks on government and public officials," may have reduced *Chaplinsky* to insignificance.

The pattern of First Amendment decisions, taken with its opinions on race relations and reapportionment, not only demonstrated the Warren Court's shifting conceptions of equality but stamped it in the popular mind as a "liberal" Court. Liberalism has been identified, in the years after World War II, with support for affirmative government and protection of civil rights; the Warren Court was notable for its efforts to insure that interventionist government and civil libertarianism could coexist. But in so doing the Warren Court redefined the locus of interventionist government in America. *Brown v. Board of Education* was a classic example. Congress and the state legislatures were not taking sufficient action to preserve the rights of blacks, so the Court intervened to scrutinize their conduct and, where necessary, to compel them to act. This role for the Court was a major change from that performed by its predecessors. "Liberal" judging in the early twentieth century, according to such defenders of interventionist government as Felix Frankfurter and LOUIS D. BRANDEIS, meant judicial self-restraint: the Supreme Court was to *avoid* scrutiny of state and federal legislation whose purpose was to aid disadvantaged persons. The Warren Court eschewed that role to become the principal interventionist branch of government in the 1950s and 1960s.

In addition to its decisions in race relations and reapportionment, two other areas of Warren Court activity helped augment its public reputation as a "liberal" Court. The first area was CRIMINAL PROCEDURE: here the Court virtually rewrote the laws of the states to conform them to its understanding of the Constitution's requirements. The most important series of its criminal procedure decisions, from a doctrinal perspective, were the INCORPORATION DOCTRINE cases, where the Court struggled with the question of whether, and to what extent, the due process clause of the FOURTEENTH AMENDMENT incorporates procedural protections in the Bill of Rights, making those protections applicable against the states. The Warren Court began a process of "selective incorporation" of Bill of Rights safeguards, applying particular protections in given cases but refusing to endorse the incorporation doctrine in its entirety. This process produced some landmark decisions, notably MAPP V. OHIO (1961), which applied FOURTH AMENDMENT protections against illegal SEARCHES AND SEIZURES to state trials, and BENTON V. MARYLAND (1969), which held that the Fifth Amendment's DOUBLE JEOPARDY guarantee applied to the states. Other important "incorporation" cases were GRIFFIN V. CALIFORNIA (1965), maintaining a RIGHT AGAINST SELF-INCRIMINATION; MALLOY V. HOGAN (1964), applying the Fifth Amendment's self-incrimination privilege to state proceedings; and DUNCAN V. LOUISIANA (1968), incorporating the Sixth Amendment's right to TRIAL BY JURY in criminal cases.

A major consequence of selective incorporation was that fewer criminal convictions were obtained in state trials. Particularly damaging to state prosecutors were the decisions in *Mapp* and *Mallory,* which eliminated from state court trials illegally secured evidence and coerced statements of incrimination. The Court also tightened the requirements for police conduct during the incarceration of criminal suspects. *Mallory v. United States* (1957) insisted that criminal defendants be brought before a magistrate prior to being interrogated. MIRANDA V. ARIZONA (1966) announced a series of constitutional "warnings" that the police were required to give persons whom they had taken into custody. *Miranda* had been preceded by another significant case, ESCOBEDO V. ILLINOIS (1964), which had required that a lawyer be present during police investigations if a suspect requested one. Further, the landmark case of GIDEON V. WAINWRIGHT (1963) had insured that all persons suspected of crimes could secure the services of a lawyer if they desired such, whether they could afford them or not.

The result of this activity by the Warren Court in the area of criminal procedure was that nearly every stage of a POLICE INTERROGATION was fraught with constitutional complexities. The decisions, taken as a whole, seemed to be an effort to buttress the position of persons suspected of crimes by checking the power of the police: some opinions, such as *Miranda,* were explicit in stating that goal. By intervening in law enforcement proceedings to protect the rights of allegedly disadvantaged persons—a high percentage of criminals in the 1960s were poor and black—the Warren Court Justices were acting as liberal policymakers.

Church and state cases were another area in which the Court demonstrated its liberal sensibility, to the concern of many observers. Affirmative state action to promote religious values in the public schools—heretofore an aspect of America's educational heritage—was likely to be struck down as a violation of the establishment clause. In ENGEL V. VITALE (1962) the Court struck down nondenominational prayer readings in New York public schools. A year after *Engel* the Court also invalidated a Pennsylvania law that required reading from the Bible in ABINGTON TOWNSHIP SCHOOL DISTRICT V. SCHEMPP (1963) and a Maryland law that required recitation of the Lord's Prayer in *Murrary v. Curlett* (1963). (See RELIGION IN PUBLIC SCHOOLS.) In *McGowan v. Maryland* (1961), however, the Court permitted the state to impose SUNDAY CLOSING LAWS. Chief Justice Warren, for the Court, distinguished between laws with a religious purpose and laws "whose present purpose and effect" was secular, even though they were originally "motivated by religious forces." The Court invoked *McGowan* in a subsequent case, BOARD OF EDUCATION V. ALLEN (1968), which sustained a New York law providing for the loaning of textbooks from public to parochial schools.

Liberalism, as practiced by the Warren Court, produced a different institutional posture from earlier "reformist" judicial perspectives. As noted, liberalism required that the Court be both an activist governmental institution and a defender of minority rights. This meant that unlike previously "activist" Courts, such as the Courts of the late nineteenth and early twentieth century, its beneficiaries would be non-elites, and unlike previously "reformist" Courts, such as the Court of the late 1930s and 1940s, it would assume a scrutinizing rather than a passive stance toward the actions of other branches of government. Had the Warren Court retained either of these former roles, *Brown, Baker v. Carr,* and *Miranda* would likely not have been decided as they were. These decisions all offended entrenched elites and required modifications of existing governmental practices. In so deciding these cases the Warren Court was assuming that activism by the judiciary was required in order to produce liberal results. With this assumption came a mid-twentieth-century fusion of affirmative governmental action and protection for CIVIL LIBERTIES.

Maintaining a commitment to liberal theory while at the same time modifying its precepts required some analytical refinements in order to reconcile the protection of civil liberties with claims based on affirmative governmental action. In *Brown* the desires of some whites and some blacks to have a racially integrated educational experience conflicted with the desires of some whites and some blacks to limit their educational experiences to persons of their own race. The Court chose to prefer the former desire, basing its judgment on a theory of the educational process that minimized the relevance of race. That theory then became a guiding assumption for the Court's subsequent decisions in the race relations area.

Similar sets of intermediate distinctions between goals of liberal theory were made in other major cases. In the REAPPORTIONMENT cases the distinction was between REPRESENTATION based on population, a claim put forth by a disadvantaged minority, and other forms of proportional representation that had been endorsed by legislative majorities. The Court decided to prefer the former claim as more democratic and then made the one-person, one-vote principle the basis of its subsequent decisions. In the school prayer cases the distinction was between the choice of a majority to ritualize the recognition of a public deity in the public school and the choice of a minority to deny that recognition as out of place. The Court decided to prefer the latter choice as more libertarian. In the criminal procedure cases the distinction was between a majoritarian decision to protect the public against crime by advantaging law enforcement personnel in their encounters with persons suspected of committing crimes, and the claims of such persons that they were being unfairly disadvantaged. The Court chose to prefer the latter claims as being more consistent with principles of equal justice.

When the Warren Court reached the end of its tenure, liberalism clearly did not merely mean deference toward the decisions of democratic and representative bodies of government. It meant deference toward these decisions only if they promoted the goals of liberal policy: equality, fairness, protection of civil rights, support for disadvantaged persons. Under this model of liberal policymaking, the Supreme Court was more concerned with achieving enlightened results than it was with the constitutional process by which these results were reached. Liberalism and judicial activism went hand in hand.

As it became clear that the Court's activism was designed to promote a modified version of liberalism, the Court became vulnerable to public dissatisfaction with liberal policies. Such dissatisfaction emerged in the 1970s. The internal contradictions of liberalism

became exposed in such areas as AFFIRMATIVE AC-
TION in higher education and forced busing in primary education, and the saving distinctions made by
the Court in earlier cases appeared as naked policy
choices whose legitimacy was debatable. If affirmative
preference, based on race, for one class of applicants
to an institution of higher learning results in disadvantage to other classes, equality of condition has not
been achieved and equality of educational opportunity has been undermined. If some families are compelled to send their children to schools where they
are racial minorities in order to achieve "racial balance" throughout the school system, the resulting
"balance" may well disadvantage more people than
it advantages. Equality and social justice have turned
out to be more complicated concepts than mid-twentieth-century liberalism assumed.

The egalitarianism and the liberalism of the Warren
Court paled in significance when compared to its activism. If contemporary America has become a "liti-
gious society," as it is commonly portrayed, the Warren Court helped set in motion such trends. Social
issues have habitually been transformed into legal
questions in America, but the Warren Court seemed
to welcome such a transformation, finding constitutional issues raised in contexts as diverse as reapportionment and prayers in the public schools. As the
Court created new sources of constitutional protection, numerous persons sought to make themselves
the beneficiaries. Sometimes the Court went out of
its way to help the organizations litigating a case, as
in the civil rights area. The result was that the lower
courts and the Supreme Court became "activist" institutions—repositories of grievances, scrutinizers of the
conduct of other branches of government, havens for
the disadvantaged.

In the academic community, Warren Court activism was from the first regarded as more controversial
than Warren Court egalitarianism. The reason was
the prominence in academic circles of a two-pronged
theory of JUDICIAL REVIEW, one prong of which
stressed the necessity of grounding judicial decisions,
in the area of constitutional law, in textually supportable principles of general applicability, and the other
prong of which resurrected Frankfurter's conception
of a limited, deferential role for the Court as a lawmaking institution. The Warren Court, according to academic critics, repeatedly violated the theory's dual
standards. Decisions like *Brown v. Board, Baker v.
Carr*, GRISWOLD V. CONNECTICUT (1965), a case discovering a RIGHT OF PRIVACY in the Constitution that
was violated by statutes forbidding the use of BIRTH
CONTROL pills, and HARPER V. VIRGINIA BOARD OF

Elections (1966), a case invalidating POLL TAX requirements on voting as violating the EQUAL PROTECTION
clause because such requirements conditioned VOT-
ING RIGHTS on wealth, had not been sufficiently
grounded in constitutional doctrine. There was no evidence that the Fourteenth Amendment was intended
to reach segregated schools and there were no judicial
decisions supporting that position. The Constitution
did not single out for protection a right to vote, let
alone a right to have one's vote weighed equally with
the votes of others. "Privacy" was nowhere mentioned
in the constitutional text. The framers of the Constitution had assumed a variety of suffrage restrictions,
including ones based on wealth. In short, leading Warren Court decisions were not based on "neutral principles" of constitutional law.

Nor had the Court been mindful, critics felt, of
its proper lawmaking posture in a democratic society
where it was a conspicuously nondemocratic institution. In *Brown* it had ostensibly substituted its wisdom
for that of Congress and several Southern states. In
Baker it had forced legislatures to reapportion themselves even when a majority of a state's voters had
signified their intention to staff one house of the legislature on grounds other than one person, one vote.
In *Engel v. Vitale* it had told the public schools that
they could not have government-formulated compulsory prayers, even though the vast majority of school
officials and parents desired them. It had fashioned
codes of criminal procedure for the police, ignoring
Congress's abortive efforts in that direction. It had
decided, after more than 200 years of defamation law,
that the entire area needed to be reconsidered in
light of the First Amendment.

A role for the Court as a deferential, principled
decision maker was, however, not sacrosanct. Few Supreme Courts had assumed such a role in the past.
All of the "great cases" in American constitutional
history could be said to have produced activist decisions: MARBURY V. MADISON (1803), establishing the
power of judicial review; MCCULLOCH V. MARYLAND
(1819) and GIBBONS V. OGDEN (1824), delineating the
scope of the federal commerce power; DRED SCOTT
V. SANDFORD (1857), legitimizing SLAVERY IN THE
TERRITORIES; the LEGAL TENDER CASES, deciding
the constitutionality of legal tender notes; POLLOCK
V. FARMERS LOAN AND TRUST (1895), declaring an
income tax unconstitutional; LOCHNER V. NEW YORK
(1905), scuttling state hours and wages legislation;
UNITED STATES V. BUTLER (1936), invalidating a major portion of the New Deal's administrative structure.
Activism was an ancient judicial art.

The Warren Court's activism differed from other

Courts' versions principally not because its reasoning was more specious or its grasp of power more presumptuous but because its beneficiaries were different. Previous activist decisions had largely benefited entrenched elites, whether slaveowners, entrepreneurs, "combinations of capital," or businesses that sought to avoid government regulation. The activist decisions of the Warren Court benefited blacks, disadvantaged suburban voters, atheists, criminals, pornographers, and the poor. The Warren Court's activism facilitated social change rather than preserving the status quo. The critics of the Court had forgotten that the role they espoused for the judiciary had been created in order to facilitate change and promote the interests of the disadvantaged. In the 1950s and 1960s the "democratic" institutions charged with that responsibility had become unresponsive, so the Warren Court had acted in their stead. It was ironic that the same critics who were shocked at the Court of the 1930s' resistance to the New Deal should protest against a Court that was reaching the results they had then sought.

Activism was the principal basis of the Court's controversiality; egalitarianism its dominant instinctual reaction; liberalism its guiding political philosophy. The combination of these ingredients, plus the presence of some judicial giants, gave the Warren Court a prominence and a visibility that are not likely to be surpassed for some time. But even though countless persons in the American legal profession today were shaped by Warren Court decisions, one can see the Warren Court receding into history. That Court seemed to have been led, in the final analysis, by a conception of American life that appeared vindicated by the first fifty years of twentieth-century experience. That conception held that American society was continually progressing toward a nobler and brighter and more enlightened future. As Earl Warren wrote in a passage that appears on his tombstone:

Where there is injustice, we should correct it;
where there is poverty, we should eliminate it;
where there is corruption, we should stamp it out;
where there is violence, we should punish it;
where there is neglect, we should provide care;
where there is war, we should restore peace;
and wherever corrections are achieved we should add them permanently to our storehouse of treasures.

In that passage appears the Warren Court sensibility: a sensibility dedicated to the active pursuit of ideals that have seemed less tangible and achievable with the years.

G. EDWARD WHITE

Bibliography

BICKEL, ALEXANDER 1970 *The Supreme Court and the Idea of Progress.* New York: Harper & Row.
BLACK, CHARLES 1970 The Unfinished Business of the Warren Court. *University of Washington Law Review* 46:3–45.
COX, ARCHIBALD 1968 *The Warren Court.* Cambridge, Mass.: Harvard University Press.
KURLAND, PHILIP 1970 *Politics, the Constitution, and the Warren Court.* Chicago: University of Chicago Press.
LEVY, LEONARD W.,ed. 1972 *The Supreme Court under Earl Warren.* New York: Quadrangle Books.
MCCLOSKEY, ROBERT 1960 *The American Supreme Court.* Chicago: University of Chicago Press.
WECHSLER, HERBERT 1959 Toward Neutral Principles of Constitutional Law. *Harvard Law Review* 73:1–23.
WHITE, G. EDWARD 1976 *The American Judicial Tradition.* New York: Oxford University Press.
—— 1982 *Earl Warren: A Public Life.* New York: Oxford University Press.

WARTH v. SELDIN

See: *Simon v. Eastern Kentucky Welfare Rights Organization*

WASHINGTON, BUSHROD
(1762–1829)

Bushrod Washington served on the United States Supreme Court for thirty-one years, but he did not hand down many important decisions. Lacking the analytical sweep of JOHN MARSHALL and the erudition and energy of JOSEPH STORY, he invariably supported their opinions which strengthened the power of the central government and encouraged the development of the economy. In fact, he was so closely allied with Chief Justice Marshall that another Justice on that Court, WILLIAM JOHNSON of South Carolina, observed that the two "are commonly estimated as a single judge."

Washington was well connected by birth. His mother came from a prominent Virginia family and his father, John, was a particularly close brother of GEORGE WASHINGTON. He graduated from the College of William and Mary in 1778 and served in the Continental Army. After the war he studied law in Philadelphia under JAMES WILSON. Returning to Virginia in 1787, he was admitted to the bar and elected to the Virginia state ratifying convention, where he supported the adoption of the United States Constitution. Following this he practiced law in Richmond, where he developed a reputation for being diligent and extremely knowledgeable. Many young men, including HENRY CLAY, came to read law under his direction. During the 1790s he joined the Federalist Party, and in 1798 JOHN ADAMS appointed him to the Supreme Court. A short time later, as the "favorite nephew" of the former President, he became executor of Washington's will and inherited Mount Vernon and his uncle's public and private papers, which he made available to Marshall for his *Life of George Washington.*

Bushrod Washington was particularly effective and conscientious in the performance of his circuit-riding duties, especially when he presided over jury trials. His tact and sense of fair play allowed him to enforce the Sedition Act of 1798 in a number of cases without engaging in the partisan politics that made SAMUEL CHASE and WILLIAM PATERSON so controversial. His most famous circuit court decision came in the case *United States v. Bright* (1809). This was the TREASON trial of a general of the Pennsylvania state militia who had been formally authorized to resist the United States Supreme Court's decision in *United States v. Peters* (1809). Following a confrontation with a federal marshal, and after President JAMES MADISON threatened to use force, the state eventually backed down, whereupon Bright and several other officers were arrested, tried, and convicted. (Madison eventually pardoned them on humanitarian grounds.) Bushrod Washington handled the trial, which took place in Philadelphia amid a highly charged atmosphere, with great skill, maintaining both decorum and the authority of the federal government. Sentencing Bright, he declared, "A State has no constitutional power . . . to employ force to resist the execution of a decree of a federal court, though such decree is deemed to have been beyond the JURISDICTION of the Court to make. . . ."

Several other decisions rendered by Bushrod Washington are of interest. In a concurring opinion in DARTMOUTH COLLEGE V. WOODWARD (1819) he tried to reign in some of the implications of Marshall's more sweeping decision. In GREEN V. BIDDLE (1823) he handed down what proved to be an unenforceable decision invalidating various Kentucky statutes adopted to protect settlers from absentee landlords. Finally, in OGDEN V. SAUNDERS (1827), he openly broke with Marshall, abandoned his own earlier circuit court decision in *Golden v. Prince* (1814), and declared that a state BANKRUPTCY ACT that had a prospective application did not violate the CONTRACT CLAUSE.

Bushrod Washington died in Philadelphia on November 26, 1829.

RICHARD E. ELLIS

Bibliography

BLAUSTEIN, ALBERT P. and MERSKY, ROY M. 1969 Bushrod Washington. Pages 243–257 in Leon Friedman and Fred L. Israel, eds., *Justices of the Supreme Court, 1789–1969.* New York: Chelsea House.

WASHINGTON, GEORGE
(1732–1799)

The people of the United States are indebted to no man so much as they are to George Washington. And the debt extends to his role in the creation of the American Constitution. As the general who led the revolutionary armies to victory and so vindicated American independence, as one of the few men who had traveled in virtually every part of the United States, including the vast Western wilderness, and as a leading citizen of northern Virginia, Washington was actively involved in the movement of affairs that culminated in the CONSTITUTIONAL CONVENTION OF 1787. When the Convention met, he became its presiding officer. During the controversy over the RATIFICATION OF THE CONSTITUTION, the opposition to a strong executive was overcome by the universal assumption that Washington would be the first man to hold the office. When the Constitution was ratified and Washington did become President, he self-consciously seized the opportunity to set precedents for the conduct of governmental affairs. And when, after two terms in that office he handed over the reins of executive authority, he did so in perfect constitutional order and retired to his country seat.

The third son of a prosperous planter, Washington learned the surveying trade in his teens, and as a surveyor he traveled widely in the area west of the Appalachian Mountains. At twenty-one he was appointed to major in the Virginia militia, and when the French and Indian War broke out in 1754 he was promoted to lieutenant colonel and placed second in command of a regiment dispatched to the Ohio Valley. On his colonel's death, Washington took command and managed, without supplies, funds, competent subordinates, or trained noncommissioned officers and troops, to achieve initial military success. He was subsequently made an aide to the British commanding general, and in 1755, at the age of twenty-three, was promoted to colonel and made commander-in-chief of all Virginia forces, the highest ranking American military officer.

In 1759, Washington married Martha Custis, the wealthiest widow in Virginia, and, adding her holdings to his own, achieved a financial independence that would subsequently permit him to engage in a career of uncompensated public service. For a decade and a half he lived the life of a gentleman planter, with the attendant civic duties of serving as a justice of the peace and as a member of the House of Burgesses.

In 1769 Washington introduced in the House of Burgesses a series of resolutions (drafted by his friend and neighbor GEORGE MASON) denying the right of the British Parliament to tax the colonies and initiating the first ASSOCIATION. After passage of the Intolerable Acts in 1774, Washington introduced in the house the Fairfax County Resolves closing Virginia's trade with Britain. He was also elected a delegate to the FIRST CONTINENTAL CONGRESS, which he attended in military uniform.

The Revolutionary War began in Spring 1775 when the Massachusetts militia forcibly resisted the attempt of British troops to seize its weapons and supplies. In June, on the motion of JOHN ADAMS, the CONTINENTAL CONGRESS adopted the Massachusetts militia as the Continental Army and appointed Washington commander-in-chief. The war lasted eight and one-half years, and Washington was the American commander for the whole period. The war was not an unrelieved military success on the American side, but the commander did learn to deal with Congress and with foreign allies, and he became, in his own person, the symbol of American national unity. Just before resigning his commission in 1783, he resisted the suggestion that the army, which had been shamefully left unpaid, should overthrow the Congress and establish its own government.

After his return to private life in 1784, Washington devoted his time to management of his property in Virginia and in the Ohio Valley. He became president of the Potomac Company, which had as its object the development of the Potomac River as a navigable waterway. And he engaged in a wide correspondence, always urging, in letters dealing with politics, the strengthening of the Union and an increase in the powers of Congress under the ARTICLES OF CONFEDERATION. In March 1785 he was host to a conference of commissioners from Maryland and Virginia that was supposed to discuss the navigation of the Potomac River but that, in the event, called for a broader conference—the Annapolis Convention—that ultimately led to the Constitutional Convention of 1787.

Pleading pressures of financial reverses and ill health, Washington was reluctant to accept election as a delegate to the Convention, but he did so at the repeated urging of JAMES MADISON and EDMUND RANDOLPH. At Philadelphia he was unanimously elected president of the Convention, although, as most of the debates were conducted in a committee of the whole house, he did not actually have to preside on most occasions. Although Washington did not take an active part in the recorded debates of the Convention, his attendance and his signature on the document as president of the Convention were offered as a guarantee of the result.

The first ELECTORAL COLLEGE under the new Constitution was elected in January 1789, and every member cast one of his two votes for George Washington. Washington learned of the result on April 14. His journey from Virginia to New York took a week, and involved parades and ceremonies in every town he passed through along the way; the affection and gratitude of the population were genuine, and Washington's task was to retain them while directing the executive affairs of the government.

Following his inauguration on April 30, Washington immediately began the business of running the executive branch of government. Everything he did set a precedent, not only for America but for the world, because his position as a republican chief executive was unique. Attention had to be given to such matters as the form of address and the conduct of social events so as to insure both the dignity of the federal executive and the republicanism of the country.

Every act in the process of governing had to be done a first time: the performance of each executive task, however routine, set the pattern for the permanent conduct of the presidency. The first bill to pass the new Congress was presented for Washington's signature on June 1: he affixed his signature, and the first statute under the Constitution became law. The first occasion for negotiating a treaty arose in August; in strict compliance with Article II, section 2, Washington appeared in person before the Senate to ask for ADVICE AND CONSENT and, when the Senate referred the matter to committee he stalked out. Since that day, Presidents have submitted treaties to the Senate after they are negotiated, but no President has asked for the Senate's advice before negotiations begin.

Statutes creating the three executive departments of state, war, and treasury were enacted during the summer of 1789. Washington appointed his fellow Virginian THOMAS JEFFERSON to be the first secretary of state, his wartime chief of artillery, General Henry Knox, to be secretary of war, and his former aide, Colonel ALEXANDER HAMILTON, to be secretary of the treasury. Although the Constitution provides only that the President may require written opinions from the principal executive officers, and that only as to their peculiar duties, Washington began the practice of meeting regularly with the three secretaries and the attorney general, Edmund Randolph, to discuss affairs of state generally. From this practice has come the notion of the American CABINET, as well as the accepted opinion that the heads of the executive departments are responsible primarily to the President, and not to Congress, for their official conduct.

But Washington had to appoint not only his cabinet officers but also every official in the executive branch down to customs inspectors and lighthouse keepers. Although the Constitution permitted Congress to vest inferior appointments in the chiefs of the departments, Congress did not immediately do so. Washington was besieged with applications from would-be federal bureaucrats. Indeed, had Congress desired to hamstring the President it might have been enough just to leave all federal appointments in his hands.

Besides the cabinet officers, the most important appointees were the Justices of the Supreme Court. The JUDICIARY ACT OF 1789 provided for six Justices. Washington nominated his friend JOHN JAY, who had been secretary of foreign affairs in the old government, to be Chief Justice. The other five nominees were drawn from different states, both to facilitate their performance of circuit duty and to make the Court representative of the whole country. Among them were three men who had been Washington's fellow delegates to the Constitutional Convention, JAMES WILSON, JOHN RUTLEDGE, and JOHN BLAIR. (See SUPREME COURT, 1789–1801.)

Once the machinery was in place, the issue became what policy the new government would follow. Washington, who had relied on Congressman James Madison for the machinery, turned to Secretary of the Treasury Hamilton for the policy. Hamilton's program was set forth in a series of reports submitted over the next two years. The program called for an alliance between the federal government and the wealthier citizens to promote the unity and prosperity of the nation. The Hamiltonian program provoked a controversy over the proper interpretation of constitutional provisions conferring power on the national government. Hamilton argued for BROAD CONSTRUCTION; Jefferson, for STRICT CONSTRUCTION. The arguments were reduced to writing at Washington's request to help him to decide whether to sign or to veto the BANK OF THE UNITED STATES ACT (1790). Washington, convinced by Hamilton's doctrine of IMPLIED POWERS, signed the act.

The French Revolution of 1789 provoked a further division between Washington's chief advisers. Most Americans initially sympathized with the French overthrow of the monarchy and the attempt to establish a republican form of government. But as the French Revolution became more extreme and expansionary, and as the conservative states of Europe mobilized to resist it, opinion became divided. Jefferson and his supporters continued to sympathize with the revolution, while Hamilton and his allies were inclined to side with the embattled British.

By 1793, the Wars of the French Revolution had become global, and American interests, particularly American shipping, were suffering the effects. Washington, with the assent of his whole cabinet, issued a PROCLAMATION OF NEUTRALITY in April 1793, warning American citizens to refrain from becoming involved on either side. Hamilton published a series of newspaper articles asserting, among other things, that the proclamation had been necessary because of the active support of France on the part of the Jeffersonians. Madison, replying in his own newspaper essays, claimed that Washington, by his unilateral issuance of the proclamation, had usurped the power of Congress to declare war and of the Senate to share in treaty making.

The first party lines in American politics under the Constitution had been drawn, and drawn on constitutional grounds. Jefferson resigned from the cabinet at the end of 1793. Thereafter, Washington's was a "Federalist" administration, with Jefferson, Madison, and the "Republicans" in opposition.

The WHISKEY REBELLION of 1794 presented the first organized resistance to the national government. Western Pennsylvania farmers, upset by an excise on whiskey that seemed unduly to burden their section of the country, threatened to use force to impede collection of the tax. Washington called 15,000 militiamen into federal service and himself set out to command the expedition. The rebellion was ultimately put down without bloodshed, and when two rebel leaders were subsequently convicted of TREASON, Washington pardoned them.

The administration's foreign policy also led to controversy at about the same time. Chief Justice Jay had been sent to Britain to negotiate a settlement of certain continuing difficulties in relations between the two countries. JAY'S TREATY contained many provisions favorable to British interests, and apparently detrimental to the economic interests of some regions of the United States, especially the South and West. The treaty also provoked constitutional controversy about the operation of the TREATY POWER. For example, would the Senate be required to advise and consent to the treaty as it was presented, or could the Senate amend a treaty? And could the President and the Senate enter into treaty commitments that would involve the expenditure of funds without the concurrence of the House of Representatives whose agreement was required for the appropriation of the funds? The treaty was approved in a partisan vote, but with a reservation suspending operation of certain objectionable provisions.

Washington chose not to seek a third term as President in the election of 1796. He was dismayed and distressed by the bitterness of the partisan rivalries that had grown up among men who had once been close colleagues, and he himself attempted always to remain above the partisan fray. WASHINGTON'S FARE-WELL ADDRESS to his countrymen contained his strictures against the spirit of party, as well as his advice on foreign affairs and on public morality.

Even after his retirement to his estate at Mount Vernon, Washington could not escape either public service or partisan intrigue. When war with France seemed inevitable in 1798, President JOHN ADAMS nominated and the Senate unanimously confirmed Washington as COMMANDER-IN-CHIEF. There immediately followed a scramble among Federalist military men for the subordinate general officer positions. Washington supported Hamilton, who ultimately became second in command. Under the circumstances it is not surprising that Washington thought of the Republicans, who had been pro-French, as dangerous men and that he supported the ALIEN AND SEDITION ACTS.

Nevertheless, when Washington died in 1799 he was eulogized by Federalists and Republicans alike. More than any other individual, Washington was responsible for America's being independent, adopting the Constitution, and having a functioning republican government.

DENNIS J. MAHONEY

Bibliography

COOKE, JACOB E. 1987 Organizing the National Government. In Levy, Leonard W., and Mahoney, Dennis J., eds., *The Constitution: A History of Its Framing and Ratification.* New York: Macmillan.
FLEXNER, JAMES THOMAS 1965–1972 *George Washington.* 4 Vols. Boston: Little, Brown.
FREEMAN, DOUGLAS SOUTHALL 1948–1957 *George Washington.* 7 Vols. New York: Scribner's.
MARSHALL, JOHN (1804–1807)1925 *The Life of George Washington.* 5 Vols. New York: Wm. H. Wise & Co.
MATTESON, DAVID M. 1970 *The Organization of the Government under the Constitution.* New York: Da Capo Press.

WASHINGTON v. DAVIS
426 U.S. 229 (1976)

This landmark decision concerns the relevance of a decision maker's motives in EQUAL PROTECTION cases. Black candidates for the Washington, D.C., police force alleged that the District's selection criteria had an adverse discriminatory effect upon the employment prospects of minorities and that the effect violated the FOURTEENTH AMENDMENT's equal protection clause and ANTIDISCRIMINATION LEGISLATION. In an opinion by Justice BYRON R. WHITE, the Supreme Court held that discriminatory effects, standing alone, are insufficient to establish an equal protection violation. Proof of purposeful discrimination is necessary. The Court also rejected the candidates' statutory claim. In an opinion that did not address the constitutional question, Justice WILLIAM J. BRENNAN, joined by Justice THURGOOD MARSHALL, dissented from the Court's disposition of the statutory issue. In a concurring opinion, Justice JOHN PAUL STEVENS discussed the relationship between discriminatory effects and proof of discriminatory intent and articulated his reasons for rejecting the statutory claim.

In settling a long-standing controversy over whether a decision maker's motives may constitute the basis for an equal protection claim, the Court climbed two interesting doctrinal hills. Prior to *Davis*, cases such as *Whitcomb v. Chavis* (1971) and *White v. Regester* (1973) expressly had suggested that unintentional disproportionate effects on a minority may constitute the basis for an equal protection claim. Justice White's opinion ignores these precedents but warns against the broad consequences of such a HOLDING. Such a rule "would raise serious questions about, and perhaps invalidate, a whole range of tax, welfare, public service, regulatory, and licensing statutes that may be more burdensome to the poor and to the average black than to the more affluent white."

In addition, contrary to *Davis*'s holding, a line of opinions dating back to FLETCHER v. PECK (1810) and reaffirmed in UNITED STATES v. O'BRIEN (1968) and PALMER V. THOMPSON (1971), clearly had stated that legislators' motives may not form the basis of constitutional attacks on statutes. Without alluding to all of the relevant precedents, the Court reinterpreted *Palmer* and suggested that some of its language had constituted mere OBITER DICTA.

As a practical matter, *Davis,* when combined with subsequent similar cases such as ARLINGTON HEIGHTS V. METROPOLITAN HOUSING DEVELOPMENT CORP. (1977) and MOBILE V. BOLDEN (1980), curtailed litigants' ability to bring successful equal protection claims. Proof of intentional discrimination is difficult to obtain and judges are reluctant to deem officials intentional wrongdoers. Indeed, it was six years after *Davis* before the Court, in *Rogers v. Lodge* (1982), sustained a finding of intentional discrimination in a racial equal protection case.

THEODORE EISENBERG

WASHINGTON v. TEXAS

See: Compulsory Process; Evidence

WASHINGTON'S FAREWELL ADDRESS
(September 17, 1796)

When President GEORGE WASHINGTON decided, in the summer of 1796, not to seek a third term, he published an address to the American people embodying his advice on how to insure the survival of the new constitutional order. The first draft was prepared by Washington himself; the final version was drafted under Washington's direction by ALEXANDER HAMILTON, incorporating suggestions from JAMES MADISON and JOHN JAY.

The first, and longest, section of the address comprises an encomium of the federal union and a warning against the dangers of factionalism, and especially of sectionalism. Washington urged that Americans regard the Union as "the support of your tranquility at home, your peace abroad, of your safety, of your prosperity, of that very liberty which you so highly prize." The central section of the address commends religion as a support for free government. Anything that weakened religious belief, he argued, would corrupt public morals, undermine the efficacy of oaths, and threaten the national capacity for self-government. The final section of the address contains Wash-

ington's advice on FOREIGN AFFAIRS and defense. Washington opposed permanent alliances and standing armies as incompatible with constitutional democracy.

Advice in the address concerning specific constitutional questions includes Washington's deprecation of the "spirit of encroachment" that would subvert the SEPARATION OF POWERS and his admonition against hasty adoption of constitutional amendments.

DENNIS J. MAHONEY

Bibliography

EIDELBERG, PAUL 1974 *A Discourse on Statesmanship: The Design and Transformation of the American Polity.* Chicago: University of Illinois Press.

WATERGATE AND THE CONSTITUTION

The Watergate scandal, starting with an illegal break-in at Democratic National Committee headquarters in June 1972 and ending with President GERALD R. FORD pardoning RICHARD M. NIXON in September 1974, produced one of the most significant constitutional crises in modern times. It raised a number of unsettling issues central to the constitutional structure of SEPARATION OF POWERS.

The two major constitutional issues Watergate brought into focus were EXECUTIVE PRIVILEGE and the scope of the IMPEACHMENT power. In September 1972 a GRAND JURY indicted the Watergate burglars but the Justice Department closed the investigation despite evidence of a wider conspiracy. Following the November election, the Watergate burglary trial began. In it defendants claimed they had been pressured to remain silent and plead guilty; that perjury was committed; and that "others" were involved. Such allegations led to the creation of a Senate Watergate Committee, headed by SAM ERVIN, which began taking testimony, revealing a White House program of political espionage that included Watergate. Witnesses suggested that the President was participating in a coverup and that the President had made tape recordings of conversations in his office. The Ervin Committee attempted to subpoena such tapes, but the President refused to surrender them, claiming executive privilege. The committee then went to the courts, which in two cases (*Nixon v. Sirica,* 1973, and *Senate Select Committee on Presidential Campaign Activities v. Nixon,* 1974, attempted to define the line between a committee's power to compel testimony in order to perform its functions and the need for privacy in presidential communications. A third case, UNITED STATES V. NIXON (1974), arose out of a criminal prosecution of the President's aides. Both the prosecutor and the defense sought to subpoena the tapes, and the President again resisted. Chief Justice WARREN E. BURGER, for a unanimous Supreme Court, conceded a "presumptive privilege" for executive communications, but ruled that respect of the integrity of the judicial process required the courts to weigh any such claim against the importance of assuring the production in court of relevant evidence and ultimately of protecting the system of criminal justice. The Court thus ordered certain tapes produced. Their disclosures, which came at the height of the House of Representatives' impeachment process, demonstrated the President's active complicity in the coverup conspiracy from the first moment. This led Nixon to resign to avoid impeachment for "high crimes and misdemeanors."

The impeachment process was fraught with constitutional difficulties. Nixon's firing of a Senate-approved special prosecutor, given sweeping powers to investigate the Watergate scandal, had produced the initial demands for his impeachment. In October the House Judiciary Committee launched an impeachment inquiry. Questions promptly arose as to what constituted an impeachable offense, and what "other high crimes and misdemeanors" might include. Must these be criminal in nature and intent, or might they be quasi-political, involving gross breach of public trust? Was maladministration impeachable, or must a statutory offense or a serious crime be demonstrated? The President's attorneys argued the latter. The committee staff indicated a President might be removed for "substantial misconduct," not necessarily of specific criminal nature. This controversy was mooted by the revelations of the disputed tapes and by the resignation, but not before the House committee recommended three ARTICLES OF IMPEACHMENT to the House at large. Rejecting two articles dealing with income tax violations and the secret bombing of Cambodia, which raised the question of the extent of presidential emergency power in FOREIGN AFFAIRS, the Committee contended that "Richard M. Nixon warrants impeachment and trial and removal from office" for other charges. These were: that he prevented, obstructed, and impeded the administration of justice; that he repeatedly engaged in conduct violating the constitutional rights of citizens, impairing the due and proper administration of justice and the conduct of lawful inquiries, or contravening the

laws governing agencies of the executive branch and the purposes of these agencies; and that he failed without lawful cause or excuse to produce papers and things as directed by duly authorized subpoenas issued by the Committee on the Judiciary of the House of Representatives. Included as substantiating detail were fourteen examples of interfering or endeavoring to interfere with conduct of investigations by the Department of Justice of the United States, the Federal Bureau of Investigation, the Watergate special prosecutor, and congressional committees; endeavoring to misuse the Central Intelligence Agency; the electronic surveillance of private citizens; the break-in of a psychiatrist's office; and the unlawful campaign financing practices of the Committee to Re-elect the President.

An unresolved constitutional issue arose in September 1974: whether a subsequent President can issue a pardon in the absence of either a conviction or an INDICTMENT. A final question will trouble historians for years: did the Constitution work in Watergate, or did the crisis demonstrate fundamental failures in the governmental system?

PAUL L. MURPHY

Bibliography

KURLAND, PHILIP 1978 Watergate and the Constitution. Chicago: University of Chicago Press.
MILLER, ARTHUR S. 1979 Social Change and Fundamental Law. Westport, Conn.: Greenwood Press.
MURPHY, PAUL L. 1979 Misgovernment by Judiciary? Watergate and the Constitution. Harvard Civil Rights/Civil Liberties Law Review 14:783–799.

WATER POLLUTION CONTROL ACT

See: Environmental Regulation

WATER POWER ACT
41 Stat. 1063 (1920)

The failure to capitalize on the vast water power resources of the country led increasingly, in the early twentieth century, to efforts to develop and regulate unused power on public lands and navigable rivers. After a number of failed attempts at national legislation, Congress finally passed the Water Power Act in 1920.

The act established a Federal Power Commission

(FPC), to be composed of the secretaries of war, agriculture, and interior, with authority to approve water power projects "for the development and improvement of navigation, and for the development, transmission, and utilization of power" on any navigable river or public lands. The act empowered the FPC to license projects for up to fifty years; it also directed preferential treatment for state or municipal projects. The rates charged for the use of water were to include only FPC expenses; moreover, the act required licensees to charge "reasonable, nondiscriminatory and just" rates and prohibited combinations or other agreements to limit output or fix prices. The act stipulated that rate-fixing and regulation be administered according to the procedures outlined in the INTERSTATE COMMERCE ACT.

The Supreme Court approved extensive federal controls in UNITED STATES v. APPALACHIAN ELECTRIC POWER COMPANY (1940).

DAVID GORDON

WATER QUALITY IMPROVEMENT ACT

See: Environmental Regulation

WATKINS v. UNITED STATES
354 U.S. 178 (1957)
SWEEZY v. NEW HAMPSHIRE
354 U.S. 234 (1957)

Watkins, a labor leader called to testify before the House Committee on Un-American Activities, had been told by the union president that he would lose his position if he claimed his RIGHT AGAINST SELF-INCRIMINATION. He thus claimed a FIRST AMENDMENT privilege when he declined to answer the committee's questions about the membership of other people in the Communist party. He also objected that these questions were beyond the scope of the committee's activities. For his refusal to answer, Watkins was convicted of contempt of Congress. The Supreme Court reversed his conviction, 8–1.

Writing for the Court, Chief Justice EARL WARREN rested decision on a narrow point: Watkins had been denied PROCEDURAL DUE PROCESS, for he had not been given a sufficient explanation of the subject of inquiry, and thus could not know whether the committee's questions were "pertinent to the questions under inquiry," as the contempt statute specified. Warren's opinion, however, strongly suggested that the Court would be prepared to confront the whole issue of LEGISLATIVE INVESTIGATIONS into political association. He remarked on the use of such investigations to subject people to public stigma, and the absence in such proceedings of effective protection of procedural fairness. "We have no doubt that there is no congressional power to expose for the sake of exposure," Warren wrote. "Who can define the meaning of 'un-American'?" Justice TOM C. CLARK, the sole dissenter, appeared to object as much to these broad OBITER DICTA as to the actual decision. He complained of the Court's "mischievous curbing of the informing function of Congress."

In *Sweezy*, a COMPANION CASE to *Watkins*, the Court held, 6–2, that a state legislative investigation could not constitutionally compel Sweezy to answer questions about the Progressive party and about a lecture he had given at the University of New Hampshire. Chief Justice Warren wrote a PLURALITY OPINION for four Justices, concluding that Sweezy's contempt conviction violated procedural due process because the state legislature had not clearly authorized the attorney general, who conducted the investigation, to inquire into those subjects. Justice FELIX FRANKFURTER, joined by Justice JOHN MARSHALL HARLAN, concurred, arguing that the state had unconstitutionally invaded Sweezy's FOURTEENTH AMENDMENT liberty—here, his "political autonomy," a plain reference to the First Amendment. Justice Frankfurter used a (for him) familiar BALANCING TEST, but articulated a COMPELLING STATE INTEREST standard for cases of invasions of political privacy. The Frankfurter opinion is notable for its early articulation of the constitutional dimension of ACADEMIC FREEDOM. It also led, the following year, to the Court's explicit recognition of the FREEDOM OF ASSOCIATION in NAACP v. ALABAMA (1958). Justice Clark again dissented, now joined by Justice HAROLD H. BURTON.

A number of members of Congress reacted angrily to these opinions and others decided the same year, such as YATES v. UNITED STATES (1957) and *Jencks v. United States* (1957). (See JENCKS ACT.) Bills were proposed in Congress to limit the Supreme Court's jurisdiction over cases involving controls of subversive activities. In the event, not much "curbing" was done, and in retrospect *Watkins* and *Sweezy* appeared to be no more than trial balloons. Two years later, in BARENBLATT v. UNITED STATES (1959), a majority of the Court backed away from the expected confrontation with Congress.

KENNETH L. KARST

WAYNE, JAMES M.
(1790?–1867)

After service as an elected official and judge in Georgia and as a Jacksonian Democrat in Congress, James Moore Wayne served thirty-two years as an Associate Justice of the United States Supreme Court. Despite this lengthy tenure he produced no significant opinions, though he consistently strove to protect national authority, corporations, and slavery. During the Civil War, his nationalist outlook induced him to remain on the Court as a Unionist.

Wayne, son of a well-to-do Savannah factor and rice planter, was educated at the College of New Jersey (Princeton), read law in New Haven and in his native Savannah, and was admitted to the Georgia bar in 1811. He was a member of the Georgia House of Representatives from 1815 to 1817, mayor of Savannah from 1817 to 1819, and successively judge of a court of common pleas and of the Superior Court. He later served in two state CONSTITUTIONAL CONVENTIONS, the second time as president. In 1829, Wayne was elected to the United States House of Representatives, where he prominently supported ANDREW JACKSON. He promoted Indian removal from his native state, backed Jackson's Bank policies, and stood by the President during the NULLIFICATION Crisis in South Carolina. He was the only member of the Georgia delegation to support the FORCE BILL. In his last term, he became chairman of the Foreign Relations Committee.

Jackson nominated Wayne to take the seat of Justice WILLIAM JOHNSON of South Carolina, and he was confirmed in 1835. Justice BENJAMIN R. CURTIS later called Wayne one of the "most high-toned Federalists on the bench," referring to Wayne's tenacious nationalism. This outlook was most apparent in COMMERCE CLAUSE cases. In the PASSENGER CASES (1849), Wayne was one of a majority that held unconstitutional state statutes regulating the ingress of ship passengers on the ground that insofar as such laws "practically operated as regulations of commerce, or as restraints upon navigation," they were unconstitutional. The power to regulate foreign and INTERSTATE COMMERCE was "exclusively vested in congress." Unlike his fellow Southerner, Chief Justice ROGER B. TANEY, he was not troubled by the implications of this position for the states' control of slavery. Wayne joined in Justice JOHN MCLEAN's nationalist dissent in COOLEY V. BOARD OF WARDENS (1851), arguing that Congress's control of interstate and FOREIGN COMMERCE was exclusive of state power.

The same nationalist spirit produced other opinions upholding federal authority. In *Dobbins v. Erie County* (1842) Wayne struck down a local tax on a federal officer. He was an enthusiastic proponent of federal admiralty jurisdiction, and in *Waring v. Clarke* (1847) he extended that jurisdiction to tidal waters of the Mississippi River well above New Orleans. In *Louisville, Cincinnati, and Charleston Railroad Co. v. Letson* (1844) Wayne rejected a rule, originally fashioned by Chief Justice JOHN MARSHALL, that restricted the access of corporations to federal courts by requiring that for purposes of DIVERSITY JURISDICTION, all their shareholders be citizens of a state different from all parties on the other side. Wayne instead adopted the rule that a corporation's CITIZENSHIP for diversity purposes is derived from the state where it was chartered and where its officers conducted business.

Wayne was sympathetic to corporate investors, as his CONTRACT CLAUSE opinions reveal. He dissented without opinion in WEST RIVER BRIDGE V. DIX (1848), in which the Court permitted a state to use its EMINENT DOMAIN powers to destroy a corporate charter. In the Ohio Bank Tax cases, Wayne consistently voted to strike down state attempts to modify tax exemptions claimed by banks. One of these cases, DODGE V. WOOLSEY (1856), produced what was probably Wayne's most memorable opinion. Condemning the effort of Ohio Democrats to destroy a tax exemption by an amendment to the state constitution, Wayne sermonized: "moral obligations never die. If broken by states and nations, though the terms of reproach are not the same with which we are accustomed to designate the faithlessness of individuals, the violation of justice is not the less."

Wayne was himself a slaveholder and no less dedicated to his section than other southern jurists such as Taney and PETER DANIEL. He considered slavery a vital component of southern society, beyond control of the federal government except for purposes of protection. But, unlike Taney, Wayne remained coolly assured about the constitutional security of slavery, and he was not blinded by the state-sovereignty dogmatism that warped his Chief's opinions in slavery cases. The Constitution itself, Wayne believed, incorporated express protections for slavery's security. In his concurrence in PRIGG V. PENNSYLVANIA (1842) Wayne went along with JOSEPH STORY's assertion that states need not support enforcement of the federal Fugitive Slave Act, but only on the ground that to admit any state role at all would be to invite Northern states to interfere with the capture and rendition of fugitives.

Wayne played a mischievous role in DRED SCOTT v. SANDFORD (1857) though his brief concurring opinion merely endorsed entirely Taney's opinion. Wayne first urged that the Chief Justice write the opinion for the Court's majority rather than Justice SAMUEL NELSON, whose opinion would evade the larger issues in the case by a narrow jurisdictional ruling, and he formally moved that the Court address itself to all issues, not just the jurisdictional ones. Scholars have suggested that Taney's opinion incorporated portions of a draft opinion that Wayne did not submit. Yet Wayne was no fanatic on the subject of slavery. On circuit, he delivered a vigorous jury charge in the trial of officers of the notorious slave ship *Wanderer*, upholding the power of the federal government to hang slavers.

The Civil War forced a severe test of Wayne's conflicting loyalties. After SECESSION, he supported his son's decision to resign his commission in the United States Army and accept appointment as Georgia's adjutant general, but Wayne elected to remain on the federal bench. Georgia retaliated by confiscating his property and declaring him an enemy alien. In 1861, Wayne denied a HABEAS CORPUS petition from a soldier who claimed that ABRAHAM LINCOLN's call for troops was illegal. In conformity with that position, Wayne joined the five-member majority in the PRIZE CASES (1863), upholding the legality of Lincoln's action in imposing a blockade around the seceding states. He wrote for the Court in EX PARTE VALLANDIGHAM (1864), refusing to review the conviction of an Ohio Copperhead congressman by a military commission. In EX PARTE MILLIGAN (1866), where the majority held that Congress could not authorize military commissions for areas outside the theater of war, Wayne joined the four-man minority who argued for congressional discretion in using military commissions. But there are indications that Wayne's Unionist views would not be extrapolated to accept all aspects of Republican Reconstruction. He joined the majority in the TEST OATH CASES (1867), holding state and federal proscriptive oaths unconstitutional. He refused to hold CIRCUIT COURTS in his circuit in areas under military occupation. His death on July 5, 1867, ended his grief at the devastation that secession, war, and Reconstruction had brought to his beloved state.

WILLIAM M. WIECEK

Bibliography

GATELL, FRANK O. 1969 James M. Wayne. In Leon Friedman and Fred L. Israel eds., *The Justices of the United States Supreme Court 1789–1969: Their Lives and Major Opinions.* New York: Chelsea House Publishers.

LAWRENCE, ALEXANDER A. 1943 *James Moore Wayne: Southern Unionist.* Chapel Hill: University of North Carolina Press.

WAYTE v. UNITED STATES
471 U.S.   (1985)

After a presidential proclamation directing young men to register for a possible draft, David Wayte did not register, but wrote letters to government officials stating that he did not intend to do so. These letters went into a Selective Service file of men who had given similar notices or who had been reported by others for failing to register. The government adopted a policy of "passive enforcement" of registration: it would prosecute only men named in this file. Government officials wrote letters warning the men to register or face prosecution, and Federal Bureau of Investigation agents urged Wayte in person to register during a grace period. He refused and was indicted for failure to register. The federal district court dismissed Wayte's indictment, holding that the government had not rebutted his preliminary showing of selective prosecution. The court of appeals reversed, holding that Wayte had not shown that the government had prosecuted him because of his protest. The Supreme Court affirmed, 7–2.

Justice LEWIS F. POWELL wrote the OPINION OF THE COURT. Claims of selective prosecution, he said, must be judged under ordinary EQUAL PROTECTION standards, which, as the Court held in WASHINGTON v. DAVIS (1976), require a showing of intentional discrimination. Here, the government's awareness that "passive enforcement" would fall disproportionately on protesters was an insufficient showing of intent to punish protest. Given the government's policy of urging compliance after receiving notice of failure to register, Wayte was not prosecuted for protesting, but for persisting in refusing registration.

Wayte's FIRST AMENDMENT challenge also focused on the enforcement system's disparate impact on protesters. Applying the formula of UNITED STATES V. O'BRIEN (1968), Justice Powell concluded that "passive enforcement" passed the test. The government interest in national security was important, and unrelated to the suppression of expression; and the enforcement system burdened speech no more than was necessary to secure registration.

Justice THURGOOD MARSHALL dissented, joined by Justice WILLIAM J. BRENNAN, arguing that Wayte had been denied effective opportunity for DISCOVERY of information concerning the motivations of high government officials for prosecuting him. Thus, he could not fully support his claim that the prosecution was designed to punish his protest. The majority dismissed this argument, saying—contrary to the dissenters' view—that Wayte had not presented the issue to the Supreme Court.

KENNETH L. KARST

WEALTH DISCRIMINATION

Wealth discrimination—the state's allocation of resources on the basis of ability to pay—has received the attention of the courts only recently. Sensitivity to the plight of the poor was an outgrowth of the CIVIL RIGHTS movement of the 1960s. Thus, the first constitutional issue raised by EQUAL PROTECTION claims of the poor was whether poverty-based discrimination is analogous to RACIAL DISCRIMINATION for purposes of the applicable STANDARD OF REVIEW.

Advocates of this analogy stress the poor's lack of political power and the public's antipathy to the poor and to programs, such as welfare, enacted to ameliorate poverty. They argue that the Supreme Court should give less deference to legislative judgments when reviewing poverty discrimination claims than it does when reviewing ECONOMIC REGULATIONS challenged by those able to pursue nonjudicial means of redress. However, at no time during the more than quarter of a century since the Court's first decision in this area, GRIFFIN V. ILLINOIS (1956), has a majority of the Court ever embraced the analogy to race for purposes of equal protection review.

The Griffin decision held unconstitutional a state's refusal to provide an INDIGENT convicted criminal defendant with a free transcript necessary to obtain meaningful appellate review. In so holding, Griffin enunciated a potentially expansive principle of "equal justice": "[A] state can no more discriminate on account of poverty than on account of religion, race, or color. . . . There can be no equal justice when the kind of trial [or APPEAL] a man gets depends on the amount of money he has."

Since Griffin, the Supreme Court has struck down poverty-based discrimination in only a few other cases, most notably DOUGLAS V. CALIFORNIA (1963) and BODDIE V. CONNECTICUT (1971). Douglas held unconstitutional a state's refusal to appoint counsel for an indigent seeking appellate review of a criminal conviction; and Boddie held unconstitutional a state's refusal to waive court access fees which deprived an indigent plaintiff of access to the only available forum for obtaining a divorce.

In the vast majority of poverty-based discrimination cases, however, the Supreme Court has treated the poor's claims, whether they involve access to the judicial process itself, equal educational opportunity, or the very means of survival, the same as any other challenged "social and economic" regulation. Thus, the Court has applied the RATIONAL BASIS standard of review to uphold a $50 bankruptcy filing fee against a debtor too poor to pay it; a state financing system that allocated educational resources according to the tax bases of school districts; and an allocation of WELFARE BENEFITS that discriminated on the basis of family size. (See United States v. Kras, 1973; SAN ANTONIO INDEPENDENT SCHOOL DISTRICT V. RODRIGUEZ, 1973; DANDRIDGE V. WILLIAMS, 1971.)

Several reasons may underlie the Court's refusal actively to scrutinize legislation adversely affecting the poor. If the Court holds a payment requirement unconstitutional as applied to the poor, someone must decide who is poor enough to qualify for this affirmative relief. Moreover, such a holding may require the legislative branch to reallocate its budget to provide the funds necessary to pay for what the poor cannot afford, something which the courts are always reluctant to do, especially in times of economic recession.

Another reason for judicial restraint lies in the need for line-drawing. If not all poverty-based inequalities or deprivations are unconstitutional—as surely they are not in a market economy—then the Court must delineate those interests that are sufficiently "vital" or "fundamental" to justify stricter judicial scrutiny when the state allocates such interests through a pricing system that deprives poor people from access to them. Obvious candidates include basic necessities such as food, housing, and other means of subsistence. Beginning with its 1971 decision in Dandridge, however, the Supreme Court consistently has refused to treat any such interests as entitled to a heightened equal protection standard of review. Moreover, in MAHER V. ROE (1977) the Court carried this refusal to apply a meaningful equal protection standard to any discriminatory "social and economic" legislation to the extreme of validating a provision prohibiting Medicaid funding of abortion although other, including pregnancy-related medical care costs, were funded and the choice to seek an abortion rather than bear a child had been held to be constitutionally protected. Moreover, Maher upheld this discrimination even though, unlike the discrimination upheld in all similar prior cases, it cost rather than saved taxpayer dollars. (See HARRIS V. MCRAE, 1980.)

The Court's refusal since 1971 to treat "vital interests" of the poor as comparable to constitutionally guaranteed rights is one matter. In *Maher,* however, the Court validated discrimination only among the poor and solely on the basis of the poor's attempt to exercise a constitutionally guaranteed right of choice otherwise available to everyone. The recent jurisprudence of wealth discrimination legitimates and reinforces a dual system of constitutional rights, leaving the poor—who disproportionately are composed of women, children, the aged, and racial minorities—with paper rights beyond their financial reach.

BARBARA BRUDNO

Bibliography

BINION, GAYLE 1982 The Disadvantaged Before the Burger Court: The Newest Unequal Protection. *Law & Policy Quarterly* 4:37–69.

BRUDNO, BARBARA 1976 *Poverty, Inequality, and the Law.* St. Paul, Minn.: West Publishing Co.

———— 1980 Wealth Discrimination in the Supreme Court: Equal Protection for the Poor from *Griffin* to *Maher.* Pages 229–246 in Ron Collins, ed., *Constitutional Government in America.* Durham, N.C.: Carolina Academic Press.

WEBB-KENYON ACT
37 Stat. 699 (1913)

Although the Supreme Court had generally refused to uphold laws that it characterized as STATE REGULATION OF COMMERCE, a series of decisions in the late nineteenth and early twentieth centuries deferred to such action. Reacting to a clear invitation in the Court's opinion in LEISY V. HARDIN (1890), holding that absent congressional authorization a state could not prevent the importation and first sale of liquor in the original package, Congress passed the Wilson Act. The law subjected intoxicating liquor "to the operation and effect of the laws of [a] State or territory enacted in the exercise of its [STATE] POLICE POWERS" despite the liquor's journey in INTERSTATE COMMERCE and the ORIGINAL PACKAGE DOCTRINE. The Court sustained that act in *In re Rahrer* (1891).

The Webb-Kenyon Act, passed over the veto of President WILLIAM HOWARD TAFT, divested liquor of its interstate character when introduced in violation of state law. Congress thus effectively allowed state prohibition laws to regulate national commerce in liquor. The Court upheld this act in CLARK DISTILLING COMPANY V. WESTERN MARYLAND RAILWAY CO. (1917).

DAVID GORDON

Bibliography

SEMONCHE, JOHN E. 1978 *Charting the Future: The Supreme Court Responds to a Changing Society, 1890–1920.* Westport, Conn.: Greenwood Press.

WEBSTER, DANIEL
(1782–1852)

As a leading lawyer and politician for forty years, Daniel Webster influenced constitutional development as few others have. When the young New Hampshire representative arrived in Washington in 1813, he immediately became a spokesman for New England interests and remained so until the mid-1820s despite an interruption of congressional service (1817–1823) upon moving to Boston. For most of the time from 1827 to his death in 1852, he was an eloquent nationalist in the Senate. Except for two periods as secretary of state under Tyler and Fillmore, he spent the last quarter-century of his life in that body, expounding the principles of a perpetual Union and a flexible Constitution. In either role, sectionalist or nationalist, he applied constitutional ideas to political issues with uncommon ability.

During the early years his Federalist partisanship and loyalty to a commercial constituency led him to oppose Republican policies of embargo and war. Using economic coercion to maintain maritime rights, he believed, intolerably stretched the power to regulate commerce, indeed, it destroyed commerce. And prosecuting an offensive war against Britain caused other constitutional errors: misuse of militia, proposals for federal conscription, encroachment on STATES' RIGHTS. Though not a delegate to the HARTFORD CONVENTION, Webster approved its resolutions. Later he sought, unconvincingly, to dissociate himself from it. His sectionalism persisted when he opposed the postwar trend toward a protective tariff (1816–1824). Again he voiced a strict constructionist interpretation of the COMMERCE CLAUSE to promote low rates desired by merchants and a system of laissez-faire in the first phase of industrialization.

In the late 1820s, he shifted to a nationalist position concurrently with JOHN C. CALHOUN's shift in the opposite direction. In behalf of rising manufacturers, he joined HENRY CLAY in advocating governmental policies to achieve economic growth and American self-sufficiency. No longer did he oppose use of the commerce power for broad goals. When South Carolina nullified the tariff of 1832, his oratorical duel with

Calhoun provided an opportunity to reiterate more comprehensively his constitutional thought, dramatically set forth in his earlier debate with ROBERT HAYNE. Beyond the tariff question, he countered the doctrines of state sovereignty and NULLIFICATION with the concept of a perpetual Union, created by the people, not the states, and composed of two spheres of authority, national and state, both responsible to the people. In event of conflict, Article VI of the Constitution required national supremacy; and the Supreme Court had long performed its proper duty of upholding that rule.

Soon slavery became the focus of politics. Ever since writing a memorial on the Missouri question in 1820, Webster had advocated a national power to prevent western extension of slavery; but he conceded Congress could not touch it in existing states and he soft-pedaled the moral question. Subsequently he opposed ANNEXATION OF TEXAS and further territorial acquisitions from Mexico, fearing they would disrupt the Union. When, in the great congressional debate of 1850, controversy reached a climax, he preferred compromise to save the Union instead of legislation against extension of slavery, constitutionally possible though it was. Antislavery forces attacked him furiously—the more so when the fugitive slave law, a part of the compromise, appeared to violate CIVIL LIBERTIES. As senator, he had inclined toward TRIAL BY JURY for suspected runaways; as secretary of state he insisted upon strict observance of the statute prescribing summary process.

He was very active in the Supreme Court as well as in Congress. Altogether, he argued 168 cases, of which twenty-five involved constitutional questions. He won about half and influenced doctrinal development even in some he lost. Regularly, he set forth nationalistic arguments to limit state power in a day when most congressional powers were dormant. More successful when JOHN MARSHALL was Chief Justice (to 1835) than when ROGER B. TANEY presided, he made a deep impression on the governmental structure. Of the cases strengthening nationalism, McCULLOCH V. MARYLAND (1819) stands out. Here, though overshadowed by WILLIAM PINKNEY, Webster contributed to a definition of the Union identical to that in his Senate speeches against nullification. And he introduced the aphorism that the power to tax involves the power to destroy. OSBORN V. BANK OF THE UNITED STATES (1824) provided opportunities to advocate expansion of federal court JURISDICTION in the whole field of corporate rights.

The first commerce case the Court heard involved the New York steamboat monopoly (GIBBONS V. OGDEN, 1824). Contending for an exclusive congressional power over INTERSTATE COMMERCE, Webster would have been satisfied with a rule of partially concurrent power. Marshall sympathized with the first option but did not rest his decision on either formula, therefore postponing a judicial guideline. Over the next twenty-five years, Webster participated in several other cases, such as the LICENSE CASES (1847) and the PASSENGER CASES (1849), in an unavailing effort to obtain an exclusive-power decision. At last, in COOLEY V. BOARD OF WARDENS (1851), his protégé, Justice BENJAMIN CURTIS, spoke for a majority in laying down a partially concurrent-power standard which preserved about as much exclusive national authority as Webster wished. *Cooley* remains good constitutional law.

Webster's nationalism was not an abstract idea. He connected it with the sanctity of property rights as the very foundation of a dynamic economy. Best illustrating this belief are the CONTRACT CLAUSE cases in which he appeared. DARTMOUTH COLLEGE V. WOODWARD (1819) is a classic in the long history of VESTED RIGHTS shielded from state interference. He relied upon the contract clause of the Constitution as if it were an early version of SUBSTANTIVE DUE PROCESS of law. Though the contract clause, even the concept of vested rights of property, has declined, the notion of active judicial defense of individual constitutional rights flourishes in the area of civil liberties. The *Dartmouth* case was only Webster's first of several dealing with the contract clause.

Webster's career reflected the junction of personal capacity with a favorable setting to establish nationhood and to invigorate a capitalist economy. Still, he may have been flawed by moral oversights and may have encouraged an inequitable distribution of wealth and privilege. Perhaps his contemporaries sensed weaknesses such as these as they passed over him in electing their presidents.

MAURICE G. BAXTER

(SEE ALSO: *Constitutional History, 1801–1829; 1829–1848.*)

Bibliography

BARTLETT, IRVING H. 1978 *Daniel Webster.* New York: W. W. Norton.

BAXTER, MAURICE G. 1966 *Daniel Webster and the Supreme Court.* Amherst: University of Massachusetts Press.

—— 1984 *One and Inseparable: Daniel Webster and the Union.* Cambridge, Mass.: Harvard University Press.

FUESS, CLAUDE M. 1930 *Daniel Webster,* 2 vols. Boston: Little, Brown.

WEEKS v. UNITED STATES
232 U.S. 383 (1914)

Weeks v. United States was the Court's single most creative decision under the FOURTH AMENDMENT. To save the amendment as a living constitutional guarantee, the Court endowed it with an enforcement feature, ordering the exclusion from federal trials of EVIDENCE obtained through unlawful seizure. Without this EXCLUSIONARY RULE, seized evidence, regardless of its origin, would always be admissible. The rule thus has provided the occasion for judicial articulation of Fourth Amendment reasonableness in later cases.

Under COMMON LAW, and for the first century of the Constitution's existence, evidence unlawfully seized by government officers was nonetheless admissible in evidence. In BOYD V. UNITED STATES (1886) the Court implicitly discarded this common law principle, but the exclusionary rule, as it has come to be called, was not explicitly enthroned until the *Weeks* decision. The reason for admitting unlawfully seized evidence, a standard still followed in nearly all other countries, is readily understood. Unlike coerced confessions, which are excluded from trial in all civilized countries because of their untrustworthiness, the fruit of an illegal search is just as reliable when taken without a shadow of authority as when taken under warrant. To exclude the evidence allows a criminal to go free. Absent the exclusionary rule, however, the Fourth Amendment might become a mere paper guarantee of freedom from UNREASONABLE SEARCHES without an effective enforcement process. Unlike other guarantees in the BILL OF RIGHTS (for example, RIGHT TO COUNSEL), the Fourth Amendment affects the pretrial stage of the case and is—apart from the exclusionary rule—not within the power of the trial court to enforce. The secrecy in which searches are planned and executed makes it impossible to seek the advance protection of an INJUNCTION, a regular practice when FIRST AMENDMENT freedoms are threatened.

The unanimous *Weeks* opinion said that if unconstitutionally seized evidence were admitted, the Fourth Amendment "might as well be stricken from the Constitution." Furthermore, if the evidence were admitted, courts become parties to the misdeeds of the police, thus compromising the integrity of the judicial process.

The opinion did not, however, make clear whether the exclusionary rule was required by the Constitution or merely was the product of the Court's supervisory power over the lower federal courts and thus subject to negation by Congress. Even if the rule is rooted in the Fourth Amendment, the question remains whether it is a personal right of the defendant or just a deterrent against unlawful searches, discardable if other deterrents can be found. The *Weeks* opinion appeared to endorse the first position; use of the evidence, said the Court, would constitute "a denial of the constitutional rights of the accused." More recent decisions, however, favor the deterrent theory. Nonetheless, one who is not himself the victim of an unlawful search but is implicated in crime by the seizure does not have STANDING to challenge admission of the evidence.

JACOB W. LANDYNSKI

WEEMS v. UNITED STATES
217 U.S. 349 (1910)

In *Weems,* the Court held that punishment is cruel and unusual if it is grossly excessive for the crime. Paul Weems, a government official in the Philippines, was convicted of falsifying pay records. Under a territorial law inherited from the Spanish penal code, Weems was sentenced to *cadeña temporal,* a punishment involving fifteen years of hard labor in chains, permanent deprivation of political rights, and surveillance by the authorities for life. Since the Philippine Bill of Rights was Congress's extension to the Philippines of rights guaranteed by the Constitution, the meaning of CRUEL AND UNUSUAL PUNISHMENT was the same in both documents.

DENNIS J. MAHONEY

WELFARE BENEFITS

Nothing in the Constitution requires the United States or any state to provide public relief to those unable to earn adequate subsistence. Throughout most of history that relief has been the responsibility of private charity or local government. But several provisions of the Constitution impose an obligation on government officials, where such relief is provided, to refrain from imposing arbitrary standards or procedures. That obligation is generally recognized by legislative bodies and, since the late 1960s, has become a special concern of the federal courts.

The courts have treated questions concerning the extension or withdrawal of public welfare benefits under the PRIVILEGES AND IMMUNITIES, EQUAL PROTEC-

TION, and DUE PROCESS clauses of the Constitution. In SHAPIRO V. THOMPSON (1969) the Supreme Court held that a one-year RESIDENCE REQUIREMENT for welfare eligibility infringed the right of interstate migration, a privilege protected by Article IV and the FOURTEENTH AMENDMENT, and also denied equal protection of the laws to indigent interstate travelers. In GRAHAM V. RICHARDSON (1971) the Court held that denial of benefits to resident ALIENS was a denial of equal protection. However, in DANDRIDGE V. WILLIAMS (1970) the Court decisively rejected argument that WEALTH DISCRIMINATION was a SUSPECT CLASSIFICATION or that welfare subsistence was a FUNDAMENTAL INTEREST. And in *Jefferson v. Hackney* (1972), the Court declined to hold that the equal protection clause required a state to compute the need for public assistance according to the same standard for each of the various welfare programs. Nonetheless in GOLDBERG V. KELLY (1970) the Court held that once benefits were granted they could not be discontinued without PROCEDURAL DUE PROCESS, including NOTICE and FAIR HEARING.

DENNIS J. MAHONEY

WELSH v. WISCONSIN
466 U.S. 740 (1984)

In *Welsh* the Supreme Court considered and rejected an exception to its rule of PAYTON V. NEW YORK (1984) that the FOURTH AMENDMENT prohibits a warrantless arrest in one's home in the absence of EXIGENT CIRCUMSTANCES. Police made a warrantless night entry of a private home to arrest a man for committing the nonjailable offense of driving while drunk. Justice WILLIAM J. BRENNAN for a 6–2 Court rejected the state's reliance on the hot pursuit doctrine because the police had not in fact engaged in a pursuit. In view of the state's classification of a first-offense drunk-driving offense as a minor crime meriting merely a fine, the Court also rejected the argument that the need to get a blood-alcohol test without delay provided an exigent circumstance.

LEONARD W. LEVY

WENGLER v. DRUGGISTS MUTUAL INSURANCE COMPANY
446 U.S. 142 (1980)

Missouri's workers' compensation law provided death benefits to all widows but only to widowers who proved actual dependence on their wives or incapac-

ity to earn a living. The Supreme Court, 8–1, held this SEX DISCRIMINATION invalid, following CRAIG V. BOREN (1976) and CALIFANO V. GOLDFARB (1977).

KENNETH L. KARST

WESBERRY v. SANDERS
376 U.S. 1 (1964)

After BAKER V. CARR (1962) held that legislative districting presented a justiciable controversy, the Supreme Court held in *Wesberry*, 8–1, that a state's congressional districts are required by Article I, section 2, of the Constitution to be as equal in population as is practicable. That section provides that representatives are to be chosen "by the People of the several States." Justice JOHN MARSHALL HARLAN dissented on both textual and historical grounds.

Later decisions make clear that no justifications can excuse substantial deviation from population equality in congressional districting.

KENNETH L. KARST

(SEE ALSO: *Reapportionment.*)

WEST COAST HOTEL COMPANY v. PARRISH
300 U.S. 379 (1937)

This decision sustaining a Washington state minimum wage statute in March 1937 signaled a seismic shift in judicial philosophy toward acceptance of the validity of social and economic legislation. Together with the WAGNER ACT CASES, the decision reflected a new, favorable judicial attitude toward the New Deal, thus defusing FRANKLIN D. ROOSEVELT's court-packing proposal.

The constitutionality of minimum wage legislation had a peculiar history. In MULLER V. OREGON (1908) and BUNTING V. OREGON (1917) the Justices had approved state laws regulating maximum working hours, including provisions for overtime wages. In 1917, the Court divided evenly on an Oregon minimum wage law. WILLIAM HOWARD TAFT, among others, confidently presumed that LOCHNER V. NEW YORK's (1905) rigorous FREEDOM OF CONTRACT doctrines no longer applied. Yet in 1923, a 5–3 majority of the Court reaffirmed the *Lochner* ruling, and in ADKINS V. CHILDREN'S HOSPITAL (1923) the Court invalidated a DISTRICT OF COLUMBIA minimum wage statute. New Chief Justice Taft sharply attacked the majority's reasoning. He found no distinction between MAXIMUM HOUR AND MINIMUM WAGE LAWS: one was the "multiplier and the other the multiplicand." Although Taft reiterated his belief that *Lochner* had been tacitly overruled, *Lochner* nevertheless persisted until the *Parrish* decision in 1937.

After *Adkins,* the Court invalidated other state minimum wage laws. The Great Depression, however, stimulated new state laws, perhaps encouraged by Justice GEORGE SUTHERLAND's OBITER DICTUM that "exceptional circumstances" might justify such legislation. But in MOREHEAD V. NEW YORK EX REL. TIPALDO (1936), a 5–4 majority held to the *Adkins* precedent and invalidated a recent New York law. The Court's opinion masked Justice OWEN J. ROBERTS's uneasiness. Roberts had supported PIERCE BUTLER, JAMES C. MCREYNOLDS, George Sutherland, and WILLIS VAN DEVANTER in *Tipaldo,* but he later revealed that the state counsel's argument that *Adkins* merely be distinguished, and not overthrown, had obliged him to follow the precedent. Six months later, Roberts provided the key vote to consider the Washington law. On the surface, the procedure was justified on the ground that the state court had upheld the statute, but the combination of the *Tipaldo* dissenters' strongly held views on constitutionality and Roberts's skepticism toward *Adkins* dictated a full-scale review of the issue.

Roberts later stated that he had decided in favor of the statutes after arguments in December 1936 and that he had successfully urged delaying the decision pending HARLAN FISKE STONE's recovery from illness in order to mass a majority. Stone returned shortly after Roosevelt submitted his court-packing proposal in early February. Chief Justice CHARLES EVANS HUGHES then withheld the announcement until March 29, perhaps to avoid appearances of political submission.

Hughes's majority opinion decisively repudiated *Lochner* and *Adkins.* He argued that the Constitution nowhere enshrined freedom of contract and that "regulation which is reasonable in relation to its subject and is adopted in the interests of the community is DUE PROCESS." Seeking to deflect the outraged protests of his more conservative brethren, Hughes invoked Taft's *Adkins* dissent: "That challenge persists and is without any satisfactory answer."

Invoking the public interest doctrine of NEBBIA V. NEW YORK (1934), Hughes asked what could be "closer to the public interest than the health of women and their protection from unscrupulous and overreaching employers?" Accordingly, Hughes held that the minimum wage statute was reasonable and not "arbitrary or capricious." That, he concluded, "is all we have to decide."

Sutherland, speaking for the dissenters, passionately reiterated his *Adkins* doctrine. More broadly, Sutherland also implicitly addressed Stone's scathing dissent in UNITED STATES V. BUTLER (1936), which had pleaded for judicial self-restraint and an end to judges' imposition of their own social and economic predilections. The notion of self-restraint, Sutherland retorted, was "ill considered and mischievous"; it belonged "in the domain of will and not of judgment." Judges were bound to enforce the Constitution, he said, according to their own "conscientious and informed convictions." Sutherland concluded that freedom of contract remained the rule. The intervening economic conditions altered nothing, for "the meaning of the Constitution," he said, "does not change with the ebb and flow of economic events." Sutherland's dissent was both an apologia and an obituary for a judicial philosophy eclipsed by new realities.

STANLEY I. KUTLER

Bibliography

MASON, ALPHEUS T. 1956 *Harlan Fiske Stone.* New York: Viking Press.

WESTON v. CITY COUNCIL OF CHARLESTON
2 Peters 449 (1829)

The Supreme Court, in an opinion by Chief Justice JOHN MARSHALL, held unconstitutional a city ordinance taxing interest-bearing stock of the United States, on the grounds that the tax burdened the ENUMERATED POWER of the United States to borrow money on its credit. The principle of the opinion, that an instrumentality of the United States is immune from taxation by state and local governments, derived from MCCULLOCH V. MARYLAND (1819).

LEONARD W. LEVY

(SEE ALSO: *Intergovernmental Immunities.*)

WEST RIVER BRIDGE COMPANY v. DIX
6 Howard 529 (1848)

The *West River Bridge* case challenged a Vermont law of 1839 authorizing county officials to expropriate the rights of way, real estate, or entire franchises of chartered companies in order to provide their communities with free public roads. County officials condemned the entire franchise and property of the West River Bridge Company, which had been given a hundred-year franchise under a charter of 1795 for a bridge near Brattleboro, an important market town. The stockholders were awarded $4,000 in damages. The company's appeal was rejected by the Vermont Supreme Court, and the case was then carried to the United States Supreme Court.

DANIEL WEBSTER, as counsel for the company, sought in his arguments to reopen virtually all the issues of CHARLES RIVER BRIDGE V. WARREN BRIDGE COMPANY (1837). He contended that rising popular disregard for franchised rights of corporations would legitimate the worst "levelling ultraisms or Antirentism or Agrarianism or Abolitionism." Eminent domain was a power inappropriate to republican government, he contended, and the bridge taking was in blatant violation of the CONTRACT CLAUSE. Nonetheless, the Court, with Justice JAMES M. WAYNE dissenting, upheld Vermont's action. Each of the three opinions filed declared that eminent domain was a power fundamental to the states, had long been exercised by them, was not restrained by the contract clause, and extended as much to franchises as to any other type of property. As the first Supreme Court ruling that dealt directly with the states' power of eminent domain and related procedural matters, *West River Bridge* complemented the *Charles River Bridge* decision; both supported the states' authority to accommodate technological change and social and entrepreneurial needs.

HARRY N. SCHEIBER

WEST VIRGINIA STATE BOARD OF EDUCATION v. BARNETTE

See: Flag Salute Cases

WHALEN v. ROE
429 U.S. 589 (1977)

Rejecting a claim based on the constitutional RIGHT OF PRIVACY, a unanimous Supreme Court upheld a New York law requiring storage in a computer file of the names and addresses of persons who obtain, by doctors' prescriptions, such drugs as opium, methadone, cocaine, and amphetamines. Justice JOHN PAUL STEVENS, writing for the Court, noted that previous decisions recognizing a right of privacy had involved two different kinds of interests: (1) "avoiding disclosure of personal matters"; and (2) "independence in making certain kinds of important decisions." Both interests were arguably implicated here; there was some risk of disclosure of a drug user's name, and that risk could have deterred the prescription or use of such drugs even when they were medically advisable. Nonetheless, and despite a district court finding that the state had not proved the necessity of storing this personal information, the Court concluded that the law was valid. The state's interest in DRUG REGULATION was vital; the legislature was entitled to experiment with reasonable means for achieving that end. Balanced against this objective, the invasions of privacy were too slight to constitute invasions of either patients' or doctors' constitutional liberties.

KENNETH L. KARST

WHEATON, HENRY
(1785–1848)

Henry Wheaton read law in his native Providence, Rhode Island, and studied civil law in France in 1805–1806. While in France he translated the new *Code Napoléon* into English. He became the first official reporter for the United States Supreme Court under an 1816 statute creating that position. From 1816 to 1827 Wheaton edited twelve volumes of United States Reports. While official reporter he argued a number of cases, including GIBBONS V. OGDEN (1824). In *Wheaton v. Peters* (1834) he unsuccessfully sued his successor, Richard Peters. The Supreme Court ruled that no individual could hold a COPYRIGHT on Supreme Court opinions. From 1827 to 1846 Wheaton held various diplomatic positions and wrote extensively on international law. His works included *Elements of International Law, History of the Law of Nations* (1842) and an essay on the African slave trade (1842). He was the foremost American expert on international law during his lifetime.

PAUL FINKELMAN

Bibliography

BAKER, ELIZABETH F. 1937 *Henry Wheaton, 1785–1848.* Philadelphia: University of Pennsylvania Press.

WHEELER, BURTON K.
(1882–1975)

A Montana Democrat, Burton K. Wheeler ranked with GEORGE NORRIS of Nebraska and William Borah of Idaho as one of the major liberal leaders of the

United States Senate, where Wheeler served from 1923 to 1946. In the 1924 presidential campaign, ROBERT M. LA FOLLETTE of Wisconsin headed the Progressive party ticket, with Wheeler as his running mate. They attracted more votes than any previous third party, and their platform provided an agenda for the New Deal. One plank urged an amendment to the Constitution providing that a two-thirds majority in both houses of Congress might override any judicial decision holding a congressional enactment unconstitutional. Although Wheeler was a critic of the Supreme Court and of JUDICIAL REVIEW, he insisted that a constitutional amendment was the only proper means of reform; accordingly, he broke with FRANKLIN D. ROOSEVELT in 1937 by opposing his Court-packing plan. It was Wheeler, an ally of Justice LOUIS D. BRANDEIS, who produced the letter by Chief Justice CHARLES EVANS HUGHES that contributed to the 10–8 vote against the bill by the Senate Judiciary Committee. Wheeler remained a liberal, though he was an isolationist in foreign affairs.

LEONARD W. LEVY

Bibliography

WHEELER, BURTON K., with PAUL F. HEALY 1962 *Yankee from the West.* New York: Doubleday.

WHISKEY REBELLION
(1794)

The "rebellion" in western Pennsylvania provided the first test of the power of the federal government to suppress insurrections and enforce obedience to its laws. Frontier farmers, who were also small distillers, resisted the whiskey excise from its passage in 1791. When the resistance erupted in violence in July 1794, President GEORGE WASHINGTON issued a proclamation ordering the rebels to submit to the law or face military coercion under an act authorizing employment of the militia in such cases. After a peace mission failed, he called up 15,000 militia from Pennsylvania and neighboring states. The army marched, and the rebellion quickly collapsed without bloodshed; two ringleaders, tried and convicted of TREASON, were subsequently pardoned by the President. Federalist leaders exulted in this crushing of rebellion, which they viewed as part of a plot against the government, while their Republican counterparts denounced the force as excessive and intended to overawe opposition to the administration.

MERRILL D. PETERSON

Bibliography

BALDWIN, LELAND D. 1939 *Whiskey Rebels: The Story of a Frontier Uprising.* Pittsburgh: University of Pittsburgh Press.

WHITE, BYRON R.
(1917–)

In 1962 President JOHN F. KENNEDY appointed Byron R. White to replace CHARLES E. WHITTAKER and become the ninety-third Justice to serve on the Supreme Court. White was forty-four years old and had no previous judicial experience. He had been a CLERK for Chief Justice FRED N. VINSON in 1946–1947, however, and was the first former law clerk subsequently appointed to that tribunal. His only other significant government experience had come during the preceding year, after President Kennedy had appointed him deputy attorney general. White had managed the Justice Department, recruited lawyers, and evaluated candidates for federal judgeships. His CIVIL RIGHTS enforcement experience included a stint in Montgomery, Alabama, where local authorities had failed to prevent mob violence against the freedom riders, an interracial group protesting racial SEGREGATION in public transportation. White restored order with the help of 400 federal marshals, providing Kennedy with a significant national victory over recalcitrant state officials.

Whatever White lacked in government experience, he made up in personal capacities. Born in rural Colorado, White came of age there during the Depression. He worked in the beet fields as a boy and later won a scholarship to the University of Colorado, where he was first in his class and an all-American football player. He played professional football, and for several months, until the European outbreak of World War II, he studied as a Rhodes scholar in England, where he first met John Kennedy. He began studying law at Yale in 1939 and again topped his class. The war interrupted his studies, and he served as a naval intelligence officer in the South Pacific, where he again encountered Kennedy. He was graduated in 1946, and after his clerkship, returned to Colorado to practice law. In 1959 he organized support for Kennedy as the Democratic nominee for President. Following Kennedy's nomination, he chaired Citizens for Kennedy, a nationwide volunteer group. His public service followed.

When White joined the WARREN COURT, its most vigorous efforts to nationalize CIVIL LIBERTIES and limit government power in favor of individual rights and egalitarian values lay just ahead. White voted regularly with the majority to invalidate discrimination against racial minorities and the politically powerless in areas such as school DESEGREGATION and REAPPORTIONMENT, and to sustain the constitutionality of federal civil rights legislation. Nonetheless, he acquired a reputation as a moderate-to-conservative Justice for his frequent dissents in major decisions, such as MIRANDA V. ARIZONA (1966), which imposed new constitutional limits on police discretion; for his willingness to uphold laws excluding communists from government positions; and for his general inclination toward judicial self-restraint.

With President RICHARD M. NIXON's four Court appointments from 1969–1971, the deferential positions White previously had articulated in dissent increasingly became majority views in the BURGER COURT. But White also dissented from decisions undermining egalitarian opinions he had joined in the Warren era. The Court had changed around him—not an uncommon occurrence for Justices serving for long periods.

The Court's shift, together with White's failure to articulate a comprehensive personal vision of an ideal balance of individual liberty and government power, has led some observers to conclude that White lacks a coherent judicial philosophy. The votes and written opinions of this independent, tough-minded jurist, however, do reveal a distinctive vision of the Supreme Court's role in constitutional law, a vision compatible with White's personal history.

One pervasive attitude in White's approach is skepticism and humility about the authority and capacity of the Court to second-guess the efforts of other government officials in dealing with difficult societal problems. White's opinions reflect deference to the good faith assessments and pragmatic judgments of police, administrative officials, and state and federal judges—particularly when he is convinced that they have readier access to relevant information than the Court does, or that government flexibility is needed. He reserves the highest deference for legislative judgments, out of respect for LEGISLATIVE POWER, especially that of the national Congress, as the most legitimate source of law in a democratic society. This second tenet emphasizes the primacy of legislative decisions in allocating the benefits and burdens of government programs, balancing individual rights and community needs, and structuring government operations.

The corollary is that White's deference disappears if good faith and pragmatism are absent. When prejudice infects government decision making, when the interests of the disadvantaged systematically are excluded from consideration in government processes, or when individual liberty is sacrificed for minimal public gain, White readily and consistently supports constitutional prohibitions. He embraces a strongly individualistic ideology that demands fair government treatment of citizens as individuals and holds ordinary citizens and government officials accountable for their individual conduct.

White's individualism produces a powerful egalitarian ethic that takes two different forms. One is constitutional invalidation of government action that treats people stereotypically, with insufficient regard for their individual worth, merits, and capacities. The other is constitutional approval of government efforts to equalize opportunities for the disadvantaged.

These general themes explain much of Justice White's participation in the Court's work. His opposition to stringent constitutional limits on law enforcement practices, absent significant abuse of a particular defendant's liberty, reflects deference to the difficulties of enforcement and the flexibility it requires, as well as to the judgment that guilty individuals have no great claim to benefit from police misconduct that has not harmed them. Deference, pragmatism, and rugged individualism underlie White's position in *Miranda* and his majority opinion in *United States v. Leon* (1984), establishing a GOOD FAITH EXCEPTION to the EXCLUSIONARY RULE. His Court opinions holding that the states must provide TRIAL BY JURY if substantial imprisonment is possible, but that the states may convict with less than unanimous verdicts and with juries of only six members, illustrate a compromise between a belief in the importance of the jury in protecting individual liberty and tolerance for pragmatic modifications of its traditional features when the modifications do not seriously undermine its basic value. The heavy weight he has placed behind sanctioning guilty individuals gives way, however, when government interferes with a fair presentation of the defendant's side, as by denying the RIGHT TO COUNSEL. In civil cases, too, in contexts as diverse as PROCEDURAL DUE PROCESS and the CONTRACT CLAUSE, he has tolerated pragmatic (and unbiased) responses to perceived governmental needs.

White's deference to national LEGISLATIVE POWER has led him to reject both FEDERALISM objections that Congress has usurped reserved state power, as in OREGON V. MITCHELL (1970) and NATIONAL LEAGUE OF CITIES V. USERY (1976), and SEPARATION OF POWERS objections that Congress has invaded the Court's or the President's power, as in his provocative dissents in NORTHERN PIPELINE CONSTRUCTION CO. V.

MARATHON PIPE LINE CO. (1982), dealing with the powers of LEGISLATIVE COURTS in BANKRUPTCY cases, and IMMIGRATION AND NATURALIZATION SERVICE V. CHADHA (1983), in which the majority struck down the LEGISLATIVE VETO. He also opposed individual rights challenges to legislative efforts that promote equality, such as the affirmative action program upheld in FULLILOVE V. KLUTZNICK (1980), and Congress's attempt to equalize campaign spending, partially invalidated over White's dissent in BUCKLEY V. VALEO (1976). In these cases, deference and attachment to egalitarian values worked together; when they are in conflict, however, White tends to put aside deference and vote to strike down federal laws that discriminate on such invidious bases as race or sex.

White is as vigorous in opposing biased or arbitrary government judgments as he is in supporting justifiable, pragmatic ones. He will not invoke the Constitution to impose affirmative obligations on government, but will do so to prevent the government from imposing unfair burdens. He is reluctant to recognize constitutional immunities for even the highest level officials, preferring to hold that no one is above the law. That frequent theme appears most prominently in his dissent in NIXON V. FITZGERALD (1982), arguing that the President is legally accountable for abuse of government power, and in his opinions interpreting the SPEECH AND DEBATE CLAUSE as fully immunizing members of Congress from inquiry into legislative conduct, but providing no immunity for nonlegislative acts.

More broadly, White has voted to invalidate government policies founded on prejudice or bad motive without more, but usually would not invalidate laws adopted with proper motives, whatever their impact. Thus, in WASHINGTON V. DAVIS (1976) White led the Court in making proof of intentional discrimination a necessary condition for finding a violation of the equal protection clause. He also would have made intent a sufficient condition, however, as he articulated in dissent in PALMER V. THOMPSON (1971). He has been both generous in finding proof of illicit intent and forceful in insisting that, once wrongdoing is shown, the harm be remedied fully, especially in cases of RACIAL DISCRIMINATION. And when the impact of governmental action significantly impairs the democratic process, as in reapportionment cases, White also has supported judicial intervention.

In FIRST AMENDMENT cases, too, White is strict about disallowing government discrimination against disfavored viewpoints, but tolerant of significant limitations on individual expression that are inevitable byproducts of legitimate government aims, a theme illustrated by his opinion in BROADRICK V. OKLAHOMA (1973). That opinion also represents White's consistent belief that the OVERBREADTH and VAGUENESS doctrines should be used only sparingly to strike statutes with a neutral and uncertain inhibiting effect on the general populace—a position readily held by a believer in hardy individualism. He is likewise unreceptive to arguments that the press needs wide immunity from libel and other actions lest fear of liability deter them from vigorous and important expression. Thus, although this Justice with considerable personal experience as the object of media attention strongly supported First Amendment limits on press liability for reporting about public officials, he vigorously dissented in GERTZ V. ROBERT WELCH, INC. (1974) from the Court's granting the powerful media constitutional immunity from liability to helpless individuals who seek redress for the ravaging of their reputations. Indeed, he generally opposes affording the press any special privileges, except in cases of prior restraint or when the press serves as the public's monitor of government. Finally, White has been relatively deferential to regulations of OBSCENITY and SUBVERSIVE ADVOCACY, the former an example of deference to strong community views which invade little important freedom and the latter an example of deference to the community's right to protect its democratic character.

White's concern for the constitutional obligation to purge arbitrariness from government decision making extends naturally to questions of procedural fairness. Although White would allow government considerable flexibility in defining procedures, he has insisted that appropriate procedures be provided if government deprives a person of a government-created liberty or property entitlement, even if the government was under no initial obligation to create it. So conceived, procedural due process promotes individualized application of law on the basis of personal responsibility and guards against arbitrary decisions.

White's emphasis on equality and fair, if flexible, process generally stops short of imposing substantive limits on government policy. His normal disinclination to go beyond constitutional text or history and recognize new fundamental liberties tends to yield, however, when a state restricts personal autonomy by a law that deviates from most other states' laws or is of minimal efficacy in achieving proper objectives. Thus, White dissented in ROE V. WADE (1973), where the Court used SUBSTANTIVE DUE PROCESS analysis to invalidate laws regulating abortion, but he concurred in GRISWOLD V. CONNECTICUT (1965), arguing that the state's atypical law against marital use of contraceptives violated substantive due process because of its "marginal utility to the declared objective" of deterring illicit sexual relationships. Similarly, he initially voted against the death penalty in *Furman v. Georgia* (1972), not because it constituted CRUEL AND UNUSUAL PUNISHMENT but because it was administered arbitrarily and too infrequently to achieve its deterrent aims. Later, he voted to uphold mandatory death penalty laws applied broadly and consistently. Still, he wrote the major opinion in COKER V. GEORGIA (1977), holding the death penalty for rape cruel and unusual, largely because most states had refrained from imposing it for crimes not producing death.

Normally, White's limited belief in NATURAL RIGHTS jurisprudence surfaces as increased scrutiny of legislative means when government policy implicates broadly accepted liberties and the threat of inequality or arbitrariness is high. Perhaps not surprisingly, given his personal experience, he not only finds family choice fundamental, but educational opportunity, too. Thus, he has been especially adamant to invalidate school SEGREGATION, inequality of expenditures among a state's school districts, and school discipline that involves corporal punishment or lacks procedural safeguards. He is equally adamant that public aid to the secular functions of parochial schools, a policy that supports educational choice and quality, does not constitute a prohibited ESTABLISHMENT OF RELIGION—a distinct minority view on the Court.

JONATHAN D. VARAT

Bibliography

ISRAEL, FRED 1969 Byron R. White. In Leon Friedman and Fred Israel, eds., *The Justices of the Supreme Court: Their Lives and Major Opinions.* Vol. 4:2951–2961. New York: Chelsea House.
LIEBMAN, LANCE 1972 Swing Man on the Supreme Court. *New York Times Magazine,* October 8, 1972.
SCHWARTZ, BERNARD 1983 *Super Chief: Earl Warren and His Supreme Court: A Judicial Biography.* New York: New York University Press.
WOODWARD, BOB and ARMSTRONG, SCOTT 1979 *The Brethren: Inside the Supreme Court.* New York: Simon & Schuster.

WHITE, EDWARD D.
(1845–1921)

Born and raised in Louisiana, the son of a slaveholding sugar planter and a Confederate veteran, Edward Douglass White was an archetype of the "New South" political leader. The masters of the region's economic and social development from the 1880s until World War I combined the interests of antebellum planters with those of northern and local capitalists eager to build railroads and tap the area's coal, iron, and timber. The South's new ruling class "redeemed" Dixie from the egalitarian schemes of Radical Republicans and carpetbaggers by supporting RUTHERFORD B. HAYES for President and accepting the national hegemony of the GOP's conservative wing. In return, these leaders of the "New South" received from the Republicans a promise to remove federal troops from the region, a free hand with respect to the Negro, and a junior partnership in the management of the nation's economic affairs. (See COMPROMISE OF 1877.)

While tending his family's plantation and building a prosperous legal practice in New Orleans, White became a chief political confidant and ally of Governor Francis Nicholls, the leader of the state's conservative Democrats, who rewarded him with an appointment to the Louisiana Supreme Court and then a seat in the United States Senate in 1891. While in Washington, the portly, florid, long-haired junior senator from Louisiana adopted a rigid STATES' RIGHTS and laissez-faire posture on most issues. However, he fervently supported high duties on foreign sugar and lavish federal bounties to the planters in his home state. White led the Senate's successful revolt against President GROVER CLEVELAND's efforts to lower the protective tariff in 1893. Nevertheless, the beleaguered head of the Democratic party nominated him to the Supreme Court a year later, following the death of SAMUEL BLATCHFORD and the Senate's rejection of two earlier nominees.

White took his seat as the junior member of the FULLER COURT at one of the important turning points in the history of the federal judiciary. The country seethed with unrest generated by the worst depression of the nineteenth century. Violent confrontations between workers and employers erupted on the nation's major railroads as well as in coal mines, steel mills, and other factories. Debt-ridden farmers formed the radical Populist Party, which demanded government control of the money supply and banking system and nationalization of the major trunk rail lines. Insurgent Democrats nominated the youthful William Jennings Bryan, who ran on a platform promising inflation of the money supply, higher taxes on the wealthy, and a curb on trusts and other monopolies. In this atmosphere of class strife and regional polarization, men of property and standing looked to the Supreme Court to defend the constitutional ark against dangerous innovations. Fuller and most of his colleagues were equal to the task of repelling the radical hordes.

Even before the economic collapse, a majority of the Justices had served warning that they would not tolerate legislative attacks on corporate property and profits. Legislative power to fix railroad rates, they warned, was not without limits; corporations were PERSONS, entitled to the judicial protection of the FOURTEENTH AMENDMENT's DUE PROCESS clause; and no rate imposed by legislative fiat could be deemed "reasonable" without final judicial review. Then, in a series of cases that reached the Court together during the depths of the depression in 1895, the Justices quashed federal efforts to prosecute the sugar trust under the SHERMAN ANTITRUST ACT in UNITED STATES V. E. C. KNIGHT CO. (1895); upheld the contempt conviction of the labor leader Eugene V. Debs for his role in the Pullman boycott in IN RE DEBS (1895); and declared unconstitutional the first federal income tax levied since the Civil War in POLLACK V. FARMER'S LOAN AND TRUST CO. (1895). These three decisions displayed the FULLER COURT's conservative colors and represented a major victory for big business, the wealthy, and the enemies of organized labor.

Like the majority of his brethren, Justice White showed no sympathy for Debs and the militant working class movement he represented. White also endorsed Fuller's reasoning in the sugar trust case, which limited the scope of the Sherman Act to monopolies of interstate trade or commerce and left to the individual states all authority to curb monopolies over production. But he joined Justice JOHN MARSHALL HARLAN, the outspoken champion of nationalism and federal power, in denouncing the majority's assault on the income tax statute. White had been a member of the Senate that passed the income tax measure as part of the tariff package in 1892, and, although he did not endorse the levy, neither did he doubt the constitutional power of Congress to adopt it. In order to invalidate the law, the majority had to ignore two weighty precedents, one dating from 1796. This was too much for White, who argued eloquently that "the conservation and orderly development of our institutions rests on our acceptance of the results of the past, and their use as lights to guide our steps in the future. Teach the lesson that settled principles may be overthrown at any time, and confusion and turmoil must ultimately result."

The income tax dissent revealed an important aspect of White's jurisprudence which remained constant during his years as an associate Justice and later as Chief Justice after 1911. Although deeply conservative and devoted to the judicial protection of private property, White was also a pragmatist capable of endorsing moderate reforms that had clear constitutional sanction and that served to cap the pressures for more radical change. Though not adverse to overturning a few precedents himself, White usually did so in the pursuit of policies that strengthened rather than weakened the dominant economic forces of corporate capitalism.

In this spirit, he endorsed the judicial imperialism inherent in Justice Harlan's opinion in SMYTH V. AMES (1898), which made the federal judiciary the final arbiter of utility rates, but he also enforced the progressive reforms of the THEODORE ROOSEVELT-WILLIAM HOWARD TAFT era which revitalized the regulatory authority of the Interstate Commerce Commission (ICC) over the nation's major railroads. In a series of decisions, culminating in White's opinion in INTERSTATE COMMERCE COMMISSION V. ILLINOIS CENTRAL RAILROAD CO. (1910), the majority sustained the ICC's fact-finding and rate-fixing powers as mandated by Congress. White's views were compatible with the interests of the railroads, which looked to the ICC to prevent financially ruinous rate wars, and with those of reformers like Roosevelt, who believed that such regulation would curb the appetite for government ownership of the carriers.

White rendered his greatest service to the conservative cause in the area of antitrust law by promoting the view that the Sherman Act prohibited only "unreasonable" restraints of trade, a perspective pregnant with possibilities for enlarged judicial control over the country's economic structure, yet wholly compatible with the desires of big business. But it took White over a decade to defeat the contrary views of other Justices, who remained more wedded to the old Jacksonian belief in competition and the dangers of monopoly.

In the wake of the *E. C. Knight* decision restricting federal antitrust efforts to INTERSTATE COMMERCE, the Department of Justice began a campaign to stamp out railroad cartels and pools designed to divide up traffic and fix rates. A majority of the Justices, led by Harlan and RUFUS W. PECKHAM, a passionate spokesman for laissez-faire economics, sustained the government's efforts in this area on the theory that the Sherman Act outlawed *all* restraints of trade, even those that might be deemed "reasonable" in view of particular business conditions such as rate wars and destructive competition. In the first of these cases, UNITED STATES V. TRANS-MISSOURI FREIGHT ASSOCIATION (1897), White wrote a long, rambling dissent which accused the majority of misreading the antitrust law, defying the traditions of the COMMON LAW with respect to restraints of trade, and jeopardizing the economic progress brought to the nation by business combinations and consolidations.

White continued to dissent in the *Joint Traffic Association Case* (1898) and in NORTHERN SECURITIES CO. V. UNITED STATES (1904), where a five-Justice majority upheld the government's suit against the Morgan-Harriman rail monopoly between Chicago and the Pacific Northwest. In each case, White argued that the antitrust law, incorporating the ancient doctrines of the common law, prohibiting only "unreasonable" restraints of trade. Technically, White was correct, but all of the methods condemned in *Trans-Missouri, Joint Traffic Association,* and *Northern Securities* would have been indictable at common law as well, because their fundamental objective had been to fix prices contrary to the public interest. This fact seems to have eluded White, who believed that the Harlan-Peckham approach threatened the demise of valuable business enterprises by virtue of judicial abdication to the prosecutorial zeal of misguided reformers in the executive branch. In this perception, he enjoyed the support of three other justices, including OLIVER WENDELL HOLMES, who also looked upon the Rockefellers, Morgans, and Harrimans as agents of social and economic progress.

Four changes in the personnel of the Court between 1909 and 1911 gave White a new majority for his doctrine a year later when the government's suits against Standard Oil and American Tobacco finally reached the Justices after years of litigation. Speaking now as Chief Justice of the United States, having been appointed to the center chair by President Taft, White sustained the government's case against the monopolists but cast aside the Harlan-Peckham interpretation of the Sherman Act. Henceforth, the majority decreed, only "unreasonable" trade restraints would be indictable under the Sherman Act and the Justices on the Supreme Court would determine where the line should be drawn between legal and illegal competitive behavior. Harlan wrote a melancholy dissent against this sharp reversal of doctrine, which seemed to teach that "settled principles may be overthrown at any time, and confusion and turmoil must ultimately result."

White's RULE OF REASON doctrine provoked a storm of protest from progressives in the Congress, who denounced the Justices for mutilating the antitrust law, arrogating to themselves too much power over the economic system, and giving big business a hunting license to continue its predatory ways. Although Congress added the CLAYTON ACT amendments to the antitrust law in 1914, specifically outlawing a substantial list of business practices, White's rule

of reason carried the day. The Court quashed the government's efforts to break up the shoe machinery monopoly in 1913 and also threw out the case against United States Steel in 1920, a year before White died. There was extraordinary historical irony in the fact that it was a Southerner and a veteran of the Rebel army who advanced antitrust doctrines that sealed the triumph of industrial capitalism and big business in American life.

For a Southerner, a Democrat, and a spokesman for states' rights in the Senate, White displayed considerable toleration for the expansion of federal economic controls by means of the COMMERCE CLAUSE and the TAXING AND SPENDING POWER. In the Senate he had taken an active role in fighting a federal law to regulate the trade in agricultural "futures," noting that it would invade the JURISDICTION of the states and create "the most unlimited and arbitrary government on the face of God's earth." As a Justice, however, he joined Harlan's path-breaking opinion in the Lottery Case, CHAMPION V. AMES (1903), which greatly expanded the NATIONAL POLICE POWER via the interstate commerce clause. A year later he wrote the Court's opinion in MCCRAY V. UNITED STATES (1904), which affirmed the power of Congress to impose a prohibitive levy upon oleomargarine and thus employ its tax powers for regulatory purposes.

White drew back, however, from the logical implications of the national police power when Congress sought to apply it to other areas of social and economic life. He was willing to permit the extension of the commerce power to federal regulation of adulterated foods and interstate traffic in prostitution, but he joined Justice WILLIAM R. DAY's opinion in HAMMER V. DAGENHART (1918), which declared unconstitutional Congress's attempt to eradicate child labor. He also rejected federal efforts to tax and regulate narcotics traffic in UNITED STATES V. DOREMUS (1919), although the majority found this use of the federal taxing power compatible with White's own views in *McCray*. He sanctioned Congress's adoption of an eight-hour day for interstate train crews which brought an end to the disastrous nationwide rail strike, but he joined three other dissenters in *Block v. Hirsh* (1921) when Holmes and the majority upheld the national legislature's power to impose rent controls upon property in the DISTRICT OF COLUMBIA during the emergency of World War I.

White displayed equal inconsistency in cases where state ECONOMIC REGULATIONS came under DUE PROCESS challenge. The one thread of coherence seemed to be his growing conservatism and abiding dislike for organized labor. He dissented in LOCHNER V. NEW YORK (1905) along with Harlan and Day, noting that "no evils arising from such legislation could be more far-reaching than those that might come to our system of government if the judiciary . . . should enter the domain of legislation, and upon grounds merely of justice or reason or wisdom, annul statutes that had received the sanction of the people's representatives." He also voted to sustain the Oregon and California maximum hours laws for women in MULLER V. OREGON (1908) and *Miller v. Wilson* (1915). But he balked at the overtime pay provisions and general maximum hours limitation in BUNTING V. OREGON (1917) and sided with the majority in the three leading cases of the period which protected employers' use of YELLOW DOG CONTRACTS against both state and federal efforts to eliminate this notorious antiunion device: ADAIR V. UNITED STATES (1908), COPPAGE V. KANSAS (1915), and HITCHMAN V. HITCHMAN COAL & COKE CO. (1917).

In 1919, White joined JOSEPH MCKENNA, WILLIS VAN DEVANTER, and JAMES C. MCREYNOLDS in dissent against the Court's opinion in the *Arizona Employers' Liability Cases* (1919), which upheld that state's law shifting the cost of industrial accidents to employers. And during his final term on the Court, he joined the majority in scuttling the anti-INJUNCTION provisions of the Clayton Antitrust Act and affirming the illegality of secondary boycotts. If not the most reactionary member of the Supreme Court with respect to organized labor, White certainly ran a close race for that honor with Justices Day, MAHLON PITNEY, and McReynolds.

White had been elevated to the chief justiceship by William Howard Taft, who coveted the position for himself and feared that a younger nominee might forever prevent that happy development. Taft realized his lifelong ambition in 1921, when White died. Predictably, White's eulogizers compared his career to that of John Marshall and other immortals of the bench, but a more accurate assessment is that constitutional law showed his imprint until 1937.

MICHAEL E. PARRISH

Bibliography

DISHMAN, ROBERT   1951   Mr. Justice White and the Rule of Reason. *The Review of Politics* 13:229–248.

HIGHSAW, ROBERT B.   1981   *Edward Douglass White: Defender of the Conservative Faith.* Baton Rouge: Louisiana State University Press.

KLINKHAMER, MARIE CAROLYN   1943   *Edward Douglass White, Chief Justice of the United States.* Washington, D.C.: Catholic University Press.

SEMONCHE, JOHN E.   1978   *Charting the Future: The Supreme Court Responds to a Changing Society, 1890–1920.* Westport, Conn.: Greenwood Press.

WHITE, UNITED STATES v.
401 U.S. 745 (1971)

During the reign of OLMSTEAD V. UNITED STATES (1927) the Supreme Court consistently ruled, in cases including ON LEE V. UNITED STATES (1952) and LOPEZ V. UNITED STATES (1963), that government informers who deceptively interrogated criminal suspects and either secretly transmitted the conversations to eavesdropping government agents with concealed recorders or secretly recorded the conversations, had committed no TRESPASS, and therefore the FOURTH AMENDMENT was inapplicable. The use of spies without complying with Fourth Amendment controls was reaffirmed in HOFFA V. UNITED STATES (1966). KATZ V. UNITED STATES (1967), however, abolished the trespass requirement for Fourth Amendment protection and focused on the personal PRIVACY interests that were entitled to protection. Some therefore thought *On Lee* was no longer good law. In *United States v. White*, however, the Court held otherwise. Though there was no clear majority for either approving or disapproving *On Lee*, four Justices voted to reaffirm that decision, and Justice HUGO L. BLACK concurred to make a majority on the ground that *Olmstead*'s trespass requirement should be retained. The *On Lee* doctrine was thus reaffirmed.

Justice BYRON R. WHITE, for the plurality, ruled that a person is not protected by the Fourth Amendment against a faithless friend, regardless of whether a trespass is involved. An expectation of such protection is not "justifiable" under the *Katz* standard. Police have always been allowed to use the evidence of faithless associates who turn to the police or are informers: "one contemplating illegal activities must realize and risk that his companions may be reporting to the police." The fact that the faithless friend was wired, transmitting the conversation to others or recording it for later replaying, makes no constitutional difference.

The dissents focused on the latter point. Justice JOHN MARSHALL HARLAN rejected the "assumption of risk" rationale of the majority, stressing that the real question was which risks the law *should* force people to assume. Whereas the use of unwired spies or contemporaneous recording to ensure reliability are both justifiable, simultaneous overhearing by third parties is different; free discourse would be seriously jeopardized if people were forced to assume the risk that their words were being simultaneously transmitted to third parties and transcribed. "Were third-party bugging a prevalent practice, it might well smother that spontaneity—reflected in frivolous, impetuous, sacrilegious, and defiant discourse—that liberates daily life." Justice Harlan emphasized that the dissenters' views would not prohibit the use of wired informers but would only bring the practice under Fourth Amendment warrant and other procedures.

Even though the principal *White* opinion did not command a majority, it kept *On Lee* in effect and freed the government from Fourth Amendment restrictions on the use of spies and informers, wired or otherwise.

HERMAN SCHWARTZ

(SEE ALSO: *Electronic Eavesdropping.*)

WHITE COURT
(1910–1921)

"The condition of the Supreme Court is pitiable, and yet those old fools hold on with a tenacity that is most discouraging," President WILLIAM HOWARD TAFT wrote in May 1909 to his old friend HORACE H. LURTON. Taft would have his day. One year later, Chief Justice MELVILLE W. FULLER spoke at the Court's memorial service for Justice DAVID J. BREWER: "As our brother Brewer joins the great procession, there pass before me the forms of Mathews and Miller, of Field and Bradley and Lamar and Blatchford, of Jackson and Gray and of Peckham, whose works follow them now that they rest from their labors." These were virtually Fuller's last words from the bench, for he died on Independence Day, 1910, in his native Maine. RUFUS W. PECKHAM had died less than a year earlier. WILLIAM H. MOODY, tragically and prematurely ill, would within a few months have to cut short by retirement one of the few notable short tenures on the Court. JOHN MARSHALL HARLAN had but one year left in his remarkable thirty-four-year tenure. By 1912, five new Justices had come to the Court who were not there in 1909: a new majority under a new Chief Justice.

The year 1910 was a significant divide in the history of the country as well. The population was nearly half urban, and immigration was large and growing. The country stood on the verge of enacting humane and extensive labor regulation. A year of Republican unrest in Congress and THEODORE ROOSEVELT's decisive turn to progressive agitation, 1910 was the first

time in eight elections that the Democrats took control of the House. In the same year, the National Association for the Advancement of Colored People was founded. It was a year of progressive tremors that would eventually shake the Supreme Court to its foundations with the appointment of LOUIS D. BRANDEIS in 1916. But the five appointments with which President Taft rehabilitated his beloved Court between 1909 and 1912 had no such dramatic impact. There was a significant strengthening of a mild progressive tendency earlier evident within the Court, but the new appointments brought neither a hardening nor a decisive break with the DOCTRINES of laissez-faire constitutionalism and luxuriant individualism embodied in such decisions as LOCHNER V. NEW YORK (1905) and ADAIR V. UNITED STATES (1908). Taft's aim was to strengthen the Court with active men of sound, if somewhat progressive, conservative principles. Neither Taft nor the nation saw the Court, as both increasingly would a decade later, as the storm center of pressures for fundamental constitutional change.

Taft's first choice when Peckham died in 1909 was his friend Lurton, then on the Sixth Circuit, and a former member of the Tennessee Supreme Court. Lurton, a Democrat, had been a fiery secessionist in his youth, and in his short and uneventful four-year tenure he combined conservationism on economic regulation, race, and labor relations. Taft's second choice was not so modest. When Taft went to Governor CHARLES EVANS HUGHES of New York to replace Brewer, he brought to the Court for the first of his two tenures a Justice who would emerge as one of the greatest figures in the history of American law, and a principal architect of modern CIVIL LIBERTIES and CIVIL RIGHTS jurisprudence. As governor of New York, Hughes was already one of the formidable reform figures of the Progressive era, and his later career as a presidential candidate who came within a whisper of success in 1916, secretary of state during the 1920s, and Chief Justice during the tumultuous years of the New Deal, mark him as one of the most versatile and important public figures to sit on the Court since JOHN MARSHALL.

Taft's choice of the Chief Justice to fill the center seat left vacant by Fuller was something of a surprise, although reasons are obvious in retrospect. EDWARD D. WHITE was a Confederate veteran from Louisiana, who had played a central role in the Democratic reaction against Reconstruction in that state and had emerged as a Democratic senator in 1891. He had been appointed Associate Justice in 1894 by President GROVER CLEVELAND and had compiled a respectable but unobtrusive record in sixteen years in the side seat. He had dissented with able force from the self-inflicted wound of POLLOCK V. FARMERS' LOAN & TRUST CO. (1895), holding unconstitutional the federal income tax, and his antitrust dissents in TRANS-MISSOURI FREIGHT ASSOCIATION (1897) and UNITED STATES V. NORTHERN SECURITIES COMPANY (1904) embodied sound good sense. He had done "pioneer work," as Taft later called it, in ADMINISTRATIVE LAW. White had a genius for friendship and, despite a habit of constant worrying, extraordinary personal warmth. OLIVER WENDELL HOLMES summed him up in these words in 1910: "His writing leaves much to be desired, but his thinking is profound, especially in the legislative direction which we don't recognize as a judicial requirement but which is so, especially in our Court, nevertheless." White was sixty-five, a Democrat, a Confederate veteran, and a Roman Catholic, and his selection by Taft was seen as adventurous. But given Taft's desire to bind up sectional wounds, to spread his political advantage, to put someone in the center seat who might not occupy Taft's own ultimate ambition for too long, to exemplify bipartisanship in the choice of Chief Justice, and on its own sturdy merits, the selection of White seems easy to understand.

Along with White's nomination, Taft sent to the Senate nominations of WILLIS VAN DEVANTER of Wyoming and JOSEPH R. LAMAR of Georgia. Van Devanter would sit for twenty-seven years, and would become one of the Court's most able, if increasingly conservative, legal craftsmen. Lamar would last only five years, and his death in 1915, along with Lurton's death in 1914 and Hughes's resignation to run for President, opened up the second important cycle of appointments to the White Court.

The Taft appointees joined two of the most remarkable characters ever to sit on the Supreme Court. John Marshall Harlan, then seventy-eight, had been on the Court since his appointment by President RUTHERFORD B. HAYES in 1877. He was a Justice of passionate strength and certitude, a man who, in the fond words of Justice Brewer, "goes to bed every night with one hand on the Constitution and the other on the Bible, and so sleeps the sleep of justice and righteousness." He had issued an apocalyptic dissent in *Pollock*, the income tax case, and his dissent in PLESSY V. FERGUSON (1986), the notorious decision upholding racial SEGREGATION on railroads, was an appeal to the conscience of the Constitution without equal in our history. The other, even more awesome, giant on the Court in 1910 was Holmes, then seventy, but still not quite recognized as the jurist whom BENJAMIN N. CARDOZO would later call "probably the greatest legal intellect in the history of the English-speaking judiciary." The other two members of the Court were JOSEPH MCKENNA, appointed by President WILLIAM MCKINLEY in 1898, and WILLIAM R. DAY, appointed by President Theodore Roosevelt in 1903.

The Supreme Court in 1910 remained in "truly republican simplicity," as Dean Acheson would recall, in the old Senate chamber, where the Justices operated in the midst of popular government, and in the sight of visitors to the Capitol. No office space was available, and the Justices worked in their homes. Their staff allowance provided for a messenger and one clerk, and their salaries were raised in 1911 to $14,500 for the Associate Justices and $15,000 for the Chief Justice. The Court was badly overworked and the docket was falling further and further behind, not to be rescued until the JUDICIARY ACT OF 1925 gave the Court discretion to choose the cases it would review.

In the public's contemporaneous view, if not in retrospect, the most important cases before the White Court between 1910 and 1921 did not involve the Constitution at all, but rather the impact of the SHERMAN ANTITRUST ACT on the great trusts. UNITED STATES V. STANDARD OIL COMPANY (1911) and *American Tobacco Company v. United States* (1911) had been initiated by the Roosevelt administration to seek dissolution of the huge combinations, and when the cases were argued together before the Supreme Court in 1911, the *Harvard Law Review* thought public attention was concentrated on the Supreme Court "to a greater extent than ever before in its history."

The problem for the Court was to determine the meaning of restraint of trade amounting to monopoly. The answer offered by Chief Justice White for the Court was the famous RULE OF REASON, under which not all restraints of trade restrictive of competition were deemed to violate the Sherman Act, but rather only those "undue restraints" which suggested an "intent to do wrong to the general public . . . thus restraining the free flow of commerce and tending to bring about the evils, such as enhancement of riches, which were considered to be against public policy." Under this test, the Court deemed Standard Oil to have engaged in practices designed to dominate the oil industry, exclude others from trade, and create a monopoly. It was ordered to divest itself of its subsidiaries, and to make no agreements with them that would unreasonably restrain trade. The court ruled that the American Tobacco Company was also an illegal combination and forced it into dissolution.

Antitrust was perhaps the dominant political issue of the 1912 presidential campaign, and the rule of reason helped to fuel a heated political debate that produced the great CLAYTON ACT and FEDERAL TRADE COMMISSION ACT of 1914. Further great antitrust cases came to the White Court, notably *United States v. United States Steel Company,* begun in 1911, postponed during the crisis of World War I, and eventually decided in 1920. A divided Court held that United States Steel had not violated the Sherman Act, mere size alone not constituting an offense.

The tremendous public interest generated by the antitrust cases before the White Court was a sign of the temper of the political times, in which the regulation of business and labor relations was the chief focus of progressive attention. In this arena of constitutional litigation, the White Court's record was mixed, with perhaps a slight progressive tinge. On the great questions of legislative power to regulate business practices and working arrangements, the White Court maintained two parallel but opposing lines of doctrines, the one protective of laissez-faire constitutionalism and freedom from national regulation, the other receptive to the progressive reforms of the day.

In the first four years after its reconstitution by Taft, the Supreme Court handed down a number of important decisions upholding national power to regulate commerce for a variety of ends. The most expansive involved federal power to regulate railroads—and to override competing state regulation when necessary. *Atlantic Coast Line Railroad v. Riverside Mills* (1911) upheld Congress's amendment of the HEPBURN ACT imposing on the initial carrier of goods liability for any loss occasioned by a connecting carrier, notwithstanding anything to the contrary in the bill of lading. FREEDOM OF CONTRACT gave way to the needs of shippers for easy and prompt recovery. More significantly, in the second of the EMPLOYERS' LIABILITY CASES (1912), the Court upheld congressional legislation imposing liability for any injury negligently caused to any employee of a carrier engaged in INTERSTATE COMMERCE. This legislation did away with the fellow-servant rule and the defense of contributory negligence, again notwithstanding contracts to the contrary. In 1914, in the famous *Shreveport Case* (HOUSTON, EAST & WEST TEXAS RAILWAY COMPANY V. UNITED STATES) the Court upheld the power of the Interstate Commerce Commission to set the rates of railroad hauls entirely within Texas, because those rates competed against traffic between Texas and Louisiana. The Court overrode the rates set by the Texas Railroad Commission in the process. And

in the most important COMMERCE CLAUSE decision of the early years of the White Court, the MINNESOTA RATE CASES (1913), the Court upheld the power of the states to regulate railroad rates for intrastate hauls, even when that regulation would force down interstate rates, so long as there had been no federal regulation of those rates. Thus, state power over rates was not invalidated because of the possibility of prospective federal regulation, and a large loophole between state and federal power was closed.

Outside the area of carrier regulation, the White Court was also friendly to national regulation by expanding the NATIONAL POLICE POWER doctrine. HIPOLITE EGG CO. V. UNITED STATES (1911) upheld the PURE FOOD AND DRUG ACT of 1906 in regulating adulterated food and drugs shipped in interstate commerce, whether or not the material had come to rest in the states. "Illicit articles" that traveled in interstate commerce were subject to federal control, the Court said, although with a doctrinal vagueness and confusion that would come back to haunt the Court in HAMMER V. DAGENHART (1918). In HOKE V. UNITED STATES (1913) the Court upheld the MANN ACT, which punished the transportation in interstate commerce of women "for the purpose of prostitution or debauchery, or for any other immoral purpose."

Taft got his opportunity for a sixth appointment—more appointments in one term than any President in our history since GEORGE WASHINGTON—when Harlan died in 1911. He filled the vacancy with MAHLON PITNEY, chancellor of New Jersey. The reasons for this appointment are obscure, but like other Taft appointments Pitney was a sound, middle-of-the-road, good lawyer with little flair or imagination. As if to prepare for the coming flap over Brandeis, the Pitney appointment ran into trouble because of the nominee's alleged antilabor positions. But Pitney prevailed, and he would serve on the Court until 1922.

If ever in the history of the Supreme Court successive appointments by one President have seemed to embrace dialectical opposites, WOODROW WILSON's appointments of JAMES C. MCREYNOLDS in 1914 and Louis D. Brandeis in 1916 are the ones. McReynolds would become an embittered and crude anti-Semite; Brandeis was the first Jew to sit on the Supreme Court. McReynolds would become the most rigid and doctrinaire apostle of laissez-faire conservatism in constitutional history, the most recalcitrant of the "Four Horsemen of Reaction" who helped to scuttle New Deal legislation in the early 1930s. Brandeis was the greatest progressive of his day, on or off the Court. McReynolds was an almost invariable foe of CIVIL LIB-

ERTIES and CIVIL RIGHTS for black people; Brandeis was perhaps the driving force of his time for the development of civil liberties, especially freedom of expression and rights of personal privacy. What brought these opposites together in Wilson's esteem, although he came to regret the McReynolds appointment, was antitrust fervor. McReynolds's aggressive individualism and Brandeis's progressive concern for personal dignity and industrial democracy coalesced around antitrust law, and this was the litmus test of the day for Wilson. Thus, possibly the most difficult and divisive person ever to sit on the Supreme Court and possibly the most intellectually gifted and broadly influential Justice in the Court's history took their seats in spurious, rather Wilsonian, juxtaposition.

Wilson's third appointment was handed him by the resignation of his rival in the presidential election of 1916. As it became plain that Hughes was the only person who could unite the Republican party, he came under increasing pressure from Taft and others to make himself available. He did. Wilson nominated JOHN J. CLARK of Ohio to replace Hughes. One of the most pregnant speculations about the history of the Supreme Court is what might have happened had Hughes remained on the bench. He might well have become a Chief Justice in 1921 instead of Taft, and under his statesmanlike influence, the hardening of doctrine that led to the confrontation over the New Deal and the Court-packing plan might not have happened.

Although two of Wilson's three appointments were staunch progressives, the Supreme Court seemed to adopt a somewhat conservative stance as it moved toward the decade of erratic resistance to reform that would follow in the 1920s. Federal reform legislation generally continued to pass muster, but there was the staggering exception of the *Child Labor Case* in 1918. And the Court seemed to strike out at labor unions, in both constitutional and antitrust decisions.

In *Hammer v. Dagenhart* (1918) the Supreme Court stunned Congress and most of the country when it invalidated the first federal CHILD LABOR ACT. The extent of child labor in the United States during the Progressive era was an affront to humanitarian sensibilities. One child out of six between the ages of ten and fifteen was a wage earner. Prohibition and regulation of child labor became the central reform initiatives of the progressive impulse. In 1916, overcoming constitutional doubts, Wilson signed the KEATING-OWEN ACT, which forbade the shipment in interstate or foreign commerce of the products of mines where children sixteen and under had been employed, or of factories where children younger than fourteen worked, or where children fourteen to sixteen had worked more than eight hours a day, six days a week. Child labor was not directly forbidden, but was severely discouraged by closing the channels of interstate commerce.

A narrow majority of the Court, in an opinion by Justice Day, held that this law exceeded the federal commerce power. Day reasoned that the goods produced by child labor were in themselves harmless, and that the interstate transportation did not in itself accomplish any harm. This reasoning was entirely question-begging, because it was the possibility of interstate commerce that imposed a competitive disadvantage in states that outlawed child labor in comparison with less humanitarian states. Moreover, the reasoning was flatly inconsistent with the opinion in *Hipolite Egg* and *Hoke*. But the majority plainly regarded the federal child labor legislation as an invasion of the domestic preserves of the states. Holmes, joined by McKenna, Brandeis, and Clarke, issued a classic dissent.

With the preparations for an advent of American involvement in World War I, the Supreme Court recognized broad federal power to put the economy on a wartime footing. The burden of constitutional resistance to reform legislation shifted to cases involving state laws. Here the main hardening in doctrinal terms came in cases involving labor unions. Otherwise, a reasonable progressivism prevailed. Thus, in BUNTING V. OREGON (1917) the Court upheld the maximum ten-hour day for all workers in mills and factories, whether men or women. However, two minimum wage cases from Oregon were upheld only by the fortuity of an equally divided Supreme Court, Brandeis having recused himself.

The most chilling warning to progressives that laissez-faire constitutionalism was not dead came in COPPAGE V. KANSAS (1915). The issue was the power of a state to prohibit by legislation the so-called YELLOW DOG CONTRACT, under which workers had to promise their employers not to join a union. The Court in *Coppage* held such laws unconstitutional: to limit an employer's freedom to offer employment on its own terms was a violation of freedom of contract.

The Supreme Court's race relations decisions between 1910 and 1921 constitute one of the Progressive era's most notable, and in some ways surprising, constitutional developments. Each of the Civil War amendments was given unprecedented application. For the first time, in the *Grandfather Clause Cases* (1915), the Supreme Court applied the FIFTEENTH AMENDMENT and what was left of the federal civil rights statutes to strike down state laws calculated to deny blacks the right to vote. For the first time, in BAILEY V. ALABAMA (1911) and UNITED STATES V. REYNOLDS (1914), the Court used the THIRTEENTH AMENDMENT to strike down state laws that supported PEONAGE by treating breach of labor contracts as criminal fraud and by encouraging indigent defendants to avoid the chain gang by having employers pay their fines in return for commitments to involuntary servitude. For the first time, in BUCHANAN V. WARLEY (1917), it found in the FOURTEENTH AMENDMENT constitutional limits on the spread of laws requiring racial separation in residential areas of cities and towns, and also for the first time, in *McCabe v. Atchison, Topeka & Santa Fe Railway* (1914), it put some teeth in the equality side of the SEPARATE BUT EQUAL DOCTRINE by striking down an Oklahoma law that said that railroads need not provide luxury car accommodations for blacks on account of low demand.

To be sure, only with respect to peonage could the White Court be said to have dismantled the legal structure of racism in any fundamental way. After the White Court passed into history in 1921, blacks in the South remained segregated and stigmatized by Jim Crow laws, disfranchised by invidiously administered LITERACY TESTS, white PRIMARY ELECTIONS, and POLL TAXES; and victimized by a criminal process from whose juries and other positions of power they were wholly excluded. But if the White Court did not stem the newly aggressive and self-confident ideology of racism inundating America in the Progressive era, neither did it put its power and prestige behind the flood, as had the WAITE COURT and FULLER COURT that preceded it—and, at critical points, it resisted. The White Court's principled countercurrents were more symbols of hope than effective bulwarks against the racial prejudice that permeated American law. But the decisions taken together mark the first time in American history that the Supreme Court opened itself in more than a passing way to the promises of the Civil War amendments.

World War I generated the first set of cases that provoked the Supreme Court for the first time since the FIRST AMENDMENT was ratified in 1791 to consider the meaning of freedom of expression. The cases, not surprisingly, involved dissent and agitation against the war policies of the United States. The war set off a major period of political repression against critics of American policy.

In the first three cases, SCHENCK V. UNITED STATES, FROHWERK V. UNITED STATES, and IN RE DEBS (1919), following the lead of Justice Holmes, the Supreme Court looked not to the law of SEDITIOUS LIBEL for justification in punishing speech but rather to traditional principles of legal responsibility for attempted crimes. In English and American COMMON LAW, an unsuccessful attempt to commit a crime could be punished if the attempt came dangerously close to success, while preparations for crime—in themselves harmless—could not be punished. With his gift of great utterance, Holmes distilled these doctrinal nuances into the rule that expression could be punished only if it created a CLEAR AND PRESENT DANGER of bringing about illegal action, such as draft resistance or curtailment of weapons production. Given his corrosive skepticism and his Darwinian sense of flux, the clear and present danger rule later became in Holmes's hands a fair protection for expression. But in the hands of judges and juries more passionate or anxious, measuring protection for expression by the likelihood of illegal action proved evanescent and unpredictable.

There were other problems with the clear and present danger rule. It took no account of the value of a particular expression, but considered only its tendency to cause harmful acts. Because the test was circumstantial, legislative declarations that certain types of speech were dangerous put the courts in the awkward position of having to second-guess the legislature's factual assessments of risk in order to protect the expression. This problem became clear to Holmes in ABRAMS V. UNITED STATES (1919), in which a statute punishing speech that urged curtailment of war production was used to impose draconian sanctions on a group of radical Russian immigrants who had inveighed against manufacture of war material that was to be used in Russia. In this case, Holmes and Brandeis joined in one of the greatest statements of political tolerance ever uttered.

In 1921, the year Edward Douglass White died and Taft became Chief Justice, Benjamin Cardozo delivered his immortal lectures, "The Nature of the Judicial Process." Cardozo pleaded for judges to "search for light among the social elements of every kind that are the living forces behind the facts they deal with." The judge must be "the interpreter for the community of its sense of law and order . . . and harmonize results with justice through a method of free decision." Turning to the Supreme Court, Cardozo stated: "Above all in the field of constitutional law, the method of free decision has become, I think, the dominant one today."

In this view, we can see that Cardozo was too hopeful, although his statement may have been offered more as an admonition than a description. The method of "free decision," exemplified for Cardozo by the opinions of Holmes and Brandeis, remained in doubt notwithstanding the inconsistent progressivism of the White Court, and would become increasingly embattled in the decades to come.

BENNO C. SCHMIDT, JR.

Bibliography

BICKEL, ALEXANDER M. and SCHMIDT, BENNO C., JR. 1984 *The Judiciary and Responsible Government 1910–1921*. Vol. IX of the Holmes Devise History of the Supreme Court. New York: Macmillan.

CARDOZO, BENJAMIN N. 1921 *The Nature of the Judicial Process*. New Haven, Conn.: Yale University Press.

CHAFEE, ZECHARIAH 1949 *Free Speech in the United States*. Cambridge, Mass.: Harvard University Press.

HIGHSAW, ROBERT B. 1981 *Edward Douglass White*. Baton Rouge: Louisiana State University Press.

SEMONCHE, JOHN E. 1978 *Charting the Future: The Supreme Court Responds to a Changing Society 1890–1920*. Westport, Conn.: Greenwood Press.

SWINDLER, WILLIAM F. 1969 *Court and Constitution in the 20th Century: The Old Legality 1889–1932*. Indianapolis: Bobbs-Merrill.

WHITE PRIMARIES

See: *Grovey v. Townsend; Nixon v. Condon; Nixon v. Herndon;* Primary Elections; *Smith v. Allwright; Terry v. Adams*

WHITING, WILLIAM

See: Commentators on the Constitution

WHITNEY v. CALIFORNIA
274 U.S. 357 (1927)

SCHENCK V. UNITED STATES (1919), ABRAMS V. UNITED STATES (1919), GITLOW V. NEW YORK (1925), and *Whitney* are the four leading FREEDOM OF SPEECH cases of the 1920s in which the CLEAR AND PRESENT DANGER rule was announced but then rejected by the majority in favor of the BAD TENDENCY test announced in *Gitlow*. In *Whitney*, Justice EDWARD SANFORD repeated his *Gitlow* argument that a state law does not violate FIRST AMENDMENT rights by employing the "bad tendency" test as the standard of reasonableness in speech cases. The state may reasonably proscribe "utterances . . . tending to . . . endanger the foundations of organized government." Here Justice Sanford added that "united and joint action involves even greater danger to the public peace and security than the isolated utterances . . .

of individuals." Miss Whitney had been convicted of organizing and becoming a member of an organization that advocated and taught CRIMINAL SYNDICALISM in violation of the California Criminal Syndicalism Act of 1919. The Court upheld the act's constitutionality.

After *Schenck*, the clear and present danger position had been reiterated in dissenting opinions by OLIVER WENDELL HOLMES and LOUIS D. BRANDEIS in *Abrams* and *Gitlow*. Brandeis, joined by Holmes, concurred in *Whitney*. Brandeis's reason for concurring rather than dissenting was that Whitney had not properly argued to the California courts that their failure to invoke the danger test was error, and that the Supreme Court might not correct errors by state courts unless those errors were properly raised below.

Brandeis's concurrence was a forceful reiteration of the value to a democracy of freedom of speech for even the most dissident speakers. The framers knew that "fear breeds repression; that repression breeds hate; that hate menaces stable government; that the path of safety lies in the opportunity to discuss freely supposed grievances . . . and that the fitting remedy for evil counsels is good ones." Brandeis reemphasized the imminence requirement of the danger rule. "To courageous, self-reliant men, with confidence in the power of free and fearless reasoning applied through the processes of popular government, no danger flowing from speech can be deemed clear and present, unless the incidence of the evil apprehended is so imminent that it may befall before there is opportunity for full discussion. If there be time . . . to avert the evil by the process of education, the remedy to be applied is more speech, not enforced silence."

Whitney is often cited for an addition by Brandeis to the original clear and present danger formula. The evil anticipated must be not only substantive but also serious. "The fact that speech is likely to result in some violence or in destruction of property is not enough to justify its suppression. There must be the probability of serious injury to the state. . . ."

The Court overruled *Whitney* in BRANDENBURG V. OHIO (1969).

MARTIN SHAPIRO

WHITTAKER, CHARLES
(1901–1973)

A considerable number of Justices who served on the United States Supreme Court resembled T. S. Eliot's famous Mr. Prufrock: "an attendant lord, one that will do [to swell a progress, start a scene or two, . . .] Deferential, glad to be of use, [Politic, cautious, and meticulous;] Full of high sentence, but a bit obtuse. . . ." Charles Whittaker, a self-made man from Kansas, appointed to the Court by President DWIGHT D. EISENHOWER, was one of these.

Whittaker joined the WARREN COURT in 1957, after earlier service on the Eighth Circuit Court of Appeals. His tenure was distinguished only by its brevity and by his own inability to develop a coherent judicial philosophy apart from the orthodox political and social conservatism of the Republican Middle West. His retirement and that of Justice FELIX FRANKFURTER in 1962 marked the beginning of the Warren Court's most liberal and activist phase.

Several DEPORTATION and coerced confession cases best exemplified Whittaker's ad hoc approach to constitutional issues and the confusion that often plagued his opinions. Writing for a majority of six Justices in *Bonetti v. Roger* (1958), he overturned the federal government's attempt to deport an ALIEN who had entered the country in 1923, joined the Communist party for a brief period during the 1930s, left the country to fight in the Spanish Civil War, and finally returned to the United States without rejoining the party. Earlier, Whittaker had voted to sustain the deportation of another alien who had resided continuously in the United States for forty years and whose only offense did not constitute a crime when he committed it (*Lehmann v. Carson*). Two years after *Bonetti*, he voted to uphold the termination of Social Security benefits to aliens deported for their membership in the Communist party during the Great Depression in *Fleming v. Nestor* (1960).

Whittaker displayed little more consistency in the coerced confession cases. In *Moore v. Michigan* (1957), he voted to reverse the murder conviction of a black teenager with a seventh-grade education and a history of head injuries, who had confessed to the crime without the benefit of a lawyer. During the next term, however, he voted, in *Thomas v. Arizona* (1958), to sustain the murder conviction of a black man in Arizona, who had confessed after a twenty-hour interrogation which included the placing of a rope around his neck by a member of the sheriff's posse.

Sometimes, Whittaker joined the Warren Court's liberal bloc, as in TROP V. DULLES (1958), where five Justices declared unconstitutional a provision of the Nationality Act of 1940 depriving wartime deserters of their CITIZENSHIP. He also joined the liberals in *Perez v. Brownell* (1958) when they dissented against the EXPATRIATION of American citizens who voted in foreign elections. (See TROP V. DULLES, 1958.) Whittaker also wrote the opinion in *Staub v. Baxley* (1958), invalidating a city ordinance that required union organizers to secure a permit before soliciting new members.

More frequently, however, Whittaker cast his vote with the Court's conservative bloc led by Justices JOHN MARSHALL HARLAN, TOM C. CLARK, and FELIX FRANKFURTER. In *Beilan v. Board of Education* (1958) he helped to sanction the firing of public school teachers who refused to answer questions about their possible affiliation with the Communist party. He approved the contempt conviction of a college professor who refused to cooperate with a state legislative committee investigating subversive groups in UPHAUS V. WYMAN (1959). He likewise voted to compel the registration of the Communist party under the Subversive Activities Control Act and to allow bar examiners in California to deny admission to a candidate who refused to answer their inquiries about his past membership in the party. (See COMMUNIST PARTY V. SUBVERSIVE ACTIVITIES CONTROL BOARD, 1961; KONIGSBERG V. STATE BAR OF CALIFORNIA, 1961.)

During his final term on the Court, Whittaker continued to affirm his conservative leanings by dissenting in MAPP V. OHIO (1961). He also joined in the Court's dismissal on jurisdictional grounds of an attack on Connecticut's anti-birth control statute in *Poe v. Ullman* (1961). After retiring from the bench, he became a legal adviser to the General Motors Corporation as well as a shrill critic of the CIVIL RIGHTS and anti-Vietnam War protest movements.

MICHAEL F. PARRISH

Bibliography

BERMAN, D. M. 1959 Mr. Justice Whittaker: A Preliminary Appraisal. *Missouri Law Review* 24:1–28.

FRIEDMAN, LEON 1969 Charles Whittaker. Pages 2893–2904 in Leon Friedman and Fred L. Israel, eds., *The Justices of the United States Supreme Court, 1789–1969: Their Lives and Major Opinions.* New York: Chelsea House.

WICKARD v. FILBURN
317 U.S. 111 (1942)

In 1941, by an amendment to the AGRICULTURAL ADJUSTMENT ACT of 1938, Congress brought the national power to regulate the economy to a new extreme, yet the Supreme Court unanimously sustained the regulation in a far-reaching expansion of the commerce power. The price of wheat, despite marketing controls, had fallen. A bushel on the world market in 1941 sold for only forty cents as a result of a worldwide glut, and the wheat in American storage bins had reached record levels. To enable American growers to benefit from government fixed prices of $1.16 per bushel, Congress authorized the secretary of agriculture to fix production quotas for all wheat, even that consumed by individual growers. Filburn sowed twenty-three acres of wheat, despite his quota of only eleven, and produced an excess of 239 bushels for which the government imposed a penalty of forty-nine cents a bushel. Filburn challenged the constitutionality of the statute, arguing that it regulated production and consumption, both local in character; their effects upon INTERSTATE COMMERCE, he maintained, were "indirect."

Justice ROBERT H. JACKSON for the Court wrote that the question would scarcely merit consideration, given UNITED STATES V. DARBY (1941), "except for the fact that this Act extends federal regulation to production not intended in any part for commerce but wholly for consumption on the farm." The Court had never before decided whether such activities could be regulated "where no part of the product is intended for interstate commerce intermingled with the subjects thereof." Taking its law on the scope of the commerce power from GIBBONS V. OGDEN (1824) and the SHREVEPORT DOCTRINE, the Court repudiated the use of mechanical legal formulas that ignored the reality of a national economic market; no longer would the reach of the COMMERCE CLAUSE be limited by a finding that the regulated activity was "production" or its economic effects were "indirect." The rule laid down by Jackson, which still controls, is that even if an activity is local and not regarded as commerce, "it may still, whatever its nature, be reached by Congress if it exerts a substantial economic effect on interstate commerce, and this irrespective of whether such effect is what might at some earlier time have been defined as 'direct' or 'indirect.'" (See EFFECTS ON COMMERCE.)

How could the wheat grown by Filburn, which he fed to his own animals, used for his own food, and kept for next year's seed, be regarded as having a "substantial economic effect" on interstate commerce? Wheat consumed on the farm by its growers, the government had proved, amounted to over twenty percent of national production. Filburn consumed a "trivial" amount, but if he had not produced what he needed for his own use in excess of his allotted quota, he would have had to buy it. By not buying wheat, such producer-consumers depressed the price by cutting the demand. His own contribution to the demand for wheat was trivial, but "when taken with that of others similarly situated," it was significant. Congress had authorized quotas to increase the price of the commodity; wheat consumed on the farm where grown could burden a legitimate congressional purpose to stimulate demand and force up the price. Thus, even if a single bushel of Filburn's infinitesimal production never left his farm, Congress could reach and regulate his activity, because all the Filburns, taken collectively, substantially affected commerce.

LEONARD W. LEVY

Bibliography
STERN, ROBERT L. 1946 The Commerce Clause and the National Economy, 1933–1946. *Harvard Law Review* 59:901–909.

WICKERSHAM, GEORGE
(1858–1936)

Appointed attorney general in 1909 by WILLIAM HOWARD TAFT, George Wickersham argued and won STANDARD OIL COMPANY V. UNITED STATES (1911) and *American Tobacco Company v. United States* (1911). He initiated more prosecutions under the SHERMAN ANTITRUST ACT in four years than his predecessor had in seven, prompting business leaders to call for his resignation. As chairman of the Wickersham Committee from 1929 to 1931, he directed an investigation of the entire system of federal jurisprudence. The commission reported on problems raised by political penetrations of courts, lax criminal law enforcement, abuses of constitutional rights, and various sociological influences contributing to crime.

DAVID GORDON

WIDMAR v. VINCENT
454 U.S. 263 (1981)

In order to avoid activity that might constitute an ESTABLISHMENT OF RELIGION, the University of Missouri at Kansas City barred a student religious group from meeting on the campus for religious teaching or worship. The Supreme Court, 8–1, held that the University, having "created a forum generally open for use by student groups," was forbidden by the FIRST AMENDMENT'S guarantee of the FREEDOM OF SPEECH to exclude the religious group. Because the exclusion was based on the content of the group's speech, it was unconstitutional unless necessary to serve a COMPELLING STATE INTEREST. The exclusion was not necessary to avoid establishment clause problems, for no state sponsorship of religion was implied when the university provided a forum generally open to all student groups.

Justice JOHN PAUL STEVENS, concurring, said that any university necessarily makes many distinctions based on speech content. Here, however, the university discriminated on the basis of the viewpoint of particular speakers, and that was forbidden by the First Amendment.

Justice BYRON R. WHITE dissented, arguing that the state could constitutionally "attempt to disentangle itself from religious worship."

KENNETH L. KARST

(SEE ALSO: *Public Forum.*)

WIEMAN v. UPDEGRAFF
344 U.S. 183 (1952)

In an opinion written by Justice TOM C. CLARK, the Supreme Court struck down an Oklahoma LOYALTY OATH for state employees that required signers to affirm that they were not and had not been for five years members of organizations designated by the attorney general of the United States as "communist front" or "subversive." Clark, who as attorney general had initiated the federal list in 1947, held that the statute violated the DUE PROCESS clause because it did not distinguish innocent membership from knowing membership in the proscribed organizations.

MICHAEL E. PARRISH

WIGMORE, JOHN HENRY
(1863–1943)

John Henry Wigmore was perhaps the foremost American legal scholar and educator of the twentieth century. A professor of law at Northwestern University Law School for fifty years (1893–1943), nearly thirty of them as its dean (1901–1929), Wigmore played the leading role in developing it into one of the nation's leading law schools. Wigmore also helped to found numerous professional and academic organizations, among them the American Institute of Law and Criminology (1909) and the American Bar Association's Sections on Criminal Law (1920) and on International and Comparative Law (1934).

Wigmore wrote an extraordinary number of books and articles on almost every field of the law, but his most significant works focused on evidence, criminal law and criminology, and international and comparative law. His great *Treatise on Evidence* (1904; third ed., 1940; subsequently revised by others) established itself as the dominant work in its field and was acclaimed as the greatest treatise on any single subject of the law. Although some critics objected to the *Treatise*'s introduction of new terms, its length and elaborate organization, and its occasional divergence from the current state of the law, most scholars welcomed it as the most systematic overview of its subject, and it had great influence on many states' revisions of their rules of EVIDENCE and on the Federal Rules of Evidence (1969–1975). Wigmore's other major works on evidence were his *Pocket Code of Evidence* (1910; third ed., 1942) and his *Principles of Judicial Proof* (1913, third ed., 1937). His other books include *A Panorama of the World's Legal Systems* (1928; second ed., 1936), *A Kaleidoscope of Justice* (1941), *Problems of Law: Its Past, Present and Future* (1920), and casebooks on evidence (1906; third ed., 1932) and on torts (1910–1912).

RICHARD B. BERNSTEIN

Bibliography

ROALFE, WILLIAM R. 1977 *John Henry Wigmore: Scholar and Reformer.* Evanston, Ill.: Northwestern University Press.

WILKES CASES
19 Howell's State Trials (1763–1768)

Counting derivative trials, the Wilkes Cases embraced at least forty cases from 1763 to 1769; all emanated ultimately from a single GENERAL WARRANT issued by the British secretaries of state on April 26, 1763, against *The North Briton*, No. 45, a periodical trenchantly critical of the Grenville administration. Numerous categories of the general warrant, which allowed its bearer to arrest, search, and seize at his discretion, had operated in England for centuries. The warrant of April 26, however, was of an atypical variety, based on custom rather than statute, which the government used against dissident publications; it resulted in the search of at least five houses, the arrest of forty-nine persons, and the seizure of thousands of manuscripts and books.

Although hundreds of such warrants had issued since the Restoration, the latest crop of victims included John Wilkes, a powerful member of Parliament and principal author of *The North Briton*. When Wilkes sued every official connected with the warrant, many of the others arrested promptly did the same.

The trials unfolded in distinct series. In *Huckle v. Money*, the first trial on July 6, 1763, CHARLES PRATT, the Chief Justice of the Court of Common Pleas, criticized the *North Briton* warrant because it specified no person, had been issued without a formal complaint under oath, and thus lacked PROBABLE CAUSE. When this case reached the full Common Pleas, Pratt extended his attack to the general search feature of the warrant, holding that it, as well as its companion power of general arrest, violated MAGNA CARTA.

The outcome of the *North Briton* trials incited suits by earlier victims of secretarial warrants. In the most famous of these trials, *Entick v. Carrington* (1765), which accrued from a general warrant against *The Monitor*, the emphasis shifted to the powers of general, confiscatory seizure in such warrants. Pratt, now ennobled as Lord Camden, condemned the use of seized personal papers against their owner as self-incriminatory. Moreover, Camden continued, because private property was inherently sacred, any invasion of it without express legal authority was a trespass even if it merely involved touching the soil or grass. He conceded that the inspection of private papers was not itself a legal trespass, but he insisted that the disclosure of the personal secrets they contained greatly magnified the harm from the physical trespass of their seizure.

Although Pratt in *Wilkes v. Wood* (1763) had condemned even general warrants authorized by statute, WILLIAM MURRAY (Lord Mansfield), in a final appeal of *Huckle v. Money*, upheld statutory warrants and denounced only those not based on parliamentary enactment. When Pratt shifted to the same grounds in *Entick*, the effect was to confine the assault on general warrants to the variant based on custom, and to preserve a greater number that derived from statute. In 1766 a resolution against general warrants did emerge from the House of Commons, but an effort to transform it into binding, comprehensive legislation failed.

WILLIAM CUDDIHY

Bibliography

HOLDSWORTH, SIR WILLIAM 1938 *A History of English Law.* 7th ed. 15 vols. Vol. 10:99–100, 658–672. London: Methuen.
NOBBE, GEORGE 1939 *The North Briton.* New York: Columbia University Press.

WILLIAMS, ROGER
(1603–1683)

Arriving in New England in 1631, Roger Williams preached in Plymouth and Salem, but almost immediately clashed with the Massachusetts authorities over issues involving both church and state. He attacked Massachusetts's right to its land on the grounds that the land had not been purchased from the Indians—only granted by the king. He claimed that the colonial churches had not broken sharply enough with the Church of England, and he denied that magistrates had power to punish in religious matters. Under sentence of banishment from Massachusetts, Williams fled to Providence in 1636 and formed a settlement there. By 1644 he had secured a patent from the English government combining his own and neighboring towns into the colony of Rhode Island and Providence Plantations.

Although always a Calvinist, Williams adhered to no church after his departure from Massachusetts except for a brief period as a Baptist; rather, he lived as a Seeker. RELIGIOUS LIBERTY was his abiding passion, and he defended it primarily for its benefits to religion. Drawing the analogy of church as garden and world as wilderness, he insisted that only a wall between the two could preserve the integrity of the church.

Williams believed that allowing the state any power in church affairs made the state the arbiter of religious truth, an area in which its lack of competence only perverted religion. To demonstrate the absurdity of state attempts to proclaim the true church, he cited history, especially the recent multiple changes in religious allegiance on the part of the English government, and he expressed the psychological insights that rulers tended to advance their own religious preferences as truth and that persecutors always justified their actions in religion's name.

Williams's political views flowed from his religious theories. For him the Israel of the Old Testament was a figurative entity and not, as Massachusetts Puritans claimed, a model for government. He saw government as a SOCIAL COMPACT drawn up between citizens for secular purposes only. Just as civil interference ruined religion, so religious interference disrupted government—by accusations of heresy against civil leaders and demands for their removal from office. He believed that governing was an art, for which Christianity did not necessarily constitute a gift.

Carrying his arguments in favor of religious liberty

to their logical and remarkably radical conclusions, Williams contended that liberty should be extended to all law-abiding citizens, including Roman Catholics (whom he abhorred), non-Christians, and even those he considered blasphemers. By opposing monopolization of Rhode Island's land by its original settlers, he strove to keep the colony open to newcomers of all religions and to enable them to settle there on an equal social and economic basis with already-established inhabitants.

Beyond Rhode Island's fidelity to his ideals of religious freedom, Williams exerted hardly any influence. His views shocked his contemporaries, and throughout his life he bore the stigma of radicalism. During the colonial years, his writings almost disappeared. Succeeding centuries, however, have restored his reputation by correctly perceiving him as a prophet and forerunner of modern religious liberty.

THOMAS CURRY

Bibliography

MILLER, PERRY 1953 *Roger Williams: His Contribution to the American Tradition.* Indianapolis: Bobbs-Merrill.
MORGAN, EDMUND S. 1967 *Roger Williams: The Church and the State.* New York: Harcourt, Brace & World.

WILLIAMS v. FLORIDA
399 U.S. 78 (1970)

The rule of *Williams* is that trial by a jury of six in a noncapital FELONY case does not violate the constitutional right to TRIAL BY JURY in a state prosecution. Trial by jury had historically meant trial by a jury of twelve, neither more nor less. Justice BYRON R. WHITE for the Supreme Court found no rationale for the figure of twelve, which he called "accidental" and "superstitious." If Congress enacted a statute providing for juries of less than twelve in federal prosecutions, the Sixth Amendment would be no bar, according to this case. A jury of six is practical: it can be selected in half the time, costs only half as much, and may reach its verdict more quickly. According to White, "there is no discernible difference between the results reached by the two different-sized juries," but in fact a jury of six hangs less frequently, significantly changes the probability of conviction, and convicts different persons. White claimed that the size of the jury should be large enough to promote group deliberation and allow for a representative cross-section of the community, and he claimed that a jury of six serves those functions as well as a jury of twelve.

In fact the Court was wrong. Only Justice THURGOOD MARSHALL dissented on the question of jury size, in an opinion that rested strictly on precedent. Williams also contended that Florida violated his RIGHT AGAINST SELF-INCRIMINATION by its notice-of-alibi rule, but he convinced only Justices HUGO L. BLACK and WILLIAM O. DOUGLAS.

LEONARD W. LEVY

(SEE ALSO: *Jury Size.*)

WILLIAMS v. MISSISSIPPI
170 U.S. 213 (1898)

Williams is a realistic snapshot of our constitutional law on race at the turn of the century. A black man was tried in Mississippi for the murder of a white, convicted by an all-white jury, and sentenced to death. He alleged that he had been denied the EQUAL PROTECTION OF THE LAWS guaranteed by the FOURTEENTH AMENDMENT, because the laws of the state were rigged in such a way as to exclude members of his race from jury service. In Mississippi, to be eligible for jury service one must be qualified to vote. To be a voter one must have paid his POLL TAX and have satisfied registration officials that he could not only pass a LITERACY TEST but also could understand or reasonably interpret any clause of the state constitution; registration officials had sole discretion to decide whether an applicant had the requisite understanding. In Mississippi at that time, a black graduate of Harvard Law School could not satisfy white officials. The state convention of 1890 clearly adopted new qualifications on the right to vote in order to insure white supremacy by disfranchising black voters. Under prior laws there were 190,000 black voters; by 1892 only 8,600 remained, and these were soon eliminated. Blacks disappeared from jury lists after 1892.

A unanimous Supreme Court, speaking through Justice JOSEPH MCKENNA, held that the state constitution and laws passed under it, prescribing the qualifications of voters and jurors, did not on their face discriminate racially. McKenna also declared that the discretion vested in state and local officials who managed elections and selected juries, while affording the opportunity for unconstitutional RACIAL DISCRIMINATION, was not constitutionally excessive. Yet McKenna said, "We gather . . . that this discretion can be and has been exercised against the colored race, and from these lists jurors are selected." The Court recognized that a law on its face might be impartial and be administered "with an evil eye and an unequal hand," but it held that "it has not been shown that their actual administration was evil; only that evil was possible under them."

LEONARD W. LEVY

WILLIAMS v. VERMONT
472 U.S. (1985)

Vermont levied a use tax on automobiles, collected upon each car's registration. No tax was imposed if the car was bought in Vermont, and a Vermont sales tax was paid. If the car was purchased outside Vermont, the use tax was reduced by the amount of any sales tax paid to the other state—but only if the registrant was then a Vermont resident. Persons who had bought cars outside Vermont before becoming Vermont residents sued in state court, challenging the constitutionality of this scheme. The Vermont courts denied relief, but the Supreme Court, 6–3, held that the discrimination against newcomers violated the EQUAL PROTECTION clause. Justice BYRON R. WHITE wrote the OPINION OF THE COURT.

As it had done for half a century, the Court avoided the much-discussed question whether a state must give a credit for payment of another state's sales tax in such circumstances. Instead, the Court followed ZOBEL V. WILLIAMS (1982) and held that the discrimination against newcomers to Vermont served no legitimate statutory purpose. As in *Zobel,* Justice WILLIAM J. BRENNAN, concurring, wrote that the discrimination threatened the "federal interest in free interstate migration." (See RIGHT TO TRAVEL.) Justice HARRY A. BLACKMUN, for the dissenters, favored a REMAND to the state courts for clarification whether the law in fact so discriminated. Even if it did, he argued, Vermont could legitimately tax in rough proportion to automobiles' use on Vermont roads.

KENNETH L. KARST

WILLIAMSON, HUGH
(1735–1819)

Hugh Williamson, mathemetician, physician, and Presbyterian minister, signed the Constitution as a North Carolina delegate to the CONSTITUTIONAL CONVENTION OF 1787. A frequent but not very influential speaker, he was the first to propose the six-year term for senators. He supported RATIFICATION in the North Carolina convention and served in the first two Congresses.

DENNIS J. MAHONEY

WILLIAMSON v. LEE OPTICAL CO.
348 U.S. 483 (1955)

Justice WILLIAM O. DOUGLAS, for an 8–0 Supreme Court, announced that "the day is gone when this Court uses the DUE PROCESS CLAUSE" to strike down state business regulation. Without any inquiry into actual legislative history, Douglas upheld an Oklahoma law regulating eyeglass sales, suggesting various hypothetical reasons why the legislature might have thought it necessary.

DENNIS J. MAHONEY

WILLOUGHBY, WESTEL W.
(1867–1945)

Westel Woodbury Willoughby taught political science at Johns Hopkins University (1894–1933) and was a founder of the American Political Science Association. He wrote nearly two dozen books, including *The Supreme Court of the United States* (1890), *The Nature of the State* (1896), *The American Constitutional System* (1904), and *The Constitutional Law of the United States* (1910; second edition, 1922).

Willoughby rejected the notion that FEDERALISM implied division of SOVEREIGNTY between the central government and the states. He described the Constitution in terms of LIMITED GOVERNMENT, but regarded the central government as possessing the ultimate authority in the country and believed that in crisis situations (such as civil war) the rights of both states and citizens must yield to the INHERENT POWER of national self-preservation. Because he thought the government must at other times be limited to constitutionally DELEGATED POWERS he was especially critical of the decisions in the INSULAR CASES.

DENNIS J. MAHONEY

WILLSON v. BLACK BIRD CREEK MARSH CO.
2 Peters 245 (1829)

Chief Justice JOHN MARSHALL's opinion for a unanimous Supreme Court cannot be reconciled with his opinions in GIBBONS V. OGDEN (1824) and BROWN V. MARYLAND (1827), neither of which he mentioned in Willson. Delaware had authorized the company to dam a navigable tidewater creek, obstructing the navigation of Willson's sloop, licensed under the same Federal Coastal Licensing Act that had proved decisive in *Gibbons.* The Court sustained the constitutionality of the state statute as a measure calculated to improve marshland property and the health of its inhabitants. The Coastal Licensing Act notwithstanding, the Court found that Congress had chosen not to govern the many small navigable creeks of the eastern coast. In effect, the Court sustained the POLICE POWER in a case involving local circumstances affecting the COMMERCE CLAUSE "in its dormant state," that is, unexercised by Congress.

Marshall's *Willson* opinion is so laconic, almost unreasoned, and uncharacteristic of the great Chief Justice that it has never been satisfactorily explained. FELIX FRANKFURTER, in his book *The Commerce Clause,* surmised that Marshall understood that a completely exclusive commerce power might overdiminish STATES' RIGHTS and that Marshall realized the need for effective state regulation of local problems. Taking into consideration "the circumstances of the case," Marshall acknowledged the state interest in enhancing property values and improving the public health. Accordingly he opened the door to the police power because the state's objectives, unlike the situations in *Gibbons* and *Brown,* were not the regulation of commerce per se. *Willson,* however, left a confused legacy for the TANEY COURT, which divided in MAYOR OF NEW YORK V. MILN (1837) and produced doctrinal chaos in the LICENSE CASES (1847) and the PASSENGER CASES (1849). Not until COOLEY V. BOARD OF WARDENS (1851) did the Taney Court find a formula that purported to reconcile Marshall's doctrines in *Gibbons* and *Willson.*

LEONARD W. LEVY

WILMOT PROVISO
(1846)

The proviso was introduced by Congressman David Wilmot (Democrat, Pennsylvania) as an amendment to a $2,000,000 appropriations bill requested by President JAMES K. POLK to finance the Mexican War. The proviso prohibited slavery in any territory acquired from Mexico, thus enabling northern Democrats, like Wilmot, to support the war without supporting slave expansion and more slave states. The proviso passed the House, but the Senate adjourned without acting on the appropriations bill. In 1847 the proviso was added to a new $3,000,000 war appropriations bill. The Senate refused to accept the proviso, and in a bitterly debated compromise, the House agreed to the appropriation without the proviso. Despite its fail-

ure in Congress, the proviso raised serious constitutional and political issues. Southerners argued that they had contributed to the war effort and ought to be allowed to settle in the conquered territories without any special disabilities. Northerners condemned the war, especially after the defeat of the proviso, as aggression by an expansionist "slave power." The proviso led to the formation of the Free Soil Party, which was committed to prohibiting SLAVERY IN THE TERRITORIES. Free Soilers ran particularly well in some northern Democratic districts.

PAUL FINKELMAN

Bibliography

MORRISON, CHAPLAIN W. 1967 *Democratic Politics and Sectionalism: The Wilmot Proviso Controversy.* Chapel Hill: University of North Carolina Press.

WILSON, JAMES
(1742–1798)

James Wilson was one of the most influential members of the founding generation. He was born in Scotland and educated as a classical scholar at the University of St. Andrews. He immigrated to America in 1765, whereupon he served as a tutor at the College of Philadelphia while he studied law with the celebrated JOHN DICKINSON. His keen and perceptive mind, superb classical education, and excellent legal training prepared him to play a major role in the creation of the new American republic. He was a frequent delegate from Pennsylvania to the Second CONTINENTAL CONGRESS, one of six men who signed both the DECLARATION OF INDEPENDENCE and the Constitution, and second only to JAMES MADISON in his contribution to the deliberations of the CONSTITUTIONAL CONVENTION. He produced what was probably the most widely distributed and discussed defense of the new Constitution in his Statehouse Speech of October 6, 1787. He was the principal figure in the efforts to secure RATIFICATION OF THE CONSTITUTION by Pennsylvania, whose approval was indispensable to the success of the whole constitutional movement. He was a major architect of the significant Pennsylvania Constitution of 1790. He was one of the six original Justices of the United States Supreme Court. He was the first professor of law appointed after the founding of the new republic, and he was the only Framer to formulate a general theory of government and law—this in his lectures on law, delivered in 1791–1792 at what would later become the University of Pennsylvania.

Wilson was and remains influential, however, not so much because of the roles he played as for the ideas he articulated, the arguments he made, and the institutional arrangements he favored. Among the principal Framers, Wilson was the most committed to, and trusting of, unmitigated majoritarian democracy. He favored the simplicity of immediate consent and self-restraint to the complexity of procedural protections and constitutional contrivances. Relying heavily on the Scottish moralists (especially Thomas Reid), Wilson argued that men are naturally social; imbued with a sense of goodness, veracity, and benevolence; and possessed of a progressive intuitive sense that can be improved with practice so as to carry society "above any limits which we can now assign." As a consequence, he trusted them to elect leaders who would govern soberly and well, especially over a large and "comprehensive Federal Republic" such as the United States. He saw no need to protect the people from themselves. Madison's "republican remed[ies] for the diseases most incident to republican government" were, he believed, unnecessary. The government would be good to the extent that its branches were prompted, through their competition with one another, to serve the people and to reflect faithfully their wishes. Wilson brought this view of government and his commitment to majoritarianism to the Federal Convention, where his influence was clearly felt. He contributed significantly to the Convention's understanding of SEPARATION OF POWERS, figured prominently in determining the institutional arrangements and powers of the legislative, executive, and judicial branches, and helped to make FEDERALISM possible with his arguments concerning the dual SOVEREIGNTY of the people.

Wilson contributed to the Convention's understanding of separation of powers by arguing that it properly consists not of functionally separated branches but of coordinate and equal branches that perform a blend of functions in order to balance, not separate, powers. As he declared, "The separation of the departments does not require that they should have separate objects but that they should act separately tho' on the same objects." Wilson was aware that the various governmental branches, even though popularly elected, would occasionally be activated by "an official sentiment opposed to that of the General Government and perhaps to that of the people themselves." On those occasions, separation of powers would be necessary to insure the fidelity of these popular agents. Wilson also contributed to the Convention's understanding by stressing that separation of powers not only prevents governmental tyranny but also contributes to governmental efficiency. Aware that the democratic process of mutual deliberation and consent can paralyze government when swift and decisive action is necessary, he argued that government would be more efficient if its different functions were performed by separate and distinct agencies.

Wilson's influence on the legislative branch was felt primarily in the House of Representatives and in his promotion of reflective, as opposed to refining, representation. He argued in the Convention that "the Government ought to possess not only first, the force but secondly, the mind or sense of the people at large. The Legislature ought to be the most exact transcript of the whole Society." Wilson regarded representation as a "chain of communication" between the people and those to whom they have delegated the powers of government. Its purpose is not to "refine" the people's sentiments; rather, it is to communicate through links "sound and strong" the exact feelings of the people. Strong as this chain might be, however, Wilson was unwilling to trust it completely. So long as the legislature was perfectly reflective of the people, no problem was presented; however, there was no way to ensure this. On occasion, the legislature might come to possess and perceive an interest distinct from, and perhaps contrary to, the public at large. On that occasion, a single legislature would be dangerous, and thus Wilson argued for a divided legislature with a numerous House of Representatives, so close in political style and feelings to those it represented that it would constitute their "exact transcript," and a popularly elected Senate organized around the principle of proportional representation, thereby providing a "double representation" for the people. Wilson was one of the first to argue that it is possible for the people, simply through the electoral process, to have two different agents or representatives speaking for them at the same time. He did not fear that this common election would erode the material distinctions, and consequently the benefits that resulted from these material distinctions, between the two branches of the legislature. He trusted in the development of a "point of honor" between the two branches: they would "be rivals in duty, rivals in fame, rivals for the good graces of their common constituents." His views on the Senate, though unsuccessful at the Convention, were largely vindicated with the passage of the SEVENTEENTH AMENDMENT.

Wilson's contributions to the shape and powers of the executive branch were perhaps most significant of all. He was the first delegate to propose "that the Executive consist of a single person." He argued that the executive, no less than the legislature, needed to be restrained and controlled. But, "in order to control the legislative authority, you must divide it. In order to control the Executive, you must unite it." The advantage of clear-cut responsibility would reinforce and assure those other "very important advantages" that are also obtained from a single executive, including energy, vigor, dispatch, firmness, consistency, and stability. Wilson was also the first delegate at the Convention to suggest that the President should be elected directly by the people. When this proposal failed to gain general support, he was then the first to propose an ELECTORAL COLLEGE scheme, a modification of which ultimately found its way into the Constitution. He also favored a relatively brief presidential tenure of three years and reeligibility. These features would insure that the President would become and remain "the Man of the People."

Wilson's "Man of the People" was to be more than simply derived from their midst; he was also to be capable of acting vigorously on their behalf. As Wilson stressed in the Pennsylvania ratifying convention, the President was to be captain of the ship of state, holding firmly to the helm and allowing the vessel to "proceed neither in one direction or another without his concurrence." He was to be powerful and independent enough to protect the people from the excesses, instabilities, and injustices of legislative dominance. Wilson's captain was to take his bearings from the people and set his course according to their dictates. Because the people would not be easily misled, Wilson, unlike THE FEDERALIST, would not have the President provide the people with direction or resist them when they were wrong.

Wilson also labored at the Convention for the establishment of a powerful judiciary. Because the judges would be appointed by the President and confirmed by the Senate, he understood the judiciary to be "drawn from the same source, animated by the same principles, and directed to the same ends" and therefore "as much the friend of the people" as the other branches. As a consequence, it could be entrusted with the power of JUDICIAL REVIEW. So entrusted, it could serve as a "noble guard" defending the fundamental principles and will of the people as expressed in the Constitution from governmental sentiments—especially legislative sentiments—which from time to time might come to oppose them.

Wilson also helped to make federalism possible by arguing in the Convention that the people could create and assign power to more than "one set of immediate representatives." The delegates could preserve the states and at the same time establish a new national government because of the dual sovereignty of the people. He argued that both the states and the national government receive their authority directly from the people and owe their responsibility directly to them. The people are the sovereign foundation of all governments. As such, they can construct two levels of government and assign different powers to them. They can take powers from the state governments and place them in the national government. Wilson employed this same argument in the Pennsylvania ratifying convention to taunt those Anti-Federalists who contended that the people could not give to the national government whatever powers and for whatever purposes they pleased. He also operated from these premises in CHISHOLM V. GEORGIA (1793), his only truly important Supreme Court decision, in which he declared that the people of the United States had formed themselves into "a nation for national purposes" and that, consequently, states as well as individual persons were subject to the JUDICIAL POWER OF THE UNITED STATES.

Wilson embraced and defended the "comprehensive Federal Republic" created by the Constitution not only because the people had chosen to construct such a level of government over them but also because he believed that a reciprocating relationship existed between the structure of government and the character of the people. A petty state would produce, he believed, petty men. The only lessons they would learn would be those of "low Vice" and "illiberal Cunning." Only a large republic would sustain and nourish the good qualities of the people. Only a large republic would produce noble citizens, worthy of the great political trust Wilson would place in them.

Central to Wilson's constitutional thought was his confidence in the good qualities of the people. In this regard, he differed from his fellow Framers, in that he relied upon what The Federalist considered "the weaker springs of human character." This difference was critical then and remains so now: Wilson's commitment to unrestrained majoritarian democracy stands in sharp contrast to the Constitution's more complex mitigated democracy that relies not so much on men as on institutions for our political salvation.

RALPH A. ROSSUM

Bibliography

ADAMS, RANDOLPH GREENFIELD, ED. 1930 *Selected Political Essays of James Wilson.* New York: Knopf.
MCCLOSKEY, ROBERT GREEN, ED. 1967 *The Works of James Wilson.* 2 Vols. Cambridge, Mass.: Harvard University Press.
ROSSUM, RALPH A. 1976 James Wilson and the "Pyramid of Government": The Federal Republic. *Political Science Reviewer* 6:113–142.

SMITH, CHARLES PAGE 1956 *James Wilson: Founding Father.* Chapel Hill: University of North Carolina Press.

WILSON, WOODROW
(1856–1924)

Dr. Thomas Woodrow Wilson was both a scholar and an active participant in American constitutional development. Trained in history and law, Wilson became one of the first practitioners of the new academic political science that was born in America toward the close of the nineteenth century. He taught at Bryn Mawr College and Wesleyan University, and became a professor at, and later president of, Princeton University.

As a political scientist, Wilson urged fundamental reforms in the American system of government. In his first book, *Congressional Government* (1885), he argued that instead of the balance of powers envisaged by the Founders, American government was dominated by the legislative branch and, in particular, by a few powerful congressional committees. Wilson advocated cabinet government as he supposed it to exist in Great Britain, dominated by a strong executive. In *Constitutional Government in the United States* (1908), Wilson argued that under the Constitution the President had authority to exercise vigorous leadership of the whole American political system. In other works, Wilson advocated the scientific study of techniques of public administration and the training of a new class of civil servants who would be independent of political influence or control. Professional administrators, Wilson believed, should be left free to devise the most efficient means of carrying into effect the general policy decisions of the political branches of the government. (See PROGRESSIVE CONSTITUTIONAL THOUGHT.)

A progressive Democrat, Wilson was elected governor of New Jersey in 1910, and President of the United States two years later, when THEODORE ROOSEVELT broke with President WILLIAM HOWARD TAFT and split the Republican party. Wilson's platform called for a "New Freedom," characterized by a vigorous ANTITRUST policy, reduced tariffs, legislation to benefit organized labor, and creation of the federal reserve banking system.

During Wilson's terms of office, the SEVENTEENTH, EIGHTEENTH, and NINETEENTH AMENDMENTS were added to the Constitution. But ordinary legislation did as much to change the distribution and use of governmental power as did formal constitutional amendments. The FEDERAL RESERVE ACT (1913) placed control of the nation's money and credit in the hands of an independent, semi-private banking system. The FEDERAL TRADE COMMISSION ACT (1914), brainchild of Boston attorney LOUIS D. BRANDEIS, created an independent REGULATORY AGENCY with specific authority to make regulations having the force of law.

Among the least creditable achievements of the Wilson administration was the introduction of official racial SEGREGATION in executive departments of the federal government for the first time since the Civil War. Wilson himself approved the change of policy, arguing that segregation was in the best interests of black federal employees, but he did not regard it as a matter of major concern.

Wilson asserted a broad conception of executive power in military and FOREIGN AFFAIRS. In 1913 the United States assumed control of the foreign policy of Nicaragua and American marines put down an insurgent movement in that country. Wilson also deployed marines twice, in 1914 and 1916, to suppress insurrections in the Dominican Republic. Between 1913 and 1917 the United States intervened continuously, and ultimately unsuccessfully, in the internal politics of Mexico. For none of these military adventures did Wilson have specific congressional authorization; he relied instead on his power as COMMANDER-IN-CHIEF of the armed forces.

Although Wilson campaigned for reelection in 1916 on the slogan, "He kept us out of war," the United States entered World War I just one month after his second inauguration. The war emergency provided the rationale for a vast expansion of federal power. The Overman Act (1917) created a virtual presidential dictatorship over the machinery of the government; the RAILROAD CONTROL ACT commandeered the private rail network and consolidated it under government auspices; the SELECTIVE SERVICE ACT authorized the drafting of millions of young men into the military; and the ESPIONAGE ACT and the SEDITION ACT provided a basis for controlling civilian dissent. In a sense, the war provided the essential basis—a strongly held vision of the public good—for many of the reforms the Progressives had long advocated. For at least two decades afterward, political activists and reformers would hark back to the sense of unity that World War I provided.

American intervention enabled Britain and France to defeat the Germans and their allies, and so the American government was entitled to a leading voice in dictating the peace terms. Wilson was unable, however, to secure ratification of the Treaty of Versailles and the League of Nations Covenant by the United

States Senate. Republicans, led by Senator HENRY CABOT LODGE, opposed these measures, which seemingly would have subordinated American SOVEREIGNTY to an international body and permanently involved the United States in European quarrels.

In 1919, exhausted by a national campaign to win support for the Versailles Treaty, Wilson suffered a debilitating stroke. For the last year of his presidency the erstwhile advocate of strong presidential leadership tried, and failed, to govern the country from his sickbed. The constitutional problem of presidential disability would not be resolved until passage of the TWENTY-FIFTH AMENDMENT.

DENNIS J. MAHONEY

Bibliography

BETH, LOREN P. 1971 *The Development of the American Constitution: 1877–1917.* New York: Harper & Row.
BRAGDON, HENRY W. 1967 *Woodrow Wilson: The Academic Years.* Cambridge, Mass.: Belknap Press.
LINK, ARTHUR S. 1947–1974 *Woodrow Wilson,* 6 vols. Princeton, N.J.: Princeton University Press.

WILSON v. NEW
243 U.S. 332 (1917)

Congress passed the ADAMSON EIGHT-HOUR ACT in 1916 to avert a threatened nationwide railroad strike and to prevent disruption of INTERSTATE COMMERCE. The act prescribed an eight-hour day for railway workers and prohibited any reduction in pay for the shorter hours. Congress thereby regulated wages (pending the report of a commission established by the act) as well as hours. A United States District Court enjoined enforcement of the act, and that decision was appealed to the Supreme Court.

Chief Justice EDWARD D. WHITE, for a 5–4 Supreme Court, sustained the act as a legitimate exercise of congressional power. Asserting that Congress's power to establish working hours was "so clearly sustained as to render the subject not disputable," White faced the issue: did the COMMERCE CLAUSE give Congress the power to set wages? Despite reservations about government interference with FREEDOM OF CONTRACT, the majority held that the Adamson Act only supplemented contracting parties' rights. Moreover, Congress might set a temporary wage standard to protect interstate commerce when private parties failed to exercise their contract rights. Although the strike threatened an emergency, the emergency created no new powers, but it might provide an occasion for exercise of the commerce power.

The dissenters contended either that the act violated the Fifth Amendment as a TAKING OF PROPERTY or that the act lay outside the scope of Congress's commerce power because wages and hours were only remotely connected with interstate commerce.

DAVID GORDON

WINSHIP, IN RE
397 U.S. 358 (1970)

A 6–3 Supreme Court, speaking through Justice WILLIAM J. BRENNAN, held here that among the constitutional rights available in juvenile proceedings is the STANDARD OF PROOF beyond a REASONABLE DOUBT. A twelve-year-old was charged with a crime which, if done by an adult, would be larceny. The applicable New York statute required only a preponderance of evidence for conviction, and three successive New York courts rejected the contention that the FOURTEENTH AMENDMENT required a higher standard of proof. Tracing the requirement back to early United States history, Brennan found "virtually unanimous adherence" to the reasonable doubt standard in COMMON LAW jurisdictions. He extolled its protective value and spoke of the "vital role" of this "indispensable" standard. "We explicitly hold that the DUE PROCESS Clause protects the accused against conviction except upon proof beyond a reasonable doubt of every fact necessary to constitute the crime with which he is charged." Moreover, Brennan could find no obstacle to extending this right to juveniles. Justice HUGO L. BLACK, dissenting, charged the majority with amending the BILL OF RIGHTS. "Nowhere in that document is there any statement that conviction of crime requires proof of guilt beyond a reasonable doubt."

DAVID GORDON

(SEE ALSO: *Jackson v. Virginia,* 1979.)

WIRETAPPING

Telephone tapping is probably the best known form of electronic surveillance. The Supreme Court originally ruled in OLMSTEAD V. UNITED STATES (1928) that neither the Fifth nor the FOURTH AMENDMENT could be used to control wiretapping. In KATZ V. UNITED STATES (1967), however, the Supreme Court declared that what people reasonably expect to keep private is entitled to constitutional protection under the Fourth Amendment.

Both before and after the *Katz* decision, wiretapping was regulated by statute. Between 1934 and 1968, Section 605 of the COMMUNICATIONS ACT prohibited virtually all wiretapping except for NATIONAL SECURITY purposes. The Justice Department construed the statute so narrowly, however, that it had little effect: federal and state officials tapped extensively, as did private parties, and there were few prosecutions.

In 1968, Congress enacted Title III of the OMNIBUS CRIME CONTROL AND SAFE STREETS ACT, which prohibits telephone tapping except by federal and state officials who obtain prior judicial approval. Before issuing such approval, the court must have PROBABLE CAUSE to believe that EVIDENCE of a specific crime listed in the statute, and relating to a particular person, will be found by tapping a specific phone. Interceptions must be minimized, and notice of the interception must ultimately be given to the target of the surveillance.

Critics claim that the minimization and judicial supervision requirements are ineffective, that wiretapping is inherently indiscriminate, and that it is of little value for major crimes. Proponents assert that the technique is useful, and that the procedural protections are effective.

Wiretapping within the United States to obtain foreign national security intelligence is governed by the Foreign Intelligence Surveillance Act (1978), which creates a special warrant procedure for judicial issuance of permission to wiretap. Both wiretap statutes have been held constitutional.

HERMAN SCHWARTZ

(SEE ALSO: *Electronic Eavesdropping.*)

Bibliography
SCHWARTZ, HERMAN 1977 *Taps, Bugs, and Fooling the People.* New York: Field Foundation.

WIRT, WILLIAM
(1772–1834)

A Virginian lawyer, William Wirt helped defend James Callender in his SEDITION trial (1800) and helped prosecute AARON BURR for TREASON (1806). As United States attorney general under JAMES MONROE and JOHN QUINCY ADAMS (1817–1829), Wirt initiated the system of preserving the "opinions of the Attorneys General" for future use. While attorney general, Wirt followed the common practice of arguing private cases. In association with DANIEL WEBSTER he helped successfully to argue DARTMOUTH COLLEGE V. WOODWARD (1819), McCULLOCH V. MARYLAND (1819), and GIBBONS V. OGDEN (1824). Wirt's national perspective in these cases was similar to his official policy as attorney general.

PAUL FINKELMAN

Bibliography
KENNEDY, JOHN P. 1850 *Memoirs of the Life of William Wirt.* Philadelphia: Lea & Blanchard.

WISCONSIN v. YODER
406 U.S. 205 (1972)

Wisconsin's school-leaving age was sixteen. Members of the Old Order Amish religion declined, on religious grounds, to send their children to school beyond the eighth grade. Wisconsin chose to force the issue, and counsel for the Amish defendants replied that while the requirement might be valid as to others, the free exercise clause of the FIRST AMENDMENT required exemption in the case of the Amish.

Chief Justice WARREN E. BURGER, speaking for the Supreme Court, was much impressed by the Amish way of life. He rejected Wisconsin's argument that belief but not action was protected by the free exercise clause, and cited SHERBERT V. VERNER (1963). Nor was the Chief Justice convinced by the state's assertion of a COMPELLING STATE INTEREST. Nothing indicated that Amish children would suffer from the lack of high school education. Burger stressed that the Amish would have lost had they based their claim on "subjective evaluations and rejections of the contemporary social values accepted by the majority."

Justice BYRON R. WHITE filed a concurring opinion in which Justices WILLIAM J. BRENNAN and POTTER STEWART joined. White found the issue in *Yoder* much closer than Burger. White pointed out that many Amish children left the religious fold upon attaining their majority and had to make their way in the larger world like everyone else.

Justice WILLIAM O. DOUGLAS dissented in part. He saw the issue as one of CHILDREN'S RIGHTS in which Frieda Yoder's personal feelings and desires should be determinative. Justice Stewart, joined by Justice Brennan, filed a brief concurrence which took issue with Douglas on this point, and noted that there was nothing in the record which indicated that the religious beliefs of the children in the case differed in any way from those of the parents.

RICHARD E. MORGAN

WOLF v. COLORADO
338 U.S. 25 (1949)

In *Wolf* the Supreme Court held that "the core" of the FOURTH AMENDMENT's freedom from UNREASONABLE SEARCHES was "basic" and thus incorporated in the FOURTEENTH AMENDMENT as a restriction on searches by state officers, but that its enforcement feature, the EXCLUSIONARY RULE (in effect for federal trials since 1914), was not. The refusal to require the exclusionary rule for state trials was largely based on considerations of FEDERALISM. The Court reasoned, first, that the exclusionary rule could scarcely be considered "basic" when the COMMON LAW rule of admissibility was still followed both in the English-speaking world outside the United States and in most of the American states, and second, that suits in tort against offending officers could be "equally effective" in deterring unlawful searches. The experience of the following twelve years proved the suit in tort to be a paper remedy rather than an effective sanction, leading the Court to overrule *Wolf* and impose the exclusionary rule on the states in MAPP V. OHIO (1961).

JACOB W. LANDYNSKI

WOLFF PACKING COMPANY v. COURT OF INDUSTRIAL RELATIONS
262 U.S. 522 (1923)

Reversing a trend of broad definitions of public utilities, the Supreme Court voided a Kansas law declaring certain businesses to be AFFECTED WITH A PUBLIC INTEREST, and thus subject to regulation. A unanimous Court could find no justification for the statute and held that affectation derived from the nature of a business, not from the declaration of a state legislature. The Court thus returned to a concept implicit in *Munn v. Illinois* (1877): that a public interest inhered in monopolistic enterprises. (see GRANGER CASES.) Chief Justice WILLIAM HOWARD TAFT defined three categories of businesses clothed with a public interest: public utilities, occupations traditionally regulated (such as innkeepers), and those "businesses which, though not public at their inception, may be fairly said to have risen to be such, and have become subject in consequence to some government regulation."

DAVID GORDON

(SEE ALSO: *Public Use; Economic Regulation and the Constitution.*)

WOLMAN v. WALTER
433 U.S. 229 (1977)

Ohio's aid plan for independent schools had six components: (1) the loan of textbooks; (2) the supply of standardized testing and scoring material; (3) the provision of diagnostic services aimed at identifying speech, hearing, and psychological problems; (4) the provision, off non-public school premises, of therapeutic, guidance, and remedial services; (5) the loan to pupils of instructional materials such as slide projectors, tape recorders, maps, and scientific gear; and (6) the provision of transportation for field trips similar to the transportation provided public school students.

Justice HARRY BLACKMUN delivered what was in part an opinion of the Supreme Court and in part a PLURALITY OPINION in which only Chief Justice WARREN E. BURGER, Justice POTTER STEWART, and Justice LEWIS F. POWELL joined.

The Court upheld the loan of textbooks, the supply of testing materials, the therapeutic services, and the provision of diagnostic services on non-public school premises. The Court found unconstitutional the provisions for lending secular instructional materials and for field trip transportation.

This case indicated the extent to which the "wall between church and state" was in fact a blurred, indistinct, and variable barrier.

RICHARD E. MORGAN

WOMEN

See: Sex Discrimination

WONG KIM ARK, UNITED STATES v.
169 U.S. 649 (1898)

This case, decided at a time when prejudice against people of Chinese ancestry was widespread, maintained the integrity of the CITIZENSHIP clause of section one of the FOURTEENTH AMENDMENT. Congressional legislation, known as the CHINESE EXCLUSION ACTS, denied citizenship to Chinese immigrants, and a treaty with China provided that no subject of China in the United States could be naturalized. Neither the exclusion acts nor the treaty applied in this case, however, because Wong Kim Ark had been born in San Francisco. When he was about twenty-one he visited his parents who had returned to China after living in the United States approximately twenty years. On his return to San Francisco, he was denied entry to the United States on the grounds that he was not a citizen. The Supreme Court held, 6–2, that the government's policy in refusing NATURALIZATION to persons of Chinese ancestry could not constitutionally be applied to anyone born in the United States whose parents, regardless of ancestry, were domiciled in this country and did not have diplomatic status.

LEONARD W. LEVY

WONG SUN v. UNITED STATES
371 U.S. 471 (1963)

In *Wong Sun* the Supreme Court held that an incriminating oral statement made by a suspect that derives immediately from his unlawful arrest is inadmissible in evidence as a FRUIT OF THE POISONOUS TREE, no less than the derivative EVIDENCE obtained from an unlawful search, as in SILVERTHORNE V. UNITED STATES (1920), or from unlawful wiretapping, as in NARDONE V. UNITED STATES (1939). However, when the taint of the earlier illegality is dissipated (as it was in this case, by a suspect voluntarily returning to make a statement several days after his arraignment and release on his own recognizance), the evidence is admissible.

In addition, *Wong Sun* contributed to the elaboration of PROBABLE CAUSE standards by holding that flight from an officer is not in itself such a strong inference of guilt as to establish probable cause for an arrest.

JACOB W. LANDYNSKI

WOOD v. STRICKLAND
420 U.S. 308 (1975)

This was an early case in the development of EXECUTIVE IMMUNITY from DAMAGES in CIVIL RIGHTS actions alleging constitutional violations. The case involved the liability of school board members for alleged violations of students' DUE PROCESS rights. The Supreme Court, in an opinion by Justice BYRON R. WHITE, clarified its holding in SCHEUER V. RHODES (1974) by expressly stating that the good faith defense of executive officials contained both subjective and objective elements. An official must subjectively believe he is doing right and must not act in "ignorance or disregard of settled, indisputable law." *Harlow v. Fitzgerald* (1982) later undermined the subjective

component of *Wood*'s test. (See NIXON V. FITZGERALD, 1982.)

THEODORE EISENBERG

WOODBURY, LEVI
(1789–1851)

Levi Woodbury was a New Hampshire lawyer, state supreme court justice (1817–1823), governor (1823–1824), United States senator (1825–1831; 1841–1842), secretary of the navy (1831–1834), secretary of the treasury (1834–1841), and United States Supreme Court Justice (1845–1851). A staunch Jacksonian Democrat, Woodbury supported territorial expansion, STRICT CONSTRUCTION, and STATES' RIGHTS, while opposing the BANK OF THE UNITED STATES, abolitionists, and high tariffs. Although a conservative, Woodbury advocated public schools, female education, and prison reform. He personally disliked slavery but believed it was constitutionally protected and that all agitation over it should cease.

On the New Hampshire bench Woodbury supported the state in DARTMOUTH COLLEGE V. WOODWARD (1819). As treasury secretary, Woodbury continued President ANDREW JACKSON's Bank War and advocated an independent treasury. He believed that Congress lacked constitutional power to recharter the Bank, and as late as 1841 he asserted that MCCULLOCH V. MARYLAND (1819) neither set a valid precedent nor determined the constitutionality of any future bank charter.

In 1830, as a senator, Woodbury criticized the Supreme Court for its "manifest and sleepless opposition . . . to the strict construction of the Constitution" which had created "a diseased enlargement of the powers of the General Government and throwing chains over States-Rights. . . ." Woodbury attempted to stop these tendencies in his brief tenure on the Supreme Court. In the LICENSE CASES (1847), Woodbury joined the majority in upholding state PROHIBITION statues. In the PASSENGER CASES (1849), he asserted, in dissent, that states could constitutionally regulate immigrants without violating the Constitution's COMMERCE CLAUSE. In LUTHER V. BORDEN (1848), he agreed with the majority that the case involved a POLITICAL QUESTION beyond the court's JURISDICTION, but he nevertheless modified his states' rights position to condemn the use of martial law in Rhode Island. In *Warning v. Clarke* (1847), he again dissented, this time to assert state jurisdiction over navigable rivers. In a rare deviation from his states' rights philosophy, Woodbury wrote the majority opinion in *Planters' Bank v. Sharpe* (1848), overturning a Mississippi statute and court decision because both impaired the OBLIGATION OF CONTRACTS in violation of the Constitution.

Woodbury's most important majority opinion was written in *Jones v. Van Zandt* (1847), where he upheld a particularly harsh interpretation of the Fugitive Slave Law of 1793. Van Zandt, an Ohio Quaker, had given a ride to a group of blacks walking on a road in Ohio. Woodbury held Van Zandt financially liable for the escape of these fugitive slaves, even though at the time Van Zandt had no notice they were fugitives. Woodbury asserted that the Constitution had "flung its shield" over slavery, giving masters a COMMON LAW right to recapture their property. Woodbury held that the Fugitive Slave Law was a constitutionally proper enforcement of this right. Somewhat inconsistently, he then asserted that slavery itself was "a political question, settled by each State for itself." In 1848 Woodbury sought the presidential nomination. He was considered a likely candidate in 1852, because his *Van Zandt* opinion gave him southern support, while as a Northerner he might get grudging support from Free Soil Democrats. He campaigned for the nomination from the bench until his death in 1851.

PAUL FINKELMAN

Bibliography

GATELL, FRANK O.   1968   Levi Woodbury. Pages 843–872 in Leon Friedman and Fred L. Israel, eds., *The Justices of the United States Supreme Court, 1789–1969: Their Lives and Major Opinions.* New York: Chelsea House.

WOODRUFF v. PARHAM
8 Wallace 123 (1869)

Woodruff produced a retreat from the broad enunciation of the ORIGINAL PACKAGE DOCTRINE in BROWN v. MARYLAND (1827). In that case Chief Justice JOHN MARSHALL had said in an OBITER DICTUM that the DOCTRINE applied "equally to importations from a sister State. . . ." In this case the city of Mobile, Alabama, had taxed various commodities and transactions including goods imported from other states and sold in their original and unbroken packages. Woodruff alleged that this tax violated the constitutional clause forbidding state IMPOSTS or duties on imports. The Court ruled unanimously that the clause applied only to goods imported from foreign countries. Because the tax did not discriminate against the products of other states, it did not burden INTERSTATE COMMERCE. In effect, the Court limited the original package doctrine to FOREIGN COMMERCE.

LEONARD W. LEVY

WOODS, WILLIAM B.
(1824–1887)

William Burnham Woods of Ohio was appointed to the Supreme Court in 1880 after eleven years of service as United States circuit judge for the Fifth Circuit. His tenure on the Supreme Court was brief (1881–1887); virtually all of his opinions for the Court dealt with private law questions that came up under DIVERSITY JURISDICTION. He is remembered primarily for his collaboration with Justice JOSEPH P. BRADLEY, first on circuit, then on the Supreme Court, in the formulation of a jurisprudence for the FOURTEENTH AMENDMENT. Although initially disposed to give the amendment a BROAD CONSTRUCTION, Woods ultimately retreated in the face of a more circumspect majority on the Supreme Court.

Woods's first meeting with Bradley, who had been assigned to the circuit upon his appointment to the Supreme Court, occurred at New Orleans in 1870. There they advanced a broad interpretation of the Fourteenth Amendment's PRIVILEGES AND IMMUNITIES clause in *Live Stock Dealers & Butchers Assn. v. Crescent City Co. & Board of Metropolitan Police* (1870), the first case, Woods noted in the report, in which the amendment was fully considered by a federal tribunal. The privileges and immunities of United States citizens, they contended, embraced all "fundamental rights," including that of pursuing any lawful employment in a lawful manner. "It is possible," Bradley admitted, "that those who framed the article were not themselves aware of the far reaching character of its terms," but its language clearly applied "as well to white as colored persons" and protected the rights of both against arbitrary state laws. Working from memoranda prepared by Bradley, Woods indicated in *United States v. Hall* (1871) that FREEDOM OF SPEECH and FREEDOM OF ASSEMBLY were among the FUNDAMENTAL RIGHTS guaranteed by the Fourteenth Amendment, opening the door for INCORPORATION of the BILL OF RIGHTS through the privileges and immunities clause. Over the dissents of Bradley and three others, however, the Supreme Court rejected each of these pioneering doctrinal formulations in the landmark SLAUGHTERHOUSE CASES (1873). Eleven years later, in BUTCHERS UNION SLAUGHTERHOUSE

Co. v. Crescent City Live Stock Co. (1884), Woods joined with Bradley and Justices Stephen J. Field and John Marshall Harlan in one last trenchant protest against the majority's emasculation of the privileges and immunities clause. Woods surrendered altogether in *Presser v. Illinois* (1886), where he spoke for a unanimous Court in holding that the Bill of Rights was a limitation only on the power of the federal government and in no way restricted the states.

Woods's initial construction of Congress's affirmative powers under the Fourteenth Amendment was especially spacious. In *Hall,* the case of first impression, Woods overruled defendants' demurrer to a conspiracy INDICTMENT under the Civil Rights Act of 1870. A federal statute punishing private action such as assault, he asserted, was certainly an "appropriate" exercise of national power, for "denying the EQUAL PROTECTION OF THE LAWS included the omission to protect, as well as the omission to pass laws for protection." (See STATE ACTION.) In UNITED STATES V. CRUIKSHANK (1874), however, Bradley led a retreat from this position. There counsel for the defendants again attacked the constitutionality of the conspiracy measure, insisting that it usurped the state's exclusive JURISDICTION over crimes such as murder. Woods disagreed and stood on the doctrine advanced in his *Hall* opinion. But Bradley conceded that protection of rights against private action was primarily the duty of the states, and his views prevailed in the Supreme Court. Woods then abandoned the *Hall* formulation. Seven years later in UNITED STATES V. HARRIS (1883), his most important Supreme Court opinion, Woods prominently displayed his penchant for following the lead of others. The results were tragic. In *Harris* he not only embraced Bradley's *Cruikshank* position but also invalidated the Klu Klux Klan Act (FORCE ACT OF 1871) on the grounds that it failed to restrict criminal liability to persons who conspired to divest rights because of the victim's race. As drafted, Woods explained for the Court, the statute covered instances even where whites assaulted whites; consequently it was "broader than is warranted" by the Thirteenth Amendment.

CHARLES W. McCURDY

Bibliography

FILLER, LOUIS 1969 William B. Woods. In Leon Friedman and Fred L. Israel (eds.), *The Justices of the United States Supreme Court 1789–1969: Their Lives and Major Opinions.* Pp. 1327–1336. New York: Chelsea House.
FRANTZ, LAURENT B. 1964 Congressional Power to Enforce the Fourteenth Amendment against Private Acts. *Yale Law Journal* 73:1353–1384.

WOODS v. CLOYD W. MILLER COMPANY
333 U.S. 138 (1948)

A unanimous Supreme Court here upheld the Housing and Rent Act of 1947 which had extended wartime price controls into peacetime. Writing for the Court, Justice WILLIAM O. DOUGLAS declared that legislation adopted under the WAR POWERS could constitutionally be continued in effect in economically essential areas of public policy even after the cessation of hostilities.

DAVID GORDON

WOODSON v. NORTH CAROLINA

See: Capital Punishment Cases, 1976

WORCESTER v. GEORGIA

See: Cherokee Indian Cases

WORKERS' COMPENSATION LEGISLATION

Workers' compensation legislation provides workers compensation for losses resulting from injury, disablement, or death when the losses result from work-related accidents, casualties, or disease. The legislation replaces tort liability with a schedule of benefits based upon the loss or impairment of the wage-earning capacity of the worker. All fifty states in the Union have workers' compensation statutes.

Under the COMMON LAW, employers often were able to defeat employees' tort actions by invoking the doctrines of contributory negligence, negligence of fellow servants, or assumption of risk. Frequently the employer did not even need these defenses, for the employee first had to prove the employer's negligence in order to recover. Accordingly, many victims of work-related injuries went uncompensated.

In order to extend the protection afforded workers and to contain costly and time-consuming litigation of industrial accidents, states enacted workers' compensation legislation with no requirement of negligence or fault as a prerequisite to liability. Employers were simultaneously protected against what were perceived to be excessively large JUDGMENTS through a limited and determinant payout. The statutes essentially substitute a system of insurance for liability based on fault.

In *Ives v. South Buffalo Railway Company* (1911) New York's highest court struck down the state's first compulsory compensation requirements as unconstitutional, on the ground that they violated the state and federal DUE PROCESS clauses. However, the Supreme Court held in NEW YORK CENTRAL RAILROAD COMPANY V. WHITE (1917) that a compulsory compensation system does not violate the United States Constitution, at least for "hazardous employment." In the case of the New York statute, New York promptly amended its constitution to authorize compulsory plans.

The general rule in this area of law is that if an injury is fully or partly covered by the statute, the statutory remedy is exclusive. Many jurisdictions do not allow compensation for injuries caused by a worker's willful misconduct or unreasonable failure to observe safety rules or use safety devices.

WILLIAM B. GOULD

Bibliography

MALONE, WEX S; PLANT, MARCUS L; and LITTLE, JOSEPH W. 1980 *Cases and Materials on Workers' Compensation and Employment Rights,* 2nd ed. St. Paul, Minn: West Publishing Co.

WORTMAN, TUNIS
(?–1822)

A New York lawyer prominent in Tammany politics, Tunis Wortman contributed significantly to the emergence of a libertarian theory of the FIRST AMENDMENT following the Sedition Act of 1798. His philosophic book, *An Enquiry, Concerning the Liberty, and Licentiousness of the Press* (1800), whose publication ALBERT GALLATIN and other Jeffersonian congressmen helped underwrite, was the era's most systematic presentation of the case for an absolutist interpretion of freedom of publication (excluding personal libels). Wortman regarded prosecutions for SEDITIOUS LIBEL as incompatible with republican government.

LEONARD W. LEVY

WRIGHT v. VINTON BRANCH OF MOUNTAIN TRUST BANK OF ROANOKE
300 U.S. 440 (1937)

Despite the decision in LOUISVILLE JOINT STOCK LAND BANK V. RADFORD (1935), Congress had to act on behalf of farmers losing their farms through fore-

closures. A revised FRAZIER-LEMKE ACT fixed a three-year stay of proceedings with the proviso that a federal bankruptcy court might shorten that period if the economic emergency ended. The new act also provided that the mortgagee retained a lien on the property. But except for a few other minor changes the act remained the same, allowing the bankrupt mortgagor to retain possession of the property and to purchase it at its newly appraised value. Justice LOUIS D. BRANDEIS, for a unanimous Supreme Court, found that the new act was free of the objectionable features of the original and did not violate the Fifth Amendment's DUE PROCESS clause. President FRANKLIN D. ROOSEVELT's court-packing plan may have influenced the Court to temper its views.

LEONARD W. LEVY

WRIGHTWOOD DAIRY CO., UNITED STATES v.
315 U.S. 110 (1942)
ROCK ROYAL CO-OP, INC., UNITED STATES v.
307 U.S. 533 (1939)

These decisions are among the more significant results of the post-1936 interpretation of the COMMERCE CLAUSE as a source of federal power extending to virtually the entire national economy. The AGRICULTURAL MARKETING AGREEMENT ACT of 1937 authorized the secretary of agriculture to fix minimum prices for all milk in INTERSTATE COMMERCE, or burdening or affecting commerce. In *Rock Royal* the price-fixing provisions governed sales by local dairy farmers to dealers who processed the milk and transported it. Those opposing federal authority contended that the regulated transactions included INTRASTATE COMMERCE whose sales were fully completed *before* any interstate commerce began. Holding the statute constitutional, the Court declared that the national power to fix production quotas and prices applied to local milk because its marketing was "inextricably intermingled with and directly affected the marketing of milk which moved across state lines." In *Wrightwood,* the milk subject to regulation under the same statute was entirely intrastate and none of it was intermingled with milk that crossed state lines. Nevertheless the Court unanimously held that it was the EFFECT ON INTERSTATE COMMERCE, not the source of the injury to it, that was "the sole criterion of Congressional power." Accordingly, the commerce power extended to intrastate transactions whose regulation made the regulation of interstate commerce effective, including intrastate transactions whose competitive price affected interstate ones. Both cases were decided on a thoroughgoing application of the SHREVEPORT DOCTRINE.

LEONARD W. LEVY

WRIT OF ASSISTANCE

See: Assistance, Writ of

WRIT OF CERTIORARI

See: Certiorari, Writ of

WRIT OF ERROR

See: Error, Writ of

WRIT OF HABEAS CORPUS

See: Habeas Corpus

WRIT OF MANDAMUS

See: Mandamus, Writ of

WRIT OF PROHIBITION

See: Prohibition, Writ of

WRITS OF ASSISTANCE CASE

See: Paxton's Case

WYMAN v. JAMES
400 U.S. 309 (1971)

In *Wyman* the Supreme Court held that a recipient of Aid to Families with Dependent Children must permit a home visit by a caseworker, when the law requires it, or forfeit her right to public assistance. The Supreme Court did not consider it to be a search in FOURTH AMENDMENT terms. Even if the visit were

a search, the Court said it was reasonable: it was made for the benefit of the child; it was "a gentle means" of assuring that tax funds are properly spent; the caseworker was not a "uniformed authority"; and the recipient had the choice of invoking her right to refuse or forfeiting the benefits. Three dissenting Justices (WILLIAM O. DOUGLAS, WILLIAM J. BRENNAN, THURGOOD MARSHALL) protested that the Court had granted more protection to a commercial warehouse than to a "poor woman's home."

JACOB W. LANDYNSKI

WYNEHAMER v. PEOPLE OF NEW YORK
13 N.Y. 378 (1856)

Although out of joint with its times, *Wynehamer* became a classic case of pre-1937 American constitutional history, exemplifying our constitutional law as a law of judicially implied limitations on legislative powers, drawn from the DUE PROCESS clause for the benefit of VESTED RIGHTS. The case involved the constitutionality of a state prohibition act. More than a dozen states had such legislation before the Civil War. The New York law involved in *Wynehamer* prohibited the sale of intoxicating liquor and the possession of liquors for sale, and it ordered the forfeiture and destruction of existing supplies as public nuisances. The fundamental issue raised by such legislation was whether property which had not been taken for a public use could be destroyed in the name of the public health and morals, without any compensation to the owner. Everywhere, except in New York, the state courts held that a mere license to sell liquor was not a contract in the meaning of the CONTRACT CLAUSE, and that a charter to make and sell liquor was subject to the RESERVED POLICE POWER to alter, amend, or repeal it. Moreover, liquor, like explosives or narcotics, was a peculiar kind of property, dangerous to the public safety, morals, and health. Legislatures could never relinquish their control over such matters, not even by a contract in the form of a charter. As Chief Justice ROGER B. TANEY had said in the 1847 LICENSE CASES, nothing in the United States Constitution prevented a state from regulating the liquor traffic "or from prohibiting it altogether."

The New York Court of Appeals, however, held the state prohibition statute unconstitutional on the grounds that it violated the due process clause of the state constitution. The various opinions of the state judges used the novel concept of SUBSTANTIVE DUE

PROCESS about half a century before the Supreme Court of the United States accepted that concept. The conventional and previously sole understanding of due process had been that it referred to regularized and settled procedures insuring mainly a fair accusation, hearing, and conviction. And, the doctrine of vested rights notwithstanding, the orthodox view of the POLICE POWER authorized the legislature, as Chief Justice LEMUEL SHAW of Massachusetts had said, "to declare the possession of certain articles of property . . . unlawful because they would be injurious, dangerous, and noxious; and by due process of law, by proceeding IN REM, to provide both for the abatement of the nuisance and for the punishment of the offender, by the seizure and confiscation of the property, by the removal, sale or destruction of the noxious article" (*Fisher v. McGirr*, 1854). Accordingly the opinion of the New York court was startling when it said, "All property is alike in the characteristic of inviolability. If the legislature has no power to confiscate and destroy property in general, it has no such power over any particular species." The court showed that the prohibition statute simply annihilated existing property right in liquors. The crucial lines of the opinion declared that the right not to be deprived of life, liberty, or property without due process of law "necessarily imports that the legislature cannot make the mere existence of the rights secured the occasion of depriving a person of any of them, even by the forms which belong to 'due process of law.' For if it does not necessarily import this, then the legislative power is absolute."

Thus even if the legislature provided all the forms of due process by laying down proper procedures for prosecuting violators of the statute, as in this case, due process had still been denied. The court, in effect, looked at the substance of the statute, found it denied persons of their property, and then held it unconstitutional for denying "due process," even if it did not deny due process. One can make sense out of this by realizing that the court had rewritten the due process clause to mean that property cannot be deprived with or without due process. The Court in effect redpenciled the due process clause out of the constitution, or as EDWARD S. CORWIN said, *Wynehamer* stands for "nothing less than the elimination of the very phrase under construction from the constitutional clause in which it occurs." The difficulty, however, is that the court had to its own mind kept and relied on the due process clause. It added a new meaning to supplement the old one. It constitutionally changed process into substance by holding that the statute's infirmity lay in what it did, not how it did

it. Due process as a substantive limitation on legislative powers was then an absurd concept. Substantive process was oxymoronic, like thunderous silence.

Another way of understanding *Wynehamer*'s substantive due process is to realize that the court believed that due process had substance. The court in effect accused the legislature of retaining the forms of due process without its substance, that is, of providing mere empty formalities and labeling them due process, because the effective deprivation of property was not by judicial process but by legislative fiat.

Wynehamer, an aberration at the time, was everywhere repudiated yet destined for ultimate acceptance by the highest court of the land and destined, too, to become the source of a major doctrine in American constitutional history.

LEONARD W. LEVY

Bibliography
CORWIN, EDWARD S. 1948 *Liberty against Government.* Chap. 3. Baton Rouge: Louisiana State University Press.
MOTT, RODNEY L. 1926 *Due Process of Law.* Pages 311–326. Indianapolis: Bobbs-Merrill.

WYTHE, GEORGE
(1726–1806)

George Wythe served almost uninterruptedly in Virginia's House of Burgesses from 1754 to 1775 and was a delegate to the First Continental Congress in 1774, later signing the DECLARATION OF INDEPENDENCE. With his pupil THOMAS JEFFERSON (JOHN MARSHALL and HENRY CLAY were also his students) and EDMUND PENDLETON, Wythe revised Virginia's laws. He was appointed to the Virginia Court of Chancery in 1778; one year later he became the first professor of law in the United States, enabling him to influence the course of American jurisprudence. His opinion in COMMONWEALTH V. CATON (1782) approved, in theory, a court's right to restrain a legislative act violative of the constitution. Wythe was a delegate to the CONSTITUTIONAL CONVENTION OF 1787 and chairman of its rules committee, but judicial duties obliged him to leave the convention early. At the Virginia convention he worked for RATIFICATION OF THE CONSTITUTION. Wythe opposed slavery and freed the slaves he inherited.

DAVID GORDON

Bibliography
CLARKIN, WILLIAM 1970 *Serene Patriot: A Life of George Wythe.* Albany, N.Y.: Alan Publications.

YAKUS v. UNITED STATES
321 U.S. 414 (1944)

The EMERGENCY PRICE CONTROL ACT of 1942 delegated power to fix prices and rents to the Office of Price Administration (OPA). Under the act, challenges to the legality of OPA regulations could not be made in federal district court enforcement proceedings, even those aimed at imposing criminal penalties, but must be made in separate proceedings in the EMERGENCY COURT OF APPEALS. The Supreme Court sustained this limitation on the district courts in civil enforcement proceedings in *Lockerty v. Phillips* (1944). In *Yakus,* the Court upheld the limitation in the context of a criminal prosecution. The Court also rejected attacks on the act as an unconstitutional DELEGATION OF POWER for failing to provide sufficient guidelines. Chief Justice HARLAN FISKE STONE, for the Court, said that the act contained specific objectives: "to stabilize prices and to prevent speculative, unwarranted and abnormal increases in prices and rents." It also mentioned standards for price-setting: administrators should consult industry and consider current prices. Because the act accorded with earlier decisions and because its standards were "sufficiently definite and precise," Stone could find no unauthorized delegation of power. Justice OWEN ROBERTS, dissenting, believed that the case presented substantially the same issue as SCHECHTER POULTRY CORPORATION v. UNITED STATES (1935) which the majority, he said, had clearly overruled. Justice WILEY RUTLEDGE also dissented, joined by Justice FRANK MUR-PHY. Rutledge argued that Congress could not constitutionally command the federal courts to enforce administrative orders, disregarding their possible unconstitutionality. The Rutledge view seems likely to prevail in the absence of a wartime emergency.

DAVID GORDON

YAMASHITA, IN RE
327 U.S. 1 (1947)

A 6–2 Supreme Court here refused to consider the claim of an enemy officer, charged with war crimes before an American military tribunal in the Philippines, that he had been denied the DUE PROCESS OF LAW guaranteed by the Fifth Amendment. The Court held that it had JURISDICTION only to consider whether the military tribunal had authority to try the accused.

When General Tomoyuki Yamashita surrendered in 1945, an American military commission tried him on charges that he permitted atrocities against both civilians and prisoners of war, in violation of the law of war. Yamashita's military counsel applied to the Supreme Court for leave to file petitions for writs of HABEAS CORPUS and prohibition, challenging the jurisdiction and legal authority of the commission. Chief Justice HARLAN FISKE STONE, for the majority, denied leave to file but wrote an opinion on the jurisdictional issues. He found that Congress had legally authorized the commission's establishment under the WAR POWERS, and that the charge was adequate to state a violation of the law of war. Stone also denied that the American Articles of War (which incorporated the law of war) forbade the admission of hearsay and opinion EVIDENCE.

Justices FRANK MURPHY and WILEY RUTLEDGE, dissenting, argued eloquently for the extension of the due process clause.

DAVID GORDON

YARBROUGH, EX PARTE
110 U.S. 651 (1884)

This is the only nineteenth-century case in which the Supreme Court sustained the power of the United States to punish private persons for interfering with VOTING RIGHTS. Yarbrough and other members of the Ku Klux Klan assaulted a black citizen who voted in a congressional election. The United States convicted the Klansmen under a federal statute making it a crime to conspire to injure or intimidate any citizen in the free exercise of any right secured to him by the laws of the United States. The Court, in a unanimous opinion by Justice SAMUEL F. MILLER, held that the United States "must have the power to protect the elections on which its existence depends, from violence and corruption." Miller's reasoning is confused. Congress had passed the statute in contemplation of its power to enforce the FOURTEENTH AMENDMENT. In UNITED STATES V. CRUIKSHANK (1876) the Court had ruled that the same statute could not reach private, rather than state, actions. Miller thought the situation different when Congress sought to protect rights constitutionally conferred, and he stressed Article I, section 4, which empowered Congress to alter state regulations for the election of members of Congress. But that provision did not apply here. In UNITED STATES V. REESE (1876) the Court had ruled that the FIFTEENTH AMENDMENT did not confer the right to vote on anyone, but only a right to be free from RACIAL DISCRIMINATION in voting. Here, however, Miller ruled that "under some circumstances," the Fifteenth Amendment, which was not the basis of the statute, may operate as the source of a right to vote. In the end Miller declared, "But it is a waste of time to seek for specific sources of the power to pass these laws." In JAMES V. BOWMAN (1903), involving the right to vote in a federal election, the Court held unconstitutional an act of Congress without reference to *Yarbrough.*

LEONARD W. LEVY

YATES, ROBERT
(1738–1801)

Judge Robert Yates, who in 1777 had served on the committee that drafted the state constitution, was a delegate from New York to the CONSTITUTIONAL CONVENTION OF 1787. A trusted, if undistinguished, follower of Governor George Clinton, Yates represented the antinationalist viewpoint then dominant in New York politics. He and JOHN LANSING consistently outvoted ALEXANDER HAMILTON and kept New York in the STATES' RIGHTS camp. But on July 10 Yates and Lansing walked out, charging that the Convention was exceeding its authority.

In the contest over RATIFICATION OF THE CONSTITUTION Yates was an active anti-Federalist. His "Brutus" letters were an able and articulate presentation of the dangers opponents feared would result from adoption of the Constitution, including annihilation of the states and usurpation by the federal courts. Yates was a delegate to the New York ratifying convention where he voted against ratification.

Yates kept notes of the debates of the federal convention from its first meeting through July 5. He did not publish the notes himself, but they were published in 1821 and are, after JAMES MADISON's, the best record of the early proceedings.

DENNIS J. MAHONEY

Bibliography

ROSSITER, CLINTON 1966 *1787: The Grand Convention.* New York: Macmillan.

YATES v. UNITED STATES
354 U.S. 298 (1957)

Following DENNIS V. UNITED STATES (1951), Smith Act conspiracy prosecutions were brought against all second-rank United States Communist party officials, and convictions were secured in every case brought to trial between 1951 and 1956. In June 1957, however, the Supreme Court, in *Yates,* reversed the convictions of fourteen West Coast party leaders charged with Smith Act violations. The Court, speaking through Justice JOHN MARSHALL HARLAN, declared that the *Dennis* decision had been misunderstood. The Smith Act did not outlaw advocacy of the abstract doctrine of violent overthrow, because such advocacy was too remote from concrete action to be regarded as the kind of indoctrination preparatory to action condemned in *Dennis.* The essential distinction, Harlan argued, was that those to whom the advocacy was addressed had to be urged to *do something*, now or in the future, rather than merely *believe* in something. Without formally repudiating the "sliding scale" reformulation of CLEAR AND PRESENT DANGER set forth in the *Dennis* opinion, the Court erected a stern new standard for evaluating convictions under the Smith Act, making conviction under the measure difficult. As to INDICTMENTS for involvement in organizing the Communist party in the United States, the Court also took a narrow view. Organizing, Harlan maintained, was only the original act of creating such a group, not any continuing process of proselytizing and recruiting. Since the indictments had been made some years following the postwar organizing of their party, the federal three-year statute of limitations had run out. The Court cleared five of the defendants, remanding the case of nine others for retrial. The ruling brought an abrupt end to the main body of Smith Act prosecutions then under way.

PAUL L. MURPHY

YBARRA v. ILLINOIS
444 U.S. 85 (1979)

Although three dissenting Justices complained that the Supreme Court majority had narrowed the STOP-AND-FRISK RULE of TERRY V. OHIO (1968), Justice POTTER STEWART for the Court did not doubt that an officer may pat down a suspect for a concealed weapon. Stewart regarded *Terry* as an exception to the requirement of PROBABLE CAUSE. Here no such cause existed to search a person suspected neither of criminal activity nor of having a weapon. A police officer, having a warrant to search a tavern and its bartender, patted down a bystander, felt no weapon, but removed from his pocket a cigarette pack containing heroin. The Court reversed the man's conviction, because the warrant did not include him, and probable cause to search him was absent.

LEONARD W. LEVY

YELLOW DOG CONTRACT

The yellow dog contract was a device used by employers prior to the New Deal era to prevent collective bargaining by employees. By a yellow dog contract a worker agreed not to join or remain a member of a labor organization and to quit his job if he joined

one. At a time in our history when the courts shaped the law so that its major beneficiary was industrial capitalism, yellow dog contracts were enforceable, even though workers had little choice in accepting their terms. Workers either signed such contracts or forfeited the opportunity of working. In effect, a yellow dog contract blackmailed an employee into promising not to join a union; his supposed free choice to accept a job or look elsewhere for work turned out to be a choice between being blackmailed or blacklisted. In one perspective, yellow dog contracts robbed workers of their FREEDOM OF CONTRACT. The courts thought otherwise, however.

In the 1890s fifteen states enacted laws that promoted COLLECTIVE BARGAINING by outlawing yellow dog contracts, and in 1898 section 10 of the ERDMAN ACT, passed by Congress, also outlawed their use by interstate railroads. In ADAIR V. UNITED STATES (1908) the Supreme Court held the Erdman Act unconstitutional. SUBSTANTIVE DUE PROCESS of law provided one ground of decision. The Court reasoned that section 10 abridged freedom of contract, a liberty the Court found in the Fifth Amendment's DUE PROCESS CLAUSE, because Congress had violated the right of workers to make contracts for the sale of their labor. In COPPAGE V. KANSAS (1915) the Court applied this reasoning to state statutes that had banned yellow dog contracts.

Having disabled both the national commerce power and the STATE POLICE POWER from forbidding yellow dog contracts, the Court then sustained the legality of such contracts. In HITCHMAN COAL AND COKE CO. V. MITCHELL (1917) the Court reversed a federal circuit court's determination that a yellow dog contract was not an enforceable contract. Justice MAHLON PITNEY for a six-member majority declared, "The employer is as free to make non-membership a condition of employment as the worker is free to join the union." The Court added that the right to make such a contract was "part of the constitutional rights of personal liberty and private property, not to be taken away even by legislation," which the Court had already voided. The extent to which these decisions thwarted unionization cannot be gauged.

Congress revived the Erdman Act's provision when it passed the Railway Labor Act of 1926, and in the NORRIS-LAGUARDIA ACT of 1932 declared yellow dog contracts to be contrary to American public policy and unenforceable "in any court of the United States." The major industrial states passed "little Norris-LaGuardia acts." By the time these statutes came before the Supreme Court, it found ways to sustain them.

LEONARD W. LEVY

YICK WO v. HOPKINS
118 U.S. 356 (1886)

This is one of the basic decisions interpreting the EQUAL PROTECTION OF THE LAWS clause of the FOURTEENTH AMENDMENT. A San Francisco ordinance made criminal the conduct of a laundry business in any building not made of stone or brick, with such exceptions for wooden structures as administrative officials might make. Officials used their discretion in a grossly discriminatory manner, licensing about eighty wooden laundries run by Caucasians and denying licenses to about two hundred applicants of Chinese extraction. The Supreme Court unanimously held, in an opinion by Justice STANLEY MATTHEWS, that the ordinance, though racially neutral on its face, was applied so unequally and oppressively by public authorities as to deny equal protection. Thus the Court looked beyond the law's terms to its racially discriminatory administration and applied the benefits of the Fourteenth Amendment to Oriental ALIENS, that is, "to all persons . . . without regard to any difference of race, of color, or of nationality."

LEONARD W. LEVY

YOUNG, EX PARTE
209 U.S. 123 (1908)

The question in this case—one of the most important of the present century—was whether a citizen might resort to a federal court to vindicate a constitutional right against state infringement and, pending a final JUDGMENT, obtain freedom from civil or criminal suits by a temporary INJUNCTION directed to an officer of the state. The Supreme Court held that, the ELEVENTH AMENDMENT notwithstanding, a federal court might issue such an injunction.

A Minnesota statute fixed railroad rates and (to deter institution of a TEST CASE) made the officers and employees of the railroads personally liable to heavy fines and imprisonment if those rates were exceeded. A STOCKHOLDER'S SUIT in EQUITY was filed in federal Circuit Court to prevent enforcement of or compliance with the statute, on the ground that it violated the FOURTEENTH AMENDMENT by depriving the railroads of property without DUE PROCESS OF LAW. The federal court issued a temporary injunction restraining the state attorney general, Edward T. Young, from taking steps to enforce the statute. When Young defied the injunction the court found him in contempt and committed him to the custody of the United States marshal.

Young petitioned the Supreme Court for a writ of HABEAS CORPUS, contending that the suit for injunction was really against the state and that, under the Eleventh Amendment, the state could not be sued in federal court without its consent. The Court denied Young's petition, Justice JOHN MARSHALL HARLAN alone dissenting.

Justice RUFUS PECKHAM, for the Court, argued that if the Minnesota law was unconstitutional, then Young, attempting to enforce it, was stripped of his official character and became merely a private individual using the state's name to further his own illegitimate end. Incongruously, the end Young was furthering was unconstitutional only because it involved STATE ACTION. The "private wrong" was a fiction adopted by the Court to circumvent the Eleventh Amendment.

Congress reacted to the *Young* decision by passing a law (substantially repealed in 1976) requiring that federal court injunctions against enforcement of state laws alleged to be unconstitutional issue only from special THREE-JUDGE COURTS and providing, in such cases, for direct APPEAL to the Supreme Court.

The doctrine of *Young* remains valid law today. Although it originally arose in connection with due process protection of economic liberty, the doctrine provides a remedy for state action infringing CIVIL RIGHTS or CIVIL LIBERTIES. But the doctrine of *Young* applies only to equitable relief, and the Eleventh Amendment remains bar to actions for monetary damages that will be paid out of the state treasury.

DENNIS J. MAHONEY

(SEE ALSO: *Osborn v. Bank of the United States, 1824; Edelman v. Jordan, 1974.*)

YOUNG v. AMERICAN MINI THEATRES, INC.
427 U.S. 50 (1976)

In *Young v. American Mini Theatres, Inc.* the Supreme Court upheld a Detroit ZONING ordinance requiring adult theaters to be located certain distances from residential areas and specified businesses. Four Justices led by Justice JOHN PAUL STEVENS argued that adult movies ranked low in the hierarchy of FIRST AMENDMENT values. Four dissenting Justices led by Justice POTTER STEWART argued that the First Amendment recognized no hierarchy for types of protected speech. Justice LEWIS F. POWELL agreed with the dissent, but voted to uphold the ordinance, arguing that the theater owners had asserted no First

Amendment interest of their own and that the First Amendment interests of others, including moviemakers and potential audiences, were not endangered.

STEVEN SHIFFRIN

YOUNGER v. HARRIS
401 U.S. 37 (1971)

Harris, indicted under California's CRIMINAL SYNDICALISM LAW, sought a federal court INJUNCTION to compel the district attorney to cease prosecution in the state court. The district court held the law unconstitutional and issued the injunction. The Supreme Court reversed, 8–1, severely limiting DOMBROWSKI v. PFISTER (1965).

Justice HUGO L. BLACK, for the Court, rested decision on two interlocking grounds. First, a state prosecution was pending; because any claim that the underlying state law was unconstitutional could be made in the state proceeding, there was no "irreparable injury" to justify an injunction. Second, the national government should avoid intruding into "the legitimate activities of the state." Although a federal court might enjoin a state prosecution commenced in bad faith to harass the exercise of FIRST AMENDMENT rights, the claim that the law was unconstitutional on its face did not satisfy this bad-faith harassment requirement. (See ABSTENTION DOCTRINES.)

After *Younger*, the California courts held the syndicalism law invalid.

KENNETH L. KARST

YOUNGSTOWN SHEET & TUBE CO. v. SAWYER
343 U.S. 579 (1952)

In a landmark restriction on presidential power, the Supreme Court in 1952 held invalid President HARRY S. TRUMAN's seizure of the steel mills. Justice HUGO L. BLACK, joined by five other Justices, delivered the opinion of the Court. Chief Justice FRED M. VINSON, dissenting with Justices STANLEY F. REED and SHERMAN MINTON, believed that military and economic emergencies justified Truman's action.

Each of the five concurring Justices wrote separate opinions, advancing different views of the President's emergency power. Only Justices Black and WILLIAM O. DOUGLAS insisted on specific constitutional or statutory authority to support presidential seizure of private property. Assigning the lawmaking function exclusively to Congress, they allowed the President a role only in recommending or vetoing laws. On existing precedent, this concept of the SEPARATION OF POWERS doctrine was far too rigid. Previous Presidents had engaged directly in the lawmaking function without express constitutional or statutory authority, often with the acquiescence and even blessing of Congress and the courts.

The other four concurring Justices (FELIX FRANKFURTER, ROBERT H. JACKSON, HAROLD BURTON, and TOM C. CLARK) did not draw such a strict line between the executive and legislative branches, nor did they try to delimit the President's authority to act in future emergencies. Frankfurter thought it inadvisable to attempt a comprehensive definition of presidential power, based on abstract principles, without admitting powers that had evolved by custom: a "systematic, unbroken, executive practice, long pursued to the knowledge of the Congress and never before questioned . . . may be treated as a gloss on 'executive Power.'" Burton withheld opinion on the President's constitutional power when facing an "imminent invasion or threatened attack," while Clark agreed that the Constitution gave the President extensive authority in time of grave and imperative national emergency.

Jackson identified three categories of presidential power, ranging from actions based on express or implied congressional authorization (putting executive authority at its maximum) to executive measures that were incompatible with congressional policy (reducing presidential power to its lowest ebb). In between lay a "zone of twilight" in which President and Congress shared authority. Jackson said that congressional inertia, indifference, or acquiescence might enable, if not invite, independent presidential action. He further argued that the ENUMERATED POWERS of the President required "scope and elasticity" and said he would "indulge the widest latitude of interpretation" when presidential powers were turned against the outside world for the security of the United States.

Considering the four concurrences and three dissents, the Steel Seizure Case was far from a repudiation of the inherent power doctrine. Nevertheless, a majority of the Court did reach agreement on important principles: presidential actions, including those of an "emergency" nature, are subject to JUDICIAL REVIEW; the courts may enjoin executive officers from carrying out presidential orders that conflict with statutory policy or the Constitution; and independent presidential powers in domestic affairs are especially vulnerable to judicial scrutiny when Congress has adopted a contrary statutory policy. The Steel Seizure Case has supplied the Supreme Court with an important precedent for curbing subsequent exercises of presidential power in areas such as the Pentagon Papers case (NEW YORK TIMES V. UNITED STATES, 1971), electronic surveillance, IMPOUNDMENT, and EXECUTIVE PRIVILEGE.

LOUIS FISHER

(SEE ALSO: *Steel Seizure Controversy; Executive Order 10340; Harry S. Truman.*)

Bibliography

MARCUS, MAEVA 1977 *Truman and the Steel Seizure Case: The Limits of Presidential Power.* New York: Columbia University Press.

WESTIN, ALAN F. 1958 *The Anatomy of a Constitutional Law Case.* New York: Macmillan.

ZABLOCKI v. REDHAIL
434 U.S. 374 (1978)

In LOVING V. VIRGINIA (1967) the Supreme Court had struck down a MISCEGENATION statute flatly forbidding interracial marriage, resting decision on both EQUAL PROTECTION and SUBSTANTIVE DUE PROCESS grounds. In *Zablocki* the Court protected the "right to marry" in a setting where race was irrelevant. Wisconsin required a court's permission for the marriage of a resident parent who had been ordered to support a child not in his or her custody. Permission would be granted only when the candidate proved compliance with the support obligation and showed that the children were not likely to become public charges. Because he could not comply with the law, Redhail was denied a marriage license. The Supreme Court held, 8–1, that this denial was unconstitutional.

The case produced six opinions. Justice THURGOOD MARSHALL, for the majority, rested on equal protection grounds. Marriage was a FUNDAMENTAL INTEREST, protected by the constitutional RIGHT OF PRIVACY. The Wisconsin law interfered "directly and substantially" with the right to marry and was not necessary to effectuate important state interests. Justice POTTER STEWART concurred on due process grounds. Justice LEWIS F. POWELL, also concurring, objected to the Court's STRICT SCRUTINY test; such an inquiry would cast doubt on such limits on marriage as "bans on incest, bigamy, and homosexuality, as well as various preconditions to marriage, such as blood tests." Using a more relaxed STANDARD OF RE-

VIEW, he nonetheless found the statute wanting on both due process and equal protection grounds. Justice JOHN PAUL STEVENS concurred, calling the law a "clumsy and deliberate legislative discrimination between the rich and poor" whose irrationality violated equal protection. Justice WILLIAM H. REHNQUIST, in lone dissent, rejected the notion that marriage was a "fundamental" right and argued for the strict judicial nonscrutiny that had become his trademark.

For all the diversity of the Justices' views, little turns on the choice between equal protection and due process grounds, or on conclusory assertions about the proper standard of review. *Zablocki* makes clear that significant state interference with the freedom to marry demands correspondingly weighty justification.

KENNETH L. KARST

(SEE ALSO: *Freedom of Intimate Association; Marriage and the Constitution.*)

ZEMEL v. RUSK
381 U.S. 1 (1965)

In *Zemel* the Supreme Court sustained (6–3) the constitutionality of the secretary of state's refusal to validate passports for travel to Cuba. Chief Justice EARL WARREN, for the majority, rejected two arguments for the petitioner: that he had a RIGHT TO TRAVEL under the DUE PROCESS clause of the Fifth Amendment; and that he had a FIRST AMENDMENT right to travel to Cuba to gather information.

DENNIS J. MAHONEY

(SEE ALSO: *Richmond Newspapers, Inc. v. Virginia, 1980.*)

ZENGER'S CASE
(1735)

Had John Peter Zenger, the printer of the *New-York Weekly Journal,* attacked the provincial assembly of New York instead of its hated royal governor, he would have been summarily convicted at the bar of the house, jailed, and forgotten by posterity. But he was tried by a jury, brilliantly defended by a great lawyer, and saved for posterity by James Alexander's report of *A brief Narrative of the Case and Tryal of John Peter Zenger* (1736). Alexander, the editor of the paper which Zenger printed, probably wrote the articles that led to the prosecution and, as a lawyer, prepared the case for Andrew Hamilton.

Scalded by the paper's weekly articles against his administration, Governor William Cosby ordered an information against its printer for SEDITIOUS LIBEL; a GRAND JURY had refused to indict, the assembly had refused to cooperate, and the local government, defending "liberty of the press," protested. Zenger, in other words, symbolized the popular party against a detested administration. Not surprisingly the jury acquitted him after brief deliberation, against the instructions of Chief Justice James DeLancey, who presided at the trial before the Supreme Court of Judicature.

The law was against Zenger. Both the prosecutor and the judge accurately informed the jury that seditious libel consisted of scandalizing the government by adversely reflecting on those entrusted with its administration, by publishing material tending to breed popular contempt for the administration, or by alienating the affections of the people for government in any way. Moreover, the truth of a libel magnified its criminality. But Hamilton's reply had greater appeal. If the people could not remonstrate against the oppressions and villainies of their governors, confining themselves always to truthful accusations, they would in no time lose their liberty and property. Hamilton did not repudiate the law of seditious libel; he argued, rather, that Zenger's statements being true were not libels. When the court rejected the proposition that truth should be a defense to a charge of seditious libel, Hamilton appealed to the jury over the court. He argued that the jury, like the press, was a bastion of popular liberty. It should ignore the court's instruction to return a special verdict on the question whether Zenger had, in fact, published the statements charged; a special verdict would leave to the court a ruling on the question of law whether those statements were criminal. Hamilton urged the jury, instead, to return a general verdict of "not guilty," thus deciding the law as well as the fact. The jury returned a general verdict of "not guilty."

The jury's general verdict was a safe way of striking at the unpopular governor and endorsing the right of the people, through the press, to criticize their government. The jury's verdict did not, however, alter the settled law. Not until the Sedition Act of 1798 (see ALIEN AND SEDITION ACTS) did truth as a defense and the power of the jury to render a general verdict in cases of seditious libel become part of American law; and, as the enforcement of that infamous statute showed, embattled libertarians came to discover that they should have repudiated the doctrine of seditious libel rather than grasp at Zengerian principles.

LEONARD W. LEVY

(SEE ALSO: *People v. Croswell*, 1804; *New York Times v. Sullivan*, 1964.)

Bibliography

KATZ, STANLEY NIDER 1972 *A Brief Narrative of the Case and Trial of John Peter Zenger . . . by James Alexander.* Cambridge, Mass.: Harvard University Press.
LEVY, LEONARD W. 1960 Did the Zenger Case Really Matter? Freedom of the Press in Colonial New York. *William and Mary Quarterly,* 3d ser., 17:35–50.

ZOBEL v. WILLIAMS

See: Privileges and Immunities; Right to Travel

ZONING

When a local government decides how to allocate land uses it acts under the POLICE POWER exercised by the states and their governmental subdivisions to regulate for the public health, safety, and welfare. The first zoning ordinances appeared early in the twentieth century as a result of urbanization and the encroachment of factories and noxious uses in residential neighborhoods. In EUCLID V. AMBLER REALTY (1926) the Supreme Court upheld a comprehensive local zoning ordinance, rejecting a SUBSTANTIVE DUE PROCESS attack. Although today's zoning ordinances are more sophisticated than the simple division of land uses upheld in *Euclid,* the basic constitutional issues raised by zoning decisions remain an unusually stable area of constitutional law.

Because a zoning ordinance is adopted by a legislative body, and because zoning amendments are legislative decisions in most states, the constitutional scrutiny applied to zoning is no different from that applied to LEGISLATION at any governmental level. The courts use the due process analysis of *Euclid* to uphold zoning if they find a reasonable relationship between the zoning and the city's police power objectives. Like other social and economic legislation, zoning comes to court clothed with a presumption of validity. A court will not question the wisdom or the motives of legislators. If a court finds any RATIONAL BASIS to support zoning as an implementation of the public health, safety, and welfare, the ordinance will be held valid. A court considers factors such as increased traffic and congestion, compatibility with adjacent uses, and impact on land values of neighboring properties. Courts often apply a fairly debatable rule: if reasonable minds can differ on the reasonableness of an ordinance, the municipal decision must be upheld. Some state courts are more willing than the federal courts to use theories of STATE CONSTITUTIONAL LAW to strike down zoning regulations.

Although a court may be reluctant to question the police power objectives of zoning, it may be more inclined to examine the effects of a zoning restriction on the value of property. Even when a zoning ordinance achieves public objectives, it may be held to be a TAKING OF PROPERTY if it denies a property owner all economic use of his land. The leading case is *Pennsylvania Coal Co. v. Mahon* (1972).

Other guarantees may also serve as bases for constitutional challenges to zoning ordinances. The FIRST AMENDMENT repeatedly forms the basis of attacks on local sign ordinances and ordinances regulating adult businesses. In the 1960s and 1970s, a series of "exclusionary zoning" cases challenged a municipal refusal to rezone to allow mobile homes, apartments, or anything other than single family homes on large lots. Arguing that such practices violated the EQUAL PROTECTION clause, landowners and hopeful future residents had varying success. The Supreme Court was originally not interested in fashioning a federal constitutional remedy. In ARLINGTON HEIGHTS V. METROPOLITAN HOUSING DEVELOPMENT CORP. (1977) it severely restricted the authority of the federal courts to find RACIAL DISCRIMINATION in exclusionary zoning. Some state courts have been more aggressive. In *Southern Burlington County NAACP v. Mount Laurel* (1975), for example, the New Jersey Supreme Court held, on both substantive due process and equal protection grounds, that a municipality cannot close its doors to the housing needs of the region, including low-cost housing. Then, in CLEBURNE V. CLEBURNE LIVING CENTER, INC. (1985) the Supreme Court gave some indication that it would examine more rigorously the exclusionary classifications in zoning ordinances.

Zoning ordinances also require landowners to ob-

tain development permission under a host of administrative procedures that vary from one JURISDICTION to another. Whether it be subdivision or site plan approval, variances, special or conditional uses, or environmental permits, the process is rife with constitutional pitfalls for local administrative bodies. The standards for approving or denying permits must be made specific in the ordinance; otherwise, a state court may hold that the ordinance unconstitutionally delegates legislative authority to an administrative body. Applicants must be given PROCEDURAL DUE PROCESS, including NOTICE and an opportunity to be heard, and, in some states, even quasi-judicial procedures. The agency's decision must be based on evidence sufficient to support it.

Perhaps the most serious danger to the constitutional status of zoning is the threat of a radical departure in the judicial relief afforded a victorious landowner. Under the SEPARATION OF POWERS doctrine, the traditional judicial relief for invalid zoning has been to grant an INJUNCTION prohibiting its enforcement and allow the municipality to rezone. A few courts in the 1970s held that confiscatory zoning amounted to taking of property for public purposes and required cities to compensate landowners. The Supreme Court has not yet decided the availability of this remedy under the federal Constitution.

Damages for a taking may be available under SECTION 1983, TITLE 42, UNITED STATES CODE. In MONELL V. DEPARTMENT OF SOCIAL SERVICES (1978) the Supreme Court held that municipalities can be sued under Section 1983, and the specter of money damages for any denial of constitutional rights in the zoning process became a reality. The damage to a landowner whose economic return is restricted by zoning and who must proceed through a time-consuming local zoning process perhaps including litigation can be substantial. The traditional constitutional deference afforded local government under its police power remains, but the possible consequences of stepping outside constitutional bounds have become severe.

Zoning ordinances now include sophisticated techniques, such as computer-based point systems for approving new development, incentive and bonus programs, and the transfer of development rights. These new techniques have not yet been extensively tested in the courts, but they raise constitutional problems similar to those raised by conventional zoning. Judicial attention in the years to come will focus on the constitutionality of these techniques and on the suitability of a damage remedy in zoning cases.

DANIEL R. MANDELKER
BARBARA ROSS

Bibliography

MANDELKER, DANIEL R. 1982 *Land Use Law.* Charlottesville, Va.: Michie Co.
WILLIAMS, NORMAN, JR. 1974 *American Land Planning Law.* Chicago: Callaghan & Co.

ZORACH v. CLAUSEN
343 U.S. 306 (1952)

This was the Supreme Court's second encounter with a RELEASED TIME program. In McCOLLUM V. BOARD OF EDUCATION (1948), the Court had invalidated an arrangement by which teachers entered public schools to provide religious instruction. *Zorach* involved New York City's released time program in which instruction was offered off school premises. According to the requests of their parents, public school children were allowed to leave school for specific periods of time to go to church facilities. Nonparticipating students remained in their regular classrooms.

Justice WILLIAM O. DOUGLAS delivered the OPINION OF THE COURT sustaining the constitutionality of New York's program. Douglas emphasized that, as opposed to *McCollum*, no public facilities were used. The schools, Douglas said, were merely rearranging their schedules to accommodate the needs of religious people.

Justices HUGO L. BLACK, ROBERT H. JACKSON, and FELIX FRANKFURTER dissented. Black and Jackson argued that children were compelled by law to attend public schools and that to release them for religious instruction used governmental compulsion to promote religion. In a slap at Douglas's presumed presidential ambitions, Jackson said, "Today's judgment will be more interesting to students of psychology and of the judicial process than to students of constitutional law."

RICHARD E. MORGAN

ZURCHER v. STANFORD DAILY
436 U.S. 547 (1978)

In *Zurcher v. Stanford Daily* the police chief of Palo Alto, California, appealed from a federal district court decision declaring that a search of a college newspaper's office conducted pursuant to a duly authorized search warrant had infringed upon FOURTH AMENDMENT and FIRST AMENDMENT rights. There was no contention that the newspaper or any of its staff was reasonably suspected of the commission of a crime, nor was it contended that weapons, contraband, or fruits of a crime were likely to be found on the premises. Rather, the police secured a warrant on a showing of PROBABLE CAUSE for the conclusion that photographic evidence of a crime was to be found somewhere on the premises. The Supreme Court thus addressed the general question of the standards that should govern the issuance of warrants to search the premises of persons not themselves suspected of criminal activity and the specific question whether any different standards should apply to press searches.

The Court ruled that the innocence of the party to be searched was of no constitutional importance. So long as there was probable cause to believe that evidence of a crime was to be found on premises particularly described, no further showing was needed. Specifically, the Court declined to "reconstrue the Fourth Amendment" to require a showing that it would be impracticable to secure a subpoena *duces tecum* before a warrant could be issued.

That the party to be searched was a newspaper the Court regarded as of some moment but not enough to prefer subpoenas over warrants. Instead, the Court observed that warrant requirements should be applied with "particular exactitude when First Amendment interests would be endangered by the search."

The Court expressed confidence that magistrates would safeguard the interests of the press. Magistrates could guard against the type of intrusions that might interfere with the timely publication of a newspaper or otherwise deter normal editorial and publication decisions. Nor, said the Court, "will there be any occasion or opportunity for officers to rummage at large in newspaper files." The Court asserted that "the warrant in this case authorized nothing of this sort." Yet, as the *Zurcher* opinion discloses, the police searched "the Daily's photographic laboratories, filing cabinets, desks, and wastepaper baskets." The Court's application of the particular exactitude standard seems neither particular nor exact.

Zurcher is the first case squarely to authorize the search and seizure of mere evidence from an innocent party; it has raised difficult questions of Fourth Amendment reasonableness as applied to searches of other innocent third parties such as lawyers and judges. By suggesting that press values be considered in an assessment of reasonableness, it opens the door for further distinctions between searches of media and nonmedia persons. By suggesting that the reasonableness of a search is a requirement that may go beyond probable cause and specificity, it reopens discussion about the relationship between the two clauses of the Fourth Amendment.

STEVEN SHIFFRIN

Appendix 1

The Call for the Federal Constitutional Convention

RESOLUTION OF CONGRESS

1787, February 21

WHEREAS there is provision in the Articles of Confederation & perpetual Union for making alterations therein by the Assent of a Congress of the United States and of the legislatures of the several States; And whereas experience hath evinced that there are defects in the present Confederation, as a means to remedy which several of the States and particularly the State of New York by express instruction to their delegates in Congress have suggested a convention for the purposes expressed in the following resolution and such Convention appearing to be the most probable means of establishing in these states a firm national government

Resolved that in the opinion of Congress it is expedient that on the second Monday in May next a Convention of delegates who shall have been appointed by the several states be held at Philadelphia for the sole and express purpose of revising the Articles of Confederation and reporting to Congress and the several legislatures such alterations and provisions therein as shall when agreed to in Congress and confirmed by the states render the federal constitution adequate to the exigencies of Government & the preservation of the Union.

Appendix 2

Articles of Confederation

Articles of Confederation and perpetual Union between the States of New Hampshire, Massachusetts Bay, Rhode Island and Providence Plantations, Connecticut, New York, New Jersey, Pennsylvania, Delaware, Maryland, Virginia, North Carolina, South Carolina, and Georgia.

ARTICLE I. The style of this Confederacy shall be "The United States of America."

ART. II. Each State retains its sovereignty, freedom, and independence, and every power, jurisdiction, and right, which is not by this Confederation expressly delegated to the United States in Congress assembled.

ART. III. The said States hereby severally enter into a firm league of friendship with each other, for their common defence, the security of their liberties, and their mutual and general welfare, binding themselves to assist each other against all force offered to, or attacks made upon them, or any of them, on account of religion, sovereignty, trade, or any other pretence whatever.

ART. IV. The better to secure and perpetuate mutual friendship and intercourse among the people of the different States in this Union, the free inhabitants of each of these States, paupers, vagabonds, and fugitives from justice excepted, shall be entitled to all the privileges and immunities of free citizens in the several States, and the people of each State shall have free ingress and regress to and from any other State, and shall enjoy therein all the privileges of trade and commerce, subject to the same duties, impositions, and restrictions as the inhabitants thereof respectively, provided that such restrictions shall not extend so far as to prevent the removal of property imported into any State, to any other State of which the owner is an inhabitant; provided also, that no imposition, duties, or restriction shall be laid by any State, on the property of the United States, or either of them.

If any person guilty of or charged with treason, felony, or other high misdemeanor in any State, shall flee from justice, and be found in any of the United States, he shall, upon demand of the governor or executive power of the State from which he fled, be delivered up and removed to the State having jurisdiction of his offence.

Full faith and credit shall be given in each of these States to the records, acts, and judicial proceedings of the courts and magistrates of every other State.

ART. V. For the more convenient management of the general interests of the United States, delegates shall be annually appointed in such manner as the legislature of each State shall direct, to meet in Congress on the first Monday in November, in every year, with a power reserved to each State to recall its delegates, or any of them, at any time within the year, and to send others in their stead, for the remainder of the year.

No State shall be represented in Congress by less than two, nor by more than seven members; and no person shall be capable of being a delegate for more than three years in any term of six years, nor shall any person, being a delegate, be capable of holding any office under the United States for which he or another for his benefit receives any salary, fees, or emolument of any kind.

Each State shall maintain its own delegates in a meeting of the States, and while they act as members of the committee of the States.

In determining questions in the United States, in Congress assembled, each State shall have one vote.

Freedom of speech and debate in Congress shall not be impeached or questioned in any court or place out of Congress, and the members of Congress shall be protected in their persons from arrests and imprisonments, during the time of their going to or from, and attendance on, Congress, except for treason, felony, or breach of the peace.

ART VI. No State, without the consent of the United States in Congress assembled, shall send any embassy to, or receive any embassy from, or enter into any conference, agreement, alliance, or treaty with, any king, prince, or state; nor shall any person holding any office of profit or trust under the United States, or any of them accept of any present, emolument, office, or title of any kind whatever from any king, prince, or foreign state; nor shall the United States in Congress assembled, or any of them, grant any title of nobility.

No two or more States shall enter into any treaty, confederation, or alliance whatever between them, without the consent of the United States in Congress assembled, specifying accurately the purposes for which the same is to be entered into, and how long it shall continue.

No State shall lay any imposts or duties, which may interfere with any stipulations in treaties entered into by the United States in Congress assembled, with any king, prince, or state, in pursuance of any treaties already proposed by Congress, to the courts of France and Spain.

No vessels of war shall be kept up in time of peace by any State, except such number only as shall be deemed necessary by the United States in Congress assembled, for the defence of such State or its trade; nor shall any body of forces be kept up by any State, in time of peace, except such number only as in the judgment of the United States in Congress assembled shall be deemed requisite to garrison the forts necessary for the defence of such State; but every State shall always keep up a well regulated and disciplined militia, sufficiently armed and accoutred, and shall provide and constantly have ready for use, in public stores, a due number of field-pieces and tents, and a proper quantity of arms, ammunition, and camp equipage.

No State shall engage in any war without the consent of the United States in Congress assembled, unless such State be actually invaded by enemies, or shall have received certain advice of a resolution being formed by some nation of Indians to invade such State, and the danger is so imminent as not to admit of a delay till the United States in Congress assembled can be consulted; nor shall any State grant commissions to any ships or vessels of war, nor letters of marque or reprisal, except it be after a declaration of war by the United States in Congress assembled, and then only against the kingdom or state, and the subjects thereof, against which war has been so declared, and under such regulations as shall be established by the United States in Congress assembled, unless such State be infested by pirates, in which case vessels of war may be fitted out for that occasion, and kept so long as the danger shall continue, or until the United States in Congress assembled shall determine otherwise.

ART. VII. When land forces are raised by any State for the common defence, all officers of or under the rank of colonel shall be appointed by the legislature of each State respectively, by whom such forces shall be raised, or in such manner as such State shall direct; and all vacancies shall be filled up by the State which first made the appointment.

ART. VIII. All charges of war and all other expenses that shall be incurred for the common defence or general welfare, and allowed by the United States in Congress assembled, shall be defrayed out of a common treasury, which shall be supplied by the several States, in proportion to the value of all land within each State, granted to or surveyed for any person, and such land and the buildings and improvements thereon shall be estimated according to such mode as the United States in Congress assembled shall from time to time direct and appoint.

The taxes for paying that proportion shall be laid and levied by the authority and direction of the legislatures of the several States within the time agreed upon by the United States in Congress assembled.

ART. IX. The United States in Congress assembled shall have the sole and exclusive right and power of determining on peace and war, except in the cases mentioned in the sixth article—of sending and receiving ambassadors—entering into treaties and alliances, provided that no treaty of commerce shall be made whereby the legislative power of the respective States shall be restrained from imposing such imposts and duties on foreigners as their own people are subjected to, or from prohibiting the exportation or importation of any species of goods or commodities whatsoever—of establishing rules for deciding, in all cases, what captures on land or water shall be legal, and in what manner prizes taken by land or naval forces in the service of the United States shall be divided or appropriated—of granting letters of marque and reprisal in times of peace—appointing courts for the trial of piracies and felonies committed on the high seas, and establishing courts for receiving and determining finally appeals in all cases of captures, provided that no member of Congress shall be appointed a judge of any of the said courts.

The United States in Congress assembled shall also be the last resort on appeal in all disputes and differences now subsisting or that hereafter may arise between two or more States concerning boundary, jurisdiction, or any other cause whatever; which authority shall always be exercised in the manner following:—Whenever the legislative or executive authority or lawful agent of any State in controversy with another shall present a petition to Congress stating the matter in question and praying for a hearing, notice thereof shall be given by order of Congress to the legislative or executive authority of the other State in controversy, and a day assigned for the appearance of the parties by their lawful agents, who shall then be directed to appoint, by joint consent, commissioners or judges to constitute a court for hearing and determining the matter in question; but if they cannot agree, Congress shall name three persons out of each of the United States, and from the list of such persons each party shall alternately strike out one, the petitioners beginning, until the number shall be reduced to thirteen; and from that number not less than seven nor more than nine names, as Congress shall direct, shall, in the presence of Congress, be drawn out by lot, and the persons whose names shall be so drawn, or any five of them, shall be commissioners or judges, to hear and finally determine the controversy, so always as a major part of the judges who shall hear the cause shall agree in the determination; and if either party shall neglect to attend at the day appointed, without showing reasons, which Congress shall judge sufficient, or, being present, shall refuse to strike, the Congress shall proceed to nominate three persons out of each State, and the Secretary of Congress shall strike in behalf of such party absent or refusing; and the judgment and sentence of the court to be appointed, in the manner before prescribed, shall be final and conclusive; and if any of the parties shall refuse to submit to the authority of such court, or to appear or defend their claim or cause, the court shall nevertheless proceed to pronounce sentence or judgment, which shall in like manner be final and decisive, the judgment or sentence and other proceedings being in either case transmitted to Congress, and lodged among the acts of Congress for the security of the parties concerned: provided that every commissioner, before he sits in judgment, shall take an oath, to be administered by one of the judges of the Supreme or Superior Court of the State where the cause shall be tried, *"well and truly to hear and determine the matter in question according to the best of his judgment, without favor, affection, or hope of reward,"* provided also that no State shall be deprived of territory for the benefit of the United States.

All controversies concerning the private right of soil, claimed under different grants of two or more States, whose jurisdictions as they may respect such lands and the States which passed such grants are adjusted, the said grants or either of them being at the same time claimed to have originated antecedent to such settlement of jurisdiction, shall, on the petition of either party to the Congress of the United States, be finally determined as near as may be in the same manner as is before prescribed for deciding disputes respecting territorial jurisdiction between different States.

The United States in Congress assembled shall also have the sole and exclusive right and power of regulating the alloy and value of coin struck by their own authority, or by that of the respective States—fixing the standard of weights and measures throughout the United States—regulating the trade and managing all affairs with the Indians, not members of any of the States, provided that the legislative right of any State within its own limits be not infringed or violated—establishing and regulating post-offices from one State to another, throughout all the United States, and exacting such postage on the papers passing through the same as may be requisite to defray the expenses of the said office—appointing all officers of the land forces in the service of the United States, excepting regimental officers—appointing all the officers of the naval forces, and commissioning all officers whatever in the service of the United States—making rules for the government and regulation of the said land and naval forces, and directing their operations.

The United States in Congress assembled shall have authority to appoint a committee, to sit in the recess of Congress, to be denominated "A Committee of the States," and to consist of one delegate from each State; to appoint such other committees and civil officers as may be necessary for managing the general affairs of the United States under their direction; and to appoint one of their number to preside, provided that no person be allowed to serve in the office of president more than one year in any term of three years—to ascertain the necessary sums of money to be raised for the service of the United States, and to appropriate and apply the same for defraying the public expenses—to borrow money, or emit bills on the credit of the United States, transmitting every half-year to the respective States an account of the sums of money so borrowed or emitted—to build and equip a navy—to agree upon the number of land forces, and to make requisitions from each State for its quota, in proportion to the number of white inhabitants in such State; which requisition shall be binding, and thereupon the legislature of each State shall appoint the regimental officers, raise the men, and clothe, arm, and equip them in a soldier-like manner, at the expense of the United States, and the officers and men so clothed, armed, and equipped shall march to the place appointed, and within the time agreed on by the United States in Congress assembled; but if the United States in Congress assembled shall, on consideration of circumstances, judge proper that any State should not raise men, or should raise a smaller number than its quota, and that any other State should raise a greater number of men than the quota thereof, such extra number shall be raised, officered, clothed, armed, and equipped in the same manner as the quota of such State, unless the legislature of such State shall judge that such extra number cannot be safely spared out of the same, in which case they shall raise, officer, clothe, arm, and equip as many of such extra number as they judge can be safely spared: and the officers and men, so clothed, armed, and equipped shall march to the place appointed, and within the time agreed on, by the United States in Congress assembled.

The United States in Congress assembled shall never engage in a war, nor grant letters of marque and reprisal in time of peace, nor enter into any treaties or alliances, nor coin money, nor regulate the value thereof, nor ascertain the sums and expenses necessary for the defence and welfare of the United States, or any of them, nor emit bills, nor borrow money on the credit of the United States, nor appropriate money, nor agree upon the number of vessels of war to be built or purchased, or the number of land or sea forces to be raised, nor appoint a commander-in-chief of the army or navy, unless nine States assent to the same; nor shall a question on any other point, except for adjourning from day to day, be determined, unless by the votes of a majority of the United States in Congress assembled.

The Congress of the United States shall have power to adjourn to any time within the year, and to any place within the United States, so that no period of adjournment be for a longer duration than the space of six months, and shall publish the journal of their proceedings monthly, except such parts thereof relating to treaties, alliances, or military operations, as in their judgment require secrecy, and the yeas and nays of the delegates of each State on any question shall be entered on the journal, when it is desired by any delegate; and the delegates of a State, or any of them, at his or their request, shall be furnished with a transcript of the said journal, except such parts as are above excepted, to lay before the legislatures of the several States.

ART. X. The Committee of the States, or any nine of them, shall be authorized to execute, in the recess of Congress, such of the powers of Congress as the United States in Congress assembled, by the consent of nine States, shall from time to time think expedient to vest them with: provided that no power be delegated to the said Committee, for the exercise of which, by the Articles of Confederation, the voice of nine States in the Congress of the United States assembled is requisite.

ART. XI. Canada, acceding to this Confederation, and joining in the measures of the United States, shall be admitted into and entitled to all the advantages of this Union; but no other colony shall be admitted into the same, unless such admission be agreed to by nine States.

ART. XII. All bills of credit emitted, moneys borrowed, and debts contracted by or under the authority of Congress, before the assembling of the United States in pursuance of the present Confederation, shall be deemed and considered as a charge against the United States, for payment and satisfaction whereof the said United States and the public faith are hereby solemnly pledged.

ART. XIII. Every State shall abide by the determinations of the United States in Congress assembled, on all questions which by this Confederation are submitted to them. And the Articles of this Confederation shall be inviolably observed by every State, and the Union shall be perpetual; nor shall any alteration at any time hereafter be made in any of them, unless such alteration be agreed to in a Congress of the United States, and be afterwards confirmed by the legislatures of every State.

AND WHEREAS it hath pleased the Great Governor of the world to incline the hearts of the legislatures we respectfully represent in Congress to approve of and to authorize us to ratify the said Articles of Confederation and perpetual Union, KNOW YE, That we, the undersigned delegates, by virtue of the power and authority to us given for that purpose, do by these presents, in the name and in behalf of our respective constituents, fully and entirely ratify and confirm each and every of the said Articles of Confederation and perpetual Union, and all and singular the matters and things therein contained: and we do further solemnly plight and engage the faith of our respective constituents that they shall abide by the determinations of the United States in Congress assembled, on all questions which by the said Confederation are submitted to them. And that the Articles thereof shall be inviolably observed by the States we respectively represent, and the Union shall be perpetual.

Appendix 3

The Constitution of the United States

In the following printed copy of the Constitution, spelling, capitalization, and punctuation conform to the text of the engrossed parchment.

We the People of the United States, in Order to form a more perfect Union, establish Justice, insure domestic Tranquility, provide for the common defence, promote the general Welfare, and secure the Blessings of Liberty to ourselves and our Posterity, do ordain and establish this Constitution for the United States of America.

ARTICLE. I.

SECTION. 1. All legislative Powers herein granted shall be vested in a Congress of the United States, which shall consist of a Senate and House of Representatives.

SECTION. 2. The House of Representatives shall be composed of Members chosen every second Year by the People of the several States, and the Electors in each State shall have the Qualifications requisite for Electors of the most numerous Branch of the State Legislature.

No Person shall be a Representative who shall not have attained to the Age of twenty five Years, and been seven Years a Citizen of the United States, and who shall not, when elected, be an Inhabitant of that State in which he shall be chosen.

Representatives and direct Taxes shall be apportioned among the several States which may be included within this Union, according to their respective Numbers, which shall be determined by adding to the whole Number of free Persons, including those bound to Service for a Term of Years, and excluding Indians not taxed, three fifths of all other Persons. The actual Enumeration shall be made within three Years after the first Meeting of the Congress of the United States, and within every subsequent Term of ten Years, in such Manner as they shall by Law direct. The Number of Representatives shall not exceed one for every thirty Thousand, but each State shall have at Least one Representative; and until such enumeration shall be made, the State of New Hampshire shall be entitled to chuse three, Massachusetts eight, Rhode-Island and Providence Plantations one, Connecticut five, New-York six, New Jersey four, Pennsylvania eight, Delaware one, Maryland six, Virginia ten, North Carolina five, South Carolina five, and Georgia three.

When vacancies happen in the Representation from any State, the Executive Authority thereof shall issue Writs of Election to fill such Vacancies.

The House of Representatives shall chuse their Speaker and other Officers; and shall have the sole Power of Impeachment.

SECTION. 3. The Senate of the United States shall be composed of two Senators from each State, chosen by the Legislature thereof, for six Years; and each Senator shall have one Vote.

Immediately after they shall be assembled in Consequence of the first Election, they shall be divided as equally as may be into three Classes. The Seats of the Senators of the first Class shall be vacated at the Expiration of the second Year, of the second Class at the Expiration of the fourth Year, and of the third Class at the Expiration of the sixth Year, so that one third may be chosen every second Year; and if Vacancies happen by Resignation, or otherwise, during the Recess of the Legislature of any State, the Executive thereof may make temporary Appointments until the next Meeting of the Legislature, which shall then fill such Vacancies.

No Person shall be a Senator who shall not have attained to the Age of thirty Years, and been nine Years a Citizen of the United States, and who shall not, when elected, be an Inhabitant of that State for which he shall be chosen.

The Vice President of the United States shall be President of the Senate, but shall have no Vote, unless they be equally divided.

The Senate shall chuse their other Officers, and also a President pro tempore, in the Absence of the Vice President, or when he shall exercise the Office of President of the United States.

The Senate shall have the sole Power to try all Impeachments. When sitting for that Purpose, they shall be on Oath or Affirmation. When the President of the United States is tried, the Chief Justice shall preside: And no Person shall be convicted without the Concurrence of two thirds of the Members present.

Judgment in Cases of Impeachment shall not extend further than to removal from Office, and disqualification to hold and enjoy any Office of honor, Trust or Profit under the United States: but the Party convicted shall nevertheless be liable and subject to Indictment, Trial, Judgment and Punishment, according to Law.

SECTION. 4. The Times, Places and Manner of holding Elections for Senators and Representatives, shall be prescribed in each State by the Legislature thereof; but the Congress may at any time by Law make or alter such Regulations, except as to the Places of chusing Senators.

The Congress shall assemble at least once in every Year, and such Meeting shall be on the first Monday in December, unless they shall by Law appoint a different Day.

SECTION. 5. Each House shall be the Judge of the Elections, Returns and Qualifications of its own Members, and a Majority of each shall constitute a Quorum to do Business; but a smaller Number may adjourn from day to day, and may be authorized to compel the Attendance of absent Members, in such Manner, and under such Penalties as each House may provide.

Each House may determine the Rules of its Proceedings, punish its Members for disorderly Behaviour, and, with the Concurrence of two thirds, expel a Member.

Each House shall keep a Journal of its Proceedings, and from time to time publish the same, excepting such Parts as may in their Judgment require Secrecy; and the Yeas and Nays of the Members of either House on any question shall, at the Desire of one fifth of those Present, be entered on the Journal.

Neither House, during the Session of Congress, shall, without the Consent of the other, adjourn for more than three days, nor to any other Place than that in which the two Houses shall be sitting.

SECTION. 6. The Senators and Representatives shall receive a Compensation for their Services, to be ascertained by Law, and paid out of the Treasury of the United States. They shall in all Cases, except Treason, Felony and Breach of the Peace, be privileged from Arrest during their Attendance at the Session of their respective Houses, and in going to and returning from the same; and for any Speech or Debate in either House, they shall not be questioned in any other Place.

No Senator or Representative shall, during the Time for which he was elected, be appointed to any civil Office under the Authority of the United States, which shall have been created, or the Emoluments whereof shall have been encreased during such time; and no Person holding any Office under the United States, shall be a Member of either House during his Continuance in Office.

SECTION. 7. All Bills for raising Revenue shall originate in the House of Representatives; but the Senate may propose or concur with Amendments as on other Bills.

Every Bill which shall have passed the House of Representatives and the Senate, shall, before it become a Law, be presented to the President of the United States; If he approve he shall sign it, but if not he shall return it, with his Objections to that House in which it shall have originated, who shall enter the Objections at large on their Journal, and proceed to reconsider it. If after such Reconsideration two thirds of that House shall agree to pass the Bill, it shall be sent, together with the Objections, to the other House, by which it shall likewise be reconsidered, and if approved by two thirds of that House, it shall become a Law. But in all such Cases the Votes of both Houses shall be determined by yeas and Nays, and the Names of the Persons voting for and against the Bill shall be entered on the Journal of each House respectively. If any Bill shall not be returned by the President within ten Days (Sundays excepted) after it shall have been presented to him, the Same shall be a Law, in like Manner as if he had signed it, unless the Congress by their Adjournment prevent its Return, in which Case it shall not be a Law.

Every Order, Resolution, or Vote to which the Concurrence of the Senate and House of Representatives may be necessary (except on a question of Adjournment) shall be presented to the President of the United States; and before the Same shall take Effect, shall be approved by him, or being disapproved by him, shall be repassed by two thirds of the Senate and House of Representatives, according to the Rules and Limitations prescribed in the Case of a Bill.

SECTION. 8. The Congress shall have Power To lay and collect Taxes, Duties, Imposts and Excises, to pay the Debts and provide for the common Defence and general Welfare of the United States; but all Duties, Imposts and Excises shall be uniform throughout the United States;

To borrow Money on the credit of the United States;

To regulate Commerce with foreign Nations, and among the several States, and with the Indian tribes;

To establish an uniform Rule of Naturalization, and uniform Laws on the subject of Bankruptcies throughout the United States;

To coin Money, regulate the Value thereof, and of foreign Coin, and fix the Standard of Weights and Measures;

To provide for the Punishment of counterfeiting the Securities and current Coin of the United States;

To establish Post Offices and post Roads;

To promote the Progress of Science and useful Arts, by securing for limited Times to Authors and Inventors the exclusive Right to their respective Writings and Discoveries;

To constitute Tribunals inferior to the supreme Court;

To define and punish Piracies and Felonies committed on the high Seas, and Offences against the Law of Nations;

To declare War, grant Letters of Marque and Reprisal, and make Rules concerning Captures on Land and Water;

To raise and support Armies, but no Appropriation of Money to that Use shall be for a longer Term than two Years;

To provide and maintain a Navy;

To make Rules for the Government and Regulation of the land and naval Forces;

To provide for calling forth the Militia to execute the Laws of the Union, suppress Insurrections and repel Invasions;

To provide for organizing, arming, and disciplining, the Militia, and for governing such Part of them as may be employed in the Service of the United States, reserving to the States respectively, the Appointment of the Officers, and the Authority of training the Militia according to the discipline prescribed by Congress;

To exercise exclusive Legislation in all Cases whatsoever, over such District (not exceeding ten Miles square) as may, by Cession of particular States, and the Acceptance of Congress, become the Seat of the Government of the United States, and to exercise like Authority over all Places purchased by the Consent of the Legislature of the State in which the Same shall be, for the Erection of Forts, Magazines, Arsenals, dock- Yards, and other needful Buildings;—And

To make all Laws which shall be necessary and proper for carrying into Execution the foregoing Powers, and all other Powers vested by this Constitution in the Government of the United States, or in any Department or Officer thereof.

SECTION. 9. The Migration or Importation of such Persons as any of the States now existing shall think proper to admit, shall not be prohibited by the Congress prior to the Year one thousand eight hundred and eight, but a Tax or duty may be imposed on such Importation, not exceeding ten dollars for each Person.

The Privilege of the Writ of Habeas Corpus shall not be suspended, unless when in Cases of Rebellion or Invasion the public Safety may require it.

No Bill of Attainder or ex post facto Law shall be passed.

No Capitation, or other direct, Tax shall be laid, unless in Proportion to the Census or Enumeration herein before directed to be taken.

No Tax or Duty shall be laid on Articles exported from any State.

No Preference shall be given by any Regulation of Commerce or Revenue to the Ports of one State over those of another: nor shall Vessels bound to, or from, one State, be obliged to enter, clear, or pay Duties in another.

No Money shall be drawn from the Treasury, but in Consequence of Appropriations made by Law; and a regular Statement and Account of the Receipts and Expenditures of all public Money shall be published from time to time.

No Title of Nobility shall be granted by the United States: And no Person holding any Office of Profit or Trust under them, shall, without the Consent of the Congress, accept of any present, Emolument, Office, or Title, of any kind whatever, from any King, Prince, or foreign State.

SECTION. 10. No State shall enter into any Treaty, Alliance, or Confederation; grant Letters of Marque and Reprisal; coin Money; emit Bills of Credit; make any Thing but gold and silver Coin a Tender in Payment of Debts; pass any Bill of Attainder, ex post facto Law, or Law impairing the Obligation of Contracts, or grant any Title of Nobility.

No State shall, without the Consent of the Congress, lay any Imposts or Duties on Imports or Exports, except what may be absolutely necessary for executing it's inspection Laws: and the net Produce of all Duties and Imposts, laid by any State on Imports or Exports, shall be for the Use of the Treasury of the United States; and all such Laws shall be subject to the Revision and Controul of the Congress.

No State shall, without the Consent of Congress, lay any Duty of Tonnage, keep Troops, or Ships of War in time of Peace, enter into any Agreement or Compact with another State, or with a foreign Power, or engage in War, unless actually invaded, or in such imminent Danger as will not admit of delay.

ARTICLE II.

SECTION. 1. The executive Power shall be vested in a President of the United States of America. He shall hold his Office during the Term of four Years, and, together with the Vice President, chosen for the same Term, be elected, as follows

Each State shall appoint, in such Manner as the Legislature thereof may direct, a Number of Electors, equal to the whole Number of Senators and Representatives to which the State may be entitled in the Congress: but no Senator or Representative, or Person holding an Office of Trust or Profit under the United States, shall be appointed an Elector.

The Electors shall meet in their respective States, and vote by Ballot for two Persons, of whom one at least shall not be an inhabitant of the same State with themselves. And they shall make a List of all the Persons voted for, and of the Number of Votes for each; which List they shall sign and certify, and transmit sealed to the Seat of the Government of the United States, directed to the President of the Senate. The President of the Senate shall, in the Presence of the Senate and House of Representatives, open all the Certificates, and the Votes shall then be counted. The Person having the greatest Number of Votes shall be the President, if such Number be a Majority of the whole Number of Electors appointed; and if there be more than one who have such Majority, and have an equal Number of Votes, then the House of Representatives shall immediately chuse by Ballot one of them for President; and if no Person have a Majority, then from the five highest on the List the said House shall in like Manner chuse the President. But in chusing the President, the Votes shall be taken by States, the Representation from each State having one Vote; A quorum for this purpose shall consist of a Member or Members from two thirds of the States, and a Majority of all the States shall be necessary to a Choice. In every Case, after the Choice of the President, the Person having the greatest Number of Votes of the Electors shall be the Vice President. But if there should remain two or more who have equal Votes, the Senate shall chuse from them by Ballot the Vice President.

The Congress may determine the Time of chusing the Electors, and the Day on which they shall give their Votes; which Day shall be the same throughout the United States.

No Person except a natural born Citizen, or a Citizen of the United States, at the time of the Adoption of this Constitution, shall be eligible to the Office of President; neither shall any Person be eligible to that Office who shall not have attained to the Age of thirty five Years, and been fourteen Years a Resident within the United States.

In Case of the Removal of the President from Office, or of his Death, Resignation, or Inability to discharge the Powers and Duties of the said Office, the Same shall devolve on the Vice President, and the Congress may by Law provide for the Case of Removal, Death, Resignation or Inability, both of the President and Vice President, declaring what Officer shall then act as President, and such Officer shall act accordingly, until the Disability be removed, or a President shall be elected.

The President shall, at stated Times, receive for his Services, a Compensation, which shall neither be encreased nor diminished during the Period for which he shall have been elected, and he shall not receive within that Period any other Emolument from the United States, or any of them.

Before he enter on the Execution of his Office, he shall take the following Oath or Affirmation:—"I do solemnly swear (or affirm) that I will faithfully execute the Office of President of the United States, and will to the best of my Ability, preserve, protect and defend the Constitution of the United States."

SECTION. 2. The President shall be Commander in Chief of the Army and Navy of the United States, and of the Militia of the several States, when called into the actual Service of the United States; he may require the Opinion, in writing, of the principal Officer in each of the executive Departments, upon any Subject relating to the Duties of their respective Offices, and he shall have Power to grant Reprieves and Pardons for Offences against the United States, except in Cases of Impeachment.

He shall have Power, by and with the Advice and Consent of the Senate, to make Treaties, provided two thirds of the Senators present concur; and he shall nominate, and by and with the Advice and Consent of the Senate, shall appoint Ambassadors, other public Ministers and Consuls, Judges of the supreme Court, and all other Officers of the United States, whose Appointments are not herein otherwise provided for, and which shall be established by Law: but the Congress may by Law vest the Appointment of such inferior Officers, as they think proper, in the President alone, in the Courts of Law, or in the Heads of Departments.

The President shall have Power to fill up all Vacancies that may happen during the Recess of the Senate, by granting Commissions which shall expire at the End of their next Session.

SECTION. 3. He shall from time to time give to the Congress Information of the State of the Union, and recommend to their Consideration such Measures as he shall judge necessary and expedient; he may, on extraordinary Occasions, convene both Houses, or either of them, and in Case of Disagreement between them, with Respect to the Time of Adjournment, he may adjourn them to such Time as he shall think proper; he shall receive Ambassadors and other public Ministers; he shall take Care that the Laws be faithfully executed, and shall Commission all the Officers of the United States.

SECTION. 4. The President, Vice President and all civil Officers of the United States, shall be removed from Office on Impeachment for, and Conviction of, Treason, Bribery, or other high Crimes and Misdemeanors.

ARTICLE III.

SECTION. 1. The judicial Power of the United States, shall be vested in one supreme Court, and in such inferior Courts as the Congress may from time to time ordain and establish. The Judges, both of the supreme and inferior Courts, shall hold their Offices during good Behaviour, and shall, at stated Times, receive for their Services, a Compensation, which shall not be diminished during their Continuance in Office.

SECTION. 2. The judicial Power shall extend to all Cases, in Law and Equity, arising under this Constitution, the Laws of the United States, and Treaties made, or which shall be made, under their Authority;—to all Cases affecting Ambassadors, other public Ministers and Consuls;—to all Cases of admiralty and maritime Jurisdiction;—to Controversies to which the United States shall be a Party;—to Controversies between two or more States;—between a State and Citizens of another State;—between Citizens of different States,—between Citizens of the same State claiming Lands under Grants of different States, and between a State, or the Citizens thereof, and foreign States, Citizens or Subjects.

In all Cases affecting Ambassadors, other public Ministers and Consuls, and those in which a State shall be Party, the supreme Court shall have original Jurisdiction. In all the other Cases before mentioned, the supreme Court shall have appellate Jurisdiction, both as to Law and Fact, with such Exceptions, and under such Regulations as the Congress shall make.

The Trial of all Crimes, except in Cases of Impeachment, shall be by Jury; and such Trial shall be held in the State where the said Crimes shall have been committed; but when not committed within any State, the Trial shall be at such Place or Places as the Congress may by Law have directed.

SECTION. 3. Treason against the United States, shall consist only in levying War against them, or in adhering to their Enemies, giving them Aid and Comfort. No Person shall be convicted of Treason unless on the Testimony of two Witnesses to the same overt Act, or on Confession in open Court.

The Congress shall have Power to declare the Punishment of Treason, but no Attainder of Treason shall work Corruption of Blood, or Forfeiture except during the Life of the Person attainted.

ARTICLE IV.

SECTION. 1. Full Faith and Credit shall be given in each State to the public Acts, Records, and judicial Proceedings of every other State. And the Congress may by general Laws prescribe the Manner in which such Acts, Records and Proceedings shall be proved, and the Effect thereof.

SECTION. 2. The Citizens of each State shall be entitled to all Privileges and Immunities of Citizens in the several States.

A Person charged in any State with Treason, Felony, or other Crime, who shall flee from Justice, and be found in another State, shall on Demand of the executive Authority of the State from which he fled, be delivered up, to be removed to the State having Jurisdiction of the Crime.

No Person held to Service or Labour in one State, under the Laws thereof, escaping into another, shall, in Consequence of any Law or Regulation therein, be discharged from such Service or Labour, but shall be delivered up on Claim of the Party to whom such Service or Labour may be due.

SECTION. 3. New States may be admitted by the Congress into this Union; but no new State shall be formed or erected within the Jurisdiction of any other State; nor any State be formed by the Junction of two or more States, or Parts of States, without the Consent of the Legislatures of the States concerned as well as of the Congress.

The Congress shall have Power to dispose of and make all needful Rules and Regulations respecting the Territory or other Property belonging to the United States; and nothing in this Constitution shall be so construed as to Prejudice any Claims of the United States, or of any particular State.

SECTION. 4. The United States shall guarantee to every State in this Union a Republican Form of Government, and shall protect each of them against Invasion; and on Application of the Legislature, or of the Executive (when the Legislature cannot be convened) against domestic Violence.

ARTICLE V.

The Congress, whenever two thirds of both Houses shall deem it necessary, shall propose Amendments to this Constitution, or, on the Application of the Legislatures of two thirds of the several States, shall call a Convention for proposing Amendments, which, in either Case, shall be valid to all Intents and Purposes, as Part of this Constitution, when ratified by the legislatures of three fourths of the several States, or by Conventions in three fourths thereof, as the one or the other Mode of Ratification may be proposed by the Congress; Provided that no Amendment which may be made prior to the Year One thousand eight hundred and eight shall in any Manner affect the first and fourth Clauses in the Ninth Section of the first Article; and that no State, without its Consent, shall be deprived of it's equal Suffrage in the Senate.

ARTICLE VI.

All Debts contracted and Engagements entered into, before the Adoption of this Constitution, shall be as valid against the United States under this Constitution, as under the Confederation.

This Constitution, and the Laws of the United States which shall be made in Pursuance thereof; and all Treaties made, or which shall be made, under the Authority of the United States, shall be the supreme Law of the Land; and the Judges in every State shall be bound thereby, any Thing in the Constitution or Laws of any State to the Contrary notwithstanding.

The Senators and Representatives before mentioned, and the Members of the several State Legislatures, and all executive and judicial Officers, both of the United States and of the several States, shall be bound by Oath or Affirmation, to support this Constitution; but no religious Test shall ever be required as a Qualification to any Office or public Trust under the United States.

ARTICLE VII.

The Ratification of the Conventions of nine States, shall be sufficient for the Establishment of this Constitution between the States so ratifying the Same.

The Word "the", being interlined between the seventh and eighth Lines of the first Page, the Word "Thirty" being partly written on an Erazure in the fiftienth Line of the first Page, The Words "is tried" being interlined between the thirty second and thirty third Lines of the first Page and the Word "the" being interlined between the forty third and forty fourth Lines of the second Page.

Attest William Jackson
Secretary

DONE in Convention by the Unanimous Consent of the States present the Seventeenth Day of September in the Year of our Lord one thousand seven hundred and Eighty seven and of the Independance of the United States of America the Twelfth. IN WITNESS whereof We have hereunto subscribed our Names.

G° WASHINGTON

Presid* and deputy from Virginia

DELAWARE
- GEO: READ
- GUNNING BEDFORD jun
- JOHN DICKINSON
- RICHARD BASSETT
- JACO: BROOM

MARYLAND
- JAMES MCHENRY
- DAN OF ST. THOS. JENIFER
- DANL. CARROLL

VIRGINIA
- JOHN BLAIR—
- JAMES MADISON JR.

NORTH CAROLINA
- WM. BLOUNT
- RICHD. DOBBS SPAIGHT
- HU WILLIAMSON

SOUTH CAROLINA
- J. RUTLEDGE
- CHARLES COTESWORTH PINCKNEY
- CHARLES PINCKNEY
- PIERCE BUTLER

GEORGIA
- WILLIAM FEW
- ABR BALDWIN

NEW HAMPSHIRE
- JOHN LANGDON
- NICHOLAS GILMAN

MASSACHUSETTS
- NATHANIEL GORHAM
- RUFUS KING

CONNECTICUT
- WM. SAML. JOHNSON
- ROGER SHERMAN

NEW YORK
- ALEXANDER HAMILTON

NEW JERSEY
- WIL: LIVINGSTON
- DAVID BREARLEY
- WM. PATERSON
- JONA: DAYTON

PENNSYLVANIA
- B. FRANKLIN
- THOMAS MIFFLIN
- ROBT. MORRIS
- GEO. CLYMER
- THOS. FITZSIMONS
- JARED INGERSOLL
- JAMES WILSON
- GOUV MORRIS

AMENDMENT I

Congress shall make no law respecting an establishment of religion, or prohibiting the free exercise thereof; or abridging the freedom of speech, or of the press; or the right of the people peaceably to assemble, and to petition the Government for a redress of grievances.

AMENDMENT II

A well regulated Militia, being necessary to the security of a free State, the right of the people to keep and bear Arms, shall not be infringed.

AMENDMENT III

No Soldier shall, in time of peace be quartered in any house, without the consent of the Owner, nor in time of war, but in a manner to be prescribed by law.

AMENDMENT IV

The right of the people to be secure in their persons, houses, papers, and effects, against unreasonable searches and seizures, shall not be violated, and no Warrants shall issue, but upon probable cause, supported by Oath or affirmation, and particularly describing the place to be searched, and the persons or things to be seized.

AMENDMENT V

No person shall be held to answer for a capital, or otherwise infamous crime, unless on a presentment or indictment of a Grand Jury, except in cases arising in the land or naval forces, or in the Militia, when in actual service in time of War or public danger; nor shall any person be subject for the same offence to be twice put in jeopardy of life or limb; nor shall be compelled in any criminal case to be a witness against himself, nor be deprived of life, liberty, or property, without due process of law; nor shall private property be taken for public use, without just compensation.

AMENDMENT VI

In all criminal prosecutions, the accused shall enjoy the right to a speedy and public trial, by an impartial jury of the State and district wherein the crime shall have been committed, which district shall have been previously ascertained by law, and to be informed of the nature and cause of the accusation; to be confronted with the witnesses against him; to have compulsory process for obtaining Witnesses in his favor, and to have the assistance of counsel for his defence.

AMENDMENT VII

In Suits at common law, where the value in controversy shall exceed twenty dollars, the right of trial by jury shall be preserved, and no fact tried by a jury, shall be otherwise re-examined in any Court of the United States, than according to the rules of the common law.

AMENDMENT VIII

Excessive bail shall not be required, nor excessive fines imposed, nor cruel and unusual punishments inflicted.

AMENDMENT IX

The enumeration in the Constitution, of certain rights, shall not be construed to deny or disparage others retained by the people.

AMENDMENT X

The powers not delegated to the United States by the Constitution, nor prohibited by it to the States, are reserved to the States respectively, or to the people.

AMENDMENT XI

The Judicial power of the United States shall not be construed to extend to any suit in law or equity, commenced or prosecuted against one of the United States by Citizens of another State, or by Citizens or Subjects of any Foreign State.

AMENDMENT XII

The Electors shall meet in their respective states, and vote by ballot for President and Vice-President, one of whom, at least, shall not be an inhabitant of the same state with themselves; they shall name in their ballots the person voted for as President, and in distinct ballots the person voted for as Vice-President, and they shall make distinct lists of all persons voted for as President, and of all persons voted for as Vice-President, and of the number of votes for each, which lists they shall sign and certify, and transmit sealed to the seat of the government of the United States, directed to the President of the Senate;—The President of the Senate shall, in the presence of the Senate and House of Representatives, open all the certificates and the votes shall then be counted;—The person having the greatest number of votes for President, shall be the President, if such number be a majority of the whole number of Electors appointed; and if no person have such majority, then from the persons having the highest numbers not exceeding three on the list of those voted for as President, the House of Representatives shall choose immediately, by ballot, the President. But in choosing the President, the votes shall be taken by states, the representation from each state having one vote; a quorum for this purpose shall consist of a member or members from two-thirds of the states, and a majority of all the states shall be necessary to a choice. And if the House of Representatives shall not choose a President whenever the right of choice shall devolve upon them, before the fourth day of March next following, then the Vice-President shall act as President, as in the case of the death or other constitutional disability of the President.—The person having the greatest number of votes as Vice-President, shall be the Vice-President, if such number be a majority of the whole number of Electors appointed, and if no person have a majority, then from the two highest numbers on the list, the Senate shall choose the Vice-President; a quorum for the purpose shall consist of two-thirds of the whole number of Senators, and a majority of the whole number shall be necessary to a choice. But no person constitutionally ineligible to the office of President shall be eligible to that of Vice-President of the United States.

AMENDMENT XIII

Section 1. Neither slavery nor involuntary servitude, except as a punishment for crime whereof the party shall have been duly convicted, shall exist within the United States, or any place subject to their jurisdiction.

Section 2. Congress shall have power to enforce this article by appropriate legislation.

AMENDMENT XIV

Section 1. All persons born or naturalized in the United States, and subject to the jurisdiction thereof, are citizens of the United States and of the State wherein they reside. No State shall make or enforce any law which shall abridge the privileges or immunities of citizens of the United States; nor shall any State deprive any person of life, liberty, or property, without due process of law; nor deny to any person within its jurisdiction the equal protection of the laws.

Section 2. Representatives shall be apportioned among the several States according to their respective numbers, counting the whole number of persons in each State, excluding Indians not taxed. But when the right to vote at any election for the choice of electors for President and Vice President of the United States, Representatives in Congress, the Executive and Judicial officers of a State, or the members of the Legislature thereof, is denied to any of the male inhabitants of such State, being twenty-one years of age, and citizens of the United States, or in any way abridged, except for participation in rebellion, or other crime, the basis of representation therein shall be reduced in the proportion which the number of such male citizens shall bear to the whole number of male citizens twenty-one years of age in such State.

SECTION 3. No person shall be a Senator or Representative in Congress, or elector of President and Vice President, or hold any office, civil or military, under the United States, or under any State, who, having previously taken an oath, as a member of Congress, or as an officer of the United States, or as a member of any State legislature, or as an executive or judicial officer of any State, to support the Constitution of the United States, shall have engaged in insurrection or rebellion against the same, or given aid or comfort to the enemies thereof. But Congress may by a vote of two-thirds of each House, remove such disability.

SECTION 4. The validity of the public debt of the United States, authorized by law, including debts incurred for payment of pensions and bounties for services in suppressing insurrection or rebellion, shall not be questioned. But neither the United States nor any State shall assume or pay any debt or obligation incurred in aid of insurrection or rebellion against the United States, or any claim for the loss or emancipation of any slave; but all such debts, obligations and claims shall be held illegal and void.

SECTION 5. The Congress shall have power to enforce, by appropriate legislation, the provisions of this article.

AMENDMENT XV

SECTION 1. The right of citizens of the United States to vote shall not be denied or abridged by the United States or by any State on account of race, color, or previous condition of servitude.

SECTION 2. The Congress shall have power to enforce this article by appropriate legislation.

AMENDMENT XVI

The Congress shall have power to lay and collect taxes on incomes, from whatever source derived, without apportionment among the several States, and without regard to any census or enumeration.

AMENDMENT XVII

The Senate of the United States shall be composed of two Senators from each State, elected by the people thereof, for six years; and each Senator shall have one vote. The electors in each State shall have the qualifications requisite for electors of the most numerous branch of the State legislatures.

When vacancies happen in the representation of any State in the Senate, the executive authority of such State shall issue writs of election to fill such vacancies: *Provided,* That the legislature of any State may empower the executive thereof to make temporary appointments until the people fill the vacancies by election as the legislature may direct.

This amendment shall not be so construed as to affect the election or term of any Senator chosen before it becomes valid as part of the Constitution.

AMENDMENT XVIII

SECTION 1. After one year from the ratification of this article the manufacture, sale, or transportation of intoxicating liquors within, the importation thereof into, or the exportation thereof from the United States and all territory subject to the jurisdiction thereof for beverage purposes is hereby prohibited.

SECTION 2. The Congress and the several States shall have concurrent power to enforce this article by appropriate legislation.

SECTION 3. This article shall be inoperative unless it shall have been ratified as an amendment to the Constitution by the legislatures of the several States, as provided in the Constitution, within seven years from the date of the submission hereof to the States by the Congress.

AMENDMENT XIX

The right of citizens of the United States to vote shall not be denied or abridged by the United States or by any State on account of sex.

Congress shall have power to enforce this article by appropriate legislation.

AMENDMENT XX

SECTION 1. The terms of the President and Vice President shall end at noon on the 20th day of January, and the terms of Senators and Representatives at noon on the 3d day of January, of the years in which such terms would have ended if this article had not been ratified; and the terms of their successors shall then begin.

SECTION 2. The Congress shall assemble at least once in every year, and such meeting shall begin at noon on the 3d day of January, unless they shall by law appoint a different day.

SECTION 3. If, at the time fixed for the beginning of the term of the President, the President elect shall have died, the Vice President elect shall become President. If a President shall not have been chosen before the time fixed for the beginning of his term, or if the President elect shall have failed to qualify, then the Vice President elect shall act as President until a President shall have qualified; and the Congress may by law provide for the case wherein neither a President elect nor a Vice President elect shall have qualified, declaring who shall then act as President, or the manner in which one who is to act shall be selected, and such person shall act accordingly until a President or Vice President shall have qualified.

SECTION 4. The Congress may by law provide for the case of the death of any of the persons from whom the House of Representatives may choose a President whenever the right of choice shall have devolved upon them, and for the case of the death of any of the persons from whom the Senate may choose a Vice President whenever the right of choice shall have devolved upon them.

SECTION 5. Sections 1 and 2 shall take effect on the 15th day of October following the ratification of this article.

SECTION 6. This article shall be inoperative unless it shall have been ratified as an amendment to the Constitution by the legislatures of three-fourths of the several States within seven years from the date of its submission.

AMENDMENT XXI

SECTION 1. The eighteenth article of amendment to the Constitution of the United States is hereby repealed.

SECTION 2. The transportation or importation into any State, Territory, or possession of the United States for delivery or use therein of intoxicating liquors, in violation of the laws thereof, is hereby prohibited.

SECTION 3. This article shall be inoperative unless it shall have been ratified as an amendment to the Constitution by conventions in the several States, as provided in the Constitution, within seven years from the date of the submission hereof to the States by the Congress.

AMENDMENT XXII

SECTION 1. No person shall be elected to the office of the President more than twice, and no person who has held the office of President, or acted as President, for more than two years of a term to which some other person was elected President shall be elected to the office of the President more than once. But this Article shall not apply to any person holding the office of President when this Article was proposed by the Congress, and shall not prevent any person who may be holding the office of

President, or acting as President, during the term within which this Article becomes operative from holding the office of President or acting as President during the remainder of such term.

SECTION 2. This article shall be inoperative unless it shall have been ratified as an amendment to the Constitution by the legislatures of three-fourths of the several States within seven years from the date of its submission to the States by the Congress.

AMENDMENT XXIII

SECTION 1. The District constituting the seat of Government of the United States shall appoint in such manner as the Congress may direct:

A number of electors of President and Vice President equal to the whole number of Senators and Representatives in Congress to which the District would be entitled if it were a State, but in no event more than the least populous State; they shall be in addition to those appointed by the States, but they shall be considered, for the purposes of the election of President and Vice President, to be electors appointed by a State; and they shall meet in the District and perform such duties as provided by the twelfth article of amendment.

SECTION 2. The Congress shall have power to enforce this article by appropriate legislation.

AMENDMENT XXIV

SECTION 1. The right of citizens of the United States to vote in any primary or other election for President or Vice President, for electors for President or Vice President, or for Senator or Representatives in Congress, shall not be denied or abridged by the United States or any State by reason of failure to pay any poll tax or other tax.

SECTION 2. The Congress shall have power to enforce this article by appropriate legislation.

AMENDMENT XXV

SECTION 1. In case of the removal of the President from office or of his death or resignation, the Vice President shall become President.

SECTION 2. Whenever there is a vacancy in the office of the Vice President, the President shall nominate a Vice President who shall take office upon confirmation by a majority vote of both Houses of Congress.

SECTION 3. Whenever the President transmits to the President pro tempore of the Senate and the Speaker of the House of Representatives his written declaration that he is unable to discharge the powers and duties of his office, and until he transmits to them a written declaration to the contrary, such powers and duties shall be discharged by the Vice President as Acting President.

SECTION 4. Whenever the Vice President and a majority of either the principal officers of the executive departments or of such other body as Congress may by law provide, transmit to the President pro tempore of the Senate and the Speaker of the House of Representatives their written declaration that the President is unable to discharge the powers and duties of his office, the Vice President shall immediately assume the powers and duties of the office as Acting President.

Thereafter, when the President transmits to the President pro tempore of the Senate and the Speaker of the House of Representatives his written declaration that no inability exists, he shall resume the powers and duties of his office unless the Vice President and a majority of either the principal officers of the executive department or of such other body as Congress may by law provide, transmit within four days to the President pro tempore of the Senate and the Speaker of the House of Representatives their written declaration that the President is unable to discharge the powers and duties of his office. Thereupon Congress shall decide the issue, assembling within forty-eight hours for that purpose if not in session. If the Congress, within twenty-one days after receipt of the latter written declaration, or, if Congress is not in session, within twenty-one days after Congress is required to assemble, determines by two-thirds vote of both Houses that the President is unable to discharge the powers and duties of his office, the Vice President shall continue to discharge the same as Acting President; otherwise, the President shall resume the powers and duties of his office.

AMENDMENT XXVI

SECTION 1. The right of citizens of the United States, who are eighteen years of age or older, to vote shall not be denied or abridged by the United States or by any State on account of age.

SECTION 2. The Congress shall have power to enforce this article by appropriate legislation.

Appendix 4

Resolution Transmitting the Constitution to Congress

IN CONVENTION

Monday, September 17, 1787

PRESENT, *The States of New-Hampshire, Massachusetts, Connecticut, Mr. Hamilton from New-York, New Jersey, Pennsylvania, Delaware, Maryland, Virginia, North Carolina, South Carolina, and Georgia.*

Resolved, That the [following] Constitution be laid before the United States in Congress assembled, and that it is the opinion of this convention, that it should afterwards be submitted to a convention of delegates, chosen in each State by the people thereof, under the recommendation of its legislature, for their assent and ratification; and that each convention assenting to, and ratifying the same should give notice thereof to the United States in Congress assembled.

Resolved, That it is the opinion of this convention, that as soon as the conventions of nine States shall have ratified this Constitution, the United States in Congress assembled should fix a day on which electors should be appointed by the States which shall have ratified the same, and a day on which the electors should assemble to vote for the President, and the time and place for commencing proceedings under this Constitution; that after such publication the electors should be appointed, and the senators and representatives elected; that the electors should meet on the day fixed for the election of the President, and should transmit their votes certified, signed, sealed, and directed, as the Constitution requires, to the secretary of the United States in Congress assembled; that the senators and representatives should convene at the time and place assigned; that the senators should appoint a president of the Senate, for the sole purpose of receiving, opening, and counting the votes for President; and that after he shall be chosen, the Congress, together with the President, should without delay proceed to execute this Constitution.

By the unanimous order of the convention.

GEORGE WASHINGTON, *President.*

WILLIAM JACKSON, *Secretary.*

Appendix 5

Washington's Letter of Transmittal

IN CONVENTION

September 17, 1787

SIR,

WE HAVE now the honor to submit to the consideration of the United States in Congress assembled, that Constitution which has appeared to us the most advisable.

The friends of our country have long seen and desired, that the power of making war, peace, and treaties, of levying money and regulating commerce, and the correspondent executive and judicial authorities should be fully and effectually vested in the general government of the Union: but the impropriety of delegating such extensive trust to one body of men is evident—Hence results the necessity of a different organization.

It is obviously impracticable in the federal government of these States, to secure all rights of independent sovereignty to each, and yet provide for the interest and safety of all—Individuals entering into society, must give up a share of liberty to preserve the rest. The magnitude of the sacrifice must depend as well on situation and circumstances as on the object to be obtained. It is at all times difficult to draw with precision the line between those rights which must be surrendered, and those which may be reserved; and on the present occasion this difficulty was increased by a difference among the several States as to their situation, extent, habits, and particular interests.

In all our deliberations on this subject we kept steadily in our view, that which appears to us the greatest interest of every true American, the consolidation of our Union, in which is involved our prosperity, felicity, safety, perhaps our national existence. This important consideration, seriously and deeply impressed on our minds, led each State in the Convention to be less rigid on points of inferior magnitude, than might have been otherwise expected; and thus the Constitution, which we now present, is the result of a spirit of amity, and of that mutual deference and concession which the peculiarity of our political situation rendered indispensable.

That it will meet the full and entire approbation of every State is not perhaps to be expected; but each will doubtless consider, that had her interest alone been consulted, the consequences might have been particularly disagreeable or injurious to others; that it is liable to as few exceptions as could reasonably have been expected, we hope and believe; that it may promote the lasting welfare of that country so dear to us all, and secure her freedom and happiness, is our most ardent wish.

With great respect,
We have the honor to be
SIR,
Your Excellency's most
Obedient and Humble Servants,
GEORGE WASHINGTON, President

By Unanimous Order of the Convention
HIS EXCELLENCY
THE PRESIDENT OF CONGRESS

Appendix 6

The Birth of the Constitution: A Chronology

1786

September 11–14	Annapolis Convention.
September 20	Report of Annapolis Convention, calling for a Constitutional Convention, submitted to Congress.
October 11	Congress sends Annapolis Convention report to committee.
November 23	New Jersey elects delegates.
December 4	Virginia elects delegates.
December 30	Pennsylvania elects delegates.

1787

January 6	North Carolina elects delegates.
January 17	New Hampshire elects delegates.
February 3	Delaware elects delegates.
February 10	Georgia elects delegates.
February 21	Congress calls Constitutional Convention.
March 3	Massachusetts elects delegates.
March 6	New York elects delegates.
March 8	South Carolina elects delegates.
March 14	Rhode Island refuses to elect delegates.
April 23–May 6	Maryland elects delegates.
May 14	Day appointed for beginning of Convention; quorum not present.
May 14–17	Connecticut elects delegates.
May 25	Quorum is present (seven states represented); Convention begins.
May 29	Governor Edmund Randolph introduces the Virginia Plan.
June 15	William Paterson introduces the New Jersey Plan.
July 16	Great Compromise approved: voting power in first house of Congress to be apportioned by population; states to have equal voting power in the second house.
August 6	Committee on Detail submits draft to Convention.
September 12	Committee on Style submits draft to Convention.
September 15	Draft Constitution approved by unanimous vote of the states represented in the Convention.
September 17	Constitution is signed; Convention adjourns.

September 26–28	Proposed Constitution debated in Congress.
September 28	Congress transmits Constitution to the states for ratification action.
September 29	Pennsylvania calls state convention.
October 17	Connecticut calls state convention.
October 25	Massachusetts calls state convention.
October 26	Georgia calls state convention.
October 31	Virginia calls state convention.
November 1	New Jersey calls state convention.
November 6	Delegates to Pennsylvania convention elected.
November 10	Delaware calls state convention.
November 12	Delegates to Connecticut convention elected.
November 19–January 7, 1788	Delegates to Massachusetts convention elected.
November 20	Pennsylvania convention begins.
November 26	Delegates to Delaware convention elected.
November 27–December 1	Delegates to New Jersey convention elected.
December 1	Maryland calls state convention.
December 3	Delaware convention begins.
December 4–5	Delegates to Georgia convention elected.
December 6	North Carolina calls state convention.
December 7	Delaware convention ratifies Constitution (30–0).
December 11	New Jersey convention begins.
December 12	Pennsylvania convention ratifies Constitution (46–23).
December 14	New Hampshire calls state convention.
December 18	New Jersey convention ratifies constitution (38–0).
December 25	Georgia convention begins.
31 December–February 12, 1788	Delegates to New Hampshire convention elected.

1788

January 3	Connecticut convention begins.
January 9	Connecticut convention ratifies Constitution (128–40).
January 9	Massachusetts convention begins.
January 19	South Carolina calls state convention.
February 1	New York calls state convention.
February 6	Massachusetts convention ratifies Constitution (187–168) and proposes amendments.
February 13–22	New Hampshire convention holds first session.
March 1	Rhode Island calls state referendum on Constitution.
March 3–31	Delegates to Virginia convention elected.
March 24	Rhode Island voters reject Constitution in referendum (2711–239).
March 28–29	Delegates to North Carolina convention elected.
April 7	Delegates to Maryland convention elected.
April 11–12	Delegates to South Carolina convention elected.
April 21	Maryland convention begins.
April 26	Maryland convention ratifies Constitution (63–11).
April 29–May 3	Delegates to New York convention elected.
May 12	South Carolina convention begins.
May 23	South Carolina convention ratifies Constitution (149–73) and proposes amendments.
June 2	Virginia convention begins.
June 17	New York convention begins.
June 18	New Hampshire convention begins second session.
June 21	New Hampshire convention ratifies Constitution (57–47) and proposes amendments.
June 25	Virginia convention ratifies Constitution (89–79) and proposes amendments.

July 2	New Hampshire's ratification received by Congress; as this is the ninth state ratification, a committee is appointed to effect the transition from government under the Articles of Confederation to government under the Constitution.
July 21	North Carolina convention begins.
July 26	New York convention ratifies Constitution (30–27) and proposes amendments.
August 2	North Carolina convention proposes amendments, but does not ratify the Constitution.
September 13	Congress sets dates for presidential election and for first meeting of Congress under the Constitution.
November 20	Virginia legislature requests Congress to call a second constitutional convention.
November 30	North Carolina calls second state convention.

1789

May 4	Representative James Madison announces, during congressional debate, his intention to introduce constitutional amendments.
May 5–6	Petitions to Congress from legislatures of Virginia and New York, asking Congress to call a second constitutional convention, are reported and filed.
June 8	Madison, in a speech in the House of Representatives, introduces amendments that will become the Bill of Rights.
July 21	Madison's proposed amendments referred to select committee of the House of Representatives.
July 28	Select committee reports back the proposed amendments; its report is tabled.
August 14–18	Congress debates proposed amendments in Committee of the Whole.
August 21–22	Delegates to second North Carolina convention elected.
August 24	House of Representatives approves and sends to the Senate seventeen proposed amendments, including the provisions of the Bill of Rights.
September 2	Senate begins debate on the Bill of Rights.
September 9	Senate approves a version of the Bill of Rights.
September 21	The Senate and House versions of the Bill of Rights are referred to a conference committee.
September 24	House of Representatives approves (37–14) conference committee version of the Bill of Rights.
September 25	Senate approves conference committee version of the Bill of Rights. Twelve amendments to the Constitution, including the ten now known as the Bill of Rights, are proposed by Congress to the states.
November 16	Second North Carolina convention begins.
November 20	New Jersey legislature ratifies the Bill of Rights.
November 21	North Carolina convention ratifies Constitution (194–77) and proposes amendments.
December 19	Maryland legislature ratifies the Bill of Rights.
December 22	North Carolina legislature ratifies Bill of Rights.

1790

January 17	Rhode Island calls state convention.
January 18	South Carolina legislature ratifies the Bill of Rights.
January 25	New Hampshire legislature ratifies the Bill of Rights.
January 28	Delaware legislature ratifies the Bill of Rights.
February 8	Delegates to Rhode Island convention elected.
February 24	New York legislature ratifies the Bill of Rights.
March 1	Rhode Island convention begins.
March 10	Pennsylvania legislature ratifies the Bill of Rights.

May 29	Rhode Island convention ratifies Constitution (34–32) and proposes amendments.
June	Rhode Island legislature ratifies the Bill of Rights. (N.B.: exact date in June of Rhode Island's ratification is unknown.)

1791

March 4	Vermont admitted to the Union.
November 3	Vermont legislature ratifies Bill of Rights.
December 15	Virginia legislature ratifies the Bill of Rights.

Appendix 7

Important Events in the Development of American Constitutional Law

1215	Magna Carta.
1225	Magna Carta reissued in the modified form that became the English statute.
1295	Parliament of three estates established, the model for all future English parliaments.
1297	Confirmatio Cartarum.
1322	That no statute could be made except by consent of both lords and commons was established and declared.
1354	The phrase "due process of law" was first used in a statute.
1387	By statute the king was forbidden to levy imposts, duties, or surcharges without consent of Parliament; the king could no longer legally raise revenue by his own authority alone.
1407	The king agreed that all revenue measures must originate in the House of Commons; this practice was followed in Article I, Section 7, of the Constitution.
1606	Edward Coke was appointed Chief Justice of Common Pleas. He was made Chief Justice of the King's Bench ("Lord Chief Justice of England") in 1613.
	First Virginia Charter.
1608	*Calvin's Case.*
1610	*Bonham's Case.*
1619	The General Assembly of Virginia met, the first representative assembly in the New World.
1620	Mayflower Compact.
1628	Petition of Right.
1629	Charter of Massachusetts Bay Company.
1635	Massachusetts General Court established a committee to write fundamental laws to limit magistrate, "in resemblance to a Magna Carta."
	Roger Williams banished by the General Court of Massachusetts. He founded Providence Plantation in 1636.
	In instructions to Governor Wyatt, the Virginia Assembly was officially recognized as a permanent institution, to meet at least annually.
1639	Fundamental Orders of Connecticut.
1641	Courts of High Commission and Star Chamber abolished; oath *ex officio* abolished.
	Massachusetts Body of Liberties.
	The Grand Remonstrance charged King Charles I with various unlawful acts and demanded that executive power be exercised by ministers in whom Parliament had confidence.
1643	Roger Williams's *The Bloudy Tenent of Persecution.*
1644	John Milton's *Areopagitica,* a plea against prior restraint and censorship, published.

1644	Massachusetts General Court became bicameral, as Assistants met separately from Assembly.
1647	Massachusetts General Laws and Liberties.
1649	Maryland Toleration Act.
1652	Roger Williams's pamphlet *The Bloudy Tenent Yet More Bloudy* published.
1653	The Instrument of Government, the short-lived written constitution of the English commonwealth, promulgated by Oliver Cromwell.
1660–1696	Navigation Acts.
1662	Royal Charter for Connecticut (constitution until 1818).
1663	Royal Charter of Rhode Island (constitution until 1842).
1664	New York granted to Duke of York as proprietary colony; the proprietor to have complete power to make laws.
1670	*Bushell's Case.*
1679	Habeas Corpus Act.
1682	Pennsylvania Frame of Government.
1687	William Penn's *The Excellent Priviledge of Liberty and Property* published; it included the first text of and commentary on Magna Carta published in America.
1689	Act of Toleration.
	English Bill of Rights.
	John Locke's *Letter Concerning Toleration.*
1690	John Locke's *Two Treatises of Government.*
1695	The last English licensing act, restricting freedom of the press, expired.
1698	Algernon Sidney's *Discourses Concerning Government.*
1701	Pennsylvania Charter of Liberties.
1720–1721	Trenchard and Gordon's essays, *Cato's Letters* and *The Independent Whig,* first published.
1733	Molasses Act.
1735	*Zenger's Case.*
1748	Montesquieu's *Spirit of the Laws.*
1754	Albany Plan of Union proposed by the Albany Congress.
1758	Emerich de Vattel's *Law of Nations and of Nature.*
1762	Massachusetts General Court voted a ban on general warrants; it was disallowed by the Governor.
1763	*Paxton's Case* (Writs of Assistance Case).
1764	James Otis, in *The Rights of the British Colonies Asserted and Proved,* denied the right of Parliament to tax the Americans and maintained that a court could judge an act of Parliament void if it was contrary to natural justice.
	The Sugar Act (American Revenue Act) was the first attempt by the British Parliament to tax the colonists for revenue purposes.
1765	*Entick v. Carrington.*
	Stamp Act.
	Stamp Act Congress.
1765–1769	William Blackstone's *Commentaries on the Laws of England* published.
1766	A county court in Northhampton County, Virginia, in an advisory opinion, declared the Stamp Act unconstitutional and therefore void.
	Declaratory Act.
1767–1768	John Dickinson's *Letters from a Farmer in Pennsylvania* published.
1768	Massachusetts Circular Letter.
1772	*Somerset's Case.*
1773	Constitutional debate in Massachusetts; Governor James Hutchinson, in a message to the General Court, asserted that supreme power must rest somewhere; the alternatives were parliamentary rule or independence. The General Court replied that sovereignty could be, and, in fact, already was, divided.
1774	Coercive Acts (Intolerable Acts), including Administration of Justice Act.
	First Continental Congress.
	The Association.
	Joseph Galloway proposes his Plan of Union.
	Thomas Jefferson's *Summary View of the Rights of British America.*
1775	Second Continental Congress convened.
	Declaration of the Causes and Necessity of Taking Up Arms.

1776	Thomas Paine's *Common Sense*.
	Declaration of Independence.
	Dickinson's draft of Articles of Confederation submitted to Congress.
1776–1780	First state constitutions written.
1777	Articles of Confederation approved by Congress and submitted to states.
1779	Congressional resolution asked states to cede their western lands to the United States.
1780	*Holmes v. Walton* (New Jersey).
1781	Articles of Confederation ratified and in force.
1783	*Quock Walker's Case* (Massachusetts).
1784	*Rutgers v. Waddington* (New York).
	James Madison's "Memorial and Remonstrance" against religious assessments.
1786	Virginia Statute for Religious Freedom.
	Ten Pound Act Cases (New Hampshire).
	Trevett v. Weeden (Rhode Island).
	Annapolis Convention.
1787	*Bayard v. Singleton*.
	Congress adopted resolution calling federal Constitutional Convention.
	John Adams's *Defense of the Constitutions of Government of the United States*.
	Constitutional Convention met in Philadelphia and drafted Constitution of the United States.
	Northwest Ordinance.
	Congress transmitted Constitution to the states for ratification.
1787–1788	*The Federalist*.
1788	Constitution ratified by required nine states.
	Congress adopted ordinance to put Constitution into effect.
1789	George Washington chosen President.
	Departments of State, War, and Treasury created.
	Jucidiary Act of 1789.
	Habeas Corpus Act.
	Bill of Rights proposed.
	President Washington appeared in person to ask the Senate's advice and consent relative to an Indian treaty, failure to act cost the Senate a role as the President's council of advice.
1790	Alexander Hamilton's Report on the Public Credit.
	Treason Act.
1791	*Champion and Dickason v. Casey*.
	Bank of the United States Act.
	Bill of Rights ratified and in effect.
	Hamilton's Report on Manufactures.
1792	*Hayburn's Case*.
	President Washington used the presidential veto power for the first time, vetoing a reapportionment bill he thought unconstitutional.
1793	*Chisholm v. Georgia*.
	First Fugitive Slave Act.
	The Supreme Court, presented with a list of questions from the president and the cabinet concerning relations with France, refused to give an advisory opinion.
	Washington's Proclamation of Neutrality in the Wars of the French Revolution.
1794	Jay's Treaty.
	Whiskey Rebellion in Pennsylvania against federal alcohol tax. Suppressed by militia of four states under federal control.
1795	*Van Horne's Lessee v. Dorrance*.
	Post Office Department created.
	Ware v. Hylton.
1796	*Hylton v. United States*.
	Washington's Farewell Address.
	XYZ Affair began three-year undeclared war with France.
1798	Alien and Sedition Acts.
	Calder v. Bull.
	Department of the Navy created.

Eleventh Amendment ratified and in effect.

Virginia and Kentucky Resolutions.

1799   Second set of Kentucky Resolutions claimed states could nullify unconstitutional acts of Congress.

1801   Electoral College tie between Thomas Jefferson and Aaron Burr resolved in House of Representatives; this led to the Twelfth Amendment.

John Marshall became Chief Justice.

Judiciary Act of 1801.

1802   Judiciary Act of 1801 repealed; Judiciary Act of 1802 enacted.

1803   *Marbury v. Madison.*

Stuart v. Laird.

Louisiana Purchase Treaty.

1804   John Pickering, United States District Court judge for New Hampshire, having been impeached by the House of Representatives of malfeasance and intemperance, was convicted by the Senate and removed from office.

Twelfth Amendment ratified and in effect.

1805   Samuel Chase, Associate Justice of the Supreme Court, having been impeached by the House of Representatives of oppressive and partisan conduct, was acquitted by the Senate.

1807   *Ex Parte Bollman and Swartwout.*

Abolition of the Slave Trade Act.

Embargo Act.

Trial of Aaron Burr (*United States v. Burr*).

1809   Massachusetts Resolutions declared the Embargo unconstitutional and not legally binding.

United States v. Judge Peters (Olmstead Case).

1810   *Fletcher v. Peck.*

1812   *New Jersey v. Wilson.*

United States v. Hudson and Goodwin.

1814   Hartford Convention.

1815   *Terrett v. Taylor.*

Second Bank of the United States Act.

1816   *Martin v. Hunter's Lessee.*

1817   Madison's veto of Bonus Bill (on constitutional grounds).

1819   Secretary of War Calhoun recommended a program of internal improvements as a defense measure.

Dartmouth College v. Woodward.

McCulloch v. Maryland.

Sturges v. Crowninshield.

1820   John Taylor of Caroline's *Construction Construed* published, arguing that the Supreme Court was destroying the independence of the states and of the other branches of the federal government.

Missouri Compromise.

1821   *Cohens v. Virginia.*

1822   Cumberland Road Bill vetoed by President James Monroe, who also recommended a constitutional amendment authorizing the United States to build and operate internal improvements.

1823   Monroe Doctrine.

Corfield v. Coryell.

1824   *Gibbons v. Ogden.*

Osborn v. Bank of the United States.

1825   John Quincy Adams (who had finished second in the Electoral College vote) elected president by the House of Representatives.

Eakin v. Raub.

1826–1830   James Kent's *Commentaries on American Law.*

1827   *Brown v. Maryland.*

Martin v. Mott.

Ogden v. Saunders.

1828	South Carolina Exposition and Protest.
	American Insurance Company v. Canter.
1829	*Willson v. Black Bird Creek Marsh Company.*
1830	Maysville Road Bill vetoed by President Andrew Jackson.
	Daniel Webster and Robert Young Hayne participated in a great debate in the Senate on the nature of the Constitution.
	Craig v. Missouri.
	Providence Bank v. Billings.
1831	William Lloyd Garrison founded *The Liberator.*
	Cherokee Nation v. Georgia (first of the Cherokee Indian Cases).
1832	Jackson's Veto of the Bank Bill.
	Vice-President John C. Calhoun, in his Fort Hill Address, explained his theory of nullification.
	South Carolina Ordinance of Nullification of the Tariff Act of 1828.
	Jackson's Proclamation to the People of South Carolina.
	Worcester v. Georgia.
1833	Force Act of 1833.
	Joseph Story's *Commentaries on the Constitution.*
	Barron v. Baltimore.
1836	First congressional "gag rule" on antislavery petitions imposed.
	Roger B. Taney became Chief Justice.
1837	Membership of Supreme Court increased from seven to nine.
	New York v. Miln.
	Briscoe v. Bank of Kentucky.
	Charles River Bridge v. Warren Bridge Company.
1839	*Bank of Augusta v. Earle.*
1841	*Groves v. Slaughter.*
1842	Reapportionment Act required representatives to be elected by district.
	Dobbins v. Erie Company.
	Swift v. Tyson.
	Prigg v. Pennsylvania.
1843	*Bronson v. Kinzie.*
1844	Texas Annexation Treaty signed; rejected by Senate.
1845	Congress, by joint resolution, approved the annexation of Texas and provided for admission of Texas as a state.
	Congress provided for uniform presidential election day.
1847	License Cases.
1848	Oregon Act.
	Treaty of Guadalupe Hidalgo.
	West River Bridge Company v. Dix.
1849	Passenger Cases.
	Luther v. Borden.
1850	Compromise of 1850.
	Nashville Convention Resolutions asserted right of secession.
	Strader v. Graham.
1850–1858	Personal Liberty Laws adopted by states: Vermont in 1850; Connecticut and Rhode Island in 1854; Maine, Massachusetts, and Michigan in 1855; Kansas in 1857; Wisconsin in 1858.
1851	*Cooley v. Board of Wardens.*
1852	*Pennsylvania v. Wheeling Bridge Company.*
	The Genesee Chief v. Fitzhugh.
1854	Kansas-Nebraska Act.
	Ohio Life Insurance & Trust Company v. DeBolt.
	In re Booth (Wisconsin Supreme Court held Fugitive Slave Act of 1850 unconstitutional).
1855	Connecticut adopted law requiring literacy test for voting.
	Court of Claims created.
1856	*Murray's Lessee v. Hoboken Land Improvement Company.*

	Wynehamer v. New York.
	Dodge v. Woolsey.
1857	*Dred Scott v. Sandford.*
1858	Lincoln-Douglas debates.
1859	*Ableman v. Booth.*
1860	Crittenden Compromise proposed.
	Senator Jefferson Davis introduced a proposal for a federal slave code.
	South Carolina Ordinance of Secession.
1861	First federal income tax imposed as a war measure.
	President Abraham Lincoln proclaimed insurrection, called for troops, suspended habeas corpus.
	Secession of ten other states; Confederate Constitution adopted.
	Kentucky v. Dennison.
1862	Abolition of slavery in the territories.
	Emancipation Proclamation.
	Homestead Act.
1863	Gettysburg Address.
	Lincoln's Proclamation of Amnesty and Reconstruction.
1864	Lincoln's pocket veto of the Wade-Davis Bill.
	Salmon P. Chase became Chief Justice.
1865	Freedmen's Bureau founded.
	Joint Committee on Reconstruction established.
	Thirteenth Amendment ratified and in effect.
	Writ of habeas corpus restored by presidential proclamation.
1866	Civil Rights Act of 1866.
	Ex Parte Milligan.
1867	First Reconstruction Act.
	Habeas Corpus Act.
	Tenure of Office Act.
1868	*Ex parte McCardle.*
	Fourteenth Amendment ratified and in effect.
	Impeachment of Andrew Johnson.
	Johnson's proclamation of general amnesty.
	Texas v. White.
1869	Wyoming adopts women's suffrage.
1870	Department of Justice established.
	Fifteenth Amendment ratified and in effect.
	Hepburn v. Griswold.
1871	Force Act of 1871.
	Knox v. Lee.
	Ku Klux Klan Act.
1872	Congress established uniform date for congressional elections.
1873	Slaughterhouse Cases.
1874	Morrison R. Waite became Chief Justice.
1875	Civil Rights Act of 1875.
1876	Disputed election: Tilden-Hayes.
	Munn v. Illinois.
	United States v. Cruikshank.
	United States v. Reese.
1877	Compromise of 1877 settled disputed election and ended Reconstruction.
1880	Chinese Exclusion Treaty.
	Strauder v. West Virginia.
1881	Kansas adopted prohibition of alcohol (first state prohibition statute).
	Springer v. United States.
	Kilbourn v. Thompson.
1882	Chinese Exclusion Act (enacted over presidential veto).
1883	Civil Rights Cases.

1884	*Juilliard v. Greenman.*
	Ex parte Yarbrough.
	Hurtado v. California.
1886	*Wabash, St. Louis & Pacific Railway v. Illinois.*
	Boyd v. United States.
	Yick Wo v. Hopkins.
1887	Interstate Commerce Act.
1888	Melville W. Fuller became Chief Justice.
1890	*Chicago, Milwaukee & St. Paul Railroad v. Minnesota.*
	Leisy v. Hardin.
	Sherman Antitrust Act.
1892	*Counselman v. Hitchcock.*
1894	Force Act of 1871 repealed.
	Reagan v. Farmers' Loan and Trust Company.
1895	*United States v. E. C. Knight Company.*
	Pollock v. Farmers' Loan and Trust Company.
	In re Debs.
1896	*Plessy v. Ferguson.*
	Allgeyer v. Louisiana.
1897	Trans-Missouri Freight Case.
	Chicago, Burlington & Quincy Railroad v. Chicago.
1898	*Holden v. Hardy.*
	Smyth v. Ames.
	Williams v. Mississippi.
1899	*United States v. Wong Kim Ark.*
1901	New Alabama constitution: literacy and property tests, plus grandfather clause, required for voting (effect was to disenfranchise blacks).
1903	*Champion v. Ames.*
	First direct primary elections (in Wisconsin).
	Panama Canal Treaty (Hay-Bunau Treaty).
1904	*Northern Securities Company v. United States*
1905	*Swift & Company v. United States.*
	Lochner v. New York.
1906	Hepburn Act.
1908	*Muller v. Oregon.*
	Adair v. United States.
	Loewe v. Lawlor.
	Ex parte Young.
	Twining v. New Jersey.
1910	Edward D. White became Chief Justice.
	Mann-Elkins Act.
1911	*United States v. Grimaud.*
	Standard Oil Company v. United States.
1913	Federal Reserve Act (Owen-Glass Act).
	Sixteenth Amendment ratified and in effect.
1914	Federal Trade Commission Act.
	Weeks v. United States.
	Shreveport Rate Case.
1916	Child Labor Act (Keating-Owen Act).
1917	Selective Service Act.
1918	Selective Draft Law Cases.
	Hammer v. Dagenhart.
1919	Eighteenth Amendment ratified and in effect.
	Schenck v. United States.
	Senate rejects Treaty of Versailles.
	Volstead Act.
	Abrams v. United States.

1920	Esch-Cummings Transportation Act.
	Missouri v. Holland.
	United States v. United States Steel Corporation.
	Nineteenth Amendment ratified and in effect.
	Palmer Raids.
1921	*Bailey v. Drexel Furniture Company.*
	Budget and Accounting Act.
	William Howard Taft became Chief Justice.
1923	*Adkins v. Children's Hospital.*
	Moore v. Dempsey.
	Massachusetts v. Mellon.
1924	Child Labor Amendment proposed by Congress.
1925	*State v. Scopes* (Tennessee).
	Pierce v. Society of Sisters.
	Gitlow v. New York.
1926	*Meyers v. United States.*
1927	*Nixon v. Herndon.*
1928	*Olmstead v. United States.*
1930	Charles Evans Hughes became Chief Justice.
1931	*Near v. Minnesota.*
1932	Norris-La Guardia Act.
	Powell v. Alabama.
1933	National Industrial Recovery Act.
	Securities Act of 1933.
	Tennessee Valley Authority Act.
	Twentieth Amendment ratified and in effect.
	Twenty-First Amendment ratified and in effect.
1934	Communications Act.
	Nebbia v. New York.
	Home Building and Loan Company v. Blaisdell.
	Securities Exchange Act of 1934.
1935	National Labor Relations Act (Wagner Act).
	Social Security Act.
	Schechter Poultry Corporation v. United States.
	Norris v. Alabama.
	Humphrey's Executor v. United States.
1936	*Brown v. Mississippi.*
	United States v. Butler.
	Ashwander v. Tennessee.
	Carter v. Carter Coal Company.
1937	Franklin D. Roosevelt announced Court-packing scheme.
	West Coast Hotel Company v. Parrish.
	Wagner Act Cases.
	Social Security Act Cases.
	United States v. Curtiss-Wright Export Corporation.
	Palko v. Connecticut.
1938	Fair Labor Standards Act.
	Food, Drug and Cosmetics Act.
	House of Representatives establishes committee to investigate un-American activities.
	Johnson v. Zerbst.
	Missouri ex rel. Gaines v. Canada.
1939	*Graves, New York ex rel., v. O'Keefe.*
	Hatch Act.
1940	Alien Registration Act (Smith Act).
	Cantwell v. Connecticut.
1941	Fair Employment Practices Commission established by executive order.
	Harlan F. Stone became Chief Justice.

	United States v. Darby Lumber Company.
1942	*Wickard v. Filburn.*
	Betts v. Brady.
	President Roosevelt approved program of relocation of Japanese Americans.
	Skinner v. Oklahoma.
1943	*McNabb v. United States.*
	Hirabayashi v. United States.
	West Virginia Board of Education v. Barnette (Second Flag Salute Case).
1944	*Korematsu v. United States.*
	Smith v. Allwright.
1946	Frederick M. Vinson became Chief Justice.
1947	*Everson v. Board of Education.*
	First Hoover Commission established.
	National Labor-Management Relations Act (Taft-Hartley Act) passed over President Harry S. Truman's veto.
	National Security Act.
1948	Executive orders banned racial segregation in the armed forces and in civilian federal employment.
	Illinois ex rel. McCollum v. Board of Education.
	Shelley v. Kraemer.
	Selective Service Act.
	Sipuel v. Board of Regents.
1949	*Wolf v. Colorado.*
1950	*American Communications Association v. Douds.*
	Internal Security Act (McCarran Act).
	Sweatt v. Painter.
	McLaurin v. Oklahoma State Regents for Higher Education.
1951	*Dennis v. United States.*
	Twenty-Second Amendment ratified and in effect.
1952	Immigration and Nationality Act (McCarran-Walter Act) became law over Truman's veto.
	President Truman ordered seizure of steel mills.
	Youngstown Sheet & Tube Company v. Sawyer (Steel Seizure Case).
1953	Earl Warren became Chief Justice.
1954	*Brown v. Board of Education of Topeka.*
	Censure of Joseph McCarthy by the United States Senate.
	Communist Control Act.
1955	*Brown v. Board of Education II* ("all deliberate speed").
1956	*Ullmann v. United States.*
1957	Civil Rights Act of 1957.
	President Dwight D. Eisenhower ordered federal troops to enforce desegregation order in Little Rock, Arkansas.
	Watkins v. United States.
	Yates v. United States.
	Mallory v. United States.
	Roth v. United States, Alberts v. California.
1958	*Cooper v. Aaron.*
1959	*Barenblatt v. United States.*
1960	Civil Rights Act of 1960.
1961	*Communist Party v. Subversive Activities Control Board.*
	Mapp v. Ohio.
	Twenty-Third Amendment ratified and in effect.
1962	*Baker v. Carr.*
	Engel v. Vitale.
1963	*Edwards v. South Carolina.*
	Gray v. Sanders.
	Gideon v. Wainwright.

1964	Civil Rights Act of 1964.
	Gulf of Tonkin Resolution.
	Wesberry v. Sanders.
	Reynolds v. Sims.
	New York Times Co. v. Sullivan.
	Heart of Atlanta Motel v. United States.
	Malloy v. Hogan.
	Escobedo v. Illinois.
1965	*Pointer v. Texas.*
	Albertson v. Subversive Activities Control Board.
	Griswold v. Connecticut.
	Voting Rights Act of 1965.
1966	*Miranda v. Arizona.*
	South Carolina v. Katzenbach.
	Harper v. Virginia State Board of Elections.
	Miranda v. Arizona.
1967	*Klopfer v. North Carolina.*
	In re Gault.
	Warden v. Hayden.
	Katz v. United States.
1968	*Duncan v. Louisiana.*
	Jones v. Alfred H. Mayer Co.
	Terry v. Ohio.
1969	*Benton v. Maryland.*
	Chimel v. California.
	Warren E. Burger became Chief Justice.
1970	*In re Winship.*
	Williams v. Florida.
1971	*New York Times Company v. United States* (Pentagon Papers Case).
	Swann v. Charlotte-Mecklenburg County Board of Education.
	McKeiver v. Pennsylvania, In re Burrus.
	Lemon v. Kurtzman.
	New York Times Co. v. United States, United States v. The Washington Post.
1972	Equal Rights Amendment proposed by Congress.
	Furman v. Georgia (Capital Punishment Cases of 1972).
	Kastigar v. United States.
	Johnson v. Louisiana.
	Apodaca v. Oregon.
	Jackson v. Georgia.
	Branch v. Texas.
	Argersinger v. Hamlin.
	Branzburg v. Hayes.
1973	*Miller v. California.*
	Roe v. Wade.
1974	Resignation of President Richard M. Nixon.
	United States v. Nixon.
1976	*Buckley v. Valeo.*
	National League of Cities v. Usery.
	Gregg v. Georgia, Proffitt v. Florida, Jurek v. Texas (Capital Punishment Cases of 1976).
1977	Panama Canal Treaties.
1978	*Ballew v. Georgia.*
	First National Bank of Boston v. Bellotti.
	Regents of University of California v. Bakke.
	District of Columbia Representation Amendment proposed by Congress.
	Simple majority of Congress voted to extend ratification deadline for Equal Rights Amendment (original proposal had required a two-thirds vote).

2128 DEVELOPMENT OF AMERICAN CONSTITUTIONAL LAW

1979	*United Steelworkers of America v. Weber.*
1982	Extended deadline for ratification of Equal Rights Amendment expired.
	Plyler v. Doe.
1983	*Immigration and Naturalization Service v. Chadha.*
1985	Deadline for ratification of District of Columbia Representation Amendment expired.
	Gramm-Rudman-Hollings Balanced Budget Act.

Glossary

abstention Any of several doctrines by which federal courts delay or avoid decision, allowing issues of state law or entire cases to be decided by state courts.*

action A court case. Before the unification of law and equity, an "action" at law was distinguished from a proceeding in equity.

advisory opinion A judicial opinion on a question of law, rendered without deciding the rights of parties to an adversary proceeding. In the federal courts, advisory opinions are barred by the "case or controversy" requirement.*

amicus curiae [Latin: friend of the court] One who, although not a party to the case, submits a brief suggesting how the case, or certain issues in the case, should be decided.*

appeal Review of a court decision by a higher court to determine whether errors of law were made. Appeal is a particular type of review, but the word is sometimes used more generally, to refer to any review of a lower court decision.*

appellate jurisdiction The legitimate authority of a higher court to hear and decide appeals from lower courts.*

bail Money deposited with a court to guarantee the appearance of a defendant for trial, permitting his release from jail until trial.*

bill of attainder A legislative finding of guilt and imposition of punishment without a court trial.*

brief A document filed on behalf of a litigant, at trial or on appeal, stating the facts of the case and arguing the legal basis for a decision in the litigant's favor.*

case law The body of law established in court decisions, as distinct from customary and statutory law. Case law is the most important component of the common law.

certification A procedure by which a lower court requests from a higher court (or a federal court requests from a state court) guidance on questions of law relative to a case pending in the lower court.*

certiorari [Latin: to be made more certain] A form of writ directing a lower court to forward the record of a case to a higher court for review; it is the primary form of discretionary appellate review by the U.S. Supreme Court.*

civil law (1) the body of law dealing with the private rights and duties of individuals, distinguished from criminal law; (2) a body of law derived from the Roman legal codes that is in force in continental Europe and elsewhere, distinguished from common law. Civil law, in the latter sense, is the basis of much of the private law of Louisiana, and it is the original source of some aspects of property law in Texas and in states formed from the Mexican Cession.

---

* Entries marked with an asterisk have a separate article in the *Encyclopedia*.

class action   A legal action brought by one or more litigants in the name of a numerous class of whom the particular litigants claim to be representative, or an action against a numerous class of defendants.*

comity   The respect owed by one court or governmental agency to the official acts of a court or agency in another jurisdiction.*

common law   The body of legal custom and accumulated precedent inherited from England, sometimes inaccurately described as "judge-made law."*

concurrent powers   Governmental powers that may be exercised either by the national or by the state government.*

concurring opinion   A separate opinion filed by a judge of a multimember court indicating agreement with the decision of a case but setting forth alternative or additional reasons for reaching the result.*

consent decree   A court order that makes legally binding an agreement between the parties to a case to settle it without further litigation.*

declaratory judgment   A judicial order determining the legal rights of the parties in a particular case, anticipating future controversy rather than remedying past injury. Equitable in form, declaratory relief is available in federal court by virtue of an act of Congress.*

de facto   [Latin: in fact]   Existing in fact, whether or not existing in law or by right.*

defendant   The party against whom an action is brought. At the appellate level the party moved against is called the appellee or respondent.

de jure   [Latin: in law]   Existing in law or by virtue of official acts; distinguished from de facto (q.v.).

dictum (pl. dicta)   [Latin: something said]   Formerly, an authoritative pronouncement. Now, commonly used as an abbreviation of "obiter dictum" (q.v.).

dissenting opinion   An opinion by a judge of a multimember court who disagrees with the court's decision in a case.*

diversity jurisdiction   The legitimate authority of federal courts to hear cases in which the parties have "diversity of citizenship," that is, when they are citizens of different states or of a state and a foreign country.*

dual federalism   A doctrine of constitutional interpretation according to which the reserved powers of the states operate as limitations on the power of the national government.*

due process of law   The fair and regular procedures established by law. Under the Fifth and Fourteenth Amendments, the government may deprive a person of life, liberty, or property only after due process. The due process clauses of the Constitution protect both procedural and substantive rights.*

equity   A system of jurisprudence parallel to and corrective of the common law, based on principles of fairness rather than on the letter of the law. In most American jurisdictions, law and equity have been merged.*

error   A form of writ issued by a higher court directing a lower court to submit a case for appellate review. The writ of error is no longer used in the federal courts, having been superseded by appeal (q.v.).*

exclusionary rule   A rule excluding evidence obtained in violation of a defendant's rights from admission at the defendant's trial as proof of guilt.*

ex parte   [Latin: from one party; from the part (of)]   (1) A hearing or other legal act at which only one side of a case is represented; (2) in the heading of a case, an identification of the party who is applying for judicial relief.*

ex post facto   [Latin: from after the fact]   A law that makes criminal, or that increases the criminal penalty for, an act committed before the law was passed.*

ex relatione   [Latin: from what has been related (by)]   Legal actions brought by the state upon information supplied by or at the instigation of a private party are said to be "ex relatione." In reports, it is abbreviated "ex rel."

federal question jurisdiction   The legitimate authority of a federal court to hear and decide cases "arising under" the Constitution, laws, or treaties of the United States.*

grand jury   An investigatory body that is usually empowered to issue indictments or presentments charging persons with crimes.*

habeas corpus   [Latin: you shall have the body]   A form of writ directing a custodial official to appear before a judge with the person of a prisoner and to give a satisfactory legal justification for having the person in custody. The writ of habeas corpus is frequently used by state prisoners to obtain federal court review of their convictions.*

immunity In criminal cases, a grant of exemption from prosecution made in return for testimony; in intergovernmental relations, the exemption of government instrumentalities from taxation by other levels of government. In general, an exemption from a legally imposed duty or liability; along with privileges, immunities are protected by Article IV and by the Fourteenth Amendment.

incorporation (1) A doctrine according to which certain specific provisions of the Bill of Rights are made applicable against state authority by virtue of the "due process" clause of the Fourteenth Amendment; (2) a doctrine according to which certain territories are made so intimately a part of the United States that certain constitutional protections become applicable to the inhabitants.*

indictment A formal statement by a grand jury charging a person with a criminal offense.*

in forma pauperis [Latin: in the manner of a poor person] A proceeding in which the court waives requirements that a litigant pay certain fees and comply with certain formal requirments, granted because the litigant cannot afford to comply but ought not to be barred from access to the court.*

injunction A form of writ prohibiting or requiring the performance of a specific act by a particular person. An injunction is a form of remedy available under a court's equity power.*

in personam [Latin: against the person] A manner of proceeding in a case so that the decision and remedy are directed against a particular person.*

in re [Latin: in the matter (of)] A way of titling the report of a case in which there are no adversary parties.*

in rem [Latin: against the thing] A manner of proceeding in a case so that the decision and remedy affect the status of property with reference to the whole world rather than to particular individuals.*

judgment The official decision by a court of a case or controversy, including the remedy ordered, excluding the reasons for the ruling.*

judicial review The power of a court to review legislation or other governmental acts, including the acts of administrative agencies. The term is used especially for court review to determine whether an act is in conformance with the Constitution.*

jurisdiction Legitimate authority. The term is sometimes limited to the legitimate authority of courts to hear and decide cases.*

jury A body of lay citizens exercising responsibility for hearing and deciding facts in the judicial system; a jury is either a grand jury (q.v.) or a petit jury (q.v.).

justiciability The status of a case or controversy indicating that it may appropriately be heard and decided by a court.*

litigant A party to a legal action.

magistrate At the time the Constitution was written and in general, a government official, especially of the executive or judicial branch. In contemporary technical usage, a judicial officer authorized to conduct certain kinds of hearings, to issue certain kinds of orders, or to try minor offenses.

mandamus [Latin: we command] A form of writ directed to a government official or a lower court directing the performance of an act appropriate to that offical's or court's duties.*

mootness The status of a case or controversy indicating that it no longer involves a legal question appropriate to be heard and decided by a court.*

nolo contendere [Latin: I do not wish to contest (it).] A plea entered by a criminal defendant equivalent in effect to a plea of guilty in the criminal case but not amounting to an admission of guilt that might be used in another case, either civil or criminal.*

obiter dictum [Latin: said by the way] Any words in a court's opinion that are not required for the decision of the case, and that are therefore, in theory, not binding as precedent. The term is often misleadingly abbreviated to "dictum" or to its plural, "dicta."*

original jurisdiction The legitimate authority of a court to hear and decide cases in the first instance. Original jurisdiction is distinguished from appellate jurisdiction (q.v.).*

ordinance Any statute. In recent times, most commonly used for enactments by cities, counties, or other local governments.

per curiam [Latin: by the court] An unsigned opinion, attributable to the whole court and not to an individual judge as author.*

petit jury The ordinary trial jury; a body of lay persons who hear evidence and decide questions of fact in a civil or criminal case.*

plaintiff The party who brings an action. At the appellate level, the moving party is called the appellant or the petitioner.

police power The general authority of government to regulate the health, safety, morals, and welfare of the public.*

political question An issue reserved for decision by the legislative and executive branches of government, and so not appropriately decided by a court.*

precedent A past decision, resolving issues of law, which is relied on in the decision of later cases.*

preemption A doctrine according to which legislation by the national government explicitly displaces or conflicts with state legislation or has so pervaded a particular area or topic of regulation as to preclude state legislation on the same subject.*

presentment A formal report of a grand jury charging a person with a criminal offense; a presentment differs from an indictment in that the former is prepared on the grand jury's own initiative while the latter is initiated by the public prosecutor. Reports of the results of grand jury investigations are often referred to as "presentments" even when they do not contain criminal charges.*

ratio decidendi [Latin: reason for being decided] The reasoning supporting the decision of a court in a particular case, establishing a precedent.*

remand The action of a higher court in returning a case to a lower court for decision or for further proceedings.*

ripeness The status of a case when circumstances have advanced to the point of sufficient specificity and concreteness to justify decision or review.*

seriatim [Latin: serially] One at a time, in sequence; used to describe the opinions of judges on multimember tribunals where custom does not permit a single "opinion of the court."*

special master A person appointed by a court to perform certain functions in a case, especially to hear evidence and to make findings of fact.*

standing The legal status of a litigant indicating that he is a proper party to litigate an issue or a case or controversy.*

stare decisis [Latin: to stand by what has been decided] A doctrine requiring that courts, in deciding cases, should adhere to the principles of law established in prior cases, called precedents (q.v.).*

state action Official action by a state or under color of state law, an essential element of a claim of right raised under the "due process" or "equal protection" clause of the Fourteenth Amendment.*

statute A law enacted by a legislature; a part of the formal, written law. Also called an "act" of Congress or of the legislature, a statute is to be distinguished from a constitution and also from customary or common law and case law.

subpoena [Latin: under penalty] An order to appear and testify at a proceeding (*subpoena ad testificandum*) or to produce physical evidence at a proceeding (*subpoena duces tecum*).*

transactional immunity Immunity from prosecution for any offense mentioned in testimony given in exchange for the grant of immunity, regardless of other evidence that may be acquired independently.

ultra vires [Latin: beyond (its) power] An action by a person, corporation, or public agency that is beyond the actor's legitimate authority.

use immunity Immunity from prosecution based upon or using evidence of an offense given by a witness in exchange for the grant of immunity. Prosecution may occur only if it is based on independently acquired evidence.

venue The place where a case is to be heard.*

vested rights Legally recognized rights, especially property rights, of which a person may not be deprived without due process of law.*

writ A court order.

Case Index

HOW TO READ A CASE CITATION

A case citation tells the reader where the decision and opinion in a case have been reported. It gives, in shorthand form, all the information necessary to find a copy of the report.

The elements of a typical citation are: the volume number, the name of the reporter or of the compilation, (the series number,) the page number of the first page of the report, (the court or jurisdiction,) and the year in which the case was decided. Any information that is unnecessary or inapplicable is omitted. Thus,

384 U.S. 346 (1966)

is the citation to the case reported in volume 384 of the United States Reports, beginning on page 346; the case (*Miranda v. Arizona*) was decided in 1966 by the Supreme Court of the United States. So far, there is only one series of volumes in the United States Reports, and all cases in the United States Reports are Supreme Court cases or matters disposed of by Supreme Court Justices. And

13 N.Y. 378 (1858)

is the citation to the case reported in volume 13 of the New York Reports beginning on page 378; the case (*Wynehamer v. People*) was decided in 1858 by the New York Court of Appeals (the highest court of New York).

Many volumes of reports, especially reports of older cases, bear the name of the reporter rather than of the jurisdiction. Some volumes of reports, especially specialized volumes, have names indicating neither the reporter nor the jurisdiction. The table that follows lists the reports in which cases cited in this *Encyclopedia* are to be found:

U.S.	United States Reports
Dall.	Dallas (= United States Reports, vols. 1–4)
Cranch	Cranch (= U.S. Reports vols. 5–13)
Wheat.	Wheaton (= U.S. Reports vols. 14–25)
Pet.	Peters (= U.S. Reports vols. 26–41)
How.	Howard (= U.S. Reports vols. 42–65)
Black	Black (= U.S. Reports vols. 66–67)
Wall.	Wallace (= U.S. Reports vols. 68–90)
S.Ct.	West's Supreme Court Reporter (cited only when the citation to U.S. Reports was unavailable at the time of compilation)

Vol. 1: pp. 1–472; Vol. 2: pp. 473–1002; Vol. 3: pp. 1003–1618; Vol. 4: pp. 1619–2090.

F.	Federal Reporter (F. 2d = Federal Reporter, 2d series)
F.Supp.	Federal Supplement
F.Cas.	Federal Cases
Ct.Cl.	U.S. Court of Claims Reports
Dane Abr.	Dane's Abridgment of American Law
Gill & J.	Gill & Johnson (Maryland)
Pick.	Pickering (= Massachusetts Reports vols. 18–41)
Metc.	Metcalf (= Massachusetts Reports vols. 42–54)
Cush.	Cushing (= Massachusetts Reports vols. 55–66)
Gray	Gray (= Massachusetts Reports vols. 67–82)
Quincy	Quincy's Reports (Massachusetts)
Hals.	Halsted's New Jersey Reports
N.J. Super.	New Jersey Superior Court Reports
Abb. Prac.	Abbott's New York Practice Reports
Hill	Hill's New York Reports
Johns.	Johnson's New York Reports
Johns. Cas.	Johnson's New York Cases
N.Y.S.	New York Supplement (N.Y.S. 2d = N.Y. Supplement, 2d series)
Martin	Martin's North Carolina Reports
Serg. & R.	Sergeant & Rawles's Pennsylvania Reports
Whart.	Wharton's Pennsylvania Reports
Bay	Bay's South Carolina Reports
P.	West's Pacific Reporter (P. 2d = Pacific Reporter, 2d series)
State Abbreviations	Reports of the state's highest court
A.C.	Appeal Cases (English)
E.R.	East's King's Bench Reports (English)
Eng. Rep.	English Reports
How. St. Tr.	Howell's State Trials (English)
Mod.	Modern English Cases

Numbers in **boldface** refer to the main entry on the subject.

A

Abbate v. United States   359 U.S. 187 (1959)   102–103

Abington Township School District v. Schempp   374 U.S. 203 (1963)   **1**, 105, 293, 609, 855, 1139–40, 1538, 1651, 1652, 1653, 1658, 1769, 2006, 2029

Ableman v. Booth   21 How. 506 (1859)   **1–2**, 4, 237, 288, 302, 812, 1694, 1860, 1865

Abood v. Detroit Board of Education   431 U.S. 209 (1977)   **4**, 1118, 1119

Abrams v. United States   250 U.S. 616 (1919)   **7–8**, 225, 294, 299, 732, 791, 896, 922–73, 1203, 1439, 1493, 1623, 1624, 1643, 1645, 1805, 2015, 2059, 2060

Adair v. United States   208 U.S. 161 (1908)   **15–16**, 325, 504, 650, 778, 814, 816, 828, 900, 1113, 1131, 1178, 1239, 1392, 1596, 1799, 1800, 2054, 2083

Adams v. New York   192 U.S. 585 (1904)   1633

Adams v. Storey   1 F.Cas. 141, No. 66 (C.C.D. N.Y. 1817)   1174

Adams v. Tanner   244 U.S. 590 (1917)   **23**

Adams v. Williams   407 U.S. 143 (1972)   73, 1780

Adamson v. California   332 U.S. 46 (1947)   **23–24**, 120, 580–81, 592, 759, 765, 868, 871, 899, 903, 972, 1198, 1287, 1377, 1474, 1475, 1476, 1477, 1618, 1930, 1973

Adderley v. Florida   385 U.S. 39 (1966)   **24**, 582, 756, 2027

Addington v. Texas   441 U.S. 418 (1979)   1248

Addyston Pipe & Steel Co. v. United States   175 U.S. 211 (1899)   62, 302, 815, 1241

Adickes v. S. H. Kress & Co.   348 U.S. 144 (1970)   313

Adkins v. Children's Hospital   261 U.S. 525 (1923)   **25–27**, 187, 536, 570, 604, 779, 934, 1230, 1239, 1245, 1279, 1280, 1284, 1356, 1599, 1620, 1748, 1764, 1772, 1799, 1838, 1848, 1851, 1936, 2045, 2046

Adler v. Board of Education   342 U.S. 485 (1952)   13, **27**, 1102, 1971

Aetna Life Insurance Co. v. Haworth   300 U.S. 227 (1937)   31

Aetna Life Insurance Co. v. Kennedy   301 U.S. 389 (1937)   2004

Afroyim v. Rusk   387 U.S. 253 (1967)   **36**, 675, 754

Agins v. Tiburon   447 U.S. 255 (1980)   631, 1750

Agnello v. United States   269 U.S. 20 (1925)   **37**, 250, 1636

Aguilar v. Felton   105 S.Ct. 3232 (1985)   **39**

Aguilar v. Texas   378 U.S. 108 (1964)   **39**, 948, 979, 1464, 1629–30, 1719

B

C

D

H

I

J

M

T

Y

Z

Name Index

*Numbers in **boldface** refer to the main entry on the subject.*

Vol. 1: pp. 1–472; Vol. 2: pp. 473–1002; Vol. 3: pp. 1003–1618; Vol. 4: pp. 1619–2090.

2156

Miranda, Ernesto, 1263, 1405
Mitchell, John N., 81, 82, 1942
Mitchell, William, 441
Mondale, Walter F., 463, 1966
Monroe, James, 21, 192, 195, 296, 323, 354, 396, 400, 751, 842, 991, 1003, 1174, 1220, 1241, **1273–74,** 1360, 1895, 1958, 1997, 2072
Montesquieu, Charles Louis de S., 58, 59, 239, 267, 364, 475, 477, 482, 709, 1177, **1274–75,** 1660, 1755, 1905, 2008
Moody, William H., 81, 633, 817, **1275–76,** 1610, 1842, 1929, 2055
Moore, Alfred, **1276,** 1826
Morgan, J. P., 1149
Morgan, Thomas J., 431
Morison, Samuel Eliot, 960
Morrill, Justin, 761, 1280
Morris, Gouverneur, 191, 364, 365, 386, 1067, 1174, 1270, 1271, **1280–81,** 1435, 1980
Morris, Robert, **1281–82**
Morrow, William W., **1282**
Mosley, Earl, 1400
Mott, Lucretia, 261, 1981
Mundt, Karl, 1284
Munro, William B., 322
Murphy, Frank, 24, 83, 154, 227, 272, 451, 581, 592, 613, 669, 712, 729, 742, 871, 972, 1012, **1286–87,** 1387, 1453, 1600, 1607, 1617, 1618, 1628, 1774, 1776, 1777, 1896, 1968, 1970, 1972, 1973, 2081, 2082
Murphy, Jack, "Murph the Surf," 1287
Murray, William (Lord Mansfield), 2, 127, 682, 762, 959, 1230, **1288,** 2064
Myrdal, Gunnar, 1703

N

Nathanson, Nathaniel, 142, 1764
Neagle, David, 1621
Neale, Thomas, 1430
Nearing, Scott, 50
Nell, William C., 262
Nelson, Samuel, 70, 235, 237, 868, 1135, 1136, 1267, **1307–1308,** 1462, 1896, 2040
Nelson, Steve, 1375
Neuborne, Burt, 126, 269, 1173
Nicholls, Francis, 2051
Nixon, L. A., 1984
Nixon, Richard M., 41, 68, 70, 77, 125, 158, 169, 173, 176, 179, 181, 193, 267, 349, 455, 456, 460, 462, 549, 559, 607, 615, 621, 629, 673, 703, 714, 747, 878, 954, 960, 967, 1150, 1185, 1210, 1261, 1284, 1288, 1300, **1320–25,** 1364, 1430, 1441, 1449, 1533, 1565, 1626, 1662, 1663, 1681, 1708, 1734, 1769, 1789, 1803, 1817, 1839, 1923, 1964, 2009, 2011, 2015, 2036, 2037, 2049
Norris, Clarence, 1326
Norris, George W., 440, 441, 443, 932, **1326,** 1494, 1874, 1927, 2047
Nortz, E. C., 850

O

Oakley, Thomas, 841
Oaks, Dallin H., 665

O'Brien, David, 584
O'Brien, John Lord, 1158
O'Connor, Sandra Day, 39, 45, 69, 159, 177, 463, 506, 1020, 1251, 1267, **1337–39,** 1406, 1460, 1556, 1669, 1814, 1874, 1895, 2006
Ogden, David B., 305
Olmstead, Gideon, 625, 1030
Olmstead, Roy, 1341
Olney, Richard, 302, 1106, **1342–43,** 1423, 1424
Ordronaux, John, 320
Ortega Y Gassett, José, 269
Otis, James, Jr., 79, 134, 356, 762, 826, 943, **1351–52,** 1370, 1961
Overton, William Ray, 1946

P

Paine, Thomas, 17, 156, 356, 377, 978, **1360,** 1613
Palmer, A. Mitchell, 82, 926, **1361–62,** 1643
Palmore, Linda, 1362
Pardee, Don Albert, **1363–64**
Parker, Isaac, 228, 811
Parker, John G., 440
Parker, John J. H., 1851
Parker, Theodore, 262, 1693
Paschal, George Washington, 1884
Paterson, William, 195, 254, 363, 383, 386, 494, 693, 744, 945, 1025, 1212, **1367–69,** 1793, 1826, 1827, 1829, 1960, 1962, 2032
Patterson, James, 960
Payne, Daniel A., 1694
Peckham, Rufus, 45, 153, 226, 302, 604, 632, 815, 817–19, 822, 916, 1009, 1175, 1185, 1231, 1234, 1239, **1371–72,** 1680, 1848, 1903, 2052, 2055, 2084
Pekelis, Alexander A., 53
Pendleton, Edmond, 334, 1191, 1223, **1373,** 1872, 2079
Pendleton, George H., 1373
Penn, Lemuel A., 875
Penn, William, 185, 476, 1196, 1309, **1374,** 1376
Peters, Richard, 692, 808, 1030, **1382,** 1826, 1827, 2047
Phelps, Edward J., **1384**
Philips, Josiah, 112
Phillips, Wendell, 4, 1693
Pickering, John, 393, 1205, **1387,** 1944
Pierce, Franklin, 167, 200, 338, 408, 409, 1166, **1388**
Pierce, William, **1389**
Pinckney, Charles, 191, 219, 272, 363, 365, 1309, **1389–90,** 1826
Pinckney, Charles Cotesworth, 1025, **1390**
Pine, David, 1761, 1923
Pinkney, William, 305, 1235, **1391,** 2043
Pitney, Mahlon, 504, 616, 764, 930, 968, 1311, **1392–93,** 1846, 1849, 2054, 2057, 2083
Pitt, William, 156, 768, **1393,** 1868
Plato, 17, 1420
Pocahontas, 1181
Polk, James K., 97, 302, 405, 408, 411, 867, 1162, **1422–23,** 1719, 1762, 2067
Pollack, Sir Frederick, 545, 922, 929
Pollak, Walter H., **1423**
Pomeroy, John N., 320, 1021, 1426
Pound, Roscoe, 94, 225, 269, 844, 1134, 1245, **1431,** 1705

Powell, Adam Clayton, Jr., 1434
Powell, Lewis F., 13, 34, 35, 46, 71, 80, 97, 146, 147, 176, 178, 181, 182, 203, 208, 215, 223, 302, 309, 315, 331, 514, 567, 591, 592, 740, 803, 809, 833, 834, 840, 851, 854, 885, 913, 948, 949, 981, 1019, 1027, 1042, 1086, 1096, 1097, 1102, 1121, 1153, 1155, 1197, 1251, 1261, 1276, 1278, 1299, 1322, 1341, 1375, 1398, **1432–33,** 1569, 1616, 1619, 1625, 1667, 1681, 1684, 1894, 1921, 2040, 2073, 2084, 2087
Powell, Thomas Reed, 583, 700, 1101, **1433,** 1854
Powys, Sir Thomas, 134
Pratt, Charles (Lord Camden), 356, 762, **1434–35,** 1574, 1868, 2064
Pratt, William, 138
Preston, Thomas, 17
Price, Monroe E., 157, 682, 1450, 1770
Price, Richard, 356
Prigg, Edward, 1692, 1783
Proxmire, William, 944, 1717
Prosser, William L., 1457
Pufendorf, Samuel, 546

Q

Quincy, Edmund, 4

R

Randolph, Edmund, 81, 98, 219, 323, 364, 366, 384, 387, 623, 692, 891, 1389, 1390, **1510,** 1513, 1826, 1899, 1976, 2033
Randolph, John, 16, 233, 392, 1189, **1510,** 1638, 1815, 1925
Rantoul, Robert, 402
Raulston, John T., 1743
Rawle, William, **1515,** 1639
Rawls, John, 1614
Read, George, **1515,** 1516
Reagan, Ronald, 69, 177, 193, 461–63, 703, 704, 858, 859, 1249, 1337, 1440, **1516–18,** 1814, 1928, 1964, 1966
Redfield, Isaac, 1746
Reed, Stanley F., 23, 64, 154, 161, 184, 214, 327, 575, 650, 742, 847, 888, 1028, 1109, 1181, 1189, 1234, 1243, 1280, 1286, **1527–28,** 1607, 1698, 1776, 1970, 1972, 2021, 2024, 2085
Rehnquist, William H., 40, 71, 97, 119, 125, 131, 132, 136, 146, 159, 170, 176, 179, 182, 198, 223, 244, 301, 302, 309, 315, 512, 553, 561, 592, 607, 635, 740, 741, 809, 825, 848, 851, 854, 948, 949, 963, 1007, 1032, 1033, 1102, 1124, 1141, 1153, 1155, 1251, 1253, 1282, 1294, 1311, 1322, 1323, 1337, 1365, 1369, 1374, 1380, 1406, 1484, **1533–35,** 1554, 1556, 1569, 1588, 1595, 1611, 1612, 1615, 1616, 1622, 1642, 1673, 1711, 1721, 1735, 1737, 1800, 1814, 1833, 1873, 1884, 1897, 1921, 1993, 2087
Reich, Charles, 268
Reid, Sally, 1668
Reid, Thomas, 2068
Reston, James, 768
Rhett, Robert B., 133

Rhodes, James, 1624

Rice, Charles E., 790, 804

Richards, David, 1335

Richardson, Elliott, 1709

Roane, Spencer, 307, 397, 1200, 1217, 1220, 1221, 1235–37, **1598**, 1815

Roberts, Owen, 64, 188, 201, 214, 313, 327, 742, 771, 845, 888, 914, 926, 932, 934, 938, 1011, 1286, 1304, 1461, 1488, 1509, 1587, **1599**, 1560, 1606, 1628, 1772, 1776, 1970, 1984, 1985, 1991, 2046

Robinson, Joseph T., 1607

Rockefeller, John D., 1721

Rodell, Fred, 322

Rodney, Caesar A., **1602**

Roe, Gilbert E., 1481

Roosevelt, Franklin D., 5, 38, 45, 69, 70, 72, 106, 111, 120, 146, 149, 169, 172, 188, 240, 244, 264, 268, 273, 292, 321, 325, 327, 348, 351, 435, 436, 439, 441–47, 450, 456, 461, 527, 530, 548, 579, 606, 614, 621, 627, 629, 702, 713, 742, 764, 851, 917, 926, 932–35, 937, 940, 941, 967, 979, 1006, 1010, 1022, 1030, 1057, 1061, 1062, 1068, 1074, 1079, 1099, 1125, 1136, 1150, 1244, 1245, 1262, 1270, 1280, 1286, 1293, 1321, 1411, 1441, 1446, 1448, 1494, 1495, 1497, 1509, 1516, 1517, 1527, 1593, 1599, **1605–1609**, 1617, 1622, 1698, 1744, 1771, 1776, 1816, 1845, 1874, 1922, 1926, 1928, 1960, 1964, 1991, 2015, 2020, 2045, 2046, 2048, 2077

Roosevelt, Theodore, 69, 81, 108, 418, 432, 434, 435, 442, 542, 712, 814, 816, 817, 872, 895, 913, 1107, 1120, 1177, 1239, 1244, 1275, 1328, 1441, 1481, 1605, **1609–1610**, 1679, 1816, 1922, 1959, 1966, 1983, 2052, 2055, 2056, 2070

Rosenberg, Ethel and Julius, 184, 1611, 1971

Rossiter, Clinton, 171, 221, 1442, **1612**

Rousseau, Jean-Jacques, 17, 475, 738, 1385, 1715

Royce, Josiah, 895

Ruckelshaus, William, 1709

Rudman, Warren B., 858

Ruffin, Edmund, 1331

Ruffin, Thomas, 400

Russell, Charles T., 1542

Russell, Francis, 335

Rutherford, Joseph F., 742

Rutledge, Edward, 378, 1826

Rutledge, John, 309, 1025, **1617**, 1826, 2034

Rutledge, Wiley B., 24, 69, 132, 581, 657, 658, 848, 855, 972, 1234, 1262, 1439, 1453, 1484, 1607, **1617–18**, 1650, 1764, 1765, 1774, 1776, 1777, 1808, 1968, 1970, 1973, 2081, 2082

S

Sacco, Nicola, 335

Sacks, Albert, 906

Sadat, Anwar, 217

Sadler, John, 1660

St. Clair, Arthur, Jr., 1241

St. John, Henry, 356

Sanford, Edward, 26, 88, 847, **1620**, 1848, 1849, 2060

Sanford, John F. A., 585, 896

Sanger, Margaret, 119, 786, 1627

Santayana, George, 895

Sawyer, Charles, 1761

Sawyer, Lorenzo, **1621**

Scalia, Antonin, 1043

Schofield, John M., 1021

Schouler, James, 320, **1627**

Schroeder, Theodore, **1627**

Schwimmer, Rosiki, 1627

Scopes, John, 50, 96, 1743

Scott, Dred, 530, 584–87, 1693

Seabrook, Whitemarsh, 1330

Selden, John, 589, **1647**

Seward, William, 4, 759, 1512, **1666**, 1692, 1809, 1873, 1891

Shapiro, David L., 650, 691, 1534

Sharpe, Granville, 356

Shaw, Lemuel, 128, 228, 334, 403, 404, 500, 515, 631, 632, 812, 1113, 1160, 1396, 1600, **1675**, 1684, 1745–47, 1749, 1809, 1859, 2079

Shays, Daniel, 1676

Shellabarger, Samuel, 236, 352

Sheppard, Sam, 806, 831

Sherman, John, 960, 1679

Sherman, Roger, 113, 378, 384, 546, 866, **1678**

Sherwood, Forest, 888

Shiras, George, 69, 226, 816, 905, 995, **1680**

Shirley, J. M., 495

Sickles, Daniel, 1724

Sidoti, Anthony, 1362

Siegel, Stanley, 1431

Sims, Thomas, 530, 1693

Sirica, John, 1323

Skinner, Quentin, 467

Smith, Abby, 261

Smith, Adam, 437, 597, 1420

Smith, Alfred E., 443

Smith, Gerrit, 3

Smith, J. Allen, 322, 548, 1481, **1698**

Smith, James Morton, 532

Smith, Joseph, 1903

Smith, William French, 81, 82, 84

Snepp, Frank W., III, 1699, 1700

Soper, Philip, 637, 638

Spaight, Richard Dobbs, 104, 1000, **1716**

Spencer, Herbert, 320, 437, 598, 1798

Spock, Benjamin, 515, 1703

Spooner, Lysander, 3

Stalin, Joseph, 1233

Stanbery, Henry S., **1720**

Stanford, Leland, 1239

Stanton, Edwin M., 77, 81, 192, 423, 863, 960, 1021, 1267, **1724**, 1768, 1877

Stanton, Elizabeth Cady, 261, 1981, 1982

Steinbeck, John, 613

Stephens, Alexander H., 319, 338, 1165, **1762**, 1901

Stevens, John Paul, 34, 35, 37, 97, 146, 177, 198, 203, 208, 223, 260, 301, 332, 512, 741, 745, 781, 804, 825, 904, 1133, 1141, 1205, 1247, 1253, 1276, 1371, 1375, 1554, 1568, 1569, 1578, 1581, 1611, 1616, 1622, 1669, 1673, 1700, **1764–66**, 1802, 1833, 1895, 2006, 2035, 2047, 2063, 2084, 2087

Stevens, Thaddeus, 4, 117, 352, 758, 960, 1255, 1757, **1765**

Stevenson, Adlai, 849

Stewart, Alvan, 3, 403

Stewart, Potter J., 1, 46, 93, 108, 132, 146, 153, 177, 182, 185, 203, 207–209, 302, 315, 534, 592, 634, 635, 640, 654, 655, 787, 799, 825, 848, 868, 875, 876, 903–905, 914, 942, 1009, 1029, 1097, 1109, 1114, 1115, 1155, 1181, 1198, 1246, 1259, 1261, 1264, 1305, 1314, 1339, 1365, 1379, 1382, 1384, 1406, 1328, 1433, 1448, 1503, 1566, 1568, 1578, 1593, 1594, 1616, 1678, 1681, 1724, 1734, **1768–70**, 1814, 1839, 1931, 1977, 2005, 2028, 2072, 2073, 2084, 2087

Stewart, Richard B., 639

Stimson, Henry L., 1608

Stone, Harlan Fiske, 33, 63, 69, 81, 92, 144, 188, 211, 213, 218, 274, 310, 326, 327, 440, 502, 536, 565, 566, 568, 580, 583, 592, 644, 736, 742, 765, 830, 847, 864, 888, 894, 895, 918, 932, 934, 1001, 1011, 1030, 1041, 1245, 1279, 1310, 1360, 1365, 1497, 1509, 1514, 1537, 1565, 1569, 1599, 1600, 1606, 1607, 1617, 1618, 1620, 1623, 1640, 1686, 1698, 1705, 1713, 1714, 1721, 1758, **1771–76**, 1814, 1836, 1846, 1848, 1849, 1876, 1932, 1939, 1968, 1991, 2046, 2081, 2082

Storing, Herbert J., 58, **1782**

Story, Joseph, 69, 95, 98, 101, 155, 160, 200, 229, 241, 253, 255, 305, 318, 319, 333, 397, 402, 404, 405, 495, 496, 498, 500, 508, 528, 535, 538, 539, 594, 601, 693, 811, 812, 828, 866, 868, 897, 957, 958, 978, 1049, 1062, 1174, 1194, 1213, 1215, 1220–22, 1231, 1240, 1242, 1382, 1436, 1452, 1560, 1639, 1692, 1751, **1782–86**, 1842, 1858, 1859, 1861, 1877, 1896, 1921, 1924, 1959, 1962, 1963, 2005, 2031, 2039

Stourzh, Gerald, 475, 892

Strader, Jacob, 1693

Strong, William, 138, 232, 234, 237, 724, 863, 1135, 1272, 1384, 1684, 1787, **1791–93**, 1997, 2000

Sullivan, L. B., 1312

Sumner, Charles, 4, 283, 351, 352, 420, 529, 960, 1122, 1601, 1692–94, 1757, 1767, 1786, **1808–1809**, 1890, 1997, 2003

Sumner, William G., 320

Sutherland, George, 26, 141, 187, 212, 218, 310, 326, 466, 469, 519, 530, 531, 656, 765, 809, 845, 871, 896, 925, 932, 934, 940, 1030, 1252, 1369, 1385, 1527, 1587, 1599, 1772, **1837**, 1848, 1849, 1960, 1991, 1992, 2046

Swartwout, Samuel, 514

Swayne, Noah, 140, 234, 236–38, 283, 836, 1135, 1228, 1260, 1272, 1328, 1792, **1840**, 1884, 1999

Swisher, Carl B., 321, 1240, **1842–43**

Synar, Michael, 859

T

Taft, Robert A., 194, 449, 1108, 1411, **1845**

Taft, William Howard, 26, 33, 67–70, 92, 141, 144, 169, 243, 244, 293, 316, 330, 432, 434, 437, 440, 453, 542, 543, 712, 820, 893, 895, 896, 930, 958, 987, 1078, 1107, 1121, 1185,

Taft—*Continued*
 1239, 1244, 1284, 1289, 1341, 1392, 1441,
 1559, 1599, 1610, 1615, 1685, 1719, 1772–
 74, 1788, 1820, 1839, **1845–55**, 1921, 1932,
 1937, 1959, 2042, 2045, 2046, 2052, 2054,
 2055, 2057–59, 2062, 2070, 2073
Talleyrand, Charles, 1205
Tallmadge, James, 1268
Taney, Roger B., 1, 2, 67, 69, 81, 88, 98, 107,
 125, 155, 159, 164, 166, 222, 229, 231, 258,
 324, 410–12, 422, 496, 535, 548, 574, 585,
 586, 590, 594, 603, 629, 641, 811, 868, 874,
 875, 916, 1005, 1025, 1159, 1162, 1166, 1185,
 1240, 1242, 1260, 1269, 1307, 1355, 1381,
 1391, 1452, 1462, 1551, 1559, 1594, 1600,
 1675, 1688, 1693, 1694, 1697, 1745, 1752,
 1783, 1785, 1786, 1789, 1811, 1816, **1857–
 67**, 1888, 1896, 1982, 2014, 2039, 2040, 2043,
 2078
Tappan, Lewis, 3
Taylor, John, 307, 319, 397, 1235–37, 1638, **1872**
Taylor, Zachary, 69, 338, 406, 408, 729, 1448,
 1691, **1873**
Ten Broek, Jacobus, 641, **1873**
Thacher, Oxenbridge, 1370
Thayer, James B., 764, 814, 895, 1035, 1038,
 1043, 1143, 1234, **1884–85**
Thayer, Webster Bradley, 335
Thomas, Lorenzo, 1877
Thomas, Norman, 50
Thompson, Francis, 44
Thompson, Seymour D., 130
Thompson, Smith, 164, 496, 874, 1101, 1213,
 1217, 1231, 1379, 1860, 1863, **1895**
Thoreau, Henry David, 260, 262, 582
Thorpe, Francis Newton, **1897**
Thorpe, Merle, 321
Thurmond, Strom, 68, 451
Tiedeman, Christopher G., 320, 430, 808, 1747,
 1799, **1898**
Tiffany, Joel, 3
Tilden, Samuel J., 124, 339, 425, 1924
Tilghman, William, 811
Tilson, John G., 434
Tocqueville, Alexis de, 84, 166, 227, 348, 978,
 1058, 1212, 1335, 1715, 1727, 1866, **1899**
Todd, Thomas, 1213, **1900–1901**, 1920
Toombs, Robert A., 1792, **1901**
Trenchard, John, 221, 1911
Tribe, Laurence H., 1614, 1803
Trimble, Robert, **1920–21**
Truman, Harry S., 44, 84, 184, 194, 216, 175,
 280, 292, 443, 448, 450–52, 541, 669–71, 713,
 719, 752, 954, 992, 1023, 1028, 1099, 1108,
 1183, 1218, 1232, 1233, 1262, 1399, 1677,
 1708, 1761, 1845, 1855, **1922–23**, 1938,
 1866, 1969, 1970, 2009, 2011, 2015,
 2085
Trumbull, Lyman, 235, 761, 1890, **1924**
Tucker, Henry St. George, **1924**
Tucker, John R., 127, 320, **1924**
Tucker, Nathaniel Beverly, 127, **1924**
Tucker, St. George, 127, 319, 692, 1220, 1389,
 1924
Tugwell, Rexford, 38, **1926**
Turgot, Robert Jacques, 18
Turnbull, Robert J., 1330

Turner, Nat, 400
Tussman, Joseph, 641
Twyn, William, 1644
Tyler, John, 55, 70, 192, 197, 297, 400, 401, 403,
 1307, 1448, **1931**, 1965, 2042
Tyndale, William, 1574

U

Upshar, Abel Parker, 319, 400

V

Vallandigham, Clement L., 1957
Van Buren, Martin, 197, 399, 408, 535, 816, 841,
 1240, 1691, 1867, **1958**
Van Devanter, Willis, 69, 187, 293, 326, 327, 633,
 932, 934, 1078, 1607, 1772, 1817, 1846,
 1847, 1849, **1959**, 1979, 1992, 2046, 2054,
 2056
Vane, Henry, 359
Vanzetti, Bartolomeo, 335
Vardaman, James, 1984
Varnum, James, 1912, 1913
Vattel, Emerich de, 473, 474, 477, 546, 1226,
 1961
Vaughan, John, 185
Vesey, Denmark, 2
Viner, Charles, 356
Vining, John, 115
Vinson, Fred, 50, 69, 102, 132, 162, 184, 292,
 453, 555, 719, 896, 1109, 1442, 1527, 1611,
 1617, 1677, 1806, 1841, 1902, 1938, **1968–
 74**, 2024, 2048, 2085
Volstead, Andrew J., 1978
Voltaire, 155
von Holst, Hermann, 16, 320, **1979**

W

Wade, Benjamin, 1990
Wagner, Robert, 1992
Waite, Henry Matson, 1994
Waite, Morrison R., 32, 129, 138, 139, 527, 540,
 596, 603, 821, 862, 863, 888, 1262, 1304,
 1377, 1381, 1528, 1559, 1567, 1684, 1775,
 1776, 1983, 1989, **1993–2003**
Walker, Robert J., 408
Walker, Timothy, 1786, **2005**
Wallace, George C., 1321
Wallace, Henry, 38
Wallace, John, 836
Walpole, Sir Robert, 156
Walworth, Reuben, 402
Walter, Sir John, 959
Ward, Nathaniel, 1225
Waring, Waties, 1946
Warren, Charles, 97, **2019**
Warren, Earl, 44, 69, 70, 92, 106, 133, 149, 162,
 163, 165, 176, 185, 453, 468, 520, 558, 581,
 584, 615, 635, 643, 646, 655, 664, 743, 744,
 756, 814, 875, 1010, 1011, 1039, 1044, 1065,
 1105, 1106, 1109, 1150, 1181, 1202, 1233,
 1263, 1264, 1334, 1336, 1376, 1401, 1402,
 1434, 1436, 1553, 1566, 1613, 1675, 1712,

Warren—*Continued*
 1757, 1777, 1810, 1818, 1819, 1843, 1879,
 1880, 1902, 1921, 1979, 1986, 2005, **2019–
 31**, 2087
Warren, Robert Penn, 44
Washington, Booker T., 712, 1984
Washington, Bushrod, 505, 602, 692, 825, 867,
 1031, 1212, 1213, 1459, 1688, 1826,
 2031
Washington, George, 19, 31, 70, 98, 128, 158,
 191, 220, 233, 243, 316, 323, 361, 363, 364,
 386, 387, 392, 394, 493, 531, 549, 569, 617,
 625, 672, 692, 751, 814, 874, 889, 908, 1000,
 1013, 1014, 1016, 1025, 1047, 1149, 1177,
 1205, 1207, 1223, 1270, 1281, 1306, 1368,
 1373, 1379, 1382, 1409, 1446, 1480, 1510,
 1512, 1514, 1515, 1617, 1690, 1825, 1827,
 1888, 1922, 1928, 1964, 1981, 2009, **2031–
 37**, 2048, 2057
Wayne, James M., 234, 501, 1242, 1260, 1783,
 2039–40, 2047
Wayte, David, 2040, 2041
Webster, Daniel, 67, 98, 101, 196, 228, 398, 401,
 405, 408, 410, 529, 530, 537, 539, 630, 647,
 842, 909, 1120, 1177, 1217, 1384, 1692, 1752,
 1785, 1809, 1862, 1888, 1963, **2042–43**,
 2047, 2072
Wechsler, Herbert, 163, 1050, 1056, 1058, 1059
Weed, Thurlow, 1873
Weyl, Walter, 1482
Wheare, K. C., 977
Wheaton, Henry, **2047**
Wheeler, Burton K., 1120, **2047–48**
White, Byron R., 15, 35, 36, 97, 101, 106, 118,
 131, 146, 147, 154, 158, 159, 165, 177, 203,
 207, 226, 286, 301, 304, 309, 315, 332, 497,
 499, 519, 591, 592, 624, 655, 730, 741, 833,
 840, 853, 855, 857, 864, 871, 942, 951, 981,
 1099, 1102, 1105, 1121, 1155, 1246, 1261,
 1263, 1264, 1305, 1308, 1310, 1314, 1354,
 1371, 1380, 1405, 1407, 1433, 1477, 1535,
 1548, 1554, 1556, 1598, 1603, 1604, 1611,
 1616, 1620, 1678, 1711, 1722, 1724, 1734,
 1735, 1833, 1839, 1873, 1874, 1931, 1977,
 2006, 2035, **2048–51**, 2054, 2063, 2065,
 2066, 2072, 2074
White, Edward D., 70, 293, 302, 632, 816, 822,
 877, 986, 1121, 1234, 1328, 1355, 1424, 1559,
 1615, 1648, 1721, 1846, 1903, **2051–60**,
 2071
Whitelock, James, 474
Whiting, William, 320, 2014
Whitman, Walt, 582, 700
Whittaker, Charles E., 185, 615, 851, 1099, 2048,
 2060–61
Wickersham, George, 439, **2062**
Wigmore, John H., 341, 1149, 1400, 1401, 1575,
 2063
Wilkes, John, 2063, 2064
William III, 1224
Williams, George H., 81
Williams, Roger, 1356, 1516, 1539, 1546, 1568,
 1650, **2064–65**
Williams, Samuel, 1659
Williamson, Hugh, **2066**
Willoughby, Westel W., 321, **2066**
Wilmot, David, 411, 1696, 2067

Subject Index

*Numbers in **boldface** refer to the main entry on the subject.*

A

Abolitionist constitutional theory, **2–4**
  due process, 2, 590
  Fifth and Tenth Amendments, 3
  personal liberty laws, 1382
  philosophy and the Constitution, 1385
  Thirteenth through Fifteenth Amendments, 2, 117
  Wilmot Proviso, 2067
Abolition of slavery, *see* Slavery; Thirteenth Amendment
Abortion, **4–6**
  appellate jurisdiction, 65
  balancing test, 95
  consent of husband denied, 6, 1354
  criticism of *Roe v. Wade*, 5
  Fourteenth Amendment, 5
  freedom of intimate association, 782
  funding, 6
  Hyde Amendment, 944
  "informed" consent requirement, 1394
  interest group litigation, 988
  parental consent in, 6, 1394
  refusal of funding for medically necessary, 904
  Roe v. Wade, 1602–1604
  substantive due process, 4–6, 904
  wealth discrimination in, 1197
Absolutism, **8–9**
  First Amendment right, 8, 9, 12, 736
  freedom of speech and press, 790–97
  subject to balancing tests, 94, 95

Abstention doctrine, **9–11**
  administrative abstention, 11
  Burford doctrine, 11
  in eminent domain, 630–32
  judicial review, 1054–61
  Pullman doctrine, 10, 11
  Supreme Court reversed injunction by district court, 2085
  Younger doctrine, 9–11
Academic freedom, **12–14**
  articulated by Justice Frankfurter, 2038
  freedom of speech, 790–97
  judicial review resisted, 13
Access to the courts, **14–15**
  Bounds v. Smith, 136
  due process, 132
  of indigents, 869, 870
  petitions for habeas corpus, 14, 879–87
  by prisoners, 1480
  right to counsel, 14, 1585–92
  wealth discrimination, 14, 132, 2041, 2042
Act of state doctrine, **15**
  in federal common law, 690
  and foreign affairs, 753
  political question, 1420–22
  separation of powers, 15
Adamson Eight-Hour Act, **24**
  replaced Erdman Act, 650
  upheld under commerce clause, 2071
Adequate state grounds, **24–25**
  appellate jurisdiction, 65, 689

Adequate state grounds—*Continued*
  Burger Court, 25
  and federal questions, 715, 716
Administrative law, **27–29**
  delegation of power, 28, 552, 553
  due process in, 29, 589–91
  interest group litigation, 988
  judicial review of, 28, 1054–61
  jurisdiction of federal agencies, 28
  separation of powers, 27, 1659–64
Administrative Procedure Act
  judicial review of regulatory agencies determinations, 1532
Administrative search, **29–30**
  in absence of search warrant, 29, 198
  and fourth amendment rights, 29
  and probable cause, 29, 198
  right of privacy vacated, 1577–81
Admiralty and maritime jurisdiction, **30–31**
  affected with a public interest, 862
  extended by Taney Court, 1483
  interstate or foreign commerce, 755, 756, 993, 994
  Judiciary Act of 1789, 1075–77
Advice and consent, **31**
  appointments, 31, 66–68
  bureaucracy, 171
  in executive agreement, 106, 107, 666
  treaties, 31, 107, 1910, 1911
Advisory opinion, **31–32**
  in adequate state grounds cases, 24
  justiciability, 1089

Vol. 1: pp. 1–472; Vol. 2: pp. 473–1002; Vol. 3: pp. 1003–1618; Vol. 4: pp. 1619–2090.

2166

D

Due process of law, procedural, *see* Procedural
  due process of law
Due process of law, substantive, *see* Substantive
  due process of law
Dyer Act (1919)
  theft from intrastate shipments, 1127

E

Economic analysis and the Constitution, **596–600**
  debtor's relief, 596
  due process, 589–91
  and eminent domain, 630–32
  interstate commerce, 993, 994
  just compensation, 1088
  welfare benefits, 2044, 2045
  see also State regulation of commerce; State
    taxation of commerce
Economic liberties and the Constitution, **600–
  602**
  Bill of Rights, 113–16
  ex post facto laws, 676, 677
  freedom of contract, 774–81
  impairment of effect of Fourteenth Amend-
    ment, 757–61
  just compensation, 1088
  period of "economic due process," 600
  takings clause of Fifth Amendment, 601
  vested rights, 601
Economic Opportunity Act (1964), **602**
Economic regulation, **602–606**
  borrowing power, 135
  Brandeis brief, 145
  challenged as due process violation, 720
  Economic Stabilization Act, 606, 607
  Interstate Commerce Act, 994
  police power, 1408
  Slaughterhouse cases, 1687, 1688
  of tax discrimination by states, 1251
  taxing and spending power, 1869–71
Economic Stabilization Act (1970), **606–607**
  delegation of power to President, 552, 553
  sweeping economic regulation, 602–606
Education Amendments of 1972 (Title IX), **607**
Education and the Constitution, **608–612**
  academic freedom, 12–14
  equal protection clause, 640–47
  federal grants-in-aid, 695–97
  right to know, 1592, 1593
  religion in public schools, 1537, 1538
  religious liberty, 1538–45
  student organizations, 609
Education of Handicapped Children Acts, **612–
  613**
  antidiscrimination legislation, 56
Effects on commerce, **613–14**
  Agricultural Marketing Agreement Act up-
    held, 2077
  and congressional power, 614
  Interstate Commerce Act, 994, 995
  Sherman Antitrust Act, 1678, 1679
  Shreveport doctrine, 1681, 1682
  Wagner Act upheld, 1992, 1993
Eighteenth Amendment, **614–15**
  National Prohibition Cases, 614
  Progressive constitutional thought, 1481, 1482

Eighteenth Amendment—*Continued*
  ratification of constitutional amendments chal-
    lenged, 1510–12
  Volstead Act, 1978, 1979
Eighth Amendment, *see* Bail; Capital punish-
    ment; Cruel and unusual punishment
  roots of, 113
Elastic clause, *see* Necessary and proper clause
Elections, regulation of, **616–17**
  Fifteenth Amendment, 725–27
  Fourteenth Amendment, 1928
  Nineteenth Amendment, 1315, 1316
  one person, one vote, 1344
  of representatives, 616
  of senators, 1665
  Twenty-Fourth Amendment, 757–61
Electoral College, **617–18**
  in election of John Quincy Adams, 21
  and equal representation, 93
  no mention in Constitution, 1409
Electronic eavesdropping, **618–22**
  Communications Act of 1934, 336, 1292
  and Fourth Amendment, 761–63, 1097, 1682
  no Fourth Amendment protection against
    "faithless friend," 2054
  held not trespassing, 1178, 1344, 1345
  legal requirements for, 1091
  and national security, 619, 621
  Omnibus Crime Control and Safe Streets Act,
    1291, 1333, 1334
Elementary and Secondary Education Act,
  622
  child benefit theory, 245
  church and state concerns, 39
Eleventh Amendment, **622–24**
  does not confer municipal immunity, 1285
  immunity of states from suit in federal court,
    79, 80, 607, 990, 1285
Elkins Act (1903), **624–25**
  to strengthen Interstate Commerce Act, 994,
    995
Ellsworth Court, *see* Supreme Court, 1789–1801
Emancipation Proclamation, **626–27**
  and abolitionist constitutional theory, 2–4
  Civil Rights Act of 1866, 281–83
  Confiscation Acts, 626
  Thirteenth Amendment, 1890, 1894
Embargo Acts (1807–1809), **627**
  commerce power, 841
  disobeyed, 1030, 1031, 1215
  Jefferson's attempt to enforce, 1215
  and sovereignty, 530
Emergency Bank Act (1933), **627–28**
  upheld in gold certificate case, 850
Emergency Court of Appeals, **628**
  criminal prosecution upheld in, 2081
  jurisdiction, 630
Emergency powers, **628–29**
  concurrent resolution, 344
  National Emergencies Act of 1976, 2016
  suspension of habeas corpus, 879–87
  War Powers Resolution of 1973, 2016
Emergency Price Control Act (1942), **629–30**
  Emergency Court of Appeals, 628
  Office of Price Administration (OPA) formed,
    629
  upheld, 2081

Eminent domain, **630–32**
  and abstention doctrine, 11
  challenged in Hawaii, 908
  and common law, 862
  due process challenges, 631
  fair return, 683
  power upheld in 1848 case, 2047, 2048
  public purpose doctrine, 1489–92
Employers' Liability Acts, **632**
  denial of workmen's compensation, 1311
  only railroad employees engaged in interstate
    commerce covered, 632
Employers Liability Cases, **632–33**
  *New York Central Railroad Company v.
    White*, 1311
Enabling Act, 1179
En banc, **633–34**
  definition, 633
  Supreme Court action, 1073
Enforcement Acts, *see* Force Acts
Entanglement test, *see* Government aid to secta-
    rian institutions
Entrapment defense, **635–36**
  exclusionary rule, 662–65
  only if due process is violated, 589–91
Enumerated powers, **636**
  dual federalism, 588
  and foreign affairs, 748
  restrictive interpretation of, 59
  Tenth Amendment, 1875, 1876
Environmental Quality Improvement Act, *see*
    Environmental regulation
Environmental regulation and the Constitution,
  637–40
  admiralty power, 30, 31
  Clean Air Act, 638
  Department of Justice, 82
  Environmental Protection Agency, 638, 1894
  interstate compacts, 996, 997
  taxing power, 1869–71
Equal Pay Act, 56
Equal protection of the laws, **640–47**
  in access to courts, 14, 132
  for aliens, 42, 2084
  Barrows v. Jackson, 102
  and Burger Court, 178, 643
  Civil Rights Act of 1866, 281–83
  Civil Rights Act of 1964, 284–86
  in distribution of contraceptives, 5, 118
  Fifth Amendment grounds, 556
  Fourteenth Amendment, 641, 757–61
  freedom of speech, 795
  for indigents, 583
  Japanese American cases, 643
  judicial legislation, 1041
  poll tax, 148
  racial discrimination, 71, 102, 642
  racial discrimination in housing, 7
  role of Justice Department, 84
  in school segregation, 132, 133, 163
  titles of nobility, 1899
  voting restriction, 592
Equal rights amendment (ERA), **647–48**
Equity, **648–50**
  and admiralty law, 30
  all deliberate speed, 44
  complaint against Beef Trust, 1842
  Erdman Act, 650

M

National Emergencies Act (1976), 2016
  see also Emergency powers
National Environmental Policy Act, *see* Environmental regulations
National Firearms Act, 1203
  excise tax on manufacturers and dealers in firearms, 1710
National Industrial Recovery Act, **1293–94**
  as administrative law, 27
  general welfare clause authority, 837, 838
  invalidation of, 28, 1622, 1623
  "little" NIRA, 217
  petroleum quotas held unconstitutional, 1363
  unauthorized by commerce clause, 1622
  unconstitutional delegation of powers, 552, 553, 1294, 1622
  unfair competition proscribed, 1293, 1622
National Labor Relations Acts, *see* Taft-Hartley Act; Wagner Act
National police power, **1295–99**
  over interstate shipment of lottery tickets, 226, 1295
  law enforcement and federal–state relations, 1126–30
  and mislabeled drugs, 1808
  registration of narcotics dealers, 575
  in state–federal law enforcement, 1126–30
  taxing power, 1297
  vitiated in *Hammer v. Dagenhart*, 893
National Prohibition Cases, *see* Amending process; Eighteenth Amendment
National Security Act (1947), **1299**
  creation of Central Intelligence Agency, 1299
  and foreign affairs powers of the President, 1299
National security and the Fourth Amendment, **1299–1300**
  balancing test, 94
  freedom of association, 337
  freedom of speech, 793, 888
  procedural due process, 888
  right to travel, 888
  wiretapping in cases of, 619
National Security Council, *see* National Security Act
Natural gas regulation, *see* Economic regulation
Naturalization, **1300–1301**
  and common law, 198
  defined by Supreme Court, 1300
  denied in oath case, 1627
  expatriation and, 675
  of group, 1301
Natural law, *see* Higher law; Natural rights
Natural rights and the Constitution, **1301–1303**
  Declaration of Independence, 545–48, 1301
  "Federalist," 708–711
  fundamental interests, 825
  and higher law, 914
  and Magna Carta, 1196
Navigable waters, *see* Subjects of commerce
Necessary and proper clause, **1305–1307**
  broad construction, 158, 1306
  Embargo Acts, 627
  full faith and credit, 824
  implied powers, 962–66
  judicial policymaking, 1044
  legislation authorized as, 824

Necessary and proper clause—*Continued*
  limits on, 1306
  national police power, 1295–99, 1306
New Jersey Colonial Charters, **1309**
  evidence of constitutionalism, 1309
New Jersey Plan, **1309–1310**
  at Constitutional Convention of 1787, 360–67
Newsman's privilege, *see* Reporter's privilege
New York Charter of Liberties and Privileges (1683), **1311–12**
  based on Magna Carta, 1195–97
Nineteenth Amendment, **1315–16**
  right of women to vote, 42
Ninth Amendment, **1316–20**
  and individual liberty, 1318
  Justice Burger's opinion in *Richmond Newspapers, Inc. v. Virginia*, 1319
No-knock entry, **1325**
  governed by Federal Code of Criminal Procedure, 1325
  in exigent circumstances, 674
Nolo contendere
  definition, **1325**
Noninterpretivism, *see* Constitutional interpretation
Nontestimonial compulsion, *see* Testimonial interpretation
Norris-LaGuardia Act (1932), **1326**
  and collective bargaining, 311
  injunctions against labor curbed, 1326
  union action not protected, 45, 1938
  yellow dog contracts invalidated, 1326
North Atlantic Treaty (1949), **1327**
Northwest Ordinance (1787), **1328–29**
  Articles of Confederation, 75–77
  as first bill of rights, 1329
  and fugitive slavery, 811
  and right of bail, 90
  territorial government based on, 1180
Notice, **1329–30**
  definition, 1329
  and ex post facto laws, 676, 677
  in procedural due process, 29, 1329
  requirement of, 823
Noxious products doctrine, **1330**
  Champion v. Ames, 226
  prohibited in interstate commerce, 1330
Nullification, **1330–31**
  and Force Acts, 746
  and Hartford Convention, 906
  and interposition, 993
  Jackson's proclamations, 1008
  Nullification Crisis of 1832, 1330
  South Carolina Ordinance of Nullification, 1712
  sovereignty, 1713–16
  Virginia and Kentucky Resolutions, 1974–75

O

Obiter dictum
  definition, **1333**
Obligation of contracts, **1333–34**
  between states and corporations, 1391
  Bronson v. Kinzie, 159
  contract clause expounded by Justice Paterson, 1960

Obligation of contracts—*Continued*
  Fletcher v. Peck, 744
  regulation of states, 46
  voiding by Congress, 850
Obscenity, **1335–37**
  Bantam Books, Inc. v. Sullivan, 100
  Brockett v. Spokane Arcades, Inc., 159
  chilling effect of laws, 159, 1259
  clear and present danger test, 227, 1335
  constitutionality of laws, 8, 9
  not constitutionally protected, 1612
  definition, 159
  definition "adjusted," 846, 1009, 1259
  fighting words, 9
  First Amendment effect, 8, 9, 733, 1259, 1724
  freedom of speech, 100, 150
  injunctions against sale, 1105
  "without redeeming social value," 1246, 1259
Office of Management and Budget, **1339–40**
  Gramm-Rudman-Hollings Act requirements, 858
  preparing a budget for the government, 168, 169
Official immunity, *see* Executive immunity; Judicial immunity; Municipal immunity, Sovereign immunity
"Okie law," 613
Omnibus Act (1868), **1343**
  southern states readmitted to Union, 1343
Omnibus Crime Control and Safe Streets Act, **1333–34**
  and electronic surveillance, 108, 619, 836, 1097
  as invasion of civil liberties, 1343
  McNabb-Mallory rule abolished, 1243
  national security permits wiretaps, 1344
One person, one vote, **1344**
  Baker v. Carr, 92, 93
  Colegrove v. Green, 309
  "county unit system" invalidated, 866
  and Warren Court, 2026
Open housing laws, **1345**
  Civil Rights Act of 1968, 286, 1345
  initiative repeal in California unconstitutional, 1535
  subject to referendum, 941
Opinion of the court, **1345–46**
  to establish precedent, 1436–38
  and judicial strategy, 1066
Oral argument, **1346**
  in amicus curiae, 54
  in federal judicial system, 1073
Ordered liberty, **1346–47**
  and fundamental rights, 829, 871
Ordinance of 1784, **1347**
  and Articles of Confederation, 75–77
Organized Crime Control Act of 1970, **1348**
  and immunity, 953, 1096
  sustained, 563, 577
Original jurisdiction, **1348**
  Article III, 251
  jurisdiction of federal courts, 1080, 1081
  of Supreme Court, 1200, 1224
Original package doctrine, **1349–50**
  applied to liquor, 1155
  import-export clause, 966, 1253
  propounded by Justice Marshall, 164